PAGE
48

ON THE ROAD

YOUR COMPLETE DESTINATION GUIDE
In-depth reviews, detailed listings
and insider tips

TOP EXPERIENCES MAP | NEXT PAGE

Yukon
Territory
p761

Northwest
Territories
p787

Nunavut
p809

British
Columbia
p620

Alberta
p548

Manitoba
p503

Saskatchewan
p528

Ontario
p50

Québec
p210

Newfoundland
& Labrador
p448

Prince Edward
Island
p420

New
Brunswick
p378

Nova
Scotia
p316

D0033499

PAGE
867

SURVIVAL GUIDE

YOUR AT-A-GLANCE REFERENCE
How to get around, get a room,
stay safe, say hello

...ine, and so are the
...o un/une (a) and adjectives th
...nouns. We've included masculine
forms where necessary, marked wit

Hello.	*Bonjour.*	bon-zhoo
Goodbye.	*Au revoir.*	o-rer-vwa
Excuse me.	*Excusez-moi.*	ek-skew-za
Sorry.	*Pardon.*	par-don
Yes./No.	*Oui./Non.*	wee/non
Please.	*S'il vous plaît.*	seel voo
Thank you.	*Merci.*	mair-s
You're welcome.	*De rien.*	der

THIS EDITION WRITTEN AND RESEARCHED BY

Karla Zimmerman,

Catherine Bodry, Celeste Brash, John Lee, Emily Matchar, Brandon Presser,
Sarah Richards, Brendan Sainsbury, Ryan Ver Berkmoes

〉Canada

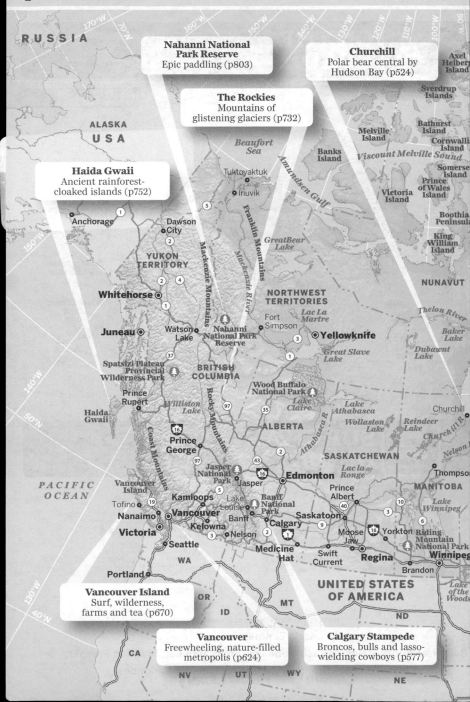

Nahanni National Park Reserve
Epic paddling (p803)

Churchill
Polar bear central by
Hudson Bay (p524)

The Rockies
Mountains of
glistening glaciers (p732)

Haida Gwaii
Ancient rainforest-
cloaked islands (p752)

Vancouver Island
Surf, wilderness,
farms and tea (p670)

Vancouver
Freewheeling, nature-filled
metropolis (p624)

Calgary Stampede
Broncos, bulls and lasso-
wielding cowboys (p577)

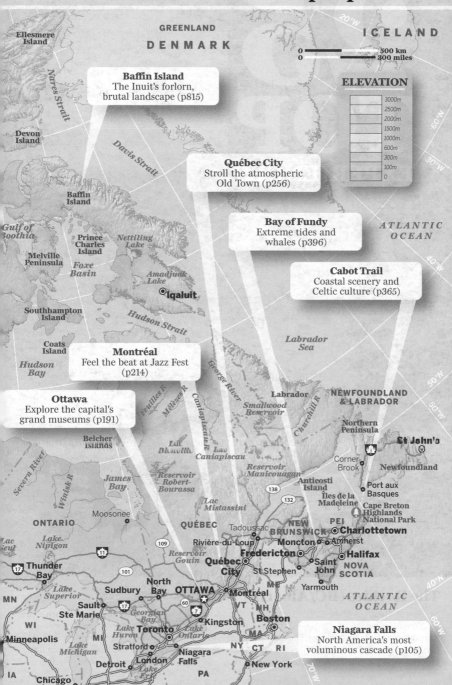

Top Experiences ›

Baffin Island
The Inuit's forlorn, brutal landscape (p815)

Québec City
Stroll the atmospheric Old Town (p256)

Bay of Fundy
Extreme tides and whales (p396)

Cabot Trail
Coastal scenery and Celtic culture (p365)

Montréal
Feel the beat at Jazz Fest (p214)

Ottawa
Explore the capital's grand museums (p191)

Niagara Falls
North America's most voluminous cascade (p105)

ELEVATION

3000m
2500m
2000m
1500m
1000m
600m
300m
100m
0

25 TOP EXPERIENCES

The Rockies (BC/Alberta)

1 The sawtooth of white-dipped mountains straddling the Alberta/BC border inspires both awe and action. Four national parks – Banff, Yoho, Kootenay and Jasper – offer opportunities for hiking, kayaking and most of all, skiing. The train provides another popular way to experience the grandeur. Luminous lakes, jumbles of wildflowers and glistening glaciers glide by as the steel cars chug up mountain passes and down river valleys en route to points east or west. Jasper National Park, above

Haida Gwaii (BC)

2 Once known as the Queen Charlotte Islands, this dagger-shaped archipelago (p752) 80km off BC's coast is a magical trip for those who make it. Colossal spruce and cedars cloak the wild, rainy landscape. Bald eagle and bear roam the ancient forest, while sea lion and orca patrol the waters. But the islands' real soul is the resurgent Haida people, best known for their war canoe and totem pole carvings. See the lot at Gwaii Haanas National Park Reserve, which combines lost Haida villages, burial caves and hot springs with some of the continent's best kayaking.

RICHARD CUMMINS

Vancouver (BC)

3 Vancouver (p624) always lands atop the 'best places to live' lists, and who's to argue? Sea-to-sky beauty surrounds the laid-back, cocktail-lovin' metropolis. With skiable mountains on the outskirts, 11 beaches fringing the core and Stanley Park's thick rainforest just blocks from downtown's glass skyscrapers, it's a harmonic convergence of city with nature. It also mixes Hollywood chic (many movies are filmed here) with a freewheeling counterculture (a popular nude beach and Marijuana Party political headquarters) and buzzing Chinese neighborhoods.

Niagara Falls (Ontario)

4 Crowded? Cheesy? Well, yes. Niagara (p105) is short, too – it barely cracks the top 500 worldwide for height. But c'mon, when those great muscular bands of water arch over the precipice like liquid glass, roaring into the void below, and when you sail toward it in a misty little boat, Niagara Falls impresses big time. In terms of sheer volume nowhere in North America beats its thundering cascade, with more than one million bathtubs of water plummeting over the edge every Bay of Fundy second.

JON DAVISON

Cabot Trail (Nova Scotia)

5 The 300km Cabot Trail (p365) winds and climbs over coastal mountains, with heart-stopping sea views at every turn, breaching whales just offshore, moose nibbling roadside and plenty of trails to stop and hike. Be sure to tote your dancing shoes – Celtic and Acadian communities dot the area, and their foot-stompin', crazy-fiddlin' music vibrates through local pubs.

YVETTE CARDOZO/ALAMY

Nahanni National Park Reserve (Northwest Territories)

6 Gorgeous hot springs, haunted gorges and gorging grizzlies fill this remote park (p803) near the Yukon border, and you'll have to fly or j-stroke in to reach them. Only about 1000 visitors per year make the trek, half of them paddlers trying to conquer the South Nahanni River. Untamed and pure-blooded, it churns 500km through the Mackenzie Mountains. Thirty-story waterfalls, towering canyons and legends of giants and lost gold round out the journey north.

Driving the Trans-Canada Highway

PHILLIP & KAREN SMITH

7 Canada's main vein stretches 7800km from St John's, Newfoundland to Victoria, BC and takes in the country's greatest hits along the way. Gros Morne National Park, Cape Breton Island, Québec City, Banff National Park and Yoho National Park are part of the path, as are major cities including Montréal, Ottawa, Calgary and Vancouver. It takes most road-trippers a good month to drive coast to coast, so what are you waiting for? Fuel up, cue the tunes, and put the pedal to the metal. Banff National Park, right

Old Québec City (Québec)

KEVIN LEVESQUE

8 Québec's capital (p256) is more than 400 years old, and its stone walls, glinting-spired cathedrals and jazz-playing corner cafes suffuse it with atmosphere, romance, melancholy, eccentricity and intrigue on par with any European city. The best way to soak it up is to walk the Old Town's labyrinth of lanes and get lost amid the street performers and cozy inns, stopping every so often for a café au lait, flaky pastry or heaping plate of poutine (fries smothered in cheese curds and gravy) to refuel.

Montréal (Québec)

9 Where else can you join more than two million calm, respectful music lovers (no slam dancing or drunken slobs) and watch the best jazz-influenced musicians in the world, choosing from 500 shows of which countless are free? Only in Montréal, Canada's second-largest city and its cultural heart. BB King, Prince and Astor Piazzolla are among those who've plugged in at the 11-day, late June Montréal Jazz Festival (p26). You might want to join them after your free drumming lesson and street-side jam session. The good times roll 24/7.

Museum of Civilization (Ontario/Québec)

10 It's one-stop shopping: the entire history of Canada in one tidy museum (p193), plus all-encompassing views of the nation's capital and parliament. Learn about everything from Aboriginal creation stories to civil rights, Basque whaling ships to Jackrabbit Johannsen, a trailblazing skier. The museum's architecture is a lesson, too: Aboriginal lore says evil spirits live in corners, so the building was created without any. While the museum overlooks Ottawa, it's actually across the river in Québec.

Manitoulin Island (Ontario)

11 The largest freshwater island in the world and floating right smack in Lake Huron's midst, Manitoulin (p152) is a slowpoke place of beaches and summery cottages. Jagged expanses of white quartzite and granite outcroppings edge the shoreline and lead to shimmering vistas. First Nations culture pervades, and the island's eight communities collaborate to offer local foods (wild rice, corn soup) and eco-adventures (canoeing, horseback riding, hiking). Powwows add drumming, dancing and storytelling to the mix. Manitoulin festival, right

The Prairies (Saskatchewan, Manitoba)

12 Solitude reigns in Canada's middle ground. Driving through the flatlands of Manitoba, Saskatchewan and Alberta turns up wheat, swaying wheat, and then more wheat, punctuated by the occasional grain elevator rising up in relief. Big skies mean big storms that drop like an anvil, visible on the horizon for kilometers. Far-flung towns for respite include arty Winnipeg, boozy Moose Jaw and Mountie-filled Regina, sprinkled with Ukrainian and Scandinavian villages. Grain elevator, above

ROLF HICKER

Bay of Fundy

13 This ain't your average bay, though lighthouses, fishing villages and other Maritime scenery surround it. The unique geography of Fundy (p396) results in the most extreme tides in the world. And they stir up serious whale-food. Fin, humpback, endangered North Atlantic right whales and blue whales swim in to feast, making a whale watch here extraordinary. Tidal bore rafting, where outfitters harness the blasting force of Fundy's waters, is another unique activity. Humpback whale, above

Northern Lights

14. Canada is has a lot of middle of nowhere places, from the Saskatchewan prairie to the Labrador coast to its Arctic villages. They may not seem like much during the day, but at night, the show begins. Drapes of green, yellow, aqua, violet and other polychromatic hues – aka the aurora borealis – light up the sky. The shapes flicker and dance, casting a spell in the north sky.
Wapusk National Park, above

Viking Trail (Newfoundland)

15 The Viking Trail (p480), aka Rte 430, connects Newfoundland's two world heritage sites on the Northern Peninsula. Gros Morne National Park, with its fjordlike lakes and geological oddities, rests at its base, while the sublime, 1000-year-old Viking settlement at L'Anse aux Meadows – Leif Eriksson's pad – stares out from the peninsula's tip. The road is an attraction in its own right, holding close to the sea as it heads resolutely north past Port au Choix' ancient burial grounds and the ferry jump-off to big bad Labrador. L'Anse aux Meadows, above

PRAMOD MISTRY

Drumheller (Alberta)

16 Dinosaur lovers get weak-kneed in dust-blown Drumheller (p611), where paleontological rcivic pride runs high thanks to the Royal Tyrell Museum, one of the planet's preeminent fossil collectors. The World's Largest Dinosaur is here, too – a big, scary, fiberglass T-rex that visitors can climb up and peer out its mouth. Beyond the dino-hoopla, the area offers classic Badlands scenery and eerie, mushroom-like rock columns called hoodoos. Scenic driving loops take you past the good stuff.

Calgary Stampede (Alberta)

17 You can always find a few cowboys kicking up dust in booming, oil-rich Calgary. But when you look down and everyone is wearing pointy-toe boots, it must be mid-July, time for the Stampede (p577). Bucking broncos, raging bulls and lasso-wielding guys in Stetsons converge for 'The Greatest Outdoor Show on Earth,' which highlights western rodeo events and chuckwagon racing. A huge midway of rides and games makes the event a family affair.

MICHAEL GEBICKI

Green Gables (PEI)

18 How did the tiny, rural town of Cavendish (p440) become one of PEI's biggest moneymakers? It's a long story – a book actually, about a red-pigtailed orphan named Anne. Lucy Maud Montgomery wrote *Anne of Green Gables* in 1908, drawing inspiration from her cousins' bucolic farmhouse. She never would have dreamed of the groupies who descend each year to lay eyes on the gentle, creek-crossed woods and other settings. Bonus for visitors: the surrounding area bursts with fresh-plucked oysters, mussels and lobsters to crack into.

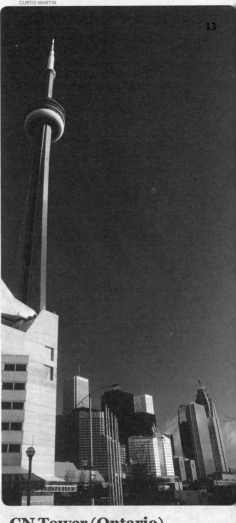

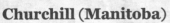

Churchill (Manitoba)

19 The first polar bear you see up close takes your breath away. Immediately forgotten are the two bum-numbing days on the train that took you beyond the tree zone onto the tundra, to the very edge of Hudson Bay. Churchill (p524) is the lone outpost here, and it happens to be smack in the bears' migration path. From late September to early November, tundra buggies head out in search of the razor-clawed beasts, sometimes getting you close enough to lock eyes. Summer lets you swim with beluga whales.

CN Tower (Ontario)

20 You can't miss the big needle (p56) poking up 553m from Toronto's skyline. It's the Western Hemisphere's highest tower, and visitors ride the glass elevator to the top to ogle Canada's largest city in all its multi-culti glory. About half of Toronto area residents were born in another country, and the city bubbles with ethnic enclaves like Little Italy, Chinatown, Little Korea, Greektown and Little India. Markets, splashy shops, bohemian quarters and arts aplenty solidify Toronto's world-class reputation.

Hockey

21 Hockey (p842) is Canada's national passion, and if you're visiting between October and April taking in a game is mandatory (as is giving a shout-out to the nation's 2010 Olympic gold medal-winning team). Vancouver, Edmonton, Calgary, Toronto, Ottawa and Montréal all have NHL teams who skate hard and lose the odd tooth. Minor pro teams and junior hockey clubs fill many more arenas with rabid fans. And if you're still looking for a fight, pond hockey brings out the sticks in communities across the land.

Vancouver Island (BC)

22 C'mon, can a place really 'have it all'? Yes, if it's Vancouver Island (p670). Picture-postcard Victoria is the island's heart, beating with bohemian shops, wood-floored coffee bars and a tea-soaked English past. Brooding Pacific Rim National Park Reserve sports the West Coast Trail, where a wind-bashed ocean meets a Paul Bunyan wilderness, and surfers line up for Tofino's waves. Then there's the Cowichan Valley, studded with welcoming little farms and boutique wineries, prime for wandering foodies. *Pacific Rim National Park Reserve, below*

Baffin Island (Nunavut)

23 The forlorn, brutal landscape of the Inuit, Baffin (p815) is home to cloud-scraping mountains and half of Nunavut's population. The island's crown jewel is Auyuittuq National Park – whose name means 'the land that never melts' – and indeed glaciers, fjords and vertiginous cliffs fill the eastern expanse. They're a siren call to hard-core hikers and climbers, and more than a few polar bears. Baffin is also a center for Inuit art. Studios for high-quality carving, printmaking and weaving pop up in many wee towns. Auyuittuq National Park, above

Fall Foliage

24 Canada blazes come autumn, which should come as no surprise in a country that's half-covered by forest. Québec's Laurentian Mountains flame especially bright from all the sugar maple trees (which also sauce the nation's pancakes). Cape Breton, Nova Scotia flares up so purty they hold a festival to honor the foliage (it's called Celtic Colours, and it's in mid-October). New Brunswick's Fundy Coast pulls in leaf peepers by the carload, too.

Rideau Canal (Ontario)

25 This 175-year-old, 200km-long canal/river/lake system (p198) connects Ottawa and Kingston via 47 locks. It's at its finest in wintry Ottawa, when it becomes the world's longest skating rink. People swoosh by on the 7km of groomed ice, pausing for hot chocolate and scrumptious slabs of fried dough called beavertails. February's Winterlude festival kicks it up a notch when townsfolk build a massive village of ice. Once it thaws, the canal becomes a boater's paradise. Winterlude festival, above

welcome to
Canada

Sighs alternate with gawps at the white-dipped mountains, mist-cloaked seascapes and epic northern roadways. And with more festivals than you can swing a moose at, you'll even forget it's cold.

Sublime Nature

The globe's second-biggest country has an endless variety of landscapes. Spiky mountains, glinting glaciers, spectral rainforests, wheat-waving prairies – they're all here, spread across six time zones. Expect wave-bashed beaches, too. With the Pacific, Arctic and Atlantic Oceans gnashing on three sides, Canada has a coastline that'd reach halfway to the moon, if stretched out.

It's the backdrop for plenty of 'ah'-inspiring moments – and the playground for a big provincial menagerie. We mean big as in polar bears, grizzly bears, whales and everyone's favorite, the ballerina-legged moose. You're pretty much guaranteed to see one of these behemoths when you leave the city behind.

Active Endeavors

Winter or summer, grand adventures lurk throughout Canada. Whether it's snowboarding Whistler's mountains, surfing Nova Scotia's swell, hiking Newfoundland's Appalachian Trail or kayaking the Northwest Territories' white-frothed South Nahanni River, outfitters will help you gear up for it. Gentler adventures abound, too, like strolling Vancouver's Stanley Park seawall, swimming off Prince Edward Island's (PEI) pink-sand beaches, or ice skating Ottawa's Rideau Canal. Before you know it, you'll be zipping up the fleece and heeding the call to action (and maybe having a go at dog-sledding, walleye fishing, snow-kiting...).

Cuisine (& Poutine)

Rarely do you hear people sigh over Canadian food the way they do, say, over Italian or French fare. So let's just call the distinctive seafood, piquant cheeses and off-the-vine fruits and veggies our little secret. Ditto for the bold reds and crisp whites the country's vine-striped valleys grow.

Canada is a local food smorgasbord. If you grazed from east to west across the country, you'd fill your plate like this: lobster with a dab of melted butter in the Atlantic provinces, poutine (golden fries soaked in gravy and cheese curds) in Québec, a bulging slice of berry pie in the Prairies and wild salmon and velvety scallops in British Columbia (BC).

It's best to leave the belt at home.

Cultural Flair

Let's see: Okanagan's icewine festival in January, Quebec City's winter carnival in February, Regina's powwow in March, Whistler's ski and snowboard fest in April, Ottawa's tulip fest in May, Montréal's jazz fest in June, Calgary's stampede in July, New Brunswick's Acadian fest in August, Toronto's film fest in September, Kitchener's Oktoberfest in October, Hamilton's Aboriginal Fest in November, Niagara's winter festival in December – yep, Canada parties all year long. Even places you might not automatically think of – say Edmonton, Winnipeg and St John's – rock with fringe festivals, live music clubs and shiny new art museums.

need to know

Currency
» Canadian dollars ($)

Language
» English
» French

When to Go?

Dry climate
Warm to hot summers, mild winters
Mild to hot summers, cold winters
Polar climate

Churchill
GO Sep-Nov

Banff
GO Jul-Sep

Vancouver
GO Jun-Aug

Montréal
GO Jun-Aug

Halifax
GO Jul-Sep

High Season
(Jun–Aug)

» Sunshine and warm weather prevail; far northern regions briefly thaw

» Accommodation prices peak (30% up on average)

» December through March is equally busy and expensive in ski resort towns

Shoulder
(May & Sep–Oct)

» Crowds and prices drop off

» Temperatures are cool but comfortable

» Attractions keep shorter hours

Low Season
(Nov–Apr)

» Places outside the big cities and ski resorts close

» Darkness and cold take over

» April and November are particularly good for bargains

Your Daily Budget

Budget less than
$90

» Dorm bed: $25-35

» Campsite: $20-30

» Plenty of markets and supermarkets for self-catering, plus fast-food options

Midrange
$90– 250

» B&B or room in a midrange hotel: $80-180

» Meal in a good local restaurant: from $20 plus drinks

» Rental car: $35-65 per day

» Attraction admissions: $5-15

High end more than
$250

» Four-star hotel room: from $180

» Three-course meal in a top restaurant: from $45 plus drinks

» Ski day-pass: $50-80

Money

» ATMs widely available. Credit cards accepted in most hotels and restaurants.

Visas

» Generally not required for stays of up to 180 days; some nationalities require a temporary resident visa.

Mobile Phones

» Local SIM cards can be used in European and Australian phones. Other phones must be set to roaming.

Driving

» Drive on the right; steering wheel is on the left side of the car.

Websites

» **Canadian Tourism Commission** (www.canada.travel) Official tourism site.

» **Environment Canada Weatheroffice** (www.weatheroffice.gc.ca) Forecasts for any town.

» **Lonely Planet** (www.lonelyplanet.com) Great for pre-planning.

» **Government of Canada** (www.gc.ca) National and regional information.

» **Parks Canada** (www.pc.gc.ca) Lowdown on national parks.

Exchange Rates

Australia	A$1	C$0.94
Europe	€1	C$1.34
Japan	¥100	C$1.25
New Zealand	NZ$1	C$0.74
UK	UK£1	C$1.64
USA	US$1	C$1.05

For current exchange rates see www.xe.com.

Important Numbers

Country code	✍ 1
International access code	✍ 011
Emergency	✍ 911
Directory assistance	✍ 411

Arriving

» **Toronto Pearson Airport**
Express buses – Every 20-30min 5am-1am; taxis – $50, 45min to downtown

» **Montréal Trudeau Airport**
Buses – Every 10-12min 8:30am-8pm; every 30-60min 8pm-8:30am; taxis – $38, 30-60min to downtown

» **Vancouver International Airport**
Trains – Every 8-20min; taxis – $30-40, 30min to downtown

» **Land Border Crossings**
Canadian Border Services Agency (www.cbsa-asfc.gc.ca/general/times/menu-e.html) updates wait times; usually 30min

Keep in Mind

Perhaps the important thing to remember is Canada's immense scale: distances can be deceivingly long and travel times slow due to single-lane highways and even a lack of highways (such as on the east and west coasts, when ferries take over). Don't try to pack too much into your itinerary and consider limiting travel to one or two regions.

Blackflies and mosquitoes can be an annoyance in the summer. Bring repellent and clothing to cover up with, especially in northern and woodsy regions.

Transportation and sleeping reservations are important in July and August.

what's new

For this new edition of Canada, our authors have hunted down the fresh, the revamped, the transformed, the hot and the happening. These are some of our favorites. For up-to-the-minute reviews and recommendations, see lonelyplanet.com/canada.

Bixi, Montréal

1 The city's ingenious solar-powered bike-sharing system makes it easy for both locals and visitors to explore the city with 3000 bikes at 300 depots scattered across downtown's core (p227).

Peak 2 Peak Gondola, Whistler

2 Powder fans can ski Whistler and Blackcomb on the same day by hopping on the new gondola. The 4.4km ride between the two takes 11 minutes (p662).

North Coast Trail, Vancouver Island

3 Giving hikers an alternative to the popular West Coast Trail, this 43km northern tip alternative winds through dense forest and alongside remote sandy coves (p703).

Art Gallery of Alberta, Edmonton

4 Opened in 2010, the silvery, post-modern building vaults the province's western Canadian and international abstract art collection into the big leagues (p552).

Haida Gwaii, BC

5 The Queen Charlotte Islands officially were renamed Haida Gwaii, or 'islands of the people', shaking off their colonial past. A huge new maritime preserve protects the islands' sea life (p753).

Blūmen Garden Bistro, Prince Edward County, Ontario

6 This arty restaurant takes advantage of the surrounding countryside's vineyards and farms by using local ingredients for its 'honest food' (p182).

Joggins Fossil Centre, Nova Scotia

7 Soon after the Joggins Fossil Cliffs became a World Heritage site, the town opened a state-of-the-art museum dedicated to the scene, with excellent cliff tours offered (p358).

Distilleries, Prince Edward Island

8 Prince Edward Distillery in Hermanville cooks up potato vodka, putting the province's abundant tubers to good use, while Myriad View Distillery in Rollo Bay produces legal, knee-buckling moonshine (p435).

Evandale Resort, New Brunswick

9 By the ferry landing on the Saint John River, this once-abandoned Victorian inn has been restored to its former opulence amid white farmhouses and wildflower fields (p387).

Canadian Museum of Nature, Ottawa

10 The natural history museum emerged massively bulked up after multiyear renovations, with plenty of new space for the dinosaurs and blue-whale skeleton (p195).

Marble Zip Tours, Newfoundland

11 Marble Mountain strung up the highest zipline in Canada, and it cruises right by a waterfall (p489).

if you like...

Adrenaline Activities

There's no excuse for sitting on your duff. Winter or summer, Canada is a land of action, and many towns gear up year-round.

Whistler If you want to ski or snowboard Canada's best, Whistler reigns supreme. Ziplining and mountain biking take over in summer (p662)

Tofino Gateway to wave-bashed Pacific Rim National Park Reserve and the 75km West Coast Trail, little Tofino packs big adventure with its surfing, kayaking and storm-watching (p697)

Banff In the heart of the Rockies, this place has it all: skiing, snowboarding, hiking, rafting, horseback riding, mountain biking – phew (p593)

Laurentians The sweet mountain villages speckling the landscape outside Montréal let you ski, luge, rock climb and refuel at maple-syrup shacks (p244)

Marble Mountain Off the beaten path, near Corner Brook, Newfoundland, there's skiing and snow-kiting in winter, caving and kayaking in summer, and ziplining year-round (p488)

Wine & Spirits

Many of Canada's wine regions are conveniently close to big cities, so it's easy to add a sip trip to your itinerary. BC's Okanagan Valley and Ontario's Niagara Peninsula are the big players, but Montréal's Eastern Townships, Ontario's Prince Edward County and Nova Scotia's countryside also fill goblets.

Winter Festival of Wine Slip, slide and slurp the season's candy-sweet icewines at the Okanagan's Sun Peaks ski resort in January (p854)

Niagara Wine Tours International Cycle backroads from winery to winery on these guided trips, tailored to all fitness levels (p114)

Taste Trail Take a self-guided driving tour through rural Prince Edward County's farms and vineyards (p181)

Myriad View Distillery Visit Canada's only legal moonshine producer and put hair on your chest with its mouth-burning, 75% alcohol elixir (p435)

Merridale Estate Cidery Sip the six apple ciders or brandy this distiller stirs up in Vancouver Island's verdant Cowichan Valley (p686)

Historic Sites

Fierce Norsemen, indigenous warriors, gold diggers...the early days of Canada were tumultuous, calamitous and waaay wild. Historic sites mark the spots.

L'Anse aux Meadows Poke around Viking vestiges that Leif Eriksson and friends left behind in Newfoundland in AD 1000 (p485)

Québec City History is palpable throughout the walled city where the French put down stakes in 1608 (p258)

Louisbourg Munch soldiers' rations and bribe guards at Nova Scotia's re-created 1744 fortress (p374)

Batoche See the moody, prairie site where Métis leader Louis Riel clashed with the Canadian army over land rights in 1885 (p546)

Klondike Sites The rush was on after prospectors struck gold in the Yukon in 1896; preserved structures in Dawson City tell the tale of those shiny, happy times (p779)

» The lighthouse at Woody Point (p481) overlooks the supernatural playground of Gros Morne National Park

Live Music

Canada rocks. From the power trio Rush to indie darlings Arcade Fire to the Celtified ravers Great Big Sea, Maple Leaf bands wield a mean guitar. Most big cities have a thriving music scene (got to keep everyone entertained during the long, cold winter).

Montréal Often compared to Seattle or Austin in the USA for its bo-ho, underground vibe, Montréal hosts Canada's most prolific indie scene, led by Arcade Fire (p241)

Evolve Festival The oceanside hills around Antigonish, Nova Scotia fill with on-the-rise alt bands for this eco-friendly, zero-waste summer fest – a sort of young, funky, jam-band Woodstock (p362)

Horseshoe Tavern Toronto's legendary venue is the place for emerging acts to cut their teeth. Buzz bands take the stage most nights (p91)

George St This cobblestoned lane in St John's is chock-full of musical pubs – supposedly more per square kilometer than anywhere in North America (p461)

Lighthouses

The romantic beacons pop up all along Canada's coast. Nova Scotia has the most, with 160 lighting its shores, but New Brunswick, Newfoundland, BC, Québec and Ontario have their fair share of fog-busters, too.

Peggy's Cove This red-and-white lighthouse dots a rolling granite outcrop near Halifax and is absolutely picture perfect – which is why it's one of the most-photographed of all time (p333)

Point Amour It'll take you 127 steps to reach the top of Atlantic Canada's tallest lighthouse, but it pays off with killer views over Labrador's black-rocked landscape and iceberg-strewn sea (p498)

Cape Enrage The 150-year old clifftop tower presides over the highest, meanest tides in the world (hence the name; p409)

Lighthouse Park Point Atkinson Lighthouse gets a whole park named after it in West Vancouver. It feels surprisingly remote for being a just splash away from the big city (p656)

Road Less Travelled

Sure there's the Sea to Sky Hwy, Icefields Pkwy and other famous thoroughfares calling out for your wheels. But here are our favorite, less-heralded scenic beauties.

Rte 132, Québec Rocky shores, glinting silver churches and wooded hills from Ste Flavie to Forillon National Park (p295)

Hwy 17 along Lake Superior's Northern Shore, Ontario Fjord-like passages, hidden beaches and primeval forests coated in mist (p295)

Old River Rd (Rte 102), New Brunswick Farmhouses, hay barns and wildflowers alongside an island-filled river (p387)

Rte 199, Québec Wee coastal road past sand dunes and fishing villages on the Îles de la Madeleine (p308)

Hwy 37A to Steward, BC Vintage toasters and converted-school-bus restaurants along with the requisite glaciers (p760)

Rte 470, southwest Newfoundland Rippled coastal ride past windswept terrain and fishing hamlets (p494)

**If you like
... long-distance**
train travel,
VIA Rail's *Canadian*
chugs from Toronto
to Vancouver on
three-night journey
through the plains
and over the mountains
(p888)

Wildlife Watching

You're guaranteed to see some mighty creatures in Canada's rugged, untamed landscape. Whales, polar bears and the goofy, twig-eating moose are perennial favorites.

Churchill Polar bears rule the tundra at Hudson Bay's edge, while beluga whales chatter in the river (p525)

Digby Neck Endangered North Atlantic right whales, blue whales, humpbacks and seals swim offshore from this spit of land in Nova Scotia (p345)

Gros Morne They say there's six moose per square kilometer in Newfoundland's premier park, plus caribou and black bear (p481)

Khutzeymateen Grizzly Bear Sanctuary Guess what creature lives here? The refuge, near Prince Rupert, BC, is home to more than 50 big guys (p751)

Witless Bay A million pairs of seabirds, including puffin, kittiwake and murre, screech and breed off Newfoundland's Avalon Peninsula (p464)

Victoria Resident pods of killer whales ride the local waves (p673)

Art

There are some whopping galleries in the major cities. Aboriginal art is always a highlight.

National Gallery of Canada A sprawling treasure trove in Ottawa, the National Gallery has your requisite Warhols and Rembrandts plus the world's largest collection of Canadian and Inuit art (p193)

Art Gallery of Ontario Toronto's big kahuna boasts rare Québecois religious statuary, First Nations and Inuit carvings, major Canadian works by the Group of Seven and the Henry Moore sculpture pavilion (p68)

UBC Museum of Anthropology Vancouver's top collection centers on soaring, beautifully carved totem poles (p633)

Sunshine Coast Gallery Crawl Artisans' wood, glass and clay studios stud the BC coast. A purple flag fluttering over a property means the artist is in (p670)

Cape Dorset This small, wintry town in Nunavut is the epicenter of Inuit art. See soapstone carvers in action at local studios and co-ops (p817)

Seafood

Bring on the bib and butter. Fresh-plucked lobster and shellfish are the east coast's catch, while wild salmon reels 'em in on the west coast.

Digby Foodies from around the globe salivate over the giant, butter-soft scallops from this Nova Scotia town. Eat them fresh from the waterfront (p346)

St Ann's Lobster Supper Crack into a crustacean in this quintessential PEI church basement, complete with chowder, steamed blue mussels and melted butter (p440)

Malpeque Head to the tiny PEI town where the namesake oysters come from, famed for their moist, briny taste that's perfect with a beer (p443)

C Restaurant Vancouver's pioneering west coast seafood restaurant knows its way around a salmon filet (p643)

Red Fish Blue Fish This takeout shack on Victoria's waterfront serves sustainably caught seafood in dishes like wild salmon sandwiches and oyster tacos (p678)

If you like... surfing,
Lawrencetown Beach in Nova Scotia gets exceptional wrapping waves. Learn to ride them at a surf school (p332)

Markets

You'll find plenty of places to putter, graze and trawl for that one-of-a-kind souvenir.

Kensington Market It's a blast rummaging through the boutiques of this Toronto neighborhood, where young bohemians buy their rasta-retro threads (p71)

Richmond Summer Night Market Taste-trip through steaming Malaysian, Korean, Japanese and Chinese food stalls or pick up Hello Kitty trinkets at this huge Asian bazaar, near Vancouver (p657)

Marché Jean Talon Farmers from the surrounding countryside bring their fruits, veggies, cheeses and sausages to Montréal's lively marketplace (p237)

Salt Spring Island Saturday Market Gobble luscious island-grown fruit and piquant cheeses while perusing locally produced arts and crafts on a day trip from Vancouver (p708)

Halifax Farmers' Brewery Market North America's oldest farmers market is a prime spot to people-watch and buy organic produce, wine, jewelry and clothing – as is its new sibling, the Seaport market (p329)

Beaches

So the water is typically freezing. That doesn't stop folks from unfurling their towels. Even if you don't go swimming, Canadian beaches are beautiful places to walk, watch birds or play Frisbee.

Basin Head Beach Many PEI locals rate this sweeping stretch of white sand as their favorite. Plus the grains 'sing' when you walk on them (p434)

Eastern Shore Beaches Several long, white-sand beaches with lifeguards, boardwalks, swimming and even surfing brush the coast near Halifax (p332)

Brackley Beach Another PEI hot spot, Brackley fills with families jumping over waves and wiggling toes in the pink sand (p436)

Long Beach Long Beach, near Tofino, takes a pounding from the Pacific's waves, but that's why surfers and beach bums flock to it (p694)

English Bay Beach This sandy curve in downtown Vancouver bustles with buskers, sunbathers and volleyballers in summer and walkers in winter (p628)

Starry Nights

In addition a sea of stars, the green-draped lights of the aurora borealis flicker in remote, far-north Canada. Prepare for a trek to get there.

Moose Factory There are no roads to this speck on the Ontario map (the historic site of the Hudson's Bay Company), there's just a small Cree settlement and eco-lodge (p171)

Torngat Mountains National Park Labrador's raw, chilly tip is about as isolated as you can get, with no towns for hundreds of kilometers (p500)

Yellowknife The Northwest Territories' far-flung, kitted-out capital lets you see the lights while dog sledding (p790)

Churchill Visit Manitoba's little piece of Hudson Bay around October and you'll have your Northern Lights with a side of polar bears (p523)

Whitehorse The Yukon's arty main town is another up-there spot with outfitters who'll take you out under the night sky (p764)

month by month

Top Events

25

1 Montréal Jazz Festival, June

2 Québec Winter Carnival, February

3 Stratford Festival, April-November

4 Calgary Stampede, July

5 Festival Acadien, August

January

Ski season is in full swing, and many mountains receive their peak snowfall. Toward the end of the month, cities begin their winter carnivals to break the shackles of cold, dark days.

 Icy Tipples
BC's Okanagan Valley (www.thewinefestivals.com) and Ontario's Niagara Peninsula (www.thewinefestivals.com) celebrate their ice wines with good-time festivals. The distinctive, sweet libations go down the hatch amid chestnut roasts, cocktail competitions and cozy alpine lodge ambience.

 Chinese New Year
Dragons dance, firecrackers burst and food sizzles in the country's Chinatowns. Vancouver (www.vancouver-chinatown.com) hosts the biggest celebration, but Toronto, Calgary, Ottawa and Montréal also have festivities. The lunar calendar determines the date. It's January 23 in 2012 and February 10 in 2013.

February

Yes it's cold, as in 'coldest temperature ever recorded' cold (that'd be Snag, Yukon on February 3, 1947 a −62.8°C). But that doesn't stop folks from being outdoors. February is a party month, filled with all kinds of wintry events.

 Québec City's Winter Carnival
Revelers watch ice-sculpture competitions, hurtle down snow slides, go ice fishing and cheer on their favorite paddlers in an insane canoe race on the half-frozen, ice-floe-ridden St Lawrence River. It's the world's biggest winter fest (www.carnaval.qc.ca).

 Winterlude in Ottawa
Another snowy bash, this one along the Rideau Canal, where skaters glide by on the 7km of groomed ice. When they're not sipping hot chocolate and eating beavertails (fried, sugared dough), the townfolk build a massive village entirely of ice (www.canadascapital.gc.ca/winterlude).

 Yukon Quest
The legendary 1600km dog-sled race goes from Whitehorse to Fairbanks, Alaska, through February darkness and -50°C temps. It's the ultimate test of musher and husky. Record time: 10 days, 2 hours, 37 minutes (www.yukonquest.com).

 **World Pond Hockey Tournament**
Small Plaster Rock, New Brunswick plows 20 rinks on Roulston Lake, rings them with straw-bale seating for 8000-odd spectators and invites 120 four-person teams to hit the puck. Teams travel from as far as the UK, Egypt and the Cayman Islands (www.worldpondhockey.com).

Northern Manitoba Trappers' Festival
The Pas puts on a weekend of frosty anarchy featuring dogsled races, snowmobiling, ice sculptures, torchlight parades and trapping games. Bundle up: the daily mean temperature is -16.1°C (www.trappersfestival.com).

March

Snow lessens and temperatures moderate from the brunt of winter. Ski resorts still do brisk business, especially mid-month when kids typically have a week-long school break.

Sugar Shacks

Québec produces three-quarters of the world's maple syrup, and March is prime time when the trees get tapped. Head out to local sugar shacks, scoop up some snow, put it on a plate and have steaming syrup from a piping cauldron poured onto it.

Regina Powwow

Students at First Nations University of Canada (www.firstnations university.ca) initiated this Saskatchewan powwow 30-plus years ago to celebrate spring and give thanks for the land's rebirth. Dancers arrive from around North America, and traditional crafts and foods abound.

Vancouver Vinos

Vancouver uncorks 1700 wines from 200 vintners at the Playhouse International Wine Festival (www.playhousewinefest.com), a rite of spring for oenophiles. You're drinking for art's sake, since the event raises funds for the city's contemporary theater company.

April

Apart from the far north, winter's chill fades and spring sprouts (though the weather can waver, so be prepared for anything). It's a good time for bargains since ski season is winding down but the summer influx hasn't yet begun.

The Bard in Ontario

Canada's Stratford, a few hours outside Toronto, nearly outdoes England's Stratford-upon-Avon. The Stratford Festival (www.stratfordfestival.ca) plays a monster season from April to November. Four theaters stage contemporary drama, music, operas and, of course, works by Shakespeare. Productions are first-rate and feature well-known actors.

World Ski & Snowboard Festival

Ski bums converge on Whistler for 10 days of adrenaline events, outdoor rock and hip hop concerts, film screenings, dog parades and a whole lotta carousing. Heed the motto: 'Party in April. Sleep in May' (www.wssf.com).

Hot Docs

Want to learn more about Ontario's Hwy 7? Millionaires who live in Mumbai's slums? Belly dancers working in Cairo? Toronto hosts North America's largest documentary film festival (www.hotdocs.ca), which screens 170-plus docos from around the globe.

May

May is a fine time for shoulder-season bargains and wildflower jumbles.

The weather is warm by day, though nippy at night. Victoria Day at month's end marks the official start of summer.

Tiptoe through the Tulips

After a long winter, Ottawa bursts with color – more than three million tulips of 200 types blanket the city for the Canadian Tulip Festival (www.tulipfestival.ca). Festivities include parades, regattas, car rallies, dances, concerts and fireworks.

Cuckoo for Cocoa

Plays about chocolate, painting with chocolate, jewelry making with chocolate – are you sensing a theme? Québec's Fête du Chocolat de Bromont (www.feteduchocolat.ca) is all about the sweet stuff. The best part: eating the chocolate. Bromont lies 75km east of Montréal.

June

Take advantage of long, warm days to hike, paddle and soak up the great outdoors (but bring repellent for black flies). Attractions don't get mega-busy until later in the month, when school lets out for the summer.

Montréal Jazz Festival

Two million music lovers descend on Montréal in late June, when the heart of downtown explodes in jazz and blues for 11 straight days. Most concerts are outdoors and free, and the party goes on round the clock (www.montreal-jazzfest.com).

Pride Toronto

Toronto's most flamboyant event celebrates all kinds of sexuality, climaxing with an out-of-the-closet Dyke March and the outrageous Pride Parade. Pride's G-spot is in the Church-Wellesley Village; most events are free. Held in late June (www.pridetoronto.com).

Elvis Festival

If you're in Penticton, BC, in late June and you keep seeing Elvis, rest assured it's not because you've swilled too much of the local Okanagan Valley wine. The town hosts Elvis Fest (www.pentictonelvisfestival.com), with dozens of impersonators and open-mike sing-alongs.

July

This is prime time for visiting most provinces, with the weather at its sunniest, a bounty of fresh produce and seafood filling plates, and festivals rockin' the nights away. Crowds are thick.

Montréal Chuckles

Everyone gets giddy for two weeks at the Just for Laughs Festival (http://montreal.hahaha.com/en), which features hundreds of comedy shows, including free ones in the Quartier Latin. The biggest names in the biz yuck it up for this one.

Calgary Stampede

Raging bulls, chuckwagon racing and bad-ass, boot-wearing cowboys unite for 'The Greatest Outdoor Show on Earth.' A midway of rides and games makes it a family affair well beyond the usual rodeo event, attracting 1.1 million yee-haw'in fans (www.calgarystampede.com).

Wacky Winnipeg

North America's second-largest fringe fest (www.winnipegfringe.com) stages creative, raw and oddball works from a global line-up of performers. Comedy, drama, music, cabaret, even musical memoirs are on tap over 12 days.

Arctic Art

The Great Northern Arts Festival (www.greatnorthart.com) in Inuvik, Northwest Territories, draws scores of carvers, painters and other creators from across the circumpolar world. It's an ideal place to buy arctic art, watch it being made, or participate in workshops.

August

The sunny days and shindigs continue. Visitors throng most provinces, and prices reflect it. It can get downright hot and humid away from the coasts.

Calling All Acadians

Acadians tune their fiddles and unleash their Franco-Canadian spirit for the Festival Acadien (www.festivalacadien.ca) in Caraquet, New Brunswick. It's the biggest event on the Acadian calendar, with singers, musicians and dancers letting loose for two weeks in early August.

Newfoundland's Big Row

The streets are empty, the stores are closed and everyone migrates to the shores of Quidi Vidi Lake for the Royal St John's Regatta (www.stjohnsregatta.org). The rowing race began in 1825 and is now the continent's oldest continuously held sporting event.

Canadian National Exhibition

Akin to a state fair in the USA, 'The Ex' (www.theex.com) features more than 700 exhibitors, agricultural shows, lumberjack competitions, outdoor concerts and carnivalia at Toronto's Exhibition Place. The 18-day event runs through Labour Day and ends with a bang-up fireworks display.

September

Labour Day in early September heralds the end of summer, after which crowds (and prices) diminish. But the weather is still decent in most places, making it an excellent time to visit. Plus moose mating season begins!

PEI International Shellfish Festival

This massive kitchen party, set on the Charlottetown waterfront, merges toe-tapping traditional music with incredible seafood. Don't miss the oyster-shucking championships or the chowder challenge (www.peishellfish.com).

Toronto International Film Festival

Toronto's prestigious 10-day celebration is a major cinematic event. Films of all lengths and styles are screened in late September, as celebs shimmy between gala events and the Bell Lightbox building. Buy tickets well in advance (www.torontointernational filmfestival.ca).

Foraging on Vancouver Island

Vancouver Island's Cowichan Wine & Culinary Festival (www.wines. cowichan.net) lets small-time cheese-makers, cider producers and organic vintners in the pretty valley showcase their wares via on-the-farm tours and tastings.

October

With fall foliage flaming bright and the weather dawning cool but comfortable, October welcomes lots of visitors. Grab a stick, because hockey season gets underway.

Celtic Colours

With foot-stompin' music amid riotous foliage, this roving festival in Cape Breton attracts top musicians from Scotland, Spain and other countries with Celtic connections. Commu-nity suppers, step dancing classes and tin whistle lessons round out the cultural celebration (www.celtic -colours.com).

Ontario's Oktoberfest

Willkommen to this nine-day beery Bavarian bash in Kitchener, supposedly the largest Oktoberfest outside of Germany. The sauerkraut, oompah bands, lederhosen and biergartens bring 500,000 people to clink steins under the tents (www.oktoberfest.ca).

November

After the fall-color events and early in the ski season, this is an offbeat time to visit. It's cold, but just a tease as to what's coming over the next three months.

Canadian Finals Rodeo

If you missed the Calgary Stampede, here's your other chance to see top cowboys test their skills with bucking broncos, steer wrestling and lasso throwdowns. Held in Edmonton mid-month (www.canadian finalsrodeo.com).

Canadian Aboriginal Festival

It's the country's biggest aboriginal event, a three-day wingding in Hamilton, Ontario, with dancing, drumming, crafts, films, traditional foods, and a lacrosse competition. Elders and healers offer traditional teachings, as well (www.canab.com).

December

Get out the parka. Winter begins in earnest as snow falls, temperatures drop, and ski resorts ramp up for the masses. 'Tis the holiday season, too. Resorts get especially busy the last few weeks of the month.

Mountain Time

Powder hounds hit the slopes from east to west. Whistler in BC, Mont-Tremblant in Québec and the Canadian Rockies around Banff, Alberta, pull the biggest crowds, but there's downhill action going on in every province (snowboarding and cross-country skiing, too).

Niagara Lit Up

The family friendly Winter Festival of Lights (www.wfol.com) gets everyone in the holiday spirit with three million twinkling bulbs and 125 animated displays brightening the town and the waterfall itself. Ice skate on the 'rink at the brink' of the cascade.

itineraries

Whether you've got six days or 60, these itineraries provide a starting point for the trip of a lifetime. Want more inspiration? Head online to lonelyplanet. com/thorntree to chat with other travelers.

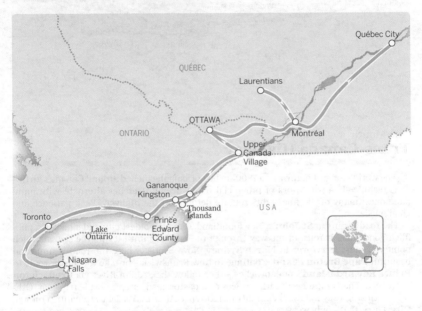

Two Weeks
The Central Corridor

> This 1450km route from Toronto to Québec City swoops up Canada's largest cities, mightiest waterfalls and prettiest islands.

Start in the multicultural mecca of **Toronto** (two days), and wallow in the wealth of architecture, art museums, restaurants and nightclubs. Spend day three at **Niagara Falls**, then begin your eastward haul. The Loyalist Parkway (Hwy 33) rambles shoreside in winery-laden **Prince Edward County** (half-day) and pulls into colonial **Kingston** (one day). From there, the misty, mansion-covered **Thousand Islands** dot the St Lawrence River; **Gananoque** (one day) makes a good break in their midst. Stop at **Upper Canada Village** (half-day), a re-created 1860s town, before heading to **Ottawa** (two days) to get your culture fix at the national museums. Save room for your next stop **Montréal** (two days), where the French *joie de vivre* seduces via Euro-cool clubs and foodie-beloved cafes. Had your fill? Swing over to the **Laurentians** (two days) to hike, cycle or ski yourself back into shape. Finish in **Québec City** (two days). The charismatic old town, walled and dramatically poised on a bluff, will leave an impression long after you return home.

One Month
Trans-Canada Highway

The world's longest highway – a 7800km belt of asphalt cinched around Canada's girth – is technically a patchwork of provincial roads. Scenic stretches alternate with mundane ones; many of the fine sights require detours off the highway. Pack patience and good music.

The road begins in **St John's**, Newfoundland, Canada's oldest city and a heckuva pub-filled good time. It rolls all the way through the province until it hits the sea, at which point you must ferry over to **North Sydney**, Nova Scotia, where the road resumes on beautiful **Cape Breton Island**. Continue to New Brunswick – or take the longer route to **Prince Edward Island**'s pink beaches – then follow the St John River via **Fredericton** to Québec. The **Gaspé Peninsula** entices as a pastoral, silver-spired side trip east. Otherwise, the highway follows the mighty St Lawrence River and reaches romantic **Québec City**. Phew, that's only week one.

Carry on the urban theme in **Montréal**, where the croissants and cafe au lait will keep you lingering, before plunging into Ontario near museum-fortified **Ottawa**. From there, follow in fur traders' footsteps to **Sudbury** and **Sault Ste Marie**, the gateway to the Algoma wilderness that inspired the Group of Seven painters. Savor the superb stretch of road skirting Lake Superior to **Thunder Bay**. And voila, there goes week two.

Next the highway enters the prairie flatlands of Manitoba, where **Winnipeg** rockets up and provides an enlivening patch of cafes and culture. The road dawdles under Saskatchewan's big skies until reaching bad-ass **Moose Jaw**, where Al Capone used to hide his bootlegged booze. In Alberta, dinosaur junkies can detour to **Drumheller**. And put on your cowboy boots before arriving in **Calgary**, a former cow town that's become one of Canada's fastest-growing cities. So passes week three...

You're in the Rockies now. They offer a dramatic change of scenery as the highway meanders through **Banff** before entering British Columbia at **Yoho National Park** and reaching its highest point (1643m) at Kicking Horse Pass. The mountains eventually give way to river country. The most memorable section leads through the **Fraser River Canyon** from where it's only a quick jaunt to mod, multicultural **Vancouver** and the ferry to **Victoria**. Snap a picture at the Mile 0 sign. You made it!

Two Weeks
Cabot & Viking Trails

> Wild, windswept and whale-riddled, this 1400km route through Nova Scotia and Newfoundland unfurls sea-and-cliff vistas you can see right from the car. But it also provides plenty of opportunities to pull over and get the blood flowing with hikes, kayak trips and art studio visits.

Start in **Halifax** and spend a few days enjoying the beer, farmers market and cosmopolitan life. Day-trip out to **Maitland** to raft the tidal bore's waves. Then hit the road east to Celtic-tinged **Cape Breton Island**. It's about a five-hour drive, and there's no ferry involved, since a causeway connects the mainland to the island. As you approach the town of Baddeck, veer off on the Cabot Trail, a well-marked 300km loop through the region. It winds and climbs over coastal mountains, with heart-stopping sea views at every turn.

Enjoy it for the next three days, popping in to little towns along the way. **Chéticamp** makes a fine stop – it's a deeply Acadian fishing community known for its arts. It's also the gateway into **Cape Breton Highlands National Park**, where you'll likely see loads of moose and nesting bald eagle. When you reach **Pleasant Bay**, you can watch whales or chant with monks at the local Tibetan monastery. **Meat Cove** is a lovely place to stretch your legs with a hike. And don't forget to get your art fix at the studios along the **St Ann's Loop** before arriving in industrial North Sydney for the ferry to Newfoundland.

It's a six-hour sail over the Cabot Strait to **Port aux Basques**. The ferry goes daily, but be sure to book in advance. Spend a day in the sleepy town and its lighthouse-dotted environs, then steer for **Gros Morne National Park**, about four hours north on the Trans-Canada Highway. The world heritage site is rich with mountain hikes, sea kayak tours, fjord-like lakes and weird rock formations. After soaking it up for three days, continue on the Viking Trail to its awe-inspiring endpoint: **L'Anse aux Meadows National Historic Site**. This was North America's first settlement, where Leif Eriksson and his Viking pals homesteaded 1000 years ago. Poke around for a few days before turning around and heading back. You'll need a couple of (long) days to retrace your path to Halifax.

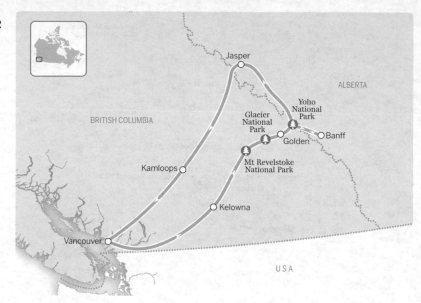

Two Weeks
The Rockies

❭ Prepare to feast on a smorgasbord of scenic delights on this 2000km trek, which loops through British Columbia and Alberta.

Start with a couple of days in mountain-meets-sea **Vancouver**, where you'll be spoiled by urban hiking, biking and other activities, plus western Canada's best cuisine scene. Make the wine pilgrimage east through rolling hills to the lake-studded **Okanagan Valley**, famous for its fruit orchards, crisp whites and bold reds. **Kelowna** (two days) makes a good sipping base in the area.

Next it's time to get high in BC's Rocky Mountains (two days). A trio of national parks pops up in quick succession, each providing plenty of 'ah'-inspiring vistas. **Mt Revelstoke** has a cool scenic drive and hikes. **Glacier** has 430 of the namesake ice sheets. And **Yoho** may be the best of all, home to looming peaks and crashing waterfalls. **Golden** is a convenient base.

Cross the border into Alberta, and park it in **Banff** (three days). You won't be able to stop the cliches from flying forth: grand! majestic! awe-inspiring! Allot plenty of time for hiking, paddling, gawking at glaciers and spotting grizzly bear (best done from a distance). Sapphire-blue Lake Louise is a must, surrounded by alpine-style teahouses that let you fuel your day-hike with scones, beer and hot chocolate.

From Banff, Hwy 93 – aka the Icefields Pkwy – parallels the Continental Divide for 230km to **Jasper** (three days). Try to keep your eyes at least partially on the road as you drive by the humungous Columbia Icefield and its numerous fanning glaciers. Foaming waterfalls, dramatic mountains and the sudden dart of a bear (or was that a moose?) are also part of the journey. Jasper itself is bigger and less crowded than Banff, and offers the requisite superb hiking, as well as horseback riding, rock climbing, mountain biking and rafting.

It's a shame to have to leave, but we must return to Vancouver. The Yellowhead Hwy (Hwy 5) plows south to **Kamloops**, a handy spot to spend the night before motoring back to the City of Glass.

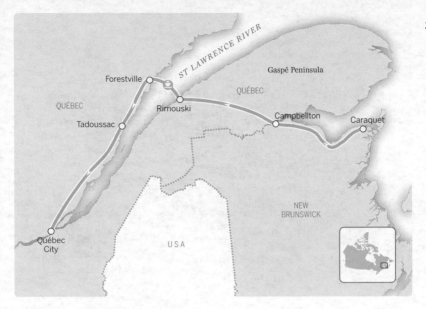

One Week
French Canadian Sampler

❭ Get a taste of Canada's French side on this 700km jaunt through New Brunswick and Québec.

Start in **Caraquet** (one day) and immerse in Acadian culture at the historic sites and via local foods like *pets de soeur* ('nun's farts' in English – try one to see if you can figure out why). If you visit in August, the fiddle-fueled Festival Acadien takes over the town.

Ramble east through **Campbellton** and cross into Québec. **Rimouski** (two days), on the St Lawrence River, is your target. Browse its intriguing museums and delicious cafes, and day trip east up the Gaspé Peninsula on Rte 132, where fluttering Acadian flags, tidy farming hamlets and rocky shores flash by.

From Rimouski, a ferry crosses the river to Forrestville, from which you can head south to welcoming **Tadoussac** (two days). Its all about whale watching in this bo-ho little town. Zodiacs go out to see the mondo blue whales that patrol the area.

Finish your trip in atmospheric **Québec City** (two days). Check in at a cozy inn, wander the Old Town's labyrinth of lanes, and stop often to sip in the corner cafes.

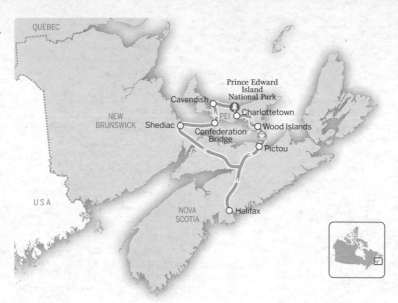

One Week
Heart of the Maritimes

> This 650km loop lassoes the core of the Maritime provinces (Nova Scotia, New Brunswick and PEI).

Eat and drink your way through **Halifax** (two days), then make a break northwest for New Brunswick. Festive **Shediac** (one day) is home to the world's biggest lobster sculpture and – no surprise – the cooked version of the creature gets served in eateries all over town. Cap off the evening at the retro drive-in movie theater.

Barrel over the 12.9km **Confederation Bridge** that links New Brunswick to PEI and begin the pilgrimage to Anne's Land. Anne, of course, is the fictional red-headed orphan of Green Gables fame, and **Cavendish** (one day) is the wildly developed town that pays homage to her.

Continue the red theme by exploring the red sandstone bluffs at **Prince Edward Island National Park** (one day); there's birdwatching, beach walking and swimming, too. Stop in PEI's compact, colonial capital **Charlottetown** (one day) before taking the ferry from **Wood Islands** back to **Pictou** (half-day) in Nova Scotia. You can stroll Pictou's boardwalk and if you're lucky, the town might be hosting its First Nations Powwow. It takes about two hours to return to Halifax from here.

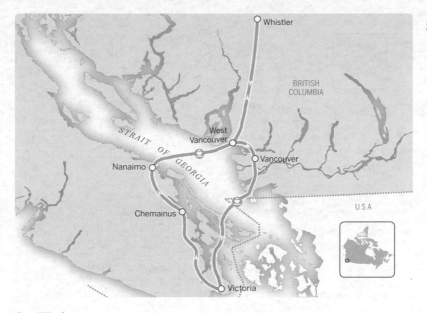

One Week
Bite of BC

❯ You don't have to drive far to experience a range of humbling, heart-leaping landscapes
in southern BC. Ocean, mountains, forests, islands – all present and accounted for in
roughly 550km.

Begin in **Vancouver** and take a couple of days to check out the indie shops, foodie
fare and forested seawall vistas of Stanley Park. On day three, drive to the **Tsawwassen
ferry terminal** for the dreamy boat trip snaking through fir-y isles to **Swartz Bay** on
Vancouver Island. Zip over to **Victoria**, spending an overnight exploring the picture-
perfect capital and its historic buildings. On day four, drive north up the island on Hwy 1,
stopping off at **Chemainus**, a former logging settlement that's reinvented itself as an art
town. Continue north for a late lunch and an overnight in **Nanaimo**, then, next morning,
catch the ferry back to the mainland's Horseshoe Bay terminal in **West Vancouver**.

From here, the Sea to Sky Hwy (aka Hwy 99) runs cliffside through formidable mountains to **Whistler**. The resort town has heaps of adrenaline activities (skiing, snowboarding, ziplining, mountain biking) and fun, ski-bum bars to occupy days six and seven. It's
130km back to Vancouver.

One Week
Klondike Hwy & Around

❭ Heed the call of the wild, and set your wheels for this epic roadway. Know it'll be a lot of driving for one week (approximately 30 hours). But the road *is* the main attraction for the trip.

Start in **Skagway**, Alaska, as the Klondike Hwy does. Soon you'll leave the cruise ships behind and enter the rugged land Jack London wrote so much about. Follow the road to lively **Whitehorse**, which has groovy arts and organic bakeries. From there continue north to offbeat **Dawson City**. Linger a few days and check out the gold rush historic sites, take a mine tour and blow a kiss to the dancing girls. Day-trip to **Tombstone Territorial Park** for its wide, steep grandeur.

Next, follow the Top of the World Hwy (Hwy 9) across mountain tops to the Alaskan border, and connect down through the US and onto the Alaska Hwy in the Yukon at **Beaver Creek**. The road between here and well-stocked **Haines Junction** is sublime, paralleling Kluane National Forest and the St Elias Mountains. The gawk-worthy Haines Hwy rolls in to **Haines**, Alaska, where you'll finish.

Travel with Children

Where to Go in Canada's Playground

Vancouver

Sandwiched between sea and mountains, build a sandcastle one day and go snowboarding the next while enjoying the comforts of a cosmopolitan city.

Canadian Rockies

Hike, ski, camp or snowshoe while looking out for moose, bear, elk and whistling marmot.

Montréal

Historic cobblestoned-streets, year-round ice-skating an inner-city beach and the Biôdome full of critters will make you understand the meaning of *joie de vivre*.

Maritime Provinces

Climb a lighthouse, sail on a pirate ship, whale watch and beach hop in summer; watch the trees turn red, orange and gold in fall.

Toronto

Stroll through parks in summer, ice-skate in winter and don't forget to visit Niagara Falls!

Deciding where to go with your kids in Canada can be a daunting decision. Mountains, prairies, beaches, ice fields and easy going cities are strewn across six time zones and even more landscape variations. Yet between sure-bet wildlife sightings, meeting real-life cowboys, learning hands-on about pirate history, roaming the plains for dinosaur fossils and ice-skating on mountain lakes, it's impossible to make a bad choice. Add the fact that Canada caters to kids better than nearly any other country in the world and you may find yourself (as many do) bringing the kids back year after year.

Canada for Kids

Canada is for kids. As if seeing moose, eagles and whales or running around in the snow, on the beach or in the woods all day wasn't fun enough, everywhere you turn those crafty Canadians have cooked up some hands-on learning experience, living history lesson or child-oriented theater.

Museums & Monuments

Most large Canadian cities have science museums that specialize in hands-on activities that get all ages involved while, at historic sites strewn across the country costumed thespians get you right into the period and often have demonstrations of everything from blacksmithing to cooking. At some of these places there are also puppet or theatrical performances for children and other events such as hayrides. Teens usually enjoy these sites as well since they are often large and diverse enough for self-exploration and touch on subjects they've studied at school.

Art museums sometimes offer craft centers and classes for kids but you'll have to call ahead to check for schedules.

Outdoor Activities

Canada is about open spaces, fresh air, wildlife, snow, sand, rivers, lakes and mountains. Outdoor activities on offer are about as endless as the land itself and there are suitable options for babies to teens.

Canadian cities encourage **cycling** and most are endowed with parks and promenades set up for even the tiniest cyclists; bike rental is available but finding a child-sized bike can be hit or miss. For a cycling-oriented holiday try the mostly flat Confederation Trail that traverses bucolic Prince Edward Island or the traffic-free Kettle Valley Trail (KVR; British Columbia) that's one of the least strenuous stretches of the Trans Canada Trail. If you've got bigger kids into **mountain biking**, Canada offers some of the best off-road options on the planet – rentals and tours are available for all levels.

The Canadian National Park system takes families into account and **hiking** trail systems invariably contain easy strolls as well as the more long-winded ones that teens might enjoy. **Horseback riding** is widely on offer and can be especially fun in cowboy country around Calgary.

Kayaking and canoeing is one of the best ways to explore this country. Most lake areas offer canoe rentals perfect for leisurely family outings, while seafront regions are packed with kayak outfits offering rentals, classes, tours and multiday trips. For a bigger adrenaline rush for older kids and teens, try some of the country's **white water rafting** or '**playboating**' spots, particularly on the Ottawa River in Beechburg.

To add waterside action, not much can beat **fishing**. While fishing lodges (often located in the best, but remote, fishing areas) can cost a fortune, you'd be surprised at how lucky you can get just casting into any lake or river if you're not out to catch a monster. Likewise, try **clamming** (PEI and BC are tops) – just ask locals where to go and bring a shovel and a bucket. If you don't find anything at least you'll have the perfect

EXTRAS BY AGE

Babies & Toddlers

» A front or back sling for baby and toddler if you're planning on hiking and a stroller for city jaunts (nearly everywhere is stroller-accessible).

» Kids' car seats: rental companies rent them but at proportionately extortionate rates; in Canada babies need a rear-facing infant safety seat while children under 18kg (40lb) must be in a forward-facing seat.

» Sandcastle or snowman making tools

6-12 years

» Children between 18kg (40lb) and 36kg (80lb) should have a booster seat. Seatbelts can be used as soon as a child is either 36kg, 145cm (4ft 9in) tall or eight years old.

» Binoculars for young explorers to zoom in on wildlife

» Field guides about Canada's flora and fauna

» A flip camera to inject newfound fun into 'boring' grown-up sights and walks

» Fold-away microscooter and/or roller blades if you're doing lots of urban street walking

» Kite (for beaches)

Teens

» Canada-related iPhone or Android apps

» Canada-related novels (find a list of Young Adult Canadian Book Award winners at www.cla.ca)

» French-Canadian phrasebook

tools for building sandcastles. **Deep-sea fishing** is offered along the coasts and can be very fun for older kids but full days on a boat can be tiresome for the little ones.

On the coasts and the Bay of Fundy, **whale watching** can be thrilling but be prepared with seasickness pills, extra snacks, sunscreen and warm clothes. If the sea is rough and your kids get seasick, the unpleasantness of the voyage can sometimes out-weigh the excitement of seeing whales. Try to aim for calm days and shorter trips unless your family members possess Viking hardiness.

The water is cold in Canada but kids don't seem to mind. **Surfing** the East and West Coast's tiny summer waves is an excellent way to start learning this sport. Rent a board or wetsuit or take a class. See the Wet and Wild list (p39) for where to go.

Once the kids are out of diapers **skiing and snowboarding** is the obvious family choice. Children under six often ski for free, ages six to 12 usually pay around 12% to 50% of the adult price while ages 12 to 18 pay a little more than 33% to 75% of the adult price. Prices change annually but in 2010–11 the Banff area offered much better children's rates than Whistler-Blackcomb. Then, of course, there is all the off-slope fun: **ice-skating, sledding and snowshoeing**. See the Winter Wonderland list (p39) for where to go.

Eating Out

Everywhere you turn in Canada you'll find fast food, fried fare and Tim Horton's, Canada's favorite stop for doughnuts, sandwiches and coffee. If you're health conscious, one of your biggest hurdles with kids will be finding more wholesome options; in small towns your only choice might be to self-cater. Fortunately there are plenty of cabin and family suite-style options that allow you to cook for yourself and some B&Bs will also let you cook. In cities every restaurant option is available from vegan to steakhouses.

Most Canadian restaurants are adept at dealing with families, offering booster seats and child-friendly servers as soon as you steer your progeny through the door. As an alternative to chicken fingers and burgers on the kids menu, you can usually ask for a half-order of something from the adult menu. Families with even the most well-behaved children may not feel comfortable at fine-dining establishments.

Children's Highlights

A History Lesson

» **Dinosaurs** Drumheller Museum, Alberta

» **First Nation** Haida Gwaii (British Columbia), Head-Smashed-in-Buffalo Jump World Heritage site (Alberta), Aboriginal Experiences (Ottawa), Wanuskewin Heritage Park (Saskatchewan)

» **European Colonization** L'Anse aux Meadows (Newfoundland), Fort Louisbourg (Nova Scotia), Fort William Historical Park (Ontario)

Winter Wonderland

» **Winter Carnivals** Québec City Winter Carnival (Québec City), Cavalcade of Lights (Toronto), Vancouver Festival of Lights (Vancouver)

» **Ice-Skating** Rideau Canal (Ottawa), Lake Louise (Alberta), Harbourfront Centre (Toronto), Lac des Castors (Montréal)

» **Skiing, Snowboarding & Sledding** Whistler-Blackcomb (British Columbia), Norquay (Banff), Mont-Sainte-Anne (Québec)

» **Dog-sledding** Yellowknife (Northwest Territories), Iqaluit (Nunavut)

Critters of the Great North

» **Moose** Nearly everywhere but especially Algonquin National Park (Eastern Ontario) and Gros Morne National Park (Newfoundland)

» **Polar Bears** Churchill (Manitoba)

» **Whales & Orcas** Vancouver Islands (British Columbia), Bay of Fundy (New Brunswick & Nova Scotia), Newfoundland

» **Bald Eagles** Brackendale (British Columbia), Cape Breton Island (Nova Scotia)

Wet & Wild

» **Rafting the Tidal Bore** Maitland, Nova Scotia

» **Beaches** Prince Edward Island & British Columbia

» **Surfing** Lawrencetown Beach, Nova Scotia & Vancouver Island, British Columbia

» **Kayaking** Johnstone Strait (Vancouver Island), Georgian Bay (Ontario),

» **Canoeing** Algonquin National Park (Ontario), Bowron Lakes (British Columbia), Kejimkujik National Park (Nova Scotia)

» **Fishing** Lunenburg Nova Scotia (lobster), Point Prim Prince Edward Island (clamming), Northern Saskatchewan (freshwater fishes), Maritime Provinces (deep-sea fishing)

Urban Adventures

» **Calgary's Cowboys & Cowgirls** Calgary Stampede, Heritage Park Historical Village, horse rides at family ranches

» **Vancouver's Outside Action** Capilano Suspension Bridge, Stanley Park

» **Ottawa's Museum Mission** Canada Agricultural Museum, Museum of Nature, Science & Technology Museum, Museum of Civilization

» **Toronto's High Heights to Underground** CN Tower to the subterranean corridors connecting downtown

» **Montréal's Culture Infusion** Old Montréal, Little Italy

» **Halifax's Pirates & the Titanic** Maritime Museum of the Atlantic, *Titanic* graveyards

Theme Park Delight

» **Paramount Canada's Wonderland** Toronto (Amusement & Water Park)

» **Galaxy Land** World's Largest Indoor Amusement Park (Edmonton)

TOP 5 PLACES TO CAMP WITH KIDS

» **Living Forest, Vancouver Island** (British Columbia; www. campingbc.com) spot orcas, fish for crabs and see eagles soar overhead

» **Arowhon Pines, Prince Albert National Park** (Saskatchewan; www.arowhonpines.ca) Gentle terrain full of wildlife; perfect for swimming and canoeing

» **Tunnel Mountain, Banf** (Alberta; www.tunnelmountain.com) Crowded but 5km from town; swim in a hot spring in a limestone cave, see plenty of wildlife and have convenient access to the Rockies

» **Takhini Hot Springs, Whitehorse** (Yukon; www.takhinihot springs.yk.ca) Horse riding, hot springs, swimming and a chance to see the northern lights

» **Dinosaur Provincial Park, Patricia** (Alberta; www.dinosaurpark. ca) Jurassic park in the Badlands; get familiar with cacti and go on fossil tours

---

» **La Ronde** Amusement Park (Montréal)

» **Calaway Park** Amusement Park & Campground (Calgary)

» **Playland** Amusement Park (Vancouver)

» **Avonlea** Anne of Green Gables (Prince Edward Island)

Planning

Traveling around Canada with the tots can be child's play. Lonely Planet's *Travel with Children* offers a wealth of tips and tricks. The website **Travel For Kids** (www. travelforkids.com) is another good, general resource.

When to Go

Festivals fill Canadian calendars year-round and most are very family-oriented. Summers are the most festival-heavy times with lots of outdoor-oriented get-togethers from jazz festivals and food and drink extravaganzas to street busker festivals and rodeos. Unless it's obviously an adult theme there are invariably activities and practicalities set up for children. Fall is a lovely time to visit Canada if you can arrange it around your children's school schedule. At this time the trees are changing colors, daytime temperatures are still manageably warm and most of the crowds have gone home.

The best time for good, fresh snow and snow sports is January to April. Santa Claus parades usually kick off the holiday season around the country in November and early December; for a list and descriptions see http://www.canada.com/Santa+Claus+pa rades+across+Canada/941414/story.html. Around the same time or just after, come the festivals of light where you can expect fireworks, concerts, more visits from Santa, children's performances, parades and Christmas tree lightings.

Accommodation

Hotels and motels commonly have rooms with two double beds. Even those that don't can bring in rollaways or cots, usually for a small extra charge. Some properties offer 'kids stay free' promotions so check on the web. B&Bs may refuse to accept pint-sized patrons while others may have special 'family suites.' Ask when booking.

Another good option are 'cabins' which are usually rented out by the week and come with kitchens, any number of bedrooms and other perks like barbecues. Because of long-term rental nature of these places, not many are listed in this book but you can find full listings with each province's visitor's guides online and in print (order them for free at each province's tourism website).

Camping is huge in Canada and many campgrounds also offer rustic cabins (bring your own bedding) that sometimes have kitchens, fire pits or barbeques. A few privately fun grounds offer more exotic options like tipis or yurts while others have swimming pools, minigolf or might be on a lake for swimming and canoeing. You'll find camping in national parks as well as near urban areas and this can be a fun budget option for families – you'll meet the most other kids this way but bring twice the bug spray.

What to Pack

Canada is very family oriented so anything you forget can probably be purchased in-country. Breastfeeding in public is legal and tolerated, although most women are discreet about it. Most facilities can accommodate a child's needs; public toilets in airports, stores, malls and cinemas usually have diaper-changing tables.

What you will need is layered clothing for everyone since it can get spontaneously cool during summer months and very, very cold during winter. Sunscreen is a must – you'd be surprised how much you can burn on the greyest of days – as are rain gear and bug spray. It's also a good idea to bring activities for lengthy car rides since getting anywhere in Canada can involve very long distances.

If you're coming from the US you might also find Canada to be more expensive these days (depending on the exchange rates) so it's frugal to bring the clothes you need from home.

Regions at a Glance

You can't go wrong in Canada. Each region has eye-popping landscapes and a slew of activities to match. Ontario, Québec and British Columbia (BC) – the most populated provinces – are the ones with the most going on. In addition to outdoor action, they hold Canada's largest cities – Toronto, Montréal and Vancouver – with multicultural museums, sophisticated eateries and wee-hours nightlife. Alberta booms in the Rockies with parks and oil-rich towns. Manitoba and Saskatchewan in the Plains hold big wildlife and arty surprises. The salty Atlantic provinces are tops for seafood munching and whale watching. And the far north is the place to lose the crowds (and roads) and get well off the beaten path.

Ontario

Cuisine ✓✓✓
Parks ✓✓
History ✓✓✓

Farms and Vineyards
At a geological and climactic nexus, Ontario is ripe with agriculture and viticulture. The province's wines are internationally recognized, drawing attention to more than its amazing produce. But that doesn't mean you should skip dinner.

Fresh Air
If you're looking for a simple stroll, a multiday backpacking trip, or some time on the water, Ontario supplies anything from small city green spaces to massive provincial parks. Throw in your binoculars and break in your hiking boots; this is the place to get outside.

Museums
With both Canada's largest city and capital city, and lands steeped in rich history, Ontario is a history-buff's Eden. Artifacts from a bygone era, geological evidence of the province's glacial past and contemporary art are all part of the mix.

p50

Québec

Culture ✓✓✓
Winter Sports ✓✓
Architecture ✓✓

Joie de Vivre

Imagine: Sipping a café au lait and eating a flaky croissant on a sidewalk terrace while the murmurs of a foreign language waft through the air. It's easy to be swept away by the Québécois zest for life, especially when their fine wines, local ingredients and luxurious lodgings are so accessible.

Snow

The Laurentians' jagged peaks offer skiing and snowboarding opportunities, but it's the region's star, Mont-Tremblant, that draws the international crowds Throw in a little French panache and it makes for one heck of an après-ski party in the boisterous village surrounding this majestic mountain.

Historic Style

Nowhere are the vestiges of Canada's colonial past more apparent than in the cobbled stones and grandiose facades of Old Montréal, and within the ancient city walls of Québec City's Old Town.

p210

Nova Scotia

Culture ✓✓
Activities ✓✓
History ✓✓

Cultural Mishmash

Tartan shops, native French speaking villages and First Nation communities are all within kilometers of each other. Throw in some African Nova Scotians and Pier 21, Canada's entry point for over a million immigrants and you have the definition of a cultural melting pot.

Coves, Cliffs & Tides

Coastal coves between evergreen islets are bird and marine mammal habitats that beg you to go paddling. On the Fundy Coast behold the highest tides in the world that constantly change the landscape. Cape Breton Island's vertiginous coastal cliffs are home to moose and nesting bald eagle.

Time Warp

Nova Scotians don't just preserve their historical vestiges, they get in period costume and do old-time activities from lace making to blacksmithing, re-creating the scene as it might have been hundreds of years ago.

p316

New Brunswick

Activities ✓✓
Fishing ✓✓✓
Wildlife ✓✓

You in a Canoe

From the tranquil Chiputneticook Lakes to the quicksilver Tobique River, New Brunswick is absolute tops for canoeing, surely the most Canadian of activities. You can even meet artisans who still make canoes the old-fashioned way, a dying art.

Tie your Flies

Baseball stars and captains of industry used to come to New Brunswick to cast their fly rods into the province's salmon- and trout-choked rivers. Why shouldn't you do the same?

Puffin Lovin'

Whether you're a hardcore bird-watcher or just want to be able to tell your friends you saw a moose, New Brunswick's got plenty of animal action to go around. Your best bet: observing rare Atlantic puffin on desolate Machias Seal Island.

p378

Prince Edward Island

Culture ✓✓
Cuisine ✓✓
Beaches ✓✓

It's All About Anne

Personified by Anne Shirley, LM Montgomery's spunky red-headed star of the *Anne of Green Gables* series, PEI is as sweet and pretty as it's portrayed in the books. Red dirt and sands mimic Anne's hair while white picket fences and fields of wildflowers paint the real-life backdrop.

Lobster Supers, Oysters and Potatoes

Vying with Idaho as potato capital of the Americas, you'll pass vine-covered hills to reach town halls serving fisherman-sized suppers of PEI's second most famous food, lobster. Then hit coves of sunlit fishing boats pulling up succulent Malpeque oysters.

White and Pink Beaches

What's your favorite color? PEI showcases sienna beach flats topped by red-and-white lighthouses, cream-colored road-eating dunes and stretches of white sands that 'sing' when you walk on them.

p420

Newfoundland

Seascapes ✓✓✓
Culture ✓✓
History ✓✓

Great Big Sea

'There's one!' someone shouts, and sure enough, a big, barnacled humpback steams through the water. Or maybe they're referring to the hulking iceberg. Whether you're hiking along shore, out in a boat or just sitting by your B&B's window, Newfoundland's sea delivers.

Strange Brew

The peculiar brogue is vaguely Irish, the slang indecipherable enough to merit its own dictionary. Plates arrive with cod tongues, bakeapple jam and figgy duff. Towns have names like Dildo and Jerry's Nose. This place is so offbeat it even has its own time zone: a *half* hour ahead of the mainland.

Viking Vestiges

They've taken a low-key approach at L'Anse aux Meadows, Leif Eriksson's 1000-year-old settlement, but the bare, forlorn sweep of land is more powerful that way. You can feel the Vikings' edge-of-the-world isolation.

p448

Manitoba

Wildlife ✓✓✓
Open Spaces ✓
Culture ✓

Polar Bears & Whales

Polar bears prowling the ice, wandering the beach, sniffing at you, that's what sub-Arctic Churchill's all about. The biggest predator in the hemisphere can be found year-round but especially in the fall when they turn up by the hundreds. Out on the water in summer, expect to see scores of shockingly white beluga whales.

Muskeg & Wheat

Drive through the south and you'll be mesmerized by kilometer after kilometer of wheat, punctuated by giant grain elevators. In the sub-arctic north, a year-round evergreen swath lives off the rich muskeg, think marshy soil from eons of plants – look for moose.

Oh Winnipeg!

The surprising oasis of great dining, fun nightlife and hip culture rises up from the prairies around it.

p503

Saskatchewan

Wildlife ✓
History ✓
Culture ✓

Alberta

Hiking ✓✓✓
Winter Sports ✓✓
Festivals ✓

British Columbia

Landscapes ✓✓✓
Cuisine ✓✓
Wildlife ✓✓✓

Moose & Critters

Backroads galore wander through the seemingly empty reaches of this huge province – but they're not empty. Saskatchewan is alive with Canada's iconic critters, especially moose, which love roadside boggy bottoms. Oh, and that big moving black blob up ahead? That's a grizzly bear. Next, spot beavers expanding their dam.

Revolution Rocks

In 1885 Louis Riel fought the law and while the law won, he and a band of followers almost beat the army at Duck Lake, a town where people of mixed races had tried living despite serial treaty violations.

The Good Twins

Regina and Saskatoon combine for plenty to do after dark – which is most of the winter. Inventive restaurants using the province's produce combine with pubs serving microbrews made with the region's grains.

p528

Banff & Jasper

Two parks, hundreds of miles of trails, and acres of easily accessible wilderness. If you're ever going to fulfill your latent hiking ambitions, these pioneering protected areas are the places to do it. Banff is the more popular park; Jasper retains a wilder, less developed feel.

Cross-country skiing

While Alberta's downhill resorts heave with skiers, the backcountry is so quiet you can almost hear the snowflakes drop. There's nothing like breaking trail at dawn in stunning places like Tonquin Valley on a pair of cross-country skis with a distant lodge beckoning across the horizon.

Edmonton International Fringe

Edinburgh invented it, but Edmonton has taken the concept of 'alternative theater' and given it a Canadian twist. Uncover new talent at the International Fringe Festival in Old Strathcona where cutting-edge performers offer comedy, satire and weirdness.

p548

Breathtaking Vistas

From jaw-dropping mountains to multifjorded coastlines and from dense old-growth forest to lush islands, BC is a vast, vista-packed idyll for landscape-lovers. Hit the backcountry on a hiking or skiing trip or just set your camera to panorama and snap away.

Dine-around Delights

From North America's best Asian dining scene in Vancouver to a cornucopia of taste-bud popping regional seafood and produce throughout the province, local flavors are a foodie focus here – accompanied, of course, by a BC wine or microbrewed beer.

Wildlife Wonderland

The Inside Passage is alive. Hop a ferry along the coast and stay glued to the deck for orca, whale, seal and much more aquatic delight. Ashore, the entire cast of animal characters is here, especially huge grizzly in the north.

p620

Yukon Territory

Wildlife ✓✓
Parks ✓✓✓
History ✓✓✓

Bears, Oh My!

The Alaska Highway cuts right across the lower third of the Yukon on its twisting journey to its namesake state. But stop to admire the wildlife and you may not bother reaching your destination, there's that much to see. In one afternoon we saw two kinds of bear, moose, bison, wolf, elk and lots of little marmot and other critters. A riot of nature!

Unimaginable Beauty

Kluane National Park is a Unesco-recognized wilderness of glaciers cleaving through granite peaks. You won't just feel small here, you'll feel minute.

Gold!

The Klondike gold rush of 1898 still shapes the Yukon with its spirited sense of adventure. Paddle your way to Dawson City, a time capsule of a town that is as lively and surprising now as then.

p761

Northwest Territories

Northern Lights ✓✓✓
Kayaking ✓✓
Winter Sports ✓

Aurora Borealis

Unusually for the pricey NWT, viewing the aurora borealis is free of charge. Spend a little extra on heated outdoor seating and 'luxury' tepees and you'll hopefully be able to withstand the Arctic temperatures which can plummet to -40°C in winter.

Nahanni National Park

The presence of literally thousands of lakes and rivers means that you can travel almost anywhere in the NWT by water; not least to Nahanni National Park, a Unesco World Heritage site that offers some of the wildest and most spectacular river kayaking in Canada. With no road access, most people go as part of an organized tour.

Dog-sledding

With zero ski resorts, the NWT specializes in more esoteric winter activities such as dog-sledding, a quintessential northern experience that has been a traditional form of Arctic transportation for centuries. Hardy canine teams can be hired in Yellowknife.

p793

Nunavut

Wildlife ✓
Aboriginal Culture ✓✓
Parks ✓✓

Arctic Outfitters

Yes, animals live up here – lots of them, in fact – it's just they're not always so easy to spot. Hook up with a professional Arctic outfitter and sally forth to remote wildlife hotspots for rare viewings of polar bear, caribou, arctic hare and copious species of bird.

Aboriginal Art

Shopping is probably the last thing on most Nunavut traveler's minds, but the quality and finesse of genuine Inuit art is one of the region's biggest cultural draws. Unlikely souvenir outlets can be found in Cape Dorset, Pangnirtung, and territorial capital, Iqaluit.

Untamed Wilderness

With annual visitation numbers that rarely hit three figures, Nunavut's four national parks guarantee a hard-nosed wilderness experience. Sky-high costs are sweetened by the moonlike emptiness of the incredible Arctic terrain.

p809

Look out for these icons:

 Our author's recommendation

A green or sustainable option

FREE No payment required

See the Index for a full list of destinations covered in this book.

On the Road

Ontario

Best Places to Eat

» Blūmen (p182)

» Bijou (p128)

» The Swan (p88)

» Zen Kitchen (p202)

» Respect is Burning (p157)

Best Places to Stay

» Gladstone Hotel (p83)

» Three Houses B&B (p127)

» Bayside Inn (p150)

» Green Door (p190)

» Thunder Bay
International Hostel (p167)

Why Go?

When it comes to culture, cuisine and sophistication, Ontario is on top of its game. When you're here, you can't help but feel a palpable connection with the rest of the planet. Forget ice fishing, conifers and bears for a minute – this is global Canada, big-city Canada, sexy, progressive, urbane Canada.

Toronto, Canada's largest city, is a blazing metropolis overflowing with multicultural arts, entertainment and eating opportunities. Ottawa, Canada's capital, is no longer a steadfast political filing cabinet: contemporary Ottawa is as hip as you want it to be.

Not far from the madding crowds, low-key agricultural towns and historic settlements define Ontario's country civility. And if you're into wildlife, excellent national parks abound. From arctic Hudson Bay in the north to the temperate Great Lakes in the south, you'll find more than enough boreal forests, undulating hills and vineyards to keep you feeling green.

When to Go
Toronto

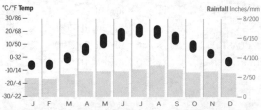

January Ice skate on the world's largest rink, the Rideau Canal in Ottawa

July Cool off on Lake Ontario's oasis, Pelee Island, with beaches and warm water

September Enjoy Ontario's harvests; follow Prince Edward County's Taste Trail for a sample

Only an hour's drive from Toronto, the **Niagara Peninsula** is usually a day-trippers' destination, though it has plenty to keep you occupied for days. Known first for the massive Niagara Falls and second for its wineries, the peninsula also offers plenty of recreational activities including biking, rafting, kayaking and sailing. Niagara-on-the-Lake bursts with boutique shopping and bistro dining, and Niagara's old downtown is in the midst of a revitalization that is attracting art galleries and coffee shops. There's so much to do here, in fact, that you could stay on the peninsula and make a day trip to Toronto!

Prince Edward County is about to steal some of Ontario's food and wine spotlight. Still relatively unknown to outsiders, this island boasts nearly identical soil conditions as France's Bordeaux region. Wineries sprawl throughout the terrain, but the food scene is equally intoxicating: cheese makers, bread bakers, and those who simply take advantage of the great growing conditions by sourcing locally-grown produce all make for a sumptuous visit.

Ontario's Top Parks

» Algonquin Provincial Park (p175)
» Killarney Provincial Park (p151)
» Fathom Five National Marine Park (p140)
» Lake Superior Provincial Park (p162)
» Pukaskwa National Park (p164)
» Quetico Provincial Park (p169)

Don't Forget

» Binoculars – spot birds, moose, otters and deer
» Your drinking arm – wineries in the south and breweries throughout
» Your appetite – Ontario is Canada's bread basket, cheese plate, and salad bowl
» Your biking muscles – with hundreds of kilometers of trails, including the Bruce Trail, Ontario is ready for you to spin your wheels from one side of the province to the other.
» Your inner history buff – every town sports a museum, and Toronto's and Ottawa's are home to some of the world's best.

Planning Your Trip

During summer and major festivals, you must reserve your accommodation in advance. If places are booked, local tourist offices can often help out.

Weather can change rapidly, so pack accordingly if you're planning any outdoor activities.

Fast Facts

» Population: 12,753,700
» Area: 1,076,395 sq km
» Capital: Toronto
» Quirky fact: The longest street in the world, Yonge St, begins in Toronto and runs 1896km to the border of Ontario and Minnesota.

Resources

» Ontario Travel Information Centre (www.ontariotravel.net) has offices throughout the province
» Toronto Tourism (www.seetorontonow.com) is run the by the Toronto Convention and Visitor's Association and is an excellent resource for the city.
» Ottawa Tourism (www.ontariotourism.ca) is Ottawa's official tourist site.

Top Wineries in Ontario

» Norman Hardie Winery & Vineyard (p181)
» Stratus (p103)
» Pelee Island Winery (p133)

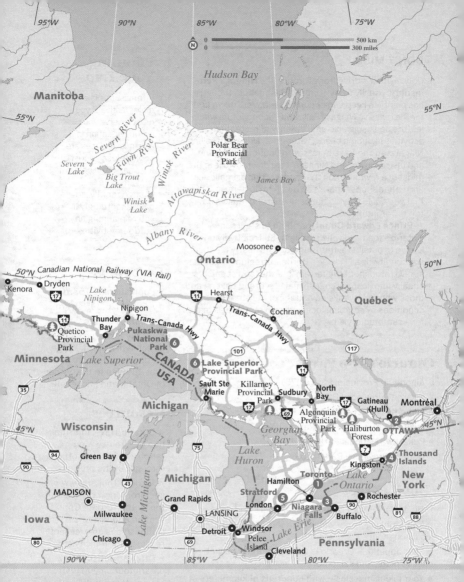

Ontario Highlights

❶ Sample what fashionistas, foodies and fun-lovers adore about **Toronto** (p55)

❷ Take in the Gothic Parliament building, amazing museums and bustling downtown market in the province's capital, **Ottawa** (p191)

❸ Get to the bottom of things on a cruise to the roaring base of **Niagara Falls** (p105)

❹ Ogle cabins perched on impossibly tiny rocks as you cruise through **Thousand Islands** (p188)

❺ Dress up for dinner and a show in emerging foodie destination **Stratford** (p125)

❻ Take a walk on the wild side in northern Ontario's **Pukaskwa National Park** (p164) and **Lake Superior Provincial Park** (p162)

History

When Europeans first stumbled through the snow into Ontario, several Aboriginal nations already called the region home. The Algonquin and Huron tribes had long occupied the southern portion of the province, but by the time European colonization took hold in the early 18th century, the Iroquois Confederacy (aka the Five Nations) held sway in the lands south of Georgian Bay and east to Québec. The Ojibwe occupied the lands north of the Great Lakes and west to Cree territory on the prairies (today's Alberta and Saskatchewan).

The first Europeans on the scene were 17th-century French fur traders, who established basic forts to facilitate trade links with the Mississippi River. With the arrival of the British Loyalists around 1775, large-scale settlement began. After the War of 1812, British immigrants arrived in larger numbers, and by the end of the 19th century Ontario's farms, industries and cities were rapidly developing. In the aftermath of both world wars, immigration from Europe boomed – Toronto has since evolved into one of the world's most multicultural cities.

An industrial and manufacturing powerhouse, Ontario is home to around 39% of Canada's population. Despite boom times in Alberta, Ontario remains the first choice of immigrants from across the globe, with solid employment prospects and Toronto's well-established immigrant support services proving a powerful draw.

Local Culture

Ontario sees itself as a civilized place – the pinnacle of multicultural Canada, detached from the rednecks out west and infinitely more sensible than the Francophiles in Québec. The good citizens of Toronto work hard and play hard, and are fond of making myopic comments like, 'This place is so awesome – why would we want to go anywhere else?' The rest of the country finds this highly irritating, a reaction celebrated in the 2007 film *Let's All Hate Toronto*.

Outside of Toronto, however, you'll find most Ontarians to be rather mild-mannered folk – they know they have a high standard of living and access to all the world's bounty, but they don't feel the need to boast about it. Rural Ontarian towns are generally unassuming (and often unspectacular), but usually have some good pubs, B&Bs and farmers' markets selling high-quality local organic produce.

More than any other province, Ontario is hockey-mad. This is the home of Wayne 'The Great One' Gretzky, and right through the year, huge slabs of prime-time radio are given over to Toronto Maple Leafs and Ottawa Senators talk-back shows, spotlighting the failings of new recruits, dissecting Leafs' coach Paul Maurice's post-match interviews and debating whether or not *this* could be the year. The 'Sens' fell just short of Stanley Cup glory in 2007, but Toronto's 1967 Stanley Cup victory looks set to remain unreprised for some time yet.

Land & Climate

From north to south, Ontario spans a whopping 1730km. It's mostly flat country (this ain't the place for downhill skiing), but is peppered with lakes and forests. The northern continental climate sees bitterly cold winters and mild summers. In southern Ontario there's a collision between cold air from the Arctic north and warm maritime air from the Great Lakes and the Gulf of Mexico. This creates steady precipitation throughout the year, heavy summer humidity and much milder winters than in the north.

That said, the entire province is blanketed with heavy snowfalls during winter. January averages are around -4°C on the Niagara Peninsula and -18°C in Ontario's northern zones. In the south, where most of the population lives, winter snow melts rapidly in spring. As summer draws closer, the strip of land bordering the USA gets increasingly hot and sticky, particularly the Niagara Peninsula. July averages are around 23°C in southwestern Ontario, 10°C in eastern Ontario and 15°C in the north.

Parks & Wildlife

Ontario contains six of Canada's national parks: in the south, Georgian Bay Islands National Park (p146), Bruce Peninsula National Park (p141), Fathom Five National Marine Park (p140) and Point Pelee National Park (p133), the southernmost point of the Canadian mainland. In the north are Pukaskwa National Park (p164)and St Lawrence Islands National Park (p189) – more than 20 islands adrift in the St Lawrence River.

There are also 104 provincial parks here, offering hiking and camping facilities. Campsites for up to six people cost between $23 and $36 per night (plus $12 booking fee), ranging from basic sites sans showers and electricity to well-located plots with showers and plug-in power. Make reservations with **Ontario Parks** (📞888-668-7275; www.ontarioparks.com).

Charismatic megafauna has largely been evicted from southern Ontario due to development and agriculture, but the further north you travel, the more likely you are to spot hairy roadside individuals (no, not lumberjacks).

ℹ Getting There & Around

AIR

Most Canadian airlines and major international carriers arrive at Toronto's Lester B Pearson International Airport. **Air Canada** (www.air-canada.com) and **WestJet** (www.westjet.com) service the province thoroughly. **First Air** (www.firstair.ca) and **Canadian North** (www.canadiannorth.ca) connect Toronto (via Ottawa) with Iqaluit in Nunavut daily.

BUS

Greyhound Canada (www.greyhound.ca) covers southern Ontario, while **Ontario Northland** (www.ontarionorthland.ca) services northern Ontario from Toronto. Booking bus tickets at least seven days in advance can sometimes halve the fare. Long-haul Greyhound routes from Toronto include Montréal ($56, eight to 10 hours, frequently), Winnipeg ($159, 31 hours, four daily) and Vancouver ($220, 65 to 70 hours, one daily).

CAR & MOTORCYCLE

When driving in Ontario, you can turn right on a red light after first having made a full stop. Note that it's now illegal to text or talk on a mobile device while driving (we learned the hard way). The big car-hire companies have offices in larger towns.

TRAIN

VIA Rail (www.viarail.ca) trains service the Ontario–Québec corridor, from Windsor all the way through to Montréal ($205, 10 to 11 hours, four daily). VIA Rail also services northern Ontario into Manitoba.

Ontario Northland (www.ontarionorthland.ca) operates train routes throughout northern Ontario. Its *Northlander* service connects Toronto with Cochrane, from where buses go to Hearst and Kapuskasing. The *Polar Bear Express* runs from Cochrane to Moosonee in northern Ontario.

ONTARIO ITINERARIES

Four Days

Prime yourself for some high times in the neighborhoods of **Toronto**, scanning the scene from atop the **CN Tower**. Two days of museums, bars, clubs, shops and world-class eateries is barely enough...

On day three, bow down before the power and grace of **Niagara Falls** then trundle up the Niagara Parkway to **Niagara-on-the-Lake** to find out what the definition of 'quaint' really is.

On day four, roam northeast to **Ottawa** and sample the cultural offerings of 'Our Nation's Capital.' Wine and dine in Prince Edward County at **Kingston** and the picturesque **Thousand Islands** en route.

Two Weeks

Feel like road trippin'? Heading northwest, take a paddle through the expansive **Algonquin Provincial Park**, visit **Manitoulin Island** for a dose of aboriginal culture, and try **Sudbury** and **Sault Ste Marie** for a history lesson on shipping and mining in northern Ontario.

Continue westward and base yourself in **Wawa** for a few days. Explore the primeval topography of **Pukaskwa National Park** and **Lake Superior Provincial Park**. Greater expanses of unexplored nature lie ahead as you roll on toward **Thunder Bay** and beyond.

If you're heading back to Toronto, rest your road-weary bones in **Elora** in Wellington County.

Wine, Wine, Wine...

Ontario's wines take huge leaps forward with every vintage. If you've got a spare day, wobble your way around the vineyards in the **Niagara Peninsula Wine Country** and see what all the fuss is about.

> **REGIONAL DRIVING DISTANCES**
>
> Toronto to Niagara Falls: 125km
> Toronto to Windsor: 380km
> Toronto to Ottawa: 440km
> Toronto to Thunder Bay: 1470km

GO Train (www.gotransit.com) is Toronto's commuter train, heading as far west as Hamilton and north to Barrie.

TORONTO

POP 5.5 MILLION

Polite yet edgy, urban yet green: Toronto is one of those places where you can get it all. A cultural leader, Toronto has a thriving art community and food scene. And while you could spend weeks pinballing between Toronto's urban virtues, it's a green city too. Parks and natural spaces fill in city gaps, and public transport is top notch.

Toronto is a city driven by the seasons. Dramatic shifts in weather elicit almost schizophrenic behavior from the locals. Washed-out by winter, reticent residents scuttle between doorways to stay out of the April wind – spring here is far from frivolous. Come back in July and it's a whole new ball game: patios overflow with laughing crowds, pubs heave and sway, people play in the parks and along the lakeshore till late. Humidity clogs the avenues and the streetlife hum approaches a roar. In October, Torontonians have a haunted look – reddening maples bring a tight-lipped, melancholy realization that winter isn't far away. Spanked across the face by bitter February, locals head underground into the PATH network of subterranean walkways. Snowy streets are no place to be – instead it's galleries, coffee shops and cozy pubs. And of course, winter is hockey season!

Toronto's many immigrants play along with this well-weathered performance, their relocated cultures transforming the city into a hyperactive human stew of ethnic, subcultural and historic districts. Far from ghettos, this patchwork of neighborhoods shapes the city's social agenda and fuels its progress. Overlaid by a typically laconic Canadian attitude, Toronto is as unpretentious and tolerant as it is complex.

The Greater Toronto Area (GTA) is a deep, loamy plain furrowed by leafy ravines – refuges for raccoons, eagles and more sweaty joggers than seems plausible. Tommy Thompson Park, an artificial wildlife oasis, juts abstractly into Lake Ontario, while the Toronto Islands rustle their leafy boughs at the city skyline.

History

In the 17th century, present-day Toronto was Seneca aboriginal land. Frenchman Étienne Brûlé was the first European here in 1615. The locals didn't relish the visit, the chilly reception they issued temporarily impeding further French development. It wasn't until around 1720 that the French established a fur-trading post in what's now the city's west end.

In 1793 the British took over and John Simcoe, lieutenant governor of the new Upper Canada, chose the site as the capital (formerly at Niagara-on-the-Lake) and founded the town of York. On April 27, 1813, during the War of 1812, American forces reached Fort York and overcame British and Ojibwe troops. The Americans looted and razed York, but held sway for only six days before Canadian troops booted them out and hounded them back to Washington.

In 1834, with William Lyon Mackenzie as mayor, York was renamed Toronto, an aboriginal name meaning 'gathering place.' The Victorian city, controlled by conservative politicians, became known as 'Toronto the Good,' a tag that only began to fade in the 1970s. Religious restraints and strong anti-vice laws were to blame: on Sundays it was illegal to hire a horse, curtains were drawn in department-store windows (window-shopping was considered sinful) and movies weren't allowed to be screened.

Like many big cities, Toronto had a great fire; in 1904 about 5 hectares of the inner city burned, leveling 122 buildings. Amazingly, no one was killed. By the 1920s, Bay St (Toronto's Wall St) was booming, in part due to gold, silver and uranium discoveries in northern Ontario.

In 1941, 80% of the population was Anglo-Celtic, but the city's cultural face changed after WWII. Well over one million immigrants have arrived since: Italian, Portuguese, Chilean, Greek, Southeast Asian, Chinese and West Indian immigrants have rolled into the city in waves. New tongues, customs and cuisines have livened the place up, curing the city's chronic case of one-eyed Anglo reserve.

ⓘ ALL ABOARD THE BIKE TRAIN

The **Bike Train** (☎416-338-5083, 866-333-4491; www.biketrain.ca) initiative provides bike racks and staff on select passenger train routes throughout Ontario. Service between Niagara and Toronto launched in 2007 with the *Greenbelt Express*, and later extended to Windsor/Essex and Montréal. The most recent addition was to Gravenhurst and Bracebridge in 2010. All three major rail carriers (GO Train, VIA Rail and Ontario Northland) participate; check the website for specific routes and rates.

In 1998 five sprawling Toronto suburbs – York, East York, North York, Etobicoke and Scarborough – fused to become the Greater Toronto Area (GTA). As the fifth-largest city in North America, contemporary Toronto is booming – a million miles from its beginnings as 'Muddy York,' Ontario's second-choice town.

◉ Sights

Downtown Toronto is an easy-to-navigate grid, bounded by a hodgepodge of bohemian, ethnic and historic neighborhoods. A plethora of Toronto sights – breweries, water parks, sports stadiums, gardens, historic sites – huddle around the Harbourfront and Financial District at the southern end of downtown. Toronto's oldest and most well-preserved buildings sit just east of here in the Old York neighborhood. The Toronto Islands are where the locals retreat to for a bit of peace and quiet.

North from the lake, modernity and history collide at Dundas Sq: shopping centers, office blocks, museums and majestic theaters all stake their claim. The mixed-bag continues along Yonge St into Bloor-Yorkville and The Annex, where you'll find gracious old mansions, museums, eccentric markets and even a faux castle.

Kensington Market, Little Italy, Queen West and West Queen West are all attractions in their own right – multicultural enclaves bubbling with human activity. Suburban East Toronto and The Beaches are less edgy but are still interesting to explore.

Car parking in Toronto is expensive and traffic congestion is an issue; public transportation is usually the best option.

HARBOURFRONT

At the foot of Yonge and York Sts on Lake Ontario is the redeveloped Harbourfront area. Once a run-down district of warehouses, factories and docklands, the area now teems with folk milling about the restaurants, theaters, galleries, artists' workshops, stores, condominiums and parklands along Queens Quay. Ferries for the Toronto Islands dock here.

Harbourfront Centre   LANDMARK
(Map p64; ☎416-973-4000; www.harbourfrontcentre.com; York Quay, 235 Queens Quay W; ⊙box office Tue-Sat 1-6pm, to 8pm show nights; 🚋509, 510; P) The 4-hectare Harbourfront Centre puts on a kaleidoscopic variety of performing arts events at the **York Quay Centre**; many are kid-focused, some are free. Performances sometimes take place on the covered outdoor concert stage by the lake. Also outside are a lakeside ice-skating rink where you can slice up the winter ice, and the ramshackle **Artists' Gardens** – seasonally rotating raised planter beds constructed by local artists in the spirit of 'guerilla gardening.' Parking costs $12 to $15.

Don't miss the free galleries, including the **Photo Passage** and the functioning **Craft Studio**.

TOP CHOICE **Power Plant Gallery** (☎416-973-4949; www.thepowerplant.org; adult/child/concession $6/free/3, admission free 5-8pm Wed; ⊙noon-6pm Tue-Sun, to 8pm Wed) is a big-reputation gallery celebrating contemporary Canadian art.

Toronto Music Garden   GARDEN
(Map p64; www.harbourfrontcentre.com; 475 Queens Quay W; admission free; ⊙dawn-dusk; 🚋509, 510) Delicately strung along the western harbourfront, the Toronto Music Garden was designed in collaboration with cellist Yo-Yo Ma. It expresses Bach's *Suite No 1 for Unaccompanied Cello* through landscape, with an arc-shaped grove of conifers, a swirling path through a wildflower meadow and a grass-stepped amphitheater where free concerts are held. Contact the Harbourfront Centre box office for performance schedules and guided tour details.

CN Tower   NOTABLE BUILDING
(Canadian National Tower, La Tour CN; Map p64; www.cntower.ca; 301 Front St W; adult/child

Greater Toronto Area (GTA)

5 km
3 miles

To Cathedral
Bluffs Park (1km)

Ellesmere Rd

Lawrence Ave E

Warden Ave

Eglinton Ave E

Pine Hills
Cemetery

Charles Saurial
Conservation
Reserve

St Clair Ave E

Danforth Ave

Kingston Rd

Danforth Rd

Don Valley Pkwy

Don Mills Rd

Edwards
Gardens

Woodbine Ave

Ivan Forrest
Gardens

Balmy
Beach

Queen St E

Kew Gardens

Kew
Beach

Woodbine
Beach Park

Lake Ontario

To David Dunlap
Observatory (13km)
Toronto Centre for
the Arts (15km)

Sunnybrook
Park

O'Connor Dr

Todmorden Mills

Monarch
Park

Gerrard St E

Queen St E

Distillery
District

Tommy
Thompson
Park

Eglinton Ave E

Mount
Pleasant
Cemetery

Riverdale
Farm

Eglinton Ave W

Lawrence Ave W

Mt Pleasant Rd

Yonge St

Avenue Rd

See Downtown
North Map (p60)

Bay St

Toronto
Islands

Wilson Ave

Bathurst St

Casa
Loma

See West
Toronto
Map (p66)

See Downtown
Toronto

See Downtown
Toronto South
Map (p64)

Downsview
Airport

Allen Expwy

Eglinton Ave W

St Clair Ave W

Davenport Rd

Queen St W

Dundas St W

Queen St W

Toronto
City Centre
Airport

To Black Creek
Pioneer Village
(7km)

Keele St

Black Creek Dr

Weston Rd

Jane St

Dundas St W

High
Park

The Queensway

Humber Bay

To Paramount Canada's
Wonderland (15km)

Weston Golf
& Country
Club

St Phillip's Rd

Scarlett Rd

St George's
Golf &
Country
Club

Royal York Rd

Bloor St W

Humber
Marshes Park

Humber
River

Lester B
Pearson
International
Airport

Macdonald –
Cartier Fwy

Eglinton Ave W

Islington
Golf
Club

Islington Ave

Rathburn Rd

Burnhamthorpe Rd

Bloor St

Kipling Ave

Queensway East

Gardiner Expwy

Lake Shore Blvd W

Browns Line

Toronto
Golf
Club

To Mountsberg
Conservation
Area (38km)

Mimico Creek

Etobicoke Creek

Dundas St E

Mimico Creek

$23/15; ☺9am-10pm Sun-Thu, to 10:30 Fri & Sat, to 11pm summer; ⑤Union) Though it's been around for more than 30 years, the funky CN Tower still warrants 'icon' status. Its primary function is as a radio and TV communications tower, but relieving tourists of as much cash as possible seems to be the second order of business. It's expensive, but riding the great glass elevators up the highest freestanding structure in the world (553m) is one of those things in life you just *have* to do. On a clear day, the views from the Observation Deck are astounding; if it's hazy, you won't be able to see a thing. Beware: two million visitors every year means summer queues for the elevator can be up to two hours long – going up *and* coming back down. For those with reservations and sacks full of cash, the award-winning revolving restaurant **360°** (Map p64; ☑416-362-5411; mains $32-65; ☺dinner, lunch & dinner summer) awaits (with 'the world's highest wine cellar'). Elevator price is waived for diners.

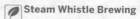

Steam Whistle Brewing

HISTORICAL BUILDING

(Map p64; www.steamwhistle.ca; 255 Bremner Blvd; 45min tour $10; ☺noon-6pm Mon-Thu, from 11am Fri & Sat, to 5pm Sun; ⑤Union, ⛟509, 510; Ⓟ) 'Do one thing and do it well,' is the motto of Steam Whistle Brewing, a microbrewery that makes only a crisp European-style pilsner. Bubbling away in a 1929 train depot, Steam Whistle continually works on being environmentally friendly, in part by using renewable energy, steam heating, all-natural (and often local) ingredients, and using super-cool ginger ale bottles that can be reused up to 40 times. During snappy tours of the premises, guides explain the brewing process in great detail. Tours depart half-hourly from 1 to 5pm and include tastings.

Rogers Centre

STADIUM

(Map p64; ☑416-341-2770; www.rogerscentre. com; 1 Blue Jays Way; 1hr tour adult/child/concession $16/10/12; ⑤Union) Technically awe-inspiring, the Rogers Centre sports stadium opened in 1989 with the world's first fully retractable dome roof. Tours include

TORONTO IN...

Two Days

Quick weekend? Take a rocket-ride up the **CN Tower** – as high as Torontonians get without wings or drugs. Lunch at **St Lawrence Market**, then head up to **Bloor-Yorkville** to splash some cash in the shops. Compensate with a thrifty dinner in **Chinatown**.

On day two check out the amazing **Royal Ontario Museum**, **Hockey Hall of Fame** or **Art Gallery of Ontario** – then take a long lunch in **Baldwin Village**. Afterwards, ride the ferry to the **Toronto Islands** to hire a bike and wheel away the afternoon. Back on the mainland, relax with a pint at the **Mill Street Brewery** in the atmospheric **Distillery District**.

Four Days

With four days to burn, rummage through the boutiques at **Kensington Market** and eat in **Little Italy**. Explore Toronto's underbelly on our **Walking Tour**, or take the streetcar east to explore **The Beaches**. Finish with dinner on the patio of **Queen Mother Café** before catching a comedy show or going clubbing in the **Entertainment District**.

Peruse the shops, bars and eateries along **Queen West** and **West Queen West**. If you're feeling more hot-dogs-and-beer, catch a baseball game at the **Rogers Centre** or hockey at the **Air Canada Centre**.

One Week

Explore some highlights beyond the downtown area: the **Scarborough Bluffs**, **Tommy Thompson Park** or the **McMichael Canadian Art Collection**. Further afield, **Niagara Falls** awaits, while the **Niagara Peninsula Wine Country** makes a worthy/woozy excursion.

TORONTO BY NUMBERS

» Canadian immigrants who settle in Toronto: 1 in 4

» Estimated number of visitors during Pride Week: 1 million

» Pint of local brew: $5

» TTC subway ride: $3

» Percentage of the US population within a day's drive of Toronto: 50%

» Height of the CN Tower: 553m

» Cheap seat at a Blue Jays game: $13

» Parkland as a percentage of Toronto's area: 18%

» Last time the Maple Leafs won the Stanley Cup: 1967

a brain-scrambling video-wall screening footage of past sporting glories, concerts and events, a sprint through a box suite, a locker-room detour (sans athletes) and a memorabilia museum. Tour times vary.

A budget seat at a Blue Jays baseball or Argonauts football game is the cheapest way to see the Rogers Centre. In between times the facility hosts everything from wedding expos to Wiggles concerts. Alternatively, go for a beer and a burger at the Renaissance Toronto, where you can watch the activities through huge windows, or rent a room with a view of the field.

Fort York   HISTORICAL SITE
(www.toronto.ca/culture/fort_york.htm; 100 Garrison Rd; admission & tour adult/child/concession $6/3/3.25; ⊙10am-5pm May-Sep, closed mid-Dec-early Jan; ⛟509, 511; Ⓟ) Established by the British in 1793 to defend the town of York (as Toronto was then known), Fort York was almost entirely destroyed during the War of 1812 when a small band of Ojibwe warriors and British troops couldn't stop US troops.

Today, a handful of the original log, stone and brick buildings have been restored. In summer, men decked out in 19th-century British military uniforms carry out preposterous marches and drills, firing musket volleys into the sky. Kids feign interest or run around the fort's embankments with wooden rifles. Tours run hourly from May to September, and a fancy new visitor's centre was being planned when we visited. It's, off Fleet St W, east of Strachan Ave.

Spadina Quay Wetlands   PARK
(Map p64; ☑416-392-1111; www.toronto.ca/harbourfront/spadina_quay_wet.htm; 479 Queens Quay W; ⊙dawn-dusk; ⛟509, 510) A former lakeside parking lot has been transformed into the 2800-sq-meter Spadina Quay Wetlands, a thriving, sustainable ecosystem full of frogs, birds and fish. When lakeside fishers noticed that northern pike were spawning here each spring, the city took it upon itself to create this new habitat. Complete with flowering heath plants, poplar trees and a birdhouse, it's a little gem leading the way in Harbourfront redevelopment. Aside from the pike, look for monarch butterflies, mallard ducks, goldfinches, dragonflies and red-winged blackbirds.

Ontario Place   AMUSEMENT PARK
(www.ontarioplace.com; 955 Lake Shore Blvd W; day pass adult/child $29/15, grounds-only admission $17/11, Cinesphere per person $8; ⊙10am-8pm late Jun-early Aug, 10am-6pm Sat & Sun only May & Sep; ⛟511; Ⓟ) A 40-hectare fun park, Ontario Place is built on three artificial islands. A 'Play All Day' pass gets you into most of the thrill rides and attractions, including **Soak City** water park, and walk-up seating at the **Cinesphere**, a spiky, space-age gooseberry screening IMAX films. Kids go berserk at soft-play areas like the H2O Generation Station and the Atom Blaster.

Additional attractions like the human-sized MegaMaze and House of Blues concerts at the **Molson Amphitheatre** (☑416-260-5600; www.hob.com/venues/cncerts/molson amp) cost extra. Discounted passes may be available after 5pm and for grounds-only admission. On rainy days, many of the rides, activities and restaurants close.

You can catch a streetcar to Exhibition Place then trudge over the Lakeshore Bridge to Ontario Place, or take the free shuttle bus from Union Station. The shuttle runs daily from June to August, and on weekends in May and September, departing every half-hour between 9am and 7pm. Parking costs $12 to $20.

Exhibition Place   LANDMARK
(☑416-263-3600; www.explace.on.ca; off Lake Shore Blvd W, btwn Strachan Ave & Dufferin St; ⛟511; Ⓟ) Every August, historic Exhibition Place is revived for its original purpose, the Canadian National Exhibition. During 'The Ex', millions of visitors flood the midway for carnival rides, lumberjack competitions and more good, honest,

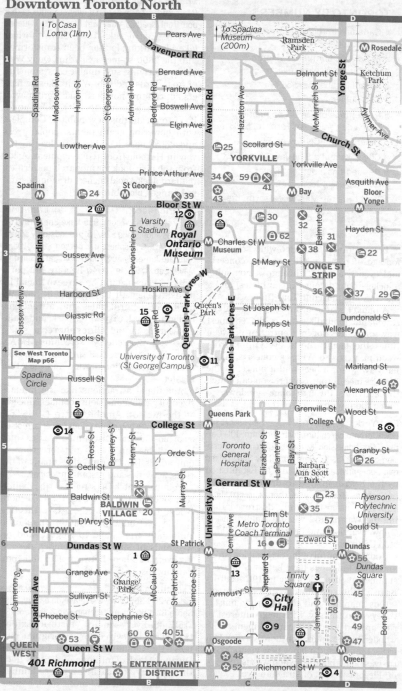

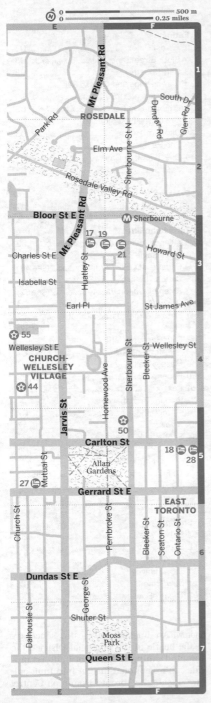

homegrown fun than a Sunday-school picnic in June. The beaux arts *Victory* statue over Princes' Gate has stood proud since 1927, when Canada celebrated its 60th birthday.

Other events held at Exhibition Place throughout the year include the Grand Prix of Toronto in July and a slew of spectator sports and indie design shows. At other times the grounds are often spookily bereft of visitors. Parking costs $12 (after 6pm it will set you back back $9).

FINANCIAL DISTRICT

The area around Union Station is busy night and day with hot-dog vendors, shivering office workers smoking in doorways, and fans heading to hockey games at the Air Canada Centre. Bay St is Toronto's Wall St – the 'Bay St Boys' do their darndest to convince themselves that this is actually New York.

Hockey Hall of Fame　　　MUSEUM
(Map p64; ☎416-360-7765; www.hhof.com; BCE Pl, 30 Yonge St; adult/child/concession $15/10/12; ◎10am-5pm Mon-Fri, 9:30am-6pm Sat, 10:30am-5pm Sun, 9:30am-6pm Jun-Aug; ⑤Union) Inside an ornate rococo gray stone Bank of Montreal building (c 1885) on the Yonge St lower concourse, the Hockey Hall of Fame gives hockey fans everything they could possibly want. Check out the collection of *Texas Chainsaw Massacre*–esque goalkeeping masks, attempt to stop Wayne Gretzky's virtual shot or have your photo taken with hockey's biggest prize – the hefty Stanley Cup (no trifling shield or pint-sized urn for these boys, oh no). Even visitors unfamiliar with this super-fast, ultra-violent sport will be impressed with the interactive multimedia exhibits and hockey nostalgia.

Cloud Forest Conservatory　　GARDEN
(Map p60; ☎416-392-7288; admission free; ◎10am-2:30pm Mon-Fri; ⑤Queen) An unexpected sanctuary, the steamy Cloud Forest Conservatory is crowded with enormous jungle leaves, vines and palms. Information plaques answer the question 'What Are Rainforests?' for temperate Torontonians, distracting accountants from their spreadsheets for a few minutes. It's a great place to warm up during winter, but avoid the area after dark – the adjacent park attracts some pretty lewd types. It's between Richmond and Temperance Sts, west of Yonge St.

FREE **Toronto Dominion Gallery of Inuit Art** MUSEUM
(Map p64; ☎416-982-8473; ground fl & mezzanine, Maritime Life Tower, 79 Wellington St W; ⊗8am-6pm Mon-Fri, 10am-4pm Sat & Sun; ⑤St Andrew) An unexpectedly calm sanctuary in the bustle of the Financial District, the Toronto Dominion Gallery of Inuit Art provides an exceptional insight into Inuit culture. Inside the Toronto-Dominion Centre,

a succession of glass cases displays otter, bear, eagles and carved Inuit figures in day-to-day scenes.

FREE **Design Exchange** INDUSTRIAL MUSEUM
(DX; Map p64; www.dx.org; 234 Bay St; special exhibit surcharge; ☺10am-6pm Mon-Fri, noon-5pm Sat & Sun) The original Toronto Stock Exchange now houses eye-catching industrial design exhibits. The permanent collection includes more than 1000 Canadian pieces that span six decades. Tours ($10) should be booked in advance.

OLD YORK

Historically speaking, the old town of York comprises just 10 square blocks. But today the neighborhood extends east of Yonge St all the way to the Don River, and from Queen St south to the waterfront esplanade. The ghosts of Toronto's past are around every corner.

TOP CHOICE **Distillery District** LANDMARK
(Map p57; ☑416-866-1177; www.the distillerydistrict.com; 55 Mill St; ☺10am-7pm Mon-Wed, to 8pm Thu-Sat, 11am-5pm Sun; ☒503, 504) The slick, 5-hectare Distillery District emerges phoenixlike from the 1832 Gooderham and Worts distillery – once the British Empire's largest distillery. Victorian industrial warehouses have been converted into soaring galleries, artists studios, pricey design shops, coffeehouses, restaurants, the Young Centre for Performing Arts and the Mill Street Brewery. Wedding parties shoot photos against a backdrop of redbrick and cobblestone; clean-cut couples shop for leather lounge suites beneath charmingly decrepit gables and gantries. In summer expect live jazz, exhibitions and food-focused events.

St Lawrence Market MARKET
(Map p64; ☑416-392-7129; www.stlawrence market.com; 95 Front St E; ☺8am-6pm Tue-Thu, to 7pm Fri, 5am-5pm Sat; ☒503, 504; ℗) Old York's sensational St Lawrence Market has been a neighborhood meeting place for over two centuries. The restored, high-trussed 1845 **South Market** houses more than 50 specialty food stalls: cheese vendors, fishmongers, butchers, bakers and pasta makers. Inside the old council chambers upstairs, the **St Lawrence Market Gallery** (☑416-392-7604; admission free; ☺10am-4pm Wed-Fri, 9am-4pm Sat) has rotating displays of paintings, photographs, documents and historical relics.

On the opposite side of Front St, the dull-looking **North Market** is redeemed by a Saturday farmers market and a Sunday antique market (get there at dawn – literally – for the good stuff). Neglected for decades, it was rebuilt around the time of Canada's centenary in 1967. A few steps further north, the glorious **St Lawrence Hall** (1849) is topped by a mansard roof and a copper-clad clock tower that can be seen for blocks.

Parking at the market costs $2 to $6.

THEATRE BLOCK & ENTERTAINMENT DISTRICT

West of the Financial District, occupying two blocks of King St W between John St and Simcoe St, is Toronto's Entertainment District (aka Clubland). The Theatre Block is just south of here – an area crowded with much ado.

401 Richmond ART GALLERY
(Map p60; www.401richmond.net; 401 Richmond St W; ☺Tue-Sat; ☒510) Inside an early-20th-

LAKE ONTARIO

It's a bit like ignoring the elephant in the corner of the room, but Torontonians consistently fail to appreciate their lake. It's not really their fault – lousy urban planning means it's usually impossible to see the water from the city, and lakeshore access has only opened up in recent decades. Chemicals, sewage and fertilizer runoff have traditionally fouled the waters and, although the situation is improving, only the brave and stupid dare to swim at city beaches. For most citizens, Lake Ontario is simply a big, gray, cold thing that stops the Americans from driving up Yonge St.

For the record, Lake Ontario is the 14th largest lake in the world and the smallest and most easterly of the five Great Lakes: 311km long, 85km wide and 244m deep. The name 'Ontario' derives from *Skanadario*, an Iroquois word meaning 'sparkling water,' and, despite the lousy planning and pollution, it still sparkles. Visit the Toronto Islands or Tommy Thompson Park and you'll soon see the lake for what it really is – stoic, powerful and very beautiful. Be sure to tell the locals all about it.

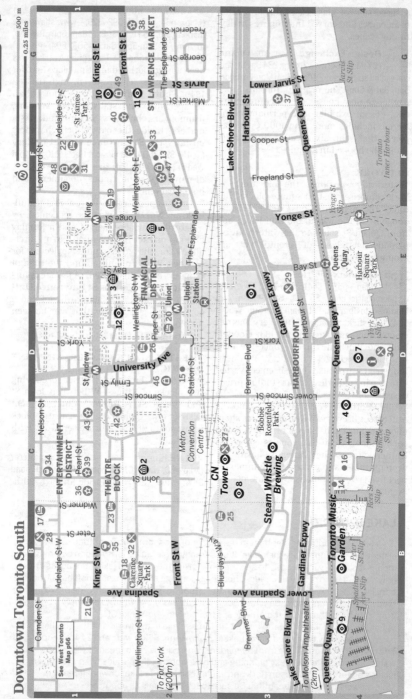

Downtown Toronto South

500 m
0.25 miles

See West Toronto
Map p66

To Fort York
(200m)

To Molson Amphitheatre
(2km)

**ENTERTAINMENT
DISTRICT**

**THEATRE
BLOCK**

**FINANCIAL
DISTRICT**

HARBOURFRONT

ST LAWRENCE MARKET

Camden St
Adelaide St W
King St W
Wellington St W
Front St W
Spadina Ave
Lower Spadina Ave
Blue Jays Way
Bremner Blvd
Lake Shore Blvd W
Gardiner Expwy
Queens Quay W
Peter St
Widmer St
John St
Pearl St
Clarence
Square
Park
Nelson St
Emily St
Simcoe St
University Ave
St Andrew
York St
Station St
Metro
Convention
Centre
CN
Tower
Steam Whistle
Brewing
Bobbie
Rosenfeld
Park
Lower Simcoe St
Bremner Blvd
Bay St
Piper St
Wellington St W
Union St
Union Station
The Esplanade
York St
Harbour St
Gardiner Expwy
Queens Quay W
Lake Shore Blvd W
Toronto Music
Garden
Spadina Ave Slip
Peter St Slip
Rees St Slip
Smith St Slip
Queens Quay W
Lombard St
Adelaide St E
St James
Park
King St E
Front St E
Frederick St
George St
The Esplanade
Market St
Jarvis St
Lower Jarvis St
Harbour St
Cooper St
Freeland St
Yonge St
Bay St
Harbour St
Queens
Quay
Harbour
Square
Park
Queens Quay W
Queens Quay E
Yonge St Slip
Park St Slip
Jarvis
St Slip
Toronto
Inner Harbour
Yonge St
King
Wellington St E
King St E
Nelson St
St James
Park

century lithographer's warehouse, restored in 1994, the 18,500-sq-meter 401 Richmond bursts forth with 130 diverse contemporary art and design galleries displaying the heartfelt works of painters, architects, photographers, printmakers, sculptors and publishers. The original floorboards creak between the glass elevator, ground-floor cafe, leafy courtyard and rooftop garden. A

ONTARIO TORONTO

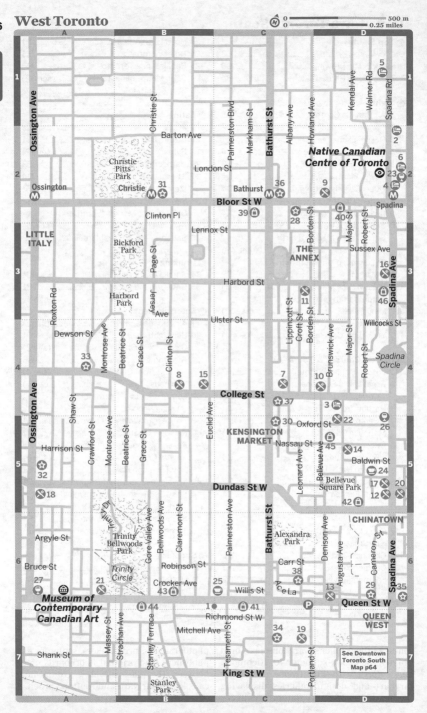

0 500 m
0 0.25 miles

Ossington Ave

Christie St

Barton Ave

Palmerston Blvd

Markham St

Bathurst St

Albany Ave

Howland Ave

Kendal Ave

Walmer Rd

Spadina Rd

5

2

Christie Pitts Park

London St

Native Canadian Centre of Toronto

6

Ossington

Christie

31

Bathurst

36

9

23

4

2

Bloor St W

39

28

Borden St

40

Major St

Robert St

Spadina

Clinton Pl

LITTLE ITALY

Lennox St

THE ANNEX

Sussex Ave

Bickford Park

Page St

16

Spadina Ave

Harbord St

Roxton Rd

Harbord Park

Jersey Ave

Lippincott St

Croft St

Borden St

11

46

Dewson St

Montrose Ave

Beatrice St

Grace St

Clinton St

Ulster St

Brunswick Ave

Major St

Robert St

Willcocks St

33

Spadina Circle

8

15

7

10

College St

37

Shaw St

Crawford St

Montrose Ave

Beatrice St

Grace St

Euclid Ave

30

Oxford St

22

26

Harrison St

3

KENSINGTON MARKET

Nassau St

45

14

32

Leonard Ave

Bellevue Ave

Baldwin St

24

18

Dundas St W

Bellevue Square Park

17

20

12

42

Argyle St

Trinity Dr

Trinity Bellwoods Park

Gore Valley Ave

Bellwoods Ave

Claremont St

Palmerston Ave

Bathurst St

Alexandra Park

Denison Ave

Augusta Ave

Cameron St

CHINATOWN

Spadina Ave

Bruce St

27

21

Trinity Circle

Robinson St

Carr St

38

13

29

35

Crocker Ave

25

Willis St

Ace La

Queen St W

Museum of Contemporary Canadian Art

Massey St

Strachan Ave

Stanley Terrace

43

44

1

41

Richmond St W

Mitchell Ave

Tesamenth St

34

19

QUEEN WEST

Shank St

Portland St

See Downtown Toronto South Map p64

Stanley Park

King St W

new lounge space livens things up. Check the website for events and tours.

Canadian Broadcasting Centre   MUSEUM
(CBC; Map p64; ☎416-205-3311; www.cbc.ca; 250 Front St W; ⊙museum & theater Mon-Fri; ⓢUnion, ⓐ504) Toronto's enormous Canadian Broadcasting Centre is the headquarters for English-language radio and TV across Canada. French-language production is in Montréal, which leaves the president (in a truly Canadian spirit of compromise) stranded in Ottawa.

You can peek at the radio newsrooms anytime or attend a concert in the world-class Glenn Gould Studio. Don't miss the miniature-sized **CBC Museum** with its amazing collection of antique microphones (the 1949 RCA 74DX is a doozy!), sound-effects machines, tape recorders and puppets from kids' TV shows. Next door the **Gra-**

ham Spry Theatre screens ever-changing CBC programming.

QUEEN STREET & DUNDAS SQUARE
Heading north on Yonge St, Dundas Sq is a makeshift public space that's never convinced locals. It's better known for the nearby landmark, the Eaton Centre, which sprawls between Queen and Dundas. Both are east of the Queen St shopping district.

Elgin & Winter Garden Theatre
                                    HISTORICAL BUILDING
(Map p60; ☎416-314-2871; www.heritagefdn. on.ca; 189 Yonge St; tours adult/concession $10/8; ⊙tours 5pm Thu & 11am Sat; ⓢDundas) A restored masterpiece, the Elgin & Winter Garden Theatre is the world's last operating double-decker theater. Constructed in 1913, the stunning Winter Garden was built as the flagship for a vaudeville chain that never really took off, while the downstairs

Elgin theater was converted into a movie house in the 1920s.

Saved from demolition in 1981, the theaters then received a $29 million facelift: bread dough was used to uncover original rose-garden frescoes, the Belgian company that made the original carpet was contacted for fresh rugs, and the floral Winter Garden ceiling was replaced, leaf by painstaking leaf. Public tours are worth every cent.

City Hall
HISTORICAL BUILDING

(Map p60; ☑311, 416-392-2489; www.toronto. ca; 100 Queen St W; admission free; ☺8:30am-4:30pm Mon-Fri; ⑤Queen; ℗) Much-maligned City Hall was Toronto's bold leap of faith into architectural modernity. Its twin clamshell towers, flying-saucer central structure, sexy ramps and funky mosaics were completed in 1965 to Finnish architect Viljo Revell's award-winning design. An irritable Frank Lloyd Wright called it a 'headmarker for a grave'; in a macabre twist, Revell died before construction was finished. Collect a self-guided tour pamphlet at the info desk; don't miss the geeky 1:1250 Toronto scale model in the lobby. Parking is $13.

Out the front is **Nathan Phillips Square**, a meeting place for skaters, demonstrators and office workers on their lunch breaks. In summer, look for the **Fresh Wednesdays** farmers market (10am to 2:30pm), free concerts and special events. The fountain pool becomes an ice-skating rink in winter.

Across Bay St is the 1899-built **Old City Hall** (Map p60; ☑416-327-5614; www.toronto. ca/old_cityhall; 60 Queen St W; admission free; ☺8:30am-4:30pm Mon-Fri), the definitive work of Toronto architect EJ Lennox, the same fellow who built Casa Loma. Now housing legal courtrooms, the hall has an off-center bell tower, interesting murals and grimacing gargoyles. The website also has an online tour, which is handy to visit before your actual visit.

Church of the Holy Trinity
CHURCH

(Map p60; ☑416-598-4521; www.holytrinityto ronto.org; 10 Trinity Sq; ☺services 10:30am & 2pm Sun, 12:15pm Wed; ⑤Dundas) On the west side of the Eaton Centre is the oasislike Trinity Sq, named after the welcoming Anglican Church of the Holy Trinity. When it opened in 1847, it was the first church in Toronto not to charge parishioners for pews. Today it's a cross between a house of worship, a small concert venue and a community drop-in center – everything a downtown church should be!

Textile Museum of Canada
MUSEUM

(Map p60; ☑416-599-5321; www.textilemuseum. ca; 55 Centre Ave; adult/child/concession/family $12/6/6/25, admission free 5-8pm Wed; ☺11am-5pm Thu-Tue, to 8pm Wed, tours 2pm Sun; ⑤St Patrick) Obscurely located at the bottom of a condo tower in a cultureless corner of town, this museum has exhibits drawing on a permanent collection of 10,000 items from Latin America, Africa, Europe, Southeast Asia and India, as well as contemporary Canada. Workshops teach batik making, weaving, knitting and all manner of needle-stuff.

CHINATOWN & BALDWIN VILLAGE

Toronto's vibrant Chinatown occupies a chunk of Spadina Ave between College and Queen Sts; a vermilion twin dragon gate marks the epicenter. West of here, occupying a block of Baldwin St between Beverley and McCaul Sts, is leafy Baldwin Village. The village has Jewish roots, but today's bohemian air stems from counterculture US exiles who decamped here during the Vietnam War.

Art Gallery of Ontario
ART GALLERY

(AGO; Map p60; ☑416-979-6648, 877-225-4246; www.ago.net; 317 Dundas St W; adult/child/concession/family $19.50/11/16/49, admission free 6-8:30pm Wed; ☺10am-5:30pm Tue, to 8:30 Wed, to 5:30 Thu-Su; ₪505) The AGO houses art collections both excellent and extensive (bring your stamina). Renovations, designed by Frank Gehry, were completed in 2008, and include a new entrance and a massive glass and wood facade. Other highlights include rare Québecois religious statuary, First Nations and Inuit carvings, major Canadian works by the Group of Seven, the Henry Moore sculpture pavilion, and a restored Georgian house, **The Grange**. There's a surcharge for special exhibits.

While you're in the 'hood, note that TIFF Cinematheque screens movies at the AGO's Jackman Hall.

YONGE STREET STRIP & CHURCH-WELLESLEY VILLAGE

North of Dundas Sq, the Yonge St Strip falls between College and Bloor Sts, peppered with sex shops, cheap eateries and strip clubs. One block east is Church St, Toronto's gay quarter. The rainbow flag-festooned Church-Wellesley Village centers on the intersection of Church and Wellesley Sts.

Maple Leaf Gardens LANDMARK
(Map p60; 60 Carlton St; SCollege) This hallowed hockey arena was built in an astounding five months during the Great Depression, and was home to the Toronto Maple Leafs for over 50 years. The Leafs lost their first game (and the last at the Gardens in 2009) to the Chicago Blackhawks in 1931, but went on to win 13 Stanley Cups before relocating to the Air Canada Centre in 1999. Over the years, Elvis, Sinatra and the Beatles have all belted out tunes here.

The Gardens were bought by grocery chain Loblaws in 2004, but have sat unchanged since. When we visited, renovations were under way (with a $60 million price tag) that will include sports facilities, a Loblaws store and a memorabilia museum. Renovations are planned to be completed by 2011, at which time the building will reopen as the Ryerson University Sports and Recreation Centre at Maple Leaf Gardens. Check www.ryerson.ca.

BLOOR-YORKVILLE
Once Toronto's version of New York's Greenwich Village or San Fran's Haight-Ashbury, the old countercultural bastion of Yorkville has become the city's *très* glamorous shopping district, done up with galleries, condos, exclusive nightspots, restaurants and cafes. Bloor-Yorkville stretches from Yonge St west to Avenue Rd, south to fashionable Bloor St, and north to Davenport Rd.

Royal Ontario Museum MUSEUM
(ROM; Map p60; ☑416-586-8000; www.rom. on.ca; 100 Queen's Park; adult/child/concession $20/14/17; ⊙10am-6pm Sat-Thu, to 9:30pm Fri; SMuseum) The multidisciplinary ROM was already Canada's biggest natural history museum, even before embarking upon the 'Renaissance ROM' building project, which should be complete by the time you read this. The new work involves a magnificent explosion of architectural crystals on Bloor St, housing an array of new galleries.

ROM's collections bounce between natural science, ancient civilization and art exhibits. The Chinese temple sculptures, **Gallery of Korean Art** and costumery and textile collections are some of the best in the world. Kids file out of yellow school buses chugging by the sidewalk and rush to the dinosaur rooms, Egyptian mummies and Jamaican bat-cave replica. Don't miss

GAY & LESBIAN TORONTO

To say Toronto is G&L-friendly is understating things. 'Gay is the new straight' is closer to the mark! During Pride Toronto, about a million visitors descend on the city. The action is at the Church-Wellesley Village, or simply the 'Gay Village.' Spread along Church St north and south of Wellesley St E is a busy commercial strip that draws mustachioed crowds, promenading and people-watching. Other gay-focused neighborhoods include the Annex, Kensington Market, Queen West and Cabbagetown.

Gay nightlife venues are abundant and although men's bars and clubs vastly outnumber lesbian venues, Toronto is also home to drag kings, women-only bathhouse nights and lesbian reading series.

In 2003 Toronto became the first city in North America to legalize same-sex marriage; apply at **City Hall** (Map p60; ☑416-392-7036; www.toronto.ca/registry-services; 100 Queen St W; license $110; ⊙8:30am-4:15pm Mon-Fri; SQueen). In September 2004 an Ontario Court also recognized the first legal same-sex divorce.

See p871 for Canada-wide G&L resources. Helpful Toronto resources:

519 Community Centre (☑416-392-6874; www.the519.org; 519 Church St; ⊙9am-10pm Mon-Fri, to 5pm Sat, 10am-5pm Sun; SWellesley)

Canadian Lesbian & Gay Archives (☑416-777-2755; www.clga.ca; 34 Isabella St; ⊙7:30-10pm Tue-Thu; SWellesley)

Queer West (www.queerwest.org) Info on west Toronto's gay scene.

This Ain't the Rosedale Library (www.thisaint.ca; 86 Nassau St; ⊙11am-8pm Mon-Wed, 10am-10pm Thu-Sat, to 6pm Sun; SWellesley)

Toronto Women's Bookstore (www.womensbookstore.com; 73 Harbord St; ⊙10:30am-6pm Mon-Wed & Sat, to 8pm Thu & Fri, noon-5pm Sun; ⬛510)

Xtra! Free G&L alternative weekly.

the cedar **crest poles** carved by First Nations tribes in British Columbia. The onsite **Institute of Contemporary Culture** explores current issues through art, architecture, lectures and moving image. There are free museum tours daily; call or check the website for times. There's a surcharge for special exhibits.

Bata Shoe Museum　　　　MUSEUM
(Map p60; 416-979-7799; www.batashoemu seum.ca; 327 Bloor St W; adult/child/concession/family $12/4/10/30, admission free 5-8pm Thu; ◎10am-5pm Tue, Wed, Fri & Sat, to 8pm Thu, noon-5pm Sun; ⑤St George) It's important in life to be well shod, a stance the Bata Shoe Museum takes seriously. Designed by architect Raymond Moriyama to resemble a stylized shoebox, the museum displays 10,000 'pedi-artifacts' from around the globe. Peruse 19th-century French chestnut-crushing clogs, Canadian Aboriginal polar boots or famous modern pairs worn by Elton John, Indira Gandhi and Pablo Picasso.

Gardiner Museum of Ceramic Art MUSEUM
(Map p60; 416-586-8080; www.gardinermuse um.on.ca; 111 Queen's Park; adult/child/concession $12/free/8, admission free 4-9pm Fri & all day 1st Fri of month; ◎10am-6pm, to 9pm Fri, to 5pm Sat & Sun; ⑤Museum) Opposite the Royal Ontario Museum, the Gardiner Museum of Ceramic Art was founded by philanthropists. Spread over three floors, collections cover several millennia; various rooms focus on 17th- and 18th-century English tavern ware, Italian Renaissance majolica, ancient American earthenware and blue-and-white Chinese porcelain. There are free guided tours on Tuesdays, Thursdays and Sundays at 2pm.

UNIVERSITY OF TORONTO & THE ANNEX

Founded in 1827, the prestigious University of Toronto (U of T) is Canada's largest university, with almost 40,000 full-time students and 10,000 faculty and staff. The central St George campus is venerable indeed.

West and north of U of T lies The Annex, a residential neighborhood populated primarily by students and professors. It overflows with pubs, organic grocery stores, global-minded eateries and spiritual venues.

Casa Loma　　　HISTORICAL BUILDING
(Map p57; 416-923-1171; www.casaloma. org; 1 Austin Tce; adult/child/concession $19/10.50/13.60; ◎9:30am-5pm, last entry 4pm; ⑤Dupont; ℗) The mock medieval Casa

Loma lords over The Annex on a cliff that was once the shoreline of the glacial Lake Iroquois, from which Lake Ontario derived. Climb the 27m **Baldwin Steps** up the slope from Spadina Ave, north of Davenport Rd.

The 98-room mansion – a crass architectural orgasm of castellations, chimneys, flagpoles, turrets and Rapunzel balconies – was built between 1911 and 1914 for Sir Henry Pellat, a wealthy financier who made bags of cash from his contract to provide Toronto with electricity. He later lost everything in land speculation, the resultant foreclosure forcing Hank and his wife to move out. Parking costs $3/9 per hour/day.

Spadina Museum　　　MUSEUM
(416-392-6910; www.toronto.ca/culture/spadina; 285 Spadina Rd; tours adult/child/concession $6/4/5, grounds admission free; ◎noon-4pm Tue-Fri, to 5pm Sat & Sun, grounds 9am-4pm Mon-Fri, noon-5pm Sat & Sun; ⑤Dupont; ℗) This gracious museum was built in 1866 as a country estate for financier James Austin and his family. Lit by Victorian gaslights, the interior contains three generations of furnishings, art and fabrics. The working kitchen hosts cooking demonstrations by costumed workers, while **Edwardian Teas** ($20 per person; ◎most Sun, call for bookings), strawberry festivals and summer concerts are held in the apple orchard. When we visited, the museum was closed for re-restoration and was set to open with new exhibits on the 1920s. Parking costs $8.25.

FREE **Provincial Legislature**
　　　　　　　　HISTORICAL BUILDING
(Map p60; www.ontla.on.ca; Queen's Park; ◎tours 9am-5pm Mon-Fri, also Sat & Sun Jun-Aug; ⑤Queen's Park) The seat of Ontario's Provincial Legislature resides in a fabulously ornate 1893 sandstone building, north of College St in Queen's Park. For some homegrown entertainment, head for the visitors' gallery when the adversarial legislative assembly is in session (Monday to Thursday March to June and September to December). Viewing is free, but security regulations are in full force. You can't write, read or applaud as the honorable members heatedly debate such pressing issues as skidoo safety. Free 30-minute tours depart from the information desk.

University of Toronto – St George Campus　　　LANDMARK
(Map p60; www.utoronto.ca; Nona Macdonald Visitors Centre, 25 King's College Circle; admission

free; ☺1hr campus tours 11am & 2pm Mon-Fri, 11am Sat & Sun; ⑤Queens Park, Museum; 🚌506, 510; 🅿) Life at the University of Toronto rotates around the grassy/muddy expanse of **King's College Circle**, where students study on blankets, kick soccer balls around and dream of graduation day in domed **Convocation Hall**.

Dating from 1919, sociable **Hart House** (✆416-978-2452; www.harthouse.utoronto.ca; 7 Hart House Circle; ☺7am-midnight) is an all-purpose art gallery, music performance space, theater, student lounge and cafe. **Soldiers' Tower** next door is a memorial to students who lost their lives during WWI and WWII. A nearby mid-19th-century Romanesque Revival building houses the **U of T Art Centre** (✆416-978-1838; www.utac. utoronto.ca; 15 King's College Circle; ☺noon-5pm Tue-Fri, to 4pm Sat), a contemporary art |gallery for Canadian and world cultures.

If you're architecturally bent or have an inclination for urban planning, check out the **Eric Arthur Gallery** (✆416-978-2253; www.ald.utoronto.ca; 2nd fl, 230 College St; ☺9am-5pm Mon-Fri, noon-5pm Sat), curated by the Faculty of Landscape, Architecture and Design.

On free campus walking tours, student guides shed light on the haunted stonemasons love triangle at the **University College**, and point out how the campus' old cannons aim toward the Provincial Legislature, a stone's throw (or one good shot) away.

Parking costs $15.

Native Canadian Centre of Toronto
COMMUNITY CENTER
(Map p66; ✆416-964-9087; www.ncct.on.ca; 16 Spadina Rd; ☺9am-8pm Mon-Thu, to 6pm Fri, noon-4pm Sat; ⑤Spadina) This community center hosts Thursday-night drum socials, seasonal powwows and elders' cultural events that promote harmony and conversation between tribal members and non-First Nations peoples. You can also sign up for workshops and craft classes, such as beading and dancing.

KENSINGTON MARKET & LITTLE ITALY
Tattered around the edges, elegantly wasted Kensington Market is multicultural Toronto at its most authentic. Eating here is an absolute joy, and shopping is a blast. The streets are full of artists, dreadlocked urban hippies, tattooed punks, potheads,

junkies, dealers, bikers, goths, musicians and anarchists. Shady characters on bicycles whisper their drug menus as they glide by; hooch and Hendrix tinge the air.

Further along College St, Little Italy is an established trendsetting strip of outdoor cafes, hip bars and stylish restaurants that are almost always changing hands – the affluent clientele is notoriously fickle. The further west you go, the more traditional things become, with aromatic bakeries, sidewalk *gelaterias* and rootsy *ristoranti*.

QUEEN WEST & WEST QUEEN WEST
Although Queen West and its extension, West Queen West, may not have many dedicated sights to speak of, they effect a siren's call nonetheless. Toronto's funkiest 'hoods, this is where the wild things are, where locals shop avariciously, dine deliciously and rock into the night.

Museum of Contemporary Canadian Art
MUSEUM
(MOCCA; Map p66; ✆416-395-0067; www.mocca. ca; 952 Queen St W; admission by donation; ☺11-6pm Tue-Sun; 🚌501; 🅿) The MOCCA is the city's only museum mandated to collect works by living Canadian and international visual artists. West Queen West has consolidated as an arts and design precinct – the perfect location for this facility. Permanent holdings only number about 400 works, curated since 1985, but award-winning temporary exhibitions promote emerging artists from Nova Scotia to British Columbia.

EAST TORONTO
The district east of Parliament St to the Don River was settled by Irish immigrants fleeing the potato famine of 1841. It became known as **Cabbagetown** because the area's sandy soil proved cabbage-conducive. Cabbagetown has possibly the richest concentration of fine Victorian architecture in North America – well worth a stroll.

Further North is Greektown (aka The Danforth, on Danforth Ave), and further east Little India (on Gerrard St E) – two versions of heaven for the food-focused.

Tommy Thompson Park
PARK
(Map p57; www.trca.on.ca; Leslie St, off Lake Shore Blvd E; ☺9am-4:30pm Sat & Sun Nov-Mar, 9am-6pm Sat & Sun Apr-Oct; 🚌501, 502, 503) A 5km-long artificial peninsula between the Harbourfront and The Beaches, Tommy Thompson Park reaches further into Lake Ontario than the Toronto Islands. This

THE BLOOR STREET VIADUCT

In his 1987 novel *In the Skin of a Lion*, Toronto author Michael Ondaatje describes the torturous man-versus-steel construction of the Bloor St Viaduct. Completed in 1918, the 490m bridge arcs 40m above the Don River, linking east and west Toronto. Structural engineer Edmund Burke cunningly included a lower deck for future rail transport in his design. When the Toronto Transit Commission (TTC) opened the Bloor–Danforth subway line in 1966, they rolled their trains straight across Burke's bridge without any structural modifications at all.

Farsighted, yes, but what Eddie Baby didn't plan on was the hundreds of miserable Torontonians who would use his bridge to hurl themselves into oblivion. At a peak rate of one every 22 days, around 500 folks decided to call it quits here. The solution? A very expensive barrier of closely spaced steel rods called the 'Luminous Veil,' installed in 2003.

'accidental wilderness' – constructed from Outer Harbour dredgings and fill from downtown building sites – has become a phenomenal wildlife success. It's one of the world's largest nesting places for ring-billed gulls, and is a haven for terns, black-crowned night heronS, turtles, owls, foxes, even coyotes.

The park is open to the public on weekends and holidays; cars and pets are prohibited. Summer schedules offer interpretive programs and guided walks, usually with an ecological theme. At the end of the park there's a lighthouse and some awesome city views.

To get here on public transportation, take any streetcar east along Queen St to Leslie St, then walk 800m south to the gates. Call the **Toronto & Region Conservation Authority** (TRCA; 416-667-6295) for information on shuttles from the gates into the park (May to mid-October). Alternatively, hire a bike or some in-line skates and follow the **Martin Goodman Trail** all the way here.

Riverdale Farm   MUSEUM
(416-961-8787; www.friendsofriverdalefarm. com; 201 Winchester St; 9am-5pm; 506; P) This farm was once the Toronto Zoo, where prairie wolves howled at night and spooked the Cabbagetown kids. It's now run as a working-farm museum, with two barns, a summer wading pool, and pens of sundry fowl and animals (geese, goats, pigs, rabbits, turkeys etc). Kids follow the farmer around as he does his daily chores, including milking the cows at 10:30am. The Tuesday farmers' market (3pm to 7pm May to October) features hippies selling organic goods and buskers playing Appalachian mountain dobros.

THE BEACHES
To residents, 'The Beach' is a rather wealthy, mainly professional neighborhood down by the lakeshore. To everyone else, it's part of The Beaches – meaning the suburb, the beaches themselves and the parklands along Lake Ontario.

Of all the beaches, **Kew Beach** (Map p57; 416-392-8186; www.toronto.ca/parks; dawn-dusk; 501) is the most popular stretch of sand, the boardwalk running east to **Balmy Beach** and west to **Woodbine Beach**.

Adjacent **Kew Gardens** offers restrooms, snack bars, a skating rink, lawn bowls and tennis courts; at the western end there's an Olympic-sized public swimming pool. For cyclists and in-line skaters, the **Martin Goodman Trail** leads past Ashbridge's Bay Park. Off Queen St E, the sunken **Ivan Forrest Gardens** leads to Glen Stewart Ravine, a wilder patch of green running north to Kingston Rd.

RC Harris Filtration Plant   LANDMARK
(416-392-2934; www.toronto.ca; 2701 Queen St E; 501; P) Commanding heavenly views of the lakefront on a priceless slab of real estate, the elegantly proportioned RC Harris Filtration Plant is a modern art-deco masterpiece that has appeared in countless movies and TV shows, as well as in Michael Ondaatje's *In the Skin of a Lion*. Originally residents disparagingly dubbed it the 'Palace of Purification,' due to hefty construction costs during the Great Depression. The operational filtration plant is currently closed to the public, but hard-core Ondaatje fans should call to see if tours are back on the agenda.

TORONTO ISLANDS

Once upon a time there were no Toronto Islands, just an immense sandbar stretching 9km into the lake. On April 13, 1858, a hurricane blasted through the sandbar and created the gap now known as the Eastern Channel. Toronto's jewel-like islands were born – nearly two-dozen isles covering 240 hectares. When you visit the close-knit, 800-strong artistic communities on gorgeous **Algonquin Island** and **Ward's Island,** expect pangs of jealousy. The islands are only accessible by a 15-minute ferry ride.

Centreville Amusement Park

AMUSEMENT PARK

(☑416-203-0405; www.centreisland.ca; day pass adult/child/family $29/21/90, grounds admission free; ⊘10:30am-8pm Jul-Aug, 10:30am-5pm Mon-Fri & 10:30am-8pm Sat & Sun Jun, 10:30am-6pm Sat & Sun May & Sep; 🚢Centre Island) From Centre Island ferry terminal, wander past the information booth to quaint Centreville Amusement Park. Squeezed together are an antique carousel, goofy golf course, miniature train rides and a sky gondola. **Far Enough Farm** zoo presents kids with plenty of opportunities to cuddle something furry and step in something sticky.

South over the Centreville bridge is a well-over head-high **hedge maze** and ticket booths for Toronto Islands **tram tours** (☑416-392-8192; 35min ride adult/child/concession $5/2/4; ⊘1-5pm Mon-Thu, to 6pm Fri-Sun). Further south are changing rooms, snack bars, bicycle rentals and a pier striking out into the lake. Just to the east is a **boathouse** (☑416-392-8192; rentals per hr $15-25; ⊘11am-5:45pm Mon-Thu, to 6:45pm Fri-Sun) where you can rent canoes, kayaks or paddleboats and explore the Islands' lagoons.

Hanlan's Point

PARK

(🚢Hanlan's Point) At the west end of Centre Island by the Toronto City Centre Airport is Hanlan's Point, named after world-champion sculler 'Ned' Hanlan (1855–1904), a member of the first family to permanently settle here. Babe Ruth hit his first professional home run here in 1914 while playing minor-league baseball – the ball drowned in Lake Ontario, the ultimate souvenir lost forever... The sport of iceboating atop the frozen lake was at its peak until the 1940s. Thanks to climate change, winters nowadays are too mild for it.

Beyond the free tennis courts and a fragile ecosystem of low-lying dunes sustaining rare species, the not-so-rare *nekkid* *humanus* roams free on the gray sand of **Hanlan's Point Beach**. Popular with gay men, the beach's 'clothing optional' status was legalized in 1999.

Ward's Island

ISLAND

(🚢Ward's Island) At the western end of Ward's Island is an 18-hole **Frisbee Golf Course** (www.discgolfontario.com; ⊘dawn-dusk). An old-fashioned boardwalk runs the length of the south shore of the island, passing the back gate of the Rectory cafe.

GREATER TORONTO AREA (GTA)

Many of the towns surrounding Toronto have been incorporated into the monstrous GTA. Exploring these areas can be rewarding, but it'll take a fat chunk of your day if you don't have a car.

High Park

PARK

(Map p57; www.highpark.org; 1873 Bloor St W; ⊘dawn-dusk; ⑤High Park, 🚌501, 506, 508; ℙ) Toronto's biggest park is the delightfully unkempt High Park – unfurl a picnic blanket, swim, play tennis, cycle around, ice-skate or just sit amongst great stands of oaks and watch the sunset. Also here is the stage for **Dream in High Park**, **Grenadier Pond** where people ice-skate in winter, the **animal paddocks** (a small children's zoo) and **Colborne Lodge** (☑416-392-6916; www.toronto.ca/culture/colborne.htm; Colborne Lodge Dr; adult/child/concession $6/2.50/2.50; ⊘noon-4pm Tue-Sun Oct-Dec, to 5pm May-Sep, Fri-Sun only Jan-Apr; ℙ), a Regency-style cottage built in 1836 by the Howard family, who donated much of High Park to the city in 1873.

High Park's north entrance is off Bloor St W at High Park Ave. Bus 30B picks up at High Park subway station, then loops through the park on weekends and holidays from mid-June to early September. Otherwise it's a 200m walk to the north gates. The 506 High Park streetcar drops off on the east side of the park. If you exit the park by Colborne Lodge at the south gates, walk down to Lake Shore Blvd W and catch any streetcar back east to downtown.

Scarborough Bluffs

PARK

(☑416-392-1111; www.torontoca/waterfront/tour/scarborough_bluffs.htm; Scarborough; ⊘dawn-dusk; ℙ) The Scarborough Bluffs are a 14km stretch of glacial lakeshore cliffs. Elizabeth Simcoe named it in 1793 after Scarborough in Yorkshire, England. Several parks provide access to cliff tops, with views across Lake Ontario.

From Kingston Rd (Hwy 2), turn south at Cathedral Bluffs Dr to reach the highest section of the bluffs, **Cathedral Bluffs Park** (65m). Erosion has created cathedral spire formations, exposing evidence of five different glacial periods. You can also access the shore at Galloway Rd further east. Below this section of bluffs off Brimley Rd, landfill has been used to form **Bluffer's Park**, a private marina and recreational area.

Unless you have wheels, getting to the bluffs can be a drag, and if you do have a car, parking is limited. One option is to take the subway to Victoria Park, then bus 12 along Kingston Rd. Ask the driver to let you off near Cathedral Bluffs Dr, east of the St Clair Ave E intersection.

Todmorden Mills   HISTORICAL SITE
(☑416-396-2819; www.toronto.ca/todmorden; 67 Pottery Rd; adult/child/concession $5.25/ 1.45/2.25; ⊘noon-4:30pm Wed-Fri, to 4pm Sat & Sun Apr-May & Sep-Dec, 10am-4:30pm Mon-Fri, noon-5pm Sat & Sun Jun-Aug; P) Sitting quietly on the Don River, Todmorden Mills is an industrial relic housed in a late-18th-century gristmill-turned-sawmill, then brewery and distillery, then paper mill. Historical exhibits loiter inside the Brewery Gallery, where eager guides show visitors around old millers' houses and the petite Don train station. The renovated **Papermill Theatre and Gallery** (gallery admission free) showcases local and emerging artists, as well as performances by the resident Eastside Players. Nature paths start near the bridge and wind back to the secluded **Todmorden Mills Wildflower Preserve** (www.hopscotch.ca/ tmwp), 9 hectares of wildflowers growing on former industrial wasteland, complete with boardwalks and viewing platforms. To get here by public transport, you can catch the subway to Broadway then bus 8, 62, 87 or 100.

🏃 Activities

They're often mummified in winter layers, but Torontonians still like to stay in shape. Outdoor activities abound, with folks cycling, blading and running along the lakeshore, hiking up the city's ravines and paddling on Lake Ontario during summer. Ice-skating and hockey are winter faves, but don't be surprised if you see hard-core cyclists on icy streets, or hockey players skating on artificial ice in mid-July.

Cycling & In-Line Skating
For cyclists and in-line skaters, the **Martin Goodman Trail** is the place to go. This paved recreational trail stretches from The Beaches through Harbourfront to the Humber River in the west – head for the lake and you'll find it. On the way you can connect to the Don Valley mountain-bike trails at Cherry St. On the **Toronto Islands**, the south-shore boardwalk and the interconnecting paved paths are car-free. You can also cycle or skate around **High Park**. If you fancy a longer trek, the Martin Goodman Trail is part of the **Lake Ontario Waterfront Trail** (www.waterfronttrail.org), stretching 450km from east of Toronto to Niagara-on-the-Lake, where you pick up the paved recreational trail on the **Niagara Parkway** (p109).

Recommended maps for cyclists include MapArt's *Toronto with Bicycle Routes* ($3.95) and the *Official Lake Ontario Waterfront Trail Mapbook* ($9.95).

Useful bicycling organisations include:

Community Bicycle Network   BIKE HIRE
(Map p66; ☑416-504-2918; www.communit ybicyclenetwork.org; 761 Queen St W; rental 1st day/2nd day/week $25/10/50; ⊘noon-6pm Mon-Sat; ☐501) What used to be a bike-share program is now strictly rentals, though staff can help with repairs and information.

Europe Bound Outfitters   BIKE HIRE
(Map p64; ☑416-601-1990; 47 Front St; ⊘10am-7pm Mon-Fri, to 6pm Sat, 11am-5pm Sun; ☐503) Mountain bikes and tandems with helmets from $30 per day.

Toronto Bicycling Network   CYCLING CLUB
(☑416-760-4191; www.tbn.on.ca) This recreational cycling club is an excellent resource, with organized rides open to nonmembers for a $5 fee.

Toronto Islands Bicycle Rental   BIKE HIRE
(☑416-203-0009; bicycles/tandems per hr $7/14, 2-/4-seat quadricycles $16/40; ⊘10am-5pm Jun-Aug, Sat & Sun only May & Sep; ☒Centre Island)

Wheel Excitement   BIKE & SKATE HIRE
(Map p64; ☑416-260-9000; www.wheelex citement.ca; 249 Queens Quay W; bicycles & in-line skates per hr/day $15/30; ⊘10am-6pm; ☐509, 510) Close to ferries for Toronto Islands; take a bike.

Hiking
Feel like stretching your legs? Delve into Toronto's city parks, nature reserves or

ravines. Alternatively, hook up with a group such as **Hike Ontario** (📞905-277-4453, 800-894-7249; www.hikeontario.com) or **Toronto Bruce Trail Club** (📞416-763-9061; www.torontobrucetrailclub.org) for hardy day hikes.

Ice-Skating
In winter there are some cool (literally) places to ice-skate downtown, including **Nathan Phillips Square** outside City Hall and at the **Harbourfront Centre**. These artificial rinks are open daily (weather permitting) from 10am to 10pm, mid-November to March. Admission is free; skate rental costs $7. Contact **Toronto Parks & Recreation** (📞416-397-2628; www.toronto.ca/parks) for information on other rinks around town, including those at **Kew Gardens** near Kew Beach and **Trinity Bellwoods Park** in West Toronto. If it's been *really* cold, you can skate on **Grenadier Pond** in High Park.

Swimming
Torontonians don't like swimming in Lake Ontario, despite the presence of a dozen city beaches tended by lifeguards from July to August. Water quality can be lousy, especially after rain; check with Toronto's **Beach Water Quality Hotline** (📞416-392-7161; www.city.toronto.on.ca/beach).

The City of Toronto operates more than a dozen Olympic-sized outdoor swimming pools, open dawn-to-dusk during summer. Check www.toronto.ca/parks/opening pools2005.htm for hours and locations.

Water Sports
Choose from sailboat, kayak, canoe and windsurfer rentals and lessons.

Harbourfront Canoe & Kayak Centre   BOATING
(Map p64; 📞416-203-2277, 800-960-8886; www.paddletoronto.com; 283a Queen's Quay W; canoes per hr/day $30/60, kayaks $20/50, tandem kayaks $30/65; ⏱noon-6pm Mon-Fri, from 10am Sat-Sun; 🚋509, 510; Ⓟ) Offers lake paddles and lessons. Parking costs $7.

Queens Quay Sailing & Powerboating   BOATING
(Map p64; 📞416-203-3000; www.qqy.ca; 275 Queens Quay W; sailboats per 3hr from $75, power boats per hr from $65; ⏱9am-9pm May-Sep, to 5pm Mon-Fri Oct-Apr; 🚋509, 510; Ⓟ) Sail and power-boat rentals and lessons. Parking costs $5 to $8.

Toronto Windsurfing Club   WINDSURFING
(📞416-461-7078; www.torontowindsurfingclub.com; 2 Regatta Rd; rental per hr $30; Ⓟ)

Windsurfing rental and lessons at Cherry Beach. Get off the 172 bus at Commissioners St and walk 10 minutes south.

Offbeat Toronto
In Toronto, if you're into something weird, obsessive or perverse, you can bet there's someone else doing it too. Some of the weirder festivals include Caribana, with its booty-licious carnival parade; Nuit Blanche, a sleepless night of kooky urban art experiences; and the Toronto Buskerfest.

Cineforum   CINEMA
(Map p66; www.cineforum.ca; 463 Bathurst St; over/under 24yr $20/10; ⏱screenings 7pm & 9pm Sat-Thu; 🚋506, 511) Though there have been a few attempts to shut it down, an off-the-wall experience (or perhaps *on*-the-wall) still awaits at Cineforum. Irascible Torontonian character Reg Hartt wraps posters around telephone poles advertising his cinema – the front room of his house where he showcases classic and avant-garde films. Animation retrospectives are his specialty, as are Salvador Dalí prints. Come prepared for idiosyncratic lectures designed to expand your consciousness (like 'What I Learned from LSD'), sometimes delivered while movies are playing. Seats 20; bring your own food and drink.

Theatre Passe Muraille   THEATER
(Theater Beyond Walls; Map p66; 📞416-504-7529; www.passemuraille.on.ca; 16 Ryerson Ave; tickets $20-35, previews $16; ⏱shows 8pm Tue-Sat; 🚋501) Theatre Passe Muraille is an alternative theater in the old Nasmith's Bakery & Stables. Since the 1960s, it has focused on radical new plays with contemporary Canadian themes. Postperformance chats with cast and producers occur often. Saturday matinees are 'Pay What You Can.'

Come as You Are   ADULT STORE
(Map p66; 📞416-504-7934, 877-858-3160; www.comeasyouare.com; 701 Queen St W; ⏱11am-7pm Mon-Wed & Sat, to 9pm Thu & Fri, noon-5pm Sun; 🚋501) Catering to all genders and orientations, Canada's pioneering co-op sex shop sells it all. Sign up for a workshop on erotic photography or Bondage 101!

Beguiling   BOOKSTORE
(Map p66; www.beguiling.com; 601 Markham St; ⏱11am-7pm Mon-Thu & Sat, to 9pm Fri, noon-6pm Sun; Ⓢ Bathurst) Need a comic book fix? Beguiling is the kind of crowded, mixed-up place that Robert Crumb would drop by

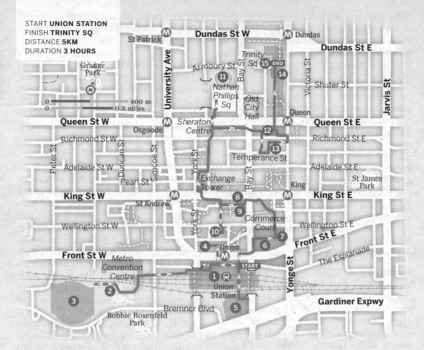

START **UNION STATION**
FINISH **TRINITY SQ**
DISTANCE **5KM**
DURATION **3 HOURS**

Walking Tour
Subterranean Toronto Blues

❯ When the weather freezes your nose off (or is too hot!), duck into Toronto's underground **PATH** (www.city.toronto.on.ca/path) system, an accidental 28km labyrinth of subterranean corridors connecting downtown sights, skyscrapers and shops.

From ➊ **Union Station**, follow the tubular SkyWalk over the railroad tracks to the ➋ **CN Tower**, next to the ➌ **Rogers Centre**. Retrace your steps to Union Station, cross beneath Front St and spiral up the staircase into ➍ **Fairmont Royal York**. Back inside the basement concourse of Union Station, follow the signs to the ➎ **Air Canada Centre** – home of the Maple Leafs and Raptors – and browse the architectural conservation displays near the Bay St doors.

Back at Union Station, then go outside into Union Station's TTC section below Front St W. Turn sharp right just inside the doors and follow the color-coded arrows to ➏ **BCE Place** and ➐ **Hockey Hall of Fame**. Wander through Commerce Court to the ➑ **Toronto-Dominion Centre**. Beyond the digital stock-market displays, go left and take the stairs up to the ➒ **Design Exchange**.

Back below the TD Centre, follow the signs for the TD Waterhouse Tower to the ➓ **Toronto Dominion Gallery of Inuit Art**. Back to the TD Centre and chase the signs toward the Standard Life Centre, the Exchange Tower then the Richmond-Adelaide Complex. The Sheraton Centre Hotel is next, before ⑪ **City Hall** – pop your head above ground to see ice-skaters in Nathan Phillips Sq.

Back underground on the PATH, follow the signs for ⑫ **The Bay** department store. Then through the basement, diverting right through a striped corridor and up some stairs out to Temperance St. It's a sprint from here to the ⑬ **Cloud Forest Conservatory**. Warm up inside, then cross the street and enter The Bay again, reconnecting with the PATH. Pursue the signs to the ⑭ **Eaton Centre** (p95), walk to the north end of the mall then take the escalators up two levels. Outside is Trinity Sq in the shadows of the ⑮ **Church of the Holy Trinity**.

(in fact, he once did). Be mesmerized by original 'zines, indie comics, pop culture books, limited edition artworks and posters. Check the website for events.

Matador   NIGHTCLUB
(466 Dovercourt Rd; ☉2am-5:30am Fri & Sat; ☎506) Matador is a hard-to-believe club just west of Ossington Ave and Little Italy, where there's been late-night dance-floor chaos for more than 40 years. Shuffle in under the rusty ballroom sign for live bands playing honky-tonk and classic rock. It's alcohol-free, but if you're up this late, chances are you won't need any more.

Tattoo Shops
Body art in Toronto is almost mainstream – you'd run out of body parts before running through the city's tattoo and piercing shops. Our favorites:

New Tribe Map p60; ☎416-977-2786; www. newtribe.ca; 2nd fl, 232 Queen St W; ☉11am-8pm Mon-Thu, to 10pm Fri & Sat, noon-6pm Sun; ☎501)

Way Cool Tattoos (Map p66; ☎416-603-0145; www.waycool-queen.com; 675 Queen St W; ☉noon-midnight Mon-Sat, to 8pm Sun; ☎501, 511)

☞ Tours
Boat
Several companies run harbor and Toronto Islands boat tours between May and September. Most sail from the Harbourfront beside Queen's Quay Terminal or York Quay Centre. For shorter excursions, just show up and buy a ticket at the quay; reservations are recommended for brunch and dinner cruises. Keep in mind that ferries to the Toronto Islands offer spectacular city views for half the price!

Great Lakes Schooner Company
                                        BOAT TOURS
(Map p64; ☎416-203-2322; www.tallship cruisestoronto.com; 90min cruise adult/child/ concession $22/11/20; ☉Jun-Aug; ☎509, 510) The dashing black three-master *Kajama*, a 1930 German trading schooner, sails from the foot of Lower Simcoe St, but there's usually a ticket kiosk beside Queen's Quay Terminal.

Mariposa Cruises   BOAT TOURS
(Map p64; ☎416-203-0178, 866-627-7672; www. mariposacruises.com; Queen's Quay Terminal, 207 Queens Quay W; 1hr tour adult/child/concession $20/13/18; ☉May-Sep; ☎509, 510) Nar-

rated harbor and two-hour buffet lunch tours (adult/child $49/25). Sunday brunch and dinner-and-dance cruises, too.

Toronto Harbour Tours   BOAT TOURS
(Map p64; ☎416-868-0400; www.torontotours. com; Pier 6, Queens Quay W; 1hr cruise adult/ child/concession $25/15/23; ☉11am-5pm Apr-May, 10am-9pm Jun-Aug, 10am-5pm Sep-Oct; ☎509, 510) Narrated tour departures every half-hour. Also offers evening cruises and various city/harbor tour combos (some including the CN Tower).

Bus
Toronto bus tours are convenient, but with TTC day passes being so cheap, a do-it-yourself tour makes perfect sense. Try the following for something organized, or if you want to get to Niagara Falls.

ROMBus   BUS TOURS
(Map p60; ☎416-586-5797; www.rom.on.ca; 100 Queen's Park; full-day tours $110-140; ⒮Museum) Monthly tours arranged around historical, cultural and architectural themes are organized by the Royal Ontario Museum.

Toronto Hippo Tours   BUS TOURS
(Map p64; ☎416-703-4476, 877-635-5510; www.torontohippotours.com; 151 Front St W; 90min tour adult/child/concession/family $38/25/33/110; ☉10am-6pm May-Nov; ⒮Union) Amphibious buses take passengers on goofily narrated hourly tours of downtown before splashing into the lake.

JoJo Tours   BUS TOURS
(☎416-201-6465, 888-202-3513; http://home. interlog.com/~jojotour; Niagara day tour $50) Budget Niagara Falls tours (May-Oct) include a stop at a winery and Niagara-on-the-Lake. Winter tours include dog-sledding and ice fishing.

Gray Line Tours   BUS TOURS
(Map p60; ☎800-594-3310; www.grayline.ca; departs Metro Toronto Coach Terminal, 610 Bay St; 3-day pass adult/child/concession/family $34.50/18/31/95; ☉9am-4pm; ⒮Dundas) Two-hour, double-decker bus tours of central Toronto – hop-on, hop-off running hourly. Buy tickets on board. Niagara Falls tours also available.

Chariots of Fire   BUS TOURS
(☎905-693-8761, 866-833-0460; www. chariots-of-fire.com; day tours $60; ☉May-Oct) Budget Niagara Falls tours including a *Maid of the Mist* boat ride and Niagara-on-the-Lake.

Special events for children take place throughout the year in Toronto; the Harbourfront Centre produces ongoing events through HarbourKIDS. The Canadian National Exhibition also has events in August.

Climb a rock wall, journey to the center of a human heart, catch a criminal with DNA fingerprinting and race an Olympic bobsled at the excellent, interactive **Ontario Science Centre** (www.ontariosciencecentre.ca; 770 Don Mills Rd; Science Centre adult/child/concession $18/11/13.50, Omnimax $12/8/9, combined ticket $25/15/19; ☉10am-7pm; **P**). Over 800 high-tech exhibits and live demonstrations wow the kids (and the adults at the back, pretending not to be interested). Also here is the giant domed Omnimax Cinema. Check the website for family events, including theme-night sleepovers ($54, reservations required). Parking is $8. To get here, take the subway to Eglinton then bus 34, or Pape then bus 25.

The interactive exhibits at the **Ontario Science Centre** and **Royal Ontario Museum** are fabulous. The **Gardiner Museum of Ceramic Art** runs regular children's clay classes.

During summer keep 'em occupied at **Ontario Place** or **Paramount Canada's Wonderland** (www.canadas-wonderland.com; 9580 Jane St, Vaughan; day pass adult/child/concession $55/32/32; ☉10am-10pm Jun-Aug, Sat & Sun only late Apr-late May & early Sep-early Oct; **P**), a state-of-the-art amusement park with over 60 rides. Highlights include some lunch-losing roller coasters, an exploding volcano, a 20-hectare Splash Works water park, and the Fantastic World of Hanna-Barbera for the young 'uns. Queues can be lengthy; most rides operate rain or shine. Wonderland is a 45-minute drive northwest of downtown Toronto on Hwy 400. Exit at Rutherford Rd, 10 minutes north of Hwy 401. Alternatively, from Yorkdale or York Mills subway stations catch GOTransit's hourly **Wonderland Express Bus** (www.gotransit.com; adult/child $5.15/2.60; ☉9am-5:30pm). Parking costs $10.

Black Creek Pioneer Village (www.blackcreek.ca; 1000 Murray Ross Pkwy, Downsview; adult/child/concession $15/11/14; ☉9:30am-4pm Mon-Fri, 11am-5pm Sat & Sun May-Dec; **P**) re-creates rural life in 19th-century Ontario. Workers in period costume attend farm animals, play fiddlin' folk music and demonstrate country crafts using authentic tools and methods. Shops sell the artisans' handiwork – everything from tin lanterns to slate boards to licorice plugs. The village is a 40-minute drive northwest of downtown. Take the subway to Finch then bus 60. Parking costs $6.

Drop by story-time at the **Toronto Public Library – Lillian H Smith Branch** (Map p60; www.torontopubliclibrary.ca; 239 College St; ☉9am-8:30pm Mon-Thu, to 6pm Fri, to 5pm Sat, also 1:30-5pm Sun Sep-Jun; 🚌506, 510) or catch a show at the innovative **Lorraine Kimsa Theatre for Young People** (Map p64; ☎416-862-2222; www.lktyp.ca; 165 Front St E; ☉box office 9am-5pm; 🚌503, 504), delivering enlightening children's plays.

A handy online resource for parents is www.helpwevegotkids.com, which lists everything child-related in Toronto, including babysitters and day-care options.

Walking & Cycling

The easiest way to experience Toronto is on foot, though cycling tours allow you to cover a bit more territory.

FREE **ROMWalks**   WALKING TOURS
(☎416-586-8097; www.rom.on.ca; ☉Wed & Sun evenings May-Sep) Volunteers from the Royal Ontario Museum lead one- to two-hour historical and architectural walking tours, rain or shine.

A Taste of the World   WALKING TOURS
(☎416-923-6813; www.torontowalksbikes.com; 2-3½hr tours $25-45) Quirky, well-qualified guides lead offbeat walking and cycling tours of Toronto's nooks and crannies, usually with a foodie focus. Reservations recommended.

FREE **Heritage Toronto**   WALKING TOURS
(☎416-338-3886; www.heritage toronto.org; ☉weekends May-Sep) Excellent historical, cultural and nature walks led by museum experts and neighborhood historical society members last from one to three hours. Reservations not required. You can also download an audio tour from the website.

✯ Festivals & Events

January–February

WinterCity Festival CULTURAL FESTIVAL
(www.toronto.ca/special_events) Toronto breaks the late-January winter shackles with this city-wide celebration of culture, cuisine and the arts. Many events are free.

April

Hot Docs FILM FESTIVAL
(www.hotdocs.ca) North America's largest documentary film festival screens more than 100 docos from around the globe.

May

Doors Open Toronto CULTURAL FESTIVAL
(www.toronto.ca/doorsopen) Architectural treasures creak open their doors and let the public sneak a peek.

June

North by Northeast FILM FESTIVAL
(NXNE; www.nxne.com) An affordable wristband gets you into 400 new music and film shows at over 30 clubs, all squeezed into one long, boozy weekend in mid-June.

Pride Toronto GAY PRIDE FESTIVAL
(www.pridetoronto.com) Toronto's most flamboyant event celebrates all kinds of sexuality, climaxing with an out-of-the-closet Dyke March and the outrageous Pride Parade. Pride's G-spot is in the Church-Wellesley Village; most events are free. Late June.

National Aboriginal Day CULTURAL FESTIVAL
(www.toronto.ca/diversity/events-aboriginal-day.htm) Canada's heritage of First Nations, Inuit and Métis cultures is celebrated on the summer solstice (June 21), with events leading up to it the week before.

Toronto Downtown Jazz Festival
MUSIC FESTIVAL
(www.tojazz.com) For 10 days in late June/early July, jazz, blues and world beats blaze in the city's streets, nightclubs and concert halls, with musical workshops, film screenings and harbor cruises.

July

Toronto Fringe Festival CULTURAL FESTIVAL
(www.fringetoronto.com) Over two weeks in early July, dozens of stages host dozens of plays ranging from utterly offbeat to deadly serious, plus a program of kids' plays too.

Honda Indy Toronto CAR RACE
(www.hondaindytoronto.com) Drivers from the international circuit compete in front of massive crowds; engine noise abounds as cars top 300km/h along Lakeshore Blvd.

Beaches International Jazz Festival
MUSIC FESTIVAL
(✆416-698-2152; www.beachesjazz.com) Going strong for almost 20 years, this high-caliber, free three-day jazz fest in late July fills stages along Queen St E, at Kew Gardens and in the Distillery District.

August

Caribana CARIBBEAN FESTIVAL
(www.caribana.com) North America's largest Caribbean festival, from late July into early August. The carnival parade, featuring florid and almost-not-there costumes, takes five hours to gyrate past – damn, that's some party!

Canadian National Exhibition
AGRICULTURAL FESTIVAL
(CNE; www.theex.com) Dating from 1879, 'The Ex' features over 700 exhibitors, agricultural shows, lumberjack competitions, outdoor concerts and carnivalia at Exhibition Place. The air show and Labour Day fireworks take the cake.

Scotiabank Buskerfest MUSIC FESTIVAL
(www.torontobuskerfest.com) For three days in late August, a ragtag troupe of Canadian and international buskers descends on St Lawrence Market: expect sword-swallowers, jugglers and musicians of unpredictable merit.

September

Toronto International Film Festival
FILM FESTIVAL
(TIFF; torontointernationalfilmfestival.ca) Toronto's prestigious 10-day celebration is one of the world's best film festivals and a major cinematic event. Films of all lengths and styles are screened in late September, as celebs shimmy between gala events and the gorgeous new Bell Lightbox. Buy tickets well in advance.

Nuit Blanche CULTURAL FESTIVAL
(www.scotiabanknuitblanche.ca) Over 130 overnight urban art experiences, all over town. Contrived 'chance encounters,' interactive dance pieces, and an all-night street market are part of the fun. Late September.

October
International Festival of Authors
WRITERS FESTIVAL

(www.readings.org) Bookish, mid-October festival corralling acclaimed authors from Canada and abroad at the Harbourfront Centre. Readings, discussions, lectures, awards and book signings. Kid-friend events, too.

November
Canadian Aboriginal Festival
CULTURAL FESTIVAL

(www.canab.com) A multiday late-November celebration at the Rogers Centre involving dancing, drumming, crafts, films, traditional teachings and a lacrosse competition. Canada's biggest aboriginal festival.

🛏 Sleeping

Hold onto your wallets, it's gonna get ugly... Finding good-value accommodations in Toronto is the most difficult and expensive part of your trip. Reservations outside of winter are mandatory – decent options are full every night from Victoria Day (around mid-May) to the last vestiges of summer. Booking ahead also limits the sting of wildly fluctuating hotel tariffs – many places charge double or triple the off-peak rates during summer and major festivals. Some hostels, guesthouses and B&Bs don't charge tax, but hotels always do. Check hotel websites for discounts.

Downtown Toronto offers historic hotels, boutique digs and lakefront properties. It can be pricey, but you don't have to spend big to be close to the action. Guesthouses and B&Bs are prolific in eastern Toronto, the Church-Wellesley Village and The Annex. Budget beds are hard to find, but there are some top-quality youth hostels around.

Toronto's thriving B&B industry caters to most budgets. Many B&Bs require a two-night minimum stay. A handy online resource is www.bbcanada.com, with around 100 city listings. Booking agencies are another way to save time and money.

Bed & Breakfast Homes of Toronto
B&B

(416-363-6362; www.bbcanada.com/asso ciations/toronto2) Anything from modest family homes to deluxe suites.

Downtown Toronto Association of Bed and Breakfast Guest Houses
B&B

(416-483-8032; www.bnbinfo.com) Rooms in various neighborhoods, mostly in renovated Victorian houses.

Toronto Bed & Breakfast Reservation Service
B&B

(705-738-9449, 877-922-6522; www.toron tobandb.com) The oldest agency in town with a dozen central listings.

HARBOURFRONT
Renaissance Toronto
HOTEL $$$

(Map p64; 416-341-7100, 800-237-1512; www. renaissancehotels.com; 1 Blue Jays Way; d/ste from $290/325; S Union; P ⊕ ✳ 🛜 🏊) Seventy of the impressive rooms here overlook the Rogers Centre playing field – if you book one, be prepared for floodlights and hollering sports fans! If you'd rather use your room for sleeping, the restaurant and bar also overlook the field. Parking costs $20 to $30.

FINANCIAL DISTRICT
Fairmont Royal York
HOTEL $$$

(Map p64; 416-368-2511, 866-440-5489; www. fairmont.com/royalyork; 100 Front St W; d from $239; S Union; P ✳ 🛜 🏊) Since 1929 the eminent Royal York has accommodated everyone from Tina Turner to Henry Kissinger. Built by the Canadian Pacific Railway, its mock-chateau design adds character to Toronto's modern skyline. Rates rise with demand. The Epic tearooms and the Library Bar are both worth a look. Parking (valet only) costs $40.

Hotel Victoria
BOUTIQUE HOTEL $$

(Map p64; 416-363-1666, 800-363-8228; www. hotelvictoria-toronto.com; 56 Yonge St; d $134-164; S King; ⊕ ✳ 🛜) The early-20th-century Hotel Victoria is one of Toronto's best small downtown hotels. Refurbished throughout, it maintains a few old-fashioned features, including a fine lobby and a warm welcome at the 24-hour reception desk. Rates include health club privileges.

DOUBLE PLAY

The Renaissance Toronto at the Rogers Centre gained infamy when, during an early Blue Jays baseball game, a couple in one of the field-view rooms – either forgetfully or pornographically – became involved in some sporting activity of their own with the lights on, much to the crowd's amusement. These days the hotel insists that guests sign a waiver stipulating there will be no such free double plays.

Strathcona Hotel
HOTEL $$

(Map p64; 416-363-3321, 800-268-8304; www. thestrathconahotel.com; 60 York St; d from $125; St Andrew;) With many refurbished rooms (and more on the way), this 65-year-old hotel is unpretentious and reasonably priced for its downtown location. Downstairs, a pub and cafe offer good deals on grub.

OLD YORK
Cosmopolitan
BOUTIQUE HOTEL $$$

(Map p64; 416-945-5455, 866-852-1777; www. cosmotoronto.com; 8 Colborne St; ste from $228; King;) Sleek and quiet, with only five rooms per floor, this Asian-inspired hotel oozes calm. Suites have lake views, bedroom-sized showers and CD players tinkling meditation music. Both the spa and downstairs wine bar, **Eight**, will further ease your sink into relaxation. Parking will cost $33.

Hostelling International Toronto
HOSTEL $

(Map p64; 416-971-4440, 877-848-8737; www. hostellingtoronto.ca; 76 Church St; dm/d $29/99; 504;) This award-winning hostel gets votes for amenities such as a rooftop deck and electronic locks. Most dorms have their own bathrooms, and new deluxe rooms (which come with breakfast) offer great private accommodation at an affordable rate. Pub crawls and quiz nights keep things lighthearted.

THEATRE BLOCK & ENTERTAINMENT DISTRICT
Canadiana Guesthouse & Backpackers
HOSTEL $

(Map p64; 416-598-9090, 877-215-1225; www. canadianalodging.com; 42 Widmer St; dm $25-33, s/d $63-82; 504;) Filling an appealing Victorian town house row, Canadiana's pluses include pancake breakfasts, movie theater, barbecue nights, gas cooking and a crop of immaculate private rooms. It's comfortable, clean and friendly, and the several-house layout makes the place feel smaller than its 200 beds. Parking is $15.

Clarence Castle
HOSTEL $

(416-260-1221, 877-215-1225; www.clarence castle.com; 8 Clarence Sq; dm/d from $28/90, 510;) If Pottery Barn designed a hostel, it might look a little bit like this one. Earth tones, matching furniture and soft lighting are topped off with a super-friendly atmosphere. The heritage building fronts a small park and sports views from a roof-top patio. Roomy doubles feel like

hotel rooms, and the pricier ones are en suite. Limited parking costs $10.

Soho Metropolitan Hotel
BOUTIQUE HOTEL $$$

(Map p64; 416-599-8800; www.soho.metropol itan.com; 318 Wellington St W; d from $475; 510;) Have a seat in the lap of luxury. With heated floors in the bathrooms, private dressing rooms, floor-to-ceiling windows and top-end linens, you'll have all the pampering you can handle. The excellent **Sen5es** restaurant is right downstairs. Parking is $30.

Hôtel Le Germain
BOUTIQUE HOTEL $$$

(Map p64; 416-345-9500, 866-345-9501; www. germaintoronto.com; 30 Mercer St; d $240-500, ste $475-900; 504;) Hip and harmonious, Le Germain resides in a quiet Entertainment District side street. Clean lines, soothing spaces and Zen-inspired materials deliver the promised 'ocean of well-being.' Aveda bath amenities, in-room Bose stereos and a rooftop terrace are bonuses. Parking costs $35.

QUEEN STREET & DUNDAS SQUARE
Les Amis Bed & Breakfast
B&B $$

(Map p60; 416-928-0635; www.bbtoronto.com; 31 Granby St; s/d with shared bathroom incl breakfast from $90/125; College;) Run by a multilingual Parisian couple, this cheery B&B offers full, gourmet vegetarian (or vegan) breakfasts. Colorful rooms are adorned with the owners' art, and a leafy back deck is a great spot to chill out. It's a short walk from the Eaton Centre. Parking costs $10.

Delta Chelsea Toronto Downtown
HOTEL $$

(Map p60; 416-595-1975, 800-268-1133; www. deltahotels.com; 33 Gerrard St W; d/ste from $100/250; College;) With nearly 1600 rooms, Toronto's largest and arguably best-value hotel caters to all people. If you're with kids, you'll appreciate the apartment-style family suites and indoor waterslide. Prices vary with season and day of the week. Parking costs $27 to $32.

CHINATOWN & BALDWIN VILLAGE
Baldwin Village Inn
B&B $$

(Map p60; 416-591-5359; www.baldwininn. com; 9 Baldwin St; d with shared bathroom $85-105; 505, 506;) This yellow-painted B&B plugs a gap in the local Baldwin Village market. Facing a leafy street filled with dim sum cafes and art galleries, the front courtyard is perfect for lounging about.

YONGE STREET STRIP & CHURCH-WELLESLEY VILLAGE

Victoria's Mansion Inn & Guesthouse

INN $$

(Map p60; 416-921-4625; www.victoriasmansion.com; 68 Gloucester St; s/d/studio from $69/99/139; S Wellesley; P ✴ 🕸 🛜) Festooned with international flags, gay-friendly Victoria's Mansion accommodates travelers in a renovated 1880s redbrick heritage building. Studios have kitchenettes and singles have been renovated. Parking is $10.

Comfort Hotel

HOTEL $$

(Map p60; 416-924-1222, 800-424-6423; www.choicehotels.ca/cn228; 15 Charles St E; d from $125; S Bloor-Yonge; P ✴) The embodiment of nameless, faceless hotel anonymity, this is the place to stay if you're on the run from the law – risk-free accommodations where you won't arouse suspicion. Renegades under 18 stay free. Parking is $19.

BLOOR-YORKVILLE

TOP CHOICE **Windsor Arms**

BOUTIQUE HOTEL $$$

(Map p60; 416-971-9666; www.windsorarmshotel.com; 18 St Thomas St; ste from $300; S Bay; P ⊖ ✴ 🛜) The Windsor Arms is an exquisite piece of Toronto history – stay the night or drop in for afternoon tea. It's a 1927 neo-Gothic mansion boasting a grand entryway, stained-glass windows, polished service and its own coat of arms. When we visited, the swish establishment was ready to open a Russian tearoom, where ornate service costs $85. Parking is $35.

Howard Johnson Inn

HOTEL $$

(Map p60; 416-964-1220, 800-446-4656; www.hojo.com; 89 Avenue Rd; d incl breakfast from $129; S Bay; P ✴ 🛜) To say HoJos is nothing flash could be the understatement of the decade, but it's the cheapest accommodations you'll find in ritzy Yorkville. Parking costs $15.

Holiday Inn Toronto Midtown

HOTEL $$

(Map p60; 416-968-0010, 888-2654329; www.holiday-inn.com/torontomidtown; 280 Bloor St W; d from $154; S St George; P ✴ 🛜) The familiar green banners outside this high-rise, brown-brick monolith do little to improve the aesthetics, but inside the rooms are better than average. The location, near U of T and the big museums, is prime. Parking costs $22.

UNIVERSITY OF TORONTO & THE ANNEX

Global Guesthouse

INN $

(Map p66; 416-923-4004; singer@inforamp.net; 9 Spadina Rd; s/d with shared bathroom $62/72, s/d with bathroom $72/82; S Spadina; P ⊖ ✴ 🛜) Built in 1889, this old-fashioned redbrick Victorian has beautiful carved gables and sits just north of Bloor St. There's a friendly owner, shared kitchen and 10 spacious rooms featuring cable TV, hippie wall hangings, wooden floors and murals. It fills up quickly, so book well in advance.

Annex Quest House

INN $$

(Map p66; 416-922-1934; www.annexguesthouse.com; 83 Spadina Rd; d from $90; S Spadina; P ⊖ ✴) Engaging the principles of *vastu*, an Indian architectural science promoting tranquility through natural materials and asymmetrical layouts (similar to feng shui), this place has some lovely rooms. Wooden floors, patterned bedspread and crafted copper bowls highlight the spaces.

Havinn

B&B $

(Map p66; 416-922-5220, 888-922-5220; www.havinn.com; 118 Spadina Rd; s/d with shared bathroom incl breakfast $59/79; S Dupont; P ⊖ ✴ @) Havinn is a haven on busy Spadina Rd, with six tidy rooms, immaculate shared bathrooms and a communal kitchen. Breakfast includes croissants, bagels, yogurt, fruit and fresh muffins. The vibe is chilled and cheery, and it's a great alternative to a hostel while being cheaper than many other B&Bs.

Madison Manor

B&B $$

(Map p66; 416-922-5579, 877-561-7048; www.madisonavenuepub.com; 20 Madison Ave; d incl breakfast $129-149; S Spadina; P ⊖ ✴) A refurbished Victorian home near the University of Toronto. All rooms have a bathroom; a few have a fireplace or balcony. You should be warned, however, that the Manor is sandwiched between a fraternity house and a pub, and readers have complained of noise on weekends. Parking costs between $10 and $15.

KENSINGTON MARKET & LITTLE ITALY

College Backpackers

HOSTEL $

(Map p66; 416-929-4777, 866-663-2093; www.collegehostel.com; 280 Augusta Ave; s/d $55/75; 🚌506, 510; ⊖ 🛜) Though it bills itself as a hostel, this new joint actually features affordable singles and doubles with shared baths, TVs and balconies. The communal kitchen is a good place to toss some pasta, but with Kensington Market's cheap eats right outside your door, why would you bother?

QUEEN WEST & WEST QUEEN WEST

Gladstone Hotel [TOP CHOICE] BOUTIQUE HOTEL **$$$**
(Map p57; ☎416-531-4635; www.glad
stonehotel.com; 1214 Queen St W; d/ste from
$195/375; 🅿501; P⊖❋🛜) From teeny bop-
per to urban explorer to Canadian forest,
the 37 artist-designed rooms at this re-
furbished hotel are stylish and fun. High-
ceilinged rooms are on the 3rd and 4th
floors (take the hand-cranked birdcage el-
evator up!), while the 2nd floor is dedicated
to studio space and exhibitions for renting
artists. The ground level has a bar and cafe,
where you can take your breakfast or hear a
band. Locally produced bathroom products
and a green roof showcase the Gladstone's
eco commitment. Go to the website to
choose the room that fits your mood. Park-
ing is $15.

Drake Hotel BOUTIQUE HOTEL **$$$**
(☎416-531-5042; www.thedrakehotel.ca; 1150
Queen St W; d $189-279; 🅿501; P⊖❋🛜) An-
other super-hip hotel on Queen West. Revamped to the tune of a cool $5 million,
this century-old hotel beckons bohemians,
artists and indie musicians (with a little
cash). Artful rooms come with vintage furnishings, throw rugs, flat-screen TVs and
luxury bath products. There's a cafe, restaurant, bar and excellent live music in the
basement to keep you entertained. Parking
costs $18

Global Village Backpackers HOSTEL **$**
(Map p64; ☎416-703-8540, 888-844-7875;
www.globalbackpackers.com; 460 King St W; dm
$27-29, d from $73; 🅿504, 511; ⊖🛜) This kaleidoscopically colored independent hostel
was once the Spadina Hotel, where Jack
Nicholson, the Rolling Stones and Leonard
Cohen lay their heads. It likely hasn't been
updated since those glory days, though despite its grubbiness it's a fave among backpackers. There's a party-centric bar and
outdoor patio.

EAST TORONTO

Au Petit Paris B&B **$$**
(Map p60; ☎416-928-1348; www.bbtoronto.com/
aupetitparis; 3 Selby St; s/d incl breakfast from
$105/140; 🅂Sherbourne; ⊖❋🛜) Hardwood
floors blend with modern decor inside this
exquisite bay-and-gable Victorian. The pick
of the four en-suite rooms are the skylit No-
mad's Suite and the Artist's Suite, with gar-
den views and extra-large bathtubs. Eating
the vegetarian breakfast on the roof patio
is a great way to start your day in the city.

Neill-Wycik College Hotel HOSTEL **$**
(Map p60; ☎416-977-2320; www.neill-wycik.
com; 96 Gerrard St E; s/d/tr/f with shared
bathroom $50/75/88/99; 🅂College; P🛜)
Pronounced 'Why-zik,' this budget trav-
eler's favorite operates from early May to
late August when the students are out.
Private bedrooms with telephones are in-
side apartment-style suites that share a
kitchen/lounge and bathroom. There are
laundry facilities, lockers, TV lounges,
a student-run cafeteria and incredible
sundeck views. No air-con = hot August
nights. Parking costs $10.

Toronto Townhouse B&B B&B **$$**
(Map p60; ☎416-323-8898, 877-500-0466;
www.torontotownhouse.com; 213 Carlton St; d
$119-169; 🅿506; P⊖❋🛜) The six quaint
rooms inside this 140-year-old heritage
row house are beautifully restored. A few
come with private balconies and en suite
bathrooms; breakfast includes homemade
granola, baked goodies, hot pancakes and
omelets.

1871 Historic House B&B B&B **$$**
(Map p60; ☎416-923-6950; www.1871bnb.com;
65 Huntley St; s/d with shared bathroom incl
breakfast from $95/105; 🅂Sherbourne; P⊖❋🛜)
What other property can claim both Buf-
falo Bill Cody and John Lennon as one-time
guests? In this historic Victorian home,
which displays its art and antiques in sun-
ny common areas, all rooms are without a
bathroom, but the coach-house suite has its
own hot tub.

Amsterdam Guesthouse INN **$$**
(Map p60; ☎416-921-9797; www.amster
damguesthouse.com; 209 Carlton St; s/d with
shared bathroom from $75/85; 🅿506; ⊖❋🛜)
Bedecked with flags above a grand front
porch, Amsterdam is a shabby-chic Victorian house. The occasional shirtless stoner
wanders through the lobby, trying to recall
which of the simple, clean and comfy rooms
(with cable TV) is theirs.

Clarion Hotel & Suites Selby HOTEL **$$$**
(Map p60; ☎416-921-3142, 800-387-4788;
www.hotelselby.com; 592 Sherbourne St; d/ste
incl breakfast from $189/239; 🅂Sherbourne;
P❋🛜♿) Ernest Hemingway stayed in
this turreted Victorian mansion while he
worked as a reporter for the *Toronto Star*
in the 1920s. The modern extension out the
back is no architectural dreamboat, but
contains family-sized suites. Parking will
set you back $17.

THE BEACHES

Accommodating the Soul   B&B **$$**
(☑416-686-0619, 866-686-0619; www.accom
modatingthesoul.com; 114 Waverley Rd; d incl
breakfast $125-145; ☎501; P ⊖ ❄ ⓐ) An early-
20th-century home boasting antiques and
fabulous gardens, these soulful accommo-
dations are a short walk from the lake. One
room has an en suite, the other two share
a bathroom. Full, hot breakfasts are served
regardless of which room you're in.

TORONTO ISLANDS

Smiley's B&B   B&B **$$**
(☑416-203-8599; www.erelda.ca; 4 Dacotah Ave,
Algonquin Island; r with shared bathroom $97,
apt per night/week $215/1152; ⊖ ❄ ⓐ; ⓢWard's
Island) Sleep the night away in 'Belvedere' –
a sunny B&B room, and dine with the hosts –
or hole-up in the studio apartment with its
own kitchen and bathroom. Either way, on
the car-free islands, relaxation is sure to
come easy.

GREATER TORONTO AREA (GTA)

Toadhall Bed & Breakfast   B&B **$$**
(☑905-773-4028; www.225toadhall.ca; 225 Lake-
land Cres, Richmond Hill; s/d/tr incl breakfast
$110/145/185; P ⊖ ⓐ) It's worth trekking
north of downtown Toronto to stay in this
solar-powered home on picturesque Lake
Wilcox, with swimming, canoeing and
windsurfing right outside the door. There's
no air-con, but cool lake breezes blow
through. Salubrious gourmet breakfasts em-
phasize organic fare (vegetarian by request).

Bonnevue Manor   B&B **$$**
(☑416-536-1455; www.bonnevuemanor.com; 33
Beaty Ave; d incl breakfast from $99; ☎501, 504,
508; P ⊖ ❄ ⓐ) One of the city's best B&Bs,
this cozy place occupies a restored 1890s
redbrick mansion west of Jameson Ave, with
divine handcrafted architectural details. Six
guestrooms exhibit warm-colored interiors; all have bathrooms. Enjoy your cooked
breakfast out on the grapevine-covered deck.

✕ Eating

Nowhere is Toronto's multiculturalism
more potent and thrilling than on the plates
of its restaurants. Eating here is a delight –
you'll find everything from Korean walnut
cakes to sweat-inducing Thai curries, New
York steaks and good ol' Canuck pancakes
with peameal bacon and maple syrup. Fusion food is the future: traditional Western
recipes invaded with handfuls of zingy

Eastern ingredients and cooked with pan-
Asian flare. British influences also linger –
fizzy lunchtime pints and formal afternoon
high teas are much-loved traditions.

Executive diners file into classy restaurants in the Financial District and Old
York, while eclectic, affordable eateries
fill Baldwin Village, Kensington Market,
Queen West and the Yonge St Strip. More
ethnically consistent are Little Italy, Greektown (The Danforth), Little India and Chinatown. Ponder your profoundest cravings,
identify your neighborhood of choice, then
dive right in!

HARBOURFRONT

Il Fornello   ITALIAN **$$**
(Map p64; ☑416-861-1028; 207 Queen's Quay W;
mains $12-24; ⊙11:30am-1am Mon-Fri, from 5pm
Sat & Sun; ☎509, 510) One of five Il Fornellos
in Toronto, this insider's-favorite is popular
not only for its seafood-favoring menu but
also its 200-seat patio overlooking Lake On-
tario. If you're not fancying fish, there are
plenty of other options, including gourmet
pizza. We like the fig pizza: mascarpone,
figs, honey and prosciutto are a few of the
ingredients. Delightful.

Harbour Sixty Steakhouse   STEAKHOUSE **$$$**
(Map p64; ☑416-777-2111; 60 Harbour St; mains
$29-52; ⊙lunch & dinner Mon-Fri, lunch Sat &
Sun; ☎509, 510) Inside the Gothically isolated 1917 Toronto Harbour Commission
building, this opulent baroque dining
room glows with brass lamps and plush
booths. Indulge yourself in an eminent variety of steaks, salmon or seasonal Florida
stone-crab claws and broiled Caribbean
lobster tail. Side dishes are big enough for
two. Reservations essential.

FINANCIAL DISTRICT

Mercatto   ITALIAN **$$**
(Map p64; ☑416-306-0467; 330 Bay St; meals $8-
14; ⊙Mon-Fri; ⓢKing) One of an effervescent
string of Italian deli-cafes, Mercatto serves
up creative panini, pasta, risotto, frittata
and pizza dishes at a central dining bench
beneath entirely out-of-place chandeliers.
Espresso in the morning or wine at night;
dine in or take out: you've got options.

Bymark   FUSION **$$$**
(Map p64; ☑416-777-1144; Toronto-Dominion
Centre, 66 Wellington St W; mains $34-50;
⊙lunch & dinner Mon-Fri, dinner Sat; ⓢSt
Andrew) Celebrity chef Mark McEwan of
North 44° brings his sophisticated menu

TORONTO'S TOP VEGETARIAN

Meat-free restaurants in Toronto run the gamut from gourmet to greasy spoon. Here's a couple for you to start out with.

» Fressen
(Map p66; ☑416-504-5127; 478 Queen St W; mains $10-14; ⊘dinner Mon-Fri, brunch Sat & Sun; ✍; 🚇501)

» Sadie's Diner
(Map p66; 504 Adelaide St W; mains $7-10; ⊘breakfast & lunch daily, dinner Wed-Sat; ✍; 🚇504, 511)

» Urban Herbivore
(Map p66; 64 Oxford St; mains $4-8; ⊘8am-8pm; ✍; 🚇510)

of continentally hewn cuisine to this hip, bi-level downtowner. His creative kitchen crew whips seasonal regional ingredients (wild truffles, quail, soft-shell crab) into sensational combinations, each with suggested wine or beer pairings. It's on street level.

OLD YORK

St Lawrence Market   MARKET $
(Map p64; South Market, 92 Front St E; items $2-10; ⊘8am-6pm Tue-Thu, to 7pm Fri, 5am-5pm Sat; 🚇503, 504) Buskers and classical trios provide an acoustic backdrop at the city's beloved market, offering a mouthwatering range of quality produce, baked goods and imported foodstuffs. The Carousel Bakery is known for its peameal bacon sandwiches, and crowds pack lunch counters outside Everyday Gourmet, Quik Sushi, and St Urbain for Montréal-style bagels. The farmers market livens up the North Market from 5am every Saturday.

Sultan's Tent & Café Maroc
                              MIDDLE EASTERN $$
(☑416-961-0601; 49 Front St E; mains $12-25; ⊘noon-3pm Mon-Fri, 5-10:30pm Mon-Sat; 🚇503, 504) Dark and atmospheric, replete with stained-glass lanterns, candles and fringed cushions, Sultan's features a Moroccan menu. The Couscous Royale ($22) is splendiferous, and for dessert try the sweet *keskesu* (sweet couscous, cinnamon, almonds, raisins and orange blossom water). Belly dancers may or may not help you digest.

Burrito Banditos   MEXICAN $
(Map p64; 120 Peter St; mains $4-8; ⊘11:30am-11pm Mon-Thu, to 4am Fri & Sat, noon-9pm Sun; 🚇501, 502) Club-hounds who haven't got lucky pile into this basement booth to assuage their disappointment with a hefty injection of chili, sour cream and salsa. There's not enough room in here for both you and your burrito – grab one to go.

Sen5es   FUSION $$$
(Map p64; ☑416-935-0400; 318 Wellington St W; breakfast & lunch $5-17, dinner $32-45; ⊘7am-2pm daily, 6-11pm Tue-Sat, lounge 5pm-1am daily; 🚇510) Sen5es' sun-drenched, airy cafe serves breakfast (try an impeccable cappuccino and chocolate croissant), while the sleek modern dining room harbors a chef's table and nocturnal offerings like goat cheese and beef ravioli or seared scallops with citrus salad and curry yoghurt. Alternatively, dine in the lounge to sample from the same amazing menu for under $25 per plate.

QUEEN STREET & DUNDAS SQUARE

TOP CHOICE **Queen Mother Café**   FUSION $$
(☑416-598-4719; 208 Queen St W; mains $9-18; ⊘11:30am-1am Mon-Sat, to 11pm Sun; 🚇Osgoode) A Queen St institution, the Queen Mother is beloved for its cozy, dark wooden booths and excellent pan-Asian menu. Canadian comfort food is also on offer – try the Queen Mum burger. Check out the display of old stuff they found in the walls the last time they renovated. The patio is hidden and one of the best in town.

Commensal   CAFE $
(Map p60; 655 Bay St; lunch/dinner $10/15; 🚇Dundas) Cafeteria-style Commensal sells 100-plus buffet dishes from breakfast to dinner, many of them priced by weight (lasagna is $2.43 per 100g). Fresh salads, hot mains with international flavors, and naturally sweetened desserts are a step above normal cafeteria food. Also accommodates most dietary restrictions.

Terroni   ITALIAN $$
Adelaide St E (☑416-203-3093; 57 Adelaide St E; meals $11-16; ⊘lunch&dinner; 🚇Queen); Queen West (☑416-504-0320; 720 Queen St W; 🚇501) Terroni is a traditional Southern Italian grocer and deli. Wood-fired pizzas, wines by the glass and fresh panini all approach perfection, served in a busy and upbeat

environment. The Adelaide St location is best; it's in an old courthouse with marble throughout. Don't bother trying to order a diet Coke at either location, though: these folks are cola purists.

CHINATOWN & BALDWIN VILLAGE
Cafe la Gaffe   CAFE $$
(Map p60; ☎416-596-2397; 24 Baldwin St; mains $10-15; ⊘lunch & dinner; ᵭ505, 506) Stripy cotton tablecloths and fresh-cut flowers adorn the tables in this little cafe. A small patio sits under leafy trees, where you can dine on market salads, a filet mignon sandwich or the hand-tossed pizzas. A small-print wine list offers an extensive selection.

Dumpling House Restaurant   CHINESE $
(Map p66; 328 Spadina Ave; 12 dumplings $4-6; ⊘lunch & dinner; ᵭ510) Watch dumplings being rolled in the window, then walk right in, sit right down and order a steaming mass of them. Impale steamed or pan-fried pork, chicken, beef, seafood or vegetarian dumplings on your chopsticks, dunk them in soy sauce and dispense with them forthwith.

Phở Hu'ng   VIETNAMESE $
Spadina Ave (Map p66; 350 Spadina Ave; mains $6-13; ⊘lunch & dinner; ᵭ510); Bloor-Yorkville (Map p60; 2nd fl, 200 Bloor St W; ⓈMuseum) Clipped service and infernally busy tables are the price you pay for Phở Hu'ng's awesome Vietnamese soups. A few dishes may be a touch

too authentic for some (what, don't you like pork intestines and blood?), but the coffee is spot-on. A fair-weather bonus is the superb patio.

Swatow   CHINESE $$
(309 Spadina Ave; mains $8-14; ⊘11am-2am; ᵭ505, 510) Catering to a late-night crowd, the menu here covers cuisine from Swatow (a city now known as Shantou, on the coast of China's Guangdong province). Nicknamed 'red cooking' for its potent splashings of fermented rice wine, the house noodles are fiery. Cash only; be prepared to queue.

YONGE STREET STRIP & CHURCH-WELLESLEY VILLAGE
7 West Café   CAFE $$
(Map p60; ☎416-928-9041; 7 Charles St W; mains $9-15; ⊘24hr; ⓈBloor-Yonge) Three floors of moody lighting, textured jade paint, framed nudes, wooden church pews and jaunty ceiling angels set the scene for a dazzling selection of pizzas, pastas and sandwiches, and 24-hour breakfasts. Make like a vampire sipping blood-red wine (by the glass or bottle) as the moon dapples shadows across the street.

Fire on the East Side   FUSION $$
(Map p60; ☎416-960-3473; 6 Gloucester St; mains $10-24; ⊘11:30am-10:30pm Mon-Fri, from 10am Sat & Sun; ⓈWellesley) A fusion kitchen works haywire variations on African, Caribbean, Acadian French and Cajun themes, from spicy crab cakes to duck confit quesadillas, and the menu changes quarterly. At night, the kitchen closes and beats from the next-door club are piped in, making it more of a lounge. It's a popular brunch spot, so reservations are essential for the weekends.

Ethiopian House   AFRICAN $$
(Map p60; ☎416-923-5438; 4 Irwin Ave; mains $12-28; ⊘noon-1am; ⓈWellesley) It's a packed and popular place with African-inspired murals on the walls, but there's no silverware in sight as *sherro wot* (seasoned chickpeas) and *gored-gored* (spiced beef) are slathered onto wonderful moist *injera* (bread).

BLOOR-YORKVILLE
Carens Wine and Cheese Bar   FUSION $$$
(Map p60; ☎416-962-5158; 158 Cumberland St; lunch $12-19, dinner $16-32; ⊘11:30am-11pm Tue-Sat; ⓈSt George) As expected, there's an amazing selection of cheese boards, and

staff can recommend wine pairings. Bright pashminas drape over chairs in case you get a chill on the intimate and stylish back patio, and Thai lanterns hang from the trees. Also, the spicy baked mac 'n cheese ($16) is some of the best we've ever had.

Bloor Street Diner
FRENCH $$

(Map p60; ☑416-928-3105; Manulife Centre, 55 Bloor St W; mains $12-19, brunch $22; ⊙noon-1am; ⑤Bloor-Yonge) Humbly named but actually pretty swanky, the recently updated Bloor Street Diner impresses with a Parisian-style patio, a distinguished wine list and a massive weekend brunch buffet (with live music). Hit the cafe section out the front in the mall for speedy take-out sandwiches.

Sassafraz
CAFE $$$

(Map p60; ☑416-964-2222; 100 Cumberland St; mains $30-45; ⊙11am-2am Tue-Sat, to midnight Mon & Sun; ⑤Bay) With a red-carpet parade of celebs filing through (Jude Law, Matthew McConaughey, Joan Collins etc), Sassafraz feels more like LA than TO. Jazz combos serenade weekend brunchers; sassy receptionists distribute clientele between the sun-drenched patio and indoor courtyard. The food? Predictably good.

Okonomi House
JAPANESE $

(Map p60; 23 Charles St W; mains $6-12; ⊙11:30am-10pm Mon-Fri, noon-10pm Sat, noon-8pm Sun; ⑤Bloor-Yonge) Okonomi House is one of the only places in Toronto (and perhaps North America) dishing up *okonomiyaki*, savory Japanese cabbage pancakes filled with meat, seafood or vegetables. Perfect cold-weather comfort food.

UNIVERSITY OF TORONTO & THE ANNEX

By the Way
FUSION $$

(Map p66; ☑416-967-4295; 400 Bloor St W; mains $8-18; ⊙9am-10:30pm Sun-Tue, to 11:30pm Wed & Thu, to 12:30am Fri & Sat; ⑤Bathurst, Spadina) An Annex fixture, this cheerful corner bistro has a fusion menu that leans towards Middle Eastern. Although there's plenty of meat on the menu, vegetarians won't go hungry. Service is A+ and the wine list features Niagara ice varietals and labels from far-flung Oregon and Australia.

Chabichau
FRENCH $

(Map p66; 196 Borden St; mains $9-19; ⊙10am-6pm Tue-Sun, from noon Mon; ⑤510) The selection of cheeses and pâté (try the duck and pistachio) grab your eyes, but don't miss the sandwiches on homemade bread or daily specials such as pork-apple stew. Simple, hearty, awesome.

Papa Ceo
FAST FOOD $

(Map p66; 654 Spadina Ave; slices $3-4; ⊙9am-4am; ⑤510) Nearly two dozen types of gourmet slices show off here, and they are all enormous – grab a chunky slab of 'bun giorno' (mozzarella, mushrooms, chicken, roast beef and corned beef) and retreat to the back tables where Italian Serie A soccer dances across TV screens.

KENSINGTON MARKET & LITTLE ITALY

Aunties & Uncles
CAFE $$

(Map p66; 74 Lippincott St; mains $8-15; ⊙9am-3pm; ⑤510) An always-bustling place with a line on the sidewalk outside the picket fence, Aunties & Uncles does yummy breakfasts with a whole lot of housemade items such as ketchup and chorizo. Plop yourself down in one of the mismatched chairs and dig into dishes like grilled brie with pear chutney and walnuts on challah.

Kalendar
CAFE $$

(Map p66; 546 College St; mains $11-20; ⊙11am-midnight Mon-Wed, to 1am Thu, to 2am Fri, 10:30am to 2am Sat, 10:30am-midnight Sun; ⑤510) It feels like France in Little Italy, with dark wood, tiled floors and a dainty sidewalk patio. The menu funks things up with different types of scrolls (crepe-style roti topped with all sorts of veggies and sauces) and nannettes – naan topped with yummies such as pesto, artichoke hearts and asiago cheese. There's a long list of cocktails to help you wash it all down.

Bar Italia
ITALIAN $$

(Map p66; ☑416-535-3621; 582 College St; mains $10-17; ⊙11am-1am Mon-Thu, to 2am Fri, 10:30am-2am Sat, 10:30am-1am Sun; ⑤506) Locals love Bar Italia, a place to see and be seen (especially from a vantage point on the coveted front patio). Grab a sandwich or *al dente* pasta, with a lemon gelato and a rich coffee afterward – and while away the entire afternoon or evening.

Caplansky's Deli
SANDWICH SHOP $$

(Map p66; 356 College St; ⑤510) Grab breakfast any time (the sandwich board leftovers are delish), or take some slices to go from this authentic deli. The friendly folks won't make you feel like chopped liver, though you're more than welcome to order some.

Jumbo Empanadas
MEXICAN $

(Map p66; 245 Augusta Ave; items $3-6; ⊙9am-8pm Mon-Sat, 11am-6pm Sun; ⑤510) They're not kidding – chunky Chilean empanadas (toasted delights stuffed with beef, chicken, cheese or vegetables) and savory corn pie with beef, olives and eggs always sell out early. A mini empanada will only set you back $1. Bread and salsas are also homemade.

QUEEN WEST & WEST QUEEN WEST

TOP CHOICE **The Swan** CAFE $$
(Map p66; 892 Queen St W; mains $18-23; ⊙noon-10pm Mon-Fri, from 10am Sat & Sun; 🚌501) This art-deco diner features a small and deceptively simple menu, with items like smoked oyster with pancetta and egg scrambles, club sandwiches, and mussels that sit iced in a vintage Coca-Cola cooler. The coffee is divine, and it's a great place to sit at the counter and read the paper on a rainy Sunday.

Pizza Libretto ITALIAN $$
(Map p66; ☎416-532-8000; 221 Ossington Ave; mains $13-16; ⊙noon-11pm Mon-Sat, from 4pm Sun; 🚌505) A bit north of Queen West in Portugal Village, Pizza Libretto crafts what is arguably the best pizza in town. The secret? A wood-fired oven built by a third-generation pizza-oven builder with stones shipped from Italy. Besides certified Neapolitan pizza and other Naples staples, the menu also includes a prix fixe lunch (salad, pizza and gelato for $15) and an all-Italian wine list. Make sure you reserve your table for weekends.

Julie's CARIBBEAN $$
(☎416-532-7397; 202 Dovercourt Rd; mains $15-19; ⊙dinner Tue-Sun; 🚌501) This West Queen West neighborhood joint has customers driving from as far away as Buffalo to enjoy trad Cuban dishes like *ropa vieja* (shredded beef in spicy tomato sauce with ripe plantains, white rice and black beans). The restaurant was once a grocery store, and every effort has been made (or rather, not made) to preserve the vibe.

EAST TORONTO

TOP CHOICE **Gilead Café** CAFE $
(4 Gilead Pl; mains $7-12; ⊙8am-5:30pm Mon-Sat; 🚌503, 504) Counter service meets haute Canadian cuisine in this Jamie Kennedy kitchen. The menu, featuring items like gourmet poutine, Canadian artisan cheese plates, and cider mayo, is written on the chalkboard daily. Ingredients are sourced from Ontario farms; if you're watching your mileage, the Gilead is a great choice for the 100-mile diet.

Siddhartha INDIAN $$
Gerrard St E (☎416-465-4095; 1450 Gerrard St E; mains $9-15; ⊙lunch & dinner; 🚌506); Queen West (☎416-703-6684; 647a King St W; ⊙lunch & dinner; 🚌504) In a neighborhood stuffed with excellent South Asian food, Siddhartha is a consistent favorite. Although it's popular for its all-you-can-eat lunch and dinner buffets, don't be afraid to order off the menu. The naan is perfect, the curries are classic and the samosas are massive. Cool your burning tongue with a Kingfisher.

Toast FUSION $$
(993 Queen St E; mains $11-25; ⊙lunch Tue-Fri, dinner Thu-Sat, brunch Sat & Sun; 🚌501, 502, 503) Beyond velvet curtains is an artsy, old-fangled bistro that's best for weekend brunch: $12 for eggs Benedict or French toast with cranberries and cream cheese. Relax on the velvet antique couch or dine at one of the Formica tables, and if there's a wait, check out the local art on the walls.

Gio Rana's Really Really Nice Restaurant ITALIAN $$$
(☎416-469-5225; 1220 Queen St E; mains $25-35; ⊙6pm-midnight Tue-Sun; 🚌501, 502, 503) Don't be deterred by outside appearances: though 'Gio's' home was once a nondescript 1950s bank building, the interior is actually (we have to say it) really, really nice. Hip without trying *too* hard, Gio's serves up southern Italian staples such as hot sausage risotto, veal, and 'sexy duck.'

Real Jerk CARIBBEAN $$
(709 Queen St E; mains $5-15; ⊙11:30am-10pm Mon & Tue, to 11pm Wed & Thu, to midnight Fri, 1pm-midnight Sat, 2-10pm Sun; 🚌501, 502, 503) This sunny Caribbean kitchen serves classic jerk chicken, oxtail and curries, 'rasta pasta' and Red Stripe beer. The vibe is beachy, with reggae beats, tropical decor and Jamaican flags everywhere.

Pan on the Danforth MEDITERRANEAN $$
(☎416-466-8158; 516 Danforth Ave; mezes $6-13, mains $15-25; ⊙noon-11pm Sun-Thu, to midnight Fri & Sat; 🚇Chester) Colorful, casual Pan serves unpretentious fare with traditional Greek flavors, like Santorini chicken stuffed with spinach and feta, with new potatoes and seared veggies. Finish with a sticky chocolate baklava.

THE BEACHES

Beacher Café CAFE $$
(☎416-699-3874; 2162 Queen St E; mains $8-17; ⊙11am-11pm Mon-Fri, 9am-10pm Sat & Sun; 🚌501)

This long-standing cafe looks like a seaside cottage and boasts a narrow but eternally sought-after sidewalk patio. The egg and pancake brunches are particularly good. Local artwork changes monthly.

King's Table SEAFOOD $
(2248 Queen St E; meals $6-12; ☉noon-10pm Tue-Sun; ⌂501) A fraternal, back-slapping feeling suffuses this storefront, which we'll crown King of The Beaches' fish-and-chip shops. Cheery tables fill up fast with diners ordering hearty halibut or salmon grills and salads.

TORONTO ISLANDS
The Rectory CAFE $$
(☎416-203-2152; 102 Lakeshore Ave, Ward's Island; mains $13-21; ☉11am-5pm Sun-Thu Oct-May, 10am-10pm daily Jun-Sep; ☸Ward's Island) Propped up next to the boardwalk, this cozy gallery-cafe serves light meals, cups of tea and weekend brunch with views of Tommy Thompson Park. Reservations recommended for brunch and dinner; quick snacks and drinks are more casual. Try to nab a seat on the lakeside patio if the sun is shining.

GREATER TORONTO AREA (GTA)
Vanipha Lanna THAI $$
(☎416-654-8068; 863 St Clair Ave W; mains $10-15; ☉dinner Tue & Sat, lunch & dinner Wed-Fri; ⌂512) Highly recommended, Vanipha Lanna emerges from the night like some kind of Asian carwash crossed with a birthday cake. Thai-Laotian food ranges from fiery seafood creations to familiar curries, plus unusual dishes like *khao moak ga* (spiced ⁯⁯ portraits of Thai royals adorn the room.

Globe Earth FUSION $$$
(☎416-551-9890; 1055 Yonge St; mains $20-30; ☉lunch & dinner Mon-Fri, brunch & dinner Sat & Sun; ⑤Rosedale) This newbie features local, seasonal foods only, which you can feast on in the lounging surrounds. A wood-burning oven adds flavor flair to flatbreads, and you can order your meat by weight. Charcuterie and deep-fried cheese curds bring things down to an approachable level, and there's a little something for everyone on the massive menu.

Drinking

Toronto usually tries to distance itself from its British heritage, but everywhere you look, perfectly decent Canadian bars are selling out to Anglo-Celtic pub chains and subjecting themselves to horrible faux-Yorkshire makeovers: plastic bookshelves, twiddle-dee-dee soundtracks, stodgy ales. Genuine Canuck watering holes are still out there though – you just need to know where to look.

The TO bar scene embraces everything from sticky-carpet beer holes to slick martini bars, downtown money-waster wine rooms and an effervescent smattering of gay and lesbian bars. Thirsty work! Strict anti-smoking bylaws prohibit nicotine-fixing in indoor public spaces – you can enjoy your martini without your favorite shirt smelling like an ashtray in the morning.

The pubs listed below open at 11am and stay open until 2am. Bars keep serving until 2am too, but don't generally open their doors until around 4pm.

Mill Street Brewery BREWERY
(55 Mill St, Bldg 63, Distillery District; ⌂503, 504) With 10 specialty beers brewed on-site in the atmospheric Distillery District, these guys are a leading light in local microbrewing. Order a sample platter so you can taste all the award-winning brews, including the Tankhouse Pale Ale, Stock Ale and Organic Lager. On a sunny afternoon, the courtyard is the place to be. Typical brewery fare is served, with beer-friendly pairings like burgers, sandwiches, and wraps.

Sweaty Betty's BAR
(Map p66; 13 Ossington Ave; ⌂501) In a city of infused vodkas and creative cocktails, Betty's refuses to mix anything with more than three ingredients. This no-nonsense ⁯⁯ essentials: having a good time and chatting people up. The tiny place is packed with hipsters on the weekends, and the living room-ish setup kinda makes it feel like a college house party.

C'est What PUB
(67 Front St E; mains $10-15; ⌂503, 504) Over 30 whiskeys and six dozen Canadian microbrews (mostly from Ontario) are on hand at this underground pub. An in-house brewmaster tightly edits the all-natural, preservative-free beers on tap. There's live music most nights at the Music Showbar next door. There's good grub as well – the menu encompasses all-local meats, including peameal bacon from St Lawrence Market next door as well as free-range bison.

Gladstone Hotel
BAR

(1214 Queen St W; ☎501) This historic hotel revels in Toronto's avant-garde arts scene. The Art Bar and Gladstone Ballroom sustain offbeat DJs, poetry slams, jazz, book readings, alt-country and blues, while the Melody bar hosts karaoke and other musical ventures. Cover varies, usually $10 or less.

Red Room
CAFE

(Map p66; 444 Spadina Ave; mains $4-8; ☎506, 510) The Red Room rules. Part pub, part diner, part funky lounge – this arty Kensington Market room is the place to drag your hungover bones for a recuperative pint of microbrew, an all-day breakfast and an earful of Brit pop. Sink into a booth and forget your misdemeanors.

Black Bull
PUB

(Map p60; 298 Queen St W; ☎501) The Black Bull may have Toronto's most desirous pub patio. Though it lacks the charm of more intimate spaces, it's in an open downtown location that manages to catch more evening sunlight than perhaps anywhere else in the city center. Line up behind the others to wait for a table, and don't give it up until the sun goes down.

Underground Garage
BAR

(Map p64; 365 King St W; ☎504, 510) Trying valiantly to keep it real in the otherwise skin-deep Entertainment District, this urban rock bar is down a steep staircase lined with Led Zeppelin, Willie Nelson and John Lennon posters. Wailing guitars, cold beer and good times – just as it should be. Doesn't usually get going until 9pm; cover under $5.

Madison Avenue Pub
PUB

(Map p66; 14-18 Madison Ave; ☎Spadina) Consuming three Victorian houses in The Annex, the Madison is positively elephantine. A 25-to-35 crowd is lured through the doors – billiards, darts, a sports bar, polished brass, antique-looking lamps lighting the curtained upper floors at night, *five* patios and plenty of hot babes.

Smokeless Joe
BAR

(Map p64; ☎416-728-4503; 125 John St; ☎501) Buried below street level in Clubland, this narrow 'where everybody knows your name' bar sells more than 250 different beers (the menu is a book). Some of the rarest brews aren't sold in stores, so stop by for a pint or three. It was one of the first places in TO to ban smoking. Thanks, Joe.

☆ Entertainment

There's no dearth of entertainment to be had in Toronto. In fact, it's a very entertaining place! Whether you're craving a jazzy quartet, an indie film, some offbeat theater or a punk-rock gig, you'll have no trouble finding it here. Toronto's incendiary club scene is thriving, as is gay and lesbian nightlife. There are free outdoor festivals and concerts going on nearly every weekend, especially in summer. In a spirit of goodwill and artistic openheartedness, many Toronto events adopt a 'Pay What You Can' (PWYC) policy. In essence, this means they're free, but artists still appreciate your pocket change.

To stay attuned to club, alt-culture and live-music options, scan the city's free street press: *Now*, *Xtra!* and *Eye Weekly*. The daily newspapers also provide weekly entertainment listings. Glossy *Toronto Life* magazine publishes a monthly 'What's On' guide.

Ticketmaster (☎416-870-8000; www.ticketmaster.ca) sells tickets for major concerts, sports games, theater and performing arts events. Buy tickets online or at various city outlets, including the Rogers Centre and Hummingbird Centre for Performing Arts. **TO Tix** (Map p60; ☎416-536-6468, ext 40; www.totix.ca; Dundas Sq, 1 Dundas St E; ⊙noon-6:30pm Tue-Sat; ☎Dundas) sells half-price and discount same-day 'rush' tickets. **TicketKing** (☎416-872-1212, 800-461-3333; www.mirvish.com) represents several venues in town, including the Royal Alexandria Theatre and the Princess of Wales Theatre.

Cinemas

Perhaps more than any other pastime, Torontonians cherish going to the movies (something to do with the weather?). Tickets cost around $14 for adults. Tuesday is discount day – expect to pay around $8.

TIFF Cinematheque
CINEMA

(Map p60; www.cinemathequeontario.ca; box office 2 Carlton St W; ⊙box office 10am-7pm Mon-Fri, closed late Aug & Sep; ☎Bloor-Yonge) Popular TIFF Cinematheque screens world cinema, independent films and retrospectives of famous directors. About 400 films are shown annually at Jackman Hall at the Art Gallery of Ontario; many screenings are now held in the new **Bell Lightbox** (Map p64; www.tiff.net; cnr King St & John St; ☎504). Nonmembers can purchase tickets at the Manulife Centre box office 30 minutes before the day's first screening.

Bloor Cinema
CINEMA

(Map p66; ☑416-516-2330; www.bloorcinema.com; 506 Bloor St W; ⊙noon-midnight; ⑤Bathurst) This art-deco theater with a two-tiered balcony screens a wonderfully varied schedule of new releases, art-house flicks, shorts, documentaries and vintage films.

Alliance Atlantis Cumberland 4
CINEMA

(www.alliancecinemas.com) Bloor-Yorkville (☑416-646-0444; 159 Cumberland St; ⑤Bay); The Beaches (☑416-646-0444; 1651 Queen St E; ◰501) The pint-sized Cumberland 4 multiplex screens a mix of independent films and hand-picked, left-of-centre Hollywood releases. There is a slightly more mainstream branch at The Beaches.

Cineplex Odeon Varsity
CINEMA

(Map p60; ☑416-961-6304; www.cineplex.com; Manulife Centre, 55 Bloor St W; ⊙noon-midnight; ⑤Bloor-Yonge) Screening a range of movies, from Hollywood blockbusters to small-budget indie releases, this state-of-the-art multiplex has VIP theaters and smaller screens.

Rainbow Cinemas
CINEMA

(Map p64; ☑416-491-9731; 80 Front St E; www.rainbowcinemas.ca; ◰503, 504) Plays first-run movies at second-run prices, right in Market Sq.

Scotiabank Theatre
CINEMA

(Map p60; ☑416-368-5600; www.paramount-toronto.com; 259 Richmond St W; ⑤Osgoode) This gargantuan multiplex shows new releases and the latest IMAX technology, including 3-D. It always screens a dozen movies or more, with some offbeat ones tossed among mainstream releases.

Polson Pier Drive-In Theatre
CINEMA

(☑416-465-4653; www.polsonpier.com; 11 Polson St; ⊙from 8:30pm Fri-Sun Apr-Oct) Double features of first-run blockbusters start around dusk at this lakeside yard; the usual fast-food suspects are on hand.

Live Music

Dust off your Iggy Pop T-shirt, don your Eddie Vedder Doc Martens and get rockin'. Alt-rock, metal, ska, punk and funk – Toronto has it all. Bebop, smoky swamp blues and acoustic balladry provide an alternative. Expect to pay anywhere from nothing to a few dollars on weeknights; up to $20 for weekend acts. Megatours play the Rogers Centre, the Air Canada Centre and the Molson Amphitheatre at Ontario Place.

ONTARIO

INDEPENDENT CONCERT HALLS

Koolhaus
LIVE MUSIC

(Map p64; 132 Queens Quay E; ◰6, 75) Inside Guvernment nightclub.

Opera House
LIVE MUSIC

(☑416-466-0313; www.theoperahousetoronto.com; 735 Queen St E; ◰501, 502, 503)

Phoenix
LIVE MUSIC

(Map p60; ☑416-323-1251; www.libertygroup.com; 410 Sherbourne St; ◰506)

ROCK, JAZZ & BLUES

Cameron House
LIVE MUSIC

(www.thecameron.com; 408 Queen St W; ◰501, 510) Singer-songwriters, soul, jazz and country performers grace the stage; artists, musos, dreamers and slackers crowd both front and back rooms. Sunday evening's Mad Bastard Cabaret ('accordion singing about love, lust and Spain') is a can't-miss.

Reservoir Lounge
LIVE MUSIC

(Map p64; www.reservoirlounge.com; 52 Wellington St E; ◰503, 504) Swing dancers, jazz singers and blues crooners call this candlelit basement lounge home. A great martini list includes a chocolate raspberry drink as well as the 'Reservoir Red,' and you can enjoy chocolate fondue strawberries while enjoying the entertainment.

Horseshoe Tavern
LIVE MUSIC

(Map p66; www.horseshoetavern.com; 370 Queen St W; ◰501, 510) Well past its 60th birthday, the legendary Horseshoe still plays a crucial role in the development of local indie rock. Not so local, The Police played here on their first North American tour – Sting did all PURPHP HI HIS HHHPHWPHP HHV HHPPHS at the door or check **Ticketmaster** (☑416-870-8000; www.ticketmaster.ca).

Dakota Tavern
LIVE MUSIC

(Map p66; www.thedakotatavern.com; 249 Ossington Ave; ◰501, ◰63) This basement tavern rocks with wooden-barrel stools and a small stage where you can catch a little bit of twang. Country music is the main sound, but you'll also hear some blues and rock.

Rivoli
LIVE MUSIC

(Map p60; www.rivoli.ca; 334 Queen St W; ◰501) Songbird Feist got her start here, and the talents keeps rolling in. Nightly live music (rock, indie and solo singer-songwriters), weekly stand-up comedy and monthly hip-hop nights are all part of the line-up. CD launches, art shows and Saturday-night DJs complete a very renaissance picture. There's also a pool hall, and the food is fabulous!

Rex
LIVE MUSIC

(Map p60; www.therex.ca; 194 Queen St W; 501) The Rex has risen from its pugilistic, blue-collared past to become an outstanding jazz and blues venue. Over a dozen different Dixieland, experimental and other local and international acts knock over the joint each week. Cheap drinks; affordable cover.

Lee's Palace
LIVE MUSIC

(Map p66; 416-532-1598; www.leespalace. com; 529 Bloor St W; Bathurst) Legendary Lee's Palace has set the stage over the years for Dinosaur Jr, Smashing Pumpkins and Queens of the Stone Age. Kurt Cobain started an infamous bottle-throwing incident when Nirvana played here in 1990. You can't miss it – look for the primary-colored mural that seems to scream out front.

Dominion on Queen
LIVE MUSIC

(www.dominiononqueen.com; 500 Queen St E; 501, 502, 503) This jazzy pub has earned a rep for sassy vocalists, trios and sextets through to full-blown swing bands. Music starts nightly around 9pm. Beers have a crafty edge, and there's plenty of *vin rouge* to soothe your big-city heartbreak.

Sneaky Dee's
LIVE MUSIC

(Map p66; 416-603-3090; www.sneaky-dees. com; 431 College St; 506, 511) Spangled with graffiti on the prominent Bathurst/College St corner, Sneaky Dee's isn't so sneaky-looking. The downstairs bar has battered booths with skeletons painted on them; upstairs is a darkened breeding ground for new TO rock talent. Fill up on Tex-Mex while downing cheap beer.

CLASSICAL & OPERA

Canadian Opera Company
LIVE MUSIC

(Map p60; 416-363-8231, 800-250-4653; www. coc.ca; Four Seasons Centre for the Performing Arts, 145 Queen St W; box office 11am-7pm Mon-Sat, to 3pm Sun; Osgoode) Canada's national opera company has been warbling its pipes for over 50 years. Tickets sell out fast; the Richard Bradshaw Amphitheatre (in the Four Seasons Centre) holds free concerts from September through June, usually at noon. Check the website for specific days.

Glenn Gould Studio
LIVE MUSIC

(Map p64; 416-205-5555; www.cbc.ca/glenn gould; Canadian Broadcasting Centre, 250 Front St W; tickets $15-40; box office 2-6:30pm Mon-Fri, to 8pm Sat; Union, 504) Glenn Gould Stu-dio's acoustics do the namesake famous pianist honors. Purchase advance tickets for evening concerts of classical and contemporary music by soloists, chamber groups, choirs and sinfonia between September and June. Young international artists are often featured.

Harbourfront Centre
LIVE MUSIC

(Map p64; 416-973-4000; www.harbourfront centre.com; York Quay Centre, 235 Queens Quay W; tickets $10-40; box office 1-6pm Tue-Sat; 509, 510) The vibrant Harbourfront Centre puts on a variety of world-class musical performances throughout the year, including Sunday family shows and free outdoor summer concerts in the Toronto Music Garden and on the Concert Stage.

Toronto Symphony Orchestra
LIVE MUSIC

(TSO; Map p64; 416-593-4828; www.tso.ca; Roy Thomson Hall, 60 Simcoe St; box office 10am-6pm Mon-Fri, noon-5pm Sat; St Andrew) A range of classics, Cole Porter–era pops and new music from around the world are presented by the TSO at Roy Thomson Hall, Massey Hall and the Toronto Centre for the Arts. Consult the website for the answers to such questions as 'What if I need to cough?' and 'Should I clap yet?'.

Other major classical and opera venues:

Sony Centre for the Performing Arts
LIVE MUSIC

(416-872-2262; www.sonycentre.ca; 1 Front St E; box office 10am-5:30pm Mon-Fri, to 1pm Sat; Union)

Massey Hall
LIVE MUSIC

(Map p60; 416-872-4255; www.masseyhall. com; 178 Victoria St; box office from noon on show days; Queen)

Roy Thomson Hall
LIVE MUSIC

(Map p64; 416-872-4255; www.roythomson. com; 60 Simcoe St; box office 10am-6pm Mon-Fri, noon-5pm Sat, 2hr pre-show Sun; St Andrew)

Toronto Centre for the Arts
LIVE MUSIC

(416-733-9388; www.tocentre.com; 5040 Yonge St; box office 11am-6pm Mon, to 8pm Tue-Sat, noon-4pm Sun; North York Centre)

Theater

Toronto is a playground for first-rate mainstream theater, centered around the Theatre Block and Dundas Sq. Upstart companies favor smaller venues around Harbourfront and in the Distillery District. Check www.onstagetoronto.ca or newspapers for current listings. Tickets for major productions are sold through **TicketKing** (☑416-872-1212, 800-461-3333; www.ticketking. com). For half-price tickets, go to **TO Tix** (Map p60; ☑416-536-6468, ext 40; www.totix.ca; Dundas Sq, 1 Dundas St E; ⊙noon-6:30pm Tue-Sat; ⑤Dundas) or ask about 'rush' tickets at box offices.

CanStage   THEATER
(Canadian Stage Company; ☑416-368-3110; www.canstage.com; 26 Berkeley St; ⊙box office 10am-6pm Mon-Sat, to 8pm show days; ⋒503, 504) Contemporary CanStage produces top-rated Canadian and international plays by the likes of David Mamet and Tony Kushner. Plays are staged at its own Berkeley Street Theatre, and the larger **St Lawrence Centre for the Arts** (Map p64; ☑416-366-7723, 1-800708-6754; www.stlc.com; 27 Front St E; ⊙box office noon-6pm Mon-Fri, 2hr prior to events; ⑤Union). CanStage also runs **Dream in High Park** (☑416-367-1652; High Park, 1873 Bloor St W; ⊙8pm Tue-Sun Jul-Sep; ⑤High Park), wonderful mid-summer productions of Shakespeare under the stars in High Park (Map p57). Show up early and bring a blanket.

Elgin & Winter Garden Theatre   THEATER
(Map p60; ☑416-314-2901; www.heritagefdn. on.ca; 189 Yonge St, Dundas Sq; ⊙box office 11am-5pm Tue-Sat; ⑤Queen) The restored double-decker Elgin & Winter Garden Theatre stages high-profile productions in an amazing setting.

Canon Theatre   THEATER
(☑416-872-1212, 800-461-3333; 244 Victoria St; www.mirvish.com ⊙box office noon-6pm Mon, to 8pm Tue-Sat, 11am-2pm Sun; ⑤Dundas) The Canon, a 1920s-era Pantages vaudeville hall is a hot ticket for musical extravaganzas.

Royal Alexandra Theatre   THEATER
(Map p64; ☑416-872-1212, 800-461-3333; www. mirvish.com; 260 King St W; ⊙box office 10:30am-6:30pm Mon, to 8:30pm Tue-Sat, 11am-3pm Sun; ⋒504) Commonly known as the 'Royal Alex,' this is one of the most impressive theaters in the city. Expect renditions of plays like Tennessee Williams' *Orpheus Descending* and splashy Broadway musicals.

Princess of Wales Theatre   THEATER
(Map p64; ☑416-872-1212, 800-461-3333; www. mirvish.com; 300 King St W; ⊙box office noon-6pm Mon, 3:30-8:30pm Tue, from noon Wed; ⋒504) Almost next door to the Royal Alex, POW theater is a 200-seat playhouse showing big-ticket items such as *Miss Saigon* and *Rock of Ages*.

Young Centre for Performing Arts THEATER
(☑416-866-8666; www.youngcentre.ca; 55 Mill St, Bldg 49, Distillery District; ⊙box office Tue-Sat 1-8pm; ⋒503, 504) The $14 million Young Centre houses four separate performance spaces, utilized by theatrical tenants including **Soul Pepper** (www.soulpepper.ca), **Moonhorse Dance Theatre** (www.danceum brella.net/clients_moonhorse.htm) and **George Brown Theatre Co** (www.georgebrown.ca/theatre). There's an on-site bookshop and bar too.

Factory Theatre   THEATER
(Map p66; ☑416-504-9971; www.factorytheatre. ca; 125 Bathurst St; ⊙box office 1-7pm Tue-Sat; ⋒511) This innovative theater company – 'Home of the Canadian Playwright' – has been busy for 35 years. The independent **SummerWorks Theatre Festival** (☑416-504-7529; www.summerworks.ca) stages plays at the Factory Theatre too, as do performers from the Toronto Fringe Festival. Sunday matinees are 'Pay What You Can.'

Gay & Lesbian Venues

Most of the following venues are in the Church-Wellesley Village. You could also try the El Convento Rico nightclub.

Fly   NIGHTCLUB
(Map p60; www.flynightclub.com; 8 Gloucester St; ⊙10pm-4am Fri & Sat; ⑤Wellesley) Off Yonge St, gay-focused Fly is a shirts-off muscle fest, with state-of-the-art sound and light, and US and international DJs spinning hard-house, tribal and trance. Music from the club is piped next door into Fire on the East Side, so you can enjoy a lounge scene before hitting the dance floor.

Woody's/Sailor   NIGHTCLUB
(Map p60; www.woodystoronto.com; 465-7 Church St; ⑤Wellesley) The city's most popular gay bar complex has a glad-bag of tricks, from drag shows, 'best ass' contests, leather sessions, billiards tables and nightly DJs. Sailor is a slick bar off to one side.

Slack's   NIGHTCLUB
(www.slacks.ca; 562 Church St; ⑤Wellesley) Bridging the divide between gays, lesbians, urban cowboys and straights all searching for a little glitz, quasi-retro Slack's opens its backlit bar to all-comers. Events include comedy, karaoke, drag shows, live music and art installations. Female DJ's spin on the weekends; the food's great too.

Black Eagle
NIGHTCLUB

(Map p60; www.blackeagletoronto.com; 457 Church St; S Wellesley) A charred-out, lawless tomb, Black Eagle lures leather-men, uniform fetishists and denim boys. Hard-core gay porn plays on big screens; the art on the walls is well hung in all senses of the expression. Check your clothes at the door for gritty theme nights (not for the mild-mannered).

Crews/Tango/Zone
NIGHTCLUB

(Map p60; 508 Church St; S Wellesley) This three-pronged joint sees women cranking up the heat at Tango, next door to the men's bar Crews (nice pun!) and the cabaret-style Zone. Show up for karaoke nights, drag queen/king shows and DJs spinning their stuff.

El Convento Rico
NIGHTCLUB

(416-588-7800; 750 College St; Fri & Sat; 506) Gender-bending Latino dance palace.

Nightclubs

Toronto's 'Clubland' convenes around Richmond St W and Adelaide St W at John St, where dozens of nightclubs come to life after dark. Nondescript doorways creak open, thick-necked bouncers cordon off sidewalks and queues of scantily clad girls start to form. Hip-hop guys drive hotted-up cars past the girls, hissing come-ons from wound-down windows. The air hangs heavy with clearly defined gender roles and anticipation. Later in the night, things get messy: drunk girls stagger, guys swing apocalyptic fists, hot-dog cart owners struggle to maintain order amongst the condiments. It's quite a scene!

Other club zones include Little Italy, Church-Wellesley Village and Queen West. Cover charges range from $5 to $15. Most clubs open around 9pm or 10pm (some don't really get going until later) and close around 4am.

Club XS
NIGHTCLUB

(www.clubxs.ca; 261 Richmond St W; Thu-Sun; 501, 505) One of Toronto's newest clubs, XS is a sexy venue where the dress code is strictly observed. With bottle service and VIP rooms (natch), XS caters to the elite. Though reservations aren't mandatory, if you want to make certain you're on the guest list you'd be wise to make them via the website.

Clinton's Tavern
NIGHTCLUB

(Map p66; www.clintonstavern.com; 693 Bloor St; S Christie) CD releases, Saturday night Shake-a-Tail parties, live music and comedy are all part of the line-up at Clinton's. It's a fun, casual crowd, and it's a bit of an antidote to the techie beats at other clubs.

Drake Hotel
NIGHTCLUB

(www.thedrakehotel.ca; 1150 Queen St W; 501) The Drake Hotel has a vibrant musical scene, with a lounge, a patio bar, and a basement underground.

Mod Club
NIGHTCLUB

(Map p66; www.themodclub.com; 722 College St; Tue-Sun; 506) Celebrating all things UK mod, this excellent Little Italy club plays electronic, indie and Brit pop, with occasional live acts like Paul Weller, The Killers and Muse taking the stage. Up-to-the-nanosecond lighting gives way to candlelit chill-out rooms.

Guvernment
NIGHTCLUB

(Map p64; www.theguvernment.com; 132 Queens Quay E; Tue-Sat; 6, 75) For diversity, nothing beats the gargantuan Guv. DJs play hip-hop, R&B, progressive house and tribal music to satisfy all appetites. Rooftop skyline views are as impressive as the Arabian fantasy lounge and art-deco bar. Koolhaus is the midsize live venue.

Sports

Torontonians weep with joy at the very mention of sport. There's professional baseball and football through the summer; ice hockey, basketball and lacrosse through the winter. **Ticketmaster** (416-872-5000; www.ticketmaster.ca) sells advance tickets, as do the box offices at the Air Canada Centre and Rogers Centre. Ticket scalping is illegal, but that doesn't seem to stop anybody (you can get some pretty sweet deals, but you didn't hear it from us...).

Toronto Blue Jays
SPORTS

(416-341-1234; www.toronto.bluejays.mlb.com; regular season Apr-Sep) Toronto's Major League Baseball team plays at the **Rogers Centre** (Map p64; 416-341-2770; www.rogerscentre.com; 1 Blue Jays Way; S Union). Buy tickets through Ticketmaster or at the Rogers Centre box office near Gate 9. The cheapest seats are way up above the field. Instead, try for seats along the lower level baselines where you have a better chance of catching a fly-ball (or wearing one in the side of the head). The Jays haven't won the World Series since 1993, but who knows, this could be their year.

Toronto Argonauts   SPORTS
(☑416-341-2700; www.argonauts.on.ca; ⊘regular season Jun-Oct) The Toronto Argonauts crack their Canadian Football League (CFL) helmets at the Rogers Centre. They haven't won the Grey Cup since 2004, but the Argos have brought home more championships than any other team (15, two ahead of Edmonton). Bring a jacket – the open-roof Rogers Centre cools off at night. Tickets through Ticketmaster or the Rogers Centre.

Toronto Maple Leafs   SPORTS
(☑416-815-5982; www.mapleleafs.com; ⊘regular season Oct-Apr) The 13-time Stanley Cup-winning Toronto Maple Leafs slap the puck around the **Air Canada Centre** (ACC; Map p64; ☑416-815-5500; www.theaircanadacentre.com; 40 Bay St; ⑤Union) in the National Hockey League (NHL). Every game sells out, but a limited number of same-day tickets go on sale through Ticketmaster at 10am and at the Air Canada Centre ticket window from 5pm. You can also buy tickets via the website from season ticket-holders who aren't attending – expect to pay around $80 and up.

Toronto Raptors   SPORTS
(☑416-815-5500; www.nba.com/raptors; ⊘regular season Oct-Apr) During hockey season, the Toronto Raptors of the National Basketball Association (NBA) also play at the ACC. The 'Raps' have been around since 1995, but haven't yet caused much of a flap. Tickets through Ticketmaster or the ACC.

Toronto Rock   SPORTS
(☑416-596-3075; www.torontorock.com; ⊘regular season Jan-Apr) Lacrosse may not immediately spring to mind when someone mentions Canadian sports, but the 13-team **National Lacrosse League** (www.nll.com) has been building momentum for two decades. Toronto's team is red hot, having won the championship five times since 1999. Games at the Air Canada Centre; tickets through Ticketmaster.

🔒 Shopping

Shopping in Toronto is more of a hobby than a necessity. Shops dot every part of the city, but you'll find concentrations of stores in monstrous malls like the **Eaton Centre** (Map p60; ☑416-598-8560; 220 Yonge St; ⊘10am-9pm Mon-Fri, 9:30am-7pm Sat, noon-6pm Sun; ⑤Queen, Dundas) or neighborhoods like Kensington Market, where young bohemians buy their rasta-retro threads. On the same side of town, eclectic Queen West and West Queen West have the lion's share of music and vintage shops.

The Annex features specialized bookstores, secondhand music shops and a hodgepodge of artistic vendors, especially along Harbord St and on Markham St (aka Mirvish Village). Chichi Bloor-Yorkville is the city center's most exclusive shopping district. This day-spa mecca was once 'Free Love' central for hippies during the 1960s. Nothing is free here nowadays, and don't expect much love from the haughty sales clerks.

Downtown, the underground PATH shops are literally bargain basements for discount clothing, everyday goods and services. Canadian and international design shops line King St W between Jarvis and Parliament Sts, an area known as the Design Strip. Also near downtown, the burgeoning Distillery District is a major draw, with design shops, art galleries and craft studios. The Yonge St Strip and Church-Wellesley Village house a mishmash of music, gay-friendly and random specialized shops.

Typical retail shopping hours are 10am until 6pm Monday to Saturday, noon to 5pm Sunday. But this varies depending on the season, the neighborhood and the amount of foot traffic.

Aboriginal Art & Canadian Crafts
Bay of Spirits Gallery   SOUVENIRS
(Map p64; www.bayofspirits.com; 156 Front St W; ⊘10am-6pm Mon-Sat; ⑤Union) The works of Norval Morrisseau – the first indigenous artist to have a solo exhibit at the National Gallery of Canada – are proudly on display in this atmospheric space, which carries aboriginal art from across Canada. Look for the Pacific West Coast totem poles (from miniature to over 4m tall), Inuit carvings and Inukshuk figurines.

Guild Shop   SOUVENIRS
(Map p60; www.theguildshop.ca; 118 Cumberland St; ⊘10am-6pm Mon-Wed, to 7pm Thu & Fri, to 6pm Sat, noon-5pm Sun; ⑤Bay) The **Ontario Crafts Council** (www.craft.on.ca) has been promoting artisans for over 70 years. Ceramics, jewelry, glassworks, prints and carvings make up most of the displays, but you could also catch a special exhibition of Pangnirtung weaving or Cape Dorset graphics. Staff are knowledgeable about First Nations art.

Arts on Queen
SOUVENIRS

(2198 Queen St E; ⊘11am-6:30pm Mon-Fri & Sun, from 9am Sat; 🚌501) It'll be hard to leave this cruisy store and gallery empty-handed. One-of-a-kind pottery, glassworks, photography and modern, fun art pieces are mostly made by Ontario-based artists, many of whom live in The Beaches.

Fashion

TOP CHOICE Preloved
CLOTHING

(Map p66; www.preloved.ca; 881 Queen St W; ⊘11am-7pm Mon-Wed, to 8pm Thu & Fri, to 7pm Sat, noon-6pm Sun; 🚌501) Preloved is all about reusing and recycling, but this is no thrift store: you can find Preloved designs on the runway. Reclaimed vintage fabrics are reassembled to create all-new, one-of-a-kind clothing. Women's items are the main focus, but kids and men will find kicky outfits as well. Items are reassuringly expensive, but not so much as to break the bank.

John Fluevog
ACCESSORIES

(Map p60; www.fluevog.com; 242 Queen St W; ⊘11am-7pm Mon-Wed & Sat, to 8pm Thu & Fri, noon-6pm Sun; 🚌501) Legendary Vancouver-based designer John Fluevog has always marched to the beat of his own drum, and this local favorite now carries bags and a line of hemp Veggie Vogs in addition to the famed granny platform boots and classic footwear. Reheeling and resoling is also done here.

Girl Friday
CLOTHING

(Map p66; www.girlfridayclothing.com; 740 Queen St W; ⊘noon-7pm Mon-Fri, from 11am Sat, noon-6pm Sun; 🚌501) Edgy, trendy and pretty, Girl Friday proves that office clothes don't need to be boring. Style never fades, and Girl Friday's pieces are trendy yet stylish enough to last. Formal dresses and jeans are up for grabs too.

Courage My Love
CLOTHING

(Map p66; 14 Kensington Ave; ⊘11am-7pm Mon-Wed & Sat, to 8pm Thu & Fri, to 6pm Sat, 1:30-5pm Sun; 🚌505, 510) Vintage clothing stores have been around Kensington Market for decades, but Courage My Love amazes fashion mavens with its secondhand slip dresses, retro pants and white dress-shirts in a cornucopia of styles. The beads, buttons, leather goods and silver jewelry are handpicked.

Annie Thompson Studio
CLOTHING

(www.anniethompson.ca 1 Wiltshire Ave; ⊘11am-6pm Tue-Sat, 1-5pm Sun; 🚌501) The motto of internationally famous designer Annie Thompson, 'Personality is a terrible thing to waste,' flows into the artistic and unique designs of her clothing, handbags and backpacks in this Queen West staple. Canadian-designed jewelry is available here too.

Books

Open Air Books & Maps
BOOKSTORE

(openairbooks@yahoo.ca; 25 Toronto St; ⊘10am-6pm Mon-Fri, to 5:30pm Sat; 🅂King) Ramshackle basement full of travel guides and maps plus books on nature, camping, history and outdoor activities.

BMV
BOOKSTORE

Bloor St (471 Bloor St W; ⊘11am-10pm Mon-Wed, to midnight Thu-Sat, noon-10pm Sun; 🅂Spadina); Dundas Sq (Dundas Sq, 10 Edward St; ⊘10am-11pm Mon-Sat, noon-8pm Sun; 🅂Dundas) The biggest (and most loved) used bookstore in Toronto.

Nicholas Hoare
BOOKSTORE

(www.nicholashoare.com; 45 Front St E; ⊘10am-6pm Mon-Wed, to 8pm Thu & Fri, 9am-6pm Sat, from noon Sun; 🅂King) One of the few shops where book covers face forward, this great little shop has loads of good reads and friendly staff.

TheatreBooks
BOOKSTORE

(www.theatrebooks.com; 11 St Thomas St; 🅂Bay) Original scripts, music, film, dance, drama theory, plus screenwriting software and DVDs.

ℹ Information

Cultural Centers

Alliance Française (📞416-922-2014; www.alliance-francaise.ca; 24 Spadina Rd; ⊘8am-9:30pm Mon-Thu, to 3:30pm Fri & Sat; 🅂Spadina)

Italian Cultural Institute (📞416-921-3802; www.iictoronto.esteri.it; 496 Huron St; ⊘9am-1pm & 2-5pm Mon-Fri; 🅂Spadina)

Japan Foundation (📞416-966-1600; www.japanfoundationcanada.org; 2nd fl, 131 Bloor St W; ⊘9am-3:30pm & 6-9pm Mon-Fri, 8am-9pm Sat; 🅂Bay)

Spanish Centre (📞416-925-4652; www.spanishcentre.com; 46 Hayden St; ⊘10am-9pm Mon-Thu, to 8pm Fri, to 3pm Sat; 🅂Bloor-Yonge)

Dangers & Annoyances

By North American standards, Toronto is extremely safe, but it's not a brilliant idea for women to walk alone after dark east of Yonge St from the Gardiner Expwy north to Carlton

St. The southern section of Jarvis St, between Carlton and Queen Sts, especially around Allan Gardens and George St, should also be avoided at night (actually it's not so great during the day either).

Many social service agencies have recently closed, creating a tide of homeless (often mentally ill) people on the streets – a real problem for Toronto. Most homeless people are more likely to be assaulted or harassed than to do so to you.

Emergency

Police, non-emergency (☑416-808-2222)

SOS Femmes (☑416-759-0138) French-language crisis line for women.

Toronto Rape Crisis Centre (☑416-597-8808)

Internet Access

Toronto's cheapest internet cafes congregate along the Yonge St Strip; Bloor St W in The Annex and Koreatown; and Chinatown's Spadina Ave. Rates start around $3 per hour. Wi-fi is becoming increasingly available at restaurants and coffee shops.

FedEx Office Queen St & Dundas Sq (505 University Ave; ☺24hr; ⑤St Patrick); The Annex (459 Bloor St W; ☺24hr; ⑤Spadina)

Net Plaza (267 College St; ☺8am-2am Sun-Fri, 24hr Fri & Sat; 🚌510)

Media

MAGAZINES & NEWSPAPERS

Eye Weekly (www.eyeweekly.com) Free alternative street press, with an arts and entertainment bent.

Globe & Mail (www.theglobeandmail.com) Elder statesman of the national daily newspapers.

Metro (www.metronews.ca) Free daily rag with bite-sized news, sports and entertainment (often left on subway seats).

Now Toronto (www.nowtoronto.com) Alternative weekly (good for events and concerts) free every Thursday.

Toronto Life (www.torontolife.com) Upscale monthly mag: lifestyle, dining, arts and entertainment.

Toronto Star (www.thestar.com) Canada's largest newspaper; a comprehensive left-leaning daily.

Toronto Sun (www.torontosun.com) Sensational tabloid with predictably good sports coverage.

Where Toronto (www.where.ca/toronto) The most informative of the free glossy tourist magazines.

Xtra! (www.xtra.ca) Free biweekly alternative gay and lesbian street press.

CILQ (107FM; www.q107.com) Classic rock broadcast from Dundas Sq.

CIUT (89.5FM; www.ciut.fm) Music and spoken-word from the U of T campus.

Edge (102.1FM; www.edge102.com) Toronto's premier new-rock station.

Medical Services

Dental Emergency Clinic (☑416-485-7121; www.dentalemergency.com; 1650 Yonge St; ☺8am-midnight; ⑤St Clair)

Hassle-Free Clinic (www.hasslefreeclinic. org; 2nd fl, 66 Gerrard St E; ⑤College) Women (☑416-922-0566; ☺10am-3pm Mon, Wed & Fri, 4-8pm Tue & Thu); Men (☑416-922-0603; ☺4-8pm Mon & Wed, 10am-3pm Tue & Thu, 4-7pm Fri, 10am-2pm Sat) STD/HIV testing and reproductive health.

Hospital for Sick Children (☑416-813-1500; www.sickkids.on.ca; 555 University, emergency 170 Gerrard St W; ☺24hr; ⑤Queens Park)

Mount Sinai Hospital (☑416-596-4200, emergency 416-586-5054; www.mtsinai.on.ca; 600 University Ave; ☺24hr; ⑤Queens Park)

Toronto General Hospital (☑416-340-3111, emergency 416-340-3946; www.uhn.ca; 190 Elizabeth St; ☺24hr; ⑤Queens Park)

Women's College Hospital (☑416-323-6400; www.womenscollegehospital.ca; 76 Grenville St; ☺24hr; ⑤College) Nonemergency women's and family health.

Money

ATMs are on every street corner. **American Express** (www.americanexpress.com/canada) branches function as travel agencies and don't handle financial transactions. Instead, tackle the banks or try **Money Mart** (www.moneymart.ca; 617 Yonge St; ☺24hr; ⑤Wellesley)

Post

Toronto no longer has a main post office, but over two dozen branch offices and outlets in drugstores are dotted throughout the city. The most central is probably the **Adelaide St Post Office** (☑866-607-6301; www.canadapost.ca; 31 Adelaide St E; ☺8am-5:45pm Mon-Fri; ⑤Queen).

Tourist Information

Ontario Travel Information Centre (☑English 800-668-2746, French 800-268-3736; www.ontariotravel.net; 20 Dundas St W; ☺10am-8pm Mon-Fri, to 6pm Sat, noon-5pm Sun; ⑤Dundas) Knowledgeable, multilingual staff and overflowing racks of brochures.

Tourism Toronto (☑416-203-2500, 800-499-2514; www.seetorontonow.com; 207 Queens Quay W; ☺8:30am-6pm Mon-Fri; ⑤Union) Contact one of the telephone agents; after hours use the automated touch-tone information menu.

ⓘ Getting There & Away

Air

Most Canadian airlines and international carriers arrive at Canada's busiest airport, **Lester B Pearson International Airport** (YYZ; Map p57; ☑866-207-1690, Terminals 1 & 2 416-247-7678, Terminal 3 416-776-5100; www.gtaa.com), 27km northwest of downtown Toronto. Terminal assignments are subject to change; call ahead or check airport entrance signs.

Air Canada and WestJet compete heavily and match fares between Toronto and Ottawa (from $69), Montréal (from $69), Calgary (from $159), Edmonton (from $159), Vancouver (from $179) and Victoria (from $224).

On the Toronto Islands, small **Toronto City Centre Airport** (TCCA; ☑416-203-6942; www.torontoport.com/airport.asp) is home to regional airlines, helicopter companies and private flyers. Air Canada Jazz flights from Ottawa land at TCCA rather than Pearson.

Bus

Long-distance buses operate from the **Metro Toronto Coach Terminal** (www.torontocoach terminal.com; 610 Bay St; Ⓢ Dundas), where the **Travellers' Assistance Services of Toronto** (☑416-596-8647; www.travellersaid.com; ◷9:30am-9:30pm) have a help desk. When making reservations, always ask for a direct or express bus. Advance tickets are cheaper but don't guarantee a seat.

See the table opposite for **Greyhound Canada** (www.greyhound.ca) routes from Toronto:

Coach Canada (www.coachcanada.com) offers similar routes (mostly) and prices.

Union Station downtown serves as the bus and train depot for **GO Transit** (www.gotransit.com), a government line that services nearby towns. It's mainly used by commuters, but does go a relatively long way west and north of Toronto.

Car & Motorcycle

Toronto is served by expressways from all directions. Expect lots of congestion. Along the lake,

the Gardiner Expwy runs west into Queen Elizabeth Way (QEW) to Niagara Falls. At the city's western border is Hwy 427, which runs north to the airport. The tolled (and often bumper-to-bumper) Hwy 401 runs east–west above the downtown area: east to Montréal, west to Windsor. On the eastern side of the city, the Don Valley Pkwy connects Hwy 401 to the Gardiner Expwy. Hwy 400 and Hwy 404 run north from Toronto.

International car-rental agencies have desks at Pearson airport, as well as city offices. Smaller independent agencies offer lower rates, but may have fewer (and older) cars. **New Frontier Rent-a-Car** (☑416-675-2000, 800-567-2837; www.newfrontiercar.com; 5875 Airport Rd, Mississauga) and **Wheels 4 Rent** (☑416-585-7782; www.wheels4rent.ca; 77 Nassau St; ☒510) rent compact cars from around $35 per day excluding taxes.

For long-distance trips, try **Auto Drive-Away Co** (☑416-225-7754, 800-561-2658; www.torontodriveaway.com; 5803 Yonge St; ☒97), which has cars for Canadian and US destinations. Also check the newspaper classified ads in either the *Toronto Sun* or the *Toronto Star* and the travel ads in *Now*.

Train

Grand **Union Station** (Map p64; ☑416-869-300; www.viarail.com; 140 Bay St) downtown is Toronto's main rail hub, with currency exchange booths and two **Travellers' Aid Society** (☑416-366-7788; www.travellersaid.com; ◷9:30am-9:30pm) help desks. VIA Rail plies the heavily trafficked Québec City–Windsor corridor and beyond. Daily departures are in the table below.

Ontario Northland (☑416-314-3750; www.ontarionorth land.ca) runs the *Northlander* train to northern Ontario, visiting Huntsville, North Bay and Temagami, and the *Polar Bear Express* to Moosonee. For the latter, take the *Northlander* to Cochrane ($131, 11 hours, once daily except Saturday) and make connections there.

Amtrak trains link Toronto's Union Station with Buffalo ($52, four hours, one daily), Chicago ($130, 15 hours, one daily) and New York City ($125, 14 hours, one daily).

GO Transit trains and buses also use the station.

VIA RAIL TRAIN INFORMATION

DESTINATION	COST	DURATION	FREQUENCY
Kingston	$81	2½hr	10 daily
London	$55	2hr	8 daily
Montréal	$130	5¼hr	6 daily
Niagara Falls	$35	2hr	2 daily
Ottawa	$119	4½hr	6 daily
Sudbury Junction	$105	7hr	1 daily
Vancouver	$795	75hr	1 daily

DESTINATION	COST	DURATION	FREQUENCY
Hamilton	$91	2hr	5 daily
London	$37	2½-3½hr	frequent
Montréal	$94	8-10hr	frequent
Niagara Falls	$30	1½-2hr	8 daily
Ottawa	$76	5½hr	10 daily
Sault Ste Marie	$127	10-11hr	3 daily
Sudbury	$69	5hr	3 daily
Thunder Bay	$184	20hr	3 daily

ⓘ Getting Around

To/From the Airport

Airport Express (☏905-564-3232, 800-387-6787; www.torontoairportexpress.com) operates an express bus connecting Pearson International with the **Metro Toronto Coach Terminal** (☏416-393-7911; www.greyhound.ca; 610 Bay St; ☺5:30am-midnight; Ⓢ Dundas) and major downtown hotels. Buses depart every 20 to 30 minutes from 5am to 1am. Allow 1½ hours to get to/from the airport. A one-way/round-trip ticket costs $17/30 (cash, credit card or US dollars). Students and seniors receive $2 off one-way fares; kids under 11 travel free. Buses leave Terminals 1/2/3 from curbside locations B3/17/25.

If you're not buried under luggage, the cheapest way to Pearson is via the TTC. From the airport, the 192 Airport Rocket bus departs Terminals 1, 2 and 3 every 20 minutes from 5:30am to 2am. It's a 20-minute ride to Kipling Station ($2.75, exact change only), where you transfer free onto the Bloor–Danforth subway line using your bus ticket. Allow an hour for the full trip. The 300A Bloor-Danforth night bus runs every 15 minutes from 2am to 5am ($3, exact change only). The 300A departs the same locations as the 192; it's 45 minutes from Pearson to Yonge and Bloor.

A taxi from Pearson into the city takes around 45 minutes, depending on traffic. The Greater Toronto Airports Authority (GTAA) regulates fares by drop-off zone ($46 to downtown Toronto). A metered taxi from central Toronto to Pearson costs around $50. If you're driving yourself to/from the airport, avoid Hwy 401 and take the Gardiner Expwy west from Spadina Ave, then head north on Hwy 427. Parking at the Terminal 1, 2 and 3 garages costs $3 per half-hour, $24 per day. Long-term parking at off-site lots costs around $13 per day or $50 per week.

Boat

From April to September, **Toronto Islands Ferries** (☏416-392-8193; www.city.toronto.on.ca/parks/island/ferry.htm; adult/child/concession $6/2.50/3.50) run every 15 to 30 minutes from 8am to 11pm. The journey (to either Ward's Island or Hanlan's Point) only takes 15 minutes, but queues can be long on weekends and holidays – show up early. From October to March, ferry services are slashed (roughly hourly), only servicing Ward's Island, plus a couple per day to Hanlan's Point. The Toronto Islands Ferry Terminal is at the foot of Bay St, off Queens Quay.

Bicycle

See p74 for bicycle-rental operators.

Car & Motorcycle

Parking in Toronto is expensive – usually $3 to $4 per half-hour, with an average daily maximum of $12 or more (or a flat rate of around $6 after 6pm). Cheapest are the municipal lots run by the **Toronto Parking Authority** (☏416-393-7275; www.greenp.com) – look for the green signs. They cost the same as metered street parking – usually $3 per hour. Some metered spaces have a central payment kiosk – purchase your time then display the receipt on your dashboard. It's illegal to park next to a broken meter; residential streets have severely restricted on-street parking.

Traffic is horrendous around the edges of town, and construction never ends – always allow extra time. Vehicles must stop for streetcars, behind the rear doors, while the streetcar is collecting or ejecting passengers. Drivers must also stop for pedestrians at crosswalks when crossing signals are flashing.

Hwy 407, running east–west from Markham to Mississauga for about 40km just north of the city, is an electronic toll road. Cameras record your license plate and the time and distance traveled. If you don't have a prepaid gizmo on your car, expect a bill in the mail (Canada, US or Zanzibar, they'll find you).

Public Transportation

The **Toronto Transit Commission** (TTC; ☏416-393-4636; www.toronto.ca/ttc) operates Toronto's efficient subway, streetcar and bus system. The regular fare is adult/child/ concession $3/0.70/1.85 (cash), or 10 tickets (or tokens) for $21. Day passes ($8.50) and weekly Metropasses ($30) are also available. Tickets or tokens are available in the subway and at some convenience stores. You can transfer to any other TTC bus, subway or streetcar for free using your paper streetcar/bus ticket or transfer ticket from automated dispensers near subway exits. Exact change is required for streetcars and buses; subway attendants are more forgiving.

Subway lines operate from approximately 6am (9am on Sunday) until 1:30am daily, with trains every five minutes. The main lines are the cross-town Bloor–Danforth line, and the U-shaped Yonge–University–Spadina line which bends through Union Station. Stations have Designated Waiting Areas (DWAs) monitored by security cameras and equipped with a bench, pay phone and intercom link to the station manager.

Streetcars are slower than the subway, but they stop every block or two. Streetcars operate from 5am until 1:30am on weekdays with reduced weekend services. The main east–west routes are along St Clair Ave (512), College St (506), Dundas St (505), Queen St (501 and 502) and King St (503 and 504). North–south streetcars grind along Bathurst St (511) and Spadina Ave (510). The 511 turns west at the lakefront toward the Canadian National Exhibition (CNE) grounds; the 510 turns east toward Union Station. The 509 Harbourfront streetcar trundles west from Union Station along Lake Shore Blvd.

Visitors won't find much use for TTC buses, which are slow and get held up in traffic. Women traveling alone between 9pm and 5am can request stops anywhere along regular bus routes; notify the driver in advance and exit via the front doors.

For more far-flung travel, the TTC system connects with GO Transit's **GO Bus** (☎416-869-3200, 888-438-6646; www.gotransit.com) routes in surrounding suburbs like Richmond Hill, Brampton and Hamilton.

Taxi

Metered fares start at $4, plus $1.60 per kilometer, depending on traffic. There are taxi stands outside hotels, museums, shopping malls and entertainment venues. Reliable companies:

Crown Taxi (☎416-240-0000; www.crowntaxi. com)

Diamond Taxicab (☎416-366-6868; www. diamondtaxi.ca)

Royal Taxi (☎416-777-9222; www.royaltaxi.ca)

AROUND TORONTO

Within 1½ hours' drive of Toronto is a crop of small towns that were once functional farming communities. The land here is fertile, but working farms have given way to urban sprawl. Stifled city-slickers still make day trips around this district though, especially on Sundays, enjoying the rolling landscapes, and walking and picnicking in conservation areas.

Not far southeast of here, Terra Cotta is one of the closest points to Toronto for access to the Bruce Trail, perfect for an afternoon's walk. The Hockley Valley area, near Orangeville, offers more of the same. The Credit River has trout fishing, and in winter the area is not bad for cross-country skiing.

David Dunlap Observatory

Just north of the Toronto city limits, the **David Dunlap Observatory** (☎905-883-0174; www.theddo.ca; 123 Hillsview Dr, Richmond Hill; adult/child/senior $10/2/5; ⊗8:30pm Sat Jun-Oct, also 8:30pm Fri Jul-Aug; P) is a major player in the cut-throat world of international stargazing. On Saturday evenings,

THE MAGNIFICENT SEVEN

The Group of Seven, a gung-ho, all-male group of Canadian landscape painters, first joined in the 1920s. Fired by an almost adolescent enthusiasm, they rampaged through the wilds of northern Ontario, capturing the rugged Canadian wilderness through the seasons in all kinds of weather. The energy they felt joyfully expressed itself in vibrant, light-filled canvases of mountains, lakes, forests and provincial townships.

Painter Tom Thomson died before the group was officially formed, but the other members – which included Arthur Lismer, JEH MacDonald, Frank Johnston, Frederick Varley and Franklin Carmichael – considered him their leading light. An experienced outdoorsman, Thomson drowned in 1917 just as he was producing some of his most powerful work. His deep connection to the land is obvious in his works hanging in the Art Gallery of Ontario in Toronto. His rustic cabin has been moved onto the grounds of the McMichael Canadian Art Collection, which, along with Ottawa's National Gallery, is the best place to view esteemed Group of Seven creations.

the observatory presents introductory talks on modern astronomy (but 'no math!'), followed by interplanetary voyeurism through Canada's biggest optical telescope (the reflector measures 1.9m). Nights without a lecture are cheaper; book ahead as there are limited tickets available. Call to check weather conditions. No kids under seven.

From Toronto, drive 30 minutes up Bayview Ave past 16th Ave to Hillsview Dr, turn left onto Hillsview Dr and drive 1km west until you see the sinister white dome on your left. Alternatively take the TTC subway north to Finch station. Walk underground to a nearby transit terminal and catch the 91 Bayview bus operated by **York Region Transit** (www.yorkregiontransit.com). This bus stops on request at Hillsview Dr, from where it's a 1km walk to the observatory. The one-way trip costs $3, with a free transfer from the subway station.

McMichael Canadian Art Collection

Handcrafted wooden buildings (which include painter Tom Thomson's cabin, moved from its original location) are set amidst 40 hectares of conservation trails at the **McMichael Canadian Art Collection** (www.mcmichael.com; 10365 Islington Ave, Kleinburg; adult/child/concession/family $15/free/12/30; ⊙10am-4pm; P). Works by Canada's best-known landscape painters, the Group of Seven, as well as First Nations, Inuit and other acclaimed Canadian artists, are on display. School groups tend to overrun the gallery on weekday mornings

To get here from Toronto (a 34km, 45-minute drive), take the Queen Elizabeth Way (QEW) west to Hwy 427, driving north past Hwy 401. Exit at Hwy 7, drive east (turn left) 6km, then turn north onto Hwy 27, then right onto Major Mackenzie Dr. At the next traffic light, turn left onto Islington Ave. Drive 1km north to the gallery gates, or park in Kleinburg then backtrack on foot. Parking is $5.

Local Conservation Areas

Southern Ontario is urban. To offset this somewhat, the government has designated many conservation areas – small nature parks for walking, picnicking and (sometimes) fishing, swimming and cross-country skiing. The **Toronto and Region Conservation Authority** (www.trca.on.ca) is responsible for the development and operation of these areas, most of which are difficult to reach without a vehicle.

West of Toronto near Milton is **Crawford Lake Conservation Area** (Steeles Ave, at Guelph Line; adult/child $6.25/4.50; ⊙10am-4pm; P), one of the most interesting conservation area in the entire system. Deep, glacial Crawford Lake is set in the woods, surrounded by walking trails. Read up on its formation at the interpretive center. Crawford Lake is 5km south of Hwy 401, down a road called Guelph Line (Hwy 1). The Bruce Trail also runs through the park.

For a quick summer escape, try **Albion Hills Conservation Area** (Hwy 50, Albion; adult/child $6/free; ⊙9am-dusk; P), a quiet, wooded area with walking trails and cross-country skiing in winter. It's on the west side of Toronto; take Hwy 427 north from the airport, then Hwy 50 for about 20km to the park.

Also in this region, near Kleinburg, is the **Kortright Centre for Conservation** (9550 Pine Valley Dr, Woodbridge; adult/child $5/3 Sat & Sun, free Mon-Fri; ⊙10am-4pm; P). There are trails here too, but it's more of a museum, with displays and demonstrations on resources, wildlife and ecology.

In the same general area as Crawford Lake is the **Mountsberg Conservation Area** (Millburough Line, Mountsberg; adult/child $6.25/4.50; ⊙10am-9pm Jun-Aug, reduced winter hours; P). It's 19km west of Milton; exit south off Hwy 401 at Guelph Line and head southwest from Campbellville. The site runs country-related educational programs, including a maple-syrup demonstration explaining the history, collection and production of this Canadian specialty, and there's a raptor center here, too. Kids can climb, scale and slide themselves silly in the Cameron Playbarn on-site.

NIAGARA PENINSULA

Jutting east from Hamilton and forming a natural divide between Lake Erie and Lake Ontario, the Niagara Peninsula is a legitimate tourist hot spot. Though many only see the Falls and Clifton Hill on a day tour from Toronto, there is lots to explore here. Consider a several-day visit to fully experience the wineries and wonders of the Peninsula.

Water flows from Lake Erie, 100m higher than Lake Ontario, via two avenues: stepping down steadily through the locks along the Welland Canal, or surging over Niagara Falls in a reckless, swollen torrent. A steep escarpment jags along the spine of the peninsula, generating some weird weather. Humid and often frost-free, this is Ontario's premier wine-growing region, the commercial focus of which is picture-postcard Niagara-on-the-Lake.

Niagara Peninsula Wine Country

The Niagara Peninsula adheres to the 43rd parallel – a similar latitude to northern California and further south than Bordeaux, France. A primo vino location, the mineral-rich soils and moderate microclimate are the perfect recipe for viticulture success. A visit to the area makes an indulgent day trip or lazy weekend, with haughty old vineyards and brash newcomers competing for your attention.

Touring the vineyards by car is the best way to go. There are two main areas to focus on: west of St Catharines around Vineland, and north of the Queen Elizabeth Way (QEW) around Niagara-on-the-Lake. Regional tourist offices stock wine-route maps and brochures, which are also available at winery tasting rooms. For more info, check out www.winesofontario.ca.

Winery Driving Tour

The following drive weaves through the best Niagara wineries. Besides tastings, most offer tours and dining; check the respective websites for more info. Parking is free at all vineyards.

Coming from Toronto, take QEW exit 78 at Fifty Rd into Winona and **Puddicombe Estate Farms & Winery** (www.puddicombe farms.com; 1468 Hwy 8, Winona; tastings $0.50; ☺9am-5pm May-Dec, 9am-5pm Mon-Fri, 10am-4pm Sat & Sun Jan-Apr), a rustic farm specializing in fruit wines (try the peach and the iced apple). Light lunches available.

Off QEW exit 74 is **Kittling Ridge Winery** (www.kittlingridge.com; 297 South Service Rd, Grimsby; tastings free; ☺10am-6pm Mon-Sat, 11am-5pm Sun, free tours 2pm Tue-Sat year-round & 11am Sun Jun-Aug). It looks like a factory, but friendly staff and award-winning ice- and late-harvest wines will win you over.

Continue east on the service road, then cut south onto rambling Hwy 81; photogenic **Peninsula Ridge Estates Winery** (pen-

insularidge.com; 5600 King St W, Beamsville; tastings $0.50, tours $5; ☺10am-6pm, tour 11:30am Jun-Nov) is unmissable on a hilltop. The lofty timber tasting room, restaurant and hilltop setting are magic.

From Hwy 81, turn right at Cherry Ave up the hill and then turn left onto Moyer Rd for the stone buildings of **Vineland Estates Winery** (www.vineland.com; 3620 Moyer Rd, Vineland; tastings $3, tours $6; ☺10am-6pm May-Oct, 11am-5pm Nov-Apr), the elder statesman of Niagara viticulture. Almost all the wines here are excellent – Riesling and cabernet franc are the flavors of the moment. The restaurant and accommodations are fabulous too.

Backtrack up to King St, and northeast at the intersection of King and Cherry you'll see the wine business of Canada's beloved hockey star, **Wayne Gretzky Estate** (www.gretzky.com; 3751 King St, Vineland; ☺10am-6pm Mon-Sat, from 11am Sun summer, 10am-5pm Mon-Sat, from 11am Sun winter).

Follow King Rd east, turn right onto Victoria Ave, then left onto 7th Ave for friendly **Flat Rock Cellars** (www.flatrockcellars.com; 2727 7th Ave, Jordan; tastings $1-2, tours $10-25; ☺10am-6pm Mon-Sat, from 11am Sun Apr-Dec, noon-5pm Mon-Fri, 10am-6pm Sat, from 11am Sun Jan-Mar). The hexagonal architecture and lake views here are almost as good as the wine!

Wander back toward the lake to 4th Ave and cheery **Creekside Estate Winery** (www.creeksidewine.com; 2170 4th Ave, Jordan Station; tastings free if purchasing, tours free; ☺10am-6pm May-Sep, to 5pm Oct-Apr, tours 2pm), where you can tour the crush pad and underground cellars. Try the sauvignon blanc.

From 7th Ave, scoot back onto the QEW and truck east into the Niagara-on-the-Lake region. Take exit 38 and head north onto Four Mile Creek Rd, which will take you to **Hillebrand Estates Winery** (www.hillebrand.com; 1249 Niagara Stone Rd, Niagara-on-the-Lake; tastings $5-10; ☺10am-9pm Jun-Aug, to 6pm Sep-May). Mass-market wines are the name of the game here, but hourly introductory tours and tasting-bar presentations are good if you're new to the wine scene.

Further north, superiority emanates from **Konzelmann Estate Winery** (www.konzelmann.ca; 1096 Lakeshore Rd, Niagara-on-the-Lake; tastings $0.50-4, tours $5; ☺10am-6pm May-Oct, 10am-5pm Mon-Sat, from 11am

THE GRAPE ONE

Hockey: it's not just about beers and brawls anymore, at least since Ontario's favorite son, NHL hockey legend Wayne 'The Great One' Gretzky, embarked on a new career as a winemaker. **Wayne Gretzky Estates** (www.gretzky.com; 3751 King St, Vineland; ◷10am-6pm Mon-Sat, from 11am Sun summer, 10am-5pm Mon-Sat, from 11am Sun winter) opened in 2009 and is producing a veritable rainbow of wines, from cab-merlot blends to ice wine to Rieslings. Before you doubt that a switch from hockey pro to viticulturist is possible, know that No 99, as it's dubbed, has won several awards. Nevertheless, we doubt Ontario's legions of rabid hockey fans will be switching from beer to wine anytime soon.

Sun Nov-Apr, tours 11am, 1 & 3pm May-Sep), one of the oldest wineries in the region and the only one to take full advantage of the lakeside microclimate. Snooty, maybe, but the late-harvest vidal and ice wines are superb.

Next on the right is **Strewn** (www.strewn winery.com; 1339 Lakeshore Rd, Niagara-on-the-Lake; tastings $0.50-2, tours free; ◷10am-6pm, tours 1:30pm), producing medal-winning vintages and home to a classy restaurant and **Wine Country Cooking School** (www. winecountrycooking.com), where one-day, weekend and weeklong classes are a gastronomic delight.

Closer to Niagara-on-the-Lake, **Sunnybrook Farm Estate Winery** (www.sunny brookfarmwinery.com; 1425 Lakeshore Rd, Niagara-on-the-Lake; tastings $1-3; ◷10am-6pm mid-May–mid-Oct, 11am-5pm Mon-Fri, from 10am Sat & Sun mid-Oct–mid-May) specializes in unique Niagara fruit and berry wines, and brews a mean 'hard' cider. It's only a little place, so tour buses usually don't stop here.

TOP **Stratus** (www.stratuswines.com; 2059 Niagara Stone Rd, Niagara-on-the-Lake; tastings $10; ◷11am-5pm May-Dec, noon-5pm Wed-Sat Jan-Apr) on Niagara Stone Rd, south of Niagara-on-the-Lake, is brilliant, the first building in Canada to earn LEED (Leadership in Energy & Environmental Design) certification. The design addresses complex recycling, organic, energy-efficient and indigenous concerns. Your wine choice is less complex: Stratus White or Stratus Red.

Heading south down the Niagara Pkwy, **Reif Estate Winery** (www.reifwinery.com; 15608 Niagara Pkwy, Niagara-on-the-Lake; 1st tasting free then $1-5, tours $5-20; ◷10am-6pm Apr-Oct, to 5pm Nov-Mar, tours 11:30am & 1:30pm May-Oct), pronounced 'Rife,' is a well-established winery. Ice wines are what you're here for.

Nearby, award-winning **Inniskillin** (www. inniskillin.com; 1499 Line 3, cnr Niagara Pkwy, Niagara-on-the-Lake; tastings $1-20, tours $5; ◷9am-6pm, tours hourly 10:30am-4:30pm May-Oct, reduced schedule Nov-Apr) is a master of the ice-wine craft.

☞ Tours

See p114 for winery tours departing Niagara-on-the-Lake.

Crush on Niagara   WINERY TOURS
(☏905-562-3373, 866-408-9463; www.crush tours.com; tours $69-99) Small-group morning and afternoon van tours departing from various pickup points in the Niagara region.

Niagara Airbus   WINERY TOURS
(☏905-374-8111, 800-268-8111; www.niagara airbus.com; tours from Niagara Falls $46-117, from Toronto $123-180) Stops at well-known wineries; some itineraries include vineyard tours, lunch and shopping in Niagara-on-the-Lake.

✺ Festivals & Events

Niagara Icewine Festival
                                        WINE FESTIVAL
(www.niagaraicewinefestival.com) A 10-day winter festival held throughout the Niagara region during mid-January, showcasing Ontario's stickiest, sweetest ice wines.

Niagara New Vintage Festival
                                FOOD & WINE FESTIVAL
(www.grapeandwine.com) Celebrating Niagara's new-season vino and regional cuisine in late June.

Niagara Wine Festival   WINE FESTIVAL
(www.niagarawinefestival.com) A weeklong event in mid-September celebrating the region's finest picks off the vine.

ICE, ICE BABY

Niagara's regional wineries burst onto the scene at Vinexpo 1991 in Bordeaux, France. In a blind taste test, judges awarded a coveted gold medal to an Ontario ice wine – international attendees' jaws hit the floor! These specialty vintages, with their arduous harvesting and sweet, multidimensional palate, continue to lure aficionados to the Niagara Peninsula.

To make ice wine, a certain percentage of grapes are left on the vines after the regular harvest is over. If birds, storms and mildew don't get to them, the grapes grow ever-more sugary and concentrated. Winemakers wait patiently until December or January when three days of consistent, low temperature (-8°C) freeze the grapes entirely.

In the predawn darkness (so the sun doesn't melt the ice and dilute the grape juice), the grapes are carefully harvested by hand, then pressed and aged in barrels for up to a year. After decanting, the smooth ice vintages taste intensely of apples, or even more exotic fruit, and pack a serious alcoholic punch.

Why are ice wines so expensive? It takes 10 times the usual number of grapes to make just one bottle. This, combined with labor-intensive production and the high risk of crop failure, often drives the price above $50 per 375mL bottle. Late-harvest wines picked earlier in the year may be less costly (and less sweet), but just as full-flavored and aromatic.

🛏 Sleeping & Eating

See www.20valley.ca for local B&B listings.

TOP CHOICE **Squirrel House Gardens**   B&B $$$
(☎905-685-1608; www.squirrelhouse niagara.ca; 1819 5th St, St Catharines; ste incl breakfast $180; P⊖@☒) Stay in a massive suite in the old barn, built in 1850 as part of this country estate. Lovingly decorated, the room opens onto a massive garden and features brick and colored cement floors, original wood beams, and French doors that open onto a deck. The grounds have a swimming pool, patio and fire pit. The delightful, arty owners are welcoming and friendly, and take as good care of you as they do for their impressive country garden.

Bonnybank   B&B $$
(☎905-562-3746,888-889-8296;www.bbcanada. com/bonnybank; RR 1, Vineland; r incl breakfast $95-135; P⊖❄☎) A stately Tudor-meets-Grimsby-sandstone house in an owl-filled wilderness setting. Call for directions, as it's not signposted and is a little off the beaten track (a good thing!).

Vineland Estates Winery   B&B $$$
(☎905-562-7088, 888-846-3526; www.vineland. com; 3620 Moyer Rd, Vineland; r incl breakfast $175, guesthouse $295; P⊖❄) The seminal Niagara winery also has a small but perfectly formed B&B for two, and a three-bedroom guesthouse.

Peninsula Ridge   FUSION $$$
(☎905-563-0900; 5600 King St W, Beamsville; mains $16-35; ⊙lunch Wed-Sun, dinner Wed-Sat) Sit outside, upstairs or down in this high-Victorian 1885 manor, serving haute cuisine that won't break the bank. Super-chef Robert Trout will start you on Prince Edward Island mussels steamed in chardonnay and coconut milk, and follow up with double-smoked, bacon-wrapped rib eye stuffed with herb mustard.

Peach Country Farm Market   MARKET $
(4490 Victoria Ave, Vineland Station; items from $2; ⊙9am-8pm Jun-Aug, to 6pm Sep & Oct) An open-fronted barn selling fresh fruit, jams, ice cream and fruit pies, all grown, picked and baked on-site by fourth-generation farmers – a roadside gem!

Pie Plate   BAKERY $
(41516 Niagara Stone Rd, Virgil; sandwiches $7-10; ⊙10am-5pm Tue-Sun) Simple but delicious lunches (we devoured the pear and brie sandwich) at reasonable prices. It wouldn't be an Ontario bakery without butter tarts, but there's also thin-crust pizzas, meat pies, salads and a few beers on tap. A great place to fill up your belly while touring the wine country.

Vineland Estates Winery Restaurant   FUSION $$
(☎905-562-7088, 888-846-3526; 3620 Moyer Rd, Vineland; mains $15-40, tasting menus

$39-70; ⊗11:30am-2:30pm & 5:30-8:30pm)
The winery's elegant restaurant proffers
unbeatable vineyard views and locally
sourced, seasonal inventions such as summer risotto with garden greens, cherry tomatoes and roasted eggplant caviar. Reservations advised.

❶ Getting There & Away

The 100km drive from Toronto to the central
peninsula takes around 1½ hours – take Hwy
403 then the QEW east from Hamilton toward
Niagara Falls. The official Wine Route is signposted off the QEW, on rural highways and along
backcountry roads.

Welland Canal Area

Built between 1914 and 1932, the historic
Welland Canal, running from Lake Erie
into Lake Ontario, functions as a shipping bypass around Niagara Falls. Part of
the St Lawrence Seaway, allowing shipping between the industrial heart of North
America and the Atlantic Ocean, eight locks
along the 42km-long canal overcome the
difference of about 100m in the lakes' water
levels.

On Lake Ontario, understated **St Catharines** (www.stcatharines.ca) is the major town of the Niagara fruit- and wine-
producing district. Remnants of the first
three canals (built in 1829, 1845 and 1887)
are visible at various points around town,
while the Welland Canals Pkwy traces
the canal along the city's eastern edge –
seeing massive container ships floating
along *above* road level is a disconcerting
experience.

Before it shifted east to Port Weller, the
original Welland Canal opened into Lake
Ontario at Lakeside Park in **Port Dalhousie** (pronounced Dal-*oo*-zey). This rustic
harbor area is a blend of old and new, with
a reconstructed wooden lock and an 1835
lighthouse alongside bars, restaurants and
ice-cream parlors. Hikers and cyclists can
stretch out along the 45km **Merritt Trail**
(www.canadatrails.ca/tct/on/merritt.html), an
established track along the Welland Canal
from Port Dalhousie to Port Colborne.

For a more up-to-date look at the canal, the FREE **Welland Canals Centre** (www.
stcatharineslock3museum.ca; 1932 Welland
Canals Pkwy; ⊗9am-5pm Jul-Aug, reduced
weekend hours in winter; P) at Lock 3, just
outside St Catharines, has a viewing plat-

form close enough to almost touch the
building-sized ships as they wait for water levels to rise or fall. You can check the
ships' schedules on the website and plan
your visit accordingly. Also here is the **St
Catharines Museum** (adult/child/conces-
sion $4.20/2.50/4), with displays on town
history and canal construction, plus a lacrosse hall of fame.

There's not much on offer in the town of
Welland other than its collection of **murals**, depicting historic, agricultural and
canal scenes. Most appear along Main St E,
but our favorite adorns the Sears building
at 800 Niagara St N – a powerful evocation
of indigenous, white and black history on
the Niagara Peninsula.

Port Colborne, where Lake Erie empties
into the canal, contains the 420m Lock 8 –
one of the longest in the world. Check it out
at **Lock 8 Park** (Mellanby St; ⊗24hr), south
of Main St. Also here is **Port Colborne
Visitors Information Booth** (www.experi
enceportcolborne.com; Lock 8 Park, Mellanby
St; ⊗8am-7pm Jul-Aug, hours vary in winter).
The quiet, good-looking town has a canal-
side boardwalk and shops and restaurants
along West St – good for an afternoon stroll
or evening meal.

Niagara Falls

POP 79,000

Niagara Falls: great muscular bands of
water arch over the precipice like liquid
glass, roaring into the void below; a vast
plume of spray boils up from the cauldron,
feathering into the air hundreds of meters
above. There are dozens of taller waterfalls in the world (Niagara ranks a lowly
50th), but in terms of sheer volume these
falls are unbeatable: more than a million
bathtubs of water plummet over the edge
every second.

By day or night, regardless of the season,
the falls never fail to awe (14 million visitors
annually can't be wrong!). Even in winter,
when the flow is partially hidden and the
edges freeze solid, the watery extravaganza
is undiminished. Very occasionally the falls
stop altogether. This first happened on Easter Sunday morning in 1848, when ice completely jammed the flow. Pious locals feared
the end of the world was nigh...

Piety, however, isn't something Niagara Falls strives for these days. It's been a
saucy honeymoon destination ever since

FORT ERIE

East of Port Colborne and south of Niagara Falls is the town of Fort Erie, where the Niagara River leaks out of Lake Erie. Across from Buffalo, New York, it's connected to the US by the Peace Bridge. The main drawcard here is the historic, star-shaped **Fort Erie** (www.oldforterie.com; 350 Lakeshore Rd; adult/child $9.25/6; ⊙10am-5pm May-Nov; P), a key player in the War of 1812, and 'Canada's bloodiest battlefield.' Also known as the Old Stone Fort, it was first built in 1764. The US seized it in 1814 before retreating. Inside there's a museum and immaculate, uniformed soldiers performing authentic military drills. Take the worthwhile guided tour (every 30 minutes), included in the admission.

Napoléon's brother brought his bride here – tags like 'For newlyweds and nearly deads' and 'Viagra Falls' are apt. More recently, a crass morass of casinos, fast-food joints, sleazy motels, cheesy tourist attractions and sex shops has bloomed parasitically around the falls in the Clifton Hill area – a Little Las Vegas! Love it or loathe it, there's nowhere quite like Niagara Falls.

The old downtown area, where you'll find the bus and train stations, is seeing revitalization along and around Queen St: millions of dollars have been pumped in to encourage growth and refurbishment. It remains to be seen whether or not it will work, but galleries and bistros are breathing new life into previously tired and shuttered buildings, and the streets are being repaved with hope. You can expect many more shops and restaurants to open in the future. Check the enthusiastic www. queeenstreetniagara.com to see what's happening.

◉ Sights & Activities

Parking access for sights and activities around the falls and Clifton Hill is expensive and limited (see p112).

THE FALLS & AROUND

Niagara Falls forms a natural rift between Ontario and New York State. On the US side, **Bridal Veil Falls** (aka the American Falls) crash onto mammoth fallen rocks. On the Canadian side, the grander, more powerful **Horseshoe Falls** plunge into the cloudy **Maid of the Mist Pool**. The prime falls-watching spot is **Table Rock**, poised just meters from the drop – arrive early to beat the crowds.

Tickets for the following four main falls tours and activities can be bought separately, or purchase the **Niagara Falls**

Great Gorge Adventure Pass (www.ni agaraparks.com; adult/child $40/28) discount pass for admission to all four attractions, plus Niagara Pkwy and Queenston sites, and all-day transportation on the Niagara Parks People Mover. Passes are available from the Niagara Parks Commission at Table Rock Information Centre and various attractions.

Maid of the Mist BOAT TOUR
(www.maidofthemist.com; 5920 River Rd; adult/child $15.60/9.60; ⊙8:45am-7:45pm Jun-Aug, 8:45am-4:45pm Mon-Fri, to 5:45pm Sat & Sun Apr, May, Sep & Oct) This brave little boat has been plowing headlong into the falls' misty veil since 1846. It's loud and wet and heaps of fun. Everyone heads for the boat's upper deck, but views from either end of the lower deck are just as good. Departures are every 15 minutes, weather permitting.

Journey Behind the Falls WALKING TOUR
(www.niagaraparks.com; 6650 Niagara Pkwy; adult/child $13/8; ⊙9am-5:30pm Mon-Fri, to 7:30pm Sat & Sun) From Table Rock Information Centre you can don a very un-sexy plastic poncho and traverse rock-cut tunnels halfway down the cliff – as close as you can get to the falls without getting in a barrel. It's open year-round, but be prepared to queue.

White Water Walk WALKING TOUR
(www.niagaraparks.com; 4330 Niagara Pkwy; adult/child $9/6; ⊙9am-7:45pm Jun-Aug, 9am-4:45pm Mon-Fri, to 5:45pm Sat & Sun Apr-May & Sep-Oct) At the northern end of town, next to Whirlpool Bridge, the White Water Walk is another way to get up close and personal, this time via an elevator down to a 325m boardwalk suspended above the rampaging torrents, just downstream from the falls.

Whirlpool Aero Car   GONDOLA
(3850 Niagara Pkwy; adult/child $12/7; ⊙9am-8pm Jun-Aug, 9am-5pm Mon-Fri, to 6pm Sat & Sun Apr-May & Sep-Oct) Dangling above the Niagara River, 4.5km north of Horseshoe Falls, the Whirlpool Aero Car was designed by Spanish engineer Leonardo Torres Quevedo and has been operating since 1916 (but don't worry – it's still in good shape). The gondola travels 550m between two outcrops above a deadly whirlpool created by the falls – count the logs and tires spinning in the eddies below. No wheelchair access.

FREE **Floral Showhouse**   GARDEN
(☎905-353-5407; www.niagaraparks.com; 7145 Niagara Pkwy; ⊙9:30am-8pm) Around 1km south of Horseshoe Falls, the showhouse offers year-round floral displays and some warm respite on a chilly day. Opposite, lodged on rocks in the rapids, the **Old Scow** is a rusty steel barge that's been waiting to be washed over the falls since 1918 – a teetering symbol of Western imperialism, perhaps?

CLIFTON HILL & AROUND
Clifton Hill is a street name, but refers to a broader area near the falls occupied by a sensory bombardment of artificial enticements. You name it – House of Frankenstein, Madame Tussaud's Wax Museum, Castle Dracula – they're all here. In most cases, paying the admission will leave you feeling like a sucker.

Daredevil Gallery   MUSEUM
(www.imaxniagara.com; 6170 Fallsview Blvd; adult/child $8/6.50; ⊙9am-9pm) The most engaging thing around here is the Daredevil Gallery attached to IMAX Niagara. Scratch your head in amazement at the battered collection of barrels and padded bubbles

in which people have ridden over the falls (not all of them successfully). There's also a history of falls 'funambulism' (tightrope walking) here.

Bird Kingdom   ZOO
(www.birdkingdom.ca; 5651 River Rd; adult/child/concession $17/12/15; ⊙9:30am-7pm May-Sep, to 5pm Oct-Apr) The jungly Bird Kingdom claims to be the world's largest indoor aviary, with 400 species of free-flying tropical birds from around the globe. You can also buddy-up with a boa constrictor in the Reptile Encounter Zone.

FREE **Ten Thousand Buddhas Sarira Stupa**   TEMPLE
(4303 River Rd; ⊙9am-5pm, main temple Sat & Sun only) If the tourist bustle is messing with your yang, find tranquility at the totally out-of-context Buddhist temple Ten Thousand Buddhas Sarira Stupa. Visitors are welcome to wander the serene complex and view the various sculptures, bells and artworks.

Konica Minolta Tower   OBSERVATION DECK
(www.niagaratower.com; 6732 Fallsview Blvd; adult/child $5.50/3.50; ⊙7am-11pm) Leering over the falls, the Minolta Tower is a bodacious vantage point, with indoor and outdoor observation galleries. On a clear day the view extends from Toronto to Buffalo, New York. There's a restaurant and hotel here, too.

Skylon Tower   OBSERVATION DECK
(www.skylon.com; 5200 Robinson St; adult/child $13/7.50; ⊙8am-midnight Apr-Oct, 11am-9pm Nov-Mar) The Skylon Tower is a 158m spire with yellow elevators crawling like bugs up the exterior. The views are real eye-poppers, and the revolving restaurant is worth a spin or two.

JAGGED EDGES

The Niagara Escarpment, the land formation that creates Niagara Falls, is a prominent feature of Ontario. Sweeping from eastern Wisconsin and along the shore of northern Lake Michigan, down through Lake Huron and across Manitoulin Island, slicing through Ontario and then curving under Lake Ontario and ending in New York State, the escarpment is a long spine of brush-covered stone. A combination of what was originally lime bed and ancient sea floor, the dolomitic limestone that makes up the land formation is more resistant than the land around it, which has eroded and left the bulge of limestone slithering around the Great Lakes.

Great waterfalls are just one result of the escarpment. Together with Lake Ontario, the geological formation has created a microclimate perfect for viticulture. The soil (a combination of limestone and clay) and the warmth created by Lake Ontario generate growing conditions very similar to those of France's Burgundy region.

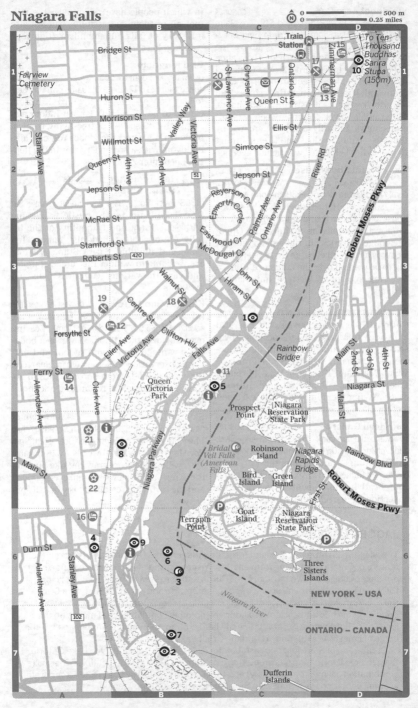

ONTARIO NIAGARA PENINSULA

500 m
0.25 miles

Fairview
Cemetery

Bridge St

Huron St

Morrison St

Willmott St

Queen St

Jepson St

McRae St

Stamford St

Roberts St 420

Stanley Ave

4th Ave

2nd Ave

Valley Way

Victoria Ave

51

Chrysler Ave

St Lawrence Ave

20

Queen St Ave

Ellis St

Simcoe St

Jepson St

Reyerson Cr

Epworth Circle

Eastwood Cr

McDougal Cr

Ontario Ave

Palmer Ave

Ontario Ave

River Rd

Train
Station

17

15

13

10

To Ten
Thousand
Buddhas
Sarira
Stupa
(150m)

Zimmerman Ave

Robert Moses Pkwy

Walnut St

19

Centre St

18

12

Forsythe St

Ellen Ave

Victoria Ave

Clifton Hill

Falls Ave

John St

Hiram St

1

Rainbow
Bridge

Main St

2nd St

3rd St

4th St

Niagara St

Ferry St

14

Clark Ave

Allendale Ave

Queen
Victoria
Park

11

5

Prospect
Point

Niagara
Reservation
State Park

Main St

Rainbow Blvd

21

8

Main St

22

16

4

Dunn St

Stanley Ave

Allanthus Ave

102

Niagara Parkway

9

6

3

Bridal
Veil Falls
(American
Falls)

Robinson
Island

Bird
Island

Green
Island

Terrapin
Point

Goat
Island

Three
Sisters
Islands

Niagara
Rapids
Bridge

First St

Niagara
Reservation
State Park

Robert Moses Pkwy

NEW YORK – USA

7

2

Niagara River

ONTARIO – CANADA

Dufferin
Islands

Niagara Falls

NIAGARA PARKWAY

The slow-roaming, leafy Niagara Pkwy meanders for 56km along the Niagara River, from Niagara-on-the-Lake past the falls all the way to Fort Erie. Along the way you'll find parks, picnic areas and viewpoints. The 3m-wide **Niagara River Recreation Trail** (www.niagaraparks.com/nature/rectrailarea.php) for cycling, jogging or walking runs parallel to the parkway – an idyllic short or long cycling excursion. The trail can easily be divided into four chunks, each of which takes around two hours to pedal. For bicycle hire, see p115. In season, fresh-fruit stands selling cold cherry cider adorn the side of the trail. Download a map online, or pick one

up in person at the Niagara-on-the-Lake Chamber of Commerce Visitors Information Centre.

FREE **Niagara Glen Nature Reserve**

NATURE RESERVE

(www.niagaraparks.com; Niagara Pkwy; ⊙dawn-dusk; P) About 8km north of the falls is this exceptional reserve, where you can get a sense of what the area was like pre-Europeans. There are 4km of walking trails winding down into a gorge, past huge boulders, cold caves, wildflowers and woods. The Niagara Parks Commission offers **guided nature walks** daily during the summer season for a nominal fee. Bring something to drink – the water in the Niagara River is far from clean.

FREE **Botanical Gardens**

GARDEN

(www.niagaraparks.com; 2565 Niagara Pkwy; ⊙dawn-dusk; P) Almost opposite Niagara Glen are the neatly pruned botanical gardens with 40 hectares of herbs, vegetables and trees – a quiet spot to chill.

Butterfly Conservatory

GARDEN

(www.niagaraparks.com; 2565 Niagara Pkwy; adult/child $11.75/8; ⊙10am-7pm Jun-Aug, 10am-4pm Mon-Fri, to 5pm Sat & Sun Nov-May, 10am-7pm Jun-Sep; P) Inside the botanical gardens, the conservatory has more than 50 species of butterflies (some as big as birds) flitting around 130 species of flowers and plants. This is also a breeding facility where you can see young butterflies released.

QUEENSTON

Queenston Heights Park

HISTORICAL SITE

(www.niagaraparks.com; 14184 Niagara Pkwy, Queenston, ⊙dawn-dusk, P) In Queenston village, a snoozy historic throwback north of the falls near the Lewiston Bridge to the US, is Queenston Heights Park, a national historic site. Here, the commanding **Brock Monument** honors Major General Sir Isaac Brock, 'Savior of Upper Canada.' The tower stairwell was closed for repairs during research, but might open by the time you visit. Self-guided walking tours of the hillside recount the 1812 Battle of Queenston Heights, a British victory that helped Canada resist becoming part of the USA.

Mackenzie Printery & Newspaper Museum

MUSEUM

(www.niagaraparks.com; 1 Queenston St, Queenston; adult/child $4.75/3.65; ⊙10am-4pm May-Sep; P) This ivy-covered museum was where the esteemed William Lyon Mackenzie

DAREDEVILS

Surprisingly, more than a few people who have gone over Niagara Falls have actually lived to tell the tale. The first successful leap was in 1901, by a 63-year-old school-teacher named Annie Taylor, who did it in a skirt, no less. This promoted a rash of barrel stunters that continued into the 1920s, including Bobby Leach, who survived the drop but met his untimely death after slipping on an orange peel and developing gangrene!

In 1984 Karl Soucek revived the tradition in a bright red barrel. He made it, only to die six months later in another barrel stunt in Houston. Also during the '80s, two locals successfully took the plunge lying head to head in the same barrel.

A US citizen who tried to jet ski over the falls in 1995 might have made it – if his rocket-propelled parachute had opened. Another American, Kirk Jones, survived the trip over the falls unaided in 2003. After being charged by the Canadian cops with illegally performing a stunt, he joined the circus.

Only one accidental falls-faller has survived – a seven-year-old Tennessee boy who fell out of a boat upstream in 1960 and survived the drop without even breaking a bone.

Take the virtual plunge at IMAX Niagara, and check out the over-the-falls barrels folks have used at the Daredevil Gallery.

once edited the hell-raising *Colonial Advocate*. Enthusiastic young staff conduct tours every half-hour.

Laura Secord Homestead   MUSEUM
(www.niagaraparks.com; 29 Queenston St, Queenston; adult/child $4.75/3.65; ◷11am-5pm May-Aug, to 4pm Wed-Sun Sep-Oct; P) The demure Laura Secord Homestead celebrates a Canadian heroine who lived here during the War of 1812. She's famous for booting it nearly 30km to warn the British soldiers of impending attack by the USA – even though she was a US citizen. The rose garden out front was planted by Laura herself.

RiverBrink Gallery   GALLERY
(www.riverbrink.org; 116 Queenston St, Queenston; adult/child/concession $5/free/4; ◷10am-5pm May-Oct; P) Further north of the homestead, this gallery houses the Samuel E Weir Collection of Canadian art, which includes early landscapes of the Niagara Peninsula and works by the Group of Seven.

Bruce Trail   NATURE TRAIL
(www.brucetrail.org) The southern end of the Bruce Trail (see the boxed text, p140), which extends 800km to Tobermory on Georgian Bay, is in Queenston. There are numerous access points in the Niagara area.

☞ Tours

See p77 for tours to Niagara Falls from Toronto; p114 for Wine Country tours from Niagara Falls.

Double Deck Tours   BUS TOUR
(☎905-374-7423; www.doubledecktours.com; cnr River Rd & Clifton Hill; tours adult/child from $69/41; ◷11am Apr-Oct) Offers a deluxe 4-hour tour on a red double-decker bus. The price includes admission to the Whirlpool Aero Car, Journey Behind the Falls *and* the Maid of the Mist.

Niagara Helicopters   HELICOPTER TOUR
(☎905-357-5672; www.niagarahelicopters. com; 3731 Victoria Ave; 10min flights adult/child $132/82; ◷9am-sunset, weather permitting) A fantastic falls encounter, but pricey and not the most environmentally sensitive option.

✫✫ Festivals & Events

Niagara Wine & Food Classic   FOOD FESTIVAL
(☎800-563-2557) A gastronomic celebration in mid-September to welcome the autumn wine harvest. Some of the region's top wines are paired with sublime cuisine.

Winter Festival of Lights   WINTER FESTIVAL
(www.wfol.com) A season of events from late November to mid-January, including more than 125 animated displays and three million tree and ground lights, the undisputed highlight of which is an over-the-top nocturnal light display along a 36km route. There's also concerts, fun runs and a cheerleading championship.

🛏 Sleeping

There are more beds than heads in Niagara Falls, but the town is sometimes completely booked up. Prices spike sharply in summer, on weekends and during holidays (Canadian and US). Check B&B availability online at www.bbniagarafalls.com; if you haven't made a reservation, look for vacancy signs. Lundy's Lane is motel central.

ACBB Hostel Niagara *TOP CHOICE*   HOSTEL $
(☎905-359-4815; www.hostelniagara.ca; 5741 McGrail Ave; dm/d $20/50; P☻📶) With a maximum of six beds per room, kitchens on every floor and loads of balconies, ACBB is a notch above the rest. There's even a ladies powder room with couches and hand creams! Owner Patrick is passionate about Niagara and hostelling, and always has time to make suggestions or draw you a map. He also bakes blueberry muffins in the mornings.

Oakes Hotel   HOTEL $$$
(☎905-356-4514, 877-843-6253; www.oakes hotel.com; 6546 Fallsview Blvd; d $119-269; P☻✳📶) A jaunty silver spire next to the Fallsview Casino, the Oakes has front-row-center views of the great cascades. For a lofty establishment, staff are remarkably down to earth. Not all rooms have falls views, but ask and ye shall receive. The pricier rooms have Jacuzzis, floor-to-ceiling windows, fireplaces, terraces and the best views. Wi-fi is an additional $13; parking is $15.

Hostelling International Niagara Falls   HOSTEL $
(☎905-357-0770, 888-749-0058; www.hostelling niagara.com; 4549 Cataract Ave; dm/d incl linen $22/48; P☻@📶) Quietly adrift in the old town, this homey, multicolored hostel sleeps around 90 people. The facilities, including a sizable kitchen, pool table, lockers and cool basement lounge, are in good shape; staff are friendly and ecofocused. It's close to the train and bus stations, and you can rent bicycles for $15 per day.

Crystal Inn   MOTEL $$
(☎905-354-1436; www.crystalinn.ca; 4249 River Rd; r $50-90; P☻✳📶) Run by the same family since it was built in 1955, this basic motel has plain but remodeled rooms. It has a great location across from the river and about a 20-minute walk to the falls. Some rooms have heart-shaped Jacuzzi tubs.

Backpacker's International Hostel   HOSTEL $
(☎905-357-4266, 800-891-7022; www.backpack ers.ca; 4219 Huron St; dm $25, d $60-65; ☻@) An independent, shabby-chic hostel housed inside a grand 19th-century home. The endearing upstairs doubles feel like small, non-specific European hotel rooms; the friendly owner is also a small, non-specific European. Rates include taxes, kitchen use, morning coffee and a muffin.

Cadillac Motel   MOTEL $$
(☎905-356-0830, 800-650-0049; www.cadillac motelniagara.com; 2 Ferry St; r $59-149; P✳) What killer architecture! Straight out of a 1950s design dreambook, the old Cadillac has resisted the urge to scrap its neon sign, funky pink-and-peach brickwork, retro plastic chairs, lewd tiling and geometric carpets. The walls are a little thin (an eavesdropper's delight), but the location is brilliant.

🍴 Eating

The old downtown section is seeing a lot of new restaurants crop up and is worth exploring. In general, though, finding food in Niagara is no problem, but be prepared for quantity rather than quality. For cuisine a cut above, you're better off heading to the Wine Country. Aside from the following there are sky-high restaurants at both the Skylon Tower and Minolta Tower.

Taps on Queen Brewhouse & Grill   BREWERY $$
(www.tapsbeer.com; 4680 Queen St; mains $9-14; ⊙noon-10pm Mon, Tue & Sun, to midnight Wed-Sat) Does a mix of stuff, from shepherd's pie to ancient grains curry (quinoa, couscous, adzuki beans, mung beans and veggies). All dishes are, naturally, best when paired with one of the brewery's tasty beers.

Edwin's   FUSION $$
(4616 Erie Ave; mains $8-10) Born in Jamaica and trained in England, the illustrious Edwin blends Caribbean and Mediterranean cuisine at this little spot near the train station. Jerk chicken, fried plantains, curried goat and salmon salad are all on offer, as is a weekend breakfast buffet ($6.99).

Flying Saucer   FAST FOOD $
(6768 Lundy's Lane; items $1-16; ⊙6am-10pm) For extraterrestrial fast food, you can't go past this diner on the Lundy's Lane motel strip. Famous $1.59 breakfasts are served until noon (eggs, fries and toast), but heftier meals in the way of steaks, seafood, fajitas,

burgers and hot dogs are also on-board. Take-out is in the saucer to the left.

Guru INDIAN $$
(☑905-354-3444; 5705 Victoria Ave; mains $11-16; ☺noon-11pm Mon-Thu, to midnight Fri-Sun) Alternate sips of cold mango lassi with forks of red-hot curry at the Guru, an unexpected gem in Clifton Hill. Dark-wood wicker chairs and Ganesh-skin tablecloths set the scene for smooth vegetable curries, tangy chicken masalas and a surprisingly global wine list.

Suishe Gardens JAPANESE $$$
(☑905-354-1500; 5701 Lewis Ave; mains $16-25; ☺dinner) Teppanyaki and teriyaki, sake and soba: Suishe does it up. Wide leather lounge chairs surround a central fireplace, while more private booths cozy up in the corners.

☆ Entertainment

IMAX Niagara CINEMA
(www.imaxniagara.com; 6170 Fallsview Blvd; adult/child $12.50/9; ☺9am-9pm) On a 20m screen with 12,000-watt woofers, IMAX blasts out the 45-minute *Falls Movie* about the history and development of the region. The amazing Daredevil Gallery is here too.

Niagara Fallsview Casino CASINO
(www.fallsviewcasinoresort.com; 6380 Fallsview Blvd; admission free; ☺24hr) This mondo-successful casino never closes. The building itself is worth a look – an amazing complex of commerce and crap-shoots, with a fantastical fountain in the lobby. Corny old-timers and has-beens like Kenny Rogers and Donny Osmond are regularly wheeled out to perform.

ⓘ Information

Accessible Niagara (www.accessibleniagara.com) Advice for the mobility-impaired.

Greater Niagara General Hospital (☑905-378-4647; www.niagarahealth.on.ca; 5546 Portage Rd; ☺24hr) Emergency room.

Info Niagara (www.infoniagara.com) Privately run website with helpful links.

Niagara Falls Public Library (www.niagarafallspubliclib.org; 4848 Victoria Ave; ☺9am-9pm Mon-Thu, to 5:30pm Fri & Sat, 1-5pm Sun) Free internet and wi-fi internet access.

Niagara Falls Tourism (☑905-356-6061, 800-563-2557; www.niagarafallstourism.com; 5400 Robinson St; ☺8am-5pm Mon-Fri, 10am-4pm Sat & Sun) Everything you need to know about Niagara, served with a smile.

Niagara Parks Commission (www.niagaraparks.com; ☺9am-11pm Jun-Aug, to 4pm Sep-May) The falls' governing body, with information desks at Maid of the Mist Plaza and Table Rock Information Centre.

Ontario Travel Information (☑905-358-3221; www.ontariotravel.net; 5355 Stanley Av; ☺8am-8pm May-Aug, to 5pm Sep-Apr) On the western outskirts of town; free tourist booklets containing maps and discount coupons.

Post office (www.canadapost.ca; 4500 Queen St; ☺8am-5pm Mon-Fri)

ⓘ Getting There & Away

Bus

The **Niagara Falls Bus Station** (☑905-357-2133, 800-461-7661; www.greyhound.ca; 4555 Erie Ave) is in the old part of town. Greyhound Canada buses depart for Toronto ($27.50, 1½ to two hours, seven daily) and Buffalo, New York ($10.50, one to 1½ hours, six daily).

Niagara Airbus (☑905-374-8111, 800-268-8111; www.niagaraairbus.com) is a door-to-door coach service with frequent connections to and from airports in Toronto (one way/return $71/112, 1½ hours) and Buffalo, New York ($81/133, 1½ hours).

Working in liaison with the Niagara Fallsview Casino, **Safeway Tours** (☑416-593-0593, 888-230-3505; www.safewaytours.net; return ticket $25) shuttles passengers between Toronto and Niagara Falls. No overnight stays; over-19s only (ID required). Call for pickup locations and times.

Train

From **Niagara Falls Train Station** (☑888-842-7245; www.viarail.ca; 4267 Bridge St) opposite the bus station, VIA trains run to Toronto ($37, two hours, two daily) and New York City ($85, 10 hours, once daily).

ⓘ Getting Around

Bicycle

The excellent **Zoom Leisure Bicycle Rentals** (☑866-811-6993) is based in Niagara-on-the Lake, but has a new office in Niagara Falls inside the Best Western on Fallsview Bvld. However, they will deliver a bike to you anywhere in the Niagara region. Longer rentals and two-wheeled wine tours are available, too. Hostelling International Niagara Falls and the ACBB Hostel also rent out bikes. Also note that the area is a Bike Train destination (see the boxed text, p56).

Car, Motorcycle & Parking

Driving and parking around the centre is an expensive headache. Park way out and walk, or follow the parking district signs and stash the car for the day (around $6 per 30 minutes, or $15 per day). The huge Rapidsview parking lot (also the Niagara Parks People Mover depot) is 3km south of the falls off River Rd.

Public Transportation

Cranking up and down the steep 50m slope between the falls and Fallsview Blvd is a quaint **Incline Railway** (www.niagaraparks.com; 6635 Niagara Pkwy; one way $2.50; ☺9am-11pm Jul-Aug, to 8pm Sep-Nov & Apr-Jun).

The **Niagara Parks People Mover** (www.niagaraparks.com; day pass adult/child $7.60/4.60; ☺every 20min 9am-9pm Mar-Oct) is an economical and efficient bus system, departing the huge Rapidsview parking lot south of the falls. Day passes can be purchased at most stops. Shuttles follow a 15km path from the parking lot north past the Horseshoe Falls, Rainbow and Whirlpool bridges and Whirlpool Aero Car, continuing along Niagara Pkwy to Queenston in peak season. Tickets include a ride on the Incline Railway.

Niagara Transit (☎905-356-1179; one way adult/child $3.50/1, day pass for 1 adult & 2 children $6; ☺every 30min 9am-1:30am Jun-Aug, reduced service May, Sep & Oct) runs two shuttle bus routes around town: the red route goes around Clifton Hill and other falls attractions, then up Lundy's Lane and back; the green route goes from Rainbow Bridge north to the Whirlpool Aero Car, then back down River Rd past the B&Bs to Clifton Hill and then on to the Rapidsview parking lot. Out of season, use Niagara Transit's regular city buses (adult/child $2.35/1.10).

Walking

Put on your sneakers and get t'steppin' – walking is the way to go! You'll only need wheels to visit outlying sights along the Niagara Pkwy.

Niagara-on-the-Lake

One of the best-preserved 19th-century towns in North America, affluent N-o-t-L is a strange fruit indeed. Originally a Neutral First Nations village, the town was founded by Loyalists from New York State after the American Revolution. It later became the first capital of the colony of Upper Canada. These days it's an undeniably gorgeous place, with tree-lined streets, lush parks and impeccably restored houses, but the atmosphere smacks of skin-deep tourist cash-in. Tour bus stampedes overrun the streets, puffing Cuban cigars and dampening the charm; the town fountain is full of coins – there are no homeless people here to plunder it. Is this a *real* town, or just gingerbread? Is there a soul beneath the surface? The annual Shaw Festival paves the way to redemption.

⊙ Sights & Activities

Queen St teems with shops of the ye olde variety selling antiques, Brit-style souvenirs and homemade fudge.

Fort George HISTORICAL SITE
(www.pc.gc.ca/fortgeorge; 51 Queens Pde; adult/child/concession/family $11.70/5.80/10/29.40; ☺10am-5pm May-Oct, Sat & Sun only Apr & Nov; P) On the town's southeastern fringe, restored Fort George dates from 1797. The fort saw some bloody battles during the War of 1812, changing hands between the British and US forces a couple of times. Within the spiked battlements are officers' quarters, a working kitchen, a powder magazine and storage houses. Ghost tours, skills demonstrations, retro tank displays and battle re-enactments occur throughout the summer. Parking costs $6, but this is reimbursed with your ticket.

FREE **Niagara Apothecary** MUSEUM
(www.niagaraapothecary.ca; 5 Queen St; ☺noon-6pm May-Sep, from 11am Jul & Aug) A functional pharmacy until 1964, the Victorian-era apothecary is now a museum fitted with great old cabinets, remedies, jars and old posters advertising snake-oil cures ('Merchant's Gargling Oil: a liniment for man and beast!').

Greaves Jams & Marmalades SOUVENIRS
(www.greavesjams.com; 55 Queen St; jams around $5; ☺9:30am-8pm summer, 9am-4pm winter) Run by fourth-generation jam-makers (try the sour cherry jam).

Niagara Historical Society Museum
MUSEUM
(www.niagarahistorical.museum; 43 Castlereagh St; adult/child/concession $5/1/3; ☺10am-5pm May-Oct, from 1pm Nov-Apr; P) The Niagara Historical Society Museum, south of Simcoe Park, has a vast collection relating to the town's past, ranging from First Nations artifacts to Loyalist and War of 1812 collectibles (including the prized hat of Major General Sir Isaac Brock).

Lincoln & Welland Regimental Museum
MUSEUM
(☎905-468-0888; www.lwmuseum.ca; cnr King & John Sts; adult/child $3/2; ☺10am-4pm Wed-Sun; P) The Lincoln & Welland Regimental Museum has wonderfully aged displays of Canadian military regalia.

☞ Tours

Grape Escape Wine Tours WINE TOUR
(☎866-935-4445;www.tourniagarawineries.com;
tours $59-124; ☉year-round) A range of wine-
flavored regional tours, by bike, van or SUV.
Tours include some kind of meal (cheese
platters on cheaper tours through to full
gourmet dinners). There's free hotel pickup/
drop-off.

Jetboat Niagara BOAT TOUR
(☎905-468-4800, 888-438-4444; www.whirl
pooljet.com; 61 Melville St; 45min tours adult/child
$58/48; ☉Apr–mid-Oct) A wet and wild ride,
full of fishtails and splashy stops – bring a
change of clothes (and maybe underwear).
Reservations required.

Niagara Wine Tours
International FOOD TOUR
(☎905-468-1300, 800-680-7006; www.niagara
worldwinetours.com; 92 Picton St; tours $65-165)
Various bicycle and gourmet lunch and dinner tours around local wineries, including
tastings.

🛏 Sleeping

Although there are over 300 B&Bs in town
(!), accommodations here are expensive and
often booked out. When the Shaw Festival
is running, lodging is even tighter, so plan
ahead.

Prince of Wales Hotel HOTEL $$$
(☎905-468-3246, 888-669-5566; www.vintage
-hotels.com; 6 Picton St; d $225-375, ste $425-
575; ⓟ☉❄❄✉@wi-fi) Prince of N-o-t-L, this
elegant Victorian hotel was knocked into

shape around 1864 and retains much of its
period primp: vaulted ceilings, timber-inlay
floors, red-waistcoated bellhops. Frills and
floral prints seem angled toward the elderly
and honeymooners, but it's the perfect spot
for anyone looking to splash out. Also on-
site are a spa, afternoon tea, and the excel-
lent Escabeche restaurant. Parking costs
$10. It's on the corner of King St.

Moffat INN $$
(☎905-468-4116; www.moffattinn.com; 60 Picton
St; d $135-195; ❄❄✉) Green trim and flower
boxes lend an Irish pub feel to the outside
of the Moffat, which bills itself as 'cottage
chic.' Twenty-four rooms are tastefully decorated, and you'll probably find the word
charming pop out of your mouth more than
once while visiting.

Skyehaven Bed & Breakfast B&B $$
(☎905-468-9696; www.skyehaven.com; 67 Mary
St; d incl breakfast $130; ⓟ☉❄❄✉) Built in 1787
(now *that's* old!), the two-story sky-blue
shuttered Skyehaven has stood the test of
time. It's a bit of a hike from the action, but
that's not a bad thing. There's a two-night
minimum on weekends.

Anchorage Motel MOTEL $$
(☎905-468-2141; www.theanchor age.ca; 186 Ri-
cardo St; d $65-95; ⓟ☉❄) Drifting in a dol-
drum of B&Bs, it might come as some relief
to drop anchor at the old Anchorage Motel,
its shingled roof bent toward the breeze and
the local marina. The shipshape rooms are
unremarkable, but who's remarking at these
prices? Definitely the best deal in town.

A SHAW THING

In 1962 a lawyer and passionate dramatist, Brian Doherty, led a group of residents in
eight performances of George Bernard Shaw's *Candida* and 'Don Juan in Hell' from
Man and Superman. Doherty's passionate first season blossomed into today's much-
esteemed **Shaw Festival** (☎905-468-2172, 800-511-7429; www.shawfest.com; ☉box
office 10am-8pm). For 45 years the festival has lured global audiences who haven't been
shy about issuing praise.

Plays run from April through to October, and the festival's visionary art direction infus-
es a variety of works and playwrights. Aside from an opening Shaw showstopper, you'll
be treated to Victorian drama, European and US plays, musicals, mystery and suspense,
and classics from Wilde, Woolf and Coward. Specialized seminars are held throughout
the season, plus informal 'Lunchtime Conversations' on selected Saturdays.

Actors tread the boards in three theaters around town – the Festival, Royal George
and Court House theaters – all of which are within walking distance of town. The
cheapest rush seats go on sale at 9am on performance days (except for Saturdays).
Students, under-30s and seniors receive discounts at some matinees; weekday matinees are the cheapest. Call the toll-free telephone number from anywhere in Canada
or the USA well in advance, or check the internet site for details.

X Eating

A few blocks from Queen St, Queen's Royal Park is a sweet spot for a picnic beside the water.

Escabeche   FUSION **$$$**
(☎905-468-3246, 888-669-5566; www.vintage -hotels.com; 6 Picton St; mains $25-48) Arguably the best restaurant on the whole Niagara Peninsula, the fine-dining room at the opulent Prince of Wales Hotel takes its food seriously. The contemporary menu offers taste inventions like a tart of locally cured prosciutto, cacciatore sausage, tomato and mascarpone, followed by roast lamb with fine mustard, fingerling potatoes and baby amber turnips in ice-wine-braised shank jus. Leave room for dessert (you've been warned).

Epicurean   CAFE **$$**
(☎905-468-0288; 84 Queen St; lunch mains $5-11, dinner $17-27; ◷lunch & dinner) By day this fare-thee-well cafeteria dishes up fresh, tasty sandwiches, salads, pies and quiches. The ambience ramps up at night with a bistro menu offering the likes of crispy-skin chicken with steamed rice, scallions and shiitake mushrooms in Thai coconut curry. The street-side patio is always full.

Fans Court   CHINESE **$$**
(135 Queen St; lunch mains $7-10, dinner $15-20; ◷noon-9pm Tue-Sun) A menu graced with Cantonese, Szechuan and pan-Asian dishes distinguishes this place from its neighbors in this most Anglo of towns. The best part about Fans, however, is not the mango pork (though that's delish), but the wonderful flowered courtyard.

ℹ Information

Chamber of Commerce Visitors Information Centre (☎905-468-1950; www.niagaraon thelake.com; 26 Queen St; ◷10am-7:30pm Apr-Oct, to 5pm Nov-Mar) A brochure-filled info center; staff can book accommodations for a $5 fee. Pick up the *Niagara-on-the-Lake Official Visitors' Guide* for maps and a self-guided walking tour.

ℹ Getting There & Around

There are no direct buses between Toronto and Niagara-on-the-Lake, so head for St Catharines or Niagara Falls then transfer.

5-0 Taxi (☎905-358-3232, 800-667-0256; www.5-0taxi.com) shunts folks between Niagara Falls and Niagara-on-the-Lake. Call for pickup

locations and times. A regular one-way taxi between the two towns costs around $45.

Cycling is an ace way to explore the area. Rent a bike from (or have one delivered to you by) the reader-recommended **Zoom Leisure Bicycle Rentals** (☎905-468-2366, 866-811-6993; www. zoomleisure.com; 2017 Niagara Stone Rd; rental per half-day/day/2 days $20/30/50; ◷9am-5pm). Free delivery.

SOUTHWESTERN ONTARIO

The heavily populated industrial and agricultural areas of southwestern Ontario have a rich history of aboriginal settlement, farming, manufacturing and urban sprawl. Arcing around Lake Ontario from Toronto to Hamilton is the 'Golden Horseshoe' – a heavily industrialized zone serving primarily as a conduit between Toronto, Detroit and Buffalo. But those who bravely venture off Hwy 401 will uncover the region's storied heritage, well-preserved limestone and red-brick buildings, tree-lined boulevards, verdant pastures and sandy shorelines. Don't miss the chance to explore brilliant little towns like Elora, St Jacobs and Fergus.

Way out west, sandy soils sustain dead-flat wheat- and corn-growing regions where you'll cheer at the sighting of even the most modest of hills. Farming gives way to sandy beaches along the north shore of Lake Erie and east shore of Lake Huron. Substantial inland cities like Kitchener-Waterloo, Guelph and London are thriving university and technological centers. Stratford plays host to the annual Shakespeare Festival, while Windsor – like Detroit, Michigan (its big brother across the river) – is an auto-manufacturing hub.

Hamilton

POP 503,000

Less than an hour's drive southwest of Toronto is the industrial town of Hamilton, where amongst the factory-filled skyline you'll also find lush trees, a tidy and bustling downtown center, and a few good sights. Blue-collar Hamilton is the center of Canada's iron and steel industry, and there's a vague whiff of sulfur in the air. Tourists usually grit their teeth and continue to Niagara Falls without entertaining thoughts of stopping, but recent cleanup efforts have improved things. If you do pull

off the freeway, there are some decent eateries, interesting museums and charming B&Bs here, and the Niagara Escarpment cuts through the southern part of town, providing sweeping Lake Ontario views.

⊙ Sights & Activities

Dundurn Castle MUSEUM
(www.hamilton.ca/museums; 610 York Blvd; adult/child/concession/family $11/5.50/9/27; ⊘10am-4pm Jul & Aug, from noon Tue-Sun Sep-Jun; P) A boxy, column-fronted, 36-room mansion, Dundurn Castle once belonged to Sir Allan Napier McNab, Canadian prime minister from 1854 to 1856. It sits on a cliff overlooking the harbor amid lovely chestnut-studded grounds, and is furnished in mid-19th-century style.

Also on-site is the **Hamilton Military Museum** (adult/child/concession/family $3.50/2.50/3/8.50), with weapons and uniforms from the War of 1812 to WWI. Admission is free with Dundurn Castle admission.

Royal Botanical Gardens GARDEN
(www.rbg.ca; 680 Plains Rd W; adult/child/concession/family incl shuttle-bus rides $12.50/7.25/9.50/32.25; ⊘10am-5pm; P) With 1000-plus hectares of flowers, natural parklands and a wildlife sanctuary, the Royal Botanical Gardens is only one of six world gardens

to be designated 'royal.' During spring, the rock garden is a highlight, with 3 hectares of rare trees, waterfalls, ponds and 125,000 flowering bulbs. Think a rose is a rose? Think again, pal. From June to October, thousands of different roses (including antique varieties) bloom in the Centennial rose garden. The arboretum is best in May when the lilacs explode into flower. The sanctuary is home to birds, deer, fox, muskrat and coyote, with trails traversing marshes and wooded ravines.

African Lion Safari ZOO
(www.lionsafari.com; ☎905-623-26209453; RR1, Cambridge; adult/child/concession $30/25/28; ⊘10am-5:30pm Jul-Aug, to 4pm May-Jun & Sep; P) About 1000 animals and birds express themselves freely in the vast, cageless African Lion Safari, about 25km northwest of Hamilton off Hwy 8. Drive your car through the park and get within kissing distance of lions, giraffes, zebras, monkeys and other African beasts. If your car-rental agency has an aversion to bird droppings, take the park tour-bus instead ($5 per person). Kids love this place.

Canadian Football Hall of Fame & Museum MUSEUM
(www.cfhof.com; 58 Jackson St W; adult/child/concession/family $7/3.50/3.50/16; ⊘9:30am-

4:30pm Tue-Sat) Despite universal mockery of 'Canadian football,' nothing stops Canadian sports fans from welling with enthusiasm for their fast-paced brand of gridiron. The Canadian Football Hall of Fame & Museum puts more than 100 years of Canadian Football League (CFL) history on display through equipment, photos and the actual Grey Cup – the CFL's holy grail.

Walking Trails   NATURE TRAILS
Hamilton's recent efforts to clean up its act means there are plenty of good parks and multiuse trails here. The 32km **Hamilton to Brantford Rail Trail** (☑905-627-1233; www.conservationhamilton.ca) and the Ontario Waterfront Trail are all within striking distance of the city; consult the tourism office for maps and directions.

🛏 Sleeping & Eating
The QEW and Hwy 403 are dotted with standard motels, which are considerably cheaper than accommodations in Toronto or Niagara-on-the-Lake.

Rutherford House B&B   B&B $$
(☑905-525-2422; www.rutherfordbb.com; 293 Park St S; s/d incl breakfast $115/120; ℗ 🖨 ❄) A short walk from downtown, the Rutherford is a gracious old tier-fronted redbrick house with two en-suite guestrooms, each with plush beds and over-the-top wallpaper. It's one of Hamilton's better B&Bs, but note that it isn't really set up for kids.

Gown and Gavel   PUB $$
(www.gownandgavel.ca; 24 Hess St S; mains $12-20; ☺11am-2am) In the cobblestone Hess Village, Gown and Gavel inhabits a large, intricate building. The food is upscale pub fare, with sandwiches and salads. Upstairs, a little-known tearoom waits to be discovered.

☆ Entertainment
Hamilton Tiger-Cats   SPORTS TEAM
(Ti-Cats; ☑905-527-2287; www.ticats.ca; Ivor Wynn Stadium, 75 Balsam Ave; ☺Jul-Nov) The 15-time CFL Grey Cup champions have been cracking heads and busting tackles since 1869. Try to catch a game against archrivals the Toronto Argonauts and hear the crowd snarl.

❶ Information
Parks Canada Discovery Centre (☑9055-526-0911; www.pc.gc.ca; 57 Discovery Dr; adult/child/concession/family $7.50/3.50/6/18; ☺10am-5pm, closed Mon Oct-May; ℗) On the lakeshore is this snazzy

new place, an urban outreach center with displays on local maritime conservation, parks and heritage sites.

Tourism Hamilton (☑905-546-2666, 800-263-8590; www.tourismhamilton.com; 34 James St S; ☺8:30am-4:30pm, closed Sat & Sun Sep-May) Downtown, this office can help with maps, brochures and the local lowdown.

❶ Getting There & Away
WestJet uses **John C Munro Hamilton International Airport** (YHM; ☑905-679-1999; www.flyhi.ca; 9300 Airport Rd, Mt Hope), 10km south of town, as a major hub for flights to other parts of Canada.

Coach Canada, Greyhound Canada and Toronto-bound Go Transit commuter buses ($9, one to two hours, every 20 minutes) and trains ($9.50, one hour, three daily) roll out of the **GO Centre** (☑905-529-0196, 888-438-6646; www.gotransit.com; 36 Hunter St E; ☺5am-11:30pm Mon-Fri, from 6:15am Sat & Sun), three blocks south of the center of town.

Brantford & Around
You'd think that a town that lays claim to a Mohawk village, the invention of the telephone and the birthplace of the greatest hockey player ever would have plenty going on, right? Well, not really. Surrounded by farmland and bisected by the lazy Grand River, 'Telephone City' Brantford is about as demure as a city of its size can get. But it does make an affordable pit stop if you're trucking between Windsor and Toronto.

Southeast of town, the Six Nations territory has been a First Nations' center for centuries. Captain Joseph Thayendanegea Brant led the Six Nations people here from upper New York State in 1784 and established a village that long served the district's First Nations tribes. European settlement and industrial growth along the Grand occurred steadily over subsequent centuries.

◉ Sights
Woodland Cultural Centre   CULTURAL CENTER
(☑519-759-2650; www.woodland-centre.on.ca; 184 Mohawk St; adult/child/concession $5/3/4; ☺9am-4pm Mon-Fri, 10am-5pm Sat & Sun; ℗) The Woodland Cultural Centre triples-up as an indigenous performance space, cultural museum and art gallery. Exhibits follow a timeline from prehistoric Iroquoian and Algonquian exhibits through to contemporary indigenous art. The attached shop stocks beautifully made basketry and

jewelry, plus books, ceramics and paintings. Call or check the website for the latest lecture, gallery talk and performance dates.

Bell Homestead National Historic Site
HISTORICAL SITE
(www.bellhomestead.on.ca; 94 Tutela Heights Rd; adult/child/concession $5.50/free/4.25; ⊕9:30am-4:30pm Tue-Sun; P) Put down your cell phone and listen up: Alexander Graham Bell changed the future of communication when he conceived the first telephone at Bell Homestead National Historic Site on July 26, 1874. Bell's first North American home has been lovingly restored to original condition. There's a cafe here, too.

FREE Brantford Sports Hall of Recognition
MUSEUM
(www.brantford.ca/gretzkycentre; 254 North Park St; ⊕9am-9pm Mon-Fri, to 6pm Sat & Sun; P) The shining gem at the heart of the Gretzky Centre is the Brantford Sports Hall of Recognition. Memorabilia from dozens of local track-and-field, football, lacrosse and wrestling stars line the walls, but who wants to know about them? What you're here for is Wayne 'The Great One' Gretzky's permanent display. Gretz honed his game on the backyard hockey rink at his childhood Brantford home before shattering the NHL record books and blitzing his way to four Stanley Cups.

Her Majesty's Chapel of the Mohawks
CHURCH
(www.mohawkchapel.ca; 291 Mohawk St; admission by donation; ⊕10am-5pm Jul-Aug, 1-5:30pm Wed-Sun May-Jun & Sep-Oct; P) Captain Brant's tomb is on the grounds of the tiny but exquisite Her Majesty's Chapel of the Mohawks, best visited on sunny afternoons when light streams through the gorgeous stained-glass windows. On the site of the original village, it's the oldest Protestant church in Ontario (1785) and the world's only Royal Indian Chapel. To get here, follow the signs off Colborne St E.

Six Nations of the Grand River Territory
FIRST NATIONS TERRITORY
Southeast of Brantford is Six Nations of the Grand River Territory – the six nations being Mohawk, Oneida, Onondaga, Cayuga, Seneca and Tuscarora – and the village of Ohsweken, a well-known aboriginal community. Established in the late 18th century, the territory gives visitors a glimpse of traditional and contemporary First Nations culture. Six Nations Tourism (www.sntourism.com; 2498 Chiefswood Rd; ⊕9am-4:30pm Mon-Fri, 10am-3pm Sat & Sun) at the corner of Hwy 54 runs the visitors center, with information on local sites, attractions and events in Six Nations.

Across the street from the visitors center, Chiefswood National Historic Site (www.chiefswood.com; 1037 Hwy 54; adult/child/concession $5/free/4; ⊕10am-3pm Tue-Sun May-Oct; P) was the home of Mohawk poet E Pauline Johnson, whose best-selling *Flint & Feather* poems reflected a blend of European and aboriginal cultures in the late 19th and early 20th centuries.

🏃 Activities
Rafting on the Grand River is a great way to see the countryside. Put flashbacks from *Deliverance* to one side and contact an operator to organize your trip.

Blue Heron Rafting
RAFTING TRIP
(☎519-754-0145; www.blueheronrafting.com) Family, romantic evening and combined bike/rafting trips from Brantford.

Grand River Rafting Company
RAFTING TRIP
(☎866-286-7722; www.grandriverrafting.ca) Operating out of Paris, just north of Brantford; guided family, moonlight, evening and overnight rafting trips.

🎊 Festivals & Events

Grand River Powwow
CULTURAL FESTIVAL
(www.grpowwow.com) A major two-day cultural event held over the fourth weekend in July. Expect colorful dancers, traditional drumming and singing, competitions, and aboriginal foods and crafts.

🛏 Sleeping & Eating
Along Colborne St E there are a handful of standard (some sub-standard) motels, plus Thai and Japanese eateries near the Queen St corner competing admirably with the usual fast-food suspects.

Bear's Inn
INN $$
(☎519-445-4133; www.thebearsinn.com; 1979 4th Line Rd, Ohsweken; r incl breakfast $60-80; P❄☀🐾) For an authentic taste of Six Nations hospitality, try Ohsweken's Bear's Inn in the heart of Six Nations of the Grand River Territory. Comfortably decked out in rustic style, rooms range from studios to suites, with cable TV and continental breakfast. Wander around the village and stock up on cheap no-name cigarettes.

ℹ Information

Brantford Visitor & Tourism Centre (☑519-751-1771, 800-265-6299; www.discover brantford.com; 399 Wayne Gretzky Pkwy; ☺9am-8pm Mon-Fri, to 9pm Sat, to 5pm Sun) Just north of Hwy 403, the sparkling tourism center is optimistic about Brantford's future, with plenty of brochures and helpful staff.

ℹ Getting There & Away

The **Brantford Transit Terminal** (☑519-756-5011; www.greyhound.ca; 64 Darling St; ☺7am-7pm Mon-Fri, 8:30am-4pm Sat) is downtown. Greyhound Canada connects to Toronto ($28, one to two hours, five daily), London ($26.40, 1½ hours, four daily) and (via Hamilton) Niagara Falls ($35, four hours, two to three daily).

Brantford Train Station (☑519-752-0867; www.viarail.ca; 5 Wadsworth St; ☺7-10:30am & 11:30am-9pm Mon-Fri, 8:30-11:10am & noon-9pm Sat & Sun) has trains to Toronto ($35, one hour, five daily) and London ($35, one hour, five daily).

Guelph

POP 115,000

Balanced by the imposing spires of the Church of our Lady Immaculate and local beer Sleeman's, Guelph is an attractive spot to chillax for a spell. A student population keeps things lively, while attractive stone buildings exude a sense of history.

◉ Sights

Church of Our Lady Immaculate   CHURCH
(www.churchofourlady.com; 28 Norfolk St; admission by donation; ☺7am-dusk; Ⓟ) Lording over downtown Guelph is the dominant stone-faced bulk of the Church of Our Lady Immaculate. It's hard to move around town without catching a glimpse of Our Lady's twin towers and elegantly proportioned rose window, which have been awing parishioners since 1888.

Macdonald Stewart Art Centre   GALLERY
(www.msac.uoguelph.ca; 358 Gordon St; suggested donation $3; ☺noon-5pm Tue-Sun; Ⓟ) Worthwhile shows are held in the Raymond Moriyama–designed galleries of the Macdonald Stewart Art Centre, specializing in Inuit and Canadian art. The **Donald Forster Sculpture Park** outside features gravity-defying cubes, beached boats and cell phones spiked onto agricultural sickles.

McCrae House   MUSEUM
(www.guelph.ca/museum; 108 Water St; adult/child/concession/family $4/free/3/10; ☺1-5pm, closed Sat Dec-Jun) The birthplace of John McCrae is a modest stone museum laying out the trials and tribulations of his life. McCrae was a Canadian soldier and author of *In Flanders Fields* – an antiwar poem written during WWI, read by all Canadian school kids.

Guelph Civic Museum   MUSEUM
(www.guelph.ca/museum; 6 Dublin St S; adult/child/concession/family $4/free/3/10; ☺1-5pm; Ⓟ) In a handsome 1847 stone house, this museum offers exhibitions, programs and events digging up the history of the city (which, incidentally, is named after the British Royal Family's ancestors the Guelphs). The 'Growing Up in Guelph' kids' exhibition makes a happy distraction. An extensive remodel will double the museum's size as well as give it LEED certification.

✗ Activities

Go paddling with **Speed River Canoe & Kayak Rentals** (☑519-822-5692; speedriver paddling@hotmail.com; 116 Gordon St; kayak/canoe rental per hr $10/12 Mon-Fri, $12/15 Sat & Sun; ☺10am-dusk Tue-Sun Jun-Aug; Ⓟ), then tackle the ice-cream store next door. This is also the starting point of a self-guided **eco-heritage walk** along the banks of the Speed and Eramosa Rivers, a 6km circuit with interpretive signs. Ask at the visitors center about guided downtown walks.

🛏 Sleeping & Eating

The **Guelph Area Bed & Breakfast Association** (www.gabba.ca) has a crop of quality B&Bs on its books. If motels are more your style, there are a couple on Woodlawn Rd W, just north of town.

Parkview Motel   MOTEL $
(☑519-836-1410; www.parkviewmotel.ca; 721 Woolwich St; r from $65; Ⓟ✲) It's nothing too special and occasionally smells like smoke, but the butter-yellow walls, larger-than-average rooms and amenities such as microwaves and TVs raise this roadside motel up a notch.

🏆 TOP CHOICE **Cornerstone**   CAFE $
(1 Wyndham St N; mains $6-10; ☺8am-midnight Mon-Fri, from 9am Sat & Sun;🖋) Thick stone walls plus scuffed wood floors equal serious comfy-ness at this well-loved vegetarian cafe. Go for coffee in the morning and return for a pint and some live music in the evening. If you're looking for a sandwich, consider the Taste of Downtown: avocado, brie, red peppers and garlic aioli ($8).

☆ Entertainment

Bookshelf   THEATER
(📞519-821-3311; www.bookshelf.ca; 41 Quebec St; cinema tickets $9; ⏰9am-9:30pm Mon-Sat, 10:30am-9pm Sun) Part lefty bookstore, part cinema, part cafe, Bookshelf is the pacemaker of Guelph's cultural heartbeat. Swing by to read the paper, catch an art-house flick or have brunch in the Artisanale Café & Bistro (brunch mains $4 to $14, dinner $16 to $22).

ℹ Information

Guelph Tourism Services (📞800-334-4519; www.visitguelphwellington.ca; 1 Carden St; ⏰9am-4:30pm Mon-Sat) In the new city hall, helpful staff can steer you in the right direction.

ℹ Getting There & Away

The **Guelph Bus Station** (📞519-824-0771; www.greyhound.ca; cnr MacDonnell & Carden Sts) has buses to Toronto ($23, 1¼ hours, 16 daily) and London ($29, 2¾ hours, three daily).

Trains to Toronto ($28, 1½ hours, three daily) and London ($35, two hours, three daily) depart from the **Guelph Train Station** (📞888-842-7245; www.viarail.ca; cnr Wyndham & Carden Sts; ⏰6am-1pm & 4pm-midnight Mon-Fri, 9am-2pm & 4pm-midnight Sat & Sun).

Kitchener-Waterloo

POP 280,000

Affectionately known as 'K-W' (but *not* 'Kay-Dub'), these twin cities have formed a symbiotic, neighborly relationship rather than doing battle. Despite their proximity, they're very different in attitude and appeal. Leafy, hilltop Waterloo is regularly voted one of Canada's 'smartest cities.' Waterloo universities churn out dot-com geniuses, many of whom find local employment at RIM (Research in Motion), home of the BlackBerry.

At the bottom of the hill, Germanic Kitchener (called Berlin before WWII – oh the shame...) is a different prospect entirely. Derelict industrial monoliths, bong shops and tattoo parlors line the city's hard-luck streets, awash with homeless alcoholics. Still, there's a toothy integrity here, and it's a surprisingly multicultural town with some good places to eat, drink and sleep.

The main throughway, King St, runs north–south from 'uptown' Waterloo downhill into 'downtown' Kitchener.

◉ Sights & Activities

Kitchener Market   MARKET
(www.kitchenermarket.ca; 300 King St E, Kitchener; ⏰7am-2pm Sat, Upper Level 9am-5pm Tue-Fri; 🅿) The building here is not the original, but Kitchener Market has been open downtown since 1839. Bread, jam, cheese, sausages and pecks of pickled peppers are cultivated and created by local Mennonite farmers, and sold alongside handcrafted quilts, rugs, clothes and toys. More conventional farmers are here too – you can pretty much get anything you need for lunch on the run.

Waterloo Region Museum   MUSEUM
(www.region.waterloo.on.ca; 10 Huron Rd, Kitchener; adult/child/concession/family $6/3/4/15; 🅿) Waterloo's newest attraction is this primary-colored building set on 24 hectares. Though it wasn't completed when we visited (and information about hours and admission prices was yet to be set), the building looked stunning and should be open in 2011. It serves as the gateway to the **Doon Heritage Crossroads** (adult/child/concession/family $7/4/5/18; ⏰10am-4:30pm May-Aug, Mon-Fri only Sep-Dec, closed Jan-Apr; 🅿), a recreated pioneer settlement where costumed volunteers walk boardwalks between a general store and workshops, doing their best to help you time-travel.

Children's Museum   MUSEUM
(www.thechildrensmuseum.ca; 10 King St W, Kitchener; admission $13; ⏰10am-4pm Mon-Fri, to 5pm Sat & Sun, closed Mon & Tue Sep-Jun; 🅿) The K-W regional Children's Museum has been well received by the young and not-so-young since it opened in 2003. Hands-on technological and educational displays have different themes every month (like 'Measure your ecological footprint' and 'Smile – the tooth and nothing but the tooth!'), while the permanent building-block display is a big hit.

Joseph Schneider Haus   HISTORICAL SITE
(www.region.waterloo.on.ca; 466 Queen St S, Kitchener; adult/child/concession/family $2.25/1.25/1.50/5; ⏰10am-5pm Mon-Sat, from 1pm Sun Jul-Aug, 10am-5pm Wed-Sat, from 1pm Sun Sep-Jun; 🅿) A national historic site, Joseph Schneider Haus was one of the first homes built in the area, and has been restored to full 19th-century splendor. Originally built for a prosperous Pennsylvanian Mennonite, the architecture is amazing, as are demonstrations of day-to-day 1800s chores and skills (everything from bead-

work to making corn-husk dolls). When we visited, a two-story washhouse was under construction.

FREE **Kitchener-Waterloo Art Gallery**
GALLERY
(www.kwag.on.ca; 101 Queen St N, Kitchener; 9:30am-5pm Mon-Wed & Fri, to 9pm Thu, 10am-5pm Sat, from 1pm Sun) The natty K-W Art Gallery is in the Centre in the Square performance hall. There's a 3500-piece art collection with a local bias, plus free public tours and seasonal studios in painting, drawing and sculpture for kids, teens and grown-ups (from $15).

Centre in the Square THEATER
(519-578-1570, 800-265-8977; www.centre -square.com; 101 Queen St N, Kitchener) This hefty performance hall hosts live musical acts like KISS and Bryan Adams, comedy, and Broadway productions like *Rent* and *Mamma Mia*.

⭐ Festivals & Events

Uptown Waterloo Jazz Festival
MUSIC FESTIVAL
(www.uptownwaterloojazz.ca) Big-time jazz, small-town environment, held in mid-July.

Waterloo Busker Carnival MUSIC FESTIVAL
(www.waterloo-buskers.com) Street performers from around the world entertain and bedazzle in last August; a must-see if you're in the area.

Oktoberfest FOOD FESTIVAL
(www.oktoberfest.ca) *Willkommen* to this nine-day beery Bavarian bash – the biggest of its kind in North America and possibly the largest outside of Germany. It's K-W's favorite event, bringing in about 500,000 people each year from early to mid-October – sauerkraut, oompah bands, *lederhosen* and *biergartens* galore. Book accommodations well in advance.

🛏 Sleeping

There are plenty of motels on Victoria St N west of King St, or along King St E south of downtown toward Hwy 401. KW Tourism can help with finding B&Bs, as can the **Waterloo Region Bed & Breakfast Association** (www.bbwaterlooregion.ca).

Walper Terrace Hotel HOTEL $$
(519-745-4321, 800-265-8749; www.walper. com; 1 King St W, Kitchener; r $99-139; P ☺ ✴ ⑨)

There's a rich sense of history at the old Walper, a classy downtown dame that's been around the block a time or two. Quality renovations haven't stifled this sense, and the friendly young staff keep the love flowing by failing to be remotely snooty. With a lovely ballroom to act out your Cinderella fantasies.

Bingemans Camping Resort CAMPGROUND $
(519-744-1002, 800-565-4631; www.binge mans.com; 425 Bingemans Centre Dr, Kitchener; tent/RV sites $35/45, cabins from $65, reservations $8; P ✳) South of Hwy 401, Bingemans is a combined water park and campground with enough pools, ponds and waterslides to warrant 'Great Lake' status. The cabins are nothing spectacular, but sleep four.

Sunbridge Crescent B&B B&B $$
(519-743-4557, www.sunbridgecres.com; 11 Sunbridge Cres, Kitchener; d incl breakfast $95-140; P ☺ ✴ ⚇ ⑨ ✳) The owners of this quiet neighborhood house have stripped out the old wallpaper, brought in new beds and quality linen, and shunted the breakfast menu into the realm of frittatas and omelets. There are four rooms here – the cheaper two share a bathroom – plus a backyard pool and hot tub.

🍴 Eating & Drinking

Concordia Club GERMAN $$
(429 Ottawa St S, Kitchener; lunch mains $7-12, dinner $12-20; 11:30am-11pm Mon-Sat, 11am-2pm Sun) Polish up your German verbs and fill up on schnitzel at Concordia, a Teutonic fave that's been around for decades. Dark wood, low ceilings, white linen and loud conversation complement the menu. There's red-hot polka action on Friday and Saturday nights, and a summer *biergarten*.

Fiedler's SANDWICH SHOP $
(197 King St E, Kitchener; items $3-6; 8am-6pm Tue-Fri, 7am-4pm Sat) Thanks to Kitchener's Euro heritage, you'll find a few continental delis like this one along King St. Not far from the market, Fiedler's is stacked full of cheeses, rye breads, sausages and salamis.

Rude Native Bistro FUSION $$$
(519-886-3600; 15 King St S, Waterloo; mains $24-29; 11:30am-2am) A fun place, with cuisine from all over the planet (think pasta, curry or jambalaya). Live music and drink specials draw an energetic crowd, and the patio is a nice place to watch the downtown action.

ℹ Information

Echo is a free weekly, available from bookstores and restaurants around town.

KW Tourism (☏519-745-3536, 800-265-6959; www.explorewaterlooregion.com; 200 King St W, Kitchener; ⊙8:30am-5pm Mon-Fri) Can help with maps and information on local walking tours, plus bike and nature trails.

Waterloo Visitor's Centre (☏519-885-2297; 10 David Bower Dr, Waterloo)

ℹ Getting There & Around

From **Waterloo International Airport** (YFK; www.waterlooairport.ca; 4881 Fountain St N, Breslau), 7km east of town, there are daily flights to Calgary and Detroit.

Greyhound Canada operates from the **Charles St Transit Terminal** (☏800-661-8747; www.greyhound.ca; 15 Charles St W, Kitchener), a five-minute walk from downtown. Buses run to Toronto ($28, 1½ to two hours, hourly) and London ($25, 1½ to two hours, three daily).

Kitchener Train Station (☏888-842-7245; www.viarail.ca; cnr Victoria & Weber Sts, Kitchener) is an easy walk north of downtown. Trains serve Toronto ($34, two hours, three daily) and London ($31, 1½ hours, three daily).

Grand River Transit (www.grt.ca; one way $2.50, day pass $5; ⊙6am-midnight) has extensive services in the K-W area.

St Jacobs & Around

For some exposure to Mennonite ways, drive 6km north of Waterloo along King St N to the historic river village of St Jacobs – don't be surprised if you pass a horse and buggy along the way. The town has become an artsy-craftsy tourist trap (wanna learn how to make a quilt?), selling its soul down the river, but the original stone buildings and fantastic market retain a steadfast charm.

About 8km north of St Jacobs up Hwy 86, Elmira is a working Mennonite town. The main street feels like it's caught in a time warp: black buggies rattle past, the scent of cattle fills the air, and bonnets, braces and buttons are *de rigueur*.

⊙ Sights & Activities

St Jacobs Farmers Market   MARKET
(www.stjacobs.com; cnr King & Weber Sts, St Jacobs; ⊙7am-3:30pm Thu & Sat, also 8am-3pm Tue Jun-Aug) This quintessential country market 3km south of town has an earthy soul fully intact. Locals from miles around flock here for the high-quality produce, smoked meat, cheese, baked treats, arts and crafts. Across the street is the smaller **Sunday Market** (⊙10am-4pm Sun Mar-Dec) – less busy than St Jacobs, but still selling quality local products.

The Mennonite Story   MUSEUM
(adult/child $4/free) Venture downstairs at the St Jacobs Visitors Centre to see the Mennonite Story, an insightful exhibition on the Mennonites, their history, culture and agricultural achievements.

St Jacob's Country Playhouse   THEATER
(☏519-747-7788; 40 Benjamin Rd E, St Jacobs; ⊙shows Wed-Sun) Family-friendly shows such as *High School Musical* and *Peter Pan* take the stage at this 385-seat playhouse.

FREE **Maple Syrup Museum of Ontario**
MUSEUM
(www.stjacobs.com; 1441 King St N, St Jacobs; ⊙10am-6pm Mon-Sat, noon-5:30pm Sun; P) Saccharine but interesting, the Maple Syrup Museum of Ontario is on the 3rd floor of the old mill by the river. Peer quizzically

---

SCENIC DRIVE: O(LD) CANADA

For a scenic, time-tripping drive through Wellington County's villages, rattling cornfields, lonesome farmhouses and rust-red barns, head north along King St N from Kitchener-Waterloo to **St Jacobs**. Take Rte 17 east to Rte 23 and turn left. Take another left on Rivers Edge Dr and rekindle youthful romance (or start a new one) at the **Kissing Bridge**. Constructed in 1880 to protect the bridge surface from the elements, it's Ontario's only remaining covered bridge. Wipe off the lipstick on the far side and turn right onto Kissing Bridge Dr, then turn left onto Rte 86 and roll into Mennonite **Elmira**. Keep driving west on Rte 86, hanging left onto Rte 10 and detouring into leafy, agricultural **Hawkesville**. Rte 10 continues south to utilitarian **St Clements**. Leave town on Rte 15 west and turn left onto Moser-Young Rd to **Bamberg**, then left again onto Rte 12 to **St Agatha** with its unmissable church steeple. Keep going south on Rte 12 through **Petersburg**, where you'll turn left onto Rte 8, which lands you back in Kitchener.

THE MENNONITES

Many people see the Mennonites as curious social hark-backs: black-clad, carriage-riding, traditional farmers eschewing modern life. True enough in an orthodox sense, but many Mennonites are less hard-line, and their history and culture go deeper than these surface impressions.

The Mennonite timeline arcs back to a 16th-century Swiss Protestant sect who were forced to move around Europe due to religious disagreements. During a stay in Holland the sect acquired its name from one of its Dutch leaders, Menno Simons. Another leader, William Penn, promised religious freedom and prosperity in the rural setting of what is now Pennsylvania in the USA. News of cheaper land and more of it in southern Ontario lured many Mennonites north in the late 19th century. The Mennonites' unwillingness to fight under the US flag hastened their exodus.

Ontario has several groups of Mennonites. The 'plain' group is known for their simple clothes and simple living. The Old Order Mennonites are the strictest and most rigid in their practices and beliefs. They are similar to the Amish, for whom even buttons on clothes are considered a vanity. They don't worship in a church but hold services in undecorated houses within the community. You might see less-strict Mennonites chatting on cell phones or tightening the Velcro on their kids' shoes (even jumping into pickup trucks!), but the basic values of their society still apply: family, humility, simplicity, modesty and pacifism.

For more detailed history and information, see www.mhsc.ca.

into display cases full of spiles, buckets, taps and tanks, and check out the short film *Liquid Gold of Spring*.

✲ Festivals & Events

Elmira Maple Syrup Festival   FOOD FESTIVAL
(www.elmiramaplesyrup.com) Spring street festivities and pancake breakfasts soaked in the good stuff. Check the website for dates; it's usually the final weekend in March or the first weekend in April.

🛏 Sleeping & Eating

Benjamin's Restaurant & Inn   HOTEL $$
(☎519-664-3731; www.stjacobs.com/benjamins; 1430 King St N, St Jacobs; d $100-145; ⓟ🐶❄🅟) A renovated 1852 inn right in the middle of St Jacobs, Benjamin's is bright, spacious and comfortable, (with mandatory quilts). The downstairs restaurant (lunch $10 to $15, dinner $18 to $32) cooks traditional chicken, seafood and steak dishes. The stone fireplace and occasional jazz group add a little life.

Stone Crock Bakery   BAKERY $
(☎519-664-3612; 1402 King St N, St Jacobs; items $2-6; ⊙6:30am-6pm Mon-Sat, 11am-5:30pm Sun) The Stone Crock Bakery is a Mennonite-run bakehouse selling fruit pies, muffins, breads, quiches and scones fresh from the oven – they taste as good as they smell.

Vidalia's Bar & Grill   FUSION $$
(☎519-664-3731; 1398 King St N, St Jacobs; mains $12-22; ⊙lunch & dinner) This place shakes things up a little bit with offerings such as onion flan and squash ravioli. Don't fret, regular burgers are also on the menu to satisfy those who are less-adventurous.

ℹ Information

St Jacobs Visitors Centre (☎519-664-3518, www.stjacobs.com; 1406 King St, St Jacobs; ⊙11am-5pm Mon-Sat, from 1:30 Sun Apr-Dec, 11am-4:30pm Mon-Sat, from 2pm Sun Jan-Mar) Has effusive staff who field questions with confidence.

Centre Wellington: Elora & Fergus

In boxing parlance, the Centre Wellington district of Wellington County is punching well above its weight. Linked by the sinuous, fish-filled Grand River, the area's main towns – seductive Elora and practical Fergus – have been proactive in keeping their old buildings, mills and farms looking as good as old. This sets the scene for crowd-pulling festivals, snug pubs and outstanding accommodations – plan to stay a few days!

◎ Sights & Activities

Wellington County Museum MUSEUM
(☎519-846-0916; www.wcm.on.ca; Rte 18, Elora; admission by donation; ◎9:30am-4:30pm Mon-Fri, noon-4pm Sat & Sun; P) Midway between Fergus and Elora, an austere, red-roofed former 'Poor House' provided refuge for the aged and homeless for almost a century before becoming the Wellington County Museum in 1957. Historical and local modern-art exhibits extend through 12 galleries, displaying an obvious pride in local history and current culture. The centerpiece is the new 'If These Walls Could Speak' exhibit, which examines the lives of those who lived or worked there.

Elora Gorge Conservation Area PARK
(www.grandriver.ca; Rte 21, Elora; adult/child $5.75/2.75; ◎late Apr–mid-Oct; P) About 2km south of Elora is the photo-worthy Elora Gorge Conservation Area, a plunging limestone canyon through which the Grand River seethes. Easy walks extend to cliff views, caves and the Cascade waterfalls – a sheet of white water spilling over a stepped cliff. For a free gorge view, head to the end of James St, off Metcalfe St in Elora. **Tubing** (rentals $15) – the gentle art of floating down the river in an inner tube – is a lazy way to spend a warm afternoon at the gorge. You can also camp here.

Elora Quarry Conservation Area PARK
(☎519-846-9742; www.grandriver.ca; Rte 18, Elora; adult/child $5.75/2.75; ◎dawn-dusk Jun-Aug; P) A short walk east of Elora are the possibly bottomless waters and 12m limestone cliffs of the Elora Quarry Conservation Area – a superb swimming hole. Hormone-fuelled teens plummet from great heights, despite signs suggesting they don't.

☞ Tours

Elora Culinary Walking Tours WALKING TOUR
(☎226-384-7000; www.eloraculinarywalkingtour.com; per person $10; ◎1pm Sat May-Sep) Sample some of Elora's culinary treats on this two-hour guided tour. Rain or shine, meet in front of the Village Olive Grove.

Elora-Fergus Studio Tour STUDIO TOUR
(☎877-242-6353; www.elorafergusstudiotour.ca; ◎late Sep) Pan-weekend self-guided tours visiting local artisans' workshops.

Festivals & Events

Elora Festival MUSIC FESTIVAL
(www.elorafestival.com) A classical, jazz, folk and arts festival held from mid-July to mid-August, with concerts at the quarry and in the town's salt barn (the acoustics are wicked!). Singers and musos from around the country crowd the schedule of Elora's premier event.

WORTH A TRIP

COUNTRY PUB CRAWL

For your pint-sloshing pleasure, four pre-1875 taverns await you in the isolated communities west of K-W. Designate a nondrinking driver (sucker!) and have yourself a fine country time.

» Blue Moon
(www.thebluemoon.ca; 1677 Snyders Rd E, Petersburg) Take Hwy 7/8 west from Kitchener to Petersburg's Georgian-style inn, built in 1848; a smokin' place for live blues, Tuesday-night jams and tasty pints of Blue Moon Pilsner.

» EJ's Tavern
(www.ejsatbaden.com; 39 Snyder Rd W, Baden) From Petersburg, take Snyders Rd west to Baden to find hand-painted ceiling tiles, an 1891 oak bar and ornamental beer taps in this impressive redbrick edifice. Cozy, family vibes.

» Kennedy's Country Tavern
(62 Erb Rd West, St Agatha) Backtrack to Petersburg, turn left onto Notre Dame Dr and head north into St Agatha. Kennedy's is an Irish pub with a lively atmosphere and honest pints – mayhem on St Patrick's Day!

» Olde Heidelberg Brewery & Restaurant
(www.oldhh.com; cnr Kressler Rd & Lobsinger Line, Heidelberg) Take Rte 12 north from St Agatha, turn right onto Berlett's Rd, left onto Wilmot Line and continue north to Heidelberg. Straight out of the 1940s, the only thing changing around here is the contents of the copper brew tanks out the back.

Fergus Scottish Festival & Highland Games

SCOTTISH FESTIVAL

(www.fergusscottishfestival.com) If it's not Scottish, it doesn't count: tugs-of-war, caber tossing, bagpipes, Celtic dancing, kilts, haggis and Scotch nosing (aka tasting). Hoots! Held over two days in mid-August.

🛏 Sleeping

With more than 100 B&Bs in Centre Wellington, you'll have no trouble finding a place to stay. Visitors centers can help with contacts, or check availability online with the **Fergus Elora Bed & Breakfast Association** (www.febba.ca).

Drew House

INN $$

(☑519-846-2226; www.drewhouse.com; 120 Mill St E, Elora; r incl breakfast from $120; P ⊖ ✳) Run by a Basque chef and a New Jersey journo, Drew House unites the old world with the new. Set on spacious grounds, the inn has both renovated stable suites (with private bathrooms) or guestrooms (with shared bathrooms) in the main house. Yard-thick stone walls whisper history as you drift into dreams, before waking to a breakfast of fresh fruit (from the St Jacobs Farmers Market), hot coffee, and bacon and eggs cooked how you love them.

Brewhouse Inn

INN $$

(☑519-843-8871; www.fergusbrewhouse.com; 170 St David St S, Fergus; r $95-125; P ⊖ ✳ @ 🛜) Two rooms above a pub give this riverside place a touch of Old World. Stone walls and river views are ambience enough, but electric fireplaces warm things up a bit. One room has a clawfoot tub, both rooms come with a continental breakfast.

Elora Mill Inn

BOUTIQUE HOTEL $$$

(☑519-846-9118; www.eloramill.com; 77 Mill St W, Elora; r $200-340; P ⊖ ✳ @ 🛜) The limestone walls and massive wooden beams of the old five-story Elora Mill stand on the edge of the river, an enduring reminder of the town's industrious past. The moody, luxurious restoration inside is fabulous, with a dining room terrace that overlooks a waterfall. Some rooms have fireplaces.

Elora Gorge Conservation Area Campground

CAMPGROUND $

(☑519-846-9742, 866-668-2267; www.gran driver.ca; Rte 18, Elora; unpowered/powered sites $32.50/40, reservations $13; P) More than 550 campsites in six distinct, riverside zones. They're overflowing during summer, especially on holiday weekends.

🍴 Eating & Drinking

Dragonfly Café

CAFE $

(15 Mill St E, Elora; mains $5-11; ⊙10am-5pm Mon-Fri & Sun, to 6pm Sat) A busy breakfast and lunch joint that had a great river-view deck under construction when we visited. Baked goods, sandwiches and organic espresso are all on the menu.

The Brewhouse

PUB $$

(170 St David St S, Fergus; mains $10-19; ⊙11:30am-1am Mon-Sat, Sun to 1pm) Wave to the fly-fishermen on the Grand River from the shady Brewhouse patio as you weigh up the benefits of a Cheddar and Wellington ale soup, bangers and mash, or curried chicken enchilada. It sports a cozy bar, European beers on tap and live music to boot.

Shepherd's Pub

PUB $$

(8 Mill St W, Elora; mains $9-13; ⊙noon-10pm) Pubby mains and cold pints of Guinness by the river. All-day breakfast fry-ups, beer-battered fish and chips, and hearty beef pies will revive you if you spent too long here the night before.

ℹ Information

The **Fergus Information Centre** (☑519-843-5140, 877-242-6353; www.elorafergus.ca; 400 Tower St S, Fergus; ⊙10am-5pm Mon-Fri, noon-4pm Sat & Sun) is a well-stocked, informative tourist office. The same can be said of the **Elora Welcome Centre** (☑519-846-2563; www.elora.info; 9 Mill St E, Elora; ⊙10am-5pm), just near the bridge.

ℹ Getting There & Away

Greyhound Canada stops on Bridge St in Fergus, and at the **Little Katy Variety Store** (185 Geddes St, Elora; ⊙9am-7pm) in Elora, heading to/from Toronto ($25, two hours, one to two daily).

Stratford

A thriving foodie scene combined with a world-famous Shakespeare festival and a downtown primped to English country-garden perfection (complete with swans), Ontario's vibrant Stratford nearly outdoes England's Stratford-upon-Avon! Never dull, the affluent township profits from the festival trade and injects 'the Bard' into all facets of life. Come for a show, but stay for the fine food, parks and encircling farmland.

⊙ Sights & Activities

Avon River
PARKS

Stratford's swan-filled Avon River (what else were they going to call it?) flows slowly past the town, with plenty of riverbank lawns on which to chill out. Just west of Stratford Tourism on the riverbank, the **Shakespearean Gardens** (⊙dawn-dusk) occupy the site of an old wool mill. Parterre gardens, manicured box hedges, herbs, roses and a bronze bust of Bill – pick up a brochure at Stratford Tourism. Further along the river is **Queen's Park**, with paths leading from the Festival Theatre along the river past Orr Dam and an 1885 stone bridge to a formal **English flower garden**.

Stratford-Perth Museum
MUSEUM

(www.stratfordperthmuseum.ca; 4275 Huron Rd; suggested donation $5; ⊙10am-4pm Tue-Sat, from noon Sun & Mon May-Aug, 10am-4pm Tue-Sat Sep-Apr; [P]) The Stratford-Perth Museum has a new home that was still being built when we visited. Draws include hockey memorabilia (with some serious hockey fans running the show), collections of 20th-century Canadiana, and historical and cultural exhibitions, and a 1km walking trail.

Gallery Stratford
GALLERY

(www.gallerystratford.on.ca; 54 Romeo St; adult/child/concession $5/free/4; ⊙10am-5pm Tue-Sun Jun-Nov, noon-4pm Tue-Sun Dec-May; [P]) In a renovated 1880s pump house, Gallery Stratford exhibits innovative contemporary art with a Canadian emphasis. If your timing's good, there are regular art studios, movie nights and family days. A community studio lets kids create their own pieces. Bring a picnic and wander over to Queen's Park afterwards.

☞ Tours

Free self-guided historic, landmark and garden audio walking tours as well as PDFs are available at www.welcometostratford.com or at Stratford Tourism.

Epicurean Trek
FOOD TOUR

(www.stratfordperthheritage.ca; ⊙May-Oct) A downloadable guide gives you over a dozen local farms, cheese makers, bakeries and markets to visit on a self-guided tour, and includes individual opening days and hours. If you have a car, great; if you want to go by bike, even better!

Boat Tours
BOAT TOURS

(☏519-271-7739; fherr@sympatico.ca; 30 York St; 30min tours adult/child/concession $7/3/6; ⊙9am-dusk May-Oct) Take in the parks, swans, riverbanks and grand gardens on Avon River tours departing below Stratford Tourism by the river. Canoes, kayaks and paddleboats can also be rented (per hour $15 to $25).

THE STRATFORD FESTIVAL

Sir Alec Guinness played Richard III on opening night of the much-lauded **Stratford Festival** (☏519-273-1600, 800-567-1600; www.stratfordfestival.ca; Festival Theatre, Queen's Park, 55 Queen St; ⊙box office 9am-5pm Mon-Sat Dec-Mar, to 8pm Mon-Fri, to 5pm Sat, to 2pm Sun Apr-Nov), which began humbly in a tent at Queen's Park. The festival, with more than 50 seasons under its belt, has achieved international acclaim. Productions are first-rate and feature respected actors, but there's a vague sense in the wider theatergoing community that the festival has become an unwieldy show-pony, straying dangerously far from its Shakespearean roots. Whatever your impression, Stratford is certainly vibrant during the festival, and there's no better excuse to don your tights and pantaloons and wax lyrical!

Aside from the plays, there's a peripheral schedule of interesting programs, including post-performance discussions, backstage tours, lectures, concerts and readings. Some are free; some charge a nominal fee.

The festival plays a monster season from April right through to November. Four theaters stage contemporary and modern drama and music, operas and, of course, works by the Bard. Mainstage productions occur at the 1800-seat Festival Theatre. The Avon Theatre is the secondary venue, putting more than 1000 bums on seats. The Tom Patterson Theatre and Studio Theatre are more intimate.

Tickets go on sale to the general public in early January, and by showtime nearly every performance is sold out (book your tickets months ahead). Spring previews and fall end-of-season shows are often discounted by 30%, with 50%-off 'rush' tickets on sale two hours before showtime.

✦ Festivals & Events

Savour Stratford Festival FOOD FESTIVAL
(📞519-271-7500; www.welcometostratfordcom)
Beer, wine and food tastings, workshops,
farm tours and special dinners all highlight Perth County's abundance in mid-
September. Prices vary with the event.

Stratford Garlic Festival FOOD FESTIVAL
(www.stratfordgarlicfestival.com) Takes place
in conjunction with the Savour Stratford
Festival in mid-September. Bring your
breath mints.

Stratford Garden Festival GARDEN FESTIVAL
(www.stratfordgardenfestival.com; Stratford
Coliseum, 20 Glastonbury Dr; admission $8) A
four-day horticultural extravaganza in
early March, featuring flora from around
the world, guest speakers and
presentations.

Stratford Festival CULTURAL FESTIVAL
(www.stratfordfestival.ca) Shakespearean
plays plus theatrical tours, lectures,
concerts and readings from April to
November.

Stratford Summer Music MUSIC FESTIVAL
(www.stratfordsummermusic.ca; tickets $10-
$40) Four weeks of classical, cabaret and
theatrical music from mid-July to mid-
August, with acclaimed musicians from
around Canada tuning up and letting
loose.

⊨ Sleeping

There is a veritable plethora of accommodations in Stratford, but locals aren't shy
about exploiting their captive theater-going
guests for top prices. The majority of rooms
are B&B-style, but there are several well-
appointed, traditional inns too. The **Stratford Festival Visitor Accommodation Bureau** (📞800-567-1600; www.stratfordfestival.
ca) can help with bookings.

TOP
CHOICE
**Three Houses Bed &
Breakfast** B&B $$$
(📞519-272-0722; www.thethreehouses.com;
100 Brunswick St; ste incl breakfast $195-225;
P⊖❄🛜▨) Two Edwardian townhouses, a
garden carriage house and an 1870s Itali-
anate house make up this meticulous, *al-
most* over-the-top 18-room inn. Owner Da-
vid has spared no detail in decorating these
light-filled spaces – even the luggage racks
match the quirky individual room designs.
A saltwater pool and secret oasis garden
add relaxing touches.

SWANS ON PARADE

Stratford's beloved swans don't
paddle around the Avon all winter;
instead, they are kept warm in winter
pens. Come early April, the release
of the birds to their summer home on
the river is a Stratford celebration.
The swans waddle down the street in
parade formation, backed by bagpipe
players marching in kilts. Check www.
welcometostratford.com for exact
dates and more information.

Swan Motel MOTEL $$
(📞519-271-6376; www.swanmotel.on.ca; Downie
St S; r $102-125; P⊖❄🛜▨) A fabulously
maintained roadside motel from the 1960s,
the Swan has spotless rooms with costume
sketches and other original artwork on the
walls, and parklike grounds with hammered-
steel sculptures and fountains. It's a favorite
with returning visitors, who appreciate the
friendly owners and quiet surrounds. About
3km south of town; look for the vintage sign
out front. Closed from November until May.

Acrylic Dreams B&B $$
(📞519-271-7874; www.acrylicdreams.com; 66 Bay
St; r incl breakfast $120-155; P⊖❄🛜) How
can you go past a name like this? Owned
by a husband-and-wife team, this renovated
1879 B&B has polished wooden floorboards
and spa amenities. Besides being artists
(there are more than a few acrylic master-
pieces on the walls), the owners also prac-
tice chair massage and reflexology. They
can accommodate all diets.

Bentley's Inn INN $$
(📞519-271-1121, 800-361-5322; www.bentleys
-annex.com; 99 Ontario St; r $130-195; P⊖❄🛜)
This modern, dark-wood furnished inn
houses commodious bi-level suites and
lofts. Skylights, kitchenettes and period
furnishings are standard, the reception-
ists are friendly and the cafe downstairs is
always pumping. Cheaper off-season rates.

Mercer Hall Inn BOUTIQUE HOTEL $$
(📞519-271-1888, 888-816-4011; www.mercerhal
linn.com; 108 Ontario St; d $120-190; P⊖❄🛜)
Another fine choice with liberal luxuries,
Mercer Hall Inn has more class than most.
Uniquely artistic rooms with handcrafted
furniture, kitchenettes, electric fireplaces
and whirlpools also come with breakfast
from the cafe downstairs.

LOCAL KNOWLEDGE

ANTONY JOHN: ORGANIC FARMER

Perth County is a remarkable nexus of rainfall patterns, soil profile and topography that results in incredible food. If this were a wine region, we'd be the equivalent of a Bordeaux or a Burgundy for our soil quality.

There is no truer expression of a region's distinct combination of geography and climate than the food grown in its soil. You can sample some of Perth County's finest here at my farm, or at a few restaurants around town.

Stratford's most flavorful eats

» **Bijou** (p128)

» **Down the Street** (p128)

Stratford General Hospital Residence

HOSTEL **$**

(SGH Residence; ☎519-271-5084; sgh.residence@hpha.ca; 130 Youngs St; s/d $55/65; ⓟ❄☒) The closest thing you'll find to a youth hostel in these parts is this renovated nurses' quarters: 360 rooms with shared bathrooms, kitchens and a heated pool.

✖ Eating & Drinking

A local chef's school as well as the surrounding farmland mean there's a plethora of good eats in town – far too many to list here. With plenty of theatergoers in town, it's best to make dinner reservations.

Bijou

FRENCH **$$$**

(☎519-273-5000; 105 Erie St; lunch $8-18, dinner $46-52; ⓢlunch Fri-Sat, dinner Tue-Sun) Classy and delightful, this French joint has a different set menu written on the chalkboard each evening. The locally sourced meals might include quail, heirloom tomato salad or Lake Huron Whitefish *ceviche*. Creaky wooden floorboards and children's artwork on the walls add a personal touch.

Down the Street Bar & Restaurant

CAFE **$$**

(☎519-273-5886; 30 Ontario St; lunch mains $12-15, dinner $19-29; ⓢ11:30am-1am Tue-Sun) Darkly atmospheric, with gorgeous gilt mirrors and old neons stirring memories of Parisian cafes, this place offers pre-theater dining, microbrews and wines by the glass. The menu is multicultural (thin-crust pizzas, goat cheese enchiladas) and late night

the bar steps up as one of Stratford's more kickin' nocturnal haunts.

York Street Kitchen

SANDWICH SHOP **$**

(41 York St; mains $7-16; ⓢ8am-8pm) This technicolor bunker at the bottom of an old riverside warehouse dishes up homestyle cooking: show-stopper sandwiches on homemade bread, brie fritters, salads, quiches and desserts. Try the 'Mennonite' sandwich: sausage, cheddar, corn relish, tomato, honey mustard, mayo and lettuce.

Raja

INDIAN **$$**

(☎519-271-3271; 10 St George St W; mains $10-18; ⓢlunch & dinner; ✈) Challenging Stratford's demure Anglo tastes with funky lashings of chili and spice, Raja plates up super curries, soups, salads, breads, vegetarian and tandoori dishes and serves them on white linen. Staff are dapper and unfailingly polite.

Let Them Eat Cake

BAKERY **$**

(82 Wellington St; mains $5-11; ⓢ7am-8pm) All-day breakfast (we couldn't deny ourselves the eggs benny pizza) as well as fresh-baked scones and muffins make this Stratford institution the perfect place to start your morning.

Tango Café & Grill

CAFE **$**

(104 Ontario St; lunch mains $5-10, dinner $10-14; ⓢ7am-4pm Mon-Thu, to 8pm Fri, 8am-8pm Sat, to 4pm Sun) Aromatic coffee has bean-fiends tangoing through the doors here, many of whom decide to stay for a tasty sandwich, omelet, burger or salad. Fair trade coffee blends include the light-roasted 'Sleepy Monk' and tongue-in-cheek 'Moonbucks.'

ⓘ Information

Stratford Public Library (www.stratford. library.on.ca; 19 St Andrew St; ⓢ1-9pm Mon, 10am-9pm Tue-Sat) Free internet access.

Stratford Tourism (☎519-271-5140, 800-561-7926; www.welcometostratford.com) Downtown (47 Downie St; ⓢ8:30am-6pm Mon-Fri, to 4:30pm Jun-Aug) Riverside (30 York St; ⓢ10am-6pm Tue-Sun Jun-Sep) Help with accommodations and all things 'Festival.' The website is an excellent information source, with loads of tour options.

ⓘ Getting There & Away

For select summer weekend matinees, **Toronto Direct** (www.stratfordfestival.ca) buses depart Toronto's York Mills TTC subway station at 9:30am, returning from Stratford at 7pm (round trip $48). Contact the Festival Theatre box office for schedules and reservations.

The **Stratford Airporter** (☎519-273-0057, 1-888-549-8602; www.stratfordairporter.com) runs eight shuttles per day to Pearson International Airport, but it's very expensive unless you have a large group to share the cost.

VIA Rail runs from **Stratford Train Station** (☎888-842-7245; www.viarail.ca; 101 Shakespeare St) to Toronto ($39, two hours, three daily) and London ($20, one hour, three daily).

London

POP 348,000

The Thames, Covent Garden, Pall Mall and Oxford St – that's London, right? You betcha, but beyond nomenclature, this version has nothing in common with its namesake. Midway between Toronto and Detroit, London Ontario is a staid, functional student town that seems hell-bent on trying to be something more than it really is. Take the students out of the picture (they remove themselves every summer) and London seems little more than a loose affiliation of tattoo parlors, homeless strugglers and Anglo street signs. Still, the music scene is rockin' and there are some cool local festivals.

⊙ Sights & Activities

Museum London   MUSEUM
(☎519-661-0333; www.museumlondon.ca; 421 Ridout St N; admission by donation; ⊙noon-5pm Tue, Wed & Fri-Sun, to 9pm Thu; P) Focusing on the visual arts and how they fit together with history, Museum London has over 5000 works of art (including the largest collection of Paul Peel paintings) and an artifact collection of over 25,000 pieces. Exhibitions and programming are created around the stories of artifacts, and outdoor installations carry the stories beyond the walls.

Also on-site is **Eldon House** (adult/child/concession/family $6/1/5/11, admission by donation Wed & Sun; ⊙noon-5pm Tue-Sun Jun-Sep, Wed-Sun May & Oct-Dec, Sat & Sun Jan-Apr), London's oldest residence, which places you in the past rather than attempting to describe it.

Museum of Ontario Archaeology   MUSEUM
(☎519-473-1360; 1600 Attawandaron Rd; www.uwo.ca/museum; adult/child/concession/family $4/2/3.25/10; ⊙10am-4:30pm May-Aug, Wed-Sun only Sep-Dec, 1-4pm Sat & Sun Jan-Apr; P) An educational and research facility affiliated with the University of Western Ontario, the Museum of Ontario Archaeology displays materials and artifacts spanning 11,000 years of aboriginal history in Ontario.

Lawson Prehistoric Indian Village (⊙May-Nov) is an active excavation of a 500-year-old village next to the museum.

Ska-Nah-Doht Village & Museum
                              HISTORICAL PARK
(☎519-264-2420; www.lowerthames-conservation.on.ca; Longwoods Rd Conservation Area; adult/child/concession $3/free/2; ⊙9am-4:30pm May-Sep, Mon-Fri only Oct-Apr; P) Re-creating a 1000-year-old Iroquois longhouse community, Ska-Nah-Doht Iroquoian Village & Museum is 32km west of London. Village structures are encircled by a maze; the museum contains artifacts thousands of years old and recounts the area's history. Outside the walls are First Nations crops and burial platforms. Meandering park trails are open until dusk. From London, take Hwy 402 to interchange 86 then follow Hwy 2 west.

Fanshawe Pioneer Village   HISTORICAL PARK
(☎519-457-1296; www.fanshawepioneervillage.ca; 1424 Clarke Rd; admission $5; ⊙10am-4:30pm Tue-Sun May-Oct; P) Explore London's history at the 30-building Fanshawe Pioneer Village on the eastern edge of town. Costumed blacksmiths, farmers and craftspeople carry out their duties in true 19th-century pioneer-village style.

At the adjoining **Fanshawe Conservation Area** you can swim, walk and camp.

Ponds & Bogs   PARKS
In the west side of town, oozy **Sifton Bog** (www.thamesriver.on.ca; ⊙dawn-dusk; P) is a peaty acid bog off Oxford St W that's home to unusual plants and animals, including lemmings, shrews, carnivorous sundew plants, white-tailed deer and nine varieties of orchid.

South of town behind the Tourism London office, off Wellington Rd S, **Westminster Ponds** (www.thamesriver.on.ca; ⊙dawn-dusk; P) is an area of woods, bogs and ponds sustaining a veritable zoo of creatures, including fox, turtles and herons.

Banting House National Historic Site
                              HISTORICAL SITE
(www.diabetes.ca; 442 Adelaide St N; adult/child/concession/family $4/free/3/8; ⊙noon-4pm Tue-Sat; P) This historic site is where Nobel Prize–winner Sir Frederick Banting devised the method for extracting insulin in the 1920s. A pilgrimage site for diabetics, the meticulously curated museum outlines the history of diabetes, and chronicles Banting's medical contributions.

Royal Canadian Regiment Museum MUSEUM
(www.royalcanadianregiment.ca; 750 Elizabeth St; adult/child/concession $5/3/4; ⏲10am-4pm Tue-Fri, from noon Sat & Sun; P) Inside the austere Wolseley Hall, the Royal Canadian Regiment Museum focuses on the oldest infantry regiment in Canada, with displays covering the North-West Rebellion of 1885 through both world wars to the Korean War.

Tours

Double Decker Sightseeing Tour BUS TOUR
(☎800-265-2602; www.londontourism.ca; cnr Wellington & Dundas Sts; 2hr tour adult/child/concession $13/5/11; ⏲10am late Jun-Aug) Top-deck London views on a London bus; departing the downtown Tourism London office.

Festivals & Events

Bluesfest International MUSIC FESTIVAL
(www.thebluesfest.ca) *My woman done left me, and my dog went with her...* Big names like Robert Cray play the blues in mid-July.

London Beer Festival BEER FESTIVAL
(www.london beerfest.ca) Put your drinkin' shoes on in mid-July.

Sunfest CULTURAL FESTIVAL
(www.sunfest.on.ca) Celebrates global arts with music, dance, crafts and cuisine in mid-July.

London Fringe Festival CULTURAL FESTIVAL
(www.londonfringe.ca) Eleven days of theater, spoken word, film and visual arts around downtown from late July to mid-August.

Sleeping

The **London & Area B&B Association** (www.londonbb.ca) lists accommodations, while Tourism London also publishes rate sheets for local hotels and B&Bs. Wellington Rd south of town and Dundas St E are predictable motel/fast-food/sex-shop strips.

ACBB London HOSTEL $
(☎519-936-7823; www.allcanbb.com; 190 Wellington St; dm/d incl breakfast $25/55; P ⊖ ❄ ☰) Just south of downtown is this top-notch backpackers joint. Good security, friendly atmosphere, custom-made beds and mattresses, outdoor decks, clean bathrooms, well-equipped kitchens, free breakfast, barbecues and internet – it's a simple formula, but rare that anyone gets it right!

Windermere Manor HOTEL $$
(☎800-997-4477; www.windermeremanor.com; 200 Collip Circle, off Windermere Rd; r/ste incl breakfast $132/154; P ⊖ ❄ ☰) Atop a green hill overlooking the Thames and the university, this modified, upper-crust 1925 manor is popular with conventioneers and visiting uni lecturers. It's a fair hike from downtown, but the on-site cafe does breakfast, lunch and dinner.

Fanshawe Conservation Area Campground CAMPGROUND $
(☎519-451-2800, 866-668-2267; www.thamesriver.on.ca; 1424 Clarke Rd; unpowered/powered sites $25/29, reservations $9; ⏲late Apr–mid-Oct; P ≋) Convenient camping within the city limits, across from Fanshawe Pioneer Village.

London Executive Suites HOTEL $$
(☎519-679-3932, 800-265-5955; www.les-hotel.com; 362 Dundas St; ste $75-120; P ❄ ☰) This former downtown apartment building has spacious rooms with balconies and kitchens. No surprises, just comfy mattresses, solid furniture and good views from the upper floors. Rates go down the longer you stay.

Eating

Bertoldi's Trattoria ITALIAN $$
(☎519-438-4343; 650 Richmond St; mains $12-20; ⏲11am-10pm Sun & Mon, to 11pm Tue-Sat) A massive place with a massive wine list, Bertoldi's does authentic Italian and also has special regional menus (we can't think of an Italian region whose cuisine we wouldn't want to taste). It doesn't take reservations but you can phone ahead on the weekends.

Covent Garden MARKET $
(130 King St; items from $2; ⏲8am-6pm Mon-Sat, 11am-4pm Sun) This humongous, barn-shaped market will whet and satisfy any appetite. There's a permanent collection of delis, bakeries, chocolate shops, fresh produce stalls and world cuisine eateries, plus seasonal vendors and a sunny, busker-fuelled buzz on the patio.

Thaifoon THAI $$
(120 Dundas St; mains $11-14; ⏲lunch Mon-Fri, dinner daily) Classing Dundas St up a bit is Thaifoon. A calm, composed atmosphere and babbling water features provide relief from the mean streets, while chili-laden curries, stir-fries, soups and salads provide a kick in the pants.

Sammy's Souvlaki FAST FOOD **$**
(cnr Richmond & Carling Sts; items $3-7;
⊘10:30am-3am) Bump elbows with taxi drivers and late-night beery hordes at Sammy's, serving take-out souvlaki, falafels, poutine, burgers and hot dogs. Burp...

🍺 Drinking & Entertainment

Check out the local rag *Scene* (www.scene magazine.com) for arts and entertainment listings.

London Music Club LIVE MUSIC
(☎519-640-6996; www.londonmusicclub.com; 470 Colborne St; admission free-$15; ⊘7pm-late Wed-Sat) Touring blues and folks acts fall over themselves to play here, a rockin' room out the back of a cream-brick suburban house. Electric blues jam on Thursday nights; acoustic open mic on Fridays.

Honest Lawyer PUB
(228 Dundas St; ⊘11am-late) Is there such a thing? Maybe not, but it's a sure-fire conversation starter at this long, narrow beer room where an upbeat crowd is usually knocking back a few. Student specials, wing nights, big-screen sports and live music on the weekends.

Call the Office LIVE MUSIC
(www.calltheoffice.com; 216 York St; ⊘5pm-late) A grungy dive bar with cheap drinks and alt-rock live bands.

CEEPS PUB
(671 Richmond St; ⊘11am-2pm) For reliable good times, head to this student-flavored party bar. Live bands, DJs, pool tables, shuffleboard, local beers on tap – hard to beat.

Up on Carling NIGHTCLUB
(www.uponcarling.ca; 153 Carling St; ⊘9pm-late Thu-Sat) A stylish, martini-soaked affair, spinning Latin, R&B, funk house and soul. Dress code enforced.

ℹ Information

London Public Library (www.londonpublic library.ca; 251 Dundas St; ⊘9am-9pm Mon-Thu, to 6pm Fri, to 5pm Sat, 1-5pm Sun) A fabulous modern setting with a cafe, reading garden, and free internet and wi-fi.

Post office (www.canadapost.ca; cnr Dufferin & Richmond Sts; ⊘8am-5pm Mon-Fri)

Tourism London (☎519-661-5000, 800-265-2602; www.londontourism.ca) Downtown (267 Dundas St; ⊘8:30am-4:30pm Mon-Fri, 10am-5pm Sat & Sun); Wellington Rd (696 Wellington Rd S; ⊘8:30am-8pm) The downtown office shares a building with the Canadian Medical Hall of Fame and its interesting/gory displays of brains, hearts and bones.

ℹ Getting There & Around

London International Airport (YXU; www.londonairport.on.ca; 1750 Crumlin Rd) is a regional base for Air Canada, WestJet and Delta with flights to Toronto and Detroit, and limited Canadian and US destinations.

Greyhound Canada rolls out of **London Bus Station** (☎800-661-8747; www.greyhound.ca; 101 York St; ⊘6:30am-9pm) to Toronto ($37, 2½ hours, 12 daily) and Windsor ($37, 2½ hours, five daily).

London Train Station (☎519-672-5722; www.viarail.ca; cnr York & Clarence Sts; ⊘5am-9:30pm Mon-Fri, from 6:30am Sat & Sun) has trains to Toronto ($58, two to three hours, eight daily) and Windsor ($53, two hours, four daily).

London Transit (www.londontransit.ca; 150 Dundas St; ⊘7:30am-7pm Mon-Fri, 8:30am-6pm Sat) has extensive bus services around town ($2.75 a ride).

St Thomas

St Thomas is a low-key farming community with a well-maintained Victorian downtown, 20km south of London on the way to Lake Erie. The **St Thomas Visitors Centre** (☎877-463-5446; www.elgintourist.com; Old Talbot St; ⊘10am-5:30pm Mon-Sat) can help with accommodations info.

For the kid in everyone, the **Elgin County Railway Museum** (www.ecrm5700.org; 225 Wellington St; adult/child $4/free; ⊘10am-4pm late May-Aug; P) is an old brick warehouse full of red hot locomotive action. Displays revisit the times when St Thomas was the undisputed 'Railway Capital of Canada.'

Unfortunately, St Thomas does have a deep, dark story to tell. Hearts were broken around the world when the famous circus elephant Jumbo met his maker when he was hit by a train here in 1885. A jumbo-sized **Jumbo statue** next to the visitors center pays tribute to the poor pachyderm.

Lake Erie Shoreline

From the Welland Canal to the Detroit River, the Lake Erie shoreline is a scenic, thinly populated strip of sandy beaches, chilled-out towns and peaceful parks – no wonder so many Ontarians have summer cottages here. Lake Erie (the shallowest and warmest of the Great Lakes) has long been considered a polluted puddle, but recent environmental efforts have brought it back from the brink. You can swim here now, but it's still wise to look before you leap (or send your kid brother in first). Don't miss a visit to the lowest of low-key holiday destinations, Pelee Island, Canada's southernmost point.

PORT DOVER & AROUND

Port Dover is a summer-centric beach town with a sandy, laid-back vibe. Sunburned mid-lifers, bikini teens and ice-cream-dripping kids patrol the main drag on summer vacation. **Port Dover Visitor Centre** (☑519-583-1314; www.portdover.ca; 19 Market St W, Port Dover; ☺10am-5pm Jun-Aug, Mon-Fri only Sep-May) has giggly staff who can help with accommodations and loan bicycles for free.

The two-story **Port Dover Harbour Museum** (☑519-583-2660; portdover.museum@norfolkcounty.on.ca; 44 Harbour St, Port Dover; admission by donation; ☺11am-6pm) is a cute, reconstructed fishing shack focusing on the Lake Erie fishing industry, sailing, shipwrecks, knot-work and the exploits of local sea-dog Captain Alexander McNeilledge ('Wear no specks, use no tobacco, take a wee dram as necessary').

Southwest along the coast are two excellent provincial parks: **Turkey Point Provincial Park** (☑519-426-3239; www.ontarioparks.com; 194 Turkey Point Rd, Turkey Point; unpowered/powered sites $28/33, admission per car $11; ☺May-Oct; P) and **Long Point Provincial Park** (☑519-586-2133; www.ontarioparks.com; 350 Erie Blvd, Port Rowan; unpowered/powered sites $28/33, admission per car $11; ☺May-Oct; P), both popular day-use and camping parks. Long Point occupies a sandy spit jagging into the lake, great for swimming, while Turkey Point's forests teem with bird nerds and nature lovers.

The most central beds in town are at the white-walled **Erie Beach Hotel** (☑519-583-1391; www.eriebeachhotel.com; 19 Walker St, Port Dover; d from $80; P☺✳☎). The best rooms overlook impossibly perfect lawns, while the pubby **dining room** (mains $10-20; ☺11am-3pm & 6-9pm) menu obsesses over perch and shrimp.

PORT STANLEY

A working fishing village in a nook of Kettle Creek, **Port Stanley** (www.portstanley.net) has a tiny, picture-perfect downtown and an agreeable atmosphere that's far from pretentious. It's the kind of place where the lady in the coffee shop issues a heartfelt 'Thank you!' and goes into great detail explaining ice-cream flavors to the kids.

The summer program at the **Port Stanley Festival Theatre** (☑519-782-4353; www.psft.on.ca; 302 Bridge St; ☺box office 10am-5pm Tue, to 3pm Wed, to 5pm Thu, noon-5pm Sat) always fills seats, while outside, the **Port Stanley Terminal Rail** (☑877-244-4478; www.pstr.on.ca; 309 Bridge St; 1hr rides adult/child $12.50/8; ☺noon, 1:30pm & 3pm Jul-Aug, weekends only May-Jun & Sep-Oct; P) chugs along a 14km portion of the historic London–Port Stanley railroad.

If you want to stay the night, try the upmarket, maritime-hewn **Inn on the Harbour** (☑519-782-7623; www.innontheharbour.ca; 202 Main St; d $125-155; P☺✳☎). Watch fishing boats come and go, offloading baskets of perch and pickerel. In back, the new **Little Inn** offers themed suites (think African Safari or Paris Boutique) for $225 per night.

LEAMINGTON & AROUND

Lakeside Leamington is the 'Tomato Capital of Ontario,' and a key ketchup producer – the Heinz factory south of town is a major employer. Greenhouses dot the acreage around town, rampaging tomato vines crowding out against the glass. The neat, window-box-strewn downtown area attracts visitors en route to Pelee Island. **Leamington Tourist Information** (☑800-250-3336; www.uptownleamington.ca; cnr Albert & Talbot Sts, Leamington; ☺9am-6pm Apr, to 7pm May-Sep, 9am-6pm Thu-Sun Oct, 9am-5pm Sat & Sun Nov) occupies a giant tomato!

SMOKE GETS IN YOUR EYES

The flat, sandy soils of northern Norfolk County between Port Dover and Port Stanley provide ideal growing conditions for alternate crops – what used to be a strictly tobacco-growing area now also supports hemp and ginseng fields. For a sniff of old 'baccy, take Hwy 3 inland to the **Delhi Tobacco Museum & Heritage Centre** (☑519-582-0278; www.delhimuseum.ca; 200 Talbot Rd, Delhi; admission by donation; ☺10am-4:30pm Mon-Fri, 1-4pm Sat & Sun Jun-Aug; P), a wooden-crate, leaf-filled multicultural museum with displays on the local history and tobacco production.

About 10km east of Leamington, **Wheatley Provincial Park** (www.ontarioparks.com; 21116 Klondyke Rd S, Wheatley; unpowered/powered sites $34/39, admission per car $13; ☺Apr-Oct; P) has good camping despite much of the beach being swept away by a monster storm in 1998. The park gets busy as a woodpecker during migrations.

Southeast of town, **Point Pelee National Park** (☏519-322-2365, 866-787-3533; www. pc.gc.ca; 407 Robson Rd, Leamington; adult/child/concession/family $8/4/7/20; ☺dawn-dusk; P), on the southernmost point of mainland Canada, is a pit stop for thousands of birds during spring and fall migrations. The fall migration of monarch butterflies is a spectacle of swirling black and orange. There are numerous nature trails, a marsh boardwalk, forested areas and sandy beaches within the park.

In Kingsville, just west of Leamington, **Pelee Island Winery** (☏800-597-3533; www. peleeisland.com; 455 Seacliff Dr, Kingsville; admission free, tours adult/child/concession $5/free/4; ☺9am-6pm Mon-Sat, 11am-5pm Sun; P) offers tours (noon, 2pm and 4pm), including a trip down to the huge wooden cellar doors, and free tastings. The grapes actually come from Pelee Island, so the name isn't a fraud!

Just east of town, **Hillman Marsh** (www. erca.org; Country Rd 37, Leamington; admission per car $5; ☺dawn-dusk; P) is another bird-filled wetland with a 4.5km walking trail and a nice little visitor center.

PELEE ISLAND
Excessively green and as southerly as Canada gets, Pelee Island (pronounced pee-loo, from the French *pelée* meaning bare, though it inherited this misnomer from Point Pelee) is a surprising little oasis 20km from the mainland on Lake Erie. Surrounded by sandy beaches and shallow water that gets bathtub-water warm in the summer, this limestone-dotted island draws birders, cottagers and those looking to take a tipple from the fruits of the island – the winery.

The island's settled history arcs back to 1788 when the Ojibwe and Ottawa nations leased it to Thomas McKee. It remained largely undeveloped until William McCormick bought it in 1823. By 1900 Pelee had 800 residents, four churches and four schools. These days there are just 275 residents and life revolves around tourism, but nothing is overly pricey, snobby, hurried or harried – perfect for a weekend of doing not much at all.

◉ Sights & Activities

Pelee Island Heritage Centre   MUSEUM
(☏519-724-2291; West Dock; adult/child/concession $3/2/2.50; ☺10am-5pm May-Oct; P) Near West Dock, the small Pelee Island Heritage Centre has one of the best natural history collections in Ontario. Engrossing displays cover indigenous to 20th-century history, geology, wildlife, industry, sailing and shipwrecks.

Explore Pelee   BIKE TOURS
(☏519-724-2285; www.explorepelee.com; tours $25-40) Led by the effervescent Anne Marie, an Explore Pelee bike tour will show you all the lovely little details about the island, from the oldest home through to the canals, pump houses and graveyard. Wine-tasting combos are available; call or email to schedule any of the tours.

Fish Point Nature Reserve   NATURE RESERVE
(www.ontarioparks.com; 1750 McCormick Rd; admission free; ☺dawn-dusk; P) Fish Point Nature Reserve is a long sandy spit – absolutely the southernmost point of Canada. A 3.2km return forest walkway leads to the point, one of the island's best swim spots. Like other spots in the region, Fish Point is a birder's Eden, with black-crowned night herons and a multitude of shorebirds.

Pelee Island Lighthouse   NOTABLE BUILDING
(www.ontarioparks.com; East Shore Rd; ☺dawn-dusk; P) The 1833 Pelee Island Lighthouse on the island's northeastern corner stopped flashing in 1909 and was derelict until restoration in 2000. It's a 10-minute return walk from the end of East Shore Rd. You can't access the lighthouse, but it's interesting (and photogenic) nonetheless.

Pelee Island Winery Wine Pavilion   WINERY
(☏800-597-3533; www.peleeisland.com; 20 East-West Rd; special tours adult/child/concession $5/free/4; ☺10am-6pm Mon-Sat, 11am-5pm Sun May-Oct; P) Enjoy the fruits of island life at the Pelee Island Winery Wine Pavilion. Regular tours are free at noon, 2pm and 4pm most days; special wine-and-cheese and wine-and-chocolate tours can be scheduled by calling.

🛏 Sleeping
There are great B&Bs here, plus cottages which are rented out by the week. Most take advantage of the western side's fantastic sunsets. **Explore Pelee** (www.explorepelee. com) can help with booking.

FINE FEATHERED FRIEND

Legend has it that one chilly winter, a couple of islanders drove their truck from Pelee across frozen Lake Erie to Leamington to have some repairs done. All went to plan until the return trip, when a thick bank of fog blew in, enshrouding the men on the ice. Night was falling, and rather than continue with no sense of direction (and maybe bump into Ohio), they decided to wait it out. Just before dawn, they heard a rooster crowing on the island. Realizing they were close to home, the happy trucksters followed the rooster's cries to Pelee and went promptly to bed. When they awoke later that day, the fog lifted to reveal a broken and rapidly disappearing ice sheet! We suspect that particular fowl lived a long and prosperous life.

TOP CHOICE **Stonehill Bed & Breakfast** B&B $
(☎519-724-2193; 911 West Shore Rd; s/d with shared bath $65/80; P⊜) Built in 1875 with limestone from the quarry in back, this old farmhouse is stone silent. Two limestone walls with airspace between them ensure no sound gets through. With waterfront views, a parklike setting and friendly hosts, a night's sleep here is probably the best bargain on the island. Check out the fossils embedded in the front steps!

Anchor & Wheel Inn MOTEL, CAMPGROUND $$
(☎519-724-2195; www.anchorwheelinn.com; 11 West Shore Rd; unpowered/powered sites $20/35, d $85-115, cottage from $150; P⊜❋) The effervescent Anchor & Wheel in the northwest corner of Pelee has a range of beds from grassy campsites through to air-conditioned guestrooms with Jacuzzis and a dockside cottage.

East Park Municipal Campground CAMPGROUND $
(☎519-724-2931; East Shore Rd; unpowered sites $20; P) Camp on the east side of the island at these basic, wooded sites – quiet, uncrowded, and you can light a campfire.

✕ Eating

Conorlee's Bakery & Delicatessen BAKERY $
(www.conorlee.bravehost.com; 5 Northshore Dr; sandwiches $5-7; ⊘breakfast & lunch daily, pizza 5-9pm Thu-Sun) An islanders' favorite, Conorlee's is a great place to grab lunch-to-go before a bike tour. Fresh-baked breads, espresso, local honey and awesome pizzas are all available, but the coolest offering is the Wine & Dinner Series (per person $38), a monthly five-course sampling of Pelee's finest. It's held at the Pelee Island Winery; check Conorlee's website for dates.

Scudder Beach Bar & Grill BURGERS $$
(325 North Shore Rd; mains $8-16; ⊘noon-10pm May-Sep) This woody bar room serves wraps and sandwiches plus gallons of cold beer; there might even be a live band on a Saturday night (otherwise it's the game on TV).

Westview Tavern PUB $
(1075 West Shore Rd; mains $8-12, ⊘lunch & dinner) Across from the ferry dock you'll find pub standbys such as fish and chips, grilled cheese and locals talking hockey.

ℹ Information

Regional visitor information centers will help you plan your visit, as will www.pelee.org. During summer, book ferries and accommodations in advance. Good luck finding internet on the island; your best bet is cell coverage. There are two ATMs, one at Scudder Beach Bar & Grill and the other at Westview Tavern. It's best to stock up on cash, however, as the machines can run out of dough on busy weekends (just like the rest of us, eh?).

ℹ Getting There & Around

From Leamington (and sometimes Kingsville), **Ontario Ferries** (☎519-326-2154; www.ontarioferries.com; adult/child/concession $7.50/3.75/6.25, car/bicycle/motorcycle $16.50/3.75/8.25; ⊘Apr–mid-Dec) services the island. Schedules depend on the day and season; reservations essential. The trip takes 1½ hours each way. Ferries also connect Pelee with Sandusky, Ohio; see the website for details. In winter you'll need to book a flight out of Windsor.

Bicycles can be rented at **Comfortech Bicycle Rentals** (☎519-724-2828; West Dock; per hr/day $8/20; ⊘9am-7pm May-Oct, to 4pm Apr & Nov) – call for reservations.

AMHERSTBURG

South of Windsor, where the Detroit River flows into Lake Erie, sits small, historic

Amherstburg. Much more happened here in the past than of late, a fact you can't help but avoid (signs in the downtown area actually say 'Olde Towne'). War of 1812 and Underground Railroad buffs will find some enthralling diversions. The **Amherstburg Visitors Information Centre** (☑519-736-8320, 800-413-9993; www.amherstburg.ca; cnr Sandwich & William Sts) is just north of town and was closed for renovations when we visited.

On earthwork embankments along the river stands **Fort Malden National Historic Site** (☑519-736-5416; www.pc.gc.ca; 100 Laird Ave; adult/child/concession/family $4/2/3.50/10; ☺10am-5pm May-Oct; P), a British fort built in 1840. Beginning with the arrival of the fur traders, the area saw a lot of friction between the French, First Nations and English, and, later, the Americans. Here, during the War of 1812, General Brock (together with his ally, Shawnee Chief Tecumseh) conspired to take Detroit.

Learn about black settlement in the area at the **North American Black Historical Museum** (☑519-736-5433, 800-713-6336; www.blackhistoricalmuseum.com; 277 King St; adult/child/concession/family $5.50/4.50/4.50/20; ☺10am-5pm Tue-Fri, from 1pm Sat & Sun; P). The Nazrey African Methodist Episcopal Church here, a national historic site, was built by former slaves and played a role in the Underground Railroad as a terminal.

Park House Museum (☑519-736-2511; www.parkhousemuseum.com; 214 Dalhousie St; adult/child/concession $3/1/2; ☺10am-5pm Jun-Aug, from 11am Tue-Fri & Sun Sep-May) is the oldest house in town, and the only one not *from* town. It was built on the other side of the river, ferried across in 1799, and is now furnished in 1850s style.

POP 209,000

At the southwestern tip of Ontario, across the Detroit River from Detroit, Michigan, Windsor is the only Canadian city *south* of mainland USA. Like Detroit, Windsor is a 'motor city,' but with the car industry feeling the pinch, this formerly neat, civilized town's future is uncertain. There are few reasons to linger in Windsor, but if you do there are some solid late-night bars and eateries here, and the riverside on a warm summer night and the Italian district on Erie St E have a happening vibe.

⊙ Sights & Activities

Caesar's Windsor
CASINO

(www.caesarswindsor.com; 377 Riverside Dr E; admission free; ☺24hr; P) The super-plush Caesar's Windsor overlooking the river provides a fat economic injection for Windsor, though the crowds have declined with passport legislation. Still, the giant screen advertises big-name shows to potential customers across the river. Minimum age 19 years.

Art Gallery of Windsor
GALLERY

(AGW; www.agw.ca; 401 Riverside Dr W; admission $5, free Wed; ☺11am-5pm Wed, Sat & Sun, to 9pm Thu & Fri; P) The jaunty glass-and-concrete prow of the AGW has an awesome permanent collection focused on contemporary Canadian sculpture and painting.

Walkerville Distillery
DISTILLERY

(☑519-973-9503; www.canadianclubwhisky.com; Canadian Club Brand Heritage Centre, 2072 Riverside Dr E; adult/child/concession $5/free/4; ☺noon-6pm Wed-Sat, to 4pm Sun May-Dec, Fri & Sat only Jan-Apr; P) Whiskey was here long before gambling. Distributed to 151 countries, Canadian Club has been sluicing out of the distillery since 1858. One-hour tours (noon, 2pm and 4pm) examine the processes and offer a taste.

THE UNDERGROUND RAILROAD

Neither subterranean nor an actual railroad, the Underground Railroad refers to the secretive web of abolitionists and humanitarians – both black and white – who shepherded, sheltered, hid and transported escaped slaves north from the US to freedom in Canada. Before the American Civil War, it's estimated that 40,000 brave souls made the dangerous journey. Predictably, this part of southwestern Ontario, so close to the US border, is rich with historic Underground Railroad sites. Many local towns have substantial African-American populations, descended from those who found sanctuary here.

Visit www.blackhistory society.ca. See also the North American Black Historical Museum, the Walls Underground Railroad Museum and Uncle Tom's Cabin Historic Site.

Walls Underground Railroad Museum

MUSEUM

(www.undergroundrailroadmuseum.com; 855 Puce Rd, Maidstone; admission $5; ⊗10am-5pm Jun-Aug; ℙ) One of the best Underground Railroad historical displays is at the Walls Underground Railroad Museum, 20km east of Windsor. The original 1846 log cabin built by John Freeman Walls, a fugitive slave from North Carolina, is still here; it functioned as a safe terminal for others searching for freedom. Walls' descendants still run the museum.

Parks & Gardens

PARKS

The best views of the glimmering Detroit skyline are from **Dieppe Gardens** (cnr Ouellette St & Riverside Dr; ⊗24hr), constructed on land once used by Detroit–Windsor ferries before the 1929 bridge and 1930 tunnel put them out of business.

Further south, the **Odette Sculpture Park** (Riverside Dr; ⊗24hr), almost under the Ambassador Bridge, features a long run of zany 3-D efforts including a family of elephants, a huge apple core and twisty swan necks.

🎪 Festivals & Events

Bluesfest International

MUSIC FESTIVAL

(www.thebluesfest.com) Working in tandem with London's Bluesfest International, and featuring the likes of Los Lobos and Steve Earle. Held in mid-July.

🛏 Sleeping & Eating

There are plenty of beds in Windsor and reservations aren't crucial. Chain hotels and local motels dominate Huron Church Rd, leading off the Ambassador Bridge.

Oullette Ave (Thai, Indian and coffee shops) and Chatham St (bars and grills) lend foodie focus to the downtown area. Erie St E is the Italian district, with oodles of affordable eateries.

Kirk's B&B

B&B $$

(☑519-255-9346, 888-251-2624; www.kirks bandb.com; 406 Moy Ave; s/d $75/99; ℙ⊖✳🛜) One block from the river, Kirk's is a three-story, old-fashioned brick affair, with a lush garden and a cat. Warm, tidy rooms have ridiculously comfortable beds.

University Place Accommodations

HOTEL $

(☑519-254-1112, 866-618-1112; www.windsorex ecutivestay.com; 3140 Peter St; r with shared bath from $39; ℙ✳🛜🍽) Though not affiliated with the university, this long- and short-term residence caters to students and their visiting families. Rooms share common kitchens, a rec room and on-site laundry, and pricier ones have en-suite bathrooms. Bike rentals are on offer for $5.

Spago Trattoria e Pizzeria

ITALIAN $$

(☑519-252-9099; 690 Erie St E; mains $10-28; ⊗lunch & dinner) Windsor has a reputation for its Italian, and this is the place to dip your tongue in some. If you're not in the mood for delicious pasta, the clean-shaven staff also deliver outstanding pizzas from the wood-fired oven.

Upstairs, the **Spago Ristorante Italiano** (mains $12-30; ⊗dinner) has a similar menu and a bar that stays open late.

Bubi's Awesome Eats

BURGERS $$

(149 Chatham St W; mains $9-16; ⊗lunch & dinner) Though Bubi's boasts big servings of garlic anything, it actually has a varied menu that appeals to someone who forgot their after-dinner breath mints: burgers, wraps, tacos and curries. It's nothing fancy, but well priced and friendly.

ℹ Information

Ontario Travel Information Centre (☑800-668-2746; www.ontariotravel.net; ⊗8:30am-8pm Jun-Aug, to 5pm Sep-May) Tunnel (☑519-973-1338; 110 Park St E) Bridge (☑519-973-1310; 1235 Huron Church Rd) Offices are near the Detroit–Windsor Tunnel entrance and the Ambassador Bridge.

Tourism Windsor Essex (☑519-255-6530, 800-265-3633; www.tourismwindsoressex. com; Ste 103, 333 Riverside Dr; ⊗8:30am-4:30pm Mon-Fri) Information on Windsor and the area; best accessed from Pitt St.

ℹ Getting There & Away

Detroit–Windsor is a major international border crossing, via either the famously expansive **Ambassador Bridge** (toll $4.75/US$4), or the **Detroit–Windsor Tunnel** (toll $4.50-4.75/US$4-4.50) connecting the two downtowns.

The **Windsor Bus Station** (☑519-254-7577; www.greyhound.ca; 300 Chatham St W; ⊗7am-9pm) runs buses to Toronto ($76, five hours, six daily) via London ($40, two hours). US-bound trips to Chicago ($80, seven to nine hours, two daily) transfer from Greyhound Canada to Greyhound in Detroit. Also here is **Transit Windsor** (☑519-944-4111; www.citywindsor.ca), running buses to Detroit ($3.75, 30 minutes, every 30 minutes) – bring your passport.

Windsor Train Station (☑888-842-7245; www.viarail.ca; cnr Walker & Wyandotte Sts;

⊘5:15am-11:30pm), 3km east of downtown, has trains to Toronto ($101, four hours, four daily) via London ($53, two hours).

Lake Huron Shoreline

Lake Huron has some of the cleanest waters of the Great Lakes, and it's wide enough that the sun actually sets on the waterline when viewed from its eastern shore. If you've been lingering around Toronto and Lake Ontario, Lake Huron's 'blueness' will be both surprising and refreshing. The coast road traces the under-populated shoreline, separated by pine forests and lakefront mansions.

About 100km northeast of Windsor is **Uncle Tom's Cabin Historic Site** (⊘519-683-2978; www.uncletomscabin.org; 29251 Uncle Tom's Rd, Dresden; adult/child/concession/family $6.25/4.50/5.25/20; ⊘10am-4pm Mon-Sat, from noon Sun Jul-Aug, closed Mon Jun, Sep & Oct; P). Uncle Tom was the fictional protagonist and namesake of the book written by Harriet Beecher Stowe in 1852, based on real-life hero Reverend Josiah Henson. The 5-hectare site displays articles relating to the story and the Underground Railroad (see p135), as well as a theater, gallery and interpretive center.

South of Grand Bend is **Pinery Provincial Park** (www.pinerypark.on.ca; 9526 Lakeshore Rd; unpowered/powered sites $34/39, yurt $85, day pass $10-18; P), with 10km of beaches and lots of trails winding through wooded sections and sand dunes (bike/kayak rental per day $40/35). Take your pick of the 1000 campsites, or rent a 'yurt' – a kind of rigid tent. No rowdyism!

Acting as a regional center, **Goderich** has bitten off more of the charming country-town pie than seems fair, with a distinctive octagonal town square forming the commercial hub. Grab the self-guided *4 Heritage Walking Tours* brochure from **Goderich Tourist Information Centre** (⊘519-524-6600, 800-280-7637; www.goderich. ca; 91 Hamilton St; ⊘9am-7pm) or the *Visitor's Guide* to help you get your bearings. Don't miss a walk along the beach boardwalks at dusk to see the swoon-worthy sunsets.

Walk the wooden floorboards at **Huron County Museum** (⊘519-524-2686; www.huroncounty.ca/museum; 110 North St, Goderich; adult/child/concession/family $5/3.50/4.50/18, combined Huron Historic Gaol ticket $7.50/4/5.50/25; ⊘10am-4:30pm Mon-

Sat, from 1pm Sun; P) for an informed look at local history, industry and transportation. Displays include everything from antique furniture and china to an old steam engine and a tank.

Follow a creepy, prison-gray corridor into the **Huron Historic Gaol** (⊘519-524-6971; www.huron county.ca/museum; 181 Victoria St, Goderich; adult/child/concession/family $5/3.50/4/18, combined Huron County Museum ticket $7.50/4/5.50/25; ⊘10am-4:30pm Mon-Sat, from 1pm Sun; P), an octagonal fortress that served as the courthouse and jail for almost 130 years (and was the site of Canada's last public hanging in 1869).

The nearby village of **Blyth** has the kind of main street Bruce Springsteen likes to sing about, and is home to the esteemed summer **Blyth Festival** (⊘519-523-9300, 877-862-5984; www.blythfestival.com; ⊘box office 9am-9pm performance days, to 5pm non-performance days). From June to August, primarily Canadian plays get an airing, from outdoor pioneer performances to indoor gut-busting comedies.

GEORGIAN BAY & LAKELANDS

A vast realm of blues and greens, Georgian Bay is a land of infinite dreaming. Summer breezes amble along curving lakes and sandy shores, while thick pines quiver at winter's frosty kiss. These ethereal landscapes inspired Canada's best-known painters, the Group of Seven, and today the bay is home to hundreds of artists who use their backyard as inspiration. Evidence of these creative enclaves is conspicuous in Owen Sound and Manitoulin Island. In Midland, the downtown has been transformed into an outdoor gallery of over 30 spectacular murals.

Summers along Georgian Bay are crowded with Canadians looking for a sandy spot to catch some sun. Wasaga, the longest freshwater beach in the world, lures thousands of visitors on sweltering summer days. Ontarians from other regions take part in the annual ritual of negotiating and dividing 'cottage time' between factions of families that have owned the same lakeside retreat for generations. Then, in fall, much of the region closes down when the trees shed their enticing autumn foliage. The watery realm sees a surprising surge in winter as the area offers some of the best skiing in Ontario. Wasaga turns into a cross-country skiing paradise, and nearby Blue Mountain has the best vertical drop in the province.

Relative to the rest of the province, this small expanse of shoreline crams in a wondrous amount of varying topographical features. Southampton, on Lake Huron, enjoys warm waters and thick sandy shores. Next door, the Bruce Peninsula's jagged limestone outcrops offer dramatic cliffs and craggy beaches. Further along, the land flattens out at industrial Owen Sound, and sharply rises once more to host Blue Mountain. The swampy waters of Midland and Penetanguishene lead to myriad islands off the coast of Parry Sound. Shimmering quartzite cliffs immerge at Killarney and continue on to Manitoulin, the largest freshwater island in the world.

This section is ordered in a similar fashion, moving counterclockwise around the bay from Southampton and arcing along the shore before reaching Manitoulin Island in the north. For a shortcut, try the Chi-Cheemaun Ferry (p142), which connects Manitoulin to the tip of Bruce Peninsula. The bay-adjacent lakelands between Midland and Parry Sound are also featured in this section. Orillia, a major stop on the Trent-Severn Waterway, offers several memorable dining options. Further north lies a vast forested domain of winding lakes called Muskoka (or 'The Muskokas'). This region, situated between the towns of Gravenhurst and Huntsville, has long been established as 'cottage country' for wealthy Torontonians.

Barrie

Barrie marks the definitive end of Toronto's vast suburban sprawl and the beginning of 'cottage country.' However, this small city set along Lake Simcoe feels more like an extension of Toronto than a pleasant lakeside enclave. It's worth stopping at the large **Ontario Travel Information Centre** (☎705-725-7280, 800-668-2746; 21 Maple View Dr; ☺8am-8pm Jun-Aug, 8:30am-5pm Sep-May) just south of Barrie along Hwy 400.

Northbound traffic on Friday afternoon can be a real killer, as is the southbound traffic on Sunday evenings (or Monday if it's a holiday weekend). Greyhound Canada and Ontario Northland provide transportation services down to Toronto and up to Sudbury, North Bay and beyond. Both companies offer express buses between Toronto and Barrie ($19, 1½ hours, one hourly).

Georgian Bay & Lakelands

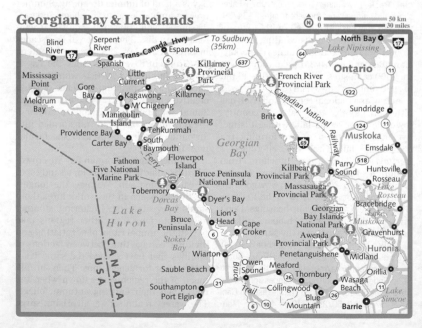

Southampton & Around

With the bulk of shopping options and bumping nightlife in nearby Port Elgin, quiet Southampton has happily sequestered itself from the beaten path of rowdy summer holidays. The quaint colony's sandy beach feels almost undiscovered at times, and a stroll down the main streets reveals mom-and-pop shops and the piecemeal architecture of Queen Anne–styled homes.

◉ Sights & Activities

Chantry Island   LANDMARK

Chantry Island, just 2km off the shoreline, is home to a lonely lighthouse and a sanctuary for migratory birds. The only way to reach the island is with **Chantry Island Tours** (☑519-797-5862, 866-797-5862; www.chantryisland.com; per person $28.25; ⊙Jun-mid-Sep). Informative outings are led by the Marine Heritage Society and provide fascinating insights into the region's nautical history as well as a chance to climb the blinking lighthouse. Book in advance as only nine people can be accommodated per tour.

Bruce County Museum   MUSEUM

(☑519-797-2080, 866-318-8889; www.bruce museum.ca; 33 Victoria St N, Southampton; adult/child/concession $8/4/6; ⊙10am-5pm Mon-Sat, from 1pm Sun) This museum has an extensive collection of artifacts relating to shipwrecks in the region. There are also rotating summer exhibits for kids.

Saugeen River   KAYAK TRIPS

The Saugeen River, which flows into Lake Huron at Southampton, is one of the best-established routes for canoeing and kayaking in southern Ontario. **Thorncrest Outfitters** (☑519-797-1608, 888-345-2925; www.thorncrestoutfitters.com; 193 High St, Southampton) runs an extensive program of short self-guided and organized trips aimed at inexperienced paddlers. It also has a variety of do-it-yourself adventures including a picturesque day trip (per canoe $50) or a three-day paddle interspersed with quiet evenings spent at historic inns (all inclusive $335). Thorncrest also operates from a base on the Bruce Peninsula at Tobermory.

Rail Trail   PARK

Cyclists will enjoy this 25km stretch of abandoned railway, which starts at the corner of Albert and Adelaide Sts and ends in the small town of Paisley.

GEORGIAN BAY & LAKELANDS

» Manitoulin Island – join a vibrant summertime powwow (p152)

» Killarney Provincial Park – kayak between shimmering quartzite cliffs (p151)

» Blue Mountain – luxurious skiing adventures (p143)

» Muskoka – deep lakes and towering pines (p147)

⌂ Sleeping

Chantry Breezes   B&B $$

(☑519-797-1818, 866-242-6879; www.chantry breezes.com; 107 High St, Southampton; r incl breakfast $110-150; ☑❀❁) This old Queen Anne manor, tucked gently behind gnarled evergreens, is a fine option for a weekend in Southampton. Seven rooms are spread out amongst endearingly cluttered antiques, and a private cottage rests at the end of a stone pathway in the backyard garden. Made-to-order breakfasts are sure to satisfy, especially if you take them on the cheerful sun porch.

Southampton Inn   INN $$

(☑519-797-5915, 888-214-3816; www.thesouth amptoninn.com; 118 High St, Southampton; r $100-130, ste $100-136; ☑❀❀❁) If the beachy blend of sand and wind isn't a good enough exfoliant, head downstairs for a full spa treatment. The upper level is dedicated to sprawling accommodations – each suite has a private sunny sitting room.

✕ Eating & Drinking

Armen's   FUSION $

(224 High St, Southampton; mains $4-8; ⊙9am-4pm daily, 5-8pm Wed-Sat) Forget the local greasy spoons and say hi to chatty Armen as he prepares a tasty sandwich from the ever-changing menu. A rotating dinner menu in June, July and August highlights global cuisine; one night it's Canadian, another it's Moroccan. It keeps your taste buds on their toes. Sneak upstairs and enjoy your fresh eats on the sunny rooftop deck.

Elk and Finch   CAFE $

(54 Albert St, Southampton; mains $7-9; ⊙8am-8pm Sun-Thu, to 9pm Fri & Sat, closed Mon & Tue in winter) This 'coffee pub' serves more than

caffeinated and alcoholic beverages: sandwiches, salads and thin-crust pizzas will fill you up. Sip your trendy brew in the wobbly house or park yourself at a table on the grassy lawn.

 Information

The small **Southampton Chamber of Commerce** (☑519-797- 2215, 888-757-2215; 201 High St, Southampton; ☺10am-4pm Mon-Sat, from noon Sun) can be found in the town hall – the large brick building with a clock tower. The **Saugeen Shores Chamber Office** (☑519-832-2332, 800-387-3456; 559 Goderich St; ☺9am-5pm Mon-Fri, 10am-4pm Sat, noon-4pm Sun), 8km down the shoreline in Port Elgin, offers a wider array of information about the region.

 Getting There & Away

Passengers arriving at Lester B Pearson International Airport in Toronto can take the **Grey Bruce Airbus** (☑519-389-4433; www.grey bruceairbus.com), which connects to Southampton and Port Elgin ($72, three hours, four daily). From the downtown bus station in Toronto, **Can-ar** (☑800-387-7097; www.can-arcoach.com) operates a bus service to Port Elgin ($35 to $40, 4¾ hours, one daily), arriving at Ralph's Hi-way Shoppette in the center of town.

Bruce Peninsula

The Bruce, as it's known, is an 80km-long limestone outcrop of craggy shorelines and green woodlands at the northern end of the Niagara Escarpment. The fingerlike protrusion separates the cool crystal waters of Georgian Bay from the warm churning water of Lake Huron.

The main base for travelers is Tobermory, a charmingly unpretentious village at the tip of the peninsula. Activity centers on the harbor area known as Little Tub, which bustles during ferry season and is all but deserted in the winter. The 100km stretch of highway from Wiarton to Tobermory is dismal at best. Consider taking a side road or two to get a taste of the rural, often rugged scenery that makes the Bruce so special.

◉ **Sights**

From Hwy 6 just south of the Bruce Peninsula National Park boundary, take Dyer's Bay Rd to the quaint village of **Dyer's Bay**. The wee village is reminiscent of Cape Cod, with pretty clapboard houses and shoreline scenery. (Do not get out of your car along Dyer's Bay Rd as the street is lined with poison ivy.) **Cabot Head Lighthouse** (admission by donation; ☺May–mid-Oct), about 7km from Dyer's Bay, contains a small museum and offers stunning views from the keeper's perch. There are other more accessible lighthouses across the peninsula, but the rugged journey is definitely all part of the fun.

The best-known, most visited feature of **Fathom Five National Marine Park** is Flowerpot Island, named after the 'flowerpots' of the area: top-heavy, precarious-looking rock formations created by wave erosion. Several small glass-bottom cruises depart from the ferry dock offering privileged views of the rusty barnacle-ridden ships below.

TRAVEL ON THE BRUCE TRAIL

For 800km, the Bruce Trail winds along the top of the Niagara Escarpment, from the Niagara Peninsula to the Bruce Peninsula. This wide, well-maintained path is excellent for hiking during summer months, while those armed with cross-country skis and snowshoes make good use of it in winter. Opened in 1967, it's the oldest hiking trail in Canada, and the longest in Ontario.

The trail winds through public and private land, as well as roadways. In Niagara you'll wander past wineries, while up north you'll have clear views of Georgian Bay's blue water from the escarpment's white cliffs. In-between, the scenery is just as unique and gorgeous.

Multiple entry points make day hikes along 'the Bruce' an appealing way to spend a sunny afternoon, and a multitude of campgrounds offer budget accommodation for those who are looking for longer trips. In towns where the trail passes through, B&Bs and inns are available to travelers.

Check www.thebruce.org for all sorts of information including trail conditions and accommodations.

☆ Activities

Visit www.explorethebruce.com for additional information about activities on the rugged peninsula.

Hiking

The **Bruce Peninsula National Park** (☎519-596-2233; day use per vehicle $11.70; ☺May–mid-Oct) flaunts some of the most incredible features along Georgian Bay: the Niagara Escarpment, 1000-year-old cedars and rare orchids. The center of most activity in the park is the **Cyprus Lake Campground & Visitor Centre** (☎519-596-2263; Cyprus Lake Rd; ☺8am-4:30pm), which offers easy hikes ranging from about 1km to 5km in length. Treks to the Grotto, Halfway Rock Point and Halfway Log Dump are the local favorites.

Kayaking

Thorncrest Outfitters (☎519-596-8908, 888-345-2925; www.thorncrestoutfitters.com; Hwy 6, Tobermory) runs a variety of kayaking trips along the Bruce, which are geared more toward intermediate paddlers. Swing by the shop in Southampton for additional paddling options. Independent paddlers can rent just about anything from this friendly outfitter.

Scuba Diving

Some of the best wreck-diving in North America exists in these coral blue waters. Meander through 22 separate wrecks, some dating back to the 1800s. Visibility in the area is exceptional; however, the water is about 1 degree short of being an ice bath. All divers must register in person at the **Parks Canada Visitor Centre** (☎519-596-2233; www.pc.gc.ca/fathomfive; Alexander St, Tobermory).

G&S Watersports (☎519-596-2200; www.gswatersports.net; 8 Bay St S, Tobermory) and **Diver's Den** (☎519-596-2363; www.diversden.ca; 3 Bay St S, Tobermory) offer gear rentals, certification courses (from $545 to $675 for open-water certification) and 'discovery' dives for beginners ($180 to $200).

🛏 Sleeping & Eating

In summer it's absolutely essential to book accommodations in advance. Visit www.bbgreybruce.com for a variety of lodging options in the area.

Camping is available in the **Bruce Peninsula National Park** (☎519-596-2233; ☺May-mid-Oct; backcountry/campground sites $8/22).

You can book backcountry sites at **Cyprus Lake Campground** (☎519-596-2263; Cyprus Lake Rd; sites $23-50); reservations for campgrounds must be made through **Parks Canada** (☎877-737-3783; www.pccamping.ca).

The following lodging and dining options are situated in the picturesque town of Tobermory, at the tip of the peninsula.

Cedar Vista Motel   MOTEL $$
(☎519-596-2395; 7370 Hwy 6; r $69-99) This super-tidy motel is on the right side of the highway just before arriving in Tobermory, and attracts a lot of repeat visitors. Free coffee in the lobby helps get you going.

Innisfree   B&B $$
(☎519-596-8190; www.bbcanada.com/innisfree; 46 Bay St; r $84-144; ☺May-Oct; P ☺) Whether it's the scent of fresh blueberry muffins, or the stunning harbor views from the sunroom and large deck, guests will adore this charming country home.

Princess Hotel   HOTEL $$
(☎519-596-8282, 877-901-8282; www.tobermory-hotel.com; 34 Bay St; r $75-130; P ☺) Trying hard, the Princess boasts harbor views from large balconies (not all rooms have both, so make sure you ask when booking).

Mermaid's Secret   CAFE $$
(7433 Hwy 6; mains $8-14) A colorful shack with a screened-in back porch that looks out to a mossy forest. The menu has it all: organic fair-trade coffee, gourmet sandwiches, fresh and smoked local fish, and homemade pastries. After you're full, check out the boutique next door.

Craigie's   FAST FOOD $$
(fish & chips $10.50; ☺7am-7pm May-Oct) This white sea shanty has been serving fish and chips in Tobermory since 1932, so by now they've pretty much perfected their recipe. The hearty breakfast menu is a solid second choice if you don't feel like battered fish in the wee hours of the morning.

ℹ Information

Bruce County Tourism (☎800-268-3838; ☺8:30am-4:30pm Mon-Fri) A telephone service providing information; there's no walk-in office.

Parks Canada Visitor Centre (☎519-596-2233; Alexander St; ☺10am-6pm Mon-Fri, from 8am Sat) Has a fantastic interpretive center, exhibits, a movie theater, several hiking trails and a soaring lookout tower.

Tobermory Chamber of Commerce (☎519-596-2452; www.tobermory.org; Hwy 6; ☺9am-5pm Sep-Jun, to 9pm Jul & Aug)

ℹ Getting There & Away

Bus services to the Bruce Peninsula run only on Friday, Saturday and Sunday from late June to early September. **First Student** (☑519-376-5712) runs services between Owen Sound and Tobermory ($28, 1½ hours, one daily Friday to Sunday June to early September) with several stops along the peninsula including Wiarton, Lion's Head (by request only) and Cyprus Lake.

Take the Chi-Cheemaun ferry from the Bruce Peninsula across the mouth of Georgian Bay to Manitoulin Island. Operated by **Ontario Ferries** (☑800-265-3163; www.ontarioferries.com; adult/child/car $16/8/34.70; ☺early May–mid-Oct), the boat connects Tobermory with South Baymouth (a two-hour journey). There are four daily crossings from late June to early September, and two daily crossings during the rest of the season, with an additional voyage on Friday evenings. Reservations are highly recommended.

Owen Sound

Owen Sound's sordid past as a shipping center is rife with slow boats and fast women. Known to sailors as 'Little Liverpool,' the skanky port became so overrun with uncouth characters that alcohol was strictly prohibited for over 60 years. By the time the embargo was lifted in 1972, Owen Sound had transformed into a thriving artists' colony. A visit to the **Owen Sound Visitor Information Centre** (☑519-371-9833, 888-675-5555; www.owensound.com; 1155 1st Ave W; ☺9am-5pm late May–mid-Oct, 9am-5pm Mon-Fri & from 11am Sat mid-Oct–late May) will point you in the direction of several natural attractions and a handful of interesting museums, including the on-site **Marine & Rail Museum** (☑519-371-3333; www.marinerail.com; 1155 1st Ave W; adult/child $5/2; ☺10am-4pm late May–mid-Oct, 10am-4pm Tue-Fri & 11am-3pm Sat & Sun mid-Oct–late May).

◉ Sights & Activities

Tom Thomson Art Gallery   MUSEUM
(www.tomthomson.org; 840 1st Ave W; adult/child $5/3; ☺10am-5pm Mon-Sat, from noon Sun Jun-Aug, 11am-5pm Tue-Fri, from noon Sat & Sun Sep-Jun) This gallery displays the work of Tom Thomson, a passionate outdoorsman and the granddaddy of modern Canadian landscape painting. His intimate and smoldering portrayal of nature is said to have inspired the formation of the Group of Seven painters. Thomson grew up in Leath, and many of his works were composed in near-

by thickets of fall leaves. Rotating exhibits also include selections from the collection of contemporary Canadian art.

Grey Roots   MUSEUM
(www.greyroots.com; 102599 Grey Rd 18, RR 4; adult/child/concession $8/4/6; ☺10am-5pm late May-Aug, closed Sun & Mon Sep-late May) Grey Roots, near Inglis Falls, highlights the rich pioneer history of the region through displays about early settlers and local heroes, and interactive presentations about the region's natural resources, climate and topography. Colorful rotating attractions truly embrace the non sequitur: past exhibits have explored Albertan dinosaurs and the history of the toilet.

Billy Bishop Heritage Museum   MUSEUM
(www.billybishop.org; 948 3rd Ave W; adult/child/student $5/2/4; ☺10am-4pm Mon-Sat & noon-5pm Sun Jul-Aug, noon-4pm Tue-Sun Sep-Jun, closed Jan & weekends Feb & Mar) Hometown hero William Avery ('Billy') Bishop, Canada's notorious flying ace in WWI, is honored at his childhood home, now the Billy Bishop Heritage Museum. A walk through the old Victorian manse reveals changing exhibits, such as ones highlighting local veterans or Canada's aviation history.

Waterfalls   PARKS
There are eight scenic waterfalls in the area, four of which are almost right in town. Rent a bike at **Jolley's Alternative Wheels** (☑519-371-1812; www.alternative wheels.com; 939 2nd Ave E; rental per day $39; ☺11:30am-6:30pm Tue-Fri, 11am-6pm Sat) to explore the nearby falls, or take a ride along Grey County Rd 1, which winds along the scenic shoreline of staggering pines between Owen Sound and Wiarton.

✸ Festivals & Events

Summerfolk Music Festival   MUSIC FESTIVAL
(www.summerfolk.org) This three-day jam session in mid-August is one of the top folk festivals on the continent. Performers – Dar Williams, Bruce Cockburn – flock to the lakeside stage from all over the world to rock out in front of a sea of eager attendees. Weekend passes start at $83.

🛏 Sleeping & Eating

If you're into B&B-ing, have a peek at www.bbgreybruce.com for a lengthy list of options in the region.

Butchart Estate B&B $$
(☎519-371-0208, 877-280-2403; www.butchart
estate.com; 919 5th Ave E; s/d $109/129; P✻)
When the Butchart family, of Butchart
Gardens fame (p683), first emigrated from
Scotland, they constructed this rambling
estate. The Queen Anne home, with a spiky
turret and brick gables, is a jumble of archi-
tectural styles, which is further exaggerat-
ed by the modern addition of a large indoor
pool and hot tub. Unfortunately, a housing
tract is going up around the lush grounds.

Diamond Motor Inn MOTEL $$
(☎519-371-2011; www.diamondmotorinn.com;
713 9th Ave E; r $60-89; P✻) A pleasant, no-
frills choice, this small motel contains
bright rooms with wooden paneling and
kitchenettes.

Rocky Racoon Café FUSION $$$
(☎519-376-2232; 941 2nd Ave E; mains $15-23;
⏱11am-11pm Mon-Sat; ✍) These organic ad-
vocates serve up wild boar and Tibetan
dumplings, with vegan and vegetarian op-
tions. You'll find plenty of South Asian fla-
vors, especially delicious curries.

Jazzmyn's Tapas & Taps FUSION $$
(267 9th St E; tapas $8-9, mains $11-16; ⏱11:30am-
2am Mon-Sat) In a deep purple room that
feels a bit like a palm-reader's foyer, draught
beer (including Creemore!) and live music,
be it Celtic tunes or angst-y folk beats, are
served in candlelit ambience. We see a good
time in your future.

🛍 Shopping

Pick up *The Art Map*, or check out www.
theartmap.com, for a list of over 50 local
artists' studios.

Owen Sound Artists' Co-op GALLERY
(www.osartistsco-op.com; 279 10th St E;
⏱9:30am-5:30pm Mon-Sat, noon-4pm Sun) The
co-op features an assortment of crafts from
regional artists. Spend countless hours
browsing the high-quality pottery, photography, basketwork, woodwork, weaving and
jewelry while listening to the experimental
melodies of new-age music.

Owen Sound Farmers' Market MARKET
(www.owensoundfarmersmarket.ca; 114 8th St E;
⏱7am-12:30pm Sat) This co-op of vendors is
one of the oldest in Ontario. Set up in an
old brick waterworks building, the weekly
displays include ripe produce, maple syrup,
soaps and baked goods among the colorful
bounty.

ℹ Getting There & Away

Greyhound Canada runs bus services between
Owen Sound and Toronto ($37, 4¼ hours, two
daily), and routes to Barrie ($35, 2½ hours, two
daily) as well. Bus services from Owen Sound up
the Bruce Peninsula ($28, 1½ hours, one daily)
are available with **First Student** (☎519-376-
5712) on Friday, Saturday and Sunday from late
June to early September.

Collingwood & Blue Mountain

Collingwood and Blue Mountain are frater-
nal twins. Quiet Collingwood's small-town
vibe feels similar to the other communities
along the bay, while Blue Mountain is a
horse of a different color. The village of Blue
Mountain is the newest avatar of Intrawest,
the same folks who brought you Whistler
in British Columbia and Mont-Tremblant in
Québec. The company's recipe for stellar ski
resorts is simple: clone the Alpine villages
of Zermatt or Gstaad and then add every
luxurious amenity imaginable. Although
construction is still under way, much of the
enclave is already complete.

◎ Sights & Activities

Blue Mountain (www.bluemountain.ca) offers
the best skiing and snowboarding in Ontario, with freestyle terrain, multiple half-
pipes, jump-on jump-off rails, 16 lifts and
over 35 runs rated from beginner to double
black diamond. A day-long lift ticket (valid
from 9am to 4:30pm) costs $57 for adults
and $39 for youths and seniors. Afternoon
(12:30pm to 4:30pm) and night (4:30pm to
10pm) tickets are available for $30. Keep
an eye out for special deals throughout the
season.

The Blue Mountain Snow School offers a
variety of lessons geared toward all levels of
experience. The beginner course for adults
is $69, which includes a day-long lift pass,
guided instruction and equipment rental
(ski or snowboard).

In summer, the resort offers loads of
activity packages in the surrounding area,
including mountain biking, sailing, climbing, hiking and windsurfing. For details
and booking information contact **Activity
Central** (☎705-443-5522; www.blueactivities.
com; ⏱9am-7pm, to 9pm Jul-Aug & mid-Dec–
mid-Mar), which has a storefront on Main
St in the village, right near the Events
Plaza.

Escape the crowds and call **Free Spirit Tours** (☎705-444-3622, 519-599-2268; www. freespirit-tours.com) for an offbeat adventure. Enjoy a sensational day of rock climbing along the Niagara Escarpment ($110), or take a stab at snowshoeing ($45) and caving ($65) in the winter months. Hiking, cycling and kayaking trips are also available.

Sleeping & Eating

Accommodations in Collingwood and Blue Mountain are rather pricey because the area is a year-long tourist hub. Blue Mountain has several choices, all running in the mid to upper price range. Collingwood has several B&Bs, or you can take your pick from the run-of-the-mill motels along Hwy 26. A stroll around the synthetically charming Blue Mountain village will reveal numerous family-friendly dining options. While they're all safe bets for a satisfying meal, none are particularly spectacular. Hurontario St in Collingwood has a selection of restaurants as well.

Beild House Country Inn   B&B $$$
(☎705-444-1522, 888-322-2394; www.beild house.com; 64 3rd St; r $280-340; P❄☎🐾) Beild House is a grand old place, built at the turn of the 20th century and now rumored to house a ghost. The experience is a bit frilly, with canopy beds and an extravagantly set table, but the rate includes breakfast, afternoon tea and a five-course dinner. There's a spa to help you unwind, and romance packages available to help you feel the love. Rates are priced for two guests.

Blue Mountain Inn   HOTEL $$$
(☎705-445-0231, 877-445-0231; www.blue mountain.ca; r $130-200; P❄@🐾) When this place was built, people were still skiing on planks of wood, but thankfully the inn has seen a facelift in recent years. Cosmetic renovations have rendered the basic rooms comfy, with white down comforters and new mattresses.

Grandma Lambe's   MARKET $
(Hwy 26; ⏰8am-6pm Sat-Thu, to 7pm Fri) You won't regret the 35km trek to Grandma Lambe's (west on Hwy 26 between Thornbury and Meaford). The store is a delicious jumble of maple syrup vintages, butter tarts, bushels of vegetables and tables piled high with pies, buns and jellies.

Café Chartreuse   FUSION $$
(☎705-444-0099; 70 Hurontario St; mains $11-18; ⏰breakfast and lunch Wed-Mon) Pancakes with warm maple butter, sandwiches on fresh-baked bread: these French-trained chefs have got it right. Stay and sample the ever-changing menu, or take a spinach spanako-pita or savory tart to go.

ℹ Information

Blue Mountain (☎705-445-0231; www. bluemountain.ca) Centralized number and website provide information on all aspects of the resort. Stop by one of the many hotels in the compound for a handy map and additional information.

Georgian Triangle Lodging Association (☎705-445-0748; ⏰9am-5pm) Centralized number for accommodations bookings.

Georgian Triangle Tourism Association (☎705-445-7722; www.visitsoutherngeor gianbay.ca; 30 Mountain Rd, Collingwood; ⏰9am-5pm)

ℹ Getting There & Around

Greyhound Canada offers services to Owen Sound ($22, one hour, two daily) and Barrie ($22, 1½ hours, two daily), departing from the bus station in Collingwood or from the Blue Mountain Inn. **Ace Cabs** (☎705-445-3300, 705-445-0300) can drive you between Collingwood and Blue Mountain ($17, 15 minutes).

Wasaga Beach

Wasaga has the distinct honor of being the longest freshwater beach in the world. It's also the closest full-fledged beach resort to Toronto, attracting thousands of visitors every summer. Most of the 14km-long expanse of soft sands and crashing waves belongs to **Wasaga Beach Provincial Park** (☎705-429-2516; day use per vehicle $15; ⏰closed mid-Oct–Apr); no camping. The beach gets so much hype during the summer, many people forget that Wasaga's pristine sand dunes transform into awesome cross-country skiing in the winter.

The **Chamber of Commerce** (☎705-429-2247, 866-292-7242; www.wasagainfo.com; 550 River Rd; ⏰9am-5pm Mon-Fri, 10am-4pm Sat & Sun) is a great resource for finding lodging. A drive down Main St or Mosley St will unveil several accommodations options; there are also many choices right on the beach.

Buses from Wasaga Beach to Barrie ($11, one hour), with continued service to Toronto ($28, 2½ hours), depart twice daily from **Daisy Mart** (☎705-429-4575; 620 River Rd W).

Midland

The small commercial center of Midland is the most interesting spot in the Huronia region. The Huron-Ouendat first settled in this area, and developed a confederacy to encourage cooperation amongst the neighboring Aboriginal peoples. Later, this alliance attracted French explorers, especially Jesuit missionaries. Much of Midland's fascinating history focuses on the bloody altercations between the Huron and the Christian stalwarts.

⊙ Sights & Activities

Martyrs' Shrine   MONUMENT
(www.martyrs-shrine.com; adult/child $4/free; ⊗8:30am-9pm late May–mid-Oct) Midland's biggest attraction is the Martyrs' Shrine, a monument to six Jesuit missionaries who met their gruesome demise at the hands of the Huron. The compound includes a large green area strewn with crosses, and an imposing cathedral-like structure. Tens of thousands of pilgrims journey to the shrine every year to visit the bones of the martyred St Jean de Brébeuf. The pope showed up in 1984.

Ste-Marie among the Hurons

HISTORICAL SITE
(☎705-526-7838; www.saintemarieamongthe hurons.on.ca; Hwy 12; adult/child $11.25/8.50; ⊗10am-5pm May-Sep) Across the street from the Martyr's Shrine lies Ste-Marie among the Hurons, a historic reconstruction of the 17th-century Jesuit mission. Costumed staff members dote on visitors, offering stories about hardship and torture with a cheerful smile.

Wye Marsh Wildlife Centre   NATURE RESERVE
(16160 Hwy 12; adult/child/concession $11/8/8.50; ⊗9am-5pm) The Wye Marsh Wildlife Centre, right beside the Ste-Marie site, provides boardwalks, trails and an observation deck over the marsh. The park features an array of unusual birdlife including the much-trumpeted trumpeter swans, back from the brink of extinction. Guided walks are included in the price, kids can feed the wildlife, and canoe tours through the marsh are an extra $5.

30,000 Island Tours   BOAT TOURS
(☎705-549-3388, 888-833-2628; www.midland tours.com; adult/child/concession/family $27/14/25/66; ⊗late May–mid-Oct) *Miss Midland* isn't a regional beauty pageant; it's actually the name of a bay cruiser operated by 30,000 Island Tours. Two-and-a-half-hour cruises depart daily at 2pm, with additional morning and dinner cruises in July and August.

Murals   ART
Midland is known for its murals, which have transformed the downtown core into an outdoor art gallery. The various frescoes animate the region's history through breathtaking designs. They were commissioned throughout the 1990s, and were mostly painted by the gifted Fred Lenz. A handy detailed map is available at the tourist office.

Huronia Museum & Huron-Ouendat Village   MUSEUM
(☎705-526-2844; www.huroniamuseum.com; 549 Little Lake Park Rd; adult/child/concession $8.60/5.40/7.55; ⊗9am-5pm) The Huronia Museum & Huron-Ouendat Village is a replica of a 500-year-old Huron-Ouendat settlement (from before the French Jesuits arrived on their soul-saving mission). With an active art program, the museum house a collection of nearly one million pieces, and an expansion is planned.

⊨ Sleeping & Eating

Galerie Gale   B&B $$
(☎705-526-8102; www.galeriegale.com; 431 King St; r $85-120; P) This inviting Tudor-style B&B is filled with the vibrant abstract artwork of its owners. Swap travel tales with the inspiring hosts over a delicious breakfast before a morning walk around the marina, just a couple of blocks away.

Little Lake Inn   INN $$
(☎705-526-2750, 888-297-6130; www.littlelake inn.com; 669 Yonge St; r $120-160; 🅿✱🔊📶) Each room at this modern B&B offers a TV, DVD player and whirlpool. The caring hosts do their best to ensure a comfortable and relaxing stay. True to its name, the inn has a quiet little lake out back.

TOP CHOICE Explorer's Cafe   FUSION $$
(☎705-527-9199; 345 King St; mains $14-21; ⊗noon-10pm Jun-Sep, closed Sun & Mon Oct-May) This fantastic restaurant features comfort food from all over the globe (including a meatloaf called 'the mattress'). The walls are covered with an incredible range of souvenirs including African tribal masks and photos from Arctic expeditions. Meals range from savory Southeast Asian noodles to spicy Caribbean cuisine, and the menu boasts the largest wine list north of Via Allegro (ie Toronto). Dubbed

'the shack in the back,' the place is set back from King St; if you're a good explorer, you'll find it.

Riv Bistro   GREEK $$

(www.rivbistro.huronia.com; 249 King St; mains $10-20; ☺lunch Tue-Fri, dinner daily) The dark-blue awning and crisp white-clothed tables are reminiscent of a faraway Greek isle (as is the rowdy mural on the wall). The Mediterranean dishes are great, too.

Cellarman's Ale House   PUB $$

(337 King St; mains $8-17; ☺noon-midnight Mon-Thu, 11:30am-2am Fri-Sat) This soft, cozy, British-style pub even has an intimate location, tucked away off King St. Hearty English fare, like bloody steaks and kidney pies, keep the locals strong during drafty winters. Live folk music.

❶ Information

The friendly and knowledgeable staff at the **Southern Georgian Bay Chamber of Commerce** (☎705-526-7884, 800-263-7745; 208 King St; ☺9am-5pm, to 8pm Jul-Aug) will point you in the right direction.

❶ Getting There & Away

Greyhound Canada buses connect Barrie with Midland ($15, one hour, two daily). **Central Taxi** (☎705-526-2626) can give you a lift up the road to Penetanguishene.

Penetanguishene

Little 'Penetang' (*pen*-uh-tang-wa-sheen), as it's often known, prefers to be called by its full moniker. The small town with the big name makes a great base for exploring the 30,000 islands that are sprinkled around Georgian Bay. The **tourist office** (☎705-549-2232; 2 Main St; ☺9am-5pm early May–mid-May, to 6pm mid-May–Jun, to 8pm Jul-Aug, 9:30am-6pm Sep) is situated right on the docks.

DiscoveryHarbour(www.discoveryharbour. on.ca; 93 Jury Dr; adult/child/student $6/4.25/ 5.25; ☺10am-5pm Jul-Aug, 10am-5pm Mon-Fri mid-May–Jun) is a reconstruction of the strategic fort erected by the British after the War of 1812. The recommended guided tours lead visitors through two replica vessels and recount the history of the garrison. The on-site **King's Wharf Theatre** (☎888-449-4463; www.kingswharftheatre.com) offers an exciting roster of performances year-round.

The area's pristine wildlife is protected in two picturesque parks. **Awenda Provincial Park** (Awenda Park Rd; day use per vehicle $11-20, camping $15-46; ☺mid-May–mid-Oct) is home to four sandy cobble beaches, 30km of easy walking trails and over 200 species of birds. According to Huron legend, **Giant's Tomb Island**, lurking just off the coast, is the resting place of the spirit Kitchikewana. Sixty islands across the sound belong to the **Georgian Bay Islands National Park** (www. pc.gc.ca/pn-np/on/georg/index.aspx; adult/child $5.80/2.90; ☺mid-May–mid-Oct).Theseglacier-scraped islands are only accessible by boat, and Beausoleil, the park's largest isle, offers backcountry camping in a rugged hardwood forest.

Catch a cruise on the **MS Georgian Queen** (☎705-549-7795, 800-363-7447; www. georgianbaycruises.com; 2½hr cruise adult/ child $25/10, 3½hr cruise $27/11; ☺May–mid-Oct) as it winds through a stunning archipelago of craggy islands. Trips depart daily during July and August; call ahead for an up-to-date schedule in the slower months.

The **Georgian Terrace** (☎705-549-2440, 888-549-2440; www.georgianterrace.ca; 14 Walter St; r incl breakfast $150-175; ℗☺❄☎) is Penetanguishene's newest lodging option. Dramatic pillars front this heritage home, which is elegant without being frilly.

Additional lodging options can be found up the road in Midland, or check out www. southerngeorgianbaybb.com.

Greyhound Canada connects Penetanguishene with Barrie ($16, 1¼ hours, two daily), or **Central Taxi** (☎705-526-2626) can give you a lift over to Midland.

Orillia

Orillia (oh-*really*-ya) proudly sits at the northern end of Lake Simcoe, which pours into Lake Couchiching. This major stop along the Trent-Severn Waterway is an amiable town that sees plenty of tourist traffic during the summer months. Triangular sails and grumbling motorboats clutter the harbor, while drivers turn off Hwy 11 for a stroll down the time-warped Mississauga St, Orillia's main drag. The **tourist office** (☎705-326-4424; 150 Front St S; ☺9am-7pm mid-May–mid-Sep, 8:30am-5pm mid-Sep–mid-May) will point you in the right direction, and during summer a manned info booth can be found on the docks.

◎ Sights & Activities

Leacock Museum   MUSEUM
(www.leacockmuseum.com; 50 Museum Dr; adult/child $5/2; ⊙9am-5pm Mon-Sat) Orillia was the home of humorist Stephen Leacock, whose sequence of stories entitled *Sunshine Sketches of a Little Town* was a spoof about country life. In 1928 he built a lavish waterfront house that has since become the Leacock Museum. In July the museum hosts the Leacock Summer Festival, a well-regarded literary festival; tickets to readings cost $8 to $13.

Island Princess   BOAT TOURS
(☎705-325-2628; www.orilliacruises.com; cruises adult $17.50-22, child $9-11; ⊙mid-Jun–mid-Oct) Like most towns in the Georgian Bay region, Orillia offers a variety of sightseeing cruises. The *Island Princess* departs daily at 2:15pm, with up to four cruises throughout the day in July and August. Lunch and dinner cruises ($40 and $50, respectively) require advance booking. If you have the time, hop up to Penetanguishene or Parry Sound for slightly more spectacular cruising options.

Casino Rama   CASINO
(Rama Rd; admission free; ⊙24hr) The Aboriginal-owned Casino Rama is also a stage for the touring circuit: think Drew Carey or Captain & Tennille. A courtesy shuttle links major accommodations chains with the kitschy casino.

Orillia Opera House   THEATER
(☎705-326-8011, 888-674-5542; www.operahouse.ca; 20 Mississauga St W) The turreted Orillia Opera House hosts a variety of productions including the likes of *Cats* and *Oklahoma!*

🛏 Sleeping & Eating

Cranberry House   B&B **$$**
(☎705-326-6871, 866-876-5885; www.orillia.org/cranberryhouse; 25 Dalton Cres S; r from $90) This B&B sits on a quiet street that feels a lot like the set for the TV show *The Wonder Years*, or maybe even a Norman Rockwell painting. Every house seems tidy and welcoming, and Cranberry House is no exception. Enjoy a comfortable stay amid polished collectibles, and a cranberry-themed breakfast (juice, pancakes etc).

Champlain Hotel Waterfront   HOTEL **$$**
(☎705-325-0770, 800-228-5151; www.choicehotels.ca/cn542; 2 Front St N; r incl breakfast

$115-175; P❄🛜) It may be a part of the Quality Inn chain, but the Champlain is Orillia's most attractive option, with white pillars, crimson brick and stately Georgian architecture.

Stone Gate Inn   HOTEL **$$**
(☎705-329-2535, 877-674-5542; www.stonegateinn.com; 437 Laclie St; r incl continental breakfast $124-154; P❄🛜🏊) It's the extra perks that set this modern inn apart from the rest: a swimming pool, full business center, hors d'oeuvres over the weekend and bathrobes in the rooms.

Paul Weber   FAST FOOD **$**
(Hwy 11; hamburger $3.29; ⊙11am-10pm) Just 12km north of Orillia on Hwy 11, this legendary grill-hut lures passers-by with cheap eats and a shmancy sky bridge to nab commuters on the far side of the highway. Endless lines of lip-lickers form for food, as though the burgers and fries have curative powers, which, of course, is the opposite of the truth. Now if only angioplasties were as cheap as the food...

Mariposa Market   MARKET **$**
(www.mariposamarket.ca; 109 Mississauga St E; quiche $3.49; ⊙7am-8pm Mon-Thu, to 9pm Fri, to 6pm Sat, 8am-5:30pm Sun Jun-Aug, 7am-6pm Mon-Sat, 8am-5:30pm Sun Sep-May) It's a bit like dining inside a Christmas stocking, but this half-bakery, half-knickknack shack is a feast for the eyes as well as the mouth. Try the assortment of savory pastries for a light lunch, grab a dessert, and shop around for candles and figurines.

❶ Getting There & Away

Greyhound Canada provides services between Orillia and Toronto ($31.20, 2½ hours, four daily). Ontario Northland also offers passenger services ($27.75, two hours, four daily).

Gravenhurst

While nearby Bracebridge is the favored destination amongst visitors, this sleepy logging town is starting to come into its own. The biggest push to put Gravenhurst on the map is the massive waterfront development called **Muskoka Wharf** (www.muskokawharf.ca), which thus far includes shops, restaurants, condos, a farmer's bazaar and a museum. For updates, check out www.gravenhurst.ca or visit the **Gravenhurst Chamber of Commerce** (☎705-687-4432; www.gravenhurstchamber.

com; 685 Muskoka Rd N; ⊙8:30am-5pm Mon-Fri, 9am-noon Sat), which hides in a gray building on the edge of town.

The museum at Muskoka Wharf, **Muskoka Boat & Heritage Centre** (☑705-687-2115; www.segwun.com; 275 Steamboat Bay Rd; adult/child/concession $7/2/5; ⊙10am-4pm Tue-Sat Jun–mid-Oct), vividly tells the region's rich history of steamships and hoteliers, and a museum-cum-boathouse displays over 20 wooden vessels.

Also housed at the new docklands is the **Muskoka Steamship Association** (☑705-687-6667, 866-687-6667; www.segwun.com; 185 Cherokee Lane; ⊙late May–mid-Oct). The fleet consists of two ships: the *Segwun*, the oldest operating steamship in North America, and the *Wenonah II*, a new cruiser with an old-school design. In a past life, the *Segwun* was a freight vessel, delivering mail to secluded enclaves in the Muskoka region. Both offer various cruising opportunities including the 'millionaires' row' tour, which follows a shoreline of grand summer homes (cruises from $18, from $49 with meals). There are also pirate cruises for kids – aarrrgh!

The **Bethune Memorial House** (☑705-687-4261; www.pc.gc.ca/bethune; 297 John St N; adult/child/concession/family $3.90/1.90/3.40/9.80; ⊙10am-4pm Tue-Sat Jun-Oct) honors Canadian doctor Norman Bethune, a communist sympathizer who spent much of his life in China as a surgeon and educator. Bethune set up the world's first mobile blood-transfusion clinic while in Spain during the Spanish Revolution. A life-sized statue of the doctor sits in front of the **Gravenhurst Opera House** (☑705-687-5550; 295 Muskoka Rd S), which presents a summer season of professional theater.

In summer, thousands flock to **Music on the Barge** (www.gravenhurst.ca; Gull Lake Park; admission by donation) to hear big-band numbers, jazz or country. Concerts start at 7:30pm each Sunday from late June to late August.

Ontario Northland runs buses between Toronto and Gravenhurst ($36.45, 2½ hours, four to five daily) on the North Bay route, which pull in to the **Gravenhurst Train Station** (☑705-687-2301; 150 2nd Ave). Ontario Northland also operates trains on the same route ($38.70, two hours, six weekly).

Bracebridge

Woodsy Bracebridge sits exactly on the 45th parallel – halfway between the North Pole and the equator. The enchanting town reveals its charms throughout the year, with towering needleleaf evergreens, gushing waterfalls, and milky snowbeds in the winter. Day trips to Algonquin Park (75km away) are definitely doable. The **Bracebridge Visitor Centre** (☑705-645-5231, 866-645-8121; 1 Manitoba St; ⊙9am-5pm Mon-Fri, from 10am Sat, also noon-4pm Sun Jun-Aug) is open year-round.

◎ Sights & Activities

Waterfalls   NATURAL ATTRACTION
There are 22 waterfalls around Bracebridge (some private). The most apparent cascade is **Bracebridge Falls**, which cuts right through town near the visitor centre. **Muskoka (South) Falls**, about 6km south of town off Hwy 11, is the highest in Muskoka at 33m, and **Wilson's Falls** and **High Falls**, both just north of town, are fan-favorites.

Mural   ART
Just north of Bracebridge, along Rte 118 in Port Carling, is a fantastic mural of an old ship. A closer glance reveals that the mural is actually a mosaic of vintage photographs – truly remarkable. Muskoka's majestic beauty serves as an inspiring backdrop for many other artists in the region. For more information, contact the **Arts Council of Muskoka** (www.artscouncilofmuskoka.com). In September, the **Muskoka Autumn Studio Tour** (www.muskokaautumnstudiotour.com) allows tourists to visit local studios.

Lady Muskoka   BOAT TOURS
(☑705-646-2628, 800-263-5239; www.ladymuskoka.com; cruises adult/child $27.50/13; ⊙mid-May–mid-Oct) Billing itself as 'Muskoka's Largest Capacity Cruise Ship' isn't that thrilling, but a cruise of Lake Muskoka along 'millionaires row' is a sumptuous tour. Cruises depart at noon daily in July and August (less often in other months), and take just under three hours. Brunch and lunch cruises are available on Saturdays, Sundays and Wednesdays (adult/child $40/20).

Muskoka Cottage Brewery   BREWERY
(www.muskokabrewery.com; 13 Taylor Rd; ⊙11am-5pm Mon-Sat) Muskoka Cottage Brewery bottles some delicious flavors including a cream ale and a couple of lagers. On summer weekends, visitors can take a free taste-testing tour.

Lake Muskoka

KAYAKING

Kayaks and canoes are available for hire from **Algonquin Outfitters** (☎705-645-9262; www.algonquinoutfitters.com; 271 Ecclestone St; ⊙10am-6pm Mon-Fri, to 5pm Sat, 11am-4pm Sun), as well as outdoor gear and clothing.

🛏 Sleeping

Riverview B&B

B&B $

(☎705-645-4022, 888-998-9961; 420 Beaumont Dr; s $35-40, d $70-80; P⊙⊕@) Homemade breakfast goodies and a genuine, warm host make a stay at this comfy B&B feel like a visit to grandma's farmhouse. The beautiful riverside home, with scarlet shutters and a towering brick chimney, is an amazing deal for solo travelers.

Inn at the Falls

HOTEL $$

(☎705-645-2245, 877-645-9212; www.innat thefalls.net; 1 Dominion St; s $110-190, d $120-200; P🌸🤝) This local landmark is a destination in itself. The original building dates back to the 1870s, and now the 'estate' includes the six neighboring cottages. A turn-of-the-20th-century vibe is maintained with iron lanterns, antique candelabras, old portraits and picket fences. The more luxurious suites have two floors and feature gargantuan beds that feel more like boats. Two dining rooms cater to vegetarians and their meat-eating friends.

Wellington Motel

MOTEL $$

(☎705-645-2238; www.wellingtonmotel.com; 265 Wellington St; r $80-120, ste $140; P🌸) This tidy redbrick motel could lose the forest-green carpets, but has extra amenities like micro-fridges, coffee-makers and huge bathrooms. Suites come with full kitchens.

✕ Eating & Drinking

Riverwalk

MEDITERRANEAN $$$

(☎705-646-0711; www.riverwalkrestaurant.ca; 1 Manitoba St; lunch mains $7-17, dinner $25-30; ⊙11:30am-2:30pm & 5:30-8pm Tue-Sat) Great food and great views – Riverwalk has it all. If you can tear your eyes away from the view, you can watch your food being prepared from the open dining room. Tasting menus ($75) feature exotic blends like seared sea scallop with sweet potato, pea sprouts and wasabi, and are surprisingly delicious. Reservations are highly recommended.

Marty's World Famous Café

CAFE $

(5 Manitoba St; www.martysworldfamous.com; mains $4-9; ⊙10am-5pm May-Oct, 8am-10pm Jul & Aug) Well, it might not be *world* famous, but Marty's is locally loved for butter tarts (try the butter tart ice cream – divine!), as well as giant apple pies, home-made pizzas, quiche and bread. Owner Marty is a character himself, and authored a cookbook that dishes all his recipe secrets. Show up early – the butter tarts sell out quickly.

Old Station

PUB $$

(88 Manitoba St; mains $10-15; ⊙11am-10pm) On summer evenings this is the most happening place in town. The patio overlooks the main drag – perfect for post-kayak recovery sessions. Dig into a prime rib sandwich and wash it back with a pint of Muskoka ale from the brewery just over the road.

ℹ Getting There & Away

Ontario Northland buses connect Bracebridge with Toronto ($39.30, three hours, up to six daily) on the North Bay route.

Huntsville

Muskoka's largest town, set amongst twisting lakes and furry pines, is the gateway to Algonquin Provincial Park (p175) in eastern Ontario. The **Chamber of Commerce** (☎705-789-4771; www.huntsville.ca; 8 West St N; ⊙9am-5pm Mon-Fri, 10am-3pm Sat) provides tons of information and has a performance schedule for the year-long **Festival of the Arts** (www.huntsvillefestival.on.ca).

For a historic perspective of the region, visit **Muskoka Heritage Place** (www.mus kokaheritageplace.org; 88 Brunel Rd; adult/child/concession $15/10/13.50; ⊙mid-May–mid-Oct), which includes an authentic pioneer village, several informative museums and a working steam train from 1902 (departs several times per day; rides included in admission).

Consider sleeping in Huntsville if you're planning an Algonquin adventure. **Au Petit Dormeur** (☎705-789-2552; www.aupetit dormeur.com; 22 Main St W; d $80-100), set in a beautiful colonial home, is a worthy option, with a complimentary gourmet breakfast served on the balcony overlooking the nearby lakes. Several quality motels are peppered throughout town, including the lakeside **Sunset Inn Motel** (☎705-789-4414, 866-874-5360; www.sunsetinnmotel.com; 69 Main St W; r $100), which includes breakfast in a sunny common room.

After a long hike in Algonquin Park, swing by **Pub on the Docks** (90 Main St; ☺11:30am-1am) for a burger and beer on the water-view patio. It's located behind Pizza Pizza.

Ontario Northland's service between Huntsville and Toronto includes buses ($44.84, 3½ hours, up to six daily) and trains ($48.15, three hours, up to seven weekly), with continuing services to North Bay and Cochrane. **Hammond Transportation** (☏705-645-5431; www.hammontranspor tation.com) offers services in July and August from Huntsville to Algonquin Park ($36, Monday, Wednesday and Friday). Buses to Algonquin depart from **Huntsville Travel** (☏705-789-6432; 77 Centre St N) at 1:15pm, and stop in the park at Oxtongue Lake (near the West Gate), the Portage Store (14km inside the West Gate) and the Lake of Two Rivers (32km inside the West Gate), leaving the Lake of Two Rivers at 2:30pm to return to Huntsville.

Parry Sound

Quiet Parry Sound is gently tucked behind myriad islands on Georgian Bay. The atmosphere is quite laid-back and serene, despite the giant set of railroad tracks soaring through the sky near the docks.

◉ Sights & Activities

TOP CHOICE **Charles W Stockey Centre** MUSEUM (☏877-746-4466; www.stockeycentre. com; 2 Bay St) The Charles W Stockey Centre incorporates the **Bobby Orr Hall of Fame** (adult/child/family $8/6/20; ☺9am-5pm Jul-Aug, 10am-6pm Tue-Sat, noon-4pm Sun Sep-Jun). For the uninitiated, local legend Bobby Orr is one of hockey's greatest heroes as he forever changed the role of defensemen with his awesome offensive prowess. At his huge modern shrine, fans can play air hockey, pretend to be a sports announcer or strap on goalie gear and confront an automated puck-firing machine.

A beautiful theater has live performances, including free summer concerts every Tuesday evening.

White Squall KAYAK TRIPS (☏705-342-5324; www.whitesquall.com; 53 Carling Bay Rd, Nobel; ☺9am-5:30pm Apr–mid-Oct, to 8pm Fri Jul-Aug) Explore the area's waterways on an exciting expedition with White Squall, based about 15km northwest of Parry Sound near Nobel (en route to Kill-

bear Provincial Park). An incredible staff of friendly and knowledgeable guides offer a range of paddling programs on Georgian Bay, from a half-day intro kayaking trip ($60) to multiday nature-fests ($695 to $995). Stop by the company's **retail store** (19 James St; ☺9:30am-5:30pm Mon-Sat, to 8pm Fri and 11am-4pm Sun Jul-Aug) in downtown Parry Sound for more information.

Lake Cruises BOAT TOURS For the less adventurous, there are cruises through the nearby 30,000 islands on the 550-passenger **Island Queen** (☏705-746-2311, 800-506-2628; www.island-queen.com; 9 Bay St; 2hr cruise adult/child $25/12.50, 3hr cruise $33/16.50; ☺Jun–mid-Oct). Two-hour trips push off at 10am daily and three-hour trips at 2pm.

The **MV Chippewa III** (☏705-746-6064, 888-283-5870; www.spiritofthesound.ca; Seguin River Parkette, Bay St; ☺Jun-Oct), a tiny green tugboat, operates a less-regular schedule of lunch restaurant cruises (adult/child $36/18 plus lunch) and dinner cruises (adult $60, child per year of age $4, dinner inclusive).

✦✦ Festivals & Events

Festival of the Sound MUSIC FESTIVAL (www.festivalofthesound.on.ca) Parry Sound hosts a nationally renowned annual festival of classical music at the Stockey Centre from mid-July to mid-August. Individual ticket prices range from $15 to $150.

🛏 Sleeping & Eating

Visit www.parrysoundbb.com for a lengthy list of quality B&Bs around town.

TOP CHOICE **Bayside Inn** B&B $$ (☏705-746-7720, 866-833-8864; www. psbaysideinn.com; 10 Gibson St; r $93-143; P☺✳@) Built in the 1880s as a luxurious private residence, this refurbished estate is full of pleasant surprises: a twisting staircase behind the fireplace and 12 beautiful bedrooms with memory-foam mattresses. All have en-suite bathrooms and are decorated in soothing colors, with fresh-cut flower bouquets to greet you. Gourmet breakfasts include the likes of gouda and maple ham omelets as well as vegetarian options.

Windhorse Bed and Breakfast B&B $ (☏705-746-8635; telfod.windhorse@gmail.com; 106 Gibson St; s/d $65/85; P☺☏) This warm and colorful artist's abode is within walking distance of downtown. Electric stoves in the rooms and perfectly soft pillows make your night's rest a good one. Arty touches like a mermaid painted on the claw-foot bathtub, and the leafy garden out back are extra perks. Breakfast is healthy and delish.

Mad Hatter Café CAFE $
(35 Seguin St; mains $6-7; ☉7am-4pm Mon-Fri, from 8:30am Sat, 10am-3pm Sun) Bustling and cheerful, this place has excellent coffee and baked goods, all of which will have you grinning like the Cheshire cat.

Wellington's PUB $$
(105 James St; mains $9-16; ☉11am-11pm) Wellington's is the 'light beer' of pubs – it looks like a bar, but it's healthier for you. The menu has some calorie-conscious options like pecan chicken.

❶ Information

Georgian Bay Visitor Information Centre
(☎705-378-5105; Hwy 69; ☉8am-5pm Mon-Thu, to 6pm Fri, to 4pm Sat, 9am-5pm Sun late May-Sep, 9am-4pm Mon-Sat, from 10am Sun Oct–late May) On the east side of the highway about 12km south of town.

Parry Sound Chamber of Commerce (☎705-746-4213; 70 Church St; ☉9am-5pm Mon-Fri Aug-Jun, to 8pm Jul & Aug) At the old train station. Pick up a copy of *Sideroads of Parry Sound*, which details a variety of quirky things to do around town.

❶ Getting There & Away

Ontario Northland buses connect Parry Sound with Toronto ($54.40, 3½ hours, twice daily) on the Sudbury route.

Killarney Provincial Park

This **park** (☎705-287-2900; Hwy 637; day use per vehicle $13, camping $29.75-42.25, backcountry camping $11) is often called the crown jewel of the Ontario park system, and is considered one of the finest kayaking destinations in the world. The Group of Seven artists had a cabin near Killarney's Hwy 6 access point (west of the park) and were instrumental in the park's establishment. In fact, the park's 100km **La Cloche Silhouette Trail** is named for Franklin Carmichael's legendary painting. The rugged trek, geared toward experienced hikers, twists through a mountainous realm of sapphire lakes, thirsty birches, luscious

pine forests and shimmering quartzite cliffs. A network of shorter, less challenging hikes also offers glimpses of the majestic terrain, including the Cranberry Bog Trail (a 4km loop) and the Granite Ridge Trail (a 2km loop).

Most people access the park from the Hwy 637 turnoff along Hwy 69, which terminates in the tiny village of **Killarney**. The popular **George Lake** access point features an information center and limited camping facilities. The total number of campsites is low, so contact **Ontario Parks** (☎519-826-5290, 888-668-7275; www.ontarioparks.com) far in advance to make a reservation. It should also be noted that there are no powered campsites in the park.

On Hwy 69, 40km south of the turnoff for Killarney, **Grundy Lake Supply Post** (☎705-383-2251; cnr Hwys 69 & 522; ☉8am-6pm May-Oct, to 9pm Jul-Aug) has everything one would need for a camping adventure, including boat rentals. For canoe rentals at the park, try **Killarney Kanoes** (☎705-287-2197, 888-461-4446; www.killarneykanoes.com; canoe rental per day $20-36; ☉7am-7pm mid-May–Oct). It mainly operates from Bell Lake, but also provides canoes at George Lake, Carlyle Lake and Johnny Lake access points. A credit card is required to reserve your equipment, and bookings must be done over the phone or on the website. There is a two-day rental minimum.

Killarney Outfitters (☎705-287-2828, 800-461-1117; www.killarney.com; Hwy 637; canoe and kayak rental per day $20-59, guided trips from $45) offers equipment rentals and a variety of guided adventures including hiking, canoeing, sea kayaking and photography workshops. The storefront location is 5km west of the George Lake Campground. The proprietors also run **Killarney Mountain Lodge** (d per person incl meals $115-215; ☉mid-May–mid-Oct), a wooden compound with loads of waterfront accommodations.

A visit to Killarney without a stop at **Herbert Fisheries** (21 Channel St; fish & chips $13; ☉11am-6:30pm Jun, to 8pm Jul-Aug, to 6:30pm Sat & Sun May & Sep-Oct) is like going to Munich's Oktoberfest and not having a beer. Make sure you give yourself plenty of time to scarf down the fish and chips; legendary queues can be up to two hours long – but trust us, it's worth it.

The park is not accessible by public transportation and is 58km west of Hwy 69 along Hwy 637.

Manitoulin Island

A trip to Manitoulin is like one giant tongue-twister. The names of its different regions sound like meditation mantras or mythical beasts: Mindemoya, Sheguiandah (shuh-*gwin*-dah), Wikwemikong. Haweaters (people born on Manitoulin) will spot you a mile away as you fumble over six-syllable words. But don't let these syllabic setbacks deter you from visiting – Manitoulin is truly an island of dreaming and secrets. Although there's little sense of being on an island (it's the largest freshwater island in the world), the jagged expanses of white quartzite and granite outcrops lead to breathtaking vistas and hidden runes.

As you cross the bridge into Little Current, consider stopping at the **Manitoulin Tourism Association** (☑705-368-3021; www.manitoulintourism.com; Hwy 6, Little Current; ⊙9am-7pm Mon-Fri, to 4:30pm Sat mid-May–Jun & Sep-Oct, 8am-8pm Jul-Aug) and pick up a free copy of the *Bluewater Visitor Guide*, which has a handy map of the island (known locally as the 'Turner's Map'). Small info booths in Gore Bay and Manitowaning are staffed during July and August (hours fluctuate according to volunteer availability).

◎ Sights & Activities

TOP CHOICE Church of the Immaculate Conception   CHURCH

(M'Chigeeng; admission free) This center for worship was built in 1972, and encapsulates both aboriginal traditions and Catholic beliefs. Built in the round, the building represents a tepee, a fire pit and the circle of life. Colorful paintings by local artist Leland Bell beautifully depict the Stations of the Cross, while magnificent carvings represent both Christ and the Great Spirit Kitche Manitou.

Great Spirit Circle Trail   CULTURE CENTER

(☑877-710-3211; www.circletrail.com; 15 Hwy 551) The eight local First Nation communities have collaborated to form a consortium offering fascinating tours of the island and local culture. Most tours stop at the **Ojibwe Cultural Foundation** (☑705-377-4902; www.ojibweculture.ca; cnr Hwys 540 & 551, M'Chigeeng; adult/child $7.50/free; ⊙9am-4pm Mon-Fri Sep-Jun, extended hours Jul-Aug), which can be explored at one's leisure (although guided tours of the museum are highly recommended). Rotating exhibits reflect a rich history of legends and skilled craftwork.

Lillian's Crafts   SOUVENIRS

(www.lilliancrafts.ca; 5950 Hwy 540, M'Chigeeng; ⊙9am-6pm) Lillian's has an excellent assortment of handcrafted items including cozy moccasins, antler carvings and a variety of powwow accessories. While you're browsing, check out her multicolored museum of porcupine quill baskets.

Cup & Saucer Trail   HIKING TRAIL

Near the junction of Hwy 540 and Bidwell Rd (18km southwest of Little Current) lies the entrance to the Cup and Saucer Trail – a must for any hiker. The 12km path leads to the highest point on the island (351m), which has marvelous views of the crinkled shoreline along the North Channel. Stop in Kagawong at **Bridal Veil Falls** and let the melodic splashes fall on your head. Check out Manitoulin's largest beach, west of the ferry landing at Providence Bay, or go frolicking in the trenchlike dunes at quiet **Carter Bay**, also on the southeastern shore.

★☆ Festivals & Events

Powwow   CULTURAL FESTIVAL

(Wikwemikong Heritage Organization; ☑705-859-2385; www.wikwemikongheritage.ca) The unceded First Nation of 'Wiky,' short for Wikwemikong, hosts a huge powwow on the first weekend in August. A $20 weekend pass grants visitors access to the festival's vibrant array of activities. Many of the events are competitive, with prize money awarded to the best dancers and drum-

---

WORTH A TRIP

WORTH THE STOP: BRITT

Stop. Do not pass Go. Do not collect $200. Get off the highway 70km north of Parry Sound and park your car (or thimble) at the TOP CHOICE **Little Britt Inn** (☑705-383-0028, 888-383-4555; www.zeuter.com/~lilbritt; 1165 Riverside Dr, Hwy 526; d $115-135). This hidden gem, on the shores of Georgian Bay, has built a reputation among foodies who travel to far-flung places for memorable meals. Make sure to pick up a copy of the *Guide to Little Britt*, a handmade rulebook to the four-room inn. The manifesto details important information like the kids' menu: fried liver with onions, broccoli and green olives, priced according to the noisiness of the brats.

mers. There's even a contest for Anishi-nabemowin-language speakers (although if you haven't figured out how to pronounce 'Anishinabemowin', you'll probably lose).

🛏 Sleeping & Eating

Southbay Gallery & Guesthouse   B&B $$
(☎705-859-2363, 877-656-8324; www.southbay guesthouse.com; 15 Given Rd, South Baymouth; r incl breakfast $69-109; ⊙May-Sep; P✳🛜🐾) A one-minute walk from the ferry docks, this delightful menagerie of colorful summery cottages is the perfect place to replenish the soul. Brenda, the kindhearted owner, serves a colorful assortment of wild fruit and organic teas at the overflowing breakfasts. Don't forget to explore the lovely gallery showing the handcrafted works of talented local artisans.

Queen's Inn   B&B $$
(☎705-282-0665, 416-450-4866; www. thequeensinn.ca; 19 Water St, Gore Bay; r $95-150; ⊙May-Dec; P) Like a pillared temple to remote elegance, this stately B&B peers over the silent cove of Gore Bay. Grab a book from the antique hutch library and idly thumb through while relaxing on the white veranda amongst potted lilacs. Families with young children should consider other options.

Auberge Inn   HOSTEL $
(☎705-377-4392, 877-977-4392; www.auberge inn.ca; 71 McNevin St, Providence Bay; dm/d incl breakfast $39/90) A newcomer to Manitoulin, enthusiastic Auberge Inn is a hostel-plus. With one bunk room and one private room, the place isn't large but it's comfortable and sociable. The house is done up in warm colors, and custom-built cedar bunks and lockers make everything smell like a delicious forest.

TOP CHOICE Garden's Gate   CAFE $$
(☎705-859-2088; Hwy 542, Tekhummah; mains $15-19; ⊙noon-10pm May-Oct; P) Manitoulin's favorite restaurant is near the junction of Hwys 6 and 542. Don't let the pastels and floral prints fool you: this place has seriously good food. With a steadfast commitment to promoting provincial products, the tantalizing menu offers a local wine selection and an assortment of wild berries. Rose, the owner, makes everything from scratch; she's always inventing desserts, which are regularly featured in the local newspaper.

Garden Shed   CAFE $
(10th Side Rd, Tekhummah; mains $3-10; ⊙breakfast & lunch) The Garden Shed takes rustic charm to a new level by placing you right inside a working greenhouse. Nibble amongst flats of greens, or sip your coffee in the light and airy shed.

☆ Entertainment

De-ba-jeh-mu-jig Theatre Group
PERFORMANCE GROUP
(www.debaj.ca) Canada's foremost Aboriginal troupe, whose name appropriately means 'storytellers,' performs moving pieces of original work transcending various types of media. Check the website for additional details about upcoming performances.

ℹ Getting There & Around
A thin, swinging bridge links the island to the mainland in the north along Hwy 6. In summer, the bridge closes for the first 15 minutes every hour to allow shipping traffic through the channel. The Chi-Cheemaun ferry operated by **Ontario Ferries** (☎800-265-3163; www.ontario ferries.com; adult/child/car $16/8/34.70; ⊙early May–mid-Oct) runs from Tobermory to South Baymouth (a two-hour journey). There are two to four daily crossings, and reservations are highly recommended. There is no land-based public transportation to or around Manitoulin.

NORTHERN ONTARIO

Northern Ontario is big. Real big. So big, in fact, that the locals measure distances in hours rather than kilometers. It's so big that six Englands could fit inside the entire region, and there would still be room for a Scotland or two.

And the region's bigness extends way beyond land size – the mining and logging industries operate on a global scale. Local mines produce over 99% of the world's silver and nickel ore, with shafts extending 25km below the earth's surface. The infinite expanses of forest have made Canada the number one provider of timber in the world.

Even the area's animals are big: bear are grizzlier, fox are foxier, and the mosquitoes are so big, they could pierce your ears with their stinger.

There's only one thing in northern Ontario that's small: its population. About 750,000 people live in the entire region, and only two towns have over 100,000 citizens

Northern Ontario

(Sudbury and Thunder Bay); the population continues to dwindle as mining jobs become scarce.

Northern Ontario's attractions are accessed from the two main highways (Hwy 17 and Hwy 11) as they weave an intersecting course like a shoelace. The oft-traveled Hwy 17 unveils northern Ontario's *pièce de résistance,* the northern crest over Lake Superior. The drive between Sault Ste Marie and Thunder Bay offers some of the most dramatic scenery in the country. Misty fjordlike passages hide isolated beaches amongst dense thickets of pine, cedar and birch. Prevailing mists cast a primeval haze over the churning waters.

Just when you thought things couldn't get more remote, the arcing path of Hwy 11 stretches deep into the north before linking back up to Hwy 17. This far-flung area offers access to the isolated James Bay. From Cochrane, a whistle-stop train shuttles passengers to Moose Factory, an aboriginal reservation and former trading hub of the legendary Hudson's Bay Company.

This section of the chapter is organized in a clockwise fashion, starting with the region's largest city, Sudbury. From Sudbury we move west along Hwy 17, passing Sault Ste Marie, Wawa and the northern arc of Lake Superior before reaching remote Thunder Bay. Then, the section follows Hwy 11 back east as it cuts through the far north, passing Cochrane and Temagami before ultimately reaching North Bay.

Canada's version of the outback is a stunning, silent expanse where ancient aboriginal canoe routes ignite under the ethereal evening lightshow of aurora borealis. If you're traveling to Ontario and you don't plan a visit, you'll regret it, big-time.

SNOWMOBILING IN ONTARIO

Ontario's system of recreational snowmobile trails is the longest in the world at 46,000km. Thousands of the province's motels and lodges cater to this subculture, and it's not uncommon to see motels advertising snowmobile parking with video security. Visit the website of the **Ontario Federation of Snowmobile Clubs** (www.ofsc.on.ca) and see what all the fuss is about.

Sudbury

POP 160,000

From the right angles, radioactive Sudbury is a pulsing oasis of cultured hipsters, offering a surprising selection of trendy dining and entertainment options. Toasty sunsets are enriched by the puff of nearby industrial chemicals, morphing the evening blazes into ethereal flares. Then, like a flickering switchboard, the industrial lights mimic the stars above.

From the wrong angles, it's easy to understand why NASA uses Sudbury's surrounding terrain to test its moon-landing machinery. If it weren't for the elephant graveyards of industrial plants, Neil Armstrong could have fooled the world by taking his 'giant leap for mankind' here instead.

You have to give props to Sudbury, though, for making something out of nothing – literally nothing: in the 1880s Sudbury was but a desolate lumber camp called Sainte-Anne-des-Pins. When the Canadian Pacific Railway plowed through in 1883, a mother lode of nickel-copper ore was discovered, transforming the dreary region into the biggest nickel producer on the globe.

Today, Sudbury's prosperity is less dependent on the copious nickel industry. Three postsecondary institutions attract students from all over, and a growing concern for the environment has encouraged people to 'go green' by reducing waste and planting trees.

To put it simply, it's hard to ignore the omnipresence of industry, despite the bevy of attractions. Although, after a couple of sunsets-on-steroids, you may begin to find that the crusty cigar-shaped smokestack, which dominates the skyline, could perhaps take its place alongside Cleopatra's Needle as another phallic homage to human progress.

Sights

If you're planning to tackle Science North and Dynamic Earth, it's worth purchasing the 'Dynamic Duo' discount coupon (adult/child $46/28), which offers admission to both museums and includes two free IMAX film passes.

Science North MUSEUM
(705-523-4629; www.sciencenorth.ca; 100 Ramsey Lake Rd; adult/child $19/16; 9am-5pm May-Jun, to 6pm Jul-Aug, 10am-4pm Sep-Apr) This huge science center is a major regional attraction conspicuously housed in two

snowflake-shaped buildings on the edge of Lake Ramsey. After passing through a tunnel dug deep within the 2.5-billion-year-old Canadian Shield, take the elevator to the top and work your way down through the spiral of exciting hands-on activities. Wander through a living butterfly garden, stargaze in the digital planetarium, explore rocks through a microscope, build an empire out of Lego or fly away on a bushplane simulator. The blue-coated staff are exceptionally friendly and can tackle the most obscure questions about the displays. Major exhibits change regularly, as do the films screened in the IMAX 3-D cinema.

Dynamic Earth   MUSEUM
(☎705-523-4629; www.dynamicearth.ca; Big Nickel Rd; adult/child $19/16; ☺9am-5pm May-Jun, to 6pm Jul-Aug, 10am-4pm Sep–mid-Nov & Apr) Most towns in northern Ontario have a mining museum, but Dynamic Earth takes the cake. The main attraction is the underground tour (with a simulated dynamite blast), and visitors will enjoy the extensive geologically themed exhibits. There's also plenty of interactive stuff for the kids and the kids-at-heart. Don't forget to grab a picture in front of the Big Nickel (a 9m-high five-cent coin), which is actually made of stainless steel.

FREE **Art Gallery of Sudbury**   ART GALLERY
(☎705-675-4871; 251 John St; ☺10am-5pm Tue-Sat, from noon Sun) Housed in the old mansion of a lumber magnate, this gallery's permanent display tells the region's history through carefully preserved artifacts, and the temporary showcase offers local artists the opportunity to express themselves.

FREE **Copper Cliff Museum**
                                  HISTORICAL BUILDING
(☎705-674-3141, ext 2460; 26 Balsam St, Copper Cliff; ☺10am-4pm Tue-Sun Jun-Aug) The Copper Cliff Museum occupies a pioneer log cabin roughly 6km west of the city center. It's filled with relics from the bygone era when settlers first entered the region to survey the land. Note the odd juxtaposition of quaint pioneer life and grumbling industry as you stare at the nearby smoke-spewing shaft affectionately known as the 'Superstack.'

FREE **Flour Mill Heritage Museum**
                                  HISTORICAL BUILDING
(☎705-673-3141, ext 2460; 245 St Charles St; ☺10am-4pm Tue-Sun Jun-Aug) Similar in style to the Copper Cliff Museum, this exhibit is sited in a 1903 clapboard house with pe-

riod implements, artifacts and furnishings. It tells the story of the three flour silos on Notre Dame Ave.

🏃 Activities

Dinosaur Valley Mini Golf   AMUSEMENT PARK
(☎705-897-6302; www.dinosaursudbury.com; 3316 St Lawrence St, Chelmsford; 18 holes adult/child $8/6; ☺8am-9pm May–mid-Sep) Sudbury is home to one of the best-known miniputt golf courses in North America. Dinosaur Valley Mini Golf has hosted international minigolf competitions on its 54-hole course, and was the recipient of Ontario's first ever 'Tourism Innovation Award.'

Wild Women Expeditions   NATURE RESERVE
(☎888-993-1222; http://wildwomenexp.com; trips from $450) Wild Women Expeditions offers women an opportunity to explore the bush. During the summer, paddling trips and cycling tours meander through the dense wilderness areas of Killarney, Temagami, Mississagi and Manitoulin Island. Throughout the rest of the year, intriguing programming such as drumming, yoga and landscape painting is offered at the base camp, 45km west of Sudbury near Narin Centre.

🛏 Sleeping

Plentiful chain motels dominate, and they're a good bet if you want something utterly predictable. There are, however, several B&Bs sprinkled about the sprawling city.

Sudbury South Suites   B&B $$
(☎705-523-0511; www.sudburysouthsuites.com; 2293 Treeview Rd; r $69-200; ☺) Set outside the city centre, this friendly B&B offers spacious accommodation and a variety of li'l perks like a gut-busting breakfast and large gurgling hot tub. Rooms are tastefully decorated and sport gussied drapes on each window.

Auberge du Village   B&B $$
(☎705-675-7732; www.aubergesudbury.com; 104 Durham St; ste $135-175; ❄☺) Lofted above a quaint *boulangerie,* these two spacious suites transport guests away from the steel jungle of factories to a quiet hamlet in Provence with soft pastels and overflowing wine.

Days Inn   HOTEL $$
(☎705-674-7517; www.daysinnsudbury.ca; 117 Elm St W; r $99; ❄@☺☒) Behind the boxlike exterior lie renovated rooms stocked with simple pleasures like a hairdryer, minifridge, and instant coffee. The central location is a plus.

✖ Eating

TOP CHOICE **Respect is Burning** ITALIAN $$$
(www.ribsupperclub.com; Durham St; lunch mains $8-12, dinner $14-24; ☺dinner Mon-Sat, lunch Tue-Sat; ☎) This self-proclaimed 'supperclub' is reason enough to visit Sudbury. Rustic Tuscan cuisine is the local specialty, and the chefs aren't shy about mixing in some experimental ingredients. Dish recommendations are virtually impossible as the ever-shifting menu promises bursting flavors with every bite. Weekend evenings are a must – delectable sample platters are on offer with late-night drinks.

Vespa Panini SANDWICH SHOP $
(359 Riverside Dr, Unit 104; mains $5-8; ☺lunch & dinner Mon-Sat; ☎) The newest avatar by the wild folks at Respect is Burning, Vespa is speedy sandwich shop that spins out flavorful bites betwixt thick pieces of freshly baked bread. It's all about homemade aioli, fresh farm produce, hanger meat from the butcher, and secret sauces.

Don's Pizza ITALIAN $
(707 Lorne St; mains $2-7; ☺lunch & dinner Tue-Fri) Don's is the don of pizza in Sudbury – you can't mess with these slices. There's no cracker-thin crust or stuffed dough nonsense here, just honest-to-goodness cornmeal pies loaded with old-school toppings. Hours vary.

Deluxe Hamburgers FAST FOOD $
(1737 Regent St; mains $3-8) McDonald's has the golden arches; Deluxe has the golden arch. McDonald's has fast food; Deluxe offers swift service. Notice a pattern? So maybe the concept wasn't original, but this blast from the past is a local institution.

☐ Drinking & Entertainment

Laughing Buddha BAR
(194 Elgin St) Sudbury's prime hangout for hipsters and slackers pulls off snobby sandwiches (like the 'Brie LT') while maintaining an uberchill vibe. Slip out to the crimson-brick courtyard and enjoy your casual lunch or one of the 100-plus types of beer (weather permitting, of course).

Towne House Tavern LIVE MUSIC
(206 Elgin St) You won't find any cover band here – this beloved institution is all about Canadian indie from punk to gospel. It's grungy and it's right along the train tracks. Naturally.

SRO NIGHTCLUB
(94 Durham St) Grab a martini from the swirling stainless-steel bar – the drinks are so large you can swim in them. Weekends are standing room only, so strap on the dance shoes and prepare to get down.

ⓘ Information

Try www.sudburymuseums.ca or www.sudburytourism.ca for the city's highlights.

Chamber of Commerce (☎705-673-7133; www.sudburychamber.ca; 49 Elm St; ☺8:30am-5pm Mon-Fri) Offers helpful information about businesses and attractions around town.

Rainbow Country Travel Association (☎705-522-0104, 800-465-6655; www.rainbowcountry.com; 2726 Whippoorwill Ave; ☺8:30am-8pm Jun-Aug, to 4:30pm Mon-Fri & 10am-6pm Sat Sep-May) It's 10km south of town.

ⓘ Getting There & Around

Sudbury's airport is in the northeast corner of the city, past Falconbridge, and is serviced by **Air Canada Jazz** (☎888-247-2262), **Bearskin Airlines** (☎800-465-2327) and **Porter Air** (www.flyporter.ca). Direct flights connect Sudbury with Toronto, Ottawa, Sault Ste Marie and Thunder Bay. Several car-rental options are available at the airport, including **Enterprise** (☎800-736-8222) and **National** (☎705-387-4747).

Ontario Northland and Greyhound Canada use the same **bus depot** (☎705-524-9900; 854 Notre Dame Ave) about 3km north of the downtown core. Ontario Northland runs between Sudbury and Toronto (5¾ hours, three daily), as does Greyhound (five hours, three daily). Greyhound Canada also connects Sudbury with Thunder Bay (14 hours, three daily) and Ottawa (7½ hours, three daily).

Most trains pull in to **Sudbury Junction Train Station** (☎800-361-1235; Lasalle Blvd), which is about 10km northeast of the town center. VIA Rail trains connect Sudbury Junction with Toronto (6¾ hours, three weekly) and stations west to Winnipeg (24 hours, three weekly). Passengers heading east toward Ottawa must catch a connecting train through Toronto. The centrally located **Sudbury Train Station** (☎800-361-1235; cnr Minto & Elgin Sts) services a small network of minor towns including White River and Chapleau by Budd car.

Over 50 city buses roam the downtown region connecting the major attractions. The **transit center** (☎705-675-3333; cnr Notre Dame Ave & Elm St) is the main transfer hub; one-way fares are $2.50.

Sudbury to Sault Ste Marie

The tree-lined jaunt between Sudbury and Sault Ste Marie offers little more than forest views out the car window. **Elliot Lake**, the largest community in the area, is the preferred location for retirees on a tight budget. The town has a clutch of fast-food joints and a mildly interesting museum about the uranium mined from the region.

Mississagi Provincial Park (☑705-848-2806, 705-865-2021; Hwy 639; day use per vehicle $13, backcountry sites $9.50, campsites $27-34; ☺mid-May–Sep), 25km north of Elliot Lake, is a secluded expanse of hemlock forests, sandy beaches, trembling aspens and chirping birds. A hike around Flack Lake reveals ripple rock – a unique geological feature formed by a billion years of wave action.

Canoeing buffs should pick up the *Area Canoe Routes* brochure at the welcome center in Elliot Lake. The pamphlet details seven unique portages around the park including the day-long **Cobre Lake Loop**, which can be interspersed with captivating hikes.

For camping reservations call **Ontario Parks** (☑519-826-5290, 888-668-7275; www.ontarioparks.com). Note that none of the campsites have electricity and the limited facilities on Semiwite Lake (the gatehouse and toilets) are solar-powered.

Sault Ste Marie

POP 75,000

'The Soo,' as it's commonly known, quietly governs the narrow rapids between Lake Huron and Lake Superior. Perched along the last 'steps' of the St Lawrence Seaway, this placid city is the unofficial gateway to the far-flung regions of western Ontario. Although the area is dominated by a veritable who's who of corporate franchises, the downtown area along the water has remained a quaint checkerboard of mom-and-pop shops.

SEEING STARS IN SAULT STE MARIE

While you're in the Soo, step outside on a clear night and look up at the stars. That's how it all started for the city's favorite daughter and Canada's first female astronaut, Roberta Bondar. Even as a young girl, Bondar wanted to be a 'spaceman,' so she clipped a coupon from the back of a cereal box and sent away for a free space helmet, only to receive a one-dimensional cut-out by return mail. She was devastated – but not deterred.

Besides getting top marks at high school, she was athlete of the year in her graduation year. At university she earned a degree in zoology and agriculture while getting her pilot's license and coaching the archery team. Continuing her education, she bagged a master's degree in experimental pathology, then a doctorate in neurobiology and (just to stay well-rounded) finished off her medical degree. For fun, she parachuted and got her scuba-diving certification. At last count she was up to six earned degrees and 29 honorary ones, on top of being chancellor of Peterborough's Trent University.

Of course, when the National Research Council of Canada decided to begin a space program, Bondar put her hand up, along with 4300 other Canadians. She was one of the six picked. As a payload scientist on board the shuttle *Discovery* in 1992, she studied the effects of weightlessness on the human body.

Upon returning to terra firma, she wrote a book about her experiences, *Touching the Earth*, which included many of her own photographs. She now earns a living through photography and as a motivational speaker based in Toronto. Her *Passionate Vision: Discovering Canada's National Parks* is a good travel souvenir. In *Canada: Landscape of Dreams*, her photographs accompany the words of famous Canadians discussing what the country means to them. Bondar's latest photography project, in progress at the time of research, features portraits of female astronauts.

Bondar is still strongly connected with her hometown and very proud of it (the feeling is mutual). The Canadian Bushplane Heritage Centre displays artifacts from her *Discovery* mission, and the Roberta Bondar Pavilion in the waterfront area is named after her. If you catch her summering in the family cottage just northwest of the city, she might even autograph one of those books for you.

Originally the area was a traditional gathering place for the Ojibwe, known as Baawitigong, or 'place of the rapids'. When French fur traders arrived, the name changed to today's Sault Ste Marie (soosaynt *muh*-ree), which roughly translates to 'St Mary's Falls.' After over a century of riding the boom-and-bust roller coaster of industry, the falls have undergone some serious manhandling and are now the gargantuan locks we see today.

◉ Sights & Activities

Algoma Central Railway   HISTORICAL SITE
(ACR; ☎705-946-7300; www.algomacentralrailway.com) The ACR is a 475km stretch of railroad that starts in the center of town and runs due north all the way to Hearst. Constructed in 1899, the iron tracks were laid down to facilitate the mass transport of raw materials from the frigid north to Sault Ste Marie's industrial plants. A couple of decades later, the region was explored by the Group of Seven, who immortalized the unspoiled scenery through vivid landscape tableaux. Today, the railway is largely used for passenger transportation and tours.

As the region's popularity grew, the **Agawa Canyon Tour Train** started up to serve the new influx of tourists. From midJune to mid-October, a daily train shuttles passengers along the pristine lakes and jagged granite of the Canadian Shield. The best time for a ride is during the last two weeks of September or the first week of October when the blazing autumn foliage turns a brilliant red and yellow. During the summer, prices are $70/00 for adults/children, increasing to $93/59 in September for the fall months. Trains depart at 8am and return at 5:30pm, with a two-hour layover in the lush Agawa Canyon, 185km north of Sault Ste Marie.

Another option is the rustic trek to the end of the line at Hearst, known as the **Tour of the Line**. It's a whistle-stop train (it stops whenever someone wants to get on or off) and entails at least one night in quiet Hearst if you're returning to Sault Ste Marie. The return cost between Sault Ste Marie and Hearst is adult/child $206/127.50, and increases to $299/186.50 in the fall as the train twists through the picturesque autumn colors. Trains depart on Wednesday, Friday and Sunday, and return the following day.

Extended wilderness adventures are available by booking accommodations at one of the many retreats dotted along the railway, known as the 'Lodges along the Line.' Check out the ACR website to plan a tailored excursion – try snowmobiling through 4000km of groomed trails in the winter, or spend a relaxing summer weekend fishing for plump trout.

All trains depart from the **train station** (129 Bay St), which also sells tickets. Check with your local accommodations before booking tickets as they may offer discount package deals.

Canadian Bushplane Heritage Centre
MUSEUM
(☎705-945-6242; www.bushplane.com; 50 Pim St; adult/child/student $10.50/2/5; ☉9am-6pm mid-May–Sep, 10am-4pm Sep–mid-May) A visit to the Soo's most dynamic museum is an excellent way to learn about the idiosyncrasies of northern Ontario culture. A 20-minute film explains the importance of bushplanes in the region, as several remote communities are not accessible by road. The jiving soundtrack captures the sense of adventure associated with this oft-used form of transportation. Stroll amongst retired bushplanes to get a sense of how tiny these flyers really are. A flight simulator takes passengers on a spirited ride along sapphire lakes and towering pines (you might even get a little wet!).

Ermatinger-Clergue National Historic Site
HISTORICAL SITE
(☎705-759-5443; 831 Queen St E; admission $3; ☉9:30am-4:30pm Jun-Aug, 9:30-4:30pm Mon-Fri Sep-Oct) This pair of stone cottages comprise the oldest buildings west of Toronto, and have been transformed into an informative museum where costumed students re-create life in 1814 with activities like churning butter and dyeing fabrics.

Sault Ste Marie Museum
MUSEUM
(☎705-759-7278; 690 Queen St E; adult/student/family $5/3/12; ☉9:30am-5pm Mon-Sat, closed Mon in winter) Constructed in the old post office, this three-story museum details the town's history through several perspectives. The Skylight Gallery is a must-see for industrial history buffs; an interactive timeline from prehistory to the 1960s incorporates the local historical society's unique collection of preserved fossils and relics. Beyond the exhibits, the structure is itself an important historical tribute to the early 1900s, when little Sault Ste Marie emerged from obscurity.

Art Gallery of Algoma   ART GALLERY

(☎705-949-9067; www.artgalleryofalgoma.on.ca; 10 East St; admission by donation; ⊙11am-6pm Wed-Sun) This gallery is housed on the ground floor of the modern brick civic center, and offers regularly rotating exhibits that often feature local artists.

Casino Sault Ste Marie   CASINO

(☎800-826-8946; 30 Bay St W; admission free; ⊙9am-4am Sun-Wed, 24hr Thu-Sat) The Soo's charity casino has a kitschy wilderness theme, where the roars of feral game have been replaced with the ambient swish of 450 slot machines. Although dwarfed by the casino across the border in Michigan, the gambling hall holds its own with two dozen gaming tables and a large restaurant.

Sault Ste Marie Canal National Historic Site   HISTORICAL SITE

(☎705-941-6262; 1 Canal Dr) Stroll through the quiet islands on the Canadian side of the waterway; the majority of freighter traffic occurs further afield in the American locks – the older Canadian locks, built in 1895, are used for recreational vessels only.

The **Attikamek walking trail** is a short, self-guided hike around South St Mary's Island. The meandering path winds through wooded knolls, encircles the trenchlike locks and dips under the International Bridge, allowing visitors to grasp the interesting juxtaposition of nature and industry.

Caribou Expeditions   NATURE RESERVE

(☎800-970-6662; www.caribou-expeditions. com; 1021 Goulais Mission Rd, Goulais Bay; tours $135-1495) Caribou Expeditions is based about 34km north of Sault Ste Marie on the quiet waters of Goulais (goo-lee) Bay. Join the team of experienced nature-lovers on a variety of kayaking expeditions – from one day to one week – along the northern crest of Lake Superior. Canoe and kayak rentals are also on offer; there's even a whale-watching sea-kayak tour down the St Lawrence River in Québec.

Treetop Adventures   ADVENTURE PARK

(☎705-649-5455; www.treetopadventures.ca; Goulais; aerial games & big zip $39) New to the region, this woodsy adventure park offers a variety of heart-pounding games like rope-walking high above the tree line and swinging through the forest on a zipline, Tarzan-style. We recommend calling ahead – at least one week ahead in summer and two days during the quieter months.

Sleeping

While the bulk of motels and chain accommodations gather further north along Great Northern Rd, there are several options peppered around the downtown core, mostly along the waterfront.

Water Tower Inn   HOTEL $$

(☎800-461-0800; www.watertowerinn.com; 360 Great Northern Rd; r from $119; ❋@❄☀❦) Set adrift in a sea of generic accommodations, this privately run hotel stands out from the rest with its cache of resort amenities, including a plethora of swimming pools and an extensive spa – a great place for the whole family.

Brockwell Chambers   B&B $$

(☎705-949-1076; www.brockwell.biz; 183 Brock St; r $85-125, ❋@❄) Antique sumptuousness is effortlessly blended with modern amenity in this decidedly adult atmosphere. Take a giant step back to the early 1900s and enjoy the delicate floral patterns, burnished candelabras and lacquered hutches.

Satelite Motel   MOTEL $

(☎705-759-2897; www.satelitemotel.com; 248 Great Northern Rd; r $59-69; ❋) The tidy custard-colored decor sets this cheery budget option apart from the usual suspects cluttered along the main northern route into town.

Algonquin Hotel   INN $

(☎888-269-7728; 864 Queen St E; r $39.60-71.50; @) 'The Gonk' has a long-standing reputation as the city's magnet for unsavory characters, but if cheap digs is your game, then there's no better place in town. Just be prepared to share your room with the spirits of drunken derelicts that called the place home some 50 years ago.

✗ Eating

Going Italian is the best bet for a savory meal as most of the locals can trace their lineage back to the Boot-land.

Panna Bar & Grill   MEDITERRANEAN $$

(472 Queen St E; lunch mains $7-14, dinner $15-28; ⊙lunch & dinner) This sleek venue puts a refreshing spin on traditional Mediterranean fare, with fusion favorites like the signature tasting platter consisting of calamari, garlic shrimp and veggie tempura. The modern menu is echoed in the smooth, minimalist decor as though Panna were plucked from a trendy urban center and plopped down amongst homely neighbors.

St Joseph Island, a quiet expanse of woodland, drifts between Canada and the USA in the northwest corner of Lake Huron. Believe it or not, it's the second-largest freshwater island in the world, the largest producer of maple syrup in Ontario, and home to a unique fleck-ridden rock called 'puddingstone.'

The island's main attraction is the **Fort St Joseph National Historic Site** (☑705-246-2664; www.pc.gc.ca/fortstjoseph; Hwy 548; adult/child $3.90/1.90; ☺9:30am-5pm Jun–mid-Oct). At one time the fort was the most remote outpost of the British landhold in North America. The preserved ruins of a 200-year-old fort are an archaeologist's dream.

Consider basing yourself in Sault Ste Marie, 50km west, and spend a quiet afternoon exploring. The island is reachable by the toll-free bridge off Hwy 17.

Muio's   DINER $
(685 Queen St E; mains $5-15) Like a shrine to the era of roller discos and drive-in movie theaters, Muio's seems to bask in its own anachronistic glory despite a recent renovation. Even the waitresses don almond uniforms and smack their gum when dropping off your homespun cookin'. The club sandwich with gravy-drenched fries is the local fave.

Mrs B's Pizzas   FAST FOOD $
(78 East St; mains $1.50-6.75; ☺lunch & dinner Mon-Sat, 1-7pm Sun) The fire-engine-red facade lures the weary masses like the call of a siren, so bop in for a slice of greasy heaven and extinguish your hunger. There's a second location at 459 Second Line W.

🍷 Drinking & Entertainment

If cheap beer is what you're after, then follow the veritable conga line of barhoppers across the International Bridge to Michigan for half-priced hooch. It's worth keeping to the Canadian side for nicer venues and a budding indie music scene. Pick up a free copy of *Fresh* magazine for the latest happenings around town.

LopLops   LIVE MUSIC
(www.loplops.com; 651 Queen St E) This inviting venue is coated in earthy tones, with the occasional splash of a neon polka dot. Grab a glass of imported wine from the glittering steel bar and enjoy an evening amid strumming guitars while eavesdropping on the restless murmurs of tortured artists. Unleash your inner diva at one of the many open mic nights or catch the latest folk and jazz music from local and visiting artists.

Docks   BAR
(89 Foster Dr) Great views and cheap booze. This lively joint squats below a nondescript restaurant that shares its name. The ample riverside patio seating makes this lodge hangout a favorite amongst the local 20-somethings. Catch live jazz on Thursday nights, or get down to the DJ's freshly mixed beats on the weekend.

❶ Information

Ontario Travel Information Centre (☑705-945-6941; 261 Queen St W; ☺8am-6pm mid-May–mid-Jun, to 8pm mid-Jun–early Sep, 8:30am-4:30pm early Sep–mid-May) Sells fishing permits and snowmobiling licenses.

❶ Getting There & Around

The **Sault Ste Marie Airport** (YAM; ☑705-779-3031; www.saultairport.com; 475 Airport Rd) is about 20km from downtown. Take Second Line (Hwy 550) 13km west, then head south for 5km along Airport Rd (Hwy 565). Flights to and from Toronto are available with Air Canada Jazz, and Bearskin Airlines offers services to several locations in Ontario and Manitoba including Ottawa, Winnipeg, Thunder Bay and Sudbury. There are several car-rental options at the airport including Enterprise and Budget. Check with your hotel before arrival as it might offer complimentary pickup service.

The **bus station** (☑705-949-4711; 73 Brock St) is downtown and serves as a terminus for local, domestic and international ground transportation. Greyhound Canada runs buses between Sault Ste Marie and Sudbury (four hours, three daily) and between Sault Ste Marie and Thunder Bay (nine hours, two daily). For $2 a ride, try the network of city buses. Call ☑705-759-5438 for more information and route details.

Join the circus of gamblers and drinkers and hop over to Sault Ste Marie's American twin. The **International Bridge Bus** (☑906-632-6882; one way $2.25) follows a regular circuit between both borders, stopping every other hour at several locations in the Soo including the Station Mall, the Cambrian Mall and the bus station. The bus runs from 7am to 7pm during the week and from 9am to 5pm on Saturday. There is no bus service on most American national holidays.

Lake Superior Provincial Park

Most people think Lake Superior got its name from of its superior size (it's the largest freshwater lake in the world), but we're pretty sure the lake gets its name from its superior beauty. Shoreline drives are sure to turn car-ride conversations into extended periods of awe-induced silence interspersed with the occasional 'wow.' Whether you're looking to become one with nature, or just want some instant gratification, **Lake Superior Provincial Park** (✆705-856-2284, 705-882-2026; www.lakesuperiorpark.ca; Hwy 17; day use per vehicle $13, backcountry sites $9.50, campsites $27.25-32.75) is the perfect introduction to the great Great Lake. The 1600-sq-km park is one of the most scenic areas along the lake, offering misty fjordlike passages, thick evergreens, and empty beaches that could have been lifted from an ad for the Caribbean.

All visitors should stop at the park's high-quality interactive museum in the **Agawa Bay Visitor Centre** (✆705-882-2026; Hwy 17; ☷9am-8pm Jul-Aug, to 5pm Jun & Sep), roughly 8.7km north of the park's southern boundary. The outdoorsy staff members are an excellent resource for making the most of your visit, however long it may be. In the quieter months visitors can stop at **Red Rock** (✆705-856-2284; ☷9am-4pm Mon-Fri), 53km north of the visitor center, for additional details.

If you're on a tight schedule, pull off Hwy 17 at the **Katherine Cove** picnic area for paradigmatic panoramas of misty sand-strewn shores. Culture junkies should make a pit stop at the **Agawa Rock Pictographs**. These animal and anthropomorphic images, painted in red ochre, are roughly 150 to 400 years old. A short-but-rugged 500m trail connects the visitor parking lot to a rock ledge where, if the lake is calm, the mysterious sketches can be viewed.

For those who have a bit more time, there are 11 excellent hiking trails to explore. The park's headline hike is the 65km **Coastal Trail**, a steep, challenging route along craggy cliffs and pebble beaches (allow five to seven days). There are five road access points for those who wish to do a smaller section.

Try the **Nokomis Trail** (5km), which loops around the iconic Old Woman Bay (so named because it is said you can see the face of an old woman in the cliffs). This moderate trek feels like a walk through the past – the wispy beardlike fog and shivering Arctic trees give off a distinctly primeval flavor.

The diverse **Orphan Lake Trail** (8km), just north of Katherine Cove, is a veritable pupu platter of the park's ethereal features: isolated cobble beaches, spewing waterfalls, elevated lookouts and dense maple forests.

Lake Superior Park also hosts a burgeoning paddling culture. Eight charted inland routes range from the mild 16km **Fenton-Treeby Loop** (with 11 short portages) to challenging routes accessible only via the Algoma Central Railway, which departs from Sault Ste Marie. Naturally Superior Adventures in Wawa and Caribou Expeditions near Sault Ste Marie run extensive paddling programs in and around the park.

There are three campgrounds just off Hwy 17: Crescent Lake (no flushing toilets), Awaga Bay and Rabbit Blanket Lake. Bookings must be made through **Ontario Parks** (✆888-668-7275; www.ontarioparks.com).

Keep an eye out for scraggly moose along the highway, especially at dusk or dawn.

Wawa

POP 3200

If you tell an Ontarian that you're heading to Wawa, they'll probably say, 'Make sure you see the goose!' They're referring, of course, to the huge gander that has been unapologetically luring travelers off the highway since the 1960s. Choosing a goose as the drive-by decoy wasn't completely unfounded; *wawa* is the Ojibwe word meaning 'wild goose.' The 1720s fur-trading post was so named because of the myriad geese that would rest by Lake Wawa during their seasonal migration.

⊙ Sights & Activities

Wawa Goose   MONUMENT

A trip through Wawa would be incomplete without seeing the notorious Wawa Goose located in front of the visitor information center. There are actually two other giant geese in town: a noticeably decrepit (and anatomically incorrect) goose lingers just up the street on the opposite side of the road, and the third bird flaps its wings above the Wawa Motor Inn.

For many years, White River was known as the coldest place in Ontario. A large kitschy thermometer was erected in town displaying the ungodly temperatures. Then it was discovered that White River had a bigger claim to fame – it was home to Winnie the Pooh. How, you may ask, is AA Milne's little critter actually from this small logging center?

It all started in 1914 when a trapper brought a baby black cub to White River after an extended hunting trip. Young Harry Colebourn, an army captain, saw the adorable bear and purchased her from the trapper for $20. He named her 'Winnipeg' after his hometown, which quickly got shortened to 'Winnie.' When Harry was called to serve in France he left his pet with the London Zoo. The friendly bear was an instant hit, winning over everyone's heart including Christopher Robin Milne, AA Milne's son. Eventually, Disney purchased Milne's tales of little Winnie and the rest is history.

When you see the giant statue of Winnie in White River, take a good look at the bear's eyes – they look slightly different from Disney's lovable honey-eater. Since Disney owns the rights to the furry bear, the giant statue in White River had to be slightly altered to avoid copyright infringement.

Naturally Superior
Adventures   NATURE RESERVE
(☎705-856-2939, 800-203-9092; www.naturallysuperior.com) Naturally Superior Adventures is based 8km southwest of Wawa. Its lodge quietly sits along Lake Superior between a craggy expanse of stone and smooth sandy beach. A day on the grounds is itself a memorable experience, as cool mists roll through in the afternoon and the evening sun gently melts into the lake. Naturally Superior guided day trips ($95) depart several times a week, while relaxed weekend kayaking trips ($350) feature an afternoon of instruction, a night at the lodge, and a night of beach camping while paddling on Lake Superior. These trips are suitable for total beginners. Intermediate paddlers can be outfitted with their own kayaks and canoes for $35 to $45 per day. Other workshops include a four-day digital photography workshop ($580), a weekend yoga retreat ($500) and guide certification courses.

🛏 Sleeping

Rock Island Lodge   CAMPGROUND $
(☎800-203-9092; www.rockislandlodge.ca; tent/tepee $20/30, d incl breakfast $72-103; ☺May-Oct; 🛜) Naturally Superior Adventures' lodge is a welcoming retreat even if you're not participating in the activities. The four basic rooms are spotless, comfortable and offer views of the lake.

Parkway Motel   MOTEL $$
(☎705-856-7020; www.parkwaymotel.com; Hwy 17; r $69-99; ✳@🛜) Don't be tricked by the rather generic motel facade – the freshly refurbished rooms sparkle with a cache of perks including DVD players (with complimentary movies), microwave ovens, plasma TVs and minifridges. There's even a hot tub out back! The comfortable motel, run by a friendly Polish couple, is situated 5km south of Wawa along the highway.

Wawa Motor Inn   MOTEL $$
(☎800-561-2278; www.wawamotorinn.com; 100-118 Mission Rd; s $71-89, d $81-99; ✳@🛜) Enter under the giant googly eyed goose for bright rooms with French doors. Log-cabinlike rooms out back are the perfect place to unleash your inner lumberjack.

✗ Eating

Kinniwabi Pines   CARIBBEAN $$
(Hwy 17; mains $15-25; ☺lunch & dinner) What would you expect to find lurking behind the facade of a highway motel in remote northern Ontario? Food from Trinidad, mon! Add some spice to your trip and try the baked pork or the stewed catfish. European and Chinese dishes are also available for those who don't care to dare their palate.

❶ Information

The **Visitor Information Centre** (☎705-856-2244, 800-367-9292; 26 Mission Rd; ☺8am-8pm Jun-Aug) offers information about the town and can provide detailed information about nearby Lake Superior Provincial Park and Pukaskwa National Park.

BIG ONTARIO

Wawa's duck decoy isn't the only 'big' thing in Ontario...

» Big Nickel – a giant piece of currency casting eclipsing shadows in Sudbury

» Big Flying Saucer – have a close encounter in the aptly named town of Moonbeam

» Big Snowman – this snazzy yeti chills out in little Beardmore

🛈 Getting There & Away

Greyhound Canada buses connect Wawa with Sault Ste Marie (three hours, three daily) and Thunder Bay (6½ hours, three daily).

Chapleau

Little Chapleau (*chap*-loh) is the gateway to the world's largest Crown game preserve, measuring a whopping 7000 sq km. For information, check out www.chapleau.ca, or stop by the **Centennial Museum & Information Centre** (☎705-864-1122; 94 Monk St; ☺9am-4pm May-Aug). You may be surprised to learn that this tiny town in the middle of the woods supports one of Canada's only municipal wireless mesh networks for the internet.

The Missinaibi River tumbles down from James Bay flowing deep within Chapleau's preserve to **Missinaibi Provincial Park** (☎705-234-2222, 705-864-3114; day use per vehicle $10; campsites $32-39; ☺May–mid-Sep). Several outfitters operate at various points along the river, including **Missinaibi Headwaters Outfitters** (☎800-590-7836; www.missinaibi.com; Racine Lake), based in the preserve.

Pukaskwa National Park

At Pukaskwa (*puck*-a-saw), bear hugs are taken literally. The **park** (☎807-229-0801, ext 242; www.parkscanada.gc.ca/pukaskwa; Hwy 627; day use adult/child $5.80/2.90, backcountry sites $9.80, campsites $15-29) features an intact predator-prey ecosystem, which continues to thrive since there is only 4km of road in the entire preserve (and 1km in winter). Pukaskwa offers many of the same topographical features as Lake Superior Provincial Park and includes a small herd of elusive caribou.

There are two ways to explore this majestic hinterland. Those pressed for time can do a trip through the frontcountry, and for those with a flexible itinerary, an adventure through the park's backcountry will be an unforgettable experience.

Pukaskwa's frontcountry is based around **Hattie Cove**, the park's only campground, about 2km from the park's entrance. The **visitor centre** (☺9am-4pm Jul-Aug) offers a wealth of information about local wildlife and the boreal forest. On most summer evenings (starting around 7pm) there are guided hikes and activities departing from the center. Three short trails depart from the campground area, offering glimpses of the pristine setting. The popular **Southern Headland Trail** (2.2km) is a spear-shaped route that pokes along a rocky route offering elevated photo ops of the shoreline and the craggy Canadian Shield. The track also acquaints hikers with bonsai-esque trees, severely stunted by harsh winds blowing off the lake. The **Halfway Lake Trail** (2.6km) loops around a small squiggly lake. Informative signs, dotted along the path, annotate the trek by offering an informed perspective on the inner workings of the ecosystem. A third route, the **Beach Trail** (1.5km), winds along Horseshoe Bay and Lake Superior revealing sweeping vistas of crashing waves and undulating sand dunes. Hattie Cove and Halfway Lake offer tranquil day-long paddling options as well.

Pukaskwa's backcountry would make the perfect setting for the next installment of *Survivor* – the 1878 sq km of untouched wilderness defines the word 'isolation.' The **Coastal Hiking Trail** (60km) is the main artery for hikers, dipping along the vast shoreline. Paddlers will be sated with three incredible routes, including the acclaimed **White River Canoe Route** (72km), which links Hattie Cove to White Lake Provincial Park. Before departing on a backcountry adventure, swing by the park's administration office and pick up the detailed guides to the preserve.

It's possible to get a taste for the rugged backcountry even if you're only here for the day. Many fit hikers opt to traverse the first 7.6km of the Coastal Hiking Trail, which culminates at the 30m-long, 25m-high White Water Suspension Bridge. The trek is arduous, even wet, and you must return the way you came (making it a 15km total), but few will complain about the stunning surroundings.

You'll probably need a water taxi if you're doing any extended hiking or paddling. **Mc-Cuaig Marine Services** (☑807-229-0193; mccuaigk@onlink.net) can pick you up or drop you off anywhere along the coast. It's best to have the boat drop you off in the wilderness and then work your way back to main camp; fickle weather can delay pickup service.

If you don't have the time to plan your own trip, Naturally Superior Adventures in Wawa and Caribou Expeditions near Sault Ste Marie offer a variety of guided excursions through Pukaskwa's backcountry.

Marathon to Nipigon

The winding path over the northern crest of Lake Superior is a pleasant jaunt with several places that make a good excuse to stretch your legs. Rocky **Neys Provincial Park** (☑807-229-1624; day use per vehicle $10), just west of Marathon, has craggy beaches, furry caribou, and sunsets that make for a perfect Kodak moment.

Drop by the town of **Terrace Bay** and catch a boat to the **Slate Islands**, home to the largest herd of woodland caribou in the world.

Consider spending the night in quiet **Rossport**, a quaint village tucked between the grumbling railroad and one of Lake Superior's only natural harbors. The **Rossport Inn** (☑877-824-4032; www.rossportinn. on.ca; 6 Bowman St; s/d $70/75, cabins $85-95; ☺mid-May–mid-Oct) has pleased passers-through since 1884, with elegant dark-wood furniture, cozy quilts and savory cuisine. Even the wallpaper peels in the most charming of ways.

Sleeping Giant Provincial Park

From Thunder Bay, 45km away, this jagged peninsula takes the shape of a large reclining man, and has been considered a rather sacred realm for millennia. The **park** (☑807-977-2526; Hwy 587; day use per vehicle $13, backcountry sites $9.50, campsites $32-42) lies at the southern tip of the craggy mass offering unforgettable views of cold Lake Superior.

The park is rugged enough to offer backcountry camping, while compact enough for a fulfilling day trip. The three-day **Kabeyun Trail** follows the dramatic west coast of the peninsula. Shorter hikes will also al-

low you to mingle with white-tailed deer, moose and porcupines. At the tip of the peninsula, where the sealed road deteriorates into a path of dirt and pebbles, you'll find the remote community of **Silver Islet**. In the mid-1880s the town exploded with the world's richest silver mine; now it would make a great set for another sequel of *Mad Max*, or any other postapocalyptic movie.

For camping reservations, contact **Ontario Parks** (☑888-668-7275; www.ontarioparks.com).

Thunder Bay

POP 109,000

First impressions of Thunder Bay can be a little jarring. After hours of driving between an ethereal coastline and majestic forests, the concrete collection of industrial relics feels quite out of place. The two distinct downtown cores act like polar magnets repelling attempts at gentrification. However, below the gritty surface, expansive Thunder Bay has a warm small-town vibe. The city itself doesn't offer heaps of attractions, but it makes for an excellent base to explore the nearby historical and natural sites.

The Ojibwe have inhabited the region for centuries, even millennia. Europeans arrived in the 1600s, but it wasn't until 1803 that things really started to get rolling. The British erected Fort William as the trading hub for the lucrative North West Company (beaver-pelt central). Soon after, a rival settlement popped up 5km up the road. Port Arthur was more mining-centric, until it became a shipping center for prairie grain. The metallic granaries continue to line the seaboard.

It was only in the late 1960s that the neighboring towns merged into one city, choosing the name Thunder Bay from the aboriginal name for the region, *Animikie*, meaning 'thunder.' Today the city makes a worthy (and obligatory) stopover for trans-Canada travelers. Consider spending a couple of days in this isolated town – you'll be surprised to find that first impressions aren't always lasting impressions.

◉ Sights & Activities

Attractions are sprinkled in a 40km radius around Thunder Bay, making it difficult for those who do not have their own means of transportation. Consider renting a car from one of the many dealerships in the stretch of commercial zoning known as Intercity.

Terry Fox Lookout & Memorial   MONUMENT
This should be your first stop in town – both to visit the valuable information center, and to learn about one of Canada's great heroes. The memorial honors the young Terry Fox, a native of British Columbia, who lost his leg and eventually his life to cancer. Before passing on, he left a powerful legacy by attempting to walk across Canada with an artificial leg to raise money for cancer research. On April 12, 1980, he started his walk in St John's, Newfoundland. On September 1, he arrived in Thunder Bay after traveling 5373km, but was forced to stop as his illness worsened. Today's memorial is erected close to where Terry ended his great 'Marathon of Hope.'

Kakabeka Falls   NATURE RESERVE
(☎807-473-9231; admission per car $3-9.50) About 25km west of Thunder Bay, just off Hwy 11-17, is Kakabeka Falls Provincial Park. The spectacular 40m waterfall is the source of many local legends. The moody chute is at its best after the thaw in early spring and it gushes year-round after heavy rains.

Fort William Historical Park   HISTORICAL PARK
(☎807-473-2344; www.fwhp.ca; 1350 King Rd; adult/child/family $13.08/9.35/35.51; ◷10am-5pm mid-May–mid-Oct) French voyageurs, Scottish gentlemen and Ojibwe scuttle about while re-enacting life in the early 1800s at this historical park. From 1803 to 1821, Fort William was the headquarters of the North West Company. Eventually the business was absorbed by the Hudson Bay Company and the region's importance as a trading center declined. Today, the large heritage center offers 42 historic buildings stuffed with entertaining and antiquated props like muskets, pelts and birch-bark canoes.

Amethyst Mine Panorama   HISTORICAL SITE
(☎807-622-6908; www.amethystmine.com; East Loon Rd; admission $6; ◷10am-5pm mid-May–Jun & Sep–mid-Oct, to 6pm Jul-Aug) Visit the mine, 40km east of Thunder Bay, and dig for your very own purple chunk of amethyst, Ontario's official gemstone. While pulling into the parking lot, you may notice that the gravel has a faint indigo hue – a testament to the fact that the area is truly overflowing with these semiprecious pieces.

Thunder Bay Museum   MUSEUM
(☎807-623-0801; www.thunderbaymuseum.com; 425 Donald St E, Fort William; adult/child $3/1.50; ◷11am-5pm mid-Jun–Aug, from 1pm Tue-Sun Sep–mid-Jun) This 100-year-old museum has enough quirks and gadgets to keep adults interested and children entertained. The well-presented artifacts offer visitors a glimpse of the region's 10,000 years of human history by incorporating displays about Ojibwe culture, fur trading, military history and recent developments.

Thunder Bay Art Gallery   ART GALLERY
(☎807-577-6427; www.tbag.ca; 1080 Keewatin St, Confederation College; adult/student $3/1.50, free Wed; ◷noon-8pm Tue-Thu, to 5pm Fri-Sun) Thunder Bay's premier gallery offers an eclectic assortment of contemporary art from First Nations artists. The use of natural imagery, haunting masks and scorching primary colors will leave lasting impressions on visitors.

Mt Mackay   NATURE RESERVE
Mt Mackay rises 350m over Thunder Bay, offering sweeping views of the region's patchwork of rugged pines and swollen rock formations. The lookout is part of the **Fort William First Nation** (☎807-622-3093; www.fwfn.com; Mission Rd; per vehicle $5; ◷9am-10pm mid-May–early Oct), and reveals its most majestic moments in the evening when the valley is but a sea of blinking lights. A walking trail leads from the viewing area to the top of the mountain. Watch your step while climbing – the shale rock can cause tumbles.

KANGAS SAUNA

(☎807-344-6761; www.kangassauna.com; 379 Oliver Rd; sauna hire from $14; ◷7:30am-9pm Mon-Fri, 8am-11pm Sat & Sun) If you're looking to be pampered, you've come to the wrong place. Think BYOB, as in 'bring your own bathing suit.' Well, actually, beer works too, as Friday night at Kangas is a well-established social event. The saunas are private and can be hired for up to five hours, so go it alone, or grab a 'conference room' for you and your 'associates.' Even if you're not in the mood to get steamy, Kangas has other amenities that might pique your interest: a public hot tub, tanning booths, a hair salon and popular stool-by-the-bar diner that's always jammed with locals.

Ouimet Canyon (☑807-977-2526; admission $2 donation; ☉mid-May–mid-Oct), just 12km off the highway, is a treacherous crevasse scoured out by ice and wind during the last Ice Age. A microclimate has formed at the bottom, 150m below, which supports a small collection of rare arctic-alpine plants. A 1km loop hugs the jagged bluffs offering views that will make your knees tremble. Camping is prohibited.

If the heart-pounding vistas of Ouimet (*wee*-met) aren't enough to get your blood rushing, stop by **Eagle Canyon Adventures** (☑807-857-1475; www.eaglecanyon adventures.ca; 275 Valley Rd, Dorion; entry $18, zip line $55, camping $30; ☉9am-9pm mid-Apr–mid-Nov). Its 183m-long bridge over the deep canyon floor is the longest suspension footbridge in Canada. Additional superlatives – like the country's longest zipline – will surely satisfy the adventurous all afternoon.

Both canyons are 45km west of Nipigon and 73km northeast of Thunder Bay.

🛏 Sleeping

As a common layover during trans-Canadian treks, Thunder Bay boasts a wide range of lodging options. A veritable who's who of international motel chains gather around the intersection of Hwys 11-17 and 61.

Thunder Bay International Hostel

HOSTEL $

(☑807-983-2042; www.thunderbayhostel.com; 1594 Lakeshore Dr; campsites $13, dm $20; @☜) Colorful bric-a-brac, including antlers and a baby grand piano, lies splayed across the shrubby lawn as though Alice in Wonderland were having a garage sale. The charismatic owners, Lloyd and Willa Jones, champion the backpacking lifestyle; in fact two of their children run hostels as well. These folks are not only kindhearted souls who care about their guests, they're also truly interesting people (ask them why their license plate says 'Borneo'). A night here is in itself an experience to be remembered. The hostel is 25km east of town.

McVicar Manor

INN $$

(☑807-344-9300; www.bbcanada.com/3918. html; 146 Court St N, Port Arthur; r $100-140; ☜) This sumptuous Victorian home has been proudly perched on its acre-sized lot for over 100 years. Ask the owners what the local unionists did to the manor in the 1960s (it involves a bomb), but don't let that scare you off – McVicar takes comfort and quality a step beyond most other B&Bs. Chocolate and roses abound, wine flows in the evening, sunflowers cheer the kitchen and the perfect homemade breakfast greets you in the stately, uncluttered dining room.

Prince Arthur Waterfront Hotel   HOTEL $$

(☑807-345-5411, 800-267-2675; www.prince arthur.on.ca; 17 Cumberland St N, Port Arthur; r $85-195; ✹@☜✹) Thunder Bay's best hotel comes at a reasonable price. The waterfront property has gone through its fair share of renovations, but the cherry-brick exterior and rickety elevator retain the old-school charm. Splurge for a room with placid views of Sleeping Giant across the bay.

Sleeping Giant Guesthouse   HOSTEL $$

(☑807-683-3995; hostelscanada2002@yahoo. ca; 139 Machar Ave, Port Arthur; dm $22; @☜) Hunker down in the 1950s-style kitchen with a complimentary cup of tea and ask Gail, the affable owner, for quirky things to do around town. She might even take you to the local dump to check out the bears that clomp around looking for food. Rooms are stocked with wooden bunk beds and pastel linoleum floors. Free bikes provide an extra bonus for those who want to explore the waterfront nearby.

🍴 Eating

Hoito Restaurant   BREAKFAST $

(www.hoito.ca; 314 Bay St, Port Arthur; mains $4-8) You'll think you've stumbled into a staff cafeteria in Finland – in fact, that's how the Hoito started, providing affordable meals to Finnish bushworkers. This Thunder Bay institution serves breakfast until 7:30pm, and lunch starts at 10:45am – though you'll probably just want to eat the notorious flattened pancakes around the clock. Don't forget to wish the Hoito a happy birthday – the restaurant celebrated 100 years in 2010, though we don't think it looks a day over 75...

Caribou Restaurant & Wine Bar FUSION $$
(807-628-8588; www.caribourestaurant.com; 727 Hewitson St; lunch mains $12-20, dinner mains $24-37; lunch Thu & Fri, dinner daily) Between the confusing haze of wide-set freeways and boxy mega-marts lies one of Thunder Bay's best dining options. The facade positively reeks of franchise banality; however, the inside is filled with one-of-a-kind touches like white-clothed tables and designer stemware.

Masala Grille INDIAN $$
(www.masalagrille.com; 170 Algoma St N, Port Arthur; mains $7-16; lunch Mon-Fri, dinner daily) Housed in a stately Victorian manse, this eclectic addition to Thunder Bay's dining scene represents the evolving community as new immigrants add a certain cosmopolitan flare to the otherwise staid city. Sample spicy platters from the subcontinent; there are a few Thai treats to tempt the palate too.

Growing Season Juice Collective CAFE $
(210 Algoma Ave S, Port Arthur; mains $4-10; lunch) Healthy blended juice is the name of the game here, but it also does scrumptious dishes to accompany your smoothie. Wash down your carrot sticks with a shot of organic wheatgrass, which just happens to be grown on-site!

Prospector Steakhouse STEAKHOUSE $$
(27 Cumberland St S, Port Arthur; mains $16-22; dinner) Appetites beware: you're about to be obliterated. Hefty carnivorous portions are dished out amid ranchlike curios. The infamous prime rib will give your arteries a workout.

Giorg ITALIAN $$
(114 Syndicate Ave N, Fort William; mains $15-22; lunch Fri, dinner Tue-Sat) The exterior is a throwback to a time when good taste and architecture weren't especially synonymous (the '70s), but the charming Italian restaurant inside ranks as one of Thunder Bay's best, with scrumptious pastas served by poised waiters.

Drinking & Entertainment

Madhouse Tavern Grill BAR
(295 Bay St, Port Arthur) A great place to relax and take a load off among warm, friendly chatter and cold beer. The dangling portraits of famous writers and artists have a swirling style similar to Dalí.

❶ Information

Both information centers have wireless internet connections, as do the city's four central libraries.

Pagoda Information Center (807-684-3670; cnr Red River Rd & Water St, Port Arthur; 9am-5pm Tue-Sat mid-Jun–Aug) This is the most central source of visitor information and happens to be the oldest tourist information bureau in all of Canada.

Tourism Thunder Bay (800-667-8386; Hwy 17; 8:30am-7:30pm mid-Jun–Aug, 9am-5pm Sep–mid-Jun) Located about 6km east of town at the Terry Fox Lookout & Memorial.

❶ Getting There & Away

Thunder Bay Airport (YQT; www.tbairport.on.ca) is served by Air Canada Jazz, Porter, Delta, WestJet, Wasaya and Bearskin airlines. The airport is about 3km southwest of the city, at the junction of West Arthur St and Hwy 61. Flight connections include Sudbury, Sault Ste Marie, Ottawa, Toronto, Winnipeg and Minneapolis.

Greyhound buses run to and from Sault Ste Marie (nine hours, three daily) and Winnipeg (nine hours, three daily). The Greyhound **bus depot** (807-345-2194; 815 Fort William Rd) lies between the two downtown areas near the Intercity Mall.

❶ Getting Around

Car-rental chains are well represented at the airport and in the commercial zoning area known as Intercity, located between the two downtown regions. The major hotels, including the Prince Arthur Waterfront Hotel, offer airport shuttles for their guests.

Thunder Bay Transit (807-684-3744; www.thunderbay.ca) covers all areas of the city and the bus drivers are helpful, which is just as well because Thunder Bay can be hard to navigate. Buses have two main hubs: the **Thunder Bay South Terminal** (cnr May & Donald Sts) and the **Thunder Bay North Terminal** (cnr Water & Camelot Sts), though at the time of research a central bus station was in the works. One-way trips cost $2.50.

Thunder Bay to Manitoba

Be your very own Captain Picard and boldly go where no man has gone before... OK, so maybe a few people have already passed through, but it sure as heck won't feel that way. Traffic thins out after Kakabeka Falls as highway vistas become noticeably dull. Then, at Shabaqua Corners, the highway forks: the northern route along Hwy 17 plows straight toward Winnipeg, Manitoba, while the southern route (Hwy 11 and Hwy 71) takes about two extra hours as it ambles through scenic landscapes. Both routes will shuttle you through prime fishing country; service stations will try to lure you in by offering free minnows with your tank of gas. Signs mark the beginning of a new time zone (you save an hour going west).

NORTHERN ROUTE

Ignace and **Dryden** have plenty of motels and basic restaurants but no compelling reason to stop. If you happen to be passing through Dryden at the beginning of July, a stop at the annual **Moose Fest** is a must. The biggest and best place to pause is **Kenora** (www.visitkenora.ca), a pulp-and-paper town and the unofficial capital of the striking **Lake of the Woods** region. This local hub services the local tourist activity, which mainly consists of summer vacation cottages and fishing trips. Accommodations options are plentiful as the usual army of franchise motels is stacked along the highway.

Canadian Native Cultural Tours (✆807-468-9124; www.mskenora.com) offers fantastic cultural and scenic tours aboard the MS *Kenora*. The **Lake of the Woods Museum** (✆807-467-2105; www.lakeofthewoodsmuseum.ca; 300 Main St S, Kenora; adult/child $3/2; ☉10am-5pm Jul-Aug, 10am-5pm Tue-Sat Sep-Jun) features the aboriginal and industrial history of the area, with a particular focus on the last 100 years when Kenora changed rapidly.

Greyhound Canada connects Kenora with Thunder Bay (6½ hours, three daily) and Winnipeg (2½ hours, three daily).

SOUTHERN ROUTE

Those who choose the longer route between Ontario and Manitoba will be rewarded with spectacular distractions. **Atikokan** is the first major stop on the southern trail after the highways diverge. The crusty mining town has several motel and lodge options, making it a good base for a day trip to the stunning and secluded **Quetico Provincial Park** (✆807-597-4602; day use per vehicle $10.75-19.50, camping per person campground $29-37, backcountry $11-21.50). The endless waterlogged preserve has but one small campground, and over 1500km of canoe routes stretching beyond the horizon into unexplored backcountry. **Canoe Canada**

Outfitters (✆807-597-6418; www.canoecanada.com; 300 O'Brien St, Atikokan) provides both self-guided and guided adventures through this dramatic wilderness.

Further west, **Fort Frances** sits right on the American border – a popular crossing for nature enthusiasts. The **Fort Frances Museum** (✆807-274-7891; www.fort-frances.com/museum; 259 Scott St; admission $3.50; ☉10am-5pm Jun-Sep, 11am-4pm Tue-Sat Oct-May) is worth a look, offering a historical introduction to the area.

Kay-Nah-Chi-Wah-Nung (✆807-483-1163; Shaw Rd, Emo; admission $10; ☉10am-6pm Wed-Sat Jun-Sep), 50km west of Fort Frances, is a sacred Ojibwe site containing the largest ancient ceremonial burial grounds in Canada.

Travelers who wish to continue along the Trans-Canada Hwy must follow Hwy 71 north after passing tiny **Emo**, since Hwy 11 veers south across the border.

Before linking back up with Hwy 17, consider making two more scenic pit stops on the eastern realm of Lake of the Woods; **Nestor Falls** and **Sioux Narrows** are serene resort towns, offering a glut of rentable cottages and houseboats.

Nipigon to Cochrane

Charge your iPod – you're going to need it to stay sane if you plan to make the trek from Nipigon to Cochrane along Hwy 11. The 615 kilometers of desolate highway offer little more than a shortcut (or a less-long-cut) across the northern part of the province. You'll pass goofy novelty items, like a giant plastic snowman, and you'll see locals with furrowed brows collectively wondering, 'What the heck are you doing here?' If you're not driven to make the trek in one day, or if you enjoy cavorting with scraggly moose, consider stopping in **Hearst** or **Kapuskasing** (*kap*-iss-*kay*-sing) – both have a decent selection of motels. Hearst is the northern terminus of the **Algoma Central Railway** and the westernmost point of Ontario Northland's train service from North Bay. Check out **Eagle's Earth** (✆705-463-2288; www.eaglesearth.com), an interactive Cree and Ojibwe cultural center, 40km west of Hearst.

Sans stops, the eight-hour car ride will give you plenty of time to ponder the following: how can there be so much roadkill and yet not another car on the road?

Cochrane

POP 5500

Time has not been kind to little Cochrane, whose raison d'être is the *Polar Bear Express* – the whistle-stop train shuttling passengers north to the remote recesses of James Bay. Cochrane doesn't pretend to be a dainty tourist destination, and in a way, that honesty is refreshing. Evidence of harsh, long winters is conspicuous in this windswept town, but despite the inhospitable winters, the largely Francophone population is warm and accommodating.

👁 Sights & Activities

Polar Bear Habitat & Heritage Village

ZOO

(☎705-272-2327, 800-354-9948; www.polarbear habitat.ca; 1 Drury Park Rd; adult/child/student $20/12/18; ⊙8am-6pm Mon-Thu, to 7pm Fri-Sun Jun-Aug, 10am-4pm Mon-Fri, to 5pm Sat & Sun Sep-May) Despite the name of the train, and the giant replica at the info center, there are no wild polar bear roaming around the region, although Nanook became Cochrane's furriest citizen (let's hope) when the Polar Bear Habitat & Heritage Village opened its doors in 2004. A loving staff cares for the scruffy beast – the oldest polar bear in captivity – who was brought to the center as a cub after poachers shot his mother. Visitors can interact with Nanook at daily 'meet the bear' sessions, or swim with him in a pool divided by a thick sheet of glass (swim session $5). Voyeurs can check out the live 'Bear Cam' on the website. An on-site mock colonial village, stocked with costumed staff, is also included in the admission cost.

Polar Bear Express

TRAIN

(☎800-268-9281; www.polarbearexpress.ca; adult/child $104.90/52.40; ⊙Tue-Sun) The *Polar Bear Express* is the only way to reach the remote communities of Moosonee and Moose Factory. The whistle-stop train departs Cochrane in the morning, and the return train pulls into the station close to midnight. The assortment of passengers is a sight in and of itself: locals, trappers, biologists, geologists, tourists, anglers and hard-core paddlers all ride the shuttle (one car is specially outfitted to transport canoes). The trip takes 4¾ hours each way, so if you return the same day you'll only have time for a short visit to Moosonee and Moose Factory. From September to June, the train is commonly known as the *Little Bear*.

🛏 Sleeping

We highly recommend booking ahead in the warmer months.

Best Western Swan Castle Inn

HOTEL $$

(☎705-272-5200; www.bestwesternontario.com; 189 Railway St; d $119; ❄@🛜❄) Cochrane's best lodging option (and unsurprisingly, the most expensive) features spacious rooms and a complimentary continental breakfast. Stop by the gym and whirlpool to get the blood flowing before a lengthy trip to Moosonee.

Station Inn

MOTEL $$

(☎705-272-3500; www.ontc.on.ca; 200 Railway St; r $115; ❄@🛜) Go one better than staying near the train station by staying on top of it. But what are the perks of a hotel-cum-station – the nice views of the tracks? Well, at least you won't be late for your train...

🍴 Eating

Dining options are limited to greasy spoons, so foodies might want to pack a sandwich if they don't want to pack an artery.

Tim Hortons

FAST FOOD $

(☎705-272-3544; 10 Victoria St (Hwy 11); mains $2-7; ⊙24hr) Before you send us hate mail for putting Timmy's in the guidebook, know this: Tim Horton was born in Cochrane and this link of his famous donut chain (started by his wife in his memory) is the busiest branch in the entire country. Truckers line up in droves at all times of the day (it's open 24 hours) to snag some sugary goodness from the remarkably efficient cashiers.

JR's Bar-B-Q Ranch

STEAKHOUSE $$

(☎705-272-4999; 63 3rd Ave; mains $9-21; ⊙lunch & dinner) The western-styled decor fits perfectly with the town's general frontier vibe. The gorge-worthy ribs are so tasty, they might convince you to plan a second trip to Cochrane.

ℹ Information

Stop by the **Cochrane Tourist Association & Board of Trade** (☎800-354-9948; www.town. cochrane.on.ca; 4 3rd Ave; ⊙9am-4:30pm Mon-Fri) to say hi to Chimo, the giant plastic polar bear, and get helpful information about the town and the adorable polar bear sanctuary.

ℹ Getting There & Away

Between Cochrane and North Bay, Ontario Northland runs buses (6¾ hours, three daily) and trains (5½ hours, six weekly). All services arrive at and depart from the **Cochrane Train Station** (☑705-272-4228). Buses also run to Timmins (1½ hours, one daily), with continued service to Sudbury (six hours, one daily).

Moose Factory & Moosonee

Moosonee and Moose Factory sit near the tundra line, and are as far north as most people ever get in eastern Canada. Expeditions further north will undoubtedly involve floatplanes, canoes, snowmobiles, dog-sleds or snowshoes. The railway reached Moosonee in 1932, about 30 years after it was established by Révillon Frères (known today as Revlon) as a trading post. A quick boat trip links Moosonee to the island of Moose Factory, which is not an industrial site that churns out large hairy beasts, but a small Cree settlement and the historic site of the Hudson's Bay Company trading hub founded in 1672.

While you ponder a lengthy journey to this ultra-remote locale, consider the following: when fur trading peaked 300 years ago, the main access to Ontario's interior was *from* the north via the Hudson and James Bays.

◉ Sights & Activities

More than 80% of people who visit come just for the day and never get to experience what the secluded area actually has to offer. Moosonee and Moose Factory could not be more different – Moosonee has a banal industrial vibe, while Moose Factory is a spirited reservation of friendly people and scores of smoke huts. The best way to experience the region is through a tour with the local Moose Cree.

Cree Cultural Interpretive Centre MUSEUM
(☺Jul-Aug) Located in Moose Factory, this centre features indoor and outdoor exhibits of artifacts, including bone tools, traditional toys, reusable diapers and dwellings from the precontact era. You'll learn about *pashtamowin*, or 'what goes around, comes around' – the Cree's version of karma, if you will. It is best to explore the center with the aid of a guide, as they can relay fascinating details and personal anecdotes about the interesting displays.

Moose Factory Centennial Museum
MUSEUM
(☺Jul-Aug) The Moose Factory Centennial Museum displays maps, furs and the Hudson's Bay Staff House, which dates from the early 1700s. Moosehide altar cloths and Cree prayer books are a feature of **St Thomas' Anglican Church**, built in 1860. The church is commonly known as the 'floating church,' because during a particularly harsh storm the wind lifted the structure up into the air and threw it down the street.

Washow James Bay Wilderness Centre
NOTABLE BUILDING
(www.moosecree.com) At the time of research, the Moose Cree were constructing the Washow James Bay Wilderness Centre. The goal of the center, 70km east of Moosonee, is to re-create several villages, each at different points in history. One camp has bark-construction dwellings typical of the precontact era, and another will feature contact-era canvas tepees. Guests travel between the main base and the villages by canoe, and activities in the area might include demonstrations of trapping and fishing. Practical details and prices had not been established at the time of research, so check the website for the latest information.

☞ Tours

Moose Cree Outdoor Discoveries & Adventures NATURE RESERVE
(☑705-658-4619; www.moosecree.com) Run by the Moose Cree First Nation, this outfit offers customized trips incorporating cultural activities (storytelling and traditional foods, for example), along with canoeing in summer and snowshoeing in winter. The friendly and laid-back staff will ask you two questions when tailoring your adventure: 'what do you want to experience?' and 'what are you not looking for?' From there, they can organize absolutely anything, just make sure to give them plenty of time. Prices vary greatly depending on whether you're one person or many, and whether you want a one-day island tour or a week-long wilderness expedition. These highly recommended trips offer a unique opportunity to experience something beyond what many train passengers see. When you finish your memorable tour, don't forget to say *mee-gwetch*, which means 'thank you' in Cree.

🛏 Sleeping & Eating

Reserve accommodations before you arrive. There are a couple of lodging options in Moosonee, though we strongly suggest staying on the island of Moose Factory.

Cree Village Ecolodge INN $$
(☎705-658-6400, 888-273-3929; www.creevillage.com; 61 Hospital Dr, Moose Factory; r from $150) The Cree ecolodge is the first lodge owned and operated by Aboriginals in the northern hemisphere. This fascinating place to stay was designed and furnished to reflect traditional Cree values. The environmentally conscious design extends to the organic wool and cotton used in the carpets, blankets and bed linen, organic soaps in every room, and some composting toilets. The lodge is also home to the first public library in Moose Factory. Breakfast, lunch and dinner are available to guests and nonguests alike, and are served in the Shabotowan Great Hall. Daily specials include locally caught fish ($19) and delicious T-bone steaks ($20).

Tidewater Provincial Park CAMPGROUND $
(☎705-336-1209; day use $10, sites $27-34; ⊘mid-Jun–Aug) This quiet park is on a small island between the mainland and Moose Factory, accessible by water taxi. There are picnic tables and fire pits – but that's about it.

❶ Getting There & Around

Moosonee and Moose Factory are not accessible by car. For information on the *Polar Bear Express* train from Cochrane, see p170. Water taxis shuttle passengers the 3km between Moosonee and Moose Factory ($10, 15 minutes). In winter the river becomes an ice bridge stable enough for cars and trucks. Van taxis from Moosonee station to docks cost $5 per person.

Timmins

POP 43,000

At one time, Timmins was the most productive gold-mining area in the western hemisphere. Today the city still heavily revolves around its lucrative silver and zinc industry, with a network of over 2000km of subterranean tunnels.

Country singer Shania Twain is the queen of her hometown, and her palace is the **Shania Twain Centre** (☎800-387-8466, 1 Shania Twain Dr; adult/student/family $9/7/32; ⊘9am-8pm Jul-Aug, 10am-5pm Sep-Jun). The shockingly large complex showcases her life and music through memorabilia, concert footage and an extensive collection of personal effects. The center is also home to North America's only authentic **gold-mine tour** (☎705-360-2619; www.timminsgoldminetour.com; adult/family $19/60; ⊘tours 9:30am, 11:30am, 1:30pm & 3pm Jul-Aug, 2 tours daily Sep-Jun). Experienced miners dress visitors up in full digging apparel and take them through the Hollinger mine, 50m underground. The journey includes a rail ride and a simulated dynamite blast. Socks and warm clothing are a must.

Timmins has the usual crew of chain motels dotted along Algonquin Blvd (Hwy 101). **Cedar Meadows Wilderness Park** (☎877-207-6123; www.cedarmeadows.com; 1000 Norman St; r $105-125, camping $15; ❀@🗢) has comfortable accommodations amid pet-able moose and elk. **Kettle Lakes Provincial Park** (☎705-363-3511; day use per vehicle $10, camping $32-39; ⊘mid-May–mid-Oct), 35km east of town, offers an innovative camping experience beside round glacial kettle lakes.

❶ Information

The city's **Chamber of Commerce** (☎705-360-1900, 800-387-8466; 76 McIntyre Rd; ⊘9am-5pm Mon-Fri, 10am-4pm Sat), in the township of Schumacher, just east of Timmins, has loads of tourist information.

❶ Getting There & Away

Ontario Northland operates buses between Timmins and North Bay (six hours, two daily) with continuing service to Toronto (10 hours, two daily). A daily bus to Sudbury (4½ hours) is also available. The **Timmins Train Station** (☎705-264-1377; 54 Spruce Ave) also services a connecting train to Matheson (1¼ hours, six weekly) so passengers can connect to the *Northlander* train line.

Temagami

Think back to your first history class – you may have learned about powerful pharaohs and Greek heroes, even ancient dynastic China, but you probably never learned about Temagami. While god-fearing Egyptians were commissioning wondrous pyramids, this region of majestic pines and hushed lakes was a thriving network of trading routes. Evidence of these ancient trails exists today as hidden archaeological sites strewn throughout the region's provincial parks.

Things get quirky in the far north. The towns have bizarre names like Porcupine and Swastika, and with an abundance of roadside oddities to lure you off the road, it can be hard to choose where to stretch your legs. The tiny town of Cobalt is your best bet. At the beginning of the 1900s, this deserted ghost town was a thriving silver mine. For 30 profitable years, the site exploded with a seemingly endless supply of precious metals, attracting over 20,000 temporary residents. The lucrative lode at Cobalt was rumored to have pulled Canada through the Great Depression and was single-handedly responsible for starting the Toronto Stock Exchange. Today, in an area littered with reminders of mining 'busts,' this abandoned expanse is a poignant souvenir of the region's fragile and hyperbolic economy.

For information about the group of preserves around Temagami, visit **Finlayson Point Provincial Park** (☎705-569-3205; day use per vehicle $13; ⊙mid-May–mid-Sep), 2km south of town on Hwy 11. Temagami's **Welcome Centre** (☎800-661-7609; www.temagamiinformation.com; 7 Lakeshore Rd; ⊙9am-4:30pm Mon-Fri) also offers information about the area and has displays about the region's history.

Check out **Obabika River Park**, or the vast **Lady Evelyn Smoothwater Provincial Park**, which has Ontario's highest point, Ishpatina Ridge (693m). There are no facilities, and campsites can only be reached by canoe. The easily accessible **White Bear Forest** has a soaring fire tower at Caribou Mountain offering a bird's-eye view of the stocky trunks below.

Affable owners Doug and Marg have been running **Northland Paradise Lodge** (☎705-569-3791; www.northland-paradise.com; 51 Stevens Rd; s/d/ste $55/85/150), their friendly lakeside lodge, since 1986. Throughout the years they've hosted a wide range of visitors from game hunters to snowmobiling enthusiasts. Nowadays Doug, a semiprofessional photographer, is busiest hunting down wild orchids and guiding trips for clients who want to shoot pictures, not animals. The comfortable motel-style rooms, with full kitchen facilities, make the perfect base for any type of adventure in Temagami. The woodsy lodge is within walking distance of the train station, and Buddy (the loveable resident dog) will greet you with a friendly lick upon your arrival.

The guided dog-sledding trips offered by **Wolf Within Adventures** (☎705-840-9002; www.wolfwithin.ca; weekend trip $395) are an incredible way to experience winter in Temagami. Embark on an exhilarating and edu-

cational adventure through snow-drenched forests and frozen lakes. You're in good hands – Francesco, the owner, was Sylvester Stallone's dog trainer for the movie *Cliffhanger*, and he'll teach you the traditional methods of travel and survival in temperatures of -50°C. In summer, the friendly guides run 10-day canoe trips through Temagami's rugged wilderness ($1450). Custom-designed adventures are available as well. All bookings at Wolf Within should be made two months in advance.

Ontario Northland connects Temagami with North Bay by bus (1¼ hours, two daily) and train (1½ hours, six weekly).

North Bay

POP 54,000

North Bay bills itself as 'just north enough to be perfect,' which begs the question: 'perfect for what?' It's just north enough to make visiting Torontonians feel like hardcore adventurers, although the 'perfection' part still eludes us. Ontario's two major highways (11 and 17) converge just outside of town, making North Bay a logical layover for trans-Canada tourists. The highways link up again near Thunder Bay, 1100km away.

☉ Sights & Activities

Dionne Quints Museum MUSEUM
(☎705-472-8480; 1375 Seymour St N; adult/child $3.50/2; ⊙10am-4pm mid-May–Jun & Sep–mid-Oct, 9am-7pm Jul-Aug) North Bay has never seen the mining-related booms and busts inherent to most towns in northern Ontario. In fact, the area was rather unremarkable until five little girls briefly turned the city into the most visited destination in Ontario after Niagara Falls. These little girls were the Dionne Quints

– identical quintuplets. Born during the Great Depression, they were exploited as a tourist attraction by the provincial government. Their fame became so widespread that they even starred in four Hollywood films. Today, the Dionne Quints Museum contains a fascinating collection of artifacts from their early years. (Their later years haven't been such a happy story – growing up in a zoo, a healthy childhood does not make.)

Lake Nipissing Waterfront   NATURE RESERVE
A walk along scenic Lake Nipissing reveals several enjoyable activities including antique **carousel rides** (705-495-8142; www.northbaycarousel.com; 230 Memorial Dr; ride $1; 10am-10pm Jul-Aug, to dusk Sat-Sun May-Jun & Sept–mid-Oct) and the **Chief Commanda II** (705-494-8167, 866-660-6686; www.chiefcommanda.com; King's Landing, Memorial Dr; mid-May–Sep). This passenger liner cruises through the Manitou Islands (adult/child $21/12), along the French River ($35/19) and down to Callander Bay at sunset ($26/14). Three-hour 'Blues Cruises' are a big hit during the summer (one per month).

🛏 Sleeping

With few quality accommodations options in the downtown area, the best bet is to choose from the endless chain of motels along Lakeshore Dr (south of Marshall St), or try one of the homier choices near Trout Lake to the east.

Gray's Log House   INN $$
(705-495-2389; www.graysloghouse.com; 5270 Hwy 63, Trout Lake; r $90) Escape the downtown bustle and retreat to this lovely log cabin near Trout Lake (5.7km after Average Joe's). Evenings can be spent chatting with the affable owner over homemade desserts, or you can snuggle up with a handmade quilt and watch the snow fall in winter.

Sunset Inn   MOTEL $$
(705-472-8370; www.sunsetinn.on.ca; 641 Lakeshore Dr; d/ste $119/169; ❋ @ 🛜) This cottagelike option along Lake Nipissing has fresh coats of paint and lovely water views. Spice up your love life and get a suite with a retro heart-shaped Jacuzzi.

✕ Eating

Average Joe's   BURGERS $$
(www.averagejoes.net; 3501 Trout Lake Rd; mains $8-23; lunch & dinner) Average Joe's is anything but average. Enjoy tasty fare from the broad menu while staring out over the serene Trout Lake. The bar keeps the gregarious locals around until 1am or 2am.

Kabuki House   JAPANESE $$
(705-495-0999; 349 Main St W; lunch mains $10-15, dinner $23-28; lunch & dinner Mon-Sat, dinner Sun) Dinner here might put a dent in your wallet, but Kabuki House has the best sushi in North Bay (although it's possible this is the only Japanese restaurant in town).

ℹ Information

North Bay Chamber of Commerce (705-472-8480; www.northbaychamber.com; 1357 Seymour St; 9am-7pm Jul-Aug, 9am-5pm Mon-Fri & 10am-4pm Sat-Sun late May-Jun & Sep-late Oct, reduced winter hours) Near the junction of Hwys 11 & 17, 5km south of downtown, beside the Quints museum.

ℹ Getting There & Away

Between Toronto and North Bay, Ontario Northland runs buses (5½ hours, four daily) and trains (five hours, six weekly). Greyhound connects North Bay with Sudbury (1¾ hours, three daily) and Ottawa (5¼ hours, three daily). The terminus for all services is the **North Bay Train Station** (705-495-4200; 100 Station Rd).

EASTERN ONTARIO

If Chicago is the 'Windy City,' and New York is the 'Big Apple,' then eastern Ontario should be called the 'Windy Apple.' This arrowhead-shaped region, between Toronto and Ottawa, has an extensive network of bountiful farmlands and windswept colonial towns. Cool misty gusts roll over the southern seaboard, and further inland the sweeping expanses of dappled branches offer juicy autumn fruits. Travelers journeying between Montréal and Toronto along Hwy 401, the nation's busiest corridor, should allow for an extra couple of days to explore this scenic and historical realm.

For a dose of colonial history, eastern Ontario is tops. Stately Kingston was once the capital of Canada, and today the picturesque city offers myriad museums annotating the nation's military history. Further east, several smaller towns, like Gananoque, Brockville and Prescott, have fostered a genteel Victorian vibe with an abundance of stately inns and estates. Even tiny Merrickville, a former Loyalist stronghold, has barely changed since the American Revolution. These horse-and-buggy townships straddle the stunning Thousand Islands region, a foggy archipelago of lonely isles peppered along the deep St Lawrence Seaway.

Eastern Ontario's natural beauty extends far beyond the misty islets of the Thousand Islands. The region's sparsely populated interior overflows with scenic parks and preserves. The internationally acclaimed Algonquin Provincial Park is the area's flagship domain, offering unparalleled hiking and canoeing through twisting sapphire lakes and towering jack pines. A similar topography extends further south to the Kawarthas and Land O' Lakes, once inhabited by ancient Aboriginal tribes.

This section picks up where the previous section left off. It begins near North Bay in northern Ontario and passes wild wooded regions while working its way south to Lake Ontario. Then, the second half of the section moves east along the St Lawrence Seaway all the way to the Québec border.

Surprisingly, there is still no major highway running directly between Toronto and Ottawa. The speediest option is to take Hwy 401 from Toronto to Prescott, and use Hwy 416 to complete the L-shaped journey. The rural, two-lane Hwy 7 is a pleasant but slower alternative.

Algonquin Provincial Park

Infamous Algonquin is a sight for sore eyes. Established in 1893, Ontario's oldest and largest park offers 7800 sq km of thick pine forests, jagged cliffs, trickling crystal streams, mossy bogs and thousands (thousands!) of lakes. An easily accessible outdoor gem, this rugged expanse is a must-see for canoeists and hikers.

Orientation

The one major road through the park, Hwy 60, runs across a small portion near the southern edge. Each kilometer of highway within the park is tagged, starting at the **West Gate** (known as 'km 0') and terminating at the **East Gate** (known as 'km 56'). Outfitters and accommodations often use the mile-markers when giving directions. For example: 'turn north off Hwy 60 at km 15.4 to reach Arowhon Pines lodge.' Numerous campgrounds and hiking trails are accessible from this well-trodden corridor. The vast, wooded interior of Algonquin is accessible via 2000km of charted canoe routes and intense hiking trails.

Several woodsy communities orbit the provincial park in all directions. The two large Muskoka towns of Bracebridge and Huntsville are within an hour's drive of the West Gate. Other small townships include

Eastern Ontario

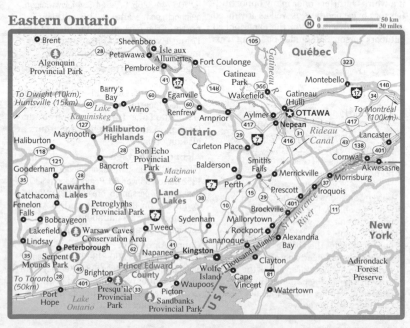

Bancroft, Harcourt and Maynooth in the southeast, while Mattawa, Petawawa and tiny Deux Rivières are north of the park.

◉ Sights & Activities

Algonquin is famous for its wildlife-watching and scenic lookouts. During spring, you're almost certain to see moose along Hwy 60, as they escape the pesky black flies to lick the leftover salt from winter de-icing. Other spotable creatures include deer, beaver, otter, mink and many bird species.

There are two small museums in the park, in addition to the rotating gallery at the visitor center. The excellent **Algonquin Logging Museum** (☎613-637-2828; km 54.5 on Hwy 60; admission free; ☺9am-5pm Jul-Oct) has extensive exhibits and interpretation of the park's logging heritage. The displays are spread along a 1.5km trail that remains open even when the reception area, bookstore and theater are closed. Exhibits at the **Algonquin Art Centre** (www.algonquin artcentre.com; km 20 on Hwy 60; admission free; ☺10am-5:30pm Jun–mid-Oct) display an array of wilderness-themed art through several media including paintings, carvings and sculpture.

If you're toying with the idea of going **canoeing**, Algonquin is a great place to give it a whirl. Outfitters offer many opportunities for novice paddlers as well as advanced wilderness adventures for the experienced outdoors person. Self-guided paddling trips

are a popular option as well. A quota system governs the number of tourists on each canoe route, so plan ahead. Canoe Lake or Opeongo Lake are popular starting points for beginners, although the launching docks are frequently crowded. Water taxis can plow through rougher waters, whisking you up to wilder regions beyond Opeongo Lake; make reservations through **Algonquin Outfitters** (☎800-469-4948, 888-280-8886; www.algonquinoutfitters.com).

Hiking is another popular pastime – there's over 140km of trails, including many shorter jaunts accessible from Hwy 60.

Scenic **horseback riding** is also very popular in and around the park. Contact **Highland Wilderness Tours** (☎613-338-2330, 866-793-9453; www.ridethewilderness.com; 1hr ride $40) or **South Algonquin Trails** (☎705-448-1751, 800-758-4801; www.southalgon quintrails.com; 4378 Elephant Lake Rd, Harcourt; 1hr ride $50); the closest park entrance is the East Gate.

The following outfitters are scattered in and around the park, providing a variety of tours and equipment rentals: canoes ($20 to $40 per day), packed food ($25 per person, per day), stoves ($3 to $6 per day) and tents ($12 per day).

Algonquin North Wilderness Outfitters
OUTFITTERS
(☎705-744-3265, 877-544-3544; www.algon quinnorth.com; Mattawa) This outfitter is north of the park at the junction of Hwy 17 and Hwy 630 in Mattawa; great for more secluded northern access.

Algonquin Outfitters OUTFITTERS
(☎800-469-4948, 888-280-8886; www. algonquinoutfitters.com) Five highly recommended locations in and around the park: Oxtongue Lake, Huntsville, Bracebridge, Opeongo Lake and Brent. Great tours are also on offer.

Algonquin Portage OUTFITTERS
(☎613-735-1795; www.algonquinportage.com; 1352 Barron Canyon Rd, Pembroke; dm $30, camping per person $5, breakfast $8) West of Pembroke on Rte 28 (the road to Achray). On-site rustic accommodations, shuttle service, food and gas available.

Canoe Algonquin OUTFITTERS
(☎705-636-5956, 800-818-1210; www.canoe algonquin.com; 1914 Hwy 518 E, Kearney) North of Huntsville; boat launching at the nearby western access points offers an instantly peaceful setting.

CRYING WOLF

Algonquin Provincial Park is very active in wolf research, and public 'howls' are an incredible way to experience the presence of these furry beasts. Wolves will readily respond to human imitations of their howling, so the park's staff conducts communal howling sessions on the occasional August evening. These events are highly organized – you could be one of 2000 people standing in the darkness waiting for the chilling wails. Wolf howls are announced only on the days they are actually held, so check the bulletin boards, the park website, or phone the visitor center – they usually take place on Thursdays.

TOP FIVE HIKES IN ALGONQUIN PROVINCIAL PARK

Whether you're visiting for a day or a month, these awesome trails are a must! Hikes depart from various mileposts (actually kilometer-posts) along Hwy 60 between the West Gate (km 0) and the East Gate (km 56).

» **Booth's Rock** (difficult 5km loop) – Follow an abandoned railway for breathtaking views of the sweeping lakes and forests (follow the road from km 40).

» **Centennial Ridges** (difficult 10km loop) – The best panoramas in the park, bar none (follow the road from km 37).

» **Lookout Trail** (difficult 1km loop) – The busiest hike in Algonquin, but for good reason: a spectacular view of untouched nature awaits (at km 40).

» **Mizzy Lake** (moderate 11km loop) – An excellent chance to see some diverse wildlife (at km 15).

» **Track & Tower** (moderate 7.7km loop) – A serene lakeside trail and an unusual elevated lookout point along an abandoned railway (at km 25).

Opeongo Outfitters　　OUTFITTERS
(☑800-790-1864; www.opeongooutfitters. com; Hwy 60) Algonquin's oldest outfitter is located just outside the park's East Gate.

Portage Store　　OUTFITTERS
(☑705-633-5622, 705-789-3645; www.por tagestore.com; km 14 on Hwy 60) Located 14km inside the park's West Gate. Bike rentals can be organized at the Lake of Two Rivers Store. Guided tours also available.

☞ Tours

A seemingly infinite number of guided tours is available to all types of adventurers. Along with the following list of specialized tour operators, note that several outfitters offer tour packages as well. Guided trips range from day hikes (starting at $50) to customized remote adventures that last as long as your stamina allows. All have their own lodge base and offer exciting dogsledding programs in the winter.

Call of the Wild　　DOG-SLED TOURS
(☑905-471-9453, 800-776-9453; www. callofthewild.ca) Offers fantastic overnight paddling and dog-sled trips.

Northern Edge Algonquin　　KAYAK TRIPS
(☑800-953-3343; www.algonquincanada.com) Features paddling trips, women's weekends, and tailored programs in winter.

Voyageur Quest　　KAYAK TRIPS
(☑416-496-3605, 800-794-9660; www.voya geurquest.com) Has lodge rentals in addition to popular paddling trips.

🛏 Sleeping & Eating

Algonquin is primarily a nature preserve, which means that most noncamping accommodations are outside the park's boundaries. Scores of accommodations are available just beyond the protected lands, including resorts, motels and hostels (check www.algonquinpark.on.ca for a lengthy list). Day-trippers can save some cash and crash in Huntsville (p149) or Bracebridge (p148), 43km and 73km from the West Gate, respectively. Both Muskoka towns have a variety of restaurants and grocery stores.

Within the park itself, there are three options: stay at one of the 11 car-accessible grounds (either in a tent or a yurt), sleep in the backcountry (accessible only by hiking or canoeing) or rest in the lap of luxury at one of the three high-end resorts. The three apmarket options have restaurants, as does the visitor center (although it's more cafeteria-style).

There are three fabulous hostels in the area, but the cheapest sleeping option at Algonquin is to camp within the park. You must contact the centralized reservation service for **Ontario Parks** (☑519-826-5290, 888-668-7275; www.ontarioparks.com) to make camping, backcountry camping and yurt reservations. There are a couple of first-come first-served sites, but reservations are strongly recommended. There are eight campgrounds with car camping (sites $32.75 to $42.75) and yurts ($85) along Hwy 60, and three additional sites (Achray, Brent and Kiosk) accessible via minor roads further north. Backcountry camping costs $11.50 per person per night.

West Gate

Wolf Den
HOSTEL $

(☎705-635-9336, 866-271-9336; www.wolfdenbunkhouse.com; 4568 Hwy 60, Oxtongue Lake; dm/s $25/42) When does a dorm room become a bunkhouse? When you put up log walls and set it in the wilderness. If you're looking for secluded luxury, you'd better book a room at one of the fancy lodges within the park. But if you're in the backpacking spirit, this hostel has an awesome buzz. Guests stay in shimmering log cabins scattered around the grounds, and a large central lodge offers a huge kitchen and stunning 2nd-floor lounge.

Riverside Motel
MOTEL $$$

(☎705-635-1677, 800-387-2244; www.algonquininn.com; Hwy 60, Dwight; r $199-$299; ❋☀) It may look like a roadside motel, but look closer: on a 4-hectare plot with its own waterfall and swimming hole, this place is something special. You can hear the river from the rooms, some of which come with kitchenettes and Jacuzzi tubs. Flower gardens and walking trails round out the offerings.

Dwight Village Motel
MOTEL $$

(☎705-635-2400; www.dwightvillagemotel.com; 2801 Hwy 60; r $79-149) You'll notice this excellent motel from the highway – the clean pine paneling of the facade is quite striking (we're not so sure about the wildlife photos on the walls inside). Spotless rooms offer all the creature comforts and the friendly owners assure a comfortable stay. It's 25km west of the park, just east of the village of Dwight.

Park Interior

The only permanent resorts within the park are the following upscale lodges, which operate between mid-May and mid-October. Each option includes breakfast, lunch and dinner in the pricing scheme. Dining rooms are open to nonguests as well.

Arowhon Pines
LODGE $$$

(☎866-633-5661; www.arowhonpines.ca; turnoff at km 15.4 on Hwy 60; r per person $193-259, private cabins per person $381-419) If you've ever wondered what it might be like to go to adult summer camp, Arowhon Pines is the answer. The all-inclusive resort has canoes, kayaks, tennis courts, hiking and gourmet meals (BWOW – Bring Your Own Wine). Cabins are a bit rustic, but you won't be spending that much time in them, anyway. The Pines is wonderfully secluded, well north of Hwy 60.

Bartlett Lodge
LODGE $$$

(☎866-614-5355; www.bartlettlodge.com; turnoff at km 23.3 on Hwy 60; cabins per person $205-238) One especially interesting cabin sets this place apart: 'Sunrise' runs completely on solar power. Bartlett Lodge is accessed by boat (provided for you) from a point 23km inside the West Gate.

Killarney Lodge
LODGE $$$

(☎866-473-5551; www.killarneylodge.com; turnoff at km 33.2 on Hwy 60; cabins per person $219-329) The bright paintwork greets you on the outside; inside, cabins are polished wood that is squeaky clean.

East Gate

Magnificent Hill
HOSTEL $

(☎705-448-9453; www.magnificenthill.ca; 1258 Magnificent Rd, Highland Grove; dm $25) Set on a 40-hectare organic farm, this rustic lodging is a huge winner. One dorm room above a woodshop sleeps a handful, while a separate 'Zen room' offers a chill-out space (not that you'd need it in this pastoral setting). Work-stay programs are available, or you can just enjoy the chickens, baby goats, and miles and miles of quiet.

Algonquin Backpackers Hostel
HOSTEL $

(☎613-338-2080, 800-595-8064; www.algonquinbackpacker.com; Hwy 62, Maynooth; HI members dm/d $17/37, nonmembers dm/d $21/45) This older hostel, southeast of the park, was once the Arlington Hotel. Tom, the knowledgeable owner, is a maven, offering invaluable advice for your Algonquin adventure.

ℹ Information

Algonquin Provincial Park is accessible year-round. Drivers can pass through the park along Hwy 60; you must pay the day-use fee to stop and look around ($15 per vehicle). The Hwy 60 corridor has limited cell-phone coverage for several kilometers on each side of the park, as well as a couple of payphones.

Algonquin Visitor Centre (☎613-637-2828; www.algonquinpark.on.ca; km 43 on Hwy 60; ⏱9am-9pm Jul-Aug, to 5pm May, Jun & Oct, 10am-4pm Sat & Sun Nov-Apr) This world-class visitor center is worth a stop in its own right. Displays and dioramas illustrate the park's wildlife, history and geology. The center also has a bookstore, cafeteria, wi-fi and a lookout with spectacular views.

Information centres ($\square$613-637-2828; www.
algonquinpark.on.ca) West Gate (⊙8am-8pm
mid-May–mid-Sep) East Gate (⊙8am-7pm Jul-
Aug, 8am-5pm mid-Sep–mid-Oct, 9am-4:15pm
Fri, Sat & Sun mid-Oct–Mar) Small info centers
at either end of the park along Hwy 60 at km 0
and km 56.

ⓘ Getting There & Away

The closest form of public transportation to
Algonquin Park is the Greyhound bus connecting
Toronto to Maynooth ($54, four hours), 44km
from the East Gate. Hammond Transportation
offers a shuttle service from Huntsville (43km
away) to the park's West Gate. Tourists can
reach Huntsville on an Ontario Northland bus.
Several resorts and hostels offer private shuttle
services into the park (prices range from about
$10 to $35).

Haliburton Highlands

This rugged expanse of needleleaf trees
feels like a southern extension of Algonquin Provincial Park. Over 240 sq km of
the densely forested region is part of the
Haliburton Forest ($\square$705-754-2198; www.
haliburtonforest.com). The privately owned
woodland, 30km north of Haliburton
town, can be accessed through its main
office on Kenneisis Lake. The recommended 'Walk in the Clouds' four-hour
guided hike ($95) takes you on a pulse-
quickening adventure along suspended
planks (20m above the ground) through
the treetops while providing a bird's-eye
view of the woods below. A visit to the
Wolf Centre is included; here visitors
can glimpse a pack of wolves (at a safe
distance, of course) as they meander
through their 6-hectare enclosure. Thick
pillows of snow in the winter encourage a
thriving snowmobiling culture, and dog-
sledding is a popular attraction as well
($185 for a full-day guided tour including
lunch).

The small town of **Bancroft** (www.
bancroftontario.com) is particularly well
known for its mineral-rich soils and the
Rockhound Jamboree – Canada's largest gem festival, held in early August.
During the yearly event, geologists lead
tours around nearby abandoned mines
to scout out stones. These 'rockhounding'
adventures are usually quite successful,
as examples of over 80% of the minerals
found in Canada are regularly dug up in
the area.

Peterborough & the Kawarthas

Peterborough, in the heart of the wooded
Kawarthas, is the best place to start your
visit through this sacred aboriginal land.
The **tourist office** ($\square$800-461-6424; www.
thekawarthas.net; 1400 Crawford Dr; ⊙9am-6pm
Mon & Tue, to 8pm Wed-Sat, Fri & Sat, to 5pm Sun
Jun-Aug, reduced winter hours) should be your
first stop – the helpful staff will point you
in the right direction, be it cultural attractions or scenic nature preserves.

Before leaving the green university town
for more secluded recesses, have a wander
around the quaint city center. Iron rail-
roads scar the urban landscape as they
plow their way through, and the impressive
hydraulic lift lock is another conspicuous
relic of a bygone era.

TOP CHOICE **Canadian Canoe Museum**
($\square$866-342-2663; www.canoemuse
um.net; 910 Monaghan Rd, Peterborough; adult/
child/family $8/6.50/20; ⊙10am-5pm Mon-Sat,
from noon Sun) is a must. Although the outside looks like a warehouse, the refurbished
interior is pure Zen, with dim lighting and
the calming sound of a trickling waterfall.
A phenomenal collection of over 200 canoes and kayaks details the lengthy history
of water navigation in the region. After an
hour at the center, you'll feel inspired to
pick up a paddle.

Day-use only **Petroglyphs Provincial
Park** ($\square$705-877-2552; Hwy 6; admission $13;
⊙10am-5pm mid-May–mid-Oct), 50km north
of Peterborough, probably has the best collection of prehistoric rock carvings in the
country. Rediscovered in 1954, this important spiritual site is home to over 900 icons
carved into the park's limestone ridges (although only a small percentage are discernible). Visitors will be pleased to find that the
site isn't overrun with other tourists.

Serpent Mounds Park ($\square$705-295-6879;
www.serpentmoundspark.com; ⊙May-Oct), south
of town of Rte 34, is the site of an ancient
aboriginal burial ground. It was closed
for renovations when we stopped by; call
for admission prices. North on Rte 38, the
Warsaw Caves Conservation Area ($\square$877-
816-7604; www.warsawcaves.com; admission
per vehicle $10; ⊙mid-May–Oct) offers hiking,
swimming, camping and spelunking in
eroded limestone tunnels.

FREE **Whetung Ojibwa Centre** ($\square$705-
657-3661; www.whetung.com; ⊙9am-
6pm) at Curve Lake, 34km north of Peter-

borough on Hwy 23, has a wonderful collection of aboriginal crafts from around the country, including the valued works of noted artist Norval Morrisseau.

Visit some of the smaller towns in the region, including Lindsay and Fenelon Falls, via 450km of scenic recreational trails, called the **Central Ontario Loop Trail** (www.looptrail.com).

Land O' Lakes

South of the Haliburton Highlands and east of the Kawarthas, the majestic Land O' Lakes region links the vast inland expanse of yawning lakes and bulky evergreens to the temperate pastures of the St Lawrence Seaway. Half of the region belongs to the Thousand Islands–Frontenac Arch reserve – Canada's 12th biosphere, appointed by Unesco in 2002.

The region's crown jewel is the serene **Bon Echo Provincial Park** (⌨613-336-2228, 888-668-7275; Hwy 41; tent & RV sites $30-37; ☺May–mid-Oct), 80km due north of Napanee. One of eastern Ontario's largest preserves, Bon Echo lures artists and adventurers alike, who come looking for a piece of untainted beauty. The park's biggest highlight is the 1.5km sheer rock face known as **Masinaw Rock**. The granite formation sharply juts out of Mazinaw Lake and features the largest visible collection of aboriginal pictographs in all of Canada. The glyphs are best seen from a canoe. For camping reservations and information, contact **Ontario Parks** (⌨519-826-5290, 888-668-7275; www.ontarioparks.com).

Frontenac Provincial Park (⌨613-376-3489; Rte 19; day use per car $13, backcountry sites $11) straddles both the lowlands of southern Ontario and the rugged Canadian Shield, giving the region a unique menagerie of wild plants and animals. The entrance and the information center are at **Otter Lake**, off Rte 19 north of Sydenham. From here, hikers and canoeists venture deep within the park, using the 160km of trails to spot copious beaver, black bear, coyote and osprey. **Frontenac Outfitters** (⌨613-376-6220, 800-250-3174; 6674 Bedford Rd, Sydenham; canoe rental per day $35; ☺8:30am-5pm Mon-Thu, 8am-6pm Fri & Sat, 8am-5pm Sun Apr-Oct) offers canoe rentals near the entrance to the park.

TRENT-SEVERN WATERWAY

This scenic **waterway** (www.trentsevern.com; ☺mid-May–mid-Oct) cuts diagonally across eastern Ontario, following the lakes and rivers of Lake Simcoe County and the forested Kawarthas. This scenic hydrohighway starts on Lake Huron and passes 45 locks before emptying out near Prince Edward County on Lake Ontario. A hundred years ago, this 386km-long aboriginal canoe route bustled with commercial vessels, and today the system is purely recreational.

Brighton & Presqu'ile Provincial Park

Pop off Hwy 401 at exit 509 to find quiet Brighton, and a curious L-shaped **park** (⌨613-475-4324; day use per vehicle summer/winter $11/7, nonhydro/hydro sites $27.75/32.75), which juts out onto Lake Ontario. Relax on the beach amongst migrating birds, or try the **Jobes Wood Trail**, a 1km circular path that's just rural enough to glimpse the diverse woodlands and wildlife. The **interpretive center** (☺mid-Jun–Aug) at the tip of the peninsula provides additional information about local flora and fauna. Overnight camping is only allowed from the end of April to the beginning of October.

Drop by Brighton's **visitor center** (⌨613-475-2775, 877-475-2775; www.brighton.ca; 74 Main St; ☺9am-4pm Mon-Thu, to 7pm Fri, 10am-4pm Sat & Sun) for more information about the town and region of Northumberland. It's worth staying overnight at the immaculate **Pine Breeze** (⌨613-475-6262, 877-369-7779; www.pinebreezebedandbreakfast.com; 93 Simpson St; r incl breakfast $95-120), a modern country home where MaryLou, the owner, puts a fantastic twist on the traditional B&B breakfast by adding ingredients from Mexico, her native country.

Prince Edward County

No, this isn't the green-gabled island inhabited by an infamous Anne – although the two windy islands do have many similar qualities. Like Prince Edward Island, Prince Edward County's undulating pastoral hills are extremely photogenic, as are the myriad water views. Both islands also have an intriguing colonial history. Ontario's little slice of the Maritimes is quietly turning into a hot spot for foodies, with new wineries and rustic gourmet restaurants popping up every season.

The Loyalist Parkway (Hwy 33) unfurls along Lake Ontario, retracing the steps of the British Loyalists who settled here after fleeing the American Revolution. The route runs unbroken for 94km from Trenton to Kingston, save the (free) five-minute ferry ride connecting the island back to the mainland at Adolphustown.

Small-but-active Picton is the unofficial capital of the island.

🛏 Sights & Activities

Sandbanks Provincial Park PARK
(☑613-393-3319; Country Rd 12; day use per vehicle $8-13, campsites $28.75-35.50; ☺mid-Apr–mid-Oct) Immensely popular Sandbanks Provincial Park is divided into two sections: the Outlet (with an irresistible strip of sandy beach) and the Sandbanks (containing most of the area's sand dunes, some over three stories high). This unvisited, undeveloped section at the end of the beach is unlike anywhere else in Ontario.

Cycling CYCLING
Traffic is light on most roads, making the island an excellent cycling destination. Pick up a detailed biking map at the tourism office ($1.50) and swing by Ideal Bike (☑613-476-1913; www.idealbike.com; 172 Main St, Picton; 24hr rental $25; ☺9am-6pm May-Oct) in Picton, to rent equipment for the day. In June, visitors can ride around picking luscious strawberries from the vine at numerous farms.

Lake on the Mountain PARK
Lake on the Mountain, near Glenora, is nothing more than a picnic site, but merits a stop to see the unusual elevated lake with no apparent source. The other side of the road offers picturesque views over Lake Ontario, hundreds of meters below.

Regent Theatre THEATER
(☑613-476-8416; www.theregenttheatre.org; 224 Main St, Picton) The restored Regent Theatre hosts a good series of summer plays, concerts and readings.

☞ Tours

Taste Trail FOOD TOUR
(www.tastetrail.ca) The Taste Trail is a great way to explore the wines and food producers of the county. Pick up a brochure at the tourism office – the self-guided tour, through restaurants, farms and wineries, is a gourmet adventure for the taste buds. The tour includes a stop at the old County Cider Company (☑613-476-1022; www.countycider.com; Country Rd 8, admission free; ☺10am-6pm mid-May–mid-Oct), which is perched on a high hill above a scenic bay and offers complimentary samples of the delicious house-brewed hard ciders. The white-gabled Waupoos Winery (☑613-476-8338; www.waupooswinery.com; Country Rd 8; tour $5, tasting $1; ☺10:30am-6pm mid-May–mid-Oct), with its patio overlooking the vines and lake, is worth a stop.

Arts Trail ARTS TOUR
(www.artstrail.ca) The Arts Trail is a self-guided tour leading txo 27 studios and galleries across the island. Ceramics, glassworks, photography, jewelry and painting are some of the mediums you'll encounter.

NORMAN HARDIE: VINTNER

Prince Edward County has the same soil composition as France's Burgundy, a mix of clay and soft (calcitic) limestone. It wasn't until recently, however, that we've been able to develop techniques to manage PEC's cooler winter climates. It's because of these techniques that winemakers are flooding the county and we're being recognized for our fine wine.

The county has always had a great agricultural history, which is now being revived. There's also been a discovery of how beautiful it is: great beaches, an arts culture, and now an emerging wine culture. PEC is only two hours from Toronto and four to Montréal, making it a perfect 'quick getaway' destination.

Top Local Eats

» Blümen Garden Bistro (p182)

» Fifth Town Cheeses (p182)

🛏 Sleeping & Eating

If you're contemplating a camping adventure during your travels, Prince Edward County is the best place to pitch your tent. The island also has an astounding number of B&Bs scattered amongst its three largest towns: Picton, Bloomfield and Wellington. The tourism office has a detailed lodging list – most options are Victorian-styled homes at an average price of around $125 per night.

Red Barns HOSTEL, B&B $$
(☑613-476-6808; www.theredbarns.com; 167 White Chapel Rd; dm/d $50/125; P❀❀) It's difficult to classify Red Barns: part hostel, part B&B, part art school, this 10-hectare retreat has it all. Artists rent studio space (there's a glass-blowing studio and a wood-shop) or participate in workshops; you'll likely be sharing with some of them. B&B rooms are in the farmhouse, while dorms share a common room in an outbuilding.

Sandbanks Provincial Park CAMPGROUND $
(☑519-826-5290, 888-668-7275; www.ontario parks.com; tent/RV from $31.50/46) Camping at Sandbanks Provincial Park is both scenic and stress-free, but sites along the sandy dunes get booked months in advance during summer. There are some extra first-come first-served options as well, so don't forget to set your alarm the night before – these sites go fast.

The park also has two rentable cottages: **Maple Rest Guest House** (per day $312) and **Jacques Family Cottage** (per day $139.75), both requiring a two-night minimum stay. Both chalets feature several bedrooms, a working fireplace, satellite TV and a full kitchen.

TOP CHOICE **Blūmen Garden Bistro** FUSION $$
(☑613-476-6841; www.blūmengarden bistro.com; 647 Hwy 49, Picton; lunch $12-16, dinner $19-23; ☺lunch & dinner) Serving high-end cuisine without the pretense, the friendly owners of Blūmen promote 'honest food.' Everything is under $30, even though many selections are worth more. Dishes, such as the pear and goat cheese turnovers, feature local ingredients and can be paired with Prince Edward County wines. As if that weren't enough, the restaurant feels like the living room of your hip, arty friends: comfortable but cool. And, true to its name, the bistro features a lovely garden, where stepping stones lead to private, candle-lit tables surrounded by fragrant flowers. Reservations recommended.

Fifth Town Cheeses CHEESERY $$
(www.fifthtown ca; 4309 County Rd 8, Picton; ice cream $4, cheese $7-18; ☺10am-5pm Mar-Jun, to 6pm Jul & Aug, to 5pm Wed-Sun Sep-Dec) Pop into this funky, solar-powered dairy for a scoop of lavender honey goat cheese ice cream, taste the spread of goat and sheep cheeses, and then leave with a sack full of them. You can enjoy your snack on the grounds, which has an eating pavilion and a cheese lover's herb garden, or take it back to your accommodation and pair it with a PEC chardonnay.

County Cider Company CAFE $$
(County Rd 8, Picton; mains $11-14 ☺lunch mid-May–mid-Mar) Served on a hilltop patio, surrounded by a vineyard and overlooking the lake, lunch consists of pizzas, burgers, salads, and wraps made up of local ingredients.

ℹ Information

Chamber of Tourism & Commerce (☑613-476-2421, 800-640-4717; www.pecchamber. com, www.thecounty.travel; 116 Main St, Picton; ☺9am-5pm Mon-Sat, 10am-4pm Sun) Offers touring brochures and cycling maps, and will help with booking B&Bs and bike rentals.

Kingston

POP 115,000

Curious Kingston wears many hats. The eccentric colonial town, known fittingly as the 'Limestone City,' is stocked with clunky halls of hand-cut stone and prim redbrick Victorian mansions. The attractive city continues to maintain its charm with a noticeable lack of modern architectural eyesores.

Further exploration reveals Kingston's quirks. The city has the largest holding of convicts in the country. Don't worry, they're not lurking in dark alleyways ready to pounce; they're locked up in the nearby penitentiary. The flagship of Canada's penal system, Kingston has a slew of prisons and the Royal Military College is conveniently nearby.

Queen's University, founded in 1841, adds a dash of hot-blooded youthfulness to the mix. An excellent assortment of dining options with student-friendly prices have opened up over the last couple of decades, and the city's nightlife is surprisingly pumping.

Once the nation's capital, Kingston was stripped of the title when Queen Victoria worried that it was too close to the American border and could not be properly defended. Today, Kingston finds itself strategically placed for the perfect tourist pit stop between Montréal and Toronto.

🛏 Sights

Conveniently, most sites are found around the central, historic downtown.

Fort Henry National Historic Site
HISTORICAL SITE

(☑613-542-7388; www.forthenry.com; Fort Henry Dr; adult/child/concession $14.25/9.95/13 mid-May–Aug, Sep $10/3/7; ☺10am-5pm mid-May–Sep) This restored British fortification, dating from 1832, dominates the town from its hilltop perch. The postcard-perfect structure is brought to life by colorfully uniformed guards trained in military drills, artillery exercises and the fife-and-drum music of the 1860s. The soldiers put on displays throughout the day; don't miss the 3pm Garrison Parade. Admission includes a guided tour of the fort's campus.

City Hall
NOTABLE BUILDING

(261 Ontario St; ☑9am-4pm Mon-Fri, also 11am-3pm Sat & Sun Jul-Aug) The grandiose City Hall is one of the country's finest classical buildings, and a relic from the time when Kingston was the capital of the United Provinces of Canada. Friendly red-vested volunteers conduct free tours on request, revealing colorful stained glass, dozens of portraits, dusty jail cells and an ornate council chamber.

Marine Museum of the Great Lakes
MUSEUM

(www.marmuseum.ca; 55 Ontario St; adult/child/family $8.50/5.50/20; ☺10am-4pm mid-May–Oct) Kingston was an important shipbuilding center, and this museum sits on the site of the old shipyard. Exhibits offer a detailed history of the fascinating vessels constructed at the yard.

Pump House Steam Museum
MUSEUM

(www.steammuseum.ca; 23 Ontario St; adult/child/concession $4.25/2.25/3.50; ☺10am-4pm late May-early Sep, 10am-4pm Mon-Fri Mar-late May) The one-of-a-kind, completely restored, steam-run pump house was first used in 1849. Today the warehouse features all things steam-related, including two full-model train sets as well as the recently restored steamboat *Phoebe*.

Bellevue House
MUSEUM

(35 Centre St; www.parkscanada.gc.ca; admission $3.90; ☺9am-6pm Jun-Aug, 10am-4pm Sep & Oct) This national historic site was once home to Sir John A Macdonald, Canada's first prime minister and a notorious alcoholic. It seems the architect was also a drunk, as the Italianate mansion is wholly asymmetrical, a pompous use of bright color abounds, and balconies twist off in various directions. There are also plenty of antiques and a sun-drenched garden, adding further charm and intrigue to the old manor.

FREE Royal Military College Museum
MUSEUM

(www.rmc.ca; Frederick Dr; ☺10am-5pm late Jun-early Sep) This museum, on the grounds of the military college off Hwy 2 E, is inside the Fort Frederick Martello Tower, the largest of the city's historic towers. The exhibits detail the history of the century-old military school and there's a donated collection of small arms from General Porfirio Diaz, president of Mexico from 1876 to 1911.

Murney Tower Museum
MUSEUM

(Macdonald Park, cnr Barrie St & King St E; adult/family $3/10; ☺10am-5pm mid-May–Sep) Now a national historic site, this swollen Martello defense structure from 1846 was constructed to supplement the riverside fortifications at Fort Henry. The Bloomfield cannon and various carronades are on sight, as well as other military artifacts.

Military Communications & Electronics Museum
MUSEUM

(www.c-and-e-museum.org; Hwy 2 E; admission by donation; ☺9am-1pm Mon-Fri, 11am-5pm Sat & Sun mid-May–Sep) Despite the driest of names, this is a comprehensive and well-designed museum offering chronological displays on communications technology and sundry military gadgets. It's on the military base.

FREE Kingston Archaeological Centre
MUSEUM

(☑613-542-3483; 72 Gilmour Ave; ☺9:30am-4pm Mon-Fri) If you've been traveling along the boring stretch of Hwy 401, you probably spotted the sedimentary rock outcrops – the only interesting thing on the road. Swing by the archaeological center to learn more about the craggy formations, and while you're there check out the archaeological record detailing the 8000-year-old human history of the area.

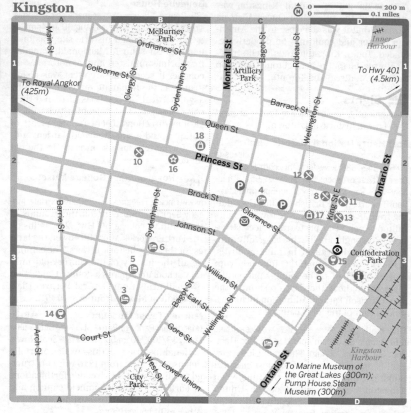

Offbeat Kingston

Penitentiary Museum   MUSEUM

(www.penitentiarymuseum.ca; 555 King St W; admission by donation; ⊙9am-4pm Mon-Fri, from 10am Sat & Sun May-Oct) The 'correctional service' is what Canadian bureaucrats call the nation's jail system, and this museum is a good way to enter a prison system without stealing a car. The museum, across from the actual penitentiary, has a fascinating collection of weapons and tools confiscated from inmates during attempted escapes.

☞ Tours

Confederation Tour Trolley   TROLLEY TOUR

(☎613-548-4453; www.kingstonchamber.on.ca; 50min tours adult/concession $14.50/12.50; ⊙mid-May–mid-Oct) A trackless mini-train departs regularly from the tourist office area for tours of downtown Kingston with cheery historical commentary.

Haunted Walk   WALKING TOUR

(☎613-549-6366; www.hauntedwalk.com; 90min tours adult/child/concession $13/7/11; ⊙8pm May-Oct, 7pm Nov & Feb-May) Tours featuring stories of hangings and grave robbers leave from 200 Ontario St, in front of the Prince George Hotel.

FREE **Interesting Places & Spaces**   AUDIO TOUR

(www.kingstonaudiotours.com) Kingston has leapt into the future of tourism by offering downloadable walking tours for your iPod. Check out the website, or stop by the Kingston Tourism office in Confederation Park.

Kingston 1000 Island Cruises   BOAT TOURS

(☎613-549-5544; www.1000islandcruises.on.ca; 1 Brock St; ⊙mid-May–mid-Oct) Has several cruises leaving from the *Island Queen* dock, on Ontario St at the foot of Brock St. A 1½-hour trip (adult/child $24/12) takes you along the Kingston shoreline with com-

Kingston

mentary on noteworthy sites. Throughout the summer there are two or three trips a day. The extended lunch and dinner cruises ($46.50 and $66 respectively) are popular.

★ Festivals & Events

Visit www.kingstoncanada.com for a complete list of events throughout the year.

Kingston Buskers Rendezvous MUSIC FESTIVAL
(www.kingstonbuskers.com) Four days of tomfoolery in July.

Limestone City Blues Festival MUSIC FESTIVAL
(www.kingstonblues.com) All-star musicians gather for a four-day jam session in August.

Sleeping

Accommodations in Kingston are top heavy, with a larger confluence of pricier stays than budget options. Motels are

strung along Princess St and along Hwy 2 on each side of town. The knowledgeable staff at the tourism office in Confederation Park can help track down additional options, including on Wolfe Island. B&B buffs should check out www.historicinnskingston.com for extra ritzy digs.

Jean's Guest House B&B $$
(☑613-546-5247; www.pnworks.com/guesthouse; 367 College St; s/d incl breakfast $60/80; 🅿⊖🔊) Parked along a quiet suburban street, this cheery option is about 2km from the city center. Awaken from a restful slumber with a colorful breakfast as Jean dotes over her famous blueberry pancakes.

Rosemount Inn B&B $$
(☑613-531-8844, 888-871-8844; www.rosemountinn.com; 46 Sydenham St; r $149-299; 🅿⊖❄🔊) Enjoy a decadent stay at this former dry goods merchant's home. Built in 1850, the massive stone building features arched doorways and intricate flooring. A small spa offers wine baths and chocolate face masks, and the full breakfast (prepared by two chefs) includes gourmet chocolate.

Queen's Inn BOUTIQUE HOTEL $$
(☑613-546-0429, 866-689-9177; www.queensinn.ca; 125 Brock St; r $89-159; ⊖❄🔊) Constructed in 1839, the Queen's Inn is one of the oldest hotels in the country. The outside has a stately limestone facade, while the interior has undergone a recent remodel. Some rooms have stone walls, dormer windows and leafy views. A downstairs pub and the downtown location make this place a worthy option. Parking is $5.

Stone's Throw B&B $$
(☑613-544-6089; www.astonesthrow.ca; 21 Earl St; r incl breakfast $129-159; 🅿⊖@) The 200-year-old home, cut from chunks of limestone, is just a stone's throw from Lake Ontario. Three dapper bedrooms, with charming exposed brick, hide behind the navy-blue shutters. Hearty, healthy breakfasts are made from local and organic ingredients.

Secret Garden B&B $$
(☑613-531-9884, 877-723-1888; www.the-secret-garden.com; 73 Sydenham St; r incl breakfast $129-192; 🅿⊖❄🔊) Whether you recline in the stately salons with dripping chandeliers overhead, or retreat upstairs to your canopied bed, don't forget to say hello to tiny Mork and Mindy, the resident dogs.

Hochelaga Inn

B&B $$

(☑613-549-5534, 877-933-9433; www.hochelaga inn.com; 24 Sydenham St; r $120-215; P🅿❄@) If the Addams family had good taste rather than a penchant for the macabre, they'd feel right at home peering out the large Gothic windows in this enchanting inn. And speaking of ghouls, it is said that the ghost of a young crying boy haunts the old nursery, which has since been converted into a cheery day spa. The lucky guests who stay in the Tower Suite could have a séance in their lofty private meditation room.

Alexander Henry

B&B $$

(☑613-542-2261; www.marmuseum.ca; 55 Ontario St; ☉Jul-Aug; P) The museum ship *Alexander Henry*, moored at the Marine Museum of the Great Lakes, becomes a summertime B&B. When we visited, this unique sleeping opportunity was closed indefinitely but call to check if it's reopened.

✕ Eating

Thank you, Queen's University, for being close by and sparking the proliferation of tasty options at student-friendly prices.

TOP CHOICE Pan Chancho

BAKERY $

(www.panchancho.com; 44 Princess St; mains $12; ☉breakfast & lunch) Enter past the large peel-wielding pig to uncover this gourmand's paradise. Light and savory lunches fuse unlikely ingredients into palate-pleasing dishes. Try the fennel and cream-cheese spread – perfect on any of the freshly baked breads. Students will get a handy 15% discount.

Luke's

FUSION $$

(☑613-531-7745; www.lukesgastronomy.com; 264 Princess St; lunch $6-12, dinner $17-25; ☉11:30am-3pm & 5:30-9pm Wed-Sat, 11am-3pm Sun) A master charcutier and child prodigy, young Luke was born in 1993 and is the genius behind the restaurant. While waiting for your meal, take a moment to read the resto manifesto, promising that each dish is lavished with a generous portion of TLC. The true essence of Luke's is distilled in the club sandwich – a unique ensemble of homemade bread, crispy bacon cured in-house, and local organic produce.

Chez Piggy

FUSION $$

(☑613-549-7673; 68-R Princess St; mains $14-26; ☉11am-midnight) Hidden in a flowery stone courtyard, the city's best-known restaurant has earned its reputation with an innovative menu, charming ambience and memorable weekend brunches. Mains include confit of Muscovy duck leg and seared Togarashi sea scallops, and the bread is freshly baked down the street at Pan Chancho. Reservations are strongly recommended on weekends.

Sleepless Goat

CAFE $

(www.thesleepless goat.ca; 91 Princess St; lunch $5-7, dinner $8-10; ☉7am-11pm Mon-Thu, to midnight Fri, 8am-midnight Sat, 8am-11pm Sun; ☑) With a name that sounds like an Alanis Morissette lyric, it's no surprise that this low-key joint attracts gaggles of artists and angsty intellectual types. A self-proclaimed co-op, the restaurant is run by a clan of savvy cooks who churn out the tastiest veggie options in town.

Kingston Brewing Company

BURGERS $$

(34 Clarence St; mains $7-14; ☉11am-2am) Chow down on tasty tavern munchies amid flickering Christmas lights and kitschy beer-themed paraphernalia, or make a meal of it and grab a patio table outside. Whatever you do, be sure to try the homemade brew: the Dragon's Breath Ale will put a fire in your belly and the White Tail Cream Ale is so popular, they've begun to bottle it.

Tango

TAPAS $$

(☑613-531-0800; www.thetango.ca; 331 King St; mains $9-20; ☉11am-2am) Kingston's attempt at downtown sophistication is a fresh combustion of DJ beats and tapas treats. Weekends are dominated by the loosened ties and popped collars of local financiers after a long week at the office. Quieter weekdays have discounted tapas and martini options.

Royal Angkor

INDIAN $

(523 Princess St; mains $5-7; ☉11:30am-3pm & 5-10pm Mon-Sat, 5-9pm Sun) When looking up 'hole in the wall' in the dictionary, you just might find a picture of this Southeast Asian eatery. It doesn't get simpler than this – a sparsely decorated sitting area and a couple of pots and pans. But who really cares about atmosphere when the homemade dishes burst with fresh ingredients and come at unbeatable prices?

🍷 Drinking & Entertainment

Grand Theatre

THEATER

(☑613-530-2050; www.kingstongrand.ca; 218 Princess St) Once an opera house, then a movie theater, and now the city's premier venue for theater, the symphony, concerts and comedy, the Grand has undergone extensive renovations since 1967, including a massive overhaul in 2008.

Toucan
PUB

(www.thetoucan.ca; 76 Princess St) Kingston's oldest Irish pub is tucked away in an old stone alley near King St. Traditional British pub fare is served alongside sweet potato fries and poutine, and the $2.99 Sunday breakfast will help with the hangover.

Tir nan Og
PUB

(www.kingston.tirnanogpubs.com; 200 Ontario St) Set inside one of the oldest and most charming buildings along the waterfront, this Irish oasis serves up live music and overflowing pints, as well as a full menu.

Grad Club
LIVE MUSIC

(www.queensu.ca/gradclub; 162 Barrie St) Housed in an imposing Victorian mansion, this Queen's campus mainstay is one of the hottest venues for live music.

Shopping

Cooke's Fine Foods
FOOD & DRINK

(www.cookesfinefoods.com; 61 Brock St) Take a look in this gourmet shop with old wooden counters and a century-old pressed-metal ceiling. There are lovely aromas and a curious assortment of goods (and shoppers).

Trailhead
OUTDOOR GEAR

(☑613-546-4757; 237 Princess St) For quality outdoor/camping equipment and supplies.

Open-Air Market
MARKET

(King St) On Tuesday, Thursday, Saturday and Sunday, a small open-air market – the oldest continuous market in Canada – takes place downtown, behind City Hall.

Information

Hotel Dieu Hospital (☑613 544 3310; 166 Brock St; ☺emergency room 8am-10pm) Centrally located.

Kingston Tourism (☑613-548-4415, 888-855-4555; www.kingstoncanada.com; 209 Ontario St; ☺9am-8pm mid-Jun–Aug, 9am-4pm May–mid-Jun & Sep-Oct, 10am-4pm Nov-Apr) A useful info center across from City Hall in Confederation Park.

Post office (www.canadapost.ca; 120 Clarence St)

Getting There & Away

The **Kingston Coach Terminal** (☑613-547-4916; 1175 John Counter Blvd) is 1km south of Hwy 401, just west of Division St. Coach Canada offers regular services throughout the day to Toronto ($29, three hours) and Montréal ($31, three hours). Buses also stop at various towns including Cornwall and Brockville. Check out www.coachcanada.com and www.megabus.com for more information.

If you're arriving by car on Hwy 401, exits 611, 613, 615, 617, 619 and 623 will lead you downtown. For car rental, try **Enterprise** (☑613-389-8969; 2244 Princess St), which offers complimentary pickup and drop-off.

The **VIA Rail-Kingston station** (☑888-842-7245; 1800 John Counter Blvd) is about 400m east of where Princess St and John Counter Blvd meet. VIA Rail runs four daily trains to Montréal ($82, 2½ hours), three to Ottawa ($52, two hours) and eight to Toronto ($84, 2½ hours). Extra trains run during the summer.

Getting Around

For information on getting around by bus, call **Kingston Transit** (☑613-546-0000). To get to town from the bus terminal, there is a city bus stop across the street; buses depart 15 minutes before and after the hour. From the train station, bus 1 stops on the corner of Princess St and John Counter Blvd, just a short walk from the bus station. Frequency is decreased on Sundays.

Cyclists will be happy to note that the Kingston area is generally flat, and both Hwys 2 and 5 have paved shoulders. Rentals are available at **Ahoy Rentals** (☑613-539-3202; www.ahoyrentals.com; 23 Ontario St; bike rental per day $25).

Wolfe Island

The most exciting part of Wolfe Island is the free mini-cruise on the **car ferry** (☑613-548-7227) that links Kingston to the island. The 25-minute trip affords views of the city, the fort and a few of the Thousand Islands. The largest island in the chain, Wolfe Island is actually bigger than Kingston; however, what was mostly undeveloped farmland is now home to 86 wind turbines. Though there is still plenty of farmland, there's no doubt that Wolfe Island's commerce is wind farming.

The island is cycle-friendly, with four routes marked with colored signs. Download a map at www.wolfeisland.com, or stop by the information center in Kingston for info on an alternate way to explore the terrain.

The 150-year-old **General Wolfe Hotel** (☑613-385-2611, 800-353-1098; www.generalwolfehotel.com; r $60-120; [P][❋][☎]) will give you another excuse to visit. The formal dining room serves award-winning cuisine (the casual dining room has pool tables and pastas, pizzas and stir fries). Try the many courses of the *table d'hôte* ($35), lavished with sirloin steak, pheasant and pork.

On the Kingston side, the ferry terminal is at the intersection of Ontario and Barrack Sts. The ferry runs continuously every hour or so from 5:45am to 1:20am daily, taking about 50 vehicles at a time. From the beginning of May to mid-October, there is a separate, 10-minute **Horne's ferry** (☑613-385-2402; passenger/car $2/13) connecting Wolfe Island to Cape Vincent, New York – don't forget your passport!

Gananoque

Pleasant Gananoque (gan-an-*awk*-way) is the perfect place to rest your eyes after a long day of squinting at the furry green islands on the misty St Lawrence. The dainty Victorian town, deep in the heart of the Thousand Islands region, teems with cruise-hungry tourists during summer and early fall. Virtually every motel chain is represented along King St E near Hwy 401, and a score of one-of-a-kind digs are found along the water's edge.

The **Chamber of Commerce** (☑613-382-3250, 800-561-1595; www.1000islands gananoque.com; 10 King St E; ☺8:30am-8pm Jun-Aug, 9am-5pm Sep-May) offers basic services like lodging recommendations. Check out www.gananoque.com for additional info.

Like most other towns in the Thousand Islands region, Gananoque is home to several river cruise operators. Shop around before choosing a company – some trips stop at several islands, others don't; some offer dinner cruises, while others specialize in quicker trips on faster boats. The **Gananoque Boat Line** (☑613-382-2144, 888-717-4837; www.ganboatline.com; 6 Water St; 1hr tours adult/child $20/11, 2½hr tours $30/11, castle cruise $36/11; ☺May–mid-Oct) is a popular choice, with several trip options including a stopover at Boldt Castle. (The castle is technically in the USA, so make sure all your papers are in order if you are planning to visit.)

If you're feeling energetic, a great way to tour the islands is by paddling. **1000 Islands Kayaking** (☑613-329-6265; www.1000ikc.com; adult/child full-day guided trip $125/65, half-day $85/45, half-day rentals s/d $35/50) has a multitude of packages, including courses and overnight trips.

The **Thousand Islands Playhouse** (☑613-382-7020, 866-382-7020; www.1000 islandsplayhouse.com; 185 South St) has pre-sented a quality lineup of mainly light summer theater since 1983.

Gananoque sports an abundance of memorable accommodations options, including several upmarket and architecturally eye-catching inns.

TOP CHOICE **Victoria Rose Inn** (☑613-382-3386, 888-246-2893; www.victoria roseinn.com; 279 King St W; d incl breakfast $155-255); ✱⊜☎, once the mayor's house and a monument to Victorian splendor, has been refurbished to its original elegance. A glassed-in veranda overlooks garden terraces, and the rooms are comfortable and spacious. A friendly family runs the Victoria Rose and is an excellent source of local information.

The large **Gananoque Inn** (☑888-565-3101; www.gananoqueinn.com; 550 Stone St S; r $179-395), with its signature green shutters, regally sits at the junction of the Gananoque River and the St Lawrence Seaway. The old carriage-works inn opened its doors in 1896, and has retained much of its charm while surreptitiously adding modern amenities like a luxurious day spa. Bike and boat rentals are offered. Half-priced rooms are available in the off-season.

Located about 4km east of Gananoque on the Thousand Islands Pkwy, **Misty Isles Lodge** (☑613-382-4232; www.mistyisles.ca; 25 River Rd, Lansdowne; r from $75) is a laid-back beachfront property boasting comfortable units with wicker furnishings. A variety of adventure outfitting is offered as well, including kayak rentals (per day $40), guided tours (day tour $69) and camping packages on some of the river's shrubby islands.

The only thing better than staying near the seaway is staying *on* the seaway! The main office for **Houseboat Holidays** (☑613-382-2842; www.gananoque.com/hhl; RR3, Gananoque; weekend/midweek/weekly rates from $650/850/1350), just 3km east of Gananoque along Hwy 2, will set you up with your very own floating hotel and provides a brief instructional course for nautical newbies.

Thousand Islands

The 'Thousand Islands' is a constellation of over 1800 rugged islands dotting the St Lawrence River from Kingston to Brockville. The lush archipelago offers loose tufts of fog, showers of trillium petals, quaking tide-pools and opulent 19th-century summer mansions, whose turrets pierce the prevailing mist.

The narrow, slow-paced **Thousand Islands Parkway** dips south of Hwy 401 between Gananoque and Elizabethtown, running along the river for 35km before rejoining the highway. The scenic journey winds along the pastoral strip of shoreline offering picture-perfect vistas and dreamy picnic areas. The **Bikeway** bicycle path extends the full length of the parkway.

In **Ivylea**, a series of soaring bridges link Ontario to New York State over several islands. Halfway across, you'll find the **Skydeck** ([phone]613-659-2335; www.1000 islandsskydeck.com; Hill Island; adult/child $9.75/5.75; [hours]9am-dusk mid-Apr–Oct), a 125m-high observation tower offering some fantastic views of the archipelago from three different balconies.

Rockport, the largest village along the Thousand Islands Pkwy, lies just beyond a cluster of stone churches. There are two large cruise lines that operate out of Rockport, both offering optional stopovers at the gorgeous, rambling **Boldt Castle**, an unfinished Gothic palace of dark spires and stone facades. The castle is technically in the USA, so make sure all your papers are in order if you are planning to visit. **Rockport Boat Line** ([phone]613-659-3402, 800-563-8687; www.rockportcruises.com; 23 Front St; [hours]May-Oct) offers a variety of cruising options including a popular two-hour cruise ($28), which departs three times per day and offers a look-see past the castle. Cruises with a stopover at the castle (adult/child/concession $30/12/26, plus admission fee adult/child US$7/4.50) allow you to explore the grounds. Lunch and dinner cruise options are also available ($39 and $59 respectively).

In Mallorytown, the **St Lawrence Islands National Park** ([phone]613-923-5261; backcountry campsites $15, plus docking fees depending on boat size) preserves a gentle green archipelago, consisting of over 20 islands scattered between Kingston and Brockville. A walking trail and interpretive center allow visitors to learn more about the lush terrain and resident wildfire. Over a dozen of the freckle-sized islands support backcountry camping (between mid-May and early September) and they are accessible only by boat (BYO boat).

Brockville

Attractive Brockville marks the eastern edge of the Thousand Islands region. The 'City of the Thousand Islands,' as it's known, has a cache of extravagant estates. Rows of Gothic spires twisting skyward make it easy to imagine that the clip-clop of carriage horses once rang through the streets. It's also the end of the Unesco World Heritage Rideau Canal.

Sights & Activities

Brockville Museum   MUSEUM
([phone]613-342-4397; www.brockvillemuseum.com; 5 Henry St; adult/child $4/2; [hours]10am-5pm Mon-Sat, from 1pm Sun mid-May–mid-Oct, 10am-4:30pm Mon-Fri mid-Oct–mid-May) Take a look at the area's history here, where you'll find displays on Brockville's railroad past, its hat-making industry and other community tidbits. The museum encompasses the Isaac Beecher house, a historic landmark and example of a typical New England home built before American independence.

Fulford Place   MUSEUM
([phone]613-498-3003; 287 King St E; adult/child/concession $5/free/4; [hours]11am-4pm Tue-Sun)

FRONTENAC ARCH BIOSPHERE RESERVE

One of only 15 Unesco-designated reserves in Canada, Frontenac Arch encompasses a small portion of the Canadian Shield that extends down through Ontario. What was once a range of towering mountains has been weathered down to rolling hills and rugged cliffs – still quite dramatic after driving through flatlands. Archeological finds in the area indicate that it was once part of a human migration route; knives from the Yellowknife region as well as shells from the Caribbean have been found in the area.

The 2700 sq km reserve has ample recreation opportunities, from biking and hiking to canoeing and diving. It's easily accessed from Hwy 401, between Gananoque and Brockville. The excellent www.explorethearch.ca will guide you to various entry points, or contact **Brockville District Tourism** ([phone]613-342-4357; www.brockvilletourism.com; 10 Market St; [hours]8am-8pm mid-May–Oct, 8:30am-4:30pm Mon-Fri Nov–mid-May).

This 35-room Edwardian mansion from the 1900s was once the home of George Taylor Fulford, the producer of the 'Pink Pill for Pale People.' Today, the sprawling place is a monument to patented prescription drugs. If that's not your cup of tea, consider enjoying the veranda for the daily afternoon tea service ($15). Admission includes a guided tour.

Brockville Arts Centre   THEATER
(☑613-342-7122, 8877-342-7122; www.brockville artscentre.com; 235 King St W) Built in 1858 as Brockville's Town Hall, what is now the Arts Centre has survived one fire and several incarnations. Today, it doubles as a theater and art gallery, where big names (Harry Connick Jr and Blue Rodeo, to name just a couple) share the space with local artists.

1000 Islands Cruises   BOAT TOURS
(%613-342-7333, 800-353-3157; www.1000islandscruises.com; Broad St; hmid-May–mid-Oct) Offers sightseeing tours of the 1000 Islands, including a 2½-hour cruise past Singer Castle ($28.50).

🛏 Sleeping & Eating

Nearby Prescott has some intriguing accommodations options, though Brockville has plenty to satisfy.

TOP CHOICE **Green Door**   B&B **$$**
(☑613-341-9325;www.bbcanadacom/104 11.html; 61 Buell St; s/d from $85/99; P ❷ ❧) The friendly owners have converted an old brick tabernacle into this comfortable B&B. Crisp sunlight dances through the ample common space during the day and evenings are spent by the piano, or snuggled up in an antique bed.

Victoria Inn   B&B **$$**
(☑613-341-1203; www.brockvillevictoriainn.ca;10 Victoria Ave; r $100-150; P ❷ ❋ ❧) With a turret that inspires Rapunzel re-enactments, the Victoria Inn charms. Choose from one of the two suites, an apartment, or a basic room.

Buell Street Bistro   FUSION **$$**
(☑613-345-2623; www.brockvillevictoriainn.ca; 27 Buell St; mains $12-20; ☉lunch & dinner Mon-Fri, dinner Sat & Sun) Three levels and a delectable patio break the space up at this locals' favorite. Seafood and pasta dishes mingle with Thai and Indian flavors – there's enough variety to please the fussiest of palates.

❶ Information

Brockville District Tourism (☑613-342-4357; www.brockvilletourism.com; 10 Market St; ☉8am-8pm mid-May–Oct, 8:30am-4:30pm Mon-Fri Nov–mid-May) Open year-round and provides ample information about attractions all along the seaway.

❶ Getting There & Away

Via Rail trains leave Brockville's **train station** (141 Perth St) for Toronto (eight daily, three hours, $101) and Ottawa (five daily, 1¼ hours, $36). Buses are more frequent to Ottawa than to Toronto, though Coach Canada runs one to two buses per day to and from Toronto ($72).

Prescott

Prescott could be Brockville's younger brother – it's smaller, scrappier, and it hasn't quite developed into a full-fledged city of its own. The 19th-century town is home to the International Bridge to Ogdensburg, New York State and, more interestingly, the **Fort Wellington National Historic Site** (☑613-925-2896; adult/child $3.90/1.90; ☉10am-5pm mid-May–Sep). The original fort was built during the War of 1812 and was used again as a strategic locale in 1838 when an American invasion seemed imminent. Some original fortifications remain, as does a blockhouse and officers' quarters. Wellington will be undergoing renovations and development of new exhibits (including a 50-ft gunboat hull); call to see what's new and open.

Prescott offers some of the most original accommodations options along the St Lawrence. **Ship's Anchor Inn B&B** (☑613-925-3573; www.shipsanchorinn.com; 495 King St W; d $99-145; P ❷ ❋) is a 175-year-old manor made of hand-cut stone, and was once the beachside abode of a crusty sea captain. The somewhat overstuffed home retains a sea shanty theme with schools of taxidermic fish and models of wooden frigates. Hearty English breakfasts, fit for a sailor, will keep you chugging along until dinnertime.

Dewar's Inn (☑613-925-3228, 877-433-9277; www.dewarsinn.com; Hwy 2; r $77-85, cottage $98-104; P ❧ ❋) – yes, like the whiskey – isn't much to look at from the road, but was constructed from the bricks of an old distillery. Dismantled in the 1920s, the Grenville Brewery was every sailor's favorite place to stop after a long journey. Scuba dives in the backyard revealed sunken bottles of old brew. Follow Hwy 2 west and you'll find the seaside inn just outside of town.

Merrickville

Tiny Merrickville can thank the Canadian Railroad for never laying down tracks through town. Had the wee burg become a stop on the line, it would have swapped its stone structures for industrial eyesores. Fortunately, today, visits can still be a step back in time, to when the area was a Loyalist stronghold ready to defend the Crown against the rebellious Americans. Merrickville was such a desirable locale that Colonel By, the master planner of the Rideau Canal, built his summer home here, and Benedict Arnold was given a tract in town as a reward for betraying the Americans.

History buffs will enjoy exploring the **blockhouse** (☑613-269-2229; cnr Main & St Lawrence Sts; admission free; ☺mid-May–mid-Oct) and boutique-browsers will love the numerous artisan workshops. Pause for a meal at **Gad's Hill** (☑613-269-2976; www.dickens-restaurant.com; 118 St Lawrence St; mains $9-17; ☺lunch & dinner), where menus are tucked inside leather-bound tomes, encouraging the pronounced Dickensian motif. Catch a dinner show while you're there; as expected, 'A Christmas Carol' is an annual event.

Morrisburg

Little Morrisburg is known far and wide for its quality historic site, **Upper Canada Village** (www.uppercanadavillage.com; adult/child/student $20/4/12; ☺9:30am-5pm mid-May–mid-Oct). Costume-clad interpreters animate this re-created town by emulating life in the 1860s. Plan to spend three or four hours at the village – that will give you plenty of time to check out the 40 buildings. Wander through Cook's Tavern, the Blacksmith's Shop, Asselstine's Woollen Factory, the Schoolhouse, the Gazette Printing Office and the many other dwellings to learn about the intricacies of colonial life. For those without transportation, the village can be reached aboard buses running between Ottawa and Cornwall, and on some Montréal to Toronto trips.

Hwy 2 along the river is slow but provides a more scenic trip than Hwy 401. The **Upper Canada Migratory Bird Sanctuary** (www.uppercanadabirdsanctuary.com; ☺mid-May–Oct) offers 8km of self-guided trails that meander through wooded thickets and lush wetlands. Over 200 bird species can be glimpsed. Inquire at the park office about the dozen camping options.

Cornwall

Cornwall is a collection of paper mills and smokestacks where Ontario and Québec collide to kiss the American border. The Three Nations Crossing to Massena, New York, is a heavily trafficked crossing. Visit www.city.cornwall.on.ca for more information about the various goings-on around town.

On Cornwall Island, the Akwesane Mohawk reservation has the **Ronathahon:ni Cultural Centre** (www.ronathahonni.com; adult/child $2/1; ☺8am-4pm Mon-Fri), an interpretive space where visitors can learn about Mohawk culture through artifacts and hands-on activities.

The **Long Sault Parkway** connects a series of parks and beaches along the river.

OTTAWA

POP 900,000

Descriptions of Ottawa read like an appealing personal ad: young, vibrant, clean, bilingual, likes kids, long walks on the river. And the attractive capital continues to impress in person.

The postcard-perfect Parliament regally anchors the downtown core at the confluence of three rivers. An inspiring jumble of pulsing districts – each with their own flavor – lies beyond the sleek government offices. In the distance, the rolling Gatineau hills tenderly hug the cloudless valley.

The city's main attraction is the vast assortment of state-of-the-art museums. From the smooth undulating walls of the ubermodern Museum of Civilization (just across the river in Gatineau) to the haunting Gothic arches of the Museum of Nature, each attraction is an inspired architectural gesture with an intriguing exhibition space.

Ottawa's cultural diversity is evident in the mix of local cuisine. Chinatown and Little Italy have been local mainstays for quite some time, but recent years have witnessed an influx of dynamic flavors from Africa, France, the Caribbean, Eastern Europe and Southeast Asia, not to mention a variety of Aboriginal choices.

OTTAWA ITINERARIES

One Day

First, shame on you for allocating only one day of your itinerary to Canada's surprisingly enchanting capital! There's no time to waste, so hop on over to **Parliament Hill** for Kodak moments with the Peace Tower, and a quick tour of the lavish, Harry Potter-esque interior. Next, swap copper towers for shimmering glass spires at the **National Art Gallery of Canada**. You'll find a carefully curated collection of stunning aboriginal art and the restored remains of a lovely wooden chapel. Pause for lunch at the **ByWard Market** where you'll uncover scores of vendors hawking fresh farm produce (and over 1000 kinds of cheese!). Sample a beavertail or an 'Obama Cookie' before making tracks toward the **Rideau Canal** – especially in winter when it becomes the largest skating rink in the world (7.8km!). For dinner try one of Ottawa's intrepid culinary experiences like the vegan paradise **ZenKitchen** or laboratory-chic **Atelier**.

Three Days

After completing the one-day itinerary, make a beeline to the gorgeous **Canadian Museum of Civilization**. Take in the awe-inducing architecture and snap your camera at the skyline views from across the river. Ogle taxidermic megafauna at the newly renovated **Canadian Museum of Nature** before catching a riveting **Senators hockey game** at ScotiaBank Place.

And on your last day – if you aren't completely museum-ed out – head to the quirky **Diefenbunker** several kilometers out of town. Clear your mind of Soviet nuclear woes on a hike in the **Gatineau Hills** nearby. In the evening, catch a show at the **National Arts Centre** or perhaps take in some live music at one of the venues clustered around the ByWard Market area.

Don't dismiss a winter visit because of frigid temperatures – the city's longest season is celebrated with myriad outdoor activities. The Rideau Canal turns into the largest skating rink in the world, and the Winterlude festival gets everyone outdoors with a gargantuan village made entirely of ice. When the thick blanket of snow melts away, auspicious tulips cheer the downtown as spring clicks to summer. Vibrant autumn leaves round out the year, as the streets are set ablaze with eye-popping reds and yellows.

Whether it's the stunning museums or the authentic eats, the rainbow of seasons or the outdoor retreats – you should definitely make a date with Ottawa.

History

Like many colonial capitals, Ottawa's birth was not an organic one. The site was chosen by Queen Victoria as a geographic compromise between Montréal and Toronto, and poof – the city was born. Canadians were initially baffled by her decision; Ottawa was far away from the main colonial strongholds. Many thought the region to be a desolate snowfield, when in fact the Ottawa area was long inhabited by Algonquin, who named the rolling river 'Kichissippi,' or 'Great River.'

For almost a century, Ottawa functioned as a quiet capital. Then, after WWII, Paris city planner Jacques Greber was tasked with giving Ottawa an urban facelift. The master planner created a distinctive European feel, transforming the city into the stunning cityscape of ample common and recreational spaces we see today.

⊙ Sights

Ottawa's best feature is its collection of stunning, state-of-the-art museums. Most of these attractions are within walking distance of one another. A couple of quick things to remember: many museums are closed on Mondays in the winter, and several attractions will let you in for free if you arrive less than an hour before closing time.

New museums are popping up all the time around the nation's capital. It's best to ask the helpful staff at the Capital Info-centre for the latest additions to the city's roster of fantastic attractions.

Parliament Hill
HISTORICAL BUILDING

(www.parliamenthill.gc.ca) Vast yawning archways dominate this stunning complex of copper-topped towers. The city's most picture-perfect attraction by far, Parliament is Canada's nexus of political activity. The primary building, **Centre Block**, supports the iconic **Peace Tower**, the highest structure in the city. Venture inside to peruse the hand-carved limestone and make a stop at the gorgeous library with its wood and wrought iron. Visitors are allowed to see the Commons and Senate while they're in session. Question Period in the House of Commons is particularly popular, occurring every afternoon and at 11am on Fridays. Admission is on a first-come first-served basis.

Free 45-minute **tours** (☏613-996-0896) run frequently; be prepared for tight security. In summer you can book tours at the conspicuous white tent; in winter there's a reservation desk inside the building. The grounds can be explored on one's own as well. Pick up a free copy of the *Walking Tour of Parliament Hill* at the information center across the street. The pamphlet details little-known facts about the buildings – learn about the gargoyles and grotesques that haunt the sculpted sandstone.

The tour schedule is quite convoluted and confusing – the best bet is to check out the parliament's website.

At 10am daily in summer, see the colorful **changing of the guard** on the front lawns. At night during summer, there's a free bilingual sound-and-light show called *Mosaika* on Parliament Hill.

After exploring the architectural allegory to nationalist Gothic, there's a bizarre little-known quirk that should not be missed. The **stray-cat sanctuary**, with its dollhouse shelters sits on Parliament Hill between the West Block and Centre Block, toward the river. Some say, loftily, that it represents the Canadian ideal of welcoming and caring for the world's needy, but then again, maybe it's just nutty.

Canadian Museum of Civilization
MUSEUM

(☏819-776-7000; www.civilization.ca; 100 Rue Laurier; adult/child/senior $12/8/10; ⊙9am-6pm Sat-Wed, to 8pm Thu-Fri) This must-see museum documents the history of Canada through a spectacular range of exhibits. The stone exterior has been sculpted into smooth ripples – like the undulating wave of a current. In fact, you won't find any corners at the museum, as it is believed in aboriginal lore that the evil spirits live in these angled nooks. Allow at least an entire afternoon to explore the museum and to take in the stunning views of the Parliament across the river.

The **Grand Hall**, with its simulated forest and seashore, illuminates the northwest coastal aboriginal cultures with towering colorful totem poles. Kids get a passport when they enter the **Canadian Children's Museum**, a vast educational and hands-on space offering glimpses into different cultures from around the world. Even adults may find that this is their favorite part of the museum. A slew of temporary exhibits supplement the already-incredible collection, and **Cineplus** adds an additional dimension, showing IMAX and Omnimax films.

National Gallery of Canada
ART GALLERY

(☏613-990-1985; www.gallery.ca; 380 Sussex Dr; adult/child under 12yr/child 12-19yr/concession/family $9/free/4/7/18, audioguide $6; ⊙10am-5pm, to 8pm Thu May-Sep, closed Mon Oct-Apr) Canada's largest art gallery is a must, housing the largest collection of Canadian and Inuit art in the world. The structure is a piece of art in itself – one of Ottawa's modern architectural gems. The striking ensemble of glass and pink granite was concocted by Moshe Safdie, a noted architect who also created Montréal's well-known 'Habitat' (a unique apartment complex). His emphatic glass spires at the museum's rear echo the ornate copper-topped towers of the Parliament nearby. The dialogue between the heavy metallic roof and the floating crystalline steeple is magical even on the dreariest of days.

On the interior, the vaulted galleries display classic and contemporary pieces with an emphasis on Canadian artists. The thoughtful chronological displays guide visitors through an annotated retelling of the nation's history. The **Inuit Gallery** on the ground level fuses ancestral themes with modern media in the dedicated **photography gallery** next door (room B102 and B103). Beyond the slew of Canadian art, galleries of US and European works will please the eye with several recognizable names and masterpieces.

There are two smooth courtyards deep within the museum's interior – both ooze Zen and tranquility, making them the perfect place to rest your eyes. Also hidden deep within is the unusual **Rideau Street Convent Chapel**. Built in 1888, this stunning

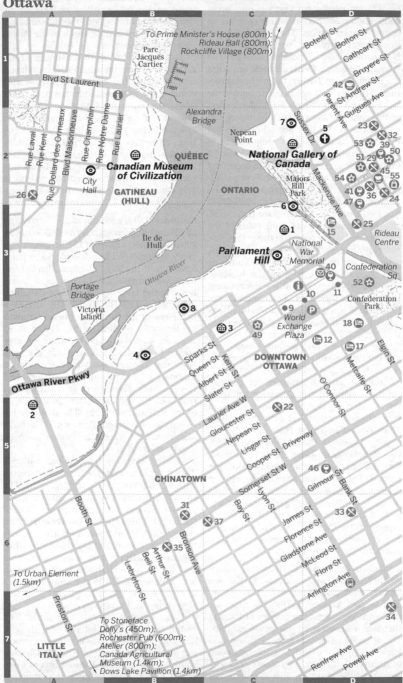

To Prime Minister's House (800m);
Rideau Hall (800m);
Rockcliffe Village (800m)

Parc Jacques Cartier

Blvd St Laurent

Boteler St
Bolton St
Cathcart St
Bruyere St

42

St Andrew St
St Patrick St

Parent Ave
Guigues Ave

23 32
53 39
51 29 50
54 45 55
41 36 24
47

Rue Laval
Rue Kent
Rue Dollard des Ormeaux
Blvd Maisonneuve
Rue Champlain
Rue Notre Dame
Rue Laurier

City Hall

Alexandra Bridge

Nepean Point

7 5

National Gallery of Canada

QUÉBEC

Canadian Museum of Civilization

GATINEAU (HULL)

ONTARIO

Majors Hill Park

Mackenzie Ave

26

6

15

25

Rideau Centre

Île de Hull

Ottawa River

1

National War Memorial

40

Confederation Sq

52

Portage Bridge

Victoria Island

8

10
9
11

Confederation Park

Ottawa River Pkwy

3

49

World Exchange Plaza

18
17

12

4

Sparks St
Queen St
Albert St
Slater St

Kent St

DOWNTOWN OTTAWA

Elgin St
Metcalfe St
O'Connor St

2

Laurier Ave W
Gloucester St
Nepean St
Lisgar St
Cooper St

22

Driveway

CHINATOWN

Somerset St W

Bay St
Lyon St

46

Gilmour St
Bank St

Booth St

31

James St

33

37

Florence St
Gladstone Ave
McLeod St
Flora St

Arthur St

Bronson Ave

Bell St

35

Lebreton St

To Urban Element (1.5km)

Arlington Ave

34

Preston St

LITTLE ITALY

To Stoneface Dolly's (450m);
Rochester Pub (600m);
Atelier (800m);
Canada Agricultural Museum (1.4km);
Dows Lake Pavillion (1.4km)

Renfrew Ave
Powell Ave

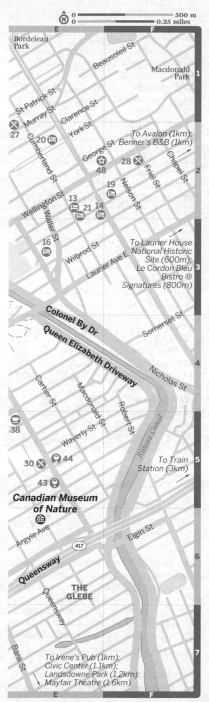

wooden chapel was saved from demolition and restored piece-by-piece inside the gallery.

The complex, a 15-minute walk north of Parliament, takes at least two hours to navigate, and that's without checking out the latest rotating exhibitions, video presentations and film archives.

Two levels of underground parking hide beneath the museum ($12 per day).

Canadian Museum of Nature   MUSEUM

(☏613-566-4700; 240 McLeod St; www.nature. ca; adult/child/family $10/8/25, free Sat morning; ☺9am-6pm Sat-Wed, to 8pm Thu-Fri) Sparkling after a massive, seemingly endless renovation, this vast museum pokes its Gothic head up just beyond the skyline, south of downtown. The gaping four-story museum houses an impressive collection of fossils, minerals and animals, a full skeleton of a blue whale, and an excellent stock of dinosaurs from Alberta. Everyone's favorite section is the realistic mammal and bird dioramas depicting Canadian wildlife. The taxidermic creatures are so lifelike, you'll be glad that they're behind a sheet of glass.

Buses 5, 6 and 14 transport passengers to McLeod St.

Canada Science & Technology Museum
MUSEUM

(☏613-991-3044; www.sciencetech.technomuses. ca; 1867 St Laurent Blvd; adult/child/senior/family $9/4/6/20; ☺9am-5pm May-Sep, 9am-5pm Tue-Sun Oct-Apr) This hands-on museum, about 6km southeast of downtown, is a wonderful place to tickle the senses. Ambient squeaks and boinks fill the air as contented visitors gingerly turn knobs and push buttons.

Clever displays are designed to teach visitors about the basic scientific laws that govern our world. Permanent collections explore optical illusions, the laws of physics, and Time, with a capital 'T.' A walk through the **Crazy Kitchen** is a must – the lopsided galley dips at a 10-degree angle causing passers-through to cling to the railings as they try to stumble from start to finish. Climb aboard the heavy-duty trains at the back of the museum to learn about the science behind coal and steam engines.

The large display on space technology has an assortment of Canadian space artifacts. The neighboring astronomy section displays mind-blowing films about the universe. On clear evenings, you can make reservations to take a peek through the large refracting telescope.

Ottawa

Canadian War Museum　　　　MUSEUM
(☎800-555-5621; www.warmuseum.ca; 1 Vimy Pl; adult/child $12/8; ⏰9am-6pm Fri-Wed, to 9pm Thu May–mid-Oct, 9am-5pm Tue-Sun, to 9pm Thu mid-Oct–Apr) This museum still has that new-car smell. The metallic building is itself an eye-catching sculptural gesture, and is worth a glance even if you don't plan on visiting the exhibits. Fascinating displays wind through the labyrinthine interior, tracing the country's military history with Canada's most comprehensive collection of military arti-facts. Many of the exhibits were constructed on a human scale, including a haunting life-sized replica of a WWI trench. Don't forget to take a second look at the facade in the evening – flickering lights pulse on and off spelling 'Lest We Forget' and 'CWM' in Morse code (in both English and French, of course).

Canada Aviation and Space Museum
　　　　　　　　　　　　　　　　MUSEUM
(☎613-993-2010;　　　www.aviation.technomuses. ca; 11 Aviation Pkwy; adult/child/family $9/5/18;

9am-5pm May-Labour Day, closed Mon-Tue Labour Day-Apr) With nearly 120 aircraft housed in the steel triangular hangar, the aviation museum almost feels bigger than Ottawa's actual airport. Stroll through the mammoth warehouse, try the flight simulator, and get up close and personal with colorful planes ranging from the Silver Dart of 1909 to the first turbo-powered Viscount passenger jet.

Call ahead to check opening hours, as they vary according to attendance levels and time of year. If you show up an hour before closing, you might be let in for free. The museum is 5km northeast (along Rockcliffe Pkwy). Take bus 129 from downtown.

Ottawa Locks & Bytown Museum MUSEUM
The series of steplike locks, between the Château Laurier and the Parliament Buildings, marks the north end of the 200km Rideau Canal, which flows all the way down to Kingston. Colonel By, the canal's visionary engineer, set up headquarters here in 1826.

Take the stairs down from Wellington St to find the **Bytown Museum** (☑613-234-4570; www.bytownmuseum.com; admission incl audioguide $6; ☉10am-5pm mid-May–mid-Oct, to 2pm mid-Oct–Nov & Apr–mid-May), sitting at the last lock before the artificial canal plunges into the waters of the Ottawa River. This well-curated collection of artifacts and documents about Ottawa's colonial past is displayed in the city's oldest stone building. The 1st floor is devoted to a nature exhibit, the 2nd floor details the arduous construction of the canal system, and, if you've got the kids in tow, don't miss the pioneer dress-up station on the 3rd floor.

Royal Canadian Mint NOTABLE BUILDING
(☑613-993-8990; www.mint.ca; 320 Sussex Dr; weekday tours adult/child $5/3, weekend $3.50/2; ☉9am-7pm Mon-Fri, to 5:30pm Sat & Sun late May-early Sep, 9am-5pm early Sep-late May) Although Canada's circulation-coin mint is in Winnipeg (see p510), the royal mint holds its own by striking special pieces like the Olympic medals for the Vancouver games. In fact, the imposing stone building, which looks a bit like the ominous Tower of London, has been Canada's major gold refiner since 1908. Excellent tours (reservations recommended) of the coin-making process are offered regularly (as often as every 15 minutes in the height of summer) – during the workweek, visitors can glimpse the transformation as sheets of metal are spun into loads of coins. Sorry, no free samples.

FREE **Currency Museum** MUSEUM
(☑613-782-8914; www.currencymuseum.ca; Bank of Canada, 245 Sparks St; ☉10:30am-5pm Mon-Sat, from 1pm Sun Jun-Aug, closed Mon Sep-May) Make sense of cents at this small museum tucked within the greenhouse lobby of the Bank of Canada building. Various displays detail the global history of money, from seashells and whales' teeth to banknotes and credit cards. Don't miss the giant Yap stone – used to display a family's wealth – sitting amid exotic foliage near the museum's entrance.

Notre Dame Cathedral-Basilica CHURCH
(385 Sussex Dr; admission free; ☉7am-6pm) Built in 1841, this shimmering tin-topped house of worship is the oldest church in all of Ottawa and the seat of the city's Catholic archbishop. Pick up the small pamphlet at the entrance outlining the church's many idiosyncratic features, including elaborate wooden carvings and the dazzling indigo ceiling peppered with gleaming stars. The cathedral is situated across from the glass spires of the National Gallery of Canada.

FREE **Supreme Court of Canada**
NOTABLE BUILDING
(☑613-995-5361; www.scc-csc.gc.ca; 301 Wellington St; ☉9am-5pm) This intimidating structure strikes an intriguing architectural balance with a modern concrete shell and a traditional copper roof. Visitors can stroll around the scenic grounds, vaulted lobby and dark oak-paneled courtroom. In summer, law students from the University of Ottawa conduct friendly and insightful tours, which depart every 30 minutes. During the rest of the year, tours must be booked in advance.

ⓘ CULTURE PASSPORT: 9 MUSEUMS, 7 DAYS

Capital-ize on Ottawa's cache of fantastic museums with the **Culture Passport** (adult/family $30/75), a discount card that grants carriers admission to the city's nine best museums. Additional perks include 20% discounts on performances at the National Arts Centre. The card can be purchased at any of the participating museums and is valid for use within seven days.

OTTAWA FOR CHILDREN

Nope, the **Canada Agricultural Museum** (🕿613-991-3044; www.agriculture.tech nomuses.ca; 930 Carling Ave at Prince of Wales Dr; adult/child $7/4; ⊗9am-5pm Mar-Oct) isn't about the history of the pitchfork – it's a fascinating experimental farm. The government-owned property, southwest of downtown, includes about 500 hectares of gardens and ranches. Kids will love the livestock as they hoot and snort around the barn. The affable farmhands will even let the tots help out during feeding time. Guided tours lead visitors to an observatory, a tropical greenhouse and an arboretum. The rolling farmland is the perfect place for a scenic summer picnic, and in winter the grounds become a prime tobogganing locale. The farm can be reached on the city's network of cycling routes.

In addition to the experimental farm, virtually all of Ottawa's museums have been designed with families in mind; several options have entire wings devoted to child's play, like the **Canadian Museum of Nature**, the **Canada Science & Technology Museum** and the **Canadian Museum of Civilization**.

FREE Library & National Archives of Canada   NOTABLE BUILDING
(🕿613-996-5115; www.collectionscanada.gc.ca; 395 Wellington St; ⊗8:30am-11pm) The mandate of this monstrous concrete institution is to collect and preserve the documentation of Canada. Behind the tiny checkered windows lies a vast anthology of records, including paintings, maps, photographs, diaries, letters, posters and 60,000 cartoons and caricatures collected over the past two centuries. Rotating exhibits are displayed on the ground floor.

Laurier House National Historic Site
HISTORICAL SITE
(🕿613-992-8142; 335 Laurier Ave; admission $3.90; ⊗9am-5pm) This copper-roofed Victorian home, built in 1878, was the residence of two notable prime ministers: Wilfrid Laurier and the eccentric Mackenzie King. The home is elegantly furnished, displaying treasured mementos and possessions from both politicos. Don't miss the study on the top floor. It's best to visit in the early morning (that is, before the chatty tour buses arrive); you'll have the knowledgeable guides all to yourself.

Prime Minister's House & Rideau Hall
NOTABLE BUILDING
You can have a quick peek at the **prime minister's house** (24 Sussex Dr), although tight security prevents visitors from exploring the grounds. **Rideau Hall** (🕿613-991-4422; 1 Sussex Dr; admission free; ⊗9am-dusk), home to the governor general, was built in the early 20th century. There are free 45-minute walking tours of the posh residence, with poignant anecdotes about the various goings-on over

the years. Tours are offered throughout the day in summer, or you can stroll the grounds all year. At the main gate, the small changing of the guard ceremony happens on the hour throughout the day from the end of June until the end of August.

Both houses are northeast along Sussex Dr. Rideau Hall is off Princess Dr, the eastern extension of Sussex Dr. Continue east along Sussex/Princess Dr to take a glance at **Rockcliffe Village**, Ottawa's swankiest neighborhood and home to prominent Canadians and most foreign diplomats.

FREE RCMP Musical Ride Centre
HISTORICAL SITE
(🕿613-998-8199; 1 Sandridge Rd; ⊗9am-4pm) While the name sounds like Disney's newest attraction starring chipper red-vested policemen, the musical ride center is actually the stage where the Mounties perfect their pageant. The public is welcome to watch the dress rehearsals and equestrian displays, though it mostly appeals to equestrian enthusiasts. Call for practice time details and the sunset ride schedule. If traveling by car, take Sussex Dr east to Rockcliffe Pkwy, and turn right on Birch St.

🏃 Activities

For a city with harsh, endless winters, its residents sure love to be outside. Tourists will find a glut of outdoor activities during all seasons.

Ice-Skating

The **Rideau Canal**, Ottawa's most famous outdoor attraction, doubles as the largest skating rink in the world. The 7.8km of groomed ice is roughly the size of 90

Olympic-sized hockey rinks. Rest stops and changing stations are sprinkled throughout, but, more importantly, take note of the wooden kiosks dispensing scrumptious slabs of fried dough called beavertails. The three skate and sled rental stations are located at the steps of the National Arts Centre, Dow's Lake and 5th Ave. The tourism office on Wellington St also has information about skate rentals.

Skiing

Several nearby skiing resorts offer a variety of alpine and cross-country trails. In the Gatineau Hills, about 20km from downtown, over 50 groomed slopes are available between **Camp Fortune** (☑819-827-1717; www.campfortune.com; 300 Chemin Dunlop, Chelsea) and **Mont Cascades** (☑819-827-0301; www.montcascades.ca; 448 Mont Cascades Rd, Cantley). Mount Pakenham, 60km west of Ottawa, offers a similar experience, and cross-country skiers will love the trails in Gatineau Park.

Ballooning

Hot-air ballooning has long been a popular leisure activity in the capital region. **Sundance Balloons** (☑613-247-8277; www.sundanceballoons.com; per person from $175) offers sunrise and sunset trips departing from several locations in the Ottawa valley.

☞ Tours

The Capital Infocentre offers several handy brochures for self-guided walking tours. The HI Ottawa Jail hostel organizes short trips around the city.

Around About Ottawa   WALKING TOURS
(☑613-599-1016; www.aroundaboutottawa.com; ⊙Mon-Fri) Two-hour guided walking tours exploring the city's historic landmarks.

Bytown Trolley Co   TROLLEY TOURS
(☑613-592-7741; cnr Sparks & O'Connor Sts; ⊙mid-Apr–mid-Oct) Offers guided hop-on hop-off tours around the capital region.

Gray Line   BUS TOURS
(☑613-565-5463; www.grayline.ca; cnr Sparks & Metcalfe Sts; 3hr city tour $38; ⊙May–mid-Oct) Tours depart from the corner-side ticket kiosk. Hop-on hop-off service (adult $26.55) is also available at 12 selected locations throughout the city (including the Museum of Civilization and the National Gallery of Canada).

Haunted Walk   WALKING TOURS
(☑613-232-0344; www.hauntedwalk.com; 73 Clarence St; walks $13-15) Has several ghoulish walking tours including visits to the old county jail. A new 'Naughty Ottawa' pub crawl is also available for those who want to get their beer on. Tickets can also be purchased at the HI Ottawa Jail hostel.

Lady Dive Amphibious   BUS TOURS
(☑613-223-6211; www.ladydive.com; cnr Sparks & Elgin Sts; tours $19-30; ⊙May-Oct) This half-bus half-boat drives around Ottawa's favorite sights and then plunges into the Ottawa River. Free hotel pickup available.

Ottawa Walking Tours   WALKING TOURS
(☑613-799-1774; www.ottawawalkingtours.com; adult/family $15/45) Run by a local high school teacher, these informative tours – great for older tourists – depart from in front of the Capital Infocentre.

Paul's Boat Lines   BOAT TOURS
(☑613-255-6781; www.paulsboatcruises.com; Ottawa Locks or Rideau Canal Dock; 1½hr Ottawa River tour adult/child $20/12, 1¼hr Rideau Canal

---

RIDEAU CANAL

On June 28, 2007, the Rideau Canal became Canada's 14th location to be named a Unesco national historic site. This 175-year-old, 200km-long canal/river/lake system connects Kingston with Ottawa through 47 locks.

After the War of 1812, there was a fear that there could be yet another war with the Americans. The Duke of Wellington decided to link Ottawa and Kingston in order to have a reliable communications and supply route between the two military centers. Although the canal is just 200km in length, its construction was a brutal affair, involving as many as 4000 men battling malaria and the Canadian Shield, working against some of the world's hardest rock. The canal climbs 84m from Ottawa over the shield then drops 49m to Lake Ontario. And guess what? It never saw any military service.

The canal did prove useful later in the century for shipping goods, and today the historical route is ideal for boating with parks, small towns, lakes and many places to stop en route.

cruise $18/10; ☉mid-May–Oct) Scenic cruises offer picture-perfect moments.

✦ Festivals & Events

The nation's capital is abuzz year-round with over 60 annual festivals and events:

Winterlude   WINTER FESTIVAL
(☎613-239-5000; www.canadascapital.gc.ca/winterlude) Three consecutive weekends in February celebrate Ottawa's winter, centering on the frozen Dows Lake and the canal. Awe-inspiring ice sculptures abound.

Canadian Tulip Festival   FLOWER FESTIVAL
(☎613-567-5757; www.tulipfestival.ca) After a long winter, the city bursts with color in May – over 200 types of tulips, mainly from Holland, blanket the city. Festivities include parades, regattas, car rallies, dances, concerts and fireworks.

Ottawa Bluesfest   MUSIC FESTIVAL
(☎613-241-2633; www.ottawabluesfest.ca) The second-biggest blues festival in the world (Chicago is the largest) brings in the big names for memorable concerts in late June.

Canada Day   NATIONAL DAY
(☎613-239-5000; www.canadascapital.gc.ca/canadaday) The best place in Canada to celebrate the nation's birthday on July 1. Noteworthy fireworks crackle and boom above the Parliament Buildings.

THE DIEFENBUNKER

During the Cold War, paranoid government officials commissioned the **Diefenbunker** (☎613-839-0007; www.diefenbunker.ca; 3911 Carp Rd, Carp; adult/child $14/8; ☉10am-6pm), a secret underground military/government refuge. The gargantuan four-floored shelter was designed to house over 300 'important persons' for 30 days during a nuclear attack. Admission includes an optional one-hour tour, whose highlights include the prime minister's suite, the CBC radio studio and the Bank of Canada vault. It's about 40km west of town, in the village of Carp. Reservations are essential. Plans are under way to open the entire 100,000 sq meter space to the public.

HOPE Volleyball Summerfest   SPORTS TOURNAMENT
(☎613-237-1433; www.hopehelps.com) A giant volleyball tournament in mid-July to raise money for local charities.

SuperEX   AGRICULTURAL FAIR
(☎613-237-2222; www.ottawasuperex.com) An enormous 10-day carnival at Lansdowne Park in mid-August. Great for kids.

Capital Pride   GAY PRIDE
(☎613-421-5387; www.prideottawa.com) A week's worth of rainbows culminating in a rowdy parade in mid-August.

🛏 Sleeping

The city has an impressive array of lodgings in all price ranges. The urban downtown district, stocked with high-rises, offers some unique upmarket lodging options in addition to the usual suspects (franchises and the like). During summer, reservations are recommended. February and May are bustling months as well, due to popular festivals.

Ottawa's two major B&B hubs are both on the east side of downtown. The Sandy Hill district – a posh pocket of heritage houses – offers several architectural gems, and the ByWard Market district has some colorful options as well. Both neighborhoods offer walkable access to the city's major attractions.

There are a good number of budget choices for this medium-sized city, including camping options starting around 10km outside the city limits; some options can be scouted in Gatineau Park across the river in Québec.

If all else fails, there are clusters of cheap motels around the city. Scores of privately owned options live on Carling Ave as it crosses under the Queensway (Hwy 417), and Rideau St E (which ultimately turns into Montréal Rd) has several options as well.

🌿 Fairmont Château Laurier
                           HISTORIC HOTEL $$$
(☎613-241-1414, 866-540-4410; www.fairmont.com/laurier; 1 Rideau St; r $250-400; ❋@✿☎❀) This opulent castle gives the Parliament a run for its money. The city's best-known hotel is a landmark in its own right. You won't want for creature comforts and the location is unbeatable. If you're cashed-up, there's no better place to stay in town. If you don't have the bucks, recline on the overstuffed chaises as though you were the toast of the town.

Hotel Indigo

BOUTIQUE HOTEL $$$

(☎613-216-2903; www.ottawadowntownhotel.com; 123 Metcalfe St; r $139-199; ✼@🖥) This boutique hotel was designed with one lofty concept in mind: Fibonacci's Sequence – a natural order governing visual aesthetics. It's a tad complicated, but basically it involves mathematical harmony; where the ratio of two quantities equals the ratio between the larger of the two quantities and the two quantities combined (whew!). Additional perks and quirks include a floor-to-ceiling mural in each room, plasma TVs, and customer information written in haiku form. Reserve at least two weeks in advance.

Barefoot Hostel

HOSTEL $

(☎613-237-0335; www.barefoothostel.com; 455 Cumberland St; dm $35.50; ✼@🖥) Barefoot is a brand-new hostel run by the lovely folks at the Swiss Hotel. Thick duvets, a wide-screen plasma TV and generous bursts of air-conditioning only begin the list of the homey details that make this place the clear budget winner. And as the name suggests, don't forget to take your shoes off when you arrive!

Bella Notte

B&B $$

(☎613-565-0497; www.bellanottebb.com; 108 Daly Ave; r incl breakfast $128-148; 🖥) This charming little gem was once the home of Alexander Campbell, a prominent politician during Canada's founding. Evenings are filled with beautiful piano-playing from the owners, who happen to be professional musicians. The hosts proudly boast an infinite breakfast – 'you can eat till you die.'

McGee's Inn

B&B $$

(☎613-262-4337; www.mcgeesinn.com; 185 Daly Ave; r $108-198; @🖥) This vast Victorian mansion has all the period trappings, from floral prints and embroidered chair caning to plush button-eyed teddy bears and varnished sewing machines. The John McGee room still contains some of the inn's original furnishings, including a cherry-wood desk and sleigh bed. Enjoy breakfast amid chirps from antique cuckoo clocks.

Arc

BOUTIQUE HOTEL $$$

(☎613-238-2888; www.arcthehotel.com; 140 Slater St; r $169-450; ✼@🖥) Arc is a savvy boutique hotel with 112 minimal-yet-elegant rooms; call it low-key, muted and restfully hip. This mellow adult atmosphere continues through the quiet bar and trendy restaurant.

Swiss Hotel – Gasthaus Switzerland Inn

INN $$

(☎613-237-0335; www.gasthausswitzerlandinn.com; 89 Daly Ave; r incl breakfast $118-188; ✼@🖥) Sabina, the Swiss owner, is effervescence personified, and her beautiful inn is a great place to call home during your visit. The old stone guesthouse has 22 rooms, all with private bathrooms. The excellent breakfast, served in the spacious dining room, features delicious imported coffees, muesli, cheese and much, much more.

Ottawa Backpackers Inn

HOSTEL $

(☎613-241-3402; www.ottawahostel.com; 203 York St; dm/s $25/60, apt from $150; @🖥) This laid-back hostel lives in a converted 19th-century house boasting fresh-faced bathrooms, sun-drenched dorms, and handy power outlets at every bed. Martin, the welcoming owner, comes from a long line of backpacking stalwarts; his parents own a popular hostel in Thunder Bay.

Hostelling International (HI) Ottawa Jail

HOSTEL $

(☎613-235-2595; www.hihostels.ca/ottawa; 75 Nicholas St; members dm/s $28/76, nonmembers dm/s $33/86; @🖥) If your experience with serving jail time is limited to a game of Monopoly, then this quirky hostel will be right up your alley – guests can sleep in the stone penitentiary's old wrought-iron cellblock. Informative walking tours are frequently organized by the friendly staff, including a spooky 'Crime and Punishment' tour of the jail itself, which is considered to be one of the most haunted buildings in town. Check out the on-site gallows where numerous criminals were hanged for their wretched crimes.

🌱 Australis Guest House

B&B $$

(☎613-235-8461; www.australisguesthouse.com; 89 Goulburn Ave; r $95-109; 🖥) The 'greenest' accommodations option in Ottawa, Australis offers 100% cotton sheets, reusable cloth napkins, all-natural cleaning products, and loos with a low-flush option.

Avalon

B&B $$

(☎613-789-3443; www.avalonbedandbreakfast.com; 539 Besserer St; d $95-125; 🖥) A refreshing departure from the usual antique-laden B&Bs, Avalon is a fresh-faced inn with a tasteful blend of trendy and homey furnishings. Enormous breakfasts (eggs Benedict!) are the norm, as are friendly licks from Apollo the dog.

LOCAL KNOWLEDGE

SUNDAY IN THE PARK WITH GORGE

'We love Sundays in Ottawa – it's the end of the work week and we have a bit of free time to roam around our green city and explore. Our favorite brunch place is the **Rochester Pub** (502 Rochester St; ✐), which offers a great selection of hearty breakfasts, including some worthy vegetarian options. It's informal to the extreme – truly a place to relax.

After breakfast, we usually hit the **Farmers Market at Lansdowne Park** (www.ottawafarmersmarket.ca) to buy our produce for the week and chat with the local farmers. It's also a great place to pick up some lunch: garlic dips, **Art-Is-In** (www.artisinbakery.com) breads, local cheeses, heirloom tomatoes, freshly picked berries and more. After snatching a few items we usually walk over to the Rideau Canal, grab a park bench, watch the runners, and tear off chunks of bread to share with the curious ducks.

For dinner, it's all about restaurants with a relaxed atmosphere, well-crafted food and a savvy wine list. While our own **ZenKitchen** fits the bill, we don't always want to eat at 'home.' One of our favorites is **Shanghai** (www.shanghaiottawa.com; 651 Somerset St W; ✐) across the street. The restaurant is widely known as the first establishment in Ottawa's Chinatown, and is now run by the artistic children of the original owners. The food is great – modern Chinese cuisine with lots of veggie options – but the real draw is the trendy decor, rotating art exhibits and fabulous weekend events (think 'Disco Bingo' and karaoke) hosted by the local diva tranny goddess China-Doll.

Dessert at **Pure Gelato** (350 Elgin St) is a must. Handmade ices come in a wide variety of flavors – there's blood orange, fig or triple chocolate. Don't worry, the long queue moves quickly.

Across the street, **Oz Kafe** (www.ozkafe.com; 361 Elgin; ✐) is a great spot for a late-night drink with a pinch of live music. It's popular with the local service industry, so you'll usually find the area's chefs mingling over martinis or munching on a veggie bento box.'

Chef Caroline Ishii and sommelier Dave Loan are co-owners of ZenKitchen, a high-end vegan restaurant in downtown Ottawa, named the city's Best New Restaurant in 2009. A reality show, The Restaurant Adventures of Caroline and Dave, followed the couple for one year as they opened the restaurant. It aired in early 2010.

Lord Elgin Hotel HOTEL **$$$**
(✆613-235-3333; www.lordelginhotel.ca; 100 Elgin St; r from $185; ✳@🔊🛒) This stately old place, built in 1941 and overhauled in 1991, has seen its share of celebrity names over the decades. The location is ideal, with numerous restaurants and sites an easy walk away – there's even a Starbucks in the lobby.

Benner's B&B B&B **$$**
(✆613-789-8320; www.bennersbnb.com; 541 Besserer St; d $95-130; 🔊) Well appointed and spacious, this 100-year-old house stands out as a comfortable option in Sandy Hill District, a 15-minute walk to downtown.

✗ Eating

Little Ottawa's smorgasbord of gastronomic choices could give Toronto a run for its money. Bounteous ByWard Market boasts 150 options squished into one condensed epicurean district. During the warm month(s), eateries spill out onto the streets, creating charming cobblestone verandas.

Follow Bank St south to the colorful Glebe neighborhood for a surplus of less-touristy pubs, restaurants and cafes between First St and Fifth St.

Take an evening stroll down Preston St, known as 'Corso Italia' – Ottawa's Little Italy – and choose from one of the many delicious options cluttering the street. The city's small but lively Chinatown is also worth a visit. Chinese restaurants spread along Somerset St W near Bronson Ave, and a tasty smattering of Vietnamese joints can be scouted west of Booth St.

Keep an eye out for chip wagons and small shawarma joints throughout the city (especially around the ByWard Market). The adventurous can try poutine: fries with cheese curds drenched in thick gravy, a passion in Québec.

🔝 **ZenKitchen** VEGAN **$$**
CHOICE (✆613-233-6404; www.zenkitchen.ca; 634 Somerset St W; mains $18-21; ⏱lunch Thu-Fri, dinner daily; ✐) Let's face it folks, this could mean

the end of the meat industry – Zen-Kitchen will baffle even the biggest of carnivores with its savvy menu of vegan-chic superlatives. The owners, Caroline and Dave, have years of culinary training between the two of 'em – they're also the stars of a hit reality TV show that documented their 'restaurant adventures.' Voted the best new restaurant in the city in 2009, this unique dining concept offers up healthful dishes that pay tribute to a colorful clash of continents. Oh, and the wine! Let's not forget about the wine! Enjoy a lip-smacking selection of expertly chosen bottles – most come from Ontario, and although the region may not have a global reputation in the industry, we guarantee you'll surprised by the quality.

Urban Element
FUSION $$$
(613-722-0885; www.theurbanelement.ca; 424 Parkdale Ave; courses from $80; 9am-5pm, meals by appointment) Housed in a vacant brick firehouse, this gustatory option wins on concept alone. Think *Iron Chef* meets Martha Stewart. Make a reservation at this kitchen-cum-classroom and cook your own three-star gourmet meal, with the help of a skilled cook, of course. The team of instructors includes a regular crew of chefs and several visiting professionals who work at the finest restaurants around town.

Atelier
FUSION $$$
(613-321-3537; www.atelierrestaurant.ca; 540 Rochester St; menu $85; dinner) The brainchild of celebrated chef and molecular gastronomy enthusiast Marc Lépine, Atelier is a white-walled laboratory dedicated to tickling the taste buds. There's no oven or stove – just Bunsen burners, liquid nitrogen and hot plates to create the unique 12-course tasting menu. Each dish is a mini science experiment that toys with texture, taste and temperature, and pushes the limit of 'normal' cuisine (think taco ice cream). This isn't fusion, it's fission.

Beckta Dining & Wine
FUSION $$$
(613-238-7063; www.beckta.com; 226 Nepean St; mains $27-37; dinner) This excellent upmarket option puts an original spin on regional cuisine. The inspired five-course tasting menu ($79) is the collective brainchild of the chef and sommelier. Ingredients are unpronounceable, which must mean they're gourmet. A second location – dubbed 'Play Food & Wine' – has recently opened in the Market district, and offers similar fare with a tapas twist.

Whalesbone Oyster House
SEAFOOD $$$
(www.thewhalesbone.com; 430 Bank St; mains $29-35; dinner) If the local chefs are purchasing their fish from Whalesbone's wholesale wing (or should we say 'fin'), then there's really no doubt that it's the best place in town for seafood. The on-site restaurant offers up a short list of fresh faves like lobster, halibut and scallops ceviche on small plates.

Boulangerie Moulin de Provence
BAKERY $
(55 ByWard Market Sq; mains $1-5; breakfast & lunch) Suddenly the Market's golden boy after a visit by President Obama, Moulin de Provence offers up glass displays filled to the brim with sugary goodness. The 'Obama Cookies' are a big hit, but we recommend going for the flaky croissants, which hold the official title as the city's best.

Brasserie Métropolitain
FRENCH $$
(www.metropolitainbrasserie.com; 700 Sussex Dr; mains $10-19; lunch & dinner) This trendy hot spot puts a modern spin on the typical brasserie with a swirling zinc countertop, flamboyant fixtures and the subtle oompah-pah from a distant accordion – you'll feel like you're dining on the set of *Moulin Rouge*. 'Hill Hour' (4pm to 7pm on weekdays) buzzes with the spirited chatter of hot-blooded politicos as they down discounted drinks and $1 oysters.

Le Cordon Bleu Bistro @ Signatures
FRENCH $$$
(613-236-2499; 453 Laurier Ave E; mains $20-30; lunch Tue-Fri, dinner daily) This sensational dining experience, housed in a Tudor-style castle, is the on-site restaurant of the prestigious Cordon Bleu culinary school. Fear not, your meal won't be cooked by fumbling students; the à la carte dinners are prepared by the well-seasoned instructors and the weekday lunches are crafted by the graduating students. Award-winning menus feature some of Canada's finest harvests, and the lengthy wine list looks more like an encyclopedia.

Chez Lucien
FRENCH $$
(137 Murray St; mains $6-14; lunch & dinner) Exposed burgundy brick, Sting playing on the free jukebox, butter-soaked escargot – somehow it all makes wonderful sense at Chez Lucien, one of Ottawa's favorite places to kick back in style.

St Hubert FAST FOOD $$
(1754 St Laurent Blvd; mains $10-18; ⊙lunch & dinner) Hubert must be the patron saint of poultry because these chicken fillets are divine. Dunk these morsels of breaded goodness in the homemade gravy to understand why the restaurant became a franchise. It's situated across the road from the Canada Science & Technology Museum, about 5km from the downtown core.

Wellington Gastropub STEAKHOUSE $$$
(www.thewellingtongastropub.com; 1325 Wellington Ave; mains $18-30, 4-course menu $60; ⊙lunch Mon-Fri, dinner Mon-Sat) Although 'gastropub' sounds like some sort of British indigestion, this up-and-comer is luring foodies to the west end of town with a savvy selection of hearty meat mains served by tatted waiters. The menu rotates daily, offering up the best local produce with a pint of crafted microbrew.

The Works BURGERS $$
(580 Bank St; burgers $9.50-13; ⊙lunch & dinner) This western-style chow house takes burgers to a new level. At the Works you can brand your juicy patty with over 60 quirky toppings, be it spinach leaves, fried eggs, brie cheese or even peanut butter. It'll fill you up without emptying your wallet.

 Sweetgrass Aboriginal Bistro
ABORIGINAL $$
(www.sweetgrassbistro.ca; 108 Murray St; mains $12-28; ⊙lunch Mon-Fri, dinner daily) Usually, you would have to travel to a distant reservation to sample bannock, corn soup or elk. This unique aboriginal kitchen will save you that grueling $200 train ride, so why not leave an extra-big tip.

Yangtze CHINESE $$
(700 Somerset St W; mains $9.75-16.50; ⊙lunch & dinner) Ottawa's mother ship of authentic Chinese cuisine is a jade palace in the heart of Chinatown. You'll love the 'bird nest' – a crunchy vermicelli basket that can hold a variety of dishes. The daily dim sum tempts the palate with an assortment of steamed appetizers.

SAVOUR OTTAWA

Check out www.savourottawa.ca for details about the burgeoning local initiative that strives to match regional restaurants with the area's farmers.

Boulanger Français BAKERY $
(119 Murray St; pastries $2-9; ⊙7am-5:30pm) The smell of freshly baked *pain au chocolat* will destroy even the smallest of diets. Pastries are prepared using tried-and-true recipes from France.

Lapointe SEAFOOD $$
(www.lapointefish.ca; 55 York St; mains $10-26; ⊙lunch & dinner) This fish market has been serving the community since 1867, and is the undisputed top vendor of fresh fish in Ottawa. The market restaurant is Lapointe's newest avatar, offering virtually every kind of fish from sashimi to breaded fish and chips.

Zak's Diner DINER $
(www.zaksdiner.com; 14 ByWard Market Sq; mains $8-13; ⊙24hr) Shoo-bop along to the '50s music that supplements the *Grease*-like atmosphere. The kitschy diner is at its best in the middle of the night when the joint fills up for post-party munchies. The club sandwich is a big hit, as are the breakfast items. Wraps are also on offer, so it's not a total time warp.

Horn of Africa AFRICAN $$
(364 Rideau St; mains $9-16; ⊙lunch & dinner;) This slightly tattered, local Ethiopian hangout warrants a visit for excellent exotic stews and dishes eaten with *injera*, an East African flatbread. A combo platter offers samples from all over the menu, including some spicy chicken and succulent vegetarian options.

Market Square FAST FOOD $
(www.bywardmarket.com; 55 ByWard Market Sq, cnr William & George Sts; meals $6-12; ⊙lunch & dinner) Anchoring the market district, this sturdy brick building is the perfect place to stop when hunger strikes. Aside from the fresh produce and cheese, there's an array of international takeaway joints offering falafel, spicy curries, flaky pastries, sushi (the list goes on). For dessert, don't miss the stand at the corner of William and George Sts selling beavertails – Ottawa's signature sizzling flat-dough dish.

🍷 Drinking

From cheery local pubs to plush, see-and-be-seen lounges, Ottawa's got it all – even the crusty joints that have been around since beer was invented. Most bars start up around 9pm, and when they shut down (usually 2am) everyone scurries over to Hull to continue the party.

Ideal Coffee
CAFE

(www.idealcoffees.com; 176 Dalhousie St) Ideal indeed; handcrafted blends are produced and roasted on-site. The decor is thin – it's all about rich, flavorful cups of joe.

Planet Coffee
CAFE

(24a York St) Skip Starbucks and grab a latte around the corner in the quiet courtyard. Sweetened ice coffees are a big hit.

Bridgehead Coffee
CAFE

(www.bridgehead.ca; 282 Elgin St) A dozen shops strong, Bridgehead is the eco-conscious alternative to the mega-chains imported from the States.

E18hteen
BAR

(www.restaurant18.com; 18 York St) If Ottawa attracted a jet-setter crowd, they'd probably come to this manse-turned-lounge.

Château Lafayette
PUB

(42 York St) Many would argue that 'the Laff' puts the 'crap' in crapulence, but this rundown relic does a good job of capturing ByWard's laid-back attitude.

Manx
BAR

(370 Elgin St) A homey velvet sea awaits you at this basement pub-style hangout. Most people come for the great selection of Canadian microbrews (including the beloved Creemore) served on copper-top tables.

Stoneface Dolly's
BAR

(www.stonefacedollys.com; 416 Preston St) Named for the owner's mother, who perfected the art of a stone-cold poker bluff, this popular joint is great place to grab a pint of Beau's or Hobgoblin – there's food throughout the day too.

D'Arcy McGee's
PUB

(www.darcymcgees.com; 44 Sparks St) Eavesdrop on MP's aides at this spirited Irish pub just a stone's throw from Parliament Hill.

Clock Tower Brew Pub
BAR

(www.clocktower.ca; 89 Clarence St) Enjoy homemade brews like Raspberry Wheat and Fenian Red amid exposed brick and ByWard bustle. There are two additional locations around town.

Social
BAR

(www.social.ca; 537 Sussex Dr) A chic, flowing lounge with slick DJ-ed beats, Social lures the trendy types with overstuffed furniture and oversized drinks – the cocktails are so large, there should be a lifeguard on duty.

Royal Oak
BAR

(www.royaloakpubs.com; 318 Bank St) Ottawa's oldest British pub is such an authentic nod to the motherland that you'll want to order blood pudding with your draught beer.

☆ Entertainment

Ottawa has a variety of publications (print and web-based) that offer the latest scoop on the various goings-on around town. *Express* is the city's free entertainment weekly. It can be found around town in various cafes, restaurants, bars and bookshops. Try www.upfrontottawa.com and www.ottawaentertainment.ca for additional info, and check out Thursday's *Ottawa Citizen* for complete club and entertainment listings.

Nightlife venues generally cluster in three zones: the ByWard Market, along Bank St in the Glebe neighborhood, and down Elgin St about halfway between the Queensway and the Parliament.

Live Music

Cover charges range from $3 to $20.

Zaphod Beeblebrox
LIVE MUSIC

(www.zaphodbeeblebrox.com; 27 York St) 'Zaphod Beeblebrox' means 'kick-ass live music venue' in an otherwise undecipherable alien tongue. Grab a Gargleblaster cocktail, and let the trippy beats (from New Age to thumping African rhythms) take you on a ride to the edge of the universe.

Fat Tuesday's
LIVE MUSIC

(www.fattuesdays.ca; 62 York St) Ottawa's little slice of New Orleans is known around town for its dueling pianos on Friday and Saturday nights. Palm readings and happy hour discounts lure the locals on the other days of the week.

Rainbow Bistro
LIVE MUSIC

(✆613-241-5123; 76 Murray St) This upstairs joint is the best place in town to catch some live blues tunes.

Irene's Pub
LIVE MUSIC

(885 Bank St) This friendly and funky lil' pub offers live Celtic, folk or blues, and a great selection of imported beers.

Theater

National Arts Centre
THEATER

(NAC; ✆613-755-1111; www.nac-cna.ca; 53 Elgin St) The capital's premier performing arts complex delivers opera, drama, and performances from the symphony orchestra. The modish complex stretches along the canal in Confederation Sq.

Gay & Lesbian Venues

If you're looking for a booming gay scene, better head to Montréal, although several venues around town have frequent gay-themed evenings. The following are the usual haunts. Check out **Capital Xtra** (www. xtra.ca) for details.

Lookout Bar
BAR

(www.thelookoutbar.com; 41 York St) This popular joint in the ByWard Market caters to a wide range of patrons, especially lesbians.

Edge
NIGHTCLUB

(212 Sparks St) A younger gay crowd grinds to Top 40 and house in this bumping nightspot.

Cinemas

Check out 'Saturday Sin-ema' at the majestic **Mayfair Theatre** (☑613-730-3403; www. mayfair-movie.com; 1074 Bank St), which looks the same as it did in the early '30s. The **Bytown Cinema** (☑613-789-3456; 325 Rideau St) has been screening independent and international movies for over 60 years.

Sports

Ottawa is a hard-core hockey town. It's worth getting tickets to a game even if you're not into hockey – the ballistic fans put on a show of their own. The NHL's Senators play at the **ScotiaBank Place** (☑613-599-0100, tickets 800-444-7367; www.senators.com; Palladium Dr, Kanata), in the city's west end.

Those on a budget can catch the Ottawa 67s, a minor-league hockey team, at the **Civic Center** (☑613-232-6767; www.ottawa67s.com; 1015 Bank St).

🛍 Shopping

The **ByWard Market** (www.byward-market. com), at the corner of George St and By-Ward St, is the best place in town for one-stop shopping. Vendors cluster around the old maroon-brick market building, erected in the 1840s. Outdoor merchants operate booths from 6am to 6pm year-round (although the winter weather drastically reduces the number of businesses). In summer, over 175 stalls fill the streets, selling fresh produce from local farms, flowers, seafood, cheese, baked goods and kitschy souvenirs. Dalhousie St, a block east of the market, has been rising in popularity with a smattering of hipster boutiques and fashion houses.

The Glebe, a colorful neighborhood just south of the Queensway, bustles with quirky antique shops and charismatic cafes. Most of the action crowds along Bank St.

ℹ Information

The **Ottawa Tourism** (www.ottawatourism.ca) website offers a comprehensive glance at the nation's capital and can assist with planning itineraries and booking accommodations. Several banks and currency exchange outlets cluster along the Sparks St mall.

Accu-Rate Foreign Exchange (☑613-238-8454; 1st fl, World Exchange Plaza, 111 Albert St; ☺9:15am-5:15pm Mon-Fri) Accommodates currency exchange, traveler's checks and EFTs.

Capital Infocentre (☑613-239-5000, TTY 866-661-3530; www.capcan.ca; 90 Wellington St; ☺9am-9pm mid-May–early Sep, to 5pm early Sep–mid-May; @☎) Sleek tourism office with a huge model of the downtown core. Located across from the Parliament Buildings.

Market Cleaners (☑613-241-6222; 286 Dalhousie St; ☺7am-9pm Mon-Fri, from 8am Sat & Sun) A laundromat and internet cafe all rolled into one.

Ottawa General Hospital (☑613-722-7000, TTY 613-761-4024; 501 Smyth Rd; ☺24hr) Southeast of downtown in Alta Vista; has an emergency room.

Post office (☑613-844-1545; www.canada post.ca; 59 Sparks St; ☺9am-4pm Mon-Fri)

ℹ Getting There & Away

Air

The state-of-the-art **Ottawa MacDonald-Cartier International Airport** (YOW; ☑613-248-2000; www.ottawa airport.ca; 1000 Airport Rd) is 15km south of the city and is, perhaps surprisingly, very small. Main airlines serving the city include Air Canada, Air Canada Jazz, American Airlines, British Airways, Northwest Airlines, KLM, Porter, US Airways and WestJet. Almost all international flights require a transfer before arriving in the capital.

Bus

The **central bus station** (☑613-238-5900; 265 Catherine St) is 20 blocks south of the Parliament, near Kent St. Several companies operate bus services from the station, the largest being Greyhound Canada.

Car & Motorcycle

Major car-rental chains are represented at the airport and offer several locations around town, especially along Laurier and Catherine Sts.

Train

The **VIA Rail Station** (☑888-842-7245; 200 Tremblay Rd) is 7km southeast of downtown, near the Riverside Dr exit of Hwy 417. VIA Rail operates five daily trains to Kingston (two hours) with continued service to Toronto (4¼ hours) and Montréal (1¾ hours). Trips to western

Ontario (including Sudbury and Thunder Bay) require a circuitous transfer in Toronto.

A satellite station operates at 3347 Fallowfield Rd in Ottawa's west end, and both stations are accessible using public transportation.

❶ Getting Around
To/From the Airport
The cheapest way to get to the airport is by city bus. Take bus 97 from the corner of Slater and Albert Sts, west of Bronson Ave (make sure you are heading in the 'South Keys & Airport' direction). The ride takes 30 minutes.

YOW Airporter (☏613-247-1779; www.yow shuttle.com; per person $15) makes an hourly round between most major hotels. Check online for exact departure times. Plan on a 35-minute ride, and call ahead to reserve a seat.

Blue Line Taxis (☏613-238-1111; www.blue linetaxi.com) and **Capital Taxi** (☏613-744-3333) offer cab service to and from the airport; the fare is $20 to $30. If you're having a hard time snagging a cab, there's always a cluster on Metcalfe St between Sparks and Queen Sts.

Bicycle
The friendly staff at **Rent-A-Bike** (☏613-241-4140; www.rentabike.ca; East Arch Plaza Bridge, 2 Rideau St; 4hr rental $25; ☉mid-Apr–Oct) will set you up with a bike and can offer tips about scenic trails.

Car & Motorcycle
There is free parking in World Exchange Plaza on weekends, and it's always the best place to park when visiting the downtown tourist office. Hourly metered parking can be found throughout downtown. During winter, overnight on-street parking is prohibited. Call the **City of Ottawa** (☏613-580-2400) for additional parking queries.

Public Transportation
Ottawa and Hull/Gatineau operate separate bus systems. A transfer is valid from one system to the other, but may require an extra payment.

OC Transpo (☏613-741-4390, 613-741-6440; www.octranspo.com) operates buses and a light-rail system known as the O-train. Public transportation can be tedious and crowded at times, as most routes involve at least one transfer and buses can be rather infrequent. Generally, the transportation network functions more rapidly and efficiently in the east end of town. Tickets cost $1.25 and all rides require a minimum two tickets. A book of six passes can be purchased at most convenience stores. Call for assistance – the agents are very helpful and can provide time estimates for the next arriving bus. Make sure to grab a transfer pass from the driver when boarding the bus; they are valid for 90 minutes.

AROUND OTTAWA

Across the river in Québec, the Ottawa Valley becomes the Outaouais (pronounced as though you were saying 'Ottawa' with a French-Canadian accent). This large, mostly rural region extends from the Ottawa River north past Maniwaki, west past Fort Coulonge, and east to Montebello.

Gatineau (Hull)
POP 242,000
Gatineau is as much a twin city to Ottawa as it is a separate town. This urban continuation has more of an industrial feel than its Ontarian neighbor. In late 2001, 'Hull' was changed to 'Gatineau' as part of an administrative reshuffling, although the locals on both sides of the river still call the city by its old moniker. Gatineau is home to most of the area's French population, although recent threats of political separation have jostled the population on both sides of the river.

◉ Sights
The most popular attraction on the Gatineau side of the river is the gorgeous Canadian Museum of Civilization (p193) – an inspiring structure with rippling stone walls offering postcard-worthy views of the parade of Parliament buildings.

> **DON'T MISS**
>
> ### BONNECHERE CAVES
>
> The Bonnechere Caves (☏613-628-2283, www.bonnecherecaves. com; Fourth Chute Rd; tours adult/child $16/12; ☉10am-4:30pm Jul-Aug, to 4pm late May-Jun & Sep-Oct), about 130km west of Ottawa, are one of the finest examples of a solution cave (a cave dissolved out of solid rock by acidic waters) in the world. Formed 500 million years ago from the floor of a tropical sea, the dank passages feature a haunting collection of prehistoric fossils including a well-defined octopus. Learn about speleology (the study of caves) from the humorous tour, which details the site's quirky history. Nimble guests will enjoy squeezing through a few extra-narrow, damp passages.

Casino du Lac Leamy
CASINO

(☎819-772-2100; 1 Boul du Casino; admission free; ☺11am-3am) Ottawa's little slice of Vegas is this posh gambling hall with docking facilities and a helipad – just in case you were thinking about bringing your helicopter. The sizable casino complex is complete with a towering hotel, dinner theater, glitzy shows, a high-class restaurant and a felt sea of gambling tables. Take the third exit after the Macdonald-Cartier Bridge from Ottawa, and don't forget to dress up.

🛌 Sleeping

Gatineau has a variety of motels and inns scattered around Hull, Gatineau Hills and quaint Aylmer. The helpful staff at the tourism office can assist you with B&B reservations.

🍴 Eating

Dining in Hull is largely influenced by French flavors; the city has two of the best and most acclaimed restaurants in the region. After 2am, when the Ontario bars close, the hard-core partygoers bounce across the river to Hull, where things roll on until 3am and later. Narrow Rue Aubry, in the middle of downtown, has several nightspots, some with live music.

Le Baccara
FRENCH $$$

(☎819-772-6210; Boul du Casino; dinner mains $30-50; ☺dinner Wed-Sun) How do you say 'shmancy' in French? The answer is 'Baccara.' This world-class dining experience in the Casino du Lac Leamy features an open-concept dining room where patrons can watch the master chefs prepare their meal. Tours are available of the cavernous wine cellar, which contains over 13,000 bottles of wine. All customers must be at least 18 years of age.

Le Troquet
CAFE $$

(☎819-776-9595; 41 Rue Laval; mains $5-15; ☺lunch & dinner) Toss in a beret or two and it'll feel like a trip to Paris. The stylish cafe teems with everyone in the know.

Café Aubry
CAFE $

(☎819-777-3700; 9 Rue Aubry; mains $10; ☺lunch & dinner Mon-Sat) This cafe serves light sandwiches at lunch and then heats things up at night (we're talkin' about a happening bar scene, not warm dinners). It's located in a tiny pedestrian mall just off Promenade du Portage.

❶ Information

Gatineau's tourist information office, **La Maison du Tourisme** (☎800-265-7822; 103 Rue Laurier at Boul St Laurent; ☺8:30am-5pm Mon-Fri, 9am-4pm Sat & Sun) is situated just over the Alexandra Bridge. The helpful staff can offer ample advice about the various regional attractions (mostly forested preserves). The information center in Ottawa proper also has heaps of information about the region. Ottawa city bus and trolley tours often include Gatineau in their circuits.

❶ Getting There & Away

The **Outaouais Bus System** (☎819-770-3242) has buses that operate along Rideau and Wellington Sts in Ottawa. From downtown, buses 8, 27 and 40 all go to the Promenade du Portage.

Gatineau Park

Gatineau Park is a deservedly popular 36,000-hectare area of woods and lakes in the Gatineau Hills of Québec. The **visitors center** (☎819-827-2020; 33 Scott Rd; ☺9am-5pm) is 12km from Ottawa's Parliament Hill, off Hwy 5.

In summer, this green expanse of cedar and maple offers 150km of hiking trails and over 90km of cycling paths. Winters are just as crowded with dozens of alpine skiing hills. Lac Lapêche, Lac Meech and Lac Phillipe have beaches for swimming (including Lac Meech's nude gay beach), which lure the land-locked locals for a refreshing dip (watch out for the occasional leech!).

Also in the park is the **Mackenzie King Estate** (☎800-465-1867; admission per car $10; ☺11am-5pm mid-May–mid-Oct), the summer estate of William Lyon Mackenzie King, Canada's prime minister in the 1920s, late 1930s and early 1940s. A capable speaker, quirky King was known for his gregarious nature; he even talked to his dead dog and deceased mother. His home, Moorside, is now a museum with a pleasant tearoom.

Fall Rhapsody (☎800-465-1867; www. canadascapital.gc.ca/gatineau) gives leaf-peepers a chance to glimpse the blazing fall foliage before the powdery snow blankets the gnarled trunks. Regular activities include organized walks, art exhibits and brunches with live music (although as the temperature drops, so does the attendance). During September and October, there are cheap buses from Ottawa to various spots in the park – it's the only time of the year that the park is accessible by quasi-public transportation. During the other seasons, tourists often use the Ottawa–Maniwaki bus route.

Wakefield

Charming and scenic, historic Wakefield is an amiable mix of heritage buildings, cafes and tourist-oriented shops. This quiet region north of Gatineau makes for a popular day trip.

Northwest of Gatineau Park, there are several outfitters who use a turbulent section of the Ottawa River for rafting adventures. The trips range from half-day to two-day adventures and run from April to October. No experience is needed, and the locations are less than two hours from the capital. Mid-week discounts are possible, although weekends tend to book up fast – reservations are required.

Esprit Rafting (☎800-596-7238; www.espritrafting.com), which is further out in the Outaouais, just off Hwy 148 in Davidson, near Fort Coulonge, uses small, bouncy self-bailing rafts. The one-day rafting trip is a favorite, while many people opt for multiday trips, which go as far as Algonquin. Round-trip shuttle service back to Ottawa is available for an additional fee. For those who want to stay a little longer, the rustic Auberge Esprit hostel, run by the folks at Esprit Rafting, includes breakfast and use of canoes and kayaks. Campsites are also available.

Try **Wilderness Tours** (☎800-267-9166) or **OWL Rafting** (☎800-461-7238; www.owl-mkc.ca) for a mix of wild and mild trips. Both companies offer meals, camping and pricey cabin accommodations, which should be booked ahead.

The **Hull-Chelsea Wakefield (HCW) Steam Train** (☎819-778-7246; www.steamtrain.ca; 165 Rue Deveault, north of central Gatineau; adult $45, during fall colors $55; ☺May–mid-Oct) connects Gatineau to Wakefield along its scenic iron strip. The 100-year-old train chugs through hushed forests on entertaining day trips. Reservations are recommended.

Québec

Best Places to Eat

» L'Express (p235)
» Le Lapin Sauté (p269)
» Manoir Hovey (p253)
» Visa Versa (p282)
» Les Saveurs Oubliées (p280)

Best Places to Stay

» Auberge Saint Antoine (p268)
» Hotel Gault (p231)
» Maison Historique James Thompson (p267)
» ALT Québec (p268)

Why Go?

Once an outpost of Catholic conservatism, an isolated island of *francophonie* languishing in a sea of anglo culture, Québec has finally come into its own, and has crafted a rich, spirited culture independent of its European motherland. The people of Québec are as vibrant and inviting as the colorful Victorian facades, lush rolling hills and romantic bistros strewn across the province.

And there's plenty to choose from. Montréal and Québec City are bustling metropolises with a perfect mixture of sophistication and playfulness, and history-soaked preserved quarters tucked away in their back pockets. The rustic allurements of old Québec are scattered among the Eastern Townships, and produce from bucolic Charlevoix graces the tables of the region's stellar restaurants. The Laurentians abound with ski resorts and peaks, while the jagged coasts of the unblemished Gaspé Peninsula and the cliffs soaring high above the Saguenay River are equally as breathtaking.

When to Go
Montréal

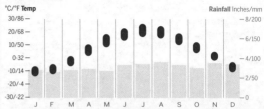

December & January Head to Mont-Tremblant – one of North America's best ski hills

February & March Maple syrup production is in full swing at local sugar shacks

July Montréal's summer-long party gets under way with the Festival International de Jazz

Local Culture

Quebecers are passionate folks; just bring up the subject of separatism if you're keen to test the theory. Life here is sipped slowly, like its strong rich coffee, which is often accompanied by a *chocolatine* (chocolate croissant) and engaging conversation with friends or family.

The Québécois drink more alcohol than the average Canadian, and predominantly liberal views contribute to a laid-back atmosphere that feeds an effervescent nightlife in Montréal and Québec City. On weekend evenings, city streets are often packed with pedestrians well into the early hours of the morning.

QUÉBEC ITINERARIES

One Day

Start with brunch in Montréal at **L'Express** and work the calories off on a hike up **Parc du Mont Royal**. Descend through **Mile End** or the **Plateau Mont-Royal** where you'll be spoiled for choice for dinner and drinks.

Three Days

Limit your time savoring **Montréal's** chilled-out vibe to one day, and then drive through the Laurentians to **Mont-Tremblant**. Leave a day to stroll within **Québec City's** walls in the **Old Upper Town**, before searching for the ultimate table d'hôte in the **Old Lower Town**.

Seven Days

Follow the three-day itinerary then ramble through **Charlevoix** en route to the **Saguenay River** for two days. Stop for lunch in **Baie St Paul** or **La Malbaie**. Spend the last two nights in welcoming **Tadoussac**, whale-watching or cruising the fjord.

What the...?

Le français québécois (Québec French), the mother tongue of nearly a quarter of all Canadians, is discernible from standard French by its accent, vocabulary and expressions, but it's the jarring use of profanity that tends to leave a more lasting impression on new learners. Frustrated Francophones have turned to the most sacred of their institutions – the once all-powerful Catholic church – for curse word inspiration, resorting to such deplorable obscenities as *tabernac* (tabarnacle), *câlisse* (chalice) and *ciboire* (ciborium).

If you want to really turn heads, practice saying *câlisse de crisse de tabernac d'ostie de ciboire de testament* (the chalice of Christ of the tabernacle of the Host of the ciborium of the testament). It's the granddaddy of all swear words.

Funnily enough, *fucké,* an adaptation of the English, is mild enough for prime time and means 'broken' or 'crazy.'

QUÉBEC À PIED

If you're visiting either Montréal or Québec City, consider leaving the car at home. Unlike other North American cities, Québec's metropolises are European in design – easily navigated on foot, with bustling sidewalks lined with outdoor cafes.

Fast Facts

» Population: 7,870,000

» Area: 1,540,687 sq km

» Capital: Québec City

» Quirky fact: The Château Frontenac in Québec City is the most photographed hotel in the world

Québec Creations

» Birthplace of: Trivial Pursuit, AM radio, Ski-Doo snowmobile, Plexiglas

» Home of: Leonard Cohen, Brian Mulroney, Jacques Villeneuve, Rufus Wainwright

» Kitschiest souvenir: Cow-shaped maple syrup lollipops

Resources

» Montréal Lifestyle: www.midnightpoutine.ca

» Spacing Montréal: spacingmontreal.ca

» Tourism Montréal: www.tourism-montreal.org

» Tourism Québec: www.bonjourquebec.com

» Tourism Québec City: www.quebecregion.com

Québec Highlights

1 Drink up the dynamic nightlife in happening **Montréal** (p214)

2 Savor the unparalleled culture, history and charm of walled **Québec City** (p256)

3 Get sprayed by whales in the Saguenay River fjord at **Tadoussac** (p283)

4 Soak up the artsy vibe and sample local delicacies in **Baie St Paul** (p277)

5 Hike the stunning peaks above the tree line in **Parc de la Gaspésie** (p297)

6 Swoosh the slopes at action-packed ski resorts such as **Mont-Tremblant** (p246)

7 Get back to nature in spectacular **Parc du Bic** (p293)

8 Sea kayak amid the remote, sculpted islands of the **Mingan Archipelago National Park** (p307)

History

Québec has had a tumultuous history and, by Canadian standards, a very long and complicated one.

At the time of European exploration, the entire region was fully settled and controlled by various Aboriginal groups, all of whom are resident today, including the Mohawks along the St Lawrence River, the Cree above them, the Innu still further north and east, and the Inuit in the remote far north.

French explorer Jacques Cartier landed in what is now Québec City and Montréal in 1535. Samuel de Champlain, also of France, first heard and recorded the word 'kebec' (an Algonquin word meaning 'where the river narrows') when he founded a settlement at Québec City some 70 years later, in 1608.

Throughout the rest of the 17th century, the French and English skirmished over control of Canada, but by 1759 the English, with a final battle victory on the Plains of Abraham at Québec City, established themselves as the winners in the Canadian colony sweepstakes. From that point onward, French political influence in the New World waned.

When thousands of British Loyalists fled the American Revolution in the 1770s, the new colony divided into Upper (today's Ontario) and Lower (now Québec) Canada; almost all the French settled in the latter region. Power struggles between the two language groups continued through the 1800s, with Lower Canada joining the Canadian confederation as Québec in 1867.

The 20th century saw Québec change from a rural, agricultural society to an urban, industrialized one, but one that continued to be educationally and culturally based upon the Catholic Church, which wielded immense power and still does (about 90% of the population today is Roman Catholic).

The tumultuous 1960s brought the so-called 'Quiet Revolution,' during which all aspects of francophone society were scrutinized and overhauled. Intellectuals and extremists alike debated the prospect of independence from Canada, as Québécois began to assert their sense of nationhood.

Formed in 1968, the pro-independence Parti Québécois came to power in 1976, headed by the charismatic René Lévesque. Since then, two referendums have returned 'No' votes on the question of separating from Canada. In the new century, the notion of an independent Québec is less attractive to a younger generation with more global concerns.

Land & Climate

Québec is quite simply stunning, from the mountainous Laurentians to the jagged, windswept coastlines of the Gaspé Peninsula. Charlevoix is flat and agricultural with checkerboard farms. The landscape of the Far North is littered with untamed forests and parkland that give way to arctic tundra at the province's northern corners.

In terms of temperature, the province is saddled with extremes. Montréal and Québec City can go from 40°C to -40°C in six months, and May could see a dump of snow. Generally, the summers are comfortably warm, although high humidity can make Montréal pretty steamy. Winters are very snowy, but usually bright, sunny and dry.

Parks

The province's protected areas can be a highlight of any trip to Québec. Aside from preserving regions of remarkable beauty, they offer a host of invigorating activities, including canoeing, kayaking, rafting, hiking, cycling and camping in the wild. Forillon National Park (p298) and Saguenay (p284), Bic (p293), Mont-Tremblant (p248) and Gaspésie (p297) Provincial Parks are among those especially recommended.

Parks Canada (☎888-773-8888; www. pc.gc.ca) administers three national parks and 28 national historic sites in Québec. The historic sites, such as forts and lighthouses, are mostly day-use areas and reveal fascinating bits of history.

The **Société des Établissements de Plein Air du Québec** (Sépaq; ☎418-890-6527, 800-665-6527; www.sepaq.com) oversees Québec's enviable array of 22 provincial parks and 16 wildlife reserves. Confusingly, they refer to their parks as 'national.' The parks provide some outstanding camping, wildlife viewing, eco-adventure and other outdoor recreation. They range from beaches and bird sanctuaries to rugged gorges.

Réserve fauniques (wildlife reserves) conserve and protect the environment but also make these spaces publicly accessible. Hunters and fishers use the reserves (permits required), but more and more visitors are discovering them as less crowded alternatives to national and provincial parks.

REGIONAL DRIVING DISTANCES:	
Montréal to Québec City	260km
Montréal to Mont-Tremblant	130km
Montréal to Trois-Rivières	134km
Montréal to Toronto	540km
Montréal to New York City	600km
Québec City to La Malbaie	140km
Québec City to Tadoussac	240km

❶ Getting There & Around

Québec is easily accessible by air, bus, car and train. It shares borders with the US states of New York, Vermont, New Hampshire and Maine. For information on border crossings, see p880.

AIR

Québec's main airport is in Montréal, although Québec City is also busy. Carriers serving the province include Air Canada, Air Canada Jazz, Air France, Porter Airlines and bargain airlines Air Transat and WestJet (for contact details, see p880). For flights in the Far North there is First Air, Air Inuit and Air Creebec. Air Canada Jazz covers the North Shore and Îles de la Madeleine from Québec City and Montréal. For contact details, see p882.

BOAT

There are numerous ferry services across the St Lawrence River, as well as to islands in the Gulf, such as the Îles de la Madeleine, and along the remote Lower North Shore toward Labrador.

BUS

Greyhound Canada, Megabus, Acadian Lines and other bus companies connect the province with Ontario and Atlantic Canada in a seamless network (see p884). From the USA, Greyhound (p881) operates three or more daily bus services between Montréal and New York City. The province is particularly well served by bus lines, including:

Autobus Maheux (www.autobusmaheux.qc.ca) Covers the northwest regions.

Autobus Viens (☑877-348-5599)

Galland (www.galland-bus.com)

Greyhound Canada (www.greyhound.ca)

Intercar (www.intercar.qc.ca)

Limocar (www.limocar.ca)

Megabus (www.ca.megabus.com)

Orléans Express (www.orleansexpress.com)

Voyageur (www.greyhound.ca)

See the Getting There & Away sections of individual destinations in this chapter for specific trip details.

CAR & MOTORCYCLE

Continental US highways link directly with their Canadian counterparts at numerous border crossings. These roads connect to the Trans-Canada Hwy (Hwy 40 within Québec), which runs directly through Montréal and Québec City.

Highways throughout the province are good. In the far eastern and northern sections, however, slow, winding, even nonpaved sections are typical and services may be few. For road conditions, a serious factor in winter, call ☑877-393-2363. Note that turning right at red lights is not permitted anywhere on the island of Montréal, in Québec City or anywhere else where signs indicate not to do so.

The ride-share agency **Allô Stop** (www.allo stop.com) offers an inexpensive way to travel within Québec by linking up drivers and paying passengers headed in the same direction. Passengers pay $6 for a one-year membership, plus a portion of the ride cost to the agency; the rest goes to the driver. There are offices in Montréal, Québec City, Sherbrooke, Chicoutimi, Tadoussac and Rimouski. See the Getting There & Away sections of those destinations for details.

TRAIN

VIA Rail (☑888-842-7245; www.viarail.ca) has fast and frequent services along the Québec City–Windsor corridor, via Montréal, and services the South Shore and Gaspésie. From the USA, **Amtrak** (☑800-872-7245; www.amtrak.com) trains run once daily between Montréal and New York City.

MONTRÉAL

POP 3.4 MILLION

Historically Montréal, the only de facto bilingual city on the continent, has been torn right in half, the 'Main' (Blvd St-Laurent) being the dividing line between the east-end Francophones and the west-side Anglos. Today French pockets dot both sides of the map, a new wave of English-speaking Canadians have taken residence in some formerly French enclaves and thanks to constant waves of immigration, it's not uncommon for Montréalers to speak not one, or two, but three languages in their daily life. With the new generation concerned more with global issues (namely the environment), language battles have become so passé.

One thing not up for debate is what makes Montréal so irresistible. It's a secret blend of French-inspired joie de vivre and cosmopolitan dynamism that has come together to foster a flourishing arts scene, an indie rock explosion, a medley of world-renowned boutique hotels, the Plateau's extraordinary cache of swank eateries and a cool Parisian vibe that pervades every *terrasse* (patio) in the Quartier Latin. It's easy to imagine you've been transported to a distant locale, where hedonism is the national mandate. Only the stunning vista of a stereotypical North American skyline from Parc du Mont Royal's Kondiaronk Lookout will ground you.

History

In May 1642, a small fleet of boats sailed up the St Lawrence River. The few dozen missionaries aboard had survived a cold winter crossing the fierce Atlantic Ocean from their native France. Finally they had reached the spot their fellow countryman, explorer Jacques Cartier, had stumbled across over a century earlier. Led by Paul Chomedey de Maisonneuve, the pioneers went ashore and began building a small settlement they called Ville-Marie, the birthplace of Montréal.

Ville-Marie soon blossomed into a major fur-trading center and exploration base, despite fierce resistance from the local Iroquois. Skirmishes continued until the signing of a peace treaty in 1701. The city remained French until the 1763 Treaty of Paris, which saw France cede Canada to Great Britain. In 1775, American revolutionaries briefly occupied the city, but left after failing to convince the Québécois to join forces with them against the British.

Despite surrendering its pole position in the fur trade to Hudson Bay in the 1820s, Montréal boomed throughout the 19th century. Industrialization got seriously under way after the construction of the railway and the Canal de Lachine, which in turn attracted masses of immigrants.

After WWI the city sashayed through a period as 'Sin City' as hordes of Americans seeking fun flooded across the border to escape Prohibition. By the time mayor Jean Drapeau took the reins, Montréal was ripe

Montréal

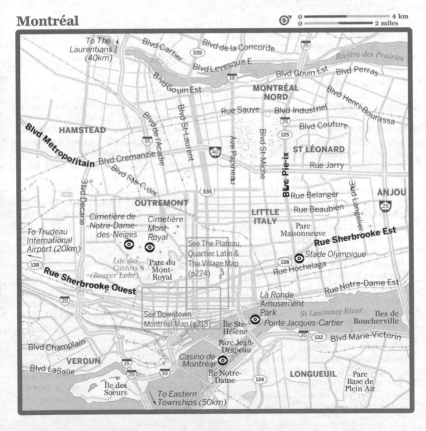

MONTRÉAL IN...

One Day

Start your day in **Mile End**, partaking in a local ritual – a long and leisurely brunch. Hike up **Mont Royal**, stopping to catch your breath and snap the cityscape from the **Kondiaronk Lookout** before ending up in the **Plateau Mont-Royal** for dinner and evening entertainment.

Two Days

Follow the one-day itinerary, and on the second day begin by exploring the cobblestoned alleys of **Old Montréal**. Get a dose of history at **Musée d'Archéologie et d'Histoire Pointe-à-Callière**, or soak up some culture at **Musée Des Beaux-Arts**. Head to **Little Italy** for dinner, then sample the club scene in **The Village**.

Four Days

Start day three at the **Olympic Park**. If the weather is behaving, follow up a visit to the **Biodôme** with a trip up the **Tour de Montréal**. Or head straight to the **Jardin Botanique** for a more fragrant affair.

On the last day, hit the **Marché Atwater** for picnic supplies, then rent bicycles for a cruise along the **Canal de Lachine** or take a jet boat ride on the **Lachine Rapids**.

After dinner at a big shot such as **Toqué!** or **L'Express**, head to the glitzy **Casino de Montréal** to blow the last of your holiday money.

---

for an extreme makeover. During his long tenure (1954–57, 1960–86), the city gained the métro system, many of downtown's high-rise offices, the underground city and the Place des Arts. Drapeau also twice managed to firmly train the world's spotlight on Montréal: in 1967 for the World Expo and in 1976 for the Olympic Games.

Montréal has been enjoying a consistently positive growth rate for the past decade, often surpassing increases in other Canadian cities. It's also a pleasant place to live: *Forbes* magazine ranked it as the 10th-cleanest city in the world in 2007.

◉ Sights

First on most itineraries is Old Montréal, where the heart of the city's history and grandeur can be chased through a labyrinth of winding laneways. Waterfront attractions in the Old Port have benefited immensely from recent rejuvenation, and across the water the attractions and trails of Parc Jean-Drapeau make a great summer escape from the urban jungle. Downtown encompasses stellar museums and universities, while the bohemian Mile End and Plateau Mont-Royal districts are perfect for meandering. The Village and Quartier Latin jolt awake at nighttime. Just outside the city, the Olympic Park and Lachine hold the greatest sightseeing appeal. From the panorama at Mont Royal it's possible to take it all in at once.

For off-the-map locations, the métro station is given.

OLD MONTRÉAL

The oldest section of the city is a warren of crooked cobblestone lanes flanked by colonial and Victorian stone houses filled with intimate restaurants, galleries and boutiques. A stroll around here will delight romantics and architecture fans, especially at night when the most beautiful facades are illuminated. And the waterfront is never far away.

Old Montréal is anchored by lively Place Jacques Cartier and dignified Place d'Armes, which are linked by busy Rue Notre-Dame. The southern end of Place Jacques Cartier gives way to Rue St-Paul, the district's prettiest and oldest street.

Basilique Notre-Dame CHURCH
(Map p218; www.basiliquenddm.org; 110 Rue Notre-Dame Ouest; adult/child $5/4; ⊘8am-4:30pm Mon-Sat, noon-4:15pm Sun) Montréal's famous landmark, Notre-Dame Basilica, is a visually pleasing if slightly gaudy symphony of carved wood, paintings, gilded sculptures and stained-glass windows. Built in 1829 on the site of an older and smaller church, it also sports a famous Casavant organ and the Gros Bourdon, said to be the biggest bell in North America. The

interior looks especially impressive during an otherwise overly melodramatic **sound and light show** (adult/child $10/5), staged from Tuesday to Saturday night.

The basilica made headlines in 1994 when singer Céline Dion was married under its soaring midnight-blue ceiling, and again in 2000 when Jimmy Carter and Fidel Castro shared pall-bearing honors at the state funeral of former Canadian Prime Minister Pierre Trudeau.

A popular place for regular Montréalers to tie the knot is the much smaller **Chapelle du Sacré Coeur** (Sacred Heart Chapel) behind the main altar. Rebuilt in a hotchpotch of historic and contemporary styles after a 1978 fire, its most eye-catching element is the floor-to-ceiling bronze altarpiece.

Place d'Armes   HISTORICAL SITE

The twin-towered Notre-Dame Basilica lords over this dignified square, where the early settlers once battled it out with the local Iroquois. A statue of Maisonneuve stands in the middle of the square, which is surrounded by some of Old Montréal's finest historic buildings. In fact, the **Old Seminary** (Map p218), next to the basilica, is the city's oldest, built by Sulpician missionaries in 1685 and still occupied today.

Behind the temple-like curtain of columns in the northwest corner lurks the **Bank of Montreal** (Map p218; 119 Rue St-Jacques Ouest; admission free; ☺10am-4pm Mon-Fri). It harbors the head office of Canada's oldest bank, founded in 1817. The opulent marble interior is worth a gander and there's a small **money museum** as well.

Looming on the square's east side is the red sandstone **New York Life Building** (1888; Map p218), which was the city's first skyscraper. Today it is dwarfed by the art-deco **Aldred Building** (1937; Map p218), which was intended to emulate the Empire State Building until the Great Crash of 1929 put an end to such lofty ambitions.

Centre d'Histoire de Montréal   MUSEUM

(Map p218; 335 Place d'Youville; adult/child $6/4; ☺10am-5pm Tue-Sun Jan-Nov) This small museum puts a human spin on city history in an engaging multimedia exhibit. You can listen to the tales of real people while sitting in a period kitchen or travel back in time while watching archival footage from the 1940s or '60s. For sweeping views, head to the rooftop.

Place Jacques Cartier & Around   HISTORICAL SITE

Gently sloped Place Jacques Cartier in the heart of Old Montréal is a beehive of activity, especially in summer when it's filled with flowers, street musicians, vendors and visitors. The cafes and restaurants lining it are neither cheap nor good, but they do offer front-row seats for the action. There is a tourist office (p243) in the northwest corner.

At the square's north end stands the **Colonne Nelson** (Nelson's Column; Map p218), a monument erected by the British to the general who defeated the French and Spanish fleet at Trafalgar. Nelson faces a small statue of Admiral Vauquelin across the street, put there as a riposte by the French.

OTHER CHURCHES WORTH EXPLORING

» The gigantic, domed **Oratoire St-Joseph** (St-Joseph's Oratory; www.saint-joseph.org; 3800 Chemin Queen Mary; admission free; ☺6am-9:30pm; ⓜCôte-des-Neiges) was built by a devoted monk named Brother André who had a knack for healing people. Crutches left by the cured still fill a chapel illuminated by thousands of votives.

» In 1987 the Anglican **Cathédrale Christ Church** (Christ Church Cathedral; Map p218; 635 Rue Ste-Catherine Ouest; admission free; ☺7am-6pm), a beautiful neo-Gothic confection, was temporarily supported by concrete stilts while a shopping mall was carved out directly underneath it.

» The **Chapelle Notre-Dame-de-Bonsecours** (Map p218; 400 Rue St-Paul Est; admission free; ☺10am-5:30pm) occupied a special spot in the heart of seamen who came here to pray for safe passage. Small ship models left here by grateful survivors still dangle from its ceiling.

» The **Cathédrale Marie-Reine-du-Monde** (Cathedral of Mary Queen of the World; Map p218; 1085 Rue de la Cathédrale; admission free; ☺7:30am-6:15pm Tue-Sun, to 7:45pm Mon) was modeled after St Peter's Basilica in Rome.

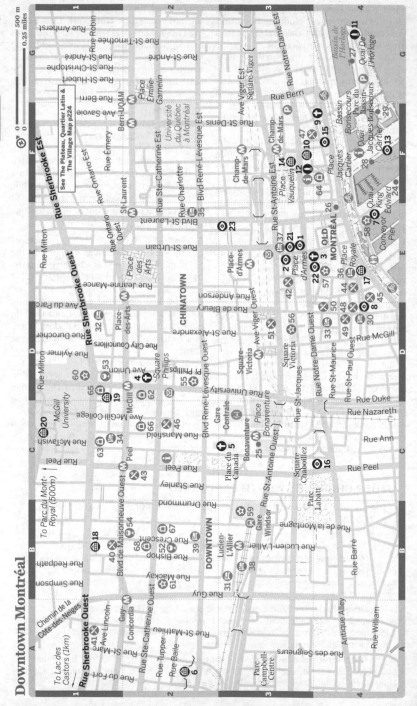

Downtown Montréal

See The Plateau, Quartier Latin & The Village Map p224

500 m
0.25 miles

To Parc du Mont-Royal (500m)

To Lac des Castors (1km)

Looking mightily majestic with its green copper roof and perky turret, the **Hôtel de Ville** (City Hall; Map p218; 275 Rue Notre-Dame Est; admission & tours free; ⊘8:30am-4:30pm, tours late Jun–mid-Aug) towers above the square's northeast end. Modeled on the city hall of Tours, France, and completed in 1878, its grandeur reflects the city's 19th-century wealth and confidence. In 1967, French President Charles de Gaulle surprised everyone by proclaiming '*Vive le Québec libre!*' (Long live free Québec!) to cheering crowds from its balcony. These four little words were enough to fan the flames of separatism, straining relations with Ottawa for years. Inside, the **Hall of Honour**, adorned with scenes of rural Québec, is worth a closer inspection.

ⓘ MONTRÉAL MUSEUM PASS

Custom-made for culture buffs, this handy **pass** ($45) is valid for three consecutive days and gets you admission to 34 museums, plus unlimited use of the bus and métro system. It's available at tourist offices, major hotels and participating museums. Note that most museums are closed on Monday.

The petite palace across the street is the **Château Ramezay** (Map p218; www.chateauramezay.qc.ca; 280 Rue Notre-Dame Est; adult/child $10/5; ◷10am-6pm Jun-Sep, 10am-4:30pm Tue-Sun Oct-May), built in 1705 as the residence of Montréal governor Claude de Ramezay. During the American Revolution, Ben Franklin stayed here, fruitlessly attempting to convince the Canadians to join the cause. Now a museum of early Québec history, its web of rooms brims with an eclectic assortment of furniture, art and objects. The mahogany-paneled **Salle de Nantes** is a feast for the eyes, and there's a pretty garden as well.

Marché Bonsecours   MARKET
(Bonsecours Market; Map p218; 350 Rue St-Paul Est; ◷10am-9pm late Jun-early Sep, to 6pm Sep-Mar) The silvery dome standing sentinel over Old Montréal like a glamorous lighthouse belongs to Bonsecours Market. After a stint as city hall, the neoclassical structure served as the city's main market hall until supermarkets drove it out of business in the 1960s. These days, the flower and vegetable stands have been replaced with fancy boutiques selling arts, crafts and clothing produced in Québec. This is not a bad place to pick up some quality souvenirs.

Old Port   LANDMARK
Montréal's Old Port has morphed into a park and fun zone paralleling the mighty St Lawrence River for 2.5km and punctuated by four grand *quais*. Locals and visitors alike come here for strolling, cycling and in-line skating. Cruise boats, ferries, jet boats and speedboats all depart for tours from various docks (see p228). In winter, you can cut a fine figure on an outdoor ice-skating rink (p228).

Historical relics include the striking white **Clock Tower** (Map p218; Clock Tower

Pier; admission free; ◷10am-9pm mid-May–Sep) at the northern end of Quai Jacques Cartier. Built in 1922 to honor sailors who died in WWI, it affords commanding views of the river and city.

A perennial family favorite is the **Centre des Sciences de Montréal** (Montréal Science Centre; Map p218; www.montrealsciencecentre.com; King Edward Pier; adult/child $12/9, with IMAX 3-D movie $20/15; ◷9am-4pm Mon-Fri, to 5pm Sat & Sun). There are plenty of buttons to push, knobs to pull and games to play as you make your way through the high-tech exhibition halls. The permanent exhibit – Mission Gaia – seeks solutions to environmental or social disasters, while idTV allows you to write your own news story with a virtual editor and report it live.

The center also includes an IMAX cinema (p239) showing vivid nature and science films in 2-D or 3-D.

Musée d'Archéologie et d'Histoire Pointe-à-Callière   MUSEUM
(Museum of Archaeology & History; Map p218; www.pacmuseum.qc.ca; 350 Place Royale; adult/child $14/6; ◷11am-6pm mid-Jun–mid-Sep, 11am-5pm mid-Sep–mid-Jun) Housed in a striking, contemporary building, this excellent museum sits near the original landing spot of the early settlers and provides a good overview of the city's beginnings. Make time for the multimedia show before plunging underground into a maze of excavated foundations, an ancient sewerage system and vestiges of the first European cemetery. Artifacts and interactive stations help bring the past to life. The **lookout tower** and restaurant can be visited free of charge.

DOWNTOWN
Montréal's modern downtown has a North American look, with wide thoroughfares chopping a forest of skyscrapers into a grid pattern. At street level you'll find some of the city's most beautiful churches, striking buildings, museums, green spaces and major shopping areas. You'll find that an almost Latin spirit pervades the cafes, restaurants and bars, especially along Rue Crescent.

FREE **Musée des Beaux-Arts**   MUSEUM
(Museum of Fine Arts; Map p218; www.mbam.qc.ca; 1380 Rue Sherbrooke Ouest; permanent collection admission free, special exhibitions adult/child $15/free, half-price Wed after 5pm; ◷11am-5pm Tue, Sat & Sun, to 9pm Wed-Fri) A must for art lovers, the Museum of

Fine Arts has amassed several millennia worth of paintings, sculpture, decorative arts, furniture, prints, drawings and photographs. European heavyweights include Rembrandt, Picasso and Monet, but the museum really shines when it comes to Canadian art. Highlights include works by Jean-Baptiste Roy-Audy and Paul Kane, landscapes by the Group of Seven and abstractions by Jean-Paul Riopelle. There are also a fair amount of Inuit and aboriginal artifacts and lots of fancy decorative knick-knacks, including Japanese incense boxes and Victorian chests. The temporary exhibits are often exceptional.

Exhibits are spread across the classical, marble-clad Michal and Renata Hornstein Pavilion and the crisp, contemporary Jean-Noël Desmarais Pavilion across the street.

Chinatown LANDMARK
Although this neighborhood, perfectly packed into a few easily navigable streets, has no sites per se, it's a nice area for lunch or for shopping for quirky knickknacks. The main thoroughfare, Rue de la Gauchetière, between Blvd St-Laurent and Rue Jeanne Mance, is enlivened with Taiwanese bubble-tea parlors, Hong Kong–style bakeries and Vietnamese soup restaurants. The public square, **Place Sun-Yat-Sen** (Map p218), attracts crowds of elderly Chinese and the occasional gaggle of Falun Gong demonstrators.

Centre Canadien d'Architecture MUSEUM
(Canadian Centre for Architecture; Map p218; www.cca.qc.ca; 1920 Rue Baile; adult/child $10/free, admission free 5:30-9pm Thu; ◷10am-5pm Wed & Fri-Sun, to 9pm Thu) Architecture buffs should make a beeline to the Canadian Centre for Architecture. It combines a museum and a research institution in one sleek, innovative complex that seamlessly integrates with the historic **Shaughnessy House**. Once the home of a wealthy businessman, the gray limestone treasure encapsulates 19th-century high-class living. The ritziest room is a lounge with intricate woodwork and a grand fireplace.

The center's galleries show prints, drawings, models and photos of remarkable buildings, both local and international. There's also a **sculpture garden** with a dozen or so works scattered about a terrace overlooking southern Montréal. It's especially impressive when illuminated at night.

Free English-language **tours** run at 1:30pm on weekends throughout the year, with additional tours every day at 10:30am and 1:30pm from July through September.

Musée McCord MUSEUM
(McCord Museum of Canadian History; Map p218; www.mccord-museum.qc.ca; 690 Rue Sherbrooke Ouest; adult/child $13/5; ◷10am-6pm Tue-Fri, to 5pm Sat & Sun year-round & Mon late Jun-early Sep) Beaded headdresses, fine china, elegant gowns, letters, photographs and toys are among the more than 1.2 million objects forming the collection of the well-regarded McCord Museum of Canadian History. Changing and permanent exhibitions tell the history of the people who built the country, zeroing in on the unique challenges they faced, from icy winters to multiculturalism. The museum is especially renowned for its **Notman Photographic Archives**, which offer an unparalleled visual record of Canada's evolution since 1840. Ask about guided tours and children's workshops.

McGill University LANDMARK
(Map p218; www.mcgill.ca; 845 Rue Sherbrooke Ouest) The closest Canada has to Ivy League, this university counts two Canadian prime ministers, six Nobel laureates and William Shatner among its alumni. These days some 30,000 students try to uphold the university's grand reputation, which is especially stellar in medicine and engineering. It was founded in 1821 with money and land donated by James McGill, a Scottish-born fur trader. The leafy campus with its Victorian edifices is a pretty place for a quiet stroll or a picnic.

The university's **Musée Redpath** (Map p218; admission free; ◷9am-5pm Mon-Fri, 1-5pm Sat & Sun, closed Fri mid-Jun–early Sep) is one of the oldest museums in Canada, and it shows. Nevertheless, it has some interesting natural history exhibits, including a life-sized dinosaur skeleton and Egyptian mummies.

Musée d'Art Contemporain MUSEUM
(Map p224; www.macm.org; 185 Rue Ste-Catherine Ouest; adult/child $10/free, admission free 5-9pm Wed; ◷11am-6pm Tue & Thu-Sun, to 9pm Wed) Canada's only major showcase of contemporary art, this museum offers an excellent survey of Canadian, and in particular Québécois, creativity. All the local legends, including Jean-Paul Riopelle, Paul-Émile Borduas and Géneviève Cadieux, are well represented. There are great temporary shows, too. Free English-language **tours** run at 6:30pm Wednesday and at 1pm and 3pm on weekends.

LOCAL KNOWLEDGE

EMMA WONTORRA: STUDENT

Being a student in Montréal is amazing because it's still a relatively cheap place to live, and there are so many free festivals all year round. Montréal is also the best place to study French. Almost anywhere you go you can speak either English or French. Even if your French is terrible, people make the effort to let you practice. And on those days when you feel lazy, you can take a break and speak English.

Student Eats

Poutine! Students are far from 'starving' when for just a few dollars, they can get all their daily calories in one plate of poutine – french fries, gravy and melty cheese curds.

Student Hangouts

Lots of students go kayaking on the St Lawrence River, cycling along Canal de Lachine, or swimming at Plage des Îles on Île Notre-Dame. During the summer semester, my friends and I take our books, pack a picnic and spend the day in Parc LaFontaine.

Secret Spot

Students from all over the city meet up at the 'tam tams' in Parque de Mont Royal every Sunday. You can eat cheap food, and watch people dance and play music. It's free entertainment!

Montréal Planetarium   NOTABLE BUILDING
(Map p218; www.planetarium.montreal.qc.ca; 1000 Rue St-Jacques; adult/child $8/4; ⊙12:30-5pm Mon, 9:30am-5pm Tue-Thu, 9:30am-9:30pm Fri, 12:30-9:30pm Sat & Sun, closed Mon early Sep–mid-Jun) The 20m-high dome of the Montréal Planetarium opens a window on the universe during narrated 50-minute shows playaed alternately in French and English. Call for the current schedule.

PARC DU MONT ROYAL AREA
Parc du Mont Royal   PARK
(off Map p218; www.lemontroyal.qc.ca) Montréalers are proud of their 'mountain,' the work of New York Central Park designer Frederick Law Olmsted. It's a sprawling, leafy playground that's perfect for cycling, jogging, horseback riding, picnicking and, in winter, cross-country skiing and tobogganing. In fine weather, enjoy panoramic views from the **Kondiaronk Lookout** near **Chalet du Mont-Royal**, a grand old stone villa that hosts big-band concerts in summer, or from the **Observatoire de l'Est** (off Map p224), a favorite rendezvous for lovebirds. It takes about 30 minutes to walk between the two. En route you'll spot the landmark 40m-high **Cross of Montréal** (1924), which is illuminated at night. It's there to commemorate city founder Maisonneuve, who single-handedly carried a wooden cross up the mountain in 1643 to give thanks to God for sparing his fledgling village from flooding.

Lac des Castors   LANDMARK
(off Map p218) Known to Anglophones as Beaver Lake, this is where locals come to rent paddleboats in summer and ice skates and sleds in winter. North of here are two vast cemeteries. The Catholic **Cimetière de Notre-Dame-des-Neiges** (Map p215) holds the remains of mayors, artists, clerics and *Titanic* victims. Further north, the protestant **Cimetière Mont-Royal** (Map p215) is smaller and more noted for its birdwatching than celebrity tombs.

Georges Étienne Cartier monument   STATUE
On the park's northeastern edge, on Ave du Parc, this statue draws hundreds of revelers every Sunday for tribal playing and spontaneous dancing in what has been dubbed 'Tam Tam Sundays' (tam-tams are bongo-like drums). It's nothing less than an institution. If the noise doesn't lead you all the way there, just follow your nose toward whiffs of 'wacky tabaccy.' This is also a good spot to pick up some unusual handicrafts sold by local artisans.

Mont Royal can be entered via the steps at the top of Rue Peel. Buses 80 and 129 make their way from the Place des Arts métro station to the Georges Étienne Cartier monument. Bus 11 from the Mont Royal métro stop traverses the park.

QUARTIER LATIN & THE VILLAGE

The Quartier Latin is Montréal's most boisterous neighborhood, a slightly grungy entertainment district made glitzy with an infusion of French panache. The area blossomed with the arrival of the Université de Montréal in 1893, which drew several prestigious cultural institutions and the wealthy French bourgeoisie in its wake. Although it fell out of fashion after the university relocated to a larger campus north of Mont Royal and suffered from an influx of crime and neglect, things began looking up again when the Université de Québec was established in 1969.

A hotbed of activity, especially during the International Jazz Festival (p230), FrancoFolies (p230) and Just for Laughs (p230), the quarter bubbles 24 hours a day in its densely packed rows of bars, trendy bistros, music clubs and record shops. The Quartier Latin fits nicely within the borders of Rue Sanguinet, Rue Sherbrooke, Rue St-Hubert and Blvd René-Lévesque. Old Montréal is just south of here, best reached via Rue St-Denis.

Over the past decade or so, Montréal's gay community has breathed new life into The Village, a once poverty-stricken corner of the east end. Today, gay-friendly doesn't even begin to describe the neighborhood. People of all persuasions wander Rue Ste-Catherine and savor the joie de vivre in its cafes, bistros and discerning eateries. The nightlife is renowned for its energy, but during the day the streets bustle with workers from the big media firms nearby. Summer is the most frenetic time as hundreds of thousands of international visitors gather to celebrate Divers/Cité (see the boxed text, p239), a major annual gay pride parade.

The spine of the (Gay) Village is Rue Ste-Catherine Est and its side streets are Rue St-Hubert in the west and Ave de Lorimier in the east.

PLATEAU MONT-ROYAL

East of Parc du Mont Royal, the Plateau is Montréal's youngest, liveliest and artiest neighborhood. Originally a working-class district, it changed its stripes in the 1960s and '70s when writers, singers and other creative folk moved in. Among them was playwright Michel Tremblay, whose unvarnished look at some of the neighborhood's more colorful characters firmly put the Plateau on the path to hipdom.

These days, many Montréalers dream of living here if only house prices would stop rising. As you stroll through its side streets, admiring the signature streetscapes with their winding staircases, ornate wrought-iron balconies and pointy Victorian roofs, you'll begin to understand why.

The Plateau is bordered roughly by Blvd St-Joseph to the north and Rue Sherbrooke to the south, Mont Royal to the west and Ave de Lorimier to the east. The main drags are Blvd St-Laurent ('The Main'), Rue St-Denis and Ave du Mont-Royal, all lined with sidewalk cafes, restaurants, clubs and boutiques. Rue Prince Arthur, Montréal's quintessential hippie hangout in the 1960s, and Rue Duluth are alive with BYOW eateries.

LITTLE ITALY & MILE END

The zest and flavor of the old country find their way into the lively Little Italy district, north of the Plateau, where the espresso seems stiffer, the pasta sauce thicker and the chefs plumper. Italian football games seem to be broadcast straight onto Blvd St-Laurent, where the green-white-red flag is proudly displayed. Soak up the atmosphere on a stroll, and don't miss the Marché Jean Talon (p237), which always hums with activity.

Dubbed the 'new Plateau' by the exodus of students and artists seeking a more affordable, less polished hangout, the Mile End district has all the coolness of its predecessor as well as two phenomenal bagel shops, upscale dining along Ave Laurier and tons of increasingly trendy hangouts at its epicenter: Rue St-Viateur and Blvd St-Laurent. The flavor here is multicultural – Hassidic Jews live side by side with immigrants from all over Europe – visible in the authentic Greek restaurants along Ave du Parc and Rue St-Urbain's neo-Byzantine Polish church, St Michael's. Many of celebrated Canadian novelist Mordecai Richler's novels are set in the Mile End, including *The Apprenticeship of Duddy Kravitz*.

OLYMPIC PARK & AROUND

Montréal hosted the 1976 Olympic summer games, which brought a host of attractions, including a beautiful botanical garden, to the area east of central Montréal, accessible from Rue Sherbrooke.

The Plateau, Quartier Latin & The Village

0 — 300 m
0 — 0.1 miles

Ave Fairmount Ouest
36
Parc AT
Lépine
Parc de
St Michel
Parc Sir
Wilfred
Laurier

18 34
35
To Mile End (500m);
Little Italy (2km)

Ave Laurier Est

53

Parc
Lahaie

Blvd St-Joseph Ouest
Blvd St-Joseph Est

Rue Drolet

Rue St-Denis

Laurier

Rue Gilford

Ave Christophe Colomb

21
42
Rue Villeneuve Est

Ave de l'Esplanade

Rue Gilford

Rue Rivard
Rue Resther
Rue St-Hubert
Rue St-André
Rue Boyer

Rue de la Roche
Rue de Brébeuf
Rue Chambord

Rue Garnier

31
12

Ave Coloniale

Mont-
Royal
37

13

Ave du Mont- Royal
Ouest

Ave du Mont-Royal Est

Rue de Lanaudière

14

46
4

Rue Clark

Parc du
Portugal

Rue de Bullion
Ave l'Hotel-de-Ville
Ave Laval
Ave Henri-Julien

Rue Marie-Anne Est

PLATEAU
MONT-
ROYAL

25
10

2
5

Ave de L'Esplanade
Rue St-Urbain

Rue Rivard
Rue St-Hubert

Parc
Jeanne-
Mance

16

Blvd St-Laurent

Rue Rachel Est

54
3

23

Parc
LaFontaine

15

Ave Duluth Est

Parc du
Mont-
Royal

32
Rue Bagg

Rue Napoléon

11
17

Rue Berri

Rue St-Christophe

Ave de Mentana
Ave du Parc
LaFontaine

Université
du Québec à
Montréal

33

27

Hôpital Hôtel
Dieu de Montréal

Rue Roy Est
Rue Roy Est

Ave des Pins Ouest
Ave des Pins Est

Rue Jeanne-Mance
Rue Ste-Famille

38
29

Ave Coloniale
Rue de Bullion
Ave Laval

Rue Drolet
24

Rue St-Denis

Sherbrooke
Rue Cherrier

19

44

6

Carré
St-Louis

Rue Sherbrooke Est

Rue de la Visitation
Ave Calixa Lavallée
Rue Plessis

Rue Milton

9

QUARTIER
LATIN

Rue St-Norbert

Rue Berri
Rue St-Hubert
Rue St-Christophe
Rue St-André

Rue Wolfe
Rue Montcalm
Rue Beaudry

52
Rue Ontario Est

20 22
39

Ave Savoie

Rue Robin

7

26

Place-
des-Arts

St-Laurent

43

Berri-
UQAM

Beaudry

49
Place
des Arts

8

48 30 40

Rue Ste-Élisabeth
Rue Sanguinet

Université
du Québec
à Montréal

Blvd de Maisonneuve Est

Place
Émilie-Gamelin
Rue Ste-Catherine Est

47 51
28
41

Rue St-Urbain

Rue Charlotte

Blvd St-Laurent

Rue Labelle
Rue St-Hubert

Rue Amherst

45
50

1

Blvd René-Lévesque Est

See Downtown Montréal
Map p218

Jardin Botanique & Insectarium GARDEN (www2.ville.montreal.qc.ca/jardin; 4101 Rue Sherbrooke Est; adult/child May-Oct $16.50/ 8.25, Nov-Apr $14/7, combination ticket with Biodôme $28/14; ⊙9am-6pm mid-May–mid-Sep, to 9pm mid-Sep–Oct, to 5pm Tue-Sun Nov–mid-Jun; ⓂPie-IX) Opened in 1931, Montréal's Botanical Garden is the world's third largest after those in London and Berlin. Approximately 22,000 species of plants grow in 30 outdoor gardens, including the tranquil **Japanese Garden**, a symphony of stone and water sprinkled with rhododendrons, water lilies and bonsai trees. Other highlights include the **First Nations Garden**, the **Chinese Garden** and the **Rose Garden**, as well as 10 greenhouses that are filled with cacti, banana trees, orchids and other magnificent tropical flowers.

Tickets also include a visit to the **Insectarium** with its intriguing collection of creepy crawlies, most of them dead and mounted, but there are also living species, including tarantulas, bees and scorpions. Not to be missed is the **Butterfly House**.

The best way to get around this huge place is by the hop-on, hop-off trolley that makes its rounds every 35 minutes or so (summer only). Free guided tours leave at 10:30am and 1:30pm daily (except Monday from November to May) from the reception center. All facilities are accessible to people in wheelchairs.

Biodôme MUSEUM
(www.biodome.qc.ca; 4777 Ave Pierre de Coubertin; adult/child $16.50/8.25, combination ticket with Jardin Botanique/Insectarium $28/14; ⊘9am-6pm mid-Jun–mid-Sep, to 5pm mid-Sep–mid-Jun; MViau) In the former Olympic Velodrome, the Biodôme beautifully recreates four ecosystems teeming with plant and animal life. A guided path leads to the hot and humid Tropical Forest where the anacondas, caimans and two-toed sloths draw the biggest crowds. From there it's off to the more temperate Laurentian woodlands with trees that change color in fall just like in the real world. A giant aquarium and a rocky cliff are at the heart of the Gulf of St Lawrence section, although the penguins of the Antarctic habitat steal the show.

A free shuttle runs between the Biodôme and the Jardin Botanique from May to September.

Olympic Park LANDMARK
The centerpiece of the sprawling Olympic Park is the multipurpose **Stade Olympique** (Olympic Stadium; Map p215; www.rio.gouv.qc.ca; 4141 Ave Pierre de Coubertin; tours adult/child $8/4; ⊘9am-6pm; MPie-IX), which seats up to 80,000 and today hosts sporting events, concerts and trade shows.

On a nice day, it's well worth boarding the bi-level funicular zooming up the **Tour de Montréal** (Montréal Tower; adult/child $15/7.50; ⊘10am-7pm Jun-Sep, to 5pm Oct-May), the world's largest inclined structure (190m at a 45-degree angle), for 360-degree views of the city, river and surrounding countryside from the glassed-in observation deck.

Down below is the Centre Sportif (p228).

PARC JEAN-DRAPEAU
Occupying the site of the hugely successful 1967 World's Fair, **Parc Jean-Drapeau** (Map p215; www.parcjeandrapeau.com) consists of two islands surrounded by the St Lawrence: Île Ste-Hélène and Île Notre-Dame. Although nature is the park's main appeal, it's also home to a Vegas-sized casino, a Formula One racetrack and an old fort museum. In summer an **information kiosk** (☎514-872-4537) opens near the métro stop Jean-Drapeau.

Drivers should take Pont (Bridge) Jacques Cartier for Île Ste-Hélène and Pont de la Concorde for Île Notre-Dame. **Ferries** (Quai Jacques Cartier) shuttle pedestrians

and bicycles to the park from the Old Port (adult/child $6/free, mid-May to mid-October). Cyclists and in-line skaters can access the park by following the signs for Cité du Havre, then for Île Notre-Dame from the Canal Lachine bike path.

Bus 167 runs between the islands.

Île Ste-Hélène LANDMARK
The northern tip of the island is occupied by **La Ronde** (Map p215; www.laronde.com; adult/child $40/20.50; ⊘11am-7pm weekends May & Sep, to 9pm weekdays Jun, to 11pm weekends Jun plus daily Jul & Aug), a giant amusement park. Owned by US-based Six Flags, the amusement park has a battery of bone-shaking thrill rides, including **Le Splash**, which will leave you soaked, **Le Monstre**, the world's highest wooden roller coaster and **Le Vampire**, a suspended coaster with five gut-wrenching loops. There's also a good assortment of kiddie rides, live shows and a minirail with good river and city views. In June and July, the park hosts the Loto-Québec International Fireworks Competition on weekends (see p230).

Near La Ronde stands an old fort built in the 19th century by the British to defend Montréal from an attack by the Americans. Inside the stone ramparts is the **Musée Stewart** (www.stewart-museum.org; adult/child $12/free; ⊘10am-5pm mid-May–early Oct), where a collection of old maps, documents, navigational equipment, firearms and other artifacts traces the early days of Canada.

Walkways meander around the island, past gardens and among the old pavilions from the World's Fair. One of them, the American pavilion in the spherical Bucky Fuller dome, has become the **Biosphère** (www.biosphere.ec.gc.ca; adult/child $12/free; ⊘10am-6pm May-Nov). Using hands-on displays, this center explains the Great Lakes-St Lawrence River ecosystem, which makes up 20% of the planet's fresh water reserves; demonstrates sustainable living and low energy consumption; and provides tours of a self-sufficient, solar-powered home. There's a great view of the river from the Visions Hall.

Île Notre-Dame LANDMARK
Created from 15 million tons of earth and rock excavated when the métro was built, Île Notre-Dame is laced with canals and pretty garden walkways. The Grand Prix du Canada Formula One race (p230) is held each year on the **Circuit Gilles**

Villeneuve, named after the Québec racecar driver who died in a crash in 1982. From mid-April to mid-November the smoothly paved track is open for cyclists and in-line skaters.

Throughout the year, the island's main draw is the huge, spaceship-like **Casino de Montréal** (Map p215; 1 Ave du Casino; admission free; ☺24hr) in the former French pavilion from the World's Fair. You can challenge Lady Luck at 3000 slot machines and 115 gaming tables. Alcohol is not allowed on the floor and you must be 18 to enter. Bridges link the pavilion to the **Jardin des Floralies**, a lovely rose garden.

On the southern tip of the island, the **Plage des Îles** (p228) draws thousands on hot summer days. Nearby is the **Bassin Olympique**, the former Olympic rowing basin, which now hosts the popular Dragon Boat Race & Festival in late July.

Habitat '67   NOTABLE BUILDING

Between Old Montréal and Île Ste Hélène lies Cité du Havre, a narrow land-filled jetty built to protect the harbor from currents and ice. Here, for the 1967 World's Fair, Moshe Safdie designed Habitat '67, an experimental housing complex. It's a hotchpotch of reinforced concrete cubes cleverly stacked at bizarre angles to provide privacy and views to each of the 150 units. The condos are among the most sought-after living space in Montréal, though they're still reasonably priced at around $350,000 for a 116-sq-meter two-cube apartment.

ELSEWHERE IN MONTRÉAL

The western suburb of Lachine is worth a visit for its history, architecture and general ambience. Not touristy, it reveals a little of Montréal's roots and culture. The side streets behind the impressive College Ste Anne nunnery and City Hall, both along Blvd St-Joseph, make for good wandering.

Canal de Lachine   LANDMARK

Completed in 1825, the Canal de Lachine stretches for 14.5km from the Old Port to Lac St-Louis and was built to circumvent the fierce Lachine Rapids of the St Lawrence River. The construction of the St Lawrence Seaway led to its closing to shipping in 1970, but its banks have since been transformed into a park that's terrific for cycling and walking. Since 2002, pleasure and sightseeing boats have plied its calm waters.

Fur Trade at Lachine National Historic Site   HISTORICAL SITE

(www.parkscanada.gc.ca/fourrure; 1255 Blvd St-Joseph; adult/child $3.90/1.90; ☺9:30am-12:30pm & 1-5pm May-Oct; Ⓜ Angrignon, bus 195) In an old stone house on the waterfront, the exhibit here tells the story of the fur trade in Canada. Lachine became the hub of Montréal's fur-trading operations because the rapids made further river navigation impossible before the canal was built.

Nearby, a **visitors center** (500 Rue des Iroquois; admission free; ☺10am-5pm mid-May-early Oct) runs guided tours and presents historical exhibits about the canal.

🏃 Activities

Cycling & In-line Skating

Montréal is a cyclist's haven. With the recent unveiling of Bixi, a self-service, solar-powered bicycle rental system with over 300 stations downtown, it's easy for anyone to reap the benefits of Montréal's more than 500km of bicycle and skating paths. If you're planning a longer cycling sojourn, you're better off visiting a rental shop for a greater selection of bikes and maps. One popular route parallels the Canal de Lachine (p227) for 14.5km, starting in Old Montréal and passing a lot of history en route. Picnic tables are scattered along the way, so pick up some tasty victuals at the fabulous Marché Atwater (p234).

The smooth **Circuit Gilles Villeneuve** on Île Notre-Dame is another cool track. It's open and free to all from mid-April to mid-November except in mid-June when it hosts the Grand Prix du Canada Formula One car race.

DON'T MISS

ESSENTIAL MONTRÉAL

» **Kondiaronk Lookout** (p222) Stupendous panoramas, especially at night

» **Mile End** (p223) The hippest new haunt in town

» **Marché Jean Talon** (p237) Eye-popping assortments of fresh produce

» **Canal de Lachine** (p227) The perfect spot for cyclists

» **Parc du Mont Royal** (p222) Sunday's 'tam tam sessions' epitomize the Plateau

For more ideas, stop by a bookstore, tourist office or any of these bicycle and in-line skate rental outlets:

Bixi (montreal.bixi.com; refundable security deposit $250, basic fees 24hr/30 days/1 year $5/28/78, usage fees 30/60/90min free/$1.50/3; ⊘24hr Apr-Nov) Three hundred pickup and dropoff stations are located every few blocks and at every main attraction throughout the city.

Ça Roule Montréal (Map p218; www.caroule montreal.com; 27 Rue de la Commune Est, Old Port; bicycles per hr/24hr $9/35, in-line skates 1st/additional hr $9/4; ⊘9am-8pm Apr-Oct)

La Maison des Cyclistes (Map p224; www. velo.qc.ca; 1251 Rue Rachel Est; ⊘8:30am-7pm Mon-Fri, from 9am Sat & Sun) Cafe, bookstore and rentals.

Ice-Skating

Atrium (Map p218; www.le1000.com; 1000 Rue de la Gauchetière Ouest; adult/child $6.50/4.50, skate rental $6; ⊘11:30am-9pm Tue-Sun, to 6pm Mon Oct-Apr, 11:30am-6pm Tue-Fri, noon-10pm Sat, noon-6pm Sun May-Sep) Take to the ice any time the mood strikes at this gigantic, state-of-the-art glass-domed indoor rink in Montréal's tallest tower.

Lac des Castors (Map p215; Parc du Mont Royal; admission free, skate rental $7; ⊘9am-6pm in winter, weather permitting) An excellent place for outdoor skating – it's nestled in the woods near a large parking lot and pavilion.

Patinoire du Bassin Bonsecours (Map p218; Parc du Bassin Bonsecours, Old Port; adult/child $5/3, skate rental $6; ⊘11am-6pm in winter, weather permitting) One of Montréal's most popular outdoor skating rinks.

Swimming

Plage des Îles   BEACH
(Île Notre-Dame; adult/child $8/4; ⊘10am-7pm late Jun-late Aug) On hot summer days, this artificial sandy beach can be a cool place to go for a swim. You won't have much privacy on days when it reaches its 5000-person capacity. The water is filtered and treated with chemicals and is considered safe, clean and ideal for kids. Kayaks, pedal boats and other water sports equipment may be rented from the Water Sports Pavilion at the beach's north entrance.

Centre Sportif   POOL
(4141 Ave Pierre de Coubertin; adult/child $5.50/4.10; ⊘6:30am-9:55pm Mon-Fri, 9am-4:25pm Sat & Sun) The best place to do laps is at Olympic Park's Centre Sportif, a huge indoor complex with six swimming pools, diving towers and a 20m-deep scuba pool.

☞ Tours

Gray Line/Coach Canada   BUS TOUR
(☎514-934-1222; www.grayline.com; adult/child $44/31; ⊘10am, noon, 1pm & 3pm early May-Sep, 10am & 1pm Oct-late May) This well-known tour operator runs three-hour Greater Montréal tours that provide a basic overview of Old Montréal, the Olympic Park, St Joseph's Oratoire and the downtown area. The six-hour tour **Deluxe Montréal** ($83/57; ⊘10am Jun-Oct) includes admission to the Tour de Montréal, Biodôme and Jardin Botanique. Tours depart from outside the Centre Info-touriste (Map p218).

Lachine Rapids Tours   BOAT TOUR
(Map p218; ☎514-284-9607; www.jetboatingmont real.com; jet boats adult/child $65/45, speedboats $25/18; ⊘10am-6pm Jun-Sep) Prepare to get wet on jet boat tours of the Lachine Rapids, bouncy half-hour jaunts around Parc des Îles leaving from Quai Jacques Cartier.

Le Bateau Mouche   BOAT TOUR
(Map p218; ☎514-849-9952; www.bateau -mouche.com; 1hr tours adult/child $23/11; ⊘11am, 2:30pm & 4:30pm mid-May–mid-Oct) Leaving from Quai Jacques Cartier, hour-long cruises aboard climate-controlled, glass-roofed boats explore the Old Port and Parc Jean-Drapeau. A 90-minute version ($27/14) departs at 12:30pm.

Guidatour   WALKING TOUR
(☎514-844-4021; www.guidatour.qc.ca; adult/ child $19.50/10.50; ⊘11am & 1:30pm Sat & Sun mid-May–late Jun, daily late Jun–mid-Oct) Guidatour's bilingual guides spice up historical tours of Old Montréal with colorful tales and anecdotes. Tours depart from the Basilique Notre-Dame (Map p218).

AML Cruises   BOAT TOUR
(Map p218; ☎514-842-9300; www.croisieresaml. com; adult/child $27/14; ⊘11:30am, 2pm & 4pm) AML runs 90-minute tours taking in the Old Port and Île Ste-Hélène. Tours depart from Quai King Edward.

Autobus Viens/Impérial   BUS TOUR
(☎514-871-4733; 2/3hr tours $35/40; ⊘10am, noon, 1pm & 3pm May-Oct, 10am & 1pm Nov-Apr) This comprehensive tour takes you to all major Montréal sights, including Old Montréal (with half-hour tours of Basilique Notre-Dame), Parc Jean-Drapeau and the

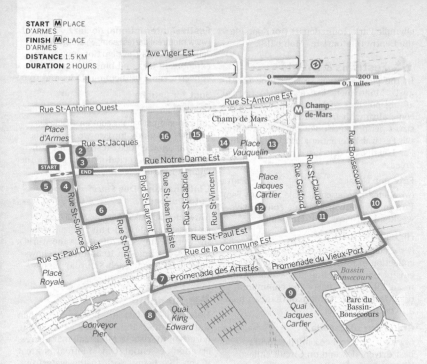

START M PLACE
D'ARMES
FINISH M PLACE
D'ARMES
DISTANCE 1.5 KM
DURATION 2 HOURS

Ave Viger Est

Rue St-Antoine Ouest

Rue St-Antoine Est

Champ-
de-Mars

Champ de Mars

Place d'Armes

Rue St-Jacques

Rue Notre-Dame Est

Place Vauquelin

START

END

Place Jacques Cartier

Blvd St-Laurent

Rue St-Jean Baptiste

Rue St-Gabriel

Rue St-Vincent

Rue St-Sulpice

Rue St-Dizier

Rue St-Paul Ouest

Rue St-Paul Est

Rue de la Commune Est

Rue Gosford

Rue St-Claude

Rue Bonsecours

Place Royale

Promenade des Artistes

Promenade du Vieux-Port

Bassin Bonsecours

Conveyor Pier

Quai King Edward

Quai Jacques Cartier

Parc du Bassin-Bonsecours

Walking Tour
Montréal

❯ Start at ❶ **Place d'Armes** (p217), where the Iroquois battled against early settlers led by Maisonneuve. You'll find him in bronze at the square's center with his back to the city's first skyscraper, the ❷ **New York Life Building** (p217), and the fantastic art-deco ❸ **Aldred Building** (p217).

Your eyes will invariably wander to the neo-Gothic ❹ **Basilique Notre-Dame** (p216), which steals the show for its outlandishly ornate interior and celebrity appeal: Céline Dion was married here in 1994, and the late Luciano Pavarotti recorded his celebrated Christmas concert here. To the west of the church lies the ❺ **Old Seminary** (p217), the city's oldest building.

Take Rue St-Sulpice and duck down ❻ **Rue Le Royer**, where the city's first condo lofts overlook the walkway. Zigzag down to the gentrified Old Port, accessible via ❼ **Promenade des Artistes**, from where the views of the Victorian facades of Rue de la Commune are phenomenal. Play around in the ❽ **Centre des Sciences de Montréal**

(p220), or get a ferry to Parc Jean-Drapeau (p226) from the ❾ **Quai Jacques Cartier**.

At Rue Bonsecours, go to the corner of Rue St-Paul, where the city's oldest stone church, ❿ **Chapelle Notre-Dame-de-Bonsecours** (p217) stands, and ⓫ **Marché Bonsecours** (p220), the former market hall turned boutique bastion sprawls west.

Peek into the artsy stalls dotting the small streets of Rue St-Amable, then round the corner and end up in ⓬ **Place Jacques Cartier** (p217). At the northern end of the street, just beyond Colonne Nelson, the breathtaking ⓭ **Hôtel de Ville** (p219) is where French President Charles de Gaulle announced 'Vive le Québec libre!' (Long live free Québec!) to cheering crowds in 1967.

Return to Rue Notre-Dame and go west past ⓮ **Vieux Palais de Justice** (Old Courthouse) and the neoclassical ⓯ **Cour d'Appel du Québec** (Québec Appellate Court) adjacent, which contrasts with the modern ⓰ **Palais de Justice** across the street. End back in Place d'Armes.

Olympic Park. Tours depart from outside the Centre Infotouriste (Map p218).

✦✦✦ Festivals & Events

In the peak summer season (June to August), Montréalers live festival to festival as big portions of the downtown district come alive with free outdoor concerts and street performances. For big ones, such as the Festival International de Jazz and Just For Laughs, expect closed roads in festival areas.

Fête des Neiges   WINTER

(www.fetedesneiges.com; ☉late Jan/early Feb) Fun in the snow over three consecutive weekends in Parc Jean-Drapeau.

Highlights Festival   MUSIC, FOOD

(www.montrealenlumiere.com; ☉late Feb) A collection of festivals showcasing local cuisine, music and fine arts, culminating in an 'all-nighter' party and communal breakfast with a frying pan that can hold a 10,000-egg omelet.

Grand Prix of Canada   CAR RACING

(www.grandprix.com; ☉Jun) The world's best drivers descend on Circuit Gilles Villeneuve on Île Notre-Dame for North America's biggest Formula One event.

Les FrancoFolies   FRENCH CULTURE

(www.francofolies.com; ☉late Jun) This annual international showcase of French-language music and theater spotlights today's biggest stars and those on the rise, held over 10 days.

Festival International de Jazz   JAZZ

(www.montrealjazzfest.com; ☉late Jun/early Jul) For 11 days the heart of downtown explodes in jazz and blues during 650 concerts, most of them outdoors and free.

Just for Laughs Festival   COMEDY

(http://montreal.hahaha.com/en; ☉Jul) Everyone gets giddy for two weeks at this international comedy festival with hundreds of shows, including free ones in the Quartier Latin.

L'International Des Feux Loto Québec   FIREWORKS

(www.internationaldesfeuxloto-quebec.com/en; ☉mid-Jun–late Aug) This international fireworks competition features the world's best pyrotechnics in 10 30-minute shows held at La Ronde each Saturday night during the competition.

🛏 Sleeping

Hotels fill up fast in the summer when warm weather and festivals galore bring hordes of tourists to Montréal, making reservations essential. Old Montréal is great if you like being close to the waterfront, although accommodations here – mostly in the form of *auberges* (inns) and a brand-new crop of ultradeluxe boutique hotels – do not come cheap unless you're visiting during the off-season. Prices are lower in the vibrant Plateau and Village neighborhoods, veritable B&B bastions that put you in the thick of the city's best nightlife.

MONTRÉAL FOR CHILDREN

Children adore Montréal. The Olympic Park area is the ultimate kid-friendly zone: the **Biodôme** (p226), home to porcupines, penguins and other local and exotic critters, is a sure winner, and the **Insectarium's** (p225) creepy crawlies are sure to provide plenty of gasps and tickles.

Budding scientists will have a field day at the **Centre des Sciences de Montréal** (p220), which has dozens of interactive stations and video games, and space travelers can catch a show at the **Montréal Planetarium** (p222). Many museums have special kid-oriented workshops and guided tours.

On hot summer days, a few hours spent at the **Plage des Îles** (p228), a big beach on Île Notre-Dame within Parc Jean-Drapeau, will go a long way toward keeping tempers cool. On nearby Île Ste-Hélène awaits **La Ronde** (p226) amusement park, where the stomach-churning roller coasters and other diversions are especially thrilling for teens. There's ice skating all year long at the grand **Atrium** (p228), which offers special kids' sessions on Sundays until 11:30am. In winter, you can take a spin on the frozen **Lac des Castors** (p222) in Parc du Mont Royal or on the popular **Patinoire du Bassin Bonsecours** (p228) outdoor rink in Old Montréal.

Many hotels can provide referrals to reliable, qualified babysitting services.

Most of the bigger hotels are west of here in downtown, close to the major museums and abundant shopping.

The following agencies can help book accommodations.

BB Select (www.bbselect.com/quebec)

BBCanada (www.bbcanada.com/quebec)

BedandBreakfast.com (www.bedandbreakfast.com/montreal-quebec.html)

Centre Infotouriste (p243)

OLD MONTRÉAL

TOP CHOICE **Hotel Gault**   BOUTIQUE HOTEL **$$$**
(Map p218; ☎514-904-1616, 866-904-1616; www.hotelgault.com; 449 Rue Ste-Hélène; r $220-750; ❉🕸) A design aficionado's haven, the Hotel Gault features a soothing minimalist palette with polished concrete floors and steel accents, original 19th-century cast-iron columns and the occasional splash of warm blondwood. Flou beds, iPod docks, flat-screen TVs and heated bathroom floors add warmth and comfort to each of the 30 serenely stark loft-style rooms.

Alternative Backpackers   HOSTEL **$**
(Map p218; ☎514-282-8069; www.auberge-alternative.qc.ca; 358 Rue St-Pierre; dm incl tax $22-24, r $75; @🕸) The owners of this hip hostel went for a chic grunge style in an 1875 building with original art, colorful walls and sunny interiors. You'll find fair trade coffee and organic breakfasts ($6) here instead of TV. The city's best option for the financially challenged.

Bonaparte   INN **$$$**
(Map p218; ☎514-844-1448; www.bonaparte.com; 447 Rue St-François-Xavier; r $145-230, ste $355; ❉🕸) This elegant property exudes refined, classic European ambience with wooden floors, Louis-Philippe furniture, French windows – some with views of the Basilique Notre-Dame – and exposed stone walls. After a satisfying three-course breakfast head up to the rooftop patio for snap-worthy views.

Le Petit Hôtel   BOUTIQUE HOTEL **$$$**
(Map p218; ☎514-940-0360, 877-530-0360; www.petithotelmontreal.com; 168 Rue St-Paul Ouest; r $138-268; ❉@🕸) The newest kid on the boutique hotel block, this 'small hotel' is indeed tiny with only 24 small, medium, large and extra-large rooms, but *très* chic with hardwood floors, colorful furniture and plenty of modern electronic gadgets.

Le Place d'Armes   HOTEL **$$$**
(Map p218; ☎514-842-1887, 888-450-1887; www.hotelplacedarmes.com; 55 Rue St-Jacques; r $126-285, ste $325-650; ❉🕸) Contemporary rooms in this ornate 19th-century property, many of which overlook the stunning Place d'Armes and Basilique Notre-Dame, carry the refreshing scents of the hotel's spa and hammam. The complimentary daily wine and cheese service in the hotel's boisterous bar is an added bonus.

DOWNTOWN

Hôtel Le Germain   HOTEL **$$$**
(Map p218; ☎514-849-2050, 877-333-2050; www.germainmontreal.com; 2050 Rue Mansfield; r $170-475; ❉@🕸) An air of calm and sophistication greets you from the moment you walk in to this unassuming former office building just a stone's throw from McGill University campus. Rooms are sexy with crisp white linens, dark, seductive Québec-crafted furniture, and see-through walls into the shower (with blinds, for shy bathers). The free continental breakfast is a classy affair, served at the in-house restaurant where, later in the day, superstar chef Laurie Raphaël presents his edgy local food creations to discerning lunch and dinner crowds.

Les Bons Matins   B&B **$$**
(Map p218; ☎514-931-9167, 800-588-5280; www.bonsmatins.com; 1401 Ave Argyle; r $129-149, ste $199-239; ❉🕸) Charming and seductive with exposed bricks and vibrant colors splashed across bed sheets and wall hangings, this classy establishment fills a series of adjoining turn-of-the-century step-ups. Breakfasts couldn't get better, with gourmet quiche, homemade waffles and Italian-style espresso. Parking is $12 per night.

HI Montréal International Youth Hostel   HOSTEL **$**
(Map p218; ☎514-843-3317, 866-843-3317; www.hostellingmontreal.com; 1030 Rue Mackay; dm $28-33, r $76-86; ❉@🕸) Large, central and well organized, this hostel has dorms sleeping four to 10 people, plus several private rooms; all rooms have air- conditioning and bathrooms. The big kitchen, cafe and common areas often buzz with activity, especially in summer when reservations are a must.

Hilton Garden Inn   HOTEL **$$**
(Map p218; ☎877-840-0010; www.hiltongardenmontreal.com; 380 Rue Sherbrooke Ouest; r $179-209;

✳@⌖) The brand-new incarnation of this popular hotel chain's budget series has garnered quite a reputation for its spacious rooms, friendly staff and excellent location. The airy rooftop swimming pool and exercise room are big pluses for families, and the free internet access and in-room fridges and microwaves only sweeten the deal. No rooms are situated near the elevator or ice machines.

Le 1 René-Lévesque HOTEL $
(Map p218; ☏514-871-9696; le1renelevesque. com; 1 Blvd René-Lévesque Est; s/d $69/89; ✳) These clean, no-frills studio suites with kitchenettes, private bathrooms and great views are some of the best deals in town considering their location at the edge of Chinatown. The hotel has a 24-hour convenience store in the lobby that sells beer (until 11pm) and free wired internet.

Montréal Y Hotel HOTEL $
(Map p218; ☏514-866-9942; www.ydesfemmesmtl. org; 1355 Blvd René-Lévesque Ouest; s/d $75/85; ✳⌖) This nonprofit hotel offers spacious, appealing rooms to both men and women, in a refreshingly noninstitutional setting. All guests have access to communal kitchens and laundry machines; the shared bathrooms are spotlessly clean.

L'Abri du Voyageur HOTEL $
(Map p224; ☏514-849-2922, 866-302-2922; www .abri-voyageur.ca; 9 Rue Ste-Catherine Ouest; r with shared bathroom $75-85, studio with bathroom $125; ✳⌖) Grandiose with high ceilings, bare-brick walls and wooden floorboards, this popular hotel (which also has apartment rentals) in Montréal's seedy 'red-light district' offers great value.

QUARTIER LATIN & THE VILLAGE
La Loggia Art & Breakfast B&B $$
(Map p224; ☏514-524-2493, 866-520-2493; www .laloggia.ca; 1637 Rue Amherst; r without bathroom $80-130, with bathroom $105-155; @⌖) Although plain-looking from the exterior, the inside of this 19th-century townhouse in the Gay Village is anything but average. The artwork of co-host, Joel, brings the five modern guest rooms alive; a sprawling breakfast buffet prepared by his partner, Rob, is served in a leafy sculpture garden behind the house.

PLATEAU MONT-ROYAL
Gingerbread Manor B&B $$
(Map p224; ☏514-597-2804; www.gingerbreadman or.com; 3445 Ave Laval; r without bathroom $79-

129, with bathroom $109-139; @⌖) Warm hosts Ephraim and Yves have taken this beautifully restored Victorian manor, replete with original crown moldings and ceiling pendants, and added tasteful classic decor and modern comforts. Breakfasts are unforgettable – don't be surprised to find quiche made with local organic vegetables one day and white-chocolate and orange French toast the next.

Auberge de la Fontaine INN $$$
(Map p224; ☏514-597-0166, 800-597-0597; www. aubergedelafontaine.com; 1301 Rue Rachel Est; r $179-219, ste $199-360; P@⌖) Located on the edge of the massive Parc LaFontaine, this charming, turreted inn is sophisticated, yet relaxed. Breakfast is a generous spread and you're free to raid the fridge for snacks and dessert all day long. Room 21 is the nicest with a dual whirlpool tub and park-facing terrace.

Opus Montréal HOTEL $$$
(Map p224; ☏514-843-6000, 866-744-6346; www.opusmontreal.com; 10 Rue Sherbrooke Ouest; r $159-239, ste $399-599; ✳@⌖) Glossy minimalist design mingles with luxurious linens to bring you to the heights of stimulation even in the most basic rooms at this hotel, occupying an art-nouveau apartment block built in 1914. The formidable location speaks for itself. Wi-fi is available in common areas only.

Anne Ma Soeur Anne HOTEL $$
(Map p224; ☏514-281-3187; www.annema soeuranne.com; 4119 Rue St-Denis; s $70-180, d $80-210; ✳⌖) Buttery croissants delivered to your door and a fresh pot of coffee brewed in your own small kitchen is the way mornings get started in this hotel. Smallish rooms feature clever beds that fold up to reveal a full dining table, but the real draw here is the central Plateau location.

Shézelles B&B B&B $$
(Map p224; ☏514-849-8694; www.shezelles. com; 4272 Rue Berri; s $75-85, d $90-100, studio $140-155; ⌖) A red door and bright yellow staircase reveal a hint of the color and flair awaiting you inside this humble abode of warm and welcoming hosts Lucie and Lyne. The giant basement studio sleeps up to six and comes with whirlpool, balcony, full kitchen and separate entrance.

Au Piano Blanc B&B $$
(Map p224; ☏514-845-0315; www.aupianoblanc. ca; 4440 Rue Berri; r without/with bathroom $80/125; P@) Owner Céline, a professional

chanteuse (no, not *that* Céline!), has drenched her enchanting B&B in a rainbow of colors, giving it a pleasingly artsy touch. Two of the five rooms have private bathrooms with romantic claw-foot tubs.

✗ Eating

Food is serious business in Montréal, and refined palettes demand high standards – there is zero tolerance for limp lettuce or an uninspired sauce. The city's top chefs have one foot in the traditions of the Old World and another foraging through the innovative atmosphere of North America's gastronomic culture, resulting in a sort of nouvelle cuisine Québécois. Thanks to the competition and proliferation of choice – over 5000 restaurants at last count – diners get more bang for their buck.

Downtown and especially the Plateau are a foodie's nirvana. More than any other street, Blvd St-Laurent epitomizes the city's gastronomic wealth, from boisterous soup parlors in Chinatown to Schwartz's smoked meat emporium to funky Plateau trendsetters. Still further north loom Mile End, the birthplace of the famous Montréal bagel, and Little Italy with its comfortable trattoria and not-to-be-missed Marché Jean Talon.

Eateries in the Plateau with a policy of *apportez votre vin* (bring your own wine; BYOW) cluster along Rue Prince Arthur at Blvd St-Laurent, and Rue Duluth Est at Rue St-Denis. For off-the-map locations, the métro station is given.

OLD MONTRÉAL

Gibby's STEAKHOUSE $$$
(Map p218; ✆514-282-1837; www.gibbys.com; 298 Place d'Youville; meals $25.50-48.50; ⊙5:30pm-late

Mon-Fri, from 5pm Sat & Sun) The setting alone, in a 200-year-old converted stable, offers eye candy galore, but it's the food, especially expertly cut steaks, that truly shines. A drink in the bar is a perfect overture to an evening of fine dining. Reservations essential.

Olive + Gourmando CAFE $
(Map p218; www.oliveetgourmando.com; 351 Rue St-Paul Ouest; meals $5-10; ⊙8am-6pm Tue-Sat; ✎) Push and shove (if necessary) through thick lunchtime crowds in this little corner cafe for a little bit of heaven, manifest in hot paninis and sultry soups using fresh, often organic produce. Leave room for the infamous chocolate brownies, infused with rich Illy coffee.

Titanic SANDWICH SHOP $
(Map p218; 445 Rue St-Pierre; dishes $9.50-15.50; ⊙7am-4pm Mon-Fri; ✎) Friendly staff here know a thing or two about delicious sandwiches and can make mouth-watering masterpieces with a baguette canvas, a mountain of brie or pâté and sprigs of fresh herbs.

Marché de la Villette CAFE $
(Map p218; 324 Rue St-Paul Ouest; dishes $7-10; ⊙9am-6pm) Gourmets on the run can stock up on foie gras ($250 per kilogram) and other deli items. Those with more time can get friendly with the locals over satisfying lunches concocted from regional products.

Ghandi INDIAN $$
(Map p218; www.restaurantgandhi.com; 230 Rue St-Paul Ouest; meals $15-20; ⊙noon-2pm Mon-Fri, 5:30-10:30pm daily) Curries are like culinary poetry at this elegant, kitsch-free Indian restaurant, which also does a mean tandoori duck and butter chicken. Portions are ample, fragrant and steamy, and the service is impeccable.

TO FOIE GRAS OR NOT TO FOIE GRAS

Québec's thirst for the rich, creamy delicacy foie gras is insatiable, despite its ban in Chicago, and disapproval from the Vatican and culinary heavyweight Wolfgang Puck.

So what's all the fuss about? All three of Canada's major foie gras producers are located in Québec, a major thorn in the side of local animal rights activists who decry the practice of *gavage* (force-feeding the animals). Producers argue that *gavage* mimics the animals' natural instinct to gorge themselves before winter.

Whether apathetic or just addicted, eating trends indicate that Quebecers are no longer waiting for Christmas, the traditional time for indulging in duck livers. Sales of tinned foie gras in supermarkets are up and takeout delis are doing a brisk foie gras trade. Montréal restaurateur Martin Picard of Au Pied de Cochon (p235) has taken it to a whole new cholesterol level by creating foie gras *poutine* – french fries slathered in gravy and melted cheese curds, the top smeared with the soft and supple foie gras paste.

L'Usine de Spaghetti Parisienne ITALIAN $
(Map p218; 273 Rue St-Paul Est; meals $9-12; ⏲11am-11pm Mon-Fri, from 5pm Sat; 🖉) Brimming with tourists and hearty piles of pasta, this Italian family-friendly restaurant is a good-value alternative to the touristy traps lining Place Jacques Cartier.

DOWNTOWN

Toqué! FRENCH $$$
(Map p218; ☎514-499-2084; www.restaurant-toque.com; 900 Place Jean-Paul-Riopelle; tasting menu $92-171; ⏲5:30-10:30pm Tue-Sat) This restaurant is consistently touted as Montréal's top restaurant, with a long list of accolades to add credence to this claim. Chef Normand Laprise's seven-course tasting menu brings fresh Québec produce to the table in a symphony of taste ingenuity and flawless presentation. Reservations essential.

Ferreira Café PORTUGUESE $$$
(Map p218; ☎514-848-0988; www.ferreiracafe.com; 1446 Rue Peel; mains $26-45; ⏲noon-3pm Mon-Fri, 5:30-11pm Mon-Wed, to midnight Thu-Sat) Munch complimentary olives while perusing the menu at this beautiful Portuguese restaurant. The chef, Marino Tavares, gives sardines, sea bass and snapper the gourmet treatment. There's also a superb port selection. Reservations essential.

Le Commensal VEGETARIAN $
(Map p218; 1204 Ave McGill College; dishes per 100g $1.69; ⏲11:30am-10pm) This small self-service vegetarian buffet chain offers plenty of healthy options for filling up on casseroles, salads and desserts. It's priced by weight, so don't load up on potatoes. There's also a Quartier Latin branch (Map p224; 1720 Rue St-Denis; open from 11am to 10:30 or 11pm, closed Monday).

Marché Atwater MARKET $
(138 Ave Atwater; ⏲7am-6pm Mon-Wed, to 8pm Thu & Fri, to 5pm Sat & Sun; 🖉; Ⓜ Atwater) This superb market brims with vendors selling mostly local and regional products, from perfectly matured cheeses to crusty breads, exquisite ice wines and tangy tapenades. It's all housed in a 1933 brick hall just west of downtown, at the intersection of Ave Atwater and Rue Ste-Catherine Ouest.

Brontë FUSION $$$
(off Map p218; ☎514-934-1801; www.bronterestaurant.com; 1800 Rue Sherbrooke Ouest; mains $22-40; ⏲6-11pm Tue-Sat) The look here is 1920s supper club meets 21st-century techno parlor. Indulge in the culinary compositions of chef Joe Mercuri that will linger in your memory long after you've paid the bill. Reservations advised.

Ong Ca Can VIETNAMESE $
(Map p224; 79 Rue Ste-Catherine Est; mains $8-13; ⏲11:30am-2pm & 6pm-late Tue-Sun) Despite its crisp white linens and intricate artwork, this bustling Vietnamese restaurant only looks pricey. The lemongrass rolls and anything involving beef get especially high marks from loyal patrons.

Boustan MIDDLE EASTERN $
(Map p218; 2020 Rue Crescent; mains $4-9; ⏲11am-4am) This little Lebanese joint scores high in popularity on the city's *shawarma* circuit. Its late hours make it a favorite with night owls in need of sustenance between bars.

QUARTIER LATIN & THE VILLAGE

Le Nil Bleu AFRICAN $
(Map p224; ☎514-285-4628; 3706 Rue St-Denis; mains $19-28; ⏲6pm-midnight; 🖉) The unusual presentation of the food here is as intriguing as the taste: imagine dollops of fragrant, spiced stews decorating the surface of a flat sourdough bread. The soft trickle of the fountain in the background makes this Ethiopian dining experience even more mystical. Reservations recommended.

Les 3 Brasseurs PUB $$
(Map p224; www.les3brasseurs.ca; 1658 Rue St-Denis; mains $11-14; ⏲11am-1am) If you'd like to cap a day of sightseeing with belly-filling fare and a few pints of handcrafted beer, stop by this convivial brewpub with its stylized warehouse looks and rooftop terrace. The house specialty is 'flamm's,' a French spin on pizza.

Liquid Nutrition JUICE $
(Map p224; liquidnutrition.ca; 1303 Rue St-Catherine Est; drinks $5-7; ⏲8am-10pm) Re-energize with innovative smoothies and protein shakes. Just woke up? Go for the *'lève tôt,'* a combination of soy milk, berries and oatmeal, or a more jolting, caffeinated 'matcha skinny' with apples and mango.

La Paryse BURGERS $
(Map p224; 302 Rue Ontario Est; mains $7-10; ⏲11am-11pm Mon-Fri, from noon Sat & Sun; 🖉) Thick and juicy – the cooks at this smart little retro diner sure know how to get burgers right. Don't sulk if you're not a meat eater

as there are plenty of tasty soups and tofu-based choices as well.

PLATEAU MONT-ROYAL

TOP CHOICE L'Express FRENCH $$
(Map p224; ☎514-845-5333; 3927 Rue St-Denis; mains $14-29; ☺8am-2am) This place is so fantastically French, you'd half expect to see the Eiffel Tower out the window, especially after guzzling too much of the excellent wines. The food's classic Parisian bistro – think steak *frites*, bouillabaisse, tarragon chicken – and so is the attitude. Reservations essential.

Schwartz's SANDWICH SHOP $
(Map p224; www.schwartzsdeli.com; 3895 Blvd St-Laurent; meals $6-17; ☺9am-12:30am Sun-Thu, to 1:30am Fri, to 2:30am Sat) Don't be deterred by the line that inevitably forms outside this legendary smoked meat parlor. Join the eclectic clientele – from students to celebrities – at the communal tables, and don't forget to order the pickles, fries and coleslaw.

Au Pied de Cochon FRENCH $$$
(Map p224; ☎514-281-1114; www.restaurant aupieddecochon.ca; 536 Ave Duluth Est; mains $13.50-40; ☺5pm-midnight Tue-Sun) French-trained chef Martin Picard quickly captured the hearts and tummies of Montréal gourmets with his avant-garde interpretations of classic country fare. No animal is safe from his kitchen. Reservations recommended.

La Sala Rosa SPANISH $$
(Map p224; 4848 Blvd St-Laurent; meals $12-15; ☺5-11pm Tue-Sun; ☑) Wash down flavorful tapas and every shade of paella with a pitcher of sangria in this unique restaurant, which shares a floor with the Spanish Social Club. Thursdays host free flamenco dance performances.

Crudessence VEGAN $$
(Map p224; www.crudessence.com; 105 Rue Rachel Ouest; mains $8-15; ☺10am-9pm) The raw, vegan *and* organic fare here is guaranteed to pique your interest, if not satisfy your hunger. Start the day with a bowl of chia, granola and almond milk, or wait for lunch to experience unbaked lasagna with macadamia nut ricotta and olive-crust pizza with 'crumesan' (Brazil nut parmesan). The busy all-organic juice bar churns out wheatgrass, smoothies and power shakes to flocks of Mile End locals.

Juliette et Chocolat CAFE $
(Map p224; www.julietteetchocolat.com; 3600 Blvd St-Laurent; meals $8-12; ☺11am-11pm, to midnight Fri & Sat; ☑) The menu at this bright and boisterous restaurant is stocked with a decent selection of savory buckwheat crepes, but true chocoholics won't be able to resist dressing their side salads with a tangy cocoa vinaigrette. Dessert is essential: the salty caramel brownies and lavender truffles are smart choices, and you can't go wrong with any of the 33 choices of drinking chocolate.

Chu Chai VEGETARIAN, THAI $$
(Map p224; 4088 Rue St-Denis; mains around $20; ☺noon-10pm) In Montréal's first vegetarian upscale eatery, zippy Thai-inspired stir-fries and coconut soups explore the potential of fragrant Kaffir lime, lemongrass and sweet basil. The fake duck could fool even the most discerning carnivore.

Le Roi du Plateau PORTUGUESE $$
(Map p224; 51 Rue Rachel Ouest; mains $12-25; ☺5-11pm Mon-Sat) Tables are squished together as tightly as the sardines on the big belching grill in this wildly popular Portuguese eatery, which lurks behind a ho-hum facade. Succulent and finger-lickin' good chicken is clearly the *roi* (king) of the menu.

Robin Des Bois FUSION $$
(Map p224; 4403 Blvd St-Laurent; mains $12.50-25; ☺8am-11pm Mon-Sat) Montréal's own Robin Hood, restaurateur Judy Servay, donates all profits and tips from this St-Laurent hot spot to local charities. Ever-changing dishes scribbled on the chalkboard could include a succulent venison steak or fried duck with apple spring rolls, delivered with a smile by volunteer staff.

Eduardo ITALIAN $$
(Map p224; 404 Ave Duluth Est; mains $9-15; ☺11am-11pm Mon-Fri, from 3pm Sat & Sun; ☑) Hopping any night of the week, this cozy little bistro dishes up Italian favorites such as simple, yet bang-on, rich and gooey stuffed cannelloni and spaghetti napoletana, all in a dimly lit, warm atmosphere.

Aux Vivres VEGAN $$
(Map p224; 4631 Blvd St-Laurent; mains $10-17; ☺noon-midnight Tue-Fri, from 11am Sat & Sun) The chefs here make vegan cuisine accessible to all with winning combinations such as the 'CLT' – a BLT with smoked coconut to replace the bacon – and creative rice bowls topped with fresh vegetables and zippy sauces.

Le Jardin de Panos MEDITERRANEAN **$$**
(Map p224; www.lejardindepanos.com; 521 Ave Du-luth Est; mains $15-22; noon-midnight) Sample a stellar selection of tastes and textures in the mixed appetizer platter on the flower-filled back courtyard of this delightful Greek eatery.

Maestro SVP SEAFOOD **$$$**
(Map p224; www.maestrosvp.com; 3615 Blvd St-Laurent; mains $14-40; 11am-10pm Tue-Fri, from 4pm Sat-Mon) A changing palette of 15 varieties of oysters is the specialty at this trendy bistro where tables are lit by a halo of halogen. If you're not into slimy mollusks, try the fried scallops, grilled shrimp or any of the pasta dishes.

Santropol SANDWICH SHOP **$**
(Map p224; www.santropol.com; 3990 Rue St-Urbain; mains $7-10; 10:30am-10pm;) Creative sweet and savory sandwiches piled high with fresh fruits and vegetables are the main draw here. Earthy soups and soy lattes are big hits with locals, too.

LITTLE ITALY & MILE END

Lucca ITALIAN **$$$**
(514-278-6502; 12 Rue Dante; mains $18-36; noon-3:30pm & 6-10:30pm Mon-Fri, 6-10:30pm Sat; De Castelnau) This hot little Italian number is on the speed dial of many Montréal foodies. The menu, put together daily from market-fresh ingredients and written on a chalkboard, ranges from classics to adventurous culinary spins. It's *la dolce vita*, Québec-style. Rue Dante is just off Blvd St-Laurent, south of Rue Jean-Talon. Reservations recommended.

La Croissanterie Figaro CAFE **$**
(www.lacroissanteriefigaro.com; 5200 Rue Hutchison; mains $8-11; 7am-1am; Place des Arts, then bus 80) Locals at this lovely cafe, self-dubbed *un petit coin perdu de Paris* (a little lost corner of Paris), keep the sidewalk patio packed solid, with a marbled, classy interior fielding the spillover. Attractive, black-clad waiters deliver steamy bowls of *café au lait;* the casual table d'hôte menu appears

---

LE BRUNCH, MAIS OUI!

Weekend brunching in Montréal is de rigueur, and usually gets started at around 10am, although at some of the city's hot spots the long lines – full of late-night revelers not long out of bed – will linger until 2pm. Here are some of our favorite places to sign up:

» **L'Express** (Map p224; 3927 Rue St-Denis; breakfast $7-20) Montréal's hottest foodie address (see also p235) serves up simple dishes like scrambled eggs and *pain perdu* (French toast) in a classic Parisian bistro atmosphere.

» **Beauty's** (Map p224; 93 Ave du Mont-Royal Ouest; breakfast $5-12) With an unwavering fan base since it opened in 1942, folks brave lines as legendary as the diner itself for pleasant chats with owner Hymie Skolnick and simple, yet outstanding breakfast staples dished up with toasted sesame bagels.

» **Café Souvenir** (1261 Ave Bernard; breakfast $5-12; Outremont) The patio is great for watching the well-heeled Outremont crowd descend for weekend brunch. Reasonably priced breakfasts come with dense, flavorful breads from nearby bakery, Première Moisson. The restaurant is located just north of the Mile End neighborhood.

» **Chez Cora** (Map p224; 1396 Ave du Mont-Royal Est; breakfast $6-12) You can't miss the cheery, yellow sunshine logo of this breakfast restaurant chain, known for its crazy concoctions and abundance of country-style kitsch, such as cutesy ceramic chickens, adorning the walls.

» **Senzala** (177 Ave Bernard; breakfast $8-13; Place des Arts, then bus 80) Bask in the sunshine on the patio at this spicy Brazilian eatery and tuck into one of the interesting variations of eggs, such as the stimulating 'Tropicana' – a poached egg atop an avocado or mango sitting in a spicy tomato sauce and garnished with plantains and baked apples. North of Ave Fairmount and west of Blvd St-Laurent.

» **Eggspectation** (Map p218; 201 Rue St-Jacques; breakfast $8-15) Famous for its huge breakfast menu (including a dozen versions of eggs Benedict), this small chain has four locations downtown, each with a different atmosphere, the best of which is this Old Montréal locale.

around 4pm. It's just off Ave Fairmount, about seven blocks west of Blvd St-Laurent.

Marché Jean Talon
MARKET $

(7075 Ave Casgrain; ☺7am-6pm Mon-Wed, to 8pm Thu & Fri, to 5pm Sat & Sun; M Jean Talon) The gem of Little Italy, this kaleidoscopic market is perfect for assembling a gourmet picnic or partaking in a little afternoon grazing. A great stop is Marché des Saveurs, devoted entirely to Québec specialties such as wine and cider, fresh cheeses, smoked meats and preserves. The market sprawls south of Rue Jean-Talon between Blvd St-Laurent and Rue St-Denis.

Alep
MIDDLE EASTERN $$

(199 Rue Jean Talon Est; mains $8-14; ☺5-11pm Tue-Sat; M De Castelnau) A tantalizing mélange of cumin, coriander and other spices envelops this impressive dining room, with decor inspired by the famous citadel in Alep, Syria. Make a meal from wonderful appetizers or the grilled kebabs.

Wilensky's Light Lunch
SANDWICH SHOP $

(Map p224; 34 Ave Fairmount Ouest; dishes $2.50-5; ☺9am-4pm Mon-Fri) Generations of meat-lovers have flocked to Moe Wilensky's corner joint to order 'The Special,' a pressed bologna and salami sandwich. It has even been immortalized in Mordecai Richler's novel *The Apprenticeship of Duddy Kravitz*. Wash it down with a cherry cola from the fountain.

Le Jardin du Cari
CARIBBEAN $

(5554 Blvd St-Laurent; mains $6-8; ☺noon-10pm Tue-Fri, 5-10:30pm Sat & Sun; ✍; M Place des Arts, then bus 80) One bite into the taut, overstuffed roti will release a gush of curried chickpeas, melt-in-your-mouth stewed chicken or goat and a slightly sweet squirt of mashed pumpkin at this little Guyanese hole in the wall. North of Ave Fairmont.

Fairmount Bagel
BAKERY $

(Map p224; 74 Ave Fairmount Ouest; bagels $0.50-$1.50, sandwiches $3.50-7; ☺24hr) The original Montréal bagel baker still churns them out 24/7, from the classic onion to the new-fangled muesli, sun-dried tomato and pesto variations.

La Maison du Bagel
BAKERY $

(263 Rue St-Viateur Ouest; bagels $0.50-$1.50, sandwiches $4-8; ☺24hr; M Place des Arts, then bus 80) Also known as St Viateur bagel shop, this place is just as famous as Fairmount Bagel, if not quite as old. Try them both and judge for yourself which one is better. It's north of Ave Fairmount and west of Blvd St-Laurent.

Maison Indian Curry
INDIAN $

(996 Rue Jean Talon Ouest; mains $8; ☺11am-10pm Wed-Mon; ✍; M Acadie) In the up-and-coming Parc-Extension neighborhood, redubbed 'Little India' by locals, the cheap and hearty dishes (of both the northern and southern varieties) at this little hole in the wall are outstanding. The lunchtime *thali* platter with three curries, rice and bread ($5) is a steal.

🍷 Drinking

The best drinking areas are found along the stylish strips of the Plateau – Blvd St-Laurent, Rue St-Denis and Ave du Mont-Royal – and along the noisy cafe terrace-lined Rue Crescent downtown. The bars along Rue Ste-Catherine in The Village are slightly gay-focused, but frequented by all types.

Bu
WINE BAR

(Map p224; www.bu-mtl.com; 5245 Blvd St-Laurent; ☺5pm-1am) Subtle just about sums up the nonabrasive crowds and cool-as-a-cucumber decor at this pleasant *bar à vins*. Knowledgeable staff can advise on the bible-like wine list, or shop around with a trio of tasters. You must order at least a snack ($4 to $9) to drink.

Le Ste-Elisabeth
PUB

(Map p224; ste-elisabeth.com; 1412 Rue Ste-Elisabeth; ☺4pm-3am Mon-Fri, from 6pm Sat & Sun) Microbrews, imported Euro beers and quality Scotch sing their sweet siren song to the low-key crowd at this popular pub. It's a pretty place with a lovely garden overlooked by an upstairs terrace.

Brutopia
BREWERY

(Map p218; www.brutopia.net; 1219 Rue Crescent; ☺3pm-3am Sat-Thu, noon-3am Fri) Boisterous and brick-lined Brutopia brews its own beer, including its outstanding India Pale Ale, in sparkling copper vats right behind the bar. A friendly young crowd invades nightly, not least for the live bands.

Le Saint Sulpice
PUB

(Map p224; www.lesaintsulpice.ca; 1680 Rue St-Denis; ☺11am-3am) On a hot summer night, a cool place to be is the huge beer garden of this always bustling hangout. There's great people-watching potential here, as well as in the cafe, with three terraces and a disco. Did we mention the place was huge?

GETTING YOUR FIX

No matter where you are in Montréal, life is never too busy for a coffee break. It's the only place in Canada where the usual franchises/chains invading most cities, such as Tim Hortons and Starbucks, have been kept at bay by an abundance of great Italian coffee bars and chilled out independently owned cafes. Whether you're searching for that neat and straight shot of Italian espresso or a more French-inspired bowl of café au lait served up with cool atmosphere, you'll find it at any one of the following:

» **Caffè Italia** (6840 Blvd St-Laurent; espressos $1.50; ⊘8am-4pm; Ⓜ Jean Talon) Nothing fancy, but phenomenal espresso and a peeping hole into the lives of the Little Italy clientele who frequent this coffee bar in droves.

» **Café Olimpico** (124 Rue St-Viateur; espressos $1.50; ⊘8am-4pm; Ⓜ Place des Arts, then bus 80) Popular with Mile End locals, this hole-in-the-wall is short on frills but huge on taste and quality; espresso shots go down like velvet. North of Ave Fairmount and west of Blvd St-Laurent.

» **Caffè ArtJava** (Map p224; 837 Ave du Mont-Royal Est; espressos $1.95; ⊘8am-4pm) Often praised as the best espresso in Montréal – fragrant and rich – and the cappuccino foam is a work of art. There's also a smaller location at University and Président Kennedy (Map p218).

Baldwin Barmacie BAR
(Map p224; baldwinbarmacie.com; 115 Ave Laurier Ouest; ⊘9pm-3am) This hip bar, with retro paisley orange textiles and bubble-shaped light fixtures, attracts a young crowd for its ambient and trip-hop music. The eclectic drinks menu includes martinis, wine and gin/vodka cocktails.

Gogo Lounge BAR
(Map p224; 3682 Blvd St-Laurent; ⊘3pm-3am) This groovy outpost, decorated in a psychedelic Austin Powers sort of way, is famous for its huge martini selection. All drinks are listed on old vinyl records. Dress nicely.

Sir Winston Churchill Pub PUB
(Map p218; www.winniesbar.com; 1455 Rue Crescent; ⊘11:30am-3am) A quintessential Crescent St watering hole, founded in 1967 by Johnny Vale, a one-time comrade of Che Guevara. The late local author Mordecai Richler used to knock back cold ones in the bar upstairs. Things get clamorous between 5pm and 8pm when it's two-for-one happy hour.

Whisky Café CIGAR LOUNGE
(www.whiskycafe.com; 5800 Blvd St-Laurent; ⊘5pm-3am Mon-Fri, from 6pm Sat, from 7pm Sun; Ⓜ Place des Arts, then bus 80) The last of a dying breed of bars in Montréal, this classy lounge offers over 150 Scotch whiskies and an impressive selection of Cuban cigars.

☆ **Entertainment**

Quiet and laid-back by day, Montréal has a secret ulterior side that bursts into life when the sun goes down. Constantly rejuvenating and ever improving, the nightlife here is without a doubt the most exciting in Canada, putting Toronto's 'Entertainment District' to shame.

The city's club scene is vibrant and exuberant with much of the action unfolding along Blvd St-Laurent, Rue Ste-Catherine Est (in The Village) and, in the western part of town, Rue Crescent. Music lovers can easily get their fill from the extensive menu of jazz and classical to pop and new age to world beats. And performing arts fans have plenty of theater and dance troupes of international renown from which to choose.

Tickets for major concerts, shows, festivals and sporting events are available from the box offices of individual venues or from **Admission** (☏514-790-1245, 800-361-4595; www.admission.com) or **Ticketmaster** (☏514-790-1111; www.ticketmaster.ca).

See p242 for publications that help you keep your finger on the pulse of the latest happenings. For details about top clubs and DJs du jour, pick up a copy of the glossy ME (Montréal Entertainment). For raves, check for flyers in record stores, bars and clubs. **Info-Arts Bell** (☏514-790-2787) is an information line for cultural events, plays and concerts.

Nightclubs

Altitude 737
NIGHTCLUB
(Map p218; www.altitude737.com; 1 Place Ville-Marie; ☉5-7pm Mon-Sat, 10pm-3am Thu-Sat) This restaurant-bar-disco combo always promises 'high times' thanks to its location at the top of Montréal's tallest office tower. Alas, attitude reigns at this altitude, but the drinks prices are surprisingly fair and the buzz electric.

Bains Douches
NIGHTCLUB
(Map p218; www.bainsdouches.ca; 390 Rue St-Jacques Ouest; ☉10pm-3am Thu-Sat) The hottest night is Thursday in this chic club – the only one of its kind in Old Montréal. Big-name DJs from as far afield as Europe draw huge crowds; the chilled mezzanine space is a great place to get lost in techno haze.

Mado Cabaret
NIGHTCLUB
(Map p224; www.mado.qc.ca; 1115 Rue Ste-Catherine Est) Outrageous drag shows and stand-up comedy; Tuesday nights are the most rollicking.

Cinemas

Multiplex theaters showing Hollywood blockbusters abound, but plenty of art and indie houses survive as well. Look up what's showing where at www.cinema-montreal. com, with reviews and details of discount admissions.

IMAX (Map p218; www.montrealscience centre.com; adult/child $12/9; ☉10am-11:30pm late Jun-late Sep, to 9:30pm late Sep-late Jun) Part of the Centre des Sciences de Montréal (p220), this is a great place to take the kids. Discounted tickets with museum admission and for double features are available.

FREE **Cinerobothéque** (Map p224; www. nfb.ca/cinerobotheque; 1564 Rue St-Denis; ☉noon-9pm Tue-Sun) Make your choice from an extensive National Film Board of Canada collection, and a robot housed in a glass-roofed archive pulls your selection from the stacks. Then settle back into individual, stereo-equipped chair units to watch your personal monitor.

Popular independent theaters include **Cinéma du Parc** (www.cinemaduparc.com; 3575 Ave du Parc; ⓂPlace des Arts, then bus 80) and **Ex-Centris Cinema** (Map p224; www. excentris.com; 3530 Blvd St-Laurent).

Theater & Dance

Centaur Theatre
THEATER
(Map p218; ☎514-288-3161; www.centaurthea tre.com; 453 Rue St-François-Xavier) Based in the beautiful Old Stock Exchange in Old Montréal, the Centaur ranks among the country's leading theater companies. Its

---

'OUT' & ABOUT IN MONTRÉAL

Montréal is one of Canada's gayest cities with the rainbow flag flying especially proudly in The Village along Rue St-Catherine between Rue St-Hubert and Rue Dorion. Dozens of high-energy bars, cafes, restaurants, saunas and clubs flank this strip, turning it pretty much into a 24/7 fun zone. The authoritative guide to the gay and lesbian scene is **Fugues** (www.fugues.com), a free monthly mag found throughout The Village. For online chat rooms, a confidential telephone service, and other English resources for the LGBTQ community, try the volunteer-run organization, **CAEO Québec** (☎514-866-5090, 888-505-1010; www.caeoquebec.org).

The big event on The Village calendar is the **Divers/Cité Festival** (www.diverscite. org), Montréal's version of Pride Week, usually held in July. It draws as many as one million people. Almost as much of a pull is the **Black & Blue Festival** (www.bbcm.org) in October, with major dance parties, cultural and art shows and a mega-party in the Olympic Stadium.

Bars and clubs worth checking out:

» **Sky Pub & Club** (Map p224; 1474 Rue Ste-Catherine Est) Huge place with rooftop terrace complete with Jacuzzi and pool.

» **Aigle Noir** (Map p224; 1315 Rue Ste-Catherine Est) For the leather-and-fetish crowd.

» **Le Drugstore** (Map p224; 1360 Rue Ste-Catherine Est) Fun seekers of every persuasion will be satisfied on at least one of the six multithemed floors.

» **Unity II** (Map p224; 1171 Rue Ste-Catherine Est) Sexy dance club humming with shirtless techno ravers, muscle queens and mellow straights.

» **Mado Cabaret** (p239)

repertoire ranges from Shakespeare classics to experimental fare by local English-language playwrights.

Cirque du Soleil   THEATER
(☎514-722-2234; www.cirquedusoleil.com) For the past two decades, this phenomenally successful troupe has redefined what circuses are all about. Headquartered in Montréal, it usually inaugurates new shows in the city every year or two. Call or check with the tourist office.

Les Ballets Jazz de Montréal   DANCE
(☎514-982-6771; www.bjmdanse.ca) This modern dance troupe has earned a sterling reputation for showcasing its classically trained dancers in experimental forms. Performances take place at various venues around town.

Les Grands Ballets Canadiens   DANCE
(Map p224; ☎514-849-8681; www.grandsballets. qc.ca; Place des Arts) Québec's leading ballet troupe stages four shows annually. They range from classical to modern programs and are both innovative yet accessible to general audiences.

Live Music
JAZZ, BLUES & ROCK
Casa del Popolo   LIVE MUSIC
(Map p224; www.casadelpopolo.com; 4873 Blvd St-Laurent; ☺from noon) Low-key and funky, this cafe-bar cum art gallery cum performance venue usually has several live music and spoken word events scheduled in three locations. The cafe serves fair trade coffee and vegetarian fare.

L'Esco   LIVE MUSIC
(Map p224; ☎514-842-7244; 4467a Rue St-Denis; ☺6pm-1am) This smoky and intimate Plateau club serves up wicked jazz or indie rock from some of Montréal's up-and-coming hipsters.

Metropolis   LIVE MUSIC
(Map p224; ☎514-844-3500; www.montreal metropolis.ca; 59 Rue Ste-Catherine Est) Of its many faces, as a skating rink, a porn movie theater and disco among others, rock venue suits this 2300-person-capacity concert hall best. The stage was graced by the likes of Radiohead, David Bowie and Coldplay earlier in their careers.

Upstairs   LIVE MUSIC
(Map p218; ☎514-931-6808; www.upstairsjazz. com; 1254 Rue Mackay; ☺noon-1am Tue-Fri, 5pm-1am Sat & Sun) Some mighty fine talent, both home-grown and imported, has tickled the ivories of the baby grand in this intimate jazz joint. Shows start at 10pm. Nice terrace and respectable dinner menu.

Foufounes Electriques   LIVE MUSIC
(Map p224; www.foufounes.qc.ca; 87 Rue Ste-Catherine Est; ☺4pm-3am) The graffiti-covered walls and industrial charm should tip you off that 'Electric Buttocks' isn't exactly a mainstream kinda place. Punk, hardcore and grunge often rule the night at this two-decades-old alternative bastion. There's cheap beer and a nice terrace.

CLASSICAL
Opéra de Montréal   LIVE MUSIC
(Map p224; ☎514-985-2222; www.operademont real.com; Place des Arts) The Montréal Opera has delighted fans of Mozart, Wagner and Bizet for almost three decades. Productions are in the original language with subtitles.

Orchestre Symphonique de Montréal   LIVE MUSIC
(Map p224; ☎514-842-9951; www.osm.ca; Place des Arts, Salle Wilfrid-Pelletier) One of Canada's most accomplished orchestras, the OSM has been helmed by such famous conductors as Otto Klemperer, Zubin Mehta and Charles Dutoit.

McGill Chamber Orchestra   LIVE MUSIC
(☎514-487-5190; www.ocm-mco.org) Founded in 1939, this fine chamber ensemble is one of Canada's oldest. Concert series are held in various venues, including the **Pollack Concert Hall** (Map p218; 555 Rue Sherbrooke Ouest) and the Place des Arts.

🏃 Sports
Hockey and Catholicism are regarded as national religions in Québec, but football also attracts a fair number of worshippers.

Montréal Canadiens   SPORTS
(Map p218; ☎514-932-2582; www.canadiens.com; Bell Centre, 1200 Rue de la Gauchetière Ouest; tickets $29-261) Bell Centre is home base for this National Hockey League team and 24-time Stanley Cup winners (the last time in 1993). Although they have struggled in recent years, Montréalers still have a soft spot for the 'Habs' and games routinely sell out. After the first drop of the puck you might be able to snag a half-price ticket from the scalpers lurking by the entrance. Bring binoculars for the rafter seats.

Montréal Alouettes   SPORTS
(☎514-871-2255; www.montrealalouettes.com; Molson Stadium, Ave des Pins Ouest; tickets $20-

Over the past decade, Montréal has emerged as one of North America's most diverse hotbeds of musical talent and ingenuity. Akin to Seattle's infamous grunge scene or Austin's live music fever, indie pop and rock music found a new home in Montréal at the turn of this century.

It may surprise that the largest French-speaking city outside Paris would foster such an important English music scene. But even with a 60% francophone population, Montréal's bohemian Plateau and Mile End – districts well known for harboring artists and musicians – have reverted to English-heavy neighborhoods. Ironically, these enclaves blossomed despite (or maybe even because of) the notorious political upheavals that plagued the city in the 1980s and '90s and drove away much of the English-speaking population, plummeting the city into economic recession.

Until a few years ago, there was virtually no music 'industry' to speak of here, and so for the broke beatnik types all pressure was off. And we can't overlook Montréal's greatest asset – its affordability, which has only encouraged 'starving' artistry – and its biggest drawback, the bitterly cold winters that have forced many a musician indoors for months at a time to create and record music.

While bands were still content with not 'getting signed,' and the fame- and money-hungry had yet to discover Montréal, this underground scene churned out some of Canada's most famous indie musicians. The Arcade Fire, perhaps the most unlikely group to reach stardom considering their preference for live shows and refusal to sign with big labels, stuck to their guns and reached international success largely through online buzz. At the same time, things were coming together for west coast natives Wolf Parade, an experimental rock group that moved to Montréal to run with their music. And perhaps as a result of living in a city where anyone can feel like an outsider – French, English and the recently arrived included – the hugely successful band the Dears tackled issues of social alienation and racism, with songs such as 'Whites Only Party' and 'You and I are a Gang of Losers.' Stars, another band that helped shape Montréal's indie pop genre, is characterized by its soft, bittersweet romantic ballads, each with a different story to tell. The Stills, a post-punk revival rock band that formed in 2000 and is comprised of both anglophone and francophone artists, rose to fame in 2003 with its first album *Logic Will Break Your Heart*.

To get a taste of Montréal's independent music scene, make sure you're in town for **Pop Montréal** (www.popmontreal.com), a mainly local indie pop/rock affair, with a little experimental and folk thrown into the mix. For five days in October, Montréalers flood the concert halls and venues of the city for *the* event of the year.

75; Ⓜ Square Victoria, then free shuttle bus) This once-defunct Canadian Football League team is the unlikely hottie of the city's sports scene, especially since winning the league's Grey Cup trophy in 2009. They have sold out every game since 1999, so order tickets early. Free shuttle buses start two hours before each game.

 Shopping

Just spending time in this stylish city, where personal appearance tops many a Montréaler's priority list, may prompt a spending spree. Hardcore shoppers will inevitably end up on Rue Ste-Catherine Ouest, which is chock-a-block with department, chain and one-of-a-kind stores, plus multilevel malls such as the **Centre Eaton**

(Map p218; Rue St-Catherine btwn Ave McGill College & Rue University; ⊗10am-9pm Mon-Fri, 9am-5pm Sat, 10am-5pm Sun). And that's just at street level. Head underground and you'll have hundreds more retailers displaying everything from turquoise to tank tops.

For shopping at a more leisurely pace, head to the Plateau. Blvd St-Laurent, Rue St-Denis and Ave du Mont-Royal are famous for their unique boutiques hawking trendy must-haves. On Rue St-Paul in Old Montréal, the focus is on tourist-oriented trinket shops with some very respectable art galleries thrown into the mix. Antiques aficionados can easily spend a day scouring the shops along Rue Notre-Dame Ouest, between Ave Atwater and Rue Guy, known as Antique Alley.

Ogilvy CLOTHING
(Map p218; www.ogilvycanada.com; 1307 Rue Ste-Catherine Ouest) Dripping with tradition, this Victorian-era department store stocks all the top international labels. Be sure to visit the historic concert hall on the 5th floor. Since 1927, a kilt-clad bagpiper has roamed the store daily at noon.

Galerie Le Chariot ART
(Map p218; 446 Place Jacques Cartier) This three-level gallery specializes in museum-quality Inuit art, primarily soapstone sculptures. Each piece has been authenticated by the Canadian government.

Guilde Canadienne des Métier d'Art Québec ART
(Map p218; www.canadianguildofcrafts.com; 1460 Rue Sherbrooke Ouest) This gallery-like space showcases only the finest in Canadian arts and crafts from all over the nation.

Parasuco CLOTHING
(Map p218; www.parasuco.com; 1414 Rue Crescent) Made right here in Montréal, Parasuco has become one of Canada's hottest labels for jeans and casual wear. Its high-energy flagship store stocks all the latest styles.

Eva B CLOTHING
(Map p224; www.eva-b.ca; 2013 Blvd St-Laurent) The '60s, '70s and '80s are alive and well at this groovy retro boutique. Stock up on styles guaranteed to make you a standout at any party. Costume rentals, too.

Les Touilleurs KITCHENWARE
(Map p224; www.lestouilleurs.com; 152 Ave Laurier Ouest) Kitchenware has never looked so sexy. Almost as impressive as the vast collection of ultra-high-quality, brand-name toasters and cake tins is the minimalist interior design.

Cheap Thrills MUSIC STORE
(Map p218; cheapthrills.ca; 2044 Rue Metcalfe) It's easy to lose track of time as you browse through this big selection of used books and music (CDs and some vinyl), both with a mainstream and offbeat bent and sold at bargain prices.

Indigo (Map p218; www.chapters.indigo.ca; Place Montréal Trust, 1500 Ave McGill College; ⊘9am-11pm) Books galore.

Word (469 Rue Milton; ⊘10am-6pm Mon-Wed, to 9pm Thu & Fri, 11am-6pm Sat; MⓂMcGill) Long-standing student hangout with used academic books and modern literature. North of Rue Sherbrooke Ouest and east of Rue University.

Ulysses (Map p224; 4176 Rue St-Denis; ⊘10am-6pm Mon-Wed, to 9pm Thu-Fri, to 5:30pm Sat, 11am-5:30pm Sun) Travel books and maps.

 Information

Emergency & Medical Services

CLSC (☑514-934-0354; 1801 Blvd de Maisonneuve Ouest) Walk-in community health center for minor ailments; costs $105 (cash only) per visit, not including tests.

Montréal Police Station (☑nonemergencies 514-280-2222)

Pharmaprix Pharmacy Mont-Royal (www.pharmaprix.ca; 5122 Chemin de la Côte-des-Neiges; ⊘24hr; MⓂCôte-des-Neiges); Downtown (1500 Rue Ste-Catherine Ouest; ⊘8am-midnight; MⓂGuy-Concordia) Check the website for additional branches.

Royal Victoria Hospital (☑514-934-1934; 687 Ave des Pins Ouest; ⊘24hr) McGill University-affiliated, with emergency room, and the best option for English-speaking patients.

Sexual Assault Centre (☑514-934-4504)

Media & Internet Resources

The *Montréal Gazette* is the main English-language daily newspaper with solid coverage of national affairs, politics and arts. The Saturday edition has useful what's-on listings, although the free alternative weeklies, the *Mirror* and the *Hour*, are better sources. Published every Thursday, they're widely available in restaurants, bars and shops. Their French counterparts are *Voir* and *Ici*.

Useful websites:

City of Montréal (ville.montreal.qc.ca) Official city website.

Montréal Clubs (www.montreal-clubs.com) Keeps the finger on the pulse of Montréal's latest nightlife hot spots.

Tourism Montréal (www.tourism-montreal.org) Official website of the Montréal tourist office with reams of information and a last-minute hotel search engine with guaranteed minimum 10% discount.

Money

You'll find currency exchange counters at the airport, the train station, the main tourist office, the casino (p227; open 24 hours) and throughout the central city, especially along Rue Ste-Catherine.

Calforex (1250 Rue Peel; ⊘8:30am-9pm Mon-Sat, 10am-6pm Sun)

National Bank of Canada Plateau Mont-Royal (www.nbc.ca; 4506 Rue St-Denis); Quartier Latin (801 Rue Ste-Catherine Est) Check the website for additional branches.

Post

Main Post Office (Map p218; 677 Rue Ste-Catherine Ouest; ☏7am-7pm Mon-Fri, 10am-5pm Sat, 11am-5pm Sun) The largest branch, but you'll find many other sites around town.

Station Place d'Armes (Map p218; 157 Rue St-Antoine, Montréal, Québec H2Y 1L0) Have poste restante (general delivery) mail sent here.

Tourist Information

Montréal and Québec province maintain a central phone service for tourist information (☏514-873-2015, 877-266-5687).

Centre Infotouriste (Map p218; www.bonjourquebec.com; 1255 Rue Peel; ☏9am-6pm Mar–mid-Jun, 8:30am-7pm mid-Jun–Aug, 9am-6pm Sep-Oct, 9am-5pm Nov-Feb) Information about Montréal and all of Québec. Free hotel, tour and car reservations, plus currency exchange.

Montréal Tourist Office (Map p218; www.tourism-montreal.org; 174 Rue Notre Dame Est; ☏9am-5pm Jan-May & early Sep-Oct, to 7pm Jun-early Sep)

Old Port Tourist Kiosk (Map p218; Quai Jacques Cartier; ☏10am-7pm Mon-Fri, to 8pm Sat & Sun May–mid-Jun, 10am-10pm mid-Jun–Aug, 10am-5pm Mon-Fri, to 7pm Sat & Sun Sep–mid-Oct)

Travel Agencies

Voyages Campus (www.travelcuts.com; 1613 Rue St-Denis; ☏9am-6pm Mon-Wed, to 7pm Thu & Fri, 11am-5pm Sat) Known as Travel Cuts outside Québec; check the website for additional branches around town.

ⓘ Getting There & Away

Air

Both domestic and international airlines land at **Pierre Elliott Trudeau International Airport** (YUL; ☏514-394-7377, 800-465-1213; www.admtl.com), formerly known as Dorval Airport, about 20km west of downtown. Facilities include lockers, a left-luggage office, ATMs and a currency exchange desk. Montréal's other airport, Mirabel, no longer handles passenger flights.

Bus

Buses to the airports and to Canadian and US destinations depart from the **Station Centrale de l'Autobus** (Central Bus Station; Map p224; 505 Blvd de Maisonneuve Est).

Several bus operators offer services in all directions. See p272 for contact details for all these companies. Voyageur runs regular and express buses to Ottawa ($36, 2¼ hours, 21 daily), while Orléans Express serves Québec City ($48, 3¼ hours, up to 24 daily) as well as the Mauricie and Gaspésie regions.

Megabus offers the best deal to Toronto ($30 to $80, 6¾ hours, eight daily). Voyageur covers the same route but takes a few more hours. Greyhound has daily services to New York City ($84, eight hours, up to seven daily). Galland goes to the Laurentian resorts and Limocar cuts through the Eastern Townships en route to Sherbrooke.

Montréal is also a stop on the eastern Canada circuit run by Moose Travel Network (p888).

Car & Motorcycle

All the major international car-rental companies have branches at the airport, main train station and elsewhere around town. See p886 for general contact information. **Auto Plateau** (☏514-398-9000, 877-281-5001; www.autoplateau.com; 3585 Rue Berri; Ⓜ Sherbrooke) is a reputable local company.

The ride-share agency **Allô Stop** (☏514-985-3032; www.allostopmontreal.com; 4317 Rue St-Denis; Ⓜ Mont-Royal) has an office in the Plateau. A sample fare is $13 to Québec City.

Train

Montréal's **Gare Centrale** (Central Train Station; Map p218; 895 Rue de la Gauchetière Ouest) is the local hub for VIA Rail. The overnight service between Montréal and Halifax is a treat aboard new modern and comfortable cars. There are six trains daily to Toronto, aboard immaculate trains fitted with wi-fi connections and a beverage service.

Amtrak runs one train daily to/from New York City (US$62, 11 hours).

ⓘ Getting Around

To/From the Airport

STM (www.stm.info), the city's public transportation system, runs two bus lines from Montréal Trudeau to downtown. Rte 747 (one-way $7 in exact change, 35 minutes) is the express service to downtown, with stops at Lionel-Groulx métro station, the central train station and Berri-UQAM métro station. The service runs every 10 to 12 minutes from 8:30am to 8pm, every half-hour from 5:30am to 8:30am and from 8pm to 1am, and hourly between 2am and 5am.

WI-FI ACCESS

Île Sans Fil (http://ilesansfil.org) offers free wi-fi access to anyone who registers. There are hot spots in Caffè ArtJava (see the boxed text, p238), Juliette et Chocolat (p235) and Santropol (p236), as well as at Le Saint Sulpice (p237), Marché Jean Talon (p237) and Titanic (p233).

You can also make the trip on bus 204 Est, from Gare Dorval (Dorval Train Station) to the Lionel-Groulx métro station. A shuttle bus runs between the airport and Gare Dorval. Buses operate from 6am to midnight; the entire journey takes about an hour and costs $2.75 (in exact change).

Drivers heading into town should take Autoroute 13 Sud, which merges with Autoroute 20 Est; this in turn takes you into the heart of downtown, along the main Autoroute Ville-Marie (the 720). The trip takes about 20 to 30 minutes when traffic runs smoothly, but up to one hour during peak times.

A taxi to/from Trudeau airport costs a flat rate of $38.

Car & Motorcycle

Though Montréal is fairly easy to navigate, public transportation is preferable to driving a car while you're just getting around town. If you choose to drive, you'll find metered street parking (with meters set back from the curb) and public garages throughout the central area, especially underneath big hotels and shopping complexes. Expect to pay about $12 to $20 per day.

Note that turning right at red lights is illegal on the island of Montréal.

Public Transportation

Montréal has a modern and convenient bus and métro system run by **STM** (www.stm.info). The métro is the city's subway system and runs quickly and quietly on rubber tires. It operates until at least 12:30am. Some buses provide service all night.

One ticket can get you anywhere in the city. If you're switching between buses, or between bus and métro, get a free transfer slip, called a *correspondence*, from the driver; on the métro take one from the machines just past the turnstiles. Transfers are valid for 90 minutes only for travel in one direction.

Tickets cost $2.75 but are cheaper by the half-dozen ($13.25). There are also 'Tourist Cards' for $7/14 for one/three days and weekly cards for $20.50 (valid Monday to Sunday). Note that bus drivers won't give change.

Taxi

Flag fall is $3.15, then it's $1.45 per kilometer. You can flag down a cab on the street or order one by phone, for instance from **Taxi Diamond** (514-273-6331) or **Taxi Co-Op** (514-636-6666).

AROUND MONTRÉAL

THE LAURENTIANS

The Laurentians, or Les Laurentides in French, are perhaps the best-kept secret of Montréal day-trippers. Just an hour's drive from the city, you'll find yourself amid gentle rolling mountains, crystal blue lakes and meandering rivers peppered with towns and villages too cute for words. A visit to this natural paradise is like putting your feet up after a long day.

Although sometimes criticized for being über commercialized, Mont-Tremblant offers outstanding skiing rivaled by only Whistler in the whole of Canada. Speckling the Laurentians are many more lower-profile resort villages, whose miniature town centers deliver an air of the Alps with their breezy patios and exclusive, independent designer clothing shops.

Expect higher prices and heavy crowds during high season, which includes the summer months and Christmas holidays. Check ahead for opening hours if you plan to visit in the winter months.

Nearly all towns in the Laurentians can be accessed via Hwy 15, the Autoroute des Laurentides. Old Rte 117, running parallel to it, is slow but considerably more scenic.

ℹ Information

Besides the tourist offices listed under individual towns, you'll find branches in many other Laurentian towns. Official hours are from 8:30am to 7pm between late June and early September and 9am to 5pm the rest of the year. Actual hours, though, may vary, depending on such factors as day of the week, the weather and the visitor influx, so call ahead.

Association Touristique des Laurentides (Laurentian Tourist Association; 450-436-8532, 800-561-6673, reservation service 450-436-3507; www.laurentides.com; 9am-5pm) Regional tourist office; can answer questions on the phone, make room bookings and mail out information. It operates a free room reservation service.

La Maison du Tourisme des Laurentides (La Porte du Nord, exit 51 off Hwy 15; 8:30am-8pm mid-Jun–mid-Sep, to 5pm mid-Sep–mid-Jun) Information office maintained by the Association Touristique des Laurentides with helpful staff and lots of maps and brochures, including the excellent *Official Tourist Guide*.

ℹ️ Getting There & Around

Galland (p272) runs buses from Montréal's Central Bus Station to the Laurentians at least four times daily. Towns serviced include St-Jérôme ($16, 1¼ hours), St-Sauveur ($20, 1½ hours), Val-David ($23, two hours) and Mont-Tremblant ($29, 2½ hours).

From mid-May to mid-October, **Autobus du P'tit Train du Nord** (www.transportduparc lineaire.com) runs two buses daily between St-Jérôme and Mont Laurier (tickets $24 to $52), stopping as needed. Bicycles are transported at no extra charge.

Drivers coming from Montréal should follow either Hwy 15 or the slower Rte 117.

ST-JÉRÔME

Some 43km north of Montréal, St-Jérôme is the official gateway to the Laurentians. Despite its administrative and industrial demeanor, it's worth a stop for its Byzantine-style **cathedral** (355 Rue St-George; admission free; ⊘7:30am-4:30pm) and nearby **La Musée D'Art Contemporain des Laurentides** (101 Place du Curé-Labelle; admission free; ⊘noon-5pm Tue-Sun), which often presents superb exhibits featuring regional artists.

St-Jérôme is also the southern terminus of the **Parc Linéaire du P'tit Train du Nord** (www.laurentians.com/parclineaire), a trail system built on top of old railway tracks and snaking 200km north to Mont Laurier, passing streams, rivers, rapids, lakes and great mountain scenery. In summer it's open to bicycles and in-line skates and you'll find rest stops, information booths, restaurants, B&Bs and bike rental and repair shops all along the way. Snow season lures cross-country skiers to the section between St-Jérôme and Val-David, while snowmobile aficionados rule between Val-David and Mont Laurier.

ST-SAUVEUR-DES-MONTS

St-Sauveur-des-Monts (or St-Sauveur, for short) is the busiest village in the Laurentians and is often deluged with day-trippers thanks to its proximity to Montréal (60km). A pretty church anchors Rue Principale, the attractive main street, flanked by restaurants, cafes and boutiques. Guided tours and information about accommodations are available at **Pays d'en Haut Tourist Office** (☑450-227-3417; www.lespaysdenhaut.com; 1014 Rue Valiquette, Ste-Adèle), and **Banque Nationale** (6 Rue de la Gare) has a branch in town. **Café Saint-Sau** (Galerie des Monts mall, Block I-2, 75 Rue de la Gare; per 15/30min $3/5; ⊘8am-5pm) has internet access.

👁 Sights & Activities

Saint-Sauveur Valley Resort   SPORTS

With about 100 runs for all levels of expertise crisscrossing the area's five major ski hills (www.mssi.ca), the downhill skiing is excellent in this region. The biggest hill, **Mont Saint-Sauveur** (www.mont saintsauveur.com; per day $25-46) is famous for its night skiing, with many slopes open until 11pm. In summer, it's transformed into the **Parc Aquatique** (Water Park; www. parcaquatique.com; 350 Rue St-Denis; adult/child per day $32/16, half-day $26/14; ⊘10am-5pm early Jun & late Aug-early Sep, to 7pm late-Jun–late Aug). Kids of all ages love getting wet in the wave pool, plunging down the wicked slides (including a couple starting near the mountaintop and reached by chairlift) or being pummeled on rafting rides. Cross-country skiers flock to the over 150km of interconnecting trails at **Morin Heights** (www.skimorinheights.com; per day $29-39).

🎭 Festivals & Events

For two weeks starting in late July, St-Sauveur's **Festival des Arts** (www.fass.ca) brings dozens of international dance troupes to town. Many performances are free.

🛏 Sleeping

Auberge Sous L'Edredon   B&B $$

(☑450-227-3131; www.aubergesousledredon. com; 777 Rue Principale; r $100-190; ❋ 🐾 🛜 ❋) A Victorian inn overflowing with character about 2km from the village center and close to a little lake and the Mont Habitant ski area. Some of the delightfully decorated rooms have fireplaces and private facilities.

Le Petit Clocher   B&B $$$

(☑450-227-7576; www.lepetitclocher.com; 216 Rue de l'Église; s $165-195, d $185-215) A gorgeous inn occupying a converted monastery on a little hillside above town. It has seven rooms decorated in French Country style, many of which have extraordinary views.

🍴 Eating

Orange & Pamplemousse MEDITERRANEAN $$

(www.orangepamplemousse.com; 120 Rue Principale; mains $12-32; ⊘8am-10pm) Tranquil with the soft sounds of a Japanese bamboo water fountain, this restaurant is a great place to devour complex pasta dishes and extraordinary grilled fish. The breakfasts are also divine.

Rio BARBECUE $$
(352 Rue Principale; mains $10-20, meals from $20; ☺5-10pm) It's a bit strange to imagine ordering a barbecue dinner in the mountains of rural Québec, but this classy diner gets rave reviews from American tourists and locals alike. Don't leave without at least a taste of the succulent, fall-off-the-bone baby back ribs.

Chez Bernard DELI $
(www.chezbernard.com; 411 Rue Principale; dishes $6-15; ☺9am-7pm Mon-Wed, to 8pm Thu-Fri, to 6pm Sat & Sun) Superb deli with local specialties, some homemade, plus full meals perfect for picnics.

La Brûlerie des Monts CAFE $
(197 Rue Principale; meals $5-10; ☺7am-9pm) *The* place in town for breakfast and sandwiches, with a great terrace. Coffee beans are roasted on-site.

VAL-DAVID

Val-David is a pint-sized village with an almost lyrical quality and a gorgeous setting along the Rivière du Nord and at the foot of the mountains. Its charms have made it a magnet for artists whose studios and galleries line the main street, Rue de L'Église. There is a **tourist information office** (www.valdavid.com; 2501 Rue de L'Église) in town.

◉ Sights & Activities

From mid-July to mid-August, the **1001 Pots Festival** (www.1001pots.com), a huge ceramic exhibit and sale, brings around 100,000 people to town. It's the brainchild of Japanese-Canadian artist Kinya Ishikawa whose utilitarian yet stylish pieces are displayed year-round at his **Atelier du Potier** (2435 Rue de L'Église; ☺10am-5pm Tue-Sun).

The great outdoors is Val-David's other main attraction. **Phénix Sports and Adventure** (☎819-322-1118; 2444 Rue de L'Église) and **Pause Plein Air** (☎819-322-6880; 1381 Rue de la Sapinière) rent bicycles, kayaks and canoes, and offer cycle-canoe packages on the Rivière du Nord.

Rock climbing is to Val-David what skiing is to other Laurentian villages, with more than 500 routes from easy walls to challenging cliffs. The mountain-climbing school **Passe Montagne** (1760 Montée 2e Rang; ☺mid-Apr–mid-Oct) offers courses for beginning and experienced rock hounds from $60.

⌂ Sleeping

Le Chalet Beaumont HOSTEL $
(☎819-322-1972; www.chaletbeaumont.com; 1451 Rue Beaumont; dm $25, r without/with private bathroom $60/75; @☎) This private hostel in a historic log cabin on a wooded hill has the look and amenities of a luxurious country retreat. Inside you'll find free sauna and internet, a well-equipped communal kitchen and bar, bicycle and ski rentals and helpful, friendly staff.

✗ Eating

Le Grand Pa MEDITERRANEAN $$$
(www.legrandpa.com; 2481 Rue de L'Église; mains $21-30; ☺11:30am-2pm & 5-10pm) This convivial restaurant attracts a winning mix of locals and visitors nibbling on creative grilled meat and fish dishes or wood-fired pizzas. A *chansonnier* serenades diners on Friday and Saturday nights. Big terrace.

La Vagabonde BAKERY $
(www.boulangerielavagabonde.com; 1262 Chemin de la Rivière; ☺8am-6pm Wed-Sun) This popular cafe and bakery serves delicious handcrafted organic breads and pastries.

ST-FAUSTIN-LAC-CARRÉ

The gateway to the Mont-Tremblant region, St-Faustin has a couple of attractions in its own right. At the maple-sugar shack **Cabane à Sucre Millette** (1357 Rue St Faustin; adult/child $7/5; ☺11:30am-8pm Tue-Sun Mar & Apr, by reservation only May-Feb), you can see production in action – sap is still culled in horse-drawn carts – and sample the results.

The **Centre Touristique Éducatif des Laurentides** (www.ctel.ca; 5000 Chemin du Lac Cordon; adult/child $6/3; ☺8am-5pm mid-Jun–early Sep, 8am-5pm Fri-Sun May–mid-Jun & early Sep–mid-Oct) is a marvelous protected area and a great place to learn about local flora and fauna. The 36km trail network includes some wheelchair-accessible sections, and there are canoe and kayak rentals as well. To get here, take exit 83 from Hwy 15 or exit 107 on Rte 117 North.

VILLE DE MONT-TREMBLANT

The Mont-Tremblant area is the crown jewel of the Laurentians, lorded over by the 960m-high eponymous mountain, dotted with pristine lakes and traversed by rivers. It's a hugely popular four-season playground, drawing ski bums from late October to mid-April, and hikers, bikers, golfers, water sports fans and other outdoor enthusiasts the rest of the year.

The area of Ville de Mont-Tremblant is divided into three sections: **Station Tremblant**, the ski hill and pedestrianized tourist resort at the foot of the mountain; **Mont-Tremblant Village**, a sweet and tiny cluster of homes and businesses about 4km southwest of here; and **St-Jovite**, the main town and commercial center off Rte 117, about 12km south of the mountain. A shuttle bus ($2.25, 6am to 8pm) connects all three.

⊙ Sights & Activities

Station Tremblant (www.tremblant.com; adult lift ticket full/half-day $62/48) is among the top-ranked international ski resorts in eastern North America according to *Ski* magazine and legions of loyal fans. Founded in 1938, it sprang from the vision of Philadelphia millionaire Joe Ryan and has been seriously slicked up since 1991 when Intrawest, the Vancouver company responsible for putting Whistler on the map, took over its administration. The mountain has a vertical drop of 645m and is laced with 95 trails and two snow parks served by 14 lifts, including an express gondola. Ski rentals start at $32 per day.

A summer attraction is the **downhill luge track** (1/3/5 rides $12.50/23/36) that snakes down the mountain for 1.4km; daredevils can reach speeds up to 50km/h. The nearby **Activity Center** (☎891-681-4848; www.tremblantactivities.com) can arrange for a wide variety of outdoor pursuits, from fishing to canoeing to horseback riding.

The southern mountain base spills over into a sparkling pedestrian tourist village with big hotels, shops, restaurants and an amusement park atmosphere. The cookie-cutter architecture doesn't quite exude the rustic European charm its planners sought to emulate, but this seems of little concern to the 2.5 million annual visitors milling along its cobbled lanes year after year.

✲ Festivals & Events

For 10 days every early July, the resort is abuzz with music fans during the **Festival International du Blues** (www.tremblantblues. com), the country's biggest blues festival.

🛏 Sleeping

HI Mont-Tremblant Hostel HOSTEL $
(☎819-425-6008; www.hostellingtremblant.com; 2213 Chemin du Village, Mont-Tremblant Village;

dm member/nonmember $24.75/28.75, s/d $63.75/71.75; @🖘) This attractive hostel right next to Lac Moore (free canoe rentals) features a big kitchen and large party room with bar, pool table and fireplace. The clean and spacious rooms often fill to capacity, especially in the ski season.

Auberge Le Lupin B&B $$
(☎819-425-5474, 877-425-5474; www.lelupin. com; 127 Rue Pinoteau, Mont-Tremblant Village; r $90-123; @🖘) This 1940s log house offers snug digs just 1km away from the ski station, with private beach access to the sparkling Lac Tremblant. The tasty breakfasts whipped up by host Pierre in his homey rustic kitchen are a perfect start to the day.

Hotel Quintessence BOUTIQUE HOTEL $$$
(☎866-425-3400; www.hotelquintessence.com; 3004 Chemin de la Chapelle, Mont-Tremblant Village; ste from $350; ✲@🖘🌊) This luxurious estate fuses Old World splendor with North American nature. From calming wood fireplaces and private balconies overlooking Lac Tremblant to heated marble floors and plunge baths, suites at this small, exclusive resort are definitely splurge-worthy.

Country Inn & Suites by Carlson HOTEL $$
(☎819-681-5555, 800-596-2375; 160 Chemin Curé des Lauriers, Station Tremblant; ste from $149; ✲@🖘🌊) With its perfect position in the heart of the pedestrian village, the large and functional rooms of this contemporary ski lodge are comfortable and convenient. All suites have full kitchens. Children under 17 stay free.

✖ Eating

Plus Minus Café FUSION $$$
(www.plusminuscafe.com; Station Tremblant; mains $29-40; ⊙6am-10pm; ✍) The healthy avant-garde menu here extends from colorful salads to elaborately designed mains incorporating high-quality lean red meats, reserve-raised wild poultry, salt-water fresh fish and funky flavor combinations such as locally grown cannabis with miso, star anise and chlorophyll.

Microbrasserie La Diable PUB $$
(www.microladiable.com; Station Tremblant; mains $10-23; ⊙11:30am-2am) After a day of tearing down the mountain, the hearty sausages, burgers and pastas served at this lively tavern at Station Tremblant fill the belly nicely, as do the tasty homebrews.

Coco Pazzo ITALIAN **$$**
(www.coco-pazzo.com; Station Tremblant; mains $12-29; ⊙noon-3pm & 5-9pm) Modern Italian with a twist is on offer at this upscale eatery, awash in a sea of soft oranges and soothing blues and overlooking the stage at Place des Lauriers.

❶ Information

Au Grain de Café (Homewood Suites par Hilton, Station Tremblant; per 10min $3; ⊙8am-9pm) Internet access.

Banque Nationale (Country Inn & Suites, Station Tremblant; ⊙10am-5pm)

Clinique Medicale Saint-Jovite (☑819-425-2728; 910 Rue de L'École, St-Jovite)

Mont Tremblant Tourism (☑800-322-2932; www.tourismemonttremblant.com) St-Jovite (48 Chemin de Brébeuf); Mont-Tremblant Village (5080 Montée Ryan, cnr Rte 327); Station Tremblant (Place des Voyageurs)

PARC DU MONT-TREMBLANT

Nature puts on a terrific show in **Parc du Mont-Tremblant** (☑819-688-2281, reservations 800-665-6527; www.parksquebec.com; Chemin du Lac Supérieur; adult/child per day $3.50/1.75), the province's biggest and oldest park – it opened in 1894. Covering 1510 sq km of gorgeous Laurentian lakes, rivers, hills and woods, the park boasts rare vegetation (including silver maple and red oak), hiking and biking trails and canoe routes. It is home to fox, deer, moose and wolves, and a habitat for more than 200 bird species, including a huge blue heron colony.

The park is divided into three sectors. The most developed area is the **Diable sector**, home to beautiful Lac Monroe. The main entrance is 28km northeast of Station Tremblant. The year-round service center, which also has equipment rentals, is another 11km from the entrance.

Diable's incredible trails range from an easy 20-minute stroll past waterfalls to day-long hikes that take in stunning views of majestic valleys. You can also take your bike out on some trails or rent canoes to travel down the serpentine Rivière Diable. The gentle section between Lac Chat and La Vache Noir is perfect for families.

Further east, the **Pimbina sector** is a 10-minute drive from St-Donat. Here you'll find an **information center** (⊙mid-May–mid-Oct & mid-Dec–Mar), canoe and kayak rentals and campgrounds with some amenities. Activities include swimming at Lac Provost and hiking and biking trails near-

by. A highlight is the **Carcan Trail**, a 14.4km route to the top of the park's second-highest peak (883m), which passes waterfalls and lush scenery on the way.

Further east is the **L'Assomption sector**, accessible via the town of St-Côme. It is the most untamed part of the park, with more trails, secluded cottages and remote camping options. In winter, you can't access this sector by car, as snow covers the roads.

The wilder interior and eastern sections are accessible by dirt roads, some of which are old logging routes. The off-the-beaten-track areas abound in wildlife. With some effort, it's possible to have whole lakes to yourself, except for the wolves whose howls you hear at night.

By late August, nights start getting cold and a couple of months later a blanket of snow adds a magic touch. That's when cross-country skiing and snowshoeing are popular activities in the Diable and Pimbina sectors.

Some of the park's many **campgrounds** (camp sites $19.25-37.75) come with amenities, but most are basic. Reservations are recommended in busy periods. Some of the nicest spots can only be reached by canoe. There's also lodging in four-person **yurts** (per night $120) and cozy two- to eight-person **cabins** ($125-230).

MONTRÉAL TO QUÉBEC CITY

There's so much charm packed into this idyllic stretch of pastoral patchwork between Québec's two metropolises that it's bursting at the borders. Kick back and stay awhile to enjoy the picture-postcard scenery of the Eastern Townships and take in the unique bilingual atmosphere that constant American tourist traffic to this area has fostered. Alternatively, the Mauricie region – from Trois-Rivières north to Lac St Jean and following the flow of the mighty St Maurice River – has been known to snatch unsuspecting visitors in search of wild, unadulterated natural beauty.

The Trans-Canada Hwy (Hwy 20) cuts a straight path to Québec City from Montréal. The Eastern Townships are nestled between here and the Vermont border, mainly along Hwy 10; Mauricie falls to the north of Hwy 20 along Hwy 40.

Eastern Townships

Lush rolling hills, crystal-clear blue lakes and checkerboard farms fill the Eastern Townships, or the 'Cantons-des-l'Est' as it's known by French inhabitants. The region begins 80km southeast of Montréal, south of Hwy 20, and finds itself squished in between the labyrinth of minor highways that stretch all the way to the Vermont and New Hampshire borders. New Englanders will feel right at home with the covered bridges and round barns that dot the bumpy landscape, sculpted by the tail end of the US Appalachian mountain range, which peters out here.

A visit during spring is rewarding, as it's the season for 'sugaring off' – the tapping, boiling and preparation of maple syrup (see the boxed text, p250). Summer brings fishing and swimming in the numerous lakes; in fall the foliage puts on a show of kaleidoscopic colors to toast with freshly brewed apple cider, which is served in local pubs. The district is also home to a fast-growing wine region that produces some respectable whites and an excellent ice wine, a dessert wine made from frozen grapes. Cycling is extremely popular in the warmer months, with nearly 500km of trails taking in sumptuous landscapes. Winter means excellent downhill skiing at the three main ski hills: Bromont, Mont Orford and Sutton.

Originally the territory of Abenakis, the townships were settled in the aftermath of the 1776 American Revolution by New England Loyalists seeking to remain under the British crown. They were joined by successive waves of immigrants from Ireland and Scotland as well as French Canadians, who today make up the vast majority of residents.

ℹ Information

Eastern Townships Tourism Association (www.cantonsdelest.com; Hwy 10 exit 68) At the turnoff for Granby/Bromont.

Montréal to Québec City & Around

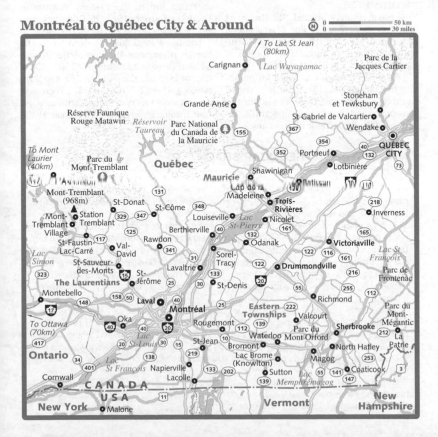

① Getting There & Away

Coming from Montréal, Hwy 10 will take you straight to the Eastern Townships to just east of Sherbrooke where it continues as Rte 112. Coming from Québec City via Hwy 20, the fastest route is via Hwy 55, which you'll pick up near Drummondville.

Limocar operates bus services between Montréal's Station Centrale de l'Autobus and Magog ($31, 1½ hours) and Sherbrooke ($36, 2½ hours) up to 15 times daily. Seven of these buses also stop in Granby ($21, one to 1½ hours), while Bromont is served twice daily ($25, 2¼ hours). Orléans Express goes to Trois-Rivières ($27, 1½ hours) in the Mauricie region eight times daily.

Autobus Viens operates three daily bus services between Montréal's central bus station and the townships of Sutton ($18, one hour) and Lac Brome ($19, 2¼ hours).

The ride-share organization **Allô Stop** (✆819-821-3637; 1204 Rue King Ouest) has a branch in Sherbrooke. Rides to Montréal/Québec City are $10/13.

BROMONT

This town revolves around **Ski Bromont** (www.skibromont.com; 150 Rue Champlain), a year-round resort on the slopes of 533m-high Mt Brome. In summer its 100km of marked trails, including 15 thrilling downhill routes, have made it a mecca for mountain bike aficionados (Bromont has hosted world championships). In winter, skiers and snowboarders take over the 104 trails, including 50 trails open for night skiing.

On weekends from April to October, Bromont's other major attraction is its giant **flea market** (16 Rue Lafontaine; admission free; ⊙9am-5pm Sat & Sun), just off Hwy 10, with more than 1000 vendors attracting thrifty treasure hunters from near and far.

Limocar buses stop at Dépanneur Shefford, 624 Rue Shefford.

LAC BROME (KNOWLTON)

Lac Brome is the name of seven amalgamated towns orbiting the eponymous lake, with Knowlton on the southern shore being the largest and most attractive. First settled by Loyalists in 1802, the town still retains an upmarket British flair and numerous 19th-century buildings. A stroll around its cute downtown, which teems with quality boutiques, art galleries, cafes and restaurants, is a fun way to spend an hour or two. Pick up a free walking tour pamphlet from the Auberge Knowlton, which has been in business since 1849, making it the oldest continuously operating inn in the Eastern Townships. There is a **tourist office** (255C Chemin Knowlton; ⊙Jun-early Sep) at exit 68 on Hwy 10.

For more local history, drop in to the **Musée Historique du Comté de Brome** (130 Rue Lakeside; adult/child $5/2.50; ⊙10am-4:30pm Mon-Sat, 11am-4:30pm Sun mid-May–mid-Sep), where exhibits include a recreated general store and courthouse (Sunday only) and, incongruously, a WWI Fokker D-VII plane.

MAPLE SYRUP & THE SUGAR SHACK

Maple syrup is Canada's most famous export, with three-quarters of the world's total output hailing from Québec. It was Aboriginal tribes who taught Europeans how to make the sweet nectar, and by the 19th century cultivating the sap and transforming it into syrup had quickly become a local tradition.

Every summer, starches accumulate in sugar maple trees, which are native to North America. As soon as the mercury dips below zero, they turn into sucrose. To tap the sugar inside the tree, inventive types have come up with a system that sucks out the sap through a series of tubes called Sysvacs. These snake through a maple grove straight to machines that cook the juice into syrup. The different grades produced depend on how long it is cooked and to what temperature (to make taffy, for example, it must cook to 26°C above boiling point).

Sugar shacks became part of the Québécois experience in the early 20th century. They remain places to experience the maple tradition at its best. The 'taffy pull' is the most fun – you scoop up some snow, put it on a plate and have some steaming syrup from a piping cauldron poured onto it. The syrup hardens as it hits the snow, and it can then be twisted onto a Popsicle stick and sucked and chewed until you feel the need to do it all over again.

Sugar shacks are only open for a month or so, in February and March. A few are mentioned in this book (see Cabane à Sucre Millette, for example, p246), but any tourist information office can recommend others.

Auberge Knowlton ([📞]450-242-6886; www.aubergeknowlton.ca; 286 Chemin Knowlton; d incl breakfast $142; [🛜]), in a landmark Victorian building, in business since 1849, has come a long way since the stagecoach days. Antique-style furniture meets modern amenities in the country-themed, spacious rooms. Breakfast is à la carte.

Le Relais (286 Chemin Knowlton; lunch mains $9-20, dinner $14-25), at Auberge Knowlton, is great place to try the juicy Brome duck paired with a glass of local wine. In summer, the tables on the upstairs terrace are much in demand.

Lac Brome is famous for its ducks, which have been bred here since 1912 on a special diet including soy and vitamins. Pick up pâté and other products at the Brome Lake Duck Farm (40 Chemin Centre; [🕐]8am-5pm Mon-Thu, to 6pm Fri, 9:30am-5pm Sat & Sun).

To get to Lac Brome from Hwy 10, take Rte 243 south. Autobus Viens stops at Dépanneur Rouge, 483 Rue Knowlton.

SUTTON

Sutton is a little Loyalist town with a pretty main street where you can shop to your heart's content or let your hair down during après-ski partying in the many bars. There is internet access at Net Connect (20 Place Sutton; per hr $5; [🕐]10am-5:30pm Mon-Sat) and information at the tourist office (www.sutton. ca; 11b Rue Principale Sud).

Sutton is surrounded by the Sutton Mountains, a string of velvety, round hills whose highest peak (Sommet Rond) rises to 968m. Not surprisingly, this makes Sutton a major winter sports hub with much of the action centered on Mont Sutton (www.montsutton. com; 671 Chemin Maple; day ticket adult/child $58/33; [🕐]9am-4pm Mon-Fri, from 8:30am Sat & Sun). There are 54 trails for plunging down the mountain; the longest run is 2.85km.

In summer, Sutton is prime hiking territory, especially in the conservation area Parc d'Environnement Naturel ([📞]450-538-4085; day fee adult/child $5/3; [🕐]Jun-Oct), where 80km of trails have been carved through the thickly forested mountains. Backpackers can unfold their tents at three primitive campgrounds (the one at Lac Spruce is the nicest).

Inside a perfectly restored heritage building, Auberge Le St-Amour ([📞]450-538-6188, 888-538-6188; www.innsutton.com; 1 Rue Pleasant; r $60-140; [@]) is a pretty inn and a great place for a weekend escape or romantic interlude. Some of the pretty rooms

have views of Mont Sutton and the breakfasts are memorable. The restaurant serves Mediterranean-influenced dinners.

Sutton is 18km south of Knowlton via Rtes 104 and 215. Autobus Viens stops at the Esso gas station, 28 Rue Principale.

VALCOURT

Valcourt would be a mere blip on the radar were it not for local resident Joseph Armand Bombardier, the father of the Ski-Doo (snowmobile), whose invention is a great source of pride to Canadians. At the Musée J Armand Bombardier (www.bombardiermuseum. com; 1001 Ave J-A Bombardier; adult/child $7/ free; [🕐]10am-5pm May-Aug, 10am-5pm Tue-Sun Sep-Apr) you can see early models of his Ski-Doo (and amusing historic clips of how they looked in action), the original workshop and a collection of contemporary and vintage snowmobiles. Tours of the plant, which also churns out ATVs and Sea-Doos, are offered as well (for an additional $12/5).

To get to Valcourt, take exit 90 off Hwy 10, then follow Rte 243. There are no buses.

MAGOG

Magog occupies a prime spot on the north shore of Lac Memphrémagog, a banana-shaped lake that stretches south for 44km, all the way across the US border. It's the biggest township, with a pretty main street and plenty of decent restaurants and hotels.

Sights & Activities

There's a beach in Magog, but in summer carving out space for your towel can be a tall order. The rest of the shore is largely in private hands, so the lake is best explored from the water. Club de Voile ([📞]819-847-3101; Plage des Cantons) is among several outfitters renting kayaks, sailboats and windsurfing equipment, while Croisières Memphréma-gog ([📞]819-843-8068; adult $22-88, child $12-88; [🕐]mid-May–Oct) offers 1¾-hour, 2½-hour and seven-hour narrated cruises. Watch for Memphré, the feisty yet elusive creature that lives, Nessie-style, at the bottom of the lake!

Sleeping

À L'Ancestrale B&B   B&B $$
([📞]819-847-5555, 888-847-5507; www.ancestrale. com; 200 Rue Abbott; r incl breakfast $105-145; [@🛜]) Wake up to a four-course gourmet breakfast at this intimate retreat, whose four rooms are dressed in a romantic, countrified way and outfitted with refrigerators and coffee makers. It's central but on a quiet street.

Auberge du Centre d'Arts Orford INN $
(☎819-843-3981; 3165 Chemin du Parc; cabin
$38, r incl breakfast $68-82) This inn on the
woodsy grounds of the Centre d'Arts makes
a good base for exploring Parc du Mont Orford. Rooms are basic but modern and comfortable. If you like roughing it, rent one of
the rustic cabins (basically tiny permanent
tents with shared facilities; summer only).

Ô Bois Dormant B&B $$
(☎819-843-0450; www.oboisdormant.qc.ca;
205 Rue Abbott; r incl breakfast $85-120; ❄ @)
Although only a short walk from the
main street, the rambling back lawn at
this towering Victorian feels like a se-
cluded resort. Rooms are cozy and bright.

La Belle Victorienne B&B B&B $$
(☎819-847-0476, 888-440-0476; www.bellevic.
com; 142 Rue Merry Nord; d $99-125; @ ☎)
A daintily elegant Victorian in central
Magog with a year-round spa.

✖ Eating

Bistro Lady of the Lake MEDITERRANEAN $$$
(www.bistrolady.com; 125 Plage des Cantons;
mains $21-31; ☉4-10pm) This popular eatery,
its success enhanced by its great lakeside
setting, serves Mediterranean with a twist.
Dishes get daring, with interesting com-
binations such as dill, almonds and fresh
trout, and the wine list is decent.

ℹ Information

CLSC Health Clinic (☎819-843-2572; 50 Rue
St-Patrice Est)

La Petite Place (108 Place du Commerce; per
hr $6; ☉8:30am-5pm Mon-Fri, to 2pm Sat)
Internet access; tucked into the basement, in
the back of the parking lot.

Tourist office (www.tourisme-memphremagog.
com; 55 Rue Cabana) Off Rte 112.

ℹ Getting There & Away

Limocar buses stop at 768 Rue Sherbrooke.

PARC DU MONT ORFORD

About a 10-minute drive north of Magog,
Parc du Mont Orford (3321 Chemin du Parc;
adult/child per day $3.50/1.50; ☉year-round),
home to snapping turtles and countless
bird species, is fairly compact and often
gets busy. Fitness freaks can hike the park's
two mountains, **Mont Chauve** (600m) and
Mont Orford (853m), while water babies
have three lakes in which to play. The big-
gest is Lac Stukely, which has a beach,
camping and boat rentals.

Winter activities include snowshoeing
and cross-country skiing in the park, as
well as downhill skiing at the **Station de
Ski Mont-Orford** (www.orford.com; lift ticket
adult/child $47/27; ☉9am-4pm). It offers a
vertical drop of 540m and 54 slopes, mostly
for beginners and intermediate skiers, plus
a snow park with half-pipe and other fun
features.

Just outside the park boundaries, the
Centre d'Arts Orford (Orford Arts Center;
www.arts-orford.org; 3165 Chemin du Parc; tickets
from $39) hosts the **Festival Orford**, a pres-
tigious series of 40 to 50 classical concerts,
from late June to mid-August.

NORTH HATLEY

North Hatley wins top honors as the cutest
of all the cute Eastern Townships. It occu-
pies an enchanting spot at the northern tip
of the crystal-clear (and monsterless) Lac
Massawippi, about 17km east of Magog.

Wealthy Americans have always loved it
here, so much so, in fact, they started build-
ing their stately vacation homes as early as
1880. A Yankee influence still makes itself
felt (there are as many cow paintings and
scented candles here as anywhere in New
England!) and there's even a 'Main St' (well,
technically 'Rue Main'). Many of the fancy
homes have been converted into B&Bs,
inns or gourmet restaurants, including the

WORTH A TRIP

ABBAYE ST-BENOÎT-DU-LAC

About 12km south of Magog, on the western lakeshore, is the **Abbaye St-Benoît-du-
Lac** (www.st-benoit-du-lac.com; admission free; ☉church 5am-8:30pm, gift shop 9-10:45am
& 11:45am-4:30pm Mon-Sat Sep-Jun, to 6pm Jul & Aug), home to about 50 Benedictine
monks. The complex is a striking blend of traditional and modern architecture, includ-
ing a hallway awash in colorful tiles and a lofty church with exposed structural beams
and brick walls. If you can, visit at 7:30am, 11am or 5pm when the monks practice
Gregorian chanting. Music CDs, cheeses and apple cider are among the products for
sale in the gift shop.

ultradeluxe Manoir Hovey. There is a small information center, internet access and great coffee at **Café North Hatley** (90 Rue Main; per 30min $2.95; ☺9:30am-5pm).

A great way to explore the delightful terrain surrounding North Hatley is on horseback; **Randonées Jacques Robidas** (www.randonneesjrobidas.qc.ca) offers rides year-round.

TOP CHOICE **Manoir Hovey** (☎819-842-2421; www.manoirhovey.com; 575 Chemin Hovey; r incl breakfast & 3-course dinner per person $145-410; ❀@☎☎) is the area's premier resort with a dining room that emphasizes refined Québécois fare prepared from fresh local ingredients (a tasting menu is $89 for nonguests). Lucky overnight guests can run wild in the expansive gardens, lined with beautiful wildflowers and overlooking the lake, or take refuge in sumptuous bedrooms hidden within the massive country house. There's a heated pool, an ice rink (in winter) and a jovial pub on-site; a whole slew of outdoor activities such as windsurfing, golfing and lake cruises can be arranged.

Pilsen (www.pilsen.ca; 55 Rue Main; mains $12-27; ☺11:30am-11pm Mon-Thu, to midnight Fri & Sat) is the liveliest restaurant in town, famous for its salmon, both grilled and smoked, and upmarket pub fare. There's a nice riverside terrace and another facing the lake.

North Hatley is east of Magog along Rte 108. Coming from Sherbrooke, take Rte 243 to Rte 108. There is no bus service.

SHERBROOKE

This bustling city is perfect for refueling on modern conveniences before returning to the Eastern Townships. The historic center sits at the confluence of two rivers and is bisected by Rue Wellington and Rue King, the main commercial arteries. It's recommended that you stick to this area, 'Vieux Sherbrooke,' where the smattering of stellar restaurants and cafes stands defiant against the blight of overdevelopment in other parts of the city. Sherbrooke lies along Hwy 10, about 25km northeast of Magog.

◉ Sights & Activities

Bishop's University　　NOTABLE BUILDING
(Rue du Collège) If you're interested in scholarly pursuits, head 5km south (or catch bus 2 or 11) to Lennoxville to see the Anglican Bishop's University, founded in 1843 and modeled after Oxford and Cambridge in England. The campus' architectural

highlight is **St Mark's Chapel** (admission free; ☺8:30am-5pm), richly decorated with carved pews and stained-glass windows.

Centre d'Interprétation de l'Histoire de Sherbrooke　　MUSEUM
(www.histoiresherbrooke.com; 275 Rue Dufferin; adult/child $4/2.50; ☺9am-5pm Tue-Fri, 10am-5pm Sat & Sun mid-Jun–Aug, 9am-5pm Tue-Fri, 1-5pm Sat & Sun Sep–mid-Jun) This center offers an engaging introduction to the town's history and rents out MP3 players for self-guided city tours on foot or by car ($10).

Cathédrale St-Michel　　HOSTEL
(130 Rue de la Cathédrale; admission free; ☺9am-noon & 2-4pm) Quietly overlooking the action from its hilltop perch is the Cathédrale St-Michel, a monumental granite edifice.

Musée des Beaux-Arts　　MUSEUM
(www.mbas.qc.ca; 241 Rue Dufferin; adult/child $8/4; ☺10am-5pm Tue-Sun late Jun-Aug, noon-5pm Tue-Sun Sep-late Jun) This museum has a good permanent collection featuring works by regional artists and also stages temporary exhibits.

Lac des Nations　　NATURE RESERVE
Further south, Rivière Magog flows into the pretty Lac des Nations, surrounded by a scenic paved trail perfect for walking, in-line skating and cycling (rentals available).

ⓘ Information

Brûlerie de Café (180 Rue Wellington; ☺10am-11pm) For free internet access.

Hospital Hôtel-Dieu (☎819-346-1110; 580 Rue Bowen Sud; ☺24hr)

National Bank of Canada (3075 Blvd Portland; ☺10am-3pm Mon & Tue, to 5pm Wed, to 8pm Thu, to 4pm Fri)

Tourist office (www.tourismesherbrooke.com; 785 Rue King Ouest; 9am-6pm Mon-Fri, 10am-5pm Sat & Sun)

ⓘ Getting There & Away

The Limocar bus terminal is at 80 Rue du Depôt.

PARC DU MONT-MÉGANTIC

At the heart of a scenic and delightfully uncrowded area, the **Parc du Mont-Mégantic** (189 Rte du Parc; day entry adult/child $3.50/1.50; ☺9am-11pm Jun-Aug, to 5pm Sat & Sun Sep-May) holds mega-sized appeal for wilderness fans and stargazers. Encounters with moose, white-tailed deer, coyote and

KIDS LOVE GRANBY

You'll score big with your kids if you take them to the **Granby Zoo** (www.zoodegranby.com; 525 Rue St-Hubert; adult/child $26.50/16.50; ⊙10am-5pm Jun, to 7pm Jul & Aug, to 5pm Sat & Sun Sep–mid-Oct). The tigers, kangaroos, elephants and some 170 other species of finned, feathered and furry friends rarely fail to enthrall the little ones. Tickets include admission to the **Parc Aquatique Amazoo**, a small water park with a churning wave pool and rides. Take exit 68 off Hwy 10.

other wildlife are pretty much guaranteed as you roam the trails of this park.

The park's **AstroLab** (☑819-888-2941, 800-665-6527; www.astrolab-parc-national-mont -megantic.org; adult/child $9/5, summit tours day $13/6, night $17/9; ⊙noon-11pm late Jun-late Aug, noon-5pm & 8-11pm Sat, noon-5pm Sun late May-late Jun & late Aug-early Oct) is an astronomy research center that explains space through interactive exhibits and a multimedia show. A highlight is a tour of the observatory at the summit. Reservations are required.

The park is approximately 60km east of Sherbrooke along Rtes 108 and 212. There is no bus service.

Mauricie

Mauricie is one of Québec's less-known regions, despite being in a strategic spot halfway between Montréal and Québec City. Stretching 300km from Trois-Rivières north to Lac St Jean, it follows the flow of the mighty St Maurice River, which for centuries has been the backbone of the area's industrial heritage. Logs were being driven down the river to the pulp and paper mills until as late as 1996. Centuries earlier, the region had given birth to the country's iron industry; the original forge is now a national historic site. Industry still dominates the lower region, but things get considerably more scenic after the river reaches La Mauricie National Park.

TROIS-RIVIÈRES

Founded in 1634, Trois-Rivières is North America's second-oldest city north of Mexico, but you'd never know it: a roaring fire that swept through in 1908 left little of the city's historic looks. Still, the city center, right on the north shore of the St Lawrence River, is not without charms and some bona fide tourist attractions. The name, by the way, is a misnomer as there are only two, not three, streams here. There are, however, three branches of the St Maurice River at its mouth, where islands split its flow into three channels.

⊙ Sights & Activities

Rue Notre Dame and Rue des Forges, the main arteries in Trois-Rivières' compact downtown, are lined with cafes and bars. A riverfront promenade leads to the oldest section of town along Rue des Ursulines.

En Prison   MUSEUM
(In Prison; www.enprison.com; 200 Rue Laviolette; adult/child $9/5; ⊙10am-6pm Jun-Aug, to 5pm Tue-Sun Sep-May) Unquestionably the most intriguing museum is En Prison, an exhibit housed in an 1822 prison that remained open for business until 1986. Ex-cons bring the harsh realities of the lock-up vividly to life during 90-minute tours that include a stop at dark and dank underground cells known as 'the pit.' The prison exhibit is affiliated with the adjacent **Musée Québécois de Culture Populaire** (www.culturepop.qc.ca; adult/child $9/5, incl En Prison $14/8; ⊙10am-6pm Jun-Aug, to 5pm Tue-Sun Sep-May), which has a renowned regional folk art collection and changing exhibits, often with a quirky pop culture bent.

Musée des Ursulines   MUSEUM
(734 Rue des Ursulines; adult/child $4/free; ⊙1-5pm Wed-Sun Mar & Apr, 10am-5pm Tue-Sun May-Oct) For a slice of the town's religious history, stop at the Musée des Ursulines. The former hospital founded by Ursuline nuns in 1639 forms a pretty backdrop for the fine collection of textiles, ceramics, books and prints related to religion. Beautiful frescoes adorn the chapel.

Cathédrale de l'Assumption   CHURCH
(362 Rue Bonaventure; admission free; ⊙7am-noon & 2-5pm) Church fans should also make a beeline to the colossal Cathédrale de l'Assumption, a soaring neo-Gothic confection with exquisite sculpture and intricate Florentine stained-glass windows.

Sanctuaire Notre Dame du Cap   CHURCH
(626 Rue Notre Dame; admission free; ⊙8:30am-8pm) In nearby Cap de la Madeleine (take

bus 2), located about 4km northeast of the center, the grand Sanctuaire Notre Dame du Cap looks like a spaceship sitting on a launch pad. Up to 1660 worshippers can congregate underneath the dome while being serenaded by a giant Casavant organ. A Marian shrine with a miracle-performing statue draws believers all year-round.

Les Forges-du-Saint-Maurice
INDUSTRIAL MUSEUM

(10,000 Blvd des Forges; adult/child $4/2; ☺9:30am-5:30pm Wed-Sun mid-May–Jun, 9:30am-5:30pm Jul & Aug, 9:30am-4:30pm Wed-Sun Sep & Oct) About 7km northwest of the center (take bus 4), Les Forges-du-Saint-Mauricie is a national historic site preserving the 18th-century birthplace of the Canadian iron industry. Costumed guides take you around the grounds and into the blast furnace, while a sound-and-light show reveals the daily operations of Canada's first ironworks.

Croisières/Cruises
CRUISE

(☏819-375-3000) Croisières/Cruises runs various cruises, mostly 90-minute spins on the St Lawrence and St Mauricie Rivers ($22). The cruises depart from the landing docks at the foot of Rue des Forges.

🛏 Sleeping & Eating

L'Emerillon B&B
B&B $$

(☏819-375-1010; www.bbcanada.com/1949.html; 890 Terrasse Turcotte; r $99-129; 🛜) This is hands-down, one of the classiest B&Bs around. A grand wooden staircase leads to the four rooms, the nicest of which features a heavenly four-poster and balcony with river views. There are two large common rooms with billiards table, telescope and piano.

Café Morgane
CAFE $

(100 Rue des Forges; dishes $3-7; ☺8am-9pm) On most afternoons, this is the busiest spot in Trois-Rivières. Espresso, herbal teas and decadent sweets infuse the airy space with delightful smells. There's a free wi-fi connection here.

Restaurant Le Grill
STEAKHOUSE $$

(350 Rue des Forges; mains $13-32; ☺11:30am-9:30pm daily, brunch Sat & Sun) Locals flock to this trendy steakhouse on the main strip in droves for the filet mignon and happening night scene. The streetside patio puts you right in the middle of all the action.

ℹ Information

Caisse Populaire (5700 Blvd Jean XXIII; ☺10am-3pm Mon-Wed & Sat, to 7pm Thu, to 4pm Fri) The only currency exchange, about 2.5km north of downtown.

Hôpital St-Joseph (☏819-697-3333; 731 Rue Ste-Julie)

Main Post Office (cnr Rue des Casernes & Rue des Ursulines)

Tourist Office (www.tourismetroisrivieres.com; 1457 Rue Notre Dame; ☺9am-8pm mid-Jun–Aug, 9am-5pm Mon-Fri, 10am-4pm Sat & Sun mid-May–mid-Jun & Sep–mid-Oct, 9am-5pm Mon-Fri mid-Oct–May)

ℹ Getting There & Away

Trois-Rivières lies about 150km northeast of Montréal and 130km southwest of Québec City and is easily accessible via Hwys 40 and 20 or Rtes 138 and 132.

The **bus station** (☏819-374-2944; 275 Rue St-Georges) is behind the Hôtel Delta. Orléans Express runs eight daily buses to Montréal ($29, 1½ to 2½ hours) and five daily to Québec City ($29, 1¾ hours).

SHAWINIGAN

There would be little reason to stop in Shawinigan were it not for the unique **Cité de l'Énergie** (City of Energy; www.citedelenergie.com; 1000 Ave Melville; adult/child $17/10, tours $12; ☺10am-6pm Jun-Aug, to 5pm Tue-Sun Sep). Built around a 1901 hydroelectric power station and the country's oldest aluminum smelter, the 'City of Energy' celebrates the region's industrial legacy with lots of different exhibits and experiences. Learn about turbines, electrochemistry, aluminum and pulp and papermaking in a multimedia show and exhibits. Race along a 'walk-through comic book' with scientists as they try to save the environment through switching to non-polluting hydrogen.

There are river and trolleybus cruises, a 115m-high observation tower and the nightly **Eclyps** (adult/child $49.50/20; ☺Jul & Aug) spectacle featuring musicians, dancers and acrobats. Throughout the summer, the National Gallery of Canada moves into the aluminum smelter with different world-class temporary exhibits. Most labeling is in English and French, but the tours are in French only. Last admissions are 2½ hours before closing.

Shawinigan is about 40km north of Trois-Rivières via Hwy 55. Orléans Express runs two buses daily from Trois-Rivières ($14, 50 minutes).

PARC NATIONAL DU CANADA DE LA MAURICIE

Moose foraging by an idyllic lake, the plaintive cry of a loon gliding across the water, bear cubs romping beneath a potpourri of birch, poplar, maple and other trees waiting to put on a spectacular show of color in the fall – these are scenes you might possibly stumble across while visiting **La Mauricie National Park** (☏819-538-3232, 888-855-6673; www.pc.gc.ca/mauricie; adult/child $7.80/3.90). What may well be Québec's best-run and best-organized park is also among its most frequented. The arresting beauty of the nature here, whether seen from a canoe or a walking trail, is everyone's eye candy, but particularly suits those who don't want to feel completely disconnected from 'civilization.'

The park covers 550 sq km, straddling northern evergreen forests and the more southerly hardwoods of the St Lawrence River Valley. The low, rounded Laurentian Mountains, which are among the world's oldest, are part of the Canadian Shield, which covers much of the province. Between these hills lie innumerable small lakes and valleys. The Canadian government created the park in 1970 to protect some of the forest that the paper industry was steadily chewing up and spitting out. At one point, two sawmills were operating in the park's current territory. But that's all in the past now.

The main entrance is at St-Jean-des-Piles (Hwy 55, exit 226), but there's another at St-Mathieu (Hwy 55, exit 217). Both are well indicated and double as **information centers** (☉7am-10pm late May-early Sep, 9am-4:30pm Sat-Thu, to 10pm Fri late May & early Sep-Oct). They are connected by the 63km-long Rte Promenade, which runs through the park. St-Mathieu is closed from late October until early May.

⚐ Activities

The numerous **walking trails**, which can take anywhere from half an hour to five days to complete, offer glimpses of the indigenous flora and fauna, brooks and waterfalls (the **Chutes Waber** in the park's western sector are particularly worth the hike), as well as panoramic views onto delicate valleys, lakes and streams.

The longest trail, **Le Sentier Laurentien**, stretches over 75km of rugged wilderness in the park's northern reaches. Backcountry campsites are spaced out every 7km to 10km. No more than 40 people are allowed on the trail at any time, making reservations essential (☏819-538-3232). There's a fee of $46 and you must arrange for your own transport to cover the 30km from the trail's end back to Rte Promenade. Topographic maps are for sale at the park.

The park is excellent for **canoeing**. Five canoe routes, ranging in length from 14km to 84km, can accommodate everyone from beginners to experts. Canoe/kayak rentals ($23.75/40 per day) are available at three sites, the most popular being **Lac Wapizagonke**, which has sandy beaches, steep rocky cliffs and waterfalls. One popular day trip has you canoeing from the Wapizagonke campground to the west end of the lake, followed by a 7.5km loop hike to the Chutes Waber and back by canoe.

The most popular winter activity is **cross-country skiing** (adult/child $9.80/4.90), with some 85km of groomed trails.

🛏 Sleeping & Eating

Camping at designated sites costs $25.50 without electricity and $29 with it; camping in the wild during canoe trips costs $15 without a campfire permit, or $23 with one.

You can also sleep in four- to 10-person dorms in one of two **outdoor lodges** (☏819-537-4555; www.pccamping.ca; per person $29-35). They are 3.5km from the nearest parking lot, so you must come in by foot, bike, canoe or ski.

There are no restaurants in the park, so the best thing is to stock up on supplies in Trois-Rivières or Shawinigan before heading north.

QUÉBEC CITY

POP 167,000

Québec, North America's only walled city north of Mexico City, is the kind of place that crops up in trivia questions. Over the centuries, the lanes and squares of the Old Town – a World Heritage site – have seen the continent's first parish church, first museum, first stone church, first Anglican cathedral, first girls' school, first business district and first French-speaking university. Most of these institutions remain in some form. The historical superlatives are inescapable: flick through the *Québec Chronicle-Telegraph* and you're reading

North America's first ice hotel may be a good example of wacky 'novelty architecture,' but every winter guests pay serious sums of money to sleep in its frosty chambers. Located half an hour's drive from central Québec City, the Hôtel de Glace first opened its cool, blue doors in 2001, following similar Scandinavian establishments.

Yes, almost everything is made of ice (hot tubs and fireplaces are two understandable exceptions). This architectural feat strikes you, like an ice mallet, as soon as you step into the entrance hall: tall, sculpted columns of ice support a ceiling where a crystal chandelier hangs, and carved sculptures, tables and chairs line the endless corridors. The reception desk, the pen you sign the guest book with, the sink in your room, even your bed are also made of ice. Visitors say the bed is not as frigid as it sounds, thanks to thick sleeping bags laid on lush deer pelts.

The 3000-sq-meter structure's public areas include exhibition rooms, a cinema, a chapel and the Absolut Ice Bar. The hotel melts in the spring and has to be rebuilt every winter, a job that takes five weeks, 12,000 tons of snow and 400 tons of ice.

The ice hotel offers several packages, starting at $600 per double, including a welcome vodka, dinner and breakfast. If you're not staying, simply take the tour for $15. The **Ice Hotel** (☏418-875-4522, 877-505-0423; www.icehotel-canada.com; 143 Rte Duchesnay, Ste Catherine de la Jacques Cartier; ☺Jan-Apr) is off Rte 376 to the west of Québec City, reached via Hwy 40, exit 295.

North America's oldest newspaper; if you have to visit L'Hôtel Dieu de Québec, console yourself with the thought that it's the continent's oldest hospital.

Once past Le Château Frontenac, the most photographed hotel in the world, visitors find themselves torn between the various neighborhoods' diverse charms. In Old Upper Town, the historical hub, many excellent museums and restaurants hide among the tacky fleur-de-lis T-shirt stores. Old Lower Town, at the base of the steep cliffs, is a labyrinth, where it's a pleasure to get lost among street performers and cozy inns before emerging on the north shore of the St Lawrence. Leaving the walled town near the star-shaped Citadelle, hip St Jean Baptiste is one of the less historical but still interesting areas, and the epicenter of a vibrant nightlife.

History

Only a Huron village, 'Stadacona,' the *kanata* (settlement) referred to in Canada's name, stood on the site of Québec City when French explorer Jacques Cartier landed in 1535, on his second voyage to the New World. He returned in 1541 to establish a permanent post, but the plan failed, setting back France's colonial ambitions for 50 years. Explorer Samuel de Champlain finally founded the city for the French in 1608, calling it Kebec, from the Algonquian word meaning 'the river narrows here.' It was the first North American city to be founded as a permanent settlement, rather than a trading post.

The English successfully attacked in 1629, but Québec was returned to the French under a treaty three years later and it became the center of New France. Repeated English attacks followed. In 1759, General Wolfe led the British to victory over Montcalm on the Plains of Abraham. One of North America's most famous battles, it virtually ended the long-running conflict between Britain and France. In 1763, the Treaty of Paris gave Canada to Britain. In 1775, the American revolutionaries tried to capture Québec but were promptly pushed back. In 1864, meetings were held here that led to the formation of Canada in 1867. Québec became the provincial capital.

In the 19th century, the city lost its status and importance to Montréal. When the Great Depression burst Montréal's bubble in 1929, Québec regained some stature as a government center. Some business-savvy locals launched the now-famous Winter Carnival in the 1950s to incite a tourism boom. Obviously, it's still working.

In 2001, the city was the site of the Summit of the Americas, which exploded into mass demonstrations against globalization. In 2008, the city marked the 400th anniversary of Québec's founding.

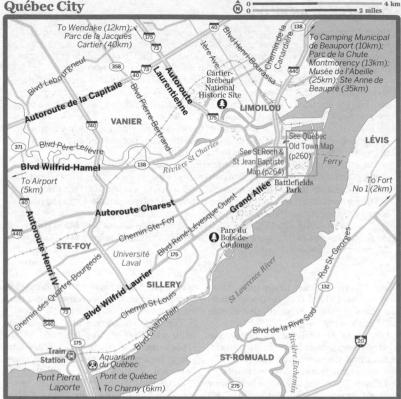

⊙ Sights

Part of the city sits atop the cliffs of Cap Diamant (Cape Diamond), and part lies below. Québec City is thus divided into Haute Ville (Upper Town) and Basse Ville (Lower Town), each with old and new sections. The Citadelle, a fort and landmark, stands proudly on the highest point of Cap Diamant. Together, the historic upper and lower areas form the appealing Vieux Québec (Old Town), which spreads over a 10-sq-km area within the stone walls.

The two main streets heading southwest from Old Upper Town are Blvd René-Lévesque and, to the south, Grande Allée, which eventually becomes Blvd Wilfrid Laurier. If you're driving to Old Upper Town, arrange parking through your hotel, or find a spot outside the walls to avoid steep prices.

OLD UPPER TOWN

Fortifications of Québec LANDMARK
The largely restored old wall is a national historic site. You can walk the 4.6km circuit on top of it all around the Old Upper Town, with much of the city's history within easy view. At the old powder magazine beside Porte St Louis, the **interpretive center** (Map p260; 100 Rue St-Louis; adult/child $4/2; ☺10am-6pm May-Aug, to 5pm Sep–mid-Oct) examines the city's defenses through displays, models and a short film. The center's enthusiastic guides run 90-minute **walking tours** (adult/child $10/5) from here and the Kiosk Frontenac (p272).

Beside Porte St Jean, another national historic site, the **Parc d'Artillerie** (2 Rue d'Auteuil; adult/child $4/2; ☺10am-6pm May-Aug, to 5pm Sep–mid-Oct) housed French military headquarters, a British garrison and a munitions factory. The interpretive center includes an early-19th-century scale model of Québec City and a children's history lesson. In the summer there are costumed guides and musket firing demonstrations.

The complex also includes a 19th-century officers' mess, a former powder magazine and **Les Dames de Soie** (2 Rue d'Auteuil; admission free; ☺11am-5pm Mon-Sat mid-Jan–Dec). This *économusée* (economuseum; a workshop-cum-museum) has a sizable doll population, including folk figures wearing costumes from different regions of Québec, a doll hospital and doll-making courses.

La Citadelle   LANDMARK

(Fort; Map p260; www.lacitadelle.qc.ca; Côte de la Citadelle; adult/child $10/5.50; ☺10am-4pm Apr, 9am-5pm May, Jun & Sep, 9am-6pm Jul-early Sep, 10am-3pm Oct) The dominating Citadelle is North America's largest fort, covering 2.3 sq km. Begun by the French in 1750 and completed by the British in 1850, it served as part of the defense system against an American invasion that never came.

Today the Citadelle is the base of Canada's Royal 22s (known in bastardized French as the Van Doos, from the French for 22, *vingt-deux*). Founded in WWI, the regiment earned three Victoria Crosses in that conflict and WWII. Admission to the site is by one-hour guided tour, which takes in the regimental museum, numerous historical sites and a cannon called Rachel. Tours depart regularly, apart from between late October and early April, when there's only one tour a day at 1:30pm. A separate tour of the **Governor General's Residence** (Map p260; tours free; ☺10am-4pm Sun May & Jun, 11am-4pm late Jun-early Sep, 10am-4pm Sat & Sun Sep & Oct) is also available.

The **changing of the guard** ceremony takes place at 10am each day in the summer months. The **beating of the retreat**, which features soldiers banging on their drums at shift's end, happens at 7pm on Friday, Saturday and Sunday during July and August. It's a small bit of Canadiana right in the heart of Québec.

LATIN QUARTER

Wedged into the northeast corner of the Old Upper Town, this area is classic Québec City, with dewy-eyed tourists drifting along narrow streets toward Le Château Frontenac.

Le Château Frontenac   HISTORICAL BUILDING

(Map p260; 1 Rue des Carrières) Said to be the world's most photographed hotel, Le Château Frontenac was built in 1893 by the Canadian Pacific Railway (CPR) as part of its chain of luxury hotels. During WWII, Prime Minister MacKenzie King, Winston Churchill and Franklin Roosevelt planned D-Day here. Leaving every hour on the hour, slightly underwhelming 50-minute hotel **tours** (adult/child $9.50/6; ☺10am-6pm May–mid-Oct, noon-5pm Sat & Sun mid-Oct–Apr) evoke polite society in the late 19th century. Facing the hotel along Rue Mont Carmel is **Jardins des Gouverneurs**, with a monument to both Wolfe and Montcalm.

Musée de l'Amérique Française   MUSEUM

(Museum of French America; Map p260; www. mcq.org; 2 Côte de la Fabrique; adult/child $8/2; ☺9:30am-5pm Jun-Sep, 10am-5pm Tue-Sun Oct-May) Next to the cathedral is the Museum of French America. Purported to be the country's oldest museum, it examines North America's Francophone diaspora, from the surrounding city to New England's '*petits* Canadas,' the Métis in western Canada and the American midwest. As well as artifacts relating to French settlement in the New World, there are interactive changing displays. The museum occupies part of the 17th-century seminary, built by Monseigneur de Laval under the order of Louis XIV.

Basilica Notre-Dame-de-Québec   CHURCH

(Map p260; 16 Rue de Buade; admission free; ☺8:30am-6pm) This cathedral towers above the site of a chapel erected by Samuel de Champlain in 1633. It became one of the continent's first cathedrals in 1674, following the appointment of the first bishop of Québec, Monseigneur de Laval, whose tomb is inside. Ever bigger replacements were constructed over the centuries, with the last

---

DON'T MISS

» **Le Château Frontenac** (p259) The world's most photographed hotel

» **Battlefields Park** (p263) Where England and France clashed

» **Place Royale** (p262) The cradle of Nouvelle France

» **Fortifications** (p258) A 4.6km of walkable walls

» **Lévis ferry** (p273) City and cliff views

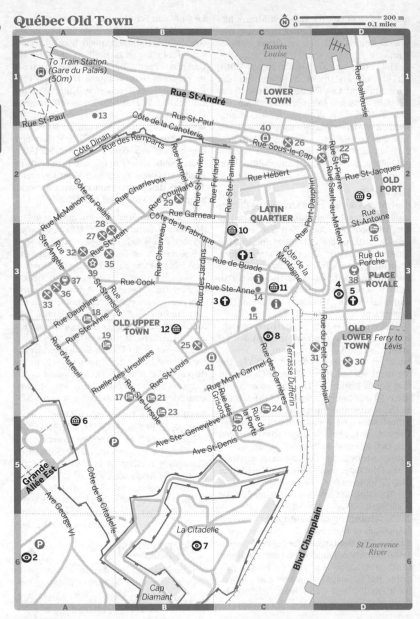

QUÉBEC QUÉBEC CITY

being completed in 1925. The grandiose interior recreates the spirit of the 17th century.

Ursuline Convent & Museum   MUSEUM
Founded in 1639, this convent is the oldest girls' school on the continent. The **museum** (Map p260; 12 Rue Donnacona; adult/child $7/free;

⊘10am-noon & 1-5pm Tue-Sat, 1-5pm Sun Apr-Sep, 1-5pm Tue-Sun Oct & Nov) recounts the generally forgotten story of the Ursuline sisters, the first order of nuns to come to North America. They were cloistered until 1965; there are some 50 nuns today, with an average age of 78. One room houses intricate gold and silver embroidery. At the same address, the lovely **chapel** (admission free; ◎10-11:30am & 1:30-4:30pm Tue-Fri, 1:30-4:30pm Sun Apr-Oct) dates to 1902 but retains some interiors from 1723.

Cathedral of the Holy Trinity CHURCH
(Map p260; 31 Rue des Jardins; admission free; ◎10am-5pm mid-May–mid-Oct, to 2pm Sun mid-Oct–mid-May) Built in 1804, the elegantly handsome Cathedral of the Holy Trinity, modeled on London's St Martin-in-the-Fields, was the first Anglican cathedral built outside the British Isles. The 47m-high bell tower competes with Basilica Notre-Dame for attention.

Musée du Fort MUSEUM
(Map p260; www.museedufort.com; 10 Rue Ste-Anne; adult/child $8/free; ◎English shows on the hour 10am-5pm Apr-Oct, 11am-4pm Feb-Mar & Nov-Dec) It's a little hokey and overpriced,

but this diorama gives an enjoyable, easy-to-grasp audio-visual survey of Québec City's battles and history. It features a 1200-sq-meter model of the city in 1750.

OLD LOWER TOWN
From Upper Town, you can reach this must-see area in several ways. Walk down Côte de la Canoterie from Rue des Ramparts to the Old Port, or edge down the charming and steep Rue Côte de la Montagne. About halfway down on the right, a shortcut, the Break-Neck Stairs (Escalier Casse-Cou) leads down to Rue du Petit-Champlain. You can also take the **funicular** ($2 each way) from Terrasse Dufferin.

Teeming **Rue du Petit-Champlain** is said to be, along with Rue Sous le-Cap, the narrowest street in North America, and is the center of the continent's oldest business district. Look out for the murals decorating the 17th- and 18th-century

QUÉBEC SIGHTS

CANINE OF THE CASTLE

Newcomers to Le Château Frontenac may be surprised to see a soppy dog bounding across the reception's thick carpets. Officially titled the canine ambassador, but known as Santol by his many friends and fans, the lucky mutt came to the Château in 2007 to promote the Mira guide dog foundation. He has his own employee name tag, business cards and email address. The hotel offers 'It's a Dog's Life' packages, from which it donates $25 to Mira. Guests can take Santol for walks. One admirer commented, 'He humanizes the hotel.' It takes a dog.

buildings, which, along with numerous plaques, statues and street performers, give this quarter its distinct, history-meets-holiday feel.

Place Royale, Old Lower Town's central, principal square, has had an eventful 402 years. When Samuel de Champlain founded Québec City, he settled this bit of shoreline first. In 1690 cannons placed here held off the attacks of the English naval commander Phips and his men. Today the name 'Place Royale' generally refers to the district.

Built around the old harbor, north of Place Royale, the **Vieux Port** (Old Port) is being redeveloped as a multipurpose waterfront area.

Musée de la Civilisation   MUSEUM
(Museum of Civilization; Map p260; www.mcq.org; 85 Rue Dalhousie; adult/child $12/4, free Tue Nov-May & 10am-noon Sat Jan & Feb; ◎10am-6.30pm late Jun-Aug, to 5pm Tue-Sun Sep-late Jun) This museum offers a dozen exhibitions in its airy halls, including permanent shows on the culture of Québec's 11 Aboriginal people, and tells the province's story from the French settlers to today's distinct society. Quirky displays, videos and interactive features bring the weighty subjects to life. The striking building incorporates some pre-existing structures; it shares an early-18th-century wall with Auberge Saint Antoine.

Église Notre-Dame-des-Victoires   CHURCH
(Our Lady of Victories Church; Map p260; 32 Rue Sous le Fort; admission free; ◎9:30am-5pm May–mid-Oct, 10am-4pm mid-Oct–May) Our Lady of Victories Church is the oldest stone church in North America, built in 1688 and devastated by cannon fire in 1759. It stands on the spot where de Champlain set up his 'Habitation,' a small stockade. Inside are copies of works by Rubens and Van Dyck. Hanging from the ceiling is a ship-shaped good-luck charm: a replica of the *Brézé*, in which the Carignan-

Salières regiment sailed to New France in 1664 to fight the Iroquois. The gold hearts above the altar date to 1855, when Mother Marcelle Mallet hung a heart there after taking a vow.

Centre d'Interprétation de Place-Royale   MUSEUM
(Map p260; 27 Rue Notre-Dame; adult/child $7/2; ◎9:30am-5pm late Jun-Aug, 10am-5pm Tue-Sun Sep-late Jun) This interpretive center touts the area as the cradle of French history in North America with a series of good participatory displays. While here, pick up a brochure on Place Royale's 27 vaulted cellars (ancient stone basements), five of which can be visited for free, including the one right here, complete with costumed barrel-maker.

OUTSIDE THE WALLS
Most visitors venture through Porte St Louis to take a peek at Québec City's most significant attraction outside the walls: Battlefields Park, site of the famous Plains of Abraham. Unfortunately, most then scuttle back to the safety of that fairy-tale land inside the walls. Some of the sights here are certainly more interesting than taking yet another snap of the Château – notably Hôtel du Parlement and Obsérvatoire de la Capitale. The St Jean Baptiste and St Roch areas, which offer a taste of everyday Québec, are a depressurization chamber after the onslaught of historical tourism in the Old Town.

St Jean Baptiste, the new part of Upper Town, is situated immediately west of the old, walled section, and is easily reached from Porte St Jean and Porte St Louis along Rue St-Jean and Grande Allée Est respectively. Battlefields Park runs south of Grande Allée, overlooking the St Lawrence. Northwest of St Jean Baptiste, and down a steep hill, is St Roch (Lower Town). All of these areas can be explored on foot or by bike, though remember that you will have to come back up the hill from St Roch.

Hôtel du Parlement
NOTABLE BUILDING

(Parliament Building; Map p264; cnr Ave Honoré Mercier & Grande Allée Est; admission free; ⊙9am-4:30pm late Jun-Sep, 9am-4:30pm Mon-Fri Sep-late Jun) Just across from Porte St Louis is the Parliament Building. The Second Empire structure, dating from 1886, houses the Provincial Legislature, known as the Assemblée Nationale. Its facade is decorated with 22 bronze statues of significant historical Québécois figures, made by much-loved Québécois sculptor Louis-Philippe Hébert. Admission (at door three) is by half-hour tour, available in French, English and Spanish.

Obsérvatoire de la Capitale
NOTABLE BUILDING

(Capital Observatory; Map p264; 1037 Rue de la Chevrotière; adult/child $5/2; ⊙10am-5pm) The Capital Observatory offers great views from 221m up on the 31st floor over St Jean Baptiste's red and green roofs and across the city to the Laurentians. Bone up on local history by reading the information panels.

Battlefields Park
HISTORIC PARK

(Map p258) With its hills, gardens and monuments, this huge park looks like any urban North American park, but where yoga groups stretch and joggers sweat, there was once a bloody battleground that determined the course of Canadian history. The part closest to the cliff is known as the **Plains of Abraham** – it was here in 1759 that the British finally defeated the French. The British general, Wolfe, died on the battlefield; Montcalm of France died the following morning, while his officers fled the city for Montréal.

Within the park are diverse sites. The reception center at the **Discovery Pavilion** (Map p260; 835 Ave Wilfrid-Laurier; admission free; ⊙8:30am-5:30pm late Jun-early Sep, 8:30am-5pm Mon-Fri, from 9am Sat, from 10am Sun early Sep-late Jun) is a good place to start. The staff offer park bus tours and multiple-attraction packages.

The pavilion contains a tourist office and the **Canada Odyssey** (Map p260; adult/child $14/4; ⊙10am-5pm), a 45-minute multimedia spectacle focusing on local life before and after the great battle. The odyssey concludes with an exhibition on the lot of the soldiers who fought in the battle and on the park itself, used in the 18th and 19th centuries for executions, pistol duels and prostitution. Admission includes a bus tour and entry to Martello Tower 1.

Visit the sprawling **Musée National des Beaux-Arts du Québec** (www.mnba.qc.ca; adult/child $15/4; ⊙10am-6pm Jun-Aug, to 5pm Tue-Sun Sep-May, to 9pm Wed year-round) for an artistic tour of Québec City's history. It houses the province's most important collections of Québécois art and Inuit sculptures, as well as international work. One gallery narrates the clash between academia and modernism in Québec's salons between 1860 and 1945; another looks at artistic responses to the British government's Durham Report (1839), which dismissed French Canadians as having 'no history and no culture.' The holdings include work by Riopelle, Borduas, Dallaire, Leduc and Québec City's greatest modernist, Peltan.

Nearby is **Martello Tower 1** (adult/child $14/4; ⊙10am-5pm late Jun-early Sep), one of four circular defense structures built by the British in the early 19th century and never used. Admission includes a bus tour and entry to the Canada Odyssey. **Martello Tower 2** (cnr Ave Taché & Ave Wilfrid-Laurier; dinner & show $39; ⊙Feb, Jul, Aug & Oct) presents fun, period whodunit dinner/theater evenings. They're mostly in French, but English texts are available.

St Jean Baptiste
NEIGHBORHOOD

Strolling along **Rue St-Jean** (Map p264) is a great way to feel the pulse of this bohemian area. The first thing that strikes you, once you've recovered from climbing Rue Ave Honoré Mercier, is the area's down-to-earth ambience. Good restaurants, hip cafes and bars and interesting shops, some catering to a gay clientele, line the thoroughfare as far as Rue Racine.

Take any side street and walk downhill (northwest) to the narrow residential streets such as Rue d'Aiguillon, Rue Richelieu and Rue St-Olivier. These miniature, scrunched-together houses, some with very nice entrances, are typical of Québec City's residential landscape. The fanciful, protruding windows are known as *oriels*.

To the southwest of Rue St-Jean, the colorful strip of storefronts along **Ave Cartier** (off map p264) has exploded during recent years with hip eateries, cafes and boutiques. It's most buzzing on hot

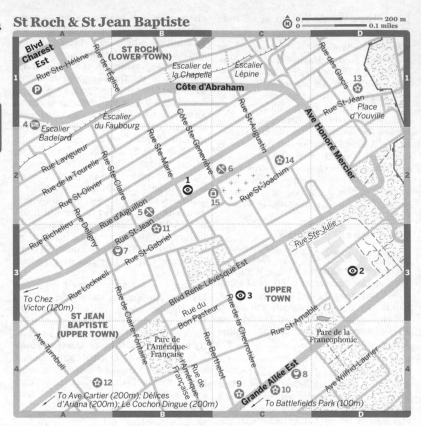

days when the dozen or so patios open up for business. The epicenter of this little restaurant district is located at the intersection of Ave Cartier and Blvd René-Lévesque Ouest.

St Roch   NEIGHBORHOOD
Walking down Côte Ste-Geneviève in St Jean Baptiste, you will come to a steep staircase, the Escalier de la Chapelle, which takes you down to St Roch. If you're cycling, Côte d'Abraham can also be accessed from Côte Ste-Geneviève.

Traditionally a working-class district for factory and naval workers, St Roch has been slowly gentrifying. On the main artery, **Rue St-Joseph**, spiffy new restaurants and bars have sprung up among the junk shops and secondhand clothes stores. Private art galleries are also found here and on **Rue St-Vallier Est**.

Cartier-Brébeuf National
Historic Site   MUSEUM
(Map p258; 175 Rue de l'Espinay; adult/child $4/2; ☺10am-5pm early May-Aug, 11am-4pm Wed-Sun Sep) On the St Charles River, northwest of the walled section of the city, this national historic site marks the spot where Iroquoian people helped Cartier and his men through the winter of 1535. The center features a full-scale replica of Cartier's ship, a reproduction of an aboriginal longhouse, and exhibits about Jesuitism, established in Canada in 1625 by Jean de Brébeuf.

Parc du Bois-de-Coulonge   PARK
(Map p258; 1215 Grande Allée Ouest; admission free) Not far west of the Plains of Abraham lie the colorful gardens of this park, a paean to the plant world and a welcome respite from downtown. Adorned with extensive horticultural displays, the woodland was the residence of the Canadian and

St Roch & St Jean Baptiste

Québécois political elite from 1854 to 1966. The main house burnt down.

🏃 Activities

Terrasse Dufferin   PARK
Outside Le Château Frontenac along the riverfront, 425m-long Terrasse Dufferin is marvelous for a stroll, with dramatic views over the river, perched as it is 60m high on a cliff. It's peppered with quality street performers vying for attention.

Cyclo Services   CYCLING
(Map p260; 289 Rue St-Paul; bicycles per hr/24hr $14/35; ☺8:30am-8pm) This shop rents bikes and organizes excellent cycle tours of the city and outskirts, available in English. It has good cycling maps covering the vicinity.

Aventure X   CLIMBING
(Map p258; 2350 Ave du Colisée; ☺10am-8pm Mon-Fri, to 6pm Sat & Sun Jun-Aug, 10am-10pm Mon-Sat, to 6pm Sun Sep-May) Offers indoor climbing and excursions to the canyons and crevices around Québec City. During the evenings and weekends, 30-minute $20 'try out' sessions are available.

☞ Tours

Guided walking tours can pack a lot of specialized knowledge into a short time. For example, on one tour a cannonball wedged into a tree right beside the sidewalk on Rue St-Louis is pointed out as strollers pass blindly by.

Les Services Historiques
Six Associes   WALKING
(☎418-692-3033; 2hr walking tours $16) Costumed guides lead excellent walking circuits such as the ever-popular 'Lust and Drunkenness,' which creaks open the rusty door on the history of alcohol and prostitution in the city. Other tours, done in English and French, focus on epidemics and crimes. A cheery bunch, they are. Reservations should be made by phone.

Boat Tours   BOAT
Operators Croisières AMV and Groupe Dufour Croisières cruise downriver to Montmorency Falls and Île d'Orléans from near Place Royale. A little further north, next to the Bassin Louise gate, Croisières Coudres operates tours to Grosse Île (p289). For city views, you can't beat the cheap ferry to Lévis.

Calèches   HORSE-DRAWN CARRIAGE
From Place d'Armes (Map p260) the horses give nice rides but are expensive at $80 for up to four people for 40 minutes. The drivers provide some commentary.

Les Tours Voir Québec   WALKING
(Map p260; www.toursvoirquebec.com; 12 Rue Ste-Anne; adult/child $23/11) These two-hour tours explore the significant areas across the Old Town, as well as less obvious aspects, such as religious communities and interior courtyards.

TOP FIVE FREEBIES

» **Les Dames de Soie** (p259) Visit the doll hospital

» **Musée de la Civilisation** (p262) Free Tuesday and Saturday morning for part of the year

» **Fou-Bar** (p271) Go for Tuesday-night jazz

» **Marché du Vieux-Port** (p271) Sample local farm fare

» **Choco-Musée Érico** (p266) Anyone for chocolate?

QUÉBEC CITY FOR CHILDREN

Certainly, this town is about history, architecture and food. While much of the old city, including accommodations and restaurants, is geared toward adults, this is not exclusively the case. Several restaurants listed in the Eating section are suitable for kids. There are good things to do with younger ones in the central core, while around the edges are sites fully designed for kids' enjoyment.

In the historic area, walking the **fortifications** (p258) suits all ages. La Citadelle (p259) ceremonies, with uniformed soldiers, are winners too. Terrasse Dufferin, with its river views and buskers, always delights children. Place d'Armes and Place Royale are also good for street performers. When the little ones have tired of climbing over cannons, there's always the cheap **ferry to Lévis** (p273), **boat cruises** (p265) or a horse-drawn **calèche** (p265; two-wheeled carriage).

Choco-Musée Érico (Map p264; www.chocomusee.com; 634 Rue St-Jean; admission free; ⊙10am-5:30pm Mon-Wed & Sat, to 9pm Thu & Fri, 11am-5:30pm Sun, extended hours warm summer evenings) is a museum and store devoted to all things chocolaty. Get a history lesson, see the kitchen, sample a chunk and try to resist the shop.

Aquarium du Québec (Map p258; 1675 Ave des Hôtels; adult/child $17/8.50; ⊙10am-5pm Jun-Aug, to 4pm Sep-May) has walrus, seals, polar bear and thousands of smaller species.

Children enjoy the 'bee safari' and adults enjoy the mead at **Musée de l'Abeille** (off Map p258; 8862 Blvd St Anne; admission free; ⊙9am-5pm Apr-late Jun & Sep, to 6pm late Jun-early Sep, 11am-5pm Oct-Mar), a beekeeping *économusée* (workshop-cum-museum) northeast of the city on Hwy 138.

Old Québec Tours BUS
(Map p260; ☎418-664-0460; www.toursvieux quebec.com; 12 Rue Ste-Anne; 2hr tours $33) Also offers a 4½-hour trip to Île d'Orléans, Montmorency Falls and Ste Anne de Beaupré ($43), and other options. They'll pick you up at your hotel.

Les Promenades Fantômes WALKING
(Map p260; www.promenadesfantomes.com; 12 Rue Ste-Anne; adult/child $18/15.50; ⊙ 8pm May-Oct) Take a nocturnal trip by the light of a swinging lantern and learn about bygone Québec City's shadowy side.

✵ Festivals & Events

Carnaval WINTER
(www.carnaval.qc.ca; ⊙Feb) This famous annual event is unique to Québec City. It bills itself as the biggest winter carnival in the world, with parades, ice sculptures, a snow slide, boat races, dances, music and lots of drinking. Activities take place all over town and the iconic slide is on the Terrasse Dufferin behind the Château. If you want to go, organize the trip early, as accommodations fill up fast, and don't forget to bring lots of warm clothes.

Fête Nationale de la St Jean Baptiste
CULTURAL
(Festival of John the Baptist; www.snqc.qc.ca, in French; ⊙23 Jun) On this night, Québec City parties hard. Originally a holiday honoring John the Baptist, this day has evolved into a quasi-political event celebrating Québec's distinct culture and nationalistic leanings. Major festivities on the Plains of Abraham start around 8pm.

Festival d'Été SUMMER
(Summer Festival; www.infofestival.com; ⊙early Jul) This festival features some 500 free shows, concerts, drama and dance performances, and 900,000 spectators wandering the streets. Most squares and parks in the Old Town host daily events; a good area to check out is Place d'Youville.

Les Grands Feux Loto-Québec
FIREWORKS
(International Fireworks Competition; www.quebec fireworks.com; ⊙late Jul-early Aug) Major fireworks displays at Montmorency Falls.

Fête de Nouvelle France CULTURAL
(Back to Colonial Times; www.nouvellefrance. qc.ca; ⊙Aug) Periodic reenactments of the last days of the French regime are conducted at various locations.

🛏 Sleeping

There are many places to stay in Québec City, and generally the competition keeps prices at a reasonable level. The best options are the small, European-style hotels scattered around the Old Town. They offer character, convenience and a bit of romance. The larger downtown hotels tend to be expensive.

As you'd expect in such a popular city, the top choices are often full. Look for a room before 2pm or reserve ahead. Midsummer and the winter Carnaval are especially busy times. Most rooms have been upgraded to include private bathrooms, unless otherwise noted here. Prices drop markedly in the low-season.

OLD UPPER TOWN

Maison Historique James Thompson

B&B $$

(Map p260; ☑418-694-9042; www.bedandbreakfast quebec.com; 47 Rue Ste-Ursule; r $75-135) History buffs will get a real kick out of staying in the 18th-century former residence of James Thompson, a veteran of the Battle of the Plains of Abraham. The beautifully restored house comes complete with the original murder hole next to the front door. Rooms are spacious and brightly infused with host Guitta's cheerful artwork; and it's easy to while away an afternoon chatting with host Greg – a wealth of knowledge on all things Québec and historical.

HI Auberge Internationale de Québec

HOSTEL $

(Map p260; ☑418-694-0775; www.aubergeinter-nationaledequebec.com; 19 Rue Ste-Ursule; dm member $24-30, nonmember $28-34, r without/with bathroom $74/89; @ 🛜) It's dauntingly large but it's the best hostel in town, with friendly staff who organize all sorts of tours, pub crawls and film nights. In the basement, rock music blares as backpackers flock to the bar in the evening (or queue for the free buffet breakfast). Despite the school groups tearing along the institutional corridors, you can usually get a decent night's sleep.

La Marquise de Bassano

INN $$

(Map p260; ☑418-692-0316, 877-692-0316; www. marquisedebassano.com; 15 Rue des Grisons; r $99-175; P @) Rooms sporting canopy beds, claw-foot tubs or a rooftop deck are part of the allure of this serene Victorian house, run by young, gregarious owners.

The sweet scent of fresh-baked croissants for breakfast will have you up before the alarm clock.

Le Clos Saint Louis

INN $$$

(Map p260; ☑418-694-1311, 800-461-1311; www. clossaintlouis.com; 69 Rue St-Louis; r incl breakfast $175-250; 🛜) It's hard to tell which trait is more evident here: the obvious care that the owners devote or simply the natural 1844 Victorian charm. The 18 spacious, lavishly decorated rooms each have a whirlpool tub in a beautifully tiled bathroom. The suites are like Victorian apartments, apart from the TV in the mini drawing room.

Fairmont Le Château Frontenac

HOTEL $$$

(Map p260; ☑418-692-3861, 800-257-7544; www. fairmont.com/frontenac; 1 Rue des Carrières; r from $360; P 🛜) More than just a hotel, more than just a landmark, the 618-room Château is the enduring symbol of Québec City. Scenes of films such as *Catch Me If You Can*, starring Leonardo DiCaprio, and Alfred Hitchcock's *I Confess* have been shot here. Previous guests include Queen Elizabeth II, President Jacques Chirac, Charlie Chaplin and Grace Kelly. Unfortunately, following in their footsteps isn't cheap.

Hôtel Acadia

HOTEL $$$

(Map p260; ☑418-694-0280, 800-463-0280; www.hotelacadia.com; 43 Rue Ste-Ursule; r $99-219; P @ 🛜) This longtime visitor fave is carved out of three adjacent historic houses and has rooms in a range of sizes, features and prices, from small 'classic' quarters to luxury spreads with fireplaces. There's a peaceful garden overlooking the old Ursuline convent.

Chez Hubert

B&B $$

(Map p260; ☑418-692-0958; www.chezhubert. com; 66 Rue Ste-Ursule; s incl breakfast $80-85, d $85-100; P) This dependable choice is in a Victorian townhouse with chandeliers, stained-glass windows and oriental rugs. The three tasteful rooms, one with a view of the Château, come with a buffet breakfast and free parking.

Manoir sur le Cap

INN $$

(Map p260; ☑418-694-1987, 866-694-1987; www. manoir-sur-le-cap.com; 9 Ave Ste-Geneviève; r from $105; P) Some rooms in this house by the boardwalk overlook the Jardin des Gouverneurs, the Château or the river. They're modern, but many have attractive stone or brick walls; a few have king-sized beds.

OLD LOWER TOWN

TOP CHOICE **Auberge Saint Antoine**

BOUTIQUE HOTEL $$$

(Map p260; ☑418-692-2211; www.saint-antoine. com; 8 Rue St-Antoine; r $179-989; ✳@🛜) History and modernity are ecstatically married in this hotel, where understated details such as a clock projected onto a wall complement one of the city's most significant archaeological sites. A daily tour takes in the 700 artifacts on display, discovered when the heated underground car park was installed. In the original, 250-year-old part of the complex, the rooms and historical suites are stacked with antique furniture and personality. The views of the Château are so good, this might well be the better hotel. When you've finished feasting your eyes, wander into the restaurant, housed in a 19th-century warehouse overlooking the St Lawrence.

Le Germain-Dominion BOUTIQUE HOTEL $$$

(Map p260; ☑418-692-2224, 888-833-5253; www.germaindominion.com; 126 Rue St-Pierre; r $169-315; ✳@🛜) This winner by local luxury chain, Groupe Germain, tucked away in a cozy spot in the heart of the Lower Town, hits high notes with fresh, modern decor (renovated in 2010), a never-ending list of amenities, and flawless customer service.

OUTSIDE THE WALLS

Prices drop drastically and rooms grow in size when you decide to stay outside the walls, and for drivers, parking suddenly becomes a less complicated affair. All of the lodgings listed are within a 15-minute drive or walk from the Old Town.

ALT Québec HOTEL $$

(☑418-658-1224, 800-463-5253; quebec.althot els.ca; 1200 Ave Germain-des-Prés; r $129-169; P@🛜) For drivers who prioritize convenience and want to leave the sometimes overwhelmingly touristy walled city behind at the end of the day, this hotel located just off Blvd Laurier (7km from the Old Town) is a rare gem. Boutique hotel service, slick, modern decor and free parking are just a few of the pluses.

Auberge Le Vincent INN $$$

(Map p264; ☑418-523-5000; www.aubergele vincent.com; 295 Rue St-Vallier Est; r $149-279; P@🛜) Style-conscious budget travelers love the rain-water showers, exposed brick walls and windows (with quadruple glazing) overlooking the downtown St Roch district in the affordable rooms at this inn. Included in the rate is excellent advice from the outstanding staff, as well as a gourmet hot breakfast with Italian-style coffee. It's a short walk to the Old Town.

Auberge JA Moisan B&B $$

(Map p264; ☑418-529-9764; www.jamoisan. com; 699 Rue St-Jean; s $120-135, d $130-145; ✳) Tucked away above the oldest supermarket in North America, the unstuffy, old-fashioned rooms of this charming 18th-century home look out over the restaurants and bars of the funky St Jean Baptiste district. After a filling breakfast (with chocolates for dessert) cooked by hosts Clément and Nathalie, it's an easy walk to the Old Town.

Camping Municipal de Beauport

CAMPGROUND $

(off Map p258; ☑418-641-6112, 877-641-6113; www.campingbeauport.qc.ca; 95 Rue de la Sérénité; tent/RV sites $28/35; ☺Jun-early Sep) This excellent campground near Montmorency Falls is green, peaceful and just a 15-minute drive from the Old Town. To get there, take Hwy 40 toward Montmorency, get off at exit 321 and turn north.

✕ Eating

Restaurants are abundant and the quality is generally high in Québec City. Central places pack in the crowds by serving an odd mix of high and lowbrow cuisine. Many of these places are reasonable value and boast unbeatable locations, but the less obvious choices usually provide superior dining experiences. For the best bargains, get the table d'hôte, especially at lunch.

OLD UPPER TOWN

Le Patriarche FUSION $$$

(Map p260; www.lepatriarche.com; 17 Rue St-Stanislas; mains $26-50; ☺11:30am-2pm Thu-Fri, 5:30-10pm daily) The nouvelle cuisine echoes the contemporary art hanging on the 180-year-old stone walls in this top-class restaurant. On the menu stocked almost entirely with local products, starters include foie gras and pan-fried frogs legs; mains range from New Brunswick salmon fillet to Appalachian deer and Québec lamb.

Paillard BAKERY $

(Map p260; www.paillard.ca; 1097 Rue St-Jean; breakfast $7; ☺7am-7pm) This light, modern New York–style cafe with long wooden tables is perfect for a quick breakfast or coffee break.

Aux Anciens Canadiens   QUÉBÉCOIS **$$$**
(Map p260; www.auxancienscanadiens.qc.ca; 34 Rue St-Louis; meals $20-89; ☺noon-9pm) Occupying the historic Jacquet house, built in 1676, this 40-year-old restaurant's name comes from the novel by Philippe Aubert de Gaspé, who lived here during his stint as sheriff of Québec. The menu preserves classic Québécois specialties and country dishes, such as 'trapper's treat' (Lac St Jean meat pie with pheasant and buffalo) and 'grandfather's treat' (boar and pig's knuckles ragout with meatballs). It's well worth negotiating the tourists for the $20 lunchtime special, which includes a beer or wine.

Chez Temporel   CAFE **$**
(Map p260; 25 Rue Couillard; meals $12.50; ☺7am-1:30am Sun-Thu, to 2:30am Fri & Sat) For a sandwich or leisurely breakfast of a perfect *café au lait* and fresh croissants, you can't beat this Parisian-style hideaway. Later in the day, it's the province of solitary book readers and wistful music.

Le Petit Coin Latin   CAFE **$$**
(Map p260; 8 Rue Ste-Ursule; meals $10-25; ☺7:30am-10:30pm) A great spot for a breakfast of fruit, croissants or eggs and ham, scoffed either inside listening to the Gallic music or outside on the terrace. Sandwiches, soups and heftier dishes such as caribou are also available.

Un Thé au Sahara   AFRICAN **$$**
(Map p260; 7 Rue Ste-Ursule; meals $14-22; ☺11:30am-2:30pm Thu-Fri, 5pm-late daily) Bring your own wine or hit the mint tea in this basic but popular Moroccan restaurant. All the classics are available: tabbouleh, hummus, couscous, brochettes and *tagine kéfta* (veal croquettes in tomato sauce).

Casse Crêpe Breton   CAFE **$**
(Map p264; cassecrepebreton.com; 1136 Rue St-Jean; crepes $3.50-7.75, meals $10; ☺7am-9:30pm; ☞) Small and unassuming, this find dishes up hot, fresh crepes of every kind. Some diners like to sit at the counter and watch the chef at work.

Chez Ashton   FAST FOOD **$**
(Map p260; 54 Côte du Palais; meals $7; ☺11am-2am Sun-Wed, to 4am Thu, to 4.30am Fri & Sat) This snack bar is one of the establishments that claims to have invented poutine (fries smothered in cheese curds and gravy; see the boxed text, p270). It's popular throughout the day and night for all varieties of poutine, burgers and subs.

OLD LOWER TOWN

Rue St-Paul and Rue du Petit-Champlain are lined with restaurants and their outdoor tables.

Le Lapin Sauté   FRENCH **$$**
(Map p260; www.lapinsaute.com; 52 Rue du Petit-Champlain; mains $15-23; ☺11am-10pm Sun-Thu, 9am-11pm Fri & Sat) If you only splash out once in Québec City, do it at this cozy restaurant specializing in country cooking. Naturally, *le lapin* (rabbit) lasagna and sausages are available, but so are duck, salmon and chicken, and there's maple syrup crème brûlée for dessert. In good weather you can sit on the flowery patio, overlooking tiny Félix Leclerc park.

Le Cochon Dingue   FRENCH **$$**
(Map p260; www.cochondingue.com; 46 Blvd Champlain; meals $10-20; ☺8am-11pm) Since 1979, this Gallic gem among touristy eateries has delighted diners with its attentive service and outside seating. A French feel pervades its checkered tablecloths and dishes, which range from *croque monsieur* to mussels and steak frites. There's a second **location** (Map p264; 46 Blvd René-Lévesque Ouest) with the same menu, in the Ave Cartier district in the southwest corner of the city.

Buffet de l'Antiquaire   QUÉBÉCOIS **$**
(Map p260; 95 Rue St-Paul; meals $8; ☺6am-10:30pm) One of the most 'real' spots in town, with local characters enjoying the soundtrack of waiters wheezing orders above the clatter of pots and pans. The Québec home-cooking on offer includes filling meat and fish dishes, and there's Boréale on tap.

L'Échaudé   FRENCH **$$$**
(Map p260; ☎418-692-1299; 73 Rue Sault-au-Matelot; mains $18-38; ☺11:30am-2:30pm & 6pm-late Mon-Fri, 6pm-late Sat, 10am-2:30pm & 6pm-late Sun) This 25-year-old bistro is a favorite with locals, although they're increasingly being outnumbered by tourists lured by its hype. There is a pleasing atmosphere to the waiters bustling between full tables, and meat lovers will enjoy dishes such as duck confit, stuffed guinea fowl and the popular steak tartare ($22).

OUTSIDE THE WALLS

Beyond the walls, there are three main eating districts. Rue St-Jean, away from the tourist haunts, houses inexpensive eateries, many with a BYOW policy. Bistros line

POUTINE, BIEN SÛR

Like all fast food, Québec's beloved poutine is perfect if you have a *gueule de bois* (hangover) after a night on the Boréale Blonde. In the calorie-packing culinary Frankenstein, the province's exemplary fries (fresh-cut, never frozen and served limp and greasy) are sprinkled with cheese curds and smothered in gravy. The dish was devised in the early 1980s and spread across Québec like a grease fire.

Poutine is a staple of the oft-seen roadside diners, *cantines* or *casse croutes*, where you can sample embellished versions such as Italienne, with spaghetti. The eateries generally have their own top-secret recipe; for example, Cantine d'Amour in Matane has its Poutine d'Amour. As a general guide, these house specialties include mincemeat and green peppers. In the main cities, La Paryse, Montréal (p234) and Chez Ashton, Québec City (p269) are good places to take the poutine challenge.

Ave Cartier between Grande Allée Ouest and Blvd René-Lévesque Ouest, attracting a local clientele. Lastly, in the artsy St Roch district a smattering of bistros and cafes featuring trendy nouveau cuisine have appeared in recent years.

Café du Clocher Penché FRENCH $$
(off Map p264; 203 Rue St-Joseph Est; mains $16-26; ⊙11:30am-2pm & 5-10pm Tue-Fri, 9am-2pm & 5-10pm Sat, 9am-2pm Sun) A light and airy bistro with a simple, understated design that mimics their unpretentious menu, this happening spot in the St Roch district is *the* place to pair modern French cuisine with a glass of wine, chosen from a vast array of high-quality European vintages.

Délices d'Ariana AFGHAN $$
(off Map p264; 102 Blvd René-Lévesque Ouest; mains $7-14; ⊙11:30am-2pm Mon-Fri, 5-10pm daily; 🖉) Frequented almost exclusively by locals in the know, this turreted restaurant is one of the best-kept secrets in Québec City. The exotic menu includes sumac-scented kebabs and traditional central Asian curries such as *borani bodenjan* (stewed eggplant in tomato sauce with homemade yogurt) and *qorma* (an onion-based dish with meat or vegetables), which accompany the *qabli pulao* (cardamom-flavored rice with fruit and nuts) perfectly.

Chez Victor BURGERS $$
(off Map p264; 145 Rue St-Jean; mains $10-15; ⊙8am-10pm; 🖉) Burgers are done to perfection – stacked high with all the fixings and paired with a mountain of crispy fresh-cut fries – at this bustling resto. Choose from over 20 burger masterpieces that use black Angus beef, deer, duck, pork, salmon, chicken, tofu and vegetarian patties as a canvas.

Le Billig CAFE $$
(Map p264; 526 Rue St-Jean; crepes $3.50-16; ⊙11am-3pm & 5-9pm Tue-Sat, 11am-3pm Sun) A Breton bistro specializing in crepes, featuring winning combinations like duck confit and onion marmalade, and buckwheat inventions such as the Roscoff, which crams in ham, asparagus, Swiss cheese, apple and béchamel sauce.

Le Hobbit PUB $$
(Map p264; 700 Rue St-Jean; mains from $13; ⊙8am-10pm) This popular St Jean Baptiste meeting point has outside seating, a casual atmosphere and good-value lunch and dinner specials. The delicious steak *frites* ($16) is among the best deals in town. Various fresh pasta dishes and salads round out the menu.

Drinking

L'Oncle Antoine PUB
(Map p260; 29 Rue St-Pierre; ⊙11am-late) In the Old Port area, in the stone cellar of one of the city's oldest surviving houses (dating from 1754), this tavern pours out several drafts *(en fût)* and Québec microbrews (the coffee-tinted stout is particularly reviving); taste four for $7.

Bar Ste Angèle BAR
(Map p260; 26 Rue Ste-Angèle; ⊙8pm-late) A low-lit, intimate hideaway, where the genial staff will help you navigate the list of cocktail pitchers and local and European bottled beers.

L'Inox PUB
(Map p264; 655 Grande Allée Est; ⊙noon-3am) The city's only brewpub is located along the tourist-heavy Grande Allée strip of restaurants and is a must-visit for beer connoisseurs.

Le Sacrilège
BAR

(Map p264; 447 Rue St-Jean) The pumping heart of St Jean Baptiste, this indie-soundtracked hangout has a conservatory and a sculpture-filled walled garden.

☆ Entertainment

Though Québec City is small, it's active after dark. The entertainment paper **Voir** (www.voir.ca), published each Thursday, has listings in French. Rue St-Jean, and to a lesser degree Grande Allée and Ave Cartier, are the happening streets. Rue St-Jean attracts a young, bohemian crowd; Grande Allée Est is the stamping ground of the posy '*m'a-tu vu?*' (did you see me?) set.

Nightclubs

Chez Maurice
NIGHTCLUB

(Map p264; 575 Grande Allée Est; ⊙9pm-3am) This Babylonian nightspot in a Victorian mansion boasts a nightclub, cigar lounge, 'ultralounge' bar and the VooDoo Grill restaurant. The disco, open Wednesday to Sunday, offers Latino, happy house and live pop music nights.

Chez Dagobert
NIGHTCLUB

(Map p264; 600 Grande Allée Est; ⊙9.30pm-3am Wed-Sun) With a huge mirror ball spinning above its terrace overlooking Grande Allée Est, Dagobert competes with Chez Maurice opposite for the attention of local clubbers. Inside, multifloors play everything from rock to dance.

Gay & Lesbian Venues

Le Drague
NIGHTCLUB

(Map p264; 815 Rue St Augustin; ⊙noon-late, shows 10:30pm Thu, 11pm Fri, 9:30pm & 11pm Sun) The city's gay and lesbian scene is small, but this 10-years-young institution is its star player: a multifaceted bar with various 'zones' with different vibes. The drag shows on Friday and Sunday nights are among the city's most raucous and hilarious nights out, whatever your sexual inclination. From Thursday to Sunday nights, there are two packed floors of dancing ($4 entry).

Theater

Grand Théâtre de Québec
THEATER

(Map p264; ☑418-643-8131; 269 Blvd René-Lévesque Est) The city's main performing arts center presents classical concerts, dance and theater, all usually of top quality. The Opéra de Québec often performs here.

Le Capitole
THEATER

(Map p264; www.lecapitole.com; 972 Rue St-Jean) A smaller spot to catch performing arts, this theater-restaurant offers cabaret and musical revues.

Live Music

Fou-Bar
LIVE MUSIC

(Map p264; 525 Rue St-Jean; ⊙3pm-3am) Laid-back and with an eclectic mix of bands, this is one of the town's classics for live music. The jazz on Tuesdays from 9pm is a winner.

Les Yeux Bleus
LIVE MUSIC

(Map p260; 1117 Rue St-Jean) The city's best *boîte a chanson* (live, informal singer/songwriter club), this is the place to catch newcomers, the occasional big-name francophone concert and Québécois classics.

🔒 Shopping

Claustrophobically narrow, and thick with gawkers, Rue du Trésor, by the Château, is nonetheless worth a wander for the easel-touting artists and their finished products.

A smattering of medieval shops can be found along Rue St Jean, stocking bodices for the maiden, capes for the knight, axe pens, gargoyle candlesticks and other essential archaic paraphernalia.

In the Old Lower Town, Rue St-Paul has a dozen shops piled with antiques, curiosities and old Québécois relics, and incongruous **Le Roquet** (Map p260; 141 Rue St-Paul), selling funky T-shirts made by local company Vêtements 90 Degrés.

Marché du Vieux-Port
FOOD & DRINK

(Map p260; 160 Quai St André) Further along, at the waterfront, is this farmers market, where you can stock up on fish, *fromage* (cheese), flowers, foie gras, iced cider and garden gnomes. It's open until 5pm daily, but peaks on summer Saturday mornings, when local farmers flock here and stalls are set up outside the building.

JA Moisan Épicier
FOOD & DRINK

(Map p264; www.jamoisan.com; 699 Rue St-Jean) Established in 1871, this is considered the oldest grocery store in North America. An old-fashioned atmosphere lingers between the herbal teas, scented toiletries, jars of coffee beans and other goodies.

Musée d'Art Inuit
ART

(Map p260; 35 Rue St-Louis) A stunning gallery selling soapstone, serpentine and basalt

Inuit sculptures from northern Québec. Prices range from $45 to several thousand dollars.

Information

Medical Services

Health Info (☑418-648-2626; ☺24hr) For consultations with nurses.

L'Hôtel Dieu de Québec (☑418-525-4444; 11 Côte du Palais; ☺24hr) A centrally located hospital with emergency services.

Tourist Information

Centre Infotouriste (Map p260; www.bonjour quebec.com; 12 Rue Ste-Anne; ☺8:30am-7:30pm Jun-Aug, 9am-5pm Sep-May) Busy provincial tourist office; also handles city inquiries. Tour operators have counters here.

Kiosk Frontenac (Map p260) A tourist information booth on Terrasse Dufferin facing Le Château Frontenac; makes reservations for all city activities and is the starting point for some tours.

Québec City Tourist Information (www. quebecregion.com; 835 Ave Wilfrid-Laurier; ☺8:30am-7:30pm late Jun-Aug, to 6:30pm Sep–mid-Oct, 9am-5pm Mon-Sat, 10am-4pm Sun mid-Oct–late Jun) This official city information office in the Discovery Pavilion is less crowded than Centre Infotouriste; it also covers the surrounding region and has a *bureau de change*.

ⓘ Getting There & Away

Air

Jean Lesage airport (www.aeroportdequebec. com) is west of town off Hwy 40, near where north–south Hwy 73 intersects it. Air Canada flies daily to Montréal, Toronto, Gaspé, the Îles de la Madeleine and Sept Îles, and to Ottawa on weekdays. There are also United, Continental and Delta flights to US destinations including Chicago, Newark, Detroit, Cleveland and Washington.

Boat

The **ferry** (☑877-787-7483) between Québec City and Lévis runs frequently between 6am and 2am. The one-way fare is $3/2 per adult/child; including the driver, cars cost $6.75 and bikes $3. The 10-minute crossing provides great views of the river, Le Château Frontenac and the Québec City skyline. The terminal is at Place Royale.

Bus

The **bus station** (Map p260; ☑418-525-3000; 320 Rue Abraham-Martin) is beside the main train station, Gare du Palais. Buses run to Montréal ($54, three to four hours) nearly every hour through the day and evening. Intercar serves Charlevoix, Saguenay and the north

shore, stopping in major towns as far as Havre St Pierre. Orléans Express buses cover the south shore and do a circuit of the Gaspé Peninsula; for Edmundston, New Brunswick, take one of the regular services to Rivière du Loup ($38, three hours) and pick up an Acadian bus there. USA-bound coaches go via Montréal (see p881).

Car & Motorcycle

Budget (☑418-692-3660; 29 Côte du Palais), **Hertz** (☑418-694-1224; 44 Côte du Palais), **Avis** (☑418-523-1075; 1100 Blvd René-Lévesque) and **Enterprise** (☑418-523-6661; 690 Blvd René-Lévesque) have central offices.

It may be worth making the trek to **Budget** (☑418-872-9885; 7115 Blvd Wilfrid Hamel) or **Discount** (☑418-522-3598, 800-263-2355; 240 3e Rue) in Ste-Foy for a good deal; the latter offers pickups and drop-offs anyway.

Kangouroute (☑418-683-9000, 888-768-8388; www.kangouroute.net; 6345 Blvd Wilfrid Hamel) is a local agency.

Budget (☑418-872-8413), **Avis** (☑418-872-2861), **Enterprise** (☑418-861-8820), **Hertz** (☑418-871-1571) and **Discount** (☑418-877-1717) have desks at the airport.

Allô Stop (www.allostop.com; 665 Rue St-Jean) gets drivers and passengers together for cheap rides to other parts of Québec. For example, a lift to Montréal costs $14.

Motorcycles are not permitted within the walls of the Old Town.

Taxi

In winter **Taxi Co-op** (☑418-525-5191) operates the Hiver Express taxis to the ski hills.

Train

Québec City has three **train stations** (☑888-842-7245), all with the same phone number. In the Lower Town, the renovated and simply gorgeous **Gare du Palais** (off Map p260), off Rue St-Paul, complete with bar and cafe, is central and convenient. Daily Via Rail trains go to Montréal (from $56, three hours) and destinations further west. Bus 800 from Place d'Youville runs to the station.

The **Ste-Foy station** (Map p258; 3255 Chemin de la Gare), southwest of downtown, is used by the same trains and is simply more convenient for residents who live on that side of the city.

The third station is inconveniently across the river in the town of **Charny**, east of Hwy 73. Trains here mainly serve eastern destinations, such as the Gaspé Peninsula and the Maritimes, but some also go to Montréal. Buses connect to Ste-Foy station. Overnight trains go to Moncton, New Brunswick (from $100, 12½ hours) every day except Tuesday. Some trains from downtown will connect to Charny.

Getting Around

To/From the Airport

A **Taxi Co-op** (☑418-525-5191) cab between town and the airport costs about $30. Tour companies **Old Québec Tours** (p273) and **Dupont Tours** (☑418-649-9226) sometimes run cheaper shuttle buses.

Bicycle

Many bike paths run through and around the city, covered by the *Plan du Réseau Cyclable* and more-detailed *Parcours Cyclables*. Cyclo Services (p265) rents bikes (one hour/day $14/35), tandems and electric bikes. Customers need to leave an identification document there.

Car & Motorcycle

In Québec City, driving isn't really worth the trouble. You can walk just about everywhere, the streets are narrow and crowded, and parking is limited. But if you're stuck driving, the tourist offices have a handy map of city-operated parking lots that don't gouge too much. The public lot beside Discovery Pavilion is affordable and close to the Old Town. Better still are the lots in St Roch, including a few off Rue St-Vallier Est, which charge about half the price of those in Upper Town. Parking there means a 10-minute hike uphill, but you can buy yourself a treat with the money you save.

Public Transportation

A ride on the city **bus system** (☑418-627-2511) costs $2.60, with transfer privileges, or $6.70 for a day pass. Buses go out as far as Ste Anne de Beaupré on the North Shore. The tourist offices will supply you with route maps and information.

Many buses serving the Old Town area stop in at Place d'Youville, just outside the wall on Rue St Jean. Bus 800 goes to Gare du Palais, the central long-distance bus and train station. Buses 800 and 801 go from downtown to Université Laval.

AROUND QUÉBEC CITY

As tempting as it may be to wander Old Québec for days, the larger Québec region is well worth exploring. Other than Lévis, the sights here are all on the north side of the river: Wendake, St Gabriel de Valcartier, Stoneham and Parc de la Jacques Cartier to the north of Québec, and the rest to the northeast. The south side also possesses some excellent places to visit, listed under South Shore (p288).

Lévis

On the 1km ferry crossing (p272) to the town of Lévis, the best views are undoubtedly on the Québec side of the vessel. The Citadelle, the Château Frontenac and the seminary dominate the clifftop cityscape. Once you disembark, riverside Lévis is a relaxing escape from the intensity of Québec City's Old Town.

Tourisme Lévis (☑418-838-6026; ⊗May-Oct), at the ferry landing, has maps and an Old Lévis package ($9), which includes return ferry and a 30-minute guided bus shuttle to several points of interest, including those listed here.

Bikes, tandems and rollerblades can be rented at the ferry terminal for cheaper rates than in Québec City.

Near the ferry landing, the **Terrasse de Lévis**, a lookout point inaugurated in 1939 by King George VI and (the then future) Queen Elizabeth II, offers excellent vistas of Québec and beyond from the top of the hill on Rue William-Tremblay.

Between 1865 and 1872, the British built three forts on the south shore to protect Québec. One, known as **Fort No 1** (41 Chemin du Gouvernement; adult/child $4/2; ⊗10am-5pm May-Aug), has been restored and operates as a national historic site with guided tours. It's on the east side of Lévis, just off Rte 132/Blvd de la Rive Sud.

In Old Lévis, the main shops and restaurants are on Ave Bégin. Alternatively, for more views of Québec, head south on the riverside path through Parc de l'Anse-Tibbits. At the marina, about 2km from the ferry landing, **La Piraterie** (4685 Rue St Laurent; sandwiches from $6, meals from $20; ⊗7am-10pm May-Sep) serves club sandwiches, brochettes, pasta and seafood.

Wendake

In Huron-Ouendat, the number eight is a letter, pronounced 'oua' (like the 'wh' in 'what'), which explains the curious name of the reconstructed Huron village **Onhoüa Chetek8e** (www.huron-wendat.qc.ca; 575 Rue Stanislas Kosca; adult/child $10/7.50; ⊗9am-5pm). It's in small Wendake, about 15km northwest of the city via Hwy 73 (exit 154).

Entry to the village is by a 45-minute tour. For an extra $7, you can supplement the tour with lunch in the log cabin, tucking into venison, caribou and mint tea, though this is one of the more theme park-like aspects of the experience.

The tour includes a longhouse, a sweat lodge, a smoker (a wigwam for smoking meat) and a shaman's hut, where you learn how dream-catchers work and how shamans exorcised sick people using bear skulls. It's the world's only Huron village, and the surrounding reserve is a relatively dynamic Aboriginal community. In 1960, it became the first reserve with its own bank; today, it provides employment for other tribes.

Entertainment such as dances ($5.25) can make it a full day. The tax-free shop sells Huron crafts and souvenirs. Bus 72 runs half-hourly from Québec ($2.60, 30 minutes).

St Gabriel de Valcartier

Announced by the 'pirate's den' slide overshadowing the packed car park, **Village Vacances** (1860 Blvd Valcartier; adult/child $31/24, evening $25/22; ⊙10am-7pm mid-Jun–mid-Aug, to 5pm early Jun & late Aug) is a water-city that looms above the village like Jabba the Hutt next to Princess Leia. With eight slides, water games, heated pools and a paddling pool, it's heaven on earth for children. Rafting, carting, diving displays and a campground are also on offer. It's northwest of Wendake, accessible via Rte 371.

Stoneham

Leaving Québec's suburbs, Rte 371 winds along Rivière Jacques Cartier and through the hills. At Stoneham, the **Station Touristique** (Mountain Resort; www.ski-stoneham. com; 600 Chemin du Hibou) offers an array of activities in a friendly resort atmosphere with lodgings and a restaurant. Stoneham is one of the province's main ski centers, switching to hiking, climbing and kayaking in summer.

Parc de la Jacques Cartier

This 600-sq-km **wilderness park** (☑418-848-3169, 800-665-6527; adult/child $3.50/1.50), just off Rte 175 about 40km from Québec, is ideal for a quick escape. In less than an hour from the city, you can be hiking or biking along trails, or canoeing along Rivière Jacques Cartier. L'Epéron

(5.5km) is a steamy forest walk with lookouts giving views down the valley, while Les Loups (10km) and Du Hibou (13km) are two tough, rewarding trails.

Some 10km from the southernmost 'Valley Sector' entrance to the park, the information center provides services such as showers. It hires out camping equipment, canoes and bikes, and organizes activities (in French) from caving to survivalist training. Simple overnight cabins and campgrounds ($18 to $37) are scattered throughout the park. In winter, there's cross-country skiing with shelter huts along some routes.

Going a little further north leads to the 7861-sq-km **Réserve Faunique des Laurentides** (Rte 175; adult/child $3.50/free), wilder and less organized but popular for fishing.

Domaine la Truite du Parc (☑418-848-3732; 4 Chemin des Anémones; camping $22, tepee $40, 4-person yurt $100), off Rte 175, 2km north of the Valley Sector entrance to the park, has riverside camping and a restaurant. Owners Pascal and Véronique's main business during winter is dog-sledding, as the huskies hanging at the door suggest.

You can organize for Intercar's Québec-Chicoutimi bus to drop you at one of the four entrances, all of which are on Rte 175.

Île d'Orléans

Before Jacques Cartier named Île d'Orléans in the Duke of Orleans' honor, it was known as L'Île de Bacchus for its wild vines. Four centuries later, Québécois troubadour Félix Leclerc, who died here in 1988, likened the island to France's famous Chartres cathedral.

Today, there are no signs of Dionysian orgies on sleepy Île d'Orléans, but there is plenty to attract day-trippers and those lucky visitors with more time to spare. The island is still primarily a pastoral farming region, with gentle landscapes and views across to both shores of the St Lawrence. One road (60km) circles it, with two more running north-south. Their edges are dotted with strawberry fields, orchards, cider producers, windmills and arts and crafts workshops and galleries. Some of the villages contain houses that are up to 300 years old, and there are wooden or stone cottages in the Normandy style.

At the island's more developed southwestern end, where the bridge crosses from the north shore, it feels at times like a floating suburb of Québec. The city soon becomes a distant memory as you head northeast.

It's worth spending $1 on a brochure at the helpful **tourist office** (☑418-828-9411, 866-941-9411; www.iledorleans.com; 490 Côte du Pont; ☺8:30am-7:30pm mid-Jun–Sep, 10am-5pm Oct–mid-Jun), which is visible soon after you cross the bridge.

◉ Sights & Activities

Domaine Steinbach   CIDERY
(www.domainesteinbach.com; 2205 Chemin Royal, St-Pierre; ☺10am-7pm May-Oct) This store stocks 30 farm products, including five ciders made using apples from the organic orchard, one with maple syrup. If the generous tasting tickles your taste buds, tuck into a cheese or duck platter ($10) on the terrace overlooking the river.

Le Vignoble Isle de Bacchus   WINE
(1071 Chemin Royal, St-Pierre; ☺10am-6pm) A tour and tasting here should be on your agenda, and there's a *gîte* (B&B) if you can't drag yourself away from the red, white and rosé.

Chocolaterie de Île d'Orléans   STORE
(www.chocolaterieorleans.com; 150 Chemin du Bout-de-Île, Ste-Pétronille; ☺11am-5pm) Using cocoa beans from Belgium, the chocolatiers at this 200-year-old house churn out tasty concoctions including almond bark and flavored truffles.

La Forge à Pique Assaut   STORE
(www.forge-pique-assaut.com; 2200 Chemin Royal, St-Laurent; ☺9am-5pm Jun-Oct, 9am-noon & 1:30-5pm Mon-Fri Oct-Jun) Artisan blacksmith Guy makes star railings and decorative objects at this *économusée*.

Croisières les Coudrier   CRUISES
(☑418-692-0107; www.croisierescoudrier.qc.ca; 1515 Chemin Royal, St-Laurent; ☺May-Oct) Offers boat tours from St-Laurent, in the southwest corner of the island, to Grosse Île (p289).

ÉcoloCyclo   CYCLING
(www.ecolocyclo.net; 1979 Chemin Royal, St-Laurent; ☺May-Oct) Hires out bikes (per hour/day $12/30).

🛏 Sleeping & Eating

If you refuse to leave, the island is blessed with memorable places to sleep and eat,

and it's an easy commute to Québec by car. The website www.gitesiledorleans.com covers 25 B&Bs on the island.

Au Toit Bleu   B&B $$
(☑418-829-1078; 3879 Chemin Royal, Ste-Famille; r $82-110) Next to Le Mitan microbrewery, this eclectic B&B uses the decor gathered on the owner's travels to beautiful effect, with African, Indian, Indonesian and Japanese rooms. Choose between a shared bathroom or your own freestanding tub, then ponder the big questions in a hammock overlooking the river.

Auberge le P'tit Bonheur   HOSTEL $
(☑418-829-2588; www.leptitbonheur.qc.ca; 186 Côte Lafleur, St-Jean; dm/s/d $23/50/70) The door is always open (literally) at this hostel in a stone manor above St Jean in the middle of the south side. With a wigwam in the garden, it's like staying in your eccentric uncle's ramshackle home. You can rent bikes, kayaks, dune buggies and cross-country skis here.

La Maison du Vignoble   B&B $$
(☑418-828-9562; 1071 Chemin Royal, St-Pierre; r $70-110) A 300-year-old farmhouse at the winery; Montmorency Falls at the backyard, vineyards at the front. Life's tough.

Camping Orléans   CAMPGROUND $
(☑418-829-2953; www.campingorleans.com; 357 Chemin Royal, St-François; campsite $39-54; ☺May-Oct; 🛜🏊) This leafy site is at the water's edge at the far end of the island from the bridge. There's a swimming pool and pub on-site.

Le Moulin de St Laurent   MEDITERRANEAN $$
(www.moulinstlaurent.qc.ca; 754 Chemin Royal, St-Laurent; mains $10-25, meals $30-40; chalets from $120; ☺11:30am-8:30pm May-Oct) You'd be hard-pressed to find a more agreeable place to dine than the terrace at the back of this early-19th-century flour mill, with tables inches from a waterfall. The well-prepared, diverse menu is continental with regional flourishes, such as trout and veal. Chalets are also available.

Resto-Pub l'O2 Île   PUB $$
(1025 Rte Prévost, St-Pierre; mains $8-18; ☺8am-10pm) The island's hottest hangout, this pub attracts locals for its long menu of decent grilled meats, pizzas and pastas.

Chez Bacchus   PUB $$
(1236 Chemin Royal, St-Laurent; mains $8-18; ☺11am-9.30pm mid-Jun–Nov, 11am-3pm Wed & Sun, to 9pm Thu-Sat Nov–mid-Jun) This

roadside gathering point for local couples, as well as drinking buddies at the bar, serves pub grub in addition to more dramatic dishes such as chicken in tarragon sauce.

Parc de la Chute Montmorency

This waterfall is 30m higher than Niagara Falls and as much of a tourist trap, if not as impressive. It's perfectly visible from the main road and can be visited free. In the winter, snowboarders make the most of the *pain de sucre* (sugar loaf) next to the plunge pool, formed by ice and snow blanketing a huge rock. The cascade was harnessed to power sawmills and cotton factories, as detailed in an exhibition in the clifftop Manoir Montmorency.

From May to November the **park** (2490 Ave Royale) charges $9.50 for parking, at both the foot and the top of the falls. From the visitor center, off Rte 138 at the base of the falls, you can take the **cable car** (adult/ child one way $9/4) to the top or climb the 487 steps. The suspended footbridge right above the waterfall provides the best views.

The park is 7km northeast of Québec. To enter for free, either park your car at the church parking lot in neighboring Beauport, then walk 1km to the falls, or catch bus 800 at Place d'Youville in Québec and transfer at the Beauport terminal, taking bus 50 to the top of the falls or bus 53 to the bottom. You can also cycle here from Québec.

Ste Anne de Beaupré

Approaching Ste Anne de Beaupré along Rte 138, the twin steeples of the 1920s **basilica** (10018 Ave Royale; admission free; ⊘8:30am-4:30pm) tower above the motels and *dépanneurs* (convenience stores). It's intriguing in that it is one of the few remaining mega-attractions related not to nature, nor artificial diversions, but to faith. Since the mid-1600s, the village has been an important Christian site; the annual late-July pilgrimage draws thousands, turning all nearby space into a random, gypsy-like camp.

Unfortunately, before you even enter the basilica, it becomes apparent that this is going to be a case study in the human ability to mix the sacred and the profane. During the summer, visitors line up at the Blessings Bureau to have a priest bless the Jesus keychain they've just bought. Inside the building, the crutches piled up against the pillars are ex-voto offerings, left behind over decades by believers who no longer needed them after praying to Ste Anne. There is impressive tile work, stained glass and glittering ceiling mosaics depicting the life of Ste Anne. Unfortunately, the next things that strike you are the signs and screens blaring 'silence' and asking pilgrims not to deface the stonework, and the security cameras and earpiece-wearing heavies. However, the basilica is grand enough and the religious theme park of a village surreal enough to justify a stop here.

Nearby is the **Cyclorama of Jerusalem** (www.cyclorama.com; 8 Rue Régina; adult/child $9/6; ⊘9am-6pm May-late Oct), not an IMAX cinema, but a wraparound, 110m painting of Jerusalem on the day Jesus was crucified.

Facing the basilica is the chapel-like **Auberge de la Basilique** (✆418-827-4475; Ave Régina; s/d $43/56; ⊘closed Nov–mid-Apr), which has a self-service restaurant.

Intercar (✆in Québec City 418-627-9108) runs two services a day from the Québec bus station up the north shore. The buses stop in town at the **Dépanneur Olco** (✆418-827-3621; 9272 Blvd Ste Anne) store, opposite Café des Artistes.

Mont Ste Anne

The slopes here, 50km from Québec, make it a top-ranking Québécois **ski resort** (www.mont-sainte-anne.com; 2000 Blvd du Beau Pré). Novices, expert skiers and snowboarders alike rave about the 50-plus trails with more than a dozen lifts. For Nordic skiing, the village of St Ferréol les Neiges, 7km east of Mont Ste Anne along Rte 360, has 224km of excellent trails.

In summer, a scenic gondola ($17 return) glides to the mountain's summit. Bicycle and hiking trails wind up to the top, with bikes available for hire at the visitor center. Throughout April there's a giant sugar shack set up here. Other activities include canyoning, rafting, golf and visits to the 65-dog 'husky village.'

The water slides and walking trails at **Camping Mont Ste Anne** (✆418-826-2323; Rang St Julien; campsites from $28) distinguish this large, green park near St Ferréol les Neiges. There are others on Rte 138 going east from Québec City through the Ste Anne de Beaupré area.

Year-round tourist village **Chalets Montmorency** (☏800-463-2612; www.chalets montmorency.com; 1768 Ave Royale; studio/1-bedroom/2-bedroom/4-bedroom chalet $89/99/170/400; ☏) is also in the St Ferréol les Neiges area.

Coming here from Québec, Intercar buses cost $11 return and the Hiver Express (p272), which picks up from hotels, costs $24 return. From late June to mid-September, the resort runs a shuttle, geared toward mountain bikers and costing $12 return.

Canyon Ste Anne

Some 6km northeast of Beaupré on Rte 138, are these 74m-high **waterfalls** (206 Rte 138; adult/child $11.50/5.50; ☺9am-5:30pm late Jun-early Sep, to 4:30pm May-late Jun & Sep-Oct) in a deep chasm. You can walk around and across them via a series of steps, ledges and bridges. Though busy, this is a pleasant spot – it's less developed and more dramatic than Montmorency Falls.

Cap Tourmente National Wildlife Area

This **bird sanctuary** (570 Chemin du Cap Tourmente; adult/child $6/2; ☺8:30am-4pm early Jan–mid-Mar, to 5pm mid-Apr–Oct) is home to 700 species, including the flocks of snow geese that migrate to its wetlands in spring and autumn. It's beyond the villages of St Joachim and Cap Tourmente, signposted along Rte 138 from Ste Anne de Beaupré.

CHARLEVOIX

Hold up a blade of Charlevoix grass and you'll see it bend in the breeze of contentment that wafts through the region's flowery farmlands. For 200 years, this pastoral strip of rolling hills has been a summer retreat for the wealthy and privileged. Rtes 138 and 362 are the main activity in towns nestled comfortably between the St Lawrence and parks such as the taiga-covered Parc des Grand Jardins, named by the English after its resemblance to their country gardens.

Unesco has classified the entire area a World Biosphere Reserve, which has resulted in worthwhile restrictions on the types of permitted developments, as well as a palpable sense of pride among residents. There's also a lot to be proud of in towns such as the almost impossibly relaxing Baie St Paul. The *ateliers* (artists studios), galleries and boutiques lining its few streets hark back to the artists who, in the late 19th century, gravitated to Charlevoix to paint landscapes as a nationalistic exercise.

Charlevoix is also known as a center for the culinary arts and was at the forefront of the organic food movement in Canada 10 years ago. The Route des Saveurs (Route of Flavors) takes in 16 farms and eateries, including the home of Éboulmontaise lamb and one of Québec's best restaurants. Local menus generally read like inventories of Charlevoix produce.

The area totals 6000 sq km yet is home to just 30,000 people. Glacier-carved crevices, cliffs and jagged rock faces overlook a unique geographical feature: the immense valley formed by a prehistoric meteor. A space rock weighing 15 billion tons, with a diameter of about 2km, smashed into the earth here at 36,000km/h some 350 million years ago, leaving a crater measuring 56km in diameter. The point of impact was the present-day Mont des Éboulements, halfway between Baie St Paul and La Malbaie, some 10km inland.

A driving route to consider taking is the 'River Drive' (Rte 362) one way and then returning through ear-popping hills on the 'Mountain Drive' (Rte 138) inland.

Le Massif

Outside of Petite Rivière St Francois is **Le Massif** (www.lemassif.com; 1350 Rue Principale), perhaps the best little-known ski center in the country. It offers the highest vertical drop (770m) and most snow (600cm) east of the Rockies and a fabulous view over the St Lawrence. The chalet at the top of the hill houses **Mer & Monts Restaurant** (☏418-632-5276, 877-536-2774; meals from $20; ☺11:30am-2pm Wed-Sun), which serves up a three-course table d'hôte highlighting regional cuisine, not heat-lamp burgers.

Baie St Paul

The clowning, juggling troupe Cirque du Soleil started out in Baie St Paul, but most of the entertainment here is of a gentler nature. The small town boasts some 30 galleries and *ateliers,* along with historic hous-

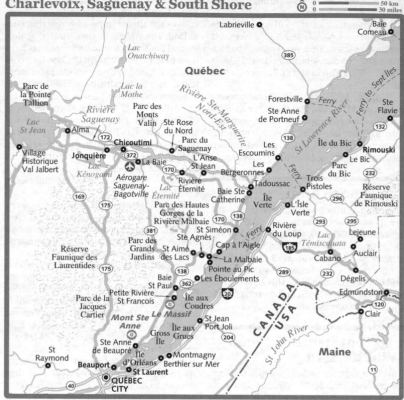

es converted into superb restaurants and *gîtes*. With its prosperous, holiday atmosphere and its location among wood-covered hills at the meeting of the St Lawrence and Gouffre Rivers, Baie St Paul is one of the North Shore's most appealing towns.

◉ Sights & Activities

Musée d'Art Contemporain   ART GALLERY
(www.macbsp.com; 23 Rue Ambroise-Fafard; adult/child $6/free; ☉noon-5pm Tue-Sun) Across the main drag, this architecturally attention-grabbing gallery houses contemporary art by local artists and some photographic exhibits on loan from the National Gallery of Canada. The gallery also organizes an international contemporary art symposium in August.

Carrefour Culturel Paul Médéric

ART GALLERY
(4 Rue Ambroise-Fafard; admission free; ☉10am-5pm) This gallery is named after a local

priest and writer who founded a youth movement here. Stay a while as it's possible to watch local artisans working in their studios.

Randonnées Nature-Charlevoix   TOURS
(randonneesnature.com; 11-1 Rue Ambroise-Fafard; adult/child $29.50/12; ☉1:30pm Jul & Aug) Nonprofit organization Randonnées Nature-Charlevoix runs two-hour tours of the meteor crater. It's based at Boutique Le Cratère, where you can learn about the world's largest inhabited crater by looking at the 3-D map and talking to guide François.

Air du Large   TOURS
(www.airdularge.com; Quay; ☉8am-5pm) Air du Large offers kayaking, sailing, climbing, canyoning, biking and paragliding. Tours are available and equipment can be hired.

📍 Sleeping

Auberge La Muse
B&B $$

(☑418-435-6839, 800-841-6839; www.lamuse. com; 39 Rue St Jean Baptiste; r $109-209; ❄) This cheerful yellow B&B has refined the art of relaxation. The superior rooms variously feature therapeutic baths, pillow-based massage technology and terraces overlooking the flower garden. If you can, avoid No 1, the slightly noisy room next to the front door.

Nature et Pinceaux
B&B $$

(☑418-435-2366; www.natureetpinceaux.qc.ca; 33 Rue Nordet; r $125-145) Atop the mountain peeking out over the river below, the views from the spacious rooms at this charming B&B are surpassed only by the phenomenal four-course breakfasts cooked by host Francine. The house is east of town, signposted off Rte 362.

La Balcon Vert
CAMPGROUND $

(☑418-435-5587; www.balconvert.com; 22 Côte du Balcon Vert; campsite/dm/d $23/23/52; ❄mid-May–early Oct) With its nightly bonfires, this hilltop hideaway is an involving place to stay, though guests should be prepared to rough it. A campground, private and shared cabins, a games room with table tennis, and a bar-restaurant nestle among the trees. The site is east of town, signposted off Rte 362.

✕ Eating

Le Mouton Noir
FRENCH $$$

(☑418-240-3030; 43 Rue Ste Anne; meals $30-36; ❄11am-2pm & 5-10pm Wed-Sun) Since 1978, the rustic-looking Black Sheep has been home to fine French cuisine. Fish, including walleye, the freshwater queen, is on offer when available, as are buffalo, caribou and steak, all enlivened by a deft touch incorporating wild mushrooms and local produce. The outdoor terrace overlooks the Gouffre. Reservations advised.

L'Orange Bistro
FRENCH $$$

(www.orangebistro.com; 29 Ambroise-Fafard; meals $26-37; ❄11am-9pm) This central, colorful restaurant's terrace overlooks the main road into town, but it's easy to forget the cars when the food's this good. Local produce on offer includes organic chicken, pork chops, veal, venison and mussels, while fresh herbs and organic vegetables edge the menu closer to perfection.

Le Saint Pub
PUB $$$

(2 Rue Racine; meals $20-30; ❄11am-2am) Ale lovers will foam at the mouth in this former brewery, where the dinner menu begins with beers and continues via beer-based sauces, dressings and marinades. For $6 you can sample four regional brews including the local malt.

Café des Artistes
CAFE $

(25 Rue St Jean Baptiste; lunch from $6.50; ❄9:30am-midnight) For excellent coffee and a light but zippy lunch, head to this pizzeria on the main strip.

ℹ Information

Charlevoix Tourist Office (www.tourisme-charlevoix.com; 444 Blvd Mgr de Laval; ❄8:30am-4:30pm Apr-late Jun, 9am-7pm late Jun-early Sep, restricted hours rest of year) On Rte 138 just west of town.

Town Tourist Office (☑418-240-3218; 6 Rue St Jean Baptiste; ❄8:30am-4:30pm Apr-late Jun, 9am-7pm late Jun-early Sep, restricted hours rest of year)

ℹ Getting There & Away

The **bus station** (☑418-435-6569; 2 Rte de l'Équere) is at La Grignotte restaurant, about a 20-minute walk from downtown at Blvd Mgr de Laval. Three Intercar buses per day go to/from Québec City ($23, 1¼ hours), with an extra Friday service. Two of the northbound services finish in La Malbaie and two continue to Baie Comeau via Tadoussac.

Parc des Grands Jardins

This **provincial park** (☑418-439-1227, reservations 800-665-6527; www.parcsquebec. com; adult/child $3.50/free) covers 310 sq km, much of it taiga. Information is available from the **Thomas-Fortin service center** (❄late May-early Oct), at the main entrance, and **Mont du Lac des Cygnes visitor kiosk** (❄mid-May–mid-Nov, Christmas holidays, Sat & Sun Feb & Mar).

Excellent hiking and rugged topography are the lure at this gem. The hills frame well over 100 small lakes. Caribou may be spotted. The half-day trek up **Mont du Lac des Cygnes** (Swan Lake Mountain) is an exceptional short hike. One of the longest and most difficult continuous trails east of the Rockies, **La Traversée** stretches 100km from the park, snaking down the great valleys in the Parc des Hautes Gorges and winding up in the Parc du Mont Grand-Fonds. An intermediate-level hiker needs about seven days for the full trek. You can rent canoes, kayaks and bikes, and stay at primitive campsites (from $19.75) or rustic, pioneer-style cottages (from $25). Bring all necessary supplies.

To get to the park, take Rte 381 north of Baie St Paul; it's 30km to the visitor kiosk and 46km to the main entrance.

Île aux Coudres

Quiet, rural Île aux Coudres is what those people disappointed by better-known Île d'Orléans are seeking. Standing on the island's more exposed southwestern side, where birds land on rocky promontories, it could be the remotest of gulf islands. This impression continues in the forested hinterlands, above the 26km road that circles the island. The hills of the north shore are never far from view, but this is nonetheless a place to forget the rest of the world.

◉ Sights & Activities

Musée Maritime   MUSEUM
(305 Rue de l'Église; adult/child $5/free; ☺9am-5pm late Jun-Aug, 9am-4pm Mon-Fri, 11am-4pm Sat & Sun mid-May–late Jun & early Sep–mid-Oct) Before or after boarding the ferry in St Joseph de la Rive, drop into Musée Maritime. It details the schooner-building history of a region where it was common to see 20 different types of commercial boat on the St Lawrence. Visitors can climb aboard some beauties in the shipyard. There's also a display on the area's famous meteorite crater.

Musée les Voitures d'Eau   MUSEUM
(203 Chemin des Coudriers; adult/child $4/2; ☺10am-5pm mid-Jun–mid-Sep, Sat & Sun late May–mid-Jun & mid-Sep–mid-Oct) The antique-shop-like Musée les Voitures d'Eau tells the island's nautical history through boat engines, buoys, anchors, plodding voiceovers and cheery explanations of the perils of the St Lawrence. There are also boats you can climb on.

Les Moulins   INDUSTRIAL MUSEUM
(36 Chemin du Moulin; admission free; ☺9:30am-5:30pm mid-May–early Oct) *Économusée* Les Moulins has two restored 19th-century mills and exhibits showing how wheat and buckwheat were ground using grindstones.

Gérard Desgagnés   BIKE RENTAL
(☎418-438-2332; 36 Chemin de la Traverse; ☺Apr-Oct) Near the tourist office, Gérard Desgagnés hires out bikes (per one hour/day $3/15) and tandems.

🛏 Sleeping & Eating

There are half a dozen restaurants and even more places to stay, from campgrounds to B&Bs and motels.

Gîte au Vent de l'Isle   B&B $$
(☎418-438-2649, 877-666-2649; 39 Chemin du Moulin; s $75-95, d $85-105) Next to Les Moulins, this B&B has four rooms with varnished wood floors, ceramic tiles in the showers and tapestries decorating the walls. Montréaler Sylvie, who speaks good English, produces muffins, fruit salad and crepes for breakfast.

ℹ Information

Tourist office (www.tourismeisleauxcoudres.com; 1024 Chemin des Coudriers; ☺9am-5pm late Jun-Oct) Near the crossroads just beyond the port.

ℹ Getting There & Away

Free **ferries** (☎877-787-7483) take 15 minutes and depart St Joseph de la Rive, on the north shore of St Lawrence, on the half hour from May to October, less frequently the rest of the year.

Les Éboulements

There are few signs of life in the tin shacks and wooden sheds peeking out at Rte 362 from the trees in this farming region. Even *ateliers* are thin on the ground, though there is the odd carving outlet between piles of wood used for a more practical purpose during the longer winters. The most activity is in the rippling hills and rock formations, formed by the 1633 earthquake that gave the area its name ('rock fall').

Award-winning restaurant **Les Saveurs Oubliées** (Forgotten Flavors; ☎418-635-9888; 350 Rang St Godefroy; mains from $27; ☺11am-9pm Wed-Mon Jun-Oct) specializes in Éboulmontaise lamb from the attached farm and organic vegetables. Stroll around the barn and ogle the shop, which sells jams, jellies, oils, vinegar, sausages and *(bien sûr)* lamb, mostly produced on the farm. The restaurant, which serves lamb in about 10 succulent ways, is open from 5:30pm. Reservations are essential.

Ste Irénée

With its cafes overlooking one of the area's best beaches, Ste Irénée is an inviting halfway house between backcountry

Les Éboulements and developed La Malbaie. Between June and September, the **Domaine Forget** (www.domaineforget.com) season of classical music, jazz and dance attracts performers from around the world. **Katabatik** (📞418-665-2332; 180 Rte 362) offers sea kayaking tours.

In a grand house built for an industrialist, **Hôtel Le Rustique** (📞418-452-8250; www.charlevoix.qc.ca/lerustique; 102 Rue Principale; s/d from $75/85) is one of Charlevoix' friendliest and most alluring B&Bs. With their pale colors and photos from owner Diane's travels, the rooms have the feel of an artist's seaside cottage. Three self-contained apartments are also available. The restaurant serves mouthwatering Charlevoix chow such as chicken breast with local Migneron cheese.

La Malbaie

Now encompassing five previously separate villages, La Malbaie was one of Canada's first holiday resorts. From the late 19th century, steamers run by the Richelieu and Ontario Navigation Company and Canada Steamship Lines docked here. Today, the steam mainly comes from cars hurtling along Rte 138, but there are signs of the region's former glory, particularly in hilly Pointe au Pic.

Arriving from St Irénée on the riverside Rte 362, the first village you come to is **Pointe au Pic**. Pointe au Pic was a holiday destination for the wealthy at the beginning of the 20th century, drawing the elite from as far away as New York. One of its famous residents was former US president William Howard Taft, who had a summer home built here. Some of these large, impressive 'cottages' along Chemin des Falaises have been converted into comfortable inns.

Sainte Agnès lies to the northwest, away from the St Lawrence. Adjoining Pointe au Pic is **La Malaie**, which begins to the west of the Malbaie River and continues to the other side.

North of La Malbaie is **Rivière Malbaie**, while **Cap à l'Aigle** and **Saint Fidèle** are east on Rte 138.

There is a **regional tourist office** (📞418-665-4454, 800-667-2276; www.tourisme-charlevoix.com; 495 Blvd de Comporté, Pointe au Pic; ⊙8:30am-4:30pm) in La Malbaie.

⊙ Sights & Activities

Manoir Richelieu   NOTABLE BUILDING
The gray country cousin of Québec City's Château Frontenac, this mega-hotel is also owned by the Fairmont chain. Nonetheless, the sprawling, copper-roofed castle-like structure, which was built in 1928 and received a $140 million facelift in 1999, attests to the area's longtime prosperity. Wander the clifftop gardens, have a drink on the terrace and drop by the gallery displaying local art. Outside, coach loads of hopefuls stream into the much-advertised **Casino de Charlevoix** (Point au Pic; admission free; ⊙10am-late).

Maison du Bootlegger   NOTABLE BUILDING
(📞418-439-3711; 110 Ruisseau des Frênes, Ste Agnès; adult/child $8/5, meal, tour & entertainment from $40; ⊙10am-6pm mid-Jun–mid-Sep) This unexpected hostelry in a conventional-looking 19th-century farmhouse was surreptitiously modified by an American bootlegger during the prohibition period. Tours reveal the marvel of secret doorways and hidden chambers intended to deter the morality squad. From 6pm, it turns into a party restaurant where meat feasts are accompanied by Al Capone beer in boot-shaped glasses and lots of boisterous entertainment.

Musée de Charlevoix   MUSEUM
(www.museedecharlevoix.qc.ca; 10 Chemin du Havre, Point au Pic; adult/child $7/free; ⊙9am-5pm Jun-late Sep, 10am-5pm Mon-Fri, 1-5pm Sat & Sun Oct-late May) Part art gallery, part museum, this waterfront museum portrays the life and times of Charlevoix through a variety of media.

Jardins   GARDEN
(625 Rue St Raphael; adult/child $6/free; ⊙9am-5pm May-Oct) In Cap à l'Aigle, a little village 2km east of La Malbaie, are the Jardins, where 800 types of lilac range up the hill between a waterfall, a footbridge and artists selling their daubs.

Katabatik   KAYAKING
(📞418-665-2332; www.katabatik.ca; Cap à l'Aigle marina; half-day tour adult/child $55/36, full day $105/70) Offers sea kayak expeditions lasting from half a day to five days.

🛏 Sleeping

Gîtes line the approach to Manoir Richelieu, hoping their guests strike it lucky in the casino. Elsewhere in Pointe au Pic, there's an enticing strip of moderately priced B&Bs on Rue du Quai at the water's edge. La Malbaie is less tourist focused, offering services, eating options and stores, but it does have some good accommodations.

Manoir Richelieu   HOTEL $
(☎418-665-3703, 866-540-4464; www.fairmont. com/richelieu; 181 Rue Richelieu, Pointe au Pic; r $111-529; ❄🖥🌊🐾) With its overwhelming size (405 rooms), dark, winding hallways, old-fashioned decor and its location – perched on a cliff beating off the howling winds from the St Lawrence River below – you may feel like you've been cast in a British murder mystery. But that's part of the allure of this creaky old castle – that and the four restaurants, spa, casino, golf course and a never-ending list of kids' amenities, including a gym, indoor and outdoor swimming pools, a movie theater and nightly treasure hunts.

Auberge des 3 Canards   INN $$
(☎418-665-3761; www.auberge3canards.com; 115 Côte Bellevue, Pointe au Pic; r from $115; ❄) With its 49 rooms boasting flat-screen TVs, vintage photos of the steamers, local art and balconies overlooking the tennis court, this 50-year-old institution is more special than it looks from Rte 138. The staff are attentive and the **restaurant** (meals $59) features impeccably presented regional cuisine. Ask how it got its name.

Gîte au Soleil Levant   B&B $
(☎418-665-4976; www.charlevoix.qc.ca/soleil-levant; 469 Rue St Étienne, La Malbaie; r $45-55) Five minutes' walk from the town center, this comfortable family home offers some privacy, with a door leading straight to the guests' lounge and bedrooms.

Camping des Chutes Fraser CAMPGROUND $
(☎418-665-2151; www.campingchutesfraser. com; 500 Chemin de la Vallée, La Malbaie; tent & RV sites $23-38, cottage $90-125; ☼camping mid-May–mid-Oct, cottages year-round) This campground with a waterfall, toward Mont Grand-Fonds park, is idyllic.

✕ Eating

Visa Versa   QUÉBÉCOIS $$$
(☎418-665-6869; 216 Rue St Étienne, La Malbaie; meals $65; ☼6-9:30pm Tue-Sun Jun-Sep, 6-9:30pm Thu-Sat Oct-May) The intriguing name comes from the split personality menu, on which owner-chefs Danielle and Eric have each created a column of choices. Decided two weeks in advance, the menu is underpinned by local produce (Éboulmontaise lamb, calf's sweetbreads with Grand-Fonds oyster mushrooms, St Urbain duck, rock Cornish stew with Charlevoix beer), but the tangy, peppery sauces keep you guessing exactly which ingredient it is that tastes so good.

Le Passe Temps   FRENCH $$$
(245 Blvd de Comporté, Pointe au Pic; meals $20-40; ☼11am-11pm Jun–mid-Sep, 5-11pm mid-Sep–Oct & May, 5-11pm Tue-Sat Nov-Apr) Sample some traditional French cuisine in a comfortable room filled with natural wood. The specialties to try are crepes and fondue.

Pains d'Exclamation   BAKERY $
(302 Rue John-Naime, La Malbaie; sandwiches $5.75; ☼7am-5:30pm Tue-Sat) This bakery makes a good lunchtime stop, mainly for the Brie, apple and walnut grilled sandwich.

Parc des Hautes Gorges de la Rivière Malbaie

Work off all that Charlevoix produce with an invigorating hike in this 233-sq-km **provincial park** (☎reservations 866-702-9202; adult/child $3.50/free; ☼7am-9pm May–mid-Oct), which boasts several unique features, including the highest rock faces east of the Rockies. Sheer rock plummets (sometimes 800m) to the calm Rivière Malbaie, creating one of Québec's loveliest river valleys.

There are trails of all levels, from ambles around the Barrage des Érables (Maple Dam) to vigorous hikes ascending from maple grove to permafrost.

A highlight is the **boat cruise** (adult/child $31/24; ☼late May-early Oct) up the river squeezed between mountains. The river can also be seen from a canoe or kayak, which are available for hire, as are bikes. Boat tickets are available at the visitor center at the park entrance, and rentals 7km further on at the dam.

Many people make it a day trip from La Malbaie, but there are basic **camp sites** ($20 to $25) available. Canoes can be used to reach the three riverside campgrounds. Bring all required supplies.

The park is about 45km northwest of La Malbaie. To reach it from La Malbaie, head northwest on Rte 138 toward Baie St Paul, then take the turn for St Aimé des Lacs and keep going for 30km.

St Siméon

Parc d'Aventure Les Palissades (1000 Rte 170; without a guide adult/child $4.35/2.60; ☺9am-5pm), 12km north of St Siméon on Rte 170, is an adventure sports center. There are 15km of trails with lookouts to admire the unusual geological formations, and access to the **Trans Canada Trail (TCT)**. The main attraction, however, is the rock climbing, with 150-plus routes, a suspension bridge, rappelling and two via ferrata cliff walks with safety cables (no experience required). Accommodations range from camping and dorms to chalets, and a lakeside spa and sauna. Québec City–based **Aventure X** (p265) runs trips here.

A **ferry** (adult/child/car $18.80/12.70/40, early April to early January) connects St Siméon with Rivière du Loup. During the summer, there are four or five daily departures, and discounts are offered for the earliest and latest trips each day. No reservations are taken; arrive at least 90 minutes before departure in summer. A motion-sickness pill may be welcome on the sometimes rough, 65-minute crossing.

Baie Ste Catherine

It's overshadowed by nearby Tadoussac, but Baie Ste Catherine is nonetheless an attractive spot, its line of multicolored roofs punctuated by glinting barns and patches of grass. Most of the activities offered in Tadoussac can also be arranged from here.

Up the hill from the ferry landing, **Pointe Noire Observation Center** (Rte 138; adult/child $5.80/2.90; ☺11am-6pm mid-Jun–early Sep, Fri-Sun early Sep-early Oct), a whale-study post at the confluence of the Saguenay and St Lawrence Rivers, features an exhibit, a slide show and films, plus an observation deck with a telescope. From the boardwalk, you can often spy belugas in the Saguenay very close to shore, especially when the tide is coming in.

Three of the four cruise companies operating out of Tadoussac pick up from Baie Ste Catherine pier en route to spotting whales (p284) on the St Lawrence or exploring the Saguenay fjord. **Groupe Dufour** (☎418-692-0222, 800-463-5250), **AML** (☎800-563-4643) and **Croisières 2001** (☎866-373-2001) all have booths around the pier.

Friendly and professional **Azimut Aventure** (☎418-237-4477, 888-843-1100; 185 Rte 138) tends to attract a clientele who is serious about sea kayaking. The excursions last hours to days, including a memorable two-day trip to L'Anse St Jean ($265), and you can rent kayaks ($35 per day).

If it's busy in Tadoussac, there are plenty of B&Bs here.

At the southern end of town, the free 10-minute ferry to Tadoussac runs across the Saguenay River. The 24-hour service departs every 20 minutes from 8:20am to 8:40pm weekdays and summer weekends, from 11am to 5:40pm Saturdays, and from 1pm to 8:20pm Sundays; at all other times, it leaves with a frequency of 40 minutes to one hour.

SAGUENAY

Some fans of the Rivière Saguenay fjord, where a dramatic, towering canyon ploughs northwest from the St Lawrence, rank it as the province's most beautiful area. The 100km river, fed by Lac St Jean, stretches from north of Chicoutimi to the captivating, winding village of Tadoussac. From its dark waters rise majestic cliffs up to 500m high. Formed during the last Ice Age, the fjord is the most southerly one in the northern hemisphere. As deep as 270m in some places, the riverbed rises to a depth of only 20m at the fjord's mouth at Tadoussac. This makes the relatively warm, fresh waters of the Saguenay jet out atop the frigid, salt waters of the St Lawrence, leading to massive volumes of krill, which in turn attract the visitor highlight of the region: whales. They and the entire waterway now enjoy protected status.

There are two main areas of the Saguenay region. The first hugs the Rivière Saguenay and consists of park and tiny, scenic villages along both sides. The second is the partially urban, industrialized section with mid-sized Chicoutimi as its pivot.

Tadoussac

For many visitors to Québec, Tadoussac is the one place in the province they visit outside Montréal and Québec City. What consistently draws the hordes to the small spot, where fewer than 1000 inhabitants gaze across the St Lawrence and at those poor souls leaving on the ferry across the Saguenay, is the whales. Not only do Zodiacs zip out in search of the behemoths, but smaller whales such as belugas and minkes can be glimpsed from the shore. Added to that are activities such as sea kayaking, 'surfbiking,' exploring the fjord by boat or on foot, or simply wandering the dunes and headlands. Some of Tadoussac's vibrancy departs with the whales between November and May, but it remains a historic, bohemian town where the locals invariably have time for a chat.

History

Tadoussac became the first fur-trading post in European North America in 1600, eight years before the founding of Québec City. The word *tatouskak,* in the Innu (Montagnais) language, means breast, and refers to the two, rounded hills by the fjord and bay. When the Hudson's Bay Company closed its doors, Tadoussac was briefly abandoned, only to be revived as a resort with the building of Hotel Tadoussac in 1864, and as an important cog in the pulp and paper wheel.

◎ Sights

Centre d'Interprétation des Mammifères Marins   MUSEUM

(CIMM; 108 Rue de la Cale Sèche; adult/child $9/4.50; ◉noon-5pm mid-May–mid-Jun & late Sep-late Oct, 9am-8pm mid-Jun–late Sep) The CIMM gives excellent background information on local sea creatures through multimedia exhibits.

Poste de Traite Chauvin   HISTORICAL SITE

(157 Rue du Bord de l'Eau; adult/child $4/free; ◉10am-6pm Jun, 9am-7pm Jul-late Sep, 9am-noon & 3-6pm late Sep–mid-Oct) The Poste de Traite Chauvin is a replica of the continent's first fur-trading post and offers some history on the first transactions between Aboriginals and Europeans. Exhibits are in French, but ask for an English guidebook.

Petite Chapelle   HISTORICAL SITE

(Rue du Bord de l'Eau; adult/child $2/0.50; ◉9am-8pm mid-Jun–early Sep, to 6pm early Sep-early Oct) Built in 1747 by the Jesuits, Petite Chapelle is one of North America's oldest wooden churches. Also known as the Indian Chapel, it contains a small exhibition on missionary life.

🏃 Activities

Whale-Watching

From May to November, tourists flock to Tadoussac for a very good reason: whale-watching. It's phenomenal, particularly between August and October, when blue whales are spotted. All over town, tickets are available for boat tours, from 12-person

Zodiacs to the 600-person *Grand Fleuve;* check out the possibilities carefully. **Otis Excursions** (☎418-235-4197; 431 Rue du Bateau Passeur) is a local company that has been running for 35 years. Its Zodiacs get closest to the waves and offer the most exciting, if roughest, rides. Young children aren't permitted, however, and the Zodiac operated by **Croisières AML** (www.croisieres aml.com, 177 Rue des Pionniers) is twice the size of the others. Wait for a calm day, when the view won't be marred by waves and a rocking boat, and go out in the early morning or evening, when the whales are livelier and there are fewer vessels around. Adult fares are $59 for a two-hour Zodiac trip and $69 for a three-hour boat trip. Zodiac passengers are given waterproofs; whatever trip you do, take lots of warm clothes.

For the adventurous, sea-kayaking supremo **Mer et Monde** (www.mer-et-monde. qc.ca; 405 Rue de la Mer, Les Bergeronnes; 3hr from $52) offers whale-watching expeditions and excursions up the fjord. Similar Azimut Aventure (p283) has a booth on the beach during the summer.

Hiking

There are four 1km paths in and around Tadoussac, marked on the map given out by the tourist office. The trails around the peninsulas **Pointe de l'Islet**, by the quay, and, at the other end of the beach, **Pointe Rouge** are the best for spying whales from the shore.

Parc du Saguenay borders the fjord on both sides of the river. The provincial park has over 100km of splendid hiking trails, views down the fjord from atop 350m-plus cliffs, plus trailside refuges where you can spend the night. There are three refuges on the 43km trail from Tadoussac to Baie Ste Marguerite, open May to October. To book a hut, contact Parc du Saguenay; its local office is at Maison des Dunes (p285). For a one-day walk on the track, **Maison Majorique** (☎418-235-4372; www.ajtadou.com; 158 Rue de Bateau-Passeur, Tadoussac) runs a shuttle ($12) back to Tadoussac from Cap de la Boule, 13km west.

Overlapping with Parc du Saguenay, and extending to the Saguenay, Charlevoix and North Shore regions, with various entry points, **Saguenay-St Lawrence Marine Park** (197 Rue des Pionniers) was the first conservation project in Québec to be jointly administered by the federal and provincial governments. This liquid park covers and protects 1138 sq km of the two rivers and their coastlines, from Gros Cap à l'Aigle to Les Escoumins and up the Saguenay as far as Cap à l'Est, near Ste Fulgence.

Parc du Saguenay's interpretation center, **Maison des Dunes** (750 Chemin du Moulin à Baude; adult/child $3.50/1.50; ☺10am-5pm Sat & Sun late May–mid-Jun, 10am-5pm mid-Jun–early Oct), is 5km out of town in another prime whale-watching location. An exhibit explains why what everyone calls 'dunes' in the area are actually marine terraces, formed by waves, not wind, as dunes are. It's a 7km walk along the shore from town, and there are 1km trails leading through the dunes to lookout points.

🎎 Festivals & Events

Tadoussac's busy summer season begins with a vengeance at the 25-year-old **Festival de la Chanson** (Song Festival; ☎418-235-2002; www.chansontadoussac.com; ☺mid-Jun), a celebration of Francophone music, mostly Québécois, and a serious party. Stages spring up all over town and accommodations fill up for the long weekend.

🛏 Sleeping

Auberge la Ste Paix   B&B **$$**
(☎418-235-4803; www.aubergelasaintepaix.com; 102 Rue Saguenay; r $98-133) Guests at this out-of-the-way, seven-room B&B spot whales while savoring gourmet breakfasts ranging from French toast to Mexican omelet's, cooked by the entertaining Montréaler Denis.

Hôtel Tadoussac   HOTEL **$$**
(☎418-235-1121; www.hoteltadoussac.com; 165 Rue du Bord de l'Eau; r from $155; ▣) This 149-room, red-and-white landmark has extensive gardens, a pool overlooking the port, and vintage photos of steamers and the hotel looking considerably smaller in 1870. Somewhat tired and dated bedrooms have plush carpets, ceiling fans and river views.

Maison Clauphi   MOTEL, B&B **$$**
(☎418-235-4303; www.clauphi.com; 188 Rue des Pionniers; B&B $95, motel r $119; ☺May-Oct) The accommodations range from motel and B&B rooms to studios and suites in this building built in 1932 by the owner's parents. Bikes and water-borne 'surfbikes' can be rented.

Domaine des Dunes   CAMPGROUND **$**
(☎418-235-4843; www.domainedesdunes. com; 585 Chemin du Moulin à Baude; tent

& RV sites $32, trailer or motorhome $45, chalet from $150) The smaller and leafier of Tadoussac's two campgrounds, 3km from town. Self-catering chalets are also available.

🍴 Eating

Chez Mathilde   FUSION **$$$**
(227 Rue des Pionniers; lunch & dinner meals from $25; ☺11am-9:30pm Jun-Oct) The stellar chef at this cute little house utilizes plenty of local produce in his creative, though limited, menu. The innovative dishes, cooked to perfection, are served up alongside a view of the port from an airy patio.

Restaurant Le Bateau   QUÉBÉCOIS **$$**
(246 Rue des Forgerons; lunch/dinner meals $11/18; ☺11am-9:30pm May-Oct) A great view comes with the buffet of traditional Québec workers' fare at this friendly restaurant. Fill up on Lac St Jean meat pie, followed by blueberry, sugar or vinegar pie.

Café Bohème   CAFE **$$**
(239 Rue des Pionniers; meals $14-20; ☺8am-10pm May-Oct) The village's hangout of choice is a prime place for a breakfast of fruit and yogurt or a *panini,* or just to sip fair trade coffee among the local intellectuals. Later in the day, choose between dishes such as smoked fish bagel and fresh pasta of the day.

La Galouine   FUSION **$$$**
(251 Rue des Pionniers; meals $22-38; ☺8am-10pm) Entered by a fairy-light-covered balcony above an organic market, this is a wholefood cafe taken up a notch. Dishes such as smoked duck salad are satisfyingly earthy, though the service is variable.

Chantmartin   FAST FOOD **$$**
(412 Rue du Bateau Passeur; meals $15-25; ☺5:30am-10pm) Despite its truck-stop-like appearance and attached line of generic motel rooms, Chantmartin is a good, rapid stop for everything from poutine and pizza to crab, prawns and roast chicken.

ℹ Information

Café Bohème (239 Rue des Pionniers; per hr $5; ☺8am-10pm) Internet access upstairs.

Tourist information office (☎418-235-4744, 866-235-4744; www.tadoussac.com; 197 Rue des Pionniers; ☺8am-9pm Jul-Sep, 9am-6pm Apr-Jun & Oct) In the middle of town with very patient staff who can help with accommodations.

ℹ️ Getting There & Away

Tadoussac is right off Rte 138. The 10-minute ferry from Baie Ste Catherine in Charlevoix is free and runs around the clock (p283). The terminal is at the end of Rue du Bateau Passeur.

Intercar (☑418-235-4653; 433 Rte 138) buses connect Tadoussac with Montréal ($99, eight hours) and Québec City ($51, four hours) twice a day and run as far northeast as Sept Îles. The bus stop is opposite Camping Tadoussac at the Petro-Canada garage.

Les Bergeronnes

The slow pace of the North Shore begins in Les Bergeronnes, which is pleasingly deserted after Tadoussac. With a handful of attractions and an excellent campground, it's worth leaving Tadoussac for it.

Archéo Topo (498 Rue de la Mer; adult/child $5.50/3.50; ⊙9am-6pm Jun & Sep, 8am-8pm Jul & Aug) is a research and exhibition center dedicated to archaeological findings along the North Shore. Outside, trails lead down to the beach.

A few kilometers northeast of Les Bergeronnes, signposted from Rte 138, the **Cap de Bon Désir Interpretation Centre** (13 Chemin du Cap de Bon Désir; adult/child $7.80/3.90; ⊙8am-8pm mid-Jun–early Sep, 9am-6pm early Sep-early Oct) has captivating marine life exhibits and scheduled activities, but the real attraction is the natural stone terrace for whale-watching.

Eight kilometers further northeast, the **Marine Environment Discovery Centre** (41 Rue des Pilotes; adult/child $7.80/3.90; ⊙9am-6pm mid-Jun–early Sep, 9am-6pm Fri-Sun early Sep-early Oct) has sophisticated facilities such as a video link with naturalist-divers foraging on the estuary floor.

Outside of Les Escoumins, 12km northeast of Les Bergeronnes on Rte 138, is Essipit, an Innu community. The **Essipit Centre** (☑418-233-2266, 888-868-6666; 46 Rue de la Réserve; ⊙7am-11pm) sells local crafts and makes reservations for a campground and chalets. The center offers whale-watching cruises at slightly lower prices than in Tadoussac (Zodiac tours from $50). Blue whales are more likely to be seen in this area.

At **Camping Paradis Marin** (☑418-232-6237; 4 Chemin Émile Boulianne; campsites from $12; ⊙mid-May–mid-Oct), off Rte 138 northeast of town, you can hear whales breathing from your tent (or wigwam) and rent kayaks.

L'Anse St Jean

Heading west up the Saguenay is a fine drive on either side of the fjord. There are more good stops on the south side and there's more access to the river, but the north shore is memorable for its rugged topography and little lakes strung along the roadside.

First stop on the south side is L'Anse St Jean, a sleepy village where the most activity seems, at first, to be in a local crafting a roll-up cigarette. However, there's a lot going on in the alternative community's *ateliers,* as well as the Parc du Saguenay trails, water-based activities and **Mont Édouard**, Saguenay's highest summit. There are marvelous fjord views at **L'Anse de Tabatière**.

◉ Sights & Activities

Croisière Personnalisée Saguenay
CRUISES
(☑418-272-2739; 15 Rue du Faubourg; ⊙Jul-Sep) Among several cruise options, this one offers one- to four-hour cruises ($35 to $65) in a seven-person motorboat, taking in the fjord and beluga whales.

Fjord en Kayak
KAYAKING
(☑418-272-3024; www.fjord-en-kayak.ca; 359 Rue St Jean Baptiste; 3hr tour $50) Offers great excursions lasting from two hours to five days.

Centre Équestre des Plateaux
HORSEBACK RIDING
(Equestrian Center; ☑418-242-3231; 34 Chemin des Plateaux; per hr $30) Has horses, ponies and even a horse-drawn sleigh for winter fun. It's signposted up the hill from Rue St Jean.

🛏️ Sleeping & Eating

L'Auberge du BoutduMonde
INN $
(☑418-272-9979; www.boutdumonde.ca; 40 Chemin des Plateaux; dm/r $25/50) It does indeed feel like it's at the end of the world, secluded on the steep hill (even by car it's a challenge). The former eco-commune, built using whatever was available, has recently been renovated by its new owners: five 20-somethings who grew up here. Yoga classes, a cultural center, a lake, a herbal garden and forest are on the doorstep. As breakfast is not served, be sure to stock up on groceries before arriving. Cash only.

Auberge des Cévennes
INN $$
(☑418-272-3180, 877-272-3180; www.auberge-des-cevennes.qc.ca; Rue St Jean Baptiste; r

$57-99) You can hear the river gurgling across the street at this lovely inn, with a **restaurant** (meals $28) overlooking the covered bridge, near to the dock.

Les Gîtes du Fjord   INN **$$**
(☑418-272-3430, 800-561-8060; www.lesgites-dufjord.com; 354 Rue St Jean Baptiste; studios/ condos/cottages from $81/116/188; ﹡) Accommodations ranging from studios to condos to hillside cabins of varying sizes and amenities. It overlooks the marina and has its own quality **restaurant** (meals $26).

Bistro de L'Anse   PUB **$$**
(319 Rue St Jean Baptiste; meals $13-22; ⊙3pm-1am mid-May–mid-Oct) The local hub where you can catch live music on Saturday nights and tuck into sandwiches, salad and pasta on the verandah.

❶ Getting There & Away

L'Autobus L'Anse St Jean (p288) runs a minibus to Chicoutimi.

Rivière Éternité

The town itself is rather lacking in anything other than unlikely collections of religious art, but it is one of the main access points for both the Saguenay-St Lawrence Marine Park and Parc du Saguenay. Contact the Rivière Éternité–based **park information office** (☑418-272-1556, 800-665-6527; 91 Rue Notre Dame; ⊙9am-6pm late Jun-early Sep, to 4pm mid-May–late Jun & early Sep-early Oct) about trips, trails, sea kayaking, sailing, Zodiac outings and numerous ᴍᴜᴍᴜᴜᴜᴜ ᴜᴜᴜᴜᴜᴜᴜᴜ.

A four-hour-return hike, including a brutally long staircase, leads to an 8m-tall statue of the **Virgin Mary**. She looms on one of the fjord's highest cliffs, protecting the sailors and boats below. Charles Robitaille erected it in 1881, having narrowly escaped death the previous winter when his horse crashed through the ice on the river. Vowing to honor the Virgin Mary for saving his life, he commissioned the 3200kg statue, which took over a week to cart and assemble.

Back in town, the **church** has a renowned collection of 250 Christmas manger vignettes. Nearby, over the wooden bridge off Rte 170, the **Halte des Artistes** is a free, drive-through park containing sculptures in little mangers.

Chicoutimi

This regional center is a pleasant place to take care of chores before returning to the Saguenay wilds. The site of a 1676 fur-trading post, it was founded as late as 1842, and became a world pulp and paper capital in the early 20th century. It looks rather industrial from the approach roads, but downtown buzzes with students from the town's university and Cégep (pre-university college).

The helpful staff at the **tourist office** (☑418-698-3157, 800-463-6565; 295 Rue Racine Est; ⊙8:30am-4:30pm Mon-Thu, to 8pm Fri, 10am-4pm Sat & Sun) speak good English.

◎ Sights & Activities

La Pulperie   INDUSTRIAL MUSEUM
(www.pulperie.com; 300 Rue Dubuc; adult/child $10/4; ⊙9am-6pm late Jun-early Sep, 10am-4pm Wed-Sun early Sep-late Jun) This was once the world's biggest pulp mill. A guided tour and exhibitions explain the mill's history and its pivotal role in the development of a town that increased its population from 708 in 1899 to 4255 in 1929. The site also features the **House of Arthur Villeneuve**, now a museum. The barber-artist painted the entire building inside and out like a series of canvases in his bright, naive folk style.

Musée de la Petite Maison Blanche
                                                     MUSEUM
(Little White House; 240 Rue Bossé; adult/child $4.50/3.10; ⊙8am-8pm Jun-Aug, 10am-4pm Sep) Nearby, also in the area known as 'the Basin,' is the spindly Musée de la Petite ᴍᴀᴜᴜᴜ ᴜᴜᴜᴜᴜᴜᴜ ᴜᴜᴜ ᴜᴜ ᴜᴜᴜᴜ. ᴛᴜᴜ ᴜᴜᴜᴜᴜ withstood water with a force equivalent to Niagara Falls in a 1996 flood that caused $16 billion of damage to Chicoutimi.

🛏 Sleeping & Eating

Auberge Racine   B&B **$$**
(☑418-543-1919; 334 Rue Racine Est; s/d $85/95; ℙ) In this 19th-century house, the delightful rooms have original details and are named after some of the first owner's three wives and 12 children.

Artis Resto Lounge   ITALIAN **$$**
(416 Rue Racine Est; mains $10-18; ⊙4pm-late Mon-Fri, 8am-3am Sat & Sun) With its popular terrace, Artis serves typical Italian fare, but is nonetheless more interesting than the pubs nearby.

❶ Getting There & Away

Intercar (☎418-543-1403; 55 Rue Racine Est) buses connect to Québec City, Montréal and Tadoussac. **L'Autobus L'Anse St Jean** (☎418-272-1397) runs a minibus down the Saguenay to L'Anse St Jean on Monday, Tuesday, Thursday and Friday.

Lac St Jean

Motorists crossing the nondescript flats between Chicoutimi and Lac St Jean may wonder if the area is popular among Québécois for quasi-political reasons alone. The region touts itself as the heartland of Québec nationalism. However, upon reaching the lake, there is a subtle beauty to this open area, where the meeting of sky and water is interrupted only by pale wooden houses and shining church spires. The area also claims to be the province's blueberry and *tourtière* (meat pie) capital; look out for chocolate-covered blueberries.

◉ Sights & Activities

Véloroute des Bleuets   TRAIL
The 272km of cycling trails around the lake combine to form the **Blueberry Bike Trail**, and nearly every town along the way has facilities to make the trip easier: rental and repair shops, B&Bs that cater to cyclists and rest areas. For maps, suggested itineraries and a list of helpful stops, visit the **Maison du Vélo** (Bicycle Tourism Information Center; ☎418-668-4541; www.veloroute-bleuets. qc.ca; 1692 Ave du Pont) in Alma.

Village Historique Val Jalbert   HISTORIC SITE
(95 Rue St Georges; adult/child $23/11.50; ⊙9:30am-5:30pm Jun-Sep, last admission 4pm) The Val Jalbert Historic Village is a ghost town that was inhabited from 1901 until a few years after the pulp mill closed in 1927. There's a trolleybus with running commentary from one of the zealous, costume-wearing guides, and a pleasant restaurant in the old mill by the dramatic waterfall. The peaceful spot also has a campground and cabins.

Mashteuiatsh   MUSEUM
North of Roberval on the lakeshore, one of the province's best-organized aboriginal villages is home to the **Musée Amérindien de Mashteuiatsh** (www.museeilnu.ca; 1787 Rue Amishk; adult/child $10/6; ⊙9am-6pm mid-May–mid-Oct, 8am-noon & 1-4:30pm Mon-Thu, to 3pm Fri mid-Oct–mid-May), featuring good exhibits on the area's Pekuakamiulnuatsh group.

⊨ Sleeping

Auberge Île du Repos   CAMPGROUND/HOSTEL
(☎418-347-5649; 105 Rte Île du Repos; campsites $18.50, dm $30, r from $55) Taking up an entire little island off Péribonka and Parc de la Pointe Taillon, Auberge Île du Repos is a resort featuring dorms, kitchen facilities, private chalet rooms, camping, a cafebar, a beach, croquet and volleyball. With the closest Intercar terminal in Dolbeau-Mistassini, some 25km northwest, it can be a little ghostly despite its cheery pink facade.

Ste Rose du Nord

On the Saguenay River's less-frequented north side, Ste Rose du Nord is a member of the Association of the Most Beautiful Villages of Québec. Wander beneath the purple cliffs to the quay with the fjord beyond and it's easy to see why.

Above the village on Rue de la Montagne, there are short walks through the trees to viewing points.

Signposted off Rte 172 between Ste Fulgence and Ste Anne du Rose, **Pourvoirie du Cap au Leste** (☎418-675-2000; www. capauleste.com; 551 Chemin du Cap à l'Est; s $77-142, d $104-192) is worth the bumpy 7km of side road for its dramatic views over a large stretch of the fjord. The frugal but charming cabins have wood burners and balconies, and the restaurant serves superb regional cuisine (meals $30); nonguests should reserve. Hiking, canoeing, kayaking, climbing and mountain biking can be organized.

You can pitch your tent on a hill at **Camping Descente des Femmes** (☎418-675-2581; 154 Rue de la Montagne; campsites $18-23) and wake up to a view over the village and onto the fjord. The showers and toilets are in a converted grange, and the owner's a hoot.

SOUTH SHORE

It's tempting to rush through the South Shore, which includes the Chaudière-Apalaches and Bas St Laurent regions, en route to the Gaspé Peninsula. However, the area has a wonderfully eclectic mix of attractions, from haunting Grosse Île to refined Rivière du Loup, which respectively tell of the colonial era's losers and winners. Other stops include a major woodcarving center, an island once used as a smugglers' stash, and museums devoted to a *Titanic*-like tragedy, Basque whalers and squeezeboxes.

Added to this are the spectacular views across the island-dotted St Lawrence to the undulating North Shore. Hwy 20 is fastest but Rte 132 is more scenic and goes through the heart of numerous riverside villages.

Grosse Île

The first stop outside Québec City's urban sprawl is one of the region's most interesting. Grosse Île served as the major **quarantine station** for immigrants arriving from Europe from 1832 to 1937. The tour of the island sheds light on this little-known aspect of North American history, through visits to the disinfecting chambers, the original hospital and immigrants' living quarters, and the memorial cemetery which holds the remains of 7500 people. The tragic histories lived out on the island are cleverly, and at times movingly, explained by guides. A 14.5m Celtic cross, the tallest in the world, commemorates the 76,000 Irish immigrants wiped out by a typhus epidemic in 1847. You'll also be told about the island's 600 species of flora, 21 of them rare.

⊙ Sights & Activities

Grosse Île National Historic Site

BOAT TOURS

(📞418-234-8841, 888-773-8888; ⊙mid-May–mid-Oct) Berthier sur Mer marina, 55km northeast of Québec City on Rte 132 (also accessible via Hwy 20), is the closest departure point for the boat tours to Grosse Île. Times and prices are determined by the boat tour operators.

It is also possible to visit the 21-island **Île aux Grues** archipelago (p289). For all trips, wear warm clothing and comfortable shoes.

Croisières Lachance CRUISES

(☑418-259-2140, 888-476-7734; www.croisieres lachance.com; 110 Rue de la Marina, Berthier sur Mer; adult/child tours $46.50/25) Offers two daily tours: a narrated return cruise and a Parks Canada–guided walk.

Croisières les Coudrier CRUISES

(☑418-692-0107, 888-600-5554; www.crois ierescoudrier.qc.ca; Pier 19, 180 rue Dalhousie,

Vieux Port, Québec City; adult/child tours $70/30) Operates tours from Québec City, Île d'Orléans and Ste Anne de Beauprè on the north shore.

Montmagny

The main reason to stop beneath the green copper steeple in Montmagny, the first town of any size east of Lévis, is to go to **Île aux Grues**. This 10km-long island, part of an otherwise uninhabited 21-island archipelago, has one of North America's largest unspoiled wetlands. Birders flock to the area in spring and autumn to spot migratory birds including snow geese. The island has a couple of **walking trails**. **Ferries** (two to four daily, April to December, free) leave from Montmagny marina for the 25-minute crossing. Other commercial excursions to the archipelago are also possible.

In Montmagny is the **Centre des Migrations** (Migration Educational Center; 53 Ave du Bassin Nord; admission free; ⊙10am-5pm Jun-Sep), an interpretive center with exhibits on migration, feathered and human, to Grosse Île and the South Shore.

The **Accordion Museum** (301 Blvd Taché; adult/child $6/2; ⊙10am-4pm late Jun-early Sep, 10am-4pm Mon-Fri early Sep-late Jun), North America's only one, gives an insight into this giant of the Gallic music scene. Squeezeboxes date back to 1820, and incorporate materials such as ivory and mother-of-pearl. In late August, the four-day **Carrefour** features performances by squeezebox aficionados from around the globe.

St Jean Port Joli

St Jean became known as a center of craftsmanship in the 1930s, a reputation it works hard to keep. Riverside Parc des Trois Berets, named after the three beret-wearing brothers who launched the town as a woodcarving capital, is the venue for an international **sculpture festival** in June.

There are scores of *ateliers,* boutiques and roadside pieces, covered by a free map available from the seasonal **tourist office** (☑418-598-3747; Rte 132). **Musée des Anciens Canadiens** (332 Rte 132 Ouest; adult/child $6/3; ⊙9am-5:30pm May-Jun, 8:30am-9pm Jul-early Sep, 9am-6pm early Sep-Oct) has over 250 wood-carved figures from René Lévesque to Harry Potter, providing a good introduction to the work of the beret-clad Bourgaults and other local notables.

Philippe-Aubert de Gaspé, author of *Les Anciens Canadiens,* is buried in the 18th-century **church.**

🛏 Sleeping & Eating

La Maison de l'Ermitage B&B $$
(☎418-598-7553; www.maisonermitage.com; 56 Rue de l'Ermitage; r incl breakfast $75-105) This eye-catching house with red-and-white towers hides artfully decorated rooms inside, which have either private or shared bathrooms. The friendly alpaca in the backyard is popular with kids.

Gîte La Merveille B&B $$
(☎418-598-3112; www.gite-lamerveille.com; 261 Rue Lionel Groulx; s incl breakfast $65, d $85-110; 🅿) In a leafy garden near the quay, this family-run hotel is one of the only ones not overlooking Rte 132.

Camping de la Demi Lieue CAMPGROUND $
(☎418-598-6108, 800-463-9558; 598 Rte 132; campsites from $26; @🅿) Huge but well equipped and closer to town than the other campgrounds.

La Boustifaille QUÉBÉCOIS $$
(547 Rte 132 Est; meals $12-20; ⏰8am-8pm May-Oct) Renowned for huge portions of local classics such as pork ragout, *tourtière* and cheese quiche, and its adjacent theater.

Pizzeria Porto Bellissimo ITALIAN $
(318 Rue de l'Église; meals $5-14; ⏰11am-8pm; 🖉) For homemade pizzas, sandwiches and decadent desserts in a bright and cheery atmosphere, this cafe in the center of town is a smart choice.

ℹ Getting There & Away

Orléans Express buses stop in the center of town at Épicerie Régent Pelletier, 10 Rte 132. There are two daily buses to/from Québec City ($33, 2½ hours).

Rivière du Loup

Its curious name (the Wolf River) either refers to seals (sea wolves), an Amerindian tribe or a 17th-century French ship, but one thing is certain: Rivière du Loup is a town of some distinction. Its key position on the fur and postal routes between the Maritimes and the St Lawrence made it the main town in eastern Québec during the 19th century. Formerly an English-speaking town, it was

planned according to the British model, with open spaces in front of grand buildings such as the Gothic silver-roofed St Patrice. Having declined in the early 20th century, it's booming again, with one of the province's highest birthrates, as well as an influx of urban runaways and graduates returning to their beautiful birthplace.

The **tourist office** (☎418-862-1981; www.tourismeriviereduloup.ca; 189 Blvd de l'Hôtel de Ville; ⏰8:30am-9pm late Jun-early Sep, 8:30am-4:30pm Mon-Fri early Sep-late Jun) has internet access and a free Old Town walking map.

⊙ Sights

Parc des Chutes LANDMARK
Short trails make the most of the small but seductive Parc des Chutes, a few minutes' walk from downtown at the end of Rue Frontenac. If you get lost, just follow the sounds of the cars and the 30m waterfalls that power a small hydroelectric power station.

Parc de la Croix PARK
A short drive into the hilly part of town leads to tiny Parc de la Croix, where an illuminated cross guards a stunning view across town and the river. To get there from downtown, take Rue Lafontaine south to the underpass leading to Rue Témiscouata. Make a left on Chemin des Raymond, then turn left at Rue Alexandre, right at Rue Bernier and left at Rue Ste Claire.

Musée du Bas St Laurent MUSEUM
(300 Rue St-Pierre; adult/child $5/3; ⏰9am-6pm late Jun-early Sep, 1-5pm Wed-Sun early Sep-late Jun) The lively Musée du Bas St Laurent has a collection of contemporary Québec art, but the main event is the 200,000 vintage photos of the local area, used in thematic, interactive exhibits that explore life on the St Lawrence.

Fraser Manor NOTABLE BUILDING
(www.manoirfraser.com; 32 Rue Fraser; adult/child $6/2; ⏰9:30am-5pm late Jun-Sep) Rivière du Loup was called Fraserville in the 19th century, named after the powerful Scottish dynasty that inhabited the grand Fraser Manor. This gives an insight into life in the upper echelons of the developing colony.

🏃 Activities

La Société Duvetnor CRUISE
(☎418-867-1660; www.duvetnor.com; 200 Rue Hayward) Offshore, a series of protected islands sport bird sanctuaries and provide habitat for other wildlife. The nonprofit group La

Société Duvetnor offers bird-watching and nature excursions to the islands. Sighting belugas is common. There are 45km of trails on the largest island, 13km-long l'Île aux Lièvres, and accommodations including a campground. Prices start at $25 for a 1½-hour cruise to Pot au l'Eau de Vie (the brandy pot), named for its use as a bootlegging way station during the prohibition era.

Croisières AML CRUISE
(☑418-867-3361, 800-563-4643; 200 Rue Hayward; 3hr tours $60; ☺mid-Jun–mid-Oct) For whale-watching there's Croisières AML. If you're crossing the river to Tadoussac, save your trip for there.

Rivière du Loup/Saint Siméon Ferry
FERRY
(www.traversedl.com; adult/child round trip $15.80/10.50) You can take a return trip on the St Siméon ferry without disembarking (three hours). Beluga whales are commonly spotted.

Petit Témis Interprovincial
Linear Park PARK
The Petit Témis Interprovincial Linear Park is a scenic bike and walking trail, mainly flat, which runs along an old train track for 135km to Edmundston, New Brunswick. The tourist office has maps and **Hobby Cycles** (278 Rue Lafontaine) rents bikes.

🛏 Sleeping

Rue Fraser is a good place to look for motels. If you're catching an early morning ferry, there are campgrounds and B&Bs near the marina.

Auberge Internationale HOSTEL $
(☐418-862-7566; www.aubergedl.ca in French; 46 Blvd de l'Hotel de Ville; dm members/nonmembers $20/24; r $52/56; Ⓟ@) This excellent, central HI hostel in an old house has small dorms with en suite bathrooms. The long-term staff create a placid, welcoming atmosphere. A continental breakfast is included with the rate.

Auberge St Patrice MOTEL $$
(☑418-867-4630; 165 Rue Fraser; r $65-115) Behind its balcony, pavilion and flowerpots, this attractive new establishment has 16 rooms of various sizes with fridges. Most of the room choices are no more than clean, basic motel rooms, although a few boast rustic allure with wooden furniture, fireplaces and exposed brick.

Au Vieux Fanal MOTEL $$
(☑418-862-5255; www.motelauvieuxfanal.com; 170 Rue Fraser; r $55-120; ☺May-Nov; ❋ ≋)

One of the best motels on the strip is this multicolored place with great views of the river and a heated swimming pool.

L'Innocent INN $
(☑418-714-2096; 460 Rue Lafontaine; r $35) This paint-splashed cafe has four simple, tiny double rooms with shared bathrooms.

🍴 Eating

Chez Antoine FRENCH $$
(433 Rue Lafontaine; lunch/dinner mains from $16/20; ☺11am-2pm & 5-9pm Mon-Fri, 5-9pm Sat & Sun) Long considered the best in town, it maintains its tradition. Specialties include Atlantic salmon, shellfish and filet mignon, served in an old white house with a classy dining room enrobed in wood paneling.

L'Innocent CAFE $$
(460 Rue Lafontaine; meals $10-15; ☺10am-10pm Mon-Fri, from 8am Sat & Sun) The hippest cafe around serving great-value daily specials to a ska soundtrack. It's the best place in town to meet locals; and if you're in a hurry, they serve coffee to go.

Picolo Piazza ITALIAN $$
(371 Rue Lafontaine; mains $13-25; ☺5-11pm Tue-Sun) Fourteen types of pizza and dishes such as the recommended sole stuffed with scallops and crab are served in a great atmosphere. Pause at the bar for a beer cocktail before taking a seat in the ramshackle conservatory.

L'Estaminet PUB $$
(299 Rue Lafontaine; mains $10-20; ☺10am-midnight or 1am) You can feast on hearty pub grub and specials, including house specialty mussels with fries, in this 'bistro du monde' with 150 types of beer.

L'Intercolonial FUSION $$
(407 Rue Lafontaine; mains $10-20; ☺11:30am-2:30pm & 5-9:30pm mid-Mar–Dec) The name refers to the train that once stopped in Rivière du Loup, but it's also a good description of a menu featuring European dishes, Asian flavors and creations that could only come from the Québécois imagination, such as salmon with pear cream.

ℹ Getting There & Away

Hwy 20 (exit 503), Rte 132 and Hwy 85 lead directly into Rivière du Loup.

Orléans Express arrives at/departs from the **bus station** (317 Blvd de l'Hôtel de Ville). It has five buses daily to/from Québec City ($42, 2¼ to four hours) and four daily to/from Rimouski ($33, 1½ hours); transfer there for New Brunswick.

Rivière du Loup is linked by **VIA Rail** (☎418-867-1525, 888-842-7245; 615 Rue Lafontaine) six times a week to Charny, Québec City ($67, 2½ hours) and Halifax ($167, 15 hours), and three times a week to Percé ($112, 11 hours). The station is only open when the trains arrive, in the middle of the night.

A ferry runs between Rivière du Loup marina and St Siméon (see p283).

Le Témis

Le Témis is the name affectionately given to a region concentrated around its main geographical feature, the 40km-long Lac Témiscouata. The sleepy, unexplored area is perfect for a Sunday drive.

Rte 185 passes mills and farms cradled between the low-lying hills, giving a foretaste of New Brunswick. **St Louis du Ha! Ha!** possibly owes its odd name to an archaic French word for something unexpected, or to the exclamation of wonder the area's colonizers uttered upon seeing such beauty. We favor another explanation: the name comes from a 15th-century French expression for 'dead end.'

Moving swiftly on, there are motels in **Cabano**, and some pleasant restaurants on the waterfront. **Fort Ingall** (☎418-854-2375, 866-242-2437; 81 Rue Caldwell; adult/child $9/7; ☉10am-4pm Mon-Fri Jun & Sep, 9am-5pm daily Jul & Aug) is a 1973 reconstruction of an 1839 British fort set up to keep out Americans who had set their sights on the area. The six buildings include the blockhouse with its 'whipping horse.' If you want to empathize with the poor soldiers who were stationed here, you can stay the night – **accommodation** (campsites $22, dorms $20).

The hourly ferry ride between Notre Dame du Lac and St Juste du Lac is a fine summer diversion. If you miss it, there are good views up the slender lake from Rte 185.

On the northeast side of the lake in Auclair, you can taste the country's first alcoholic drinks made from a maple sap base at *économusée* **Domaine Acer** (145 Rte du Vieux Moulin; guided tours $4; ☉9am-5pm Apr–mid-Oct, 9am-5pm Mon-Fri mid-Oct–Mar). Made on-site, the aperitifs' name comes from *acer*, the Latin for maple. The gift shop also sells maple jelly, which is delicious on toast. Tours take in the aging cellars and demonstrate how maple sap is turned into syrup. There are English signs throughout the facility and some guides speak a little English.

Île Verte

For some respite from the road, which thins to one lane after Rivière du Loup but is busy as far as Rimouski, take the 15-minute ferry crossing to Île Verte.

Summer cottages have only recently begun creeping onto the 11km-long island, which has a permanent population of 45. It's popular for birding, cycling, whale-watching and, in the winter, ice fishing.

In the last 10 years, the island has gained some culinary celebrity for *l'agneau de pré-salé* (salt water lamb). This comes from sheep that graze on the flats during low tide. The animals have more muscle and less fat than other sheep, and their meat is more tender and flavorful. The specialty can be tried on the island at the 'salt water lamb ambassador,' **La Maison d'Agathe** (meals from $31; ☉end Jun-early Sep).

The river's oldest **lighthouse** (1809) contains a museum and you can stay in the adjacent cottages, **Les Maisons du Phare** (☎418-898-2730; s/d incl breakfast $57/74; ☉mid-May–mid-Oct). There's also a campground.

Ferries (☎418-898-2843; tickets $7) shunt between the island and mainland according to tides.

Consider renting a bike and leaving the car on the mainland. Reservations are recommended.

Trois Pistoles

On the northern outskirts of Trois Pistoles, a village memorable only for pretty much every business name referring to its Basque heritage, rises the blue-and-red **Parc de l'Aventure Basque en Amérique** (66 Ave du Parc; adult/child $7/3; ☉noon-4pm late May-late Jun, 10am-8pm late Jun-late Sep). Inside, an exhibition tells the story of the Basque whalers who were the first Europeans after the Vikings to navigate the St Lawrence, predating Jacques Cartier. The exhibits are in French only, but an English booklet is available. In July, the museum hosts the **International Basque Festival**, with music, a small parade and games.

Outside is Canada's only **pelote court**, or *fronton*, where the Basque sport, one of the world's oldest bat and ball games, is played.

Pelote aficionados travel from as far afield as Montréal to use the court; *palas* (bats), *pelotes* (balls) and the court can be rented for $5 per hour.

Inquire at the Parc de l'Aventure Basque en Amérique about guided excursions to **Île aux Basques** (☑418-851-1202; Marina; adult/child $2/free; ☉Jun-early Sep), 5km offshore, with its 16th-century Basque ovens, 2km of trails and bird refuge. Admission is by tour only; **Kayak des Îles** (☑418-851-4637; Ave du Parc) runs sea-kayaking expeditions.

Camping & Motel des Flots Bleus Sur Mer (☑418-851-3583; Rte 132; tent & RV $20, r $60; ☉May–mid-Oct), 5km west of town, is a small, quiet campground with a neighboring bare-bones motel.

On a hill above the church near hiking rails and waterfalls, **La Rose des Vents** (☑418-851-4926, 888-593-4926; 80 2ème Rang Ouest; s/d incl breakfast $60/80), a lovely old place with a modified roofline, has a breakfast room with huge windows gazing at the North Shore.

Parc du Bic

This 33-sq-km park, half covered by water, is both one of the smaller parks in Québec and among the most beautiful. A striking sight even from Rte 132, its rotund headlands that shelter bays and islands have provided sanctuary for aboriginal peoples dating back 9000 years, colonial vessels and a multitude of flora and fauna. There are 700 types of plants, thousands of marine birds, seals (between July and October), deer and one of North America's highest-density porcupine populations.

The **park** (☑418-736-5035; 3382 Rte 132; adult/child $4.80/2.50; ☉late May–mid-Oct & mid-Dec–Mar) has an excellent interpretation center. The activities on offer, most of which the helpful staff can organize, include excellent hiking, mountain biking, sea kayaking, guided walks and drives, wildlife observation by day and night, snowshoeing and Nordic skiing. The two-hour-return trail to **Champlain Peak** (346m) rewards with views across to Îlet au Falcon; the park runs a shuttle there.

The park has three campgrounds, igloos, a hut and even a luxurious yurt. Avoid the noisy campground by Rte 132.

Rimouski

A fairly large, oil-distribution town, Rimouski has a prosperous air and some of the best cafes and museums found between here and Gaspé. The student population gives it some atmosphere, making it a reasonable place to do chores or wait for a ferry.

On Place des Veterans, at the intersection of Rue St Germain and Ave de la Cathédrale, is the busy but helpful **tourist office** (☑418-723-2322; www.tourisme-rimouski.org; 50 Rue St Germain Ouest; ☉8:30am-7:30pm mid-Jun–early Sep, 9am-noon & 1-4:30pm Mon-Fri early Oct–mid-Jun).

⊙ Sights & Activities

Musée de la Mer MUSEUM
(www.shmp.qc.ca; 1034 Rue du Phare; adult/child $14.50/8; ☉9am-6pm Jun-Aug, to 5pm Sep-early Oct) Seven kilometers east of town is the Musée de la Mer, which narrates the *Empress of Ireland* tragedy, the worst disaster in maritime history after the *Titanic*. In the 14 minutes it took for the ship to disappear into the St Lawrence after colliding with a Norwegian collier, 1012 people lost their lives. The disaster was all but forgotten in the outbreak of WWI two months later.

On the same campus, you can join a guided tour and climb 128 steps up **Pointe au Père Lighthouse** (adult/child $4/3), the highest in eastern Canada. The former keeper's cottage has displays on navigating the river and diving to the *Empress*, 45m down.

The wreck itself is considered one of the world's premier **scuba diving** sites. However, this is a dangerous dive; several inexperienced divers have died. Currents, visibility and water temperature are serious challenges.

Musée Régional de Rimouski ART GALLERY
(www.museerimouski.qc.ca; 35 Rue St Germain Ouest; adult/child $5/3; ☉9:30am-8pm Wed-Fri, to 6pm Sat-Tue Jun-Sep, noon-5pm Wed-Sun Oct-May) In a renovated stone church, this gallery has contemporary art exhibitions and regular events including film nights.

Le Canyon des Portes de l'Enfer LANDMARK
(Chemin Duchénier; adult/child $9/5) For hiking, mountain biking and a view of a canyon and waterfalls from the province's highest suspended bridge (62m), head to Le Canyon des Portes de l'Enfer, near St Narcisse de Rimouski, 30km south of town along Rte 232.

🛏 Sleeping

Accommodations can be found on the waterfront and around Ave de la Cathédrale.

Auberge de la Vielle Maison　　INN $
(📞418-723-6010; 35 Rue St Germain Est; r incl breakfast $60-85; P🐾🛜) The rooms here are more attractive than the faded red exterior, overlooking a posse of pubs and clubs, suggests. Bathrobes and hardwood floors edge it toward the desired country home effect.

Auberge de l'Évêché　　INN $$
(📞418-723-5411; 37 Rue de l'Évêché Ouest; s/d incl breakfast $88/99; 🛜) Above a *chocolaterie* opposite the town hall, these eight rooms with TVs are attractively decorated with vintage photos.

🍴 Eating

Le Crêpe Chignon　　CAFE $$
(www.crepechignon.com; 140 Ave de la Cathédrale; meals $17-21; ⏰8am-10pm) This bright light on the Rimouski dining scene serves delicious savory and dessert crepes. The only drawback is there's often a wait for a table.

La Brûlerie d'Ici　　CAFE $
(91 Rue St Germain Ouest; sandwiches $6; ⏰8am-11pm) A hip hangout offering Guatemalan and Ethiopian coffees, bites from bagels to banana bread, wi-fi and live music during the summer.

Central Café　　CAFE $$
(31 Rue de l'Évêché Ouest; mains $12-16; ⏰11am-10pm Mon-Sat, 4-10pm Sun) Set in a two-story house built in 1947, this is where locals go to pig out on burgers, pasta, pizza and smoked-meat sandwiches.

❶ Getting There & Away

Boat

A **ferry** (📞418-725-2725, 800-973-2725) links Rimouski with Forestville on the North Shore. From May to early October, two to four boats make the 1¾-hour journey every day. The one-way fare is $25/19 per adult/child. A car is $40. Reservations are accepted.

The **Relais Nordik** (📞418-723-8787, 800-463-0680; www.relaisnordik.com; 17 Ave Lebrun) takes passengers on its weekly cargo ship to Sept Îles, Île d'Anticosti, Havre St Pierre, Natashquan and the Lower North Shore. It departs Rimouski marina at noon on Tuesday from early April to mid-January and gets to Blanc Sablon at 7pm Friday. Prices start at $244 for the full journey and range up to $714 for a deluxe cabin containing a porthole, toilet and

shower. Meals are available (breakfast/lunch/dinner $6.50/14/19) onboard and cars can be taken, although this is extremely costly ($411 each way) and a bicycle is more convenient at the brief stopovers. Reservations are best made months in advance.

Bus

Orléans Express buses leave from the **bus station** (90 Rue Léonidas) to Québec City ($60, four hours, four daily), Rivière du Loup ($33, 1½ hours, four daily) and Gaspé ($81, seven hours, three daily).

Car

Allô Stop (📞418-723-5248; www.allostop.com; 106 Rue St Germain Est) hooks up drivers with those that are requiring lifts to locations including Québec City ($16) and Montréal ($32).

Train

For VIA Rail services, the **train station** (57 Rue de l'Évêché Est) is only open when trains pull in, which is usually after midnight. Nine trains per week travel to/from Montréal ($140, eight hours).

GASPÉ PENINSULA

The promontory, which is known locally as 'La Gaspésie', is one of those remote rural areas that generates all manner of myths among folk who, generally speaking, have never been there. You can take these urban myths with a pinch of sea salt plucked from the St Lawrence gulf, but they do prove that Gaspé has well and truly etched itself into the Québécois imagination.

The remnants of a colorful colonial past can be seen on a coastline that bulges into the gulf, overlooking rusting shipwrecks and migratory whales. Like the whales, Normans, Bretons, Basques, Portuguese and Channel Islanders were attracted by the rich fishing grounds. English, Scottish and Irish fugitives from upheavals such as the Great Famine and American independence settled on the south shore, leaving isolated anglophone communities where the accents have more in common with the Old World lilts than classic Canadian cadence. Flags that were erected by the descendents of Acadian settlers flutter above Rte 132.

Between the small communities' colorful farm buildings and silver spires, the landscape is also striking. There's the famous pierced rock in Percé, of course, and

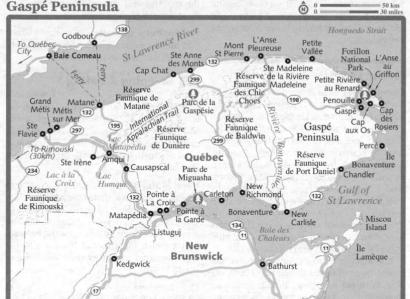

there are endless beaches overshadowed by glacier-patterned cliffs. The mountainous, forested hinterlands, home to the breathtaking Parc de la Gaspésie, are crossed by few routes, among them the Matapedia Valley drive, the International Appalachian Trail and Rte 198, one of the province's quietest roads.

In contrast with the brooding north shore, the southern Baie des Chaleurs, named after its relatively warm waters, has a flat, calm landscape. Come here to unwind after the emotional experience of the rest of Gaspé. Throughout the peninsula, the tourist season runs from about June to mid-September. Outside those times, things seriously wind down and, from November to mid-May, the main activity you'll see will be the waves crashing against the rocks.

Ste Flavie

The gateway to Gaspé is also one of the peninsula's most touristy towns. Nonetheless, it's a relaxing place to pause before tackling the rocky landscape that soon rises above Rte 132.

On Rte 132, the large **Tourisme Gaspésie office** (☎418-775-2223, 800-463-0323; 357 Rte de la Mer; ◷8am-8pm mid-Jun–mid-Sep,

8:30am-4:30pm mid-Sep–mid-Jun) is Gaspé's main tourist office. If you're here in the off-season, pick up the pamphlet listing winter facilities.

The 19th-century windmill **Vieux Moulin** (141 Rte de la Mer; admission free; ◷8am-9pm) offers tastings of Shakespeare's favorite tipple, mead, and has a small museum containing colonial and prehistoric aboriginal artifacts.

The star of the town's art trail is the **Centre d'Art Marcel Gagnon** (www.marcelgagnon. net; 564 Rte de la Mer; admission free; ◷7:30am-10pm May–mid-Oct, to 9pm mid-Oct–Apr). Outside, the extraordinary sculpture *The Great Gathering* has more than 100 stone figures filing out of the St Lawrence. Unfortunately, the gallery, displaying work by Gagnon and his son, feels a little too commercial, with all manner of *Great Gathering* souvenirs for sale.

Upstairs, the **auberge** (☎418-775-2829, 866-775-2829; r incl breakfast $79-109) has understatedly artistic rooms with private bathrooms. The **restaurant** (meals $13-25; ◷7:30am-8:30pm) serves pizza, pasta and a plethora of seafood with a great view.

Also overlooking the St Lawrence, **Capitaine Homard** (180 Rte de la Mer; meals $15-35; ◷11am-11pm May-Sep) has been the local 'kilometer 0' since 1968. It serves exquisite seafood beneath a Davy Jones' Locker–like ceiling, and offers internet access, camping and chalets.

Grand Métis

One of Gaspé's most revered attractions, the **Jardins de Métis** (www.refordgardens.com; 200 Rte 132; adult/child $16/free; ☺8:30am-5pm Jun & Oct, to 6pm Jul-Sep) comprises more than 90 hectares of immaculately tended gardens boasting 3000 varieties of plants. Begun in 1910, the gardens are also known as the Reford Gardens (after Elsie Reford, who inherited the land from her uncle, Lord Mount Stephen, founder of the CPR, and whose 37-room villa is now a museum). The International Garden Festival blooms here from late June to September. The villa and cafe serve lunch and English teas.

About 10km east of Grand Métis are the beach towns of **Métis Beach** and **Métis sur Mer**. With big lawns and British names on their street signs and mailboxes, they resemble American towns. Traditionally a retreat for the Anglophone bourgeoisie, the area has an 85% English-speaking population.

Matane

Matane is a commercial fishing port famous for its shrimp. While it's hardly the peninsula's prettiest town, it is popular for salmon fishing and for sampling local hauls in the markets and restaurants.

The **tourist office** (☎418-562-1065; www. tourismematane.com; 968 Ave du Phare Ouest; ☺9am-6pm Jun & Sep, to 9pm Jul & Aug) is based in a lighthouse alongside a maritime museum.

◉ Sights & Activities

Observation Center   FISHING
(260 Ave St Jerômé; adult/child $3/free; ☺7:30am-9:30pm mid-Jun–Aug, 8am-8pm Sep) Salmon weighing up to 19kg swim up the Rivière Matane to spawn in June. The observation center at the dam is worth a visit before or after dinner. It sells permits to fish the 100km river starting right in town.

Absolu Écoaventure   HIKING
(www.ecoaventure.com) This outfitter organizes advanced and beginners' hikes on part of the International Appalachian Trail (see the boxed text, p304), which cuts through the wild, rugged Réserve Faunique de Matane. Reserve online.

Poissonnerie Boréalis   MARKET
(985 Rte 132; ☺8am-6pm) A good choice for fish, fresh or smoked.

🛏 Sleeping & Eating

Camping Rivière   CAMPGROUND $
(☎418-562-3414; 150 Rte Louis Félix Dionne; tent & RV sites $22-30) Southwest of downtown, this campground has 145 secluded, private sites among the trees. From town, head south toward Amqui, on Rue Henri Dunant.

Hôtel Motel Belle   HOTEL $$
(☎418-562-2323; www.hotelbelleplage.com; 1310 Rue Matane sur Mer; s $62-118, d $67-149; 🐾) You can order smoked salmon and white wine to your room and dine on the balcony. Pretty swish for a motel! It's close to the ferry terminal and away from the noise of Rte 132.

La Seigneurie   B&B $$
(☎418-562-0021; 621 Ave St Jérôme; r $99-119) This friendly B&B occupies a grand property dating from 1919 with attic rooms, a grand piano and a freestanding bath in the 'lovers' room.'

Le Rafiot   SEAFOOD $$
(1415 Ave du Phare Ouest; mains $9-40; ☺11am-2pm Mon-Fri, 5-9pm daily) At this casual bistro with maritime-themed decor, seafood duos and trios abound.

ℹ Getting There & Away

Buses (☎418-562-4085; 521 Rte 132) arrive at and depart from the Irving gas station, 1.5km east of the town center. Two Orléans Express buses a day go to Gaspé ($39, five hours) and Rimouski ($26, 1½ hours).

A **ferry** (☎877-562-6560) links Matane with Baie Comeau and Godbout (see p283). The ferry terminal is off Rte 132, about 2km west of the town center.

Cap Chat

Cap Chat is a typical Gaspé village...apart from those 133 windmills beating above the white houses. This is Canada's largest wind farm and the world's most economical, producing 100 megawatts of electricity. Covering a 100km area, the dreamlike critters perch on hilltops above the start of the St Lawrence gulf. Dominating the gang is the world's largest vertical-axis windmill, which, alas, is no longer used.

If you'd like to take a one-hour tour, including the biggest windmill, contact **Éole Cap-Chat** (www.eolecapchat.com; tours $10; ⊙9am-5pm late Jun-Oct). Look for the signs on Rte 132 just west of Cap Chat. English tours are available.

Right off Rte 132 east of the bridge at Cap Chat, **Camping au Bord de la Mer** (☑418-786-2251; 173 Rue Notre Dame Est; tent & RV sites $20-26) is a simple campground offering river views.

Ste Anne des Monts

A regional service center at the turnoff for Parc de la Gaspésie, Ste Anne des Monts is the place to stock up, refuel and get a sea fix before heading inland to the wilderness.

The **tourist bureau** (☑418-763-7633; 96 Blvd Ste Anne Ouest; ⊙8am-8pm late Jun-Sep) is on Rte 132, next to the Orléans Express bus stop.

Off Rte 132 east of town, the funky HI member **Auberge Festive Sea Shack** (☑418-763-2999; www.aubergefestive.com; Ruisseau Castor; campsites $13-17, dm member/nonmember $25/29, cabins from $70; @⊚) is a highlight on the 'party hostel' circuit. Bands play at the beach bar and water lovers take out kayaks or gaze at the St Lawrence from the outdoor Jacuzzi.

La Seigneurie des Monts (☑418-763-5308; www.seigneurie-des-monts.com; 21 1-ère Ave Est; r $99-119), built in 1864, exudes a vintage atmosphere in its creaky floorboards, 'hip and horn' dropping sawno, antiquarian books and chaise longue.

Parc de la Gaspésie

From Ste Anne des Monts, Rte 299 runs south to this outstanding, rugged **park** (☑418-763-7494, 866-727-2427; www.sepaq.com/pq/gas/en; adult/child $3.50/free), 802 sq km of spectacular scenery dotted with lakes and two of Québec's most beautiful mountain ranges, the Chic Choc and McGerrigle Mountains, which together include 25 of the province's 40 highest summits. Some of Québec's most scenic camping spots are here, as well as 140km of hiking tracks, including one of the best sections of the International Appalachian Trail. What's more, the only herd of caribou south of the St Lawrence River lives in the park. If you're

lucky, you'll see the animals in the distance, but stay on the paths to protect them and the fragile vegetation.

At the park's **Interpretation Center** (⊙8am-10pm early Jun–mid-Sep), the staff are extraordinarily helpful in planning a schedule to match your time and budget. They also rent hiking equipment.

◎ Sights & Activities

Québec's second-highest peak, **Mont Jacques Cartier** (1270m), is also its highest accessible summit. Hiking the mountain takes about 3½ hours return, passing through alpine scenery with fantastic views and a good chance of spying woodland caribou. Other fabulous walks include the strenuous trek to the top of **Mont Albert** and the less-known, exhilarating half-day return trip up **Mont Xalibu**, with alpine scenery, mountain lakes and a waterfall on the way. **Mont Ernest Laforce** is good for moose, which also often feed at **Lac Paul** in the morning and evening.

⌦ Sleeping & Eating

Ste Anne des Monts makes a convenient base for the park. Overnight tent and RV sites cost $25 in the four campgrounds. The busiest serviced grounds are near the Interpretation Center; try for a spot at the quietest, Lac Cascapédia. Two- to eight-person **chalets** (from $138) are also available.

Gîte du Mont Albert   INN $$
(☑418-763-2288, 866-727-2427; r & cottages per person incl breakfast from $73; ⊙Jan-Oct; ✳@⊚) This is a large, comfortable lodge next to the Interpretation Center for those who like their nature spliced with luxury. Facilities include a pool, sauna and first-class restaurant with mountain views through the floor-to-ceiling windows.

❶ Getting There & Away

A bus runs from the Ste Anne des Monts tourist information center to the Interpretation Center. It leaves at 8am daily from late June to the end of September, returning at 4:45pm; the round-trip fare is $6/4 per adult/child. There is a daily service between the Interpretation Center and Mont Jacques Cartier trailhead ($14/10), and five daily shuttles between Mont Jacques Cartier campground and the trailhead ($6/4).

Driving to Mont St Pierre from the Interpretation Center, taking Rte 299 and the coastal Rte 132 is faster, safer and more scenic than the tree-lined track through the park.

Réserve Faunique des Chic Chocs

This reserve surrounds and bleeds into Parc de la Gaspésie. Mainly a site for hunting and fishing, it also attracts geological expeditions. Agates are common and you can go gem collecting at **Mont Lyall Mine** (adult/child $8/5; ☺9am-5pm Jun-Sep). To reach the main entrance, go south on Rte 299, 12km past the Gîte du Mont Albert, then east for 1.5km on the Rte du Lac Ste Anne toward Murdochville.

Mont St Pierre

The scenery becomes ever more spectacular east of Ste Anne des Monts. The North Shore, across the St Lawrence, disappears from view, and the road winds around rocky cliffs and waterfalls, every curve unveiling a stretch of mountains cascading to the sea.

Appearing after a dramatic bend in the road, Mont St Pierre takes its name from a 418m mountain with a cliff that's one of the best spots on the continent for **hang gliding** and **paragliding**. At the end of July, the 10-day hang-gliding festival **Fête du Vol Libre** fills the sky with hundreds of sails. Near the eastern end of town and south of Camping Municipal, rough roads climb Mont St Pierre, where there are take-off stations and excellent views. If you're not hoofing it up the mountain, which takes an hour, you must have an ATV.

Beneath the scree slopes of Mont St Pierre, **Camping Municipal** (✆418-797-2250; 103 Rte 2; tent & RV sites $23-30; ☺Jun–mid-Sep; ☒) is well equipped, with laundry facilities, a pool and a tennis court.

Parc de la Gaspésie and Réserve Faunique des Chic Chocs can be reached via Rte 2, which turns to gravel a few kilometers south of town. Take a map and watch out for logging trucks. If you're heading to the Interpretation Center, take the main roads (see p297).

East of Mont St Pierre

Eastbound, the landscape increases in majesty. Rte 132 winds around the base of cliffs, past telegraph poles protruding from mounds of scree, and surges over headlands. Watch for the viewpoints and picnic areas and be prepared for some strain on the engine and brakes.

Next to the lighthouse at **Ste Madeleine de la Rivière Madeleine** is a cafe with internet access, a fishing center and a museum about the local paper mill that employed over 1200 workers at its peak in 1921. As the road dips in and out of towering green valleys around **Grande Vallée**, there are more waves in the strata-lined cliff faces than in the calm bays on the other side of the road.

Petite Vallée is a quaint waterfront village, particularly around the blue-and-white **Théâtre de Vieille Forge** (✆418-393-2222; 4 Rue de la Longue-Pointe), the venue for much of the **Festival en Chanson** (☺late Jun-early Jul). This has become one of Québec's most important folk-song festivals, but has retained an intimate feel. Kids and even the local butcher participate impromptu on stage.

So you thought this was a peaceful area? Miniscule **St Yvon** was hit by a wayward torpedo in WWII.

For those not visiting Forillon National Park, Rte 197 runs south just past Petite Rivière au Renard, avoiding the end of the peninsula.

At **Cap des Rosiers**, the gateway to Forillon, the village's history of Irish, French and Channel Island settlers can be read in the epitaphs in the clifftop **Cimetière des Ancêtres**. The **lighthouse** is the highest in Canada.

Forillon National Park

Covering Gaspé's northeastern-most tip, this small **park** (www.pc.gc.ca/forillon; adult/child $7.80/3.90; ☺reception 10am-5pm early Jun–mid-Oct, park 24hr) feels a fitting place to end a journey along the top of the peninsula. Its rugged sea cliffs attract seabirds, including great blue herons, and whales and seals make frequent appearances offshore. Inland are rolling, forest-covered hills, where you might come across moose, deer, fox and, increasingly, black bears.

There are two main entrances with visitors centers where you can pick up maps: one at L'Anse au Griffon, east of Petite Rivière au Renard on Rte 132, and another on the south side of the park at Penouille.

◉ Sights & Activities

The north coast consists of steep limestone cliffs, some as high as 200m, and long pebble beaches, best seen at **Cap Bon Ami**. Keep a lookout through the telescope there for whales and seals. In the **North Sector**, south of Cap des Rosiers, you'll find a great picnic area with a small, rocky beach. The south coast features more beaches, some sandy, with small coves. **Penouille Beach** is said to have the warmest waters. The rare maritime ringlet butterfly flourishes in the salt marshes here, and the end of the curving peninsula is a prime sunset-watching spot.

The trails that meander through the park range from easy, 30-minute loops to a rigorous 18km trek that takes 6½ hours one way. The gentle hike east to **Cap Gaspé** provides seashore views. The International Appalachian Trail ends in the park, where the Appalachians plunge into the sea.

Parks Canada organizes activities (at least one a day in English) including a whale-watching cruise, sea kayaking, fishing, scuba diving and horseback riding.

🛏 Sleeping

Auberge Internationale Forillon HOSTEL $
(📞418-892-5153; www.aubergeforillon.com; 2095 Blvd Grande Grève, Cap aux Os; dm member/nonmember $20/24, r $42/50; ⊗May-Nov) This HI hostel makes a great base for explorers, with friendly staff who dole out walking advice. The restaurant offers overpriced, fairly average grub. The building could feel institutional when full, but that view across the bay is the ultimate redeeming feature. A *dépanneur* (convenience store), and bike and kayak rental, are nearby.

Forillon Campgrounds CAMPGROUND $
(📞866-787-6221; www.pccamping.ca; tent/RV sites $26/30; ⊗late May-Sep) The park contains 367 campsites in three campgrounds, and it often fills to capacity. Petit Gaspé is the most popular ground, as it is protected from sea breezes and has hot showers. Cap Bon Désir is the smallest, with 41 tent-only sites.

ℹ Getting There & Around

Transportation is limited. Orléans Express buses between Rimouski and Gaspé stop in the park daily during the summer, at locations including Cap des Rosiers and Cap aux Os. A drawback is that this still leaves a walk along Rte 132 to the hiking trails and campgrounds, though the bus driver may drop passengers within the park. During the summer, a shuttle runs between Penouille reception center and the beach ($1.50).

Gaspé

The most scenic aspect of the peninsula's nominal capital is its view of Forillon. However, it boasts two interesting attractions and could be a better place than touristy Percé to adjust to civilization after a few days in the park.

This was where Jacques Cartier first landed in July 1534. After meeting the Iroquois of the region, he boldly planted a wooden cross and claimed the land for the king of France.

⊙ Sights

Musée de la Gaspésie MUSEUM
(80 Blvd Gaspé; adult/child $7/4; ⊗9am-5pm Jun-Oct, 9am-5pm Tue-Fri, 1-5pm Sat Nov-May) Here you can get to grips with the peninsula's history, evoking its maritime heritage through artifacts such as a 17th-century hourglass. Most involving is the exhibition on Jacques Cartier, the former ship's boy who persuaded the French navy to back his 'voyage to that kingdom of the New World.' Outside, a bronze **monument** commemorates Cartier's landing.

Site d'Interpretation de la Culture Micmac de Gespeg MUSEUM
(783 Blvd Pointe Navarre; adult/child $8/3; ⊗9am-5pm Jun-Sep) Northwest of town, next to the **Notre Dame des Douleurs** church, a Catholic pilgrimage site, is this center which explains the culture and history of the local Mi'kmaq group through an exhibition, English and French tours (10am, 11am, 2pm and 3:30pm) and workshops.

🛏 Sleeping & Eating

Motel Adams MOTEL $$
(📞418-368-2244, 800-463-4242; www.moteladams.com; 20 Rue Adams; r $86-154; 🅿❄🛜) Central with 96 large units and a bar, restaurant. Orléans Express buses stop here.

Motel Plante MOTEL $$
(📞418-368-2254, 888-368-2254; 137 Rue Jacques-Cartier; r $80-130; @🛜) Atop a small hill overlooking downtown Gaspé with basic suites and studios with kitchens.

Café des Artistes CAFE $
(101 Rue de la Reine; sandwiches $7-11; ⊗7am-10pm) There's world music on the stereo, a list of teas and coffees as long as Gaspé and grub ranging from croissants to pizza.

Bistro Bar Brise-Bise CAFE **$$**
(135 Rue de la Reine; meals $10-20; ⊙11am-10pm) Devour pizzas, burgers and mussels while enjoying nightly entertainment.

ℹ Getting There & Away

Daily Air Canada flights link the small airport south of town with Îles de la Madeleine and Montréal via Québec City. VIA Rail trains from Montréal, via Charny at Québec City, run through the Matapédia Valley and along the south side of the peninsula to Gaspé (from $181, 18 hours) three nights a week.

Percé

Just when Gaspé's charms seemed to lurk deep in its national parks rather than in its towns, along comes Percé and its famous Rocher Percé (Pierced Rock). The 88m-high, 475m-long chunk of multihued limestone has inspired descriptive entries in travel journals dating back to Samuel de Champlain's captain's log of 1603.

One of Canada's best-known landmarks, the rock rears out of the sea near North America's largest migratory bird refuge, **Île Bonaventure**. Both sit in a patch of gulf that, from 1784, attracted schools of European cod fishers. Having stained a lobster bib, you can work off the fishy pounds with a hike in the hills, part of the Appalachians, that shelter the peninsula's most appealing town.

The **tourist office** (☑418-782-5448, 800-463-0323; 142 Rte 132; ⊙9am-5pm late May & Oct, to 6pm Jun & Sep, 8am-8pm Jul & Aug) is in the middle of town.

⊙ Sights & Activities

The town's landmark attraction, **Rocher Percé**, is accessible from the mainland at low tide only; a timetable is posted at the tourist information office. Signs warning of falling rocks should be taken seriously – each year, some 300,000kg of debris detach from the big rock. There used to be two holes in it, but one arch collapsed in 1845; in 2003, 100,000kg of debris fell at once. To get there, follow Rue du Mont Joli to the end and descend the stairs. Île Bonaventure cruises generally include the rock.

Access to the **Parc National** (4 Rue du Quai; adult/child $3.50/free; ⊙9am-5pm Jun–mid-Oct) campus, overlooking the rock, includes the reception, some of the surrounding waters, Île Bonaventure and an interpretation center covering local history, birdlife and geology.

A **boat trip** to meet over 100,000 gannets on green Île Bonaventure (see the boxed text, p302) is an active antidote to gorging on Percé's tempting fish platters. Head toward the dock and you'll come across the tour operators' booths and touts. Ask whether you can disembark at the island, or just sail around it. The bigger boats can't get as close to the attractions.

Club Nautique de Percé (199 Rte 132) offers kayak, bike and scuba diving tours and rentals. The heated pool might suit those who don't wish to brave the seas.

Above town are some great hikes around southern Gaspé's most rugged, hilly area. Hike up the 3km path to **Mont Ste Anne** (340m), beginning above the church, to enjoy the view and detour to **La Grotte** (The Cave). Another 3km trail leads to the **Great Crevasse**, a deep crevice in the mountain near Auberge du Gargantua. The tourist office gives out a useful map.

☞ Tours

Les Traversiers de l'Île BOAT
(☑418-782-5526; Rue du Quai; ⊙mid-Jun–Sep) One of three cruise companies, it offers a lobster fishing excursion and tours (adult/child $22/7) of Île Bonaventure, where you have the option of disembarking and walking the island's trails.

Taxi Percé JEEP
(☑418-782-2102; 16 Rue St Michel; ⊙Jun-Sep) Gives 2½-hour jeep tours of beauty spots such as Mont Ste Anne, La Grotte and Le Pic d'Aurore ($25), saving you the hike.

🛏 Sleeping

Accommodations here are fair bargains, though prices spike during midsummer, when visitor traffic is heavy, and booking ahead or finding a bed by early afternoon is recommended. The tourist office can help you find a place. Numerous motels and campgrounds, several with write-home-about views, lie close at hand. Tranquil Rue de l'Église has convenient, quality guesthouses with character. The following accommodations are open between May and October.

Gîte au Presbytère B&B **$$**
(☑418-782-5557; www.perce-gite.com; 47 Rue de l'Église; s/d incl breakfast $72/109) With a well-tended garden by the massive church,

this sizable, bright old rectory with gleaming hardwood floors is one of the best options. Friendly and gracious host Michel is a wealth of tourist knowledge and has an extra-soft spot for children.

Hôtel La Normandie
HOTEL $$

(☑418-782-2112, 800-463-0820; www.norman dieperce.com; 221 Rte 132 Ouest; r $89-399) The classiest spot in town, the retreatlike Normandie's amenities include the beach, room balconies, a dining room for seafood and expansive lawns with panoramic views of the rock.

Le Macareux
MOTEL $$

(☑418-782-2414, 866-602-2414; cnr Rte 132 & Rte des Failles; s/d from $35/70; P☎) Behind a breezy seaside exterior, the sparkling rooms with TVs and shared bathrooms are good value. Downstairs, the souvenir shop offers a 15% discount on boat tours.

La Maison Rouge
HOSTEL $

(☑418-782-2227; www.lamaisonrouge.ca; 125 Rte 132; dm/r $25/75; @) The red house of the title is actually a converted barn with three 10-bed dorms. Private rooms are in the adjacent 19th-century ancestral home, with its welcoming open fire. Laundry facilities and bike rental are available.

Le Coin du Banc
INN $

(☑418-645-2907; 315 Rte 132; s/d/chalet from $55/60/85) Beneath the low ceilings and horseshoe-adorned doorways of a 130-year-old farmhouse, the rooms with shared bathrooms have a *Heidi*-like charm. The restaurant, composed of four diminutive dining rooms, serves turbot, cod lingue and scallops. It's 11km north west of Percé.

✗ Eating

Percé has budget eateries, but if you're hankering to splash out and sample some seafood, this is the place to do it. For picnic breads, try the **bakery** (9 Rue Ste Anne).

La Maison du Pêcheur
SEAFOOD $$

(☑418-782-5331; maisondupecheur.restoque bec.com; 155 Place du Quai; pizzas $13-23, meals $18-40; ☉11am-2:30pm & 5-10pm Jun-Oct) In a former fishermen's shack that became a commune in the 1960s (graffiti remains on the ceiling), this award-winning restaurant serves seafood, including lobster, and 15 types of pizza (even octopus!) baked in a maplewood-heated stove. There's web access downstairs in bistro-cafe

L'Atlantique. Reservations are strongly recommended.

Auberge du Gargantua
FRENCH $$$

(☑418-782-2852; Rte des Failles; meals $15-50) Signposted off Rte 132, at the top of a road being reclaimed by the bush, it feels like time has passed this hilltop cabin by. The rustic restaurant serves French specialties and panoramic views, and there are nearby walking trails for an after-dinner stroll. Reservations are advised.

Resto du Village
CAFE $$

(162 Rte 132; meals $20; ☉8am-9:30pm Jun-Sep, restricted hours rest of year) This casual, long-running fave cafe is recommended anytime for a coffee or meal in the warm atmosphere. The menu includes seafood and vegetarian dishes.

❶ Getting There & Away

Orléans Express buses stop outside the tourist office en route to Gaspé (55 minutes), where you can transfer to Forillon National Park, and west to Rimouski ($81, 8½ hours).

Trains from Montréal and Gaspé (see p299) stop on Rue de l'Anse à Beaufils, 10km southwest of Percé (about $15 by taxi).

New Carlisle

One of the main English towns, Loyalist-founded New Carlisle has New Brunswick–style clapboard houses and Protestant, Anglican and Presbyterian churches on grid-arranged streets. Incongruously, René Lévesque (p211) grew up here, on 16 Rue Mount Sorrel.

The **Palladian Hamilton Manor** (☑418-752-6498; www.manoirhamilton.com; 115 Rue Gérard Lévesque; tour $5, r incl breakfast $80; ☉mid-May–Dec; @) was built in 1852 by the town's first mayor. It's a wonderful portrait of colonial life, from the picture of Queen Victoria and the bread oven to the maids' attic quarters, and the guest rooms are decked out in 19th-century decor. From Wednesday to Sunday between June and September, afternoon tea is served in porcelain cups and saucers. The *petit théâtre* screens classic films in the living room.

Bonaventure

Founded by Acadians in 1791, Bonaventure is a nondescript, spread-out town but it's

GANNET GATHERING

Of the hundreds of feathered species found in Québec, none is closer to the hearts of Québécois than the northern gannet *(fou de bassan)*. Île Bonaventure is home to 110,000 of them, one of the world's largest colonies and certainly the most accessible. But it's not their sheer numbers or the squawking din that makes seeing them memorable. Adult gannets are strikingly beautiful, with blazing white plumage and, at the base of a handsome gray-blue bill, piercing blue eyes surrounded by a black patch. During mating season, their heads turn pale yellow, as if glowing from within.

Mature gannets have a wingspan of about 2m, which is evident in their graceful flight, sometimes seeming never to require a single flap. Seeing them return to their life-long mate, evidently without a moment's confusion despite the mob, and indulge in a little friendly caressing is both touching and amusing.

And then there's the birds' dive-bomb approach to hunting. They strike from a distance of about 20m, plunging straight down, sending spray all over the place and, more often than not, resurfacing from as deep as 5m with a mouthful of fish.

Visiting them on the island, where you can get close without disturbing them, is a highlight of any already engaging Île Bonaventure cruise.

worth a stop to learn about the Acadians' 'Great Upheaval' or to drift up the Rivière Bonaventure, one of Québec's cleanest.

The **tourist office** (✆418-534-4014; Rte 132; ☉9am-4pm Jun & Sep, to 7pm Jul & Aug) has internet access.

The small **Musée Acadien** (95 Ave Port Royal; adult/child $8/5; ☉9am-6pm late Jun–early Sep) houses artistic interpretations of the Acadian plight with bilingual explanations. It hosts popular outdoor Acadian music concerts on Wednesday evenings during the summer.

Northeast of town, the almost 500,000-year-old **Grotte de St Elzéar** (✆418-534-3905, 877-524-7688; 136 Chemin Principal; adult/child $37/27; ☉tours 8am-3pm mid-Jun–mid-Oct) is one of Québec's oldest caves. You descend into the cool depths (bring warm clothes) and view the stalactites, stalagmites and moon milk (a mysterious, semiliquid deposit found in caves). Book English tours in advance. To get there, follow the signs after Cime Aventure.

The young, dynamic **Cime Aventure** (✆418-534-2333; www.cimeaventure.com; 200 Chemin Arsenault) leads canoe/kayak trips lasting from two hours ($35) to six days ($1335), mostly on the scenic, tranquil Rivière Bonaventure. It also runs one of the province's best campgrounds (campsites from $23), with tepees (from $69), eco-lodges reached by treetop walkways (from $139) and a rustic resto-bar. To get there from Rte 132, take Ave Gran Pré, which turns into Chemin de la Rivière.

Cime Aventure is signposted to the left of Chemin de la Rivière, just after you cross Rivière Bonaventure.

Overlooking the marina, the boatshed-like **Café Acadien** (✆418-534-4276; 168 Rue Beaubassin; meals $25; ☉10am-9pm) is great for breakfast, serving crepes and salmon, bacon and eggs. Bagels and Acadian, Cajun and Italian food are also on the menu. There are some **rooms** (singles/doubles including breakfast $50/60) upstairs.

New Richmond

The **British Heritage Village** (351 Blvd Perron Ouest; adult/child $10/7; ☉9am-5pm mid-Jun–mid-Sep), in English-speaking New Richmond, shows what the village would have looked like in the late 1700s, recreating a Loyalist settlement of the time. You can take a carriage ride around buildings including a military museum, forge, school and general store.

Carleton

One of the best spots on the Baie des Chaleurs, Carleton is much loved by Gaspésien day-trippers for its sandbars, bird-watching and walking in 550m-plus mountains.

There's a **tourist office** (✆418-364-3544; 629 Blvd Perron; ☉8am-8pm Jun-Sep) in the Hôtel de Ville. From the quay, boats depart for fishing or sightseeing excursions. At the **bird observation tower** on the Banc de Carleton, beyond the marina, you can see herons, terns, plovers and other shore birds along the sandbar. Walking paths and Rue de la Montagne climb to the blue metal-roofed oratory on top of **Mont St Joseph** (555m), which provides fine views over the bay to New Brunswick.

🛏 Sleeping & Eating

Camping de Carleton CAMPGROUND $
(☑418-364-3992; Pointe Tracadigash; tent & RV sites $21-47; ☉Jun-Sep) Occupying a spit of land running between the Baie des Chaleurs and the calm inner bay, with access to miles of beach, which you can camp on.

Le Marin d'Eau Douce SEAFOOD $$
(215 Rte du Quai; mains from $16, meals $32-37; ☉11:30am-2:30pm & 5-9:30pm) An inviting dockside eatery right on the water that serves fresh seafood and other specialties using local ingredients.

Gîte Pignon sur Rue B&B $
(☑418-364-3170; 741 Blvd Perron; s/d incl breakfast $50/70) Keep an eye on New Brunswick from the deck of this home, which has pleasant rooms with shared bathroom and a bike for guests' use.

Le Héron CAFE $$
(561 Rte 132; meals $15-25; ☉8am-midnight) Since 1963, locals and visitors have been enjoying the food and view at this greasy spoon. It's got all the basics plus a kids' menu, seafood and even frog legs!

❶ Getting There & Away

Orléans Express buses stop at 561 Blvd Perron; get tickets inside Le Héron. Buses go to Rimouski and Gaspé twice daily. The **VIA Rail station** (Rue de la Gare) is 1km from the center of town, back against the mountains.

Parc de Miguasha

The small peninsula 7km south of Rte 132, near Nouvelle, was the second place in Québec to be named a Unesco World Heritage site. It's the world's premier fossil site for illustrating the Devonian period, or the 'age of fish,' when sea creatures started evolving into tetrapods, which could walk on land. In the museum, fossils show fish with bones in their fins that are similar to the bones that humans have in their arms and legs.

Inquire at the **information centre** (☑418-794-2475; 231 Rte Miguasha Ouest;

adult/child $11.50/5.50, less for park only; ☉9am-6pm Jun-Aug, to 5pm Sep-early Oct, 8:30am-4:30pm Mon-Fri early Oct-May) about guided walks through the museum and along the fossil-filled cliffs. Do not collect your own fossils!

Pointe à la Garde

Among the trees in otherwise nondescript Pointe à la Garde is an extraordinary wooden chateau with red metal roofs topping its emerald green towers. Owner Jean explains: 'I wanted to live in a castle, so I built one. Everybody thought I was crazy, now they think I'm lucky.' Inspired by annual trips to Europe and the 175 pictures of castles decorating the complex, he recently added a library to the ever-evolving building, begun in 1983, and his friend is constructing a taller chateau next door.

The basic rooms and dorms at **Château Bahia** (☑418-788-2048; 152 Blvd Perron; dm $24, s/d from $33/66; ☉May-Oct; @), with both private and shared bathrooms, are split between the castle's towers and an annex (castellated, of course). Candlelit banquets ($15) take place in the great hall and prices include a wild-berry pancake breakfast.

Pointe à La Croix/Listuguj

The bay now peters out in a swampy mix of mist-covered islands and weeds, overlooked by Listuguj, the Mi'kmaw part of Pointe à La Croix. Crossing the bridge to Campbellton, New Brunswick is uneventful apart from English and French swapping places on the road signs. As so many people travel to bigger Campbellton for work, New Brunswick time (one hour ahead) is often unofficially used in Pointe à La Croix.

A few kilometers west of town, the **Battle of the Restigouche National Historic Site** (Rte 132; adult/child $3.90/1.90; ☉9am-5pm Jun-early Oct) details the 1760 naval battle in the nearby Restigouche River estuary, which finished off France's New World ambitions. The interpretive center with simulated ship explains the battle's significance to the British and displays salvaged articles and even parts of a sunken French frigate.

CANADIAN APPALACHIAN

The 1034km Canadian segment of the 4574km International Appalachian Trail (IAT) was added to the American portion in 2001 and, though still not well known, it forced the 'International' prefix. Crossing the peaks and valleys of the Appalachian Mountains, one of the world's oldest chains, North America's longest continuous hiking trail stretches from Mt Springer, Georgia, USA to Forillon National Park at the tip of the Gaspé Peninsula.

The Canadian section begins on the Maine/New Brunswick border, crosses New Brunswick, including the province's highest peak, Mt Carleton, and enters Québec at Matapédia. The 644km Québec part of the trail winds up the Matapédia Valley to Amqui, where it swings northeast for the highlight of this section, Parc de la Gaspésie and the surrounding reserves. It then descends from the mountains to Mont St Pierre and follows the coast for 248km to its final destination, Cap Gaspé.

The trail is clearly marked and well maintained, apart from in the Matapédia Valley, and there are shelters and campgrounds along the way. Some portions should only be attempted by experienced hikers, and everyone should seek advice about matters such as black bears. More information and maps are available at tourist offices and park information offices in locations such as Matapédia, by calling ☎418-562-7885 and by visiting www.sia-iat.com.

Matapédia Valley

Driving through the Matapédia Valley gives a taste of the terrain that challenges walkers on the International Appalachian Trail. The trees covering the hillsides only stop for rivers, cliffs and lines of huge pylons charging through the wilderness. If it's raining, the mist-swathed forests look like the highlands of a Southeast Asian country. The Rivière Matapédia, famous for its salmon fishing, attracted former US presidents Nixon and Carter.

MATAPÉDIA

Matapédia is squaring up to Causapscal as a center for outdoor pursuits, but, thankfully, it has a long way to go before it resembles a tourist town. A gateway for the International Appalachian Trail (see the boxed text), it has a **reception center** (www.sia-iat.com; Rte 132; ☯mid-Jun–mid-Oct), which doubles as the local tourist office. A free map, available here, covers trails on the hilltop plateau to the west, such as a 10km walk via St Alexis to the **Horizon du Reve lookout**.

Nature-Aventure (☎418-865-3554; ☯mid-May–mid-Nov) leads rugged paddles of varying difficulty along local rivers, including the Matapédia ('the accessible') and the Restigouche ('the magnificent'). Packages include two-hour tours ($40), and excursions lasting one/two/three/four/five days ($85/235/315/415/515).

CAUSAPSCAL

As its monolithic statue of 'the king of our rivers' suggests, Causapscal is crazy about salmon. The largest **salmon** caught here weighed over 16kg. Other outdoor activities on the town's doorstep include **hiking**, with trails meandering through the surrounding hills. The town itself has a beautiful stone church and many old houses with typical Québécois silver roofs, though odors from nearby sawmills sometimes spoil the picturesque scene.

There is a **tourist office** (53 Rue St Jacques; ☯8am-8pm late Jun-early Sep, closed Sep) and, for (expensive) fishing permits, an office of **CGRMP** (1 Rue St Jacques Nord; ☯Jun-Sep).

Rivière Matapédia is the healthiest river for salmon; 13kg beauties are regularly netted there at the beginning of the season. There are covered bridges south of town and, in the center, a pedestrian-only suspension bridge across the Matapédia. Anglers go there to cast their lines where the Matapédia and Causapscal meet.

Check out the **Matamajaw Historic Site** (www.sitehistoriquematamajaw.com; 53 Rue St Jacques; adult/child$7/6; ☯9am-5pm mid-Jun–Sep) to see how the chaps in the fishing club used to relax in wood-paneled luxury after a hard day on the river. On the other side of Rte 132 is a salmon pool.

Appealingly old-fashioned **Auberge La Coulée Douce** (☎418-756-5720, 888-756-5270; www.lacouleedouce.com; 21 Rue Boudreau; r $65-99, chalets $109-159) is perfect for fishers, and for those who simply want to sit in the comfortable dining room listening to ripping fishing yarns.

The Orléans Express bus linking Gaspé and Rimouski stops at 560 Rue St Jacques Nord.

NORTH SHORE

The Côte Nord (North Shore) comprises two regions: Manicouagan (stretching to Godbout) and Duplessis (east to the Labrador border). Statistics here are as overwhelming as the distances you have to drive to cross the areas. The two regions encompass an awesome 328,693 sq km (the size of New Zealand, Belgium and Switzerland combined). In this vast expanse live just over 100,000 hardy souls, mostly on the 1250km of coastline, making the area's population density just 0.3 persons per square kilometer.

The further northeast you go, the greater the distance between villages, the fewer the people, the deeper the isolation and the wilder the nature. This part of the Canadian Shield was heavily glaciated, resulting in a jumble of lakes and rivers.

Baie Comeau

This unattractive city owes its existence to Robert McCormick, former owner of the *Chicago Tribune,* who in 1936 decided to build a colossal pulp and paper factory here. This enterprise necessitated harnessing the hydroelectric power of the Manicouagan and Outardes Rivers, which in turn begat other hydro-dependent industries such as aluminum processing.

Baie Comeau is at the beginning of Rte 389, which runs north past the **Manicouagan Reservoir**, the fifth-largest meteorite crater in the world, to Labrador City and Wabush. Along the way is a fascinating landscape of lake-filled barrens, tundra and, about 120km north of the hydroelectric complex Manic Cinq, the **Groulx Mountains**, where the peaks reach as high as 1000m.

A year-round **ferry** (☎877-562-6560; 14 Rte Maritime) makes the 2½-hour journey to Matane daily (per adult/child/car $15/10/35), providing the easternmost link to the south shore. Making a reservation the day before is recommended.

Godbout

The principal activity in this comatose village is the arrival of the ferry. Originally a 17th-century trading post, it flourished thanks to its salmon-filled rivers, the Godbout and Trinité, which are among the best in Québec for salmon fishing.

The **tourist information office** (☎418-568-7462; 115 Rue Pascal Comeau; ⊙7am-7pm late Jun–mid-Sep) is at the ferry terminal. The **Musée Amérindien et Inuit** (134 Rue Pascal Comeau; adult/child $4/2; ⊙9am-10pm late Jun-late Sep) owns a nice collection of Inuit and aboriginal sculptures. If you feel like **swimming**, hit the beach below the museum.

Hébergement Cormier (☎418-568-7535; 156 Rue Pascal Comeau; s/d $25/30) has neat rooms above a convenience store and cafe overlooking the ferry terminal. It can organize fishing permits for nonresidents, kayaking and whale-watching.

The **ferry** (117 Rue Pascal Comeau) links Godbout with Matane.

Pointe des Monts

This marks the point where the coast veers north and the St Lawrence graduates from river to gulf. The 1830 **lighthouse** here, one of Québec's oldest, has lorded over dozens of shipwrecks, despite its function. Sitting on a picturesque spit of land, it has been converted into a **museum** (1830 Chemin du Vieux Phare Casier; adult/child $6/free; ⊙9am-5pm mid-Jun–mid-Oct) explaining the lives of the keepers and their families.

Next to the lighthouse, chalets are rented out daily and weekly at **Le Gîte du Phare de Point** (☎418-939-2332, 866-369-4083; 1937 Chemin du Vieux Phare Casier; chalets daily/weekly from $95/538; ⊙mid-May–mid-Oct), and packages on offer include fishing and birding. The on-site restaurant serves first-rate local specialties (meals $26 to $35); reservations are advised for nonguests.

Baie Trinité

If you've developed a morbid interest in the St Lawrence's history of shipwrecks, stop at **Centre National des Naufrages** (National Shipwrecks Center; www.centrenaufrages.ca; 27 Rte 138; adult/child $8/6; ⊙9am-7pm mid-Jun–mid-Sep), 34km northeast of Godbout on Rte 138.

Rivière Pentecôte

The local pronunciation of this blissful village's name is a classic example of the nasal Québécois accent. In the village, the pier beneath the Pentecostal church attracts fishers, who cast in the confluence of the St Lawrence and Pentecôte Rivers.

Between the village and Pointe aux Anglais, 12km south, is a long public **beach** where campers can stay in the wooded dunes for free and spend a day sighting whales offshore. The beach is sandy, sprawling and clean, one of the North Shore's finest. There are no services, but you can shower at a cafe 5km north of Pointe aux Anglais, **Le Routier de Pentecôte** (☑418-799-2600; 3011 Rte 138; s/d \$35/55; ☺7am-8pm). It also has cheap rooms and is the local Intercar bus stop.

Even more pleasant is the basic campground at the pier, **Abri des Campeurs** (☑418-766-5590; Site Historique de Rivière Pentecôte; campsite \$12).

Sept Îles

The last town of any size along the North Shore and one of Canada's busiest ports, Sept Îles is a quietly attractive place with alphabetically ordered streets. Exploring its excellent museums and archipelago is the perfect cure for the fatigue of long-distance driving.

The main **tourist office** (☑418-962-1238, 888-880-1238; 1401 Blvd Laure Ouest; ☺7:30am-9pm May-Sep, 8:30am-5pm Mon-Fri Oct-Apr) is on the highway west of town. A smaller, seasonal office is at the port.

◉ Sights

Musée Régional de la Côte Nord   MUSEUM
(www.mrcn.qc.ca; 500 Blvd Laure; adult/child \$5/free; ☺9am-5pm late Jun-early Sep, 10am-noon & 1-5pm Tue-Fri, 1-5pm Sat & Sun early Sep-late Jun) This museum is a must-visit. It tells the history of the North Shore and its 8000 years of human habitation through a mix of gadgets and artifacts such as 17th-century maps.

Musée Shaputuan   MUSEUM
(290 Blvd des Montagnais; adult/child \$5/free; ☺9am-5pm late Jun-early Sep, 9am-5pm Mon-Fri early Sep-late Jun) This is the North Shore's best aboriginal museum. The atmospheric circular exhibition hall, divided into four sections symbolizing the seasons, follows the Montagnais (Innu) people as they hunt caribou or navigate the treacherous spring rivers. Photography, traditional clothes, sculptures and mythological tales are incorporated.

Le Vieux Poste   HISTORICAL SITE
(Blvd des Montagnais; adult/child \$3/free; ☺9am-5pm late Jun-late Aug) Seventeenth-century fur-trading post Le Vieux Poste has been reconstructed as a series of buildings showing the lifestyles of the hunters who called the forest home.

🏃 Activities

There is a small archipelago off Sept Îles. The largest island, **Île Grande Basque**, is a pretty spot to spend a day, walking on the 12km of trails or picnicking on the coast. During the summer, **Croisière Petit Pingouin** (☑418-968-9558) and **Les Croisières du Capitaine** (☑418-968-2173) run regular 10-minute ferry crossings between the island and Sept Îles port (adult/child \$20/15), as well as archipelago cruises. Tickets are available at the port, Parc du Vieux Quai. Camping is possible with a permit, available from the cruise companies and the tourist office. For guided kayaking tours of the islands, contact **Vêtements des Îles** (☑418-962-7223; 637 Ave Brochu). Île du Corossol is a bird refuge.

🛏 Sleeping & Eating

You'll find several motels along Rte 138 (Blvd Laure).

Le Tangon   HOSTEL \$
(☑418-962-8180; www.aubergeletangon.net; 555 Rue Cartier; campsites \$10, dm member/nonmember \$18/22, s with shared bathroom \$26-30, d \$44-48; P@🛜) The wooden balcony is an uplifting sight after miles of Rte 138. Inside, this HI hostel has friendly faces in reception, power showers, small dorms and a homely lounge and kitchen.

Gîte de l'Étale   B&B \$
(☑418-962-1777; 745 Rue de la Rive; r \$69-79, chalet \$79-89) This friendly B&B, in a tranquil spot 7km east of town, has beach views, smart rooms and buffet breakfasts featuring local specialties.

Pub St Marc   GASTROPUB \$\$
(588 Ave Brochu; meals \$14-25; ☺11am-10pm Mon-Fri, 4pm-midnight Sat & Sun) With an outdoor patio with heat lamps, this mel-

low bar near the hostel serves a dozen draft beers, pasta and salads.

Les Terrasses du Capitaine SEAFOOD $$$
(295 Ave Arnaud; meals from $25; ⊘11am-2pm Mon-Fri, 4:30-9pm daily) Behind the fish market, this is the best place in town to taste local catches.

ⓘ Getting There & Away

Air Labrador (☑800-563-3042; www.airlabrador.com) serves the Lower North Shore, Labrador, Newfoundland, Québec City and Montréal.

The **Relais Nordik** (☑418-723-8787, 800-463-0680; www.relaisnordik.com) ferry travels to Île d'Anticosti and along the Lower North Shore (see p294).

Intercar (☑418-962-2126; 126 Rue Mgr Blanche) runs a daily bus to/from Baie Comeau ($44, four hours) and, Monday to Friday, another to/from Havre St Pierre ($37, 2¾ hours).

Aboriginal-owned **Tshiuetin Rail Transportation** (☑418-962-5530; www.tshiuetin.net; 1005 Blvd Laure) operates a twice-weekly service to/from Schefferville, 568km north, one of the province's most remote spots, though once a thriving mining town. The scenery en route is phenomenal. Cutting through forests, the tracks pass over gorges, dip inside valleys, curve around waterfalls and rapids, slice through a section of mountain and jut along stretches of lakes, rivers and hills as far as the eye can see. The train crosses a 900m-long bridge, 50m over Rivière Moisie and past the 60m-high Tonkas Falls. You can stop in the wilderness to camp and fish, then catch the next service back.

Mingan

Beyond Sept Îles, the landscape reaches the primeval state it has previously hinted at. The warm blanket of trees lining the road is whisked away and stretches of muskeg come into view. Certainly, the sky is bigger than it was before, but these plains could not be described as empty. The stones rearing out of the ground become increasingly large and the moors are dotted with blue lakes and rocky rivers hurling themselves into the St Lawrence.

Mingan is a former fishing and trading post, populated partly by a dynamic Innu community that calls the village Ekuanitshit. The small Catholic church **Église Montagnaise** (15 Rue Nashipetimit; admission free; ⊘8am-7pm) contains a striking mix of Catholicism and aboriginal culture. A tepee form enshrines the crucifix, the pulpit is made of antlers, and tasseled cloth covers the altar, showing hunting scenes.

Mingan Archipelago National Park

By far the region's main attraction, this **park** (adult/child $5.80/2.90; ⊘Jun-Sep) is a protected string of 40 main offshore islands stretching more than 85km from Longue Pointe de Mingan to 40km east of Havre St Pierre. The islands' distinguishing characteristics are the odd, erosion-shaped stratified limestone formations along the shores. They're dubbed 'flowerpots' for the lichen and small vegetation that grow on top. Perched there might be the goofy puffin (*macareux moine* in French), a striking cross between a parrot and penguin and one of some 200 bird species here.

The **Reception & Interpretation Centre** (☑418-949-2126; Longue Pointe de Mingan; ⊘8am-6:30pm Jun-Sep) has a lot of information. In the same building is the nonprofit **Cetacean Interpretation Centre** (adult/child $7.50/3.50), which gives as much of an insight into the science of studying whales as it does the mysterious mammals themselves.

Half a dozen tour companies leave from Havre St Pierre and Longue Pointe de Mingan. In general, the smaller the boat, the better the experience. Trips last between three and five hours and cost $38 to $60.

The archipelago is one of the country's best kayaking destinations, with exceptional topography, flora and fauna. **Agaguk** (☑418-538-1588, 866-538-1588) and **Odysée Minganie** (☑418-949-2438) run kayak tours, suitable for inexperienced paddlers, from Havre St Pierre and Longue Pointe de Mingan respectively. Agaguk also rents out equipment.

Camping (sites from $15.70) is allowed on some of the islands, but you must register at the Reception & Interpretation Center or the Havre St Pierre tourist information office.

Havre St Pierre

This fishing town is worth a stop on the way northeast, mainly because it has the last garage for 124km. It has a lot of charm, despite being an industrial zone, where iron oxide- and titanium-rich rock from nearby mines is shipped to processing plants in Tracy-Sorel. It was founded in 1857 by six Acadian families who left the Îles de la Madeleine and set up here in Inuit territory.

The **tourist information office** (☑418-538-2512; 1010 Promenade des Anciens; ☺9am-9pm mid-Jun–mid-Sep) is also a hub for Mingan Archipelago tours.

Auberge Boréale (☑418-538-3912; www.aubergeboreale.com; 1288 Rue Boréale; r $55) has nine cool, blue-and-white rooms and a pretty sea view.

The 2nd-floor **Gîte Chez Françoise** (☑418-538-3778; www.gitechezfrancoise.has.it; 1122 Rue Boréale; s/d from $58/62; @) has four artistically decorated rooms.

Both sleeping options offer **bike rental**.

The Intercar bus (see p307) stops at **Variétés Jomphe** (843 Rue de l'Escale).

Île d'Anticosti

This 7943-sq-km island has only recently begun to unfold its beauty to a growing number of visitors. A French chocolate maker named Henri Menier (his empire became Nestlé) bought the island in 1895 to turn it into his own private hunting ground. With its thriving white-tailed deer and salmon populations, it has long been popular with hunters and fishers. Now wildlife reserves are attracting nature lovers to the heavily wooded, cliff-edged island with waterfalls, canyons, caves and rivers.

In Port Menier, the closest thing to a village on the island, there is a **tourist office** (☑418-535-0250; 36 Chemin des Forestiers; ☺Jun-Sep) and a few restaurants and B&Bs; accommodations should be arranged before arrival. From here, the island's lone road ventures to the interior.

Though it's possible to reach and tour the island yourself, it requires much planning. Most visitors go with a small-group tour; Sépaq (p213) offers two- and seven-day packages with flights. The Havre St Pierre tourist office has more information. Relais Nordik (p294) provides the only regular transportation.

Natashquan

Natashquan is still getting used to its connection to the rest of the province. Rte 138 reached the village in 1996, and it has been paved only since 1999. Romantics are drawn here for the experience of reaching the end of the road at Pointe Parent, 7km further on, and for Natashquan's peaceful, windswept beauty.

The **tourist information office** (☑418-726-3054; 24 Chemin d'En Haut; ☺8am-7pm late Jun–mid-Oct, 9am-5pm mid-Oct–late Jun) doubles as an interpretive center.

Natashquan is the birthplace of the great Québécois singer-songwriter Gilles Vigneault. An exhibition in the **Vieille École** (Old School; 32 Chemin d'en Haut; adult/child $4/2; ☺8:30am-6pm late Jun-early Sep) looks at the local characters who inspired his songs.

Les Galets is a cluster of white huts with bright red roofs, huddled together on a windblown peninsula. Fishers used to salt and dry their catch here, an important communal activity. Aside from enjoying the surrounding beaches, you can hike inland trails through isolated, peaceful woods full of waterfalls and lookouts; the tourist office has a free map.

ÎLES DE LA MADELEINE

Everything about the Magdalen Islands, a stringy archipelago that resembles a Mandelbrot set on maps, is head turning. Located 105km north of Prince Edward Island, its six largest islands are connected by the 200km-long, classically named Rte 199, which curves between lumpy, verdant blotches of land on sand spits that seem about to be reclaimed by the omnipresent ocean. Between the islands' 350km of beach are iron-rich, red cliffs, molded by wind and sea into anthropomorphic forms and caves just crying out to be explored by kayak. Surprisingly, despite their exposed position, the isles are a comforting place, where the horizon is normally interrupted, along with the thought that you're in the open sea, by another wing of the archipelago.

The Magdalens look like desert islands as you circle above their crescent beaches on one of the tiny airplanes that fly here. In fact, 13,000 lucky blighters live here, and that figure quadruples in the summer. As on the Gaspé Peninsula, the islands' isolated communities, descended from Acadian refugees and shipwrecked sailors, have developed in ways that would make an anthropologist zip between them faster than the wind whips the sand spits. In the

Anglophone minority, for example, some members of Grosse Îles' 600-strong, Irish-descended community report that they often struggle to understand the accent on Île d'Entrée, where the 130 residents mostly have Scottish roots.

A great way to meet the islanders, who generally don't lock their scattered, brightly painted houses when they go out, is at *boîtes à chansons*. The archipelago has a vibrant nightlife, and on Cap aux Meules you can normally catch wistful Acadian songs being strummed on summer evenings. During the day, if you're not busy in rock pools or trying to keep your bike upright on a blustery sand spit, other forms of creativity can be enjoyed in the seafood restaurants, *économusées* and boutiques. The islands are teeming with artists, often encountered looking for inspiration in a *pot-en-pot* (a local specialty, with mixed fish, seafood and sauce baked in a pie crust) or a Pas Perdus (one of three beers brewed on Cap aux Meules).

The islands fall in the Atlantic Time Zone, one hour ahead of mainland Québec.

❶ Getting There & Around

The airport is on the northwest corner of Île du Havre aux Maisons. Air Canada Jazz offers daily flights from Montréal, Québec City and Gaspé; **Pascan** (☎888-313-8777; www.pascan.com) flies from the two cities, Sept Îles and Bonaventure.

The cheapest and most common arrival method is by ferry from Souris, Prince Edward Island, to Île du Cap aux Meules. **CTMA Ferries** (☎418-986-3278, 888-986-3278; www.ctma.ca) makes the five-hour cruise from April through January. From July to September, boats go once or twice a day, at other times, less frequently. In midsummer, reservations are strongly recommended. The fare is $45.75/23 per adult/child aged five to 12. Bikes cost $11, cars $85.50.

Between June and October, CTMA also operates a two-day cruise from Montréal via Québec City, Tadoussac and Chandler. It's a great way of seeing the St Lawrence River, and you could always take your car and return by road.

There is no public transportation. **Le Pédalier** (☎418-986-2965; 500 Chemin Principale), in Cap aux Meules, rents bicycles. Hertz and local companies have airport car-rental outlets; book as far ahead as possible.

Île du Cap aux Meules

With more than half the archipelago's population and its only Tim Hortons, the islands' commercial center is disappointingly developed compared with its neighbors. Nonetheless, it's still 100% Madelinot and, with its amenities, accommodations and lively nightlife, it makes an ideal base.

The **main tourist office** (☎418-986-2245, 877-624-4437; www.tourismeilesdelamadeleine. com; 128 Chemin Principale; ☺7am-9pm late Jun-Aug, 9am-8pm Sep, 9am-5pm & when ferries arrive Oct-Nov, 9am-5pm Mon-Fri Dec-late Jun), near the ferry terminal, is a helpful source of information about all the islands.

◉ Sights & Activities

On the west side of the island, you can see the red cliffs in their glory. Their patterns of erosion can be glimpsed from the clifftop path between La Belle Anse and Fatima. Southwest, the lighthouse at **Cap du Phare** (Cap Hérissé) is a popular place to watch sunsets, and a cluster of bright boutiques and cafes overlooks a shipwreck at **Anse de l'Étang du Nord**. In the middle of the island, signposted on Chemin de l'Église near the junction with Rte 199, **Butte du Vent** offers views along the sandbanks running north and south.

Aerosport Carrefour d'Aventures KAYAKING
(☎418-986-6677; www.aerosport.ca; 1390 Chemin Lavernière) Young, enthusiastic thrill-seekers run this company that offers kayak expeditions and cave visits. When the wind is right, you'll have an unforgettable experience if you opt for the power kite buggy ride.

À l'Abri de la Tempéte BREWERY
(☎418-986-5005; 286 Chemin Coulombe; tours $5; ☺tours 11am-7pm Jun-Sep) Finish the day at this microbrewery on the beach.

Vert et Mer KAYAKING
(☎418-986-3555; www.vertetmer.com; 169 Chemin Principale) This eco-outfit offers excursions including sea kayaking and yurt lodging on Île Brion (p311).

MA Poirier BUS TOUR
(☎418-986-4467; 375 Chemin Petipas; tours from $99) Runs seven-hour guided bus tours of the main sights throughout the islands.

🛏 Sleeping & Eating

Pas Perdus PUB, INN $$
(Not Lost; ☎418-986-5151; 169 & 185 Chemin Principale; mains $12-20; s/d/tr with private bathroom $40/50/65; ☺11am-8pm) Munching on a shark burger on the *terrasse* at Pas Perdus, watching the traffic on Rte 199 cruise by, or

in the red interior among curvy mirrors, is a sure way to feel the islands' bohemian pulse. Everyone drops by to surf the internet or sip a Pas Perdus from the nearby micro-brewery. You can actually get a decent night's sleep in the bright bedrooms above the restaurant now the musical entertainment has shifted next door (185 Chemin Principale). This venue hosts live acts most summer nights and, on Monday, films about the islands (7pm) and a free jam session (10pm). Pas Perdus is on the east side of the island, just west of the tourist office.

La Factrie SEAFOOD **$$**
(521 Chemin du Gros Cap; mains $15-30; ⏰11am-10pm Mon-Sat, 4-10pm Sun May-Sep) Serves top-notch seafood in a cafeteria above a lobster processing plant; only in Îles de la Madeleine! Try lobster in salad, boiled, thermidore, sandwich or crepe form.

Parc de Gros-Cap HOSTEL, CAMPGROUND **$**
(☎418-986-4505, 800-986-4505; www.parc-degroscap.ca; 74 Chemin du Camping; tent & RV sites $20-27, dm member/nonmember $23/27, r member $46-70, nonmember $50-76; ⏰May-Sep; @🛜) Situated on the Gros Cap peninsula overlooking a bay dotted with fishers in waders, this could be the HI network's most tranquil retreat. It has a family atmosphere and is a good place to organize activities such as sea kayaking.

Café la Côte CAFE **$$**
(499 Chemin Boisville Ouest; mains $9-20; ⏰8am-10pm Jun-Sep) Near the fishermen statue in L'Etang du Nord, this beach-hut–like place is perfect for breakfast or a quick lunch of seafood or pasta. The adjoining *boîte à chansons* puts on outdoor Acadian music shows on summer evenings.

Camping Le Barachois CAMPGROUND **$**
(☎418-986-6065; 87 Chemin du Rivage; tent & RV sites $19-26; ⏰May-Sep) This 120-site campground, surrounded by trees, lake and sea, has great sunsets.

Île du Havre Aubert

Heading south from Cap aux Meules to the archipelago's largest island, Rte 199 glides between dunes backed by the blue Atlantic and Baie du Havre aux Basques, popular with kite surfers.

The liveliest area of **Havre Aubert** town is La Grave, where the rustic charm of a fishing community remains in the old houses, small craft shops and restaurants. Beyond, walk along the **Sandy Hook** to feel like you're at the end of the world (apart from during the sand castle contest in August).

The excellent **Musée de la Mer** (1023 Rte 199; adult/child $5/2; ⏰10am-6pm late Jun-early Sep, reduced hours rest of year) covers Madelinot history from Jacques Cartier's impressions of walruses onwards.

Économusée **Artisans du Sable** (907 Rte 199; ⏰10am-5:30pm) sells chessboards, candlesticks and other souvenirs...all made of sand.

At **Le Site d'Autrefois** (3106 Chemin de la Montagne; adult/child $10/4; ⏰9am-5pm Jun-Aug, 10am-4pm Sep), flamboyant fisherman Claude preserves Madelinot traditions through storytelling, singing and a model village.

On rainy days, the 'petting pool' in the small **aquarium** (146 Chemin de la Grave; adult/child $6.50/2; ⏰10am-6pm Jun–mid-Oct) makes a popular stop.

Chez Denis à François (☎418-937-2371; www.aubergechezdenis.ca; 404 Chemin d'en Haut; s incl breakfast $55-115, d $75-135), opposite the (highly undersubscribed) jail, was built using lumber salvaged from a shipwreck. The spacious, Victorian-style rooms have ceiling fans, fridges, sofas and private bathrooms.

Café de la Grave (969 Rte 199; meals $9-15; ⏰11:30am-midnight late Apr–mid-Oct) is more than a local institution, it's one of the islands' vital organs. *Pot-en-pot, croque monsieur,* soups and cakes meet an appreciative crowd in the ex-general store.

Île du Havre aux Maisons

The home of the airport is one of the most populated islands but certainly doesn't feel it. Particularly to the east of Rte 199, it's probably the most scenic area, best seen from Chemin des Buttes, which winds between green hills and picture-perfect cottages. A short climb from the car park on Chemin des Échoueries near Cap Alright, the cross-topped **Butte Ronde** has wonderful views of the lumpy coastline.

🛏 Sleeping & Eating

Domaine du Vieux Couvent HOTEL **$$**
(☎418-969-2233; www.domaineduvieuxcouvent.com; 292 Rte 199; meals from $27; r incl break-

fast $125-275; ⊘late Feb–mid-Dec; 🔊) Smack-dab in the middle of the archipelago, the Domaine boasts the swankiest digs in Îles de la Madeleine. Every room overlooks the ocean through a wall of windows. The very popular **restaurant** (⊘6-9pm May-Oct, to 10pm Jul & Aug) is a must-visit for adventurous foodies, who can sample local dishes made with seafood, veal, boar, wild fruits and cheeses from the islands.

La Butte Ronde
B&B $$
(☏418-969-2047; www.labutteronde.com; 70 Chemin des Buttes; r incl breakfast $100-145) With ticking clocks, classical music, beautiful rooms decorated with photos of Tuareg nomads, and a sea-facing conservatory, this grand home has a calming, library-like air.

Grosse Île

This island is home to most of the archipelago's English-speaking minority, their Newfoundlandlike accents telling of their Celtic roots. The Anglophone community has an uneasy relationship with its Francophone neighbors and you'll hear comments such as, 'We want our English signs back.'

At the end of a windswept sandbank interrupted only briefly by Île de Pointe aux Loups, Grosse Île begins with a **salt mine**, which excavates at a depth of 300m below sea level.

In **Trinity Church**, Pointe de la Grosse Île, Anglicanism reflects island life. The stained-glass window depicts Jesus clad in a woolen jumper and boots, saying, 'Come with me and I will make you fishers of men.'

Between Pointe de la Grosse Île and Old Harry, the 684-hectare East Point bird reserve boasts the archipelago's most impressive beach, **Plage de la Grande Échouerie**. The 10km sweep of pale sand extends northeast from Pointe Old Harry; there are car parks there and en route to Old Harry from East Cape.

The museum at the **Council for Anglophone Magdalen Islanders** (787 Chemin Principale; admission free; ⊘8am-4pm Mon-Fri) in Old Harry is housed in a former schoolhouse built in 1921. The anglophone relics include 19th-century sailors' tombstones from **Île Brion**, 16km north. Brion is now an ecological reserve with 140 species of birds and much interesting vegetation.

Seacow Rd in Old Harry leads to the site where walrus were landed and slaughtered for their oil. Nearby, **St Peter's by the Sea**, built in 1916 using wood from shipwrecks, is bounded by graves of Clarkes and Clarks. The surname evolved as it was misspelt on formal documents.

QUÉBEC'S TIMBUKTU

Beyond Natashquan, the coastline known as the **Lower North Shore** stretches some 400km northeast to the Labrador border. Connected to the rest of the province only by the weekly Relais Nordik ferry (p294), Air Labrador flights (p307) and, during the winter, by snowmobile, the area remains an enigma to most Québécois. Montréalers can correct visitors' pronunciation of the remote villages' names, but only because they've heard them in weather reports.

The area's 10 anglophone villages and four francophone settlements, mostly founded by Newfoundlander fishermen and Acadians from Îles de la Madeleine, are completely cut off from each other. Innu communities also dot the coast. This makes a disjointed experience for Relais Nordik passengers who wander onshore when the ferry docks for a few hours, in the middle of the night in some places. The ferry, the region's lifeline for supplies, takes 3½ days to travel from Rimouski to **Blanc Sablon**, 2km west of the Labrador border. Ice prevents it from sailing between January and April.

Kegaska, 50km east of Natashquan, is known for its crushed-seashell-covered roads. **Harrington Harbour**, 100km further on, is considered one of Québec's prettiest villages, with brightly colored houses perching on rocks around a small, windsheltered bay. Rte 138 begins again at **Vieux Fort**, 65km from Blanc Sablon, which has had a European presence since the 16th century and an Aboriginal one for more than 8000 years. A **ferry** (☏866-535-2567; www.labradormarine.com) links Blanc Sablon to St Barbe, Newfoundland, and Rte 510 connects it to several coastal villages in Labrador (see p496).

Île de la Grande Entrée

Even by Madelinot standards, Grand Entry is a remote outpost, its 650 residents' homes seemingly outnumbered by the masts at the fishing port.

Club Vacances Les Îles (☎418-985-2833, 888-537-4537; 377 Rte 199; tent & RV sites $19-24) is a hive of activity, offering sea kayaking, windsurfing, caving, nature walks, archipelago tours, seafood tasting, fishers' storytelling, even mud baths. It has a campground and a ho-hum cafeteria; the bedrooms are for tour packages only.

On-site, the **Seal Interpretation Center** (adult/child $7.50/4; ☺10am-6pm Jun-Sep) delves into the world of seals and, particularly in the 'controversy corner,' seal clubbing.

The center overlooks **Île Bordeau**, which has a hiking trail and is reached via Chemin du Bassin Ouest, near the end of Rte 199.

In **Galerie-Boutique Marie Marto** (889 Rte 199) the beachcombing artist sells objects made of natural materials.

Délices de la Mer (907 Chemin Principale; meals $25; ☺11am-8pm Jun-Sep), formerly the office of the local fishing cooperative, serves affordable seafood such as lobster-garnished bread and chips.

FAR NORTH

This area truly represents the final frontier of Québec, where the province runs barren and eventually disappears into the depths of the Arctic Ocean. Here lies the great Far North, where remote villages, a strong Aboriginal presence and stunning geography entice those wanting to drop right off the tourist radar. The earth brims with valuable resources, such as silver, gold and copper, caribou run free and the waters teem with fish.

The North is an immense region, the most northerly sections of which are dotted with tiny Inuit and First Nations settlements accessible only by bush plane. The developed areas largely owe their existence to massive industrial operations – mining, forestry and hydroelectricity. While accessing the really far North (the Inuit communities in Nunavik) requires expensive flights, other areas of the Abitibi-Témiscamingue and James Bay regions can easily, with time, be reached by car and bus, and will provide a taste of Canada's true North.

Abitibi-Témiscamingue

What's it like up here? In over 65,140 sq km, the people barely outnumber the lakes. But despite the shortage of humans, this sparsely populated area occupies a special place in the Québécois imagination. The last area to be settled and developed on a major scale, it stands as a symbol of dreams and hardships.

The traditional land of the Algonquins, Abitibi-Témiscamingue is an amalgamation of two distinct areas, each named after different tribes. Témiscamingue, accessible only via northern Ontario and one long road south of Rouyn-Noranda, sees few tourists. It's more diversified in its vegetation and landscape, with valleys and the grand Lac Témiscamingue. Most of Abitibi's slightly more visited terrain is flat, which makes the stunning valleys and cliffs of Parc d'Aiguebelle all the more striking.

Abitibi-Témiscamingue was colonized following the usual pattern of resource exploitation. Before the 19th century, the only Europeans in the area were hunters and fur traders. Then forestry and copper mining brought more development. In the 1920s gold fever struck and thousands flooded the region in search of their fortune. Boomtowns bloomed around deposits.

Today, this vast region of Québec retains an oddly exotic air, partially due to its remoteness. Generally, visitors are seeking solitude in its parks or are en route to still more epic northern destinations.

RÉSERVE FAUNIQUE LA VÉRENDRYE

Relatively accessible, this immense **park** (☎819-736-7431, 800-665-6527; www.sepaq.com; Hwy 117; adult/child $3.50/free; ☺mid-May–mid-Sep) is best as a canoeing destination. Very satisfying circuit routes of varying lengths have been mapped and there are stunning **campgrounds** (sites $19-40) sprinkled around the lakes' edges. Even in a heat wave in midsummer, you may well have entire lakes virtually to yourself. And you don't need to be an expert or an athlete to enjoy the peace in this park. Aside from camping, there are chalets for rent, with rates starting at $280 per week per person. The waterfalls at Lac Roland are worth seeing. Though not evident, this is not a true wilderness as the central lakes are actually part of a massive reservoir and are very shallow.

The park is accessed at four points, all on Hwy 117. Coming from the Laurentians, **Le Domaine** (☑819-435-2541), 58km past the village of Grand Remous, has information, canoe rentals and services. Staff are so friendly you may receive an unexpected Christmas card!

During the 180km drive across the reserve from the south end to Val d'Or, there are no villages – make sure your tank is full.

VAL D'OR

Born in 1933 around the Sigma gold mine, Val d'Or today looks like a mining boomtown of yesterday, with wide avenues and a main street (Ave 3-ème) that one can easily imagine was frenzied in gold-rush days. That main street retains its traditional rough edge. The Sigma mine still operates, though it's no longer the city's economic engine. The **tourist office** (☑819-824-9646; 1070 3-ème Ave Est; ☺9am-5pm) is on Hwy 117 at the eastern end of town.

La Cité de l'Or (www.citedelor.com; 90 Ave Perreault; adult/child $25/12; ☺underground tours 8:30am-5:30pm late Jun-early Sep) offers guided excursions 91m underground to show what gold mining's all about. On the same site is the **Village Minier de Bourlamaque** (adult/child $12/5), a restored mining village with 80 log houses. Call to reserve tours in advance, and don't forget to bring warm clothes if you're going underground.

Air Creebec flies into Val d'Or from Montréal. Autobus Maheux (p272) covers the region with buses to Montréal (seven hours), Matagami (3½ hours) and Chibougamau via Senneterre (six hours).

PARC D'AIGUEBELLE

As the Abitibi landscape can be a tad on the dull side, the stunning scenery in this **provincial park** (☑819-637-7322; 1737 Rang Hudson; adult/child $3.50/free; ☺year-round) comes as a doubly pleasant surprise. Suddenly there are magnificent canyons and gorges, massive rocky cliffs with fascinating geological formations and excellent, rugged hiking trails (some 60km worth) flanked by trees 200 years old.

This small park (only 268 sq km) has three entrances – via Mont Brun (well marked on Hwy 117 west of Val d'Or; this is the closest to the suspended bridge); Destor (off Rte 101 between Rouyn-Noranda and La Sarre); and Taschereau (south from Rte 111 between La Sarre and Amos). There are

lovely **campgrounds** (sites from $23) near all three, as well as canoe and kayak rentals.

James Bay

This area truly represents Québec's hinterland, where precious metals flow freely beneath a seemingly endless forest of boreal spruces that sprout from the earth. On many evenings, the northern lights dye the sky a kaleidoscope of pinks and blues, which eventually give way to blazing orange sunsets. Only 30,000 people live here, in the world's largest administrative municipality (350,000 sq km), which is roughly the size of Germany. Almost half of them are Cree living on eight reserves separated by hundreds of kilometers.

The near mythic Rte de la Baie James ends at Radisson, a small village 1400km north of Montréal and 800km north of Amos. A 100km extension branches westward to Chisasibi, a Cree reserve near James Bay. This area is defined by the immense James Bay hydroelectric project, a series of hydroelectric stations that produces half of Québec's energy resources. Many visitors make the trek just to get a glimpse of these.

While temperatures sporadically attain 30°C in July or August, it is essential to bring warm clothes for the evenings. The usual July daytime temperature is around 17°C. In winter – which can come as early as October – the temperatures are often below -15°C and can reach -40°C.

Most people access the region via Abitibi. Rte 109 runs 103km north to Matagami, the last town before Rte 109 becomes the Rte de la Baie James and continues 620km to Radisson. To reach the eastern sector, where Chibougamau is the largest town, you're better off starting from the Lac St Jean region. From Chibougamau, a grueling 424km gravel road (Rte du Nord) joins the Rte de la Baie James at Kilometer 274. It's also possible to drive from Senneterre to Chibougamau (351km) on the paved Rte 113, passing through several Cree villages on the way. The Chibougamau region is of little interest.

MATAGAMI

For a dreary town in the middle of nowhere, this place sure feels busy. Since 1963, when the town was founded, it has been the site of a copper and zinc mine. It is also

Québec's most northerly forestry center. Both of these industries are still going strong here, and shift workers are always coming and going. Plus, almost everyone driving through on Rte 109 on the way to Radisson stops here for the night.

Hôtel-Motel Matagami (☎819-739-2501; 99 Blvd Matagami; r from $95; ✳) is considered the top place in town. It's decent enough and always seems to be crowded – mainly because of the restaurant, which is open from 5am to 10pm daily.

Motel Le Caribou (☎819-739-4550, 866-739-4550; 108 Blvd Matagami; s/d $65/75; ✳) is a bit more run-down than the hotel, but is fine for a night. The dingy bar in front draws long-faced, jowly clientele.

Every day but Saturday, the Autobus Maheux bus travels to/from Val d'Or (3½ hours) stopping at Hôtel-Motel Matagami.

ROUTE DE LA BAIE JAMES

This road, an extension of Rte 109 to the James Bay hydroelectric projects, is paved, wide and kept in good shape.

At Kilometer 6, a **tourist office** (☎819-739-2030) operates 24 hours a day throughout the year. You must at least slow down here and announce yourself through a speaker; for safety reasons, everyone traveling north is registered. It's worth stopping and going inside, however, as you can pick up several booklets and pamphlets that detail the geological and geographical features along the way and offer information about forest fires. There are bilingual information panels all along the road and emergency telephones at Kilometers 135, 201, 247, 301, 361, 444 and 504.

At Kilometer 38, you'll reach the route's only **campground** (sites $22-26; ☺mid-Jun–early Sep).

Everyone needs to stop at Kilometer 381, the so-called Relais Routier, the only gas station and service stop on the road. It's open 24 hours a day. There's a cafeteria and a **motel** (s/d $80/170) of sorts.

RADISSON

Named after explorer Pierre-Esprit Radisson, this village was set up in 1973 to house the workers on the James Bay hydroelectric project. It looks and feels larger than its population of 350 would suggest, partly because it was built to accommodate fluctuating numbers of workers (who work for eight days, then fly home for six)

and because some families have decided to settle permanently here and create a real village.

The scenery around Radisson is spectacular, with views of the majestic Rivière La Grande from the built-up area around the larger-than-life LG2 hydroelectric power station (also called Robert Bourassa station), just outside town. The **tourist office** (☎819-638-8687; 98 Rue Jolliet; ☺8am-8pm Jun-Oct) is at the village's entrance. At other times, contact the **town hall** (☎819-638-7777; 101 Place Gérard Poirier).

Everyone who makes it here takes a free, guided tour of the power station (get details at the tourist office). The main offices of **Hydro Québec** are in the Pierre Radisson Complex. After an introduction to hydroelectricity, you'll be taken inside and outside the massive LG2. This, together with LG2A, the world's largest underground power station (as tall as a 15-story building but buried 140m deep in the bedrock), produces 25% of the province's energy and ranks among the top handful in size globally.

Eight power stations stretch out over the 800km length of Rivière La Grande; thus, the same water is used eight times, for a total energy output of 15,244 megawatts. It took 20 years, 185,000 laborers and 70 million work hours to complete construction at a cost of some $23.5 billion. The most impressive element is the Robert Bourassa spillway, backed by the enormous Réservoir Robert Bourassa, which is three times the size of Lac St Jean. Stretching out almost 1km in length, this 'giant staircase' of a spillway features a series of 10 steps blasted out from rock, each 10m high with a landing the size of two football fields.

There are several functional motels and **Camping Radisson** (☎819-638-8687; 198 Rue Jolliet; ☺mid-Jun–Sep) on a hill behind the tourist office.

CHISASIBI

Located near where Rivière La Grande meets James Bay, 100km west of Radisson, Chisasibi is a Cree village well worth visiting. The surrounding environment, windswept taiga doused by the arctic breezes from James Bay, is haunting.

The town as it looks now has existed only since 1981. Before this, the residents lived on the island of Fort George, 10km from town, where the Hudson's Bay Company had set up a fur-trading post in 1837. A vestige of the old-fashioned way of life survives in the many tepees seen in backyards, mainly used for smoking fish.

Fort George Island Tours (☎819-855-2626; fgtours@cancom.net) offers excellent guided excursions of varying lengths to Fort George, where most of the original structures, including churches, schools and cemeteries remain. Traditional meals can be ordered. The **Mandow Agency** (☎819-855-3373; mandow@chisasibi.ca) also arranges fishing trips, canoe trips, cultural exchanges and winter activities. Email them with your desire and they may well be able to set it up.

Motel Chisasibi (☎819-855-2838; s/d $97/122) offers the only commercial accommodations.

Nunavik

The desolate expanse of Québec's northern limits, Nunavik, is a tad smaller than France, yet fewer than 10,000 people live here in 14 villages. Hundreds of kilometers of tundra separate them from each other, with no roads to join them. Almost 90% of the population is Inuit; the remainder includes Cree, Naskapis and white Québécois. This surreal territory stretches from the 55th to the 62nd parallel, bordered by Hudson Bay to the west, the Hudson Strait to the north and Ungava Bay and the Labrador border to the east.

Because Nunavik can only be accessed by plane, few casual tourists make the trip. Yet those willing to make their own local contacts can travel independently. Be prepared for high prices for goods and services. On average, food prices are close to double what they are in Québec City.

Land & Climate

There is a great geographic diversity. Even the tundra has many rich shades of beauty and the region is far from a desolate plain of snow and ice. In the southwest, beaches and sand dunes stretch as far as the eye can see. In the northeast, the formidable Torngat Mountains extend in a series of bare, rocky peaks and untamed valleys 300km along the border of Labrador. The province's highest peak, Mont d'Iberville (1652m), is here.

There are also five meteorite-formed craters in Nunavik (of the 144 known on earth). The largest – indeed one of the largest on earth – is called **Pingualuit**, a 1.4-million-year-old cavity with a diameter of 3.4km and a depth of 433m (the height of a 145-story building) in parts. The lake that's formed inside the crater contains water considered among the purest in the world. In terms of transparency, it's second only to Japan's Lake Masyuko. Pingualuit lies 88km southwest of Kangiqsujuaq.

Floating above this unusual terrain are the magical **northern lights** (aurora borealis), which can be seen an average of 243 nights each year.

Local Culture

Socially, the villages hold great interest. The Inuit are generally friendly and approachable. It's their adaptability that's helped them make such a radical transition in their lifestyles in so short a time. But the differences between Inuit communities and contemporary North American towns may give the unprepared a jolt of culture shock.

The villages range in population from 160 (Aupaluk) to 2050 (Kuujjuaq). Half the population is under 18, as you might guess by the sheer number of little ones running around. Everybody gets by alright here money-wise, but some struggle with the serious social problems of domestic violence, drug abuse and alcoholism (even though most villages are 'dry').

After Inuktitut, the most widely spoken language here is English. More youngsters are learning French than their parents did, but elders can rarely speak anything other than Inuktitut.

ⓘ Getting There & Around

First Air provides (costly) service between Montréal and Kuujjuaq ($980 to $1260 one-way, 2¼ hours, twice weekly). Air Inuit flies the same route as well as from Montréal to Puvirnituq ($1600, 3½ hours, daily). From there, flights go to other villages such as Whapmagoostui-Kuujjuarapik ($620, two hours, daily). Air Creebec flies to other communities.

Nova Scotia

Best Places to Eat

» Fid (p327)

» Jane's on the Common
(p327)

» Fleur de Sel (p338)

» Red Shoe Pub (p365)

» Lobster suppers (at town
halls and churches around
the province)

Best Places to Stay

» Waverley Inn (p325)

» Desbarres Manor (p375)

» Lightkeeper's Kitchen &
Guest House (p358)

» Cranberry Cove Inn
(p374)

» Digby Backpackers
Hostel (p346)

Why Go?

At first glance, Nova Scotia appears sweet as a storybook:
lupin-studded fields, gingerbread-like houses, picture-
perfect lighthouses and lightly lapping waves on sandy
shores make you want to wrap it all up and give it to a
cuddly kid as a gift. Then another reality creeps up on
you: this is also the raw Canada of fishermen braving icy
seas, coal miners, moose, horseflies and hockey. Even so,
locals remain the most down-to-earth folk you'll ever
meet; Scottish, Acadian or First Nation, they all enjoy a
drink, a song, a dance and a new face to share it with.
During daylight hours it's easy to discover empty coastal
beach trails and wilderness paths through mixed forest to
vistas with briny breezes. For something more cosmopolitan, head to Halifax for world-class dining and a rocking
music scene.

When to Go

Halifax

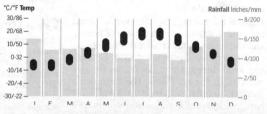

June to August
Wildflowers car-
pet the country
while whales
come close to
feed

**September &
October** Trees
aflame with golds
and reds provide
a backdrop to fall
music festivals

**August to
November** Put on
a thick wetsuit,
hood and booties
to surf icy hur-
ricane swells

History

From time immemorial, the Mi'kmaq First Nation lived throughout present-day Nova Scotia. When the French established the first European settlement at Port Royal (today's Annapolis Royal) in 1605, Grand Chief Membertou offered them hospitality and became a frequent guest of Samuel de Champlain.

That close relationship with the French led to considerable suspicions by the British after they gained control of Nova Scotia, and rewards were offered for Mi'kmaw scalps. Starting in 1755, most French-speaking Acadians were deported to Louisiana (where they became 'Cajuns') and elsewhere for refusing to swear allegiance to the British Crown (see the boxed text, p353).

Nova Scotia was repopulated by some 35,000 United Empire Loyalists retreating from the American Revolution, including a small number of African slaves owned by Loyalists and also freed black Loyalists. New England planters settled other communities and, starting in 1773, waves of Highland Scots arrived in northern Nova Scotia and Cape Breton Island.

Most Nova Scotians trace their ancestry to the British Isles, as a look at the lengthy 'Mac' and 'Mc' sections of the phone book easily confirms. Acadians who managed to return from Louisiana after 1764 found their lands in the Annapolis Valley occupied. They settled instead along the French Shore between Yarmouth and Digby and, on Cape Breton Island, around Chéticamp and on Isle Madame. Today Acadians make up some 18% of the population, though not as many actually speak French. African Nova Scotians make up about 4% of the population. There are approximately 20,000 Mi'kmaq in 18 different communities concentrated around Truro and the Bras d'Or lakes on Cape Breton Island.

Local Culture

With nearly 8000km of coastline, Nova Scotia has a culture that revolves around the sea. Historically, this has been a hard-working region of coal mines and fisheries. The current culture is still very blue collar, but with the decline of the primary industries, many young Nova Scotians are forced to leave their province in search of work.

Perhaps because of the long winters and hard-working days, an enormous number of Nova Scotians play music. Family get-togethers, particularly Acadian and Scottish, consist of strumming, fiddling, foot-tapping and dancing.

❶ Getting There & Away

Air

Most flights go to/from Halifax but there's also an international airport in Sydney on Cape Breton. Airlines include Air Canada, Air Canada Jazz, Westjet, United and Continental. There are multiple flights daily between Halifax and cities such as Toronto, Montréal, Ottawa, Saint John, Moncton and Boston (Massachusetts). In summer and fall there's a weekly direct flight to London.

Bus

Acadian Lines (☎902-454-9321, 800-567-5151; www.acadianbus.com) provides a bus service through the Maritimes and connects Voyageur buses from Québec and Ontario, and Greyhound from the USA (see p884). From Halifax, destinations include Charlottetown ($70, 5½ hours, two daily), Moncton ($57, four hours, three daily) and Bangor (Maine; $105, 11 hours, daily), where there are connections for Boston and New York. All fares for Acadian Lines are tax-inclusive, and there are discounts for children aged five to 11 years (50%), students (15%) and seniors (25%).

Contactable through Acadian Lines, **Trius Lines** (☎902-454-9321, 800-567-5151) travels along the South Shore from Halifax to Yarmouth ($50, 5½ hours, daily) with connections to the ferries. There are discounts for students (15%) and seniors (25%) and for purchasing return tickets.

Boat

NEW BRUNSWICK Bay Ferries (☎888-249-7245; www.bayferries.com; adult/child under 6yr/child 6 13yr/senior $40/5/25/30, car/motorcycle/bicycle $80/50/10) has a three-hour trip from Saint John (New Brunswick) to Digby. Off-season discounts and various packages are available.

NEWFOUNDLAND Marine Atlantic (☎800-341-7981; www.marine-atlantic.ca) operates ferries year-round to Port aux Basques (Newfoundland) from North Sydney (adult/child/car $29/14/81.50). Daytime crossings take between five and six hours, and overnight crossings take about seven hours. Cabins and reclining chairs cost extra. In summer, you can opt for a 14-hour ferry ride (adult/child $80/40.25, car/motorcycle $165/83.50) to Argentia on Newfoundland's east coast. Reservations are required for either trip.

PRINCE EDWARD ISLAND Northumberland Ferries (☎902-566-3838, 888-249-7245; www.peiferry.com; adult/child $16/free, car/motorcycle/bicycle incl passengers $64/40/20)

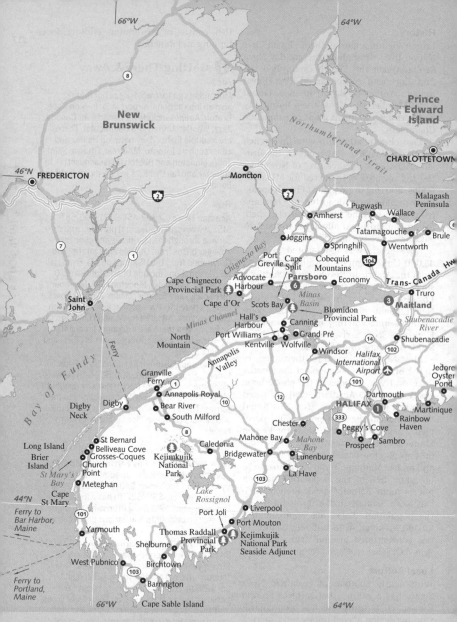

Nova Scotia Highlights

1 People-watch along the waterfront and take in an unforgettable meal in **Halifax** (p320)

2 Sample French soldiers' rations or a general's feast c 1744 at **Louisbourg National Historic Site** (p374)

3 Crash through the waves of the tidal bore at **Maitland** (p354)

4 Experience the misty peace of kayaking through the deserted islands and protected coves around **Tangier** (p377)

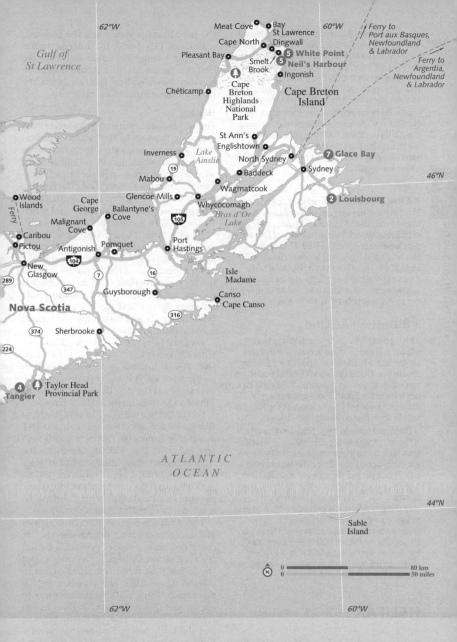

Eat hot chowder after looking for eagles and whales from **White Point to Neil's Harbour** (p369)

Search the sand flats exposed by extreme Fundy tides for semiprecious stones around **Parrsboro** (p356)

Voyage under the ocean floor to the coal mines of **Glace Bay** (p373) while listening to the yarns of a retired miner

cruises between Wood Islands (Prince Edward Island; PEI), and Caribou, near Pictou, up to nine times daily (1¼ hours). You only pay when leaving PEI so it's slightly cheaper to arrive by ferry then exit PEI via the Confederation Bridge (see p424). No reservations are required, but it's wise to show up half an hour before the sailing.

USA Ferry service between Bar Harbor (Maine) and Yarmouth has been running since the 1950s but it was halted in 2010 due to funding issues. It's expected that the service will start up again in 2011 with a new boat so check online for details.

Train

VIA Rail (www.viarail.ca) runs services between Montréal and Halifax (one-week advance purchase adult/child $182/80, 21 hours, daily except Tuesdays) with stops in Amherst (advance purchase adult/child $137/69, 17 hours from Montréal) and Truro (advance purchase adult/child $148/74, 18 hours from Montréal). Students pay the same as adults with no need for advance purchase; adult discount fares may sell out so it's best to book as early as possible.

ℹ Getting Around

Renting a car is by far the easiest way to get around and can be more economical than taking the bus. Shuttle buses (p330) are another alternative. Distances are very manageable; you can easily stay in the Annapolis Valley and do day trips to the South Shore and vice versa. The longest drive most people will do is the four-hour haul to Cape Breton Island from Halifax.

The direct route to most places will be on a 100-series highway (eg 101, 102, 103), which have high speed limits and limited exits. There is usually a corresponding older highway (eg 1, 2, 3) that passes through communities and has varying speed limits, but none higher than 80km/h. The Trans-Canada Hwy (Hwy 104/105) cuts directly across the province from Amherst to Sydney without passing through Halifax. Other back roads snake across rural Nova Scotia, usually numbered 200 to 299 when traveling vaguely east–west and 300 to 399 going north–south. You'll find more potholes than gas stations along these.

HALIFAX

POP 360,000

Halifax is the kind of town that people flock to, not so much for the opportunities, but for the quality of life it has to offer. Sea breezes off the harbor keep the air clean, and parks and trees nestle between heritage buildings, cosmopolitan eateries and arty shops. Several universities ensure that the population is young and the bars and nightclubs full. Stroll the historic waterfront, catch some live music and enjoy the best of what the Maritimes have to offer. In summer, never-ending festivals ignite the party ambience that much more.

History

Pirates, Indians, warring colonialists and exploding ships make the history of Halifax read like an adventure story. From 1749, when Edward Cornwallis founded Halifax along what is today Barrington St, the British settlement expanded and flourished. The destruction of the French fortress at Louisbourg in 1760 increased British dominance and sealed Halifax as Nova Scotia's most important city.

Despite being home to two universities from the early 1800s, Halifax was still a rough and ready sailors' nest that during the War of 1812 became a center for privateer blackmarket trade. As piracy lost its government endorsement, Halifax sailed smoothly into a mercantile era, and the city streets (particularly Market and Brunswick Sts) became home to countless taverns and brothels.

On April 14, 1912, three Halifax ships were sent in response to a distress call: the 'unsinkable' *Titanic* had hit an iceberg. Over 1500 people were killed in the tragedy and many were buried at Fairview Cemetery, next to the Fairview Overpass on the Bedford Hwy.

Soon after, during WWI in 1917 the *Mont Blanc,* a French munitions ship carrying TNT and highly flammable benzol, collided with another ship. The 'Halifax Explosion,' the world's biggest man-made explosion prior to A-bombs being dropped on Japan in 1945, ripped through the city. More than 1900 people were killed and 9000 injured. Almost the entire northern end of Halifax was leveled.

The downtown area, three universities and older residential neighborhoods are contained on a compact peninsula cut off from mainland Halifax by an inlet called the North West Arm. Almost all sights of interest to visitors are concentrated in this area, making walking the best way to get around. Point Pleasant Park is at the extreme southern end of the peninsula, and the lively North End neighborhood – home to African Nova Scotians, art-school students and most of Halifax' gay bars – stretches from the midpoint to the northern extreme.

Two bridges span the harbor, connecting Halifax to Dartmouth and leading to highways north (for the airport) and east. The

MacDonald Bridge at the eastern end of North St is closest to downtown. The airport is 40km northwest of town on Hwy 102.

◉ Sights

DOWNTOWN HALIFAX

Historic Properties
NOTABLE BUILDINGS

The Historic Properties is a group of restored buildings on Upper Water St, built between 1800 and 1905. Originally designed as huge warehouses for easy storage of goods and cargo, they now house boutiques, restaurants and bars and are connected by the waterfront boardwalks. Artisans, merchants and buskers do business around the buildings in the summer.

The 1814 **Privateer's Warehouse** is the area's oldest stone building. The privateers were government sanctioned and sponsored pirates who stored their booty here. Among the other vintage buildings are the wooden **Old Red Store** – once used for shipping operations and as a sail loft – and **Simon's Warehouse**, built in 1854.

Alexander Keith's Nova Scotia Brewery
BREWERY

(☎902-455-1474; www.keiths.ca; Brewery Market, 1496 Lower Water St; adult/child $16/8; ⊗11am-8pm Mon-Thu, 11am-9pm Fri & Sat, noon-4pm Sun) A tour of this brewery takes you to 19th-century Halifax via costumed thespians, quality brew and dark corridors. Finish your hour-long tour with a party in the basement pub with beer on tap and ale-inspired yarns. Note that you'll need your ID. (Kids are kept happy with lemonade.)

Maritime Museum of the Atlantic
MUSEUM

(☎902-424-7490; www.museum.gov.ns.ca/mma, 1675 Lower Water St; adult/child $8.50/4.50; ⊗9:30am-5:30pm Wed-Mon, to 8pm Tue) Part of this fun waterfront museum was a chandlery, where all the gear needed to outfit a vessel was sold. You can smell the charred ropes, cured to protect them from saltwater. There's a wildly popular display on the *Titanic* and another on the Halifax Explosion. The 3-D film about the *Titanic* costs $5. Outside at the dock you can explore the CSS *Acadia,* a retired hydrographic vessel from England.

The last WWII corvette **HMCS Sackville** (adult/child $3/2; ⊗10am-5pm) is docked nearby and staffed by the Canadian Navy.

Pier 21 Centre
MUSEUM

(☎902-425-7770; www.pier21.ca; 1055 Marginal Rd; adult/child $8.50/5; ⊗9:30am-5:30pm) Named by CBC (Canadian Broadcasting

» Population: 932,966

» Area: 55,491 sq km

» Capital: Halifax

» Quirky fact: Has the only tidal power plant in the western hemisphere

Company) as one of the Seven Wonders of Canada, Pier 21 was to Canada what Ellis Island was to the USA. Between 1928 and 1971 over a million immigrants entered Canada through Pier 21. Their stories and the historical context that led them to abandon their homelands are presented in this museum. Researchers fanned out across Canada to get first-hand testimonials from immigrants who passed through Pier 21. These moving videos are shown in screening rooms off a railcar – bring your hankie.

Citadel Hill National Historic Site
HISTORICAL SITE

(☎902-426-5080; off Sackville St; adult/child $11.70/5.80; ⊗9am-6pm) Canada's most visited national historic site, the huge and arguably spooky Citadel, is a star-shaped fort atop Halifax' central hill. Construction began in 1749 with the founding of Halifax; this version of the Citadel is the fourth, built from 1818 to 1861. Guided tours explain the fort's shape and history. The grounds inside the fort are open year-round, with free admission when the exhibits are closed.

Art Gallery of Nova Scotia
ART GALLERY

(☎902-424-7542; www.agns.gov.ns.ca; 1723 Hollis St; adult/child $12/3; ⊗10am-5pm Fri-Wed, to 9pm Thu) Don't miss the permanent, tear-jerking Maud Lewis Painted House exhibit that includes the 3mx4m house that Lewis lived in most of her adult life. The main exhibit in the lower hall changes regularly, featuring anything from ancient art to the avant-garde. Free tours are given at 2pm Sunday year-round (daily during July and August).

Halifax Public Gardens
GARDEN

At the corner of Spring Garden Rd and South Park St, these are considered the finest Victorian city gardens in North America. Oldies bands perform off-key concerts in the gazebo on Sunday afternoons in summer, tai chi practitioners go through their paces, and anyone who brings checkers can play on outside tables.

Titanic Burial Grounds HISTORICAL SITES
When the *Titanic* sank, the bodies not buried at sea were brought to Halifax. Today there are 19 graves at Mount Olivet Catholic Cemetery (7076 Mumford Rd), 10 in the Baron de Hirsch Jewish Cemetery at the north end of Windsor St, and 121 in the adjacent Fairview Lawn Cemetery; 40 graves are still unidentified. J Dawson, whose name was the basis for Leonardo DiCaprio's character in the film *Titanic,* is at Fairview Cemetery.

FREE **Anna Leonowens Gallery** ART GALLERY
(☑902-494-8184; 1891 Granville St; ⊙11am-5pm Tue-Fri, noon-4pm Sat, show openings 5:30-7:30pm Mon) Off the pedestrian area on Granville St, this gallery shows work by students and faculty of the Nova Scotia College of Art & Design. The gallery is named for the founder of the college, who was immortalized in *The King and I* for her relationship with the King of Siam.

St Paul's Church CHURCH
(☑902-429-2240; 1749 Argyle St; ⊙9am-4pm Mon-Fri) Established in 1749 for the founding of Halifax, Anglican St Paul's Church once served parishioners from Newfoundland to Ontario. Across the square, Halifax' **City Hall** is a true gem of Victorian architecture.

St Mary's Cathedral Basilica CHURCH
(☑902-423-4116; 1508 Barrington St; ⊙free tours 10am & 2pm Jul-Sep) You can't miss this cathedral which purportedly has the largest free-standing spire in North America.

Old Town Clock NOTABLE BUILDING
At the top of George St, at Citadel Hill, the Old Town Clock has been keeping time for 200 years. The inner workings arrived in Halifax from London in 1803 after being ordered by Prince Edward, the Duke of Kent.

NORTH END
The North End has been a distinct neighborhood for almost as long as Halifax has existed. In the early 1750s this 'North Suburbs' area became popular and subsequently grew because of its larger building lots.

Churches
St George's Round Church (☑902-423-1059; http://collections.ic.gc.ca/churchandcommunity; 2222 Brunswick St) was built in 1800 and is a rare circular Palladian church with a main rotunda 18m in diameter. Tours are by arrangement. Tours of the 1756 **Little Dutch**

Church (2405 Brunswick St), the second-oldest building in Halifax, can also be arranged through St George's. The **Cornwallis St Baptist Church** (5457 Cornwallis St) has been serving African Nova Scotians since the 1830s. Walk by on Sunday morning and hear the gospel music overflow its walls.

FREE **Maritime Command Museum**
MUSEUM
(☑902-427-0550, ext 6725; 2725 Gottingen St; ⊙9:30am-3:30pm Mon-Fri) The admiral of the British navy for all of North America was based in Halifax until 1819 and threw grand parties at Admiralty House, now the Maritime Command Museum. Apart from the beautiful Georgian architecture, the museum is worth a visit for its eclectic collections: cigarette lighters, silverware and ships' bells, to name a few.

OUTSIDE THE CITY CENTER
Point Pleasant Park NATURE RESERVE
Some 39km of nature trails, picnic spots and the **Prince of Wales Martello Tower** (a round 18th-century defensive structure) are all found within this 75-hectare sanctuary, just 1.5km from the city center. Trails around the perimeter of the park offer views of McNabs Island, the open ocean and the North West Arm. Bus 9 along Barrington St goes to Point Pleasant, and there's ample free parking off Point Pleasant Dr.

McNabs Island NATURE RESERVE
Fine sand and cobblestone shorelines, salt marshes, abandoned military fortifications and forests paint the scenery of this 400-hectare island in Halifax harbor. Staff of the **McNabs Island Ferry** (☑902-465-4563; www.mcnabsisland.com; Government Wharf; round-trip adult/child $12/10; ⊙24hr) will provide you with a map and an orientation to 30km of roads and trails on the island. For camping reservations contact the **Department of Natural Resources** (☑902-861-2560; www.parks.gov.ns.ca/mcnabs.htm). The ferry runs from Fisherman's Cove in Eastern Passage, a short drive through Dartmouth. When the ferry staff are not too busy, they'll pick you up in Halifax for the same fare.

🏃 **Activities**
Cycling
Cycling is a great way to see sites on the outskirts of Halifax – you can take bikes on the ferries to Dartmouth or cycle over the MacDonald Bridge.

Pedal & Sea Adventures (☑902-857-9319, 877-772-5699; www.pedalandseaadventures.com; per day/week incl tax from $35/140) will deliver the bike to you, complete with helmet, lock and repair kit. It also leads good-value tours (one-/two-day trips including taxes and meals cost $105/235) and offers self-guided tours from $69.

Hiking

There are both short and long hikes surprisingly close to downtown. **Hemlock Ravine** is an 80-hectare, wooded area that has five trails, suitable for all levels. To get there take the Bedford Hwy from central Halifax then turn left at Kent Ave – there is parking and a map of the trail at the end of this road. See www.novatrails.com for more detailed trail descriptions and directions to other trailheads. There's also hiking in Point Pleasant Park and on McNabs Island.

☞ Tours

Bluenose II   HARBOR TOURS
(☑902-634-1963, 800-763-1963; www.schoonerbluenose2.ca; Lower Water St) This replica of the famous two-masted racing schooner, the *Bluenose*, seen on the back of Canada's 10¢ coin, runs harbor tours when it's in town. It was completely restored in 2010 – check the website for pricing.

Tall Ship Silva   HARBOR TOURS
(☑902-429-9463; www.tallshipsilva.com; Queen's Wharf at Prince St; ⊙noon, 2pm, 4pm, 6pm & 10:30pm daily May-Oct) Lend a hand or sit back and relax while taking a one-hour ($12 per person), 1½-hour (adult/child $20/14) or evening party two-hour ($20 per person) cruise on Halifax' square masted tall ship.

Tattle Tours   WALKING TOURS
(☑902-494-0525; www.tattletours.ca; per person $10; ⊙7:30pm Wed-Sun) Lively two-hour tours depart from the Old Town Clock and are filled with local gossip, pirate tales and ghost stories. Walking tours are also available on demand – ask at any VIC.

Salty Bear Adventure Tours
                                             BUS TOURS
(p887) A sociable backpacker's choice for touring the province.

Great E.A.R.T.H Expeditions   ECO TOURS
(☑902-223-2409;   www.greatearthexpeditions.com; half-/full-day tours from $60/90) Eco half- and full-day tours led from Halifax can include hiking, kayaking or historical themes.

DON'T MISS

HALIFAX HIGHLIGHTS

» **Halifax Farmers' Brewery Market** (p329) Have breakfast here on Saturday mornings

» **Dartmouth Ferry** (p331) Enjoy a breezy budget cruise

» **Maritime Museum of the Atlantic** (p321) Learn all about the Halifax Explosion and the *Titanic*

» **Citadel Hill National Historic Site** (p321) For history and a view

» **Live music** (p329) At a variety of pubs or venues

Longer four-day tours up the Cabot Trail and through Kejimikujic are also on offer.

Murphy's Cable Wharf
                                             HARBOR TOURS
(☑902-420-1015; www.murphysonthewater.com; 1751 Lower Water St) This tourism giant runs a range of tours on Halifax Harbour, from deep-sea fishing and two-hour scenic cruises to the popular 55-minute **Harbour Hopper Tours** (adult/child $26/15) on an amphibious bus.

☆ Festivals & Events

Halifax is most vibrant during its jovial festivals. Check out volunteering opportunities through festival websites.

Nova Scotia Tattoo   CULTURAL
(www.nstattoo.ca; tickets $27-65; ⊙early Jul) The world's 'largest annual indoor show' is a military-style event with lots of marching bands.

Atlantic Jazz Festival   MUSIC
(www.jazzeast.com; ⊙mid-Jul) A full week of free outdoor jazz concerts each afternoon, and evening performances ranging from world music to classic jazz trios (tickets $15 to $30).

Halifax International Busker Festival   BUSKING
(www.buskers.ca; ⊙early Aug) Comics, mimics, daredevils and musicians from all over the world perform along the Halifax waterfront.

Atlantic Fringe Festival   THEATER
(www.atlanticfringe.com; ⊙mid-Sep) Offbeat and experimental theatre from both emerging and established artists.

NOVA SCOTIA HALIFAX

To Little Dutch
Church (50m)

To Fresh Start B&B (750m);
Maritime Command
Museum (750m)

34

10

43
17

3

Cornwallis St

Brunswick St

Maitland St

Gottingen St

Creighton St

Barrington St

Maynard St

41

To Jane's on
the Common
(500m)

Agricola St

Cogswell St

Scotia
Square

Halifax
Common

28

6

1

To Heartwood Vegetarian
Cuisine & Bakery (1km)

Duke St

2

Art Gallery
of Nova Scotia

39

Hollis St

Upper Water St

**Citadel Hill National
Historic Site**

9

Brunswick St

George St

Argyle St

21

38

30

12

37

Granville St

Barrington St

Bell Rd

32

40

42

4

Summer St

Sackville St

Market St

Grafton St

24

8

Blowers St

11

5

29

25

Spring Garden Rd

20

Dresden Row

Birmingham St

Queen St

35

26

South Park St

Brenton St

Clyde St

To Dalhousie University,
Howe Hall (400m)

Tower Rd

Brenton St
Pl

Morris St

College St

Robie St

To Point Pleasant
Park (1.4km)

Atlantic Film Festival FILM
(www.atlanticfilm.com; tickets $10-15; ☉mid-Sep) Ten days of great flicks from the Atlantic region and around the world.

Halifax Pop Explosion MUSIC
(www.halifaxpopexplosion.com; wristbands $50; ☉mid-Oct) Some 130 concerts are spread out over 12 clubs during a five-day period and include hip-hop, punk, indie rock and folk. A wristband gets you into as many shows as you can manage to see.

🛏 Sleeping

TOP CHOICE Waverley Inn INN $$
(☎902-423-9346, 800-565-9346; www.waverleyinn.com; 1266 Barrington St; d incl breakfast $130-240; P@) Every room here is furnished uniquely and nearly theatrically with antiques and dramatic linens. Both Oscar Wilde and PT Barnum once stayed here and probably would again today if they were still living. The downtown location can't be beat.

Pebble Bed & Breakfast B&B $$
(☎902-423-3369, 888-303-5056; www.thepebble.ca; 1839 Armview Tce; r $110-225; P) Bathroom aficionados will find heaven at this luxurious B&B. The tub and shower are in a giant room that leads to a terrace overlooking a leafy garden. The bedrooms are equally generous with plush, high beds and a modern-meets-antique decor. Irish owner Elizabeth O'Carroll grew up with a pub-owning family and brings lively, joyous energy from the Emerald Isle to her home in a posh, waterside residential area.

Halliburton INN $$$
(☎902-420-0658; www.thehalliburton.com; 5184 Morris St; r $145-350; P☺@) Pure, soothing class without all that Victorian hullabaloo can be found at this exceedingly comfortable and well-serviced historic hotel right in downtown.

Lord Nelson Hotel HOTEL $$$
(☎902-423-5130, 800-565-2020; www.lordnelsonhotel.com; 1515 South Park St; d $140-360; P@) When rock stars (such as the Rolling Stones) come to Halifax, they stay here. It's an elegant yet not stuffy 1920s building right across from Halifax Public Gardens. Rates drop dramatically in the off-season.

Prince George Hotel HOTEL $$$
(☎902-425-1986, 800-565-1567; www.princegeorgehotel.com; 1725 Market St; d $170-300; P@)

A suave and debonair gem, central Prince George has all the details covered. Garden patios are a great place to take a drink or a meal or even work as an alternative to indoor meeting areas. Parking is $15.

Marigold B&B   B&B **$**
(☎902-423-4798; www.marigoldbedandbreakfast.com; 6318 Norwood St; r $70; P) Feel at home in this artist's nest full of bright floral paintings and fluffy cats. It's in a tree-lined residential area in the North End with easy public transport access.

Fresh Start B&B   B&B **$$**
(☎902-453-6616, 888-453-6616; freshstart@ns.sympatico.ca; 2720 Gottingen St; r $90-130; P @) Run by two retired nurses, this majestic yet lived-in-feeling Victorian is in a quiet part of the North End. Rooms with en-suite bathrooms are the best value. Gay friendly.

Halifax Backpackers Hostel   HOSTEL **$**
(☎902-431-3170, 888-431-3170; www.halifaxbackpackers.com; 2193 Gottingen St; dm/d/f $20/57.50/80; P) Co-ed dorms at this hip, 36-bed North End hostel hold no more than six beds. It draws a funky young crowd and everyone congregates at the downstairs cafe to swill strong coffee, eat cheap breakfasts and mingle with the eclectic local regulars. City buses stop right in front, but be warned: it's a slightly rough-edged neighborhood.

Discovery Centre
MUSEUM

(☎902-492-4422; www.discoverycentre.ns.ca; 1593 Barrington St; adult/child $8.50/6; ⊙10am-5pm Mon-Sat, 1-5pm Sun) Hands-on exhibits, live shows and movies make science fun for all ages.

Museum of Natural History
MUSEUM

(☎902-424-7353; http://museum.gov.ns.ca/mnh/index.htm; 1747 Summer St; adult/child $5.75/3.75; ⊙9am-5pm Tue-Sat, to 8pm Wed, noon-5pm Sun year-round, 9am-5pm Mon Jun-Sep) Daily summer programs introduce children to Gus the toad and demonstrate the cooking of bugs. Exhibits on history and the natural world will keep parents engaged, too.

Theodore Too Big Harbour Tours
HARBOR TOURS

(☎902-492-8847; www.theodoretoo.com; 1751 Lower Water St; adult/child $20/15; ⊙11am, 12:30pm, 2pm, 3:30pm & 5pm daily mid-Jun–Sep) One-hour tours on this funny-looking cartoon character boat of book and television fame are particularly good for under-sixes.

HI Nova Scotia
HOSTEL $

(☎902-422-3863; www.hihostels.ca; 1253 Barrington St; member/nonmember dm $27/32, r $57; ⊙check-in 2pm-midnight) Expect a dark and dormy night and a bright and cheery do-it-yourself breakfast at this exceptionally central 75-bed hostel. Staff is friendly, the shared kitchen lively and the house Victorian. Reserve ahead in summer.

Dalhousie University
HOSTEL $

(☎902-494-8840; www.dal.ca/confserv; s/tw $45/70; ⊙mid-May–mid-Aug; P☂) Dorm rooms with shared bathrooms are nearly sterile (read: posterless and beer-bottle-free). Most people stay at **Howe Hall** (6230 Coburg St), which is adjacent to all the included university amenities and is a short walk to the Spring Garden Rd area. Check the website for other halls that may be available and for student and senior rates.

✗ Eating

Bars and pubs (p328) often serve very good food; kitchens close around 10pm.

TOP CHOICE Fid
FUSION $$

(☎902-422-9162; www.fidcuisine.ca; 1569 Dresden Row; mains lunch $14-16, dinner $22-27; ⊙lunch Wed-Fri, dinner Tue-Sun; ✗) Slow-food proponent Dennis Johnston buys all his ingredients from the local farmers' market, then concocts dishes such as monkfish with shell peas, asparagus, maple-glazed pork belly with sweet potato and a beautiful pad thai. It's a great place to sample regional foods; the menu changes weekly and carries vegetarian options.

TOP CHOICE Jane's on the Common
CANADIAN $$

(☎902-431-5683; 2394 Robie St; mains lunch $11-13, dinner $16-19; ⊙lunch Tue-Fri, dinner Tue-Sun, brunch Sat & Sun) The shiny black diner-style tables fill up early at this increasingly popular eatery. Try a delectable starter such as the arugula, apple and ricotta tart or seared scallops in a curried apricot vinaigrette, then move on to to-die-for mains such as a smoked pork chop stuffed with spinach, sage and cheddar. Divine!

Bish
CANADIAN $$$

(☎902-425-7993; 1475 Lower Water St; mains $30-36; ⊙dinner Mon-Sat) If a sizzling platter of shellfish including king crab, scallops and lobster doesn't up the ante of Maritime cuisine, not much will. There's no better place to celebrate or get very, very romantic than waterside Bishop's Harbour.

Da Maurizio
ITALIAN $$$

(☎902-423-0859; 1496 Lower Water St; mains $28-34; ⊙dinner Mon-Sat) Many locals cite this as their favorite Halifax restaurant. The ambience is as fine as the cuisine; exposed brick and clean lines bring out all the flavors of this heritage brewery building. Reservations strongly recommended.

Epicurious Morcels
FUSION $$

(☎902-455-0955; Hydrostone Market, 5529 Young St; mains around $12; ⊙11:30am-8pm Tue-Thu, 10:30am-8pm Fri & Sat, 10:30am-2:30pm Sun) The specialties here are smoked salmon, *gravlax* (dill-cured salmon) and unusual but extremely tasty homemade soups. The rest of the internationally inspired menu is also fantastic.

Halifax has a thumping and thriving gay and lesbian scene with most of the nightlife action concentrated around Gottingen St. In the city center, **Reflections Cabaret** (☎902-422-2957; 5184 Sackville St) is a wild disco that attracts a mixed crowd. It opens at 4pm, but the action really starts after 10pm (it stays open until 3am).

Lesbian travelers can stop by **Venus Envy** (☎902-422-0004; 1598 Barrington St; ⊕10am-6pm Mon-Wed & Sat, 10am-7pm Thu & Fri, noon-5pm Sun) to network, browse books and check out fun toys. Squeaky clean **Seadog's Sauna & Spa** (☎902-444-3647; www.seadogs.ca; 2199 Gottingen St; ⊕4pm-1am Mon-Thu, from 4pm Fri through 1am Mon) is the largest private men's club east of Québec City and has all the spa fixings. The same folks have opened **Menz Bar** (2182 Gottingen St; ⊕3pm-2am), which offers its own Menz Pale Ale on tap. A map of the heart of the gay community is available on the Seadog's website.

Halifax Pride Week (www.halifaxpride.com) takes place every year around the second week of July. Don't miss the Dykes versus Divas softball game that usually kicks off the week.

Morris East
ITALIAN $$

(☎902-444-7663; 5212 Morris St; 10in pizzas $14-17; ⊕lunch Tue-Sat, dinner Tue-Sun) You'll find creative wood-fired pizzas (try the peach, rosemary aioli and prosciutto) on your choice of white, whole-wheat or gluten-free dough, and snazzy cocktails (like basil, lime and vodka punch) at this cosmopolitan cafe.

Brooklyn Warehouse
CANADIAN $$

(☎902-446-8181; 2795 Windsor St; mains lunch $8-14, dinner around $18; ⊕lunch Mon-Fri, dinner Mon-Sat; 🖉) This North End hot spot is loaded with vegetarian and vegan options (the eggplant moussaka stack is excellent), has a huge beer and cocktail menu, and has an atmosphere that feels like a modern, hip version of *Cheers* – but with way better food.

Il Mercato
ITALIAN $$

(☎902-422-2866; 5650 Spring Garden Rd; mains $10-24; ⊕11am-11pm) This long-standing Italian favorite doesn't take reservations; come early or late on weekends, or wait a short while.

Chives Canadian Bistro
CANADIAN $$$

(☎902-420-9626; 1537 Barrington St; mains $17-35; ⊕dinner) With a menu that changes with what's seasonally available using mostly local ingredients, the food is fine dining while the low-lit cozy ambience is upscale casual.

Sushi Nami Royal
JAPANESE $$

(☎902-422-9020; 1535 Dresden Row; lunch bento boxes from $10; ⊕lunch Mon-Sat, dinner Mon-Sun) Bento box lunch specials with a choice of chicken, pork, eel and more served with rice salad, miso soup and a sushi or tempura option are one of Halifax' better bargains. The sushi is excellent as well.

Wooden Monkey
CANADIAN $$

(☎902-444-3844; 1707 Grafton St; mains $14-23; ⊕11am-10pm; 🖉) This dark, cozy nook with outdoor sidewalk seating on sunny days adamantly supports local organics and is a fab place to get superb gluten-free and vegan meals as well as humane meat dishes.

Heartwood Vegetarian Cuisine & Bakery
VEGETARIAN $

(☎902-425-2808; 6250 Quinpool Rd; light meals from $5; ⊕10am-8pm Mon-Sat; 🖉) Try the local organic salad bar or amazing baked goods along with a cup of fair-trade coffee.

Scotia Square Mall Food Court
FAST FOOD $

(cnr Barrington & Duke Sts) If you're not fussed about ambience, get surprisingly authentic Indian, Korean, Italian food and more for around $5 a plate at this food court. Favorites here are **Ray's Falafel** (⊕8am-6pm Mon-Wed, 8am-9pm Thu & Fri, 9am-6pm Sat) and **Cafe Istanbul** (⊕8am-6pm Mon-Wed, 8am-9pm Thu & Fri, 9am-6pm Sat).

🍷 Drinking

Halifax rivals St John's, Newfoundland, for the most drinking holes per capita. The biggest concentration of attractive bars is on Argyle St, where temporary streetside patios expand the sidewalk each summer. Pubs and bars close at 2am (a few hours earlier on Sunday).

Lower Deck

PUB

(☎902-422-1501; 1869 Lower Water St) A first stop for a real Nova Scotian knee-slapping good time. Think pints in frothy glasses, everyone singing, and live music all spilling out over the sidewalks on summer nights. When someone yells 'sociable!' it's time to raise your glass.

Economy Shoe Shop

PUB

(☎902-423-8845; 1663 Argyle St) This has been the 'it' place to drink and people-watch in Halifax for almost a decade. On weekend nights actors and journalists figure heavily in the crush. It's a pleasant place for afternoon drinks and the kitchen dishes out tapas until last call at 1:45am.

Onyx

BAR

(☎902-428-5680; 5680 Spring Garden Rd) A sultry place for a chic cocktail, the Onyx has a backlit white onyx bar that serves a huge selection of fine wines, single malt whiskeys and nine signature fresh fruit mojitos, among other options. Imbibe small plates of Asian-French cuisine made with local ingredients.

Cabin Coffee

CAFE

(☎902-422-8130; 1554 Hollis St; ⊙6:30am-6pm Mon-Fri, 7:30am-5pm Sat, 9am-5pm Sun) As cozy as a cabin living room, this place serves excellent coffee as well as light meals and all-day breakfasts from $4.

☆ Entertainment

Check out the *Coast* to see what's on – a free weekly publication available around town, it's the essential guide for music, theater, film and events.

Live Music

Halifax seems to be fueled on music, with folk, hip-hop, alternative country and rock gigs around town every weekend. Cover charge depends on the band.

Paragon

LIVE MUSIC

(☎902-429-3020; 2037 Gottingen St) The choice venue for touring bands and big-name local acts.

Carelton

LIVE MUSIC

(☎902-422-6335; 1685 Argyle St) Catch acoustic sets then enjoy the reasonable meals including a late-night menu.

Bearly's House of Blues & Ribs

LIVE MUSIC

(☎902-423-2526; 1269 Barrington St; cover $3) The best blues musicians in Atlantic Canada play here at incredibly low cover charges.

Wednesday karaoke nights draw a crowd and some fine singers.

Seahorse Tavern

LIVE MUSIC

(☎902-423-7200; 1665 Argyle St) The place to see punk, indic and metal bands.

Nightclubs

Dome

NIGHTCLUB

(☎902-422-5453; 1740 Argyle St) Dubbed the 'Liquordome,' with four establishments under one roof. The Attic has live music; the others are nightclubs open until 3am.

Theater

The two professional theaters in and around Halifax – Neptune Theatre and Eastern Front Theatre in Dartmouth – take a break in summer, with their last shows typically playing in May. However, Shakespeare by the Sea provides diversion through the summer.

Neptune Theatre

THEATER

(☎902-429-7070; www.neptunetheatre.com; 1593 Argyle St) This downtown theater presents musicals and well-known plays on its main stage (from $35), and edgier stuff in the studio (from $15).

Shakespeare by the Sea

THEATER

(☎902-422-0295; www.shakespearebythesea.ca; Point Pleasant Park; suggested donation $15; ⊙Jun-Sep) Fine performances of the Bard's works at the Cambridge Battery, an old fortification, in the middle of Point Pleasant Park. Check the website for a map and details.

Sports

Halifax Mooseheads junior hockey team plays at Halifax Metro Centre (☎902-451-1221; 5284 Duke St; tickets $15).

🛍 Shopping

Halifax has some truly quirky shops to discover in the city center between Spring Garden Rd and Duke St.

Halifax Farmers' Brewery Market

FOOD & DRINK

(☎902-492-4043; 1496 Lower Water St; ⊙8am-1pm Sat Jan–mid-May, 7am-1pm Sat mid-May–Dec) North America's oldest farmers' market, in the 1820s Keith's Brewery Building, is the ultimate shopping experience. Head here to people-watch and buy organic produce, locally crafted jewelry, clothes and more. In fact, the market has become so popular it's going to be expanded in 2011 to the newly built **Seaport Market**, a second location near Pier 21 – it will be a daily event with more vendors and cafes and more parking.

Nova Scotian Crystal   CRAFTS
(☑888-977-2797; 5080 George St; ☺9am-6pm Mon-Fri, 10am-5pm Sat & Sun) As much of a show as a place to shop. Watch glass blowers form beautiful crystal glasses and vases then pick the ones you want in the classy adjacent shop.

ⓘ Information

Bookstores

Book Room (☑902-423-8271; 1546 Barrington St; ☺9am-7:30pm Wed-Fri, 9am-5pm Mon, Tue & Sat, noon-5pm Sun) Around for nearly 160 years, it stocks a good selection of maps and travel guides, plus books by local authors.

John W Doull Bookseller (☑902-429-1652; 1684 Barrington St; ☺10am-6pm Mon & Tue, 9:30am-9pm Wed-Fri, 10am-9pm Sat) This secondhand store has more books than many libraries.

Internet Access

Many cafes, restaurants and public spaces have wi-fi.

Spring Garden Road Memorial Library (☑902-490-5723; 5381 Spring Garden Rd; ☺10am-9pm Tue-Thu, 10am-5pm Fri & Sat) Computers on a first-come, first-served basis.

Internet Resources

Destination Halifax (www.halifaxinfo.com) Halifax' official tourism site has information on everything from events to package bookings.

Halifax Regional Municipality (www.halifax. ca) Info on everything from bus schedules to recreation programs.

Studio Map (www.studiorally.ca) An up-to-date guide to art and craft studios across the province, plus a shortlist of spot-on recommendations for eateries and B&Bs.

Medical Services

Family Focus (☑902-420-2038; 5991 Spring Garden Rd; consultation $65; ☺8:30am-9pm Mon-Fri, 11am-5pm Sat & Sun) Walk-in or same-day appointments.

Halifax Infirmary (☑902-473-3383/7605; 1796 Summer St; ☺24hr) For emergencies.

Money

Bank branches cluster around Barrington and Duke Sts.

Post

Lawton's Drugs (☑902-429-0088; 5675 Spring Garden Rd; ☺8am-9pm Mon-Fri, 8am-6pm Sat, noon-5pm Sun) Post office inside.

Main Post Office (☑902-494-4670; 1680 Bedford Row; ☺7:30am-5:15pm Mon-Fri) Pick up mail sent to General Delivery, Halifax, NS B3J 2L3 here.

Tourist Information

Check out posters for performances and events on the bulletin boards just inside the door of the Spring Garden Road Memorial Library.

Tourism Nova Scotia (☑902-425-5781, 800-565-0000; www.novascotia.com) Operates Visitor Information Centres (VICs) in Halifax and other locations within Nova Scotia province, plus a free booking service for accommodations, which is useful when rooms are scarce in midsummer. It publishes the *Doers & Dreamers Guide* that lists places to stay, attractions and tour operators.

Visitor Information Centre (VIC) Argyle St (☑902-490-5963; cnr Argyle & Sackville Sts; ☺8:30am-8pm Jul & Aug, to 7pm May, Jun & Sep, to 4:30pm Mon-Fri rest of year); Halifax International Airport (☑902-873-1223; ☺9am-9pm); Waterfront (☑902-424-4248; 1655 Lower Water St; ☺8:30am-8pm Jun-Sep, to 4:30pm Wed-Sun Oct-May)

ⓘ Getting There & Away

Air

Most air services in Nova Scotia go to/from Halifax and there are multiple daily flights to Toronto, Calgary and Vancouver. See p317 for more information.

Bus

Acadian Lines (☑902-454-9321, 800-567-5151; www.acadianbus.com; 1161 Hollis St) The Acadian terminal is at the train station next to the Westin Hotel. Its buses travel daily to Truro (1½ hours) and Amherst (2¾ hours) and connect to Montréal and New York. It also goes to Digby (four hours), with stops throughout the Annapolis Valley, and to Sydney (6½ hours), stopping in Antigonish (3½ hours).

Trius Lines (☑902-454-9321, 800-567-5151) Has a daily route from Halifax to Yarmouth (4½ hours) that serves towns along the South Shore. Call Acadian for information on prices and departure points.

Shuttle

Private shuttle buses compete with the major bus companies. They usually pick you up and drop you off; with fewer stops, they travel faster, but the trade-off is a more cramped ride.

Cloud Nine Shuttle (☑902-742-3992, 888-805-3335; www.thecloudnineshuttle.com) Does the Yarmouth–Halifax–Yarmouth (3½ hours each way) route, stopping along the South Shore; airport pickup or drop-off is an extra $5.

Campbell's Shuttle Service (☎800-742-6101; www.campbell-shuttle-service.com) Goes to Yarmouth.

Inverness Shuttle Service (☎902-945-2000, 888-826-2477; www.invernessshuttle.com) Travels between Halifax and Chéticamp on Cape Breton Island every day but Saturday and Monday (six hours).

Kathleen's Shuttle & Tours (☎903-834-2024; www.digbytoursandshuttle.webs.com) Halifax airport to Digby and Annapolis areas.

PEI Express Shuttle (☎902-462-8177, 877-877-1771; www.peishuttle.com) Goes to Charlottetown (PEI), with early morning pickups.

Scotia Shuttle (☎902-435-9686, 800-898-5883; www.scotiashuttle.com) Travels to Sydney on Cape Breton Island (five hours, daily).

Train

One of the few examples of monumental Canadian train station architecture left in the Maritimes is found at 1161 Hollis St. Options with **VIA Rail** (www.viarail.ca) include overnight service to Montréal (20½ hours, daily except Tuesdays).

❶ Getting Around
To/From the Airport

Halifax International Airport is 40km northeast of town on Hwy 102 toward Truro. **Airbus** (☎902-873-2091; one-way/return $19/27) runs between 5am and 11pm and picks up at major hotels. If you arrive in the middle of the night, as many flights do, your only choice is a taxi, which costs $54 to downtown Halifax. There are often not enough taxis so it's prudent to reserve one in advance. Try **Satellite Taxi** (☎902-445-3333), which has 24-hour airport service.

Car & Motorcycle

Pedestrians almost always have the right-of-way in Halifax. Watch out for cars stopping suddenly!

Outside the downtown core you can usually find free on-street parking for up to two hours. Otherwise, try private **Impark** (1245 Hollis St; per hr/12hr $1.50/8) or the municipally owned **Metro-Park** (☎902-830-1711; 1557 Granville St; per hr/12hr $2.25/15). Halifax' parking meters are enforced from 8am to 6pm Monday to Friday.

It costs considerably more to rent a car at the airport than in town. All the major national chains (see p886) are represented there and also have offices in Halifax.

Public Transportation

Metro Transit (☎902-490-6600; one-way fare $2.25) runs the city bus system and the ferries to Dartmouth. Transfers are free when traveling in one direction within a short time frame. Maps and schedules are available at the ferry terminals and at the information booth in Scotia Sq mall.

Bus 7 cuts through downtown and North End Halifax via Robie St and Gottingen St, passing both hostels. Bus 1 travels along Spring Garden Rd, Barrington St, and the south part of Gottingen St before crossing the bridge to Dartmouth. '**Fred**' is a free city bus that loops around downtown every 30 minutes in the summer.

Taking the **ferry to Dartmouth** (one-way fare $2.25; every 15 to 30 minutes from 6am to 11:30pm) from the Halifax waterfront is a nice way of getting on the water, even if it's just for 12 minutes. Woodside, where another ferry goes in peak periods, is a good place to start a bike ride to Eastern Passage or Lawrencetown.

AROUND HALIFAX

Dartmouth

Founded in 1750, one year after Halifax, Dartmouth is Halifax' counterpart just across the harbor. It is more residential than Halifax, and the downtown area lacks the capital's charm and bustle, but it can make a pleasant base since getting to Halifax by bus or ferry is so easy.

Even if you don't stay here, don't miss a harbor cruise via the ferry, the oldest saltwater ferry system in North America. Alderney Gate houses Dartmouth's ferry terminal.

The city swells during the **Nova Scotia Multicultural Festival** (www.mans.ns.ca) in late June. This weekend festival on the waterfront celebrates diversity with great performances and even better food.

Dartmouth Heritage Museum (☎902-404 6300; www.dartmouthheritagemuseum.ns .ca; 26 Newcastle St; admission $3; ☺10am-5pm Tue-Sun mid-Jun-Aug, 1:30-5pm Wed-Sat Sep–mid-Jun) displays an eclectic collection in **Evergreen House**, the former home of folklorist Helen Creighton (who traversed the province in the early 20th century recording stories and songs). Tickets include admission on the same day to the 1786 **Quaker House** (59 Ochterloney St; ☺10am-5pm Tue-Sun Jun-Aug), the oldest house in the Halifax area, which was built by Quaker whalers from Nantucket who fled the American Revolution.

Entertainment can be found at **Eastern Front Theatre** (☎902-463-7529; www.easternfronttheatre.com; Alderney Gate, Dartmouth; tickets $25), which debuts several works by Atlantic playwrights each year.

Close to both bus routes and the ferry, **Caroline's B&B** (☑902-469-4665; 134 Victoria Rd; s/d $50/60; ☺Apr-Dec) is run by a charming woman. Check out the cool mosaics on the walls.

Shubie Campground (☑902-435-8328, 800-440-8450; www.shubiecampground.com; Jaybee Dr, off Waverley Rd), the only campground accessible from Halifax on public transportation, is privately run and municipality owned. Facilities include showers and a laundromat.

Haligonians head to Dartmouth just for the massive buttery chocolate croissants at **Two If By Sea** (66 Ochterloney St; chocolate croissants $3; ☺7am-6pm Mon-Fri, 8am-5pm Sat &Sun) – but be warned they are usually sold out by about 1pm. Even sans pastries, it's a hip place to stop for coffee and people-watching on a sunny day, with a distinctly Dartmouth atmosphere.

Eastern Shore Beaches

When downtown-dwellers venture over the bridge to Dartmouth on a hot summer's day, it's most likely en route to a beach. There are beautiful, long, white-sand beaches all along the Eastern Shore, and although the water never gets very warm, brave souls venture in for a swim or a surf, particularly if the fog stays offshore.

The closest – and therefore busiest – of the Eastern Shore beaches, **Rainbow Haven**, is 1km long. It has washrooms, showers, a canteen and a boardwalk with wheel-chair access to the beach. Lifeguards supervise a sizable swimming area.

The most popular destination for surfers, cobblestone **Lawrencetown Beach** faces directly south and often gets big waves compliments of hurricanes or tropical storms hundreds of kilometers away. It boasts a supervised swimming area, washrooms and a canteen. To surf, learn to surf or just enjoy the view, stay at **Lawrence town Beach House** (☑902-827-2345; www.lawrencetownbeachhouse.com; dm/d $28/75), a comfy hostel with 10 beds and three private rooms beautifully nestled in the beach grass above one of the only stretches of real sand. There are several places in the area to rent surf boards (around $15 per day) and wetsuits (also $15 per day). Surf lessons are around $75 for 1½ hours including equipment; try **Dacane Sports** (☑902-431-7873; www.hurricanesurf.com), **Nova Scotia Surf School** (www.quiksilvercamps.com) or the all-women-run **One Life Surf School** (☑902-880-7873; www.onelifesurf.com).

With more than 3km of white sand backed by beach grass, **Martinique** is the longest beach in Nova Scotia and one of the prettiest in the area. Even if you find the water too cold for a swim, this is a beautiful place to walk, watch birds or play Frisbee.

Sambro

Just 18km south of Halifax, **Crystal Crescent Beach** is on the outskirts of the fishing village of Sambro. There are actually three beaches here in distinct coves; the third one out – toward the southwest – is clothing-optional and gay friendly. An 8.5km **hiking trail** begins just inland and heads through barrens, bogs and boulders to Pennant Point. To get here, take Herring Cove Rd from the roundabout in Halifax all the way to Sambro, then follow the signs.

Prospect

As pretty as Peggy's Cove, Prospect doesn't attract a fraction of the tourist traffic. An undeveloped **trail** starts at the end of Indian Point Rd and leads 3km along the coast past plenty of perfect picnic spots. There's not a lot of room to park at the trailhead, so you may need to leave your vehicle on the roadside into the village.

Prospect Village B&B (☑902-850-1758, 877-850-1758; www.prospectvillagebb.ca; 1758

DON'T MISS

FISHERMAN'S COVE

If you're heading up the Eastern Shore from Dartmouth or Halifax, detour onto Hwy 322 to Fishermen's Cove in Eastern Passage, a Popeye-esque fishing port with some of the region's best seafood samplings. **Wharf Wraps** (104 Government Wharf Rd; fish & chips $12; ☺10am-6pm Jun-Sep) has an outdoor seating area and deservedly famous (and huge) portions of fish and chips, or head next door to the **Fish Basket** (100 Government Wharf Rd; ☺9am-6pm) for fish and lobster by the pound or a delicious fresh lobster sandwich ($8) for the road.

Prospect Bay Rd; r $135-160) is in a restored nunnery that nearly glows on the misty shores. The warm owners use organics for everything from soaps to the ingredients of their tasty breakfasts.

Peggy's Cove

Peggy's Cove is one of the most visited fishing towns in Canada but for a good reason: the rolling granite cove highlighted by a perfect red-and-white lighthouse exudes a dreamy seaside calm even through the parading tour buses. Most visitors hop off their air-con bus, snap a few pictures, then get right back on the bus. If you stick around you'll find it surprisingly easy to chat with the friendly locals (there are only 45 of them) and settle into a fishing village pace. At 43km west of Halifax on Hwy 333 it makes a mellow day trip from the city.

It's best to visit before 10am in the summer as tour buses arrive in the middle of the day and create one of the province's worst traffic jams. There's a free parking area with washrooms and a **tourist information office** (☏902-823-2253; 109 Peggy's Cove Rd; ⏱9am-7pm Jul & Aug, to 5pm mid-May–Jun, Sep & Oct) as you enter the village. Free 45-minute walking tours are led from the tourist office daily from mid-June through August.

◉ Sights & Activities

Peggy's Cove Lighthouse   NOTABLE BUILDING
(⏱9:30am-5:30pm May-Oct) The highlight of the cove is this picture-perfect lighthouse, which for many years was a working post office where visitors could send postcards to be stamped with a famed lighthouse-shaped postmark. Unfortunately water damage from storms has shut the long-running post office.

DeGarthe Gallery   ART GALLERY
(☏902-823-2256; admission $2; ⏱on demand) See paintings here by local artist William deGarthe (1907–83), who sculpted the magnificent 30m-high *Fishermen's Monument* into a rock face in front of the gallery.

🛏 Sleeping & Eating

Peggy's Cove Bed & Breakfast   B&B $$
(☏902-823-2265, 877-725-8732; www.nsinns. com; 19 Church Rd; r $100-145) The only place to stay in the cove itself, this B&B has an enviable position with one of the best views in Nova Scotia, overlooking the fishing docks and the lighthouse; it was once home to art-

ist William deGarthe. You'll definitely need advance reservations.

Oceanstone Inn & Cottages   INN $$
(☏902-823-2160, 866-823-2160; www.oceanstone.ns.ca; 8650 Peggy's Cove Rd, Indian Harbour; r $95-145, cottages $185-265; ◉) Whimsically decorated cottages are a stone's throw from the beach and just a short drive from Peggy's Cove. Guests can use paddleboats to venture to small islands. Rhubarb, the inn's dining room, is considered one of the best seafood restaurants in the region.

Wayside Camping Park   CAMPGROUND $
(☏902-823-2271; wayside@hfx.eastlink.ca; 10295 Hwy 333, Glen Margaret; tent/RV sites $20/32) Ten kilometers north of Peggy's Cove and 36km from Halifax, this camping park has lots of shady sites on a hill. It gets crowded in midsummer.

☆ Entertainment

Old Red School House   THEATER
(☏902-823-2099; www.beales.ns.ca; 126 Peggy's Point Rd; suggested donation $10) This performance venue puts on comedies and music performances through the high season. A few shows per season are serviced by shuttle vans that offer round-trip to Halifax hotels. Check the website for details.

SOUTH SHORE

This is Nova Scotia's most visited coastline and it's here you'll find all those quintessential lighthouses, protected forested coves with white beaches and plenty of fishing villages turned tourist towns. The area from Halifax to Lunenburg is cottage country for the city's elite and is quite popular with day-tripping tourists and locals. Hwy 3 – labeled the 'Lighthouse Route' by tourism officials – can be slow as a result. Take this scenic route if you're not pressed for time and want to check out antique shops or artisans' wares en route. Travel times can be halved by taking Hwy 103 directly to the closest exit for your destination.

Chester

Established in 1759, the tiny town of Chester has today become a choice spot for well-to-do Americans and Haligonians to have a summer home. It's had a colorful history as the haunt of pirates and Prohibition-era bathtub-gin smugglers and it keeps its color today via the many artists' studios about town. There's a large **regatta** in the tranquil harbor in mid-August.

Sights & Activities

FREE **Lordly House Museum** MUSEUM
(902-275-3842; 133 Central St; 10am-4pm Tue-Sat) A fine example of Georgian architecture from 1806, the Lordly House Museum has three period rooms illustrating 19th-century upper-class life and Chester history. The museum is also an artists' studio.

Tancook Island NATURE RESERVE
This island (population 190) is a 45-minute ferry ride from Chester's government wharf (round-trip $5, four services daily Monday to Friday, two daily on weekends; schedule at http://freepages.history.rootsweb.com/~tancook/ferry.htm). **Walking trails** crisscross the island. Settled by Germans and French Huguenots in the early 19th century, the island is famous for its sauerkraut. The last ferry from Chester each day overnights in Tancook Island.

Sleeping & Eating

Mecklenburgh Inn B&B B&B $$
(902-275-4638; www.mecklenburghinn.ca; 78 Queen St; r $95-155; May-Jan) This casual four-room inn, built in 1890, has a breezy 2nd-floor veranda; some rooms have private adjacent balconies, most have private bathrooms. The owner is a cordon bleu chef so expect an excellent breakfast.

Graves Island Provincial Park
CAMPGROUND $
(902-275-4425; www.parks.gov.ns.ca; campsites $24) An island in Mahone Bay connected by a causeway to the mainland has 64 wooded and open campsites. RVs usually park in the middle of the area, but some shady, isolated tent sites are tucked away on the flanks of the central plateau. It's 3km northeast of Chester off Hwy 3.

Kiwi Café CAFE $
(902-275-1492; 19 Pleasant St; light lunches $4-13; 8am-4pm) A New Zealand chef prepares excellent soups, salads, sandwiches and baked goods that you can eat in or take away in recyclable containers. There's also beer, wine and a friendly atmosphere all painted kiwi green.

Rope Loft PUB $$
(902-275-3430; 36 Water St; mains around $15; food served 11:30am-9pm Sun-Thu, to 10pm Fri & Sat, pub open daily to 11pm) You couldn't find a better setting than this bayside pub. Hearty pub food is served indoors or out.

Entertainment

Chester Playhouse THEATER
(902-275-3933; www.chesterplayhouse.ca; 22 Pleasant St; tickets around $25) This older theater space has great acoustics for live performances. Plays or dinner theater are presented most nights, except Mondays in July and August, with occasional concerts during spring and fall.

Information

Tourist office (902-275-4616; Hwy 3; 10am-4pm Jul & Aug, 10am-6pm Jun & Sep, 10am-5pm May & Oct) In the old train depot near the Chester turnoff.

Mahone Bay

The sun shines more often here than anywhere else along this coast. With more than 100 islands only 100km from Halifax, it's a great base for exploring this section of the South Shore. Take out a kayak or a bike or simply stroll down Main St, which skirts the harbor and is scattered with shops selling antiques, quilts, works by local painters and pottery.

Sights & Activities

FREE **Mahone Bay Settlers' Museum**
MUSEUM
(902-624-6263; 578 Main St; 10am-5pm Tue-Sun Jun–mid-Oct) Exhibits on the settlement of this area by 'Foreign Protestants' in 1754 and local architecture.

FREE **Amos Pewter** SHOPPING
(800-565-3369; www.amospewter.com; 589 Main St; 9am-6:30pm Mon-Sat, 10am-5:30pm Sun Jul & Aug, 9am-5:30pm Mon-Sat, noon-5:30pm Sun May, Jun, Sep & Oct) Watch demonstrations of the art of pewter making then buy wares at the attached store.

Tours

Historic Mahone Bay Walking Tours
WALKING TOURS
(per person $5; 1pm Fri, Sat & Sun) In July and August, 1¼-hour walking tours are led from the VIC to many of Mahone Bay's historic homes. Times change year to year so check with the VIC.

South Shore Boat Tours BOAT TOURS
([902-543-5107; www.southshoreboattours.com; Jul & Aug) Offers boatbuilding and nature tours (1¾ hours, adults $35).

✯ Festivals & Events

Mahone Bay Regatta REGATTA
(www.mahonebayregatta.wordpress.com) On the weekend prior to the first Monday in August, this regatta features workshops in boatbuilding and daily races.

🛏 Sleeping & Eating

Edgewater B&B B&B $$
([902-624-9382, 866-816-8688; www.bbcanada.com/edgewater; 44 Mader's Cove Rd; r $120-165; Jul-Oct) Overlooking the water on the outskirts of town towards Lunenburg, the three rooms here are decorated in modern yet sea-feeling grays and beiges. There's also a big two-story cottage ($225 per night) – essentially a house – that's perfect for groups or families.

Hammock Inn the Woods B&B B&B $$
([902-624-0891; www.hammockinnthewoods.com; 198 Woodstock Rd; d $75-95) Up a quiet road from Main St, there are two beckoning hammocks nestled in a wooded garden and the house is a restful blend of modern plush and country comfort. The healthy breakfasts are cooked using organic produce and there's free yoga every morning. A loft apartment should be available in 2011.

Three Thistles B&B B&B $$
([902-624-0517; www.three-thistles.com; 389 West Main St; r $90-130) Owner Phyllis Wiseman uses environmentally conscious cleaning agents and cooks with organic foods. Rooms are sparkling and clean and there's a back garden that stretches to a wooded area.

Kiwi Kaboodle Backpackers Hostel
HOSTEL $
([902-531-5494, 866-549-4522; www.kiwikaboodle.com; Hwy 3; dm $28; 🐾) Three kilometers from the attractions of Mahone Bay and 7km from Lunenburg, this friendly nine-bed hostel is superbly located. Owners offer town pickup as well as economical tours (www.novascotiatoursandtravel.com), shuttle service and excellent area tips. Plans are in the works for bike rentals and tours as well as a private room.

La Have Bakery DELI $
(cnr Edgewater & Main Sts; sandwiches from $4; 9am-6pm; 🐾) This bakery is famous for its hearty bread and sandwiches are made on thick slabs of it. Gluten-free breads are available as well as burgers and pizza.

Gazebo Café RESTAURANT $$
([902-624-6484; 567 Main St; mains $15-20; lunch & dinner Apr-Oct; 🐾) This bistro-style eatery has water views and fantastic local favorites prepared with flair rather than a deep-fat fryer. Vegetarian options are available.

ℹ Information

Biscuit Eater Booktrader & Cafe ([902-624-2665; 16 Orchard St; internet per hr $5; 9am-5pm Wed-Sat, 11am-5pm Sun; 🐾) The best place to check email, with a fair trade coffee and a light organic meal. Free wi-fi.

Mahone Bay (www.mahonebay.com) Links to restaurants and accommodations.

VIC ([902-624-6151; 165 Edgewater St; 10am-5pm Sat & Sun May, 9am-6pm Jun & Sep, 9am-7pm Jul & Aug, 10am-5pm Oct) Has do-it-yourself walking-tour brochures.

Lunenburg

The largest of the South Shore fishing villages is historic Lunenburg, the region's only Unesco World Heritage site and the first British settlement outside Halifax. The town is at its most picturesque viewed from the sea around sunset when the boxy, brightly painted old buildings literally glow behind the ship-filled port. Look for the distinctive 'Lunenburg Bump,' a five sided dormer window on the 2nd floor that overhangs the 1st floor.

Lunenburg was settled largely by Germans, Swiss and Protestant French who were first recruited by the British as a workforce for Halifax then later became fishermen. Today Nova Scotia has been hard hit by dwindling fish stocks, but Lunenburg's burgeoning tourism trade has helped shore up the local economy.

◉ Sights & Activities

Fisheries Museum of the Atlantic MUSEUM
([902-634-4794; www.fisheries.museum.gov.ns.ca; 68 Bluenose Dr; adult/child $10/3; 9:30am-5:30pm May-Oct) The knowledgeable staff at the Fisheries Museum of the Atlantic includes a number of retired fisherfolk who can give firsthand explanations of the

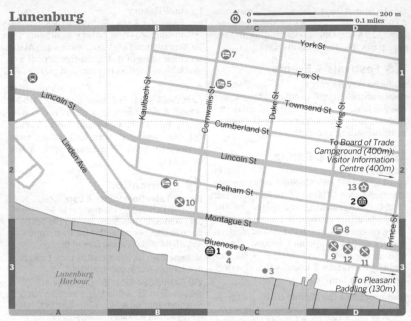

fishing industry. A cute aquarium on the 1st floor lets you get eye-to-eye with halibut, a 6kg lobster and other sea creatures. Film screenings and talks are scheduled throughout the day.

Knaut-Rhuland House   MUSEUM
(☎902-634-3498; 125 Pelham St; admission $3; ☉11am-5pm Tue-Sat, 1-5pm Sun Jun-Sep) Knaut-Rhuland House is considered the finest example of Georgian architecture in the province. This 1793 house has costumed guides who point out its features.

Bike Barn   CYCLING
(☎902-634-3426; www.bikelunenburg.com; 579 Blue Rocks Rd; hybrid/tandem bikes per day $25/40) About 2km east of town, the Bike Barn rents bikes. On a small peninsula, this area is a cyclist's dream, with few hills, great ocean views and little vehicle traffic. Owners Merrill and Al will gladly help you plan your trip.

Pleasant Paddling   KAYAKING
(www.pleasantpaddling.com; 86 Bluenose Dr; rentals 2hr/half-day/full-day $30/50/70, tours half-/full-day $65/110) Offers rentals and tours in double or single kayaks; knowledgeable folks and a beautiful place to paddle.

☞ Tours
Numerous fishing, sailing and whale-watching tours depart from the wharf adjacent to the Fisheries Museum on Bluenose Dr. Book on the dock or at the VIC.

Bluenose II

SAILING

(☎902-634-1963, 800-763-1963; www.blue nose2.ns.ca; 2hr cruises adult/child $20/10) This classic replica of the *Bluenose* racing schooner is sometimes in Halifax and sometimes in Lunenburg. It was closed in 2010 for refitting but should reopen in 2011. Check the website for details.

Gray Line Lunenburg
Town Walking Tours

WALKING TOURS

(☎902-634-3848) Enthusiastic and very experienced Eric Croft leads leisurely tours during the day or spooky lantern-lit ones at night; call for more information.

Trot in Time

CART TOURS

(adult/child $20/8; ☺Jun–mid-Oct) Take a half-hour tour of town in a horse-drawn cart. Leaves from outside the Fisheries Museum of the Atlantic.

✯ Festivals & Events

Boxwood Festival

MUSIC

(www.boxwood.org; festival pass $50; ☺last week of Jul) Flautists and pipers from around the world put on stellar public concerts.

Lunenburg Folk Harbour Festival

MUSIC

(☎902-634-3180; www.folkharbour.com; ☺Aug) Singer-songwriters from Canada and beyond, plus traditional music and gospel.

Nova Scotia Folk Art Festival

FOLK ART

(www.nsfolkartfestival.com; ☺1st Sun of Aug)

🛏 Sleeping

Make reservations as far ahead as possible, especially during summer festivals. Kiwi Kaboodle Backpackers Hostel (p335), 7km north of town, is the best budget option.

Sail Inn B&B

B&B $$

(☎902-634-3537, 877-247-7075; www.sailinn.ca; 99 Montague St; r $80-140; @) Rooms have a view over the waterfront and are bright, airy and modern with an antique twist. You get a free sail on the owner's 15m ketch with your stay. Don't miss checking out the old well on the ground floor that's been turned into a lighted fish pond.

1775 Solomon House B&B

B&B $$

(☎902-634-3477; www.bbcanada.com/5511. html; 69 Townsend St; r $100-125; @) A wonderfully antique place with undulating wooden floors and low door jams (watch your head!), this B&B has the nicest and most helpful owner ever. Rooms are cozy amid the ageing walls and you'll be talking about the breakfasts for the rest of your trip. The only drawback is the minuscule bathrooms.

Lennox Tavern B&B

B&B $$

(☎902-634-4043, 888-379-7605; www.lennox inn.com; 69 Fox St; r $85-140) This place feels authentically old, with electric candles lighting the halls and massive plank-wood floors. The inn is the oldest in Canada and you get to eat breakfast in what was once the tavern.

NOVA SCOTIA LUNENBURG

A PIRATE'S TREASURE

Oak Island, near Mahone Bay, is home to a so-called 'money pit' that has cost over $2 million in excavation expenses and six lives. There is still not a shred of information about what the pit is or what might be buried there.

The mystery began in 1795 when three inhabitants of the island came across a depression in the ground. Knowing that pirates had once frequented the area, they decided to dig and see what they could find. Just over half a meter down they hit a layer of neatly placed flagstone; another 2.5m turned up one oak platform, then another. After digging to 9m, the men temporarily gave up but returned eight years later with the Onslow Company, a professional crew.

The Onslow excavation made it down 27.5m; when the crew returned the next morning, the shaft had flooded and they were forced to halt the digging. A year later, the company returned to dig 33.5m down in a parallel shaft, which also flooded. It was confirmed in 1850 that the pit was booby-trapped via five box drains at Smith Cove, 150m from the pit. The beach was found to be artificial.

Ever since, people have come to seek their fortune from far and wide at the 'money pit.' Only a few links of gold chain, some parchment, a cement vault and an inscribed stone have been found.

1826 Maplebird House B&B   B&B **$$**
(☑902-634-3863, 888-395-3863; www.maple
birdhouse.ca; 36 Pelham St; d $115; @☒)
Decorated country style with teddy bears
a-go-go, this house in the heart of town
manages to remain cozy, not frilly. The
lovely, large rear garden overlooks the
harbor and has a barbecue for guests.

Board of Trade Campground
CAMPGROUND **$**
(☑902-634-8100/3656; lbt@aliantzinc.ca;
11 Blockhouse Hill Rd; tent/RV sites $23/30;
@) This campground, beside the VIC,
has great views and a lot of gravel RV
sites. Grassy tent sites are closely packed
together and lack shade.

✖ Eating & Drinking

Try some offbeat Lunenburg specialties.
Solomon Gundy is pickled herring with on-
ions. Lunenburg pudding – pork and spices
cooked in the intestines of a pig – goes well
with Scotch and water.

Fleur de Sel   RESTAURANT **$$$**
(☑902-640-2121; 53 Montague St; mains lunch
$8-12, dinner $28-36; ⊙11am-2pm & 5-10pm;
☑) This is by far the most elegant eating
option in the region. French-inspired seafood, meat and vegetarian dishes use organic produce and are served in the classic,
bright dining area.

Fish Cake Café   RESTAURANT **$$**
(☑902-634-9995; 100 Montague St; lunch $10-
15; ⊙9am-4pm) Specializing in (surprise!)
fish cakes, including delicious ones made
with salmon and scallops with lime-
ginger aioli and red-onion chutney. Also
available are sandwiches, daily specials,
soups, original cocktails and decadent
desserts.

Salt Shaker Deli   DELI **$**
(☑902-640-3434; 124 Montague St; meals
$8-15; ⊙11am-9pm Tue-Sat, 11am-3pm Sun)
With a clean-cut modern atmosphere, a
waterfront deck and amazing food, it's
no wonder this new deli-restaurant is al-
ways packed. Try the thin-crust pizzas or
a pound of mussels cooked to the style of
your choosing.

Magnolia's Grill   RESTAURANT **$**
(☑902-634-3287; 128 Montague St; mains $8-
16; ⊙lunch & dinner) Try one of the many
soups of the day at this diner-style lo-
cal's favorite. Seafood (including Solomon
Gundy) and an extensive wine list are
available.

☆ Entertainment

Lunenburg Opera House   THEATER
(☑902-634-4010; 290 Lincoln St; tickets $5-20)
This rickety old 400-seat theater is ru-
mored to have a resident ghost. Built as an
Oddfellows Hall in 1907, it's now a favorite
venue for rock and folk musicians. Check
the posters in the window for what's com-
ing up.

ⓘ Information

Explore Lunenburg (www.explorelunenburg.
ca) Local history and tourism information.

Lunenburg Public Library (☑902-634-8008;
19 Pelham St; ⊙10am-6pm Tue, Wed & Fri,
10am-8pm Thu, 10am-5pm Sat) Free internet
access.

VIC (☑902-634-8100, 888-615-8305; 11
Blockhouse Hill Rd; ⊙9am-6pm May-Oct, 9am-
8pm Jul & Aug) Walking-tour maps and help
with accommodations.

ⓘ Getting There & Away

Trius Lines buses serve Lunenburg on their
once-daily Halifax–Yarmouth route; the best
source of information on Trius' prices and de-
parture locations is **Acadian Lines** (☑902-454-
9321, 800-567-5151; www.acadianbus.com). For
alternative shuttles, see p330.

Liverpool

There is plenty to do in Liverpool and it's
well situated for exploring several gorgeous
beaches as well as Kejimkujik National Park
(68km north) and its Seaside Adjunct (15km
southwest). That said, it lacks the seaside
quaintness of the villages north of here.

◉ Sights & Activities

Rossignol Cultural Centre   MUSEUM
(☑902-354-3067; www.rossignolculturalcen
tre.com; 205 Church St; adult/child $5/3;
⊙10am-5:30pm Mon-Sat) Local character
Sherman Hines' most fabulous endeavor
is a must-see for anyone who enjoys the
offbeat. There are lifelike halls of taxi-
dermy animals, cases of gorgeous aborig-
inal beadwork, walls of Hines' beautiful
photography (including his Mongolian
adventures) and a room dedicated to
outhouses around the world. If you love
it so much you don't want to leave, an
authentic Mongolian yurt (with en-suite
bathroom) is for rent adjacent to the
museum for a $100 per night donation.
Admission to the museum includes en-
try to the **Sherman Hines Museum of**

Photography (☑902-354-2667; www.sher manhinesphotographymuseum.com; 219 Main St; ☺10am-5:30pm Mon-Sat).

Perkins House Museum   MUSEUM
(☑902-354-4058; www.museum.gov.ns.ca/peh; 105 Main St; adult/child $2/1; ☺9:30am-5:30pm Mon-Sat, 1-5:30pm Sun Jun–mid-Oct) Perkins House Museum displays articles and furniture from the colonial period. Built in 1766, it's the oldest house belonging to the Nova Scotia Museum.

Queen's County Museum   MUSEUM
(☑902-354-4058; www.queenscountymuseum. com; 109 Main St; admission $1; ☺9:30am-5:30pm Mon-Sat, 1-5:30pm Sun Jun–mid-Oct, 9am-5pm Mon-Sat mid-Oct–May) This museum has First Nations artifacts and more materials relating to town history as well as some writings by early citizens.

FREE Fort Point   LIGHTHOUSE
At Fort Point a cairn marks the site where Frenchman Samuel de Champlain landed in 1604. You can blow the hand-pumped foghorn in the **lighthouse** (☑902-354-5260; 21 Fort Lane; ☺10am-6pm mid-May–mid-Oct), at the end of Main St.

Hank Snow Country Music Centre
                                            MUSEUM
(☑902-354-4675; www.hanksnow.com; 148 Bristol Ave; admission $3; ☺9am-5pm Mon-Sat, noon-5pm Sun late May-early Oct) The Hank Snow Music Centre sheds light on Nova Scotia's status as a northern Nashville. In the old train station, it captures the history of Snow, Wilf Carter and other crooners and yodelers.

🎊 Festivals & Events

Privateer Days   HISTORICAL
(www.privateerdays.com; ☺early Jul) A celebration of piracy and history.

🛏 Sleeping & Eating

Geranium House   B&B $
(☑902-354-4484; 87 Milton Rd; r $60) This B&B on a large wooded property next to the Mersey River has three rooms with shared bathroom, ideal for cyclists and families.

Lane's Privateer Inn   INN $$
(☑902-354-3456, 800-794-3332; www.lanes privateerinn.com; 27 Bristol Ave; r incl breakfast $95-150; @) Originally the home of a swash-buckling privateer, this 211-year-old inn now looks more 1980s than anything else, but it's still a clean and pleasant place to stay. There's also a gourmet food store and a **dining room** (mains $9 to $25; open 7am to 10pm).

Woodpile Carving Cafe   CAFE $
(☑902-354-4494; 181 Main St; light meals $4-10; ☺8am-4pm Mon-Sat) This atmospheric cafe, a local favorite, has the owner's wood-carving workshop right in its center. Grab a specialty coffee, soups, sandwiches and salads.

☆ Entertainment

Astor Theatre   THEATER
(☑902-354-5250; www.astortheatre.ns.ca; 59 Gorham St) The Astor is the oldest continuously operating performance venue in the province. Built in 1902 as the Liverpool Opera House, it presents films, plays and live music.

ℹ Information

Tourist office (☑902-354-5421; 28 Henry Hensey Dr; ☺9:30am-5:30pm Jul & Aug, 10am-5pm mid-May–Jul & Sep–mid-Oct) Near the river bridge; has a walking-tour pamphlet.

Kejimkujik National Park

Less than 20% of Kejimkujik's 381-sq-km wilderness is accessible by car; the rest is reached either on foot or by canoe. Birdwatchers can hope to see plenty of water fowl, barred owls and pileated woodpeckers, while wildlife ranges from porcupines to black bear. On a less joyful note, biting insects are rampant; watch out for mosquitoes the size of hummingbirds and eel-like leeches in the lakes.

Get an entry permit and reserve back-country sites at the **visitor center** (☑902-682-2772, 800-414-6765; www.parkscanada. gc.ca/keji; Hwy 8; adult/child $5.80/2.90; ☺8:30am-9pm mid-Jun–early Sep, to 4pm rest of year, closed weekends Nov-Mar).

🏃 Activities

The main **hiking** loop is a 60km trek that begins at the east end of George Lake and ends at the Big Dam Lake trailhead. A shorter loop, ideal for an overnight trek, is the 26km Channel Lake Trail that begins and also ends at Big Dam Lake. September to early October is prime hiking time; the bugs in the spring would drive you mad. More than a dozen lakes are connected by a system of portages, allowing canoe trips of up to seven days. A topographical map

($10) may be required for ambitious multi-day trips.

Rent canoes and other equipment in the park at **Jakes Landing** (902-682-5253; 8am-9pm Jun-Sep). One-hour hire of a double kayak, canoe or rowboat is $8, kayak or bike is $7; 24-hour hire is $35/30 and one-week hire is $130. It's open during the off-season by appointment.

Sleeping & Eating

Forty-five backcountry campsites ($24.50 per person including firewood) are scattered among the lakes of Kejimkujik. You must book them in advance by telephone or stopping at the park's visitor center. There's a 14-day maximum; you can't stay more than two nights at any site.

Mersey River Chalets   CABINS $$
(902-682-2447, 877-667-2583; www.mersey riverchalets.com; 2537 River Rd; tepees $70, d $110, cabins $150-205;) Comfy cabins have pine floors, wood-burning stoves and very private porches complete with barbecue; rooms in the lodge have private decks with lake views; and cozy tepees have fully equipped kitchens. Free canoes and kayaks are available for guests.

Caledonia Country Hostel   HOSTEL $
(902-682-3266, 877-223-0232; www.caledonia countryhostel.com; 9960 Hwy 8, Caledonia; dm/d $25/60;) In the heart of Caledonia – the only town near the park that has an internet cafe, a VIC, a gas station and a grocery store – this spotless hostel has beds on the 2nd floor of an adorable Victorian-style home. Cozy nooks with TV, books, old-style upholstered chairs and country linens abound. The owners also have tours and shuttle services available.

Raven Haven Hostel & Family Park
    HOSTEL & CAMPGROUND $
(902-532-7320; www.annapoliscounty.ns.ca; 2239 Virginia Rd, off Hwy 8, South Milford; dm member/nonmember $20/22, tent/RV sites $20/24, cabins $68; mid-Jun–early Sep) This HI hostel and campground is 25km south of Annapolis Royal and 27km north of the national park. The four-bed hostel is in a cabin near the white-sand beach and rustic two-bedroom cabins have equipped kitchens but no linens. There are 15 campsites but the camping in the park is better. Canoes and paddleboats can be rented.

Jeremy's Bay Campground   CAMPGROUND $
(902-682-2772, 800-414-6765; campsites $25.50) Of the 360 campsites within the park, 30% are assigned on a first-come, first-served basis. There is only one shower area for the whole camp so be prepared to wait for a stall. It costs $10 to reserve a site.

M&W Restaurant & Variety Store   RESTAURANT $
(902-682-2189; Hwy 8; mains $4-12; 9am-8pm mid-May–mid-Oct) Only 500m from the park entrance this place serves 'hungry camper' breakfasts ($6) as well as lunch and dinner. It's also a general store stocked with camping supplies (including firewood) and a Laundromat.

Seaside Adjunct (Kejimkujik National Park)

The 'Keji Adjunct' protects angelic landscapes of rolling low brush, wildflowers, white sandy coves and the granite outcrops spreading between Port Joli and Port Mouton (ma-*toon*) Bay. The only access from Hwy 103 is along a 6.5km gravel road. Pay your park fee and grab a trail map at the helpful **Park Office** (adult/child $6/3; 8:30am-8pm mid-Jun–Sep, 8:30am-4pm Oct–mid-Jun) at the parking lot. From there, two mostly flat trails lead to the coast. **Harbour Rocks Trail** (5.2km return) follows an old cart road through mixed forest to a beach where seals are often seen. A loop trail around **Port Joli Head** is 8.7km.

The Port Joli Basin contains **Point Joli Migratory Bird Sanctuary** with waterfowl and shorebirds in great numbers (*Nova Scotia Birding on the Lighthouse Route* is an excellent resource available at VICs). It's only easily accessible by kayak. The **Rossignol Surf Shop** (902-683-2550; www. surfnovascotia.com; White Point Beach Resort) in nearby White Point rents kayaks (half-/full-day $30/45), surfboards and bodyboards ($20/40), and offers kayak tours ($65/110) and surfing lessons ($65).

Thomas Raddall Provincial Park (902-683-2664; www.parks.gov.ns.ca; campsites $24; mid-May–Oct), across Port Joli Harbour from Keji Adjunct, has large, private campsites with eight walk-in ones. The forested campground extends out onto awesome beaches.

Port Mouton International Hostel (📞902-947-3140; www.wqccda.com/PMhostel; 8100 Hwy 3; dm $30; @), only five minutes from Keji Adjunct, is run on a volunteer basis by the community in a former school. There are 30 beds (plus one private room), a good kitchen and a washer and dryer. Call in advance or if you arrive between 10am and 5pm you can check in at the crafts store next door.

Shelburne

Shelburne's beautiful historic waterfront area bobs with sailboats and has 17 pre-1800 homes – it feels like a historical recreation but it's real. The wonderfully maintained, low-in-the-earth buildings once housed Loyalists who retreated here from the American Revolution. In 1783 Shelburne was the largest community in British North America with 16,000 residents, many from the New York aristocracy, who exploited the labor of Black Loyalists living in nearby Birchtown (see the boxed text, p341). Shelburne's history is celebrated with **Founders' Days** during the last weekend of July.

◎ Sights & Activities

Shelburne has started organizing a slew of activities from mid-June to mid-August including daily demonstrations around town by folks in period costumes of old-style cooking, sewing, music, military exercises, carving and more; schedules change daily but start around 1pm. Check at the VIC for

more information. Admission to the following museums is $3, but you can buy a pass for all four for $8.

Built in 1784, **Ross-Thomson House** (📞902-875-3141; www.rossthomson.museum.gov.ns.ca; 9 Charlotte Lane; admission free 9:30am-noon Sun; ◎9:30am-5:30pm Jun–mid-Oct) belonged to well-to-do Loyalist merchants who arrived in Shelburne from Cape Cod. Furniture, paintings and original goods from the store are on display. The house is surrounded by authentic period gardens.

Another c 1787 Loyalist house is now the **Shelburne County Museum** (📞902-875-3219; cnr Maiden Lane & Dock St; ◎9:30am-5:30pm) with a collection of Loyalist furnishings, displays on the history of the local fishery and a small collection of Mi'kmaw artifacts.

The **Muir-Cox Shipyard** (📞902-875-1114; www.historicshelburne.com/muircox.htm; 18 Dock St; ◎9:30am-5:30pm Jun-Sep) has been in almost continuous operation since 1820, turning out barques, yachts and fishing boats. It's still active year-round, but the interpretive center is seasonal. Likewise, Shelburne dories (small open boats once used for fishing from a mother schooner) are still made to order at the **Dory Shop Museum** (📞902-875-3219; www.museum.gov.ns.ca/dory; 11 Dock St; ◎9:30am-5:30pm Jun-Sep) for use as lifeboats.

There's a **trail** for hiking or biking the 6km to Birchtown across from Spencer's Garden Centre at the far south end of Main

---

BLACK LOYALIST BIRCHTOWN

Just as Shelburne was once the largest settlement in British North America, so Birchtown was once the largest settlement of freed African slaves in North America. After the American Revolution, about 3500 Black Loyalists were rewarded by the British with land for settlements near Shelburne, Halifax, Digby and Guysborough. Nine years later, in 1792, after barely surviving harsh winters and unequal treatment, 1200 of them boarded 15 ships bound for Sierra Leone, in West Africa, where they founded Freetown. An additional 2000 from the USA settled in the Maritimes after the War of 1812, and others came from the Caribbean in the 1890s to work in the Cape Breton Island coal mines.

The future was no brighter. Underfunded, segregated schools existed until the 1950s. Birchtown's **Black Loyalist Heritage Society Historical Site & Museum** (📞902-875-1381, 888-354-0722; www.blackloyalist.com; 104 Birchtown Rd; ◎11am-6pm Tue-Fri, noon-6pm Sat, noon-5pm Sun) includes a museum and a walking trail that leads to a 'pit house' which archaeologists think was once a temporary shelter. There is also a **trail** for hiking or cycling the 6km to Shelburne.

A self-guided tour of African heritage in Nova Scotia is available online (www.gov.ns.ca/nsarm/virtual/africanns/).

St. Historic 1½-hour **walking tours** (per person $10; ⏰2pm Tue-Fri, 7pm Tue & Thu) depart from the VIC.

🛌 Sleeping

TOP CHOICE **Cooper's Inn B&B**   B&B $$
(☎902-875-4656, 800-688-2011; www.thecoopersinn.com; 36 Dock St; r $100-150; ◉) Part of this waterfront building dates to 1784 and was brought here from Boston. Now it's a relatively modern but still charmingly heritage-style inn with six rooms and a flower-filled garden where you can drink your complimentary bottle of Jost wine at sunset.

Water Street Lighthouse B&B   B&B $
(☎902-875-2331; www.shelburnelighthouse.com; 263 Water St; r $60-80; ◉) Not really luxurious, but comfy and friendly, this is a great B&B to shack up your bike for the night. A lighthouse theme runs through the house.

The Islands Provincial Park   CAMPGROUND $
(☎902-875-4304; www.parks.gov.ns.ca; off Hwy 3; campsites $18) Across the harbor from Shelburne are 65 campsites in mature forest and a beach for swimming.

🍴 Eating & Drinking

TOP CHOICE **Charlotte Lane**   RESTAURANT $$$
(☎902-875-3314; 13 Charlotte Lane; mains $16-35; ⏰lunch & dinner Tue-Sat) People drive from Halifax to eat here, and then rave about it; evening reservations are highly recommended. Swiss chef Roland Glauser is constantly revising an extensive annotated wine list to accompany his ever-changing menu of local seafood, meat and pasta dishes.

Bean Dock   CAFE $
(☎902-875-1302; sandwiches from $4; ⏰10am-4pm Mon-Fri, to 8pm Wed, 10am-4pm Sat) Snuggle over to a wood table overlooking the bay for coffee, grilled sandwiches and light mains from fish cakes and salad ($9) to sun-dried tomato pasta salad ($7). The giant Adirondack chair out front is worth chatting about.

ℹ Information

VIC (☎902-875-4547; 31 Dock St; ⏰8am-8pm Jul & Aug, 11am-5pm mid-May–Jun & Sep) Has copies of a self-guided historic district walking tour.

Barrington to West Pubnico

At Barrington you can choose to take the fast, not-very-scenic Hwy 103 to Yarmouth or meander along about 100km of interesting coastline via Hwy 3. It's worth taking a detour to **Cape Sable Island** (not to be confused with Sable Island, p376), a puddle-flat appendage that is Nova Scotia's southernmost point. Many of the island's windy, white-sand beaches are designated as 'important bird areas,' and a few are piping plover nesting grounds. The whole island tends to get banked in fog which might explain why its lighthouse is 31.1m tall, the tallest in Nova Scotia.

Not to be confused with all the other nearby Pubnicos, West Pubnico is an old Acadian community. **Le Village Historique Acadien** (☎902-762-2530; Old Church Rd; adult/child $16/11; ⏰10am-6pm mid-Jun–Sep) re-creates an Acadian village, with a blacksmith shop, a timber-frame house and a fish store.

Yarmouth

Yarmouth is the biggest town in southern Nova Scotia due mostly to the ferry that linked the province to Bar Harbor (Maine) since the 1950s. Sadly, the ferry service stopped in 2010, although there were plans for starting it up again in 2011 with a new boat; if not, Yarmouth could be in for some tough times. The only really pretty area is out beyond town around the lighthouse, but like anywhere in the province, stay awhile and the people will win you over.

◉ Sights & Activities

First settled by New Englanders from Massachusetts in 1761, Yarmouth reached its peak of growth and prosperity in the 1870s. The Collins Heritage Conservation District protects many fine Victorian homes built around that time. Check at the VIC for a self-guided walking tour.

FREE **Yarmouth Light**   NOTABLE BUILDING
(☎902-742-1433; Hwy 304; ⏰9am-9pm) Yarmouth Light is at the end of Cape Forchu, a left on Hwy 304 from Main St. The lighthouse affords spectacular views and there's a tearoom below. Stop at **Stanley Lobster Pound** (Hwy 304; ⏰11am-7pm Mon-Sat, 2-7pm Sun), where you can get a fresh-

Yarmouth

⊚ **Sights**

1 Art Gallery of Nova Scotia.................. B1
    Pelton-Fuller House.....................(see 2)
2 Yarmouth County Museum B1

⊜ **Sleeping**

3 Clementine's B&B B2
4 MacKinnon-Cann House
    Historic Inn...................................B2

⊗ **Eating**

5 Rudder's Brew Pub.............................A1

NOVA SCOTIA YARMOUTH

cooked lobster at market-value price to take and eat on the beach.

Art Gallery of Nova Scotia ART GALLERY
(☏902-749-2248; www.artgalleryofnovascoatia. com; 341 Main St; adult/child $5/1; ⊘noon-8pm) Practical Yarmouth is the unexpected home to the refreshingly cosmopolitan Art Gallery of Nova Scotia. The new three-story building has well-selected works from mostly Maritime artists.

Yarmouth County Museum MUSEUM
(☏902-742-5539; http://yarmouthcountymus eum.ednet.ns.ca; 22 Collins St; adult/student $5/2; ⊘9am-5pm Mon-Sat, 2-5pm Sun) This museum, in a former church, contains five period rooms related to the sea. A regular single admission ticket (adult/student $3/0.50) includes **Pelton-Fuller House** (⊘9am-5pm Mon-Sat Jun-Oct) next door, which is filled with period artwork, glassware and furniture.

🛏 Sleeping & Eating

TOP
CHOICE **MacKinnon-Cann House Historic Inn** INN **$$**
(☏902-742-0042; www.mackinnoncanninn. com; 27 Willow St; r $140-185; ⊘☀@) Each one of the six rooms here represent a decade from the Victorian 1900s to the groovy '60s. Each room depicts the decade at its most stylish while managing to stay calming and comfortable. Two rooms can be joined to create a family suite and the inn is gay friendly.

Clementine's B&B B&B **$$**
(☏902-742-0079; 21 Clements St; d $95; @) Open for over 20 years, Clementine's hasn't

faded a bit. Rooms with shared bathrooms are unpretentiously decorated and breakfasts are famous throughout Yarmouth. The B&B is a few minutes' walk to Main St.

Rudder's Brew Pub PUB **$$**
(☏902-742-7311; 96 Water St; pub menu $8-14, dinner mains $14-32) The 300 seats at this waterfront pub and restaurant fill fast. A mean ale is brewed on-site and there's a wide-ranging menu. Drinks are poured until the wee hours on busy summer nights.

❶ Information

VIC (☏902-742-5033; 228 Main St; ⊘7:30am-9pm Jul & Aug, to 4:30pm May, Jun, Sep & Oct) Also has a money-exchange counter.

Yarmouth Public Library (☏902-742-2486; 405 Main St; ⊘10am-8pm Mon-Thu, 10am-5pm Fri, 10am-4pm Sat, 1-4pm Sun) Free internet access.

❶ Getting There & Away

The **Trius Lines** (☏902 454 0321, 800 567 5151) bus leaves from the Rodd Colony Hotel at 6:20am Mondays to Saturdays or 11:20am Sundays and holidays and travels along the southwestern shore. For information on private shuttles, see p330. If the ferry starts running again, Yarmouth will also be the departure point to Maine.

ANNAPOLIS VALLEY & FRENCH SHORE

Heading up the French Shore you'll be regularly waved to by the Stella Maris, the single-starred, tricolored Acadian flag. Admire the many elaborate Catholic churches, stop at a roadside eatery to sample Acadian rappie pie (a type of meat pie topped with grated pastelike potato from which all the starch has been drawn) and take a walk along a fine-sand beach. If you stay longer, don't miss the chance to sample the region's foot-tapping music performances that take place frequently in summer.

Continuing northeast, the Annapolis Valley was the main breadbasket for colonial Canada and still produces much of Nova Scotia's fresh produce, especially apples. Recently wineries have taken advantage of the sandy soil. Make sure to get to the Fundy coast at Annapolis Royal and eastwards for tidal vistas over patchwork farmland, red sands and undulating hills.

Cape St Mary to Meteghan

A long, wide arc of fine sand, just 900m off Hwy 1, **Mavilette Beach** is great for collecting seashells, and the marsh behind it is good for bird-watching. At the southern edge of Meteghan, the largest community on the French Shore, **Smuggler's Cove Provincial Park** is named for its popularity with 19th-century pirates. A hundred wooden stairs take you down to a rocky beach and a good cave for hiding treasure. There are picnic sites containing barbecue pits at the top of the stairs, with a view across St Mary's Bay to Brier Island.

La Maison D'Amité B&B (☑902-645-2601; www.houseoffriendship.ca; 169 Baseline Rd; r from $175; @) is perched dramatically on a cliff close to the beach on six private hectares. The huge, American-style home has cathedral ceilings and sky-high windows with views on all sides.

Church Point to St Bernard

The villages of Church Point, Grosses-Coques, Belliveau Cove and St Bernard, on the mainland directly across St Mary's Bay from Digby Neck, make up the heart of the French Shore. This is where Acadians settled when after trekking back to Nova Scotia following the deportation they found their homesteads in the Annapolis Valley already occupied. Now linked by Hwy 1 – pretty much the only road in town – these are small fishing communities.

The oldest of the annual Acadian cultural festivals, **Festival Acadien de Clare** (www.festivalacadiendeclare.ca), is held during the second week of July at Church Point. In July and August the musical *Évangéline*, based on Henry Wadsworth Longfel-

low's romantic poem about the Acadian deportation, is presented in the **Théâtre Marc-Lescarbot** (☑902-769-2114; adult/child $25/15), also at Church Point. Performances are given in English on Saturday, in French with headset translation Tuesday and Friday, and outdoors in French on Wednesday.

◉ Sights & Activities

Hinterland Adventures & Gear　　KAYAKING
(☑902-837-4092; www.kayakingnovascotia.com; 54 Gates Lane, Weymouth; rentals per hr/day $7/40, guides per hr $10, half-/full-day tours $45/115) Running tours for over 15 years, this respected kayaking outfit specializes in paddling tours of St Mary's Bay and the Sissiboo River.

Église Ste Marie　　CHURCH
(☑902-769-2808; Hwy 1; admission incl guide $2; ⊙9am-5pm mid-May–mid-Oct) The town of Church Point, also commonly known as Pointe de l'Église, takes its name from Église Ste Marie, which towers over the town. Built between 1903 and 1905, the church is said to be the tallest and biggest wooden church in North America. An informative guide will show you around. Adjacent is the **Université Ste Anne**, the only French university in the province and a center for Acadian culture, with 300 students.

Belliveau Beach　　BEACH
Belliveau Beach, near the southern end of Belliveau, is reached by turning right onto Major's Point. The beach is made up of masses of sea-polished stones broken only by small clumps of incredibly hardy fir trees. Just behind the beach, a cemetery and monument recall the struggles of the early Acadian settlers of the French Shore.

St Bernard Church　　CHURCH
(☑902-837-5637; Hwy 1; ⊙tours Jun-Sep) St Bernard is also known for its church, a huge granite structure built by locals who added one row of blocks each year between 1910 and 1942. It has incredible acoustics which are showcased each summer through the **Musique Saint-Bernard** (www.musiquesaintbernard.ca; adult/child $15/5) concert series.

🛏 Sleeping & Eating

Chez Christophe Guesthouse & Restaurant　　INN & RESTAURANT $$
(☑902-837-5817; www.chezchristophe.ca; 2655 Hwy 1; breakfast $10, dinner mains $12-36; ⊙6am-9pm Tue-Sun) Locals drive from Yarmouth and Digby to dine at this restaurant in Grosses-Coques. Master chef Paul Comeau

has turned the house that his grandfather built in 1837 into a guesthouse (rooms $70 to $85) and restaurant; this is probably the most renowned Acadian restaurant in Nova Scotia. There's live Acadian music from 6pm to 8pm Thursday nights through June and nearly every night in July and August.

Roadside Grill RESTAURANT $
(☎902-837-5047; 3334 Hwy 1; meals $7-15; ☺8am-9pm Jul & Aug, 9am-7pm Sep-Jun) A pleasantly old-fashioned local restaurant in Belliveau Cove – try the steamed clams or the rappie pie. It also rents three small cabins (singles/doubles $55/70) with cable TV and microwaves. There's live Acadian music Tuesday nights from 5:30pm to 7:30pm June through August.

Digby Neck

Craning out to take a peek into the Bay of Fundy, Digby Neck is a giraffe's length strip of land that's a haven for whale- and seabird-watchers. At the far western end of the appendage are Long and Brier Islands, connected by ferry with the rest of the peninsula.

Plankton stirred up by the strong Fundy tides attracts finback, minke and humpback whales and this is the best place in the world to see the endangered North Atlantic right whale. Blue whales, the world's largest animal, are also sighted on occasion plus you're almost certain to see plenty of seals.

Bring plenty of warm clothing (regardless of how hot a day it seems), sunblock and binoculars; motion-sickness pills are highly recommended.

LONG ISLAND

Most people head straight to Brier Island, but Long Island has better deals on whale-watching as well as a livelier community. At the northeastern edge of Long Island, **Tiverton** is an active fishing community.

FREE **Island Museum** (☎902-839-2853; 3083 Hwy 217; ☺9:30am-7:30pm Jul & Aug, to 4:30pm late May-Jun & Sep–mid-Oct), 2km west of the Tiverton ferry dock, has exhibits on local history and a tourist information desk.

One of the best whale-watching tours in the province is found just near the Tiverton ferry dock. **Ocean Explorations Whale Cruises** (☎902-839-2417, 877-654-2341; www.oceanexplorations.ca; half-day tours adult/child $59/40; ☺Jun-Oct), led by biologist Tom Goodwin, has the adventurous approach of getting you low to whale-level in a Zodiac. Shimmy into an orange coastguard-approved flotation suit and hold on tight! Goodwin has been leading whale-watching tours since 1980 and donates part of his proceeds to wildlife conservation and environmental education organizations. Discounts are given for groups of three or more; tour times depend on weather and demand.

A 4km round-trip trail to the **Balancing Rock** starts 2km southwest of the museum. The trail features rope railings, boardwalks and an extensive series of steps down a rock bluff to the bay. At the end there's a viewing platform where you can see a 7m-high stone column perched precariously just above the pounding surf of St Mary's Bay.

Near the center of Long Island, **Central Grove Provincial Park** has a 2km hiking trail to the Bay of Fundy. There's camping at quirky **Whale Cove Campground** (☎902-834-2025; www.whalecovecampground.com; Hwy 217; serviced/unserviced sites $30/25, cabin or trailer $35-62; ⊜) in Tiddville, about 5km before Freeport; there's a cabin and a trailer to rent if you don't have gear.

At the southwestern end of Long Island, **Freeport** is central for exploring both Brier and Long Islands.

Lavena's Catch Café (☎902-839-2517; 15 Hwy 217; mains $5-15; ☺lunch & dinner) is a country-style cafe directly above the wharf at Freeport; it's the perfect spot to enjoy a sunset and you might even see a whale from the balcony. There's occasional live music in the evenings.

BRIER ISLAND

Westport was the home of Joshua Slocum, the first man to sail solo around the world, and is the only community on Brier Island. It's a quaint little fishing village and a good base to explore the numerous excellent, if rugged and windy, hiking trails around the island; don't miss a trip to the West Lighthouse. Columnar basalt rocks are seen all along the coast and agates can be found on the beaches.

The **Brier Island Backpackers Hostel** (☎902-839-2273; www.brierislandhostel.com; 223 Water St; dm adult/child $20/10; ☜) is a tiny, spotless place about 1.5km to the left as you come off the ferry. The common room and kitchen area has big windows with views over the water. There's a general store, gas station and basic **cafe** (mains

$5-8; ◷8am-9pm Mon-Sat, 10am-8pm Sun) next door, owned by the same people. You can book excellent whale-watching tours (2½ to five-hours depending on where the whales are) here with eco-conscious **Brier Island Whale & Seabird Cruises** (☑902-839-2995, 800-656-3660; www.brierisland whalewatch.com; adult/child $49/27; ◷Jun-Oct).

Atop cliffs 1km east of Westport, **Brier Island Lodge** (☑902-839-2300, 800-662-8355; www.brierisland.com; r $90-150; 🖥) has four rooms, most of which have ocean views. Its **restaurant** (mains $14-33; ◷breakfast & dinner) is the best dining option, with views on two sides, perfect service and fabulously fresh seafood. Boxed lunches are available.

ⓘ Getting There & Away

Two ferries connect Long and Brier Islands to the rest of Digby Neck. The Petit Passage ferry leaves East Ferry (on Digby Neck) 25 minutes after the hour and Tiverton on the hour; ferries are timed so that if you drive directly from Tiverton to Freeport (18km) there is no wait for the Grand Passage ferry to Westport. Both ferries operate hourly, 24 hours a day, year-round. Round-trip passage is $5 for a car and all passengers. Pedestrians ride free.

Digby

Known for its scallops, mild climate and daily ferry to Saint John, New Brunswick (p380), Digby is nestled in a protected inlet off the Bay of Fundy. Settled by United Empire Loyalists in 1783, it's now home to the largest fleet of scallop boats in the world.

Digby has been a tourist mecca for more than a century and it's a good base from which to explore Digby Neck and some lesser-known hiking trails in the area. If you're here in passing, the best things to do are to stroll the waterfront, watch the scallop draggers come and go, and eat as much of their catch as your belly can hold. If you're in town mid-August, reserve even more space in your gut for the delicious **Digby Scallop Days** (www.townofdigby.ns.ca) festival.

The only real sight in town is the **Admiral Digby Museum** (☑902-245-6322; www.admuseum.ns.ca; 95 Montague Row; admission by donation; ◷9am-5pm Tue-Sat, 1-5pm Sun mid-Jun–Aug, 9am-5pm Tue-Fri Sep–mid-Oct, 9am-5pm Wed & Fri mid-Oct–mid-Jun), a mid-19th century Georgian home which contains exhibits of the town's marine history and early settlement.

🛏 Sleeping & Eating

TOP CHOICE **Digby Backpackers Hostel**

HOSTEL $

(☑902-245-4573; www.digbyhostel.com; 168 Queen St; dm/r $28/65; ◷@) Arguably the nicest hostel in Nova Scotia. Saskia and Claude keep their solid four-bed dorm rooms spotless and can be known to spontaneously take the whole hostel out to see the sunset from a hiking trail. The heritage house has plenty of communal areas including a deck with a barbecue, and there's a lively vibe. Internet access, a light breakfast and towels are included in the price.

Bayside Inn B&B B&B $$

(☑902-245-2247, 888-754-0555; www.bayside inn.ca; 115 Montague Row; r $60-100; @) In continuous operation since the late 1800s, the historic 11-room Bayside is Digby's oldest inn. Centrally located in town, it has views over the scallop fleet and Fundy tides. It was remodeled in 2010.

Digby Pines Golf Resort & Spa HOTEL $$$

(☑902-245-2511, 800-667-4637; www.digbypines.ca; 103 Shore Rd; r $160-440; ◷May-Oct; ◷@) At the posh Pines you almost expect Jay Gatsby to come up and slap you on the back with a hearty 'old sport.' Rooms are elegantly furnished with dark woods and lush beds but are small for the price. The family-friendly grounds include everything from a golf course, spa and swimming pool to walking trails and a playground. Ask for a water-view room.

Boardwalk Café CAFE $

(☑902-245-5497; www.boardwalkcafe.netfirms.com; 40 Water St; mains $8-15; ◷lunch daily, dinner Thu & Fri) This little waterfront cafe serves delicious light mains such as chicken rappie pie and salad ($8) or shrimp jambalaya ($9). Dinner is a more upscale experience with mains around $18.

Royal Fundy Seafood Market CAFE $$

(☑902-245-5411; 144 Prince William St; mains $6-14; ◷11am-8pm) Get your seafood from the source at this little fishmonger-cum-cafe. Local seafood is made into all the usual fried suspects as well as soups.

ⓘ Information

VIC (☑902-245-2201; Shore Rd; ◷8:30am-8:30pm mid-Jun–mid-Sep, 9am-5pm mid-Sep–Oct & May–mid-Jun) A large provincial tourist office, 2km from the ferry wharf, with hundreds of brochures.

Western Counties Regional Library (☎902-245-2163; 84 Warwick St; ☺12:30-5pm & 6-8pm Tue-Thu, 10am-5pm Fri, 10am-2pm Sat) Free internet access.

ℹ Getting There & Away

Acadian Lines (☎902-454-9321, 800-567-5151; www.acadianbus.com) buses from Halifax ($40, four hours, daily) stop at the **Irving gas station** (☎902-245-2048; 77 Montague Row). For ferry information, see p317.

Bear River

This country haven for offbeat artists is only minutes from the coast but enjoys inland, fogless temperatures. There's a strong Mi'kmaq presence here that mixes in with the Scottish, giving Bear River a unique vibe. Some buildings near the river are on stilts while other historic homes nestle on the steep hills of the valley. A few wineries are also starting to pop up just out of town.

◉ Sights & Activities

Bear River Vineyards WINERY
(☎902-467-4156; www.wine.travel; 133 Chute Rd) All estate-produced, award-winning wines made at this adorable little winery use solar energy, biodiesel, wind power and the natural slope of the property. Stop by to take a free tour and tasting (July to September) or stay longer at friendly hosts Chris and Peggy's one-room B&B ($130 per night) to enjoy wine-making workshops and retreats.

Annapolis Highland Vineyards WINERY
(☎902-467-0917; www.novascotiawines.com; 2635 Clementsvale Rd; ☺10am-5pm Mon-Sat, noon-5pm Sun) A more commercial winery – don't miss the gold-medal White Wedding dessert wine if you come in for a free tasting here. Delicious fruit wines are available.

Bear River First Nation FIRST NATION
Bear River First Nation is a five-minute drive from the heart of town: turn left after crossing the bridge, then take a left where the road forks. In a beautiful building, with a wigwam-shaped foyer, the **Heritage & Cultural Centre** (☎902-467-0301; 194 Reservation Rd; admission $3; ☺10am-6pm mid-May–mid-Oct) offers demonstrations of traditional crafts and hands-on workshops. A 1km **trail** starts behind the center and highlights plants with traditional medicinal uses.

🛏 Sleeping & Eating

Inn Out of the Fog INN $$
(☎902-467-0268; www.innoutofthefog.com; 1 Wharf Rd; r $75-95) Sparkling tapestries and old kimonos grace the brightly painted walls of this whimsically artistic inn housed in an historic marine warehouse. The sunny gardens surrounding the inn are bubbling with flowers and chirping birds. Don't miss the shop downstairs.

Bear River Cafe CAFE $
(☎902-467-3008; 1870 Clementsvale Rd; mains $7-14; ☺10am-5pm Tue-Sun) This cafe is a great place to chat with locals, drink a cup of coffee over a slice of pie and enjoy the view of Bear River.

🛍 Shopping

Flight of Fancy SOUVENIRS
(☎902-467-4171; Main St; ☺9am-7pm Mon-Sat, 11am-7pm Sun Jul & Aug, 9am-5pm Mon-Sat, 11am-5pm Sun Sep-Jun) An exquisitely curated craft store and gallery with work by more than 200 artists and craftspeople. If you want to buy one unique treasure to take away from Nova Scotia, this is a good place to find it.

Bear Town Baskets SOUVENIRS
(☎902-467-3060; 44 Maple Ave, Bear River First Nation; ☺10am-10pm) Baskets sold here are made by a retired chief of the Bear River First Nation. Follow the signs to the studio in his front yard where he makes traditional ash baskets.

Annapolis Royal & Around

The community's efforts of village restoration have made this one of the most delightful places to visit in the region. In fact, Annapolis Royal (population 800) is one of the only well-trodden towns of its size in Nova Scotia without a Tim Hortons (a ubiquitous fast-food franchise).

KINGS TRANSIT

The local **Kings Transit** (☎902-628-7310, 888-546-4442; www.kingstransit.ns.ca) bus line runs every other hour from 6am to around 7pm from Weymouth to Bridgetown, stopping in every little town along the way. Tickets cost around $3.50 depending on the distance traveled.

NOVA SCOTIA BEAR RIVER

The site was Canada's first permanent European settlement, Port Royal, founded by French explorer Samuel de Champlain in 1605. As the British and French battled, the settlement often changed hands. In 1710 the British had a decisive victory and changed the town's name to Annapolis Royal in honor of Queen Anne.

Most sights are on or near long, curving St George St. A waterfront boardwalk behind King's Theatre on St George St provides views of the village of Granville Ferry across the Annapolis River.

◉ Sights & Activities

Fort Anne National Historic Site
HISTORICAL SITE
(☏902-532-2397; www.parkscanada.gc.ca/fortanne; Upper St George St; adult/child $4/2; ☺9am-6pm) This historic site in the town center preserves the memory of the early Acadian settlement plus the remains of the 1635 French fort. Entry to the extensive grounds is free, but you'll also want to visit the museum where artifacts are contained in various period rooms. An extraordinary four-panel tapestry, crafted in needlepoint by more than 100 volunteers, depicts 400 years of history.

Annapolis Royal Historic Gardens GARDEN
(☏902-532-7018; www.historicgardens.com; 441 St George St; adult/student $8/7; ☺8am-dusk) Annapolis Royal Historic Gardens covers a rambling 6.5 hectares with various themed gardens such as an Acadian kitchen garden one might have seen in the late 1600s and an innovative modern one. Munch on blueberries, ogle the vegetables and look for frogs. The Secret Garden Café offers lunches and German-style baked goods.

Delap's Cove Wilderness Trail
NATURE RESERVE
Over the North Mountain from Annapolis Royal, Delap's Cove Wilderness Trail lets you get out on the Fundy shore. It consists of two loop trails connected by an old inland road that used to serve a Black Loyalist community, now just old foundations and apple trees in the woods. Both the loop trails are 9km return.

Port Royal National Historic Site
HISTORICAL SITE
(☏902-532-2898; 53 Historic Lane; adult/child $4/2; ☺9am-6pm) Some 14km northwest of Annapolis Royal, Port Royal National Historic Site is the actual location of the first permanent European settlement north of Florida. The site is a replica of de Champlain's 1605 fur-trading habitation, where costumed workers help tell the story of this early settlement.

FREE **Tidal Power Project** INDUSTRIAL MUSEUM
(☏902-532-5454; ☺10am-6pm) A hydroelectric prototype at the Annapolis River Causeway, Tidal Power has been harnessing power from the Bay of Fundy tides since 1984 (see the boxed text). An interpretive center includes models, exhibits and a video.

☞ Tours
Be escorted by an undertaker-garbed guide for a tour of the Fort Anne **graveyard** (Fort Anne National Historic Site; adult/child $7/1; ☺9:30pm Tue, Thu & Sun Jun-Sep). Everyone carries a lantern to wind through the headstones and discover this town's history through stories of those who've passed away. Proceeds go to the Annapolis Royal Historical Society.

TAPPING THE TIDES

With 14 billion tonnes of sea water flowing in and out of the Bay of Fundy every day (the equivalent of the flow of every river on Earth combined), it seems only logical to try to convert this power into usable energy. Annapolis Tidal began in 1984 as a pilot project and it employs the largest straight-flow turbine in the world, generating more than 30 million kilowatt-hours of electricity per year – enough for 4500 homes.

Nowadays, the newer instream tidal systems (underwater windmills anchored to the seafloor) are preferred, and Nova Scotia has been chosen to house the first major instream tidal power plant in North America. In collaboration with the Irish company OpenHydro, plans are under way to build one of the world's largest single underwater turbines within the 6km-wide Minas Passage.

Once the first one-megawatt-producing, doughnut-shaped unit has been built and tested, as many as 300 more could be constructed in the Bay of Fundy. The combined efforts of these 300-plus turbines could power over 200,000 homes; about one-fifth of the province's population.

Starting from the lighthouse on St George St, **daytime tours** (adult/child $7/1; ⊙2pm Mon-Fri), run by the same group, focus on the Acadian heritage of Annapolis Royal or the architecture of the historic district.

🛏 Sleeping

TOP CHOICE **Queen Anne B&B** B&B $$
(☎902-532-7850, 877-536-0403; www. queenanneinn.ns.ca; 494 St George St; r $120-180, carriage house $209; 🛜) Arguably the most elegant property in Annapolis Royal, this B&B is the perfect balance of period decor and subtle grace. It's so beautiful, with the Tiffany lamp replicas, manicured grounds and sweeping staircases, that it might seem stuffy were it not for the friendly owners who make you feel like you could (almost) kick your feet up on the antique coffee table.

Bailey House B&B B&B $$
(☎902-532-1285, 877-532-1285; www.baileyhouse.ca; 150 Lower St George St; r $135-145; 🛜) The only B&B on the waterfront, Bailey House is also the oldest inn in the area. The friendly owners have managed to keep the vintage charm (anyone over 6ft might hit their head on the doorways!) while adding all the necessary modern comforts and conveniences. The B&B is gay friendly.

Croft House B&B B&B $
(☎902-532-0584; www.crofthouse.ca; 51 Riverview Lane; r $75; 🛜) This farmhouse stands on about 40 hectares of land, across the river and about a five-minute drive from Annapolis Royal. One of the enthusiastic owners is a chef, and he whips up a fine breakfast with organic ingredients.

Dunromin Campground CAMPGROUND $
(☎902-532-2808; www.dunromincampsite.com; Hwy 1, Granville Ferry; serviced/unserviced sites $26/39, tepees/caravans $50/55, cabins $65-110; @🛜) This offbeat campground has some secluded riverside sites as well as nifty options such as a tepee (for up to six people) and a gypsy caravan. You can rent canoes for $10 per hour.

🍴 Eating

Many of the B&Bs, such as the Queen Anne, are open for elegant lunches and dinners.

Leo's SANDWICH SHOP $
(☎902-532-7424; 222 St George St; mains $6-12; ⊙9am-8pm Mon-Sat, noon-4pm Sun) In a flower-filled garden, Leo's is very popular with locals; be prepared to wait for a delicious sandwich.

Ye Olde Pub PUB $
(☎902-532-2244; 9-11 Church St; mains $5-15; ⊙11am-11pm Mon-Sat, noon-8pm Sun) On sunny days eat gourmet pub fare on the outdoor terrace; when it's cooler slip into the dark and cozy old bar. Try the marinated scallop appetizer ($7).

☆ Entertainment

King's Theatre THEATER
(☎902-532-7704; www.kingstheatre.ca; 209 St George St; movies $6, live shows $14-22) Right on the waterfront, this nonprofit theater presents musicals, dramas and concerts most evenings in July and August, and occasionally during the rest of the year. Hollywood films are screened on most weekends and independent films most Tuesdays, year-round.

🔒 Shopping

Farmers & Traders Market MARKET
(cnr St George & Church Sts; ⊙10am-3pm Wed, 8am-noon Sat) Annapolis Royal's thriving community of artists and artisans offer their wares alongside local farmers at this popular market. There's live entertainment most Saturday mornings.

ℹ Information

Annapolis Royal (www.annapolisroyal.com) Links to history, festivals and everything else.

VIC (☎902-532-5769; 209 St George St; ⊙10am-6pm mid-May–mid-Oct) At the King's Theatre; pick up a historic walking tour pamphlet.

ℹ Getting There & Away

Acadian Lines (☎902-454-9321, 800-567-5151; www.acadianbus.com) buses stop at the **Port Royal Wandlyn Inn** (☎902-532-2323; 3924 Hwy 1) from Halifax (3½ hours, daily), en route to Digby (30 minutes).

Kentville

During the colorful spring bloom of the valley, the **Annapolis Valley Apple Blossom Festival** (www.appleblossom.com) in early June brings folks together with concerts, a parade, barbecues and art shows. Kentville is the county seat for this area, with a number of government offices and stately old homes.

◉ Sights & Activities

FREE **Agriculture Research Station**
MUSEUM
(☎902-678-1093; off Hwy 1; ⊙8:30am-4:30pm) At the eastern end of town, the Agriculture

Research Station includes a museum on the area's farming history and the apple industry in particular. Guided museum tours are offered during summer.

FREE **Old King's County Museum** MUSEUM (☑902-678-6237; 37 Cornwallis Ave; ⊙9am-4pm Mon-Sat) Local artifacts, history and an art gallery can be seen at the Old King's County Museum.

ℹ Information

Tourist office (☑902-678-7170; 125 Park St; ⊙9:30am-7pm Jul & Aug, to 5:30pm Sep-early Oct & mid-May–Jun) West of the town center.

ℹ Getting There & Away

Acadian Lines (☑902-678-2000; www.acadianbus.com; 66 Cornwallis St) Has an office in the old train station; buses run to Halifax (two hours, twice daily).

North of Highway 1

The North Mountain, which ends at the dramatic Cape Blomidon, defines one edge of the Annapolis Valley. On the other side of the mountain are fishing communities on the Bay of Fundy. The valley floor between Hwy 1 and the North Mountain is crisscrossed with small highways lined with farms and orchards. It's a great place to get out your road map – or throw it out – and explore. To start the adventure, turn north on Hwy 358 just west of Wolfville (at exit 11 of Hwy 101). The historic town of Canning is en route to Scots Bay, where Hwy 358 ends and a dramatic hiking trail leads to views of the Minas Basin and the Bay of Fundy.

PORT WILLIAMS

Only a blink away from Wolfville on Hwy 358 is **Tin Pan** (☑902-691-0020; 978 Main St; mains $3-9; ⊙breakfast, lunch & dinner Mon-Sat), a favorite for motorbikers who congregate here Saturday mornings for hearty breakfasts.

Prescott House Museum (☑902-542-3984; www.prescott.museum.gov.ns.ca; 1633 Starr's Point Rd; adult/student $3/2; ⊙9:30am-5:30pm Mon-Sat, 1-5:30pm Sun Jun–mid-Oct), c 1814, is one of the finest examples of Georgian architecture in Nova Scotia and former home of the horticulturalist who introduced many of the apple varieties grown in the Annapolis Valley. To get here, turn right on Starr's Point Rd at the flashing light in Port Williams, 2km north of Hwy 1, and follow it for 3.25km.

CANNING

From November to March, hundreds of **bald eagles** gather in the Canning area, attracted by local chicken farms – a photographer's and nature-lover's dream. Just west of Canning on Hwy 221 **Blomidon Estate Winery** (☑902-582-7565; www.blomidonwine.com; 10318 Hwy 221; tastings $4; ⊙10am & 6pm Jun-Sep) offers tastings and free tours. Further along Hwy 358, stop at the **Look-Off**. About 200m above the Annapolis Valley, this is the best view of its rows of fruit trees and picturesque farmhouses.

Art Can Gallery & Café (☑902-582-7071; www.artcan.com; 9850 Main St; mains $11; ⊙10am-5pm Tue-Thu, to 10pm Fri & Sat, to 4pm Sun) is an art-store-cum-cafe. Enjoy fair-trade coffee and delicious baked goods with views over the valley. Check the website for the availability of art classes and workshops.

SCOTS BAY

The hike to the end of **Cape Split** starts in Scots Bay. This is probably the most popular hiking trail in Nova Scotia. It's about 14km return, taking five hours with little elevation change if you follow the easier inland route. To do that, follow the trail along the fence as you leave the parking area, and then choose the trail on your right when you come to a fork. (The trail on the left leads to a coastal route, which is poorly marked and subject to erosion. Give yourself extra time and consider carrying a compass if you want to explore that route.) The hike ends in a grassy meadow on cliffs high above the Bay of Fundy. Here you can see the tides creating waves called tidal rips. The unique geography of the Bay of Fundy results in the most extreme tides in the world: at its peak, the flow of water between Cape Split and the Parrsboro shore is equal to the combined flow of all the rivers in the world.

Take time before or after the hike to look for agates along the beach at Scots Bay.

Blomidon Provincial Park (☑902-582-7319; www.parks.gov.ns.ca; off Hwy 358; campsites $24) is on the opposite side of Cape Blomidon from Scots Bay. There are a number of routes to get here from Hwy 358, all well signed. One route begins 15km south of Scots Bay and involves driving 10km along the Minas Basin. The campground is set atop high cliffs that overlook the basin. There's a beach and picnic area at the foot of the hill and a 14km system of hiking trails within the park.

Further southeast on the Bay of Fundy (take any route west from Hwy 358 until you hit Hwy 359, then take it over the North Mountain), **Hall's Harbour** is a great spot to spend an afternoon hiking along the beach and in the surrounding hills. It's also one of the best places in Nova Scotia to eat lobster.

Pick your own lobster at **Hall's Harbour Lobster Pound** (☑902-679-5299; ◒noon-8pm Jul & Aug, to 7pm May, Jun, Sep & Oct). The price is determined by the market – a whole lobster will rarely cost below $28. Seafood baskets with scallops or clams cost $16.

On the road back toward Kentville in Centreville, stay the night or stop for tea at **Delft Haus B&B Inn & Goodchild's Tea Room** (☑902-678-4333; www.delfthaus. com; 1942 Hwy 359; r $90-145; ◎), a storybook white Victorian house on an acre of gardens. The tearoom serves light meals (sandwiches from $4.50), free trade tea and coffee, and a great selection of ice cream.

Wolfville

Wolfville is a college town with several wineries nearby so as you'd expect there are plenty of drinking holes, good eating establishments and culture all around. The students and faculty of Acadia University make up about 50% of the town's 7000 residents. Just outside of town you'll find Acadian dikes, scenic drives and enough hiking to keep you here for days. If you're in town early fall, rock out to modern roots music at the annual **Canadian Deep Roots Festival** (www.deeprootsmusic.ca).

◉ Sights

Waterfront Park   PARK

(cnr Gaspereau Ave & Front St) Waterfront Park offers a stunning view of the tidal mudflats, Minas Basin and the red cliffs of Cape Blomidon. Displays explain the tides, dikes, flora and fauna, and history of the area. This is an easy spot to start a walk or cycle on top of the dikes.

L'Acadie Vineyards   WINERY

(☑902-542-8463; www.lacadievineyards.ca; 310 Slayter Rd; ◒10am-5pm May-Oct) Overlooking Gaspereau Valley just south of Wolfville, this geothermal winery grows certified organic grapes to make traditional method sparkling and dried grape wines. You can also stay in one of three country-style two-

bedroom, kitchen-equipped cottages ($150 per night), which of course include a free bottle of wine.

Gaspereau Vineyards   WINERY

(☑902-542-1455; www.gaspereauwine.com; 2239 White Rock Rd; ◒10am-5pm mid-May–Oct, tours noon, 2pm & 4pm daily mid-May–Oct) In Gaspereau, 3km south of Wolfville, this is one of the province's best-known wineries with award-winning ice wine.

Muir Murray Winery   WINERY

(☑902-542-0343; www.muirmurraywinery.com; 90 Dyke Rd; ◒10am-5pm late Jul-Sep, tastings 11am, 1pm & 3pm daily) Three kilometers east of Wolfville, this is the area's newest winery in a barn-like structure overlooking fields. A tearoom is planned that will serve lunch. We particularly liked the Cape Split Leon Millot.

Randall House Museum   MUSEUM

(☑902-542-9775; 171 Main St; admission by donation; ◒10am-5pm Mon-Sat, 2-5pm Sun mid-Jun–mid-Sep) Randall House Museum relates the history of the New England planters and colonists who replaced the expelled Acadians.

⚡ Activities

Locals fought to save the home of hundreds of chimney swifts, birds that migrate annually to Wolfville from Peru. As a result, the chimney of a now-demolished dairy has become the focal point of the **Robie Tufts Nature Centre**, opposite the public library on Front St. Drop by in the late evening in spring or summer to see the birds swooshing down for a night's rest.

Rent bikes at **Valley Stove & Cycle** (☑902-542-7280; 234 Main St; half-/full-day $25/30).

🛏 Sleeping

TOP CHOICE **Garden House B&B**   B&B $$

(☑902-542-1703; www.gardenhouse.ca; 220 Main St; r $65-110; ◈) This antique house retains its old-time feel in the most comfortable way. Creaky floors, a rustic breakfast table decorated with wildflowers, and the fact that everyone is encouraged to take off their shoes, creates a lived-in vibe you instantly feel a part of. Bathrooms are shared.

Blomidon Inn   INN $$

(☑902-542-2291, 800-565-2291; www.theblom idon.net; 195 Main St; d $110-160, ste $160-290; ❄@◈) Lofty Victorian architecture and

RAISING A GLASS TO NOVA SCOTIA WINES

The wine-making tradition in Nova Scotia goes back to the early 1600s and it's possible that this was the first place in North America where wine grapes were grown. Today wineries are springing up everywhere (there are six distinct wine-growing regions in the province), although most are found in the Annapolis Valley and on the Malagash Peninsula. These are mellow regions to pop in for some tastings between hikes and sightseeing.

The French hybrid grape l'Acadie Blanc grows particularly well in Nova Scotia and has become the province's signature grape; it makes a medium-bodied, citrusy white wine that pairs well with scallops or smoked salmon. New York Muscat also grows well and is often used for dry white and ice wines.

Most restaurant wine lists in the province will include several for you to choose from. It's easy to find Jost, Gaspereau and Blomidon wines, but it's worth seeking out the smaller vineyards, some organic, that make excellent and often award-winning blends.

In its fourth year in 2011, the 10-day **Ice Wine Festival** in early February is celebrated through wine pairing and culinary events in Halifax and at wineries around the province.

old-world extravagance make this a very uppercrust-feeling inn. On 2.5 hectares of perfectly maintained gardens, the rooms are just as well groomed. Check the website for package deals.

Gingerbread House Inn   INN $$
(☎902-542-1458; www.gingerbreadhouse.ca; 8 Robie Tufts Dr; d $115-135, ste $145-215; ☜) The exterior of this unique B&B is like a big pink birthday cake with lacy white edging. Rooms, several of which have a hot tub, are like your own candle-lit spa.

✖ Eating & Drinking

Acton's   RESTAURANT $$
(☎902-542-7525; 268 Main St; mains lunch $11-18, dinner $18-32; ☺lunch & dinner) Acton's fame spreads as far as Yarmouth as one of the finest restaurants in the region. Spectacular salads and new twists on old favorites are the house specialties.

Tempest   RESTAURANT $$$
(☎902/866-542-0588; 117 Front St; mains lunch $8-18, dinner $22-30; ☺lunch & dinner) Tasty fine dining that borrows from all sorts of cuisines, with dishes such as chicken satay with coconut and daikon or sambuca flambéed prawns served on polenta.

Coffee Merchant & Library Pub
    CAFE & PUB $
(☎902-542-4315; 472 Main St; ☺11:30am-midnight Mon-Sat) Downstairs the cafe serves up good fair-trade coffee and baked goods, while you can get a pint and a square meal at the cozy upstairs pub.

Ivy Deck   RESTAURANT $$
(☎902-542-1868; 8 Elm Ave; mains $9-17; ☺lunch & dinner, closed Mon Nov-Jun) Try a salad with flowers intermingled among the lettuce or salmon and shrimp penne. There's a pleasant outside deck.

❶ Information

Tourist office (☎902-542-7000; 11 Willow Ave; ☺9am-9pm Jul-Sep, 9am-5pm May, Jun & Oct) A very helpful office at the east end of Main St.

Wolfville (www.wolfville.info) Information on Wolfville, Acadia University and exploring Nova Scotia.

Wolfville Memorial Library (☎902-542-5760; 21 Elm Ave; ☺11am-5pm & 6:30-8:30pm Tue-Thu, 11am-5pm Fri & Sat, 1-5pm Sun) Free internet access.

❶ Getting There & Away

Acadian Lines (☎902-454-9321, 800-567-5151; www.acadianbus.com) buses stop at Acadia University in front of Wheelock Hall off Highland Ave. **Kings Transit** (☎902-678-7310, 888-546-4442; www.kingstransit.ns.ca) buses run between Cornwallis and Wolfville and stop at 209 Main St.

Grand Pré

Grand Pré, 25km northwest of Windsor at the outskirts of Wolfville, is now a very small English-speaking town. In the 1750s, however, it was the site of one of the most tragic but compelling stories in eastern

Canada's history that you learn about at the Grand Pré National Historic Site.

◉ Sights & Activities

Grand Pré National Historic Site

HISTORICAL SITE

(☎902-542-3631; 2205 Grand Pré Rd; adult/child $7.80/3.90; ◷9am-6pm May-Oct) At Grand Pré National Historic Site a modern interpretive center explains the historical context for the deportation from Acadian, Mi'kmaw and British perspectives and traces the many routes Acadians took from and back to the Maritimes.

Beside the center, a serene **park** contains gardens and an Acadian-style stone church. There's also a bust of American poet Henry Wadsworth Longfellow, who chronicled the Acadian saga in *Evangeline: A Tale of Acadie,* and a statue of his fictional Evangeline, now a romantic symbol of her people.

Beyond the park, you can see the farmland created when the Acadians built dikes along the shoreline as they had done in northwest France for generations. There are 12 sq km below sea level here, protected by just over 9km of dike.

Domaine de Grand Pré

WINERY

(☎902-542-1753; www.grandprewines.ns.ca; 11611 Hwy 1; tours $7; ◷tours 11am, 3pm & 5pm, free tastings 10am-6pm) Many people travel to town to visit Domaine de Grand Pré vineyards and winery. The tours take about 45 minutes or you can do tastings and stroll through the vines by yourself.

🛏 Sleeping & Eating

TOP CHOICE The Olde Lantern Inn & Vineyard

INN $$

(☎902-542-1389, 877-965-3845; www.old lanterninn.com; 11575 Hwy 1; r $100-155; 🛜) Clean lines and attention to every comfort (such as butter-soft sheets) makes this a great place to stay. The vineyard grounds overlook Minas Basin where you can watch the rise and fall of the Fundy tides.

Le Caveau

RESTAURANT $$

(☎902-542-1753; 11611 Hwy 1; mains $16-32; ◷lunch & dinner) Considered to be the finest Northern European–style restaurant in the province, this Swiss restaurant is on the grounds of Domaine de Grand Pré. The beautiful outdoor patio is paved with fieldstones and shaded with grapevines.

Evangeline

RESTAURANT $

(☎902-542-2703; pie $3-5; ◷8am-7pm) The restaurant on the same grounds as the Evangeline Inn & Motel is famous for its homemade pie and exceptional local fare; it's always packed.

🛍 Shopping

Tangled Garden

FOOD & DRINK

(☎902-542-9811; 11827 Hwy 1; ◷10am-6pm) Impossible to classify, this is probably the best-smelling shopping experience in Nova Scotia. Buy a bottle of herb-infused vinegar or jelly to take away, or stroll the gardens and meditative labyrinth while licking herb-flavored ice cream.

THE ACADIANS

When the French first settled the area around the Minas Basin, they called the region Arcadia, a Greek and Roman term for 'pastoral paradise.' This became Acadia, and by the 18th century the Acadians felt more connection with the land here than with the distant Loire Valley they'd come from.

To the English, however, they would always be French, with whom rivalry and suspicion was constant. The Acadians refused to take an oath of allegiance to the English king after the Treaty of Utrecht granted Nova Scotia to the British, considering it an affront to their Catholic faith. When hard-line lieutenant governor Charles Lawrence was appointed in 1754, he became fed up with the Acadians and ordered their deportation. The English burned many villages and forced some 14,000 Acadians onto ships.

Many Acadians headed for Louisiana and New Orleans; others went to various Maritime points, New England, Martinique in the Caribbean, Santo Domingo in the Dominican Republic, or back to Europe. Not once were they greeted warmly with open arms. Some hid out and remained in Acadia. In later years many of the deported people returned but found their lands occupied. In Nova Scotia, Acadians resettled the Chéticamp area on Cape Breton Island and the French Shore north of Yarmouth. New Brunswick has a large French population stretching up the east coast past the Acadian Peninsula at Caraquet.

Windsor

Windsor was once the only British stronghold in this region but today it's just a graying little town eking out an existence between the highway and the Avon River. Windsor is a place to enjoy bluegrass music – think lots of fast banjo picking. Avon River Park hosts two bluegrass festivals, one in June and one in July, and is a hangout for aficionados all summer long. The **tourist office** (☑902-798-2690; 31 Colonial Rd; ⊙8:30am-6:30pm Jul & Aug, 9am-5pm Sat & Sun Jun, Sep & Oct) is just off exit 6 from Hwy 101. The dike beside the tourist office offers a view of the tidal river flats.

While in town check out **Haliburton House** (☑902-798-2915; 414 Clifton Ave; adult/student $3.60/2.55; ⊙10am-5pm Mon-Sat, 1-5pm Sun), once home of Judge Thomas Chandler Haliburton (1796–1865), writer of the Sam Slick stories. Many of Haliburton's expressions, such as 'quick as a wink' and 'city slicker,' are still used.

Stay the night at the **Clockmaker's Inn** (☑902-792-2573, 866-778-3600; www.the clockmakersinn.com; 1399 King St; d $100-190; 🛈), a French chateau-style mansion with curved bay windows, lots of stained glass and sweeping hardwood staircases. It's gay friendly and afternoon tea is served everyday, as is breakfast.

CENTRAL NOVA SCOTIA

Hiking, rafting and rockhounding are the activities of choice around this mildly touristed region. For those traveling overland from the rest of Canada this is your first taster of Nova Scotia – do not let it pass you by on bleak Hwy 104.

Called the 'Glooscap Trail' in provincial tourism literature, the area is named for the figure in Mi'kmaw legend who created the unique geography of the Bay of Fundy region. Unfortunately, stories and representations of Glooscap are easier to come across than genuine acknowledgments of present-day Mi'kmaq people.

Shubenacadie

Shubenacadie, or simply 'Shube,' is best known for the **Shubenacadie Provincial Wildlife Park** (☑902-758-2040; http://wild lifepark.gov.ns.ca; 149 Creighton Rd; adult/child $4.25/1.75; ⊙9am-7pm mid-May–mid-Oct, 9am-3pm Sat & Sun mid-Oct–mid-May), the place to commune with Nova Scotia's wildlife (you can hand-feed the deer and, if you're lucky, pet a moose). The animals were either born in captivity or once kept as 'pets,' and as a result cannot be released into the wild – they live in large enclosures. Turn off Hwy 102 at exit 11 and follow Hwy 2 to the park entrance.

Maitland

Tiny Maitland is the place to go rafting on the white water that is created by the outflow of the Shubenacadie River meeting the blasting force of the incoming Fundy tides, but it's also one of the oldest towns in Canada.

Wave heights are dependent on the phases of the moon (see the boxed text, p355); get information from your rafting company about the tides for your chosen day since your experience (either mild or exhilarating) will be dictated by this. Outboard-powered Zodiacs plunge right through the white water for the two to three hours that the rapids exist. Prepare to get very, very wet – no experience is needed.

⊙ Activities

Shubenacadie River Runners RAFTING (☑902-261-2770, 800-856-5061; www.tidalbore rafting.com; 8681 Hwy 215; half-/full-day adult $55/75, child $50/70) The biggest rafting company is hyper-organized and professional in every way.

Shubenacadie River Adventures RAFTING (☑902-261-2222, 800-878-8687; www.shubie. com; 10061 Hwy 15; day rafting with barbecue adult/child $75/70) Also offers mud sliding.

🛏 Sleeping

There are a handful of places to sleep in Maitland but the few eating options have unpredictable opening hours – bring your own food or a full belly.

🔺TOP CHOICE **Tidal Life Guesthouse** B&B $ (☑902-261-2583; www.thetidallife.ca; 9568 Cedar St; dm $35, r $90-120; 🛈) This place is a backpackers-B&B hybrid in an old beauty of a house with grand airy rooms and large windows overlooking grassy fields. Artistically designed communal spaces are everywhere, including a hammock on the back porch. All options include a big healthy breakfast and bathrooms are shared.

THE POWER OF THE BORE

The **tidal bore** phenomenon occurs when the first surge of the extreme Bay of Fundy tides flows upriver at high tide. Sometimes the advancing wave is only a ripple, but with the right phase of the moon it can be a meter or so in height, giving the impression that the river is flowing backwards. It's not a very thrilling spectacle but you can see it from the lookout on Tidal Bore Rd, off Hwy 236 just west of exit 14 from Hwy 102 on the northwest side of Truro. Staff in the adjacent Palliser Motel **gift shop** (☏902-893-8951) can advise when the next tidal bore will arrive. There's another viewpoint in Moncton, New Brunswick (p410).

Cresthaven by the Sea   B&B $$
(☏902-261-2001, 866-870-2001; www.cresthavenbythesea.com; 19 Ferry Lane; r $140-150) Stay here for what is possibly the best view in Canada over the Fundy tides. The immaculate white Victorian sits on a bluff right over the point where the Shubenacadie River meets the bay. All the rooms have river views and the lower ones are wheelchair accessible.

Truro

Several major highways converge here, along with a VIA Rail line so it's no wonder Truro is known as the hub of Nova Scotia. It's also a bus transfer point. While the town does look somewhat like an aging shopping mall, it's exceptionally well serviced and can make a good stop to pick up that nagging item you need or just stock up on food.

◉ Sights & Activities

Victoria Park   PARK
(Park St off Brunswick St) Escape Truro's busy streets at Victoria Park, 400 hectares of green space in the very center of town, including a deep gorge and two waterfalls. The park attracts dozens of bird species.

✸ Festivals & Events

Truro International Tulip Festival
          CANADIAN
(www.townoftruro.ca; ⊙mid-May) A great family gathering with bluegrass concerts and a big antique market.

Millbrook Annual Powwow   CULTURAL
(☏902-897-9199; www.millbrookfirstnation.net; ⊙2nd weekend of Aug) The best time to visit Truro is when Millbrook First Nation hosts its annual powwow. Campsites and showers are available; drugs and alcohol are prohibited.

🛏 Sleeping & Eating

Baker's Chest B&B   B&B $$
(☏902-893-4824, 877-822-5655; www.bakerschest.ca; 53 Farnham Rd; r/ste $100/125; ☏) A newly restored classic older home with contemporary decor and a fitness room and hot tub. The famous tearoom was closed in 2010 but keep your fingers crossed for a reopening.

Wooden Hog   RESTAURANT $$
(☏902-895-0779; 627 Prince St; mains lunch $8, dinner $11-17; ⊙9am-4pm Mon, 9am-9pm Tue-Fri, 11am-9pm Sat) Named for the huge, sculpted Harley that hangs off the back wall, this is a popular restaurant with local and Mexican specialties plus decadent desserts.

ℹ Information

Tourist office (☏902-893-2922; Victoria Sq, cnr Prince & Commercial Sts; ⊙9am-5pm May & Jun, 8:30am-7:30pm Jul & Aug, 9am-5pm Sep & Oct) This place offers internet access and a terrific guide to the tree sculptures around town. The trees were carved after the region was attacked by Dutch elm disease more than 30 years ago.

ℹ Getting There & Away

The **bus station** (☏902-895-3833; 280 Willow St; ⊙8am-10:30pm) is busy with **Acadian Lines** (☏902-454-9321, 800-567-5151; www.acadianbus.com) buses en route to Amherst ($23, two hours, three times daily) and Sydney ($52, five hours, three times daily).

Economy to Five Islands

Highway 2 hugs the shore of the Minas Basin, the northeast arm of the Bay of Fundy, and this is the first sizable community that you'll arrive at. There's great **hiking** and several interesting sites around Economy.

◉ Sights & Activities

Hiking

The most challenging hikes are around Economy Falls. The **Devil's Bend Trail** begins 7km up River Phillip Rd toward the Cobequid Mountains. Turn right and park; the 6.5km (one-way) trail follows the river to the falls. The **Kenomee Canyon Trail** begins further up River Phillip Rd, at the top of the falls. A 20km loop, it takes you up the river to its headwaters in a protected wilderness area. Several streams have to be forded. There are designated campsites, making this a good two-day adventurous trek.

The **Thomas Cove Coastal Trail** is actually two 3.5km loops with great views across the Minas Basin and of the Cobequid Mountains. They begin down Economy Point Rd, 500m east of the Cobequid Interpretation Centre. Follow the signs to a parking area. Finally, just 7km west of Economy, there are several hikes in **Five Islands Provincial Park** (☎902-254-2980; parks.gov.ns.ca). The 4.5km **Red Head Trail** is well developed with lookouts, benches and great views.

Cobequid Interpretation Centre   MUSEUM
(☎902-647-2600; 3248 Hwy 2, near River Phillip Rd; admission free; ⊙9am-4:30pm Mon-Fri year-round, to 6pm Sat & Sun Jul & Aug) Stop here for good exhibits on the area's ecology and history. Climb a WWII observation tower for a bird's-eye view of the surrounding area and pick up hiking information from the staff.

🛏 Sleeping & Eating

Four Seasons Retreat   RESORT $$
(☎902-647-2628, 888-373-0339; www.fourseas onsretreat.ns.ca; 320 Cove Rd, Upper Economy; 1-/2-bedroom cottages $109/210; 🛜🐾) Fully equipped cottages are surrounded by trees and face the Minas Basin. In summer there's a hot tub near the pool; in winter – or on a chilly night – there are woodstoves.

Mo's at Five Islands   HOSTEL & CAFE $
(☎902-254-8088; www.mosatfiveislands.com; 951 Hwy 2, Five Islands; dm $28; 🛜) You can usually count on an interesting crowd at this spotless hostel and at the large homey cafe out front (light meals from $4). The owner also owns one of the five islands (of the synonymous town) and holds a running race each year from the mainland to the island when the tide goes out high enough – the race and the hostel are named after Moses and his parting of the Red Sea.

High Tide B&B   B&B $$
(☎902-647-2788; www.hightidebb.com; 2240 Hwy 2, Lower Economy; d $85-95; 🛜) This friendly, modern bungalow has great views. Janet, one of the owners, will have you down on the beach for a clam boil in no time.

That Dutchman's Farm   CAFE $
(☎902-647-2751; www.thatdutchmansfarm.com; 112 Brown Rd, Upper Economy; lunch $8; ⊙11am-5pm late Jun-early Sep) The yummy cafe here offers sandwiches, soups and plates of the eccentric farmer's own gouda. You can tour the farm for a small fee.

Several takeaway stands selling fried clams pop up along the highway near Five Islands Provincial Park in the summer.

Parrsboro

Rockhounds come from far and wide to forage the shores of Parrsboro, the largest of the towns along the Minas Basin. The Fundy Geological Museum has wonderful exhibits and good programs that take you to the beach areas known as Nova Scotia's 'Jurassic Park.' For more serious rock lovers, the annual **Gem & Mineral Show** is in mid-August.

◉ Sights & Activities

Fundy Geological Museum   MUSEUM
(☎902-254-3814; www.museum.gov.ns.ca/fgm; 162 Two Islands Rd; adult/child $6/3.50; ⊙9:30am-5:30pm) This award-winning museum got a $1 million makeover in 2010 and uses interactive exhibits to help its visitors 'time travel' to a time when the fossils littering Parrsboro's beaches were alive. You can see a lab where dinosaur bones are being cleaned and assembled. Beach tours (times, length and frequency are dependent on the tides) are included in the admission price and focus on minerals or fossils.

Partridge Island   NATURE RESERVE
Steeped in history, Partridge Island is the most popular shoreline to search for gems, semiprecious stones and fossils. The island is 4km south of town on Whitehall Rd. From the end of the beach a 3km **hiking trail** with explanatory panels climbs to the top of the island (connected to the mainland by an isthmus) for superb views of Cape Blomidon and Cape Split.

RODD & HELEN TYSON: GEOLOGISTS & MINERAL DEALERS

Rodd Tyson is considered one of the most successful mineral dealers in Canada. He and his wife Helen moved to Parrsboro several years ago and opened a small shop that displays some of their finest pieces.

Why Parrsboro?

The tides and rains are moving things all the time so on any given day we could still potentially find something in one of several places suitable for our own private collection.

Where to Go

Partridge Island is the easiest place to go. Just remember to wear good footwear, be careful of the cliffs and be vigilant about checking the tides so you don't get stuck somewhere.

What to Look For

You're looking for color. Stilbite is amber-gold, chabazite is orange, agates have banded colors and patterns, and jasper is a deep brick red or forest green. You won't find much amethyst here no matter what anyone tells you, unless it's pretty pale. It's illegal to take fossils.

Ottawa House Museum   MUSEUM
(☑902-254-2376; 1155 Whitehall Rd; admission $2; ☺10am-6pm) Just before the beach is Ottawa House Museum, a 21-room mansion that was once the summer home of Sir Charles Tupper (1821–1915), who served as both premier of Nova Scotia and prime minister of Canada. The museum has exhibits on the former settlement on Partridge Island, shipbuilding and rum-running.

🛏 Sleeping & Eating

Riverview Cottages   INN $
(☑902-254-2388; www.riverviewcottages.ca; 3575 Eastern Ave, cottages $55-90; ☑) These country-cute, completely equipped cottages are a steal. You can canoe and fish on the bordering river and there's a big lawn perfect for a barbecue.

Evangeline's Tower B&B   B&B $$
(☑902-254-3383; 866-338-6937; www.evangelinestower.ca; 322 Main St; d $70-150; 🛜) This gay-friendly Victorian home has three rooms; one can be a two-room suite for families. Mountain bikes are available.

Bare Bones   RESTAURANT $$
(☑902-254-3507; 121 Main St; mains $10-22; ☺11am-9pm Mon-Sat, 1-9pm Sun) Bare Bones serves far and away the best food in town. Enjoy steamed mussels, sandwiches like a lobster bacon club or curry apple chicken, and larger mains like baby back ribs or pan-seared scallops.

☆ Entertainment

Ship's Company Theatre   THEATER
(☑902-254-3000, 800-565-7469; www.shipscompany.com; 18 Lower Main St; tickets $12-28; ☺Jul-mid-Sep) This innovative theater company performs new Canadian and Maritime works 'on board' the MV *Kipawo*, the last of the Minas Basin ferries, now integrated into a new theater. There's high-quality theater for kids, improv comedy, readings and concerts.

🛍 Shopping

Parrsboro Rock & Mineral Shop
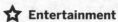
(☑902-254-2981; 39 Whitehall Rd; ☺9am-9pm Mon-Sat, to 5pm Sun May-Nov) Browse the collection of prehistoric reptile fossils, semiprecious stones from Parrsboro and around the world, and even a one-of-a-kind fossilized footprint of the world's smallest dinosaur found by the proprietor, Eldon George. If Eldon is there don't miss the chance to chat with him – he's one of Parrsboro's favorite characters.

Tysons' Fine Minerals   ROCKS & MINERALS
(☑902-254-2376; 249 Whitehall Rd; ☺10am-variable) This place is more like a museum than a shop with some of the most sparkling, massive and colorful minerals on display you're likely to see anywhere. Sometimes Helen takes visitors in to see the Tysons' private collection which is even more breathtaking.

🛈 Information

Cape d'Or

This spectacular cape of sheer cliffs was misnamed Cape d'Or (Cape of Gold) by Samuel de Champlain in 1604 – the glittering veins he saw in the cliffs were actually made of copper. Mining took place between 1897 and 1905 and removed the sparkle.

TOP CHOICE **Lightkeeper's Kitchen & Guest House** (☑902-670-0534; www.capedor.ca; s/d with ocean view $80/110; 🕾) This original lighthouse-keeper's residence is now a laid-back four-room guesthouse in what is perhaps one of the most perfect spots in Nova Scotia (even more so when the sun's out). Take the side road off Hwy 209 to Cape d'Or then hike down the dirt trail. A cosmopolitan **restaurant** (mains lunch $9-16, dinner $22-28; ☉noon-7pm; ☑) pumps out low-volume techno music and serves original seafood, meat and vegetarian creations.

Cape Chignecto Provincial Park & Advocate Harbour

The **Cape Chignecto Coastal Trail** is a rugged 60km loop with backcountry – nay, old-growth – campsites. Allow four days and three nights for the hike. The **Mill Brook Canyon Trail** (15km return) and the hike to **Refugee Cove** (20km return) are other challenging overnight hikes. There are some easier hikes and more are being developed – the newest is the **Eatonville Trail** (5.6km return) that begins at a new 'Phase 2' entrance to the park about 15km north of the main entrance. Some hikers have tried to avoid the ups and downs of the trails by taking shortcuts along the beach at low tide and been cut off by the Bay of Fundy tides. Get a tide table and follow advice from park staff to avoid being trapped on the cliffs.

Park visitors must register and leave an itinerary at the **Visitor Centre** (☑902-392-2085; www.capechignecto.net; 1108 West Advocate Rd; hiking permits day/annual $5/25, campsites $24; ☉8am-7pm Mon-Thu, to 8pm Fri & Sat). Camping in the backcountry requires reservations. In addition to 51 wilderness campsites at six points along the coastal trail and 27 walk-in sites near the visitor center, there is also a bunkhouse ($53.40, up to four people) and a wilderness cabin ($53.40, up to four people).

Advocate Harbour is the nearest town, about 2km southeast of the park entrance. It's a breathtaking place with a 5km-long beach piled high with driftwood that changes dramatically with the tides. Behind the beach, salt marshes reclaimed with dikes by the Acadians are now replete with birds.

Kayak through Cape Chignecto Provincial Park with **Nova Shores Adventures** (☑866-638-4118; www.novashores.com; Hwy 33, Advocate Harbour; 1-day tours $85, 2-day tours incl overnight and food $350; 🕾). You'll often see seals and bears. The outfit also offers a beautiful, sea-view room ($110 per night) in its Victorian home headquarters.

TOP CHOICE **Wild Caraway Restaurant & Cafe** (☑902-392-2889; www.wildcaraway.com; 3721 Hwy 209; meals around $20, r $80; 🕾) Wild Caraway Restaurant is an excellent place to stop or stay in Advocate Harbour. The invitingly cozy, well-tended Victorian overlooks the often foggy harbor.

Joggins

Joggins, between Amherts and Advocate Harbour on Chignecto Bay, is famous for its Unesco World Heritage fossil cliffs, said to be the best place on Earth to see what life was like over 300 million years ago in the late Carboniferous (Coal Age). The wealth of fossils in the 15km of seaside cliffs are preserved in their original setting and include rare land species. The big new **Joggins Fossil Centre** (www.jogginsfossilcliffs.net; 100 Main St; adult/child $8/6; ☉9:30am-5:30pm) is the place to start your visit and explains through displays and film what you can see in the cliffs below. The

---

AGE OF SAIL HERITAGE CENTRE

Stop for tea, baked goods and a tour at the **Age of Sail Heritage Centre** (☑902-348-2030; Rte 209; adult $3; ☉10am-6pm Jun-Sep) in Port Greville, about 20km to the west of Parrsboro on Rte 209. It captures the area's shipbuilding heritage. The site also includes a restored 1857 Methodist church and a working blacksmith shop.

best time to visit the cliffs is at low tide when all of the beaches can be accessed – otherwise you'll be cut off from some of the more interesting sites by high water. Recommended guided tours are available at the Fossil Centre, starting from $5 and leaving on an irregular schedule depending on the tides; you can reserve in advance on the website.

Amherst

Amherst is the geographic center of the Maritimes and a travel junction for travelers to Nova Scotia, PEI and New Brunswick. There's little reason to dawdle here as you're just a short drive from either the Bay of Fundy shore or the Northumberland Strait (between Nova Scotia and PEI), but the historic downtown does have some stately buildings and there's bird-watching at the 490-hectare **Amherst Point Migratory Bird Sanctuary** nearby (off Exit 3 from the Trans-Canada Hwy). The massive **VIC** (☎902-667-8429; ☺8:30am-8pm) is at exit 1 off Hwy 104, just as you cross the border from New Brunswick.

Acadian Lines (☎902-454-9321, 800-567-5151; www.acadianbus.com) has bus services to Halifax that leave from the **Irving Mainway gas station** (☎902-667-8435; 213 S Albion St). The Trans-Canada Hwy east of Amherst charges a toll of $4. It's an incentive to use scenic Hwy 2 through Parrsboro instead of dull – but fast – Hwy 104. The Sunrise Trail (Hwy 6) through Pugwash and Tatamagouche to Pictou also avoids the toll.

SUNRISE TRAIL

It's claimed that the Northumberland Strait between Nova Scotia's north shore and PEI has some of the warmest waters north of the US Carolinas, with water temperatures averaging slightly over 20°C during summer. It's a prime area for beach-hopping, cycling and exploring friendly countryside towns.

Wallace

Wallace is perfect territory for birding and beachcombing. The tourist information center is at the **Wallace Museum** (☎902-257-2191; Hwy 6; ☺9am-5pm Mon-Sat, 1-4pm Sun) where collections of baskets woven by the Mi'kmaq, period dresses and shipbuilding memorabilia are displayed.

Wallace Bay Wildlife Bird Sanctuary (1km north of Hwy 6 on Aboiteau Rd) protects 585 hectares, including tidal and freshwater wetlands. In the spring, keep your eyes peeled for bald eagles nesting near the parking lot, which is on the left just before the causeway.

Wentworth

The Wentworth Valley is a detour off the shore, 25km south of Wallace via Hwy 307, and is particularly pretty in fall when the deciduous trees change color. The 24-bed, cabin-like **Wentworth Hostel** (☎902-548-2379; www.hihostels.ca; 249 Wentworth Station Rd; HI member/nonmember dm $20/25, r $40/45) is 1.3km west of Hwy 4 on Valley Rd, then straight up steep, dirt Wentworth Station Rd. The rambling farmhouse, built in 1866, has been used as a hostel for half a century. It's central enough to be a base for both the Sunrise Trail and much of the Minas Bay shore. Trails for hiking and mountain biking start just outside the door. It gets particularly booked-up in winter for the cross-country and downhill skiing nearby.

Tatamagouche

The Malagash Peninsula, which juts out into protected Tatamagouche Bay, is a low-key, bucolic loop for a drive or bike ride. Stop at the local winery for tastings, explore beaches galore or take a peek in some interesting museums found just inland. Tatamagouche is the largest on the Northumberland Shore coast west of Pictou and makes a great base for exploring. The **Fraser Cultural Centre** (☎902-657-3285; 362 Main St; ☺10am-5pm Mon-Fri, 10am-4pm Sat, 11am-3pm Sun mid-Jun–Sep) has tourist information, internet access and local history displays.

☉ Sights & Activities

Jost Winery   WINERY
(☎902-257-2636; www.jostwine.com; off Hwy 6, Malagash; ☺tours noon & 3pm mid-Jun–mid-Sep) Take a free tour of the scenically located Jost Winery. While regular wine is free to taste, the ice wine costs $5 – if you want to try all three ice wine varieties, ask to have three small glasses for the price of one large one. Winery signs direct you about 5km off Hwy 6.

Mills

In a gorgeous setting on the stream that once provided it with power, the **Balmoral Grist Mill** (☎902-657-3016; 660 Matheson Brook Rd; adult/child $3/2; ☺9:30am-5:30pm Mon-Sat, 1-5:30pm Sun) still grinds wheat in summer. From Tatamagouche, turn south on Hwy 311 (at the east edge of town) and then east on Hwy 256.

From the Balmoral Grist Mill, drive further east on Hwy 256, and then north on Hwy 326, to get to the **Sutherland Steam Mill** (☎902-657-3365; off Hwy 326, Denmark; adult/child $3/2; ☺9:30am-5:30pm Mon-Sat, 1-5:30pm Sun). Built in 1894, it produced lumber, carriages, wagons and windows until 1958.

Beaches

Blue Sea Beach on the Malagash Peninsula has warm water and fine sand, and a marsh area just inland that's ideal for bird-watching. There are picnic tables and shelters to change in. Small cottages crowd around **Rushton's Beach**, just east of Tatamagouche in Brule, but it's worth a visit to look for seals (turn left at the end of the boardwalk and walk toward the end of the beach) and birdlife in the adjoining salt marsh.

Tatamagouche Centre   RETREAT CENTER
(☎800-218-2220; www.tatacentre.ca; Loop 6) This gay-friendly center, which is affiliated with the Uniting Church, offers retreats and short courses on everything from organic gardening to yoga (two-day course including lodging $250), plus guided excursions to First Nations powwows.

🎊 Festivals & Events

Oktoberfest   FOOD & DRINK
(☎902-657-2380; tickets $10-20; ☺Sep) The wildly popular Oktoberfest is held the last weekend in September – yes, September.

🛏 Sleeping & Eating

Train Station Inn   INN $$
(☎902-657-3222, 888-724-5233; www.trainstation.ca; 21 Station Rd; carriages $89-179) It's a museum, it's a kooky gift shop, it's a restaurant, it's a hotel and...it's a stationary train. Each unique carriage suite is an eight-year-old boy's dream decorated with period train posters, toy trains and locomotive books. The dreamer behind the inn, James LeFresne, grew up across the tracks and saved the train station from demolition when he was just 18. Dine on delicious seafood, meat and salads in the c 1928 dining car or have a blueberry pancake breakfast ($6) in the station house. Free self-guided tours are available from the gift shop.

Sugar Moon Farm   FARM $
(☎902-657-3348, 866-816-2753; www.sugarmoon.ca; Alex Macdonald Rd, off Hwy 311, Earltown; mains $8-13; ☺9am-5pm Thu-Mon Jul & Aug, 9am-5pm Sat & Sun Sep-Jun) The food – simple, delicious pancakes and locally made sausages served with maple syrup – is the highlight of this working maple farm and woodlot. Check online for dates of the monthly 'Chef's Night': one Saturday night where a prix fixe meal ($69) is served.

🛍 Shopping

Lismore Sheep Farm   SOUVENIRS
(☎902-351-2889; 1389 Louisville Rd, off Hwy 6; ☺9am-5pm) A working farm with more than 300 sheep, this is a fun destination even if you don't buy a rug, blanket or socks. From May to October, the barn is open (adult/child $2/1) for visitors to pat the lambs and learn all about producing wool.

Pictou

Many people stop in Pictou (*pik*-toe) for a side trip or as a stopover via ferry to/from PEI, but it's also an enjoyable base for exploring Northumberland Strait. Water St, the main street, is lined with interesting shops and beautiful old stone buildings but unfortunately the sea views are blighted by a giant smoking mill in the distance. The town is known as the 'Birthplace of New Scotland' because the first Scottish immigrants to Nova Scotia landed here in 1773.

◉ Sights & Activities

You can picnic and swim at Caribou/Munroe's Island Provincial Park (see p361).

Hector   SHIP
A replica of the ship *Hector* that carried the first 200 Highland Scots to Nova Scotia is tied up for viewing during the summer. **Hector Heritage Quay** (☎902-485-4371; 33 Caladh Ave; adult/student $5/2; ☺9am-5pm Mon-Sat, noon-5pm Sun mid-May–early Oct) captures the experience of the first Scottish settlers through a re-created blacksmith shop, a collection of shipbuilding artifacts and displays about the *Hector* and its passengers. There are guided tours at 10am and 2pm.

Northumberland Fisheries Museum

MUSEUM

(☎902-485-4972; 71 Front St; adult/student $4/2; ⊙10am-6pm Mon-Sat) In the old train station, this museum explores the area's fishing heritage. Exhibits include strange sea creatures and the spiffy *Silver Bullet,* an early 1930s lobster boat.

✪ Festivals & Events

Pictou Landing First Nation Powwow

CULTURAL

(☎902-752-4912; ⊙1st weekend of Jun) Across the Pictou Harbour (a 25-minute drive through New Glasgow), this annual powwow features sunrise ceremonies, drumming and craft demonstrations. Camping and food are available on-site, which is strictly alcohol- and drug-free.

Lobster Carnival

FOOD & DRINK

(☎902-485-5150; www.townofpictou.com; ⊙2nd week of Jul) Begun in 1934 as the Carnival of the Fisherfolk, this four-day event now offers free entertainment, boat races and lots of chances to feast on lobster.

Hector Festival

MUSIC

(☎902-485-8848; www.decostecentre.ca; ⊙mid-Aug) Free daily outdoor concerts, Highland dancing and piping competitions and a *Hector* landing reenactment.

🛏 Sleeping & Eating

Pictou Lodge

HOTEL $$

(☎902-485-4322,888-662-7484;www.maritimeinns.com; 172 Lodge Rd, off Braeshore Rd; r/cottages from $139/159; ☒) This atmospheric 1920s resort is on more than 60 hectares of wooded land between Caribou/Munroe's Island Provincial Park and Pictou. Beautifully renovated ocean-side log cabins have original stone fireplaces. Motel rooms are also available. There's a life-sized checkerboard, paddle boats, a private beach and the best restaurant in town.

Customs House Inn

INN $$

(☎902-485-4546; www.customshouseinn.ca; 38 Depot St; r incl breakfast $80-170; @🖤) The tall stone walls here are at once imposingly chic and reassuringly solid. The chunky antique decor is as sturdy and elegant as the walls and many rooms have waterfront views. Identical twin brothers run this inn so don't be alarmed if the innkeeper seems to be everywhere at once!

Willow House Inn

B&B $$

(☎902-485-5740; www.willowhouseinn.com; 11 Willow St; r with shared/private bathroom $60/120; 🖤) This historic c 1840 home is a labyrinth of staircases and cozy, antique rooms. The owners whip up great breakfasts as well as conversation and tips for what to do around town.

Caribou/Munroe's Island Provincial Park

CAMPGROUND $

(☎902-485-6134; www.parks.gov.ns.ca; 2119 Three Brooks Rd; campsites $24) Less than 5km from Pictou, this park is set on a gorgeous beach. Sites 1 to 22 abut the day-use area and are less private; Sites 78 to 95 are gravel and suited for RVs. The rest are wooded and private.

Carver's Coffeehouse & Studio

CAFE $

(☎902-382-3332; 41 Coleraine St; light meals around $8; ⊙8am-9pm) This bright and inviting cafe is also the carving studio for Keith Matheson, who did the detail work on the *Hector.* Anne, his partner, runs the cafe, which specializes in decadent desserts, traditional Scottish oatcakes, and strong coffee with free refills.

Pressroom Pub & Grill

RESTAURANT $$

(☎902-485-4041; 50 Water St; mains $8-15; ⊙11am-midnight) Often so busy that it resembles a pressroom, the Pressroom serves up standard salads, sandwiches, wraps or chowder to enjoy on the big outdoor patio.

☆ Entertainment

deCoste Centre

MUSIC & THEATER

(☎902-485-8848; www.decostecentre.ca; 91 Water St; tickets about $18; ⊙box office 11:30am-5pm Mon-Fri, 1-5pm Sat & Sun) Opposite the waterfront, this impressive performing arts center stages a range of live shows. Experience some top-notch Scottish music during a summer series of ceilidhs (*kay*-lees) at 2pm from Tuesday to Thursday (adult/child $15/7).

ℹ Information

Pictou Public Library (☎902-485-5021; 40 Water St; ⊙noon-9pm Tue & Thu, noon-5pm Wed, 10am-5pm Fri & Sat) Free internet access.

Town of Pictou (www.townofpictou.com) Links to sights and festivals.

VIC (☎902-485-6213; Pictou Rotary; ⊙8am-9:30pm Jul & Aug, 9am-7pm May, Jun & Sep–mid-Dec) A large information center situated northwest of town to meet travelers arriving from the PEI ferry.

❶ Getting There & Away

Ferries to/from PEI leave and arrive from Pictou. For more information, see p317.

New Glasgow

The largest town on the Northumberland Shore, New Glasgow has always been an industrial center; the first mine opened in neighboring Stellarton in 1807. Still, it's a pleasant town with plenty of aging architecture, a river running through the center and some good places to eat. The few major local attractions are in Stellarton, a 5km drive south.

◉ Sights & Activities

Crombie Art Gallery   ART GALLERY

FREE (☎902-755-4440; 1780 Abercrombie Rd; ⊙tours on the hour 9-11am & 1-4pm Wed Jul & Aug) This private gallery in the personal residence of the founder of the Sobey supermarket chain has an excellent collection of 19th- and early-20th-century Canadian art, including works by Cornelius Krieghoff and the Group of Seven.

Museum of Industry   MUSEUM

(☎902-755-5425; www.industry.museum.gov.ns .ca; Hwy 104 at Exit 24; adult/child $7/3; ⊙9am-5pm Mon-Sat, 10am-5pm Sun) This is a wonderful place for kids. There's a hands-on water power exhibit and an assembly line to try to keep up with.

✖ Eating

The Bistro   RESTAURANT $$

(☎902-752-4988; 216 Archimedes St; mains $18-27; ⊙dinner Tue-Sat) The only constant on the menu is creativity in spicing and sauces. The menu changes daily according to what's available and in summer everything is organic. Try the Thai grilled salmon or pork tenderloin with black mission-fig butter. Enjoy the local art on display that's also for sale.

Café Italia   RESTAURANT $

(☎902-928-2233; 62 Provost St; pizza & salad $8; ⊙7:30am-10pm Mon-Thu, 7:30am-midnight Fri, 11:30am-10pm Sat) Between noon and 1pm you might have to wrestle a local for a booth at this small trattoria. Choose from salads, homemade pasta and thin-crust pizza. It is open during the morning for coffee and snacks, but not for breakfast.

Antigonish

Beautiful beaches and hiking possibilities north of town could easily keep you busy for a couple of days, but Antigonish (an-tee-guh-*nish*) town is lively enough and has some great places to eat. Catholic Scots settled and established St Francis Xavier University and today the university still dominates the ambience of the town. Antigonish is known for the Highland Games held each July since 1861.

◉ Sights & Activities

St Francis Xavier University   NOTABLE BUILDING

The attractive campus of 125-year-old St Francis Xavier University is behind the Romanesque **St Ninian's Cathedral** (120 St Ninian St; ⊙7:30am-8pm). The **Hall of the Clans** is on the 3rd floor of the old wing of the Angus L MacDonald Library, just beyond the St Ninian's Cathedral parking lot. In the hall, crests of all the Scottish clans that settled this area are displayed. Those clans gather each July for the Antigonish Highland Games.

Antigonish Landing   NATURE RESERVE

A 4km hiking/cycling trail to the nature reserve at Antigonish Landing begins just across the train tracks from the museum, then 400m down Adam St. The landing's estuary is a good bird-watching area where you might see eagles, ducks and ospreys.

✯ Festivals & Events

Antigonish Highland Games   CULTURAL

(www.antigonishhighlandgames.ca; ⊙mid-Jul) An extravaganza of dancing, pipe-playing and heavy-lifting events involving hewn logs and iron balls.

Evolve   MUSIC

(www.evolvefestival.com; ⊙late Jul) Five stages of funk, bluegrass, hip-hop and more, plus workshops on everything from puppetry to media literacy.

🛏 Sleeping & Eating

Antigonish Highland Heart B&B   B&B $$

(☎902-863-1858, 800-863-1858; www.bbcanada .com/3241.html; 135 Main St; r $85-95; 🐾) Smiling Shebby, the friendly owner of this c 1854 house, brightens her centrally located home with special touches such as rag dolls on the beds.

TOP CHOICE **Gabrieau's Bistro** RESTAURANT **$$**
(☎902-863-1925; 350 Main St; mains lunch $8-13, dinner $16-30; ☺7:30am-9:30pm Mon-Sat; ☑) Grab a coffee and pastry in the morning or any of a number of imaginative vegetarian dishes, salads, meats and seafood for lunch or dinner. Locals credit chef Mark Gabrieau for setting the culinary high-watermark in Antigonish. The cedar roasted salmon with nasturtium butter and a white wine velouté infused with lemongrass and roseberries is divine.

Sunshine on Main Café CAFE **$**
(☎902-863-5851; 332 Main St; mains $8-13; ☺7am-9pm Sun-Thu, 7am-9:30pm Fri & Sat) A great place to stop if you're tiring of fried food, this bright cafe serves healthy breakfasts, lunches and dinners using plenty of organic ingredients.

ℹ Information

Antigonish Public Library (☎902-863-4276; 274 Main St; ☺10am-9pm Tue & Thu, 10am-5pm Wed, Fri & Sat) Free internet access. Enter off College St.

VIC (☎902-863-4921; 56 West St; ☺10am-6pm mid-Jun–early Oct, to 8pm Jul & Aug) Brochures, local calls and free internet access. It's in the Antigonish Mall parking lot at the junction of Hwys 104 and 7.

ℹ Getting There & Away

Acadian Lines (☎902-454-9321, 800-567-5151; www.acadianbus.com) bus services stop at Bloomfield Centre at St Francis Xavier University.

Around Antigonish

POMQUET
About 16km east of Antigonish, this tiny Acadian community is on a stunning beach with 13 dunes that keep growing; waves dump the equivalent of more than 4000 truckloads of sand on the beach each year. Many bird species frequent the salt marshes behind the dunes. Comfortable **Sunflower B&B** (☎902-386-2492; www.bbcanada.com/5382.html; 1572 Monk's Head Rd; r $85-115; ☜) is right on the water.

Cape George

It's a pleasant day cruising this 72km route that loops up Hwy 245 from Antigonish to Malignant Cove and around Cape George. It's been dubbed a 'mini-Cabot Trail' (see p363) but really the two routes are quite different; Cape George is much less mountainous and forested but has more beaches.

From a well-marked picnic area close to **Cape George Point Lighthouse**, a 1km walk leads to the lighthouse itself. It's automated and not that big, but there are lovely views to Cape Breton Island and PEI. Signs at the picnic area point to longer hikes through forests and coastal areas, including one 32km loop.

You can also start exploring these trails from the wharf at **Ballantyne's Cove**, one of the prettiest communities in Nova Scotia. To walk from the wharf to the lighthouse and back again is an 8km trip. Also stop in at the **Ballantyne's Cove Tuna Interpretive Centre** (☎902-863-8162; 57 Ballantyne's Cove Wharf Rd; admission free; ☺10am-7:30pm Jul-Sep) for displays on both the fish and the fishery. A fish-and-chips van parks nearby.

CAPE BRETON ISLAND

Floating over the rest of Nova Scotia like an island halo, Cape Breton is a heavenly, forested realm of bald eagles, migrating whales, palpable history and foot-tapping music. Starting up the Ceilidh Trail along the western coastline, Celtic music vibrates through the pubs and community centers, eventually reaching the Cabot Trail where more eclectic Acadian-style tunes ring out around Chéticamp.

The 300km Cabot Trail continues around Cape Breton Highlands National Park. It winds and climbs around and over coastal mountains, with heart-stopping ocean views at every turn, narrow bridges roads (watch out!) and plenty of trails to stop and hike.

Take a side trip to Glace Bay to learn firsthand about the region's coal-mining history, Fortress Louisbourg in the east to get a taste of 18th-century military life or at the Highland Village Museum in Iona to get some visuals of what life was like for early Scottish immigrants. The region around Bras d'Or Lake offers opportunities to explore the past and present of the Mi'kmaq First Nation and in Baddeck you can learn everything you ever wanted to know about Alexander Graham Bell.

Most tourists visit in July and August, and many restaurants, accommodations and VICs are only open from mid-June to September. **Celtic Colours** (www.celtic-colours.com; ☺Oct), a wonderful roving music festival that attracts top musicians from Scotland, Spain and other countries with Celtic connections, helps extend the season into the fall – a superb time to visit.

Port Hastings

Cape Breton Island ceased to be a true island when the Canso Causeway was built across the Strait of Canso in 1955. A big and busy VIC (☑902-625-4201; 96 Hwy 4; ☻9am-8pm) is on your right as you drive onto Cape Breton Island. This is definitely worth a stop: there are few other information centers on Cape Breton, especially outside of July and August; the staff is very well informed; and one wall is covered with posters advertising square dances and ceilidhs.

Ceilidh Trail

Take a hard left immediately after leaving the Port Hastings VIC to get on the Ceilidh Trail (Hwy 19), which snakes along the western coast of the island. Then put on your dancing shoes: this area was settled by Scots with fiddles in hand and is renowned for its ceilidh music performances, square dances and parties.

For a great introduction to local culture, visit the Celtic Music Interpretive Centre (☑902-787-2708; www.celticmusicsite.com; 5473 Hwy 19; admission $12; ☻9am-5pm Mon-Fri Jun-Aug). Half-hour tours (which can be self-guided if you arrive when no guides are available) include a fiddle lesson and a dance step or two. Square dances are advertised around the admissions desk – try a Saturday dance at the community hall in West Mabou or a Thursday evening dance in Glencoe Mills. Ceilidhs at the music center itself are held at 11:30am Monday to Friday during summer.

Creignish B&B (☑902-625-5709; www.bbcanada.com/159.html; 2154 Hwy 19; s/d/f $30/60/75) is a 'recycled school house' that's been turned into a guesthouse/artist's haven. Wildflowers, shells and bones are everywhere and there's even a 1000lb stuffed tuna hanging on the ceiling. 'Improvised' arts and crafts classes are offered and owner Sandra can point you to the best-hidden secrets of Cape Breton Island. Rooms are large and comfortable, and the B&B is only a 10-minute drive from the causeway.

MABOU

Although it looks unlikely at first glance, micro Mabou is the not-so-underground hot spot of Cape Breton's Celtic music scene. Among lush hills and quiet inlets you can hike away your days and dance away your nights – and don't forget to scorch your tonsils with single malt whiskey at the distillery down the road.

◉ Sights & Activities

Mabou is more a place to experience than to see specific sights. Take any turn off Hwy 19 and see where it takes you.

Glenora Inn & Distillery   INN & DISTILLERY
(☑902-258-2662, 800-839-0491; www.glenora distillery.com; Hwy 19; guided tours incl tasting $7; ☻tours on the hour 9am-5pm mid-Jun–mid-Oct) Glenora Inn & Distillery is the only distillery making single malt whiskey in Canada. After a tour and a taste of the rocket fuel, stop for a meal at the gourmet pub (there are daily lunchtime and dinner ceilidhs) or even for the night; cave-like rooms ($125 to $150 per night) are perfect for sleeping it off if you've been drinking the local beverage but the chalets ($175 to $240) are a better choice if you want brighter surroundings. It's 9km north of Mabou. Tours are held on the hour.

Cape Mabou Highlands   NATURE RESERVE
Within the Cape Mabou Highlands an extensive network of hiking trails extends between Mabou and Inverness toward the coast west of Hwy 19. The trails are sometimes closed when the fire danger is high but otherwise hikes ranging from 4km to 12km start from three different trailheads. An excellent trail guide ($5) is available at the grocery store across the road from the Mull Café & Deli when the trails are open. Maps are also posted at the trailheads.

⊨ Sleeping & Eating

Clayton Farm B&B   B&B $$
(☑902-945-2719; 11247 Hwy 19; s/d $75/90; ▣) This 1835 farmhouse sits on a working red angus ranch and is run by hard-working Isaac Smith. Paraphernalia of old Cape Breton life and of Isaac's family are casually scattered throughout the common areas and comfortable guest rooms. It's rustically perfect.

Duncreigan Country Inn   INN $$
(☑902-945-2207, 800-840-2207; www.dunc reigan.ca; Hwy 19; r incl breakfast $120-195; ☏) Nestled in oak trees on the banks of the river, this inn has private, spacious rooms,

some that have terraces and water views. Bikes are available to guests and there's a licensed dining room (mains $10 to $23) that serves breakfast to guests or dinner by reservation.

TOP CHOICE **Red Shoe Pub** PUB $$
(☎902-945-2996; www.redshoepub. com; 11533 Hwy 19; mains $9-22; ☺11:30am-midnight Wed, 11:30am-2am Thu-Sat, noon-midnight Sun) Straddling the spine of the Ceilidh Trail, this pub is the beating heart of Mabou. Gather round a local fiddle player (often from the Rankin family) while enjoying a pint and a superb meal – the desserts, including the gingerbread with rum-butterscotch sauce and fruit compote, are divine. Don't be afraid to stay on after dinner to get to know some locals and maybe a few travelers too. Check the website for performances.

INVERNESS

Row upon row of company housing betrays the history of coal mining in Inverness, the first town of any size on the coast. Its history and people are captured evocatively by writer Alistair MacLeod. His books are for sale at the **Bear Paw** (☎902-258-2528; Hwy 19), next to the Royal Bank.

Beginning near the fishing harbor there are kilometers of sandy **beach** with comfortable water temperatures in late summer. A **boardwalk** runs 1km along the beach. In the old train station just back from the beach, the **Inverness Miners' Museum** (☎902-258-3822; 62 Lower Railway St; admission by donation; ☺9am-5pm Mon-Fri, noon-5pm Sat & Sun) presents local history. **Inverness County Centre for the Arts** (☎902-258-2533; www.invernessarts.ca; 16080 Hwy 19; ☺10am-5pm) is a beautiful establishment with several galleries and an upmarket gift shop featuring work by local and regional artists. It's also a music venue with a floor built for dancing – of course!

Macleods Inn B&B (☎902-253-3360; www.macleods.com; Broad Cove Rd, off Hwy 19; r $70-125; ☜) is a high-end B&B for a not-so-high-end price about 5km north of Inverness. The house is big and modern but the decoration is in keeping with Cape Breton heritage.

Cabot Trail & Cape Breton Highlands National Park

One of Canada's most dramatic parks and its lively surrounds are accessible via the famous Cabot Trail. The drive is at its best along the northwestern shore of Cape Breton and then down to Pleasant Bay. Be sure to take advantage of the many pull-offs for scenic views and otherwise keep your eyes on this very circuitous road. Of course it's even better if you can explore on foot, hiking through a tapestry of terrain to reach vistas looking out over an endless, icy ocean.

CHÉTICAMP

While Mabou is the center of Celtic music, lively Chéticamp throws in some folky notes and French phrases to get your feet moving to Acadian tunes. The town owes much of its cultural preservation to its geographical isolation; the road didn't make it this far until 1949. Today it's a gateway to Cape Breton Highlands National Park, and has some top-notch museums and live-music opportunities – there's always something going on. The 1893 Church of St Pierre dominates the town with its silver spire and colorful frescoes, but the rest of this seaside town is modern and drab.

Chéticamp is also known for its crafts, particularly hooked rugs, and as a pioneer of the cooperative movement. Check out the rug displays at Les Trois Pignons and take notice of all those co-ops around town: the Credit Union, Co-op grocery store, Co-op Artisanale Restaurant.

JOE'S SCARECROW THEATRE

About 25km south of Chéticamp, stop at this quasi-macabre outdoor **collection** (☎902-235-2108; 11842 Cabot Trail; admission by donation; ☺8:30am-9pm mid-Jun–early Oct) of life-sized, stuffed figures, from a dead-looking Richard Nixon in a housedress to a cartoon duck head with the body of Michael Jackson. Often the figures are arranged holding hands in a circle as if they're awaiting the mother ship. The area started when Joe Delany made some scarecrows out of Mi-Carême costumes (see p366) and folks touring the Cabot Trail began stopping to take pictures.

Visitor information and internet access are available at Les Trois Pignons.

◉ Sights & Activities

Whale Cruisers
WHALE-WATCHING

(☎902-224-3376, 800-813-3376; www.whalecruisers.com; Government Wharf; adult/child $32/15) Several operators sell tours from the Government Wharf, across and down from the church. Captain Cal is the most experienced and offers three-hour expeditions up to four times daily. It's wise to reserve your trip a day in advance in midsummer.

Les Trois Pignons
MUSEUM

(☎902-224-2642; www.lestroispignons.com; 15584 Cabot Trail; admission $5; ⊙9am-5pm) This excellent museum explains how rug hooking went from being a home-based activity to an international business. Artifacts, including hooked rugs, illustrate early life and artisanship in Chéticamp. Almost everything here – from bottles to rugs – was collected by one eccentric local resident.

Centre de la Mi-Carême
MUSEUM

(☎902-224-1016; www.micareme.ca; 12615 Cabot Trail; admission $5; ⊙9am-5pm) Mi-Carême, celebrated in the middle of Lent, is Chéticamp's answer to Mardi Gras. Locals wear masks and disguises and visit houses; trying to get people to guess who they are. This museum covers the history of the celebration and displays traditional masks.

🛏 Sleeping & Eating

Accommodations are tight throughout July and August. It's advisable to call ahead or arrive early in the afternoon.

Chéticamp Outfitters Inn B&B
B&B $$

(☎902-224-2776; www.cheticampns.com/cheticampoutfitters; 13938 Cabot Trail; r $65-100, chalet with kitchen $110; 🛜) Just 2km south of town, this place offers a range of well-priced choices in Acadian style. Views stretch from the sea to the mountain, wildflowers burst from every corner of the garden, and you might even see a passing moose. Very full breakfasts are served in the panoramic dining area by energetic hosts.

Laurence Guest House B&B
B&B $$

(☎902-224-2184; 15408 Cabot Trail; r $70-100) This gay-friendly, heritage B&B faces the waterfront and is within walking distance of most attractions. Four rooms furnished with antiques all have private bathrooms.

Co-op Artisanale Restaurant
RESTAURANT $$

(☎902-224-2170; 15067 Main St; mains $8-16; ⊙9am-9pm) This restaurant specializes in Acadian dishes such as a stewed chicken dinner ($13) and *pâté à la viande* (meat pie) for $8. Delicious potato pancakes ($8) with apple sauce, molasses or sour cream are the only vegetarian option.

All Aboard
RESTAURANT $$

(☎902-224-2288; mains $8-15; ⊙11am-midnight) The local's favorite for seafood and more has very reasonable prices. It has a fresh, nautical ambience and some creative extras on the menu such as a maple vinaigrette for the salads. You'll find it at the south entrance to Chéticamp.

☆ Entertainment

Doryman's Beverage Room
BAR

(☎902-224-9909; 15528 Cabot Trail) This drinking establishment hosts 'sessions' (cover $8) with a fiddler and piano players from Mabou each Saturday (2pm to 6pm); an acoustic Acadian group plays at 8pm Sunday, Tuesday, Wednesday and Friday.

CAPE BRETON HIGHLANDS NATIONAL PARK

One-third of the Cabot Trail runs through this extensive park of woodland, tundra, bog and startling sea views. Established in 1936 and encompassing 20% of Cape Breton's landmass, it is the jewel in Nova Scotia's island cap.

There are two park entrances: one at Chéticamp and one at Ingonish. Purchase an **entry permit** (adult/child/up to 7 people in a vehicle $7.80/3.90/19.60) at either park entrance. A one-day pass is good until noon the next day. Wheelchair-accessible trails are indicated on the free park map available at either entrance.

The **Chéticamp Information Centre** (☎902-224-2306; www.parkscanada.gc.ca; 16646 Cabot Trail; ⊙8am-8pm Jul & Aug, 9am-5pm mid-May–Jun, Sep & Oct) has displays and a relief map of the park, plus a bookstore. Ask the staff for advice on hiking or camping. It's usually staffed from 8am to 4pm, Monday to Friday November to April.

The **Ingonish Information Centre** (☎902-285-2535; 37677 Cabot Trail; ⊙8am-8pm Jul & Aug, 9am-5pm mid-May–Jun, Sep & Oct) on the eastern edge of the park is much smaller than the one at Chéticamp and has no bookstore.

Activities

HIKING

Two trails on the west coast of the park have spectacular ocean views. **Fishing Cove Trail** gently descends 330m over 8km to the mouth of rugged Fishing Cove River. You can opt for a steeper and shorter hike – 2.8km – from a second trailhead about 5km north of the first. Double the distances if you plan to return the same day. Otherwise, you must preregister for one of eight backcountry sites ($9.80) at the Chéticamp Information Centre. Reviews of trails in and near the park are available at www. cabottrail.com.

Most other trails are shorter and close to the road, many leading to ridge tops for impressive views of the coast. The best of these is **Skyline Trail**, a 7km loop that puts you on the edge of a headland cliff right above the water. The trailhead is about 5.5km north of Corney Brook Campground.

Just south of Neil's Harbour, on the eastern coast of the park, the **Coastal Trail** runs 11km round-trip and covers more gentle coastline.

CYCLING

Don't make this your inaugural trip. The riding is tough, there are no shoulders in many sections and you must be comfortable sharing the incredible scenery with RVs. Alternatively, you can mountain bike on four inland trails in the park. Only **Branch Pond Lookoff Trail** offers ocean views.

Sea Spray Outdoor Adventures (☎902-383-2732; www.cabot-trail-outdoors.com; 1141 White Point Rd; rentals per day/week $40/145; ⏰9am-5pm Jun–mid-Oct) in Smelt Brook near Dingwall rents bikes and will do emergency repairs on the road. It also offers help planning trips and leads organized cycling, kayaking and hiking tours.

Sleeping

Towns around the park offer a variety of accommodations. **Cape Breton Highlands National Park** (tent/RV sites from $17.60/29.40) has six drive-in campgrounds with discounts after three days. Most sites are first-come, first-served, but wheelchair-accessible sites, group campsites and backcountry sites can be reserved for $9.80. In the smaller campgrounds further from the park entrances, just pick a site and self-register. To camp at any of the three larger ones near the park entrances, register at the closest information center.

The 162-site **Chéticamp Campground** is behind the information center. There are no 'radio free' areas, so peace and quiet is not guaranteed.

Corney Brook (20 sites), 10km further north, is a particularly stunning campground high over the ocean. There's a small playground here, but it would be a nerve-racking place to camp with small kids. **MacIntosh Brook** (10 sites) is an open field 3km east of Pleasant Bay. It has wheelchair-accessible sites. **Big Intervale** (10 sites) is near a river 11km west of Cape North.

Near the eastern park entrance, you have a choice of the 256-site **Broad Cove Campground** at Ingonish and the 90-site **Ingonish Campground**, near Keltic Lodge at Ingonish Beach. Both have wheelchair-accessible sites. These large campgrounds near the beach are popular with local families in midsummer.

WILY COYOTES

Coyote attacks are rare worldwide but in fall 2009 a woman was killed by these wild dogs on the Skyline Trail; in August 2010 a teenage girl was attacked and injured in her sleeping bag. Fifteen trappers are now on-call to deal with complaints about aggressive animals and any found near communities will be killed. There's also a $20 bounty on coyote pelts during trapping season and it's estimated that the population will be halved by 2011 – not good news for the coyotes.

Awareness is the best safety method:

» Don't hike alone

» Sleep in a tent

» Carry a solid walking stick

» Dispose of food properly so animals can't access it

» If you see a coyote, back away slowly, act big and make noise

» Report incidents to Parks Canada at ☎877-852-3100

From late October to early May, you can camp at the Chéticamp and Ingonish Campgrounds for $22, including firewood. In truly inclement weather, tenters can take refuge in cooking shelters with woodstoves.

PLEASANT BAY

A perfect base for exploring the park, Pleasant Bay is a carved-out bit of civilization hemmed on all sides by wilderness. It's an active fishing harbor known for its whale-watching tours and Tibetan monastery. If you are in the area on Canada Day (July 1), try to be in the stands for the annual monks vs townspeople baseball game. There are lots of fish-and-chip and burger places around town but no really special places to eat.

◉ Sights & Activities

Gampo Abbey   BUDDHIST MONASTERY
(☏902-224-2752; www.gampoabbey.org; ◉tours 1:30-3:30pm Mon-Fri mid-Jun–mid-Sep) This abbey, 8km north of Pleasant Bay past the village of Red River, is a monastery for followers of Tibetan Buddhism. Ane Pema Chödrön is the founding director of the abbey and a noted Buddhist author, but you aren't likely to see her here as she is often on the road. You can visit the grounds any time during the day but you get a more authentic experience with a tour – a friendly monk escorts you.

Pollett's Cove   HIKING
The popular, challenging 20km-return hiking trail to Pollett's Cove begins at the end of the road to Gampo Abbey. There are great views along the way and perfect spots to camp when you arrive at the abandoned fishing community. This is not a Parks Canada trail, so it can be rough underfoot.

**Captain Mark's Whale &
Seal Cruise**   WHALE-WATCHING
(☏902-224-1316, 888-754-5112; www.whaleand sealcruise.com; adult $25-39, child $12-19; ◉mid-May–Sep) Two to five daily tours (depending on the season) can be taken in the lower-priced 'Cruiser' motorboat or closer to the action in a Zodiac. Captain Mark promises not only guaranteed whales but also time to see seabirds and seals as well as Gampo Abbey. There's a discount of 25% if you reserve a spot on the earliest (9:30am) or latest (5pm) tour. Tours leave from the wharf next to the Whale Interpretive Centre.

Whale Interpretive Centre   MUSEUM
(☏902-224-1411; www.whalecentre.ca; 104 Harbour Rd; adult/child $4.75/3.75; ◉9am-5pm Jun–

mid-Oct) Stop here before taking a whale-watching tour from the adjacent wharf. Park entrance permits are for sale here, and internet access is available at the C@P site downstairs.

🛏 Sleeping

Scottish Hillside B&B   B&B $$
(☏877-223-8111, 902-224-21156; scottishhillside bnb@hotmail.com; 23562 Cabot Trail; r $85-135; ☏) Run by a friendly young family, this new Victorian-style home sits right on the Cabot Trail and is a comfortable and convenient base for hiking and whale-watching. Ornately decorated rooms are big and the buffet-style breakfasts feature everything from local fruit to authentic oatcakes.

Cabot Trail Hostel   HOSTEL $
(☏902-224-1976; www.cabottrail.com/hostel; 23349 Cabot Trail; dm/r $27/59; @☏) Bright and basic, this very friendly 18-bed hostel has a common kitchen and barbecue area. The office for Cabot Trail Whale Watching is here.

BAY ST LAWRENCE

Bay St Lawrence is a picturesque little fishing village at the very north edge of Cape Breton Island.

Captain Cox (☏902-383-2981, 888-346-5556; Bay St Lawrence Wharf; adult/child $25/12) has been taking people to see whales aboard the 35ft *Northern Gannet* since 1986. He does trips at 10:30am, 1:30pm and 4:30pm in July and August. Call for spring and fall schedules.

Jumping Mouse Campground (☏902-383-2914; jumpingmousecamping@gmail.com; 3360 Bay St Lawrence Rd; campsite $25, cabin $40; ◉Jun-Sep) is an ecofriendly campground with 10 oceanfront sites (no cars allowed). Reservations are accepted for multinight stays and for a beautifully built four-bunk cabin. There are hot showers, a cooking shelter, frequent whale sightings and the whole place is nearly bug-free.

To enjoy Aspy Bay and its spectacular beach just for an afternoon, stop at nearby **Cabot's Landing Provincial Park** (www. parks.gov.ns.ca).

MEAT COVE

The northernmost road in Nova Scotia finishes at the steep, emerald coast of Meat Cove, 13km northwest of Bay St Lawrence (the last 7km of the road is gravel). As well as watching for frolicking whales in unbelievably clear water, keep an eye on the earth for orchids – some rare species aren't found anywhere else in Nova Scotia. Stop by the **Meat Cove Welcome Center** (📞902-383-2284; 2296 Meat Cove Rd; ⏱8am-8:30pm Jul-Sep) to get excellent information on hiking trails, check email and grab a bite to eat (sandwiches to lobster suppers). Leave your car here if there's no room at the trailhead.

From Meat Cove, a 16km **hiking trail** continues west to Cape St Lawrence lighthouse and Lowland Cove. Spend an hour gazing over the ocean, and you're guaranteed to see pods of pilot whales. They frolic here all spring, summer, and into the fall. Carry a compass and refrain from exploring side paths; locals have gotten lost in this area.

🛏 Sleeping & Eating

Meat Cove Lodge   B&B $
(📞902-383-2672; 2305 Meat Cove Rd; d/f $40/50; ⏱Jun–mid-Sep) Just across from the welcome center, this flower- and bric-a-brac-surrounded house is so cute and sunken into the landscape that it looks like part of a Hobbit's shire.

Meat Cove Campground   CAMPGROUND $
(📞902-383-2379/2658; 2475 Meat Cove Rd; campsites $25, cabins $60; ⏱Jun-Oct) Meat Cove Campground is spectacular, perched on a grassy bluff high above the ocean out in the middle of nowhere. A few new cabins (bring your own bedding) with no electricity or plumbing share the magnificent view. The adjacent **Chowder Hut** (mains $7-16; ⏱11am-8pm) serves mostly basic seafood dishes. Bring loose change for the coin-operated showers ($1 for 12 minutes); firewood is $3 for nine pieces. Be prepared for high winds.

Hine's Ocean View Lodge   HOSTEL $
(📞902-383-2512; www.hinesoceanviewlodge.ca; r $60; 🛜) If there's no room at Meat Cove Lodge, backtrack to this even more isolated spot, high up its own road, that has plain near-dormitory style rooms and a shared kitchen; cash only.

INGONISH

At the eastern entrance to Cape Breton Highlands National Park are Ingonish and Ingonish Beach, small towns lost in the background of motels and cottages. This is a long-standing popular destination, but there are few real attractions other than the **Highlands Links golf course** (📞902-285-2600, 800-441-1118; www.highlandslinksgolf.com; round $91), reputed to be one of the best in the world, and the beach. There are sev-

eral hiking trails and an information center nearby in the national park (see p366).

Ingonish Beach is a long, wide strip of sand tucked in a bay surrounded by green hills.

🛏 Sleeping & Eating

Keltic Lodge   HOTEL $$$
(📞902-285-2880, 800-565-0444; www.signatureresorts.com; Ingonish Beach; r $155-280, cottages $315-395; P 🅿 @ 🛜 🏊) The finest digs in the area are scattered within this theatrical Tudor-style resort erected in 1940. It shares Middle Head Peninsula with the famous **golf course** and the **Ingonish Campground**. The lodge is worth visiting even if you're not a guest for its setting and the **hiking trail** to the tip of the peninsula just beyond the resort. You must have a valid entry permit to the national park, as the lodge, the golf course and the hiking trail are all within park boundaries.

Driftwood Lodge   INN $
(📞902-285-2558; www.driftwoodlodge.ca; 36125 Cabot Trail, Ingonish; r $50, ste with kitchen $80-95) This funky cabin-meets-hotel establishment, 8km north of the Ingonish park entrance, is a steal. The owner works at the park and is a mine of info about hiking and activities. There's a fine-sand beach just below the lodge.

Main Street Restaurant & Bakery
RESTAURANT $$
(📞902-285-2225; 37764 Cabot Trail, Ingonish Beach; lunch around $10, dinner $10-20; ⏱7am-9pm Tue-Sat) By far the best breakfast stop (from $6) near the park and also a great stop for lunch and dinner. Sandwiches and ▨▨▨▨▨ ▨▨▨▨ ▨▨▨ ▨▨▨▨▨ ▨▨▨▨ ▨▨▨▨ ▨▨▨▨ bread and there are very reasonable full-lobster suppers for dinner.

WHITE POINT TO NEIL'S HARBOUR

On your way south to Ingonish, leave the Cabot Trail to follow the rugged, wind-swept White Point Rd via Smelt Brook to the fishing villages of **White Point** and **Neil's Harbour**. These are gritty, hard-working towns but there is some nice architecture, colorful homes, and illuminated, slightly disorienting views of Cape North to Meat Cove when the sun hits them at the end of the day. These are villages where there are as many fishing boats as houses – the area feels distinctly off the beaten tourist track.

Stay the night at homey **Two Tittle** (📞902-383-2817, 866-231-4087; www.twotittle.com;

2119 White Point Rd; r $60-90; 🛜), which smells like supper and whose grandparent-like proprietors are in most evenings watching *Wheel of Fortune*. Don't miss the short but gorgeous walk out back to the Two Tittle Islands the B&B is named for and look out for whales and eagles.

The perfect stop for lunch or dinner is **Chowder House** (chowder from $6, suppers from $14; ⊙11am-8:30pm), out beyond the lighthouse at Neil's Harbour. It's famous for its chowder but also serves great-value suppers of snow crab, lobster, mussels and more. There are plenty of dining locals who like to chat with folks from away while they splatter themselves with seafood juice.

ST ANN'S LOOP

Settle into the artsy calm of winding roads, serene lakes, eagles soaring overhead and a never-ending collection of artists' workshops that dot the trail like Easter eggs. Although you could skip the drive around St Ann's Bay and take a $5 ferry to Englishtown, you'd be missing a leg of the Cabot Trail that is unique unto itself. If you explore deeper you'll discover walking trails to waterfalls and scenic vistas, Mi'kmaw culture and a decidedly interesting mish-mash of characters.

Gaelic College of Celtic Arts & Crafts (☎902-295-3411; www.gaeliccollege.edu; 51779 Cabot Trail; 5-day course incl lodging $705-805; ⊙9am-5pm Jun–mid-Oct), at the end of St Ann's Bay, teaches Scottish Gaelic, bagpipe playing, Highland dancing, weaving and more. The college's **Great Hall of the Clans Museum** (admission $3) traces Celtic history from ancient times to the Highland clearances.

Don't leave the area without stopping in at an **artist's workshop** or two; you'll find pottery, leather and pewter workers, hat shops and more. The artists are easy to find – just keep an eye out for the signs along the main road.

🛏 Sleeping & Eating

J Kerr's B&B   B&B $$
(☎902-929-2114; 43627 Cabot Trail, Breton Cove; 🛜) For 26 years Joan Kerr has offered her home to travelers for whatever the traveler decides to pay – and so far she's not discouraged. Rainbow paintings grace the walls and Joan cooks up a million-dollar breakfast in the morning.

Chanterelle Country Inn & Cottages
                                          INN $$$
(☎902-929-2263, 866-277-0577; www.chanterelleinn.com; 48678 Cabot Trail, North River; r $145-225; ⊙May-Nov; @🛜☑) Unparalleled as an environmentally friendly place to stay, the house and cabins are on 60 hectares overlooking rolling pastures and bucolic bliss. Meals (breakfast and dinner) are served on the screened-in porch. If you're not staying here, you can reserve for dinner at the highly reputed restaurant (mains $20 to $28, prix-fixe four courses veg/nonveg $38/45; open 6pm to 8pm May to November).

Clucking Hen Deli & Bakery   CAFE $
(☎902-929-2501; 45073 Cabot Trail; mains $4-14; ⊙7am-7pm Jul-Sep, to 6pm May, Jun & Oct) A sign reads 'no fowl moods in here.' Listen to the local 'hens' cluck away while you eat a delicious meal of homemade breads, soup and salad.

Bras d'Or Lake Scenic Drive

The highlands meet the lowlands along the shores of this inland saltwater sea where eagles nest and puffins play. At 1099 sq km, it's the biggest lake in Nova Scotia and all but cleaves Cape Breton Island in two.

BADDECK

An old resort town in a pastoral setting, Baddeck is on the north shore of Bras d'Or Lake, halfway between Sydney and the Canso Causeway. It's the most popular place to stay for those who intend to do the Cabot Trail as a one-day scenic drive.

⊙ Sights & Activities

TOP CHOICE **Alexander Graham Bell National Historic Site**   MUSEUM
(☎902-295-2069; www.parkscanada.gc.ca; 559 Chebucto St; adult/child $7.80/3.90; ⊙9am-6pm) The inventor of the telephone is buried near his summer home, Beinn Bhreaghm, which is visible across the bay from Baddeck. The excellent museum of the Alexander Graham Bell National Historic Site, at the eastern edge of town, covers all aspects of his inventions and innovations. See medical and electrical devices, telegraphs, telephones, kites and seaplanes and then learn about how they all work. You'll come out feeling much smarter than when you went in.

Interpretive Centre   MUSEUM
(☎902-295-1675; www.brasdor-conservation.
com; 532 Chebucto St; admission by donation;
☉11am-7pm Jun–mid-Oct) Bras d'Or Lakes &
Watershed Interpretive Centre explores the
unique ecology of the enormous saltwater
lake.

🛏 Sleeping & Eating

Broadwater Inn & Cottages   INN $$
(☎902-295-1101, 877-818-3474; www.broadwater.
baddeck.com; Bay Rd; r $90-140, ste $199, cottag-
es $95-200; ☎) In a tranquil spot 1.5km east
of Baddeck, this c 1830 home once belonged
to JAD McCurdy, who worked with Alexan-
der Graham Bell on early aircraft designs.
The rooms in the inn are full of character,
have bay views and are decorated with
subtle prints and lots of flair. Modern self-
contained cottages are set in the woods and
are great for families. Only the B&B rooms
include breakfast. It's gay friendly.

Mother Gaelic's   B&B $
(☎902-295-2885, 888-770-3970; www.mother
gaelics.com; 26 Water St; d $90, with shared
bathroom $50-75; ☎) Named for the owner's
great-grandmother, who was a bootleg-
ger patronized by Alexander Graham Bell,
this sweet cottage opposite the waterfront
has the feel of an uncluttered summer
home.

Lynwood Inn   INN $$
(☎902-295-1995; www.lynwoodinn.com; 441
Shore Rd; r $100-230; P☎) Rooms in this
enormous inn go far beyond the hotel standard with Victorian wooden beds, muted
color schemes and airy spacious living
spaces. There's a family-style restaurant
downstairs that serves breakfast, lunch and
dinner (breakfast is not included in room
rates).

Highwheeler Cafe & Deli   CAFE $
(486 Chebucto St; sandwiches $8; ☉6am-8pm)
This place bakes great bread and goodies
(some gluten-free), makes big tasty sandwiches (including vegetarian), quesadillas,
soups and more. Finish off on the sunny
deck licking an ice-cream cone. Box lunches
for hikers are also available.

Baddeck Lobster Suppers   DINING HALL $$$
(☎902-925-3307; 17 Ross St; dinners $30; ☉4-
9pm Jun-Oct) In the former legion hall, this
high production, arguably high-priced insti-
tution gets live lobsters in the pot then fresh
to you lickety-split. Meals come with just

HIGHLAND VILLAGE MUSEUM   371

Explore Scottish heritage through the
Highland Village Museum (☎902-
725-2272; www.highlandvillage.museum.
gov.ns.ca; 4119 Hwy 223; adult/child
$9/4; ☉9:30am-5:30pm), a living histo-
ry museum perched on a hilltop over-
looking the Bras d'Or lakes. Costumed
Scotspeople demonstrate day-to-day
activities of early settlers' lives and
there are Celtic-inspired workshops
from spring through fall – check the
website for scheduling.

about everything and, although not spec-
tacularly prepared, could fuel you for days.

☆ Entertainment

Baddeck Gathering Ceilidhs   LIVE MUSIC
(☎902-295-2794; www.baddeckgathering.com; St
Michael's Parish Hall, 8 Old Margaree Rd; adult/child
$10/5; ☉7:30pm Jul & Aug) Nightly fiddling and
dancing. The parish hall is just opposite the
VIC right in the middle of town.

ℹ Information

VIC (☎902-295-1911; 454 Chebucto St; ☉9am-
7pm Jun-Sep)

Visit Baddeck (www.visitbaddeck.com) Maps,
tour operators, golf courses etc.

WAGMATCOOK & AROUND

Stop in the Mi'kmaw community of Wag-
matcook just west of Baddeck to visit the
Wagmatcook Culture & Heritage Centre
(☎902-295-2999/2402; www.wagmatcook.com;
Hwy 105; ☉9am-8pm May-Oct, call for hours
Nov-Apr). This somewhat empty cultural at-
traction offers an entryway into Mi'kmaw
culture and history.

TOP CHOICE **Bear on the Lake Guesthouse**
(☎902-404-3636; www.bearonthe
lake.com; 10705 Hwy 105; dm/r $30/75; ☎), be-
tween Wagmatcook and the next town of
Whycocomagh, is a super-fun place over-
looking the lake. Everything is set up for
backpacker bliss from the drive share board
to the big sunny deck and inviting commu-
nal areas. This place is so popular another
six-bed dorm was being added on when we
passed; there are also rooms with private
sitting areas on the top level of the house.
Everyone falls in love with effervescent Kat
who manages the place.

Also on Hwy 105, 12km southwest of Baddeck, is **Herring Choker Deli** (☑902-295-2275; sandwiches around $4; ⊗8am-6pm). Arguably the region's best pit stop, the deli serves gourmet sandwiches, soups and salads.

North Sydney

North Sydney itself is nondescript, though there are some fine places to stay nearby.

Reserve accommodations if you're coming in on a late ferry or going out on an early one. Most North Sydney motels and B&Bs are open year-round, and it's understood that guests will arrive and leave at all hours. Most places to stay are along Queen St about 2km west of the ferry terminal.

🛏 Sleeping & Eating

Highland View Organic Farm & Cottages   COTTAGES **$$**
(☑902-794-1955, 800-440-5251; www.highland viewcottages.com; 20 Allen Lane, George's River; cottages $150-160) Ten kilometers away in the farming community of George's River, stay in luxurious Nova Scotia pine-wood cabins on an organic farm overlooking the Bras d'Or lakes. Owners Cyril and Loretta are phenomenally knowledgeable about their natural surroundings and will proudly teach you about everything from beekeeping to medicinal plants.

Heritage Home B&B   B&B **$**
(☑902-794-4815, 866-601-4515; www.bbcanada. com/3242.html; 110 Queen St; r $60-95; 🐾) This exceptionally well decorated and maintained Victorian home is an extremely elegant place to stay for the price. Most rooms have private bathrooms.

Alexandra Shebib's B&B   B&B **$**
(☑902-794-4876, 866-573-8294; 88 Queen St; r $50-70; 🐾) This B&B is simple, friendly and excellent value. Rooms have shared bathrooms.

Black Spoon   RESTAURANT **$$**
(☑902-241-3300; 320 Commercial St; mains $10-17; ⊗11am-8pm Mon-Thu, 11am-9pm Fri & Sat) At this amazingly chic black and beige bistro dine on local faves with a twist, like breaded haddock with mango salsa, or colorful salads like the grilled vegetable salad with goat cheese. There's also espresso drinks, cocktails and a reasonable wine list.

ℹ Getting There & Away

For information about **Marine Atlantic ferry** (☑800-341-7981; www.marine-atlantic.ca) services to Newfoundland, see p467 and p494.

Acadian Lines (☑902-454-9321, 800-567-5151; www.acadianbus.com) buses to Halifax (adult/child $64/32) and points in between can be picked up at the Ultramar gas station on Blower's St. **Transit Cape Breton** (☑902-539-8124; adult/child $3.75/3.25) runs bus 5 back and forth between North Sydney's Commercial St and Sydney at 8:40am, 12:40pm, 2:40pm and 5:40pm Monday to Saturday.

Sydney

POP 24,115

The second-biggest city in Nova Scotia and the only real city on Cape Breton Island, Sydney is the embattled core of the island's collapsed industrial belt. The now-closed steel mill and coal mines were the region's largest employers and now the city feels a bit empty. Although Sydney itself is nothing special, it is well serviced and you get more bang for your buck staying here as a base to explore Louisbourg and the Cabot Trail than you would in more scenic areas.

Downtown, Charlotte St is lined with stores and restaurants and there's a pleasant boardwalk along Esplanade, while the North End historic district has a gritty charm.

◉ Sights & Activities

Architecture   NOTABLE BUILDINGS
There are eight buildings older than 1802 in a two-block radius in North End Sydney. Three are open to the public:

St Patrick's Church Museum (☑902-562-8237; 87 Esplanade; admission free; ⊗9am-5pm), the oldest Catholic church on Cape Breton Island.

The 1787 **Cossit House** (☑902-539-7973; www.cossit.museum.gov.ns.ca; 75 Charlotte St; adult/concession $2/1; ⊗9am-5pm Mon-Sat, 1-5pm Sun Jun–mid-Oct), the oldest house in Sydney.

Jost Heritage House (☑902-539-0366; 54 Charlotte St; admission free; ⊗9am-5pm Mon-Sat, 1-5:30pm Sun), just down the road from Cossit House, which features a collection of model ships and an assortment of medicines used by an early-20th-century apothecary.

Cape Breton Centre for Heritage & Science

MUSEUM

(☎902-539-1572; 225 George St; admission free; ⊙9am-5pm Mon-Sat) In the Lyceum, this center explores the social and natural history of Cape Breton Island.

☞ Tours

Ghosts & Legends of Historic Sydney

WALKING TOURS

(☎902-539-1572; per person $10; ⊙7pm Jul & Aug) This recommended walking tour leaves from St Patrick's Church, does the loop of historic buildings and finishes with tea and scones at the Lyceum.

🛏 Sleeping & Eating

Most establishments in Sydney are open year-round.

TOP CHOICE Colby House

B&B $$

(☎902-539-4095; www.colbyhousebb. com; 10 Park St; r $100-120; @❅) It's worth staying in Sydney for the affordable luxe of this exceptional B&B. The owner used to travel around Canada for work and she decided to offer everything she wished she'd had while on the road. The result is a mix of heritage and modern design, the softest sheets you can imagine, guest bathrobes, plenty of delicious-smelling soaps, chocolates next to the bed and so many other comfort-giving details we can hardly begin to list them.

Gathering House B&B

B&B $$

(☎902-539-7172, 866-539-7172; www.gathering house.com; 148 Crescent St; r $60-150; P@) This welcoming, ramshackle Victorian home is close to the heart of town. Shared bathrooms get awfully busy when the B&B is full.

Flavors

RESTAURANT $$

(☎902-562-6611; 6 Pitt St; lunch/dinner around $10/20; ⊙8:30am-8:30pm Mon-Sat;☑) What the setting lacks in feng shui (small tables and a strange street-side patio setup), the restaurant makes up for in delicious food prepared from locally sourced ingredients. Start with mains like maple-seared salmon or roast pork loin with wild blueberry sauce then finish with a homemade ice cream sandwich with coconut cookies rolled in toffee bits. Vegan and gluten-free options are also available.

Allegro Grill

RESTAURANT $$

(☎902-562-1623; 222 Charlotte St; mains $9-25; ⊙lunch Mon-Sat, dinner Tue-Sat) Seafood and meat lovers, go here. This simple-looking spot serves not-so-simple specialties including their famous, handmade turkey andouille sausages

☆ Entertainment

A lot of touring bands make the trek to Sydney. Fiddlers and other traditional musicians from the west coast of the island also perform here or at the Savoy in Glace Bay. Gigs are about $12.

Upstair's at French Club

NIGHTCLUB

(☎902-371-0329; 44 Ferry St) This groovy little North End club features rock, Celtic, jazz and movie nights.

Chandler's

BAR

(☎902-539-3438; 76 Dorchester St) This standard, cavernous bar has top-end local and Canadian talent on stage.

ℹ Information

VIC (☎902-539-9876; 74 Esplanade; ⊙9am-7pm Jul & Aug, to 5pm Jun, Sep & Oct) On the waterfront just behind the world's largest illuminated fiddle.

ℹ Getting There & Away

The Sydney airport is none too busy. **Air Canada Jazz** (☎902-873-5000, 888-247-2262; www. aircanada.com) flies between Sydney and Halifax while **Air Saint-Pierre** (☎902-562-3140, 877-277-7765; www.airsaintpierre.com) flies to Saint Pierre ($175 one-way, two hours) from early July to early September, on Thursdays and Sundays.

The **Acadian Lines** (☎902-454-9321, 800-567-5151; www.acadianbus.com) bus depot is at 99 Terminal Dr. There are also a number of shuttle services to Halifax.

Glace Bay

Glace Bay, 6km northeast of Sydney, would be just another fading coal town were it not for its exceptional **Cape Breton Miners' Museum** (☎902-849-4522; www.miners museum.com; 42 Birkley St; tour & mine visit adult/child $12/10; ⊙10am-6pm); it's off South St less than 2km east from the town center. The highlight of this museum is the adventure under the seafloor to visit closed-down mines with a retired miner as a guide. The museum's **restaurant** (mains $8-14; ⊙noon-8pm) is highly recommended and offers seafood, sandwiches and burgers; there's a daily lunch buffet from noon to 2pm.

The town's grand 1920 **Savoy Theatre** (☎902-842-1577; www.savoytheatre.com; 116 Commercial St) is the region's premier entertainment venue.

Louisbourg

Louisbourg, 37km southeast of Sydney, is famous for its historic fortress. The town itself has plenty of soul, with its working fishing docks, old-timers and a friendly vibe.

◉ Sights & Activities

Starting from the trailhead at the lighthouse at the end of Havenside Rd, a rugged 6km **trail** follows the coast over bogs, barrens and pre-Cambrian polished granite. Bring your camera to capture the views back toward the fortress at the national historic site.

Louisbourg National Historic Site

HISTORICAL SITE

(☎902-733-2280; 259 Park Service Rd; adult/child $17.60/8.80; ⊙9am-5:30pm) Budget a full day to explore this extraordinary historic site that faithfully re-creates Fortress Louisbourg as it was in 1744 right down to the people – costumed thespians take their characters and run with them. Built to protect French interests in the region, it was also a base for cod fishing and an administrative capital. Louisbourg was worked on continually from 1719 to about 1745. The British took it in a 46-day siege in 1745 but it would change hands twice more. In 1760, after British troops under the command of General James Wolfe took Québec City, the walls of Louisbourg were destroyed and the city was burned to the ground.

In 1961, with the closing of many Cape Breton Island coal mines, the federal government funded the largest historical reconstruction in Canadian history as a way to generate employment, resulting in 50 buildings open to visitors. Workers in period dress take on the lives of typical fort inhabitants.

Free guided tours around the site are offered throughout the day. Travelers with mobility problems can ask for a pass to drive their car up to the site; there are ramps available to access most buildings. Be prepared for lots of walking, and bring a sweater and raincoat even if it's sunny when you start out.

Though the scale of the reconstruction is massive, three-quarters of Louisbourg is still in ruins. The 2.5km **Ruins Walk** guides you through the untouched terrain and out to the Atlantic coast. A short **interpretive walk** opposite the visitor center discusses the relationship between the French and the Mi'kmaq and offers some great views of the whole site.

Three restaurants serve food typical of the time. **Hotel de la Marine** and the adjacent **L'Épée Royale** (grilled cod with soup $14, 3-course meal $20) are where sea captains and prosperous merchants would dine on fine china with silver cutlery. Servers in period costume also dish out grub at **Grandchamps House** (meals $9-15), a favorite of sailors and soldiers. Wash down beans and sausage with hot buttered rum ($4). Otherwise buy a 1kg ration ($4) of soldiers' bread at the **Destouches Bakery**. There's also a small coffee shop between the restaurants serving hot drinks and a few snacks.

🛏 Sleeping & Eating

TOP CHOICE **Cranberry Cove Inn**   INN $$

(☎902-733-2171, 800-929-0222; www.cranberrycoveinn.com; 12 Wolfe St; r $105-160; ⊙May-Nov; 🛜) From the dark pink facade to the period-perfect interior of mauves, dusty blues and antique lace, you'll be transported back in time through rose-colored glasses at this stunning B&B. Each room is different and several have Jacuzzis and fireplaces.

Stacey House B&B   B&B $

(☎902-733-2317; www.bbcanada.com/thestaceyhouse; 7438 Main St; r $60-90; ⊙Jun–mid-Oct; 🛜) Interesting knickknacks such as worn teddy bears, dolls and model ships are harmoniously placed throughout this pretty house.

Spinning Wheel B&B   B&B $

(☎902-733-3332, 866-272-3222; www.spinningwheelbedandbreakfast.com; d with shared bathroom $65-75, d with private bathroom $90; ⊙May-Nov; 🛜) Try this place if everything else in town is full (which it will be during high season). It's not a looker but the cleanliness, friendly hosts and made-to-order breakfasts more than make up for it.

TOP CHOICE **Beggar's Banquet**   RESTAURANT $$$

(☎888-374-8439; Point of View Suites, 15 Commercial St Extension; meals $35; ⊙6-8pm late Jul-Sep) Finally here's a chance for you to get into period costume and gorge on a feast of local seafood in a replicated 18th-century tavern. There's a choice of four delicious and copious mains including crab and lobster.

Grubstake RESTAURANT $$
(☎902-733-2308; 7499 Main St; mains lunch $7-14, dinner $16-28; ⊗lunch & dinner) This informal restaurant is the best place to eat in town. The menu features burger platters at lunch and pastas and fresh seafood for dinner.

☆ Entertainment
Louisbourg Playhouse THEATER
(☎902-733-2996; 11 Lower Warren St; tickets $15; ⊗8pm late Jun–early Sep) A cast of young, local musicians entertain all summer long in this 17th-century-style theater.

ℹ Information
Tourist information office (☎902-733-2720; 7535 Main St; ⊗9am-7pm) Right in the center of town.

EASTERN SHORE

If you want to escape into the fog, away from summer tourist crowds, this is the place to do it. Running from Cape Canso at the extreme eastern tip of the mainland to the outskirts of Dartmouth, the Eastern Shore has no large towns and the main road is almost as convoluted as the rugged shoreline it follows. If you want to experience wilderness and are willing to hike or kayak, this is your heaven

Guysborough
Guysborough was settled by United Empire Loyalists after the American Revolution. The 26km Guysborough Trail, part of the Trans Canada Trail (TCT), is great for biking and hiking. The **Old Court House Museum** (☎902-533-4008; 106 Church St; admission free; ⊗9am-5pm Mon-Fri, 10am-4pm Sat & Sun) displays artifacts related to early farming and housekeeping, and also offers tourist information and guides to hiking trails.

🛏 Sleeping & Eating
TOP CHOICE **Desbarres Manor** INN $$$
(☎902-533-2099; www.desbarresmanor. com; 90 Church St; r from $149) This tastefully

renovated 1830 grand mansion with massive, opulent rooms is reason enough to come to Guysborough. With extraordinary service, fine dining and a range of activities on offer from canoeing and walking to golfing, it's one of the most luxurious properties in Nova Scotia.

Boylston Provincial Park CAMPGROUND $
(☎902-533-3326; www.parks.gov.ns.ca; off Hwy 16; campsites $18) The 36 shaded sites here are never all taken. From the picnic area on the highway below the campground, a footbridge leads to a small island on the coast about 12km north of Guysborough.

Rare Bird Pub RESTAURANT & PUB $$
(☎902-533-2128; www.rarebirdpub.com; 80 Main St; mains $9-17; ⊗11am-2am) The Bird is a quintessential stop for a swig of local ale, a pot of mussels, rockin' live east coast music on weekends and fiddlers on the wharf below on Wednesdays. Check the website for schedules.

Canso
Mainland North America's oldest seaport is a cluster of boxy fishermen's houses on a treeless bank of Chedabucto Bay. Long dependent on the fishery, Canso has been decimated by outward emigration and unemployment since the northern cod stocks collapsed around 1990.

The cape surrounding the village has some very off-the-beaten-track opportunities for hiking, kayaking, bird-watching and surfing. The tourist office is at the 1885 Whitman House Museum (☎902-366-2170; 1297 Union St; admission free; ⊗9am-5pm late May-Sep), which holds reminders of the town's history and offers a good view from the widow's walk on the roof.

⊙ Sights & Activities
Grassy Island National Historic Site
HISTORICAL SITE
(☎902-366-3136; 1465 Union St; admission $3; ⊗10am-6pm Jun–mid-Sep) An interpretive center on the waterfront tells the story of Grassy Island National Historic Site, which lies just offshore and can be visited by boat until 4pm. In 1720 the British built a small fort to offset the French who had their headquarters in Louisbourg but it was totally destroyed in 1744. Among the ruins today there's a self-guided **hiking trail** with eight interpretive stops explaining the

history of the area. The boat to Grassy Island departs from the center upon demand, weather permitting.

Chapel Gully Trail
NATURE TRAIL

This is a 10km boardwalk and hiking trail along an estuary and out to the coast. It begins near the lighthouse on the hill behind the hospital at the eastern end of Canso. A large map is posted at the trailhead.

✻ Festivals & Events

TOP CHOICE Stan Rogers Folk Festival
MUSIC

(www.stanfest.com; ⊙1st weekend of Jul) Most people come to Canso for the Stan Rogers Folk Festival, the biggest festival in Nova Scotia, which quadruples the town's population when six stages showcase folk, blues and traditional musicians from around the world. Accommodations are pretty much impossible to get unless you reserve a year ahead. Locals set up 1000 campsites for the festival; check the website for details and try to get a campsite away from the festival site if sleep is a priority.

🛏 Sleeping

Whitman Wharf House B&B
B&B $$

(☑902-366-2450; www.whitmanwharf.com; 1309 Union St; d $95-105; ⊙mid-May–mid-Oct; 🐾) The only place to stay in town outside of festival times is the excellent, wellness-oriented Whitman Wharf House B&B. There's a seaside cottage feel about this place and a shared bathroom that could almost be considered a spa. The owners are happy to help you organize your preferred activity.

Sherbrooke

The pleasant little town of Sherbrooke, 123km west of Canso and 63km south of Antigonish, is overshadowed by its historic site, which is about the same size.

The local tourist office is at **Sherbrooke Village** (☑902-522-2400; www.museum.gov. ns.ca/sv; Hwy 7; adult/child $9/3.75; ⊙9:30am-5:30pm Jun–mid-Oct), which re-creates everyday life from 125 years ago through buildings, demonstrations and costumed workers. There are 25 buildings to visit in this living museum that effectively helps its visitors step back in time.

On a quiet farm, **Days Ago B&B** (☑902-522-2811, 866-522-2811; www.bbcanada.com/daysago; 15 Cameron Rd; r $65-75; 🐾) will lull you with its slower pace. There's a sunporch for sitting on, or you can take out a kayak. Rooms in the house are shared while the loft-style chalet ($80 to $90) has its own bathroom.

You'll find coffee at Godsend **Village Coffee Grind** (coffees $3.25, sandwiches from $4; ⊙8am-5pm Mon-Fri, 9am-4pm Sat & Sun) on the town's minuscule main drag.

WORTH A TRIP

SABLE ISLAND

This ever-shifting, 44km-long spit of sand lies some 300km southeast of Halifax and has caused more than 350 documented shipwrecks. But what makes Sable Island most famous is that it's home to one of the world's only truly wild horse populations.

The first 60 ancestors of today's Sable Island horses were shipped to the island in 1760 when Acadians were being deported from Nova Scotia by the British. The Acadians were forced to abandon their livestock and it appears that Boston merchant ship owner Thomas Hancock helped himself to their horses then put them to pasture on Sable Island to keep it low profile. The horses that survived became wild.

Today the island works as a research center; scientists come every year, mostly to study the birds, seals and horses. Since 2003, natural gas fields run by Exxon have been working only 10km from the island but so far there has been little environmental conflict.

It's complicated and expensive but not impossible to visit Sable Island as a layperson – in fact, about 50 to 100 adventurous souls make it there each year. Contact **Sable Island Station** (☑902-453-9350; gforbes@ca.inter.net), in conjunction with Environment Canada, for information about where to get necessary permissions and independently arrange transport.

Taylor Head Provincial Park

A little-known scenic highlight of Nova Scotia, this spectacular **park** (☎902-772-2218; www.parks.gov.ns.ca; 20140 Hwy 7; ⊗mid-May–mid-Oct) encompasses a peninsula jutting 6.5km into the Atlantic. On one side is a long, very fine, sandy beach fronting a protected bay. Some 17km of hiking trails cut through the spruce and fir forests. The **Headland Trail** is the longest at 8km round-trip and follows the rugged coastline to scenic views at Taylor Head. The shorter **Bob Bluff Trail** is a 3km round-trip hike to a bluff with good views. In spring you'll see colorful wildflowers, and this is a great bird-watching venue. Pack the picnic cooler and plan on spending a full day hiking, lounging and (if you can brave the cool water) swimming here.

Tangier

About 10km southwest of Taylor Head Provincial Park, Tangier is one of the best settings for kayaking in the Maritimes. Highly recommended **Coastal Adventures Sea Kayaking** (☎902-772-2774; www.coastaladventures.com; off Hwy 7; ⊗mid-Jun–early Oct) offers introductions to sea-kayaking (half-/full-day $75/110), rentals (half-/full-day $35/50) and guided trips. The establishment also has a cozy, excellent-value B&B, **Paddlers Retreat** (s $50, d $60-80).

Murphy's Camping on the Ocean (☎902-772-2700; www.murphyscampingontheocean.ca; 291 Murphy's Rd; tent/RV sites $22/33, trailer rental $65-85; ☎) gets you out of your tent and into the water to collect mussels; you eat your labors at a beach barbecue to the music of yarns told by Brian the owner. There are RV sites, an RV rental, secluded tent sites and a very rudimentary room above the dock that can sleep four people. Boat rental is $75 per hour and there's also drop-off and pick-up services for camping on the islands.

Don't miss a snack stop at **J Willy Krauch & Sons Ltd** (☎902-772-2188; 35 Old Mooseland Rd off Hwy 7; ⊗10am-5pm Mon-Fri, 9am-5pm Sat & Sun), famed for making the tastiest smoked fish in the province. Choose from a variety of salmon, eel, mackerel and more – don't forget to bring some crackers.

Jedore Oyster Pond

The tiny **Fisherman's Life Museum** (☎902-889-2053; www.museum.gov.ns.ca/flm; 58 Navy Pool Loop; adult/child $3/1.50; ⊗9:30am-5:30pm Mon-Sat, 1-5:30pm Sun), 45km toward Halifax from Tangier, should really be renamed. The man of the house used to row 16km to get to his fishing grounds, leaving his wife and 13 daughters at home. The museum really captures women's domestic life of the early 20th century. Costumed local guides offer tea and hospitality.

New Brunswick

Best Places to Eat

» Rossmount Inn
Restaurant (p395)

» North Head Bakery
(p400)

» Saint John's Old City
Market (p404)

Best Places to Stay

» Carriage House Inn (p384)

» Bear's Lair (p390)

» Rossmount Inn (p393)

» Fairmont Algonquin
(p393)

Why Go?

In the early 20th century, New Brunswick was a Very Big Deal. Millionaire businessmen, major league baseball players and US presidents journeyed here to fish salmon from its silver rivers and camp at rustic lodges in its deep primeval forests. But over the decades, New Brunswick slipped back into relative obscurity. Today, some joke that it's the 'drive-thru province,' as vacationers tend to hotfoot it to its better-known neighbors Prince Edward Island (PEI) and Nova Scotia.

But why? The unspoiled wilderness is still here. There are rivers for fly-fishing, coastal islands for kayaking, snowy mountains for skiing, quaint Acadian villages for exploring. So do yourself a favor, and don't just drive through. Prince Edward Island will still be there when you're done, we promise.

When to Go
Fredericton

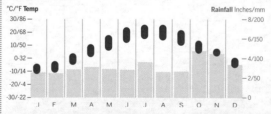

July-September St Andrews By-The-Sea bustles with crowds of whale-watchers

August Acadians unleash their Franco-Canadian spirit for the Festival Acadien in Caraquet

November-March Cross-country skiers hit the groomed trails of Fundy National Park

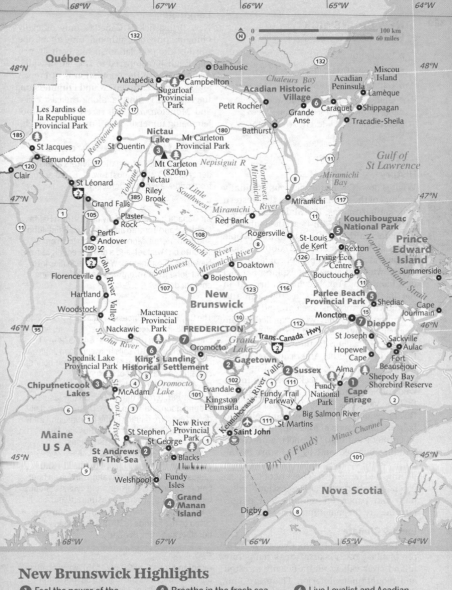

New Brunswick Highlights

❶ Feel the power of the highest tides in the world from the lighthouse at **Cape Enrage** (p409)

❷ Browse the streets in picturesque **St Andrews By-The-Sea** (p392), **Gagetown** (p387) and **Sussex** (p407)

❸ Dip your canoe paddle in the lakes of **Chiputneticook** (p392) and **Nictau** (p388)

❹ Breathe in the fresh sea air and unwind on peaceful, isolated **Grand Manan Island** (p398)

❺ Stretch out on the sandy beach at **Kouchibouguac National Park** (p415) or **Parlee Beach** (p413)

❻ Live Loyalist and Acadian history at **King's Landing Historical Settlement** (p386) and **Acadian Historic Village** (p418)

❼ Taste the first strawberries of the season and other delicacies at weekly farmers' markets in **Fredericton** (p384) and **Dieppe** (p411)

NEW BRUNSWICK FAST FACTS

» Population: 730,000

» Area: 73,400 sq km

» Capital: Fredericton

» Quirky fact: Home to the world's biggest fake lobster (Shediac), axe (Nackawic) and fiddlehead (Plaster Rock).

History

What is now New Brunswick was originally the land of the Mi'kmaq and, in the western and southern areas, the Maliseet Aboriginals. Many places still bear their aboriginal names, although the Aboriginal people (who today number around 17,000) are now concentrated on small pockets of land.

Following in the wake of explorer Samuel de Champlain, French colonists arrived in the 1600s. The Acadians, as they came to be known, farmed the area around the Bay of Fundy. In 1755 they were expelled by the English, many returning to settle along the Bay of Chaleur. In the years following, the outbreak of the American Revolution brought an influx of British Loyalists from Boston and New York seeking refuge in the wilds of New Brunswick. These refugees settled the valleys of the St John and St Croix Rivers, established the city of Saint John and bolstered the garrison town at Fredericton.

Through the 1800s lumbering and shipbuilding boomed and by the start of the 20th century other industries, including fishing, had developed. That era of prosperity ended with the Great Depression. Today, pulp and paper, oil refining and potato farming are the major industries.

Land & Climate

The province encompasses a varied geography of moist, rocky coastal areas, temperate inland river valleys and a heavily forested and mountainous interior. There are four distinct seasons. Summers are generally mild with occasional hot days. The Fundy shore is prone to fog, particularly in the spring and early summer. The primary tourist season lasts from late June to early September. Many tourist facilities (beaches, organized tours and some accommodations in resort areas) shut down for the remainder of the year.

Language

New Brunswick is Canada's only officially bilingual province, although only about one third of the population speaks both French and English (compared to 17% nationwide). Around 34% of the population is of French ancestry, concentrated around Edmundston, the Acadian Peninsula, along the east coast and Moncton. You will rarely have a problem being understood in English or French.

Getting There & Around

There are tourist information centers at all border crossings and in most towns. These are open from mid-May to mid-October only.

Air

Air Canada has several daily flights from Halifax, Montréal and Toronto into Moncton, Saint John and Fredericton. Moncton has service from Toronto on WestJet; and a daily direct flight from Newark on Continental. WestJet also flies into Saint John from Toronto. See p880 for airline contact details.

Boat

The Bay Ferries' **Princess of Acadia** (☑506-649-7777, 888-249-7245; www.bayferries.com; adult/child 0-5yr/child 6-13yr/senior $40/5/25/30, car/bicycle $80/10) sails between Saint John and Digby, Nova Scotia, year-round. The three-hour crossing can save a lot of driving.

From Saint John between late June and early September, ferries depart twice a day, usually around noon and 11pm. From Digby, twice daily departures are usually in the morning and mid-afternoon. During the rest of the year, ferries run once or twice daily in both directions.

Arrive early or call ahead for vehicle reservations, as the ferry is very busy in July and August. Even with a reservation, arrive an hour before departure. Walk-ons and cyclists should be OK any time. There's a restaurant and a bar.

For Fundy Isles ferries, see the section dedicated to the islands (p396). Book ahead where possible and/or arrive early.

Bus

Acadian Lines (☑800-567-5151; www.acadianbus.com) services the major transportation routes in New Brunswick, with service to Nova

REGIONAL DRIVING DISTANCES

Edmundston to Saint John: 375km

Fredericton to Miramichi: 180km

St Andrews By-The-Sea to Moncton: 254km

Four Days

Spend the first day at **King's Landing Historical Settlement**. Land in **Fredericton** on Saturday morning – peruse the stalls at the **WW Boyce Farmers' Market**, and nip into the **Beaverbrook Art Gallery** to see a few old masters and contemporary Canadian art. Follow the **Old River Road** through Gagetown to the port city of **Saint John**, stopping at a few pottery studios on the way. Hit Saint John on a Saturday night – catch some live Maritime music at **O'Leary's pub** or a play at the **Imperial Theatre**. The next morning, head west along the Fundy coast to catch the ferry to **Grand Manan Island**. Take your pick of whale-watching tours, hiking, cycling or relaxing on the verandah with a book.

One Week

Back on the mainland from Grand Manan, take the scenic route east through **St Martins**, **Sussex** and **Fundy National Park**. Stop for a dip in the ocean at **Parlee Beach** near Shediac, then head north toward Bouctouche. Get a taster of Acadian culture at **Le Pays de la Sagouine**, then round out the experience with a visit to the modern village of **Caraquet** and a time trip to the early 19th century at **Acadian Historic Village**. Alternatively, head up to the **Miramichi** for a few days of salmon fishing and tubing on the famed river.

Outdoor Adventures

Start with a couple of days camping by the ocean, kayaking along the dunes and exploring the cycling and hiking trails at **Kouchibouguac National Park**. Spend a day or a week hiking the northern end of the **International Appalachian Trail** up over Mt Carleton, around **Grand Manan** or along the **Fundy Trail Parkway**. Take a sea-kayaking expedition in **Passamaquoddy Bay**, then spend a week canoe-tripping through the **Chiputneticook Lakes**. Do a week-long cycling trip up the **St John River Valley** or day trips around Grand Manan, **Fredericton** and **Sussex**. Leave a couple of days for whale-watching and a boat excursion to **Machias Seal Island** to see the puffins.

Canoe maps for the Nepisiquit, Restigouche, Southwest Miramichi, St Croix and Tobique Rivers are available from **Service New Brunswick** (www.snb.ca; $7 each). It also distributes a guide to the New Brunswick Trail ($13) and a snowmobile trail map (free).

Scotia, PEI and into Québec as far as Rivière-du-Loup where they connect with **Orléans Express** (888-999-3977; www.orleansexpress.com) buses for points west.

Acadian also runs south to Bangor, Maine from Saint John ($55, 3½ hours) with onward service to Boston and New York. For information on the daily bus service between Bangor and Calais, see p391.

Car & Motorcycle

For drivers, the main access points into New Brunswick are through Edmundston, Maine at Calais and Houlton, Nova Scotia or PEI. If you're going to PEI, there's no charge to use the Confederation Bridge eastbound from Cape Jourmain – you pay on the way back. Traffic is generally light, although crossing the Maine border usually means a delay at customs.

Train

VIA Rail (888-842-7245; www.viarail.ca) operates passenger services between Montréal and Halifax six times a week. Main New

Brunswick stops are Campbellton, Miramichi and Moncton. Fares from Montréal to Moncton for a coach/sleeper are $211/449 (16½ hours).

FREDERICTON

POP 50,500

This sleepy provincial capital does quaint very well. The St John River curves lazily through Fredericton, past the stately government buildings on the waterfront and the university on the hill. Its neatly mown, tree-lined banks are dotted with fountains, walking paths and playing fields. On warm weekends, 'The Green,' as it's known, looks like something out of a watercolor painting – families strolling, kids kicking soccer balls, couples picnicking.

On a flat, broad curve in the riverbank, the small downtown commercial district

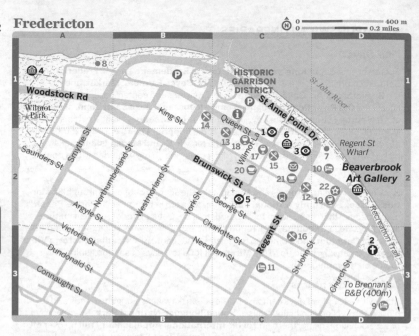

Fredericton

is a neat grid of redbrick storefronts. Surrounding it are quiet residential streets lined with tall, graceful elms shading beautifully maintained Georgian and Victorian houses and abundant flower beds. A canopy of trees spreads over the downtown, pierced here and there by church spires.

◉ Sights

The two-block strip along Queen St between York and Regent Sts is known as the Historic Garrison District. In 1875, Fredericton became the capital of the newly formed province of New Brunswick and the garrison housed British soldiers for much of the late 18th and early 19th centuries. It's now a lively multiuse area with impressive stone architecture.

Old Government House   HISTORICAL BUILDING
(www.gnb.ca/lg/ogh; 51 Woodstock Rd; admission free; ⊘10am-4pm Mon-Sat, from noon Sun mid-May–Aug) This magnificent sandstone palace was erected for the British governor in 1826. The representative of the queen moved out in 1893 after the province refused to continue paying his expenses, and during most of the 20th century the complex was a Royal Canadian Mounted Police (RCMP) headquarters. It now evocatively captures a moment in time with tours led by staff in period costume. New Brunswick's current lieutenant governor (Graydon Nicholas, a member of the Maliseet Nation and the first aboriginal lawyer in Atlantic Canada) lives on the 3rd floor.

Beaverbrook Art Gallery   MUSEUM
(www.beaverbrookartgallery.org; 703 Queen St; adult/senior/student/family $8/6/3/18, pay as you wish Thu after 5:30pm; ⊘9am-5:30pm, to 9pm Thu, noon-5pm Sun Sep-Jun, closed Mon in winter) This relatively small but excellent gallery was one of Lord Beaverbrook's gifts to the town. The exceptional collection includes works by international heavyweights and is well worth an hour or so. Among others you will see Constable, Dali, Gainsborough and Turner, Canadian artists Tom Thompson, Emily Carr and Cornelius Kreighoff as well as changing contemporary exhibits of Atlantic art.

Officers' Square   HISTORICAL SITE
(www.downtownfredericton.ca; btwn Carleton & Regent Sts; ceremonies 11am & 4pm mid-July–3rd week Aug, additional performances 7pm Tue & Thu) Once the military parade ground, the Garrison District's Officers' Square now hosts a full-uniform changing of the guard ceremony in summertime. Also in summer the Calithumpians Outdoor Summer Theatre performs daily at 12:15pm weekdays and 2:30pm weekends. The free historical skits are laced with humor. Summer evenings bring jazz, Celtic and rock concerts – see the website for schedules.

York Sunbury Historical Museum   MUSEUM
(www.yorksunburymuseum.com; Officers' Sq; adult/student/child $3/1/free; ⊘10am-5pm mid-Jun–Aug, 1-4pm Tue-Sat Apr–mid-Dec) Housed

in the 19th-century officers' quarters on the west side of Officers' Sq, this museum's collection preserves the city's past. Displays feature military pieces used by local regiments and by British and German armies from the Boer War and both world wars, furniture from a Loyalist sitting room and a Victorian bedroom, and aboriginal and Acadian artifacts. Don't miss the Coleman Frog, a 42lb creature of Fredericton legend. Real or plaster? Decide for yourself.

Soldiers' Barracks   HISTORICAL BUILDING
(cnr Queen & Carleton Sts; admission free; ⊘Jun-Sep) See how the common soldier lived in the 1820s (lousy food, too much drink) at this grim stone barracks in the Garrison District. The adjacent 1828 Guard House was also unpleasant (plank beds, thin straw mattresses), but the conditions for those held in cells were truly nasty. Threaten your kids! The lower section of the barracks is now used as artisan studios.

Old Loyalist Burial Ground   CEMETERY
(Brunswick St at Carleton St; ⊘8am-9pm) This Loyalist cemetery, dating back to 1784, is an atmospheric, thought-provoking history lesson of its own, revealing large families and kids dying tragically young. The Loyalists arrived from the 13 colonies after the American Revolution of 1776.

Christ Church Cathedral   CHURCH
(www.christchurchcathedral.com; off Queen St at Church St; admission free) Built in 1853, this cathedral is a fine early example of the 19th-century revival of decorated Gothic architecture and has exquisite stained glass. It was modeled after St Mary's in Snettisham, Norfolk.

🏃 Activities

Small Craft Aquatic Centre   BOATING
(off Woodstock Rd; ⊘mid-May–early Oct) This small center, on the St John River beside Old Government House, rents out canoes, kayaks and rowboats at $10 an hour. On offer are weekly passes, guided canoe and kayak tours, one-hour to three-day river ecology trips, and instruction in either canoeing or kayaking.

Lighthouse on the Green   HIKING, BIKING
(cnr Regent St & St Anne Point Dr) There are 70km of recreational trails around town and along the river that either begin or intersect at this riverfront lighthouse, which doubles as an info center and small museum. Pick up a map inside. In summer, enjoy

weekend concerts and Wednesday night yoga on the lighthouse deck.

Tours

Heritage Walking Tours (free; ☉10am, 2:30pm & 5pm daily Jul-Oct) Enthusiastic young people wearing historic costumes lead good, free hour-long tours of the river, the government district or the Historic Garrison District, departing from City Hall.

Haunted Hikes (adult/child $13/8; ☉9:15pm Mon-Sat Jul-Aug) Given by the same, suddenly ghoulish thespians; depart from the Coach House at 796a Queen St.

✿ Festivals & Events

NotaBle Acts Summer Theatre Festival (www.nbacts.com; ☉end Jul-early Aug) Showcases new and noted playwrights with street and theater presentations.

Harvest Jazz & Blues Festival (www.harvestjazzandblues.com; ☉early Sep) Weeklong event transforms the downtown area into the 'New Orleans of the North' when jazz, blues and Dixieland performers arrive from across North America.

Silver Wave Film Festival (www.swfilmfest.com; ☉early Nov) Three days of New Brunswick, Canadian and international films and lectures organized by the NB Filmmaker's Cooperative.

⌂ Sleeping

There are a number of budget and midrange motels on the Fredericton Bypass and parallel Prospect St.

TOP CHOICE Carriage House Inn B&B **$$** (☎506-452-9924, 800-267-6068; www.carriagehouse-inn.net; 230 University Ave; r with breakfast $99-129; P⊖❀🛜) In a shady Victorian neighborhood near the Green, this beautifully restored 1875 Queen Anne was built for a lumber baron and former Fredericton mayor. The grand common room has polished hardwood floors, antiques, comfy sofas, fireplaces and a grand piano. Upstairs, the guest rooms have high ceilings, four-posters, period wallpapers and vintage artwork. There is a deep verandah for lounging. The friendly owners are happy to give local tips.

Brennan's B&B B&B **$$** (☎506-455-7346; www.bbcanada.com/3892.html; 146 Waterloo St; r incl breakfast $95-135; P⊖❀@) Built for a wealthy merchant family in 1885, this turreted white riverfront mansion is now a handsome four-room B&B. The better rooms have hardwood floors and water views.

Crowne Plaza Lord Beaverbrook

HOTEL **$$$**

(☎506-455-3371; www.cpfredericton.com; 659 Queen St; r $120-260; P❀🛜🏊) Always bustling with weddings, conventions and business travelers, this 1948 downtown hotel is another one of Lord Beaverbrook's legacies to the city. The lobby has a touch of vintage glamour, and the 168 rooms are modern and comfortable. Check out the beaver mosaics on the facade.

Town and Country Motel MOTEL **$** (☎506-454-4223; 967 Woodstock Rd; s & d $90, tw $100; P❀) In a quiet riverside setting, you'll find sparkling clean and bright modern rooms with kitchenettes and big picture windows framing a gorgeous view of the river. It's on the walking/cycling path 3km west from the city center.

Fredericton International Hostel HOSTEL **$** (☎506-450-4417; fredericton@hihostels.ca; 621 Churchill Row; r HI members/nonmembers $25/30; ☉office 7am-noon & 6-10pm; P⊖@) This dark, rambling residence hall is part university student housing, part travelers' lodging. The big, slightly creepy basement has a laundry and pool tables.

✕ Eating

For a small city, Fredericton offers a wide, cosmopolitan cross-section of restaurants, most in the walkable downtown.

WW Boyce Farmers' Market

FARMERS MARKET **$**

(www.boycefarmersmarket.com; 665 George St; ☉6am-1pm Sat) This Fredericton institution is great for picking up fresh fruit, vegetables, meat, cheese, handicrafts, dessert and flowers. Many of the 150 or so stalls recall the city's European heritage, with everything from German-style sausages to French duck pâtés to British marmalade. There is also a restaurant where Frederictonians queue to chat and people-watch.

Racine's FUSION **$$$** (www.racinesrestaurant.ca; 536 Queen St; mains $17-33; ☉dinner) Faux leather tablecloths and touches of neon green lend an urban mod look to this trendy downtown bistro. The internationally influenced menu is heavy on seafood and grilled meats – Malpec oysters on the half-shell, curried crab cakes,

Szechuan-spiced duck, filet mignon with herb butter – all artfully displayed on white plates like abstract paintings.

Schnitzel Parlour — GERMAN $$$

(📞506-450-2520; www.facklemanschocolate heaven.com; 3136 Woodstock Rd; mains $19-22; ⊗dinner Tue-Wed & Fri-Sat, chocolate shop open from 11am) Specializing in hearty, old-fashioned German fare, this cozy countryside restaurant has richly spiced goulash (the secret ingredient is chocolate), wild boar stew and six kinds of schnitzel on homemade *spätzle* (soft egg noodles). BYOB wine. The on-site **Chocolaterie Fackleman** sells truffles and traditional central European tortes. The restaurant is about 8km west of town on Woodstock Rd.

Blue Door — FUSION $$$

(📞506-455-2583; www.thebluedoor.ca; 100 Regent St; mains $8-20; ⊗11:30am-10pm) This local hot spot serves upscale fusion dishes like gorgonzola bruschetta, maple-miso cod and chicken curry in a dim, urban-chic dining room. Retro cocktails like Singapore slings and Harvey Wallbangers are real favorites.

Caribbean Flavas — CARIBBEAN $$

(www.caribbeanflavas.ca; 123 York St; mains $16-23; ⊗lunch Mon-Fri, dinner Mon-Sat) A bright nook dishing up the tastes and colors of the Caribbean. Great for a casual, flavorful meal. No alcohol.

Chez Riz — INDIAN $$

(📞506-454-9996; 366 Queen St; mains $16-20; ⊗lunch Mon-Fri, dinner Mon-Sat) Delicious Indian and Pakistani cuisine in a darkly stylish, romantically lit cave of a place

Drinking

Fredericton has embraced coffee culture in several appealing venues. In the evenings, the bars, pubs and rooftop patios of King and Queen Sts come alive.

Garrison District Ale House — PUB

(www.thegarrison.ca; 426 Queen St; ⊗Mon-Sat) Dim lighting and a leather-and-wood decor make this popular Queen St pub feel like an old-school British hunting club. Preppy crowds munch burgers and sip a wide variety of craft brews.

Lunar Rogue Pub — PUB

(www.lunarrogue.com; 625 King St; ⊗daily) This jolly locals' joint has a good beer selection and a fine assortment of single malts. The patio is wildly popular during the warmer weather.

Second Cup — CAFE

(440 King St in Kings Place Mall; ⊗6:30am-10pm Mon-Sat, 9am-10pm Sun) Warm lighting, world beat music and the aroma of fresh roasted coffee beans draw a loyal clientele of office workers, passersby and aspiring novelists toiling away on their laptops.

Boom! Nightclub — NIGHTCLUB

(www.boomnightclub.ca; 474 Queen St; $5 cover charge; ⊗Wed-Sun) A hip gay bar and dance club welcoming folks of all stripes.

Trinitea's Cup — CAFE

(www.theatreinthecup.ca; 87 Regent St; ⊗8am-5:30pm Mon-Wed, to 8pm Thu-Sat, noon-5pm Sun) It's always 1955 inside this storefront tea parlor, serving traditional English cream teas, soups and sandwiches.

☆ Entertainment

For the scoop on concerts, art gallery openings and other happenings around town, pick up a copy of *here* (www.herenb.com), a free entertainment weekly available all over town.

Outdoor Summer Concerts — LIVE MUSIC

(www.tourismfredericton.ca; admission free; ⊗Tue-Fri & Sun) In summer, downtown venues from Officers' Sq to the Lighthouse on the Green feature live local music ranging from highland bagpipes and drums to country and blues. Check the website for schedules.

Playhouse — THEATER

(www.theplayhouse.nb.ca; 686 Queen St) The Playhouse stages concerts, theater, ballet and shows throughout the year.

ℹ Information

Dr Everett Chalmers Hospital (📞506-452-5400; 700 Priestman St)

Fredericton Public Library (12 Carleton St; ⊗10am-5pm Mon-Sat, to 9pm Wed & Fri) Free internet access is first-come, first-served.

Main Post Office (📞506-444-8602; 570 Queen St; ⊗8am-5pm Mon-Fri) General delivery mail addressed to Fredericton, NB E3B 4Y1, is kept here.

Police, Ambulance & Fire (📞911) For emergencies.

Visitors Center (📞506-460-2129, 888-888-4768; www.tourismfredericton.ca; City Hall, 397 Queen St; ⊗8am-4:15pm Mon-Fri Oct-May, longer hours in summer) Free city parking passes provided here.

ℹ️ Getting There & Away

AIR Fredericton International Airport (www.yfcmobile.ca) is on Hwy 102, 14km southeast of town. See p380 for flight details.

BUS The new **Acadian Lines Terminal** (www.acadianbus.com; 150 Woodside Lane) is a few kilometers southwest of downtown. Schedules and fares to some destinations include: Moncton ($44, 2¼ hours, two daily), Charlottetown, PEI ($68, 5½ hours, two daily), Bangor, Maine ($55, 7½ hours, one daily) and Saint John ($29, 1½ hours, two daily).

CAR & MOTORCYCLE Cars with out-of-province license plates are eligible for a free three-day parking pass for downtown Fredericton May to October, available at the Fredericton Tourism Office at 11 Carleton St. In-province visitors can get a one-day pass. Avis, Budget, Hertz and National car-rental agencies (see p886) all have desks at the airport.

ℹ️ Getting Around

A taxi to the airport costs $16. Bicycle rentals are available at **Radical Edge** (☎506-459-3478; www.radicaledge.ca; 386 Queen St; per hr/day $7.50/25).

The city has a decent bus system, **Fredericton Transit** (☎506-460-2200); tickets cost $2 and include free transfers. Service runs Monday through Saturday from 6:15am to 11pm. Most city bus routes begin at King's Place Mall, on King St between York and Carleton.

UPPER ST JOHN RIVER VALLEY

The St John River rises in the US state of Maine, then winds along the western border of the province past forests and beautiful lush farmland, drifts through Fredericton between tree-lined banks and flows around flat islands between rolling hills before emptying into the Bay of Fundy 700km later. The broad river is the province's dominant feature and for centuries has been its major thoroughfare. The valley's soft, eye-pleasing landscape makes for scenic touring by car, or by bicycle on the Trans Canada Trail (see p840), which follows the river for most of its length.

Two automobile routes carve through the valley: the quicker Trans-Canada Hwy (Hwy 2), mostly on the west side of the river, and the more scenic old Hwy 105 on the east side, which meanders through many villages. Branching off from the valley are Hwy 17 (at St Léonard) and Rte 385 (at Perth-Andover), which cut northeast through the Appalachian highlands and lead to rugged Mt Carleton Provincial Park.

King's Landing Historical Settlement

One of the province's best sites is this worthwhile recreation of an early-19th century **Loyalist village** (☎506-363-4999; www.kingslanding.nb.ca; adult/child/family $16/11/38; ⊙10am-5pm mid-Jun–mid-Oct), 36km west of Fredericton. A community of 100 costumed staff create a living museum by role-playing in 11 houses, a school, church, store and sawmill typical of those used a century ago, providing a glimpse and taste of pioneer life in the Maritimes. Demonstrations and events are staged throughout the day and horse-drawn carts shunt visitors around. The prosperous Loyalist life reflected here can be tellingly compared to that at the Acadian Historic Village in Caraquet (p418). The **King's Head Inn**, a mid-1800s pub, serves traditional food and beverages, with a nice authentic touch – candlelight. The children's programs make King's Landing ideal for families, and special events occur regularly. It's not hard to while away a good half-day or more here.

About 10km south, busy, resortlike **Mactaquac Provincial Park** (day use per vehicle $7) has swimming, fishing, hiking, picnic sites, camping, boat rentals and a huge **campground** (☎506-363-4747; 1256 Hwy 105; tent/RV sites $22/24; ⊙late-May–mid-Oct).

Hartland

This tiny country hamlet has the granddaddy of New Brunswick's many wooden covered bridges. The photogenic 390m-long **Hartland covered bridge** over the St John River was erected in 1897 and is a national historic site. The picnic tables overlooking the river and the bridge at the tourist information center are five-star lunch spots (fixings at the grocery store across the road). Otherwise, the village has a rather forlorn atmosphere.

Rebecca Farm B&B (☎506-375-1699; 656 Rockland Rd; d incl breakfast $100-130; P🍴❄🅿), about 4km from the town center, is a scrupulously maintained 19th-century farmhouse that sits in the midst of gorgeously hilly potato fields.

The main Hwy (Rte 7) between the capital and the port city of Saint John barrels south through a vast expanse of trees, trees and more trees. A far more scenic route (albeit about twice as long) follows the gentle, meandering St John River through rolling farmland and a couple of historic villages down to the Fundy coast.

Start on the north side of the river in Fredericton, and follow Rte 105 south through Maugerville to Jemseg. At Exit 339, pick up Rte 715 South which will take you to the **Gagetown ferry landing** (admission free; ☺24hr year-round). This is the first of a system of eight free cable ferries that crisscross the majestic St John River en route to the city of Saint John. You will never have to wait more than a few minutes for the crossing, which generally takes five to 10 minutes.

When you reach the opposite bank, head north a couple of miles to visit the pretty 18th-century village of **Gagetown** – well worth a look-see. Front St is lined with craft studios and shops and a couple of inviting cafes. Stop into the excellent **Queen's County Museum** (69 Front St; admission $2; ☺10am-5pm mid-May–mid-Jun) housed in Sir Leonard Tilley's childhood home, built in 1736. The top-notch staff will show you through the exhibits spanning pre-colonial aboriginal history in the area, 18th-century settler life, and up to WWII. **Gagetown Cider Company** (☎506-488-2147; 127 Fox Rd; ☺1-6pm) offers tours by appointment.

Explore scenic Gagetown Creek by boat. **Village Boatique** (☎877-488-1992; 50 Front St) has canoe/kayak rentals for $10/15 per hour, $50/75 per day. Homey **Step-Aside Inn** (☎506-488-1808; stepamau@nbnet.nb.ca; 58 Front St; s/d incl breakfast $80/95; ☺May-Dec; ✿❀☎) has four bright rooms with views of the river. To eat, grab a smoked meat sandwich and a beer at the **Old Boot Pub** (48 Front St; ☺lunch & dinner) on the riverfront.

From Gagetown, head south on Rte 102, known locally as 'the Old River Road,' denoting its status as the major thoroughfare up the valley in the kinder, simpler era between the decline of the river steamboats and the construction of the modern, divided highway. The grand old farmhouses and weathered hay barns dotted at intervals along the valley belong to that earlier age. The hilly 42km piece of road between Gagetown and the ferry landing at **Evandale** (admission free; ☺24hr year-round) is especially picturesque, with glorious panoramic views of fields full of wildflowers, white farm houses and clots of green and gold islands set in the intensely blue water of the river.

A hundred years ago, tiny Evandale was a bustling little place, where a dance band would entertain riverboat passengers stopping off for the night at the **Evandale Resort** (☎506-468-2222; ferry landing; r $120-190), than restored to its Victorian grandeur with six rooms and a fine-dining restaurant. On the other side of the water, Rte 124 takes you the short distance to the **Belleisle ferry** (admission free; ☺24hr year-round). The ferry deposits you on the rural Kingston Peninsula, where you can cross the peninsula to catch the **Gondola Point Ferry** (admission free; ☺24hr year-round) and head directly into Saint John.

Florenceville & Around

The tidy and green riverside village of Florenceville is ground zero of the global french fry industry. It's home to the McCain Foods frozen foods empire, which is sustained by the thousands of hectares of potato farms that surround it in every direction. Started by the McCain brothers in 1957 and still owned by the family, the company produces one-third of the world's french fry supply at its Florenceville factory and 54 like it worldwide. That adds up to one million pounds of chips churned out every hour and $5.8 billion in annual net sales.

Worth a stop is the **Potato World Museum** (www.potatoworld.ca; Rte 110; regular tour adult/child $5/4, experiential tour $10/8; ☺9am-6pm Mon-Fri Jun-Aug, to 5pm Sat & Sun, 9am-5pm Mon-Fri Sep & Oct). It's a cheesy name, but the museum is a tasteful, top-class interactive exposition of the history of the humble potato in these parts and its continuing centrality to the provincial economy. In this

MOOSE ON THE LOOSE

Every year, there are around 300 collisions involving moose on the roads in New Brunswick. These accidents are almost always fatal for the animal and about five people a year die this way. Eighty-five percent of moose-vehicle collisions happen between May and October and most occur at night. Slow down when driving after dusk and scan the verges for animals, using your high beams when there is no oncoming traffic. High-risk zones are posted.

area, school kids are still given two weeks off in the autumn to help bring in the harvest. The museums' new experiential tour lets you get your hands dirty – literally – by planting potato seeds and cutting your own french fries. If all the spud talk leaves you peckish, slip into a potato barrel chair at the on-site **Harvest Cafe** (lunch $5-7; ⊙11am-4pm Mon-Fri). The museum is 2km off Hwy 2 at Exit 152 toward Centreville on Rte 110.

Just outside Florenceville is the **Tannaghtyn B&B** (📞506-392-6966/866-399-6966; www.tannaghtyn.ca; 4169 Rte 103 off Rte 110, Connell; r incl breakfast $95-140; P❋☎), set high on a ridge with a spectacular view of the St John River and the green and gold patchwork of farms on the opposite side. Both stylish and cozy, the house is furnished with dramatic Canadian art, comfy sofas, beds made up with linens dried in the fresh country air, and there's a hot tub under the stars. Besides the Harvest Cafe, Florenceville has a half-dozen middle-of-the-road restaurants serving three meals a day.

Acadian Lines (www.acadianbus.com; 8738 Main St) buses stop at the Irving gas station in Florenceville.

Mt Carleton Provinvial Park & the Tobique Valley

From his workshop on the forested banks of the Tobique River at the foot of Mt Carleton, Nictau canoe-maker Bill Miller rhapsodizes that 'If you telephone heaven, it's a local call.' He may be right.

The 17,427-hectare **provincial park** offers visitors a wilderness of mountains, valleys, rivers and wildlife including moose, deer, bear and, potentially, the 'extinct' but regularly seen eastern cougar. The main feature of the park is a series of rounded glaciated peaks and ridges, including Mt Carleton, which at 820m is the Maritimes' highest. This range is an extension of the Appalachian Mountains, which begin in the US state of Georgia and end in Québec. Mt Carleton is little known and relatively unvisited, even in midsummer. It could be the province's best-kept secret.

The park is open from mid-May to October; entry is free. Hunting and logging are prohibited in the park, and all roads are gravel-surfaced. The nearest town is **Riley Brook**, 30km away, so bring all food and a full tank of gas.

🏃 Activities
Canoeing
The Mt Carleton area boasts superb wilderness canoeing. In the park itself, the Nictau and Nepisiguit chains of lakes offer easy day-tripping through a landscape of tree-clad mountains. For experienced canoeists, the shallow and swift Little Tobique River rises at Big Nictau Lake, winding in tight curls through dense woods until it joins the Tobique itself at Nictau. The more remote Nepisiguit River flows out of the Nepisiguit Lakes through the wilderness until it empties into the Bay of Chaleur at Bathurst, over 100km away.

The lower reaches of the Tobique, from Nictau, through minute Riley Brook and down to Plaster Rock is a straight, easy paddle through forest and meadow that gives way to farmland as the valley broadens, with a couple of waterfront campgrounds along the way. The easy 10km between Nictau and the Bear's Lair landing in Riley Brook makes for a relaxing afternoon paddle.

Don McAskill at **Bear's Lair** (📞506-356-8351; www.bearslairhunting.com; 3349 Rte 385, Riley Brook) has boats for $40 a day and can provide expert knowledge on canoeing in these parts. He also offers a shuttle service between your put-in and take-out point (eg boat delivery to Mt Carleton Provincial Park and transport of your vehicle down to Riley Brook is $45). In the park, **Guildo Martel** (📞506-235-2499) rents canoes and kayaks for the day on the edge of Big Nictau Lake at Armstrong Campground.

Fiddles on the Tobique (506-356-2409; late Jun) is a weekend festival held annually in Nictau and Riley Brook. It is a magical idea: a round of community hall suppers, jam sessions and concerts culminating in a Sunday afternoon floating concert down the Tobique River from Nictau to Riley Brook. Upward of 800 canoes and kayaks join the flotilla each year – some stocked with musicians, some just with paddlers – and 8000 spectators line the river banks to watch. By some accounts, the event has been damaged by its own popularity, devolving into a boisterous booze cruise. Others call it a grand party and good fun.

On land, **Bill Miller** (506-356-2409; www.millercanoes.com; 4160 Rte 385, Nictau) welcomes visitors to his cluttered canoe-making workshop in Nictau (population 12), where he and his father and grandfather before him have handcrafted wooden canoes since 1922. Also worth a stop is the **Tobique Salmon Barrier** (admission free; 9am-5pm), signposted from the road at Nictau, located at the confluence of the Little Tobique and Campbell Rivers. There is a spectacular view from the Department of Fisheries office situated on a bluff overlooking the water. From here, officers keep a 24-hour watch on the Atlantic salmon, which are trucked up by road from below the Mactaquac Dam at Fredericton and held here until spawning time, in order to protect their dwindling numbers from poachers.

Hiking

The best way to explore Mt Carleton is on foot. The park has a 62km network of trails, most of them are loops winding to the handful of rocky knobs that are the peaks. The International Appalachian Trail (IAT; see p304) passes through here.

The easiest peak to climb is Mt Bailey; a 7.5km loop trail to the 564m hillock begins near the day-use area. Most hikers can walk this route in three hours. The highest peak is reached via the Mt Carleton Trail, a 10km route that skirts over the 820m knob, where there's a fire tower. Plan on three to four hours for the trek and pack your parka; the wind above the tree line can be brutal.

The most challenging hike is the Sagamook Trail, a 6km loop to a 777m peak with superlative vistas of Nictau Lake and the highlands area to the north of it; allow three hours for this trek. The Mountain Head Trail connects the Mt Carleton and Sagamook Trails, making a long transit of the range possible.

All hikers intending to follow any long trails must register at the visitors center or park headquarters before hitting the trail. Outside the camping season (mid-May to mid-September), you should call ahead to make sure the main gate will be open, as the Mt Carleton trailhead is 13.5km from the park entrance. Otherwise park your car at the entrance and walk in – the Mt Bailey trailhead is only 2.5km from the gate.

WORLD CLASS (POND) HOCKEY

As anyone who has been in the country for more than five minutes knows, Canadians love their hockey. For many, this affection (obsession?) is wrapped up in happy childhood memories of bright winter afternoons chasing a puck up and down a frozen pond or backyard rink.

Every February, the small forest town of Plaster Rock (population 1200), 84km from Mt Carleton, hosts the **World Pond Hockey Tournament** (www.worldpond hockey.com; Rte 109, Plaster Rock; admission free; 2nd week Feb). Twenty rinks are plowed on Roulston Lake, which is ringed by tall evergreens, hot-chocolate stands and straw-bale seating for the 8000-odd spectators drawn to the four-day event. The tournament is wildly popular, with 120 amateur four-person teams traveling in from places as far flung as England, Egypt and the Cayman Islands. Anyone can register to play, but they will have to defeat the Boston Danglers, who scrambled over squads like the Skateful Dead, the Raggedy Ass River Boys and the Boiled Owls to put a lock on the championship trophy several years running.

If you want to play, register early. If you want to watch, pack your long johns and a toque (wool hat) and book your accommodations early. If the motels are full, the organizers keep a list of local folks willing to billet out-of-towners in their homes for the weekend.

🛏 Sleeping & Eating

There is lodging, a general store, gas station and restaurant in Riley Brook. The park has four public-use **campgrounds** (☑506-235-0793; www.friendsofmountcarleton.ca). In addition to Armstrong Brook (p390), there are the semiwilderness campgrounds of Franquelin and Williams Brook, with outhouses and fire pits (bring your own water), and the ultraremote Headwaters campground on the slopes of Mt Carleton.

The town of Plaster Rock, situated 54km downriver toward the Trans-Canada Hwy (Rte 385), also has several serviceable motels and a couple of casual restaurants.

TOP CHOICE **Bear's Lair** INN $
(☑506-356-8351; www.bearslairhunting.com; 3349 Rte 385, Riley Brook; r $60; P⛱) If any place in the province captures the essence of life in the north woods, this is it. A cozy log hunting lodge set on the banks of the Tobique River, it is busiest during fall hunting season, but is also a supremely relaxing base for hikers, canoeists and wildlife enthusiasts. The high-ceilinged main lodge is adorned with numerous taxidermied specimens and photographs of happy hunters and fishers with the one that didn't get away. There is also a pool table, big-screen TV, floor-to-ceiling stone fireplace, a few dining tables and huge picture windows framing a serene view of the river slipping by just a few meters away. The cozy log-walled guest rooms are spick and span and nicely accented with plaid fabrics. A long, deep verandah invites lounging after dinner. The lodge's friendly owners offer meals (great homemade pie for dessert), canoe/ kayak rentals and guided hunting trips.

Armstrong Brook Campground

CAMPGROUND $
(☑506-235-0793; tent & RV sites $9-14; ⊙mid-May–Oct) The park's largest campground has 89 sites nestled among the pines on the north side of Nictau Lake, 3km from the entrance. It has toilets, showers and a kitchen shelter, but no sites with hookups. RV drivers often have their noisy generators running, so tenters should check out the eight tent-only sites along Armstrong Brook on the north side of the campground.

ℹ️ Information

At the entrance to the park is a **visitors center** (☑506-235-0793; www.friendsofmountcarleton. ca; off Rte 385; ⊙8am-8pm daily May-Oct) for maps and information. There is also another **office** (☑506-235-6040; dnr.Mt.carleton@gnb.ca; 11 Gagnon St), the park headquarters, in St Quentin.

Grand Falls

With a drop of around 25m and a 1.6km-long gorge with walls as high as 80m, the falls merit a stop in this otherwise un-scenic town. The Grand Falls are best in spring or after heavy rain. In summer, much of the water is diverted for generating hydroelectricity, yet the gorge is appealing any time.

In the middle of town, overlooking the falls, the **Malabeam Reception Centre** (25 Madawaska Rd; admission free; ⊙10am-6pm May, Jun & Sep, 9am-9pm Jul & Aug) doubles as a tourist office. Among the displays is a scale model of the gorge showing its extensive trail system.

A 253-step stairway down into the gorge begins at **La Rochelle** (1 Chapel St; tour adult/ child $4/2, self-guided tour per family $5; ⊙mid-May–mid-Oct), across the bridge from the Malabeam Reception Centre and left on Victoria St. Boats maneuver for 45-minute trips (adult/family $11/27) up the gorge. These run up to eight times a day but only in midsummer when water levels are low (it's too dangerous when the river is in full flood). Buy the boat ticket at La Rochelle first, as it includes the stairway to the base of the gorge.

There are dramatically situated tent and RV sites at the **Falls and Gorge Campground** (☑877-475-7769; 1 Chapel St; unserviced/serviced sites $18/25; ⊙Jun–mid-Sep). **Côté's** (☑877-444-2683; www.cotebb-inn.com; 575 Broadway Blvd West; r with breakfast $95-175) is a homey, five-room B&B with a patio and hot tub. **Le Grand Saut** (www.legrand sautristorante.com; 155 Broadway Blvd; mains $11-22; ⊙lunch & dinner), a popular, two-tiered spot with an inviting deck out front, serves up salads, pastas, pizzas and steaks.

Acadian Lines (www.acadianbus.com; 555 Madawaska Rd) buses stop at the Esso station, just west of downtown. Hwy 108 (known locally as the Renous Hwy) cuts across the province through Plaster Rock to the east coast, slicing through forest for nearly its entirety. It is most tedious, but fast. Watch out for deer and moose.

Edmundston

Working-class Edmundston, with a large paper mill, a utilitarian town center and a mainly bilingual French citizenry, doesn't bother much with tourism. Nevertheless, it makes a convenient stopover for those traveling east from Québec. The first port of call for most folks is the **Provincial Tourist Office** (Hwy 2; ☉10am-6pm late-May–early Oct, 8am-9pm Jul & Aug) about 20km north at the Québec border. Halfway between the border and Edmundston in the small community of St Jacques is the **New Brunswick Botanical Garden** (www.jardinbotaniquenb. com; off Rte 2; adult/child $14/7; ☉9am-6pm May-Sep, to 8pm Jul & Aug). Here there are 80,000 plants to brighten your day, all accompanied by classical music! Kids might prefer the neat temporary exhibitions, such as a butterfly garden. Edmundston is the eastern terminus of the **Petis Témis Interprovincial Linear Park** (www.petit-temis.com, in French), a 134km cycling/hiking trail between Edmundston and Rivière-du-Loup, Québec. It follows an old railbed along the Madawaska River and the shores of Lake Témiscouata, passing by several small villages and campgrounds along the way.

Get out of gritty Edmundston and sleep next to the botanical gardens at **Auberge Les Jardins** (☏506-739-5514; www.lesjardins inn.com; 60 Rue Principale, St Jacques; r $79-180; ☎☒), a gracious inn whose 17 rooms are each decorated with a different Canadian flower or tree theme. There's also a modern motel in back, and a wood-and-stained-glass **dining room** that's considered one of the best restaurants in the province (check out the fabulous wine list). Several motels line the highway and old Hwy 2 (Blvd Acadie). For eats, head to **Bei Ali** (☏506 739 3329; 174 Victoria St, cnr Blvd Hébert; mains $6-14; ☉24hr). A city landmark since the 1950s, this is a total classic right down to the seasoned, uniformed waitresses. The you-name-it menu includes acceptable Italian, Chinese, seafood and basic Canadian fare.

Acadian Lines (www.acadianbus.com; 191 Victoria St) buses depart from the downtown bus terminal.

WESTERN FUNDY SHORE

Almost the entire southern edge of New Brunswick is presided over by the ever-present, constantly rising and falling, always impressive waters of the Bay of Fundy.

The resort town of St Andrews By-The-Sea, the serene Fundy Isles, fine seaside scenery and rich history make this easily one of the most appealing regions of the province. Whale-watching is a thrilling area activity. Most commonly seen are the fin, humpback and minke, and less so, the increasingly rare right whale. Porpoises and dolphins are plentiful. And let's not overlook the seafood – it's bountiful and delicious.

St Stephen

Right on the US border across the river from Calais, Maine, St Stephen is a busy entry point with small-town charm and one tasty attraction. It is home to Ganong, a family-run chocolate business operating since 1873, whose products are known around eastern Canada. The five-cent chocolate nut bar was invented by the Ganong brothers in 1910, and they can also be credited with developing the heart-shaped box of chocolates seen everywhere on Valentine's Day.

The **tourist office** (cnr Milltown Blvd & King St; ☉10am-6pm Jun & Sep, 8am-9pm Jul & Aug) is in the former train station. The old Ganong chocolate factory on the town's main street is now the **Chocolate Museum** (www. chocolatemuseum.ca; 73 Milltown Blvd; adult/ child/family $7/6/22; ☉9:30am-6:30pm Mon-Sat, 11am-3pm Sun Jul-early Sep, 10am-5pm Mon-Fri Mar-Jun, 10am-4pm Mon-Fri Sep-Nov), with tasteful (and tasty) interactive displays of everything from antique chocolate boxes to manufacturing equipment. The adjacent shop (open daily year-round) sells boxes of Ganong hand-dipped chocolates and is free to visit. Try the iconic chicken bone (chocolate-filled cinnamon sticks) or the old-fashioned Pal-O-Mine candy bar. The museum also offers a **guided heritage walking tour** (adult/child/family $13/10/40) of St Stephen from mid-May to mid-October. Once a year, during **Chocolate Fest** (www.chocolate -fest.ca; ☉1st week Aug), the town celebrates all things chocolate with a parade, tours of the factory with unlimited sampling of the goods, and games for the kids.

There are five very comfortable rooms complemented by a quiet garden at **Blair House** (☏506-466-2233, 888-972-5247; www. blairhouseinn.nb.ca; 38 Prince William St; s incl breakfast $75-100, d $80-109; ☒☺☀☎), a fabulous Victorian home. You can walk the main street easily from here. There are also a few run-down motels on the outskirts of town if you are desperate.

Home cooking is served up at **Carman's Diner** (☑506-466-3528; 164 King St; mains $4-16; ☺7am-10pm), a 1960s throwback with counter stools and jukeboxes (that sometimes work) at the tables.

The Red Rooster Country Store doubles as the **Acadian Lines** (www.acadianbus.com; Hwy 1 at 5 Old Bay Rd) bus stop, 4km east of town. There's daily service to Saint John ($29), which connects to Moncton ($55) and Halifax ($88). There's also a daily bus to Bangor ($38), but you have to purchase tickets in person. In Bangor, immediate connections are available to Boston and New York.

Across the border in Calais, Maine, **West's Coastal Connection** (☑800-596-2823) buses connect to Bangor. They usually leave from Carmen's Hometown Pizzeria on Main St, but call ahead to confirm. In Bangor, buses use the Greyhound terminal and connect to Bangor airport. Greyhound passes cannot be used from Calais.

St Andrews By-The-Sea

St Andrews is a genteel summer resort town. Blessed with a fine climate and picturesque beauty, it also has a colorful history. Founded by Loyalists in 1783, it's one of the oldest towns in the province. Busy with holidaymakers and summer residents in July and August, the rest of the year there are more seagulls than people.

The town sits on a peninsula pointing southward into the Bay of Fundy. Its main drag, Water St, is lined with restaurants and souvenir and craft shops.

◉ Sights

Huntsman Aquarium AQUARIUM
(www.huntsmanmarine.ca; 1 Lower Campus Rd; adult/child $5/3; ☺10am-5pm mid-May–late Sep) Part of the independent not-for-profit Huntsman Marine Science Research Centre, this popular aquarium was in temporary digs during the time of research while a newer, bigger aquatic center was being built. The aquarium features most specimens that are found in local waters, including seals (feedings at 11am and 4pm) and sharks. Kids love the touch pool. The research center also offers week-long summer field courses for amateur enthusiasts (both students and adults).

Minister's Island HISTORICAL BUILDING
(www.ministersisland.ca; adult/child $15/10; ☺May-Oct) This picturesque tidal island was once used as a summer retreat by William Cornelius Van Horne, builder of the Canadian Pacific Railway and one of Canada's wealthiest men. Covenhoven, his splendid 50-room Edwardian cottage, is now open to visitors – check out the towerlike stone bathhouse, the tidal swimming pool and the chateau-like barn. The island can be visited at low tide, when you can drive (or walk, or bike) on the hard-packed sea floor. A few hours later it's 3m under water. Be careful! During high tide, a ferry departs from Bar Rd. To get to Minister's Island from downtown St Andrews, follow 127 north for about 1km and then turn right on Bar Rd.

WORTH A TRIP

CHIPUTNETICOOK LAKES

Tucked away on New Brunswick's southwest border with the USA state of Maine is a little-known but spectacular chain of wilderness lakes. Stretching for 180km along the international border, the forest-ringed Chiputneticook Lakes offer canoeing enthusiasts the chance to slip away into the wild for a few weeks. The nonprofit **St Croix International Waterway Commission** (www.stcroix.org; 5 Rte 1, St Stephen) maintains a network of backcountry campsites on the islands and lakeshores along the chain and publishes a detailed map of the waterway ($10). It includes the St Croix River, a popular three- to four-day paddling route beginning south of the lakes. There are a couple of fishing lodges on Palfrey Lake accessible via Rte 630. Day-trippers can use the scenic lakeshore campsites at **Spednik Lake Provincial Park** (free; maintained by volunteers) where there is a hiking trail through the woods, primitive toilets and fire rings. Bring your own water. Take Rte 3 north from St Stephen then bear left on Rte 630 to reach the park gate. Canoe rentals are available in Saint John and Fredericton. Note: the lakes are not patrolled by the park service, and paddlers should be experienced and well-equipped.

Kingsbrae Garden
GARDEN

(www.kingsbraegarden.com; 220 King St; adult/senior & student/family $12/9/28, plus $2 per person for a personal guided tour; ⊙9am-6pm mid-May–mid-Oct) Extensive, multihued Kingsbrae Garden is considered one of the best horticultural displays in Canada. Check out the wollemi pine, one of the world's oldest and rarest trees.

Sunbury Shores Arts & Nature Centre
ART GALLERY, ART CLASSES

(www.sunburyshores.org; 139 Water St; admission free; ⊙9am-4:30pm Mon-Fri, noon-4pm Sat year-round, noon-4pm Sun May-Sep) This nonprofit educational and cultural center offers courses in painting, weaving, pottery and other crafts for a day, weekend or week, as well as natural science seminars. Various changing exhibits run through summer.

St Andrews Blockhouse
HISTORICAL BUILDING

(Joe's Point Rd; admission free; ⊙9am-8pm Jun-Aug, 9am-5pm early Sep) The restored wooden Blockhouse Historic Site is the only one left of several that were built here for protection in the war of 1812. If the tide is out, there's a path that extends from the blockhouse out across the tidal flats.

Sheriff Andrew House
HISTORICAL BUILDING

(cnr King & Queen Sts; admission by donation; ⊙9:30am-4:30pm Mon-Sat, 1-4:30pm Sun Jul-Sep) This 1820 neoclassical home has been restored to look like a middle-class home in the 1800s, attended by costumed guides.

Atlantic Salmon Interpretive Centre
MUSEUM, AQUARIUM

(www.salarstream.ca; Chamcook Lake No 1 Rd off Rte 127; adult/student/child $5/4/3; ⊙9am-5pm) This handsome lodge has an in-stream aquarium, offers guided tours and shows displays devoted to the life and trials of the endangered wild Atlantic salmon, once so plentiful in provincial rivers and bays.

🏃 Activities

Eastern Outdoors
BIKING, KAYAKING

(☎506-529-4662; www.easternoutdoors.com; 165 Water St; mountain bike rentals per hr/day $20/35, kayak rentals per day $55; ⊙mid-May–Oct) This St Andrews-based outfitter offers sea-kayak trips ranging from two-hour sunset paddles ($39) to multiday camping expeditions ($99 per day).

Twin Meadows Walking Trail
WALKING

The 800m Twin Meadows Walking Trail, a boardwalk and footpath through fields and woodlands, begins opposite 165 Joe's Point Rd beyond the blockhouse.

👉 Tours

Several companies offering boat trips and whale-watching cruises have offices by the wharf at the foot of King St. They're open from mid-June to early September. The cruises, which cost about $55, do take in the lovely coast seabirds are commonplace and seeing whales is the norm. The ideal waters for watching these beasts are further out in the bay, however, so if you're heading for the Fundy Isles, do your trip there.

Jolly Breeze
(☎506-529-8116; www.jollybreeze.com; adult/child $53/38; ⊙tours 9am, 12:45pm, 4:30pm mid-Jun–Oct) Antique-style tall ship that sails around Passamaquoddy Bay looking for seals and whales.

Quoddy Link Marine
(☎506-529-2600; adult/child $55/35; ⊙tours 1-3 times daily late Jun-Oct) Serious whale-watchers should hop aboard this catamaran, staffed by trained marine biologists.

🛏 Sleeping

🔝 Rossmount Inn
INN $$

(☎506-529-3351; www.rossmountinn.com; 4599 Rte 127; r incl breakfast $112-138; ⊙Apr-Dec; ❋) Flags flap in the breeze in front of this stately yellow summer cottage, perched atop a manicured slope overlooking Passamaquoddy Bay. Inside, the 18 rooms have a stylish mix of antiques and modern decor, with hand-carved wooden furniture and snowy white linens. Many people consider the hotel restaurant to be the town's best. Rossmount Inn is about 3km north of downtown St Andrews on Rte 127.

Fairmont Algonquin Hotel
HOTEL $$$

(☎506-529-8823, 888-270-1189; www.fairmont.com/algonquin; 184 Adolphus St; r $159-459; ❋❋❋❋) The doyenne of New Brunswick hotels, this Tudor-style 'Castle-by-the-Sea' has sat on a hill overlooking town since 1889. With its elegant verandah, gardens, rooftop terrace, golf course, spa and tennis courts, it's worth a look even if you're not spending the night. Note the doormen dressed in kilts. There are a couple of places for a drink, be it high tea or gin.

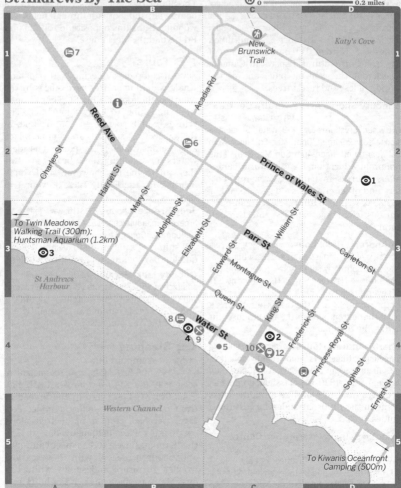

Picket Fence Motel   MOTEL **$**
(⌨506-529-8985; www.picketfencenb.com; 102 Reed Ave; s/d $75/85; ✳🛜) Modern, neat-as-a-pin motel rooms within walking distance of the main drag. Ultrafriendly management to boot.

Treadwell Inn   B&B **$$$**
(⌨506-529-1011, 888-529-1011; www.treadwellinn.com; 129 Water St; r incl breakfast $145-250; 🌐✳🛜) Big, handsome rooms in an 1820 ship chandler's house, some with private decks and ocean views.

Kiwanis Oceanfront Camping

CAMPGROUND **$**
(⌨877-393-7070; www.kiwanisoceanfront camping.com; 550 Water St; tent/RV sites $31/38; ⏰early Apr–mid-Oct) Situated at the far eastern end of town on Indian Point, this is mainly a gravel parking area for trailers, although some grassy spots do exist.

✗ Eating

In keeping with its genteel atmosphere, St Andrews has embraced the custom of afternoon cream tea. For lunch and dinner,

St Andrews By-The-Sea

there are a range of nice choices, mostly clustered around Water St.

Rossmount Inn Restaurant

NEW CANADIAN **$$$**

(☑506-529-3351; www.rossmountinn.com; 4599 Rte 127; mains $16-28; ☺dinner) The Swiss chef-owner makes wonderful use of local bounty in this warm, art-filled dining room. The ever-changing menu might include foraged goose tongue greens and wild mushrooms, periwinkles (a small shellfish) and New Brunswick lobster, each playing a part in complex, exquisite dishes. Imagine, say, lobster with nasturtium flower dumplings and vanilla bisque, or foie gras with cocoa nibs and bee balm–poached peach. Reservations crucial.

Clam Digger

SEAFOOD **$**

(4468 Hwy 127, Chamcook; mains $6-15; ☺lunch & dinner) Cars park three-deep outside this teeny red-and-white seafood shack, a summertime tradition in these parts. Order your clam platter or juicy, dripping cheeseburger, and claim one of the red-painted picnic tables. Don't forget an ice-cream cone! It's in Chamcook, about 9 km north of St Andrews.

Garden Cafe

CAFE **$$**

(www.kingsbraegarden.com; 220 King St; lunch $9-15, cream tea $13, plus admission to Kings-

brae Garden; ☺10am-6pm mid-May–mid-Oct) At Kingsbrae Garden (p393), the terrace cafe serves high tea and sandwiches and salads for lunch with a glass of wine or local ale.

Gables

SEAFOOD **$$$**

(☑506-529-3440; 143 Water St; mains $10-20; ☺8am-11pm Jul & Aug, 11am-9pm Sep & Jun) Seafood and views of the ocean through a row of tall windows dominate this comfortable place. To enter, head down the alley onto a gardenlike patio on the water's edge.

Sweet Harvest Market

CAFE **$**

(182 Water St; all items under $11; ☺8am-5pm Mon-Sat, 9am-3pm Sun) Cheerful counter staff create wholesome soups, salads, sandwiches and sweets that are way beyond average standard, and chowder that is truly outstanding. The coffee's good, too.

▼ Drinking

Afternoon cocktails at the Fairmont Algonquin are a must. In the evenings, several downtown pubs serve up beer, music and camaraderie.

Shiretown Pub

PUB

(www.kennedyinn.ca; 218 Water St; ☺11am-2am) On the ground floor of the delightfully creaky Kennedy Inn, this old-school English pub draws a mixed-age crowd of partiers. Early afternoons mean sipping New Brunswick–brewed Picaroon's bitter on the porch, while late nights bring live music and raucous karaoke.

Red Herring Pub

PUB

(211 Water St; ☺noon-2am daily) A fun, slightly divey downtown bar with pool tables, live music and frosty Canadian beers.

ℹ Information

The main **tourist office** (www.townofstandrews. ca; 46 Reed Ave; ☺8am-8pm Jul & Aug, 9am-5pm mid-May–Jun & Sep-early Oct) has free walking-tour brochures that include a map and brief description of 34 noteworthy places, and free internet access.

ℹ Getting There & Around

Acadian Lines (www.acadianbus.com) buses depart from the **HMS Transportation** (www. hmstrans.com; 260 Water St) building once daily for Saint John ($28) and once daily for Bangor, Maine ($38). HMS Transportation also rents cars ($60 per day with 200 free kilometers; you must arrange your own collision insurance coverage).

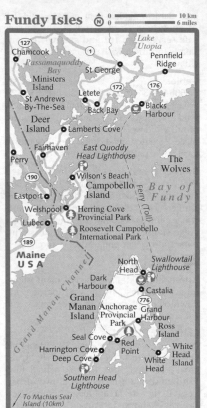
0   10 km
0   6 miles

Fundy Isles

NEW BRUNSWICK FUNDY ISLES

FUNDY ISLES

The thinly populated, unspoiled Fundy Isles are ideal for a tranquil, nature-based escape. With grand scenery, colorful fishing wharves tucked into coves, supreme whale-watching, uncluttered walking trails and steaming dishes of seafood, everyday stresses fade away and blood pressure eases. The three main islands each has a distinct personality. They offer a memorable, gradually absorbed peace. Out of the summer season, all are nearly devoid of visitors and most services are shut.

Deer Island

Deer Island, the closest of the three main Fundy Isles, is a modest fishing settlement with a lived-in look. The 16km-by-5km island has been inhabited since 1770, and 1000 people live here year-round. It's well

forested and deer are still plentiful. Lobster is the main catch and there are half a dozen wharves around the island.

Deer Island can be easily explored on a day trip. Narrow, winding roads run south down each side toward Campobello Island and the ferry (drive defensively).

◉ Sights & Activities

At Lamberts Cove is a huge lobster pound used to hold live lobster (it could well be the world's largest). Another massive pound squirms at Northern Harbor.

At the other end of the island is the 16-hectare Deer Island Point Park where Old Sow, the world's second-largest natural tidal whirlpool, is seen offshore a few hours before high tide. Whales pass occasionally.

At the end of Cranberry Head Rd is a deserted beach. Most land on the island is privately owned, so there are no hiking trails.

☞ Tours

Whales usually arrive in mid-June and stay until October. Ask at any motel or restaurant about seasonal whale watching tours.

Seascape Kayak Tours   KAYAKING
(☎506-747-1884,   866-747-1884;   www.seascapekayaktours.com; 40 NW Harbour Branch Rd, Richardson; half-/full-day trips $75/150) Guided paddling excursions around Deer Island and Passamaquoddy Bay. Multiday island-jumping camping trips also available.

☙ Sleeping & Eating

Sunset Beach Cottage & Suites   INN **$$**
(☎506-747-2972; www.cottageandsuites.com; 21 Cedar Grove Rd, Fairhaven; r from $80, cottage from $120; ☺May-Oct; ☒) On a secluded cove, this two-story unit has five tidy, basic suites with carpet and unstylish plaid bedding. Upper floors have better views. The private barbecues and the pool and hot tub overlooking the bay are major draws. The furnished cottage is nice for families.

45th Parallel Motel & Restaurant
                       MOTEL, SEAFOOD **$**
(☎506-747-2222; www.45thparallel.ca; 941 Hwy 772, Fairhaven; mains $6-25; ☺7:30am-9pm Jul & Aug, 11am-7pm May-Jun & Sep, weekends only Oct-Apr; ℗☻) The specialty is seafood at this small, rustic, country classic with a homey feel and great food. Ask to see Herman, the monster lobster. The creaky-but-clean motel rooms are a fine bargain, too, with singles at $48 and doubles for $62.

Deer Island Point Park
CAMPGROUND $

(506-747-2423; www.deerislandpointpark.com; 195 Deer Island Point Rd; tent sites $22; Jun-Sep) Set up your tent on the high bluff and spend an evening watching the Old Sow whirlpool. The campground is directly above the Campobello ferry landing.

ℹ Information

There's a summertime **tourist information kiosk** (www.deerisland.nb.ca; daily in summer) at the ferry landing.

ℹ Getting There & Away

A free government-run ferry (25 minutes) runs to Deer Island from Letete, which is 14.5km south of St George on Hwy 172 via Back Bay. The ferries run year-round every half-hour from 6am to 7pm, and hourly from 7pm to 10pm. Get in line early on a busy day.

East Coast Ferries (www.eastcoastferries.nb.ca; end Jun–mid-Sep), a private company, links Deer Island Point to Eastport, Maine, an attractive seaside town. It leaves for Eastport every hour on the hour from 9am to 6pm; it costs $13 per car and driver, plus $3 for each additional passenger.

For service to Campobello, see p398.

Campobello Island

The atmosphere on Campobello is remarkably different from that on Deer Island. It's a gentler and more prosperous island, with straight roads and better facilities. The wealthy have long been enjoying Campobello as a summer retreat. Due to its accessibility and proximity to New England, it feels as much a part of the USA as of Canada, and most of the tourists here are Americans.

Like many moneyed families, the Roosevelts bought property in this peaceful coastal area at the end of the 1800s and it is for this that the island is best known. The southern half of Campobello is almost all park and a golf course occupies still more.

Come to the island prepared. There's a single grocery store, two ATMs, a liquor store and a pharmacy, but no gas station – the 1200 residents of Campobello must cross the bridge to Lubec, Maine to fill their tanks. They generally use the same bridge to go elsewhere in New Brunswick, as the Deer Island ferry only operates in the summer.

⊙ Sights & Activities

Roosevelt Campobello International Park
PARK

(www.fdr.net; Hwy 774; admission free; sunrise-sunset year-round) The southernmost green area of Campobello Island is the 1200-hectare Roosevelt Campobello International Park. The park's biggest visitor attraction is the **Roosevelt Cottage** (tours late May–early Oct), the 34-room lodge where Franklin D Roosevelt grew up (between 1905 and 1921) and visited periodically throughout his time as US president (1933–45). The tomato-red Arts and Crafts–style structure is furnished with original Roosevelt furniture and artifacts. Adjacent **Hubbard House**, built in 1898, is also open to visitors. The grounds around all of these buildings are open all the time, and you can peek through the windows when the doors are closed.

The park is just 2.5km from the Lubec bridge, and from the Roosevelt mansion's front porch you can look directly across to Eastport, Maine. You'd hardly know you were in Canada.

Unlike the manicured museum area, most of the international park has been left in its natural state to preserve the flora and fauna that Roosevelt appreciated so much. A couple of gravel roads meander through it, leading to beaches and 7.5km of nature trails. It's a surprisingly wild, little-visited part of Campobello Island. Deer, moose and coyote call it home and seals can sometimes be seen offshore on the ledges near Lower Duck Pond, 6km from the visitors center. Look for eagles, ospreys and loons.

Herring Cove Provincial Park
PARK

(admission free) Along the international park's northern boundary is Herring Cove Provincial Park. This park has another 10km of walking trails as well as a campground and a picnic area on an arching 1.5km beach. It makes a fine, picturesque place for lunch.

Wilson's Beach
BEACH

Ten kilometers north of Roosevelt Park, Wilson's Beach has a large pier with fish for sale, and a sardine-processing plant with an adjacent store. There are various services and shops here in the island's biggest community.

East Quoddy Head Lighthouse
LIGHTHOUSE

Four kilometers north of Wilson's Beach is East Quoddy Head Lighthouse. Whales browse offshore and many people sit along the rocky shoreline with a pair of binoculars enjoying the sea breezes.

☞ Tours

Island Cruises WHALE-WATCHING
(☎506-752-1107, 888-249-4400; www.bayof
fundywhales.com; 62 Harbour Head Rd, Wilson's
Beach; adult/child $49/39; ☉Jul-Oct) Offers
2½-hour whale-watching cruises.

🛏 Sleeping & Eating

There are very few restaurants on Campobello, and the pickings across the bridge in
Lubec, Maine aren't much better. For self-
catering, there's a Valufoods supermarket
in Welshpool.

Herring Cove Provincial Park CAMPING $
(☎506-752-7010; www.tourismnewbrunswick.ca;
136 Herring Cove Rd; tent/RV sites $22/24; ☉late
May-late Sep) This 76-site park on the east
side of the island, 3km from the Deer Island
ferry, has some nice secluded sites in a forest setting, plus there's a sandy beach and
ample hiking.

Pollock Cove Cottages COTTAGES $$
(☎506-752-2300; senewman@nbnet.nb.ca; 2455
Rte 774, Wilson's Beach; r $75-175; P @) Simple,
clean one- and two-bedroom cottages with
million-dollar views.

Owen House B&B B&B $$
(☎506-752-2977; www.owenhouse.ca; 11 Welsh-
pool St, Welshpool; d incl breakfast with shared
bathroom $107-112, with private bathroom $121-
210) A classic seaside vacation home of yes-
teryear, complete with antique spool beds
made up with quilts, cozy reading nooks
and lots of windows on the ocean.

Family Fisheries Restaurant SEAFOOD $
(Hwy 774, Wilson's Beach; mains $5-23; ☉8am-
7:30pm, later in summer) Part of a fresh fish
market, this ultracasual seafood shack
specializes in fish and chips, lip-smacking
chowders and lobster rolls.

ℹ Information

For further information try the **Campobello
Island Tourism website** (www.campobellois
landtourism.com). There's a visitors center at
Roosevelt Campobello International Park.

ℹ Getting There & Away

East Coast Ferries (www.eastcoastferries.
nb.ca) connects Deer Island to Campobello
Island, costing $16 per car and driver plus $3 per
additional passenger. The ferry departs every
half-hour between 9am and 7pm. It's a scenic
25-minute trip from Deer Island past numerous
islands, arriving at Welshpool, halfway up the
16km-long island.

Grand Manan Island

Cue the Maritime fiddle music. As the ferry
from the mainland rounds the northern tip
of Grand Manan Island (population 2700),
Swallowtail Lighthouse looms into view,
poised atop a rocky, moss-covered cliff.
Brightly painted fishing boats bob in the
harbor. Up from the ferry dock, the tidy village of North Head spreads out along the
shore; a scattering of clapboard houses and
shops surrounded by well-tended flower
gardens and tall, leafy trees.

Grand Manan is a peaceful, unspoiled
place. There are no fast-food restaurants,
no trendy coffeehouses or nightclubs, no
traffic lights and no traffic. Just a ruggedly
beautiful coastline of high cliffs and sandy
coves interspersed with spruce forest and
fields of long grass. Along the eastern shore
and joined by a meandering coastal road
sit a string of pretty and prosperous fishing villages. There is plenty of fresh sea air
and that rare and precious commodity in
the modern world: silence, broken only by
the rhythmic ocean surf. Some people make
it a day trip, but lingering is recommended.

The ferry disembarks at the village of
North Head at the north end of the island.
The main road, Rte 776, runs 28.5km down
the length of the island along the eastern
shore. It connects all of Grand Manan's settlements en route to the lighthouse perched
atop a bluff at South Head. You can drive
from end to end in about 45 minutes. The
western side of Grand Manan is uninhabited and more or less impenetrable: a sheer
rock wall rising out the sea, backed by
dense forest and bog, broken only at Dark
Harbour where a steep road drops down to
the water's edge. A hiking trail provides access to this wilderness.

◉ Sights

Swallowtail Lighthouse LIGHTHOUSE
Whitewashed Swallowtail Lighthouse
(1860) is the island's signature vista, cleaving to a rocky promontory about 1km
north of the ferry wharf. Access is via
steep stairs and a slightly swaying suspension bridge. Since the light was automated
in 1986, the site has been left to the elements. Nevertheless, the grassy bluff is a
stupendous setting for a picnic. It has a
wraparound view of the horizon and seals
raiding the heart-shaped fishing weirs (an
ancient type of fishing trap made from
wood posts) below.

All of the approximately 30 weirs dotting the waters around Grand Manan are named, some dating back to the 19th century. They bear labels such as 'Ruin,' 'Winner,' 'Outside Chance' and 'Spite,' evoking the heartbreak of relying on an indifferent sea for a living. A tear made by a marauding seal in a net can free an entire catch of herring in a single night.

Grand Manan Historical Museum   MUSEUM
(www.grandmananmuseum.ca; 1141 Rte 776, Grand Harbour; adult/student & senior $5/3; ⊙9am-5:30pm Mon-Sat) This museum makes a good destination on a foggy day. Its diverse collection of local artifacts provides a quick primer on island history. Here you can see a display on shipwreck lore and the original kerosene lamp from nearby Gannet Rock lighthouse (1904). There is also a room stuffed with 200-plus taxidermied birds (including the now-extinct passenger pigeon). The museum hosts a number of evening lectures and community classes and activities.

Seal Cove   HISTORICAL SITE
Seal Cove is the island's prettiest village. Much of its charm comes from the fishing boats, wharves and herring smoking sheds clustered around the tidal creek mouth. For a century, smoked herring was king on Grand Manan. A thousand men and women worked splitting, stringing and drying fish in 300 smokehouses up and down the island. The last smokehouse shut down in 1996. Although herrings are still big business around here, they're now processed at a modern cannery. Today, the sheds house an informal Sardine Museum (admission by donation; ⊙most days). On display are the world's largest sardine can (alleged) and an authentically smelly exhibit on the smoking process.

Roland's Sea Vegetables   MARKET
(www.rolandsdulse.com; 174 Hill Rd; ⊙9am-6pm) Grand Manan is one of the few remaining producers of dulse, a type of seaweed that is used as a snack food or seasoning in Atlantic Canada and around the world. Dark Harbour, on the west side of the island, is said to produce the world's best. Dulse gatherers wade among the rocks at low tide to pick the seaweed, then lay it out on beds of rocks to dry just as they've been doing for hundreds of years. Buy some at this little roadside market, which sells various types of edible local seaweeds from nori to sea lettuce to Irish moss. Sandy, Roland's son, recommends sprinkling powdered dulse on fried eggs or baked fish.

🏃 Activities

Sea Watch Tours   PUFFIN-WATCHING
(☎506-662-8552, 877-662-8552; www.seawatchtours.com; Seal Cove fisherman's wharf; adult/child $85/45; Mon-Sat late Jun–mid-Aug) Make the pilgrimage out to isolated Machias Seal Island to see the Atlantic puffins waddle and play on their home turf. Access is limited to 15 visitors a day, so reserve well in advance. Getting onto the island can be tricky, as the waves are high and the rocks slippery. Wear sturdy shoes.

Whales-n-Sails Adventures   WHALE-WATCHING
(☎506-662-1999, 888-994-4044; www.whales-n-sails.com; North Head fisherman's wharf; adult/child $65/45; ⊙late Jun-late Sep) A marine biologist narrates these exhilarating whale-watching tours aboard the sailboat *Elsie Menota*. You'll often see puffins, razorbills, murre and other seabirds.

Hiking Trails   HIKING
Seventy kilometers of hiking trails crisscross and circle the island. Grab the comprehensive guide to the *Heritage Trails and Footpaths on Grand Manan* ($5), available at most island shops. Stay well away from the cliff edges! Unstable, undercut ground can give way beneath your feet. For an easy hike, try the shoreline path from Long Pond to Red Point (1.6km/one hour round-trip; suitable for children). In Whale Cove, the Hole-in-the-Wall is an often photographed natural arch jutting into the sea. It's a short hike from the parking area.

Adventure High   KAYAKING
(☎506-662-3563; www.adventurehigh.com; 83 Rte 776, North Head; tours $45-975; ⊙May-Oct) This outfitter offers tours of the Grand Manan coastline ranging from two-hour sunset paddles to multiday Bay of Fundy adventures.

🛏 Sleeping

Inn at Whale Cove   INN $$
TOP CHOICE   (☎506-662-3181; www.whalecovecottages.ca; Whistle Rd, North Head; s/d $120/130; ⊙May-Oct) 'Serving rusticators since 1910,' including writer Willa Cather, who wrote several of her novels here in the 1920s and '30s. The main lodge (built in 1816) and half a dozen vine-covered and shingled cottages retain the charm of that earlier era. They are fitted with

WHOSE ROCK IS IT ANYWAY?

Though Canada and the US share nearly 9000km of border, they manage to play nicely most of the time. So nicely, in fact, that today the sole remaining land dispute between the two countries is over an uninhabited 8-hectare chunk of rock called Machias Seal Island, and a neighboring (and even smaller) island so undistinguished it's referred to only as 'North Rock.' Foggy, barren and treeless, Machias Seal Island is best known as a nesting site for Atlantic puffins. North Rock is best known for...being a rock. Yet the two tiny islands are part of a dispute that dates back to the 1783 Treaty of Paris, which attempted to draw a border between the newly formed USA and what was then called 'British North America.' Machias Seal Island, approximately equidistant between Maine and New Brunswick's Grand Manan Island, was not directly addressed in the treaty (imagine that!), and has remained part of a 'gray zone' ever since. Canada operates a lighthouse on the island and attempts to maintain it as a bird sanctuary, while some American puffin boat tour operators challenge Canadian sovereignty. One, the late Captain Barna Nelson of Jonesport, Maine, would parade around the island once a year, waving an American flag. Canada and the US have had the opportunity to resolve the border dispute in international courts, but have declined.

polished pine floors and stone fireplaces, antiques, chintz curtains and well-stocked bookshelves. Some have kitchens.

Shorecrest Lodge INN $
(☎506-662-3216; www.shorecrestlodge.com; 100 Rte 776, Seal Cove; r $65-89; ☺May-Oct; ☏⌂) Near the ferry landing, this big, comfy farmhouse has 10 sunny rooms with quilts and antique furniture. A rec room has a TV and a toy train set for the kids. The Austrian owners cook up fresh seafood dinners (mains $18 to $28) and takeout lunches – nonguests can call ahead to order.

Anchorage Provincial Park CAMPGROUND $
(☎506-662-7022; Rte 776 btwn Grand Harbour & Seal Cove; tent/RV sites $22/24; ☺mid-May–mid-Sep) Family-friendly camping in a large field surrounded by tall evergreens, located 16km from the ferry. There's a kitchen shelter for rainy days, a playground, laundry and long pebbly beach. Get down by the trees to block the wind. Anchorage adjoins some marshes, which comprise a migratory bird sanctuary, and there are several short hiking trails.

Hole-in-the-Wall Campground
CAMPGROUND $
(☎506-662-3152, 866-662-4489; www.grandmanancamping.com; 42 Old Airport Rd, North Head; tent sites $25; ☺early May-late Oct) These spectacular cliff-top campsites are secluded among the rocks and trees, with fire pits, picnic tables and breathtaking views. Choose an inland site if you sleepwalk or suffer from vertigo. Showers and laundry facilities are available, as well as a couple

of spotless, simple cabins, furnished with bunk beds and a microwave.

Compass Rose B&B $$
(☎506-662-8570, off-season 613-471-1772; www.compassroseinn.com; 65 Rte 776, North Head; r incl breakfast $99-139; ☺1 Jun-30 Sep) Cheerful, comfortable guest rooms with a seashore motif and harbor views. Within walking distance of the ferry dock, it has one of the island's most atmospheric restaurants attached.

✗ Eating

The never abundant options are nearly nonexistent in the off-season (from October to early June). That said, there is some fine eating on Grand Manan. Reservations are essential for dinner due to limited table space island-wide.

TOP CHOICE **Inn at Whale Cove** NEW CANADIAN $$$
(☎506-662-3181; www.whalecovecottages.ca; Whistle Rd, North Head; mains $22-28; ☺dinner late Jun–mid-Oct, weekends May-Jun) Absolutely wonderful food in a relaxed country setting on the cove. The menu changes daily, but includes mouth-watering upscale meals such as Provençal-style rack of lamb, scallop ravioli and a to-die-for hazelnut crème caramel for dessert. Come early and have a cocktail by the fire in the cozy, old-fashioned parlor.

North Head Bakery BAKERY $
(www.northheadbakery.ca; 199 Rte 776, North Head; items $1-5; ☺6:30am-5:30pm Tue-Sat May-Oct) Scrumptious Danish pastries, fruit pies and artisanal breads made with organic

flour make this cheerful red and white bakery the first stop for many folks just off the ferry. Sit at the lunch counter with a coffee and sandwich and watch the parade.

Wharf Restaurant   CANADIAN $
(1 Ferry Wharf Rd, North Head; mains $5-10; ⏱breakfast, lunch & dinner) In a hangarlike corrugated metal building by the ferry dock, this no-frills restaurant offers three squares, plus ice cream, candy bars and other snacks.

ℹ Information

For further information on the area try the **tourist information office** (www.grandmanannb. com; 130 Rte 776, North Head; ⏱8am-4pm Mon-Fri, 9am-noon Sat).

ℹ Getting There & Away

The only way to get on and off the island from Blacks Harbour on the mainland to North Head on Grand Manan is by the **government ferry** (☎506-662-3724; www.coastaltransport. ca; ticket office at North Head ferry terminal). Service (adult/child $10.90/5.40, automobiles $32.55, bicycles $3.70, seven departures daily in summer) is first-come, first-served at Blacks Harbour; plan on arriving at least 45 minutes before departure. In July and August especially there can be long queues for vehicles to board, but cyclists and pedestrians can walk on at any time. No ticket is required for the trip over; book and pay for your return trip in North Head the day before you plan to leave for the mainland. The crossing takes 1½ hours. Watch for harbor porpoises and whales en route.

The ferry dock is within walking distance of several hotels, restaurants, shops and tour operators. To explore the whole of the island you should bring your own car, as there is no rental company on Grand Manan. Alternatively, **Leighton Spicer** (☎506-662-4904) drives the island's only taxi and meets most ferries. **Adventure High** (☎506-662-3563; www.adventurehigh. com; 83 Rte 776, North Head; ⏱8am-9pm) rents bicycles for $16/22/99 a half-day/day/week.

New River Provincial Park

Just off Hwy 1, about 35km west of Saint John on the way to St Stephen, this large park has one of the best beaches along the Fundy shore, a wide stretch of sand bordered on one side by the rugged coastline of Barnaby Head. During camping season the park charges a $7 fee per vehicle for day use, which includes parking at the beach and Barnaby Head trailhead.

You can spend an enjoyable few hours hiking Barnaby Head along a 6km network of nature trails. The **Chittick's Beach Trail** leads through coastal forest and past four coves, where you can check the catch in a herring weir or examine tidal pools for marine life. Extending from this loop is the 2.5km **Barnaby Head Trail**, which hugs the shoreline most of the way and rises to the edge of a cliff 15m above the Bay of Fundy.

The park's **campground** (☎506-755-4042; newriver@gnb.ca; 78 New River Beach Rd; tent/RV sites $22/24.50; ⏱mid-May–early Oct) is across the road from the beach and features 100 secluded sites, both rustic and with hookups, in a wooded setting. Drawbacks are the gravel emplacements and traffic noise.

SAINT JOHN

POP 68,000

Saint John is the economic engine room of the province, a gritty port city with a dynamism missing from the demure capital. The setting is spectacular – a ring of rocky bluffs, sheer cliffs, coves and peninsulas surrounding a deep natural harbor where the mighty St John and Kennebecasis Rivers empty into the Bay of Fundy. It can take a bit of imagination to appreciate this natural beauty, obscured as it is by the smokestacks of a pulp mill, oil refinery and garden variety urban blight. The city is surrounded by an ugly scurf of industrial detritus and a tangle of concrete overpasses. But those who push their way through all this to the historic core are rewarded with beautifully preserved redbrick and bandstone 19th-century architecture and glimpses of the sea down steep, narrow side streets.

Originally a French colony, the city was incorporated by British Loyalists in 1785 to become Canada's first legal city. Thousands of Irish immigrants arrived during the potato famine of the mid-1800s and helped build the city into a prosperous industrial town, important particularly for its wooden shipbuilding. Today, a large percentage of the population works in heavy industry, including pulp mills, refineries and the Moosehead Brewery.

Downtown (known as Uptown) Saint John sits on a square, hilly peninsula between the mouth of the St John River and Courtenay Bay. Kings Sq marks the nucleus of town, and its pathways duplicate the pattern of the Union Jack.

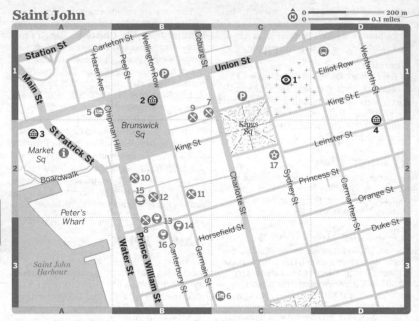

West over the Harbour Bridge (50¢ toll) is Saint John West. Many of the street names in this section of the city are identical to those of Saint John proper, and to avoid confusion, they end in a west designation, such as Charlotte St W. Saint John West has the ferries to Digby, Nova Scotia.

◉ Sights

New Brunswick Museum MUSEUM
(www.nbm-mnb.ca; 1 Market Sq; adult/student/family $6/3.25/13; ⊘9am-5pm Mon-Wed & Fri, to 9pm Thu, 10am-5pm Sat, noon-5pm Sun, closed Mon Nov–mid-May) This is a quality museum with a varied collection. There's a captivating section on marine wildlife with an outstanding section on whales, including a life-sized specimen. There are also hands-on exhibits, models of old sailing ships and an original copy of *The Night Before Christmas* written in author Clement Clarke Moore's own hand, which was sent to his godfather Jonathan Odell's family in New Brunswick.

Reversing Rapids OVERLOOK
The Bay of Fundy tides and their effects (p409) are a predominant regional characteristic. The falls here are part of that and are one of the best-known sites in the province. However, 'reversing falls' is a bit of a misnomer. When the high Bay of Fundy

tides rise, the current in the river reverses, causing the water to flow upstream. When the tides go down, the water flows in the normal way. Generally, it looks like rapids. **Reversing Rapids Visitors Centre** (200 Bridge Rd; ⊘8am-7pm mid-May–mid-Oct), next to the bridge over the falls, can supply a 'Reversing Falls Tide Table' brochure that explains where in the cycle you are.

Loyalist House HISTORIC BUILDING
(120 Union St; adult/child/family $5/2/7; ⊘10am-5pm Mon-Fri May-Jun, daily Jul–mid-Sep) Dating from 1810, the Georgian-style Loyalist House is one of the city's oldest unchanged buildings. It's now a museum, depicting the Loyalist period, and contains some fine carpentry.

Loyalist Burial Ground CEMETERY
This mood-inducing cemetery, with fading tombstones from as early as 1784, is just off Kings Sq, in a park-style setting in the center of town.

Carleton Martello Tower HISTORICAL BUILDING
(454 Whipple St; adult/child $3.90/1.90; ⊘10am-5:30pm Jun-early Oct) Built during the War of 1812, this round stone fort features a restored barracks and other historical displays, but the real reason to go is the panoramic view over Saint John and the Bay of Fundy from the hilltop locale.

Saint John Jewish Historical Museum
MUSEUM

(91 Leinster St; admission by donation; ⊙10am-4pm Mon-Fri May-Oct, 1-4pm Sun Jul & Aug) This modest museum traces the history of Saint John's once-thriving Jewish community, whose members included Louis B Mayer of Metro-Goldwyn-Mayer (MGM) Hollywood fame.

🏃 Activities

Reversing Falls Jet Boat Rides BOAT TOUR
(☎506-634-8987; www.jetboatrides.com; Fallsview Ave; adult/child $37/27; ⊙Jun–mid-Oct) Offers two types of boat trips. One is a leisurely one-hour sightseeing tour to the Reversing Falls and around the harbor. The other is a 20-minute 'thrill ride' through the white-water at Reversing Rapids. Count on getting soaked

Irving Nature Park PARK
(admission free; ⊙8am-dusk early May-early Nov) For those who have vehicles and an appreciation for nature, Irving Nature Park is a must for its rugged, unspoiled coastal topography. It's also a remarkable place for bird-watching, with hundreds of species regularly reported. Seals may be seen on the rocks offshore. Seven trails of varying lengths lead around beaches, cliffs, woods, mudflats, marsh and rocks. Good footwear is strongly recommended. It's well worth the 5km drive southwest from downtown to get here. Take Hwy 1 west from town and turn south at Exit 107, Bleury St. Then take a right on Sand Cove Rd and continue for 2km until you get to the entrance.

Harbour Passage WALKING
Beginning on a boardwalk at Market Sq (behind the Hilton Hotel), Harbour Passage is a red-paved walk and cycle trail that leads around the harbor, up Bennett St and down Douglas Ave to the Reversing Falls bridge and lookout. Informative plaques line the route and it's about an hour's walk one-way. Much of the path is slated to be under construction through 2012. Ask ahead about its progress before setting out for a stroll.

Gibson Creek Canoeing CANOEING
(☎506-672-8964; www.gibsoncreek.ca; tours per day $65) This company offers guided canoe trips through the numerous intertidal marshes and peaceful rivers close to the city.

👉 Tours

As a popular stop for cruise ship travelers, Saint John has a surprisingly large range of tour options. Whale-watching, unfortunately, is not an attraction in Saint John, save for the very occasional, very wayward minke.

Saint John Transit Commission BUS TOUR
(☎506-658-2855; www.saintjohntransit.com) Runs two-hour bus tours (adult/child $20/5) around the city mid-June to early October. Departures and tickets from Reversing Rapids Visitors Centre, Barbour's General Store at Market Sq and Rockwood Park Campground. Two tours daily.

Words, Walks & Workshops WALKING TOUR
(☎506-672-8601; walks free-$5; ⊙7pm Tue Jun-Sep) For nearly 30 years David Goss, travel

and outdoor columnist, has led themed walks throughout city and natural environments. The walks have so much flair that locals as well as visitors frequent the fun. Departure locations and hours vary; check with the visitors center.

Roy's Tour
TAXI TOUR

(www.roystours.webs.com; tours per group per hr $50) Knowledgeable local Roy Flowers narrates personalized five- to six-hour taxi tours of the city and surrounds.

🛏 Sleeping

Saint John motels sit primarily along Manawagonish Rd, 7km west of uptown. There are also a couple of upscale chain hotels uptown.

Mahogany Manor
TOP CHOICE

B&B $$

(☎506-636-8000, 800-796-7755; www. sjnow.com/mm; 220 Germain St; d incl breakfast $95-110; P☺@🛜) On the loveliest street in Saint John, this gay-friendly, antique-filled Victorian is a wonderful place to temporarily call home. Five rooms are a comfy mix of antiques and plush, modern bedding. The upbeat owners know more about the city than you'll absorb – even which meal to order at which restaurant!

Homeport
B&B $$

(☎506-672-7255, 888-678-7678; www.homeport. nb.ca; 60 Douglas Ave; r incl breakfast $95-175; P☺❄🛜) Perched above once-grand Douglas Ave, this imposing Italianate-style B&B was once two separate mansions belonging to shipbuilder brothers. It has a boutique hotel vibe, with a stately parlor, a full bar and 10 sunny guest rooms. Try to snag one with a clawfoot tub. It's about 1km west of the uptown peninsula.

Chipman Hill Suites
APARTMENTS $$

(☎506-693-1171; www.chipmanhill.com; 9 Chipman Hill; ste $49-299; P☺❄🛜) What a great concept! Chipman has taken historic properties around downtown, renovated them into mini-apartments with kitchens while retaining all the character, and rents them out by the day, week or month. Size and features determine price, but all are a steal.

Rockwood Park
CAMPING $

(☎506-652-4050; www.rockwoodparkcamp ground.com; Lake Dr S; tent/RV sites $22/32; ☺mid-May–early Oct; 🛜) A couple of kilometers north of the downtown area is huge Rockwood Park, with small lakes, a wood-land crisscrossed by walking paths, and a campground in a small open field. Bus 6 to Mt Pleasant from Kings Sq goes within a few blocks Monday to Saturday.

University of New Brunswick Summer Residences
RESIDENCE HALL $

(☎506-648-5755; www.unbsj.ca/hfs; off Sandy Point Rd near Rockwood Park; s/d $34/47, ste $72; 🛜) From May to August, the University of New Brunswick's Saint John campus offers simple rooms and rather Spartan kitchenette suites in two residence halls. The university is 6km north of the city center (take bus 15 from Kings Sq).

🍴 Eating

Old City Market
TOP CHOICE

MARKET $

(www.sjcitymarket.ca; 47 Charlotte St; ☺7:30am-6pm Mon-Fri, to 5pm Sat) Wedged between North and South Market Sts, this sense-stunning food hall has been home to wheeling and dealing since 1876. The interior of the impressive brick building is packed with produce stalls, bakeries, fishmongers and butcher shops, as well as numerous counters selling a range of delectable prepared meals. Locals head to the lunch counter at Slocum and Ferris (lunch under $6). Look out for bags of dulse, a dried Atlantic seaweed that's eaten like potato chips in these parts.

Opera Bistro
FUSION $$$

(☎506-642-2822; 60 Prince William St; mains $23-33; ☺lunch & dinner) One of Saint John's trendiest spots, this European-run bistro puts an international spin on Maritime ingredients. Ambitious dishes – local halibut with blueberry salsa, New Brunswick cheese soup with sesame croutons – can be a bit hit or miss, so try ordering small plates to share. Lunch means fancy sandwiches (including a Bay of Fundy lobster BLT!) and salads. The dining room, all exposed brick and minimalist plastic chairs, is stylish but unpretentious.

Thandi
INDIAN $$$

(☎506-648-2377; www.singhdining.com; 33 Canterbury St; mains $17-33; ☺lunch & dinner Mon-Fri, dinner Sat & Sun) A+ for atmosphere – exposed brick, heavy timbers and warm lighting with a stylish backlit bar downstairs and cozy fireplaces upstairs. The food is good, too – try Indian classics like lamb korma or shrimp vindaloo, or fusion specialties like tandoori strip loin or snapper with mango salsa.

Bourbon Quarter & Magnolia Cafe

CAJUN **$$**

(☎506-214-3618; Prince William St; mains $8-30; ☺dinner Bourbon Quarter, breakfast & lunch Magnolia Cafe) Cajun food in Canada? Hip, young Saint Johners don't seem to find anything odd about the idea, flocking to eat fried oysters and muffuletta sandwiches at this recently opened pair of adjacent New Orleans–style restaurants. Bourbon Quarter is more formal, Magnolia a casual lunch spot. Both have live music.

Taco Pica

MEXICAN, GUATEMALAN **$$**

(96 Germain St; mains $10-17; ☺lunch & dinner Mon-Sat) A fusion of authentic Guatemalan and Mexican fare is served in this colorful cantina. An economical introduction to the cuisine is *pepian,* a simple but spicy beef stew that is as good as you'll find in any Guatemalan household.

Billy's Seafood Company

SEAFOOD **$$$**

(www.billysseafood.com; 49 Charlotte St; mains $16-30; ☺lunch & dinner) Since we are on the east coast after all...this popular casual restaurant at the top of the City Market does seafood with flair.

☙ Drinking & Entertainment

There isn't much of a nightclub scene here, but pub culture and live music thrive in a handful of atmospheric waterfront bars in the uptown core. For weekly goings on, pick up the free *here* (www.herenb. canadaeast.com) entertainment paper, available around town.

Big Tide Brewing Company

BREWERY

(www.bigtidebrew.com; 47 Princess St; ☺Mon-Sat) This subterranean brewpub is a cozy spot for a pint (try the Confederation Cream Ale or the Whistlepig Stout), a plate of beer-steamed mussels or a friendly game of trivia.

Java Moose

CAFE

(www.javamoose.com; 84 Prince William St; 🛜) Get your caffeine fix at this home-grown coffeehouse with a groovy North Woods vibe.

Infusion

CAFE

(www.infusiontearoom.ca; Old City Market; 🛜) In the Old City Market, this warmly lit urban-chic cafe offers dozens of rare and exceptional teas, along with sandwiches and other light fare.

Happinez Wine Bar

BAR

(www.happinezwinebar.com; 42 Princess St; ☺Wed-Sat) For a quiet tipple in a sleek urban environment, duck into this intimate little wine bar.

O'Leary's

PUB

(www.olearyspub.com; 46 Princess St) Shoot the breeze with local barflies at this pleasantly divey downtown institution.

Imperial Theatre

THEATER

(☎506-674-4100; www.imperialtheatre.nb.ca; 24 Kings Sq S) Now restored to its original 1913 splendor, this is the city's premier venue for performances ranging from classical music to live theater.

❶ Information

Main Post Office (41 Church Ave W, Postal Station B, E2M 4X6) In Saint John W, send general delivery mail here.

Police, Fire & Ambulance (☎911) For emergencies.

Saint John Library (1 Market Sq; ☺9am-5pm Mon & Sat, 10am-5pm Tue & Wed, 10am-9pm Thu & Fri) Free internet access.

Saint John Regional Hospital (☎506-648-6000; 400 University Ave; ☺24hr)

Visitor & Convention Bureau (☎506-658-2990, 888-364-4444; www.tourismsaintjohn. com; Market Sq; ☺9:30am-8pm mid-Jun–Aug, to 6pm Sep–mid-Jun) Knowledgeable, friendly staff. Ask for the self-guided walking-tour pamphlets.

❶ Getting There & Away

AIR The airport is east of town on Loch Lomond Rd toward St Martins. See p380 for flight information.

BOAT There's a daily ferry service between Saint John and Digby, Nova Scotia (for more information, see p380).

BUS The **bus station** (300 Union St; ☺7:30am-9pm Mon-Fri, 8am-9pm Sat & Sun) is a five-minute walk from town. There are multiple daily Acadian Lines services to Fredericton ($29, 1½ hours) and Moncton ($33, two hours). There's a daily direct bus to Bangor, Maine ($55, 3½ hours), but you'll need to buy your ticket in person.

❶ Getting Around

TO/FROM THE AIRPORT City bus 22 links the airport and Kings Sq. A taxi costs around $35.

BUS Saint John Transit (☎506-658-4700) charges $2.50. The most important route is the east–west bus service, which is either bus 1 or 2 eastbound to McAllister Dr and bus 3 or 4 westbound to Saint John West near the ferry terminal.

It stops at Kings Sq in the city center. Another frequent service is bus 15 or 16 to the university.

CAR & MOTORCYCLE Discount Car Rentals (☑506-633-4440; www.discountcar.com; 255 Rothesay Ave) is opposite the Park Plaza Motel. Avis, Budget, Hertz and National all have car-rental desks at the airport.

Parking meters in Saint John cost $1 an hour from 8am to 6pm weekdays only. You can park free at meters on weekends, holidays and in the evening. Park free any time on back streets such as Leinster and Princess Sts, east of Kings Sq. The **city parking lot** (11 Sydney St) is free on weekends.

EASTERN FUNDY SHORE

Much of the rugged, unspoiled Eastern Fundy Shore from Saint John to Hopewell Cape remains essentially untouched. Indeed, hikers, cyclists, kayakers and all nature lovers will be enchanted by this marvelous coast, edged by dramatic cliffs and tides. It's not possible to drive directly along the coastline from St Martins to Fundy National Park; a detour inland by Sussex is necessary, unless you're prepared to hike.

St Martins

A 40km drive east of Saint John, St Martins is a winsome seaside hamlet surrounded by steep cliffs and flower-studded pastureland. Once a sleepy wooden shipbuilding center, it now draws hikers, bikers and scenic-drive takers to the 11km **Fundy Trail Parkway** (www.fundytrailparkway.com), which winds along a jaw-dropping stretch of coastline. In town, check out the impressive red sandstone sea caves of Mac's Beach, accessible by foot when the tide is low. The village's twin covered bridges are a popular photo op, so bring your camera.

River Bay Adventures (☑506-663-9530; www.riverbayadventures.com; tours from $45) runs two- to three-hour guided sea-kayaking trips to the caves and islands along the coast. It also rents kayaks (half-/full day $30/50).

Count on simple, homey rooms and a warm welcome at **Minihorse Farm B&B** (☑506-833-6240; www.stayatminihorsefarm.com; 280 West Quaco Rd; r incl breakfast $70; �l May-Oct; �l@☎), an old farmhouse by the sea. Yes, there are miniature horses to pet.

Ask the owners how to get to the nearby hidden beach.

St Martin's Country Inn (☑506-833-4534, 800-566-5257; www.stmartinscountryinn.com; 303 Main St; r $95-165; �l☀☎), the towering mansion overlooking the bay, is the most deluxe place in town and also offers delectable meals in its delightful, caught-in-time dining room.

Right on Mac's Beach, the resort-style **Seaside Restaurant** (81 Mac's Beach; mains $8-13; �l lunch & dinner) serves fish and chips, scallops, chowder and more. Now you know you are on holiday.

Fundy National Park

This **national park** (www.pc.gc.ca/fundy; daily permit adult/child/family $7.80/3.90/19.60) is one of the country's most popular. Highlights are the world's highest tides, the irregularly eroded sandstone cliffs and the wide beach at low tide that makes exploring the shore for small marine life and debris such a treat. The park features an extensive network of impressive hiking trails.

Activities

Cycling

Mountain biking is permitted on six trails: Goose River, Marven Lake, Black Hole, East Branch, Bennett Brook (partially open) and Maple Grove. Surprisingly, at last report there were no bicycle rentals in Fundy National Park or in nearby Alma. Contact the visitors centers to find current information on this.

Hiking

Fundy features 120km of walking trails where it's possible to enjoy anything from a short stroll to a three-day trek. Several trails require hikers to ford rivers, so be prepared.

The most popular backpacking route is the **Fundy Circuit**, a three-day trek of 45km through the heart of the park. Hikers generally spend their first night at Marven Lake and their second at Bruin Lake, returning via the Upper Salmon River. First, stop at the visitors center to reserve your wilderness campsites ($10 per night; call ahead for reservations).

Another overnight trek is the **Goose River Trail**. It joins the Fundy Trail, accessible by road from St Martins. This undeveloped three-day trek is one of the most difficult in

On a Saturday in summer, do what loads of Saint Johners do and take the **Gondola Point Ferry** (signposted off Hwy 1 at Exit 141; admission free) to the bucolic Kingston Peninsula, then follow Rte 845 east to the **Kingston Farmers' Market** (Rte 845, Kingston; ☺8am-1pm Sat). Sample the fresh fruits and vegetables and various ethnic foods on offer or stop for lunch at the restored 1810 **Carter House Tea Room** (874 Rte 845; cakes & tea $4-8; ☺9:30am-4:30pm Tue-Sat) which is, of course, haunted – by a ghost who likes to tidy up and rearrange the books. Leave the city folk behind, continuing on Rte 845 into the bustling community of Hampton, where you pick up Rte 121, which follows the north side of the Kennebecasis River through farm country and the villages of Norton and Apohaqui into **Sussex** (population 4200).

Sussex is a working farming community nestled in a green valley dotted with dairy farms. The old-fashioned main street could be a movie set for a heartwarming 1950s coming-of-age story (but please, enough with the outdoor murals!). The well-preserved railway station houses the tourist information center, a small museum devoted to the area's military regiment, and Sully's Ice Cream Parlour.

If you stick around until evening, keep up the 1950s time trip with a double-bill at the **Sussex Drive-In** (www.sussexdrivein.com; Rte 2; adult/child $10/6; ☺dusk Fri-Sun May-Sep). You can pitch your tent at the attached **Town & Country Campark** (tent/RV site $24/31). You can also bed down at **Jonah Place B&B** (☎506-433-6978, 866-448-8800; www.jonahplace.com; 977 Main St; r incl breakfast $89-195; ⊜@⊛).

The classy and cozy **Broadway Cafe** (☎506-433-5414; 73 Broad St; mains lunch $8, dinner $18-35; ☺10am-3pm Mon-Tue, 10am-9pm Wed-Sat) is the place to eat in town.

Gasthof Old Bavarian (☎506-433-4735; 1130 Knightville Rd; mains $10-24; ☺noon-10pm Fri-Sun Jun-Sep, noon-8pm Feb-May & Oct-Dec, closed Jan) is the place for a truly memorable meal in the countryside. On a country road in a quiet valley settled by German and Dutch farmers, this place could have been transported – beer steins and all – from the Black Forest. The decor is Bavarian hunting lodge, with low timbered ceilings, heavy wooden furniture and cheerful blue and white checked tablecloths. The plates of schnitzel and sausages made on the family farm are plain beautiful, decorated with purple cabbage, fresh-picked greens and creamy white dumplings, with hearty flavors to match. Despite being more or less in the middle of nowhere, this place is always packed for dinner, so reservations are recommended. It's cash only.

Hang a left out of Gasthof's back onto the Knightville Rd, then left again onto Country View Rd at Anagance Ridge, then right onto Rte 890 into Petitcodiac. This stretch of road affords breathtaking vistas of rolling green countryside that'll make you want to roll up, move here and raise chickens. If you can work up an appetite, stroll through the greenhouses and have a healthy organic lunch or tea and cake at **Cornhill Nursery and Cedar Cafe** (www.cornhillnursery.com; 2700 Rte 890; mains $8-12; ☺lunch Jun-Sep). From Petitcodiac you can rejoin Hwy 1, heading east to Moncton or west back to Fundy Park and Saint John. The views of the valley from Hwy 1 between Hampton and Sussex are also lovely.

NEW BRUNSWICK FUNDY NATIONAL PARK

the province. While you can cycle to Goose River, the trail beyond can only be done on foot.

Enjoyable day hikes in Fundy National Park include the **Coppermine Trail**, a 4.4km loop which goes to an old mine site; and the **Third Vault Falls Trail**, a challenging one-way hike of 3.7km to the park's tallest falls. In summer, rangers lead a variety of family-friendly educational programs, including night hikes.

Skiing
In the winter, 25km of park trails are groomed for fantastic cross-country skiing, with additional snowshoeing tracks through the forest.

Swimming
The ocean is pretty bracing here; luckily, there's a heated saltwater **swimming pool** (adult/child $3/1.50; ☺11am-6:30pm late Jun-early Sep) not far from the park's southern entrance.

SCENIC DRIVE: FUNDY TRAIL PARKWAY

This magnificent **parkway** (www.fundytrailparkway.com; adult/child/family $4/2.50/13; ☺6am-8pm mid-May–Oct) traverses a rugged section of what has been called the only remaining coastal wilderness between Florida and Newfoundland. The 11km-long parkway to Big Salmon River put an end to the unspoiled wilderness part. There is now a lovely stretch of pavement with numerous viewpoints, picnic areas and parking lots. Eventually, it will extend to Fundy National Park. Nova Scotia is visible across the bay. There is also a separate 16km-long very steep and hilly hiking/biking trail.

On Saturday, Sunday and holidays a free hourly **shuttle bus** operates from noon to 6pm, ferrying hikers up and down the trail between the parkway entrance and Big Salmon River. In the off-season, the main gate is closed, but you can park at the entrance and hike or pedal in.

At Big Salmon River is a superfluous **interpretive center** (☺8am-8pm mid-May–mid-Oct) with exhibits and a 10-minute video presentation. A suspension bridge leads to a vast wilderness hiking area beyond the end of the road. Hikers can make it from Big Salmon River to Goose River in Fundy National Park in three to five days. At last report, no permits or permissions were required to do so. But beyond Big Salmon River, be prepared for wilderness, rocky scree and even a rope ladder or two.

You can spend the night here too, at **Hearst Lodge** (r incl breakfast & dinner per person $99; ☺mid-Jun–Sep), a cabin-on-steroids built by newspaper magnate J Randolph Hearst.

🛏 Sleeping

The park has three campgrounds and 13 wilderness sites. **Camping reservations** (☎877-737-3783; www.pccamping.ca; reservation fee $10.80) must be made at least three days in advance. The park entry fee is extra and is paid upon arrival.

With bathhouses and showers, **Chignecto North** (tent/RV sites $25/35) is a good pick for families. The 131-site **Headquarters Campground** (tent/RV sites $23/35) is near the visitors center. It's the only area open for winter camping. Along the coast, 8km southwest of the visitors center, is **Point Wolfe Campground** (tent sites $25) and its 181 sites with sea breezes and cooler temperatures. To reserve a backcountry site ($10), call either of the visitors centers.

Fundy Highlands Inn & Chalets

CABINS, MOTEL $$

(☎506-887-2930, 888-883-8639; www.fundy highlandchalets.com; 8714 Hwy 114; motel $69-89, cabins $79-105; ☺May-Oct) Simple but charming little cabins, all with decks, kitchenettes and superlative views, and a small, well-kept motel.

ℹ Information

Headquarters Visitors Centre (☎506-887-6000; ☺10am-6pm mid-Jun–early Sep, 9am-4pm early Sep–mid-Jun) At the south entrance.

Wolfe Lake Information Centre (☎506-432-6026; Hwy 114; ☺10am-6pm late Jun-early Sep) North entrance.

Alma

The tiny village of Alma is a supply center for the park. It has accommodations, restaurants, a small gas station, grocery store, liquor outlet and laundry. Most facilities close in winter, when it becomes a ghost town. Down on the beach is a statue of Molly Kool, the first female sea captain on the continent.

Fresh Air Adventure (☎506-887-2249, 800-545-0020; www.freshairadventure.com; 16 Fundy View Dr; tours from $50; ☺late May–mid-Sep) offers myriad kayaking tours in and around Fundy, from two-hour trips to multiday excursions.

For accommodations, **Parkland Village Inn** (☎506-887-2313; www.parklandvillageinn. com; 8601 Hwy 114; r incl breakfast $95-140) is a busy 60-year-old inn with comfy, newly renovated rooms, some with killer Bay of Fundy views. At the inn, **Tides Restaurant** (8601 Hwy 114; mains $12-21; ☺lunch & dinner mid-May–Oct) is a beachy, fine-dining place that does top-rate seafood and excellent ribs. The casual take-out patio has fish and chips and cold beer.

Cape Enrage & Mary's Point

From Alma, old Rte 915 yields two sensational, yet relatively isolated, promontories high over the bay.

See the 150-year-old lighthouse at the windblown, suitably named **Cape Enrage** (www.capenrage.org; off Rte 905; adult/child $4/2.50; ⊙9am-5pm late May–mid-Oct, to 8pm Jul & Aug). The cape was restored and is still expertly run by local high-school students and volunteer mentors from the area. Onsite guides offer **climbing** (per 2hr $65) and **rappelling** (per 2hr $65) off the steep rock faces. Or you can simply wander the beach looking for fossils (low tide only!). When all that activity gets you hungry, head to the **Cape House Restaurant** (⊙lunch & dinner) in the original lighthouse keeper's house, where you can enjoy the dramatic view while dining on pan-seared local scallops, foraged fiddlehead ferns and lobster mac n' cheese.

At Mary's Point, 22km east, is the **Shepody Bay Shorebird Reserve** (Mary's Point Rd, off Hwy 915; admission free). From mid-July to mid-August hundreds of thousands of shorebirds, primarily sandpipers, gather here. Nature trails and boardwalks lead through the dikes and marsh. The interpretive center is open from late June to early September, but you can use the 6.5km of trails any time.

Hopewell Rocks

At Hopewell Cape, where the Petitcodiac River empties into Shepody Bay, are the **Hopewell Rocks** (www.thehopewellrocks.ca; off Hwy 114; adult/child/family $8.50/6.25/23, shuttle extra $2; ⊙9am-5pm mid-May–mid-Oct, later hours in summer; 🚻). The 'rocks' are bizarre sandstone erosion formations known as 'flowerpots,' rising several stories from

the ocean floor. Some look like arches, others like massive stone mushrooms, still others like enormous ice-cream cones. Crowds come from all over the world to marvel at their Dr Seussian vibe, making the rocks New Brunswick's top attraction (and certainly one of its most crowded). You can only walk amid the rocks at low tide – check the tide tables at any tourist office or area hotel. At high tide, the rock towers are still visible from the trails that wind through the woods above.

The park features a large interpretive center with educational displays, two cafes, picnic areas and several kilometers of well-trafficked trails. In high season, the massive parking lot is choked with cars and the staircases down to the beaches suffer human traffic jams.

Another way to visit the rocks is by kayak. **Baymount Outdoor Adventures** (☎877-601-2660; www.baymountadventures.com; tours adult/child $59/49; ⊙Jun-Sep) offers two-hour paddling tours.

There are several motels in the Hopewell Rocks vicinity, including the family-run **Hopewell Rocks Motel** (☎506-734-2975; www.hopewellrocksmotel.com; 4135 Hwy 114; r incl breakfast high/low season $105/55; 🚻💻), with 39 tidy rooms, a heated pool and an adjacent lobster restaurant.

SOUTHEASTERN NEW BRUNSWICK

The southeastern corner of New Brunswick province is a flat coastal plain sliced by tidal rivers and salt marshes. Moncton, known as 'Hub City,' is a major crossroads with two well-known attractions where nature appears to defy gravity. Southeast, toward Nova Scotia, are significant historical and bird life attractions.

> ### THE TIDES OF FUNDY
>
> The tides of the Bay of Fundy are the highest in the world. A Mi'kmaq legend explains the tide as the effect of a whale's thrashing tail sending the water forever sloshing back and forth. A more prosaic explanation is in the length, depth and gradual funnel shape of the bay itself.
>
> The contrasts between the high and ebb tide are most pronounced at the eastern end of the bay and around the Minas Basin, with tides of 10m to 15m twice daily 12½ hours apart. The highest tide ever recorded anywhere was 16.6m, the height of a four-story building, at Burncoat Head near Noel, Nova Scotia.

0 — 400 m
0 — 0.2 miles

Moncton

◎ Sights
1 Tidal Bore Park D2

🛏 Sleeping
2 Auberge au Bois Dormant Inn A1
3 C'mon Inn B2
4 Hotel St James C3

🍴 Eating
5 Bogart's D2
6 Cafe Archibald B1
7 Calactus C2
8 Pump House D2

🍷 Drinking
9 Café Cognito C3
  Old Cosmo .... (see 9)
10 Paramount Lounge C3

✪ Entertainment
11 Capitol Theatre C3

Moncton

POP 64,100

Moncton is like that fun-loving friend you'd love to introduce to the cute German exchange student you know. You think they'd have some good times together, but you're concerned your European friend might be put off by Moncton's dowdy strip-mall wardrobe and well, let's face it, unmemorable physical features. So, you emphasize the town's vivacious personality, appreciation of music and fine food and the fact that he speaks two languages.

Once a major wooden shipbuilding port, Moncton is now the fastest-growing city in the Maritimes with an economy built upon transportation and call centers drawn here by the bilingual workforce. It's a pleasant, suburban city, with a small redbrick downtown along the muddy banks of the Petitcodiac River. There are some decent restaurants, bars and a bustling Acadian farmers' market. Apart from that, there is little to detain the visitor.

◎ Sights

TOP CHOICE **Dieppe Farmers' Market** MARKET
(www.marchedieppemarket.com; cnr Acadie Ave & Gauvin Rd, Dieppe; ⊗7am-1pm Sat) A great place to get a taste of New Brunswick's vibrant Acadian culture is this weekly market. Stalls overflow with locally made cheeses, cottage wines and homemade preserves as well as Acadian dishes such as *tourtière* (a meat pie), *fricot à la poule* (home-style chicken stew) and rabbit pie. Nibble sweet pastries such as *plogues* and *guaffres* while browsing the craft stalls. To get there from downtown, head 2km east on Main St, which becomes Champlain, to Acadie Ave. Look for the yellow roof.

Magnetic Hill AMUSEMENT PARK
(www.magnetichill.com; cnr Mountain Rd & Hwy 2; per car $5; ⊗8am-8pm mid-May–mid-Sep) At Magnetic Hill, incredibly one of Canada's best-known (though not best-loved) attractions, gravity appears to work in reverse. Start at the bottom of the hill in a car and you'll drift upward. You figure it out. After hours and out of season, it's free. It's a goofy novelty, worth the head-scratching laugh, but all the money-generating, spin-off hoopla now surrounding the hill is nothing special. Family-oriented attractions include a zoo, faux village hawking ice cream and souvenirs, and a water park. Magnetic Hill is about 10km northwest of downtown off Mountain Rd.

Tidal Bore Park PARK
(east end of Main St; admission free; ⊗24hr) The tourist literature talks up the twice-daily return of the waters of the tidal Petitcodiac River. In theory, the tide comes in as one solid wave, unfurled like a carpet across the muddy riverbed in one dramatic gesture. As the tide advances up the narrowing bay it starts to build up on itself, pushed from behind by the powerful tides in the Bay of Fundy, the world's highest. The height of this oncoming rush can allegedly vary from just a few centimeters to about 1m. In reality, it usually just looks like a big mud seep, and is, well...boring.

Casino New Brunswick CASINO
(www.casinonb.ca; 21 Casino Dr; ⊗slots 10am-3am) The province's first full-service casino, this 24,000-sq-foot gambling palace brings a touch of Vegas to Moncton. Since opening in 2010, it's been packing in crowds with its 500 slot machines, poker room, numerous bars and buffets, and an entertainment venue boasting big-name performers such as the Beach Boys and Bill Cosby. The casino is about 9km northwest of the town center off Mountain Rd.

⟳ Tours

Roads to Sea BUS TOUR
(⚑506-850-7623; www.roadstosea.com; ⊗May-Oct) Roads to Sea offers 3½-hour bus tours ($85) to Hopewell Rocks, an eight-hour guided trip that takes in the Rocks, Fundy National Park, Cape Enrage and a few covered bridges and lighthouses ($160), as well as a 1½-hour tour of the Moncton sights ($45).

⏰ Sleeping

Reservations are a good idea as the city is a major conference destination and often gets packed solid. Most of the chain hotels are clustered around Magnetic Hill.

Hotel St James BOUTIQUE HOTEL $$$
(⚑888-782-1414; www.hotelstjames.ca; 14 Church St; r $159-289; ❁) On the 2nd floor of a 19th-century brick shop building, this downtown boutique hotel has 10 stylish, urban-chic guest rooms that wouldn't look a bit out of place in Montréal or New York. Swank design touches include mod tile walls, crisp white linens, huge flat-screen TVs and iPod docks. There's a popular pub and restaurant downstairs.

C'mon Inn HOSTEL $
(⚑506-854-8155, 506-530-0905; moncton hostel@yahoo.ca, 4/1 leet St, dm $33, r $70; ❁) Moncton's only hostel is housed in a rambling Victorian two blocks from the bus station. The five-bunk dorm rooms and private singles and doubles with shared bathroom are nothing fancy, but they are clean and comfortable. There is a kitchen for guest use and lots of space for lounging on the verandahs.

Auberge au Bois Dormant Inn B&B $$
(⚑506-855-6767, 866-856-6767; www.auberge -auboisdormant.com; 67 John St; s incl breakfast $85-110, d $95-120; ❁❄@❁) A gracious Victorian renovated with crisp modern flair. Some rooms have private balconies. This gay-friendly establishment is situated along a quiet, tree-lined residential street and puts on a three-course breakfast spread.

✖️ Eating

Little Louis'   FRENCH, NEW CANADIAN **$$$**
(☎506-855-2022; www.littlelouis.ca; 245 Collishaw St; mains $22-28; ☉dinner) The odd location of this nouvelle cuisine bistro – upstairs in a faceless industrial strip mall – only adds to its speakeasy vibe. The atmosphere is cozy, with low lights, white tablecloths and jazzy live music. Local foodies rave about dishes like foie gras with apple wine jelly, or crispy steelhead trout with shiitake and saffron-vanilla butter. Whatever you do, always start with raw local oysters on the half shell with fresh horseradish. The wine list racks up awards on a regular basis.

Bogart's   ITALIAN **$$$**
(www.bogartsmoncton.com; 589 Main St; mains $20-32; ☉lunch&dinner Mon-Fri, dinner Sat&Sun) A local favorite, this chic downtown joint specializes in modern, Italian-accented dishes like lobster risotto and rosemary-glazed beef tenderloin. The decor is a smart and snappy mix of tomato orange, dark chocolate brown wood and fresh creamy linens. Settle in for live after-dinner music on summer weekends.

Calactus   VEGETARIAN **$$**
(☎506-388-4833; 125 Church St; mains $10-13; ☉lunch & dinner) Shangri-la for vegetarians! Enjoy the freedom to order anything off the globally inspired menu, which contains everything from falafel plates, to tofu cheese pizza, to fried Indian pakoras. The natural wood, warm earth colors and burbling fountain create a soothing atmosphere.

Cafe Archibald   FRENCH, CANADIAN **$$**
(221 Mountain Rd; mains $8-12; ☉lunch & dinner) At this stylish bistro, crepes are the house specialty, whipped up in the open stainless steel kitchen and served at redwood and zebra print banquettes or on the inviting screened-in porch. Alternatively, feast on the wild mushroom and basil pizza with a leafy salad.

Pump House   BREWERY **$$**
(www.pumphousebrewery.ca; 5 Orange Lane; mains $8-15; ☉lunch & dinner) The Pump is where the locals unwind and you can get a good burger, steak-based meal or wood-fired pizza. Of the brews made on the premises, the Muddy River stout is tasty, or try the beer sample tray.

🍷 Drinking & Entertainment

Moncton has a lively little rock and indie music scene, with several bars and clubs clustered around central Main St. The free *here* (www.herenb.canadaeast.com) has the rundown on the city's vibrant (read: raucous) nightlife. Try **Paramount Lounge** (www.paramountlounge.com; 800 Main St) for cheap, fun local punk and indie shows, or the **Old Cosmo** (700 Main St) for Molson-fueled partying on a packed outdoor patio. You can also sip a glass of wine during the interval at the grand **Capitol Theatre** (www.capitol.nb.ca; 811 Main St), a 1922 vaudeville house that has been restored to its original glory. It is the venue for concerts and live theater throughout the year. Get your morning Joe at downtown's **Café Cognito** (www.cafecognito.ca; 700 Main St; ☉7:30am-5:30pm Mon-Fri, 9am-4pm Sat), a tiny European-style cafe with exposed brick walls and a handful of bistro tables.

ℹ️ Information

Moncton Hospital (☎506-857-5111; 135 MacBeath Ave) Emergency room.

Moncton Public Library (644 Main St; ☉9am-8:30pm Tue-Thu, 9am-5pm Fri & Sat) Free internet access.

St George St After Hours Medical Clinic (☎506-856-6122; 404 St George Blvd; ☉5:30-8pm Mon-Fri, noon-3pm Sat, Sun & holidays) No appointment is required to see a doctor. Adjacent to Jean Coutu Pharmacy.

Visitors Information Center (www.gomoncton.com; Bore Park, Main St E; ☉8:30am-6:30pm daily May-Sep, 9am-5pm Mon-Fri Oct-Apr)

ℹ️ Getting There & Away

AIR Greater Moncton International Airport (www.gmia.ca) is about 6km east of Champlain Place Shopping Centre via Champlain St. For flight information see p380.

BUS Acadian Lines stops at the **bus station** (www.acadianbus.com; 92 Lester St), walking distance from downtown. Buses go multiple times a day to Fredericton ($44, two hours), Saint John ($33, two hours), Charlottetown, PEI ($40, three hours) and Halifax ($55, four hours).

CAR & MOTORCYCLE If you need wheels, Avis, Budget, Hertz and National all have car-rental desks at the airport, or try **Discount Car Rentals** (☎506-857-2323; www.discountcar.com; 1543 Mountain Rd).

Parking can be a hassle in Moncton: the parking meters ($1 per hour) and 'no parking' signs extend far out from downtown. The municipal parking lot at Moncton Market on Westmorland St charges $1/8 per hour/day and is free on Saturday, Sunday and evenings after 6pm. Highfield Sq Mall on Main St provides free parking for its clients, and who's to say you aren't one?

TRAIN The **train station** (www.viarail.ca; 1240 Main St) is just west of central downtown. With VIA Rail, the *Ocean* goes through northern New Brunswick, including Miramichi and Campbellton, and into Québec, on its way to Montréal (from $129). The train to Halifax departs six days a week (from $38).

❶ Getting Around

The airport is served by bus 20 from Champlain Pl nine times on weekdays. A taxi to the center of town costs about $15.

Codiac Transit (www.codiactranspo.ca) is the local bus system, with 40 wi-fi equipped buses going all over town. Single tickets are $2.

Sackville

Sackville is a small university town that's in the right place for a pit stop – for birds and people. The **Sackville Waterfowl Park**, across the road from the university off East Main St, is on a major bird migration route. Boardwalks with interpretive signs rise over portions of it. The **Wildlife Service** (17 Waterfowl Lane, off E Main St; admission free; ◷8am-4pm Mon-Fri) has information and a wetlands display at one of the entrances. Enthusiasts should also see the **Tantramar Wetlands Centre** (www.weted.com; 223 Main St; admission free; ◷8am-4pm Mon-Fri) with its walking trail and educational office, behind the high school.

Mel's Tea Room (17 Bridge St, mains $4-10, ◷breakfast, lunch & dinner) has been operating in the center of town since 1919, now with the charm of a 1950s diner, including a jukebox and prices to match.

Fort Beauséjour National Historic Site

Right by the Nova Scotia border, this **national historic site** (www.pc.gc.ca/fortbeausejour; adult/child/family $3.90/1.90/9.50; ◷interpretive center 9am-5pm Jun–mid-Oct) 1.5km west of the visitors center preserves the remains of a French fort built in 1751 to hold the British back. It didn't work. Later it was used as a stronghold during the American Revolution and the War of 1812. Only earthworks and stone foundations remain, but the view is excellent, vividly illustrating why these crossroads of the Maritimes were fortified by two empires.

To find out more, visit the **New Brunswick Visitor Centre** (☎506-364-4090; 158 Aulac Rd; ◷9am-9pm Jul & Aug, 10am-6pm mid-May–early Oct), off Hwy 2 in Aulac, at the junction of roads leading to all three Maritime provinces.

NORTHUMBERLAND SHORE

New Brunswick's Northumberland Shore stretches from the Confederation Bridge to Kouchibouguac National Park, dotted with fishing villages and summer cottages. Shediac, on lobster lovers' itineraries, is a popular resort town in a strip of summer seaside and beach playgrounds. A good part of the population along this coast is French-speaking, and Bouctouche is an Acadian stronghold. Further north, Kouchibouguac National Park protects a large swath of scenic coastal ecosystems.

Cape Jourimain

Near the bridge to PEI, the **Cape Jourimain Nature Centre** (www.capejourimain.ca; Rte 16; admission free; ◷8am-8pm May-Oct) sits in a 675-hectare national wildlife area that protects this undeveloped shoreline and its migratory birds. Seventeen kilometers of trails wind through salt marshes, dunes, woods and beach. A four-story lookout provides views of the surroundings and Confederation Bridge.

There's a **New Brunswick Visitor Centre** (Hwy 16; ◷8am-9pm Jul & Aug, 9am-6pm mid-May–Jun & Sep-early Oct) by the bridge.

For information on crossing the Confederation Bridge into PEI, see p381.

Shediac

Shediac, a self-proclaimed lobster capital, is a busy summer beach town and home of the annual July lobster fest. The many white lights sprinkled around town all summer lend a festive air. Don't fail to have your picture taken with the 'World's Largest Lobster' sculpture – you can't miss it!

It seems on any hot weekend that half the province is flaked out on the sand at **Parlee Beach**, turning the color of cooked lobster. South at Cap Pelé are vast stretches of more sandy shorelines. Terrific **Aboiteau Beach** is over 5km of unsupervised sand, while others have all amenities and lifeguards.

Shediac Bay Cruises (506-532-2175, 888-894-2002; www.lobstertales.ca; adult/child $59/39; Pointe-du-Chene wharf) has a unique concept. They take passengers out on the water, pull up lobster traps, then show you how to cook and eat 'em.

Shediac is ringed with shantytown-like RV campgrounds whose only appeal is their proximity to Parlee Beach. More upscale lodgings are found at **Maison Tait** (506-532-4233; www.maisontaithouse.com; 293 Main St; r incl breakfast $179-219;), a luxurious 1911 mansion with nine sun-drenched rooms, and **Auberge Gabriele Inn** (506-532-8007, 877-982-7222; www.aubergegabrieleinn.com; 296 Main St; r $99-169;), with simple, country-chic rooms above a popular restaurant.

Tops for dining out are **Paturel's Shore House** (506-532-4774; Rte 133; mains $18-23; 4-10pm) for fresh seafood, or the restaurant at Maison Tait for fine dining and romantic ambiance. Grab fresh seafood and strawberry daiquiris at always-packed **Captain Dan's** (www.captaindans.ca; mains $10-24; lunch & dinner) at the busy Pointe-du-Chene wharf. After dinner, catch a flick at the wonderfully retro **Neptune Drive-In** (www.neptunedrivein.ca; 691 Main St).

Bouctouche

This small, surprisingly busy waterside town is an Acadian cultural focal point with several unique attractions. The **visitor information center** (Hwy 134; 9am-5pm Jun-Sep) at the town's south entrance features a boardwalk out over the salt marsh.

MR BIG

Kenneth Colin (KC) Irving was born in Bouctouche in 1899. From a modest beginning selling cars, he built up a business Goliath spanning oil refining, shipyards, mass media, transportation, pulp and paper, gas stations, convenience stores and more. The name is everywhere. At least 8% of the province's workforce is employed by an Irving endeavor. KC died in 1992, leaving his three sons to carry on the vast Irving Group empire.

Sights & Activities

Le Pays de la Sagouine HISTORICAL VILLAGE (www.sagouine.com; 57 Acadie St; adult/child/family $16/10/37; 9:30am-5:30pm last week Jun-1st week Sep) Sitting on a small island in the Bouctouche River, this reconstructed Acadian village has daily programs in English and French. There are interactive cooking and craft demos, historical house tours and live music, as well as several cafes in which to sample old-fashioned Acadian cuisine. In July and August there's a supper theater at 7pm Monday to Saturday ($53).

Irving Eco Centre PARK (www.irvingecocentre.com; 1932 Hwy 475; admission free; interpretive center 10am-8pm Jul & Aug, shorter hours May, Jun, Sep & Oct) On the coast 9km northeast of Bouctouche, this nature center protects and makes accessible 'La Dune de Bouctouche,' a beautiful, long sandspit jutting into the strait. The interpretive center has displays on the flora and fauna, but the highlight is the **boardwalk** that snakes above the sea grass along the dunes for 2km. The peninsula itself is 12km long, taking four to six hours to hike over the loose sand and back. There are several naturalist-led tours daily. There's a 12km hiking/cycling trail through mixed forest to Bouctouche town, which begins at the Eco Centre parking lot ($4).

KC Irving (1899–1992), founder of the Irving empire, was from Bouctouche, and there's a large bronze statue of him in the town park.

Olivier Soapery INDUSTRIAL MUSEUM (www.oliviersoaps.com; 831 Rte 505, St-Anne-de-Kent) This old-fashioned soap factory advertizes its 'museum' on what seems like every highway in New Brunswick. It's really more of a store, with tons of luscious-smelling hand-molded soaps, but it does have regular talks on the soap-making process and a few interesting historical displays.

Sleeping & Eating

Le Vieux Presbytère INN $$ (506-743-5568; www.vieuxpresbytere.nb.ca; 157 Chemin du Couvent; s $90-130;) This former priest's residence was once a popular religious retreat for Acadians from across the province. The best rooms are in the older part of the building, with high molded ceilings and simple, sunny decor.

Chez les Maury   CAMPING $
(☎506-743-5347; fermemaury@hotmail.com;
2021 Rte 475; ⊗May-Oct) On the grounds of
a family-run vineyard, this small, basic
campground has toilets, showers and a
tiny private beach across the way.

Restaurant La Sagouine   ACADIAN $
(43 Blvd Irving; mains $8-17; ⊗breakfast, lunch &
dinner) Fried clams or a traditional Acadian
dinner – get a seat on the outdoor patio.

Kouchibouguac National Park

Beaches, lagoons and offshore sand dunes
extend for 25km, inviting strolling, bird-
watching and clam-digging. The park
encompasses hectares of forest and salt
marshes, crisscrossed or skirted by bike
paths, hiking trails and groomed cross-
country ski tracks. Kouchibouguac (*koosh-
e-boo-gwack*), a Mi'kmaq word meaning
'river of long tides,' also has moose, deer
and black bear. For more information try
the **visitors center** (www.pc.gc.ca/kouchibou
guac; 186 Hwy 117; park admission per day adult/
child/family $7.80/3.90/19.60; ⊗9am-5pm mid-
May–mid-Oct, 8am-8pm Jun-Sep).

🏃 Activities

Cycling & Kayaking
Kouchibouguac has 60km of bikeways –
crushed gravel paths that wind through
the park's backcountry. **Ryan's Rental
Centre** (☎506-876-3733), near the South
Kouchibouguac campground, rents out bicycles at $6.00 per hour/day and canoes/
kayaks at $30/50 per day. From Ryan's
you can cycle a 23km loop and never be
on the park road. The calm, shallow water
between the shore and the dunes, which
run for 25km north and south, makes for
a serene morning paddle.

Hiking
The park has 10 trails, mostly short and
flat. The excellent **Bog Trail** (1.9km) is a
boardwalk beyond the observation tower,
and only the first few hundred meters are
crushed gravel. The **Cedars Trail** (1.3km)
is less used. The **Osprey Trail** (5.1km)
is a loop trail through the forest. **Kelly's
Beach Boardwalk** (600m one way) floats
above the grass-covered dunes. When you
reach the beach, turn right and hike 6km
to the end of the dune. Take drinking water.

Swimming
For swimming, the lagoon area is shallow,
warm and safe for children, while adults
will find the deep water on the ocean side
invigorating.

🛏 Sleeping & Eating
Kouchibouguac has two drive-in campgrounds and three primitive camping areas
totaling 359 sites. The camping season is
from mid-May to mid-October and the park
is very busy throughout July and August,
especially on weekends. **Camping reservations** (☎877-737-3783; www.pccamping.
ca; reservation fee $10.80) are taken for 60%
of the sites. Otherwise, get on the lengthy
'roll call' waiting list – it can take two or
three days to get a site. The park entry fee
is extra.

South Kouchibouguac (with/without
electricity in summer $27/32) is the largest
campground, 13km inside the park near
the beaches in a large open field ringed by
trees, with sites for tents and RVs, showers
and a kitchen shelter. On the north side
of Kouchibouguac River, **Cote-a-Fabien**
(campsites $16; first-come, first-served only) is
the best choice for those seeking a bit of
peace and privacy. There is water and vault
toilets, but no showers. Some sites are on
the shore, others nestled among the trees,
with a dozen walk-in sites (100m; wheel
barrows provided for luggage) for those
who want a car-free environment. The
Osprey hiking trail starts from here.

The three primitive campgrounds have
only vault toilets. **Sipu** and **Petit-Large**
have water pumps. All cost $10 per person
per night. Note that **Pointe a Maxime** is
the most difficult to get to (access by water
only), but this does not translate into remote seclusion. There is a constant stream
of passing motorized boat traffic from the
fishing wharf nearby.

There are a couple of snack bars and a
restaurant in the park, but you should stock
up on groceries in nearby St-Louis de Kent.

ⓘ Getting There & Away
It is difficult to get to and around the park without a car or bicycle. The distance from the park
gate to the campgrounds and beaches is at least
10km. The nearest bus stop is in Rexton, 16km
south of the park, where Acadian Bus Lines
stops at the **Acadian Lines** (www.acadianbus.
com; 126 Main St) bus stops at the Circle K gas
station. There is one bus a day heading south to

Moncton ($16), and one a day heading north to Miramichi ($23).

miramichifolksongfestival.com; ☺early Aug), the oldest of its kind in North America.

MIRAMICHI RIVER VALLEY AREA

In New Brunswick, the word Miramichi connotes both the city and the river, but even more: an intangible, captivating mystique. The spell the region casts emanates partially from the Acadian and Irish mix of folklore, legends, superstitions and tales of ghosts. It also seeps from the dense forests and wilderness of the area and from the character of the residents who wrestle a livelihood from these natural resources. The fabled river adds its serpentine cross-country course, crystal tributaries and world-renowned salmon fishing. The region produces some wonderful rootsy music and inspires artists including noted writer David Adams Richards, whose work skillfully mines the temper of the region.

Miramichi

The working-class river city of Miramichi is an amalgam of the towns of Chatham, Newcastle, Douglastown, Loggieville, Nelson and several others along a 12km stretch of the Miramichi River near its mouth. Miramichi, with its Irish background, is an English-speaking enclave in the middle of a predominantly French-speaking region. The **tourist information center** (199 King St; ☺Jun-Sep) is downtown at Ritchie's Wharf, a down-at-heel riverfront boardwalk park.

Though surrounded by two paper mills and sawmills, central Newcastle is pleasant enough. In the central square is a statue to Lord Beaverbrook (1879–1964), one of the most powerful press barons in British history and a major benefactor of his home province. His ashes lie under the statue presented as a memorial to him by the town. Beaverbrook's boyhood home, **Beaverbrook House** (www.beaverbrookhouse.com; 518 King George Hwy; admission free; ☺9am-5pm Mon-Fri, 10am-5pm Sat, 1-5pm Sun mid-Jun–Aug), built 1879, is now a museum.

Miramichi is a mill town, not a tourist center, but traditional folk music enthusiasts might want to pay a visit for the **Irish Festival** (www.canadasirishfest.com; ☺mid-Jul) and the **Miramichi Folksong Festival** (www.

🛏 Sleeping & Eating

Enclosure Campground CAMPGROUND **$**
(☑506-622-8638, 800-363-1733; 8 Enclosure Rd; tent/RV sites $26/30; ☺May-Oct) Southwest of Newcastle off Hwy 8 is another of Lord Beaverbrook's gifts, a former provincial park called the Enclosure. This riverside park includes a nice wooded area with spacious quasi-wilderness sites for tenters.

Governor's Mansion B&B **$$**
(☑506-622-3036, 877-647-2642; www.governorsmansion.ca; 62 St Patrick's St, Nelson; r incl breakfast $69-109) On the south side of the river overlooking Beaubears Island is the creaky-but-elegant Victorian Governor's Mansion (1860), onetime home of the first Irish lieutenant governor of the province.

Cunard CHINESE **$$**
(www.cunardrestaurant.com; 32 Cunard St, Chatham; mains $9-15; ☺lunch & dinner) Surprisingly decent Canadianized Chinese food like chicken chow mein and honey-garlic spareribs in a classic, lacquer-and-dragon-print dining room.

Saddler's Cafe FUSION **$$**
(www.saddlerscafe.com; 1729 Water St, Chatham; mains $9-18; ☺lunch & dinner Tue-Sat) Creative sandwiches and international-inspired mains like pineapple rice in a cute downtown storefront.

ℹ Getting There & Away

Acadian Lines (www.acadianbus.com; 201 Edward St) buses depart from the Best Value Inn. Daily buses leave for Fredericton ($38, 2½ hours), Saint John ($55, five hours) and Campbellton ($44, three hours).

The **VIA Rail station** (www.viarail.ca; 251 Station St at George St) is in Newcastle. Trains from Montréal and Halifax stop here.

Miramichi River Valley

The Miramichi is actually a complex web of rivers and tributaries draining much of central New Brunswick. The main branch, the 217km-long Southwest Miramichi River, flows from near Hartland through forest to Miramichi where it meets the other main fork, the Northwest Miramichi. For over a hundred years, the entire system has inspired reverent awe for its tranquil beauty and incredible Atlantic salmon fly-fishing.

Famous business tycoons, international politicians, sports and entertainment stars and Prince Charles have all wet lines here. Even Marilyn Monroe is said to have dipped her legs. The legendary fishery has had some ups and downs with overfishing, poaching and unknown causes (perhaps global warming) affecting stocks, but they now seem back at sustainable levels. The **tourist office** (www. doaktown.com) is in the Salmon Museum in Doaktown, the center of most valley activity.

◉ Sights

Atlantic Salmon Museum   MUSEUM
(www.atlanticsalmonmuseum.com; 263 Main St; adult/child $5/3; ☉9am-5pm mid-Apr–mid-Oct) Learn about historic Doaktown's storied fishing history and check out the salmon and trout aquarium at this lodgelike museum.

Metepenagiag First Nation Heritage Park   HISTORICAL SITE
(☎506-836-6118, 800-570-1344; www.meteena giag.com; 2202 Hwy 420, Redbank) On the Esk River, the new Metepenagiag First Nation Heritage Park has interpretive tours of Mi'kmaq culture and history on a 3000-year-old archaeological site. Call for info.

🏃 Activities

Sport fishing remains the main activity, but is tightly controlled for conservation. Licenses are required and all anglers must employ a registered guide. A three-day license for non-residents is $60. All fish over 63cm must be released. Salmon fishing on the Miramichi is primarily hook and release, to preserve the precious and endangered species. Most of the salmon served up in the province is in fact, salmon farmed in the Bay of Fundy.

WW **Doak & Sons** (www.doak.com; 331 Main St) is one of Canada's best fly-fishing shops. It sells a huge number of flies annually, some made on the premises. A wander around will get an angler pumped.

Despite the presence of the king of freshwaters, there are other pastimes to enjoy. The **Miramichi Trail**, a walking and cycling path along an abandoned rail line, is now partially complete, with 75km of the projected 200km useable. At McNamee, the pedestrian Priceville Suspension Bridge spans the river. It's a popular put-in spot for canoeists and kayakers spending half a day paddling downriver to Doaktown. Several outfitters in Doaktown and Blackville offer equipment rentals, shuttle services and guided trips for leisurely canoe, kayak or

even tubing trips along the river. Try **Gaston Adventure Tours** (bgaston@nbnet.nb.ca; falls tour $180, canoe tours $60-180), with personalized fishing trips and falls tours run by Bev Gaston of the Atlantic Salmon Museum.

🛏 Sleeping & Eating

Beautiful rustic lodges and camps abound, many replicating the halcyon days of the 1930s and '40s. Check out www.miramichi rivertourism.com for links to more accommodations and fishing outfitters. Restaurants are few and far between – plan to pack in your own supplies.

O'Donnell's Cottages & Expeditions
                         MOTEL, COTTAGES **$$**
(☎506-365-7636, 800-563-8724; www. odonnellscottages.com; 439 Storeytown Rd; r $99-169) Cozy log cabins on the riverbank, with a variety of outdoor activities on offer.

NORTHEASTERN NEW BRUNSWICK

The North Shore, as it is known to New Brunswickers, is the heartland of Acadian culture in the province. The region was settled 250 years ago by French farmers and fishers, starting from scratch again after the upheaval of the Expulsion, frequently intermarrying with the original Mi'kmaq inhabitants. The coastal road north from Miramichi, around the Acadian Peninsula and along Chaleurs Bay to Campbellton passes through small fishing settlements and peaceful ocean vistas. At Sugarloaf Provincial Park, the Appalachian Mountain Range comes down to the edge of the sea. Behind it, stretching hundreds of kilometers into the interior of the province, is a vast, trackless wilderness of rivers and dense forest, rarely explored.

Tracadie-Sheila

Unmasking a little known but gripping story, the **Historical Museum of Tracadie** (Rue du Couvent; adult/child $3/1; ☉9am-6pm Mon-Fri, noon-6pm Sat & Sun in summer) focuses on the leprosy colony, based here from 1868 to as late as 1965. It's the only place in Canada providing details on a leprosarium. The nearby cemetery has the graves of 60 victims of Hansen's Disease (leprosy).

Caraquet

The oldest of the Acadian villages, Caraquet, was founded in 1757 by refugees from forcibly abandoned homesteads further south. It's now the quiet, working-class center of the peninsula's French community. Caraquet's colorful, bustling fishing port, off Blvd St Pierre Est, has an assortment of moored vessels splashing at the dock. East and West Blvd St Pierre are divided at Rue le Portage.

The **tourist office** (www.ville.caraquet.nb.ca; 51 Blvd St Pierre Est; ☉9am-5pm mid-Jun–mid-Sep) and all of the local tour operators are found at the **Carrefour de la Mer** complex, with its Day Adventure Centre, restaurant and views down on the waterfront near the fishing harbor.

◉ Sights & Activities

Acadian Historic Village   HISTORIC PARK
(www.villagehistoriqueacadien.com; 14311 Hwy 11; adult/child/senior/family $16/11/14/38; ☉10am-6pm early Jun-Sep) Acadian Historic Village, 15km west of Caraquet, is a major historic reconstruction set up like a village of old. Thirty-three original buildings relocated to the site and animators in period costumes reflect life from 1780 to 1880. A good three to four hours is required to see the site, and then you'll definitely want to eat. For that, there are old-fashioned sit-down Acadian meals at La Table des Ancêtres, the 1910 historical menu at the Château Albert dining room, and several snack bars. The village has a program for kids ($35), which provides them with a costume and seven hours of supervised historical activities.

✴ Festivals & Events

The largest annual Acadian cultural festival, **Festival Acadien** (www.festivalacadien. ca), is held here the first two weeks of August. It draws 100,000 visitors; over 200 performers including singers, musicians, actors, dancers from Acadia and other French regions (some from overseas) entertain. Especially picturesque is the annual blessing of the fleet, when a flotilla of fishing vessels cruises the harbor with ribbons and flags streaming from their rigging. The culminating Tintamarre Parade is a real blowout.

▣ Sleeping & Eating

TOP CHOICE **Hotel Paulin**   HOTEL $$
(☏506-727-9981, 866-727-9981; www. hotelpaulin.com; 143 Blvd St Pierre W; r incl breakfast $128, incl breakfast & 4-course dinner for 2 from $195) Scrimp elsewhere and splurge on a night at the exquisite Hotel Paulin. This vintage seaside hotel overlooking the bay was built in 1891 and has been run by the Paulin family since 1907. The rooms are sunny and polished, done up in crisp white linens, lace and antiques. If you are staying elsewhere, make reservations for dinner; the hotel has earned a reputation for fine cuisine. An example: fiddlehead (a green, immature fern) soup followed by Acadian chicken fricot with herb dumplings (table d'hôte $45).

Château Albert   INN $$$
(Acadian Historic Village; www.villagehistorique acadien.com/chateauanglais.htm; r incl dinner & theater package for 2 $257) For complete immersion in the Acadian Historic Village, spend the night in early-20th-century style – no TV, no phone, but a charming, quiet room restored to its original 1909 splendor (with a modern bath). The original Albert stood on the main street in Caraquet until it was destroyed by fire in 1955. Packages are available including dinner in the period dining room downstairs and a tool around in a model T Ford.

Maison Touristique Dugas
                     INN, CAMPGROUND $
(☏506-727-3195; www.maisontouristiquedugas. ca; 683 Blvd St Pierre W; campsites $20-28, r with out bathroom $55, d with bathroom & cooking facilities $70, cabins $70-100) A few miles west of Caraquet, five generations of the friendly Dugas family have run this rambling, something-for-everyone property. The homey, antique-filled 1926 house has 11 rooms with shared bathrooms. There are five clean, cozy cabins with private bathrooms and cooking facilities in the backyard, a small field for RVs beyond that, and a quiet, tree-shaded campground for tenters.

Le Caraquette   CANADIAN $$
(89 Blvd St-Pierre; mains $8-14) Overlooking the harbor, this casual family-run restaurant serves Maritime standards like fried clams and mayonnaise shrimp salad along with French-Canadian specialties like *poutine* (stuffed potato dumplings) and smoked meat sandwiches.

ⓘ Getting There & Away

Public transportation around this part of the province is very limited as Acadian Lines buses don't pass this way. Local residents wishing to connect with the bus or train in Miramichi or Bathurst use a couple of van shuttles. Ask for details at the tourist office.

Take a run out to the very northeastern tip of the province – a chain of low, flat islands pointing across the Gulf of St Lawrence to Labrador. Rte 113 cuts across salt marsh and scrub arriving first in **Shippagan**, home of the province's largest fishing fleet, where crab is king. Visit the sea creatures at the **Aquarium & Marine Centre** (www.aquariumnb.ca; 100 Aquarium St; adult/child $8/5; ⊘10am-6pm late May–Sep). Kids will love the touch tanks full of sea creatures, and the seals (fed at 11am and 4pm). Hop the bridge to **Lamèque**, a tidy fishing village that has hosted the **Lamèque International Baroque Festival** (☑506-344-5846, 800-320-2276; www.festivalbaroque.com; ⊘last week Jul) for over 30 years. Note the red, white and blue Acadian flags flying from nearly every porch. Rte 113 continues north to **Miscou Island**. Stop to walk the boardwalk trail over a cranberry bog before the road dead-ends at the lighthouse.

Campbellton

Campbellton is a pleasant but unremarkable mill town on the Québec border. There are really only two reasons to come here: transiting to or from Québec; or to hike, ski and camp at Sugarloaf Provincial Park. The lengthy Restigouche River, which winds through northern New Brunswick and then forms the border with Québec, empties to the sea here. The Bay of Chaleur is on one side and dramatic rolling hills surround the town on the remaining sides. Across the border is Matapédia and Hwy 132 leading to Mont Joli, 148km into Québec.

Dominated by Sugarloaf Mountain, which rises nearly 400m above sea level and looks vaguely like one of its other namesakes in Rio, **Sugarloaf Provincial Park** (www.sugarloafpark.ca; 596 Val d'Amours Rd; admission free) is off Hwy 11 at Exit 415. From the base, it's just a half-hour walk to the top – well worth the extensive views of the town and part of the Restigouche River. Another trail leads around the bottom of the hill.

The last naval engagement of the Seven Years' War was fought in the waters off this coast in 1760. The Battle of Restigouche marked the conclusion of the long struggle for Canada by Britain and France. The helpful provincial **tourist office** (☑506-789-2367; 56 Salmon Blvd; ⊘10am-6pm mid-May–Jun & Sep-early Oct, 8am-9pm Jul & Aug) is next to City Centre Mall.

Sugarloaf Provincial Park (☑506-789-2366; www.sugarloafpark.ca; 596 Val d'Amours Rd; tent/RV sites $22/29; ⊘mid-May–early Oct) has 76 campsites in a pleasant wooded setting 4km from downtown Campbellton. You can also crash comfortably at **Campbellton Lighthouse Hostel** (☑506-759-7044; campbellton@hihostels.ca; 1 Ritchie St; dm $21; ⊘mid-Jun–Aug; 🖱). This clean, recently renovated hostel is in a converted lighthouse by the Restigouche River, near the Acadian bus stop and Campbellton's 8.5m **salmon sculpture**. Alternatively, **Maison McKenzie House B&B** (☑506-753-3133; www.bbcanada.com/4384.html; 31 Andrew St; r without bathroom incl breakfast $75-100; P🅿🖱) is a homey 1910 house handy to downtown. For $60, they'll rent you a kayak and drop you off upriver.

ⓘ Getting There & Away

Acadian Lines (www.acadianbus.com; 46 Water St) stops at the Pik-Quik convenience store, near Prince William St. The bus departs daily for Fredericton ($71, six hours) and Moncton ($65, six hours). Twice a day (once in the morning and once in the afternoon), an **Orléans Express** (www.orleansexpress.com) bus leaves from the Pik-Quick for Gaspé ($38, six hours) and Québec City ($89, seven hours).

The **VIA Rail station** (www.viarail.ca; 99c Roseberry St) is conveniently central. There's one train daily, except Wednesday, going south to Moncton ($50, four hours) and Halifax ($64, 10 hours), and one daily, except Tuesday, heading the other way to Montréal ($146, 12 hours).

Prince Edward Island

Best Places to Eat

» Lot 30 (p428)

» Lobster Suppers At town halls and churches around the province

» Shipwright's Café (p443)

» Ship to Shore (p443)

» The Pearl (p443)

Best Places to Stay

» Fairholm Inn (p425)

» Barachois Inn (p438)

» Great George (p427)

» Maplehurst Properties (p432)

» Willow Green Farm B&B (p444)

Why Go?

Move over Mounties, Canada's got a spunky, red-headed feminine side. In Prince Edward Island (PEI) little Anne Shirley, Lucy Maud Montgomery's immortal heroine of the *Anne of Green Gables* series, is larger than her fictional britches. Ironically, the island itself is a red-head – from tip to tip sienna-colored soil peeks out from under potato plants, and the shores are lined with rose and golden sand. Meanwhile the Green Gables-esque landscape is a pastoral green patchwork of rolling fields, tidy gabled farmhouses and seaside villages.

Yet despite the pervasive splendor of the province, the first thing most visitors notice, and fall in love with, is PEI's charm and relaxed atmosphere. The 'Gentle Island' really lives up to its nickname and the least authentic things you'll find here are the orange nylon braids of little girls in tourist spots dressed up as 'Anne.'

When to Go

Charlottetown

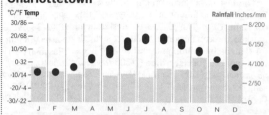

June Enjoy the spring calm before the crowds hit; the rolling hillsides are abloom with wildflowers.

July & August The entire island is in festival mode with live music and lobster suppers nightly.

September Traditional music, food mark Charlottetown's PEI International Shellfish Festival.

PEI FAST FACTS

» Population: 141,000

» Area: 5700 sq km

» Capital: Charlottetown

» Quirky fact: Kilos of potatoes produced per year: 1.3 billion

Local Culture

The defining feature of island culture is its rural roots – most islanders are just one or two generations removed from the family farm or fishing boat, or are still there working it. There are descendants of the original Mi'kmaq population and small pockets of French-speaking Acadians in the eastern and western parts of the province. Most islanders, however, trace their heritage to the British Isles.

History

Its Aboriginal inhabitants, the Mi'kmaq, knew the island as Abegeit – 'Land Cradled on the Waves.' Although Jacques Cartier of France first recorded PEI's existence in 1534, settlement didn't begin until 1603. Initially small, the French colony grew only after Britain's expulsion of the Acadians from Nova Scotia in the 1750s. In 1758 the British took the island, known then as Île St Jean, and expelled the 3000 Acadians. Britain was officially granted the island in the Treaty of Paris of 1763.

To encourage settlement, the British divided the island into 67 lots and held a lottery to give away the land. Unfortunately, most of the 'Great Giveaway' winners were speculators and did nothing to settle or develop the island. The questionable actions of these absentee landlords hindered population growth and caused incredible unrest among islanders.

One of the major reasons PEI did not become part of Canada in 1867 was because union did not offer a solution to the land problem. In 1873 the Compulsory Land Purchase Act forced the sale of absentee landlords' land and cleared the way for PEI to join Canada later that year. But foreign land ownership is still a sensitive issue in the province. The population has remained stable, at around 140,000, since the 1930s.

In 1997, after much debate, PEI was linked to New Brunswick and the mainland by the Confederation Bridge – at almost 13km, it's the world's longest artificial bridge over ice-covered waters.

Land & Climate

PEI stretches 224km tip to tip; it's 6km wide at its narrowest point, and 64km at its widest. The island is a low-lying hump of iron-rich red sandstone and earth. Its highest point rises 152m above sea level, at Springton – smack dab in the middle of the province.

July and August are the warmest and driest months. In winter the snow can be meters deep, but it rarely hinders the major roadways. The last of the white stuff is usually gone by May.

❶ Getting There & Around

Apart from a couple of shuttle services (see p424), there is no intra-island public transportation.

AIR

Charlottetown's airport is 8km from town and serves all flights entering and leaving the province.

Air Canada has daily flights to Charlottetown from Halifax and Toronto, and from Montréal in the high season (June to September). WestJet offers direct flights to Charlottetown from Toronto and Montréal. From June to September, Northwestern Airlines and Delta Airlines each run one daily direct flight to Charlottetown from Detroit and Boston, respectively. See p880 for these airlines' contact details. **Sunwing** (☎877 786-9464; www.flysunwing.com) flies from Toronto during the summer.

BICYCLE

Cyclists and pedestrians are banned from the Confederation Bridge (see p424) and must use the 24-hour, demand-driven shuttle service (bicycle/pedestrian $8/4). On the PEI side, go to the bridge operations building at Gateway Village in Borden-Carleton; on the New Brunswick side, the pickup is at the Cape Jourimain Nature Centre at exit 51 on Rte 16 (p413).

While your easiest option to get around the island is by car, bicycle is also a fine choice. The flat and well-maintained Confederation Trail (see the boxed text, p431) runs the length of the island through some beautiful countryside and small towns.

BOAT

Northumberland Ferries (☎902-566-3838, 888-249-7245; www.peiferry.com) runs the ferry service that links PEI's Wood Islands to Caribou, Nova Scotia, from May to December. There are up to nine daily sailings in each direction during the summer, and five in the fall and spring

Prince Edward Island Highlights

1 Wiggle your feet and hear a squeak at the 'singing sands' of **Basin Head Provincial Park** (boxed text, p434)

2 Eat your fill of fresh island lobster with all the fixings in **New Glasgow** (p438) or **St Ann** (p440)

3 Be taken away into the pages of *Anne of Green Gables* while visiting the Green Gables House in **Cavendish** (p441)

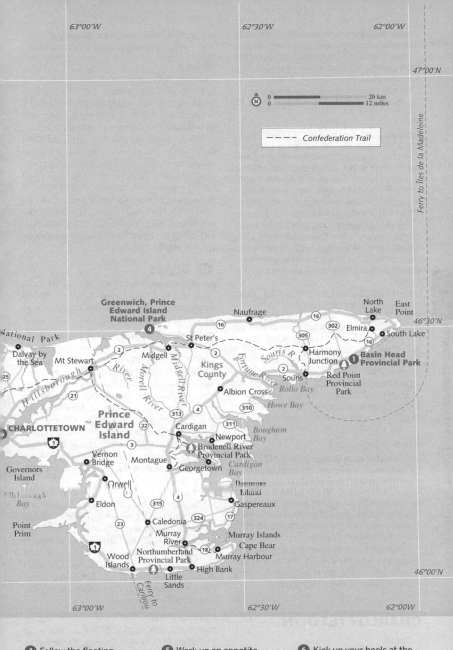

④ Follow the floating boardwalk across the salt marsh and over the sand dunes onto the empty beach at **Greenwich** (boxed text, p437)

⑤ Work up an appetite peddling through the countryside on the **Confederation Trail** (boxed text, p431)

⑥ Kick up your heels at the Benevolent Irish Society's weekly *ceilidh* (social gathering with folk music) in **Charlottetown** (p424)

(car/pedestrian/motorcycle $69/18/45). Note that vehicle fees include all passengers for the 1¼-hour trip. You only pay as you're leaving PEI; the trip over from Nova Scotia is free. The ferry operates on a first-come, first-served basis.

For information on the ferry service between Souris and Îles de la Madeleine, Québec, see p309.

BUS

Acadian Coach Lines (☑800-567-5151; www. acadianbus.com; 156 Belvedere Ave, Charlottetown) has service to Charlottetown three times per day from Moncton, New Brunswick ($38 one way, three hours), with stops at Borden-Carleton and Summerside en route. There is one bus per day to Halifax ($64 one way, 5½ hours), with a transfer in Amherst, Nova Scotia.

Advanced Shuttle (☑877-886-3322; Nassau St, University Ave, Charlottetown) is a convenient service from Charlottetown or Summerside to Halifax or any point along the way (adult/student $52/47). The van has a bicycle carrier.

The **Beach Shuttle** (☑902-566-5259; www. princeedwardtours.com; Founders' Hall, 6 Prince St, Charlottetown), running between Charlottetown and Cavendish several times per day (one way $15, same-day return $25, June to September), also makes a daily run from Charlottetown to the evening stage show in Summerside.

East Connection (☑902-892-6760, 902-393-5132) departs Charlottetown daily around noon for Souris, arriving at 1pm in time for the 2pm ferry. The shuttle van leaves Souris at 1:30pm, arriving at Charlottetown an hour later.

CAR & MOTORCYCLE

The **Confederation Bridge** (☑902-437-7300, 888-437-6565; www.confederationbridge.com; car/motorcycle $43/17; ⊙24hr) is the quickest way to get to PEI from New Brunswick and East Central Nova Scotia. Unfortunately, the 1.1m-high guardrails rob you of any hoped-for view. The toll is only charged on departure from PEI, and includes all passengers.

If you're planning to travel one way on the bridge and the other by ferry, it's cheaper to take the ferry to PEI and return via the bridge.

See p430 for car rental information.

CHARLOTTETOWN

POP 38,114

It's been said that Charlottetown is too small to be grand and too big to be quaint. In fact, PEI's capital is just about the perfect size with a collection of stylish eateries and a lively cultural scene. Couple this with quiet streets for strolling, abundant greenery and a well-preserved historical core, and you have plenty of small-town appeal.

History

Charlottetown is named after the exotic consort of King George III. Her African roots, dating back to Margarita de Castro Y Sousa and the Portuguese royal house, are as legendary as they are controversial.

While many believe the city's splendid harbor was the reason Charlottetown became the capital, the reality was less glamorous. In 1765 the surveyor-general decided on Charlottetown because he thought it prudent to bestow the poor side of the island with some privileges. Thanks to the celebrated 1864 conference, however, Charlottetown is etched in Canadian history as the country's birthplace.

⊙ Sights

All of the major sights are within the confines of Old Charlottetown, which makes wandering between them as rewarding as wandering through them.

Province House National Historic Site

HISTORIC SITE

(☑902-566-7626; 165 Richmond St; admission $3.40; ⊙8:30am-5pm) Charlottetown's centerpiece is the imposing, yet welcoming, neoclassical Province House. The symmetry of design is carried throughout, including two brilliant skylights reaching up through the massive sandstone structure. It was here in 1864, within the Confederation Chamber, that 23 representatives of Britain's North American colonies first discussed the creation of Canada (p833). Along with being the 'birthplace of Canada,' the site is home to Canada's second-oldest active legislature.

Several rooms have been restored, and in July and August you may find yourself face to face with Canada's first prime minister: actors in period garb wander the halls and regularly coalesce to perform reenactments of the famous conference. Enjoy the *Great Dream,* a 17-minute film about the monumental 1864 conference.

Founders' Hall

MUSEUM

(☑902-368-1864, 800-955-1864; 6 Prince St; adult/child $7/3.75; ⊙8:30am-8pm) Opened in 2001, this high-tech multimedia exhibit, housed in an old train station, deluges your senses with facts and fun about Canada's history since 1864. It's sure to entertain children and the child in you.

Beaconsfield House   NOTABLE BUILDING
(☎902-368-6603; 2 Kent St; adult/student/family $4.25/3.25/14; ☺10am-5pm) With its crowning belvedere, intricate gingerbread trim and elegant 19th-century furnishings, Beaconsfield House is the finest Victorian mansion in Charlottetown. Have a wander or sit on the verandah and be stunned by the view.

Government House   NOTABLE BUILDING
(☎902-368-5480; admission free; ☺10am-4pm Mon-Fri Jul & Aug) Within the sprawling gardens of Victoria Park is Government House. This striking colonial mansion, with its grand hall, Palladian window and Doric columns, has been home to PEI's lieutenant governors since 1835. In 2003 the Hon JL Bernard broke with an almost 170-year-old tradition and opened its doors to the public.

St Dunstan's Basilica   NOTABLE BUILDING
(☎902-894-3486; 45 Great George St; admission free; ☺9am-5pm) Rising from the ashes of a 1913 fire, the three towering stone spires of this neo-Gothic basilica are now a Charlottetown landmark. The marble floors, Italianate carvings and decoratively embossed ribbed ceiling are surprisingly ornate.

ᘓ Tours

Self-guided walking tour booklets are available for just a loonie ($1) at the tourist office.

Confederation Players   WALKING TOURS
(☎902-368-1864; 6 Prince St; adult/child $10/5) There is no better way to tour Charlottetown. Playing the fathers and ladies of Confederation, actors garbed in 19th-century dress educate and entertain through the town's historic streets. Tours leave from Founders' Hall, and there are three variations on the theme: historic Great George St, Island Settlers and the haunts of local ghosts.

Peake's Wharf Boat Cruises   BOAT CRUISES
(☎902-566-4458; 1 Great George St; 70min cruise $20; ☺2:30pm, 6:30pm & 8pm Jun-Aug) Observe sea life, hear interesting stories and witness a wonderfully different perspective of Charlottetown from the waters of its harbor. An excellent seal-watching trip ($28) departs at 2:30pm, returning at 5pm.

Harbour Hippo Hippopotabus
    BUS & BOAT TOURS
(☎902-628-8687; Lower Prince St Wharf; 1hr tour adult/child $24/16) Want to explore historic Charlottetown but afraid the kids will get bored? Hop on this amphibious bus that takes you to all the sights on land, then floats in the water.

Abegweit Tours   BUS TOURS
(☎902-894-9966; 157 Nassau St; adult/child $11/2) One-hour double-decker bus tours through Charlottetown leave from the Confederation Centre. The six-hour north shore tour (adult/child $80/40) will pick you up if you're staying in town. It also does a pilgrimage to the home turf of Anne of Green Gables (adult/child $65/32.50).

✹✹ Festivals & Events

Charlottetown Festival   THEATER
(☎902-566-1267; www.confederationcentre.com/festival.asp; ☺mid-May–mid-Oct) This theatrical festival features free outdoor performances, a children's theater and dance programs.

Old Home Week   CULTURAL
(☎902-629-6623; www.peiprovincialexhibition.com; ☺mid-Aug) Held at the Provincial Exhibition grounds, this event features carnival rides, musical entertainment, games of chance, harness racing and traditional livestock shows.

PEI International Shellfish Festival   FOOD
(☎866-955-2003; www.peishellfish.com; ☺3rd weekend Sep) Now one of the island's largest festivals, this massive kitchen party, set on the Charlottetown waterfront, merges great traditional music with incredible seafood. Don't miss the oyster-shucking championships or the chowder challenge.

ᘫ Sleeping

Old Charlottetown's charms and proximity to major sights and restaurants makes it the most enviable area to rest your head. During summer, Charlottetown hums with activity, so it's wise to book ahead. In the off-season, accommodations are plentiful and most places reduce their rates. Parking is freely available at, or close to, all accommodations.

TOP **Fairholm Inn**   B&B $$$
CHOICE (☎902-892-5022, 888-573-5022; www.fairholm.pe.ca; 230 Prince St; ste incl breakfast $129-289) This historic inn was built in 1838 and is a superb example of the picturesque movement in British architecture. Take tea while enjoying the morning sun in the beautiful conservatory, wander the gardens or hole up with a book in the library. Luxurious English fabrics, beautiful PEI artwork and grand antiques fill each suite. Light a fire, soak in your tub and sink back into the elegant days of the 19th century.

Charlottetown

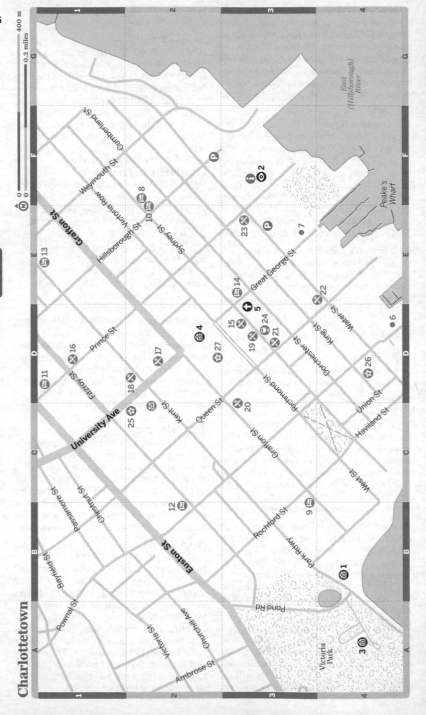

TOP CHOICE **Great George** INN **$$$**
(☎902-892-0606, 800-361-1118; www.
innsongreatgeorge.com; 58 Great George St; d
incl breakfast $175-219, ste $269-899; P✳@☎)
A colorful collage of celebrated buildings
along Charlottetown's most famous street
has rooms ranging from plush and historic
to bold and contemporary – but all are
simply stunning. It's both gay- and family-
friendly. A babysitting service is available,
as is a fitness room.

Fitzroy Hall B&B B&B **$$$**
(☎902-368-2077; www.fitzroyhall.com; 45 Fitzroy
St; d $110-190, ste $225-300) A perfect blend
of elegance and comfort, this house is as
grand as they come, while the welcome is
warm and down to earth. The innkeepers
have put some serious thought into how to
make their guests comfortable: the answer
is found with refined antiques, muted color
schemes, and details like hidden alcoves
with fridges and hot pots for guests to keep
cold drinks or make tea.

Charlotte's Rose Inn INN **$$**
(☎902-892-3699, 888-237-3699; www.charlottes
rose.ca; 11 Grafton St; r incl breakfast $155-205,
apt $180; P⊜✳@☎) Miss Marple must be
around here somewhere. This decadent Victorian has true English flair with bodacious
rose-printed wallpaper, lace canopies, big
fluffy beds and grand bathrooms. There's a

fire in the parlor for guests to enjoy along
with complimentary tea and cakes. A modern loft apartment can accommodate five
and has its own private rooftop deck.

TOP CHOICE **Spillett House B&B** B&B **$**
(☎902-892-5494; www.spilletthouse.
pe.ca; 157 Weymouth St; s/d without bathroom
incl breakfast $50/60) This lovely heritage
home is scrupulously clean, with polished
hardwood floors and antique furnishings,
homemade quilts on the beds and lace curtains on the windows. Kids are welcome
and there are storage facilities for bicycles.

Charlottetown Backpackers B&B **$**
(☎902-367-5749; www.charlottetownbackpackers.
com; 60 Hillsborough St; dm/r incl breakfast $32/79;
☎) Impossible to miss with its bright red and
white paint job and happy hostellers milling
about on the lawn. This superbly happening
backpackers has cozy single-sex or mixed
dorms, a good kitchen plus a quirky common room with a turntable and a rather epic
vinyl collection. Be prepared for spontaneous
barbecues and pub outings.

REGIONAL DRIVING DISTANCES

North Cape to East Point: 273km
Halifax to Charlottetown: 227km
Charlottetown to Montréal: 1199km

Aloha Tourist Home   B&B **$$**

(📞902-892-9944, 866-892-9944; www.aloha amigo.com; 234 Sydney St; r incl breakfast $40-150; 🐾) A welcoming choice that's really a heritage B&B complete with antiques and comfy beds, but without the hefty price tag. The serve-yourself breakfasts are gourmet, the location central and the owner is sweet and helpful. Lower-end rooms have shared bathrooms.

✕ Eating

Thanks largely to the Culinary Institute at Charlottetown's Holland College, which keeps churning out talented chefs, the city has a heaping helping of fine eateries. During summer, Victoria Row's pedestrian mall and the waterfront are hot spots for diners and drinkers. Pubs are also a great place to go for good-value eating.

TOP CHOICE Lot 30   RESTAURANT **$$$**

(📞902-629-3030; 151 Kent St; lunch mains $22-55; ⊘from 5pm Tue-Sun) Anyone who's anyone goes to Lot 30 but show up unknown and in jeans and you'll be treated just as well. Tables are in view of each other so you can see the ecstatic expressions of food bliss on the merry diners' faces; dishes from beurre blanc to curry are spiced to perfection. For a treat, try the excellent-value five-course tasting menu ($55) – small servings of a starter, three mains and a dessert sampler. Servers are wine-pairing masters, the eclectic ever-changing menu is made with local seasonal ingredients and the chef is happy to cater to food allergies and special needs. It really is a Charlottetown highlight.

TOP CHOICE Leonard's   CAFE **$**

(University Ave; sandwiches from $5; ⊘9am-5pm Tue-Sat) Find absolute comfort in this little cafe full of cushioned seating and soothing country-style muted hues. Treat yourself to excellent German pastries, salads and creative sandwiches as well as all-day breakfasts made with free-range eggs, a great cheese selection and cold cuts like Black Forest ham. Wash it down with farmers' market teas and espresso.

Water Prince Corner Shop   RESTAURANT **$$**

(📞902-368-3212; 141 Water St; meals $10-17; ⊘9:30am-8pm) When locals want seafood they head to this inconspicuous, sea-blue eatery near the wharf. It is deservedly famous for its scallop burgers but it's also the best place in town for fresh lobster. You'll probably have to line up for a seat or order takeout lobster, which gets you a significant discount.

Sirinella   RESTAURANT **$$**

(📞902-628-2271; 83 Water St; lunch mains $8-17, dinner $15-28; ⊘lunch & dinner Mon-Fri, dinner Sat) Cross the threshold of this diner-looking restaurant and you are transported to seaside Italy. It's nothing fancy, just little round, white clothed tables, some Mediterranean oil paintings and incredibly authentic Italian fare.

Off Broadway   RESTAURANT **$$**

(📞902-566-4620; 125 Sydney St; lunch mains $9-14, dinner $15-28; ⊘11am-11pm Mon-Sat, to 10pm Sun) Slip into an art-deco booth, draw the burgundy curtains and pretend you're escaping the paparazzi. The dark yet chic ambience is matched by fine entrees such as lobster crepes or seafood coconut curry. Don't leave without taking a cocktail or dessert in the even more elaborate upstairs lounge.

Sim's Corner   RESTAURANT **$$**

(📞902-894-7467; 86 Queen St; mains $12-40; ⊘4-9pm Sun-Thu, to 10pm Fri & Sat) Feeling successful, hip and carnivorous? Head to this urban-chic spot where plush lounge-style seating spills onto the sidewalk. Food is of the steakhouse and seafood variety and you're un-cool without a glass in hand from the wine bar.

Claddagh Room   RESTAURANT **$$$**

(📞902-892-6992; 131 Sydney St; mains $19-45; ⊘5-10pm Mon-Thu, to 10:30pm Fri & Sat) Locals herald the Claddagh Room as one of the best seafood restaurant in Charlottetown. Trust 'em! The Irish-inspired Galway Bay Delight features a coating of fresh cream and seasonings over scallops and shrimp that have been sautéed with mushrooms and onions, then flambéed with Irish Mist liqueur.

Pilot House   RESTAURANT **$$**

(📞902-894-4800; 70 Grafton St; mains $19-37; ⊘11am-10pm Mon-Sat) The oversized wood beams and brick columns of the historic Roger's Hardware building provide a bold setting for fine dining or light pub fare. A loyal clientele tucks into lobster stuffed chicken, vegetarian pizza or seafood torte. Lunch specials start at $10.

Formosa Tea House   RESTAURANT **$**

(📞902-566-4991; 186 Prince St; mains $6-7; ⊘11:30am-3pm & 5-8pm) Savory Taiwanese vegetarian dishes are served in this cozy Victorian, fitted out with warm wood paneling and intimate booths upholstered in red, green and gold and accented with Chinese art. Recommended are the spicy vegetables and fried rice chased with a steaming mug of hot almond milk.

Farmers' Market   MARKET $
(📞902-626-3373; 100 Belvedere Ave; ☺9am-2pm Sat, also Wed Jul & Aug) Come hungry and empty-handed. Enjoy some prepared island foods or peruse the cornucopia of fresh organic fruit and vegetables. The market is north of the town center off University Ave.

🍷 Drinking

Charlottetown has an established and burgeoning drinking scene. Historic pubs dot the old part of town. Most bars and pubs have a small cover charge (about $5) on weekends, or when there is live music. People spill into the streets at 2am when things wrap up.

TOP CHOICE Gahan House   PUB
(📞902-626-2337; 126 Sydney St; ☺11am-10pm or 11pm Sun-Thu, to midnight or 1am Fri & Sat) Within these historic walls the pub owners brew PEI's only homegrown ales. Sir John A's Honey Wheat Ale is well worth introducing to your insides, as is the medium- to full-bodied Sydney Street Stout. The food here is also great – enjoy with friends old and new.

42nd St Lounge   BAR
(📞902-566-4620; 125 Sydney St; ☺4:30pm-midnight) Climb the stairs for a cocktail or a nightcap. Above Off Broadway (p428), the 42nd St Lounge sets the same glamorous tone, with lots of richly colored velvet, gilt-framed mirrors and deep, cozily grouped sofas set against exposed brick walls. It usually closes around midnight but will stay open until the crowd thins out.

☆ Entertainment

From early evening to the morning hours, Charlottetown serves up a great mix of theater, music, island culture and fun. To tap into the entertainment scene, pick up a free monthly copy of *Buzz*.

Cinemas

City Cinema   CINEMA
(📞902-368-3669; 64 King St) A small independent theater featuring Canadian and foreign-language films.

Theater

Confederation Centre of the Arts   THEATER
(📞902-566-1267, 800-565-0278; www.confederationcentre.com; 145 Richmond St) This modern complex's large theater and outdoor amphitheater host concerts, comedic performances and elaborate musicals. *Anne of Green Gables – The Musical* has been entertaining audiences here as part of the Charlottetown Festival since 1964, making it Canada's longest-running musical. You'll enjoy it, and your friends will never have to know.

Live Music

Throughout Charlottetown and PEI various venues host traditional ceilidhs (*kay*-lees). They are sometimes referred to as 'kitchen parties' and usually embrace gleeful Celtic music and dance. If you have the chance to attend one, don't miss it. The Friday edition of the *Guardian* newspaper lists times and locations of upcoming ceilidhs.

Olde Dublin Pub   PUB
(📞902-892-6992; 131 Sydney St; admission $8) A traditional Irish pub with a jovial spirit and live entertainment nightly during the summer months. Celtic bands and local notables take the stage and make for an engaging night out.

Baba's Lounge   BAR
(📞902-892-7377; 81 University Ave; admission $8) Located above Cedar's Eatery, this welcoming, intimate venue hosts great local bands playing their own tunes. Occasionally there are poetry readings.

Benevolent Irish Society   HALL
(📞902-963-3156; 582 North River Rd; admission $10; ☺8pm Fri mid-May–Oct) On the north side of town, this is a great place to catch a ceilidh. Come early, as seating is limited.

ℹ️ Information

Main Post Office (📞902-628-4400; 135 Kent St)

Police, Ambulance & Fire (📞911)

Polyclinic Professional Centre (📞902-629-8810; 199 Grafton St; ☺5:30-8pm Mon-Fri, 9:30am-noon Sat) Charlottetown's after-hours, walk-in medical clinic. Non-Canadians must pay a $40 fee.

Queen Elizabeth Hospital (📞902-8894-2111; 60 Riverside Dr; ☺24hr) Emergency room.

Royal Canadian Mounted Police (📞902-368-9300; 450 University Ave) For nonemergencies only.

Visit Charlottetown (www.visitcharlottetown.com) A helpful website with upcoming festival information, city history and visitor information.

Visitors Centre (☑902-368-4444, 888-734-7529; www.peiplay.com; ☺9am-8pm Jun, to 10pm Jul & Aug, 8:30am-6pm Sep–mid-Oct, 9am-4:30pm Mon-Fri mid-Oct–May; @) Located in Founders' Hall, this visitors center is the island's main tourist office. It has all the answers, a plethora of brochures and maps, and free internet access.

Getting There & Away

Air

Charlottetown Airport is 8km north of the city center at Brackley Point and Sherwood Rds. A taxi to/from town costs $12, plus $4 for each additional person.

Bus

For information, see p424.

Car & Motorcycle

With next to no public transportation available, rental cars are the preferred method for most travelers going to/from Charlottetown. During the summer cars are in short supply, so make sure you book ahead.

Nationwide companies such as Avis, Budget, National and Hertz have offices in town and at the airport. Note that the airport desks are strictly for people with reservations.

Getting Around

Bicycle

Riding is a great way to get around this quaint town. **MacQueen's Bicycles** (☑902-368-2453; www.macqueens.com; 430 Queen St; per day/week $25/125) rents a variety of quality bikes. Children's models are half price. **Smooth Cycle** (☑902-566-5530; www.smoothcycle.com; 330 University Ave; per day/week $25/110) also provides super service. Both of these operators also offer excellent customized island-wide tours of the Confederation Trail.

Car & Motorcycle

The municipal parking lots near the tourist office and Peak's Wharf charge $6 per day. One Loonie gets you two hours at any of the town's parking meters, which operate between 8am and 6pm on weekdays.

Public Transportation

Trius Tours (☑902-566-5664) operates the anemic city transit within Charlottetown (one-way fare $1.80). One bus makes various loops through the city, stopping sporadically at the Confederation Centre between 9:20am and 2:40pm.

Taxi

Fares are standardized and priced by zones. Between the waterfront and Hwy 1 there are three zones. Travel within this area is about $11, plus $3 per extra person. **City Taxi** (☑902-892-6567) and **Yellow Cab PEI** (☑902-566-6666) provide good service.

EASTERN PEI

You can make your own tracks across Kings County, the eastern third of the province and PEI's most under-touristed region. From stretches of neatly tended homesteads to the sinuous eastern shore with protected harbors and beaches, natural spaces and country inns, majestic tree canopies seem to stretch endlessly over the scenic heritage roads. The 338km Points East Coastal Drive winds along the shore, hitting the highlights, but the best thing to do is to hop on a bike: these sections of the Confederation Trail are some of the most beautiful on the island.

Orwell

Situated 28km east of Charlottetown, via Hwy 1, is **Orwell Corner Historic Village** (☑902-651-8510; off Hwy 1; adult/under 12yr $7.50/free; ☺9am-5pm Jul–early Sep, 9am-5pm Mon-Fri mid-May–Jun & early Sep–Oct), a living re-creation of a 19th-century farming community, complete with bonneted school teacher and blacksmith. Come on a Wednesday and take part in a traditional ceilidh (admission $10; ☺8pm). The **Sir Andrew MacPhail Homestead**, a further 1km down the road, is open for tea on summer afternoons.

Point Prim

This skinny bucolic spit of land is covered in wild rose, Queen Anne's lace and wheat fields through summer and has views of red sand shores on either side. At the tip is the province's oldest lighthouse (adult/child $7/2; ☺9am-6pm); we think it's one of the prettiest spots on the island. Climb up the steep lighthouse steps to pump the foghorn and for panoramas over the south coast on sunny days.

Many folks come out this way for the Seaweed Experience (☑866-887-3238; adult/child $60/30, minimum 4, maximum 8; ☺Mon, Tue, Thu & Fri) where you can harvest seaweed and learn about which types are edible or have medicinal qualities, all led by a local family who have been in the industry for generations, plus a knowledgeable marine botanist.

There are lots of cottages for rent by the week but the only one offering shorter-term stays is **Gerritson's Cottage** (☑902-659-2418; 1993 Point Prim Rd; cottage $130), with one modern, fully equipped cottage right on the coast that's set up with a barbecue and a swing set for the kids. Inside are a TV and microwave. It's perfect for families.

Eat at **Chowder House** (chowder with a biscuit $8; ☉11am-7pm), a homey cafe near the lighthouse reminiscent of Cape Cod circa 1950; it serves a mean chowder and homemade pie.

Wood Islands

Wood Islands is the jumping-off point for ferries to Nova Scotia. A **visitor information center** (☑902-962-7411; Plough Waves Centre, cnr Hwy 1 & Rte 4; ☉10:30am-9pm) is up the hill from the terminal.

If you'll be waiting a while at the terminal, **Wood Islands Provincial Park** and its 1876 lighthouse are well worth the short walk. Munch a rock crab sandwich or a lobster roll at **Crabby's Seafood** (snacks $4-7; ☉noon-6pm Jun-Sep) near the ferry terminal.

Murray River & Around

From Wood Islands, Rte 4 heads east along the Northumberland Strait, veering inland at High Bank toward the lively and surprisingly artsy fishing settlement of Murray River. The coastal road becomes Rte 18, keeping the sea in view as it rounds Cape Bear, passing the lighthouse before looping back through the village of Murray Harbour and into Murray River. This stretch of flat, empty road offers superbly serene scenery and excellent cycling possibilities. Cyclists can follow the coastal road from Murray River, then loop back on the extension of the Confederation Trail at Wood Islands.

Alternatively, feel the wind in your hair aboard **Cruise Manada** (☑902-838-3444, 800-986-3444; www.cruisemanada.com; adult/under 13yr $22/11.50; ☉mid-May–Sep). It offers two-hour boat tours on the Murray River, passing mussel farms to the Murray Islands, home to hundreds of seals.

At Little Sands, 9km from the Wood Island Ferry, **Rossignol Estate Winery** (☑902-962-4193; Rte 4; ☉10am-5pm Mon-Sat, 1-5pm Sun May-Oct) has free tastings and specializes in fruit wines. The divine Blackberry Mead has won a string of gold medals and the Wild Rose Liquor made from rose hips is also well worth a try; call ahead for winter hours.

For an excellent hearty meal, head to **Brehaut's Restaurant** (☑902-962-3141; Murray Harbour; dinner under $8; ☉8am-9pm Mon-Sat, 11am-9pm Sun). There are cozy booths and nooks filled with happy diners in this big, red wooden house. The seafood chowder gets rave reviews.

Panmure Island

Duck off Hwy 17 and ride the tarmac to the tip of Panmure Island, known for its variety of beaches: white sand and cold water line the ocean side while pink sands and warmer water run along the St Mary's Bay side. Joined to the main island by a causeway, the island offers sweeping vistas of sand dunes and ocean surf, grazing horses

---

CYCLING THE CONFEDERATION TRAIL

Following the rail-bed of Prince Edward Island's erstwhile railway, the 357km-long Confederation Trail is almost entirely flat as it meanders around hills and valleys. There are some sections of the trail that are completely canopied in lush foliage, and in late June and the early weeks of July the trail is lined with bright, flowering lupines. There's perhaps no better way to enjoy the fall's change of colors than by riding the trail.

The 279km tip-to-tip route from Tignish (p447), near North Cape, to Elmira (p433), near East Point, is a rewarding workout, passing through idyllic villages, where riders can stop for meals or rest for the night. Note that the prevailing winds on PEI blow from the west and southwest, so cycling in this direction is easier. Branches connect the trail to the Confederation Bridge (p424), Charlottetown (p424), Souris (p433) and Montague (p432).

Provincial **tourist offices** (www.gov.pe.ca/visitorsguide) have excellent route maps and their website offers a plethora of planning and trail information. The bicycle rental shops in Charlottetown (p430) also run superb island-wide tours.

and a gaily painted **lighthouse** (902-838-3568; tours $5; 9:30am-5pm Jul & Aug, hours vary Jun & Sep). You can climb the tower for $4. There's an annual **Pow Wow** (902-892-5314; www.ncpei.com/powwow-trail.html; mid-Aug) held each year with drumming, crafts and a sweat tent – it attracts around 5000 visitors, so don't expect any secluded beaches!

Bring a picnic for the supervised beach at **Panmure Island Provincial Park** (902-838-0668; Hwy 347; campsites $21; Jun-mid-Sep). The park campground has every amenity for its 44 sites (most unserviced) tucked under the trees and along the shore. For something more luxurious stay at the grand **Maplehurst Properties** (902-838-3959; www.maplehurstproperties.com; Rte 347; d $109-190, cottage $125-190; May-Nov). Marsha Leftwich has mustered every glimmer of her native Southern hospitality to create this exceptional B&B that drips with gorgeous chandeliers as well as fresh baked muffins and treats.

Montague & Around

The fact that Montague isn't flat gives it a unique, inland feel. Perched on either side of the Montague River, the busy little town is the service center for Kings County; its streets lead from the breezy, heritage marina area to modern shopping malls, supermarkets and fast-food outlets.

In the old train station on the riverbank there's an **Island Welcome Center** (902-838-0670; cnr Rtes 3 & 4; 9am-4:30pm late May-late Jun & late Aug-mid-Oct, 8am-7pm late Jun-late Aug). Here, you can hop on the Confederation Trail, which follows the former rail line; rent bikes at **Pines Bicycle Rentals** (902-838-3650; 31 Riverside Dr; rentals half-/full day $20/30; 8am-8pm). Alternatively, buy a ticket for **Cruise Manada** (902-838-3444, 800-986-3444; www.cruisemanada.com; adult/under 13yr $22/11.50; mid-May-Sep), at its second location, which offers popular two-hour boat tours to PEI's largest seal colony.

On the other side of the river, the statuesque former post office and customs house (1888) overlooks the marina, and houses the **Garden of the Gulf Museum** (902-838-2467; 564 Main St S; adult/under 12yr $3/free; 9am-5pm Mon-Fri early Jun-late Sep). Inside are several artifacts illustrating local history.

Just north of town, development meets nature at **Brudenell River Provincial Park** (902-652-8966; off Rte 3; tent sites $21, RV sites $24-28; late May-mid-Oct), which is a park and resort complex. Options range from kayaking with **Outside Expeditions** (902-652-2434; www.getoutside.com; half-/full-day tours $55/100) to nature walks and, as Winston Churchill put it, 'a good walk ruined' – ie golf – on two championship courses. You can also take a one-hour horseback trail ride through the sun-dappled forest and onto the beach with **Brudenell Riding Stables** (902-652-2396; 1hr ride $25; Jun-Sep).

Sleeping & Eating

Knox's Dam B&B   TOP CHOICE   B&B $$
(902-838-4234, 866-245-0037; knoxdambandb@hotmail.com; cnr Rtes 353 & 320; r incl breakfast $85-100; mid-May-Oct;) This cheerful, red Victorian country home is constantly serenaded by the babble and flow of Knox's dam on the Montague River. Guest rooms are thoughtfully appointed with soft linens, the old-fashioned elegance of a claw-foot tub and modern amenities such as satellite TV. Rooms overlook the prize-winning flower gardens or the bountiful vegetable patch; there's good trout fishing at the dam and your hosts couldn't be kinder.

Boudreault's White House   B&B $
(902-838-2560, 800-436-3220; 342 Lower Montague Rte 17; r incl breakfast $50-65; May-Oct;) Three small, cozy rooms heaped with fresh towels and country quilts share a bathroom in friendly Zita's homey abode. You're given maps, menus and activity ideas for the area, then are pretty much left on your own. There's bicycle storage and kids are welcome.

Windows on the Water Café   RESTAURANT $$
(902-838-2080; cnr Sackville & Main Sts; dinner mains $15-27; 11:30am-9:30pm May-Oct) Enjoy a flavorful array of seafood, chicken and vegetarian dishes on the deck overlooking the water and, sort of, the road. Try the sole stuffed with lobster and scallops ($15) and leave room for a freshly baked dessert.

Georgetown

The many heritage buildings in Georgetown are testament to the town's importance as a shipbuilding center in the Victorian era. Today it's a sleepy place that's gaining popularity as a tourist spot thanks to its great places to eat and waterfront setting. It's also the site of **Tranquility Cove Adventures** (✆902-969-7184; www.tranquilitycoveadventures.com; Fisherman's Wharf, 1 Kent St; full/half-day tours $90/50) that leads excellent lobstering, fishing and clamming trips and promises to let you live the life of a fisherman for a day. Be prepared for physical work, getting wet, then filling up on your fresh catch. Check the website for details on even more exciting packages.

📂 Sleeping & Eating

Georgetown Inn & Dining Room
INN & RESTAURANT **$$**
(✆902-652-2511, 877-641-2414; www.georgetownhistoricinn.com; 62 Richmond St; r incl breakfast $85-155; 🛜) Right in the center of Georgetown, this place is as equally well-known for its PEI-themed rooms (including a Green Gables room) as for its fine casual island-fare dining.

Clamdigger's Beach House & Restaurant
RESTAURANT **$$**
(✆902-652-2466; 7 West St; mains $12-40; ◷11am-9pm) Some claim this place serves PEI's best chowder but no matter what your opinion, you can't help but ooh and aah about the water view from the deck or through the dining room's giant windows.

Cardigan Lobster Suppers
LOBSTER SUPPER **$$**
(✆902-583-2020; Rte 311; adult/child $34/20; ◷dinner Jun-Oct) In nearby Cardigan, enjoy a fine sunset lobster supper in a heritage building on Cardigan Harbor.

Souris

Wrapped around the waters of Colville Bay is the bustling fishing community of Souris (*sur*-rey). It owes its name to the French Acadians and the gluttonous mice who repeatedly ravaged their crops. It's now known more for its joyous annual music festival than for the hungry field rodents of old. The **PEI Bluegrass & Old Time Music Festival** (✆902-569-3153; www.bluegrasspei.com/rollobay.htm; Rte 2; ◷early Jul) draws acts from as far away as Nashville. Come for just a day, or camp out for all three.

This is a working town that's a friendly jumping-off point for cycling the coastal road (Rte 16) and the Confederation Trail, which comes into town. The town is also the launching point for ferries to the Îles de la Madeleine in Québec (see p308).

📂 Sleeping & Eating

Inn At Bay Fortune
INN & RESTAURANT **$$**
(✆902-687-3745; www.innatbayfortune.com; 758 Rte 310; r from $135, ste $200-335; meals from $60; ❋🛜) Find some of PEI's most upscale rooms at this waterside inn about 12km south of Souris, as well as one of the island's best restaurants. Chef Warren Barr (who planes to hand his whisk to a new chef in 2011) has created a menu that captures the essence of PEI flavors; highlights include tartar of PEI scallops with strawberry and balsamic salsa or crispy beef short ribs with roasted organic shiitake mushrooms. Rooms are modern with country flair; the most fun rooms, tiny units in a tower with nearly 360-degree views, are the least expensive. The price goes up with size, culminating in private cottages.

McLean House Inn
INN **$$**
(✆902-687-1875; www.mcleanhouseinn.com; 16 Washington St; r $105-120, ste $190, incl breakfast; 🛜) The view from, and the atmosphere of, this beautiful mansard-roofed house make it perfect for a lazy afternoon. Head to the sunroom, grab some wicker and sink into a book. Ask for the Colville Bay room (No 303).

Dockside B&B
B&B **$$**
(✆902-687-2829, 877-687-2829; www.colvillebay.ca; 37 Breakwater St; d $70; 🛜) Simple but large and airy double rooms are in a modern house situated steps from the ferry dock. Breakfast is served in a bright, glassed-in porch with a view of the harbor.

Bluefin Restaurant
RESTAURANT **$**
(✆902-687-3271; 10 Federal Ave; meals $10-14; ◷6:30am-7pm Mon-Sat, 6am-8pm Sun from 7am) Near McLean House Inn, this place is a local favorite known for its heaped servings of traditional island food. Its lunch special runs from 11am to 1pm.

East Point & Around

Built the same year Canada was unified, the **East Point Lighthouse** (✆902-357-2106; adult/child $5/4; ◷10am-6pm mid-Jun–Aug) still stands guard over the northeastern shore of PEI. After being blamed for the 1882 wreck of the British *Phoenix*, the lighthouse was moved closer to shore. The eroding shoreline is now chasing it back. There's a gift shop and a little cafe next to the lighthouse that serves good-value lobster rolls ($5), hearty chowder and nice sandwiches.

The wooded coast and lilting accents of the north shore make for an interesting change of pace. Giant white windmills march across the landscape. **North Lake** and **Naufrage** harbors are intriguing places to stop and, if you feel so inclined, join a charter boat in search of a monster 450kg tuna.

The **railway museum** (☑902-357-7234; Rte 16A; adult/student/family $3/2/10; ☉10am-6pm Jul & Aug, to 5pm Fri-Wed mid-Jun–late Jun & early Sep–mid-Sep) in Elmira includes a quirky miniature train ride (adult/student/family $7/4/15) that winds through the surrounding forest. The station marks the eastern end of the Confederation Trail (see boxed text, p431).

St Peter's to Mt Stewart

The area between these two villages is a hotbed for cycling. The section of the Confederation Trail (see boxed text, p431) closest to St Peter's flirts with the shoreline and rewards riders with an eyeful of the coast. In Mt Stewart three riverside sections of the Confederation Trail converge, giving riders and hikers plenty of attractive options within a relatively compact area. Both the Confederation Trail and a **provincial tourist office** (☑902-961-3540; Rte 2; ☉8am-7pm late Jun-late Aug, 9am-4:30pm mid-Jun–late Jun & late Aug-Oct) are found next to the bridge in St Peter's.

🛏 Sleeping & Eating

Inn at St Peters   INN & RESTAURANT **$$$**
(☑902-961-2135, 800-818-0925; www.innatstpeters.com; 1168 Greenwich Rd; d $220-265; lunch mains from $17, dinner mains from $22; ☉breakfast, lunch & dinner; 🛜) Even with its luxuri-ous rooms and stunning water views, the main reason to come to this inn is to dine on some of PEI's finest fare at the sunset-facing restaurant. Rooms are simply and elegantly decorated with antique furniture, but even if you don't stay here we highly recommend stopping in for a meal (even you, sweaty bikers).

Tir na Nog Inn   INN **$$**
(☑902-961-3004, 866-961-3004; www.tir-nanoginn.com; 5749 Hwy 2; r incl breakfast $65-115; P🛜) In a beautifully restored Victorian home in St Peter's, enjoy gracious lodgings and gourmet breakfasts, and a deep veran-dah facing the bay.

Midgell Centre   HOSTEL **$**
(☑902-961-2963; 6553 Rte 2, Midgell; dm & s with shared bathroom $20; ☉mid-Jun–mid-Sep) Al-though designed for guests of the Christian center, the austere rooms are available to visitors. Depending on the set-up, you may be in a dorm or private room. Communal kitchens in each building add value to this great budget option, near St Peter's and Greenwich.

Rick's Fish 'n' Chips & Seafood House
          RESTAURANT **$**
(☑902-961-3438; Rte 2, St Peter's; meals $5-15; ☉11am-10pm) Make a beeline for the lip-smacking battered fish and fresh-cut fries. For variety, try the vegetarian burgers, mussels done several ways, or fine pizza.

CENTRAL PEI

Central PEI contains a bit of all that's best about the island – verdant fields, quaint villages and forests undulating north to the dramatic sand dune-backed beaches of Prince Edward Island National Park. Anne of Green Gables, the engaging heroine of Lucy Maud Montgomery's 1908 novel, has spawned a huge global industry focused on

---

DON'T MISS

BASIN HEAD PROVINCIAL PARK

While this **park** (off Rte 16; admission free) is home to the **Basin Head Fisheries Museum** (☑902-357-7233; adult/student $4.50/2; ☉9am-5pm Jun & Sep, to 6pm Jul & Aug), its star attraction is the sweeping sand of golden **Basin Head Beach**. Many is-landers rank this as their favorite beach and we have to agree. The sand is also famous for its singing – well, squeaking – when you walk on it. Unfortunately, the sand only performs when dry so if it's been raining, it's no show. Five minutes of joyous 'musical' footsteps south from the museum and you have secluded bliss – enjoy!

DISTILLERIES

In the last few years two distinctly different distilleries have opened on PEI, echoing the province's fame for bootlegging during prohibition. Even today many families distill their own moonshine and this is what is often mixed in punch and cocktails at country weddings and parties.

Prince Edward Distillery (☑902-687-2586; www.princeedwarddistillery.com; Rte 16, Hermanville; ⊙11am-6pm) specializes in potato vodka that even in its first year of production turned international heads that have called it among the finest of its class. Stop in for tours (without/with tasting $2/10) of the immaculate distillery and to taste the different vodkas (potato, grain and blueberry) as well as the newer products such as bourbon, rum and a very interesting and aromatic gin.

Myriad View Distillery (☑902-687-1281; www.straightshine.com; 1336 Rte 2, Rollo Bay; ⊙11am-6pm Mon-Sat, 1-5pm Sun) produces Canada's first and only legal moonshine. The hardcore Straight Lightning Shine is 75% alcohol and so potent it feels like liquid heat before it evaporates on your tongue. Take our advice and start with a micro-sip! A gulp could knock the wind out of you. The 50% alcohol Straight Shine lets you enjoy the flavor a bit more. Tours and tastings are free and the owner is happy to answer any questions.

It's about a 10-minute drive on Hwy 307 between the two places.

the formerly bucolic hamlet of Cavendish. However, this being PEI, even its most savagely developed patch of tourist traps and commercial detritus is almost quaint – freshly painted and flower bedecked.

For those entering central PEI via the Confederation Bridge, it's worth stopping at the **Gateway Village Visitor Information Centre** (☑902-437-8570; Hwy 1; ⊙8:30am-8pm), just off the bridge on the PEI side, for its free maps, brochures, restrooms and an excellent introductory exhibit called 'Our Island Home' (open May to November). Staff can point you to the Confederation Trail (see boxed text, p431), which lurks nearby.

Victoria

A place to wander and experience more than 'see,' the shaded, tree-laden lanes of this charming little fishing village scream out character and charm. The entire village still fits neatly in the four blocks laid out when the town was formed in 1819. Colorful clapboard and shingled houses are home to more than one visitor who was so enthralled by the place they decided to stay. There's a profusion of art, cafes and eateries, as well as an excellent summer theater festival.

◉ Sights & Activities

By the Sea Kayaking   SEA KAYAKING
(☑902-658-2572, 877-879-2572; www.bythe seakayaking.ca; kayak rentals per hr/day $25/50)

Paddle round the bay on your own or on a guided tour, then take a dip off the beach at **Victoria Harbour Provincial Park** (admission free), where there are change rooms available. The outfit also operates popular 'I Dig Therefore I Clam' clamming expeditions ($70) and bike rentals (per hour/day $15/30).

Victoria Playhouse   THEATER
(☑902-658-2025, 800-925-2025; www.victoria playhouse.com; 20 Howard St; tickets $26; ⊙8pm Jun-Sep) The ornate red velvet and gold theater at Victoria Playhouse presents a series of plays over the summer, with concerts [illegible] on Monday nights.

Lighthouse Museum   MUSEUM
(admission by donation; ⊙9am-5:30pm late Jun–Aug) This museum has an interesting exhibit on local history. If it's closed, get the key from the shop across the road.

⬛ Sleeping & Eating

Orient Hotel B&B   B&B $$
(☑902-658-2503, 800-565-6743; www.theorient hotel.com; 34 Main St; r $85-105, ste $125-160, incl breakfast; ☎) A delightful Victorian confection of buttercup yellow, red and blue, this historic seaside inn is a perfect jewel. **Mrs Proffitt's Tea Room** (⊙11:30am-4pm Wed-Mon) serves afternoon cream tea and light lunches.

Victoria Village Inn INN & RESTAURANT $$
(📞902-658-2483; www.victoriavillageinn.com; 22 Howard St; r incl breakfast $80-150; 🐾) Next to the theater, this inn has relaxed rooms in a slightly disheveled heritage home with one great family suite. The restaurant (mains $19 to $27, open 5pm to 10pm) has a deliciously decadent menu including creative delicacies such as lobster and asparagus risotto. Vegetarian selections and theater packages are also available.

TOP
CHOICE **Landmark Café** CAFE $$
(📞902-658-2286; 12 Main St; mains $12-25; ⏱11:30am-10pm mid-May–Sep) People come from miles around for the wonderful imaginative food at this family-run cafe. Prepared with wholesome ingredients, every colorful menu item from lasagnas and homemade soups to Cajun stir-fries and feta-stuffed vine leaves is a winner. Enjoy the photos on the wall of the family's annual exotic trips and their equally multicultural music selection, softly pumping through the cafe.

Island Chocolates CHOCOLATE $
(📞902-658-2320; 13 Main St; chocolates $1.25 each; ⏱10am-8pm Mon-Sat, noon-8pm Sun) We dare you to eat only one of the sublime handmade Belgian chocolates at this place! Cafe tables on the front porch and inside the warmly lit, old-fashioned shop are inviting for morning coffee or a sumptuous chocolate dessert. Also offers two-hour chocolate-making workshops ($45) by reservation.

Prince Edward Island National Park

Heaving dunes and red sandstone bluffs provide startling backdrops for some of the island's finest stretches of sand; welcome to **Prince Edward Island National Park** (📞902-672-6350; www.pc.gc.ca/pei; day pass adult/child $7.80/3.90). This dramatic coast, and the narrow sections of wetland and forests behind it, is home to diverse plants and animals, including the red fox and endangered piping plover.

The park is open year-round, but most services only operate between late June and the end of August. Entrance fees are charged between mid-June and mid-September, and admit you to all park sites, except the House of Green Gables (p441). If you're planning to stay longer than five days, look into a seasonal pass. The park

maintains an information desk at the Cavendish Visitor Centre (p442).

The following sights and sleeping and eating options are organized from east to west, first covering the park-run facilities, then the private operations inside and out of the park.

⊙ Sights & Activities

Beaches lined with marram grasses and wild rose span almost the entire length of the park's 42km coastline. In most Canadians' minds, the park is almost synonymous with the beaches. **Dalvay Beach** sits to the east, and has some short hiking trails through the woods. The landscape flattens and the sand sprawls outward at **Stanhope Beach**. Here, a boardwalk leads from the campground to the shore. Backed by dunes, and slightly west, is the expansive and popular **Brackley Beach**. On the western side of the park, the sheer size of **Cavendish Beach** makes it the granddaddy of them all. During summer this beach sees copious numbers of visitors beneath its hefty dunes. If crowds aren't your thing, there are always the pristine sections of sand to the east. Lifeguards are on duty at Cavendish, Brackley and Stanhope Beaches in midsummer. A new bike lane now runs all the way along this coast.

🛏 Sleeping

Parks Canada operates three highly sought-after **campgrounds** (📞800-414-6765; tent/RV sites $28/36; ⏱early Jun–late Aug), which are spread along the park's length. They all have kitchen shelters and showers. For an additional fee of $10, you can reserve a campsite, but you must do so at least three days in advance by phone or via www.pccamping.ca. You can request a campground, but not a specific site; you must accept whatever is available when you arrive. While 80% of sites can be booked in advance, the remaining sites are first-come, first-served, so it's wise to arrive early.

Stanhope Campground, on Gulfshore East Pkwy, is nestled nicely in the woods behind the beach of the same name. There is a well-stocked store on-site.

Robinsons Island Campground, also on Gulfshore East Pkwy, is open from late June. The most isolated of the three sites, it's set at the end of Brackley Point. It's not too much fun if the wind gets up.

The proximity of **Cavendish Campground**, off Rte 6, to the sights makes it the most popular. It has exposed oceanfront sites and ones within the shelter and shade of the trees. Don't be lured by the view – it's nice, but sleep is better.

The communities listed following also provide excellent options for accommodations in or around the park.

Dalvay by the Sea

Standing proudly near the east end of the park, and overlooking the beach named after it, is Dalvay, an historic mansion. Built in 1895 this majestic building is now owned by Parks Canada, and operated as an **inn** (✆902-672-2048, 888-366-2955; www.dalvayby thesea.com; Gulfshore East Pkwy; r $174-344, cottages $404-444, incl breakfast; ❄☎☂). It's easily the most luxurious and stunning accommodations on the north shore. Each plush room's view and antique furnishings are refreshingly unique. The majestic dining room (dinner mains $18 to $36, open breakfast, lunch and dinner July and August) prepares remarkable dishes ranging from hazelnut- and sage-crusted rack of lamb to fresh island lobster. It is open to nonguests, and both lunch and afternoon tea (from 2pm to 4pm) are reasonably priced. The inn also rents bicycles (per hour/day $9/26).

Brackley Beach

There's a **Welcome Centre** (✆902-672-7474; cnr Rtes 6 & 15; ☉8am-9pm) 4km before the park entrance. **North Shore Rentals** (✆902-672-2022; Shaw's Hotel, Rte 15, 99 Apple Tree Rd; bikes per hr/day $7/22) rents bicycles, kayaks and canoes for exploring the area. For some evening variety, catch a movie at **Brackley Beach Drive-In** (✆902-672-3333; www.drivein.ca; 3164 Rte 15; adult/child $9/6; ☉May-Sep). Check the website for what's playing.

Shaw's Hotel & Cottages (✆902-672-2022; www.shawshotel.ca; Rte 15, 99 Apple Tree Rd; d $75-170, cottages $120; ☉cottages year-round, inn Jun-Oct; ❄☎☂), open since 1860, is Canada's oldest family-operated inn; it hearkens back to an earlier era, when families of sufficient means decamped to the seaside for the summer. The hotel occupies 30 hectares of the family farm, with a private lane leading to Brackley Beach, a 600m walk away. Rooms in the inn have old-fashioned simplicity and elegance. One- to four-bedroom cottages, ranging from rustic to modern, are scattered around the property. A children's program runs in July

WORTH A TRIP

GREENWICH

Massive, dramatic and ever-shifting sand dunes epitomize the amazing area west of Greenwich. These rare parabolic giants are fronted by an awesome beach – a visit here is a must. Preserved by Parks Canada in 1998, this 6km section of shore is now part of Prince Edward Island National Park.

Avant-garde meets barn at the **Greenwich Interpretation Centre** (✆902-961-2514; Hwy 13; ☉9:30am-4:30pm mid-May–late Jun & Sep–mid-Oct, to 7pm late Jun-Aug) where an innovative audio-visual presentation details the ecology of the dune system and the archaeological history of the site. The highlight though is getting out into the tree-eating dunes. Four walking trails traverse the park; the **Greenwich Dunes Trail** (4.5km return, 1½ hours) is especially scenic.

and August, with hay rides, games, trips to the beach and a supervised supper hour. The **dining room** (✆902-672-2022; mains $22-33; ☉8-10am & 5:45-9:30pm) is open to outside guests; reservations are recommended for the popular Sunday evening buffet ($40; held in July and August).

While over-the-top springs to mind, **Dunes Café & Gallery** (✆902-672-2586; Rte 15; dinner mains $16-25; ☉11:30am-10pm) is a nice change of pace. Honestly, where else on the island can you enjoy Vietnamese rice-noodle salad in the shade of a giant Buddha? Come in for a coffee, a meal or just to roam the eclectic mix of Asian and island art in the sprawling glass gallery and garden.

Rustico

The seafront Acadian settlement at Rustico dates back to 1700, and several fine historic buildings speak of this tiny village's former importance. Most prominent is **St Augustine's Church** (1830), the oldest Catholic church on PEI. The old cemetery is on one side of the church, the solid red-stone **Farmer's Bank of Rustico** is on the other. The bank operated here from 1864 to 1894; it was a forerunner of the credit-union movement in Canada. Beside the bank is **Doucet House**, an old Acadian dwelling that was relocated here. A **museum** (📞902-963-2194; adult/student \$4/2; ⊙9:30am-5:30pm Mon-Sat, 1-5pm Sun) describing the settlement of the community and the establishment of the bank is now housed in the two secular buildings.

In a prime location just across the street from the towering old church, **Barachois Inn** (📞902-963-2906, 800-963-2194; www.barachoisinn.com; 2193 Church Rd; d incl breakfast \$125-399; ❊🛜) is one of the finest B&Bs on PEI. The grand Acadian-style mansion is decorated not only with the standard sublime selection of antiques, but also very eclectic paintings, which makes walking around the many common areas like touring an art museum. Bathrooms are nearly equal in size to the enormous rooms, and hidden in the basement of the newer annex (built to copy the older building to perfection) is an exercise room, sauna and conference area.

New Glasgow

New Glasgow is a quiet town that spreads elegantly across the shores of the River Clyde. This is the favorite lobster supper getaway for folks from Charlottetown, although it's becoming equally respected for its luscious preserves.

🛏 Sleeping & Eating

My Mother's Country Inn   B&B **$$**
(📞902-964-2508, 800-278-2071; www.mymotherscountryinn.com; Rte 13; d \$85-225, cottages \$125-250, incl breakfast) Here is another reason to linger in New Glasgow: an oasis within 20 hectares of rolling hills, brisk streams and enchanting woodlands, this is pure, rural delight. The house is the essence of country style with sea green and ochre painted walls, bright pastel quilts, wood floors and plenty of light. A big red barn just begs to be photographed beside a storybook brook.

Around PEI National Park

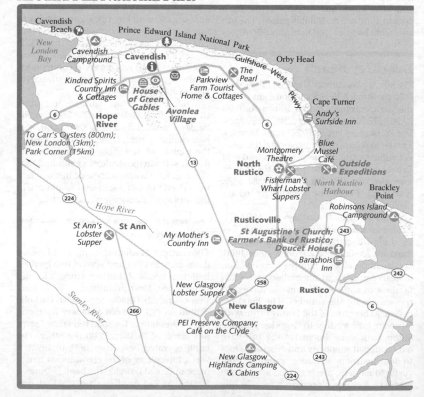

New Glasgow Highlands Camping & Cabins
CAMPING **$**

(📞902-964-3232; www.campcabinpei.com; Rte 224; tent/RV sites $30/35, cabins $55; ⊙May-Oct; ☒) The 20-odd sites here are properly spaced in the forest, each with its own fire pit. For rainy days there are simple cooking facilities in the lodge. Add a laundry, a small store, a heated swimming pool and a mystifying absence of bugs, and you're laughing. There are also bright cabins, each with two bunks, a double bed, a sofa and a picnic table but no linen or pillows; bathrooms are shared. Be sure to book ahead and don't even think about making late-night noise – peace is the word.

Café on the Clyde
RESTAURANT **$$**

(📞902-964-4300; dinner mains $13-20; ⊙9am-8pm) This is one of the better casual dining options near the national park as long as the tour buses haven't arrived before you have. Sun reflects in off the River Clyde and makes this place glow. The vegetarian wraps with a hint of feta truly hit the spot and finish the meal with the house specialty, raspberry cream cheese pie. The cafe is an addition to the famous **PEI Preserve Company** (⊙9am-5pm, to 9pm mid-Jun–late Sep). While the preserves are a tad pricey, we think they're worth every penny; if you're not going to buy, at least come in to browse the free samples. Don't pass the orange ginger curd or the raspberry champagne preserves.

New Glasgow Lobster Supper
LOBSTER SUPPER **$$**

(📞902-964-2870; Rte 258; lobster dinners $26-35; ⊙4-8:30pm) You can make a right mess with the lobster here, while also gorging on an endless supply of great chowder, mussels, salads, breads and homemade desserts.

St Ann

St Ann is so small you hardly even know you've arrived. Yet on a summer evening, follow the traffic and wafts of lobster steam to

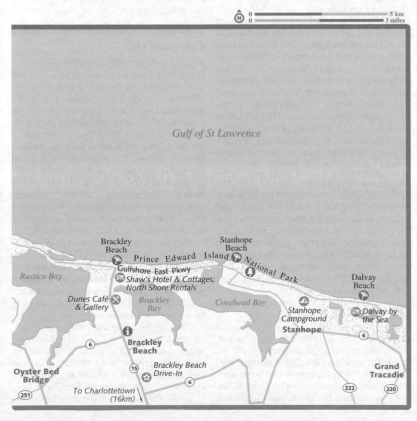

St Ann's Lobster Supper (☑902-621-0635; Rte 224; supper $26-34; ⊙4:30-8:30pm), which rivals New Glasgow as PE Islanders' favorite lobster supper.

North Rustico

Within a few minutes of arrival, it is pretty obvious that this is not simply a tourist town. Rickety, boxy fishermen's houses painted in navies, brick reds and beiges, line a deep harbor that is simply packed with fishing vessels. A walk east from the pier along the boardwalk, and out to North Rustico Harbour, is a great way to take in the sights, sounds and smells of this little village.

🏃 Activities

If your idea of ocean activity is reeling in a big one, look for the plethora of **deep-sea fishing operators** (3-3½hr trip adult/child $38/24) along Harbourview Dr.

Outside Expeditions   BIKING & KAYAKING
(☑902-963-3366, 800-207-3899; www.get outside.com; 374 Harbourview Dr) Situated at the far end of the harbor in a bright-yellow fishing shed, the 1½-hour introductory 'Beginner Bay' tour ($39) begins with a lesson in kayaking techniques. The most popular trip is the three-hour 'Harbour Passage' tour ($59), which operates three times daily (9am, 2pm and 6pm). It also offers guided 'Land of Anne' bicycle tour ($65), and bike rentals (per half/full day $20/35). Trips are operated in the off-season, whenever at least four people want to go.

Montgomery Theatre   THEATER
(☑902-963-3963; www.themontgomerytheatre. com; North Rustico Village; tickets $25-32) Opened in 2008 in honor of the 100th anniversary of the publication of *Anne of Green Gables,* this theater presents plays from the life and times of Lucy Maud Montgomery. Performances are in a renovated 19th-century church that Montgomery herself attended. Seats sell out fast, so book in advance!

🛏 Sleeping & Eating

Andy's Surfside Inn   INN $
(☑902-963-2405; Gulfshore West Pkwy; d with shared bathroom incl light breakfast $45-75; 🛜) Inside the national park, 2.7km toward Orby Head from North Rustico, is this large rambling house overlooking Doyle's Cove. It has been an inn since the 1930s, and the kitchen

is open to those who want to bring home a few live lobsters. Sit back on the porch, put your feet up and thank your lucky stars.

Blue Mussel Café   CAFE $$
(☑902-963-2152; Harbourview Dr; burgers from $14, mains $18-45; ⊙11:30am-8pm) This place is relatively small and expensive, but its bayside location, pan-fried scallops and steamed mussels will leave a big impression. Grab a table on the covered deck facing the bay. It's en route to Outside Expeditions.

Fisherman's Wharf Lobster Suppers   LOBSTER SUPPER $$$
(☑902-963-2669; 7230 Main St; lobster dinners $30; ⊙noon-9pm) During the dinner rush in July and August this huge place has lines of people out the door. It's a fun, casual, holiday-style restaurant offering excellent value – that is if you don't wreck your shirt! Come hungry, as there are copious servings of chowder, tasty local mussels, rolls and a variety of desserts to go with your pound of messy crustacean. If things go your way, you may get a table with an ocean view.

Cavendish

Anyone familiar with *Anne of Green Gables* might have lofty ideas of finding Cavendish as a quaint village bedecked in flowers and country charm; guess again. While the Anne and Lucy Maud Montgomery sites are right out of the imagination-inspiring book pages, Cavendish itself is a mishmash of manufactured attractions with no particular town center. The junction of Rte 6 and Hwy 13 is the tourist center and the area's commercial hub. When you see the service station, wax museum, church, cemetery and assorted restaurants, you know you're there. This is the most-visited community on PEI outside of Charlottetown and, although an eyesore in this scenic region, it is kiddie wonderland. To get out of the world of fabricated and fictional free-for-all, head to beautiful **Cavendish Beach**; it gets crowded during summer months but with perfect sand and a warm (ish) ocean in front, you wont really care.

If you haven't read the 1908 novel, this is the place to do it – not just to enjoy it, but to try and understand all the hype. The story revolves around Anne Shirley, a spirited 11-year-old orphan with red pigtails and a creative wit, who was mistakenly sent from Nova Scotia to PEI. The aging Cuthberts (who were brother and sister) were expecting a strapping boy to help them with farm chores. In the end, Anne's strength of character wins over everyone in her path.

◉ Sights

House of Green Gables HISTORIC SITE
(☑902-672-7874; Rte 6; adult/under 17yr/family $5.75/3/14.50; ☺9am-8pm) Cavendish is the home town of Lucy Maud Montgomery (1874–1942), author of *Anne of Green Gables*. Here she is simply known as Lucy Maud or LM. Owned by her grandfather's cousins, the now-famous House of Green Gables and its Victorian surrounds inspired the setting for her fictional tale. In 1937 the house became part of the national park and it's now administered as a national heritage site.

The site celebrates Lucy Maud and Anne with exhibits and audio-visual displays. The trails leading from the house through the green, gentle creek-crossed woods are worthwhile. The 'Haunted Wood' and 'Lover's Lane' have maintained their idealistic childhood ambience.

Avonlea Village THEME PARK
(☑902-963-3050; www.avonlea.ca; Rte 6; adult/child/family $19/15/65; ☺9am-5pm) Delve deeper into Anne fantasy at this theme park where costumed actors portray characters from the book and perform dramatic moments and scenes from Green Gable chapters. Beyond the theatrical exploits, the park offers you cow-milking demonstrations, a ride in horse-drawn wagon and other period farm activities. Check the website for the day's schedule.

Site of Lucy Maud Montgomery's Cavendish Home HISTORIC SITE
(☑902-963-2231; Rte 6; adult/child $4/2; ☺9am-6pm) This is considered hallowed ground to Anne fans worldwide. Raised by her grandparents, Lucy Maud lived in this house from 1876 to 1911 and it is here that she wrote *Anne of Green Gables*. The land is now owned and tended to by Lucy Maud's grandson who also runs a small on-site museum and bookshop.

🛏 Sleeping & Eating

While accommodations are numerous, remember that this is the busiest and most expensive area you can stay. There are more bargains and more bucolic settings east, toward North Rustico.

Kindred Spirits Country Inn & Cottages INN $$
(☑902-963-2434, 800-461-1755; www.kindredspirits.ca; Rte 6; d $55-285, ste $125-285; 🅿✳🛜🏊) A huge, immaculate complex, this place has something for everyone from a storybook-quality inn-style B&B to deluxe suites. Rooms are every Anne fan's dream with dotty floral prints, glossy wood floors and fluffy, dreamlike beds. Downstairs the lounge has a fireplace that'll make you wish it would snow and couches perfect for snuggling up with a mug of cocoa.

A YEN FOR ANNE

Cuter than Pokémon and able to leap cultures in a single bound, *Akage no An* (Red-haired Anne) has secured her place in Japanese pop culture. The novel was introduced to Japan in the 1950s and quickly found its way into the school curriculum with the idea that its wholesomeness and positive themes would build hope after the devastation of WWII. Anne remained steadfast in Japanese culture by capturing their hearts with her courage and free spirit. Today, visiting PEI is many a Japanese girl's dream.

Japanese homage to Anne has appeared in many forms. She became an animated character in 1979 and a musical version of *Akage no An* toured Japan in the '80s and '90s. In 1981, 23 Anne enthusiasts visited PEI and later established the 'Buttercups,' an Anne fan club; today the club has more than 200 members. 'Philosophy of Anne' books are available to young Japanese readers wanting to get more understanding of Anne and the 'School of Green Gables,' a social work and nursing college in Okayama, tries to instill Anne ideology in its students. But the biggest Anne shrine of them all was 'Canadian World,' a PEI theme park that re-created Green Gables down to the patchwork quilts and a little red-haired Canadian girl. Unfortunately the park, located in an out-of-the-way collapsed mining town, became too much like Canada – lots of open spaces and too few people – and went bankrupt.

Parkview Farm Tourist Home & Cottages   B&B $$

(📞902-963-2027, 800-237-9890; www.peion line. com/al/parkview; 8214 Rte 6; r with shared bathroom incl light breakfast $60-65, 2-bedroom cottages $160-225; 🐾) This fine choice is set on a working dairy farm, 2km east of Cavendish. Ocean views, bathrooms and the prerequisite flowered wallpaper and frills abound in this comfortable and roomy tourist home. Each of the seven cottages, which are available May to mid-October (but the B&B is open year-round), contains a kitchen and a barbecue, as well as a balcony to catch those dramatic comings and goings of the sun.

TOP CHOICE **The Pearl**   RESTAURANT $$

(📞902-963-2111; 7792 Cavendish Rd; mains $22-32, brunch $8-12; ⊘from 4:30pm daily, 10am-2pm Sun) This shingled house, which is surrounded by flowers just outside Cavendish is an absolutely lovely place to eat. There are plenty of unusual and seasonally changing options like ice wine–infused chicken liver pâté on a Gouda brioche for starters and locally inspired mains such as delicious butter-poached scallops.

Carr's Oysters   RESTAURANT $$

(📞902-886-3355; Stanley Bridge Wharf, Rte 6; mains $14-32; ⊘10am-7pm) Dine on oysters straight from Malpeque Bay or lobster, mussels and seafood you've never even heard of like quahogs from this place's saltwater tanks. There are also plenty of fish on offer from salmon to trout. The setting over the bay is sociable and bright and there's also on on-site market selling fresh and smoked sea critters.

ℹ️ Information

Cavendish Visitor Centre (📞902-963-7830; cnr Rte 6 & Hwy 13; ⊘9am-9pm)

ℹ️ Getting Around

The **Cavendish Red Trolley** (⊘10am-6pm late Jun–Aug) runs hourly along Hwy 6 and through Cavendish, making various stops, including the Cavendish Visitor Centre, Cavendish Beach and the House of Green Gables (all-day ticket $3).

New London & Park Corner

New London and Park Corner both have strong ties to Lucy Maud Montgomery, and are thus caught up in the everything-Anne pandemonium.

In New London, 10km southwest of Cavendish, is the **Lucy Maud Montgomery Birthplace** (📞902-886-2099; cnr Rtes 6 & 20; admission $3; ⊘9am-5pm). The house is now a museum that contains some of her personal belongings, including her wedding dress.

Almost 10km northwest of New London is the village of Park Corner and the **Lucy Maud Montgomery Heritage Museum** (📞902-886-2807; 4605 Rte 20; admission $4; ⊘9:30am-6pm). It's believed to be the home of Lucy Maud's grandfather and there's a lot of Anne paraphernalia. Take a guided tour; there's a guarantee that if you're not absolutely fascinated, you don't pay the admission.

Almost 500m down the hill from here, surrounded by a luscious 44-hectare property, is the charming home Lucy Maud liked to call **Silver Bush**. It was always dear

---

LOCAL KNOWLEDGE

JOHN BIL: CHEF & OYSTER SHUCKING CHAMPION

Three-time oyster shucking champion of Canada and chef and owner of Ship to Shore restaurant in Darnley, John Bil has been called 'one of the island's shellfish shamans' by the New York Times.

Tell us about the local oysters. I think of oysters like wine. Our oysters here are the best in the world because of the species, the climate, water salinity and the fact that people really give a shit about quality and how they raise them. Oysters from different areas even around the island taste different. For example North shore oysters are saltier because they grow in the open Atlantic where there's more salinity; South shore oysters are sweeter. Which type you prefer depends on your preference but I like them salty.

Any other types of seafood visitors should try? Soft-shell clams, also called seamer clams, although they aren't served many places any more. Locals know about them and love them but they are scarcer and more expensive since they're seasonal and hand dug from the wild.

to her and she chose the parlor for her 1911 wedding. Silver Bush hosts the **Anne of Green Gables Museum** (☑902-886-2884; 4542 Rte 20; adult/under 17yr $3/1; ⊙9am-5pm mid-May–Jun & Sep-early Oct, to 6pm Jul & Aug). It contains such items as her writing desk and autographed first-edition books.

✗ Eating

TOP CHOICE **Ship to Shore** RESTAURANT **$$**
(☑902-836-5475; 2684 Rte 20, Darnley; mains $9-29; ⊙noon-11pm) If you love shellfish, you'd be doing yourself a disservice not eating here. The menu is simple and straightforward, focusing on the flavors of the best and freshest seafood you're likely to find anywhere. Some you simply won't find elsewhere. Be warned: this place looks like a regular old roadhouse from the outside but open the door and you're in for a special treat.

Blue Winds Tea Room RESTAURANT **$$**
(☑902-886-2860; 10746 Rte 6, New London; meals under $14; ⊙11am-6pm Mon-Thu, to 8pm Fri-Sun) Just 500m southwest of Lucy Maud's birthplace, this is a pretty tearoom surrounded by English gardens. Of course like everything else in this region, they've got to be 'Anne,' so order a raspberry cordial or some New Moon Pudding, both recipes have been taken from Lucy Maud's journals.

Kensington & Around

Kensington is a busy market town about halfway between Cavendish and Summerside. It's a good place to replenish supplies and the closest service center for those attending the **Indian River Festival** (www indian riverfestival.com) when some of Canada's finest musicians (from Celtic to choral) play in the wonderfully acoustic St Mary's Church, from June through September.

Home Place Inn & Restaurant (☑902-836-5686, 866-522-9900; www.thehomeplace. ca; 21 Victoria St East; d incl breakfast $89-109, ste $149; ☎) exudes country elegance at its finest. In the morning you may be awakened with scents of freshly baking cinnamon rolls and there's a licensed pub and restaurant on the premises.

In nearby Margate, **Shipwright's Café** (☑902-836-3403; cnr Rtes 6 & 233; dinner mains $25-35; ⊙11:30am-3:30pm Mon-Fri, from 5pm daily) is housed in an 1880s farmhouse overlooking rolling fields and flower gardens. It earns rave reviews for its seafood dishes and vegetarian fare concocted from organic

MALPEQUE

So where is this place where all the oysters come from? You might ask. The tiny hamlet of Malpeque takes you off the beaten path, past shadeless, rolling farmland to a tiny bay simply jammed-packed with fishing boats and their colorfully painted storage barns. Don't miss lunch at **Malpeque Oyster Barn** (Malpeque Wharf; half-dozen oysters $14; ⊙11am-9pm Mon-Sat, noon-9pm Sun), one of PEI's more authentically ambient cafes, in the top of a fisherman's barn and overlooking the bay and its oyster-filled action. Downstairs is a seafood monger where you can pick up fresh local sea critters to take away (a dozen oysters are around $6).

herbs and vegetables from the gardens. Try the 'Salute to Our Greenhouse' salad, a paella endowed with the island's best seafood and creations with PEI beef.

WESTERN PEI

Malpeque and Bedeque Bays converge to almost separate the western third of PEI from the rest of the province. This region sits entirely within the larger Prince County, and it combines the sparse pastoral scenery of Kings County's interior with some of Queens County's rugged coastal beauty.

The cultural history here stands out more than elsewhere on the island. On Lennox Island a proud Mi'kmaq community is working to foster knowledge of its past, while French Acadians are doing the same in the south, along Egmont and Bedeque Bays.

Summerside

While it lacks the elegance and cosmopolitan vibe of Charlottetown, Summerside is a simpler, seaside-oriented place with everything you need in one small, tidy package. Recessed deep within Bedeque Bay and PEI's second-largest 'city,' this tiny seaside village possesses a modern waterfront and quiet streets lined with leafy trees and grand old homes. The two largest economic booms in the province's history,

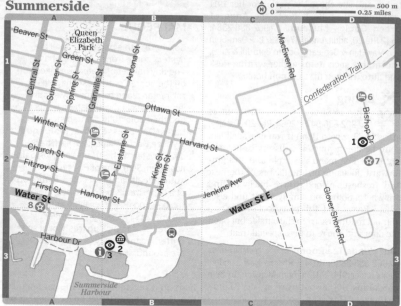

shipbuilding and fox breeding, shaped the city's development in the 19th and early 20th centuries. Like Charlottetown, its outskirts are plagued by unsightly development – you'll find most of Summerside's interesting bits along, or near to, Water St, which runs parallel to the waterfront.

◉ Sights & Activities

The Confederation Trail (see boxed text, p431) makes its journey right through town and passes behind the library on Water St.

Spinnaker's Landing   BOARDWALK
This redeveloped waterfront is the highlight of Summerside. A continually expanding boardwalk allows you to wander and enjoy the harbor and its scenic surrounds. There are some very nice eateries, a stage for live music in the summer and numerous shops. A mock lighthouse provides adults with a nice lookout and some local information, while a large model ship is a dream playground for kids. Backing all of this is the modern **Eptek Exhibition Centre** (☎902-888-8373; 130 Harbour Dr; admission by donation; ◷10am-4pm), which features local and traveling art exhibitions.

**College of Piping &
Celtic Performing Arts**   MUSIC
(☎902-436-5377; 619 Water St E; ◷9am-9pm late Jun–Aug) In celebration of Celtic dance and music, this school provides visitors with free 20-minute miniconcerts from Monday to Friday at 11:30am, 1:30pm and 3:30pm – expect bagpipes, singing and dancing. Inspired? Put on some warm clothes and make sure you enjoy the two-hour **ceilidhs** (adult/student $12/7; ◷7pm) that take place every night in the covered amphitheater.

⊨ Sleeping

TOP CHOICE **Willow Green Farm B&B**   B&B **$$**
(☎902-436-4420,   888-436-4420; www.willow greenfarm.com; 117 Bishop Dr; d incl breakfast $50-115; ☜) With the Confederation Trail at its back door, and the College of Piping & Celtic Performing Arts out its front door, this rambling farmhouse is an incredibly great-value place to stay; you feel like you're in the country but actually you're in the central Summerside. Rooms are bright, and the bold country interior is a refreshing change from busy period decors. Read beside the wood stove or check out some of the more interesting farm animals.

Summerside

⊙ **Sights**

Comme Chez Nous B&B   B&B $$

(📞902-436-8600; anwe@pei.sympatico.com; 161 Fitzroy St; r incl breakfast $90-115; 🛜) This lovingly restored early-20th-century house sits on a quiet residential street within easy walking distance of restaurants and attractions. The guest rooms feature crisp, sumptuous fabrics and richly polished antiques, as well as big windows and flatscreen TVs with headphones. The easygoing hosts serve a gourmet breakfast in the wood-paneled dining room, and will also prepare a four-course dinner feast for guests by reservation.

Silver Fox Inn   B&B $$

(📞902-436-1664, 000-505-4033, www.silverfox inn.net; 61 Granville St; d $80-155; 🛜) With opulent details like antique lace curtains and navy and gold striped wall paper, this Queen Anne revival B&B feels like a stylish 1920s or '30s re-creation of the Victorian era.

✖ Eating

Deckhouse Pub & Restaurant

RESTAURANT $$

(📞902-436-0660; 150 Harbour Dr; mains $7-17; ⊙11am-11pm Jun–mid-Sep) Step off the Spinnaker's Landing boardwalk and onto one of the Deckhouse's two outdoor decks for a great meal in harborfront surroundings. Live music adds to the atmosphere on weekends. It's well known for its hand-battered fish-and-chips.

Brothers Two Restaurant   RESTAURANT $$

(📞902-436-9654; 618 Water St E; mains $11-26; ⊙11:30am-9pm Mon-Thu, 11:30am-9pm Mon-Fri, 4-10pm Sat, 4-8pm Sun) Brothers Two's service, pasta, steak and fresh seafood have made it a local favorite for more than 30 years. The vegetarian stir-fry and island blue mussels steamed in garlic and white wine are both excellent. If you want in on the laughter coming from below, check out Feast Dinner Theatres (p445).

🍷 Drinking & Entertainment

Jubilee Theatre   THEATER

(📞902-888-2500, 800-708-6505; www.jubilee theatre.com; 124 Harbour Dr) This modern theater is in the same complex as the Eptek Exhibition Centre and is the venue for *Anne and Gilbert* (adult from $29, child $15; runs July to September), a musical that picks up where the ever-popular *Anne of Green Gables* musical in Charlottetown leaves off, and will likely be playing for the next hundred or so years at least. The Jubilee also hosts the Summer on the Waterfront Festival (July to mid-September), which showcases local and well-known Canadian musical acts.

Feast Dinner Theatres   THEATER

(📞902-888-2200, 888-748-1010; 618 Water St E; dinner & show $36; ⊙6:30pm Mon-Sat Jun-Dec) Most locals start to giggle when they speak of their last time at Feast Dinner Theatres. You will find it below Brothers Two Restaurant and it is the longest-running theater restaurant in Atlantic Canada. Music, script and improvisation combine with audience participation to make for a truly memorable evening. And that's not all. The food's not too shabby, either.

Heritage Pub & Restaurant   PUB

(📞902-436-8484; 250 Water St) This traditional watering hole is the only live-music venue in town (no cover charge). Local bands play on Friday, and occasionally on Saturday.

❶ Information

Provincial Tourist Office (📞902-888-8364; Hwy 1A; ⊙9am-4:30pm late May–late Jun & late Aug–mid-Oct, to 7pm late Jun–late Aug) Pick up a copy of the useful walking-tour pamphlet, which details the town's finer 19th-century buildings.

❶ Getting There & Away

Acadian Coach Lines (p424) stops at the **Irving gas station** (📞902-436-2420; 96 Water St) in the center of town and has services to Charlottetown ($12, one hour), Moncton ($33, two hours) and Halifax ($60, 3½ hours). On request, bus shuttles pick up at the Esso station on Hwy 1A at the end of Water St E.

Région Évangéline

The strongest French Acadian ancestry on the island is found here, between Miscouche and Mont Carmel. Some 6000 residents still speak French as their first language, although you'll have trouble discerning this region from others in the province. There is one notable exception: the red, white, blue and yellow star of the Acadian flag hangs proudly from many homes. It was in Miscouche, on August 15, 1884, that the Acadian flag was unfurled for the very first time. The yellow star represents the patron saint of the Acadians, the Virgin Mary. Renewed efforts are under way to preserve the unique Acadian culture on the island. See the Nova Scotia (p353) and New Brunswick (p378) chapters for more information on Acadians.

A favorite stop on this stretch is the **Bottle Houses** (☎902-854-2987; Rte 11, Cape Egmont; adult/child $5/2; ☹9am-8pm), the artful and monumental recycling project of Edouard Arsenault. Over 25,000 bottles of all shapes and sizes (that Edouard collected from the community) are stacked in white cement to create a handful of buildings with light-filled mosaic walls.

The very worthwhile **Acadian Museum** (☎902-432-2880; 23 Maine Dr E; admission $5; ☹9:30am-7pm), in Miscouche, uses 18th-century Acadian artifacts, texts, visuals and music to enlighten visitors about the tragic and compelling history of the Acadians on PEI since 1720. The introspective video introduces a fascinating theory that the brutal treatment of the Acadians by the British may have backhandedly helped preserve a vestige of Acadian culture on Prince Edward Island.

Tyne Valley

This area, famous for its Malpeque oysters, is one of the most scenic in the province. The village, with its cluster of ornate houses, gentle river and art studios, is definitely worth a visit.

Green Park Provincial Park, 6km north of the village, hosts the **Green Park Ship-building Museum & Historic Yeo House** (☎902-831-7947; Rte 12; adult $5; ☹9am-5pm). The museum and restored Victorian home, along with a recreated shipyard and partially constructed 200-tonne brigantine, combine to tell the story of the booming shipbuilding industry in the glory days of the 19th century.

The park has 58 **campsites** (☎902-831-7912; off Rte 12; campsites $23-25, with hookups $30, cabins with shared bathroom $45; ☹mid-Jun–mid-Sep) spread within a mixed forest. The dozen cabins just beyond the campground are a steal.

Doctor's Inn (☎902-831-3057; www.peisland.com/doctorsinn; 32 Allen Rd; d with shared bathroom incl breakfast $60-75) is an old country home that makes for a comfortable stay, but when we passed the owners were considering stopping the B&B and focusing on the restaurant; phone ahead first. The dining room (three-course meal guests/nonguests $45/55, open by reservation) is known to prepare the finest meals in the region. Cooked over a wood stove, the *tournedos rossini* (beef tenderloin and liver pâté with a red-wine sauce), *sole almandine* (fillet of sole coated with white wine and toasted almonds) and organic vegetables from the garden are all superb. It is closed on Friday. You can also take a tour of the gardens and purchase fresh produce.

Not surprisingly, the specialty at **Landing Oyster House & Pub** (☎902-831-3138; 1327 Port Hill Station Rd; mains $8-13; ☹lunch & dinner) is 15 deep-fried oysters – definitely indulge. Live bands (cover $3 to $5) play here on Friday night, and also on Saturday during July and August.

Lennox Island

Set in the mouth of Malpeque Bay, sheltered behind Hog Island, is Lennox Island and its 250 Mi'kmaq (mig-*maw*) Aboriginal people. While working hard to promote awareness and understanding of their past, both in and out of their own community, they are also making renewed efforts to preserve their culture. The island is connected by a causeway, making it accessible from the town of East Bideford off Rte 12.

The **Lennox Island Aboriginal Ecotourism Complex** (☎866-831-2702; 2 Eagle Feather Trail; adult/student $4/3; ☹10am-6pm Mon-Sat Jul & Aug, noon-6pm Mon-Sat late Jun

& early Sep) opened its doors in June 2004. Inside there are small, changing exhibits and information about the two excellent **interpretive trails** around the island. These trails consist of two loops, forming a total of 13km, with the shorter one (3km) being accessible to people in wheelchairs – for $4 a local will guide you, explaining the medicinal qualities of the plants, and lead you to a beaver dam. Also ask at the center if anything else is on offer, since it seems to change frequently.

Tignish

Tignish is a quiet town tucked up near the North Cape; it sees only a fraction of PEI's visitors. The towering **Church of St Simon & St Jude** (1859) was the first brick church built on the island. Have a peek inside – its ceiling has been restored to its gorgeous but humble beginnings, and the organ (1882) is of gargantuan proportions. Of its 1118 pipes, the shortest is 15cm, while the longest is nearly 5m!

The Confederation Trail begins (or ends!) two blocks south of the church on School St. The **Tignish Cultural Centre** (☑902-882-1999; 305 School St; admission free; ⊘8am-4pm Mon-Fri), near the church, has a good exhibition of old maps and photos, tourist information and a library with internet access.

North Cape

The drive toward North Cape seems stereotypically bucolic, until the moment your eyes rise above the quaint farmhouses to see the heavens being churned by dozens of sleek behemoth-sized white blades. Strangely, expecting the surreal sight takes nothing away from it.

The narrow, windblown North Cape is not only home to the **Atlantic Wind Test**, but also to the longest **natural rock reef** on the continent. At low tide, it's possible to walk out 800m, exploring tide pools and searching for seals. The expanded **interpretive center** (☑902-882-2991; admission $6; ⊘9:30am-8pm), at the northern end of Rte 12, provides high-tech displays dedicated to wind energy, and informative displays on the history of the area. The aquarium is always a hit with kids. The **Black Marsh Nature Trail** (2.7km) leaves the interpretive center and takes you to the west side of the cape – at sunset these crimson cliffs simply glow against the deep-blue waters.

Above the interpretive center, the atmospheric **Wind & Reef Restaurant & Lounge** (☑902-882-3535; mains $9-29; ⊘lunch & dinner) attracts visitors and locals out for a treat. The menu and view are equally vast and pleasing.

West Coast

In Miminegash, stop into the **Seaweed Cafe** (meals $5-12) that serves a special seaweed pie ($4.50), although nothing about this fluffy, creamy creation reeks of the beach.

Inland at O'Leary is the **Prince Edward Island Potato Museum** (☑902-859-2039; 1 Dewar Lane; admission $6; ⊘9am-5pm Mon-Sat, 1-5pm Sun). It's a bit like a giant school science fair project with hallways of information panels and pictures on the walls.

Between Miminegash and West Point, Rte 14 hugs the shore and provides stunning vistas. It's perhaps the finest drive on the island. Off Hwy 14, the striking black-and-white-striped **West Point Lighthouse** (☑902-859-3605, 800-764-6854; www.westpoint lighthouse.com; ⊘8am-9:30pm), dating from 1875, has been restored. Between 1875 and 1955 there were only two lighthouse keepers. Today the staff is made up of their descendants. There's a small museum (admission $4; ⊘9am-9pm), where you can climb the tower for a breathtaking view. Part of the former lighthouse keepers' quarters have been converted into a nine-room **inn** (d $100-145); the Tower Room ($145) is actually in the old lighthouse tower. The **restaurant** (meals $8-18; ⊘8am-8pm mid-May–Sep) is locally famous for its clam chowder.

Cedar Dunes Provincial Park (☑902-859-8785; tent sites $23-25, RV sites $26-27) has tent space in an open grassy field adjacent to West Point Lighthouse. Its red-sand beach is an island gem.

Newfoundland & Labrador

Best Places to Eat

» Lighthouse Picnics (p465)
» Norseman Restaurant (p486)
» Nicole's Cafe (p478)
» Bacalao (p459)

Best Places to Stay

» Tuckamore Lodge (boxed text, p489)
» Artisan Inn (p469)
» Tickle Inn (p486)
» The Cliffhouse (p468)

Why Go?

Canada's easternmost province floats in a world of its own. Blue icebergs drift by. Puffins flap along the coast. Whales spout close to shore. The island even ticks in its own off-beat time zone (a half-hour ahead of the mainland) and speaks its own dialect (the *Dictionary of Newfoundland English* provides translation, me old cock).

Outside the good-time capital St John's, it's mostly wee fishing villages that freckle the coast, some so isolated they're reached only by boat. They offer plenty of hiking and kayaking escapes where it will just be you, the local family who's putting you up for the night and the lonely howl of the wind.

If you're looking to get off the beaten path – to see Viking vestiges, eat meals of cod tongue and partridgeberry pie, and share fish tales over shots of rum – set a course for this remote hunk of rock.

When to Go

St John's

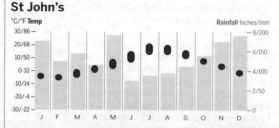

June Icebergs glisten offshore, though the weather can be wet and foggy

July & August Whales swim by, festivals rock most weekends, and the province is at its sunniest

December & January Skiers hit the slopes as Marble Mountain receives most of its 5m of snow

History

The Paleoindians walked into Labrador 9000 years ago. They hunted seals, fished for salmon and tried to stay warm. The Vikings, led by Leif Eriksson, washed ashore further south at L'Anse aux Meadows in Newfoundland in AD 1000. They established North America's first European settlement – 500 years ahead of Columbus – but conflicts with natives and harsh conditions eventually sent them back to Iceland.

John Cabot (Italian-born Giovanni Caboto) sailed around the shores of Newfoundland next. It was 1497, and he was employed by England's Henry VII. He returned to Bristol a hero, with news of finding a new and shorter route to Asia. While Cabot was badly mistaken, his stories of cod stocks so prolific that one could nearly walk on water spread quickly throughout Europe.

Soon the French, Portuguese, Spanish and Basques were also fishing off Newfoundland's coast. There were no permanent settlements on the island, and fishing crews returned to Europe with their bounties at the end of each season. The English fishers' primary base was St John's, while the French congregated around Placentia and the Port au Port Peninsula. In the end it was the 1713 Treaty of Utrecht that ceded all of Newfoundland to England.

The land remained a British colony for most of the next two centuries, with life revolving around the booming fishing industry. Newfoundland's Aboriginal people, the Beothuk, did not fare well after settlement began. Diseases and land conflicts contributed to their demise by 1830.

Ever true to its independent spirit, Newfoundland was the last province to join Canada, doing so in 1949. While Labrador was always part of the package, it wasn't until 2001 that it became part of the provincial name.

Language

One recent visitor described the local accent as Irish meets Canadian while chewing a mouthful of cod. Well said.

Two hundred years ago, coastal fishing families from Ireland and England made up almost the entire population. Since then, as a result of living in isolated outposts, their language has evolved into almost 60 different dialects. Strong, lilting inflections, unique slang and colorful idioms pepper the language, sometimes confounding even residents.

The authoritative source is the **Dictionary of Newfoundland English** (www.heritage.nf.ca/dictionary). In the meantime, here are a few translations:

Long may yer big jib draw. Good luck.

Newfoundland Pronounced 'new-fun-*land*' (emphasized the same way as 'understand').

Oweshegettinonbys? Pronounced 'how's she getting on, boys?' ie how are you?

Where you longs to? Where are you from?

Land & Climate

They don't call it The Rock for nothing. Glaciers tore through, leaving behind a rugged landscape of boulders, lakes and bogs. The interior remains barren, while the island's cities and towns congregate at its edges near the sea.

Newfoundland's most significant landscape feature is actually offshore. The Grand Banks, which swing around the southeast coast, are an incredibly fertile marine feeding ground. The continental shelf here sticks out like a thumb to intercept the south-flowing waters of the frigid Labrador Current right at the point where it mingles with the warm north-flowing waters of the Gulf Stream. The mix of warmth and nutrient-rich arctic waters creates an explosion of plankton that feeds everything from the smallest fish to the biggest humpback. This is why fishing was supreme here for so many years, and why it remains a top place to view whales and seabirds.

Labrador is more sparse than Newfoundland, puddled and tundralike, with mountains thrown in for good measure.

Temperatures peak in July and August, when daytime highs average 20°C. These are also the driest months; it rains or snows about 15 days out of every 30. Wintertime temperatures hover at 0°C. Fog and wind

NEWFOUNDLAND FAST FACTS

» Population: 510,900

» Area: 405,720 sq km

» Capital: St John's

» Quirky fact: Newfoundland has 82 places called Long Pond, 42 called White Point and one called Jerry's Nose

Newfoundland & Labrador Highlights

① Share the waves with whales and puffins at **Witless Bay Ecological Reserve** (p464)

② Hoist a drink, hear live music, take a ghost tour and soak up the history of North America's oldest city, **St John's** (p451)

③ Explore Leif Eriksson's 1000-year-old Viking pad at the sublime **L'Anse aux Meadows National Historic Site** (p485)

④ Hike the mountains and kayak the fjordlike lakes at **Gros Morne National Park** (p481)

⑤ Try out the outport life in **Fogo** (p478)

⑥ Learn Basque whaling history then walk alongside ancient whale bones at **Red Bay** (p499)

⑦ Get your French fix – wine, chocolate éclairs and baguettes – in **St-Pierre** (p472)

⑧ Snap a photo with the captain in **Dildo** (p467)

Map labels:

Labrador

Québec

Newfoundland

ATLANTIC OCEAN

Gulf of Saint Lawrence

Strait of Belle Isle

Hare Bay

Notre Dame Bay

Bonavista Bay

Trinity Bay

Conception Bay

St George's Bay

Cabot Strait

Fortune Bay

Port Hope Simpson

Mary's Harbour

Red Bay

Belle Isle

Cape Onion

L'Anse aux Meadows National Historic Site

St Lunaire-Griquet

St Anthony

Pinware

Forteau

Old Fort Bay

Blanc Sablon

St Barbe

Plum Point

Main Brook

Conche

Grey Islands

Roddickton

Port au Choix

Northern Peninsula

Hawke's Bay

Portland Creek

The Arches

Fleur de Lys

Baie Verte

La Scie

Change Islands

Cow Head

Sally's Cove

Gros Morne National Park

Baie Verte Peninsula

Twillingate Island

Fogo Island

Rocky Harbour

Norris Point

Springdale

Moreton's Harbour

Farewell

Boyd's Cove

Trout River

Woody Point

Glenburnie

Lewisporte

Lark Harbour

Deer Lake

Grand Lake

Gander

Bonavista Bay

Port au Port Peninsula

Corner Brook

Marble Mountain

Grand Falls-Windsor

Burnside

Bonavista

Elliston

Lourdes

Stephenville

Red Indian Lake

Terra Nova National Park

Salvage

Trinity

Port au Port West

Barachois Pond Provincial Park

Maelpaeg Lake

Bonavista Peninsula

Cape Anguille

Isle aux Morts

Rose Blanche

Head of Bay d'Espoir

Bay du Nord Wilderness Reserve

Clarenville

Heart's Content

Heart's Delight

Harbour Grace

ST JOHN'S

Cape Ray

Burgeo

Grey River

François

St Alban's

Pool's Cove

Cupids

Dildo

Brigus

Witless Bay Ecological Reserve

Port aux Basques

Sandbanks Provincial Park

Ramea

Hermitage

Harbour Breton

Burin Peninsula

Argentia

Avalon Peninsula

La Manche PP

South Coast Outports Ferry

Ile de Miquelon

Grand Bank

Marystown

Placentia

Avalon Wilderness Reserve

Ferryland

St-Pierre & Miquelon (FRANCE)

Fortune

Cape Burin

St Lawrence

St Mary's Ecological Reserve

St Mary's

Chance Cove PP

Ile St-Pierre

St Vincent's

Mistaken Point Ecological Reserve

Argentia-North Sydney (NS) Ferry

Port aux Basques-North Sydney (NS) Ferry

Goose Bay-Cartwright-Lewisporte Ferry

Trans-Canada Hwy

100 km

60 miles

PLANNING YOUR TRIP

» Book ahead for rental cars and accommodations. If you're arriving during the mid-July to early August peak, secure a car by April or May and don't wait much longer to book a room. **Newfoundland & Labrador Tourism** (www.newfoundlandlabrador. com) has listings.

» Driving distances are lengthy so have realistic expectations of what you can cover. For instance, it's 708km between St John's and Gros Morne National Park. The **Road Distance Database** (www.stats.gov. nl.ca/DataTools/RoadDB/Distance) is a good reference.

» Know your seasons for puffins (May to August), icebergs (June to early July) and whales (July to August). Icebergs, in particular, can be tricky to predict. Check **Iceberg Finder** (www. icebergfinder.com) to get the drift.

plague the coast much of the year (which makes for a lot of canceled flights).

Parks & Wildlife
Whales, moose and puffins are Newfoundland's wildlife stars, and most visitors see them all. Whale-watching tours depart from all around the province and will take you close to the sea mammals (usually humpback and minke). Puffins – the funny-looking love child of the penguin and parrot – are Atlantic Canada's most abundant bird; about 95% of North America's population breeds off the island (see the boxed text, p471). Moose nibble shrubs near roadsides throughout the province, so keep an eye out while driving. Some visitors also glimpse caribou near the Avalon Wilderness Reserve (p465), which is special because usually these beasts can only be seen in the High Arctic. Large caribou herds also roam in Labrador.

ℹ Getting There & Around

AIR

St John's Airport (YYT; www.stjohnsairport. com) is the main hub for the region, though **Deer Lake Airport** (YDF; www.deerlakeairport.com) is an excellent option for visitors focusing on the Northern Peninsula. Airlines flying in include **Air Canada** (www.aircanada.com), **Provincial** (www. provincialairlines.com), **Porter** (www.flyporter. com) and **Continental** (www.continental.com).

Marine Atlantic (☎800-341-7981; www. marine-atlantic.ca) operates two massive car/passenger ferries between North Sydney, Nova Scotia and Newfoundland. There's a daily, six-hour crossing to Port aux Basques (western Newfoundland) year-round, and a thrice-weekly, 14-hour crossing to Argentia (on the Avalon Peninsula) in summer. Reservations are recommended, especially to Argentia.

Provincial Ferry Service (www.gov.nl.ca/ferryservices) runs the smaller boats that travel within the province to various islands and coastal towns. Each service has its own phone number with up-to-the-minute information; it's wise to call before embarking.

BUS

DRL (☎709-263-2171; www.drl-lr.com) sends one bus daily each way between St John's and Port aux Basques (13½ hours), making 25 stops en route. Other than DRL, public transportation consists of small, regional shuttle vans that connect with one or more major towns. Although not extensive, the system works pretty well and will get most people where they want to go.

CAR

The Trans-Canada Hwy (Hwy 1) is the main cross-island roadway. Driving distances are deceptive, as travel is often slow-going on heavily contorted, single-lane roads. Watch out for moose, especially at dusk. High-risk zones are signposted (the yellow-and-black graphic of an antlered beast crumpling a car is a definite Newfoundland photo op).

ST JOHN'S

POP 100,646

Encamped on the steep slopes of a harbor, with jelly-bean-colored row houses toppling up from hilly streets, St John's is often described as looking like a mini San Francisco. And like its American counterpart, it's home to artists, musicians, inflated real estate prices and young, iPhone-using denizens. Yet the vibe of Newfoundland's largest city and capital remains refreshingly small-town, with locals happy to share conversation and a sudsy drink with newcomers. At some point, they'll be sure to let you know St John's is North America's oldest city.

REGIONAL DRIVING DISTANCES:

St John's to Port aux Basques: 905km
St John's to Gros Morne: 708km
Gros Morne to St Anthony: 372km

Five Days

Start in St John's by visiting **Signal Hill** and **Cape Spear**. Both are historic sites, but they also offer walking trails and views where you just may see an iceberg, whale or both. At night sample St John's eateries, funky shops and music-filled pubs.

After a couple of days of 'big city' life, move onward through the Avalon Peninsula. Cruise to see whales and puffins at **Witless Bay Ecological Reserve**, plan a picnic in **Ferryland** or visit the birds at **Cape St Mary's**.

Spend the last day or two soaking up the historic eastern communities of **Trinity** and **Bonavista** and the cliffside hikes in between.

Ten Days

Do the five-day itinerary and then go west, possibly via a quick flight to **Deer Lake**, and reap the reward of viewing the mighty fjords of **Gros Morne National Park** and the monumental Viking history at **L'Anse aux Meadows**. With a few extra days you could sail across the Strait of Belle Isle and slow waaay down among the wee towns and bold granite cliffs of the **Labrador Straits**.

Highlights include view-gaping from Signal Hill, walking the seaside North Head Trail and listening to live music and hoisting a pint (or shot of rum) in George St's pubs. Many visitors take advantage of the city's beyond-the-norm eating and lodging options by making St John's their base camp for explorations elsewhere on the Avalon Peninsula. Cape Spear, Witless Bay Ecological Reserve and Ferryland are among the easy day trips.

History

St John's excellent natural harbor, leading out to what were once seething seas of cod, prompted the first European settlement here in 1528. Sir Humphrey Gilbert landed in town 55 years later, and proudly claimed the land for Queen Elizabeth I. The many Spanish, French and Portuguese settlers living around the harbor were not amused. During the late 1600s and much of the 1700s, St John's was razed and taken over several times as the French, English and Dutch fought for it tooth and nail. After Britain's ultimate victory on Signal Hill in 1762, things finally settled down and St John's started to take shape throughout the 1800s.

Since then four fires have ripped through the city, the last in 1892. Each time locals rebuilt with their pride and, more importantly, their sense of humor, intact.

Despite the centuries of turmoil, the harbor steadfastly maintained its position as the world trade center for salted cod well into the 20th century. By mid-century, warehouses lined Water St, and the merchants who owned them made a fortune. Come the early 1960s, St John's had more millionaires per capita than any other city in North America. Many called it the Codfish Republic, a riff on Central America's Banana Republics, and said these merchants got rich off the backs of the outport fishing communities, which only seemed to get poorer.

Today the city's wharves still act as service stations to fishing vessels from around the world and the occasional cruise ship, though the cod industry suffered mightily after the 1992 fishing moratorium (see the boxed text, p473). The offshore oil industry now drives the economy.

⊙ Sights

Most sights are downtown or within a few kilometers, though prepare for some serious uphill walking.

Signal Hill National Historic Site

HISTORIC PARK

(☎709-772-5367; www.pc.gc.ca/signalhill; Signal Hill Rd; grounds admission free; ⊙grounds 24hr) A trip up Signal Hill, the city's most famous landmark, is worth it for the glorious view alone, though there's much more to see.

An **interpretive center** (adult/child $3.90/1.90; ⊙10am-6pm, reduced hours mid-Oct–mid-May) features interactive displays on the site's history. The last North American battle of the Seven Years' War took place here in 1762, and Britain's victory ended France's renewed aspirations for control of eastern North America.

You can see cannons and the remains of the late-18th-century British battery at **Queen's Battery & Barracks** further up the hill. The tiny castle topping the hill is **Cabot Tower** (admission free; ⊙9am-9pm Jun-early Sep, to 5pm rest of year, closed mid-Jan–Mar), built in 1900 to honor both John Cabot's arrival in 1497 and Queen Victoria's Diamond Jubilee. Here Italian inventor Guglielmo Marconi gleefully received the first wireless transatlantic message from Cornwall, England in 1901. There are guides and displays in the tower; an amateur radio society operates a station here in summer.

In midsummer, several dozen soldiers dressed as the 19th-century Royal Newfoundland Company perform a **tattoo** (www.rnchs.ca/tattoo; admission $5; ⊙11am & 3pm Wed-Thu & Sat-Sun Jul–mid-Aug) on O'Flaherty Field next to the interpretive center. It wraps up with the firing of historic cannons.

An awesome way to return to downtown is along the **North Head Trail** (1.7km) which connects Cabot Tower with the harborfront Battery neighborhood. The walk departs from the tower's parking lot and traces the cliffs, imparting tremendous sea views and sometimes whale spouts. Because much of the trail runs along the bluff's sheer edge, this walk isn't something to attempt in icy, foggy or dark conditions.

The site sits 1.5km from downtown, up Signal Hill Rd.

The Rooms   MUSEUM
(⌇709-757-8000; www.therooms.ca; 9 Bonaventure Ave; adult/child $7.50/2.50; ⊙10am-5pm Mon-Sat, to 9pm Wed, noon-5pm Sun, closed Mon mid-Oct–May) Not many museums offer the chance to see a giant squid, hear avant-garde sound sculptures and peruse ancient weaponry all under one roof. But that's The Rooms, the province's all-in-one historical museum, art gallery and archives. Frankly, the building is much more impressive to look at than look in, since its frequently changing exhibits are sparse. But whoa! The views from this massive stone-and-glass complex, which lords over the city from a breath-sapping hilltop, are eye-poppers; try the 4th-floor cafe for the best vistas. There's free admission Wednesday evenings.

Johnson Geo Centre   MUSEUM
(⌇709-737-7880; www.geocentre.ca; 175 Signal Hill Rd; adult/child $11.50/5.50; ⊙9:30am-5pm Mon-Sat, noon-5pm Sun) Nowhere in the world can geo-history, going back to the birth of the earth, be accessed so easily as in Newfoundland, and the Geo Centre does a grand job of making snore-worthy geological information perk up with appeal via its underground, interactive displays.

The center also has an exhibit on the *Titanic,* and how human error and omission caused the tragedy, not just an iceberg. For instance, the ship's owners didn't supply her with enough lifeboats so as not to 'clutter the deck,' and the crew ignored myriad ice warnings. What any of this has to do with geology remains unclear, but who cares? It's fascinating.

Trails with interpretive panels wind around outside. The Geo Centre is up Signal Hill Rd, about 1km beyond downtown.

Basilica of St John the Baptist   CHURCH
(⌇709-754-2170; www.thebasilica.ca; 200 Military Rd; admission free; ⊙8am-3pm Mon-Fri, to 6pm Sat, to 12:30pm Sun) Built in 1855, the soaring twin spires of the basilica pierce the sky and are visible all the way from Signal Hill. Its design marks the revival of classical architecture in North America. Inside, 65 unique stained-glass windows illuminate the remarkable polychromatic Italianate ceiling and its gold-leaf highlights. The honor of being named a 'basilica' was bestowed on the church by Pope Pius XII on its centennial anniversary. Free half-hour tours are offered 10am to 5pm Monday to Saturday in July and August, according to demand.

Anglican Cathedral of St John the Baptist   CHURCH
(⌇709-726-5677; www.stjohnsanglicancathedral .org; 16 Church Hill; admission free; ⊙10am-noon & 2-4pm Mon-Fri, 10am-noon Sat Jul & Aug) Serving Canada's oldest parish (1699), the Anglican cathedral is one of the finest examples of ecclesiastical Gothic architecture in North America. Although originally built in the 1830s, all but its exterior walls were reduced to ashes by the Great Fire of 1892. It was rebuilt in 1905. The Gothic ribbed ceiling, graceful stone arches and long, thin, stained-glass windows are timeless marvels. A gargoyle dating from the 12th century – a gift from the Diocese of Bristol – stands guard over the south transept. Students offer tours, organists play **concerts** (⊙1:15pm Wed) and elderly church ladies serve tea and crumpets (see the boxed text, p456).

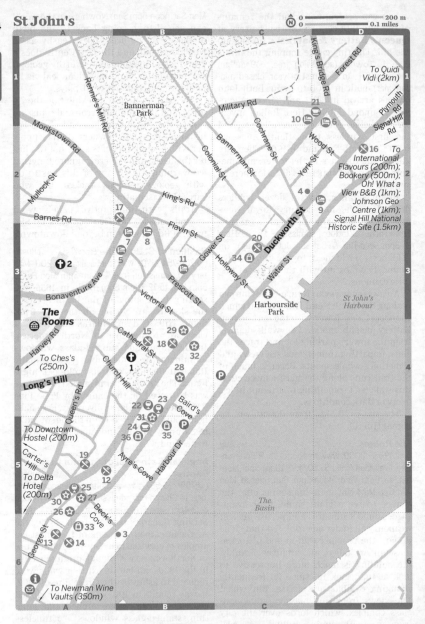

Quidi Vidi   BREWERY & HISTORICAL SITE

Over Signal Hill, away from town, is the tiny picturesque village of Quidi Vidi. Make your first stop **Quidi Vidi Brewery** (☎709-738-4040; www.quidividibrewery.ca; 35 Barrows Rd; tours $10; ⊙10am-4:30pm Mon-Sat, noon-4pm Sun), which cooks up Newfoundland's most popular microbrews. Located in an old fish-processing plant on the small wharf, it's a scenic place to slake one's thirst. The fee includes ample tastings and a bottle to sip while touring. Be sure to try

St John's

the Iceberg brand, made with water from the big hunks.

Nearby you'll find the oldest cottage in North America, the 1750s-era **Mallard Cottage** (☎709-570-7100 / RARROWS RD; ⊗9:30am-4:30pm May-Sep), now a charmingly cluttered antique/junk shop. Profits go to maintenance.

The 1762 **Quidi Vidi Battery** (☎709-729-2977; www.seethesites.ca; Cuckhold's Cove Rd; admission $3; ⊗10am-5:30pm late May–mid-Oct) atop the hill was built by the French after they took St John's. The British quickly claimed it, and it remained in military service into the 1800s. Period-garbed interpreters dole out historical information.

Inland from the village, **Quidi Vidi Lake** is the site of the city-stopping St John's Regatta. **Royal St John's Regatta Museum** (☎709-576-8921; cnr Lakeview Ave & Clancy Dr, off Forest Rd; admission free; ⊗Jul & Aug) is on the 2nd floor of the boathouse. Opening hours vary. A popular walking trail leads around the lake.

Quidi Vidi is about 2km from the northeast edge of downtown. Take Plymouth Rd, go left on Quidi Vidi Rd, then right on Forest Rd (which becomes Quidi Vidi Village Rd). For the brewery, bear right onto Barrows Rd. For the battery, veer off on Cuckold's Cove Rd. For the regatta museum,

---

ℹ **THE RENTAL CAR CRUNCH**

Be warned: rental car fleets are small (thanks to the island's remoteness and short tourist season), which means loads of visitors vie for limited vehicles in midsummer. Costs can rack up to $100 per day (including taxes and mileage fees). Reserve well in advance – April or May is recommended if you're traveling during the mid-July to early August peak – and confirm the booking before you arrive.

TEA TOMB

All around the Anglican Cathedral you'll see signs for 'tea in the crypt.' Sound spooky? It is a bit when you first arrive at the church's basement, what with all the women in flowery dresses and sensible shoes flurrying to and fro. But give it a chance, and **high tea** ($8; ⊗2:30-4:30pm Mon-Fri mid-Jul–early Sep) here becomes more than home-baked cookies and mini-scones. It's a chance to chat with the older generation about jam recipes, tips for summer holidays and the way things used to be (actually, you'll be listening and eating, and they'll do all the talking). The crypt, by the way, has never been used for burials.

take a left off Forest Rd onto Lakeview Ave. You can also walk from Signal Hill via the Cuckold's Cove Trail, which takes about 30 minutes.

Newman Wine Vaults   HISTORICAL SITE
(☑709-739-7870; www.historictrust.com; 436 Water St; admission by donation; ⊗10am-5:30pm mid-Jun–Aug) Dating from the 1780s, these dark, cool wine vaults are where the Newman company aged its port until 1996 (when EU regulations forced the process back to Portugal). Tour guides relay stories such as how English noblemen, who wanted to be buried in their homeland, got shipped back after death in barrels of port, since the alcohol preserved their bodies. There are no tastings, but you can purchase bottles. The vaults often host literary events.

CA Pippy Park   PARK
(www.pippypark.com) The feature-filled, 1343-hectare CA Pippy Park coats downtown's northwestern edge. Recreational facilities include walking trails, picnic areas, playgrounds, a golf course and a campground. **Memorial University**, the province's only university, is here too.

The university's **botanical garden** (☑709-737-8590; www.mun.ca/botgarden; adult/child $6/2.50; ⊗10am-5pm May-Sep, reduced hours rest of year) is at Oxen Pond, at the park's western edge off Mt Scio Rd. There's a cultivated garden and a nature reserve. Together, these and the park's **Long Pond** marsh give visitors an excellent introduction to Newfoundland's flora, habitats (including boreal forest and bogs) and animals (look for birds at Long Pond and the occasional moose). Take the 3km **Long Pond Walk** for the full effect.

The **Fluvarium** (☑709-754-3474; www.fluvarium.ca; Nagle's Pl; adult/child/family $7/4/20; ⊗9am-5pm Mon-Fri, from 10am Sat & Sun late Jun-early Sep, reduced hours rest of year), a glass-sided cross-section of a 'living' river, is located across the street from the campground. Viewers can peer through large windows to observe the undisturbed goings-on beneath the surface of Nagle's Hill Brook. Numerous brown trout and the occasional eel can be seen. If there has been substantial rain or high winds, all visible life is completely lost in the murkiness.

To get here from downtown, take Bonaventure Ave north to Allandale Rd and follow the signs; it's about 2km.

🏃 Activities

For whale-watching and sea kayaking, see p456. Golf and cross-country skiing enthusiasts can partake in CA Pippy Park.

Excellent walking trails zigzag across the area. The **Grand Concourse** (www.grandconcourse.ca) is an ambitious 95km-long trail network throughout St John's and environs. Many hikes are in the CA Pippy Park and Quidi Vidi Lake areas. Definitely make time for the sea-hugging North Head Trail on Signal Hill. The concourse website has route details for all walks.

The epic **East Coast Trail** (www.eastcoasttrail.com) stretches 220km from Fort Amherst south to Cappahayden; a further 320km is to be developed. It's part easy coastal walking, part tough wilderness trail. The website has details on free weekly guided hikes; on some you can also volunteer to do trail cleanup. An excellent stretch runs along the coast from Cape Spear (p463).

👉 Tours

Boat

For most tours, you need to head south of town to Witless Bay (see p464).

Iceberg Quest (☑709-722-1888; www.icebergquest.com; Pier 7; 2hr tours adult/child $55/25) Departs from St John's harbor and makes a run down to Cape Spear in search of icebergs in June, whales in July and August.

O'Brien's (☎709-753-4850, 877-639-4253; www.obriensboattours.com; 126 Duckworth St; 2hr tours adult/3-10yr/11-17yr $55/25/30) See whales, puffins and icebergs at Witless Bay. Boats launch from Bay Bulls 31km south, but O'Brien's has a shuttle service (round-trip $25) that picks up from hotels throughout St John's. Buy tickets at O'Brien's shop.

Outfitters (☎709-579-4453, 800-966-9658; www.theoutfitters.nf.ca; 220 Water St; half-/full-day tours $69/169) Popular kayak tours at Bay Bulls, with shuttle service (round-trip $25) from Outfitters' store downtown.

Bus

Ann's Tours (☎709-682-0754; www.anns tours.ca) Ann offers a variety of tours covering the Irish Loop ($160 including whale-watch boat, seven hours) and Cape St Mary's ($110, seven hours), plus shorter city jaunts and customized tours.

HI St John's Tours (☎709-754-4789; www.hihostels.ca; 8 Gower St) The hostel arranges Cape Spear/Ferryland/Witless Bay tours ($99, five hours) daily, if enough people sign up.

Legend Tours (☎709-753-1497; www.legend-tours.ca; 3hr tours $59) This award-winning operator covers St John's, Cape Spear and the northeast Avalon Peninsula. The commentary is richly woven with humor and historical tidbits. Call to reserve; they'll pick you up at your hotel or B&B.

Cultural

Cape Race Cultural Adventures (www.caperace.com; 10-day package per person $2600) Immerse yourself in life as a local. You get the keys to three houses (in St John's, Heart's Delight and Bonavista), a car and a guidebook to do it yourself.

Walking

The visitors center has brochures for self-guided walking tours in town.

TOP CHOICE **St John's Haunted Hike** (www.hauntedhike.com; tours $10; ⊘9.30pm Sun-Thu Jun–mid-Sep) The black-caped Reverend Thomas Wyckham Jarvis Esq leads these super-popular explorations of the city's dark corners. He'll spook you with tales of headless captains, murderers and other ghosts. Departure is from the Anglican Cathedral's west entrance.

East Coast Trail (www.eastcoasttrail.com) Check the website for free guided hikes.

☆ Festivals & Events

St John's Days (www.stjohns.ca; ⊘late Jun) A long weekend of jazz and blues concerts, parades, street dances and sporting events to commemorate the city's birthday.

Sound Symposium (www.soundsymposium.com; ⊘early Jul) Held every other year, it's a big, avant-garde week of concerts, workshops, dance, theater and film experiments; next symposiums are in 2012 and 2014.

George Street Festival (www.georg estreetlive.ca; ⊘late Jul) The mighty George St becomes one big nightclub for a fabulous week of daytime and nighttime musical performances.

Newfoundland & Labrador Folk Festival (www.nlfolk.com; ⊘1st weekend Aug) This intimate, three-day event in Bannerman Park celebrates traditional Newfoundland music, dancing and storytelling.

ST JOHN'S FOR CHILDREN

St John's will keep the wee ones entertained, rain or shine. **CA Pippy Park** (p456) is a kids' haven, with a huge playground, lots of trails and, of course, the Fluvarium. The ever-hungry ducks at the pond in **Bowring Park** (Waterford Bridge Rd) love company, as do the sea creatures at the **Ocean Sciences Centre** (p463). Just knowing a cannon will blast at the end of the tattoo should keep kids riveted at **Signal Hill** (p452). The various **boat tours** (p456) are also a great bet, but inquire if there are icebergs and whales in the area first. While geology may not initially spark their interest, the fact that the **Johnson Geo Centre** (p453) is underground may do the trick. Older kids will enjoy the ghostly tales of the **St John's Haunted Hike** (see p457).

Downtown Busker Festival (www.downtown stjohns.com; ⊙1st weekend Aug) Jugglers, magicians, acrobats, comedians and more take their performances to the streets.

Royal St John's Regatta (www.stjohns regatta.org; ⊙1st Wed Aug) The streets are empty, the stores are closed and everyone migrates to the shores of Quidi Vidi Lake. This rowing regatta officially began in 1825 and is now the oldest continuously held sporting event in North America.

🛏 Sleeping

Scores of B&Bs offer a place to rest your head in the heart of St John's; they're usually better value than the hotels and motels. They fill fast, so book ahead. Many have a two-night minimum stay requirement. The ones listed here all serve a hot breakfast. The city's 16% tax is not included in prices listed unless stated otherwise. Parking is available at or near all accommodations. For more lodging options, see the city's website (www.stjohns.ca/visitors/accommodation/index.jsp).

Balmoral House   B&B $$
(☎709-754-5721, 877-428-1055; www.balmoral house.com; 38 Queen's Rd; d $99-179; ⊜✿@) While the Balmoral is a typical B&B in many ways (cherub statues, long wooden antique tables), its owners live off-site and breakfast is self-serve, so it's more relaxed and private than many B&Bs. The beds are bestowed with super-comfy mattresses.

Abba Inn   B&B $$
(☎709-754-0058, 800-563-3959; www.abbainn. com; 36 Queen's Rd; d from $85-185; ⊜✿@🛜) The Abba shares the same building as the Balmoral, and it even shares reservations (ie if one is full, it'll hook you up with the other). Both B&Bs have similar amenities and ambience.

Cantwell House   B&B $$
(☎709-754-8439, 888-725-8439; www.cantwell house.nf.net; 25 Queen's Rd; r from $85-110; ⊜@) Take tea from a seat on Cantwell's deck and stare out over a colorful collage of row houses to the blue harbor. The B&B's friendly atmosphere combines with a sense of privacy amid Victorian ambience.

HI St John's   HOSTEL $
(☎709-754-4789; www.hihostels.ca; 8 Gower St; dm $28-33, r $75-89; ⊜@🛜) It's everything a good hostel should be: well located near the

action, spic 'n' span facilities, not too big (16 beds in all), and helpful. A whiteboard lists everything of interest happening in town each day. The hostel also books reasonably priced tours.

Oh! What A View B&B   B&B $$
(☎709-576-7063; www.ohwhataview.com; 184 Signal Hill Rd; r from $90; ⊜@) It's a 20-minute hike (uphill) from the town center, but oh, it really is a stunning view. Several common balconies take in the harbor below. The rooms are bright and modern, if a bit small. Ask for room No 8 with its Juliet balcony or No 3 with its straight shot of the water.

Narrows B&B   B&B $$
(☎709-739-4850, 866-739-4850; www.thenarrows bb.com; 146 Gower St; d $95-175; ⊜🛜) Warm colors mix with elegant trims and large wooden beds in the rooms of this welcoming B&B. There are modern amenities throughout and a gorgeous sitting room and balcony where guests can mingle and swap whale stories.

Bluestone Inn   B&B $$
(☎709-754-7544, 877-754-9876; www.thebluestone inn.com; 34 Queen's Rd; d $89-189; ⊜🛜) Built from the same historic stone as Cabot Tower and Government House, this B&B provides towering plasterwork ceilings, fireplaces and original artwork in its rooms. It was for sale at press time, so changes may be in the offing.

Downtown Hostel   HOSTEL $
(☎709-754-7658; www.hostels.com; 25 Young St; dm/r $22/55; ⊜🛜) It's a toss-up who has more character: the energized owner Carola or the building itself. Crooked homemade furniture resists the steeply plunging floors, and electrical cords and world maps adorn the walls. It's about 1km northwest of George St, off Carter's Hill.

At Wit's Inn   B&B $$
(☎709-739-7420, 877-739-7420; www.atwits inn.ca; 3 Gower St; d $109-139; ⊜✿@🛜) Polished floorboards, plasterwork ceilings, ornate fireplaces, bright-colored walls and beds you'll have trouble leaving make this B&B memorable. The living and dining rooms are as swank as they are comfy.

Leaside Manor   B&B $$
(☎709-722-0387, 877-807-7245; www.leaside manor.com; 39 Topsail Rd; r $129-249; ⊜✿@🛜) The higher-end rooms in this old merchant's home have a canopied bed, fireplace

and Jacuzzi, which explains why the *Globe and Mail* designated Leaside as one of Canada's 'most romantic destinations.' It's about a half-hour walk from downtown; to be closer, inquire about the downtown apartments.

Delta Hotel
(☎709-739-6404; www.deltahotels.com; 120 New Gower St; r $189-249; ❅@🖳🏊) The Delta is the main, amenity-laden business hotel in town; it's located next to the convention center. Parking costs $11.

Courtyard St John's
(☎709-722-6636; www.marriott.com/yytcy; 131 Duckworth St; r $159-189; P❅@🏊) It's the Marriott chain's typical property, with comfy beds. Some rooms have harbor views (about $10 extra). Wi-fi access is lobby only.

✖ Eating
Thai, Japanese, Indian, Latin and even vegetarian restaurants pop up along Water and Duckworth Sts, providing a variety you won't find elsewhere in the province. Stroll along here and you're sure to find something to sink your teeth into.

Bistro Sofia   CAFE $$
TOP CHOICE (☎709-738-2060; 320 Water St; sandwiches $7-9, mains $19-28; ⊙8am-11pm; 🖳) Bistro Sofia cooks up high-quality food and serves it casually in a bright, classy coffee shop ambience. Order at the counter, plop down at a roomy table, and wait for your lunch (grilled sandwiches plumped to perfection) or dinner (braised lamb shank or steak and frites) while sipping coffee or wine.

Hungry Heart   CAFE $
(☎709-738-6164; www.hungryheartcafe.ca; 142 Military Rd; mains $7-12; ⊙10am-2pm Mon-Sat) Eat in this warm-toned cafe and you're helping abused women and others in need to train in food service and get back on their feet. Try the curry mango chicken or pulled pork sandwiches. Saturday brunch brings out the cheese scones with peameal bacon and cherry bread pudding. Lots of baked goodies, too.

🌿 Bacalao   SEAFOOD $$$
(☎709-579-6565; www.bacalaocuisine.ca; 65 Lemarchant Rd; mains $28-35; ⊙noon-2:30pm Tue-Fri, from 11am Sat & Sun, 6-10pm Tue-Sun) Cozy Bacalao sources local, sustainable ingredients for its 'nouvelle Newfoundland cuisine.' Dishes include salt cod *du jour* and caribou in partridgeberry sauce, washed down by local beer and wines. Located 1.5km west of downtown; take Water St south to Waldegrave St, then Barters Hill Rd.

International Flavours   PAKISTANI $
(☎709-738-4636; 4 Quidi Vidi Rd; mains $8-12; ⊙noon-7pm Tue-Sat; ✍) Pakistani owner Talat ladles out a whopping spicy plateful of dahl or curry with basmati rice for her daily set meal (one with meat, the other without). She's just beyond downtown, a few minutes' walk up Signal Hill Rd.

Sprout   VEGETARIAN $
(☎709-579-5485; 364 Duckworth St; mains $6-12; ⊙11:30am-8pm Tue & Wed, to 9pm Thu & Fri, 9am-9pm Sat, 9am-3pm Sun; ✍) It's almost unheard of in Newfoundland: full-on vegetarian food. So savor your marinated tofu burger, spinach-pesto-melt sandwich and

---

SCRUNCHEONS, TOUTONS & FLIPPER PIE: A GASTRONOMIC GUIDE

Get ready for a whole new culinary vocabulary when you enter Newfoundland. Lesson number one: having a 'scoff' is local parlance for eating a big meal.

Two of Newfoundland's favorite dishes are fish 'n' brewis and jigg's dinner. Fish 'n' brewis is a blend of salted fish, onions, scruncheons (aka fried pork fat) and a near-boiled bread. Jigg's dinner is a right feast comprising a roast (turkey or possibly moose) along with boiled potatoes, carrots, cabbage, salted beef and pea-and-bread pudding. A touton is fried dough that you dip in gooey molasses.

Cod tongues are the tender, fleshy bits between the lower jaws served battered and fried, while cod cheeks are just that: cheeks from the fish. Fishcakes are a blend of cod, potato and onion mashed together and fried – delicious. Seal flipper pie, on the other hand, is for the brave; the strong flavor of seal meat is definitely an acquired taste.

To finish off your meal, try figgy duff, a thick fig pudding boiled in a cloth bag.

And the final lesson in gastro terminology: when you're done eating, pat your stomach and say, 'I'm full as an egg.'

brown rice *poutine* (fries served under gravy and bean curd) before leaving town.

Auntie Crae's CAFE $
(709-754-0661; www.auntiecraes.com; 272 Water St; sandwiches $6-7; 8am-6pm Tue-Sat) Come to this specialty food store for a cuppa joe, baked goods, groceries or a prepared sandwich. Relax with your goodies in the adjoining Fishhook Neyle's Common Room.

Casbah FUSION $$
(709-738-5293; 2 Cathedral St; mains $13-23; 11:30am-2:30pm Thu & Fri, from 10:30am Sat & Sun, 5:30-11pm daily) Fun, sassy waiters serve fun, sassy food in colorful Casbah. They keep everyone happy by offering small, medium and large plates, which might contain maple-roasted pumpkin soup or halibut burger with wasabi mayo.

Blue on Water SEAFOOD $$$
(709-754-2583; www.blueonwater.com; 319 Water St; mains $27-35; 7:30am-10pm Mon-Fri, 9am-11pm Sat, 9am-9pm Sun) This hip restaurant does inventive takes on seafood dishes such as cod tongues and scruncheons and maple salmon with organic veggies. Brunch includes banana pancakes topped with rum-roasted walnuts. If nothing else, grab a drink in Blue's loungelike bar next door.

Classic Cafe East CAFE $$
(709-726-4444; www.classiccafeeast.com; 73 Duckworth St; sandwiches $8-11, mains $13-21; 8am-10pm) Yes, many tourists eat here, but it's still a swell place to soak up harbor views and fork into Newfie standards like toutons, fish 'n' brewis, seafood chowder and fishcakes, plus omelettes and sandwiches.

India Gate INDIAN $$
(709-753-6006; www.indiagate.250x.com; 286 Duckworth St; mains $12-16; 11:30am-2pm Mon-Fri, 5-10pm daily;) This is the local Indian favorite, with loads of vegetarian options. Fill up at the weekday all-you-can-eat lunch special for $15.

Sun Sushi JAPANESE $$
(709-726-8688; 186 Duckworth St; sushi rolls $4.50-7.50; noon-10pm, closed Sun) This unadorned spot tops the townsfolks' list for reasonably priced sushi. The spicy tuna wins raves.

Ches's FAST FOOD $
(709-726-2373; www.chessfishandchips.ca; 9 Freshwater Rd; mains $7-12; 11am-2am Sun-Thu, to 3am Fri & Sat) Ches's and its fish and chips are an institution in Newfoundland. No frills, just cod that will melt in your mouth.

Drinking

George St is the city's famous party lane. Water and Duckworth Sts also have plenty of drinkeries, but the scene is slightly more sedate. Bars stay open until 2am. Expect many places to charge a small cover (about $5) on weekends or when there's live music. Don't forget to try the local Screech rum.

TOP CHOICE Duke of Duckworth PUB
(www.dukeofduckworth.com; McMurdo's Lane, 325 Duckworth St) 'The Duke,' as it's known, is an unpretentious English-style pub that represents all that's great about Newfoundland and Newfoundlanders. Stop in on a Friday night and you'll see a mix of blue-collar, white-collar, young and old, even band members from Great Big Sea plunked down on the well-worn, red-velour bar stools. The kitchen cooks the ultimate in chicken pot pie, fish and chips and other comfort foods, and 14 beers (including the local Quidi Vidi) flow through the taps.

Trapper John's Museum & Pub PUB
(www.trapperjohns.com; 3 George St) It's not the most refined pub in town, but it sure is

---

GETTING SCREECHED IN

Within a few days of your arrival in St John's, you'll undoubtedly be asked by everyone if you've been 'screeched in,' or in traditional Newfoundland slang, 'Is you a screecher?' It's not as painful as it sounds, and is, in fact, locals' playful way to welcome visitors to the province.

Screeching derives from the 1940s when new arrivals were given their rites of passage, and from pranks played on sealers heading to the ice for the first time. Today the ceremony takes place in local pubs, where you'll gulp a shot of rum (there's actually a local brand called Screech), recite an unpronounceable verse in the local lingo, kiss a stuffed codfish and then receive a certificate declaring you an 'Honorary Newfoundlander.' Sure it's touristy, but it's also good fun. The more the merrier, so try to get screeched in with a crowd.

the most fun place to become an Honorary Newfoundlander, which happens after you kiss Stubby the Puffin (a variation on the usual codfish). The animal traps enshrined throughout grant the 'museum' status.

Hava Java
COFFEE SHOP
(216 Water St; ⊙7:30am-11pm Mon-Fri, 9am-11pm Sat & Sun) The atmosphere at this place is refreshingly antifranchise and pro-tattoo; it just focuses on making the best coffee in town.

Bookery
COFFEE SHOP
(42 Powers Ct; ⊙10am-6pm Wed-Sat, noon-5pm Sun) Yes, it's a bookstore (with a fantastic selection of local authors), but it also pours rich hot chocolate and java. A clock-crazy antique shop sits upstairs. It's a 10-minute walk up Signal Hill Rd.

Grapevine
WINE BAR
(206 Water St) Dark, swanky Grapevine is a wine and cocktail bar with great music and martinis.

Celtic Hearth
(www.theceltichearth.com; 298 Water St; ⊙24hr) Get your Guinness and pub grub 24/7; it's underneath Bridie Molloy's.

Coffee Matters
(www.coffeematters.ca; 1 Military Rd; ⊙7am-11pm Mon-Fri, from 8am Sat & Sun; 🔊) The city's swankiest coffee and tea shop.

☆ Entertainment
The Scope (www.thescope.ca) has the daily lowdown. Perhaps because this is such an intimate city, word-of-mouth and flyers slapped on light poles are also major vehicles for entertainment information. Venues ⏰⏰⏰⏰ ⏰⏰⏰⏰⏰⏰⏰⏰ – ⏰⏰⏰⏰ ⏰ ⏰⏰⏰⏰⏰⏰ ⏰⏰⏰ ⏰⏰⏰⏰⏰

Live Music
Cover charges range from $5 to $10. **Mighty Pop** (www.mightypop.ca) lists cool upcoming shows.

Ship Pub (📞709-753-3870; 265 Duckworth St) Attitudes and ages are checked at the door of this little pub, tucked down Solomon's Lane. You'll hear everything from jazz to indie, and even the odd poetry reading. Wednesday is folk music night.

Bridie Molloy's (www.bridiemolloys.com; George St) This polished Irish pub hosts an older crowd and offers Irish and Newfoundland music six nights per week.

Rose & Thistle (📞709-579-6662; 208 Water St) Pub where well-known local folk musicians strum.

Fat Cat (www.fatcatbluesbar.com; George St; ⊙closed Mon) Blues radiates from the cozy Fat Cat nightly during the summer months.

Rock House (📞709-579-6832; George St) When indie bands visit town, they plug in here.

Theater
Resource Centre for the Arts (📞709-753-4531; www.rca.nf.ca; 3 Victoria St) Sponsors indie theater, dance and film by Newfoundland artists, all of which plays downtown in the former longshoremen's union hall (aka LSPU Hall).

Shakespeare by the Sea Festival (www.sbts.info; tickets $15; ⊙early Jul–mid-Aug) Live outdoor productions are presented at Signal Hill, Bowring Park and other venues. Buy all tickets on-site; cash only.

Nightclubs
St John's true nightclubs, which only open on Friday and Saturday night (from 11pm to 4am or so), cater to energetic straight and gay crowds. Cover charges vary, but are typically between $5 and $10.

Zone (216 Water St) This is the premier gay dance bar in Newfoundland. Straights are equally welcome to soak up the fun energy; located above Hava Java.

Liquid Ice (186B Water St) If you like your house, drum and bass or hip-hop, wade into this gay-friendly nightspot.

🔒 Shopping
You'll find traditional music, berry jams ⏰⏰⏰ ⏰⏰⏰⏰ ⏰⏰⏰ ⏰⏰ ⏰⏰⏰ ⏰⏰⏰⏰⏰ ⏰⏰⏰ ⏰⏰⏰⏰⏰⏰⏰ ⏰⏰ Water and Duckworth Sts.

Fred's
MUSIC STORE
(📞709-753-9191; www.freds.nf.ca; 198 Duckworth St) This is the premier music shop in St John's. It features local music such as Hey Rosetta, Buddy Wasisname, Ron Hynes, The Navigators and Great Big Sea.

Living Planet
CLOTHING
(📞709-739-6810; www.livingplanet.ca; 197 Water St) For quirky tourist T-shirts and buttons even locals are proud to wear.

Downhome
SOUVENIRS
(📞709-722-2070; 303 Water St) It's touristy, but it does have a fine selection of local goods such as jams, woolen wear and the coveted *How to Play the Musical Spoons* CD.

Outfitters
OUTDOOR GEAR

(209-579-4453; www.theoutfitters.nf.ca; 220 Water St) A camping and gear shop where you can get the local outdoorsy lowdown (check the bulletin board).

Information

Internet Access

There is a public internet terminal for use at the visitors center (free access for 15 minutes). Several coffee shops and bars have free wi-fi, including Bistro Sofia, Hava Java and Duke of Duckworth.

Media & Internet Resources

City of St John's (www.stjohns.ca) The 'Tourism' category has descriptions of and links to attractions, accommodations, eateries and events.

Downhome (www.downhomelife.com) A folksy, *Reader's Digest*–style monthly for the region.

St John's Telegram (www.thetelegram.com) The city's daily newspaper.

The Scope (www.thescope.ca) Free alternative newspaper covering local arts and politics.

Medical Services

Health Sciences Complex (209-777-6300; 300 Prince Phillip Dr) A 24-hour emergency room.

Water St Pharmacy (209-579-5554; 335 Water St; ⊙closed Sun)

Money

Banks stack up near the Water St and Ayre's Cove intersection.

CIBC (215 Water St)

Scotia Bank (245 Water St)

Post

Central post office (209-758-1003; 354 Water St)

Tourist Information

Visitors Centre (209-576-8106; www. stjohns.ca; 348 Water St; ⊙9am-4:30pm) Excellent resource with free provincial and city roadmaps, and staff to answer questions and help with bookings.

Getting There & Away

Air

Air Canada (www.aircanada.com), **WestJet** (www.westjet.com), **Provincial Airlines** (www. provincialairlines.com) and **Porter Airlines** (www.flyporter.com) are the main carriers. **Continental Airlines** (www.continental.com) schedules the only direct flight from the USA. Air Canada offers a daily flight to and from London.

Bus

DRL (209-263-2171; www.drl-lr.com) sends one bus daily each way between St John's and Port aux Basques ($112, cash only, 13½ hours) via the 905km-long Hwy 1, making 25 stops en route. It leaves at 7:30am from Memorial University's Student Centre, in CA Pippy Park.

Car & Motorcycle

Avis, Budget, Enterprise, Hertz, National and Thrifty (see p886) have offices at the airport. **Practicar** (209-753-2277; www.practicar.ca; 909 Topsail Rd) is a 20-minute drive from the airport but often has lower rates.

Share Taxis

These large vans typically seat 15 and allow you to jump on or off at any point along their routes. You must call in advance to reserve. They pick up and drop off at your hotel. Cash only.

Foote's Taxi (209-832-0491, 800-866-1181) Travels daily down the Burin Peninsula as far as Fortune ($45, five hours).

Newhook's Transportation (209-682-4877, in Placentia 709-227-2552) Travels down the southwestern Avalon Peninsula to Placentia, in sync with the Argentia ferry schedule ($30, two hours).

Shirran's Taxi (209-468-7741) Plies the Bonavista Peninsula daily, making stops at Trinity ($45, 3½ hours) and Bonavista ($40, four hours), among others.

Getting Around

To/From the Airport

St John's Airport (YYT; www.stjohnsairport. com) is 6km north of the city on Portugal Cove Rd (Rte 40). A government-set flat rate of $22.50 (plus $3 for each extra passenger) is charged by taxis to go from the airport to downtown hotels and B&Bs; **Citywide Taxi** (709-722-7777) provides the official service. However, when you make the trip in reverse – ie from town to the airport – taxis run on meters and should cost around $20.

Car & Motorcycle

The city's one-way streets and unique intersections can be confounding. Thankfully, citizens are incredibly patient. A loonie ($1) will get you an hour at the parking meters that line Water and Duckworth Sts. **Sonco Parking Garage** (cnr Baird's Cove & Harbour Dr; ⊙6:30am-11pm) charges $1.50 for 30 minutes or $11 per day.

Public Transportation

The **Metrobus** (www.metrobus.com) system covers most of the city (fare $2.25). Maps and schedules are online and in the visitors center. Bus 3 is useful; it circles town via Military Rd and Water St before heading to the university.

Taxi

Except for the trip from the airport, all taxis operate on meters. A trip within town should cost around $7. **Jiffy Cabs** (☑709-722-2222; www.jiffycabs.com) provides dependable service.

AROUND ST JOHN'S

North of St John's

Right out of *20,000 Leagues Under the Sea*, the **Ocean Sciences Centre** (☑709-737-3708; www.mun.ca/osc; admission free; ◷10am-5pm Jun-early Sep) is operated by Memorial University and examines the salmon life cycle, seal navigation, ocean currents and life in cold oceanic regions. The outdoor visitors' area consists of local sealife in touch tanks. It's about 8km north of St John's, just before Logy Bay. From the city, take Logy Bay Rd (Rte 30), then follow Marine Dr to Marine Lab Rd and take it to the end.

Secluded and rocky, **Middle Cove** and **Outer Cove** are just a bit further north on Rte 30 – they're perfect for a beach picnic.

North at the head of **Torbay Bight** is the enjoyably short **Father Troy Path**, which hugs the shoreline. The view from **Cape St Francis** is worth the bumpy gravel road from Pouch Cove. There's an old battery and you may just luck out and see a whale or two.

West of St John's

West of town on Topsail Rd (Rte 60), just past **Paradise** is **Topsail Beach** with picnic tables, a walking trail and panoramic views of Conception Bay and its islands.

Bell Island (www.bellisland.net) is the largest of Conception Bay's little landmasses, and it makes an interesting day trip. It's a 14km drive northwest from St John's to Portugal Cove to the **ferry** (☑709-895-6931) and then a 20-minute crossing (per passenger/car $2.25/6.25, hourly 6am to 10:30pm). Bell Island has the distinction of being the only place on the continent to have been nailed by German forces in WWII. Its pier and 80,000 tonnes of iron ore were torpedoed by U-boats in 1942. At low tide, you can still see the aftermath. The island sports a pleasant mélange of beaches, coastal vistas, lighthouses and trails. Miners here used to work in shafts under the sea at the world's largest submarine iron mine. The **Iron Ore**

Mine & Museum (☑709-488-2880; adult/child $10/3; ◷11am-6pm Jun-Sep) details the operation and gives visitors the chance to go underground; dress warmly.

South of St John's

CAPE SPEAR

A 15km drive southeast of town leads you to the most easterly point in North America. The coastal scenery is spectacular, and you can spot whales through much of the summer. The area is preserved as the **Cape Spear National Historic Site** (☑709-772-5367; www.pc.gc.ca/capespear; Blackhead Rd; adult/child $3.90/1.90; ◷grounds year-round) and includes an **interpretive center** (◷8:30am-9pm summer, 10am-6pm Sep–mid-Oct), the refurbished 1835 **lighthouse** (◷10am-6pm mid-May–mid-Oct) and the heavy gun batteries and magazines built in 1941 to protect the harbor during WWII. A **trail** leads along the edge of the headland cliffs, past 'the most easterly point' observation deck and up to the lighthouse. You can continue all the way to Maddox Cove and Petty Harbour along the East Coast Trail; even walking it a short way is tremendously worthwhile.

Heed all signs warning visitors off the rocks by the water, as rogue waves have been known to sweep in.

You reach the cape from Water St by crossing the Waterford River south of town and then following Blackhead Rd for 11km.

GOULDS & PETTY HARBOUR

In **Goulds**, at the junction of Rte 10 and the road to Petty Harbour, is **Bidgood's** (www.bidgoods.ca; Bidgood's Plaza; ◷9am-9pm Mon-Sat, 11am-5pm Sun). It's just a normal-looking supermarket, except for the fresh seal flipper (in pies, jars or jerky-like strips) and caribou steak purveyed at the back of the store. For the faint of heart, partridgeberry and bakeapple jams are the other Newfoundland specialties on hand.

Its back lapping up against steep rocky slopes, movie set-beautiful **Petty Harbour** is filled with weathered boats, wharves and sheds on precarious stilts.

AVALON PENINSULA

Flung out to the east of Newfoundland and tethered to it by nothing more than a narrow isthmus, it doesn't seem like this little afterthought of a peninsula would be the province's powerhouse. But looks can be deceiving, because not only does the Avalon hold half of Newfoundland's population, it also houses four of the province's six seabird ecological reserves, one of its two wilderness reserves and 28 of its 41 national historic sites.

The landscape along the coastline's twisting roads is vintage fishing-village Newfoundland. Many visitors day-trip to the peninsula's sights from St John's, which is easily doable, but there's something to be said for burrowing under the quilt at night, with the sea sparkling outside your window, in Cupids, Branch or Dildo (you read right).

Much of the **East Coast Trail** (www.east-coasttrail.com) runs through the area; keep an eye out for free guided hikes. The ferry to Nova Scotia leaves from Argentia.

Southeastern Avalon Peninsula

This area, sometimes called the South Shore, is known for its wildlife, archaeology, boat and kayak tours and unrelenting fog. Scenic Rtes 10 and 90, aka the **Irish Loop** (www.theirishloop.com), lasso the region.

WITLESS BAY ECOLOGICAL RESERVE
This is a prime area for whale-, iceberg- and bird-watching, and several boat tours will take you to see them from the towns of **Bay Bulls** (31km south of St John's) and around **Bauline East** (15km south of Bay Bulls).

Four islands off Witless Bay and southward are preserved as the **Witless Bay Ecological Reserve** (www.env.gov.nl.ca/parks) and represent one of the top seabird breeding areas in eastern North America. Every summer, more than a million pairs of birds gather here, including puffins, kittiwakes, storm petrels and the penguinlike murres. Tour boats sail to the islands, hugging the shore beneath sheer cliffs and giving you a shrieking earful as well as an eyeful.

The best months for trips are late June and July, when the humpback and minke whales arrive to join the birds' capelin (a type of fish) feeding frenzy. If you really hit the jackpot, in early summer an iceberg might be thrown in too.

Tours from Bay Bulls (ie the big operators O'Brien's and Gatherall's) visit Gull Island,

which has the highest concentration of birds. Tours that depart to the south around Bauline East head to nearby Great Island, home to the largest puffin colony. Bauline East is closer to the reserve, so less time is spent en route, but you see the same types of wildlife on all of the tours.

Kayaking is also popular in the area. You don't just see a whale while paddling, you feel its presence.

You can't miss the boat operators – just look for signs off Rte 10. Sometimes the smaller companies cancel tours if there aren't enough passengers; it's best to call ahead to reserve and avoid such surprises. The following are recommended tour companies, all operating from mid-May through mid-September. Most depart several times daily between 9:30am and 5pm.

Colbert's Seabird Tours (☎709-334-2098; Rte 10, Bauline East; 1hr tours adult/5-15yr $30/15) It's a 10-minute ride on a 40ft boat to see the puffins and whales.

Gatherall's (☎800-419-4253; www.gatheralls. com; Northside Rd, Bay Bulls; 1½hr tours adult/1-8yr/9-17yr $56/8/18.50) A large, fast catamaran gives you as much time at the reserve as O'Brien's. It's also more stable and a wise choice for people prone to seasickness.

Molly Bawn Tours (☎709-334-2621; www. mollybawn.com; Rte 10, Mobile; 1hr tours adult/5-16yr $30/25) These tours cruise over the waves on a small, 35ft boat. Mobile is halfway between Bay Bulls and Bauline East.

O'Brien's (☎709-753-4850, 877-639-4253; www.obriensboattours.com; 2hr tours adult/3-10yr/11-17yr $55/25/30) O'Brien's, on the south side of Bay Bulls, is the granddaddy of tours and includes storytelling, music and more on its nice, big boat. A more expensive but exhilarating option is the two-hour tour in a high-speed Zodiac ($85). There's a shuttle service from St John's (round-trip $25).

Outfitters (☎709-579-4453, 800-966-9658; www.theoutfitters.nf.ca; Bay Bulls; half-/full-day tours $69/169) Popular half-day kayak tours leave at 9am and 2pm; full-day tours depart at 9:30am and travel beyond the inner bay of Bay Bulls to the top of the eco reserve. There is a shuttle service (round-trip $25) from St John's that leaves from Outfitters at 220 Water St.

Stan Cook Sea Kayak Adventures
(☎709-579-6353, 888-747-6353; www.wildnfld.ca;
Harbour Rd, Cape Broyle; 2½/4hr tours $59/89)
Located further south near Ferryland, this
company offers great guided tours for
beginners and advanced paddlers.

LA MANCHE PROVINCIAL PARK

Diverse bird life, along with beaver, moose
and snowshoe hare, can be seen in this
lush park only 53km south of St John's.
A highlight is the 1.25km trail to the remains of La Manche, a fishing village that
was destroyed in 1966 by a fierce winter
storm. Upon arrival, you'll see the beautiful newly built suspension bridge dangling over the narrows – it's part of the
East Coast Trail. The trailhead is situated
at the park's fire-exit road, past the main
entrance.

There is excellent **camping** (☎709-685-
1823; www.nlcamping.ca; Rte 10; campsites $15-
23, per vehicle $5; ◷mid-May–mid-Sep), with
many sites overlooking large La Manche
Pond; the latter is good for swimming.

FERRYLAND

Ferryland, one of North America's earliest
settlements, dates to 1621, when Sir George
Calvert established the Colony of Avalon.
A few Newfoundland winters later he was
scurrying for warmer parts. He settled in
Maryland and eventually became the first
Lord Baltimore. Other English families arrived later and maintained the colony despite it being razed by the Dutch in 1673
and by the French in 1696.

The seaside surrounds of the **Colony of
Avalon Archaeological Site** (☎709-196-
3200; www.colonyofavalon.ca; Rte 10; adult/child
$9.50/7.50; ◷10am-6pm mid-May–mid-Oct)
only add to the rich atmosphere, where
you'll see archaeologists unearthing everything from axes to bowls. The **Visitors
Centre** (☎709-432-3207) houses interpretive displays and many of the artifacts that
have been recovered.

The village's former courthouse is now
the small **Historic Ferryland Museum**
(☎709-432-2711; Rte 10; admission $2; ◷10am-
4pm Mon-Sat, 1-4pm Sun late-Jun–early Sep).
The towering hill behind the museum
was where settlers climbed to watch for
approaching warships, or to escape the
Dutch and French incursions. After seeing
the view, you'll understand why the settlers named the hill 'the Gaze.'

TOP Lighthouse Picnics (☎709-363-
CHOICE 7456; www.lighthousepicnics.ca; Lighthouse Rd, off Rte 10; per person $25; ◷11:30am-
5pm Tue-Sun Jun-Sep) has hit upon a winning
concept: it provides a blanket and organic
picnic meal (say, a curried chicken sandwich, mixed-green salad and lemonade
from a Mason jar) that visitors wolf down
while sitting in a field overlooking the
ocean. It's at Ferryland's old lighthouse; you
have to park and hike 2km to reach it, but
ooh is it worth it. Reserve in advance.

AVALON WILDERNESS RESERVE

Dominating the interior of the region is the
1070-sq-km **Avalon Wilderness Reserve**
(☎709-635-4520; www.env.gov.nl.ca/parks; free
permit required). Illegal hunting dropped the
region's caribou population to around 100
in the 1980s. Twenty years later, there are
thousands roaming the area. Permits for
hiking, canoeing and bird-watching in the
reserve are available at La Manche Provincial Park (p465).

Even if you don't trek into the wilds, you
still might see caribou along Rte 10 between Chance Cove Provincial Park and St
Stevens.

MISTAKEN POINT ECOLOGICAL RESERVE

This **ecological reserve** (www.env.gov.nl.ca/
parks), which Unesco has short-listed for
World Heritage site designation, protects
575-million-year-old multicelled marine
fossils – the oldest in the world. The only
way to reach it is via a free, ranger-guided,
45-minute hike from the **Edge of Avalon
Interpretive Centre** (☎709-438-1100; www.
edgeofavalon.ca; Rte 10; ◷mid-May–mid-Oct) in
Portugal Cove South.

You can also drive the bumpy gravel
road between here and Cape Race. At
the end, a lighthouse rises up beside an
artifact-filled, replica 1904 Marconi wireless station. It was the folks here who received the fateful last message from the
Titanic.

The 'Mistaken Point' name, by the way,
comes from the blinding fog that blankets
the area and has caused many ships to lose
their way over the years.

ALONG ROUTE 90

The area from St Vincent's to St Mary's provides an excellent chance of seeing whales,
particularly humpbacks, which feed close

to shore. The best viewing is from **St Vincent's beach**. Halfway between the two villages is **Point La Haye Natural Scenic Attraction**, a dramatic arm of fine pebbles stretching across the mouth of St Mary's Bay – it's perfect for a walk.

FREE **Salmonier Nature Park** (🕿709-229-7189; www.env.gov.nl.ca/snp; Rte 90; admission free; ⊙10am-5pm Jun-early Sep, to 3pm early Sep–mid-Oct) rehabilitates injured and orphaned animals for release back into the wild. A 2.5km trail through pine woods takes you past indigenous fauna and natural enclosures with moose, caribou and cavorting river otters. There's an **Interpretive Centre** and touch displays for children. The park is on Rte 90, 12km south of the junction with Hwy 1.

Conception Bay

Fishing villages stretch endlessly along Conception Bay's scenic western shore, a mere 80km from St John's. Highlights include Brigus, in all its Englishy, rock-walled glory combined with North Pole history, and Cupids, a 1610 settlement complete with an archaeological dig to explore. **Northern Avalon Tourism** (www.baccalieutourism.com) provides information on accommodations and hiking trails.

BRIGUS

Resting on the water and surrounded by rock bluffs is the heavenly village of **Brigus** (www.brigus.net). Its idyllic stone-walled streams meander slowly past old buildings and colorful gardens before emptying into the serene Harbour Pond. During WWI, American painter Rockwell Kent lived here, before his eccentric behavior got him deported on suspicion of spying for the Germans in 1915. The path toward his old cottage makes a great walk.

Captain Robert Bartlett, the town's most famous son, is renowned as one of the foremost Arctic explorers of the 20th century. He made more than 20 Arctic expeditions, including one in 1909, when he cleared a trail in the ice that enabled US commander Robert Peary to make his celebrated dash to the North Pole. Bartlett's house, **Hawthorne Cottage** (🕿709-528-4004; www.pc.gc.ca/hawthornecottage; cnr Irishtown Rd & South St; adult/child $4/3.50; ⊙9:30am-5:30pm mid-May–early Oct), is a national historic site and museum.

On the waterfront, below the church, is the **Brigus Tunnel**, which was cut through rock in 1860 so Robert Bartlett could easily access his ship in the deep cove on the other side.

Every perfect village needs a perfect eatery. At **North St Cafe** (🕿709-528-1350; 29 North St; light meals $6-9; ⊙11am-6pm May–mid-Oct), quiche, fishcakes, scones and afternoon tea are all on order. Brigus has a couple of B&Bs, but we suggest sleeping down the road in Cupids.

CUPIDS

Merchant John Guy sailed here in 1610 and staked out England's first colony in Canada. It's now the **Cupids Cove Plantation Provincial Historic Site** (🕿709-528-3500; www.seethesites.ca; Seaforest Dr; adult/child $11.50/5.50; ⊙10am-5pm mid-May–early Oct). Admission includes entry to the new **Cupids Legacy Centre**, stuffed with silver coins, bottle shards and some of the other 150,000 artifacts unearthed on-site. You also get to tour the active **archaeological dig**, where they're still finding treasures.

Afterward, head to the town's northern edge and hike the **Burnt Head Trail**. Climb to the rocky headlands, past blueberry thickets and stone walls that once fenced settlers' gardens, and look out over the same sea-buffeted coast that drew Guy.

The trail departs from an old Anglican church that has been converted into the divine **Cupid's Haven B&B and Tea Room** (🕿709-528-1555; www.cupidshaven.ca; 169 Burnt Head Loop; r $99-149; ☕🖨). Each of the four rooms has a private bathroom, vaulted ceilings and Gothic arched windows that let light stream in.

HARBOUR GRACE & AROUND

A mixed crowd of historic figures has paraded through Harbour Grace over the past 500 years. Notables include the pirate Peter Easton and aviator Amelia Earhart. Learn about them at the red-brick customs house that is now the small **Conception Bay Museum** (🕿709-596-5465; www.hrgrace.ca/museum.html; Water St; adult/child $3/2; ⊙10am-4pm mid-Jun–early Sep). You can visit the airstrip Amelia launched from in 1932 – **Harbour Grace Airfield** (www.hrgrace.ca/air.html; Earhart Rd) – when she became the first woman to cross the Atlantic solo.

It's hard to miss the large ship beached at the mouth of the harbor. This is the **SS Kyle** (1913), wrecked during a 1967 storm.

TOP PLACES FOR A SEASIDE HIKE

» North Head Trail, St John's (p453)

» Skerwink Trail, Trinity, Eastern Newfoundland (p469)

» Burnt Head Trail, Cupids, Avalon Peninsula (p466)

» Boney Shore Trail, Red Bay, Labrador (p499)

» Copper Mine Trail, near Corner Brook (p491)

» Turpin's Trail, Fogo Island, Central Newfoundland (p478)

Locals liked the look of it so much they paid to have it restored instead of removed.

Clinging to cliffs at the northern end of the peninsula are the remote and striking villages of **Bay de Verde** and **Grates Cove**. Hundreds of 500-year-old rock walls line the hills around Grates Cove and have been declared a national historic site. Further offshore, in the distance, is the inaccessible **Baccalieu Island Ecological Reserve**, which is host to three million pairs of Leach's storm petrel, making it the largest such colony in the world.

Trinity Bay

Thicker forests, fewer villages and subdued topography typify the shores of Trinity Bay and give the west coast of the peninsula a much more serene feeling than its eastern shore.

HEART'S CONTENT

The **Cable Station Provincial Historic Site** (☎709-583-2160; www.seethesites.ca; Rte 80; adult/child $3/free; ☺10am-5:30pm late May-early Oct) tells the story of the first permanent transatlantic cable that was laid here in 1866. The word 'permanent' is significant, because the first successful cable (connected in 1858 to Bull Arm, on Trinity Bay) failed shortly after Queen Victoria and US President James Buchanan christened the line with their congratulatory messages.

DILDO

Oh, go on – take the obligatory sign photo. For the record, no one knows definitively how the name came about; some say it's from the phallic shape of the bay.

Joking aside, Dildo is a lovely village and its shore is a good spot for whale-watching. The **Dildo Interpretation Centre** (☎709-582-3339; Front Rd; adult/child $2/1; ☺10am-4:30pm late May–mid-Sep) has a whale skeleton and exhibits on the ongoing Dorset Eskimo archaeological dig on Dildo Island. It's not terribly exciting, but outside are excellent photo opportunities with Captain Dildo and a giant squid. Across the street, **Kountry Kravins 'n' Krafts** (☎709-582-3888; ☺9am-8pm Mon-Sat, 10am-6pm late May–mid-Sep) sells fruit pies and knick knacks (including many 'Dildo' logoed items – always a fine souvenir for folks back home).

Two flawlessly restored oceanside houses comprise **Inn by the Bay** (☎709-582-3170; www.dildoinns.com; 78 Front Rd; d $89-199; ☺May-Dec; ☺☺), the most luxurious spot to stay on the northern Avalon Peninsula. Within the B&B, the elegant **Veranda Sunroom** (mains $15-19) is open to guests for dinner.

Cape Shore

The ferry, French history and lots of birds fly forth from the Avalon Peninsula's southwesterly leg. Newhook's Transportation (p462) connects the towns of Argentia and Placentia to St John's.

ARGENTIA

Argentia's main purpose is to play host to the **Marine Atlantic ferry** (☎800-341-7981; www.marine-atlantic.ca; adult/5-12yr $80.50/40.25, per car/motorcycle $165/83.50), which connects Argentia with North Sydney in Nova Scotia – a 14-hour trip. It operates from mid-June to late September with three crossings per week. The boat leaves North Sydney at 1am Tuesday, 9:30pm Wednesday and 1:30am Saturday. It returns from Argentia at 8pm Tuesday, 3:30pm Thursday and 7:30pm Saturday. Cabins (four-berth $153) are available. Vehicle fares do not include drivers.

A provincial **visitors center** (☎709-227-5272; Rte 100) is 3km from the ferry on Rte 100. Its opening hours vary to coincide with ferry sailings.

PLACENTIA

In the early 1800s, **Placentia** (www.placentia tourism.ca) – then Plaisance – was the French capital of Newfoundland, and the

French attacks on the British at St John's were based here. Near town, lording over the shores, is **Castle Hill National Historic Site** (☑709-227-2401; www.pc.gc.ca/castlehill; adult/child $3.90/1.90; ☺10am-6pm mid-May–mid-Oct), where remains of French and British fortifications from the 17th and 18th centuries provide panoramic views over the town and the surrounding waters.

The fascinating graveyard next to the Anglican church holds the remains of people of every nationality who have settled here since the 1670s. The **O'Reilly House Museum** (☑709-227-5568; 48 Orcan Dr; admission $2; ☺11:30am-7:30pm mid-Jun–Aug), within a century-old Victorian home, gives you more of an inside look at the town and its past luxuries. Wander past the other notable buildings, including the **Roman Catholic church** and the **stone convent**. A boardwalk runs along the stone-skipper's delight of a beach.

Breakfast is a highlight at the five-room **Rosedale Manor B&B** (☑877-999-3613; www.rosedalemanor.ca; 40 Orcan Dr; r $79-109; ☻☏), cooked by the pastry chef owner with organic eggs and grains. It's a 10-minute drive from the Argentia ferry.

CAPE ST MARY'S ECOLOGICAL RESERVE & AROUND

At the southwestern tip of the peninsula is **Cape St Mary's Ecological Reserve** (www.env.gov.nl.ca/parks; admission free), one of the most accessible bird colonies on the continent. Birders swoon over it, and it's impressive even for those who aren't bird crazy. Stop at the **Interpretive Centre** (☑709-277-1666; ☺9am-5pm mid-May–mid-Oct) and get directions for the 1km trail to Bird Rock. It's an easy footpath through fields of sheep and blue irises, and then suddenly – whammo – you're at the cliff's edge facing a massive, near-vertical rock swarmed by squawking birds. There are 70,000 of them, including gannets, kittiwakes, murres and razorbills. The reserve is isolated, so you'll have to travel for lodging.

TOP CHOICE The **Cliffhouse** (☑709-338-2055; www.thecliffhouse.ca; Rte 100; r $90), in the wee town of Branch 22km away, is strongly recommended. Set high on a hill, you can see the ocean and spouting whales from everywhere: the front yard's Adirondack chairs, the porch, the front picture window and all three guest rooms. It's owned by a local family – Chris is a naturalist at the reserve, wife Priscilla is the town mayor and mum Rita cooks breakfast.

Near the reserve turnoff is **Gannet's Nest Restaurant** (☑709-337-2175; Rte 100; mains $8-15; ☺8am-8pm), frying some of the province's crispiest fish and chips and baking a mean rhubarb pie.

EASTERN NEWFOUNDLAND

Two peninsulas seem to grasp awkwardly out to sea and comprise the sliver that is Eastern Newfoundland. The beloved, well-touristed Bonavista Peninsula projects northward. Historic fishing villages freckle its shores, and windblown walking trails swipe its coast. The **Discovery Trail Tourism Association** (www.thediscoverytrail.org/english/hikediscovery) provides the hiking lowdown; several trails are less than 5km, and they go to a maximum of 17km. **Clarenville** (www.fallfordiscovery.com) is the Bonavista Peninsula's access point and service center, though there's not much for sightseers.

To the south juts the massive but less-traveled Burin Peninsula, another region of fishing villages. These towns are struggling harder to find their way in the post-cod world. The ferry for France – yes, France, complete with wine, éclairs and Brie – departs from Fortune and heads to the nearby French islands of St-Pierre and Miquelon, a regional highlight.

Trinity

POP 250

Let's set the record straight: Trinity is the Bonavista Peninsula's most popular stop, a historic town of crooked seaside lanes, storybook heritage houses and gardens with white picket fences. Trinity Bight is the name given to the 12 communities in the vicinity, including Trinity, Port Rexton and New Bonaventure.

While Trinity is movie-set lovely, some visitors have complained that its perfection is a bit boring. But if you like historic buildings and theater along with your scenery – and you're keen for a whale-watch tour – this is definitely your place. It's a tiny town and easily walkable.

First visited by Portuguese explorer Miguel Corte-Real in 1500 and established as a town in 1580, Trinity is one of the oldest settlements on the continent.

Sights & Activities

Trinity Historic Sites HISTORICAL SITE
(☎709-464-3599; adult/under 12yr $12/free; ⊙10am-5:30pm late May-early Oct) One admission ticket lets you gorge on seven buildings scattered throughout the village.

The **Trinity Historical Society** (www.trinityhistoricalsociety.com) runs four of the sites. The **Lester Garland House** (West St) was rebuilt to celebrate cultural links between Trinity and Dorset, England – major trading partners in the 17th, 18th and 19th centuries. The **Cooperage** (West St) brings on a real live barrel-maker; the **Green Family Forge** (West St) is an iron-tool-filled blacksmith museum and the **Trinity Museum** (Church Rd) displays more than 2000 pieces, including North America's second-oldest fire wagon.

The provincial government operates the other trio of **sites** (www.seethesites.ca), which include costumed interpreters. The **Lester Garland Premises** (West St) depicts an 1820s general store; the **Interpretation Centre** (West St) provides a comprehensive history of Trinity; and **Hiscock House** (Church Rd) is a restored merchant's home from 1910.

Fort Point HISTORICAL SITE
Further afield is Fort Point (aka Admiral's Point), where you'll find a pretty lighthouse and four cannons, the remains of the British fortification from 1745. There are 10 more British cannons in the water, all compliments of the French in 1762. An interpretive trail tells the tale. It's accessible from Dunfield, a few kilometers south on Rte 239.

Skerwink Trail HIKING TRAIL
The Skerwink Trail (5km) is a fabulous (though muddy) loop that reveals picture-perfect coastal vistas. It's accessible from the church in Trinity East, off Rte 230.

Tours

Boat tours leave from the wharf behind the Dock Restaurant.

Atlantic Adventures BOAT
(☎709-464-2133; www.atlanticadventures.com; 2½hr tours $55; ⊙10am & 2pm late May-early Sep) Whale-watching tours on a big sailboat.

Trinity Eco-Tours BOAT
(☎709-464-3712; www.trinityeco-tours.com; Main St; 3hr tours $80; ⊙10am, 1pm & 5pm mid-May–Oct) Whale-watching tours via Zodiac boat. The company also offers guided kayak tours (two-hour tours $59), as well as shipwreck dives for experienced divers.

Trinity Historical Walking Tours WALKING
(☎709-464-3723; www.trinityhistoricalwalkingtours.com; Clinch's Lane; adult/child $10/free; ⊙10am Mon-Sat late Jun-Aug) These entertaining and educational tours start behind Hiscock House.

🛏 Sleeping & Eating

There are numerous fine inns and B&Bs. Space gets tight in summer, so book ahead. Several snack shop and grocery stores have popped up and are good places to pick up a sandwich or cheese plate ($5 to $9), which you can take to the picnic tables near the Lester Garland Premises.

Artisan Inn & Campbell
House B&B B&B $$
(☎709-464-3377, 877-464-7700; www.artisaninntrinity.com; High St; r incl breakfast $125-169, apt $250; ⊙May-Oct; ⊜🛜) Adjacent to each other and managed by the same group, these places are gorgeous. The three-room inn hovers over the sea on stilts; the flower-surrounded, three-room B&B also provides ocean vistas. The inn's Twine Loft restaurant serves a multicourse, prix-fixe meal ($34) of local specialties; check the menu posted out front, which changes daily.

Eriksen Premises B&B $$
(☎709-464-3698, 877-464-3698; www.trinityexperience.com; West St; r incl breakfast $95-160; ⊙May-Oct; ⊜) This Victorian home offers elegance in accommodations and dining (mains $14 to $22, open lunch and dinner). It also books two nearby B&Bs: Kelly's Landing (four rooms) and Bishop White Manor (nine rooms).

Village Inn INN $$
(☎709-464-3269; www.oceancontact.com; Taverner's Path; r incl breakfast $90-130) It's kind of like grandma's house – the 10 rooms are a bit faded but they're big and bright, with antique furnishings and weathered floorboards. The dining room (mains $9 to $16, open for dinner) makes traditional meals. The whole shebang is for sale, as the current owners are retiring, so changes may be afoot.

Dock Restaurant SEAFOOD $$
(☎709-781-2255; Dock Lane; mains $9-19; ⊙9am-9pm May-Oct) This scenic spot sits next to the wharf and prepares great chowder and seafood, plus it serves Moo Moo's ice cream (from the popular eponymous shop in St John's).

Entertainment

Rocky's Place Lounge LIVE MUSIC
(☎709-464-3400; High St) Rocky's hosts bands from time to time, but even if the mics are quiet it's a friendly place to hoist a brew.

Rising Tide Theatre THEATER
(☎709-464-3232; www.risingtidetheatre.com; Water St; tickets $25; ⊙Tue-Sun late Jun-early Sep) Alongside the Lester Garland Premises is the celebrated Rising Tide Theatre, which hosts the 'Seasons in the Bight' theater festival and the **Trinity Pageant** (adult/child $15/free; ⊙2pm Wed & Sat), an entertaining outdoor drama on Trinity's history.

Information

RBC Royal Bank (West St; ⊙10:30am-2pm Mon-Thu, to 5pm Fri) No ATM.

Town of Trinity (www.townoftrinity.com) Tourism info.

Getting There & Around

Trinity is 259km from St John's and is reached via Rte 230 off Hwy 1. **Shirran's Taxi** (☎709-468-7741) makes the trip daily from St John's ($45).

Bonavista

POP 3770

'O buona vista!' (Oh, happy sight!), shouted John Cabot upon spying the New World from his boat on June 24, 1497. Or so the story goes. From all descriptions, this pretty spot is where he first set foot in the Americas. Today Bonavista's shoreline, with its lighthouse, puffins and chasms, continues to rouse visitors.

Sights & Activities

Cape Bonavista Lighthouse LIGHTHOUSE
(☎709-468-7444; www.seethesites.ca; Rte 230; adult/child $3/free; ⊙10am-5:30pm late May-early Oct) Cape Bonavista Lighthouse is a brilliant red-and-white-striped lighthouse dating from 1843. The interior has been restored to the 1870s and is now a provincial historic site. A **puffin colony** lives just offshore; the birds put on quite a show around sunset.

Dungeon Park PARK
(Cape Shore Rd, off Rte 230; admission free) Nowhere is the power of water more evident than at the Dungeon, a deep chasm 90m in circumference that was created by the collapse of two sea caves, through which thunderous waves now slam the coast.

Ryan Premises HISTORIC SITE
(☎709-468-1600; www.pc.gc.ca/ryanpremises; Ryans Hill Rd; adult/child $3.90/1.90; ⊙10am-6pm mid-May–mid-Oct) Ryan Premises National Historic Site is a restored 19th-century saltfish mercantile complex. The slew of white clapboard buildings honors five centuries of fishing in Newfoundland via multimedia displays and interpretive programs.

Ye Matthew Legacy HISTORICAL SITE
(☎709-468-1493; www.matthewlegacy.com; Roper St; adult/child $7.50/3; ⊙10am-6pm Jun-early Oct) An impressive full-scale replica of the ship on which Cabot sailed into Bonavista is at Ye Matthew Legacy. At press time, the site was at risk of closing due to lack of funding for repairs.

Natural Wonders HIKING
(☎709-468-2523; www.puffins.ca; 42 Campbell St; 2hr tours adult/child $30/20; ⊙Jun-Sep) Hike with a naturalist to see puffins and learn about local plants and ecology.

Sleeping

Check www.bonavista.net for further lodging options.

HI Bonavista HOSTEL $
(☎709-468-7741, 877-468-7741; www.hihostels.ca; 40 Cabot Dr; dm $26-30, r $74-79; @ wi-fi) This tidy white-clapboard hostel is new on the scene, offering four private rooms, two shared dorm rooms, free bike use and kitchen and laundry facilities. It's a short walk from the center. The gregarious owners also run Shirran's Taxi, which provides transport from St John's ($40 each way).

White's B&B B&B $$
(☎709-468-7018; www.bbcanada.com/3821.htm; 21 Windlass Dr; r incl breakfast $75-85; non-smoking @ wi-fi) Low-key White's has three rooms to choose from, all with either private bathroom or en suite. Enjoy the bike rentals, barbecue use and ocean view.

Harbourview B&B B&B $
(☎709-468-2572; 21 Ryans Hill Rd; r incl breakfast $70; ⊙May-Sep; non-smoking) The name doesn't lie: you get a sweet view at this simple, four-room B&B, plus an evening snack (crab legs) with owners Florence and Albert.

Eating & Entertainment

TOP CHOICE **Walkham's Gate** CAFE $
(☎709-468-7004; www.walkhamsgatepub.ca; mains $5-9; ⊙24hr; wi-fi) One side is a

coffee shop with whopping pies and hearty soups, the other side a congenial pub tended by music-lover Harvey. Located in the town center, near the courthouse.

Garrick Theatre   THEATER
(www.garricktheatre.ca; 18 Church St) The artfully restored Garrick shows mainstream and indie films and hosts live music performances.

🛈 Information
Bonavista Community Health Centre (☎709-468-7881; Hospital Rd)

Town of Bonavista (www.bonavista.net) Tourism info.

Scotiabank (☎709-468-1070; 1 Church St)

🛈 Getting There & Around
Bonavista is a scenic 50km drive north of Trinity along Rte 230. **Shirran's** (☎709-468-7741) drives up daily from St John's ($40).

Burin Peninsula

It's not exactly lively on the Burin Peninsula, as the besieged fishing economy has made its presence felt. Still, the coastal walks inspire, and the region is a low-key place to spend a day or two before embarking toward the baguettes of France (aka St-Pierre).

Marystown is the peninsula's largest town; it's jammed with big-box retailers but not much else. **Burin** is the area's most attractive town, with a gorgeous elevated boardwalk over the waters of its rocky shoreline. **St Lawrence** is known for fluorite mining and scenic coastal hikes. In Grand

Bank, there's an interesting self-guided walk through the historic buildings and along the waterfront. Just south is fossil-rich **Fortune**, the jump-off point for St-Pierre.

👁 Sights & Activities
Provincial Seamen's Museum   MUSEUM
(☎709-832-1484; www.therooms.ca/museum; Marine Dr, Grand Bank) The impressive-looking Seamen's Museum depicts both the era of the banking schooner and the changes in the fishery over the years. It's set to reopen in 2011 after renovations.

FREE **Burin Heritage Museums**   MUSEUM
(☎709-891-2217; www.burincanada.com; Seaview Dr, Burin; admission free; ⊙9am-6pm Mon-Fri, 10:30am-6pm Sat & Sun) Displays in two historic homes tell of life's highs and lows in remote outports.

Fortune Head Ecological Reserve
                                      ECO RESERVE
(www.env.gov.nl.ca/parks; off Rte 220; admission free; ⊙24hr) The reserve protects fossils dating from the planet's most important period of evolution, when life on earth progressed from simple organisms to complex animals some 550 million years ago. The reserve is about 3km west, by the Fortune Head Lighthouse. Kids will appreciate the **Interpretation Centre** (☎709-832-2810; adult/child $5/3; ⊙9am-5pm mid-Jun–Aug) with fossils to touch; it's in town by the St-Pierre ferry dock.

Hiking Trails   HIKING TRAIL
Ask at the Burin Heritage Museum about locating the **Cook's Lookout** trailhead. It's a 90 minute walk from town to the

---

WORTH A TRIP

ELLISTON: ROOT CELLARS & PUFFINS

The Root Cellar Capital of the World, aka Elliston, lies 6km south of Bonavista on Rte 238. The teeny town was struggling until it hit upon the idea to market its 135 subterranean veggie storage vaults, and then presto – visitors came a knockin'. Actually, what's most impressive is the **puffin colony** just offshore and swarming with thousands of chubby-cheeked, orange-billed birds. A quick and easy path over the cliffside brings you quite close to them and also provides whale and iceberg views.

Stop at the **Visitor Centre** (☎709-468-7117; www.rootcellars.com; Main St) as you enter town, and the kindly folks will give you directions to the site. They also can arrange **guided walking tours** ($4) of the cellars.

Work up an appetite while you're here, because **Nanny's Root Cellar Kitchen** (☎709-468-7099; ⊙8am-10pm) in historic Orange Hall cooks a mighty fine lobster, Jigg's dinner and other traditional foods, plus she's licensed.

From the adjoining hamlet of **Maberly** a gorgeous 17km **coastal hiking trail** winds over the landscape to Little Catalina.

panoramic view. Off Pollux Cres in St Lawrence, the rugged, breath-draining **Cape Trail** (4km) and **Chamber Cove Trail** (4km) shadow the cliff edges and offer amazing vistas to rocky shores and some famous WWII shipwrecks. Another good (and easier) trail is the **Marine Hike** (7km) that traces Admiral's Beach near Grand Bank. It leaves from Christian's Rd off Rte 220.

🛏 Sleeping & Eating

Options are spread thinly. For those heading to St-Pierre, Grand Bank and Fortune are the best bases. Grand Bank has better lodging but it's further, at 8km from the ferry dock. Fortune has a sweet bakery by its dock. For more choices check **The Heritage Run** (www.theheritagerun.com).

Thorndyke B&B   B&B $$
(☎709-832-0820, 877-882-0820; www.thethorn dyke.ca; 33 Water St, Grand Bank; r incl breakfast $95; ☺mid-May–Oct; ☺) This handsome old captain's home overlooks the harbor. Antique wood furnishings fill the four light and airy rooms (each with private bathroom). The hosts will provide dinner with advance notice.

Fortune Inn B&B   B&B $$
(☎709-832-1774, 888-275-1098; www.granny smotorinn.ca; Bayview St, Fortune; r incl breakfast $89; ☺mid-Jun–mid-Sep; ☺) Antiques, shmantiques – who needs 'em? The rooms in this ex-apartment building are cheaply furnished (linoleum floors, drab colors, shared bathrooms), but they're clean and functional and, most importantly, they're only a 750m walk from the St-Pierre ferry.

Inn by the Sea B&B   B&B $$
(☎709-832-0202, 888-932-0202; www.theinnby thesea.com; 22 Blackburn Rd, Grand Bank; s/d incl breakfast $79/89; ☺Jun–mid-Oct; ☺@☎) Each of the four rooms here has a plump queen-sized bed, private bathroom and desk with laptop hookup.

Sharon's Nook & the Tea Room   CAFE $
(☎709-832-0618; 12 Water St, Grand Bank; mains $7-10; ☺7:30am-9pm Mon-Sat, 11am-7:30pm Sun) This countrified eatery serves up lasagna, chili, sandwiches and heavenly cheesecake.

◉ Getting There & Around

The Burin Peninsula is accessed via Rte 210 off Hwy 1. The drive from St John's to Grand Bank is 359km and takes just over four hours. **Foote's Taxi** (☎709-832-0491, 800-866-1181) travels from St John's down the peninsula as far as Fortune ($45, five hours).

ST-PIERRE & MIQUELON
POP 6000

Twenty-five kilometers offshore from the Burin Peninsula floats a little piece of France. The islands of St-Pierre and Miquelon aren't just Frenchlike with their berets, baguettes and Bordeaux, they *are* France, governed and financed by the *tricolore*.

Citizens here take their national pride very seriously – some even feel it's their duty to maintain France's foothold in the New World. Locals kiss their hellos and pay in euros, while sweet smells waft from the myriad pastry shops. French cars – Peugeots, Renaults and Citroëns – crowd the tiny one-way streets. It's an eye-rubbing world away from Newfoundland's nearby fishing communities.

St-Pierre is the more populated and developed island, with most residents of its 5300 living in the town of St-Pierre. Miquelon is larger geographically but has only 700 residents overall.

The fog-mantled archipelago has a 20th-century history as colorful as its canary-yellow, lime and lavender houses (see the boxed text, p474). Going further back, Jacques Cartier claimed the islands for France in 1536, after they were discovered by the Portuguese in 1520. At the end of the Seven Years' War in 1763, the islands were turned over to Britain, only to be given back to France in 1816. And French they've remained ever since.

◉ Sights & Activities

In St-Pierre, the best thing to do is just walk around and soak it up – when you're not eating, that is. Pop into stores and sample goods you'd usually have to cross an ocean for. Or conduct research as to the best chocolate croissant maker. A couple of **walking trails** leave from the edge of town near the power station.

Île aux Marins   HISTORICAL BUILDINGS
(3hr tours adult/child €19.50/12.50; ☺9am & 1:30pm May-Sep) The magical Île aux Marins is a beautiful abandoned village on an island out in the harbor. A bilingual guide will walk you through colorful homes, a small schoolhouse museum and the grand church (1874). Book tours at the visitors center. You can also go over on the boat (€3) *sans* guide, but be aware most signage is in French.

For hundreds of years, Newfoundland's waters – especially the Grand Banks to the south and east – were known as a place where you could dip your bucket and then hoist it back up filled with fat, slippery codfish. By 1992 that changed. Fish stocks had been declining over the years, and the government decided to take action. With the swipe of a pen, it made cod fishing illegal within a 320km radius of provincial shores. Suddenly, 20,000 fishers and plant workers were out of work overnight.

It was supposed to be a temporary measure, but the hoped-for cod rebound never happened. Almost two decades later, scientists warn that stocks remain critically low and could take years to come back. Fisherfolk say that while it may be true, they are being unfairly penalized. Just outside the 320km no-fishing zone, they reason, big trawlers from other countries continue to scoop up cod, and that's why stock numbers remain depleted.

Whether the moratorium is right or wrong, the impact on the local way of life has been staggering. Families who fished for generations have had to scramble to find new livelihoods. Many end up leaving the province to get work, fostering a trend known as 'outmigration.' Several regions have seen their populations drop by more than 20% since 1992.

Fort McMurray, Alberta, exerts the biggest pull, where people get seasonal jobs in the oil sands industry. Although the earnings are good, the lifestyle prompts a new set of problems: families are split, drugs are prevalent and money that's easily come by is also easily spent.

Newfoundland has struggled to cope with these changes. Some communities have converted their boats and fish plants to process crab and shrimp instead of cod. The province also has developed its own oil industry offshore from St John's. Finally, many communities are generating jobs by turning to tourism, an industry that was practically nonexistent prior to the codfish moratorium.

L'Arche Museum MUSEUM
(☎508-410-435; www.arche-musee-et-archives.net; Rue du 11 Novembre; adult/child €4/2.50; ⊙10am-noon & 1:30-5pm Tue-Sun Jun-Sep) The well-done exhibits cover the islands' history, including Prohibition times. The showstopper is the **guillotine** – the only one to slice in North American Islander; dropped the 'blade of justice' just once, in 1889, on a murderer. The museum also offers bilingual **architectural walking tours** (€6.50 to €8.50).

Miquelon & Langlade ISLANDS
The island of Miquelon, 45km away, is less visited and less developed than St-Pierre. The village of **Miquelon**, centered on the church, is at the northern tip of the island. From nearby **l'Étang de Mirande** a walking trail leads to a lookout and waterfall. From the bridge in town, a scenic 25km road leads across the isthmus to the wild and uninhabited island of **Langlade**. There are some wild horses, and around the rocky coast and lagoons you'll see seals and birds. **Chez Janot** (www.chezjanot.fr; adult/child €60/35; ⊙Jun-Sep) offers full-day, bilingual tours by Zodiac covering both islands. Book at the visitors center.

Several landmarks merit a look:

Cemetery (Ave Commandant Roger Birot) The cemetery with its above-ground mausoleums provides an atmospheric wander.

Les Salines (Rue Boursaint & the waterfront) Old-timers hang out around this scenic cluster of multihued fishing shacks.

Fronton (Rue Maître Georges Lefèvre & Rue Gloanec) Watch locals play the Basque game of *pelote* (a type of handball) at the outdoor court here.

✹ Festivals & Events
From mid-July to the end of August, folk dances are often held in St-Pierre's square.

Bastille Day (⊙Jul 14) The largest holiday of the year.

Basque Festival (⊙mid-Aug) A weeklong festival with music, marching and invigorating street fun.

🛏 Sleeping & Eating
There are about a dozen accommodations on St-Pierre; all include continental breakfast. Book ahead in summer. Great eateries

ST-PIERRE'S BOOZY BACKSTORY

When Prohibition dried out the USA's kegs in the 1920s, Al Capone decided to slake his thirst – and that of the nation – by setting up shop in St-Pierre.

He and his mates transformed the sleepy fishing harbor into a booming port crowded with imported-booze-filled warehouses. Bottles were removed from their crates, placed in smaller carrying sacks and taken secretly to the US coast by rumrunners. The piles of Cutty Sark whiskey crates were so high on the docks, clever locals used the wood both to build and heat houses. At least one house remains today and is known as the 'Cutty Sark cottage'; most tours drive by. At press time, the visitors center was setting up a new tour that would cover all the island's Prohibition sites.

St-Pierre still imports enough alcohol to pickle each and every citizen a few times over. It remains legendary to Newfoundland mainlanders as the home of cheap alcohol, including a type of grain alcohol that reputedly cleans engines or can be mixed with water to create a local moonshine. Not surprisingly, it is illegal in Canada.

abound, not surprisingly; make reservations to ensure a table. Several bars and restaurants are on Rue Albert Briand.

Auberge Quatre Temps B&B
B&B $$

(☎508-414-301; www.quatretemps.com; 14 Rue Dutemple; s/d €64/72; @☎) Let's start by saying there's a bar inside and it's open all day. There's also bike rental and a fine restaurant (open to the public but reservations are required). All six rooms have their own bathroom. Quatre Temps is a 15-minute schlep from the ferry dock, but don't let that deter you.

Nuits St-Pierre
B&B $$

(☎508-412-720; www.nuits-saint-pierre.com; 10 Rue du Général Leclerc; r €95-155; ☎☎) St-Pierre's most upscale lodging opened in 2010, aiming for the honeymoon crowd. The five rooms, each with private bathroom and downy, above-the-norm beds, are named after famous French authors. There's free pickup from the airport or ferry.

Bernard Dodeman B&B
B&B $

(☎508-413-060; www.pensiondodeman.com; 15 Rue Paul Bert; s/d €45/50; ☎☎) The Dodeman's three simple rooms share two bathrooms and a communal TV parlor. It's a 15-minute walk from the ferry, on a hill above town.

Brasserie de l'île
FRENCH $$

(☎508-410-350; 6 Rue Maître Georges Lefèvre; mains €15-18; ☎noon-2pm & 7:30-10:30pm) The candlelit wood bar, gauzy curtains, crooners on the stereo and cocktail list lend a sexy vibe to this restaurant. Staff chalk the daily specials on the board, say, of fresh-plucked fish or Moroccan tagines. A fine wine selection, of course, washes it down.

TOP CHOICE Patisserie Guillard
BAKERY $

(23 Rue Marechal Foch; pastries €0.50-1; ☎7:30am-12:30pm Mon-Sat) Holy mother! These cream-plumped chocolate éclairs, macaroons and gateaux are the reason you came to France, right?

Le Feu de Braise
FRENCH $$

(☎508-419-160; www.cheznoo.net/feu-de-braise; upstairs, 14 Rue Albert Briand; mains €11-19; ☎noon-2pm & 6:30-11pm) French and Italian-influenced food hits the tables in this warm, diner-esque restaurant. Standouts include the thin-crust pizza and homemade pastas.

ℹ Information

Americans, EU citizens and all visitors except Canadians need a passport for entry. Those staying longer than 30 days also need a visa. Other nationalities should confirm with their French embassy if a visa is needed prior to arrival. Canadians can enter with a driver's license.

Business Hours Most shops and businesses close between noon and 1:30pm. Some stores also close on Saturday afternoons, and most are closed on Sunday.

Customs To merit the duty-free waiver on alcohol, you must stay on the islands at least 48 hours.

Language French, but many people also speak English.

Money Many merchants accept the loonie, though they return change in euros. If you're staying more than an afternoon, it's probably easiest to get euros from the local ATMs.

Telephone Calling the islands is an international call, meaning you must dial 011 in front of the local number. Phone service links in to the French system, so beware of roaming charges on your mobile.

Time Half an hour ahead of Newfoundland Time.

Tourist Information (www.st-pierre-et-miquelon.com) The visitors center, near the ferry dock, provides a map showing all the banks, restaurants etc. Staff also provides information on the islands' hotels and tours and make bookings for free.

Voltage 220V; Canadian and American appliances need an electrical adapter.

❶ Getting There & Away

Air

Air Saint-Pierre (www.airsaintpierre.com) flies to St John's, Montréal and Halifax. There are two to three flights weekly to each city. Taxis to/from the airport cost around €5.

Boat

From Fortune on Newfoundland, **St-Pierre Tours** (709-832-0429, 800-563-2006; www.spmexpress.net; 5 Bayview St) operates the ferries (adult/child return $107/53.50, 1½ hours). From mid-June to mid-September, one departs daily at 11:30am, returning from St-Pierre at 2:15pm. From mid-July to early September, there's a day-trip service departing at 7:15am and returning at 2:15pm (except Sunday). Call for off-season times. The boats carry foot passengers only. Leave your car in the parking lot by the dock (per day $8).

❶ Getting Around

Much can be seen on foot. Roads are steep, so prepare to huff and puff. **Auberge Quatre Temps** (14 Rue Dutemple) rents bicycles (per half/full day €10/15). Local ferries head to Miquelon and Langlade; check with the visitors center for schedules and costs.

CENTRAL NEWFOUNDLAND

Central Newfoundland elicits fewer wows per square kilometer than the rest of the province, but that's because huge chunks of the region are pure bog land and trees. The islands of Notre Dame Bay – particularly Twillingate, when icebergs glide by – are exceptional exceptions.

Terra Nova National Park

Backed by lakes, bogs and hilly woods, and fronted by the salty waters of Clode and Newman Sounds, **Terra Nova National Park** (709-533-2801; www.pc.gc.ca/terranova; adult/child/family per day $5.80/2.90/14.70) is spliced by Hwy 1 running through its interior. It's not nearly as dramatic as the province's other national parks, though it does offer moose, bear, beaver and bald eagles, as well as relaxed hiking, paddling, camping and boat tours.

Make your first stop the **Visitors Centre** (709-533-2942; Hwy 1; ⏰9am-7pm late June-early Sep, 10am-5pm rest of season mid-May-early Oct), which has oodles of park information, ranger-guided programs and marine displays with touch tanks and underwater cameras. It's 1km off Hwy 1 at Salton's Day-Use Area, 80km east of Gander.

◉ Sights & Activities

Terra Nova's 14 hiking trails total almost 100km; pick up maps at the visitors center. Highly recommended is the **Malady Head Trail** (5km), which climaxes at the edge of a headland cliff offering stunning views of Southwest Arm and Broad Cove. **Sandy Pond Trail** (3km) is an easy loop around the pond – your best place to spot a beaver. The area is also a favorite for **swimming**, with a beach, change rooms and picnic tables. In winter, the park grooms trails here for cross-country skiing.

The epic **Outport Trail** (48km) provides access to backcountry campgrounds and abandoned settlements along Newman Sound. The loop in its entirety is rewarding, but be warned: parts are unmarked, not to mention mucky. A compass, a topographical map and ranger advice are prerequisites for this serious route.

Ocean Quest Adventures (p476) rents gear for **cycling** and **kayaking**. Inquire about the **Sandy Pond-Dunphy's Pond Route** (10km), a great paddle with only one small portage.

About 15km from the park's western gate, the **Burnside Archaeology Centre** (709-677-2474; www.burnsideheritage.ca; Main St; admission $2; ⏰9am-6pm Jul-Oct) catalogs artifacts found at local Beothuk sites; ask about **boat tours** (per person $40) to the more far-flung settlements. Also in the region is **Salvage**, a photographer's-dream fishing village with well-marked walking trails. It's near the park's north end on Rte 310, about 26km from Hwy 1.

☞ Tours

Departures are from the Visitors Centre.

Coastal Connections BOAT
(709-533-2196; www.coastalconnections.ca; 2½hr tours adult/child $65/35; ⏰9:30am & 1pm mid-May-early Oct) Climb aboard for a trip through

Newman Sound, where you'll pull lobster pots, examine plankton under the microscope and engage in other hands-on activities. It's common to see eagles, less so whales.

Ocean Quest Adventures BOAT
(☎709-422-1111; www.oceanquestadventures.com; ☺mid-May–Oct) Ocean Quest will take you cod fishing ($60, including gear). It also rents kayaks and bicycles.

🛌 Sleeping

Camping is the only option within the park itself. Those with aspirations of a bed should head to Eastport; it's near the park's north end on Rte 310, about 16km from Hwy 1. For camping reservations (recommended on summer weekends), call **Parks Canada** (☎877-737-3783; www.pccamping.ca; reservation fee $10.80) or go online.

Backcountry camping CAMPGROUND $
(free permit required, campsites $16) There are several backcountry sites around the Outport Trail, Beachy Pond, Dunphy's Island and Dunphy's Pond, reached by paddling, hiking or both. Register at the Visitors Centre.

Newman Sound Campground
CAMPGROUND $
(campsites $24-30) This is the park's main (noisier) campground, with 343 sites, a grocery store and laundromat. It's open for winter camping, too.

Malady Head Campground CAMPGROUND $
(campsites $17-22) Located at the park's northern end, Malady Head is smaller, quieter and more primitive (though it does have showers).

Doctor's Inn B&B B&B $$
(☎709-677-3539; www.doctors-inn.nf.ca; 5 Burden's Rd, Eastport; r $75-100; ☺Jun-Sep; ☻) Yes, there really is a doctor in this big old rambling house, as well as a flowery patio, gazebo and five fine rooms with private bathroom. It's certainly the brightest spot in an otherwise dreary little town.

Gander

POP 9600

Gander sprawls across the juncture of Hwy 1 and Rte 330, which leads to Notre Dame Bay. It is a convenient stopping point and offers a couple of sights for aviation buffs.

Gander essentially germinated from its airport. The site was chosen by the British in the 1930s because of its proximity to Eu-

rope and its fogless weather. Most recently, Gander gained attention for its hospitality to the thousands whose planes were rerouted here after the September 2001 terrorist attacks in the USA.

There is a **Visitors Centre** (www.gandercanada.com; ☺8am-8pm mid-Jun–Sep, 8:30am-5pm Mon-Fri Oct–mid-Jun) on Hwy 1 at the central entry into town.

For aviation fanatics, the **North Atlantic Aviation Museum** (☎709-256-2923; www.naam.ca; Hwy 1; adult/child $5/4; ☺9am-6pm Jun-Dec, to 4pm Mon-Fri Jan-May) has exhibits detailing Newfoundland's air contributions to WWII and the history of navigation. Just east on Hwy 1 is the sobering **Silent Witness Monument**, a tribute to 248 US soldiers whose plane crashed here in December 1985.

Sinbad's Hotel & Suites (☎709-651-2678; www.steelehotels.com; Bennett Dr; r $93-123) has clean, comfortable hotel rooms within the center of Gander. For meals, make it **Giovanni's Cafe** (☎709-651-3535; 71 Elizabeth Dr; mains $5-9; ☺7am-5pm Mon-Thu, 8:30am-5pm Fri & Sat, 11:30am-4:30pm Sun), with coffee, wraps, sandwiches and salads.

The **Gander Airport** (YQX; www.ganderairport.com) gets a fair bit of traffic. **DRL** (☎709-263-2171; www.drl-lr.com) buses stop at the airport en route to St John's (four hours) and Port aux Basques (nine hours).

Twillingate Island & New World Island

POP 5835

This area of Notre Dame Bay gets the most attention, and deservedly so. Twillingate (which actually consists of two barely separated islands, North and South Twillingate) sits just north of New World Island. The islands are reached from the mainland via an amalgamation of short causeways. It's stunningly beautiful, with every turn of the road revealing new ocean vistas, colorful fishing wharves or tidy groups of pastel houses hovering on cliffs and outcrops. An influx of whales and icebergs every summer only adds to the appealing mix.

⊙ Sights & Activities

Prime Berth/Twillingate Fishing Museum MUSEUM
(☎709-884-5925; Walter Elliott Causeway; admission $5, tour $7.50; ☺10am-5pm Jul & Aug) Make this your first stop. Run by an engaging fish-

erman, the private museum, with its imaginative and deceivingly simple concepts (a cod splitting show!), is brilliant, and fun for mature scholars and school kids alike. It's the first place you see as you cross to Twillingate.

Long Point Lighthouse
LIGHTHOUSE

(☎709-884-2247; admission free) Long Point provides dramatic views of the coastal cliffs. Travel up the winding steps, worn from lighthouse keepers' footsteps since 1876, and gawk at the 360-degree view. Located at the tip of the north island, it's an ideal vantage point for spotting icebergs in May and June.

Little Harbour Trail
HIKING TRAIL

In Little Harbour, en route to the town of Twillingate, a 5km trail leads past the vestiges of a resettled community and rock arch to secluded, picturesque **Jone's Cove**.

Durrell Museum
MUSEUM

(☎709-884-2780; Museum St, off Durrell St; adult/child $2/1; ☉9am-5pm Jun-Sep) Don't neglect to take a tour of the exceptionally scenic Durrell and its museum, dwelling atop Old Maid Hill. Bring your lunch; there are a couple of picnic tables and a spectacular view.

Auk Island Winery
WINERY

(☎709-884-2707; www.aukislandwinery.com; 29 Durrell St; tastings $3, with tour $5; ☉9:30am-5:30pm, to 8:30pm Thu & Fri Jul-early Sep) Visit the grounds that produce Moose Joose (blueberry-partridgeberry), Funky Puffin (blueberry-rhubarb) and other fruity flavors using iceberg water and local berries.

Twillingate Museum
MUSEUM

(☎709-884-2825; www.tmacs.ca; off Main St; admission by donation; ☉9am-5pm mid-May–early Oct) Housed in a former Anglican rectory, the museum tells the island's history since the first British settlers arrived in the mid-1700s. It also displays articles brought back from around the world by local sea captains. Another room delves into the seal hunt and its controversy. There's a historic **church** next door.

☞ Tours

Fun two-hour tours (per adult/child $44/22) to view icebergs and whales depart daily from mid-May to early September.

Twillingate Adventure Tours
BOAT

(☎709-884-5999; www.twillingateadventure tours.com; off Main St) Depart from Twillingate's wharf at 10am, 1pm and 4pm (and sometimes 7pm).

Twillingate Island Boat Tours
BOAT

(☎709-884-2242; www.icebergtours.ca; Main St) Depart from the Iceberg Shop (itself worth a peek, with its iceberg pictures and crafts) at 9:30am, 1pm and 4pm.

☆ Festivals & Events

Traditional music and dance, some of which goes back to the 16th century, merrily take over Twillingate during the weeklong **Fish, Fun & Folk Festival** (www.fishfunfolkfestival. com; ☉late Jul).

☶ Sleeping

Despite having about a dozen lodging options, Twillingate gets very busy in the summer. Book early.

Captain's Legacy B&B
B&B $$

(☎709-884-5648; www.captainslegacy.com; Hart's Cove; r $89-114; ☉mid-May–Oct; ☜☎) A real captain named Peter Troake once owned this historic 'outport mansion,' now a gracious four-room B&B overlooking the harbor.

Paradise B&B
B&B $$

(☎709-884-5683, 877-882-1999; www.capturegaia. com/paradiseb&b.html; 192 Main St; r $80-99; ☉mid-May–Sep; ☜☎) Set on a bluff overlooking Twillingate's harbor, Paradise offers the best view in town. You can wander down to the beach below, or relax on a lawn chair and soak it all up. Oh, the three rooms are comfy too. Angle for room No 1. Cash only.

Harbour Lights Inn B&B
B&B $$

(☎709-884-2763; www.harbourlightsinn.com; 189 Main St; d $109-139; ☉May–mid-Oct; ☜☎) South African Ingvild Lussy-Thomsen runs this historical and popular nine-bedroom home. It's located right on the harbor and contains amenities such as TVs and Jacuzzis.

☒ Eating & Entertainment

R&J Restaurant
SEAFOOD $$

(☎709-884-2212; 110 Main St; mains $8-14; ☉8am-11pm) Sink your teeth into fish 'n' brewis, shrimp, scallops or battered fish. Pizzas and burgers are also available.

All Around the Circle Dinner Theatre
THEATER

(☎709-884-5423; Crow Head; adult/child $29/15; ☉6pm Mon-Sat Jun–mid-Sep) Six of Newfoundland's best will not only cook you a traditional meal, they'll also leave you in stitches with their talented performances. It's just south of the Long Point Lighthouse.

ℹ Information

Town of Twillingate (www.townoftwillingate.ca)
Twillingate Tourism (www.twillingate.com)

ℹ Getting There & Away

From the mainland, Rte 340's causeways almost imperceptibly connect Chapel Island, tiny Strong's Island, New World Island and Twillingate Island.

Fogo Island & Change Islands

POP 2995

Settled in the 1680s, Fogo is an intriguing and rugged island to poke around. Keep an eye on this place: it recently embarked on an ambitious, arts-oriented sustainable tourism plan that's quite progressive for the region. The rare Newfoundland pony roams the Change Islands, which float to the west.

◉ Sights & Activities

On Fogo, the village of **Joe Batt's Arm**, backed by rocky hills, is a flashback to centuries past. A **farmers' market** takes place at the ice rink on Saturday mornings.

Nearby is **Tilting**, perhaps the most engaging village on the island. The Irish roots run deep here and so do the accents. The inland harbor is surrounded by picturesque fishing stages and flakes, held above the incoming tides by weary stilts. There's also the great coastal **Turpin's Trail** (9km) that leaves from Tilting, near the beach at **Sandy Cove**.

On the opposite end of the island is the village of **Fogo** and the indomitable **Brimstone Head** (see the boxed text, p479). After you take in the mystical rock's view, do another great hike in town: the **Lion's Den Trail** (5km), which visits a Marconi radio site. Keep an eye out for the small group of caribou that roams the island.

As part of the new development plan, the island is stringing **art studios** along its walking trails, and inviting painters, filmmakers and photographers from around the world for residencies. Ask about the **digital cinema**'s current location. And by all means see what the **World's End Theatre Company** (www.worldsendtheatre.org; ⊙mid-Jul–mid-Aug) has going on. The troupe stages original works, telling local stories, in pubs, churches and outdoor venues around the island.

The Change Islands are home to the **Newfoundland Pony Refuge** (☏709-621-4400; 12 Bowns Rd; admission free; ⊙by appointment), established to increase numbers of the native, endangered Newfoundland pony. Only 88 registered beasts of breeding age remain in the province, and this is the largest herd. The small creatures are renowned as hardy workers (especially in winter) with gentle temperaments.

✯✯ Festivals & Events

Great Fogo Island Punt Race (www.fogoislandregatta.com; ⊙late Jul) Locals row traditionally built wooden boats (called punts) 16km across open sea to the Change Islands and back.

Brimstone Head Folk Festival (www.town-fogo.ca; ⊙mid-Aug) A three-day hootenanny; Irish and Newfoundland music.

🛏 Sleeping & Eating

The high-end, 29-room, ecofriendly Fogo Island Inn is scheduled to open in 2012.

Peg's B&B   B&B $$
(☏709-266-2392; www.pegsbb.com; 60 Main St, Fogo; r $75-85; ⊙May-Oct; ⊛🛜) Right in the heart of Fogo village, Peg's four-room place offers up a friendly atmosphere and harbor views.

Foley's Place B&B   B&B $$
(☏709-658-7288, 866-658-7244; www.foleysplace.ca; 10A Kelley's Island Rd, Tilting; r $85; ⊛🛜) The four rooms in this traditional, 100-year-old home are brightly colored, furnished in modern style and have en suite bathrooms.

🌿 Nicole's Cafe   CAFE $$
(☏709-658-3663; www.nicolescafe.ca; 159 Main Rd, Joe Batt's Arm; mains $15-20; ⊙9am-9pm) Nicole uses ingredients from the island – sustainably caught seafood, root vegetables and wild berries – for her contemporary take on dishes like Jigg's dinner, caribou pâté and the daily vegetarian plate. It's a sunny spot with big wood tables and local artwork and quilts on the walls.

ℹ Information

Change Islands (www.changeislands.ca)
Fogo Tourism (www.fogoisland.net)

ℹ Getting There & Away

Rte 335 takes you to the town of Farewell, where the ferry sails to the Change Islands

ROUND OR FLAT?

Despite Columbus' stellar work in 1492 (when he sailed the ocean blue without falling off the earth's edge), and despite modern satellite photos that confirm his findings of a rounded orb, the folks at the Flat Earth Society aren't buying it. A spinning, spherical world hurtling through space would only lead to our planet's inhabitants living a confused and disorientated life, they say.

In 'reality,' the stable and calming flat earth is said to have five striking corners: Lake Mikhayl in Tunguska (Siberia); Easter Island; Lhasa (Tibet); the South Pacific island of Ponape; and Brimstone Head on Fogo Island, right here in Newfoundland. So climb up the craggy spine of Brimstone Head, stare off the abyss to earth's distant edge and judge for yourself if the earth is round or flat. If nothing else, you're guaranteed a stunning view of Iceberg Alley.

(20 minutes) and then onward to Fogo (45 minutes). Five boats leave between 7:45am and 8:30pm. Schedules vary, so check with **Provincial Ferry Services** (☎709-621-3150, 709-627-3448; www.gov.nl.ca/ferryservices). The round-trip fare to Fogo is $16.50 for car and driver, and $5.50 for additional passengers. It's $6.50 to the Change Islands.

Lewisporte

POP 3308

Stretched-out Lewisporte, known primarily for its ferry terminal, is the largest town on Notre Dame Bay. Other than for the boat to Labrador, there really isn't much reason to visit, though as a distribution center it does have all the goods and services.

If you have to spend the night, the stark **Brittany Inns** (☎709-535-2533, 800-563-8386; Main St; r $90-110; ❋ ☎) is about as good as you're going to get. Several of the 34 rooms have kitchenettes.

Oriental Restaurant (☎709-535-6993; 131 Main St; meals $6-11; ⊗11:30am-11pm) is a straightforward place, and you get a chance at a few vegetables.

DRL (☎709-263-2171; www.drl-lr.com) stops at Brittany Inns en route to St John's and Port aux Basques.

Between mid-June and mid-September, the **MV Sir Robert Bond** (☎709-535-0810, 866-535-2567; www.labradormarine.com) runs a weekly vehicle-and-passenger service to the Labrador towns of Cartwright (adult/child/car $73/36.50/118, 24 hours) and Happy Valley-Goose Bay (adult/child/car $118/59.25/194, 39 hours, including a four-hour stop in Cartwright). The boat leaves Lewisporte on Friday at 2pm.

Grand Falls-Windsor

POP 13,560

The sprawl of two small pulp-and-paper towns has met and now comprises the community of Grand Falls-Windsor. The Grand Falls portion, south of Hwy 1 and near the Exploits River, is more interesting for visitors. The five-day **Salmon Festival** (www.salmonfestival.com; ⊗mid-Jul) rocks with big-name Canadian bands.

⊙ Sights

Mary March Provincial Museum MUSEUM
(☎709-292-4522; www.therooms.ca/museum; cnr St Catherine & Cromer Aves; adult/child $2.50/free; ⊗9am-4:45pm Mon-Sat, from noon Sun May–mid-Oct) This is worth visiting. Exhibits concentrate on the recent and past histories of Aboriginal peoples in the area, including the extinct Beothuk tribe. Take exit 18A south to reach it. Admission includes the loggers' museum, and vice versa

Loggers' Life Provincial Museum MUSEUM
(☎709-292-0492; www.therooms.ca/museum; exit 17, Hwy 1; adult/child $2.50/free; ⊗9am-4:45pm late May–mid-Sep) Here you can experience the life of a 1920s logging camp – smells and all.

Salmonid Interpretation Centre PARK
(☎709-489-7350; www.exploitsriver.ca; adult/child $6/2.50; ⊗8am-8pm mid-Jun–mid-Sep) Watch Atlantic salmon start their mighty struggle upstream to spawn. Unfortunately, they do so under the pulp mill's shadow. To get there, cross the river south of High St and follow the signs.

🛏 Sleeping & Eating

Hill Road Manor B&B B&B $$
(☎709-489-5451, 866-489-5451; www.hillroad manor.com; 1 Hill Rd; r $109-119; ☎) Elegant furnishings, cushiony beds that will have you

gladly oversleeping and a vibrant sunroom combine for a stylish stay. Kids are welcome.

Kelly's Pub & Eatery   BURGERS **$**
(☎709-489-9893; 18 Hill Rd; mains $7-11; ☺9am-2am) Hidden neatly behind the smoky pub is this great countrified spot. It makes the best burgers in town and the stir-fries are not too shabby either.

❶ Information

Town of Grand Falls-Windsor (www.grand fallswindsor.com)

❶ Getting There & Away

DRL (☎709-263-2171; www.drl-lr.com) has its bus stop at the Highliner Inn on the Hwy 1 service road. The drive to St John's is 430km, to Port aux Basques it's 477km.

Central South Coast

Rte 360 runs 130km through the center of the province to the south coast. It's a long way down to the first settlements at the end of **Bay d'Espoir**, a gentle fjord. Note there is no gas station on the route, so fill up on Hwy 1. **St Alban's** is set on the west side of the fjord. You'll find a few motels with dining rooms and lounges around the end of the bay.

Further south is a concentration of small fishing villages. The scenery along Rte 364 to **Hermitage** is particularly impressive, as is the scenery around **Harbour Breton**. It's the largest town (population 2080) in the region and huddles around the ridge of a gentle inland bay.

Southern Port Hotel (☎709-885-2283; www.southernporthotel.ca; Rte 360, Harbour Breton; r $90-93; ☎) provides spacious, standard-furnished rooms; even-numbered ones have harbor views. Two doors down is **Scott's Snackbar** (☎709-885-2406; mains $7-15; ☺10:30am-11pm Sun-Thu, to 1am Fri & Sat), serving burgers and home-cooked dishes; it's licensed.

Thornhill Taxi Service (☎709-885-2144, 866-538-3429) connects Harbour Breton with Grand Falls ($40, 2½ hours), leaving at 7:15am. Government passenger ferries serve Hermitage, making the western south-coast outports (see p495) accessible from here.

NORTHERN PENINSULA

The Northern Peninsula points upward from the body of Newfoundland like an extended index finger, and you almost get the feeling it's wagging at you saying, 'Don't you dare leave this province without coming up here.'

Heed the advice. This area could well be crowned Newfoundland's star attraction. The province's two World Heritage–listed sites are here: Gros Morne National Park, with its fjordlike lakes and geological oddities, rests at the peninsula's base, while the sublime, 1000-year-old Viking settlement at L'Anse aux Meadows stares out from the peninsula's tip. Connecting these two famous sites is the **Viking Trail** (www.vikingtrail.org), aka Rte 430, an attraction in its own right that holds close to the sea as it heads resolutely north past the ancient burial grounds of Port au Choix and the ferry jump-off point to big, brooding Labrador. It's no wonder many people base their entire Newfoundland trip around this extraordinary region and usually end up coming back for more, year after year.

The region continues to gain in tourism, yet the crowds are nowhere near what you'd get at Yellowstone or Banff, for example. Still, it's wise to book ahead in July and August.

It's a five- to six-hour drive from Deer Lake at the peninsula's southern edge to L'Anse aux Meadows at its northern apex. Towns and amenities are few and far between so don't wait to fuel up.

Deer Lake

There's little in Deer Lake for the visitor, but it's an excellent place to fly into for trips up the Northern Peninsula and around the west coast.

B&Bers can hunker down at plain-and-simple **Lucas House** (☎709-635-3622; 22 Old Bonne Bay Rd; r $60-70; ☺May-Sep; ☻@); it's a five-minute ride from the airport. The biggest show in town is 56-room, dog-eared **Deer Lake Motel** (☎709-635-2108; www.deerlakemotel.com; Hwy 1; r $89-139; ✻☎), which sits on Hwy 1 across from the **Visitors Centre** (☺9am-7pm) and the **DRL** (☎709-263-2171; www.drl-lr.com) bus stop at the Irving gas station. A taxi from the airport to any of these spots costs about $7.

Deer Lake Airport (YDF; www.deerlakeairport.com) is a stone's throw off Hwy 1. It's a well-equipped little place with ATMs, food, free wi-fi and internet access, and a staffed tourism desk. Flights arrive regularly from St John's, Halifax, Toronto and even London. Avis, Budget and Hertz rent cars at the airport; for costs and contact information, see p886.

Gros Morne National Park

This **national park** (☎709-458-2417; www.pc.gc.ca/grosmorne; adult/child/family per day $9.80/4.90/19.60; ☺year-round) stepped into the world spotlight in 1987, when Unesco granted it World Heritage designation. To visitors, the park's stunning flat-top mountains and deeply incised waterways are simply supernatural playgrounds. To geologists, this park is a blueprint for our planet and supplies evidence for theories such as plate tectonics. Specifically, the bronze-colored Tablelands are made of rock that comes from deep within the earth's crust. Nowhere in the world is such material as easily accessed as in Gros Morne (it's usually only found at unfathomable ocean depths). Such attributes have earned the park its 'Galapagos of Geology' nickname.

There is enough to do in and around the park to easily fill several days. The hiking, kayaking, camping, wildlife-spotting and boat tours are fantastic.

Several small fishing villages dot the shoreline and provide amenities. Bonne Bay swings in and divides the area: to the south is Rte 431 and the towns of **Glenburnie**, **Woody Point** and **Trout River**; to the north is Rte 430 and **Norris Point**, **Rocky Harbour**, **Sally's Cove** and **Cow Head**. Centrally located Rocky Harbour is the largest village and most popular place to stay. Nearby Norris Point and further-flung Woody Point also make good bases.

◉ Sights

The park is quite widespread – it's 133km from Trout River at the south end to Cow Head in the north – so it takes a while to get from sight to sight. We've listed the following places from south to north. Don't forget to stop in the park's visitors centers (see p484), which have interpretive programs and guided walks.

Tablelands   GEOGRAPHIC FEATURE
(Rte 431, near Trout River) Dominating the southwest corner of the park are the unconquerable and eerie Tablelands. This massive flat-topped massif was part of the earth's mantle before tectonics raised it from the depths and planted it squarely on

Gros Morne, L'Anse aux Meadows, Port aux Choix, Red Bay and Grenfell Historic Properties can be visited on the joint **admission pass** (adult/child/family $44/22/88), valid for seven days. It'll save you a few dollars if you're intending to see them all.

the continent. Its rock is so unusual that plants can't even grow on it. You can view the barren golden phenomenon up close on Rte 431, or catch it from a distance at the stunning **photography lookout** above Norris Point. West of the Tablelands, dramatic volcanic sea stacks and caves mark the coast at **Green Gardens**.

Bonne Bay Marine Station   AQUARIUM
(☎709-458-2550; www.bonnebay.mun.ca; Rte 430, Norris Point; adult/child/family $6.25/5/15; ☺9am-5pm late May-early Sep, by appointment rest of year) At the wharf in Norris Point is the Bonne Bay Marine Station, a research facility that's part of Memorial University. Every half-hour there are interactive tours, and the aquariums display the marine ecological habitats in Bonne Bay. For children, there are touch tanks and a rare blue lobster lurking around.

SS Ethie   SHIPWRECK
(Rte 430, past Sally's Cove) Follow the sign off the highway to where waves batter the rusty and tangled remains of the SS *Ethie*. The story of this 1919 wreck, and the subsequent rescue, was inspiration for a famous folk song.

Western Brook Pond   TRAIL & TOUR
(Rte 430) Park your car in the lot off the highway, then take the 3km flat, easy path inland to Western Brook Pond. 'Pond' is a misnomer, since the body of water is huge. Many people also call it a fjord, which is technically incorrect, since it's freshwater versus saltwater. Here's the thing everyone agrees on: it's flat-out stunning. Western Brook's sheer 700m cliffs plunge to the blue abyss and dramatically snake into the mountains. The best way to experience it is on a boat tour (see Bon Tours, p482).

FREE **Broom Point Fishing Camp**
                              HISTORICAL SITE
(Rte 430, Broom Point; admission free; ☺10am-5:30pm mid-May–mid-Oct) This restored

fishing camp sits a short distance north of Western Brook Pond. The three Mudge brothers and their families fished here from 1941 until 1975, when they sold the entire camp, including boats, lobster traps and nets, to the national park. Everything has been restored; it's staffed by guides.

Shallow Bay   BEACH

The gentle, safe, sand-duned beach at Shallow Bay seems out of place, as if transported from the Caribbean by some bizarre current. The water, though, provides a chilling dose of reality, rarely getting above 15°C.

The Arches   PARK

These scenic arched rocks on Rte 430 north of Parsons Pond are formed by pounding waves and worth a look-see.

Activities

Hiking and kayaking can also be done via guided tours.

Hiking

Twenty maintained trails of varying difficulty snake through 100km of the park's most scenic landscapes. The gem is the **James Callahan Gros Morne Trail** (16km) to the peak of Gros Morne, the highest point at 806m. While there are sections with steps and boardwalks, this is a strenuous seven- to eight-hour hike, and includes a steep rock gully that must be climbed to the ridgeline of the mountain. Standing on the 600m precipice and staring out over **10 Mile Pond**, a sheer-sided fjord, can only be described as sublime.

Green Gardens Trail (16km) is almost as scenic and challenging. The loop has two trailheads off Rte 431, with each one descending to Green Gardens along its magnificent coastline formed from lava and shaped by the sea. Plan on six to eight hours of hiking or book one of the three backcountry camping areas, all of them on the ocean, and turn the hike into an overnight adventure. A less strenuous day hike (9km) to the beach and back is possible from this trail's Long Pond Trailhead.

Shorter scenic hikes are **Tablelands Trail** (4km), which extends to Winterhouse Brook Canyon; **Lookout Trail** (5km), which starts behind the Discovery Centre and loops to the site of an old fire tower above the tree line; **Lobster Cove Head Trail** (2km), which loops through tidal pools; and **Western Brook Pond Trail**, the most popular path.

The granddaddies of the trails are the **Long Range Traverse** (35km) and **North Rim Traverse** (27km), serious multiday treks over the mountains. Permits and advice from park rangers are required.

If you plan to do several trails, invest $20 in a copy of the *Gros Morne National Park Trail Guide,* a waterproof map with trail descriptions on the back, which is usually available at the visitors centers.

Kayaking

Kayaking in the shadow of the Tablelands and through the spray of whales is truly something to be experienced. **Gros Morne Adventures** (single/double per day $50/60) provides rentals for experienced paddlers. See below for contact details.

Skiing

Many trails in the park's impressive 55km cross-country ski-trail system were designed by Canadian Olympic champion, Pierre Harvey. Contact the Main Visitor Centre, p484) for trail information and reservations for backcountry huts.

☞ Tours

Most tours operate between June and mid-September; book in advance. Kayaking is best in June and July.

Bon Tours   BOAT

(☏709-458-2016; www.bontours.ca; Ocean View Motel, Main St, Rocky Harbour) Bon runs the phenomenal **Western Brook Pond boat tour** (2hr trip per adult/child/family $52/25/120) at 10am, 1pm and 4pm. The dock is a 3km walk from Rte 430 via the easy Western Brook Pond Trail. If you haven't purchased a **park pass** ($9.80), you must do so before embarking. It's best to buy tickets ahead of time at Bon's office in the Ocean View Hotel, though you can also do so at the boat dock (where it's cash only). It's about a 25-minute drive from Bon's office to the trailhead.

Bon also runs **Bonne Bay boat tours** (2hr trip per adult/child/family $39/16/90) departing from Norris Point wharf, as well as a water taxi ($12 round-trip, foot passengers and bikes only) from Norris Point to Woody Point.

Gros Morne Adventures   MULTISPORT

(☏709-458-2722, 800-685-4624; www.grosmorneadventures.com; Norris Point wharf) It offers daily guided sea kayak tours (two/three hours $50/60) in Bonne Bay, plus full-day and multiday kayak trips and hiking, skiing and snowshoeing tours. Check the website for many additional options.

Long Range Adventures MULTISPORT
(☏709-458-2828, 877-458-2828; www.longrange adventures.com; Sally's Cove) Another multi-adventure outfitter offering daily guided sea kayaking (2½-hour tour $55), hiking and mountain-bike tours, plus winter activities. Locally owned Long Range also runs **Gros Morne Hostel/Island Traveller Tours** (www.grosmornehostel.com), a budget sister company with excursions taking in Twillingate and St John's from Deer Lake (three-day tour from $279) and others that continue on through the Northern Peninsula (seven-day tour from $749).

Festivals & Events

Gros Morne Theatre Festival (☏709-243-2899; www.theatrenewfoundland.com; tickets $15-30; ⊘late May–mid-Sep) Eight productions of Newfoundland plays, staged both indoors and outdoors at various locations throughout the summer.

Writers at Woody Point Festival (☏709-453-2900; www.writersatwoodypoint.com; tickets $20; ⊘mid-Aug) Authors from across Newfoundland, Canada and the world converge at the Woody Point Heritage Theatre to do readings.

🛏 Sleeping

Rocky Harbour has the most options. Woody Point, Norris Point and cute Cow Head are also good bets. Places fill fast in July and August.

Middle Brook Cottages CABINS $$
(☏709-453-2332; www.middlebrookcottages. com; off Rte 431, Glenburnie; cabins $115-129; ⊘mid-Mar–Nov; ☺📶♨) These all-pinewood, spick-and-span cottages are both perfectly romantic and perfectly kid-friendly. They have kitchens and TVs, and you can splash around the swimming hole and waterfalls behind the property.

Aunt Jane's Place B&B B&B $
(☏709-453-2485; www.grosmorne.com/victor ianmanor; Water St, Woody Point; r without/with bathroom $65/75; ⊘mid-May–mid-Oct; ☺) This historic house oozes character. It sits beachside, so you may be woken early in the morning by the heavy breathing of whales.

Gros Morne Cabins CABINS $$
(☏709-458-2020; www.grosmornecabins.com; Main St, Rocky Harbour; cabins $119-189; 📶♨) While backed by tarmac, most of these beautiful log cabins are fronted by nothing but ocean (ask when booking to ensure a view). Each has a full kitchen, TV and pullout sofa for children. Bookings can be made next door at Endicott's variety store.

Red Mantle Lodge HOTEL $$
(☏709-453-7204, 888-453-7204; www.redma ntlelodge.ca; Rte 431, near Woody Point; r $129-159; ❄📶) Located up a steep hill looking down on Woody Point, with 17 of its 18 rooms facing the bay, the Red Mantle gives off a new ski lodge vibe. Rooms have high ceilings, wood floors and mellow, earth-toned decor; ask for an upstairs one to minimize noise. The licensed bar-restaurant is handy for an evening drink.

Anchor Down B&B B&B $$
(☏709-458-2901, 800-920-2208; www.thean chordown.com; Pond Rd, Rocky Harbour; r $75-90; @) The home and its five rooms are pretty simple, but guests have raved about excellent hospitality and cooking from the friendly hosts.

Gros Morne Hostel HOSTEL $
(☏709-458-2828, 877-458-2828; www.gros mornehostel.com; Sally's Cove; dm $25, r with/without bathroom $65/50; @) The Long Range Adventures folks rent out extra rooms in their house. It's tight quarters, but the hosts' goodwill smooths out the roughness. Free bike use for guests.

Park Campgrounds CAMPGROUND $
(☏877-737-3783; www.pccamping.ca; campsites $19-26, reservation fee $10.80) Four developed campgrounds lie within the park: **Berry Hill** (⊘mid-Jun–mid-Sep), the largest, is most central; **Lomond** (⊘late May–mid-Oct) is good and closest to the southern park entrance; **Trout River** (⊘mid-Jun–mid-Sep) is average and closest to the Tablelands; and **Shallow Bay** (⊘mid-Jun–mid-Sep) has ocean swimming (and mosquitoes). There's also a **primitive campground** (⊘year-round) at superb Green Point. Numerous **backcountry campsites** ($10) are spread along trails; reserve them at the Main Visitor Centre (p484).

🍴 Eating

Rocky Harbour and Woody Point have the most options. There's a good chip van in Sally's Cove.

TOP CHOICE **Java Jack's** CAFE $$
(☎709-458-3004; www.javajacks.ca; Main St, Rocky Harbour; mains $9-19; ☉7:30am-8:30pm mid-May–late Sep, closed Tue; ☑) Art-filled Jack's provides Gros Morne's best cof-fees, wraps and soups by day. By night, the upstairs dining room fills hungry, post-hike bellies with fine seafood, caribou and veg-etarian fare. Greens come fresh from the property's organic garden.

Earle's Video & Convenience CANADIAN $
(☎709-458-2577; Main St, Rocky Harbour; mains $8-14; ☉9am-11pm) Earle is an institution in Rocky Harbour. Besides selling groceries and renting videos, he has great ice cream, pizza, moose burgers and traditional New-foundland fare that you can chomp on the patio.

Lighthouse Restaurant SEAFOOD $$
(☎709-453-2213; Water St, Woody Point; mains $9-15; ☉11:30am-9pm Mon-Wed, from 9am Thu-Sun May-Sep) The ladies at this diner cook up a storm out back and deliver Gros Morne's best fish and chips, cod tongues and other Newfie dishes, along with cold beer.

Old Loft Restaurant SEAFOOD $$
(☎709-453-2294; www.theoldloft.com; Water St, Woody Point; mains $15-21; ☉11:30am-9pm Jul & Aug, to 7pm May, Jun & Sep) Set on the water in Woody Point, this tiny place is popular for its traditional Newfoundland meals and seafood.

ℹ Information

Park admission includes the trails, Discovery Centre and all day-use areas.

Discovery Centre (☎709-453-2490; Rte 431, Woody Point; ☉9am-5pm late May–mid-Oct, to 9pm Wed & Sun Jul & Aug) Has interactive exhibits and a multimedia theater explaining the area's ecology and geology. There's also an information desk with maps, daily interpretive activities and a small cafe.

Main Visitor Centre (☎709-458-2066; Rte 430, near Rocky Harbour; ☉9am-9pm late Jun-early Sep, to 5pm mid-May–late Jun & early Sep–mid-Oct) As well as issuing day and backcountry permits, it has maps, books, Viking Trail materials and an impressive inter-pretive area.

Park Entrance Kiosk (Rte 430; ☉10am-6pm mid-May–mid-Oct) Near Wiltondale.

Rocky Harbour (www.rockyharbour.ca)
Western Newfoundland Tourism (www.facebook.com/gowesternnewfoundland.com)

ℹ Getting There & Around

Deer Lake Airport is 71km south of Rocky Harbour. For shuttle bus services to Rocky Harbour, Woody Point and Trout River, see Corner Brook (p490).

Port au Choix

Port au Choix, dangling on a stark peninsu-la 13km off the Viking Trail, houses a large fishing fleet, quirky museum and worthy archaeological site that delves into ancient burial grounds.

◉ Sights & Activities

Port au Choix National Historic Site
HISTORICAL SITE
(☎709-861-3522; www.pc.gc.ca/portauchoix; Point Riche Rd; adult/child $7.80/3.90; ☉9am-6pm Jun-early Oct) The Port au Choix National Historic Site sits on ancient burial grounds of three different Aboriginal groups, dating back 5500 years. The modern visitors cen-ter tells of these groups' creative survival in the area and of one group's unexplained disappearance 3200 years ago.

Phillip's Garden, a site with vestiges of Paleo-Eskimo houses, is a highlight. Two trails will take you there. One is the **Phil-lip's Garden Coastal Trail** (4km), which leaves from Phillip Dr at the end of town. From here you hopscotch your way over the jigsaw of skeletal rock to the site 1km away.

If you continue, it's another 3km to the **Point Riche Lighthouse** (1871). A plaque next to the tower recounts the many French and English conflicts in the area between the 1600s and 1900s. In 1904, France relinquished its rights here in exchange for privileges in Morocco (ah, the days when the world was a Monopoly board). The lighthouse is also ac-cessible via the visitors center road.

Another way to reach Phillip's Garden is the **Dorset Trail** (8km). It leaves the visi-tors center and winds across the barrens past stunted trees, passing a Dorset Paleo-Eskimo **burial cave** before finally reaching the site and linking to the Coastal Trail.

Ben's Studio GALLERY
(☎709-861-3280; www.bensstudio.ca; 24 Fisher St; admission free; ☉9am-5pm Mon-Fri Jun–mid-Sep) At the edge of town is Ben Plough-man's capricious studio of folk art. Pieces like *Crucifixion of the Cod* are classic. His engaging and humorous manner comple-ments the ever-evolving whale museum he's creating, which includes an impressive, wired-together whale skeleton.

🛏 Sleeping & Eating

Jeannie's Sunrise B&B   B&B $

(📞709-861-2254, 877-639-2789; www.jeanniessunrisebb.com; Fisher St; r $55-89; 😊🛜) Jeannie radiates hospitality through her spacious rooms, bright reading nook and demeanor as sweet as her breakfast muffins. Rooms at the lower end of the price spectrum share a bathroom.

Anchor Cafe   SEAFOOD $$

(📞709-861-3665; Fisher St; mains $12-18; 🕙11am-9pm) You can't miss this place – the front half is the bow of a boat – and don't, because it has the best meals in town. The luncheon specials offer good value and the dinner menu has a wide array of seafood.

St Barbe to L'anse Aux Meadows

As the Viking Trail nears St Barbe, the waters of the gulf quickly narrow and give visitors their first opportunity to see the desolate shores of Labrador. Ferries take advantage of this convergence and ply the route between St Barbe and the Labrador Straits (see p496). At Eddies Cove, the road leaves the coast and heads inland.

As you approach the northern tip of the peninsula, Rte 430 veers off toward St Anthony, and two new roads take over leading to several diminutive fishing villages that provide perfect bases for your visit to L'Anse aux Meadows National Historic Site. Route 436 hugs the eastern shore and passes through (from south to north) St Lunaire-Griquet, Gunners Cove, Straitsview and L'Anse aux Meadows village. Route 437 heads in a more westerly direction through Pistolet Bay, Raleigh and Cape Onion.

👁 Sights & Activities

L'Anse aux Meadows National Historic Site   HISTORICAL SITE

(📞709-623-2608; www.pc.gc.ca/lanseauxmeadows; Rte 436; adult/child $11.70/5.80; 🕙9am-6pm Jun-early Oct) The premise may seem dull – visiting a bog in the middle of nowhere and staring at the spot where a couple of old sod houses once stood – but somehow this Viking site lying in a forlorn sweep of land turns out to be one of Newfoundland's most stirring attractions.

Its historic significance is absolute: it's the home of the first Europeans to land in North America. They were Vikings from Scandinavia and Greenland, who sailed over some 500 years before Columbus. That they settled, constructed houses, fed themselves and even smelted iron out of the bog to forge nails, attests to their ingenuity and fortitude. That it was all accomplished by a group of young-pup 20-somethings, led by Leif Eriksson, son of Eric the Red, is even more impressive.

The remains of the Vikings' waterside settlement from circa AD 1000 – eight wood-and-sod buildings, now just vague outlines left in the spongy ground – are what visitors can see, plus three replica buildings inhabited by costumed docents. The latter have names such as 'Thora' and 'Bjorn' and simulate Viking chores such as spinning fleece and forging nails.

Allow two or three hours to walk around and absorb the ambience, as well as to browse the interpretive center. While there, be sure to see the introductory film, which tells the captivating story of Norwegian explorer Helge Ingstad, who rediscovered the site in 1960, ending years of searching.

Also worthwhile is the 3km **trail** that winds through the barren terrain and along the coast surrounding the interpretive center.

Norstead   HISTORICAL VILLAGE

(📞709-623-2828; www.norstead.com; Rte 436; adult/child/family $10/6/30; 🕙9:30am-5:30pm Jun-late Sep) Can't get enough of the long-bearded Viking lifestyle? Stop by Norstead, just beyond the turnoff to the national historic site. It's a recreation of a Viking village with costumed interpreters (more than at L'Anse aux Meadows) smelting, weaving, baking and telling stories around real fires showing life at four buildings. Granted a bit savvy but they pull it off with class. There's also a large-scale replica of a Viking ship on hand.

DON'T MISS

TOP PLACES TO GET AWAY FROM IT ALL

» Fogo Island, Central Newfoundland (p478)

» Cape Onion, Northern Peninsula (p486)

» Conche, Northern Peninsula (boxed text, p489)

» François, South Coast Outports (p495)

» Torngat Mountains, Northern Labrador (p500)

🛏 Sleeping

Straitsview, Gunners Cove and St Lunaire-Griquet are all within 12km of the national historic site.

Tickle Inn   B&B $
(☎709-452-4321; www.tickleinn.net; Rte 437, Cape Onion; r with shared bathroom $65-85; ⊙Jun-late Sep; ➜) This delightful seaside inn, built in 1890, is surrounded by a white picket fence, oodles of grass and your own private beach. Sit in the parlor, feel the warmth of the Franklin woodstove and enjoy great home-cooked meals. The location is wonderfully remote.

Valhalla Lodge B&B   B&B $$
(☎709-623-2018, 877-623-2018; www.valhalla-lodge.com; Rte 436, Gunners Cove; r $90-100; ⊙mid-May–late Sep; ➜🛜) Set on a hill overlooking the ocean, the five-room Valhalla is only 8km from the Viking site. Put your feet up on the deck and watch icebergs in comfort. This very view inspired Pulitzer Prize–winning author E Annie Proulx while she wrote *The Shipping News* here.

Viking Village B&B   B&B $
(☎709-623-2238; www.vikingvillage.ca; Hay Cove, L'Anse aux Meadows village; r from $72; ➜🛜) A timbered home with ocean views, Viking Village offers comfy, quilted rooms just 1km from the Viking site. Ask for one of the rooms with balcony access and watch the sun rise.

Snorri Cabins   CABINS $$
(☎709-623-2241; www.snorricabins.com; Rte 436, Straitsview; cabins $89; ⊙Jun-Sep; 🛜) These modern cabins offer simple comfort and great value. They're perfect for families, with a full kitchen, sitting room and a pull-out sofa. There's a convenience store on-site.

St Brendan's Motel   MOTEL $
(☎709-623-2520; www.stbrendansmotel.com; Rte 436, St Lunaire-Griquet; s/d $75/80; ⊙Jun-mid-Oct; 🛜) This 11-room motel doesn't look like much, but the rooms (with TV, coffeemaker and refrigerator) are snug and the setting peaceful.

✕ Eating

TOP CHOICE **Norseman Restaurant & Art Gallery**   SEAFOOD $$$
(☎709-623-2018; www.valhalla-lodge.com; Rte 436, L'Anse aux Meadows village; mains $19-38; ⊙noon-9pm mid-May–late Sep) A casual, water-front room which may well be the best restaurant in Newfoundland. Relish the butternut squash soup, peruse a few veg-

etarian options or sink your teeth into tender Labrador caribou tenderloin. Norseman chills all its drinks with iceberg ice. Patrons who order lobster hand-pick their dinner by donning rubber boots and heading out front to the ocean, where the freshly caught crustaceans await in crates.

Daily Catch   SEAFOOD $$
(☎709-623-2295; www.thedailycatch.ca; 112 Main St, St Lunaire-Griquet; mains $11-20; ⊙11am-9pm) Set on the water overlooking a pretty bay, the Daily Catch is a stylish little restaurant serving finely prepared seafood and wine. The basil-buttered salmon gets kudos. Fish cakes, crab au gratin and cod burgers also please the palate.

Northern Delight   SEAFOOD $$
(☎709-623-2220; Rte 436, Gunners Cove; mains $9-15; ⊙8am-9pm) Dine on local favorites such as turbot cheeks and pan-fried cod, fresh lobster and mussels, or just have a 'Newfie Mug-up' (bread, molasses and a strong cup of tea). There's live music on some evenings.

St Anthony

Yeehaw! You've made it to the end of the road, your windshield has helped control the insect population and you have seen two World Heritage sites. After such grandeur, St Anthony may be a little anticlimactic. It's not what you'd call pretty, but it has a rough-hewn charm. And the hiking and whale- and iceberg-watching are inspiring.

Grenfell is a big name around here. Sir Wilfred Grenfell was a local legend and, by all accounts, quite a man. This English-born and educated doctor first came to Newfoundland in 1892 and, for the next 40 years, traveling by dog-sled and boat, built hospitals and nursing stations and organized much-needed fishing cooperatives along the coast of Labrador and around St Anthony.

◉ Sights & Activities

Grenfell Historic Properties
     HISTORICAL BUILDING
(www.grenfell-properties.com; West St; adult/child/family $10/3/22; ⊙9am-6pm mid-Jun–mid-Sep) A number of local sites pertaining to Wilfred Grenfell are subsumed under Grenfell Historic Properties. The **Grenfell Interpretation Centre**, opposite the hospital, is a modern exhibit recounting the historic and sometimes dramatic life of Grenfell.

Its **handicraft shop** has some high-quality carvings and artwork, as well as embroidered parkas made by locals – proceeds go to maintenance of the historic properties.

Grenfell Museum   MUSEUM
(☺9am-6pm mid-Jun–mid-Sep) Admission to the Properties also includes Grenfell's beautiful mansion, now the Grenfell Museum. It's behind the hospital, about a five-minute walk from the waterfront. Dyed burlap walls and antique furnishings envelop memorabilia, including a polar bear rug and, if rumors are correct, the ghost of Mrs Grenfell.

Fishing Point Park   PARK
The main road through town ends at Fishing Point Park, where a lighthouse and towering headland cliffs overlook the sea. The **Iceberg Alley Trail** and **Whale Watchers Trail** both lead to clifftop observation platforms – the names say it all.

A **visitors center–cafe & craft shop** is also out here; in the side room there's a **polar bear display** (admission $2). Creatures like this guy have been known to roam St Anthony from time to time as pack ice melts in the spring.

☞ Tours
Northland Discovery Tours WHALE-WATCHING
(☎709-454-3092, 877-632-3747; www.discover northland.com; 2½hr tours adult/child $55/20; ☺9am, 1pm & 4pm late May-late Sep) Northland offers highly recommended cruises for whale or iceberg viewing that leave from the dock behind the Grenfell Interpretation Centre on West St. If you tend to get seasick, medicate before this one.

🛏 Sleeping & Eating
Fishing Point B&B   B&B $$
(☎709-454-3117, 866-454-2009; www.bbcana da.com/6529.html; Fishing Point Rd; r $85; ☺🐾) This tiny place clings to the rocks en route to the lighthouse and offers the best harbor view in St Anthony. Get up early, enjoy a bountiful breakfast and watch the boats head out to sea. The three rooms each have their own bathroom.

THE SEAL HUNT DEBATE

Nothing ignites a more passionate debate than Canada's annual seal hunt, which occurs in March and April off Newfoundland's northeast coast and in the Gulf of St Lawrence around the Îles de la Madeleine and Prince Edward Island.

The debate pits animal rights activists against sealers (typically local fishers who hunt seals in the off-season), and both sides spin rhetoric like a presidential press secretary. The main issues revolve around the following questions.

Are baby seals being killed? Yes and no. Whitecoats are newborn harp seals, and these are the creatures in the horrifying images everyone remembers. But it's illegal to hunt them and has been for 20 years now. However, young harp seals lose their white coats when the seals are about 12 to 14 days old. After that, they're fair game.

Are the animals killed humanely? Sealers say yes, that the guns and/or clubs they use kill the seals humanely. Animal activists dispute this, saying seals are shot or clubbed and left on the ice to suffer until the sealers come back later and finish the job.

Is the seal population sustainable? The Canadian government says yes, and sets the yearly quota based on the total seal population in the area (estimated at 6.9 million). For 2010, the harp seal quota was 330,000. The 2009 quota was 280,000. Activists say the quotas don't take into account the actual number of seals killed in the hunt, such as those that are 'struck and lost,' or discarded because of pelt damage.

Is the seal hunt really an important part of the local economy? Activists say no, that it represents a fraction of Newfoundland's income. The province disagrees, saying for some sealers it represents up to one-third of their annual income. And in a province with unemployment near 15%, that's significant.

In 2009 the European Union banned the sale of seal products, which hurt the industry considerably. For further details on the two perspectives, see the websites of the **Canadian Sealers Association** (www.sealharvest.ca) and the **Humane Society of the United States** (www.protectseals.org).

Wildberry Country Inn INN $$
([✆]709-454-2662, 877-818-2662; www.wild berryadventures.com; Rte 430; r incl breakfast $75-95) Owner Lyndon Hodge hand-built this small, rustic lodge himself, and it's a winner. Hodge attempts to tread gently on the land (for instance, the on-site restaurant sources only local ingredients), and he knows the region like the back of his hand having lived here all his life. It's a bit of a trek from St Anthony, about 20km northwest on Rte 430.

Lightkeeper's Cafe CAFE $$
([✆]877-454-4900; Fishing Point Park; meals $8-20; [⊙]11:30am-8pm early Jun-Sep) This little gem of an eatery sits in the shadow of the lighthouse and is often graced by the sight of icebergs and whales. The chowder and scallops are legendary.

❶ Getting There & Away

Flying to St Anthony is technically possible, but the airport is nearly an hour away. If you're leaving St Anthony by car, you have two options: backtrack entirely along Rte 430, or take the long way via Rte 432 (see the boxed text, p489) along the east coast and Hare Bay. This will meet up with Rte 430 near Plum Point, between St Barbe and Port aux Choix.

WESTERN NEWFOUNDLAND

Western Newfoundland presents many visitors with their first view of The Rock, thanks to the ferry landing at Port aux Basques. It's big, cliffy, even a bit forbidding with all those wood houses clinging to the jagged shoreline against the roaring wind. From Port aux Basques, poky fishing villages cast lines to the east, while Newfoundland's second-largest town, Corner Brook, raises its wintry head (via its ski mountain) to the northeast.

Corner Brook

POP 20,100

Newfoundland's number-two town is pretty sleepy, though skiers, hikers and anglers will find plenty of action. The handsome Humber Valley, about 10km east, is where it's going on. Centered on the Marble Mountain ski resort, the area experienced a huge development boom – even Oprah was rumored to be buying one of the luxury condos – until the bottom fell out of the international economy. Maybe the vibe will ratchet up again one of these days. For now, the valley offers adventure sport junkies places to play, while the city itself sprawls with big-box retailers and a smoke-belching pulp and paper mill.

◉ Sights & Activities

Marble Mountain SKIING
([✆]709-637-7616; www.skimarble.com; Hwy 1; day pass $49; [⊙]10am-4:30pm Tue-Thu, 9am-9:30pm Fri, 9am-4:30pm Sat-Sun mid-Dec–early Apr) Marble Mountain is the lofty reason most visitors come to Corner Brook. With 35 trails, four lifts, a 488m vertical drop and annual snowfall of 5m, it offers Atlantic Canada's best skiing. There are snowboarding and tubing parks, as well

---

DRIFTING DOWN ICEBERG ALLEY

Each year 10,000 to 40,000 glistening icebergs break off Greenland's glaciers and enter the Baffin and Labrador currents for the three-year trip south to Newfoundland's famed 'Iceberg Alley.' This 480km-long, 98km-wide stretch of sea runs along the province's north and east coasts and is strewn with 'bergs in late spring and early summer. Fogo and Twillingate Islands in Notre Dame Bay and St Anthony on the Northern Peninsula are some of the best places for sightings. Even St John's is graced with a few hundred of the blue-and-white marvels most years (though sometimes the waters remain barren due to climate and current shifts).

To see where the behemoths lurk, check www.icebergfinder.com, the provincial tourism association's website showing where icebergs are floating; you can get weekly email updates on their locations and plan your trip accordingly. Also, the Canadian government's website www.ice-glaces.ec.gc.ca provides daily iceberg bulletins.

Locals harvest some smaller 'bergs, and if you ask in restaurants you may get a piece along with your drink. Considering the glacial ice may be more than 15,000 years old, it is indeed an ice cube to savor.

RTE 432 & THE FRENCH SHORE

Surprises await along lonely Rte 432. First is **Tuckamore Lodge** (☎709-865-6361, 888-865-6361; www.tuckamorelodge.com; r incl breakfast $140-180; ❷@☎), a wood-hewn, lakeside retreat with ridiculously comfortable beds and home-cooked meals, located smack in the middle of nowhere. You'll pass about 20 moose on your way out to it. Owner Barb Genge arranges all manner of activities (fishing, bird-watching, hunting, photography classes) with first-rate guides.

The little towns along the coast are known as the **French Shore** (www.frenchshore. com) for the French fishermen who lived in the area from 1504 to 1904. Top of the heap is **Conche** with its intriguing gaggle of sights: a **WWII airplane** that crashed in town in 1942, the seaside **Captain Coupelongue walking trail** past old French gravemarkers, and a crazy-huge **tapestry** in the local interpretation center. A woman named Delight runs the sunny **Bits-n-Pieces Cafe** (☎709-622-5400; mains $9-14; ⊙8am-8pm, to 9pm Thu-Sat), ladling out cod cakes, Thai chicken and other fare that's, well, delightful. Two simple rooms above the cafe comprise the **Stage Cove B&B** (www.stagecovebandb.ca; r $90; ☎) if you want to spend the night. It's about 68km from Tuckamore Lodge; take Rte 433 to unpaved Rte 434.

---

as night skiing on Friday, plus there's Oh My Jesus (you'll say it when you see the slope).

When the white stuff has departed, the **Steady Brook Falls Trail** (500m) leads from the ski area's rear parking lot, behind the Tim Hortons, to a cascade of water that tumbles more than 30m.

Marble Zip Tours   ZIP-LINE
(☎709-632-5463; www.marbleziptours.com; Thistle Dr; 3hr tours adult/child $79/69) It's the highest zip-line in Canada. Strap in near the mountaintop, and zigzag platform to platform down a gorge traversing Steady Brook Falls. It'll take your breath away. Tours depart three to four times daily. The company also arranges rock climbing, caving and fishing tours. The office is past Marble Mountain's lodge, behind the Tim Hortons.

My Newfoundland Adventures
                                            MULTISPORT
(☎709-638-0110, 800-686-8900; www. mynewfoundland.ca) If skiing doesn't get the adrenaline flowing, you must try snow-kiting (a windsurfing-meets-snowboarding endeavor). Or there's snowshoeing, ice fishing and even ice climbing. Canoeing, salmon fishing and caving all take place in the warmer seasons. There again, pretty much anything is possible with these patient folks; no experience is required. The office is at Marble Mountain's base by the Tim Hortons.

Blow-Me-Down Cross-Country Ski Park   CROSS-COUNTRY SKIING
(☎709-639-2754; www.blowmedown.ca; Lundigran Dr; day pass $13; ⊙sunrise-9pm early Dec-Apr) It has 50km of groomed trails; ski rentals (per day $12) are available. It's located about 6km southwest of downtown.

Captain James Cook Monument   PARK
(Crow Hill Rd) While this clifftop monument is admirable – a tribute to James Cook for his work in surveying the region in the mid-1760s – it's the panoramic view over the Bay of Islands that is the real payoff. Cook's names for many of the islands, ports and waterways you'll see, such as the Humber Arm and Hawke's Bay, remain today. The site is northwest of downtown via a convoluted route. Ready? Take Caribou Rd to Poplar Rd to Country Rd, then go right on Atlantic Ave, left on Mayfair Ave and follow the signs.

Railway Society of Newfoundland
                                            MUSEUM
(☎709-634-2720; Station Rd, off Humber Rd; admission $2; ⊙9am-9pm Jun-Aug) Within historic Humbermouth Station, the Railway Society of Newfoundland has a good-looking steam locomotive and some narrow-gauge rolling stock that chugged across the province from 1921 to 1939.

🛏 Sleeping

Bell's Inn   B&B $$
(☎709-634-1150, 888-634-1150; www.bellsinn. ca; 2 Ford's Rd; r $80-110; ❷☎) Gordon Bell's rambling green house tops a hill that's

Corner Brook

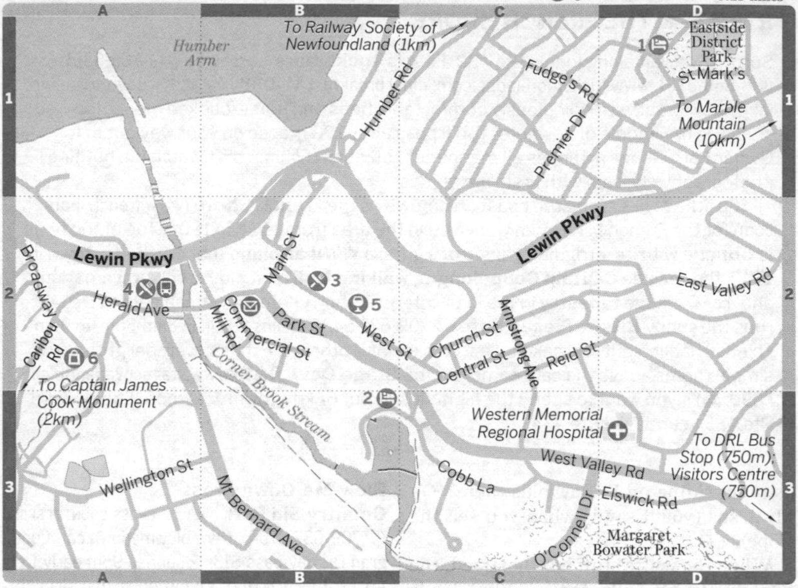

a 15-minute walk from downtown. The eight smallish, comfy rooms all have private bathroom; Nos 1 and 4 have harbor views. Sip your morning coffee on the breezy veranda.

Glynmill Inn HOTEL **$$**
(☎709-634-5181, 800-563-4400; www.glynmillinn.ca; 1 Cobb Lane; r $102-130; ❄@📶) Lawns, gardens and graciousness surround the Tudor-style Glynmill. It was built originally for the engineers supervising the pulp mill's construction in the 1920s, at that time the largest project in the history of paper making. The inn retains an elegant if somewhat faded ambience.

Two riverside B&Bs provide peace in the valley, a stone's throw from the ski area (about 10km east of Corner Brook).

Edgewater B&B (☎709-634-3474; www.visittheedge.com; 14 Forest Dr, Steady Brook; r $65-85; 🚭@📶) Four rooms.

Wilton's B&B (☎709-634-5796; www.wiltonsbandb.com; 57 Marble Dr, Steady Brook; r $69-89; 🚭📶) Three rooms.

✗ Eating & Drinking

Thistle's Place CAFE **$**
(☎709-634-4389; www.thistledownflorist.com; Millbrook Mall, Herald Ave; sandwiches $6-11; ⏲9am-5pm Mon-Sat; @📶) Walk through the front flower shop to reach the smoked meat, curried chicken and whole-wheat vegetable wraps at the wee cafe out the back.

Gitano's MEDITERRANEAN **$$**
(☎709-634-5000; www.thistledownflorist.com; Millbrook Mall, Herald Ave; tapas $7-13, mains $18-25; ⏲11:30am-2pm Mon-Fri, 5-10pm daily, to midnight Sat; 📶) Behind Thistle's and owned by the same family, Gitano's dishes up Spanish-themed mains such as *estofado* (stewed sweet potatoes, chickpeas and figs over couscous) and tapas (try the saltfish cakes) as well as pastas. Live jazz wafts through the supper club-esque room on weekends.

Bay of Islands Bistro NEW CANADIAN **$$$**
(☎709-634-1300; www.bayofislandsbistro.com; 13 West St; sandwiches $11-17, mains $30-37; ⏲11:30am-11pm, to midnight Sat, closed Mon; 📶) Inventive meals grace the plates at this hip bistro – say bacon and fava bean cushioned halibut for dinner, or a lobster and cornbread sandwich for lunch. Vegetarians will be pleased that they even get a couple of choices.

Corner Brook

Brewed Awakening   CAFE $$
(www.brewedawakening.ca; 35 West St; ⊙7am-10pm Sun-Wed, 7:30am-11pm Thu-Sat; 🛜) This small, funky, art-on-the-wall coffee shop pours fair-trade, organic java done right. It's attached to a bike shop that runs local cycling and caving tours.

🛍 Shopping
Newfoundland Emporium   SOUVENIRS
(☏709-634-9376; 7 Broadway) Step over Flossie, the owner's massive Newfoundland dog, to get at the local crafts, music, antiques and books found here.

ℹ Information
CIBC Bank (9 Main St)

Post office (14 Main St)

Visitors Centre (www.cornerbrook.com; cnr Confederation Dr & West Valley Rd; ⊙9am-5pm) Just off Hwy 1 at exit 5. Has a craft shop.

ℹ Getting There & Away
Corner Brook is a major hub for bus services in Newfoundland. **DRL** (☏709-263-2171; www.drl-lr.com) stops on the outskirts of town at the **Irving gas station** (Confederation Dr), just off Hwy 1 at exit 5 across from the visitors center.

All other operators use the **bus station** (☏709-634-2659; Herald Ave) in the Millbrook Mall building. The following are shuttle vans. Prices are one way. You must make reservations.

Burgeo Bus (☏709-886-6162, 709-634-4710) Runs to Burgeo ($38 cash only, two hours) departing at 3pm Monday through Friday. Leaves Burgeo between 8am and 9am.

Eddy's (☏709-643-2134) Travels to/from Stephenville ($20, 1¼ hours) twice daily on weekdays, once daily on weekends.

Gateway (☏709-695-2222, 709-695-7777) Runs to Port aux Basques ($33, three hours) on weekdays at 3:45pm. Departs Port aux Basques at 7:45am.

Martin's (☏709-453-7269) Operates weekdays, departing for Woody Point ($16, 1½ hours) and Trout River ($18, two hours) at 4:30pm. Returns from Trout River at 9am.

Star Taxi (☏709-634-4343) Picks up from various hotels en route to Deer Lake Airport ($22, 45 minutes) three to five times daily.

Viking 430 Shuttle (☏709-458-8186) Runs to Rocky Harbour ($20, two hours) via Deer Lake on weekdays at 4:15pm. Departs Rocky Harbour at 9am.

Around Corner Brook
BLOMIDON MOUNTAINS
The Blomidon Mountains (aka Blow Me Down Mountains), heaved skyward from a collision with Europe around 500 million years ago, run along the south side of the Humber Arm. They're tantalizing for hikers, providing many sea vistas and glimpses of the resident caribou population. Some of the trails, especially ones up on the barrens, are not well marked, so topographical maps and a compass are essential for all hikers.

Many trails are signposted off Rte 450, which runs west from Corner Brook along the water for 60km. One of the easiest and most popular is **Blow Me Down Brook Trail** (5km), which begins west of Frenchman's Cove at a parking lot. The trail can be followed for an hour or so; for more avid hikers it continues well into the mountains, where it becomes part of the International Appalachian Trail (IAT). The moderately difficult **Copper Mine Trail** (7km), by York Harbour, provides awesome views of the Bay of Islands and also links to the IAT.

Further on, **Blow Me Down Provincial Park** (☏709-681-2430; www.nlcamping.ca; Rte 450; campsites $15, per vehicle $5; ⊙late May-early Sep) has beaches and scenery.

STEPHENVILLE
As the drive into town past deserted hangars, piles of rusted pipes and tract housing portends, Stephenville is in the running for Newfoundland's least appealing town. There's not much reason to stop, except for the **Stephenville Theatre Festival** (www.stf.nf.ca). It sweeps into town during July and August toting along the Bard, Broadway and – to stir the pot – some cutting-edge Newfoundland plays.

ℹ️ NEWFOUNDLAND APPALACHIAN

Think the **International Appalachian Trail** ends in Québec just because it runs out of land at Cap Gaspé (see the boxed text, p304)? Think again. It picks up in Newfoundland, where another 1200km of trail swipes the west coast from Port aux Basques to L'Anse aux Meadows. The province has linked existing trails, logging roads and old rail lines through the Long Range Mountains, part of the Appalachian chain. It's a work in progress, but some of the most complete sections are around Corner Brook and the Blomidon Mountains. See www.iatnl.ca for trail details.

PORT AU PORT PENINSULA

The large peninsula west of Stephenville is the only French-speaking area of the province, a legacy of the Basque, French and Acadians who settled the coast starting in the 1700s. Today, the culture is strongest along the western shore between **Cape St George** and **Lourdes**. Here children go to French school, preserving their dialect, which is now distinct from the language spoken in either France or Québec.

In **Port au Port West**, near Stephenville, the gorgeous **Gravels Trail** (3km) leads along the shore, passing secluded beach after secluded beach. Nearby in Felix Cove, stop at **Alpacas of Newfoundland** (www.alpacasofnfld.ca; admission free; Rte 460; ⏱9am-6pm) and meet the fluffy namesake critters on a farm tour.

BARACHOIS POND PROVINCIAL PARK

This popular **park** (☎709-649-0048; www.nlcamping.ca; Hwy 1; campsites $15, per vehicle $5; ⏱mid-May–mid-Sep), sitting just south of Rte 480 on Hwy 1, is one of the few in the province to offer a backcountry experience. From the campground, the **Erin Mountain Trail** (4.5km) winds through the forest and up to the 340m peak, where there are backcountry campsites and excellent views. Allow two hours for the climb.

Not far away are a couple of leisurely nature trails and a nice swimming area.

Port aux Basques

POP 4320

It's all about the ferry in Port aux Basques. Most visitors come here to jump onto the Rock from Nova Scotia, or jump off for the return trip. That doesn't mean the town isn't a perfectly decent place to spend a day or night. Traditional wood houses painted brightly in aqua, scarlet and sea-green clasp the stony hills. Laundry blows on the clotheslines, boats moor in backyard inlets and locals never fail to wave hello to newcomers.

Port aux Basques (occasionally called Channel-Port aux Basques) was named in the early 16th century by Basque fishers and whalers who came to work the waters of the Strait of Belle Isle.

The town is a convenient place to stock up on food, fuel and/or money before journeying onward.

👁 Sights & Activities

Several scenic fishing villages lie to the east (see p493).

Grand Bay West Beach   BEACH

(Kyle Lane) Located a short distance west of town, the long shore is backed by grassy dunes, which are breeding grounds for the endangered piping plover. The **Cormack Trail** (11km) leaves from here and flirts with the coast all the way to John T Cheeseman Provincial Park.

Scott's Cove Park   PARK

(Caribou Rd) This park, with its restored boardwalk, candy-colored snack shacks and boat-shaped amphitheater, is the place to mingle with townsfolk and listen to live music.

Railway Heritage Centre   MUSEUM

(☎709-695-7560; off Hwy 1; museum $2, railcars $5; ⏱10am-8pm Jul & Aug) The center has two things going on. One is a museum stuffed with shipwreck artifacts. Its showpiece is the astrolabe, a striking brass navigational instrument made in Portugal in 1628. The device is in remarkable condition and is one of only about three dozen that exist in the world. Restored railway cars are the center's other facet.

🛏 Sleeping

With all the ferry traffic, reservations are a good idea.

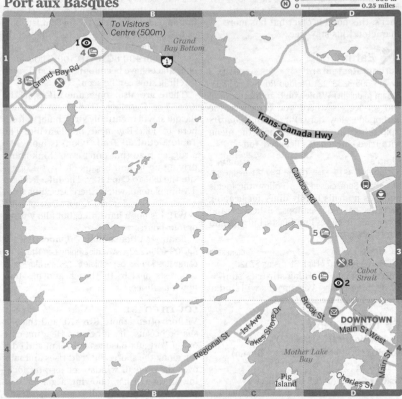

Radio Station B&B　　　　　B&B **$**

(☎709-695-2906; www.radiostationbedandbreak
fast.intuitwebsites.com; 100 Caribou Rd; r $69-
79; ☺May-Oct) Up on the bluff overlooking
the harbor, the five-room Radio Station
is the closest lodging to the ferry (a 10-
minute walk). Three rooms have their own
bathroom, the other two share, and there's
a kitchen for guest use.

Caribou B&B　　　　　　　B&B **$**

(☎709-695-3408; www.bbcanada.com/2225.
html; 42 Grand Bay Rd; r $70-80; ☺May-Sep;
☺☎) There's nothing fancy going on here,
but the five rooms are clean, bright and carpeted; two share a bathroom.

St Christopher's Hotel　　　HOTEL **$$**

(☎709-695-3500, 800-563-4779; www.stchrisho
tel.com; Caribou Rd; r $93-140; ✳☎) This is the
most professional digs in town, with a small
fitness room and a fine seafood restaurant
called the Captain's Room (meals $10 to $16,

Port aux Basques

⊚ Sights

1 Railway Heritage Centre	A1
2 Scott's Cove Park	D3

⊟ Sleeping

3 Caribou B&B	A1
4 Hotel Port aux Basques	A1
5 Radio Station B&B	D3
6 St Christopher's Hotel	D3

⊗ Eating

7 Alma's	A1
8 Harbour Restaurant	D3
9 Tai Hong	C2

open breakfast, lunch and dinner). Odd-
numbered rooms have harbor views.

Hotel Port aux Basques　　　HOTEL **$$**

(☎709-695-2171, 877-695-2171; www.hotelpab.

com; 1 Grand Bay Rd; r $85-120, ste $130; ❀❀)
The closest competition to St Christopher's, this hotel is older but has more
character. Kids stay free.

✗ Eating

Harbour Restaurant   CANADIAN $
(☎709-695-3238; 121 Caribou Rd; mains $8-15;
☺8am-midnight) While you'll get better food
and service elsewhere, you can't beat the
harborside view here. Pizzas and *donairs*
(spiced beef in pita bread) share the menu
with fried chicken. It's licensed, too.

Alma's   CANADIAN $
(☎709-695-3813; Mall, Grand Bay Rd; mains $7-
13; ☺8am-8pm, closed Sun) Follow the locals
into this no-frills family diner for heaping
portions of cod, scallops, fishcakes and
berry pies. It serves breakfasts, burgers and
sandwiches, too.

Tai Hong   CHINESE $
(☎709-695-3116; 77 High St; mains $7-12;
☺11am-10:30pm) Tai Hong stir-fries standard Chinese fare. Vegetarians will find a
couple of fried rice options.

❶ Information

Bank of Montréal (83 Main St)

Hospital (☎709-695-2175; Grand Bay Rd)

Post office (3 Main St)

Visitors Centre (☎709-695-2262; www.
portauxbasques.ca; Hwy 1; ☺6am-8pm mid-
May–mid-Oct) Information on all parts of the
province; sometimes open later to accommodate ferry traffic.

❶ Getting There & Away

The **Marine Atlantic ferry** (☎800-341-7981;
www.marine-atlantic.ca) connects Port aux
Basques with North Sydney in Nova Scotia
(adult/child/car $29/14.50/81.50). It operates
year-round, typically with two sailings daily
during winter and three or four sailings between
mid-June and mid-September. Crossings take
about six hours. The ferry terminal has no ATMs,
food or car rentals.

DRL (☎709-263-2171; www.drl-lr.com) has
its stop at the ferry terminal. Buses leave at 8am
for Corner Brook ($38, 3½ hours) and St John's
($112, 13½ hours); cash only.

Around Port aux Basques

CAPE RAY
Adjacent to John T Cheeseman Provincial
Park 14km north of town is Cape Ray. The

coastal scenery is engaging, and the road
leads up to the windblown **Cape Ray Lighthouse** (admission free; ☺8am-8pm late Jun-
early Sep, closed Mon). This area is the southernmost known Dorset Paleo-Eskimo site,
dating from 400 BC to AD 400. Thousands
of artifacts have been found here and some
dwelling sites can be seen.

There are also some fine **hikes** in the
area. The **Cormack Trail** (from Port aux
Basques) will eventually stretch north from
here to Flat Bay near Stephenville. The
Table Mountain Trail (12km) is more like
a rugged road (but don't even think about
driving up it) and begins on Hwy 1 opposite the exit to Cape Ray. The hike leads to
a 518m plateau, where there are ruins from
a secret US radar site and airstrip from
WWII. It's not a hard hike, but allow three
or four hours.

John T Cheeseman Provincial Park
(☎709-695-7222; www.nlcamping.ca; Rte 408;
campsites $15-23, per vehicle $5; ☺late May–mid-
Sep) rests next to the beach and has top-
notch facilities.

SOUTH COAST
Visitors often ignore Rte 470, and that's a
shame because it's a beauty. Heading east
out of Port aux Basques for 45km and edg-
ing along the shore, the road rises and falls
over the eroded, windswept terrain, looking as though it's following a glacier that
plowed through yesterday.

Isle aux Morts (Island of the Dead) got
its label compliments of the many shipwrecks that occurred just offshore over
some 400 years. Named after a family famous for daring shipwreck rescues, the
Harvey Trail (7km) twists along the rugged
shore and makes a stirring walk. Look for
the signs in town.

Another highlight is the last settlement
along the road, **Rose Blanche**, an absolutely splendid, traditional-looking village nestled in a cove with a fine natural harbor – a
perfect example of the classic Newfoundland fishing community. From here follow
the signs to the restored **Rose Blanche
Lighthouse** (www.roseblanchelighthouse.ca;
adult/child $3/2; ☺9am-9pm May-Oct). Built in
1873, it's the last remaining granite lighthouse on the Atlantic seaboard. Nearby, the
Friendly Fisherman Cafe (☎709-956-2022;
mains $8-14; ☺11am-9pm) serves huge por-
tions of fish and chips with a view out over
the coastal scenery.

For those without a vehicle, **Gateway** (☎709-695-3333) offers flexible van tours from Port aux Basques that visit Rose Blanche. Prices start at $90 and go up depending on how many villages you want to visit en route.

SOUTH COAST OUTPORTS

If you have the time and patience, a trip across the south coast with its wee fishing villages – called outports – is the best way to witness Newfoundland's unique culture. These little communities are some of the most remote settlements in North America, reachable only by boat as they cling to the convoluted shore. An anomaly is Burgeo (population 1600), connected by an easy road trip; it has an unspoiled, isolated feel, yet good amenities for travelers. Ramea (population 620) is another uncomplicated option. It's an island just offshore from Burgeo with lodging and activities.

Other outports along the coast include Grey River, François and McCallum. But hurry: the villages are dwindling fast as government pressure and lack of employment force residents to relocate to more accessible areas. The community of Grand Bruit was the latest to call it quits. Down to just 18 residents, they packed up and left for good in 2010.

◉ Sights & Activities

When the sun is out and the sea shimmers between endless inlets and islands Burgeo is a dream. Climb the stairs to **Maiden Tea Hill** and look out in admiration. The 7km of white-sand beaches at **Sandbanks Provincial Park** may be the best in the entire province (at least the piping plover who dawdle there think so).

Boat tours (2hr per person $25) and **sea-kayak rentals and tours** (per half-day single/double kayak $40/50, guide per hr $20) are available from Burgeo Haven B&B.

Author Farley Mowat lived in Burgeo for several years, until he penned *A Whale for the Killing* and pissed off the locals. The book tells the story of how Burgeo's townsfolk treated an 80-tonne fin whale trapped in a nearby lagoon. Let's just say the whale's outcome was not a happy one. Locals can point out the lagoon and Mowat's old house, though expect to get an earful about it.

The other outports are great areas for remote **camping**, **hiking** and **fishing**; ask locals or at the Visitors Centre in Port aux Basques about arranging a guide. Tiny **François**, surrounded by towering walls of rock, is particularly gorgeous.

🛏 Sleeping & Eating

Burgeo Haven B&B   B&B $$
(☎709-886-2544; www.burgeohaven.com; 111 Reach Rd, Burgeo; r $80-100; @🛜) Right across from Maiden Tea Hill, this large house backs onto an inlet and offers a serene setting. Some of the five rooms here have views.

Ramea Retreat   HOSTEL, B&B $
(☎709-625-2522; www.ramea.easternoutdoors. com; 2 Main St, Ramea; dm/r incl breakfast $30/59; ☺May-Nov; 🛜) The owners have 10 hostel beds at their lodge, where they arrange kayaking, bird-watching, hiking and fishing tours. In addition, they rent rooms in various vintage clapboard houses scattered around Ramea.

Gillett's Motel   MOTEL $$
(☎709-886-1284; www.gillettsmotel.ca; 1 Inspiration Rd, Burgeo; r $92; 🛜) The sole motel in town is, well, motel-like, with all the usual room amenities. It's just fine, as is the on-site Galley Restaurant (meals $7 to $15), where you'll eat cod likely caught that morning.

Sandbanks Provincial Park   CAMPGROUND $
(☎709-886-2331; www.nlcamping.ca; off Rte 480, Burgeo; campsites $15, per vehicle $5; ☺late May-mid Sep) Two thirds of the 26 camp sites here are nestled in the forest, while the remainder are in a grassy area. The flies can be brutal.

Joy's Place   CANADIAN $
(☎709-886-2569; Reach Rd, Burgeo; mains $6-11; ☺11am-11pm) Near Burgeo Haven B&B, Joy whips up fried chicken, Chinese dishes, burgers and pies in addition to her ever-present fish dishes.

ℹ Information

Burgeo (www.burgeonl.com)

ℹ Getting There & Away

Lonely, 148km-long Rte 480 shoots off Hwy 1 south of Corner Brook and then runs straight into Burgeo. Note there is no gas station and barely any civilization, just glacier-cut boulders and ponds and a whole lotta moose.

The Burgeo Bus (p491) shuttle van runs between Corner Brook and Burgeo just once per day.

Access to the other towns is by boat only. While the ferries run all year, the routes described here are for mid-May through September. Schedules change, so check with **Provincial Ferry Services** (☏709-292-4302; www.tw.gov.nl.ca/ferryservices). Note that the ferries do not take vehicles (except Burgeo to Ramea).

With careful planning a trip through the islands is doable.

Burgeo to Ramea ($3.75, 1½ hours) Departs twice per day; times do vary but there is usually one at around 11am and another in the evening.

Burgeo to Grey River to François ($7.50, five hours) Goes daily (except Tuesday and Thursday) at 1:45pm.

François to McCallum to Hermitage ($6.75, four hours) Departs on Thursday, but only at 7am.

At Hermitage, you'll have to suss out transportation back to Rte 360. You can then hook up with **Thornhill Taxi Service** (☏709-885-2144, 866-538-3429), which runs between Harbour Breton and Grand Falls, and connects with DRL in the latter.

LABRADOR

POP 27,000

It's called the Big Land, and with 293,000 sq km sprawling north toward the Arctic Circle, it's easy to see why. Undulating, rocky, puddled expanses form the sparse, primeval landscape. If you ever wanted to see what the world looked like before humans stepped on it, this is the place to head. Adding to the Great Northern effect, four huge caribou herds, including the world's largest (some 750,000 head), migrate across Labrador to their calving grounds each year.

Inuit and Innu have occupied Labrador for thousands of years, and until the 1960s the population was still limited to them and a few longtime European descendants known as 'liveyers.' They eked out an existence by fishing and hunting from their tiny villages that freckled the coast. The interior was virgin wilderness.

Over the past few decades, the economic potential of Labrador's vast natural resources has earned it a new degree of attention. Companies have tapped into the massive iron-ore mines in Wabush and Labrador City and the hydroelectric dam at Churchill Falls.

The simplest way to take a bite of the Big Land is via the Labrador Straits region, which connects to Newfoundland via a daily ferry. From there, a solitary road – the stark, rough Trans-Labrador Hwy – connects the interior's main towns. The aboriginal-influenced northern coast is accessible only by plane or supply ferry.

Labrador is cold, wet and windy, and its bugs are murderous. Facilities are few and far between throughout the behemoth region, so planning ahead is essential. Note that the Labrador Straits (not including the Québec portion) are on Newfoundland Time, while the rest of Labrador (starting at Cartwright) is on Atlantic Time, ie 30 minutes behind Newfoundland. Québec is on Eastern Time, which is an hour behind Atlantic Time. These variations can make ferry and airplane schedules a headache.

Labrador Straits

And you thought the Northern Peninsula was commanding? Sail the 28km across the Strait of Belle Isle and behold a landscape even more windswept and black-rocked. Clouds rip across aqua-and-gray skies, and the water that slaps the shore is so cold it's purplish. Unlike the rest of remote Labrador, the Straits region is easy to reach and exalted with sights such as Red Bay and Battle Harbour and a slew of great walking trails that meander past shipwreck fragments and old whale bones.

'Labrador Straits' is the colloquial name for the communities that make the southern coastal region of Labrador. Note that your first stop in the area will not actually be in Labrador at all, as the ferry terminal and airport are both in Blanc Sablon, Québec. Once in Labrador, Rte 510 is the road that connects the Straits' communities. South of Red Bay, it is sealed and open all year. From Red Bay north, it's hard-packed gravel and often closed in winter, depending on conditions. Check with the Department of Transportation & Works (☏709-729-2300; www.roads.gov.nl.ca).

BLANC SABLON TO L'ANSE AU CLAIR

After arriving by ferry or plane in Blanc Sablon and driving 6km northeast on Rte

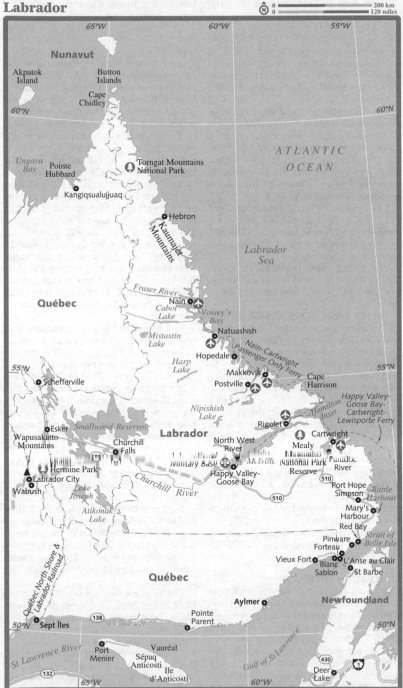

510 you come to Labrador and the gateway town of L'Anse au Clair. Here you will find the Straits' excellent **Visitors Centre** (☎709-931-2013, 877-931-2013; www.labradorcoastaldrive.com; Rte 510, L'Anse au Clair; ◷9am-5pm mid-Jun–mid-Oct) in an old church that doubles as a small museum. Be sure to pick up hiking trail information for the region.

The town makes a good pre-ferry base. Norm at **Beachside Hospitality Home** (☎709-931-2338; normanletto@yahoo.ca; 9 Lodge Rd; r with shared bathroom $48-58) plays the accordion for guests in the evening. Quilts await on the beds, while homemade jams await in the kitchen at this three-bedroom, two-bathroom B&B.

The modern, well-kept **Northern Light Inn** (☎709-931-2332, 800-563-3188; www.northernlightinn.com; 56 Main St; s/d $89/109; ✱⊛) is a tour-bus favorite. Even-numbered rooms have harbor views.

The **dining room** (mains $12-18; ◷7am-9pm Sun-Thu, to 10pm Fri & Sat) at the Northern Light Inn is your best bet for food in town.

The **MV Apollo** (☎709-535-0810, 866-535-2567; www.labradormarine.com; adult/child/car $7.50/6/15.25) sails the two hours between St Barbe in Newfoundland and Blanc Sablon between May and early January. The boat runs one to three times daily between 8am and 6pm. Schedules vary from day to day. In July and August, it's not a bad idea to reserve in advance (though there's a $10 fee). Note that the ferry terminal in Blanc Sablon operates on Newfoundland Time and not Eastern Time.

Provincial Airlines (www.provincialairlines.com) has flights to Blanc Sablon from St John's and St Anthony. Just to confuse you, departure times from the airport are on Eastern Time versus Labrador Straits (ie Newfoundland) Time.

Rental cars are available at the airport from **Eagle River Rent-a-Car** (☎709-931-3300, 709-931-2352).

FORTEAU TO PINWARE

Continuing northeast on Rte 510 you'll pass Forteau, L'Anse Amour, L'Anse au Loup, West St Modeste and Pinware.

Forteau-based Labrador Adventures (☎709-931-2055; chancock@tourlabrador.ca; tours $15-85) provides truly knowledgeable guides for Straits-oriented hikes or day tours by SUV. It also arranges all-inclusive overnight packages (from $240). This is a terrific way to see the area, especially if you're short on time or car-less.

In Forteau, the **Overfall Brook Trail** (4km) shadows the coast and ends at a 30m waterfall.

Six houses in total comprise the village of L'Anse Amour, but it holds more than its fair share of sights. **L'Anse Amour Burial Mound** (L'Anse Amour Rd), a pile of stones placed here by the Maritime Archaic Aboriginals, is the oldest burial monument in North America. A small roadside plaque marks the 7500-year-old site.

On the same road is **Point Amour Lighthouse** (☎709-927-5825; www.seethesites.ca; L'Anse Amour Rd; admission $3; ◷10am-5:30pm mid-May–late Sep). Taking four years to build and with 127 steps to climb, this is the tallest lighthouse in Atlantic Canada. When you reach the top, you will be rewarded with a spectacular 360-degree view of the coastline. The lighthouse keeper's house has exhibits on maritime history. The HMS *Raleigh* went aground here in 1922 and was destroyed in 1926. The **Raleigh Trail** (2km) takes you by the site and warship fragments on the beach.

Past L'Anse au Loup is the **Battery Trail** (4km), which meanders through a stunted tuckamore forest to the summit of the Battery, unfurling panoramic sea views.

The road veers inland at Pinware, and skirts along the western side of the Pinware River, until it crosses a one-lane iron bridge, and then runs along the eastern side, high above the rushing whitewater. This stretch of the Pinware is renowned for its **salmon fishing**. About 10km before reaching Red Bay, the land becomes rocky and barren, except for the superfluity of blueberries and bakeapples (and pickers) in August.

Forteau's **Grenfell Louie A Hall B&B** (☎709-931-2916; www.grenfellbandb.ca; Willow Ave; r $60-70; ◷May-Oct) is in the old nursing station where generations of Labrador Straits folk were born. The five simple rooms (a couple with sea views) share two bathrooms.

The **Seaview Restaurant** (Rte 510; mains $8-17; ◷9am-8pm) is nearby in Forteau. Chow down on the famous fried chicken and tender caribou. A grocery store and jam factory are also on-site.

Up and over the hills in L'Anse au Loup, **Dot's Bakery** (☎709-927-5311; Rte 510; breakfasts $4-6.50, pizzas $23; ◷7am-11pm

SCENIC DRIVE: QUÉBEC'S ROUTE 138

Yes, we know: it's the Newfoundland & Labrador chapter, but this drive is most easily accessed from Québec.

Route 138 (the Québec incarnation of Labrador's Rte 510) runs down the Lower North Shore, the name given to the wild, remote chunk of La Belle Province that extends south of Blanc Sablon. From the ferry landing until the road ends abruptly 65km later at Vieux Fort, Rte 138 makes a beautiful swing past several roadside **waterfalls** and lookouts from which to see the crashing surf and offshore **puffin colonies**.

For those wanting to do more than just drive through the region, **Tourism Lower North Shore** (www.tourismlowernorthshore.com) provides information on attractions and accommodations. For information on communities further south in Québec (reachable by boat or plane only), see the boxed text, p311.

Mon-Sat) caters to all your needs with her donuts, pies, breakfast dishes and pizzas.

RED BAY

Spread between two venues, **Red Bay National Historic Site** (☏709-920-2051; www.pc.gc.ca/redbay; Rte 510; adult/child/family $7.80/3.90/19.60; ☺9am-6pm early Jun–mid-Oct) uses different media to chronicle the discovery of three 16th-century Basque whaling galleons on the seabed here. Well preserved in the ice-cold waters, the vestiges of the ships tell a remarkable story of what life was like here some four centuries ago. Red Bay was the largest whaling port in the world, with more than 2000 people residing here. Have a look at the reconstructed *chalupa* (a small Basque dingy used for whale hunting) and some of the other relics in the museum. Then hop in a small boat ($2) to nearby **Saddle Island**, where there is a self-guided interpretive trail around the excavated land sites. Allow at least two or three hours for the museum and island.

Across the bay, the amazing **Boney Shore Trail** (2km) skirts along the coast and passes ancient whale bones (they pretty much look like rocks) scattered along it. The **Tracey Hill Trail** climbs a boardwalk and 670 steps to the top of American Rockyman Hill for a bird's-eye view of the harbor; it takes about 20 minutes each way.

Between the trails and the historic site, a 15m, 400-year-old **North Atlantic right whale skeleton** sprawls through the **Selma Barkham Town Centre** (admission $2; ☺9am-5pm Jul–mid-Sep).

Basinview B&B (☏709-920-2022; blancheearle@hotmail.com; 145 Main St; r $50-

80) is a simple four-room, shared bathroom home right on the water.

Remember, Red Bay is the end of the paved road. It's hard-packed gravel from here all the way to Labrador City.

BATTLE HARBOUR

Sitting on an island in the Labrador Sea is the elaborately restored village and salt-fish premises of **Battle Harbour** (☏709-921-6216; www.battleharbour.com; adult/child $9/4.50; ☺mid-Jun–mid-Sep). Now a national historic district, it used to be the unofficial 'capital' of Labrador during the early 19th century, when fishing schooners lined its docks. Another claim to fame: this is the place where Robert E Peary gave his first news conference after reaching the North Pole in 1909.

It's accessed by boat ($60 round-trip) from Mary's Harbour (departures 11am and 6pm, one hour) and you can come for the day or spend a few nights. Accommodations are spread among various heritage homes and cottages, operated by the **Battle Harbour Inn** (☏709-921-6325; www.battleharbour.com; r incl breakfast $125-155; ☺mid-Jun–mid-Sep). A store and **restaurant** (mains $9-18; ☺served at 8am, noon & 6pm) are on-site.

MARY'S HARBOUR TO CARTWRIGHT

After departing Mary's Harbour you'll pass through Port Hope Simpson 53km up the gravel road, and then there's nothing for 186km until Cartwright.

Cartwright-based **Experience Labrador** (☏877-938-7444; www.experiencelabrador.com; ☺Jul & Aug) runs kayaking trips that range from day paddles (six-hour tour $120) to multiday trips (three-day tour $840) along the northern coast, where you glide by the endless sands of the Wonderstrands that

BONKERS FOR BAKEAPPLES

You keep hearing about it: bakeapple jam, bakeapple pie, bakeapple syrup. But what's a bakeapple?

We'll tell you this much: it's not a red fruit that's been placed in the oven. Rather, a bakeapple (sometimes called a cloudberry) is an orangey-yellow fruit similar in shape and size to a large raspberry. It grows wild on small plants in moist northern tundra and bog lands – ie Labrador. The taste is often compared to apricot and honey.

Bakeapples ripen in mid-August, and that's when aficionados from Newfoundland pile over to the Labrador Straits and start picking. Get your fill – breakfast, lunch and dinner – at Forteau's **Bakeapple Folk Festival** (adult/child $5/3; ☻mid-Aug), a three-day event featuring music, dance, crafts and buckets of the eponymous fruit. Or buy bakeapple products at the Seaview Restaurant, where they're made on-site (see p498).

mesmerized the Vikings so long ago. The company also offers hiking, fishing and berry-picking tours.

The federal government recently created the **Mealy Mountains National Park Reserve** from 11,000 sq km of caribou-crossed boreal forest between Cartwright and Happy Valley–Goose Bay. Once the park gets up and running, paddlers, snowshoers, cross-country skiers and hikers will have access to an unblemished wilderness.

The simple **Cartwright Hotel** (☎709-938-7414; www.cartwrighthotel.ca; 3 Airport Rd, Cartwright; r $88-130; ☎) has 10 rooms, a **dining room** (mains $7-17; ☻6am-10pm) and a lounge.

Other than that, Cartwright is about the ferry. Passenger boats depart for the remote villages that sprinkle the Northern Coast. Vehicle ferries stop here on their route between Goose Bay and Lewisporte (see p479). **Labrador Marine** (☎709-535-0810, 866-535-2567; www.labradormarine.com) has the schedules.

Rte 510 continues west to Happy Valley-Goose Bay. Contact the **Department of Transportation & Works** (☎709-729-2300; www.roads.gov.nl.ca) for the latest conditions.

Northern Coast

North of Cartwright up to Ungava Bay there are a half-dozen small, semitraditional Inuit communities accessible only by sea or air along the rugged, largely unspoiled mountainous coast. Torngat Mountains National Park is the (literal) high point.

In 1993 on the shores of Voisey's Bay, near Nain, geologists discovered stunningly rich concentrations of copper, cobalt and especially nickel. A giant mine has been built to extract the goods, and it is expected to pump $11 billion into the provincial economy over 30 years. This likely will open up the north – for better or worse.

◉ Sights & Activities

The first port of call on the Northern Coast is **Makkovik**, an early fur-trading post and a traditional fishing and hunting community. Both new and old-style crafts can be bought.

Further north in **Hopedale** visitors can look at the old wooden Moravian mission church (1782). This **national historic site** (admission $5; ☻8:30am-8pm Jun-Sep) also includes a store, residence, some huts and a museum collection; it's all operated by the **Agvituk Historical Society** (☎709-933-3777).

Natuashish is a new town that was formed when the troubled village of Utshimassit (Davis Inlet) was relocated to the mainland in 2002. The move was made after a 2000 study showed that 154 of 169 youths surveyed had abused solvents (ie sniffed gasoline) and that 60 of them did it on a daily basis.

The last stop on the ferry is **Nain**, and it's the last town of any size as you go northward. Fishing has historically been the town's main industry, but this is changing due to the Voisey's Bay nickel deposit.

From Nain, you can try to arrange boat transportation to otherworldly **Torngat Mountains National Park** (☎709-922-1290; www.pc.gc.ca/torngat) at Labrador's wintry tip. The park headquarters is in town, and staff can direct you to local Inuit guides. The mountains are popular with climbers because of their altitude (some of the highest peaks east of the Rockies) and isolation. The **Kaumajet Mountains**, south of the park, also make for an out-of-this-world hiking experience.

🛏 Sleeping & Eating

Most travelers use the ferry as a floating hotel. For those wishing to get off and wait until the next boat, it usually means winging it for a room, as only Postville, Hopedale and Nain have official lodging.

Atsanik Lodge HOTEL $$
(☎709-922-2910; atsaniklabrador@msn.com; Sand Banks Rd, Nain; r $138-165; 🛜) This large, 25-room lodge and its restaurant (meals $14 to $19) are your best bet in Nain.

Amaguk Inn HOTEL $$
(☎709-933-3750; Hopedale; r $130-180; 🛜) This 18-room inn also has a dining room (meals $11 to $16), and a lounge where you can get a cold beer.

ℹ Getting There & Away

Provincial Airlines (www.provincialairlines.com) serves most of the northern coast's villages from Goose Bay.

The passenger-only MV *Northern Ranger* plies this section of coast from mid-June to mid-November. It leaves once per week, making the three-day (one way) journey between Happy Valley-Goose Bay and Nain, stopping in Makkovik, Hopedale and Natuashish along the way. Check with **Labrador Marine** (☎709-535-0810, 866-535-2567; www.labradormarine.com) for the ever-evolving schedule and fares.

Central Labrador

Making up the territorial bulk of Labrador, the central portion is an immense, sparsely populated and ancient wilderness. Paradoxically, it also has the largest town in Labrador, **Happy Valley-Goose Bay** (www.happyvalley-goosebay.com), home to a military base. The town (population 7570) has all the usual services, but unless you're an angler or hunter, there isn't much to see or do and it is very isolated.

Goose Bay was established during WWII as a staging point for planes on their way to Europe, and has remained an aviation center. The airport is also an official NASA alternate landing site for the space shuttle.

◉ Sights & Activities

FREE **Northern Lights Building** MUSEUM
(☎709-896-5939; 170 Hamilton River Rd; admission free; ⊙10am-5:30pm Tue-Sat) The Northern Lights Building hosts a military museum, interesting lifelike nature scenes and simulated northern lights.

FREE **Labrador Interpretation Centre** MUSEUM
(☎709-497-8566; www.therooms.ca/museum; 2 Portage Rd, North West River; admission free; ⊙noon-4:30pm Jun–mid-Sep, 1-4pm Wed-Sun rest of year) Officially opened by Queen Elizabeth II in 1997, the Labrador Interpretation Centre is the provincial museum, which holds some of Labrador's finest works of art. It's in North West River, via Rte 520.

🛏 Sleeping & Eating

Everything listed here is in Happy Valley-Goose Bay.

Royal Inn & Suites HOTEL $$
(☎709-896-2456; www.royalinnandsuites.ca; 5 Royal Ave; r incl breakfast $94-149; ✳🛜) The good-looking Royal has a variety of rooms to choose from; many of them have kitchens. The 'inn' side has wi-fi; the suites side has hard-wired high-speed access.

Davis' B&B B&B $
(☎709-896-5077; www.bbcanada.com/davisbb; 14 Cabot Crescent Rd; r $50-70; 🛜) Family atmosphere and caribou sausages await you at Davis' four-room home. It's near restaurants and amenities.

El Greco PIZZAS $$
(☎709-896-3473; 133 Hamilton River Rd; pizzas $16-22; ⊙4pm-1am Sun-Wed, to 3am Thu-Sat) This is a decent joint serving pizzas. It's near the Royal Inn.

ℹ Getting There & Away

Air

Air Canada (www.aircanada.com) flies to St John's and Gander. **Provincial Airlines** (www.provincialairlines.com) flies to St John's, Deer Lake and most towns around Labrador.

Boat

You can reach Goose Bay by two different ferries: the vehicle carrier MV *Robert Bond* (p479) and the passenger-only MV *Northern Ranger* (p501).

Car & Motorcycle

From Happy Valley-Goose Bay you can take gravel Rte 500 west to Churchill Falls and then on to Labrador City. The drive to Labrador City takes about 10 hours. There are no services until Churchill Falls, so stock up. The road can also be very, very rough. Rte 510 is the newly built gravel road heading southeast toward Cartwright (383km) and L'Anse au Clair (623km). Before leaving, contact the **Department of Transportation & Works** (☎709-729-2300; www.roads.gov.nl.ca) for the latest conditions.

Trucks can be rented at the airport from **National** (☎709-896-5575), but due to road conditions, you cannot buy insurance.

Labrador West

POP 9000

Just 5km apart and 15km from Québec, the twin mining towns of Labrador City (population 7250) and Wabush (population 1750) are referred to collectively as Labrador West, and this is where the western region's population is concentrated. The largest open-pit iron ore mine in the world is in Labrador City, and another-mine operates in Wabush. The landscape is massive and the celestial polychromatic artwork can expand throughout the entire night sky.

◎ Sights & Activities

Gateway Labrador MUSEUM
(☎709-944-5399; www.gatewaylabrador.ca; adult/child $3/2; ☉9am-9pm mid-Jun–Aug, reduced hours rest of year) In the same building as the visitors center is Gateway Labrador and its Montague Exhibit Hall, where 3500 years of human history and culture, including the fur trade, are represented with intriguing artifacts and displays.

Wapusakatto Mountains SKIING
The Wapusakatto Mountains are 5km from town, popping up off the vast landscape interspersed with flat northern tundra. A good, cold dry snow falls from late October to late April, so the ski season here is much longer than anywhere else in Canada. For trail information and fees for world-class cross-country skiing (the Canadian national team trains in the region), check with the **Menihek Nordic Ski Club** (☎709-944-5842; www.meniheknordicski.ca); for alpine skiing, check with the **Smokey Mountain Ski Club** (☎709-944-2129).

Grande Hermine Park PARK
(☎709-282-5369; admission $3; ☉Jun–mid-Sep) From Wabush, 39km east on Rte 500 is Grande Hermine Park, which has a beach and some fine scenery. The **Menihek hiking trail** (15km) goes through wooded areas with waterfalls and open tundra. Outfitters can take anglers to excellent fishing waters.

Mines MINE TOURS
(tours $10; ☉1pm Wed & Sun Jul-Sep) If big holes and trucks the size of apartment buildings make your heart flutter, you can tour the mines by contacting the visitors center.

🛏 Sleeping & Eating

PJ's Inn by the Lake B&B $
(☎709-944-3438; www.pjsinnbythelake.com; 606 Tamarack Dr, Labrador City; r $70-95; 🛜) Pete and Jo's home is your home: they'll let you use their treadmill, rowing machine and/or guitar. The B&B's six rooms each have their own bathroom; the Green Room has a Jacuzzi.

Wabush Hotel HOTEL $$
(☎709-282-3221; www.wabushhotel.com; 9 Grenville Dr, Wabush; r $119-124; ✳🛜) Centrally located in Wabush, this chalet-style 68-room hotel has spacious and comfortable rooms. The dining room (meals $9 to $21, open 6:30am to midnight) has a popular dinner buffet.

Carol Inn MOTEL $$
(☎709-944-7736, 888-799-7736; 215 Drake Ave, Labrador City; d $110; ✳🛜) All 20 rooms here have a kitchenette. There's also a fine dining room (meals $20 to $30, open 5:30pm Tuesday to Saturday), pub (meals $8 to $12, open 8am to midnight) and small pizza franchise.

ℹ Information

Destination Labrador (www.destination labrador.com)

Visitors Centre (☎709-944-5399; www.labradorwest.com; 1365 Rte 500) Just west of Labrador City, in the Gateway Labrador building.

ℹ Getting There & Away

Air
Air Canada (www.aircanada.com), **Provincial Airlines** (www.provincialairlines.com) and **Air Inuit** (www.airinuit.com) fly into the twin cities' airport (in Wabush).

Car & Motorcycle
Fifteen kilometers west from Labrador City along Rte 500 is Fermont, Québec. From there Rte 389 is mainly paved (with some fine gravel sections) and continues south 581km to Baie Comeau. Happy Valley-Goose Bay is a rough 10-hour drive east on Rte 500.

Budget (☎709-282-1234) has an office at the airport; rental cars may not be driven on Rte 500.

Manitoba

Best Places to Eat

» Tall Grass Prairie (p513)
» Segovia (p514)
» Reykjavik Bakery (p519)
» Gypsy's Bakery (p526)

Best Places to Stay

» Fort Garry Hotel (p512)
» River Gate Inn (p512)
» Solmundson Gesta Hus
Bed & Breakfast (p519)

Why Go?

The two prominent stars of Manitoba are Winnipeg, with its big-city sophistication and Churchill, with its profusion of natural wonders. But it's what lies between that truly defines this often misunderstood province. Open spaces of this prairie province seem to stretch forever – gently rolling fields of grain and sunflowers and wildflowers reach all the way north to Arctic tundra.

It's a land without pretence that imbues the unpretentious spirit of the locals. Its magnitude only fully appreciated while standing on the edge of a vivid yellow canola field counting three different storms on the horizon, or on the edge of Hudson Bay's rugged coastline counting polar bears while belugas play in the distance. Wander its empty roads, stop in its evocative little towns, find the subtle dramas in the land and expect surprises, whether it's a moose mewling in a bog or a future pop legend performing on stage.

When to Go
Winnipeg

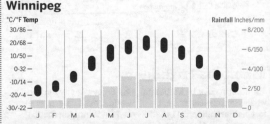

May Wildflowers line the roads and signal the end of a long winter.

June–August Days *can* be balmy but cool nights rule; at Churchill, 18°C is considered hot.

September Fall comes early and days are crisp; by October the north is under snow.

Manitoba Highlights

1 Revel in polar bears, beluga whales and even an ancient fort in **Churchill** (p524), the surprising sub-Arctic city that's difficult to get to

2 Hike and paddle Manitoba's best natural setting, **Riding Mountain National Park** (p521)

3 Enjoy big-city fun and world-class talent, prairie-style in **Winnipeg** (p505)

4 Discover small-town Manitoba in gems like charming **Neepawa** (p520), where time seems to stand still in some past idyllic era

5 Yeehaw with half the province at Canada's longest-running **Country Fest** (p522), just north of Riding Mountain National Park

6 Contemplate nature virtually surrounded by Lake Winnipeg at **Hecla-Grindstone Provincial Park** (p519)

7 Drive, lonely roads and stop for natural wonders like **Pisew Falls** (p524)

History

Tired of being labeled soft, early European explorers shunned the more hospitable south and braved the cold, rugged north coast of Hudson Bay. Indigenous Dene got involved in the fur trade soon after Hudson's Bay Company (HBC) established trading posts here in the 17th century.

British agricultural settlers moved to the future site of Winnipeg in 1811, creating constant friction with existing Métis over land rights. When HBC sold part of the land to the feds, Métis leader Louis Riel launched a rebellion and formed a provisional government. Negotiations between Riel and the federal government resulted in Manitoba joining the federation as Canada's fifth province in 1870.

Land & Climate

Manitoba's geography is as wide-ranging as you'll find anywhere in the country. Southern agricultural flatlands blend into green woodlands embracing Canada's largest lakes. Glacial footprints of potholed lakes, stubby vegetation and scraped-bare lands of the Canadian Shield characterize the north. Everywhere you go, the skies are massive.

The climate is just as variable and totally unpredictable. Average northern temperatures range from -50°C to summer highs of 20°C. Southern summers average 25°C dropping to -15°C during winter. Notoriously strong winds all year create summer dust storms, even the occasional tornado, and winter blizzards where wind chills make it feel 30 degrees colder than it is. Spring flooding is common in southern areas, and there is nothing like an intense prairie summertime thunderstorm.

Parks & Wildlife

It can't be overstated: every kind of popular Canadian animal can be seen here. Moose, beaver, bear, lynx, deer, caribou, fox, rabbit and so on. And of course the real stars: Churchill's polar bears.

Riding Mountain National Park is a microcosm of Manitoba ecology, while Wapusk National Park defines raw wilderness. *Manitoba Provincial Parks Guide*, published by **Manitoba Parks** (☑800-214-6497; www.manitobaparks.com; vehicle admission per day/year $6/25, tent sites $7-14, RV sites $11-18), is available at visitor information centers. Reserve ahead with the **Parks Reservation System** (☑888-482-

TOURIST INFO

Travel Manitoba (☑800-665-0040; www.travelmanitoba.com) is an invaluable resource. In addition to seasonal booths (⊙8am-9pm late May–early Sep) at major highway entrances into the province, it also operates the Explore Manitoba Centre (p517) in Winnipeg.

Bed & Breakfast of Manitoba (www.bedandbreakfast.mb.ca) lists dozens of B&Bs.

505

MANITOBA

2267; www.manitobaparks.com), as campgrounds often fill up.

ℹ Getting There & Around

Major **airlines** connect Winnipeg with the main Canadian cities and US Midwest hubs. Calm Air serves northern communities; Kivalliq Air flies Winnipeg to Churchill and Nunavut; and Bearskin Airlines flies to Ontario. For contact details, see p882.

Manitoba shares more than a dozen US–Canada vehicle border crossings with North Dakota and Minnesota. There are several routes into Saskatchewan, but only the Trans-Canada Hwy (Hwy 1) leads into Ontario. Southern Manitoba's tight road network disappears heading north, where Hwy 10 or Hwy 6 are the only options and services are few (watch your gas gauge).

VIA Rail's *Canadian* (p888) passes through Winnipeg and southern communities three times a week. Also out of Winnipeg, the two- or three-times-a-week sclerotic service to subarctic Churchill. See p527 for more details.

WINNIPEG

POP 657,900

Winnipeg surprises. Rising above the prairie, it's a metropolis where you least expect it. Cultured, confident and captivating, it's more than just a pit-stop on the Trans-Canada haul, it's a destination in its own right. Wander its historic neighborhoods

MANITOBA FAST FACTS

» Population: 1,178,500

» Area: 552,369 sq km

» Capital: Winnipeg

» Quirky fact: Manitobans are the highest per capita consumers of 7-Eleven slurpees in the world

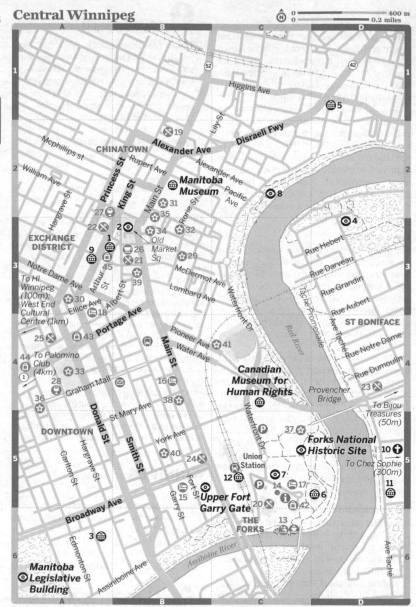

and lap up a vibe that enjoys being the butt of a *Simpsons* joke ('That's it! Back to Winnipeg!'), inspired Guy Maddin's haunting and hallucinatory 2007 film *My Winnipeg* and revels in one of the world's best fringe theater festivals.

History

An aboriginal hub for 6000 years and center of the 19th-century fur trade rivalry between HBC and North West Company, the confluence of the Assiniboine and Red Rivers had little choice in any other official

MANITOBA

name than the Europeanized *win nipee* (Cree for 'muddy waters').

French settlers established the neighborhood of St Boniface, birthplace of the controversial Métis leader Louis Riel.

The railroad's arrival in 1886 solidified Winnipeg's commercial importance, later rendered moot by the opening of the Panama Canal. Winnipeg subsequently stagnated, although a landmark general strike in 1919 helped raise union recognition across Canada. Today it has a diverse economy and modest growth. Its two most notable brands are Canwest, the conser-

vative company that runs scores of major newspapers, and Old Dutch, the potato chip maker.

◉ Sights & Activities

Winnipeg is mostly concentrated around the walkable downtown area; other sights are reached most easily by vehicle.

'Portage and Main' marks the center of downtown and is famous for incredibly strong winds and frigid temperatures – Randy Bachman and Neil Young wrote a song about it, 'Prairie Town,' with the chorus repeating the line 'Portage and Main, 50 below.'

OH POOH!

Winnie the Pooh actually gets his name from Winnipeg. In WWI a Canadian soldier had a bear cub as a mascot. While passing through London on the way to the front, he gave it to the London Zoo for safe-keeping where it became known by an abbreviated version of the soldier's hometown of Winnipeg. In the 1920s AA Milne visited the zoo with his son Christopher Robin and subsequently named his fictional bear Winnie the Pooh.

To the north, 1900s limestone architecture marks the warehouse-and-arts Exchange District. South of downtown is The Forks and across the Red River is the French neighborhood of St Boniface; west of there is the very scrollable Osborne Village and Corydon Ave.

DOWNTOWN

Manitoba Legislative Building

NOTABLE BUILDING

(Map p506; ☑204-945-5813; 450 Broadway Ave; admission free; ⊙9am-6pm Mon-Fri, tours hourly Jul–early Sep) Designed during Winnipeg's optimistic boom of the early 20th century, this building flaunts neoclassical beaux-arts design, limestone construction and governmental importance above the Red River. Surrounded by impeccable lawns and gardens, ancient gods and contemporary heroes are immortalized, including the Louis Riel monument facing St Boniface. 'Eternal Youth and the Spirit of Enterprise' – aka Golden Boy – shines his 23½-carat gold-covered splendor atop the oxidized copper dome.

Winnipeg Art Gallery

ART GALLERY

(WAG; Map p518; ☑204-786-6641; www.wag.ca; 300 Memorial Blvd; adult/child $8/4; ⊙11am-5pm Tue, Wed & Fri-Sun, to 9pm Thu) This ship-shaped gallery plots a course for contemporary Manitoban and Canadian artists, including the world's largest collection of Inuit work. Relax in the lovely rooftop cafe.

Plug In Institute of Contemporary Arts

ART GALLERY

(Map p506; ☑204-942-1043; www.plugin.org; 460 Portage Ave) Contemporary art rules at this gallery with new quarters near WAG. Check for hours.

Dalnavert Museum

MUSEUM

(Map p506; ☑204-943-2835; www.mhs.mb.ca/info/museums/dalnavert; 61 Carlton St; adult/child $5/3; ⊙10am-5pm Wed-Fri, 11am-6pm Sat, noon-4pm Sun) Restored to its original 1895 Queen Anne Revival architectural style, this museum is the former home of Sir Hugh John MacDonald, son of Canada's first prime minister. It's furnished with original pieces.

Upper Fort Garry Gate

HISTORICAL SITE

(Map p506; 130 Main St) Saved from Philistine developers, the original 1830s oak, stone and mortar walls stand where four different forts have stood since 1738. Good informative plaques and shady benches amidst the urban bustle.

THE FORKS

Strategically important and historically significant, the meeting place of the muddy and small Assiniboine River and the muddy and large Red River has been drawing people for millennia.

It's the focus for many visitors and combines several distinct areas. Parks Canada runs a historic site amidst beautifully landscaped parks. Nearby, old railway shops have been converted into the **Forks** (☑204-957-7618; www.theforks.com), a very touristy collection of shops, cafes and restaurants in renovated old buildings.

Meanwhile, Winnipeg's next major attraction, the **Canadian Museum for Human Rights** (Map p506; www.humanrightsmuseum.ca), is set to open in 2012 on a high-profile site near Provencher Birdge. Housed in a stunning new glass building, the $310 million complex will be the first national museum outside of Ottawa. The focus will be human rights, as they relate to Canada, its culture and the rest of the world.

WINNIPASS

To save loonies, buy a **Winnipass** (www.heartlandtravel.ca/winnipass; adult $30), with access to six of Winnipeg's major attractions.

Forks National Historic Site HISTORIC PARK
(Map p506; ☑204-983-6757; www.parkscanada.
ca/forks) In a beautiful riverside setting,
modern amenities for performances and
interpretive exhibits outline the area's history. Footpaths line the riverbank; plaques
offer historical context.

The rivers routinely overflow during
spring runoff and flooded pathways are
not uncommon, an event as exciting as it
is dangerous. Follow the waterways with
a canoe from **Splash Dash** (Map p506;
☑204-783-6633; rental per 30/60min $10/18;
☺11am-9pm Jun-Aug).

Tours are available by foot and by boat
(see p511).

Wintertime fun involves **ice skating** on
the river and **cross-country skiing** the
pathways.

Winnipeg Railway Museum MUSEUM
(Map p506; ☑204-942-4632; www.wpgrailway
museum.com; 123 Main St, adult/child $5/3;
☺11am-4pm daily May-Oct, 11am-4pm Sat & Sun
Apr & Oct) Winnipeg's gorgeous and unde-
rused Union Station (opened in 1911 and
designed by the same firm that did New
York's Grand Central Terminal) houses a
small collection of historic Canadian railway cars, gear and model trains.

EXCHANGE DISTRICT

Restored century-old brick buildings are
the backdrop to the **Exchange District**
(www.exchangedistrict.org), Winnipeg's most
vibrant neighborhood downtown. Hipsters,
scenesters and vagrants congregate amid
heritage buildings housing restaurants,
clubs, boutiques and art galleries. Declared
a National Historic Site; walking tours (see
p511) provide context.

The grassy haven of **Old Market Square**
is the neighborhood focal point. There's live
music at the new, controversially modern
Cube (Map p506).

Manitoba Museum MUSEUM
(Map p506; ☑204-956-2830; www.manitoba
museum.ca; 190 Rupert Ave; main galleries adult/child $8.50/7, combined ticket
$19/13.50; ☺10am-5pm daily Jun-Aug, 10am-
4pm Tue-Fri, 11am-5pm Sat & Sun Sep-May) Nature trips through the sub-Arctic, history
trips into 1920s Winnipeg, cultural journeys covering the past 12,000 years – if it
happened in Manitoba, it's here. Amidst
the superb displays are a planetarium
and an engaging science gallery. A new
exhibit shows what Churchill was like as

a tropical jungle, a mere 450 million years
ago.

The Exchange District abounds in galleries.

Ace Art ART GALLERY
(Map p506; ☑204-944-9763; www.aceart.org;
290 McDermot Ave; ☺noon-5pm Tue-Sat) With
several other galleries, focuses on contemporary art.

Artspace ART GALLERY
(Map p506; ☑204-947-0984; 100 Arthur St;
☺9am-6pm Tue-Sat) A renovated warehouse
provides studios and galleries for Winnipeg's talents.

Graffiti Gallery ART GALLERY
(Map p506; ☑204-667-9960; www.graffiti
gallery.ca; 109 Higgins Ave; ☺noon-5pm Mon-
Sat) Aims to redirect young artists from
vandalism to sanctioned public art.

Urban Shaman ART GALLERY
(Map p506; ☑204-942-2674; www.urban
shaman.org; 290 McDermot Ave; ☺noon-5pm
Tue-Sat) A noted gallery displaying contemporary Canadian aboriginal art.

ST BONIFACE

Canada's oldest French community outside
of Québec sits just across the Red River
from The Forks.

Visitor information centers have an excellent historical self-guided walking map.
Taché Promenade follows the Red River
along Ave Taché, past many of St Boniface's
historical sites.

St Boniface Basilica HISTORICAL SITE
(Map p506; 151 Ave de la Cathédrale) Mostly destroyed by fire in 1968, the original facade
still stands as a 100-year, imposing, God-
fearing reminder of the basilica, that once
stood here. A more current structure was
rebuilt on the ruins and Louis Riel (p510)
rests in the cemetery.

St Boniface Museum MUSEUM
(Map p506; ☑204-237-4500; msbm.mb.ca;
494 Ave Taché; adult/child $5/4; ☺9am-5pm
Mon-Fri, noon-4pm Sat & Sun mid-May–Sep,
9am-noon Mon-Fri, noon-4pm Sun Oct–mid-May)
Next to the Basilica, a mid-19th-century
convent is Winnipeg's oldest building and
the largest oak-log construction on the
continent. The museum inside focuses on
the establishment of St Boniface, the birth
of the Métis nation, and the Grey Nuns'
3000km journey.

Fort Gibraltar HISTORIC PARK

(Map p506; ☑204-237-7692; www.fortgibraltar. com; 866 Rue St Joseph; adult/child $5/4; ☉10am-6pm Wed-Sun mid-May–Aug) Behind the wooden walls sits this re-created 1809 fur trade fort. Along with inspired interpreters, real clothes, tools, furs, bunks, bannock and blacksmith shops create 1810 life at The Forks, the fort's original location.

GREATER WINNIPEG

Royal Canadian Mint MUSUEM

(Map p518; ☑204-257-3359; www.mint.ca; 520 Blvd Lagimodière; tours adult/child $5/3; ☉9am-5pm daily Jun-Aug, 9am-5pm Mon-Fri Sep-May) Producing loonies to the tune of billions of dollars, this high-tech mint produces money for Canada and 60 other nations. Tour the pyramid-shaped glass facility to see how money is made (the greatest action occurs on weekdays). It is 9km southeast of the centre.

Riel House HISTORICAL SITE

(Map p518; ☑204-257-1783; www.parkscanada. ca/riel; 330 River Rd; adult/child $4/2; ☉10am-5:30pm mid-May–early Sep) After Louis Riel's 1885 execution for treason (p510), his body was brought to his family home before being buried in St Boniface Basilica. Riel grew up on this farm in a cabin by the river; the 1880s house now on display housed his descendents as recently as the 1960s! Now surrounded by subdivisions, the house is 9km south of the center.

Living Prairie Museum NATURE RESERVE

FREE (Map p518; ☑204-832-0167; www.liv ingprairie.ca; 2795 Ness Ave; ☉10am-5pm Jul & Aug, 10am-5pm Sun May & Jun) Protects 30 acres of original, unploughed, now-scarce, tall prairie grass. Self-guided tours from the nature center show the seasons of wildflowers across what was once an ocean of color across the Prairie Provinces and which supported millions of bison.

Fort Whyte NATURE RESERVE

(Map p518; ☑204-989-8355; www.fortwhyte.org; 1961 McCreary Rd; adult/child $6/4; ☉9am-5pm Mon-Fri, 10am-5pm Sat & Sun) A vast, trail-laced natural site with an eco-focus, you can spot bison, deer and other wildlife here. Learn about sod houses and rent seasonal **activity gear** (buggy/snowshoes/canoe/row-boat per hour $12/1/10/10). Even better, in winter, toboggans are free. It's 13km southwest of the center.

Ross House HISTORICAL BUILDING

(Map p518; ☑204-943-3958; www.mhs.mb.ca; Joe Zuken Heritage Park, 140 Mead St N; admission free; ☉10am-5pm Wed-Sun Jun-Aug) The small log cabin where William Ross ran the west's first post office is in a pretty setting and documents pioneer life in the 1850s.

SPIRIT OF PRAIRIE: LOUIS RIEL

Born in 1844 on the Red River near today's Winnipeg, Louis Riel became a leader of the Métis, people like him who are a mixture of Aboriginal and European backgrounds. He literally battled for the rights of the Métis, who were often trampled by the westward expansion of Canada. He helped lead the Red River Rebellion, which brought Manitoba into the Canadian Confederation in 1870 and gave the Métis political power, but which also drove Riel to political exile in the US.

In 1884 he returned to Canada, this time to Saskatchewan to lead Aboriginal and Métis people fighting for their rights at Batoche. A mesmerizing speaker, by now Riel had also proclaimed himself a religious prophet and was prone to mood swings. In 1885 he almost defeated the Canadian military but instead was tried for treason and hanged.

Riel's legacy is complex. His French roots make him a powerful name in Quebec and his reputation in Manitoba only grows. The third Monday of February was made a provincial holiday in his honor in 2008.

You can find numerous legacies of Riel in Manitoba and Saskatchewan:

» His birthplace and the family house where he was taken after his execution (p510).

» His grave (p509).

» A seasonal play which dramatizes his trial for treason (p533).

» Batoche, the haunting site of his last battle (p546).

Right in The Forks, kids learn by doing at **Manitoba Children's Museum** (Map p506; ☎204-924-4000; www.childrensmuseum.com; 45 Forks Market Rd; admission $7; ⊙9:30am-6pm), where 'hands off' is not part of the program. The colorful, interactive exhibits encourage tykes to act as train conductors, astronauts and TV producers. Huge new exhibits – including a cool playground next door – were scheduled to open in 2011.

Also in The Forks, the much-heralded **Manitoba Theatre for Young People** (Map p506; ☎204-942-8898; www.mtyp.ca; 2 Forks Market Rd; tickets $10-12; ⊙Oct-May) uses colorful sets for enthusiastic performances for kids without being too treacley for adults.

Kids get the chance to play pilot or air traffic controller at the **Western Canadian Aviation Museum** (Map p518; ☎204-786-5503; www.wcam.mb.ca; 958 Ferry Rd; adult/child $7.50/3; ⊙10am-4pm Mon-Sat, 1-4pm Sun) amidst planes from the past 90 years.

Some 1800 animals populate **Assiniboine Park Zoo** (Map p518; ☎204-986-2327; www.zoosociety.com; 460 Assiniboine Park Dr; adult/child $5/2.50; ⊙10am-6pm Jul & Aug, shorter hr other times), which specializes in animals that are indigenous to harsh climates. However a recent scheme to build a Polar Bear Conservation Centre has generated a lot of controversy for its plans to capture wild bears and sell them to other zoos.

Kids also love the critters and activities at Fort Whyte (p510).

Manitoba Museum's Science Gallery (p509) is a hit with kids, as is Oak Hammock Marsh (pinned) with its interactive exhibits and computer games.

👉 Tours

Destination Winnipeg and Tourisme Riel have themed self-guided tours; also check out **Routes on the Red** (www.routesonthered.ca), which has a variety of downloadable tours for the Winnipeg area.

Historic Exchange District Walking Tours (☎204-942-6716; www.exchangedistrict.org; adult/child $7/free; ⊙call for times) Themed and history tours departing from Old Market Sq.

Muddy Water Tours (☎204-898-4678; www.muddywatertours.com; adult/child $10/4; ⊙call for times & locations) Numerous entertaining and historically-themed walking tours, including the popular 'Murder, Mystery & Mayhem' and 'Pestilence, Shamans & Doctors' depart on regular schedules all summer. 'Symbols, Secrets & Sacrifices Under the Golden Boy' is a much-acclaimed look at the hidden meanings in the capital.

Paddlewheel Riverboats (Map p506; ☎204-944-8000; www.paddlewheelcruises.com; cnr Alexander Ave & Waterfront Dr; adult/child $18/9.25; ⊙May-Oct) Afternoon (1pm), sunset and moonlight paddlewheel cruises.

Splash Dash (Map p506; ☎204-783-6633; adult/child $10/9; ⊙10am-sunset mid-May-mid-Oct) Has 30-minute tours of the river from The Forks.

The Forks Walking Tours Parks Canada offers two walks: **6000 Years in 60 Minutes** (☎204-983-6757; www.parkscanada.ca/forks; adult/child $4/free; ⊙10am, 1pm & 3pm Tue, Thu & Sun Jul & Aug), which uses costumed tour guides tell the local 6000-year history, and **The Forks Uncovered** (⊙10am, 1pm & 3pm Mon, Fri & Sat Jul & Aug), an archeological-themed walk. Tours leave from the Explore Manitoba Centre.

🎊 Festivals & Events

Festival du Voyageur (☎204-237-7692; www.festivalvoyageur.mb.ca; ⊙mid-Feb) Winnipeg's signature event. Everyone gets involved in the 10-day festival celebrating fur traders and French *voyageurs*. Centered around Fort Gibraltar, enjoy concerts, dog-sled races and *joie de vivre*.

Winnipeg Pride (www.pridewinnipeg.com; ⊙early Jun) Ten-day gay and lesbian celebration.

Winnipeg Fringe Festival (☎204-943-7464; www.winnipegfringe.com; ⊙mid-Jul) North America's second-largest fringe fest; the comedy, drama, music and cabaret are often wildly creative, raw and great fun. Watch for perennial star Jason Brasher.

Winnipeg Folk Festival (📞204-231-0096; www.winnipegfolkfestival.ca; ⊙mid-Jul) More than 200 concerts on seven stages in Birds Hill Provincial Park.

Folklorama (📞204-982-6230; www.folklorama.ca; ⊙early Aug) Longest-running multicultural event of its kind in the world. Performances, story-telling and more in pavilions representing various cultures across town.

Manito Ahbee (📞204-956-1849; www.manitoahbee.com; ⊙early Nov) A huge celebration of Aboriginal culture that draws participants from across the globe.

🛏 Sleeping

You'll find plenty of chain motels on main routes around Winnipeg and near the airport, but there's no reason not to stay downtown, where you can easily explore on foot.

Fort Garry Hotel `TOP CHOICE` HOTEL $$
(Map p506; 📞204-942-8251, 800-665-8088; www.fortgarryhotel.com; 222 Broadway Ave; r $120-200; ❄@🛜≋) Winnipeg history radiates from this locally owned 1913 limestone legacy that's like something out of a movie. Built as one of Canada's chateau-style railway stopovers, the grand foyer embodies the hotel's spirit: look for historical photographs lining the walls. Upstairs the rooms are comfortable if a tad fusty, although that only adds to the charm. Vintage touches include coffee requests you clip to your door. The free breakfast buffet is a delight.

River Gate Inn B&B $$
(Map p518; 📞204-474-2761; www.rivergateinn.com; 186 West Gate r $80-140; P❄@🛜≋) The mansion you'd enjoy if you lived in Winnipeg and were rich. This 1919 estate has a large pool surrounded by huge elms, various porches and common rooms plus amenities like free beverages and snacks around the clock. The five rooms contain traditional decor. A pleasant stroll will take you over the river to the Corydon and Osbourne Village neighborhoods.

Humphry Inn HOTEL $$
(Map p506; 📞204-942-4222, 877-486-7479; www.humphryinn.com; 260 Main St; r $80-$160; P❄@🛜≋) Formerly a Hampton Inn, this modern, six-story hotel is perfectly located downtown. Rooms are large and nicely appointed with fridges and microwaves, get one facing east for good views. The free breakfast buffet is large.

Norwood Hotel HOTEL $$
(Map p518; 📞204-233-4475, 888-888-1878; www.norwood-hotel.com; 112 Marion St; r $80-120; P❄@🛜) A friendly, family-owned five-story modern hotel. Containing 52 spacious rooms with a newish, soothing decor. It's just a short walk across the St Mary's Road Bridge to The Forks and downtown.

Malborough Hotel HOTEL $$
(Map p506; 📞204-942-6411, 800-667-7666; www.themarlborough.ca; 331 Smith St; r $70-100; ❄🛜≋) Goth-Renaissance design and open common spaces characterize this heritage building. Though parts of it smell, the building is 90 years old and it has a prime location. Renovations are ongoing (the pool now has a slide!), you may wish to see a few of the 148 rooms before deciding.

Inn at the Forks HOTEL $$$
(Map p506; 📞204-942-6555, 877-377-4100; www.innforks.com; 75 Forks Market Rd; r $150-250; ❄@🛜) With a vaguely *Mad Men*-esque look, modern style comes to Winnipeg's oldest real estate. Funky bathrooms and solid colors are in 117 spacious rooms. Enjoy river views and the services of a high-end spa.

HI Winnipeg HOSTEL $
(Map p506; 📞204-772-3022, 866-762-4122; www.hihostels.ca; 330 Kennedy St; dm/r $33/77; P❄@🛜) A remodeled old hotel downtown offers budget travelers 100 beds – two levels of dorms and another with private rooms. There's a restaurant and a slightly dodgy pub; tours to Churchill are on offer.

Backpackers Winnipeg Guest House International HOSTEL $
(Map p506; 📞204-772-1272, 800-743-4423; www.backpackerswinnipeg.com; 168 Maryland St; dm/r $27/55; P❄@🛜) Creaky-floored Victorian turned hostel lives on a quiet, tree-lined street west of the center. The musty basement has a crowded games room and small showers, but it's comfy and safe.

🍴 Eating

Winnipeg is an excellent place to dine, with an interesting and diverse choice. The Exchange District, St Boniface, Osborne Village and the Corydon Ave strip are loaded with choices. On a summer's evening you can stroll the areas and be spoiled for choice.

In the Exchange District, there's a small **farmers market** (Map p506; ☉10am-2pm Thu & Sat Jul-Sep) on Old Market Sq. To really explore the bounteous produce of the province, however, head 14km south to the **St Norbert Farmers' Market** (Map p518; www.stnorbertfarmersmarket.ca; 3514 Pembina Hwy; ☉8am-3pm Sat Jun-Oct), which has scores of vendors selling seasonal produce, prepared foods, crafts and more.

DOWNTOWN

VJ's Drive-In   FAST FOOD $
(Map p506; ☎204-943-2655; 170 Main St; mains $4-9; ☉10am-1am) Across from Union Station, VJ's is a fave for take-out fixes. There may be a line at lunchtime, but overstuffed chili dogs, greasy cheeseburgers and bronze-hued fries consistently voted the best in Winnipeg won't disappoint. Seating is limited to outdoor picnic tables.

Wagon Wheel   SANDWICH SHOP $
(Map p506; ☎204-942-6695; 305 Hargrave St; mains $5-9; ☉6am-6pm Mon-Fri) Small, basic and a Winnipeg institution: there are no frills and lots of Formica at this downtown diner. The turkey is roasted daily for the knockout toasted club sandwiches; soups are delicious.

THE FORKS

The commercial area of The Forks has a number of indifferent restaurants aimed at the masses scattered in and around the **Market Building** (Map p506) and Johnston Terminal. However you can also do well at the former, which has vendors selling prepared foods that are ideal for picnics outside plus an array of stalls with well-priced and tasty multiethnic foods.

✍ Tall Grass Prairie   BAKERY $
(Map p506; ☎204-957-5097; www.tallgrassbakery.ca; 1 Forks Market Rd; mains from $4) Spread over two stalls in the Market Building, this local legend uses organic Manitoba fare to create lovely baked goods, sandwiches and prepared meals.

Sydney's   FUSION $$
(Map p506; ☎204-942-6075; www.sydneysattheforks.com; One Forks Market Rd; lunch mains $15-20, dinner menu $50; ☉11:30am-2pm & 5-10pm Mon-Sat) On the 2nd floor of the Market Building, Sydney's is head and shoulders above the other restaurants here in every way. At night the global fare is served prixe fixe from a four-course menu that features dishes such as diverse as smoked salmon, escargot, wild scallops and steak.

EXCHANGE DISTRICT & AROUND

On a summer evening, sitting outside at a funky place on the lively, historic streets of the Exchange District is a treat. The Kings Head pub has good pub food. Further north are the smells and tastes of Winnipeg's small Chinatown.

✍ Mondraggón   CAFE $
(Map p506; ☎204-946-5241; www.mondragon.ca; 91 Albert St; mains $6-11; ☉11am-2pm Mon, 10am-10pm Tue-Sat; ✍) Still true to the Exchange District's funky roots, the Mondragón is run by a workers collective and sells the kind of left-wing books you won't find on Amazon. The cafe is vegan and the creative menu of fresh fare changes daily. A small market within is named for Sacco & Vanzetti.

Kum-Koon Garden   CHINESE $$
(Map p506; ☎204-943-4655; 257 King St; dishes $2-4; ☉11:30am-10pm) Excellent dim sum draws legions of loyal fans to this Chinatown anchor. Service can be as abrupt as the whack of the blade on a duck in the kitchen but you'll barely notice as you navigate the huge menu. Mains are big enough for several people, the reason you see everybody leave with bags of little boxes.

Oui   FRENCH $$$
(Map p506; ☎204-989-7700; 283 Bannatyne Ave; mains $25-30; ☉lunch Tue-Fri, dinner Tue-Sat) In a high-ceilinged, high-profile corner space in a 1907 warehouse, Oui has a classic French bistro menu that includes steak and frites, *fruits de mer* (seafood) and many other solid meaty mains. Salads are oh-so-fresh (*tres bon!*). Tables wrap around the sidewalk and you can lounge about with one of the many creative cocktails.

Fyxx   CAFE $
(Map p506; ☎204-944-0045; 92½ Albert St; mains from $6; ☎) This edition of the local coffeehouse chain has all the funk you'd expect from the Exchange District. Brews are excellently crafted and the sandwiches are horribly good.

Alycia's

CAFE **$$**

(☎204-582-8789; 559 Cathedral Ave; mains $9-14; ☺8am-8pm Mon-Sat) One of those must-visit places without any real draw except that it's Winnipeg's favorite Ukrainian restaurant. Everything is deliciously bad for you; daily made pierogy have a tendency to sell out. The borscht will cure those -50°C blues.

ST BONIFACE

The charming old neighborhood of St Boniface has some fine little restaurants, which, not surprisingly, reflect the local French accent. None are more than a 20-minute walk over the river from the center.

Step 'N Out

FUSION **$$**

(☎204-956-7837; www.stepnout.ca; 157 Blvd Provencher; lunch mains $9-12, dinner $18-25; ☺lunch & dinner Tue-Fri, dinner Sat) Cluttered but quaint, including the flowery outdoor terrace, this romantic place has an ever-changing menu handwritten daily. The eclectic menu mixes Asian and Western cuisines taking advantage of seasonal produce. The wine list is fine.

Chez Sophie

FRENCH, ITALIAN **$$**

(Map p506; ☎204-235-0353; www.chezsophie.net; 248 Av de la Cathédrale; meals $9-15; ☺11am-9pm Tue-Sat) A neighborhood fixture for decades – corner store, launderette – has become a favorite neighborhood bistro. It's cozy and has a well-priced classic French menu of salads, crepes, quiche and more hearty fare such as mussels and frites. Pizzas and pasta add Italian flair.

Resto Gare

FRENCH, FUSION **$$**

(☎204-237-7072; www.chezsophie.net; 630 Rue des Muerons; mains $13-25) Good crusty bread tells you you've made a good choice at this old train station near Blvd Provencher. Diners can choose the vast deck or a romantic booth in an attached old train car. Chef Scott Bagshaw is a local legend and he has creative takes on old standards plus a palette of global specials. There's live jazz on Thursday nights.

OSBORNE VILLAGE

Some of Winnipeg's trendiest restaurants are in this neighborhood close to the center.

Segovia

MEDITERRANEAN **$$**

(☎204-477-6500; www.segoviatapasbar.com; 484 Stradbrook Ave; small mains $8-12; ☺11:30am-2pm Wed-Sat, 5pm-midnight Wed-Mon) Winnipeg's restaurant of the moment is a tapas place as authentic as the house-made aioli. Set in a stylishly renovated old home in a quiet spot just off noisy Osborne St, Segovia has a long list of wines and cocktails you can savor on the patio while enjoying – and sharing – exquisite little dishes.

Baked Expectations

CAFE **$$**

(☎204-452-5176; www.bakedexpectations.ca; 161 Osborne St; mains $8-16; ☺noon-midnight) The cakes may weaken your knees as you enter this stylish palace of desserts. However, the foodie foreplay is just as good, with excellent burgers, pastas, omelettes and more. There's a cute kids menu but really, the baked goods in the display cases are to die for.

CORYDON AVENUE & LITTLE ITALY

All manner of places line the genteel climes of trendy Corydon Ave, which runs through one of Winnipeg's oldest and nicest neighborhoods. About in the middle is a string of cafes that comprise Little Italy, most with terraces perfect for having a cup of strong coffee and solving the world's woes.

Colloseo

ITALIAN **$$**

(☎204-284-4977; 670 Corydon Ave; mains $13-20; ☺11am-10pm Mon-Sat, from 3pm Sun) Classic, timeless Italian fare – from pizza to pasta to chicken to seafood – is on offer at this long-time favorite. The inside has a certain 1970s formality to it, all dark with heavy colors and furniture. Outside, a vast side patio is shaded by trees and enlivened with murals of the old country.

Tandoori Hut

INDIAN **$$**

(☎204-415-4021; 645 Corydon Ave; mains $9-16) At first unassuming in a simple brick building, in summer there's a stairway to heaven, a vast rooftop deck where you can savor Winnipeg's best Indian food under the stars. You'll find all the Indian standards here but made with excellent, fresh ingredients and with enough spice to chase those flatland blues away.

Drinking

Decent places for a drink are found throughout Winnipeg and most have a cheery neighborhood charm. Look for the local Fort Garry draft microbrews. Several of the places listed under Eating are good for a drink, such as Oui and Segovia.

TOP CHOICE **King's Head Pub** PUB
(Map p506; ☑204-957-7710; 120 King St)
Vaguely British, the gregarious sidewalk
tables are the place to be in the Exchange
District on a balmy evening. Inside it's all
rough and tumble wood. The long menu
does pub standards like burgers and fish
and chips quite well.

Tavern United BAR
(Map p506; ☑204-944-0022; 260 Hargrave St)
The inside is huge and the rooftop patio is
massive, with views across downtown. It
bustles with a sports-bar vibe.

Toad in the Hole Pub & Eatery PUB
(☑204-284-7201; 108 Osborne St) Casual pub
with local Osborne Village crowd.

☆ Entertainment

Winnipeg's rather impressive arts and cultural scene earns the town well-deserved
applause.

Live Music

The **Centennial Concert Hall** (Map p506;
☑204-956-1360; 555 Main St) is home to the
Winnipeg Symphony Orchestra (☑20
4-949-3999; www.wso.mb.ca; tickets $20-60;
☺Sep-May) and the highly acclaimed **Manitoba Opera** (☑204-942-7479; www.manito
baopera.mb.ca; tickets $30-99; ☺Nov-Apr), com-
plete with subtitles.

Almost every bar/club in town has live
bands at least once a week, fitting for a
town that produced Neil Young.

Times Chang(d) High & Lonesome Club
(Map p506; ☑204-957-0982; 234 Main St)
Honky-tonk/country/rock/blues weekend
bands jam and beer and whiskey flow
at this small, rough, raunchy and real
throwback.

Windsor Hotel (Map p506; ☑204-942-7528;
187 Garry St) The well-worn Windsor is
Winnipeg's definitive live blues bar.
There's open stage some nights; bands
perform at weekends.

West End Cultural Centre (☑204-783-
6918; www.wecc.ca; 586 Ellice Ave) A former
church, current intimate music venue
that celebrates music that includes folk
and jazz. Many an emerging artist has
gotten their big break thanks to the deep
commitment to new music on the part of
the wonderful volunteers who run this
place.

Nightclubs

Like most major cities, venues in Winnipeg
change constantly. Check the papers or
www.winnipegnightlife.ca to see what's hot
now and remember, many places are only
open Friday and Saturday nights.

Recommended spots:

Alive in the District (Map p506; ☑204-989-
8080; www.aliveinthedistrict.com; 40 Bannatyne
Ave) Cool and glitzy place in the Exchange
District. There's a dress code (no mohawks!).

Mystique (Map p506; ☑204-943-2623; 441
Main St) The regal old Imperial Bank is
now the home of a glam club that's devoted to 'the four elements of clubbing':
earth, wind, fire and water.

Whiskey Dix (Map p506; ☑204-944-7539;
436 Main St) Dress nice and get here by
10:30pm on weekends to enter this very
popular club. Outside there's a vast and
hugely popular ever-thumping terrace
(complete with fire cannon), inside high
ceilings open up the crowded dance
floor.

Palomino Club (☑204-772-0454; 1133
Portage Ave) The Pal: rowdy, fun, dance to
AC/DC or local fave Atomic Candy.

Theater & Cinema

Cinémathèque (Map p506; ☑204-925-3457;
www.winnipegfilmgroup.com; 100 Arthur St)
Shows Canadian and international films,
from art flicks to classics.

Manitoba Theatre Centre (Map p506;
☑204-942-6537; www.mtc.mb.ca; 174 Market
Ave) This company produces popular
shows on the main stage and more-
daring works at the MTC Warehouse (140
Rupert Ave).

Prairie Theatre Exchange (Map p506;
☑204-942-5483; www.pte.mb.ca; 393 Portage Ave) In the Portage Place mall, this
community-based group stages innovative
and challenging productions.

Royal Winnipeg Ballet (Map p506;
☑204-956-2792; www.rwb.org; 380 Graham
Ave) An excellent international reputation
means performances at Centennial Concert Hall are popular.

Venues

Burton Cummings Theatre (Map p506;
☑204-956-5656; 364 Smith St) Guess who

saved this 1907 former movie house? It now shows live theater and concerts.

MTS Centre (Map p506; ☎204-987-7825; www.mtscentre.ca; 260 Hargrave St) Modern downtown arena that hosts concerts and sports.

Pantages (Map p506; ☎204-989-2889; www.pantagesplayhouse.com; 180 Market Ave) Legendary venue dating back to vaudeville sees acts of all kinds through the year.

Scotiabank Stage (Map p506; www.theforks.com) Concerts and plays outdoors at The Forks.

 Sports

Winnipeggers love their teams. Get to a game for a true sample of real culture.

Manitoba Moose
(Map p506; ☎204-780-7328; www.moosehockey.com; ☺Sep-Mar) The American Hockey League (AHL) affiliate for the NHL Vancouver Canucks marks time until the much-desired return of the Jets. Matches are in the MTS Centre.

Winnipeg Blue Bombers
(☎204-784-2583; www.bluebombers.com; 1430 Maroons Rd; ☺Jun-Oct) Fanatical crowds cheer the CFL Bombers at Canad Inns Stadium.

Winnipeg Goldeyes
(Map p506; ☎204-982-2273; www.goldeyes.com; Mill St; ☺May-Sep) It's hard to get much better than cheap, small-league summer evening ballgames by the river in Canwest Stadium.

 Shopping

The Exchange District groans with art galleries and funky stores. Osborne Village and Corydon Ave are excellent places to browse (especially around Lilac along the latter). Even The Forks manages to break with the tourist schmaltz at a few antique shops in the **Johnston Terminal** (Map p506) building.

Portage Place   MALL
(Map p506; ☎204-925-4636; www.portageplace.mb.ca; Portage Ave, at Vaughan St) This three-city-block indoor shopping mall houses 160 stores downtown.

Bijou Treasures   ACCESSORIES
(Map p506; ☎204-233-9722; 190 Blvd Provencher) Local jewelers use worldwide gemstones in Franco-Manitoban designs.

Mountain Equipment Co-Op   OUTDOOR GEAR
(MEC; Map p506; ☎204-943-4202; www.mec.ca; 303 Portage Ave) Canada's favorite outdoor store rents gear.

Red River Books   BOOKSTORE
(Map p506; ☎943-956-2195; 92 Arthur St) Literally piles of secondhand books, a treasure trove of literature.

ⓘ Information

Internet Access
Millennium Library (☎204-986-6450; www.millenniumlibrary.com; 251 Donald St; ☺10am-9pm Mon-Thu, to 5pm Fri & Sat; ☎) Free wi-fi and internet computers.

Media
Uptown Magazine (www.uptownmag.com) Free alternative weekly.

JETTING HOME?

What is constantly on the minds of most locals, always makes the call-in airwaves, and always finds space on the front, editorial and sports' pages is the possible return of Winnipeg's old NHL ice hockey team, the Jets. In 1996 Winnipeg lost its beloved franchise to the improbable locale of Phoenix. Only a Brooklynite who suffered the defection of the Dodgers can understand the heartbreak. A combination of booster Americans and dreams of TV revenues lured the Jets to the brown fields of Arizona where – surprise! – hockey has never caught on. In deep financial trouble, the Phoenix Coyotes, as they are now known, may be ready to flee the desert to someplace colder, someplace where they actually like hockey.

Winnipeg is certainly ready for their return. You see people everywhere adorned with the angular, pure 1970s Jets logo. The MTS Centre (home to the minor-league Beavers) boasts glitzy skyboxes and a long procession of community luminaries and politicians stand ready to help finance the team. So all that's left is this: when will the team of Gordie Howe return?

Winnipeg Free Press (www.winnipegfreepress.com) The main daily, it has a good Friday entertainment tabloid.

Medical Services

St Boniface General Hospital (Map p506; ☎204-233-8563; 409 Ave Taché; ⊙24hr)

Money

Custom House Currency Exchange (☎204-987-6000; 243 Portage Ave; ⊙9am-4pm Mon-Sat)

Post

Many drugstores have postal outlets with extended hours.
Main Post Office (☎800-267-1177; 266 Graham Ave)

Tourist Information

Destination Winnipeg (☎204-943-1970, 800-665-0204; www.destinationwinnipeg.ca; 259 Portage Ave; ⊙8:30am-4:30pm Mon-Fri).

Explore Manitoba Centre (☎204-945-3777, 800-665-0040; 25 Forks Market Rd; ⊙10am-5pm Sep-May, to 6pm Jun-Aug) Provincial information center at The Forks; has Parks Canada and Winnipeg info.

Tourisme Riel (☎204-233-8343; www.tourismeriel.com; 219 Blvd Provencher; ⊙9am-5pm daily Jun-Aug, 9am-5pm Mon-Fri Sep-May) St Boniface visitor information center, specializes in Francophone attractions. Usually has a summer booth at the base of Esplanade Riel, the pedestrian bridge over the river.

Getting There & Away

Air

Winnipeg International Airport (YWG; Map p518; www.waa.ca; 2000 Wellington Ave) has a flash new terminal and is a convenient 10km west of downtown. It has service to cities across Canada and to major hubs in the US. Regional carriers (see p505) handle remote excursions.

Bus

Greyhound buses stop at a new **terminal** (Map p518; 2015 Wellington Ave) at Winnipeg International Airport. Services include Regina ($87, nine hours, two daily), Thunder Bay ($88, nine hours, two daily) and Thompson ($110, nine hours, two daily). A free shuttle takes bus passengers downtown to 299 Fort St.

Train

VIA Rail's transcontinental *Canadian* departs **Union Station** (Map p506; 123 Main St) three times weekly in each direction. The dismal service to Churchill runs tow or three times a week via Thompson and may take 40 hours or more.

ⓘ Getting Around

Walking is easy and enjoyable from downtown to any of the surrounding neighborhoods. In crummy weather, under- and above-ground walkways connect downtown buildings; Destination Winnipeg has a map.

To/From the Airport

A downtown taxi costs $20; some hotels have free shuttles. Winnipeg Transit's bus 15 runs between the airport and downtown every 20 minutes and takes 30 minutes.

Car & Motorcycle

Downtown street parking (free after 6pm) and parking lots are plentiful. Break-ins are common at Union Station, so enclosed lots downtown are a better option if you're taking the train.

If you're transiting Winnipeg by road, the Trans-Canada Hwy (Hwy 1) goes right through downtown. You can bypass this on looping Hwy 100, although suburban roads east and south of the city are often jammed.

Public Transportation

Winnipeg Transit (☎204-986-5700; www.winnipegtransit.com; adult/child $2.35/1.85) runs extensive bus routes around the area, most converging on Fort St. Get a transfer and use exact change. Its free *Downtown Spirit* runs four routes serving the center.

Water Taxi

See the city from a new perspective on the water taxi run by **Splash Dash** (Map p506; ☎204-783-6633; 1 way/day pass $3/15; ⊙noon-11pm daily Jul-Aug, noon-6pm Sat & Sun Sep-mid-Oct) between The Forks, the Legislature Building, Osborne Village, St Boniface and the Exchange District

AROUND WINNIPEG

Lower Fort Garry

Huge stone walls on the banks of the Red River bank surround the only stone **fort** (☎204-785-6050; www.parkscanada.ca/garry; 5925 Hwy 9; adult/child $8/4; ⊙9am-5pm mid-May–Sep) still intact from the fur-trading days. Impeccably restored and reflective of the mid-19th century, costumed interpreters add color. The lovely park-like site is 32km northeast of Winnipeg.

Oak Hammock Marsh

Smack in the middle of southern Manitoba's wetlands is **Oak Hammock Marsh** (☎204-467-3300; www.oakhammockmarsh.ca; Rte 200, at Hwy 67; adult/child $6/4; ☉10am-4:30pm Nov-Aug, to 8pm Sep & Oct), home and migratory stopping point for hundreds of thousands of birds and one of the best sanctuaries around. Springtime has diversity and autumn sees 200,000 to 400,000 geese. Boardwalks, telescopes, remote-controlled cameras and canoes get you close.

LAKE WINNIPEG

The southern end of Canada's fifth-largest lake has been a resort destination since the 1920s. Sandy white beaches, constant sunshine and the ocean-like size of the lake made a visit like 'going to the coast' for all Winnipeggers. It's a tremendously popular summer destination; in winter, when snowy white beaches line the frozen lake, it's virtually deserted.

Popular places such as Winnipeg Beach on the western shore and Grand Beach on the east are typical...well...beach towns. Not that they have zero appeal, but they're predictable centers of summer fun, right down to the arcades, beach boardwalks, ice-cream shops, take-out burger joints and crowds of families, teenagers and vacationers sunning and splashing.

There is hiking in **Grand Beach Provincial Park** (☎204-754-2212; Hwy 12; tent/RV sites $14/18), where hundreds of species of birds use the lagoon behind the beach and the nearby dunes reach 12m. It's also one of Manitoba's busiest campgrounds, meaning it can get loud.

Most land around and between Lake Winnipeg and Lakes Manitoba and Winnipegosis, aka Interlake, is privately owned and cottage rentals are possible. Plenty of small towns and villages are lived in year-round so standard motels and B&Bs can be found everywhere.

Gimli

On the surface it could be another clichéd tourist trap, but beneath the kitsch and tackiness is historic Gimli (Icelandic for 'Home of the Gods'). Settled as 'New Iceland' in 1875, this neat little town has retained its fascinating heritage.

The **Lake Winnipeg Visitor Centre** (☎204-642-7974; 97 1st Ave; ☉10am-6pm May-

Sep) answers visitor questions and displays the natural history of Lake Winnipeg. It's part of the **New Iceland Heritage Museum** (📞204-642-4001; www.nihm.ca; 94 1st Ave; adult/child $5/4; ⏱10am-4pm Mon-Fri, 1-4pm Sat & Sun), itself packed with history and artifacts telling the story of an unlikely people settling an unlikelier part of Canada. On the beach overlooking the lake, the huge **Viking statue** reinforces the town's Icelandic heritage.

Worth visiting simply for its creaky-floored history, **HP Tergesen & Sons** (📞204-642-5958; 82 1st Ave; ⏱10am-6pm Mon-Sat) is a busy general store that's been in continuous operation since 1899.

It's all Iceland during **Islendingadagurinn** (📞204-642-7417; www.icelandicfestival.com; ⏱early Aug), a provincially popular fest including *Islendingadance*, Icelandic games, live music (no Björk) and, of course, an Iceland-themed parade with a lot of blonde people.

Just outside of town, **Autumnwood Motel & RV Resort** (📞204-642-8565; www.autumnwoodresort.com; 19150 Gimli Park Rd; r $90-120; ❄) has 18 standard rooms with polychromatic decor nestled in a quiet location among trees. **Lakeview Resort** (📞204-642-8835; www.lakeviewhotels.com; 10 Centre St; r $120-150; ❄@) is a popular, architecturally challenged 99-room resort by the lake.

Pickerel, a mild lake fish, is served fresh at simple joints along the lake.

TOP CHOICE **Reykjavik Bakery** (Lighthouse Mall, Centre St; ⏱7am-6pm) sells sensational baked goods that are popular in Iceland. Try the *kleina*, a sort of trapezoidal donut.

Hecla-Grindstone Provincial Park

On an island away from the tacky hustle of Lake Winnipeg's beaches sits a natural oasis featuring Manitoba the way it's meant to be seen. The islands, marshes and forests are full of deer, moose, beaver and bear. Stop at **Grassy Narrows Marsh**, which has trails close to the park's entrance leading to shelters and towers perfect for habitat viewing.

Almost too picture-perfect to be real, Hecla Village has been a lived-in Icelandic settlement since 1876. You can go on a 1km **self-guided tour** of the old lakefront buildings. The **Heritage Home Museum** (Village

Rd; admission free; ⏱10am-4pm mid-May–early Sep) lets you look inside a household from the 1930s.

Solmundson Gesta Hus Bed & Breakfast (📞204-279-2088; www.heclatourism.mb.ca; r $75-90; ❄) is a beautiful historic home with a hot tub surrounded by manicured gardens.

Hecla Oasis Resort (📞204-279-2041, 800-267-6700; www.heclaoasis.com; r $140-200; @🛜) is affiliated with Radisson Hotels. It's a glitzy change to the local vibe, the 90 rooms are stylish and are built on a golf course. Time shares *are* available.

The **park office** (📞204-378-2945; www.manitobaparks.com; Hwy 8; tent/RV sites $14/18) provides information for visitors.

SOUTHEASTERN MANITOBA

Heading east from Winnipeg, the flat expanse typical of the prairies blends with forests and lakes typical of the Great Lakes region. While most visitors speed through toward Kenora and beyond, the eastern region of Manitoba has the same rugged woodland terrain as neighboring Ontario.

Mennonite Heritage Village

In the middle of sunflower country, southeast of Winnipeg, lies Mennonite Steinbach. This idyllic late-19th-century **village** (📞204-326-9661; www.mennoniteheritagevillage.com; Hwy 12; adult/child $10/2; ⏱10am-6pm Mon-Sat, noon-6pm Sun Jul & Aug, to 5pm May, Jun & Sep, to 4pm Tue-Fri Oct-Apr) has an excellent museum and makes for an evocative stroll. **Livery Barn Restaurant** (mains $6-9; ⏱10am-4pm Mon-Sat, 11:30am-4pm Sun May-Sep) serves borscht and *kielkje* (homemade egg noodles often served with ham), along with other unpronounceable albeit hearty Mennonite foods.

Whiteshell Provincial Park

Foreshadowing the green forests, clear lakes and Canadian Shield of northern Ontario, pine-covered hills erupt from the plains immediately inside this **park** (www.manitobaparks.com).

FLOWERS OF THE PRAIRIE: SMALLTOWN MANITOBA

Manitoba's welter of rural roads are ideal for random explorations. Many lead to small towns that make the journey worthwhile. Here's a few of our favorites:

Carman Gorgeous river setting an hour southwest of Winnipeg with a 5km trail around town.

Minnedosa Perfect little Main St with an ice-cream stand called Dairy Isle and a bowling alley.

Morden Southern town with brick buildings, a grain elevator, the Canadian Fossil Discovery Centre and the Manitoba Baseball Hall of Fame; enough said.

Neepawa Tree-lined streets and old houses are reason enough why this town is often voted Manitoba's prettiest. Look for U-pick berry farms here.

Norway House A large Cree community steeped in history on Lake Winnipeg's isolated northern shore.

Snow Lake Fun little town on the shores of Snow Lake, just north of Hwy 10, with mining museum and roadside bear crap.

Stonewall Hanging baskets, peaceful atmosphere and limestone-quarry swimming hole, an hour north of Winnipeg.

Victoria Beach Greenest village ever. Cottage-centric with limited vehicle access (walk or bike) and Lake Winnipeg's sandiest beaches, located on the eastern shore.

Unfortunately, the park is fairly commercialized; resorts and stores are found every few kilometers and larger centers have **park offices** (⊘8am-noon & 1-4pm Mon-Fri; Falcon Lake ☑204-349-2201; Rennie ☑204-369-5246; Seven Sisters ☑204-348-4004; West Hake Lake ☑204-346-2245). There is still a sense of spirituality and you can get away via hiking trails of varying lengths – the longest being the six-day, 60km Mantario – and canoe routes, the most popular being the tunnels of **Caddy Lake**.

The cute log-house **Natural History Museum** (☑204-348-2846; Nutimik Lake; ⊘9am-5pm late May–early Sep) has displays on park history. A definite don't-miss is the **petroforms interpretive tour** (☑204-348-2806; tour free; ⊘11am & 2pm Jun-Aug) teaching spiritual connections with age-old rock formations.

There are hundreds of **campsites** (sites $12-19) throughout the park. **Falcon Lakeshore Campground** with trees and seclusion is only a short walk from the lake's beaches.

Big Whiteshell Lodge (☑204-348-7623; www.bigwhiteshelllodge.com; Hwy 309; cottages $100-190) has cottages in a quiet, woodsy location on the shores of Big Whiteshell Lake at the end of Rte 309.

WESTERN MANITOBA

Between Winnipeg and Saskatchewan, Manitoba is a seemingly endless sea of agriculture until you decide to make a few detours here and there to often overlooked natural delights and some atmospheric towns.

Spruce Woods Provincial Park

Un-Manitoban shifting sand dunes in this 27,000-hectare **park** (☑204-827-8850; www.manitobaparks.com; Hwy 5) provide a home for unlikely cacti and creatures including Manitoba's only lizard: the 20cm-long northern prairie skink. Stretch your legs on the 1.6km trail to the dunes at Spirit Sands.

Brandon

POP 44,900

Manitoba's second-largest center is an attractive residential city with a historic downtown bisected by the Assiniboine River.

The redbrick home of Brandon's first mayor and named accordingly, **Daly House Museum** (☑204-727-1722; 122 18th St; adult/child/family $5/4/10; ⊘10am-noon & 1-5pm daily Jun-Sep, 10am-noon & 1-5pm Tue-Sat Oct-May) is chock full of Victoriana and local history.

On CFB Shilo, an active military base east of Brandon, the **Royal Canadian Artillery Museum** (☎204-765-3000; Hwy 340; admission free; ⊙10am-5pm Mon-Fri year-round, 10am-5pm Sat & Sun Jun-Aug) displays uniforms, guns, ammunition and 60-plus vehicles dating from 1796 through the cold war. Sadly there's no hands-on cannon demonstrations.

Chain motels line the exits from Hwy 1, and local eateries can be found downtown. Regular Greyhound buses plying the highway pause at the downtown **depot** (☎20 4-727-0643; 141 6th St).

Riverbank Discovery Centre (☎20 4-729-2141; www.tourism.brandon.com; 545 Conservation Dr; ⊙8:30am-5pm Mon-Fri, noon-5pm Sat & Sun) is both a tourist office and a hub for riverside walking paths.

International Peace Garden

The setting – a very quiet B-level Manitoba–North Dakota border crossing – is certainly appropriate for this cross-border **garden** (☎204-534-2510; www.peacegarden. com; Canada Hwy 10/US281; per vehicle $10; ⊙daylight hours mid-May–mid-Sep), which honors the peaceful relations between Canada and the US. Yet nothing is as simple since 9/11 (you have to go through customs and immigration of either country just to reach the garden) and there is added poignancy here as the twin towers marking the 49th parallel eerily and unintentionally evoke thoughts of the World Trade Center.

Just west, **Turtle Mountain Provincial Park** (☎204-945-6784; www.manitobaparks. com; Hwy 10) has vistas from rolling hills, lakes and fine places to camp and picnic.

Riding Mountain National Park

Rising like a vision above the plains, **Riding Mountain National Park** (☎204-848-7275; www.parkscanada.ca/riding; adult/child $8/4) is more than 3000 sq km of boreal forest, deep valleys, lofty hills and alpine lakes. It rewards those with an hour or a week. You might even see a bear or a moose.

Most of the park is wilderness; **Wasagaming**, on the south shore of eponymously named Clear Lake, is such a perfect little summer town that it would be a cliché if it weren't so, well, perfect.

The beautiful 1930s **Visitors Centre** (☎204-848-7275; Wasagaming Rd; ⊙9:30am-5pm late May–Jun & Sep–mid-Oct, to 8pm Jul & Aug) contains impressive dioramas, the invaluable *Visitor's Guide* and backcountry permits.

◉ Sights & Activities

Highway 10 cuts a 53km course down the middle of the park. It's fine if the only time you have is for a quick transit, but the park is at its best on any of the 400km of **walking**, **cycling** and **horseback-riding trails**. Hikes range from the 1km-long Lakeshore Trail to a 17km trek through forest and meadows to a cabin used by naturalist Grey Owl. **Elkhorn Riding Adventures** (☎204-848-4583; trail rides from $30) beside Elkhorn Resort offers a chance to honor the park's name atop a horse.

Canoeing/kayaking is excellent and offers shoreline glimpses at wildlife, though Clear Lake gets windy and also allows motorboats. Rentals are available from **Clear Lake Marina** (☎204-848-1770; www.theclearlakemarina.com; Wasagaming Pier; per hr $12).

🛌 Sleeping & Eating

Backcountry camping is possible; check with the visitors center. Motels and cabins are plentiful in Wasagaming; some open year-round.

There are 600 **campsites** (sites $16-40) in the park. **Wasagaming Campground** is the most popular. **Lake Audy** has abundant wildlife and **Whirlpool Lake** has lakeside walk-in sites within thick forest a 50m hike from the parking lot.

For a little bit of dudeness in the wilderness, **Elkhorn Resort** (☎204-848-2802; www. elkhornresort.mb.ca; Mooswa Dr W, Wasagaming; r $110-225; ⊝☒) offers genteel comfort. Better yet, **Idylwylde Cabins** (☎204-848-2383; www.idylwylde.ca; 136 Wasagaming Dr; cabins from $100; ⊝☒) offers short walks to the ice-cream stands in town and you can stay here for less than a week during the off-season.

❶ Getting There & Away

You can drive through the park on Hwy 10 for free if you solemnly promise not to stop. Better to pay the fee and make a day of it.

Around Riding Mountain National Park

Just north of the park, two summer fests around Dauphin are huge fun. **Country Fest** (📞204-622-3700, 800-361-7300; www. countryfest.ca; ☉late Jul) uses a gorgeous forested amphitheatre for four days of music, drinking, camping and a whole lotta yeehaw. **Canada's National Ukrainian Festival** (📞877-747-2683; www.cnuf.ca; ☉early Aug) features folk dancing, drinking, lacy costumes, cultural displays and the chance to munch pierogy, cabbage rolls and kielbasa.

NORTHERN MANITOBA

'North of 53' (the 53rd parallel), convenience takes a backseat to rugged beauty as lake-filled timberland dissolves into the treeless tundra of the far north. Here cell phones are useless and you're left to your own wits for adventure and even survival. Churchill is justifiably the big draw and reason enough for a journey that leaves the life you know far behind.

The Pas

A traditional meeting place of Aboriginal and European fur traders, The Pas (pronounced pah) is a useful stop for services on northern trips.

The **Northern Manitoba Trappers' Festival** (📞204-623-2912; www.trappersfestival.com; ☉mid-Feb) is one of the best-known parties of The Pas and Manitoba, featuring dog-sled races, snowmobiling, ice sculptures, torchlight parades and trapping games in a weekend of frosty anarchy.

Boreal forests surround amazingly clear waters and there's camping with pelicans at **Clearwater Lake Provincial Park** (📞204-624-5525; www.manitobaparks.ca; campsites $14-18) near the airport. The scenic Caves Trail follows deep crevices and eroding cliffs.

Motels are strung out along Hwy 10. Downtown **Wescana Inn** (📞204-623-5446; www.wescanainn.com; 439 Fischer Ave; r from $80; ❀) has basic rooms. **Miss The Pass** (📞204-623-3130; 158 Edwards St; mains from $6; ☉7am-7pm Mon-Sat) has the kind of tasty, hearty fare that will ready you for adventure.

VIA Rail's Winnipeg–Churchill train stops at the **train station** (380 Hazelwood Ave).

Flin Flon

A worthy pause on a northern routing along lonely, pretty Hwy 10 into Saskatchewan, Flin Flon (www.cityofflinflon. com) still has some of the 1930s character from when it was a mining boomtown. Straddling the border, it has a full slate of services.

WORTH A TRIP

CASTLES OF THE NEW WORLD

Barn-red or tractor-green; striking yet simple; function and form: characterizing prairie landscapes like the wheat they hold, grain elevators were once flagships of prairie architecture.

Introduced in 1880, more than 7000 of the vertical wooden warehouses lined Canadian train tracks by 1930. Their importance was invaluable, as the prairies became 'the breadbasket of the world' and their stoic simplicity inspired Canadian painters, photographers and writers who gave them life.

Today's concrete replacements are as generic as their fast-food-chain neighbors. For a glimpse of the vanishing past, make the detour to **Inglis Grain Elevators National Historic Site** (📞204-564-2243; www.ingliselevators.com; admission free; ☉10am-6pm Wed-Sat, noon-5pm Sun Jun, plus Mon & Tue Jul & Aug). A stunning row of elevators has been restored to their original splendor. Inside the creaky interiors exhibits capture the thin lives where success or failure rested with the whims of commodity brokers.

Inglis is 20km north of the Yellowhead Hwy (Hwy 16) near the Saskatchewan border.

Thompson

Carved out of the boreal forest by mining interests in the 1950s, Thompson is a necessary evil for northern itineraries. There's no way around it, the town lacks charm although the boom in minerals means that it has 24-hour fast-food chains, a Wal-Mart and plenty of services.

At the entrance to town, the **Visitor Information Centre** (☎204-677-2216; www. heritagenorthmuseum.ca; 162 Princeton Dr; ☻9am-5pm Mon-Sat, noon-5pm Sun Jun-Sep, shorter hr other times) runs the log-cabin **Heritage North Museum** (adult/child $3.25/1). Although small, it is stuffed with local wildlife and history.

McReedy Campground (☎204-778-8810; 114 Manasan Dr; campsites $17; ☻May-Sep) is set up for RVs and has a few campsites in the trees; it's just north of the river.

Centrally located, **Interior Inn** (☎204-778-5535; www.interiorinn.ca; 180 Thompson Dr N; r from $80; ✴☎) is typical of the raw-edged motels that abound in town.

Calm Air (p883) flies throughout Manitoba including Churchill to/from **Thompson Airport** (YTH; ☎204-778-5212; www.thompsonairport.ca), 10km north of town. Two daily Greyhound buses to/from Winnipeg ($105, nine hours) and other Hwy 6 destinations use the **bus station** (☎204-677-0360; 81 Berens Rd) near the visitors center.

Thompson is the end of paved roads, many people catch the lethargic VIA Rail Churchill train from here. The **station** (1310 Station Rd), in an industrial area, is not a safe spot to leave your vehicle. McReedy Campground offers vehicle storage ($8 per day) and shuttles to the train.

Pisew Falls

Around 80km southwest of Thompson along Hwy 6, **Pisew Falls Provincial Park** (www.manitobaparks.ca) is a must-stop for anyone passing. A short boardwalk runs from the parking area down to lookouts on the surging waters of the 13m falls. Water shoots over the wide precipice and then gushes through a rocky gorge while mist fills the air.

A trail from here leads to remote **Kwasitchewan Falls**. The partial looping route runs 22km there and back and offers prime backcountry hiking and camping.

Churchill

POP 950

Churchill lures people to the shores of Hudson Bay for polar bears, beluga whales, a huge old stone fort and endless sub-Arctic majesty. But while these are reason enough to be on any itinerary, there's something less tangible that makes people stay longer and keeps them coming back: a hearty seductive spirit that makes the rest of the world seem – thankfully – even further away than it really is.

History

Permafrost springs upwards about an inch per millennia chronicling old shorelines and leaving nearby evidence of aboriginal settlements up to 3000 years old. In European exploration, Churchill is one of the oldest places in Canada. HBC's – said to stand for 'Here Before Christ' – first outpost was built here in 1717. It was a stop in attempts to find the fabled Northwest Passage by explorers such as Samuel Hearne and Lord Churchill, former HBC governor and the town's namesake.

Churchill's strategic location ensured a military presence over centuries. The railway's arrival and opening of the huge port in 1929 has made the town a vital international grain shipping point for the prairie provinces.

◉ Sights

The town itself is a typical assemblage of tattered northern structures. Wander the streets, stop and peruse the beach (!), visit the museum and then get out onto the land and water for nature at its most magnificent.

TOP CHOICE **Eskimo Museum**　　MUSEUM
(☎204-675-2030; 242 La Verendrye Ave; suggested donation $2; ☻1-5pm Mon, 9am-noon & 1-5pm Tue-Sat Jun-Oct, 1-4:30pm Mon-Sat Nov-May) This museum is really just a bunch of stuff in an unexciting room with linoleum floors, but like Churchill it sucks you in and soon an hour or two has passed. The obvious standouts – stuffed polar bear and musk ox, narwhal horns and original hide-covered kayaks – are immediate attention-grabbers, but closer inspection reveals tiny arrowheads, big harpoon blades and hundreds of carvings showing intricate scenes of everyday life (look for the one titled First Airplane). A huge range of Northern books are for sale.

FOR EVERY SEASON...

In climatological terms, Churchill has three seasons: July, August and winter. For visitors, it has four: bird and flower, beluga whale, polar bear and northern lights.

Bird (peak season: mid-May–Sep) Two hundred-plus species use Churchill as nesting grounds, including rare Ross' gulls, or as a stopover on their way further north. Granary Ponds by the port, Cape Merry or Bird Cove are good viewing spots.

Wildflower (Jun-Aug) As the ice melts and the sun hits the soil for the first time in months, Churchill explodes in colors and aromas.

Beluga Whale (mid-Jun–Aug) Curious as dolphins and voluble as the label 'sea canaries' implies, about 3000 of these glossy white, 4m-long creatures summer in Churchill River. From Cape Merry they look like whitecaps; go snorkeling, kayaking or view them from a boat.

Polar Bear (Sep–early Nov) Peak season is late in the year, but sightings begin in July.

Northern Lights (Oct-Mar) The aqua-turquoise-yellow dance of the aurora borealis is nothing short of spectacular.

Parks Canada
MUSEUM

(☎204-675-8863; train station; ⊘9am-8:30pm Jun-Nov, but closes 5pm some days and Dec-May) There's a small but essential museum and nature centre in the train station along with the Parks Canada info desk. It has a good model of the fort and excellent info on the many creatures you've come far to see. There are talks on the area almost daily in season.

Fort Prince of Wales National Historic Site
HISTORICAL SITE

Parks Canada (☎204-675-8863; www.parks canada.ca; ⊘Jul & Aug) administers three sites in the area documenting Churchill's varied history. Transportation to the sites across the water is handled by licensed tour operators and the entry fee is included in tour costs.

It took 40 years to build and its cannons have never fired a shot, but the star-shaped stone Fort Prince of Wales has been standing prominently on rocky Eskimo Point across the Churchill River since the 1770s.

As English-French tensions mounted in the 1720s, HBC selected the site for presence and strategy, but surrendered during the first French attack in 1782, making it an Anglo Maginot Line forerunner. It's a boggy, buggy place with sweeping views and a real sense that duty here was best avoided.

Four kilometers south of the fort, **Sloop's Cove** was a harbor for European vessels during Churchill's harsh winters. The only indications of early explorers are simple yet profound: names such as Samuel Hearn, local 18th-century governor and first to make an overland trip to the Arctic Ocean, are carved into the seaside rocks.

TOP CHOICE **Cape Merry** has a lone cannon and crumbling walls but the location astounds with vistas across the bay and river. In season, those aren't white caps, they're belugas. A pretty 2km-walk northwest of town, get bear advice before setting out.

Wapusk National Park
PARK

(☎204-675-8863, 888-748-2928; www.parks canada.ca/wapusk) Established primarily to protect polar bear breeding grounds (*wapusk* is Cree for 'white bear'), this remote park extends along Hudson Bay's shores 45km southeast of Churchill. Its location between boreal forests and arctic tundra gives it importance for monitoring the effects of climate change. Visits center on polar bears and are only possible through licensed operators.

York Factory National Historic Site
HISTORICAL SITE

(⊘varies Jun-Sep) Even more remote, around 250km southeast of Churchill, this HBC trading post, near Hayes River, was an important gateway to the interior and active for 273 years until 1957. The stark-white buildings are an amazing sight contrasting with their seemingly middle-of-nowhere setting.

York Factory is accessible only by air or boat.

Courses

Churchill Northern Studies Centre
RESEARCH

(CNSC; ☎204-675-2307; www.churchillscience.ca; Launch Rd; courses from $900) CNSC, on the old rocket range 23km east of town, is an active base for researchers from around the world. Learning vacations feature all-inclusive (dorms, meals and local transportation) multiday courses with real scientists working on projects involving belugas, wildflowers, birds and polar bears. There are also courses in winter survival, northern lights and astronomy. An impressive new center is set to open in 2011.

⤵ Tours

Independent exploration is not encouraged in Churchill, not just for reasons of safety but primarily due to expertise. Local guides have a wealth of knowledge that guide you to wildlife and provide vital context for exploring the area.

Polar-Bear Tours

Polar bear basically overshadow Churchill's other draws. In summer, you may see them as part of other tours on land and even swimming in the river. Later in the year is the real deal however with bears on the ice and snow aplenty. Special lightweight vehicles riding high on huge tires to protect the tundra venture out on day-trips (about $350 per person). Heated cabins and open-air porches allow you to get good views at the marauding bears.

Great White Bear Tours (☑204-675-2781, 866-765-8344; www.greatwhitebeartours.com; 266 Kelsey Blvd)

Lazy Bear Lodge (☑204-675-2869, 866-687-2327; www.lazybearlodge.com; tours from $400) Offers one- and two-day tours.

Tundra Buggy Adventure (☑204-949-2050, 800-663-9832; www.tundrabuggy.com; 124 Kelsey Blvd) Longer overnight trips

assemble caravans of tundra vehicles into mobile camps, complete with cabins and common areas (from $3000).

Land & Sea Tours

Several outfits offer land tours of the area in summer. These typically take in Cape Merry, CNSC and the disused missile site plus novelties such as a crashed plane and a grounded ship. The cost averages $75 for several hours and you may well see a bear or two.

TOP CHOICE **Sea North Tours** (☑204-675-2195; www.seanorthtours.com; 39 Franklin St; tours from $100) Mike Macri leads beluga whale tours aboard a custom viewing boat, zodiac inflatables and by kayak. Belugas are naturally curious and will be as curious about you as you are about them. You can even go snorkeling with pods of these gentle, 4m-long creatures. Many trips include a visit to Prince of Wales Fort.

Lazy Bear Lodge (☑204-675-2869, 866-687-2327; www.lazybearlodge.com; 313 Kelsey Blvd; tours from $125) Summer day tours include kayaking, birding and spotting wildlife.

Nature 1st (☑204-675-2147; www.nature1sttours.ca; tours from $85) Hiking, trekking and driving are combined in various nature tours that explore the four distinct ecosystems around Churchill.

Wapusk Adventures (☑204-675-2887; www.wapuskadventures.com; 321 Kelsey Blvd; tours from $90) Dave Daley is a legendary dog-sledder and in winter you can learn from the master as you mush your way around the frozen wilderness.

MONARCHS OF THE TUNDRA

Massive and graceful, ferocious and majestic, carnivorous and curious, polar bears are Churchill's most popular yet most misunderstood creatures. They're resilient enough to spend winters hunting ring seals on the frozen ocean, and smart and strong enough to get them through meter-thick ice. They return to land when the ice melts, where they wait and mate, then the females give birth in dens while the males head north waiting for the ice to reform. Churchill is right on their migration path.

Each year, polar bears arrive sooner, stay later and are more plentiful near town – climate change figures prominently in the reasons for this. Shorter winters mean the polar ice melts sooner and freezes later, making the hunting season shorter. About 900 of the world's roughly 20,000 polar bears live in the Churchill area, a population considered the most endangered as it lives the furthest south.

Weighing upwards of 600kg (those bears you saw roadside in the south rarely top 300kg), polar bears have razor-sharp claws and can run 50km/h. They are naturally curious and will attack humans out of hunger or boredom. Read Parks Canada's *You Are in Polar Bear Country* guide and heed the Polar Bear Alert signs around town. Those warning gunshots heard around the clock are the polar-bear patrols in action.

🛏 Sleeping

Obviously rates rise dramatically in polar-bear season when demand is high and people book a year in advance. Group cancellations do occur, so a lodge fully booked now may have rooms later, though it's not guaranteed. Don't expect luxury in Churchill but you will be comfortable and all places are walkably central. Camping is generally not possible as there's rules against feeding yourself to the bears.

The CNSC (p525) has a volunteer program where visitors exchange six work-hours per day for room and board at the research center.

Tundra Inn MOTEL $$
(📞204-675-2850, 800-265-8563; www.tundrainn.com; 34 Franklin St; r from $100, bear season from $180; @) The 31 motel-style rooms are large and comfortable with highspeed internet plus fridges and microwaves. There's a laundry and shared kitchen with cereal and toast in the morning.

Lazy Bear Lodge INN $$
(📞204-675-2869, 866-687-2327; www.lazybearlodge.com; 313 Kelsey Blvd; r from $110, bear season from $200; ☺Jun-Nov; 🛜) Locally and solidly built, this log construction lodge (as in everything possible was made with logs) offers tours and packages and has one of two decent places to eat in town. The 33 rooms aren't huge, but you'll sleep well in creaky character.

Polar Inn MOTEL $$
(📞204-675-8878; www.polarinn.com; 153 Kelsey Blvd; r from $100, bear season from $180; 🛜) Basic motel-style units come with fridges. There are also studios with small kitchens and full apartments. Make-it-yourself continental breakfast is included.

Basic but clean options (rooms from $80, $150 in bear season) include:

Bear Country Inn MOTEL $$
(📞204-675-8299; bearcinn@mts.net; 126 Kelsey Blvd)

Churchill Motel MOTEL $$
(📞204-675-8853; churchillmotel@hotmail.com; 120 Kelsey Blvd)

🍴 Eating & Drinking

Most places will feature caribou and/or musk ox on the menu, which will sate your inner carnivore and provide tick on the game-eating list. Definitely seek out Arctic char, a delicious local fish that is a sort of a cross between salmon and trout.

Tourists support several restaurants here, although quality varies greatly.

🏆 Gypsy's Bakery CANADIAN $$
CHOICE (📞204-675-2322; 253 Kelsey Blvd; mains $7-25; ☺7am-9pm) The Da Silva family runs the best place to eat in Churchill. Luscious baked goods await in display cases (the cream cheese cin-bun? OMG!) and you can order from a full cafeteria-style menu. The char is especially good, but so are the sandwiches, burgers and more. Departing by train? Load up on take-out vittles here in lieu of the skimpy, yucky Via Rail offerings.

Lazy Bear Café CANADIAN $$
(📞204-675-2869; 313 Kelsey Blvd; mains $8-25; ☺noon-10pm) Attached to the lodge of the same name, log-built tables and chairs set the scene for standard meals and local cuisine. Famous for knockout milkshakes, which you can enjoy on the screened porch.

Pier Bar BAR
(📞204-675-8807; Kelsey Blvd; mains $7-18; ☺noon-1am) The Seaport Hotel's attached bar is popular with younger summer workers and most anyone looking for a beer. Watch for Tom Petty covers by the local band C Flats. The adjoining Reef Dining Room is good if you get the munchies.

🛍 Shopping

Northern (📞204-675-8891; 171 Kelsey Blvd) is the town's grocery and department store. Buy more bug juice here and ponder the milk at a cool $5.09 a liter.

Trading-post **Arctic Trading Company** (📞204-675-8804; www.arctictradingco.com; 141 Kelsey Blvd; ☺9am-6pm Mon-Sat) has locally made carvings, clothing, paintings and caribou-antler cribbage boards.

Dangers & Annoyances

In summer it's war with swarms of mosquitoes and black flies. Pack bug repellent with *at least* 30% DEET. Head-nets are a possibility, but they're often sold out in town. Always have warm clothing handy as it can get cold fast in summer.

Getting bitten by a polar bear is much worse (see the boxed text, p525).

ℹ Information

Emergencies
Ambulance (📞204-675-8880)
Fire (📞204-675-2222)
Polar Bear Alert (📞204-675-2327)
Police (📞204-675-8821)

Internet Access
Library (☎204-675-2731; Town Centre Complex; ⊙1-5pm Mon-Sat)

Internet Resources
Everything Churchill (www.everything churchill.com)

Town of Churchill (www.churchill.ca)

Medical Services
Churchill Regional Health Authority (☎204-675-8881; Town Centre Complex)

Money
Royal Bank (☎204-675-8894; La Verendrye Ave)

Post
Post Office (☎204-675-2696; La Verendrye Ave)

Tourist Information
Chamber of Commerce (☎204-675-2022; 211 Kelsey Blvd; ⊙11am-3pm Mon-Sat Jul-Nov) Near the train station.

Parks Canada (☎204-675-8863; train station; ⊙9am-8:30pm Jun-Nov) An essential first stop, but closes at 5pm some days and December to May.

❶ Getting There & Away

There is no road to Churchill; access is by plane or train only. A popular option is exploring Manitoba to Thompson and then catching a train or plane from there.

Air
Calm Air (☎800-839-2256; www.calmair.com) serves Thompson and Winnipeg. **Kivalliq Air** (☎877-879-8477; www.kivalliqair.com) serves Winnipeg and villages across Nunavut. Return fares for Winnipeg average $950 to $1000; for Thompson it's about $550/270 return/one-way. **Churchill Airport** (YYQ; ☎204-675-8868) is 11km east of town; most accommodations offer drop-off/pickup, a taxi is a pricy $20.

Train
Via Rail's Churchill train is an embarrassment. Slow and late, it even manages to run out of food and drink. It runs two to three times per week and takes upwards of 40 hours from Winnipeg and 20 from Thompson (you can drive from Winnipeg to Thompson in seven). However, there is a mesmerizing quality to the endless empty tracts of trees, muskeg and lakes from Thompson. You could fly one way and putter down the tracks the other (the American owner of the tracks, Omni-Trax, gets no awards for maintenance).

Fares average round-trip economy coach/ sleeper (recommended) from Winnipeg $350/950 and Thompson $125/470. One-way fares are about half.

The renovated historic **station** (☎204-675-2149; Hendry St) triples as a Parks Canada office and natural museum.

❶ Getting Around

Most locals walk or cycle around the compact town but you should proceed carefully and be bear aware. **Polar Inn** (☎204-675-8878; 15 Franklin St; per day $20) rents bicycles. **Tamarack Rentals** (☎204-675-2192; www.tamarackrentals.ca; 299 Kelsey Blvd; per day $75-95) rents pick-up trucks and will meet you at the airport.

Saskatchewan

Best Places to Eat

» Fainting Goat (p534)

» Blue Bird Cafe (p536)

» Souleio (p542)

» Park Cafe (p542)

Best Places to Stay

» Radisson Plaza Hotel
Saskatchewan (p533)

» The Convent (p538)

» Hotel Senator (p542)

» Sturgeon River Ranch
(p546)

Why Go?

To paraphrase an old line, there are no boring parts of Saskatchewan, just boring visitors. Yes much of it is flat, there's not a lot of people here, the two major towns define the vaguely complimentary 'nice' and so on. But that simply means that the savvy visitor is ready to dig deep to discover the province's inherent appeal.

Start with all that flat: those rippling oceans of grain have a mesmerizing poetry to their movement, the song birds and crickets providing accents to the endlessly rustling wind. If you're ready for the tranquility of solitude, pick any unpaved road and set off.

Get to know the people. Not just the plain-spoken residents of today but the people who populate Saskatchewan's story, whether eking out a living off the land, fermenting revolution or taming a frontier. The rewards won't be as dramatic but will be richly satisfying in their own way.

When to Go

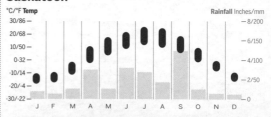

Saskatoon

May Spring wildflowers beautifully line the roads and signal the end of the long winter

June to August Days *can* be balmy although cool nights are the norm

September Fall, with its dramatic colors, comes early and days are crisp

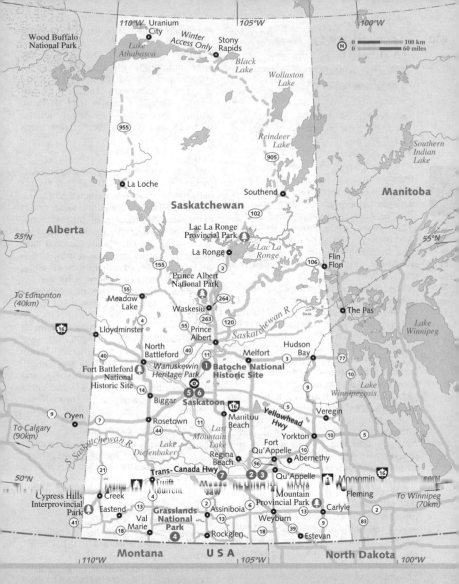

Saskatchewan Highlights

1 Honor the brave revolutionaries at **Batoche** (p546), where Riel almost beat the Canadian army

2 Quaff a fine **Bushwakker brew** (p534) made with local barley in Regina

3 Don a watermelon hat at an insane **Roughriders game** (p535) in Regina with some of Canadian football's most ardent fans

4 Let the wind whistle through your ears at **Grasslands National Park** (p538)

5 Stroll the river in **Saskatoon** (p539), the Paris of the Prairies and a very enjoyable city

6 Hunt ripe **Saskatchewan berries** (p544) around Saskatoon during the brief summer when nature bursts forth

7 Dig deep into **Moose Jaw** (p536) to experience its underground past from the days of Al Capone

SASKATCHEWAN FAST FACTS

» Population: 960,400

» Area: 586,561 sq km

» Capital: Regina

» Quirky fact: Hoodies are known throughout the province as 'bunny hugs' and no one knows why

History

The story of Saskatchewan is filled with hardship, perseverance, triumph and tragedy. The Aboriginal people lived here for 10,000 years before Europeans first arrived in the middle of the 17th century. The Cree, Dene and Assiniboine people lived a simple life, gaining all they needed from the land.

The relationship between these two cultures was often on shaky ground: Europeans wanted more land for farming, which resulted in conflicts that often translated into bloodshed. The evidence of these struggles is found throughout Saskatchewan, with many historic battle sites to see, such as Fort Batoche where Métis leader Louis Riel (p510) was captured.

As more Europeans arrived in the region, the strain on cultural relations and the ecosystem increased. In 1865 there were an estimated 60 million buffalo in Saskatchewan; by 1876 that number had dropped to just 500 due to mass slaughter by homesteaders and hunters.

By 1890 most Aboriginals lived on reserves and with immigration fueled by the railroad, Saskatchewan became a province in 1905. After the Great Depression of the 1930s and the onset of WWII, wheat production reached its highest levels. Today many grains are grown plus canola (the bright yellow flowers you see in summer).

Land & Climate

The warm (sometimes up to 35°C) and short Saskatchewan summer makes for great traveling weather and excellent thunderstorm viewing. There's nothing like watching a storm roll in: the azure-blue sky turns dishwater gray and finally to hockeypuck black, then the rain starts to fall thick and fast. Just watch out though, as that rain can turn to hail – this is, after all, the 'Land of the Living Skies.'

Winter can arrive in October and stay finger-numbingly cold (down to as low as -40°C) until April; it doesn't snow a lot, but it will snow early and it will stick around. There's a reason that all those parking spaces have electrical outlets: so people can plug in their engine block heaters.

Parks

Saskatchewan has two contrasting national parks: Prince Albert National Park (p546) in the north is a forested sanctuary of lakes, untouched land and wildlife. Outdoor activities such as canoeing, hiking and camping are all at their shining best here. Deep in the south lies Grasslands National Park (p538); unlike its northern cousin, Grasslands is devoid of trees. This park of rolling hills in a plethora of greens, with accents of wildflowers and oodles of solitude, is a splendid place to feel very small in the grand scheme of things.

There are also numerous **provincial parks** (306-953-3751, 800-205-7070; www. saskparks.net; passes 1-day/3-day/week/annual $7/17/25/50, tent sites $11-17, RV sites $16-26). Camping is available in most parks, and some have backcountry sites. Some parks have a reservation system through the website.

ⓘ Getting There & Around

This is a province people drive through on the way to someplace else. The Trans-Canada Hwy (Hwy 1) runs across the south and through Regina, offering a mesmerizing tableau of grain. The Yellowhead Hwy (Hwy 16) cuts diagonally across the province and is rather pretty northwest of Saskatoon. Some sample distances: Saskatoon to Regina, 260km; Saskatoon to Winnipeg, 780km; Regina to Calgary, 760km. Roads cross into Montana and North Dakota in the USA.

Many roads are not paved and rather consist of graded gravel. These are fine (except for your paint) during dry and not snowy weather.

Buses to Alberta or Winnipeg and beyond are handled by **Greyhound Canada** (800-661-8747; www.greyhound.ca). Within the province, **Saskatchewan Transportation Company** (STC; 800-663-7181; www.stcbus.com) serves more than 200 communities. In summer, monthly passes for people under 26 are only $40.

VIA Rail's *Canadian* (p888) passes through Saskatoon three times weekly.

REGINA

POP 180,300

Regina has come far since its days as a hunting ground for the Cree people, who called it Wascana, meaning 'pile of bones.' Huge sums have gone into making the provincial capital an oasis in the prairie; lush parks like Wascana Centre cover former grasslands. Still, this compact city will never be a vital destination, rather it makes a convenient stop as you cross Saskatchewan. You can walk to most areas of interest, including the gentrified Cathedral Village area just west of downtown, and you'll never be more than a few blocks away from Albert St, the main north–south spine.

◎ Sights & Activities

Wascana Centre   PARK
The geographic and cultural center of Regina is Wascana Centre. Where once a small river flowed, the creation of **Wascana Lake** in 1908 gave birth to the focal point of this prairie town. This enormous park is a great place to be on a nice day, with walking trails, a bandstand and heaps of green space. A huge project in 2004 deepened the lake and banished foul-smelling weeds. Now the clear waters provide mirrored accents to vistas that include the stunning Provincial Legislature. Look for animals such as mink, hare, beaver and even the odd moose.

Wascana Place (☑306-522-3661; www.wascana.sk.ca; 2900 Wascana Dr; ◎8am-4pm Mon-Fri) has some park information and useful maps. **Marina Rentals** (☑306-757-2628; Wascana Marina; canoe/kayak/pedal boat rentals per hr $15/10/15; ◎noon-8pm mid-May–mid-Sep) rents canoes, kayaks and pedal boats. **Spruce Island** is a bird sanctuary visible from the shore.

Provincial Legislature   NOTABLE BUILDING
(☑306-787-2376; Legislative Dr; admission free; ◎8am-9pm late May-early Sep, to 5pm early Sep-late May) Finished in 1912, the arresting Leg stands in proud beaux-arts style in the midst of Wascana Centre. Ponder the rich marble and ornate carvings on free tours (held every half-hour). The great lawn out front is perfect for Frisbee or political demonstrations – whichever you prefer.

Royal Saskatchewan Museum   MUSEUM
(☑306-787-2815; www.royalsaskmuseum.ca; 2445 Albert St; admission by donation; ◎9am-5:30pm May-early Sep, to 4:30pm early Sep-May)

Located in Wascana Centre, the Royal provides a great insight into the people and geography that come together to make Saskatchewan. The three main galleries all have their own flavor, focusing on the earth, animals and Aboriginal peoples. Prairie dioramas tell the story of the native fauna and the cultures that lived off the harsh land. Sweat lodges, dinosaurs and deer all make an appearance.

MacKenzie Art Gallery   ART GALLERY
FREE (☑306-584-4250; www.mackenzieartgallery.ca; 3475 Albert St; ◎10am-5:30pm Mon-Thu, to 9pm Fri, noon-5:30pm Sat & Sun) This gallery, in a south corner of the Wascana Centre, is worth the walk. Historical Canadian and contemporary art are the focus and there's a passel of special exhibits. Go find one of Joe Fafard's cow statues outside.

Saskatchewan Science Centre   MUSEUM
(☑306-522-4629; www.sasksciencecentre.com; 2903 Powerhouse Dr; adult/child $8/4, with IMAX or planetarium $13/6; ◎9am-6pm Mon-Fri, to 9pm Wed, 11am-6pm Sat & Sun) Science class was never this much fun. Check out this science center to try your hand at scoring a goal against a virtual goaltender, blow bubbles the size of a car or find out the secret to burping. Very hands on and a big hit with kids; it has an IMAX theater and an observatory.

Regina Plains Museum   MUSEUM
FREE (☑306-780-9435; www.reginaplainsmuseum.com; 2nd fl, 1835 Scarth St; ◎10am-4pm Mon-Fri) The city's history museum packs a lot into a small space; the big draw is the glass wheat field, where thousands of individual blades of glass form an inverted chandelier of wheat. Special exhibits offer fascinating glimpses of the lives of early citizens.

RCMP Heritage Centre   MUSEUM
(☑306-522-7333; www.rcmpheritagecentre.com; 5907 Dewdney Ave W; adult/child $12/10; ◎9am-

TOURIST INFO

Tourism Saskatchewan (☑877-237-2273; www.tourismsaskatchewan.com) will send out excellent maps and guides and has info centers near the provincial borders on Hwys 1 and 16. Tourist offices in larger towns have province-wide info as well.

6pm daily Jun-Aug, 10am-5pm Mon-Fri, noon-5pm Sat & Sun Sep-May) Exhibits chart the past, present and future of the iconic Canadian Mounties (coverage of the Arctic patrols is excellent). This is also part of the RCMP (Royal Canadian Mounted Police) training center, where recruits learn the ropes (check out the jutting jaws at the cadet inspections at 12:45pm Monday to Friday). It's interesting stuff, but it doesn't stray too far from the Dudley Do-Right stereotype and you won't find much mention of recent scandals that have rocked the force.

Saskatchewan Sports Hall of Fame & Museum   MUSEUM
(☎306-780-9232; www.sshfm.com; 2205 Victoria Ave; suggested donation $2; ⊙9am-5pm Mon-Fri year-round, 1-5pm Sat & Sun late May-early Sep) With an emphasis on grassroots athletes, this museum tells the story of people like Gordie Howe, one of more than 425 Saskatchewans to have played in the NHL (a Canadian provincial record).

🎉 Festivals & Events

For a listing of events, go to www.tourism regina.com. Some festival highlights:

Regina

First Nations University of Canada Annual Powwow
CULTURAL
(☎306-790-5950; www.firstnationsuniversity.ca; ⊗last weekend of Mar) With dancers from around North America and traditional aboriginal crafts and foods.

Trial of Louis Riel
HISTORICAL DRAMA
(☎306-728-5728; www.rielcoproductions.com; ⊗Jul) Actual transcripts from Riel's 1885 trial – which resulted in his hanging (p510) – are the basis of this unpolished play which was first performed in 1967. Guy Michaurd as Riel is a standout.

Queen City Ex
FESTIVAL
(Buffalo Days; ☎306-781-9200; www.thequeencityex.com; ⊗early Aug) Saskatchewan's favorite festival; people dress up in pioneer garb for six days of concerts, pancake breakfasts, amusement-park rides, a beard-growing contest and parades.

🛏 Sleeping
Victoria Ave east of town and Albert St south of town have plenty of chain motels but you can find interesting choices in the centre.

Radisson Plaza Hotel Saskatchewan
HOTEL $$$
(☎306-522-7691; www.hotelsask.com; 2125 Victoria Ave; r $150-300; ⊛❋@🏊) Overlooking Victoria Park downtown, this 1927 grand dame is the classiest digs in Regina. Bellhops, polished brass and plush carpets are just some of the sensory cues that say 'you have arrived.' The 224 rooms have a wel-

come light touch to the palette. Ponder your single-malt by the flicker of the fireplace in the Monarch's Lounge.

Dragon's Nest B&B
B&B $$
(☎306-525-2109; www.bbcanada.com/8361.html; 2200 Angus St; r $70-140; ⊛❋🏊) This cool three-room B&B is run by a feng shui consultant, so it's all lined up the way it's supposed to be. Rooms are decked out in stylish modern furniture; offbeat touches abound, including the large dragon statue over the entrance. Breakfasts are large.

Turgeon International Hostel
HOSTEL $
(☎306-791-8165; www.hihostels.com; 2310 McIntyre St; dm members/nonmembers $24/28; ⊗Feb-Dec, reception 8-10am & 6-10pm; @🏊) Conveniently situated near Cathedral Village and Wascona Centre, this vintage Victorian house has been converted into an 18-bed hostel. There is a very homey feel to this place, the only budget choice in town.

Regina Inn Hotel
HOTEL $$
(☎306-525-6767; www.reginainn.com; 1975 Broad St; r $120-170; ❋@🏊) OK, it looks like the architect might have been thinking five-year-plan when it was time to design the neo-Soviet exterior but look closer and you see a rarity for Saskatchewan: balconies for all 235 rooms. Sure, using one might freeze your parts off in winter but in summer they are a treat. Be sure to get one of the renovated rooms which have demure decor.

Wingate by Wyndham HOTEL **$$**
(⏰306-584-7400; www.wingatebywyndhamre
gina.com; 1700 Broad St; r incl breakfast $90-160;
✳@🛜) Seven stories of modern hotel right
in the centre; the Wingate has 118 large,
comfortable rooms but note that west-fac-
ing ones view a parking garage (it's bright-
er facing east – views include the flaming
exhausts of a refinery). Breakfast includes
make-your-own waffles.

Holiday Inn Express HOTEL **$$**
(⏰306-667-9922; www.hiexpress.com; 1907
11th Ave; r incl breakfast $90-170; ✳@🛜) In
the middle of downtown, this five-story
hotel has 78 generic rooms. But you're not
staying here for the decor – it's the easy
walk to pretty much the best Regina has
to offer that's the appeal. Breakfast is
modest.

🍴 Eating

Within a 10-minute walk of downtown and
Cathedral Village are several good places
to eat.

TOP CHOICE **Fainting Goat** FUSION **$$**
(⏰306-352-4628; www.thefaintinggoat.
ca; 2330 Albert St; mains $11-24; ⏲11am-midnight
Tue-Sat) Food sourced from across Saskatch-
ewan is transformed into Mediterranean
and North African wonder by the creative
family behind this bistro-cum-cultural cen-
ter. The patio out back is far from Albert St
noise, which allows you to hear the frequent
live folk music that much better. Local art
lines the walls.

Copper Kettle PIZZA **$**
(⏰306-525-3545; www.ckpizza.ca; 1953 Scarth
St; mains $10) Regina's favorite pizza joint
is actually quite large and stylish, with
a wide patio across from Victoria Park. The
choice of toppings boggles the mind
although you'll be all atwitter if you opt
for the sausage, mushroom and sun-dried
tomato number. The pizzas have a good,
crispy crust.

13th Ave Coffee House CAFE **$**
(⏰306-522-3111; www.13thavecoffee.com; 3136
13th Ave; mains $10; ⏲11am-9pm Tue-Sat; 🅿)
Plantain chips emerging erect from the
Jivin Jerk Bowl (spicy tempeh and lots of
veggies) show that this isn't just another
coffee place. Sure the java is good but the
long veggie menu makes for fun exploring.
A Cathedral Village anchor, it has a fine pa-
tio out front.

Crushed Grape CAFE **$$**
(⏰306-352-9463; 2118 Robinson St; mains $16-
25; ⏲noon-11pm Tue-Sat, 10am-4pm Sun) In an
unassuming bland brick building in Cathedral Village, this bistro comes alive inside
with local art and on many nights live jazz.
As the name implies, there's a great list of
wines by the glass. The menu is inventive,
the Sunday brunch excellent. Many vie for
patio tables in summer.

La Bodega MEDITERRANEAN **$$**
(⏰306-546-3660; www.labodegaregina.com; 2228
Albert St; small mains $10-16) The three-level
patio here wraps around a huge old tree
like a treehouse. Sharing little plates of food
and good wine amidst twinkling lights is the
peak of Regina romance. In winter, there's a
beautiful backlit ice bar carved outside.

Fireside Bistro FUSION **$$**
(⏰306-761-2305; www.firesidebistro.ca; 2305
Smith St; mains $14-26) Stationed on a quiet
suburban street, this converted Victorian
former guesthouse has style. Steaks, pasta
and seafood highlight the broad menu;
outside on the superb patio you can enjoy
casual fare like fine burgers. Don't forget to
ask about the ghost.

🍷 Drinking

Albert St in the center is a good place to
carouse. Dewdney Ave, just north of downtown in the otherwise lackluster Old Warehouse District, has a fun strip of pubs and
clubs. Wherever you are, look for Bushwak-
kers, the excellent local microbrewery.

TOP CHOICE **Bushwakker Brewpub** PUB
(⏰306-359-7276; www.bushwakker.com;
2206 Dewdney Ave) In a 1913 warehouse that
is as impressive as its beer, Bushwakker is
reason enough to cross the tracks to the Old
Warehouse District. Works by local artists
are on display, there's live music many nights,
and the pub menu features good sandwiches,
burgers and pizza. But the real draw are the
scores of house brews, including the addic-
tive seasonal Blackberry Mead and the sensational Trephination Double IPA.

O'Hanlon's PUB
(⏰306-566-4094; 1947 Scarth St) Sharing
the same fine patio with Copper Kettle,
O'Hanlon's has a grungy Irish pub vibe.
There's an excellent array of Irish and British beers and local microbrews on tap. On
weekends there's live music which you'll
love if you like offshoots of Modest Mouse.
Serves food late.

Cathedral Village Free House   BAR
(☎306-359-1661; www.thefreehouse.com; 2062
Albert St) A huge back deck is the place to
be on an even slightly warm night. The pub
menu is served late and goes beyond the
usual fish-and-chips cliché. Microbrews are
on tap – watch for $5 specials. Live music
includes acoustic early in the week, morphing to hard-edged stuff at weekends.

Drink   BAR
(☎306-543-7475; www.thedrinknightclub.ca;
2044 Dewdney Ave) Hip and happening on
either the right or the wrong side of the
tracks in the Old Warehouse District; DJs,
theme nights and much debauchery ensue
come Saturday night.

☆ Entertainment
The band shell at the northern end of Wascana Centre hosts **Sunday concerts** (www.
wascana.sk.ca; admission free; ☺2-4pm Jun-Aug).

Theater
Globe Theatre   THEATER
(☎306-525-6400; www.globetheatrelive.com;
1801 Scarth St; tickets $20-50; ☺Sep-May) The
local cast of players puts on contemporary
theatrical presentations in the round. Constantly garnering rave reviews, this is a recognized cultural arts institution in Regina.

Conexus Arts Centre   THEATER
(☎306-565-4500; www.conexusartscentre.ca;
200 Lakeshore Dr) Home of the symphony
orchestra and touring musicians, the Arts
Centre looks vaguely like vintage Saskatchewan grain elevators.

Sports
Saskatchewan Roughriders   FOOTBALL
(☎306-525-2181, 888-474-3377; www.saskriders.com; Mosaic Stadium, 2940 10th Ave; ☺Jun-Nov) Not to be confused with the Ottawa
Rough Riders, the Green Riders, as they're
known to legions of rabid locals, have
achieved cult status within the Canadian
Football League (CFL). Mosaic Stadium
usually sells out to mobs of fans who don,
of all things, watermelon hats.

Regina Pats   HOCKEY
(☎306-543-7800; www.reginapats.com; Brandt
Centre, Exhibition Park; ☺Sep-Mar) The
younger, tougher, more eager players of the
Western Hockey League (WHL) make for
an exciting brand of hockey. Fanatic fans,
crashing and bashing – everything a hockey game should be. It's about 3km west of
the center.

Cinemas
On the lower level of the library, **Central Library Repertory Cinema** (☎306-777-6027;
www.reginalibrary.ca; 2311 12th Ave; adult/child
$6/3) shows art films. There's an IMAX theater at the Saskatchewan Science Centre.

Casinos
Casino Regina   CASINO
(☎306-565-3000; 1880 Saskatchewan Dr;
☺9am-4am) In a sad commentary on priorities, the beautiful old train station has been
converted into a vast casino, where you can
derail your budget on games of chance.

ℹ Information
Free wi-fi is available throughout the downtown
and Cathedral Village areas.

Central Library (☎306-777-6000; 2311 12th
Ave; ☺9:30am-9pm Mon-Thu, to 6pm Fri, to
5pm Sat, 1:30-5pm Sun) Free internet access.

Main Post Office (☎866-607-6301; 2200
Saskatchewan Dr)

Prairie Dog (www.prairiedogmag.com) Feisty,
free and fun biweekly newspaper with good
entertainment listings.

Regina General Hospital (☎306-766-4444;
1440 14th Ave; ☺24hr) Emergency room.

Tourism Regina (☎306-789-5099, 800-661-5099; www.tourismregina.com; 1925 Rose St;
☺9am-5pm Mon-Fri) Useful local guides and
maps.

ℹ Getting There & Away
Regina International Airport (YQR; ☎306-761-7555; www.yqr.ca; 5200 Regina Ave), 5km west of
downtown, has service to major Canadian destinations and Minneapolis and Chicago in the US.

The new **bus station** (☎306-787-3340; 1717
Saskatchewan Dr) is downtown and has lockers.
Greyhound Canada runs east to Winnipeg ($93,
nine hours, two daily) and west to Calgary ($71,
11 hours, two daily). **STC** (☎306-787-3340; www.
stcbus.com) runs buses in all directions, including
three daily to Saskatoon ($40, three hours).

ℹ Getting Around
The airport is a 10-minute cab ride ($10) from
downtown; there is no public transit service.

Regina Transit (☎306-777-7433; www.regina
transit.com; adult/child $2.50/2, day pass $7)
operates city buses. Most routes converge on
11th St downtown.

Metered street **parking** ($1 to $2 per hour,
from 8am to 6pm) downtown is limited to two-hour stays; there are many paid parking garages.

Co-op Taxi (☎306-525-2727) comes when
you call.

Qu'Appelle Valley

Heading northeast from Regina, along Hwy 10, you are in for a treat. The beauty in Saskatchewan lies in its contrasts, and the Qu'Appelle Valley is just one of those provincial oddities. The wide valley stretches out in front of you, with lakes and little towns dotted along the way, and the Qu'Appelle River guides you, with its blue water reflecting the surrounding green hills. Don't be afraid to get off the main road and explore – you'll be glad you did.

At **Abernethy**, turn south of Hwy 10 and after 9km you'll reach **Motherwell Homestead National Historic Site** (☑306-333-2116; www.parkscanada.gc.ca/motherwell; adult/child $8/4; ⊙9am-5pm late May-early Sep), a fascinating early Saskatchewan farm where you can make hay with huge draft horses and meet lots of characters dressed up in period costume. A small cafe serves homemade lunches.

Regina Beach

Less than an hour's drive northwest of Regina, this small beach town is an idyllic summer spot. Kids play merrily by the clear, blue Last Mountain Lake while picnickers enjoy a shady waterfront park.

WORTH A TRIP

MANITOU BEACH

Underground springs have created the 'Lake of Healing Waters' (as it was called by the Cree), 180km north of Regina and 120km southeast of Saskatoon, near the town of Watrous. **Manitou Lake** (www.watrousmanitou.com) has Dead Sea–style waters, chockablock with minerals and salts, making the water three times the density of the ocean – in other words, you float.

If you're leery of the pungent lake, you can take a soak at the **Manitou Springs Resort & Mineral Spa** (☑306-946-2233, 800-667-7672; www.manitousprings.ca; cnr Lake Ave & Watrous St; baths $11). Get a room ($115 to $170) and you can take the plunge repeatedly.

TOP CHOICE Blue Bird Cafe (☑306-729-2385; 108 Centre St; mains from $7; ⊙10am-8pm May-Sep) is an old-time classic with wooden floors and screen doors. The fish-and-chips are legendary: lighter-than-air crispy batter on tender white fish. Equally evocative ice cream stands are nearby.

Take Hwy 11 for 32km then turn north on Hwy 54 for 16km to Regina Beach.

SOUTHERN SASKATCHEWAN

Along the Trans-Canada Hwy (Hwy 1) is iconic Saskatchewan, the sort of wide open prairie that country songs are written about. As you explore the rabbit warren of unpaved, lonely back roads, it's easy to feel divorced from modern life. It's not hard to imagine thousands of bison charging over the nearby hill, aboriginal villages in the valley or the North West Mounted Police (NWMP) patrolling the prairie on horseback. There is diversity among this immensity, with rolling grassland, short sharp hills and badlands befitting a classic Western.

Moose Jaw

POP 32,200

> 'Moose Jaw isn't a city or a municipality or even a geographic location! Moose Jaw is a damn virus that has permanently afflicted Regina and for which there is no known cure!'

So said a Regina newspaper editor about 100 years ago and, indeed, if there was ever a town that could say it had a sordid past, Moose Jaw is it. From simple beginnings as a Canadian Pacific Railway outpost, the town steadily grew in both size and infamy. It was rebellious, ripe with brothels, had brushes with the KKK and known for rampant corruption and even slavery.

In the 1920s it was a haven for Al Capone and his gang, who used the town as a base for smuggling whiskey into the US.

Small Canadian towns looking to extract riches from a dubious past can take heart in today's Moose Jaw, which dubs itself 'Little Chicago.' Its attractions, remarkably well preserved art-deco buildings, numerous murals and friendly locals make it unmissable.

◉ Sights & Activities

Main St and the historic downtown should be your focus. Expect to spend a couple of hours wandering about.

Western Development Museum MUSEUM
(WDM; ☑306-693-5989; www.wdm.ca; 50 Diefenbaker Dr; adult/child $8.50/2; ⊗9am-5pm daily, closed Mon Jan-Mar) If you can drive it, fly it, pedal it or paddle it, odds are you'll find an example of it at this branch of the WDM. Dedicated to transport within Saskatchewan, it has planes, trains, automobiles and even the odd wagon.

FREE Yvette Moore Gallery ART GALLERY
(☑306-693-7600; www.yvettemoore.com; 76 Fairford St W; ⊗10am-5pm) Just west of Main St in a proud heritage building, this renowned local artist displays her evocative and hyper-realistic works portraying Saskatchewan and its people. The cafe is an artful place for lunch.

Temple Gardens Mineral Spa SPA
(☑306-694-5055; www.templegardens.sk.ca; 24 Fairford St E; adult/child Mon-Thu $7/6, Fri-Sun $16/11; ⊗9am-11pm Sun-Thu, to midnight Fri & Sat) A modern complex houses a vast indoor-outdoor pool filled with steaming mineral water from deep below the prairie. The spa offers a long list of treatments.

☞ Tours

Over three dozen **murals** capturing, sadly, some tamer moments in Moose Jaw's history adorn walls around town. The information center has a superb walking-tour map with descriptions. **Moose Jaw Trolley Company** (☑306-693-8637; adult/child $13/6; ⊗10:30am, 11:45am, 2pm, 3:15pm & 4:30pm) runs tours from the visitor center aboard fake streetcars.

🛏 Sleeping & Eating

Many chain motels are found north of town on Hwy 1. Yvette Moore Gallery has one of several good cafes downtown.

Temple Gardens Mineral Spa Resort HOTEL $$
(☑306-694-5055, 800-718-7727; www.templegardens.sk.ca; 24 Fairford St E; r $120-260; ❄@🛜≋) Right downtown, the hotel attached to the spa offers swank accommodation and access to a casino (this is Moose Jaw after all). Most rooms have balconies or terraces, top-end ones have Jacuzzis fed with the spa's water.

DON'T MISS

THE REAL UNDERWORLD

A tunnel all the way to China can be found in the **Tunnels of Moose Jaw** (☑306-693-5261; www.tunnelsofmoosejaw.com; 18 Main St; tours adult/child $14/7.50, both tours $23/12; ⊗10am-7pm Jun-Sep, hours vary rest of year). Buried deep under the town's streets is a series of passages that have both a tragic and fascinating history. Take a tour and learn about the hardship and discrimination heaped upon Chinese workers on their 'Passage to Fortune'; forced to work and live underground, they toiled in steamy laundries trying to pay for their freedom. Fast-forward a few decades to make the 'Chicago Connection.' Al Capone is rumored to have visited MJ in the 1920s to oversee his bootlegging operation – a caper that was masterminded in these very tunnels.

Capone's Hideaway Motel MOTEL $
(☑306-692-6422; www.caponeshideawaymotel.com; 1 Main St; r $60-90; ❄🛜) Across from the defunct train station where Al and the boys might have once arrived, this old motel is more novelty than lodging. The anonymous furnishings will appeal to anyone on the lam while the dead flowers in pots seem appropriate for a place named after a guy who liked to rub out his rivals.

Deja Vu Cafe CANADIAN $
(☑306-692-6666; 16 High St E; mains $10; ⊗11am-10pm) Located downtown in an especially impressive heritage building, this restaurant specializes in two things: wings in myriad flavors (anyone for 'garlic inferno'?) and milkshakes in even more flavors (from tutti-frutti to black licorice).

Hopkins Dining Parlor CANADIAN $$
(☑306-692-5995; www.hopkinsdining.com; 65 Athabasca St W; mains $14-30; ⊗4-10pm Sun & Mon, 11:30am-10pm Tue-Sat) This three-story heritage house is a relaxed eatery with hearty Canadian fare that ranges from prime rib to wings. If you accidentally miss dessert, the large gift shop has fudge.

ℹ Information

Look for the huge anatomically correct moose statue beside the impressive **visitor center**

(☎306-693-8097; www.moosejawtourism.com; Thatcher Dr E at Hwy 1; ⊙9am-6pm). A summer annex, the 'Little Chicago Info Booth,' operates from a bus on Main St near the tunnels.

ℹ️ Getting There & Away

STC runs five daily trips to Regina ($15, one hour) from the downtown **bus station** (☎306-692-2345; 63 High St E).

Cypress Hills Interprovincial Park

The eastern edge of this **provincial park** (☎306-662-4411; www.cypresshills.com) straddling the Alberta–Saskatchewan border is a vertical oasis of topography that ignores the provincial border. The contrast between the billiard-table prairie and the rolling hills is arresting. Green grassy hills give way to trees and lakes, an arboreal apparition arising from the landscape. Deer, moose and other wildlife flourish in this forested corner of the province.

CENTRE BLOCK

Approaching from the east you arrive in the holiday hub for weekending locals. Ice-cream stands jam between souvenir shops. Set among trees, the popular **campground** (sites $17-32) gets full over weekends and on holidays. The park entrance is 37km south of Hwy 1 on Hwy 21.

WESTERN BLOCK

Much less visited than the Centre Block and therefore much more appealing, the Western Block spills over into Alberta. Here amid beautiful rolling green hills you'll find **Fort Walsh National Historic Site** (☎306-662-3590; www.parkscanada.ca/fortwalsh; adult/child $8/4; ⊙9:30am-5:30pm late May-early Sep). Established in 1875 and operational for eight years, this outpost had a small yet significant role in the history of the west. After the Battle of the Little Bighorn (aka Custer's Last Stand), Chief Sitting Bull and 5000 of his followers arrived in the Cyprus Hills area. The NWMP moved its headquarters to Fort Walsh as a result, and actually maintained peaceful relations with the Sioux, while they were in Canada.

Camping in the Western Block is serene and backcountry. The entrance is 50km south of Hwy 1 on Hwy 271. Gap Rd, which connects to the Centre Block, has deteriorated into a dodgy 4WD track.

Eastend

Isolated in southwest Saskatchewan, Eastend is tumbleweed quiet but not without charm. Nestled into a small valley about 80km south of Hwy 1, the town's few streets are lined with older buildings. The metaphor-aware **visitor center** (☎306-295-4144; www.dinocountry.com; Red Coat Dr; ⊙9am-5pm Mon-Fri) has a dinosaur skeleton on display.

In fact, one of the most complete *Tyrannosaurus rex* skeletons found anywhere was discovered in Saskatchewan in 1994. The **T-Rex Discovery Centre** (☎306-295-4009; www.trexcentre.ca; T-Rex Dr; adult/child $9/6; ⊙9am-9pm Jul & Aug, to 5pm Sep-Jun) is a glitzy working lab carved into the hillside. There are a variety of tours available, along with dinosaur dig options if you feel the need to, er, bone up.

Val Marie

At the gateway to Grasslands National Park is the hamlet of Val Marie, tiny, rough around the edges and endearing.

For a holier than thou sleeping experience, **The Convent** (☎306-298-4515; www.convent.ca; Hwy 4; s/d incl breakfast $55/75) offers beds amid classic brickwork and beautiful hardwood floors. Built in 1935, this former residential school has beautifully restored rooms, a labyrinth of staircases and even a confessional (in case you break a vow or two during the night). It has a basic restaurant, too.

The town is 140km south of Hwy 1 on Hwy 4.

Grasslands National Park

Feel at home on the range in this verdant **park** (www.parkscanada.ca/grasslands; admission free, primitive campsites $16) between Val Marie and Killdear right on the US border. Here, treeless, rolling grassy hills meet the endless sky. Take a drive through on the self-drive tour or, better yet, camp out – just don't expect shade. That musky odor you smell may not be your tentmate but could be one of the 75 resident bison.

The **visitor center** (☎306-298-2257; Hwy 4 & Centre St, Val Marie; ⊙8am-5pm daily Jun-Aug, to 4:30pm Mon-Fri Apr-May & Sep-Oct) has good advice on places to camp and ways to experience the full majesty of the park.

Moose Mountain Provincial Park

Moose Mountain is a massive plateau dotted with glacially created lakes, ponds and sloughs and topped with aspen; some of it is preserved in this **park** (☑306-577-2600; www.tpcs.gov.sk.ca/moosemountain; Hwy 9), about 70km south of Hwy 1 and 150km southeast of Regina. This is another popular recreation area in the summer and services abound. For camping fees, see p530.

Kenosee Inn (☑306-577-2099; www.kenoseeinn.com; Hwy 9; r $95-160, cabins $100-170; @) is an unpolished hotel nestled among the trees on the shores of Lake Kenosee. Skip the standard hotel rooms and go for a cabin: they're a bit rustic, but the smell of cedar intermixed with the aroma of steaks on the barbecue will remind you of what a holiday on the lake is really supposed to be like.

Yorkton

Strong Eastern European roots – especially to the strikingly similar Ukraine – flavor Yorkton. A large branch of the **Western Development Museum** (WDM; ☑306-783-8361; Hwy 16 W; adult/child $5/2; ☺9am-5pm Mon-Fri year-round, noon-5pm Sat & Sun May-Aug) highlights these settlers, as well as ones from 50 other countries, as they carved an existence out of the rough landscape. Indoor and outdoor displays tell their story.

Fifty-five feet up in the air across the ceiling of the dome at **St Mary's Ukrainian Catholic Church** (☑306-783-4549; 155 Catherine St) is a breathtaking work of art. Painted from 1939 to 1941 by Stephen Meuhsh, this fresco rivals anything in the great cathedrals.

Canadian filmmakers and producers compete for Canada's Golden Sheaf Awards at the acclaimed **Yorkton Short Film & Video Festival** (☑306-782-7077; www.yorktonshortfilm.org; ☺late May), now in its eighth decade. Winning films have included 2010's *Silent Bombs: All for the Motherland*, a Saskatchewan-produced documentary about Soviet nuclear testing in Kazakhstan.

Yorkton is 187km east of Regina on Hwy 10 and 333km east of Saskatoon on Hwy 16.

For more information, see www.tourismyorkton.com.

Veregin

A century ago in mother Russia lived a group of people called the Doukhobours. Oppressed because of their pacifist leanings and opposition to the Orthodox church, 7500 Doukhobours immigrated to Canada in 1899. Their benefactor? Leo 'War and Peace' Tolstoy.

Learn the whole story at the **National Doukhobour Heritage Village** (☑306-542-4441; www.ndhv.ca; Hwy 5; adult/child $5/1; ☺10am-6pm mid-May–mid-Sep), a living artifact of life in the province in the early 1900s. Against a backdrop of historic grain elevators, a compound of buildings furnished in period style are open to the public. If you're lucky, they'll be baking bread and lunch will follow.

Veregin is about 70km northeast of Yorkton via Hwys 9 and 5, or across various unpaved roads traversing the fertile farms.

SASKATOON

POP 208,100

> 'Sundown in the Paris of the Prairies. Wheat Kings have all their treasures buried.'

The Tragically Hip summed it up pretty well. Saskatoon, the Paris of the Prairies, is full of hidden treasures. The South Saskatchewan River winds through the lively downtown, enhancing the city's genteel air, a quality missing from its rival Regina to the south. This is the most-cultured stop between Winnipeg and Edmonton.

Despite the town's legacy as an 1883 settlement by Ontario's Temperance Colonization Society, it knows how to heat up cold winter days and short summer nights.

◉ Sights

The river is crossed by a gaggle of bridges that, er, span the history of such structures, including the rickety 1907 **Victoria Bridge** and the soaring 1908 **Canadian Pacific Railway Bridge**. The banks are lined with paths that link serene parks throughout the centre including **Kiwanis Memorial Park** and the newly opened **Riverfront at River Landing**.

Western Development Museum   MUSEUM
(WDM; ☑306-931-1910; www.wdm.ca; 2610 Lorne Ave S; adult/child $8.50/2; ☺9am-5pm) If you

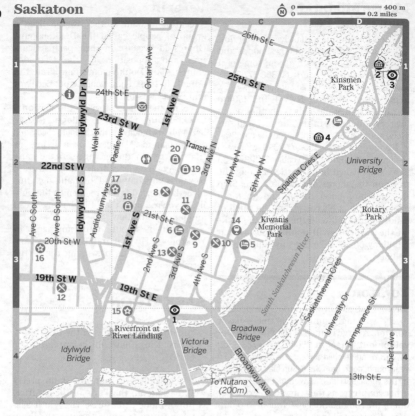

only go to one museum in Saskatchewan, this branch of the WDM should be it. With stunning detail and nothing overlooked, this is a faithful re-creation of Saskatoon c 1910. On the longest indoor street of any museum in Canada you can roam through the buildings – from a dentist's office that looks like it was taken from a horror film to the pharmacy where hundreds of vintage bottles line the shelves – and find countless treasures. There are trains, steam tractors, a sod house, buggies, sleighs and even a jail. Beyond the street is the excellent exhibition 'Winning the Prairie Gamble,' chronicling the rise from hardship that gave birth to the province. The museum is 4km south of town.

Gearheads won't want to miss the **Transportation Gallery** where dozens of cars are on display, including a 1912 Peerless and a 1972 Cadillac.

Meewasin Valley & Centre

NATURE RESERVE & PARK

As the South Saskatchewan cuts a wide swath through the center of town, the depression that it forms has come to be called Meewasin Valley. 'Meewasin' is the Cree word for beautiful, and it more than lives up to its name. Trees populate the riverbanks, while pathways, including the 60km **Meewasin Trail**, extend from the downtown paths and wind through forests and shore forming an urban network of trails. Popular with walkers, cyclists and wandering travelers, the trails have picnicking areas.

Further north, gaze out at **Mendel Island**, keeping your eyes peeled for the abundant wildlife that calls this inner-city island home.

The informative **Meewasin Valley Centre** (306-665-6887; www.meewasin.com; 402 3rd Ave S; admission free; 9am-5pm Mon-Fri year-round, 10:30am-5pm Sat & Sun Jun-Aug) is

Saskatoon

run by the authority that manages the natural areas of the valley. It tells the history of the river and the city, and has maps and superb self-guided walking tours. In summer it often offers excellent local **walking tours**.

Ukrainian Museum of Canada　MUSEUM
(☎306-244-3800; www.umc.sk.ca; 910 Spadina Cres E; adult/child $4/2; ⊙10am-5pm Tue-Sat, 1-5pm Sun) This museum tells the story of Ukrainian immigration to Canada. With an emphasis on traditional clothing and contemporary artwork, it provides a good insight into the world of Ukrainian Canadians. Check out the gift shop for *pysanka* (decorated wooden eggs).

FREE **Mendel Art Gallery**　ART GALLERY
(☎306 078 7810; www.mundvl.c.a; 950 Spadina Cres E; ⊙9am-9pm) A short walk northeast along the river from the downtown area brings you to this gallery. With a focus on local artists and frequently changing exhibits, it's a pleasant addition to a stroll by the river. The conservatory has a Zen garden to quiet the soul.

Saskatchewan Railway Museum　MUSEUM
(☎306-382-9855; www.saskrailmuseum.org; 202 Ave M S; adult/child $4/3; ⊙noon-5pm Thu-Mon late May-early Sep) The railroad opened up Saskatchewan to settlers and it was a vital lifeline for getting grain to market. The small collection here does a good job of showing how things were when rails, not roads, were the most important links in the province. It's west of the center on Hwy 7, then 2km south on Hwy 60.

☛ Tours

Shearwater Boat Cruises　BOAT CRUISE
(☎888-747-7572; www.shearwatertours.com; Spadina Cres E; adult/child from $17/10; ⊙12:30-7pm late May-early Sep) Open-top boats cruise the river all summer long. Ponder the bridges while enjoying a cool one from the bar. The dock is behind the Mendel Art Gallery.

✸✸ Festivals & Events

Sasktel Saskatchewan Jazz Festival
　MUSIC
(☎800-638-1211; www.saskjazz.com; tickets $5-50; ⊙late Jun-early Jul) Come show your soul patch at this jazzy festival. Various venues around town with lots of good acts from near and far.

Taste of Saskatchewan　FOOD & DRINK
(☎306-975-3175; www.tasteofsaskatchewan.ca; Kiwanis Memorial Park; admission free; ⊙mid-Jul) More than 30 local restaurants sell various high-caloric treats over a week; performers help you work up an appetite.

Saskatoon Fringe Theatre Festival
　THEATER
(☎306-664-2239; www.saskatoonfringe.org; tickets from $10; ⊙late Jul/early Aug) Live theater – for people who don't even like live theater. Rough-edged acts, music and stuff for kids.

Shakespeare on the Saskatchewan
　THEATER
(☎306-652-9100; www.shakespeareonthe saskatchewan.com; adult/child from $24/10; ⊙Jul & Aug) We few, we happy few who get to enjoy the best of the Bard on the riverbank.

Saskatoon Ex   CARNIVAL
(☑306-931-7149; www.saskatoonexhibition.ca; adult/child $13/free; ☉mid-Aug) Live music, racing pigs, chuck wagon races and rides to reacquaint you with your lunch.

Sleeping

The northern parts of Circle Dr near the airport and Hwy 16 are lined with chain motels.

TOP CHOICE **Hotel Senator**   HOTEL $$
(☑306-244-6141; www.hotelsenator.ca; 243 21st St E; r $90-160; ✳@☎) Dating from 1908, the much-modified former Flanagan Hotel is creaky but well maintained. Many of the 38 rooms are shaped unusually but that just adds to the charm that is the antidote for every mind-numbingly familiar chain. You can get a sense of the ornate past in the smallish lobby area. The pub is a good place to while away the night.

Delta Bessborough Hotel   HOTEL $$
(☑306-244-5521, 800-268-1133; www.delta hotels.com; 601 Spadina Cres E; r from $130; ✳@☎☒) In the grand tradition of the famed Canadian railway hotels, the Bessborough is easily up to the castle standard; it is the architectural exclamation point on the Saskatoon skyline. The interior reflects a luxe ethos that was especially fanciful when the hotel opened in Depression-era 1935. The 225 rooms come in many shapes and sizes. Sadly things have slipped a bit and the back gardens are shabby where there should be a stunning riverfront cafe.

Park Town Hotel   HOTEL $$
(☑306-244-5564; www.parktownhotel.com; 924 Spadina Cres E; r $100-170; ✳@☎☒) With prime real estate right beside the river and near the parks, this architecturally suspect hotel is a good place to soak up the local natural ambience. The 172 comfortable rooms and indoor pool are a plus. Ask for a room on the east side for river views.

Gordon Howe Campground   CAMPGROUND $
(☑306-975-3328; www.saskatoon.ca; 1640 Ave P S, south of 11th St; tent/RV sites $17/28; ☉mid-Apr–mid-Oct; @) There are enough trees amid the 135 sites to give you a bit of privacy and the tent sites are fairly large. It's named in honor of Mr Hockey himself, Saskatoon native Gordie Howe, and is about 2km southwest of the center.

Eating & Drinking

The center has many good choices for food and drink but venture just south of the river on Broadway Ave in Nutana for myriad choices with a cool neighborhood feel.

The **Saskatoon Farmers Market** (☑306-384-6262; www.saskatoonfarmersmarket.com; cnr Ave B South & 19th St W; ☉8am-2pm Sat) is in the nascent River Landing area. It has a small indoor area with stalls open daily through the year, but the main action is outside on summer Saturdays.

TOP CHOICE **Souleio**   CAFE $
(☑306-979-8102; www.souleio.com; 265 3rd Ave S; mains from $8; ☉7am-7pm Mon-Sat) The foodie's choice in the province, Souleio works with and promotes local producers. There is a large and drool-worthy deli and grocery area. Dine in or take-out paninis, soups, salads and daily hot specials.

Park Cafe   CAFE $
(☑306-652-6781; 515 20th St W; mains $8; ☉8am-4pm) Heading north into the wild and need a breakfast that will fuel your adventure? This award-winning, unassuming joint serves up breakfast platters that are legend. The hash browns are works of art.

Yard & Flagon Pub   PUB $$
(☑306-653-8883; 718 Broadway Ave; mains from $12) Hop on up to the rooftop deck and enjoy views of the rooftops of the historic Nutana neighborhood. Inside, the vintage feel continues with a well-worn 'ye olde tyme' shtick. The menu has all the classics and the burgers and wings are good foundations for pints.

John's   STEAKHOUSE $$$
(☑306-244-6384; 401 21st St E; mains $15-55; ☉11:30am-11pm Mon-Fri, 4:30-11pm Sat) For the carnivores among us, this is the place to go – big thick steaks, prime rib and decadently delicious lobster. Cavernous, dark and posh, it is a good place for a casual lunch in winter. Make sure you take a walk through the wine cellar to pick that perfect shiraz to go with your sirloin.

2nd Ave Grill   CANADIAN $$
(☑306-244-9899; www.2ndavegrill.com; 10-123 2nd Ave S; mains $10-30) Dark and a little clubby, this casual restaurant has a broad menu that features steaks, burgers, pasta, salads and much more prepared well by the sure-handed kitchen. There are no surprises, but then again that's a compliment. The bar is a popular after-work spot.

Red Pepper
ASIAN FUSION $

(☎306-477-1977; 145 3rd Ave S; mains $7-10; ⊙11am-9pm Mon-Sat) At this literal hole-in-the-wall with vinyl booths, the roar of woks competes with the cheerful chatter of patrons. Excellent Asian food (from Korea across China through Thailand and on to Malaysia) pours forth from the kitchen on plates older than you are.

Jake's on 21st
CAFE $

(☎306-373-8383; 307 21st St E; mains $8-10; ⊙8am-5pm Mon-Fri; 🛜@) The throaty hiss of the espresso machine speaks volumes about Jake's. Great coffee, a hipster vibe, lots of sandwiches and baked goods; deservedly popular for a weekday lunch.

☆ Entertainment
Nightclubs & Live Music

Broadway Ave in Nutana is the go-to place for nocturnal entertainment. **Credit Union Centre** (☎306-975-3155; www.creditunioncentre.com; 3535 Thatcher Ave) is the local place for big-name concerts; it's 12.5km north of downtown.

Lydia's Pub
LIVE MUSIC

(☎306-652-8595; 650 Broadway Ave) Right in Nutana on Broadway Ave, this popular double-story watering hole packs 'em in. Live music is a feature most nights. With 15 beers on tap and another 40 by the bottle, you'll find one you like – sooner or later.

Bud's
LIVE MUSIC

(☎306-244-4155; 817 Broadway Ave) Classic blues and good ol' rock and roll are the standards here. There is a weekly jam night if you feel like getting up and locking in the groove.

Fez
NIGHTCLUB

(☎306-665-7479; 834B Broadway Ave) These guys like to rock all night, with cover bands, local bands and cheap drinks keeping the fans entertained.

Spadina Freehouse
LIVE MUSIC

(☎306-668-1000; 608 Spadina Cres E) In a gentrified part of the center north of the river, this place doesn't inspire from the outside. But it has a swell selection of brews and live music that runs from soul to rock. In summer the terrace out front will make you forget the architecture behind.

Theater & Cinemas
Persephone Theatre
THEATER

(☎306-384-7727; www.persephonetheatre.org; 100 Spadina Cres E; tickets from $22) This perennial theatric standout has proud new quarters in the Remai Arts Centre at River Landing. Comedy, drama and musicals are all regulars.

Broadway Theatre
CINEMA

(☎306-652-6556; www.broadwaytheatre.ca; 715 Broadway Ave; adult/child $10/5) This historic Nutana cinema shows cult classics, art films and occasional local live performances.

Saskatchewan Native Theatre Co
THEATER

(☎306-933-2262; www.sntc.ca; 220 20th St W; ⊙Feb-Jun) Contemporary stage productions by Canadian Aboriginal artists highlight cultural issues both through comedy and drama.

TCU Place
THEATER

(☎306-975-7770; www.tcuplace.com; 35 22nd St E) There's a variety of concerts, lectures, dance performances and plays held here through the year. The **Saskatoon Symphony** (☎306-665-6414; www.saskatoonsymphony.org; tickets $15-55) plays regularly.

Sports
Saskatoon Blades
HOCKEY

(☎306-938-7800; www.saskatoonblades.com; Credit Union Centre; ⊙Sep-Mar) This WHL team plays a fast, rough and sharp style of hockey.

🔒 Shopping

Broadway Ave in Nutana is lined with funky shops and boutiques. Downtown, **Midtown Plaza Mall** (☎306-653-8844; www.midtownplaza.ca; 201 1st Ave S) is a large enclosed mall with all the expected chains.

White Cat
BOOKSTORE

(☎306-652-2287; 129 2nd Ave N) An excellent used book store that's ideal for stocking up before you head north to the tundra.

Vinyl Exchange
MUSIC

(☎306-244-7090; 128 2nd Ave N) This used-record and CD shop will sort you out with hard-to-find tunes to fill out your collection. It's worth a browse just to see the descriptions about the artists. Take the Tragically Hip for example: 'a beloved Canadian institution – we, however, prefer universal healthcare.'

Turning the Tide
BOOKSTORE

(☎306-955-3070; 525 11th St E) Literally a revolutionary bookstore, this small Nutana shop just off Broadway Ave specializes in the kinds of books shunned by mainstream media and burned by others.

❶ Information

Central Library (☎306-777-6000; 311 23rd St E; ⏱10am-9pm Mon-Thu, to 6pm Fri & Sat year-round, 1-5:30pm Sun Sep-May) Free internet access.

Main Post Office (☎866-607-6301; 215 Ontario Ave)

Planet S (www.planetsmag.com) Irreverent and free biweekly newspaper with good entertainment listings.

Saskatoon City Hospital (☎306-655-8000; 701 Queen St; ⏱24hr)

Tourism Saskatoon (☎306-242-1206, 800-567-2444; www.tourismsaskatoon.com; 101-202 4th Ave N; ⏱8:30am-5pm Mon-Fri Sep-May, to 5:30 daily Jun-Aug) A tourism info booth on the corner of Ave C North and 47th St W (near the airport and Hwy 16 north of the center) has the same summer hours.

❶ Getting There & Away

AIR John G Diefenbaker International Airport (YXE; ☎306-975-8900; www.yxe.ca; 2625 Airport Dr) is 5km northeast of the city, off Idylwyld Dr and Hwy 16. There's service to major Canadian cities plus Minneapolis in the US.

BUS STC covers the province extensively from the **bus station** (☎306-933-8000; 50 23rd St E); three daily buses head south to Regina ($40, three hours) and north to Prince Albert ($25, two hours). Greyhound Canada runs two buses to Winnipeg ($138, 12 hours), one to Calgary ($77, eight hours) and three to Edmonton ($74, seven hours) daily.

TRAIN Unfortunately, the **train station** (Chappell Dr) is in the middle of nowhere (8km from downtown); the thrice-weekly VIA Rail *Canadian* leaves about midnight westbound and in the morning eastbound.

❶ Getting Around

A taxi to the airport costs $15. A direct line to **Blueline Taxi** (☎306-653-3333) is available at the train station, with a trip to downtown costing $20.

City buses (☎360-975-7500; www.saskatoon.ca; adult/child $2.75/1.65) converge on the transit hub of 23rd St E (between 2nd and 3rd Aves N).

Bike Doctor (☎306-664-8555; 623 Main St; per day $25) rents bikes.

AROUND SASKATOON

Wanuskewin Heritage Park

Although most of the museums in Saskatchewan devote a portion of their displays to the history of the province's first inhabitants, this **heritage park** (☎306-931-6767; www.wanuskewin.com; Penner Rd, off Hwy 11; adult/child $8.50/4; ⏱9am-8pm late May-early Sep, to 5pm early Sep-late May) is devoted solely to that purpose. About 17km north of Saskatoon, alongside the South Saskatchewan River, the 116-hectare site presents and interprets the area's rich 7000-year-old aboriginal history. At Wanuskewin (wah-nus-*kay*-win; Cree for 'seeking peace of mind') you can wander **interpretive trails** through grassy hills and valley meadows discovering some of the 19 pre-contact sites here. The museum itself is well presented, with large interactive displays where guests are encouraged to feel buffalo furs and poke their heads into a tepee.

Virtually invisible from the surrounding prairie, the Opamihaw ('the one who flies') Valley has been left untouched and reveals why this was a spiritual and sacred place. Cultural **dance performances** take place on summer afternoons, and you can even camp out in a tepee for the night (adult/child $125/75). The on-site **cafe** (mains $5-12) serves bison pot pie, rabbit stew, bannock

---

MAKE MERRY WITH BERRIES

Valley Rd runs west of the river going south of Saskatoon. Flat as you'd expect fertile riverland to be, it is lined with some of the best berry farms in Saskatchewan. In summer it has a bounty of stands selling baskets bursting with berries from red to blue to purple to black.

Among the many U-pick farms, the best known is the highly commercial **Berry Barn** (☎306-978-9797; 830 Valley Rd; ⏱10am-8pm Apr–mid-Dec), 7km south of town. It has the expected over-cluttered gift shop but also a pretty cafe that bustles all summer long (avoid long waits and book). However, the reason to come is to pick the juicy Saskatoon berries, plump dark-blue numbers that are like sweet boysenberries. Fill a bucket for $10 and reward yourself with a luscious piece of berry pie to go. Prime picking occurs in July and August.

(unleavened fire-baked bread), Saskatoon-berry desserts and crowd-pleasers like chicken tenders and burgers.

Bring water, wear your walking moccasins and take some bug repellant – the mosquitoes are bison-sized.

NORTHERN SASKATCHEWAN

North of Saskatoon, despite disproportional geographic distribution, you are in fact in what is regarded as the north. From here, the driving options funnel into one northern route as the scenery changes from right under your feet. Gone are the vast wheat fields of the south, replaced with rugged boreal forests and a lake at every corner. There is a cultural shift up here, too – that independent spirit that carved a life out of the rugged landscape is still bubbling just below the surface.

The Battlefords

Linked by bridge across the North Saskatchewan River, the Battlefords (Battleford and North Battleford) seem only slightly removed from a century ago when they embodied the hard-scrabble existence of early prairie settlers.

The re-created town at North Battleford's branch of the **Western Development Museum** (WDM; ☎306-445-8083; www.wdm.ca; Hwy 16, at Hwy 40; adult/child $8.50/2; ☺9am-5pm daily, closed Mon Jan-Mar) is an engrossing insight into the tremendous amount of labor required by the pioneers to convert prairie to farmland. Walking along the boardwalk-covered streets and through the preserved houses, it's easy to imagine how hard life would have been. Kids will love the telephone system that connects the buildings – give it a crank and you never know who you might talk to.

You get a good bang for your buck at the **Fort Battleford National Historic Site** (☎306-937-2621; www.parkscanada.ca/battleford; adult/child $8/4; ☺9am-5pm late May-early Sep). The costumed guides and **cannon firings** (11am, 1pm and 3pm) give life to the NWMP fort, built in 1876.

Art lovers will be enthralled by the fantastic **Allen Sapp Gallery** (☎306-445-1760; www.allensapp.com; 1 Railway Ave; suggested donation $2; ☺11am-5pm daily Jun-Sep, 1-5pm

Wed-Sun Oct-May). Sapp's work, depicting his Cree heritage, is a breathtaking mix of landscapes and portraits all painted in a realist style.

Motels and campgrounds abound in the Battlefords, which are 140km northwest of Saskatoon on the Yellowhead Hwy (Hwy 16).

For more information, see www.battlefordstourism.com.

Prince Albert
POP 34,100

Prince Albert (PA) has a dilapidated yet evocative old brick downtown in a pretty location beside the North Saskatchewan River. This is the gear-up spot for trips to the forested and lake-riddled north. Started in 1776 as a fur-trading post, it became a real town named after Queen Victoria's husband in 1904.

The ebullient **Tourism & Convention Bureau** (☎306-953-4385; www.princealberttourism.com; 3700 2nd Ave W; ☺9am-6pm daily late May-early Sep, to 4pm Mon-Fri early Sep-late May) has walking and driving tour brochures of the town, Prince Albert National Park and other points north.

Across the parking lot, the small **Rotary Museum of Police & Corrections** (☎306-953-4385; 3700 2nd Ave W; admission free; ☺10am-6pm Jun-Aug) tells the story of Prince Albert's prison, the prisoners and the RCMP who were there to guard them. The display of homemade weapons is especially shocking – check out the knife made out of the maker's rib!

The **Historical Museum** (☎306-764-2992; cnr Central Ave & River St E; admission $2; ☺10am-6pm Jun-Aug), right on the river in the old fire station, traces the history of the town and has a surprisingly large and varied collection.

Chain motels are mostly on 2nd Ave W (Hwy 2), the main commercial spine.

In a sea of fast food, **Amy's on Second** (☎306-763-1515; 2990 2nd Ave W; mains $8-25; ☺11am-9pm Mon-Sat) is an island of culinary pleasure. The signature soup made from locally sourced wild rice shouldn't be missed.

Catch excellent small-town hockey enthusiasm with almost-big-league talent at a **Prince Albert Raiders** (www.raiderhockey.com) game at the **Art Hauser Centre** (☎306-764-4263; 690 32nd St E).

STC runs three daily buses to Saskatoon ($24, two hours) and one daily to places north from the downtown **bus station** (☎306-953-3700; 99 15th St E).

Prince Albert National Park

This **national park** (☎306-663-4522; www.parkscanada.ca/princealbert; adult/child $8/4) is a jewel in the wild. Just when you thought the vast prairie would never end, the trees rise up from the earth signaling the beginning of the boreal forest. This park puts the wild back into wilderness with expanses of untracked land, lakes and rivers. There is a multitude of potential adventures to be had here, from hikes to canoe trips to even chilling out on a beach. It's one of those special places you will never forget, whether it is **Grey Owl's cabin** (a 20km hike) or simply the feeling that you are truly on the edge of the known world.

Waskesiu is a quaint outpost and your base for exploration within the park. With a few small streets, a couple of shops and some rustic cafes, it's the perfect lakeside wilderness town. The **Chamber of Commerce** (☎306-663-5410; www.waskesiulake.ca; 35 Montreal Dr; ☺9am-5pm mid-May–early Sep) can help with accommodations. Also useful is the park **visitor center** (Waskesiu Dr; ☺8am-8pm mid-May–early Sep).

Waskesiu Marina (☎306-663-5994; www.waskesiumarina.com; kayaks per hr from $15) rents canoes, kayaks and motor boats. **Canoeski Discovery** (☎306-653-5693; www.canoeski.com; tours per day around $250) offers multiday paddling trips, many with themes, such as 'loon magic.'

There are many park **campgrounds** (☎877-737-3783; www.pccamping.ca; RV/backcountry/tent sites $36/16/26). The wooded **Beaver Glen**, in Waskesiu, accommodates RVs and fills up quickly. If you're tenting it, there are myriad options and you are sure to find some seclusion.

Among the lodges up here, **Sturgeon River Ranch** (☎306-469-2356; www.sturgeonriverranch.com; Big River; from $200 per day), just outside the western border of the park, is well regarded for its nature focus. Guests enjoy horseback rides deep into the wilderness. Rides are also available in the east for people staying in Waskesiu (from $100).

Note that the park's natural expanse is hard to access without a car.

La Ronge & Around

La Ronge is the southern hub of the north and your last chance to find any gear you

---

DON'T MISS

BATOCHE NATIONAL HISTORIC SITE

A virtual civil war was fought here in 1885 when Louis Riel led the Métis in defending their land from a force of Canadian troops. Heavily outmanned (800 to 200), they still almost won.

The children of French fur traders and aboriginal mothers, the Métis were forced from Manitoba in the mid-1800s and moved to Batoche to make a home for themselves. Frustrated by continual betrayal of treaties by the government in Ottawa, the Métis and many Cree declared their independence from Canada. This soon brought a military force led by Major General Frederick Middleton, who fought here for four days before winning. Riel was captured (and later hung for treason; see p510) while another Métis leader, Gabriel Dumont, had to flee to the US and join Buffalo Bill's Wild West Show.

The local community was devastated. Batoche had been prosperous but within a few years almost nothing was left except for the church you see today. The **historic site** (☎306-423-6227; www.parkscanada.ca/batoche; Rte 225; adult/child $8/4; ☺9am-5pm mid-May–mid-Sep) is an excellent place to wander and ponder the events of 1885. Signs and an engaging booklet provide context while costumed docents add color. The waves of prairie grass bend in the wind, which rustles the ancient trees that show where shops and houses once stood. An improved visitor center is set to open in 2011.

Batoche is halfway between Saskatoon and Prince Albert, west of Hwy 11 (about 70km north of Saskatoon). Keep your eyes peeled on the local roads for old **domed Ukrainian churches** such as the one near Wakaw on Hwy 312.

might need before heading into the wild. It's a rough, basic little town that is popular with anglers, hunters and other random characters.

Be sure to check out **Robertson's Trading Post** (☑306-425-2080; 308 La Ronge Ave; ⊗8am-5pm Mon-Sat). If you're in the market for a bear trap, a wolf hide or a case of baked beans, you're in the right place. The walls are filled with nostalgic memories of the frontier days, which weren't that long ago up this way. You can buy pretty much anything you'd ever need here and some stuff that you never would. It's still a functioning trading post, so bring your pelts here.

Lac La Ronge Provincial Park (☑306-425-4234, 800-772-4064; Hwy 2) surrounds huge, island-filled Lac La Ronge, which is great for fishing and canoeing. You can hike among stubby pines and over barren rocks or marshes with boardwalks. The park has six year-round campgrounds and hundreds of hectares of backcountry camping. For more information on accommodations, see p530. Services are only open from mid-May to early September.

The **Visitor Information Centre** (☑306-425-3055; www.townoflaronge.ca; 207 La Ronge Ave; ⊗8am-8pm daily late May-early Sep, to 5pm Mon-Fri late May-early Sep) has local info and good advice for heading north. Another good source of info is www.northern.sask.info.

Transwest Air (☑800-667-9356; www.transwestair.com) offers charter flights in floatplanes to points north of La Ronge. STC has a daily bus to Prince Albert ($40, three hours) and Saskatoon ($55, 6½ hours).

The Far North

It's always surprising to remember that even when you're in La Ronge, almost half of Saskatchewan is still to the north. This is frontier territory, the end of the paved

Each summer a few thousand people trek into the woods west of Prince Albert National Park for the **Ness Creek Festival** (www.nesscreek.com; festival pass $100; ⊗3rd weekend of Jul), a four-day gathering that can be described as a sort of mini-Burning Man of the north – with mosquitoes. Over 200 bands play folk and new music to a temporary community that camps in big fields by a tree-lined lake. There's an eco-bent to everything and a merry vibe overlaid with a live-and-let-live mantra. The highlight is a parade that grows organically to include everyone in a mass of singing and dancing Saturday night.

road, but if your car is in good condition and you're not skittish about getting off the grid, then this is prime adventure country. The geography changes drastically here, as the tall skinny trees give way to shorter vegetation. The thousands of lakes and the rugged terrain are evidence of the last glacial retreat.

You'll pass through tiny burgs such as Southend and the vast Reindeer Lake before arriving at the winter-only section at Stony Rapids, some 12 hours north of La Ronge. Self sufficiency is the key: make sure you fill up with fuel whenever you can, be prepared to camp and be cautious.

Before starting your journey, check with the visitor center in La Ronge for updated road information and tips on camping, fuel and things to see. This desolate land inspires plenty of tales, including no end of fish stories thanks to the large and prolific **walleye** that fill the lonely lakes.

Alberta

Best Places to Eat

» Da-De-O (p559)

» Catch (p579)

» Coyote's Deli & Grill (p597)

» Last Chance Saloon (p612)

Best Places to Stay

» Prince of Wales Hotel (p616)

» Moraine Lake Lodge (p603)

» Fairmont Banff Springs (p595)

» Centro Motel (p577)

Why Go?

In Alberta first impressions often lie. Here, landlocked in central Canada's spectacular hinterland, the Wild West sidles up to the Middle East and blue-eyed sheiks in Stetsons break bread with eco-conscious snowboarders in second-hand Gortex. But, to get a true feel for Canada's most caustic and contradictory province you need to avert your gaze momentarily from its Saudi Arabian–sized oil deposits and take a look through a wider lens. Sitting awkwardly alongside Fort McMurray's tar sands lies the world's third-oldest national park (Banff), its second-largest protected area (Wood Buffalo), numerous Unesco World Heritage sites and enough dinosaur remains to warrant a *Jurassic Park* sequel.

Alberta's urban areas are of patchier interest. Get-rich-quick Calgary is a young, audacious and constantly evolving metropolis that still feels strangely soulless to some, while archrival Edmonton is a cultural dark horse with more annual festivals than any other Canadian city.

When to Go
Edmonton

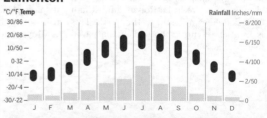

July Prime time for festivals with Edmonton Street Performers and the Calgary Stampede

July-September Banff and Jasper trails are snow-free, making a full range of hikes available

December-February Winter sports season in the Rocky Mountains

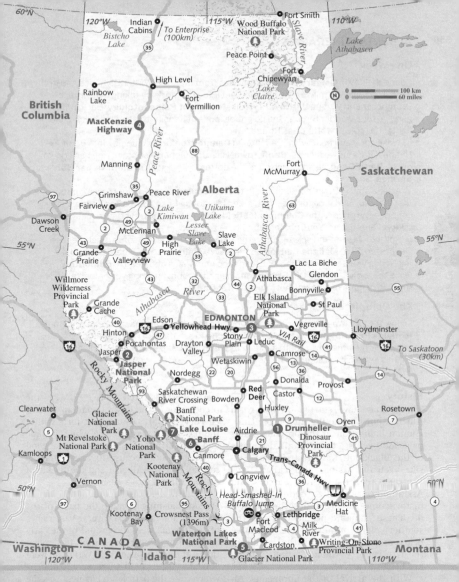

Alberta Highlights

1 Explore the Jurassic remnants of **Drumheller** (p611) and call into the **Royal Tyrrell Museum of Palaeontology** (p612)

2 Get up early and make fresh tracks on a rugged cross-country skiing trail in chilly, wintery **Jasper National Park** (boxed text, p608)

3 Take in a festival and unlock the bohemian bonhomie of historic **Old Strathcona** (boxed text, p550) in Edmonton

4 Head north on the **MacKenzie Highway** (p619) into a pure, untamed, boreal wilderness

5 Get above the tree line on the **Carthew-Alderson Trail** (p616) in Waterton Lakes National Park

6 Relax in **Banff Upper Hot Springs** (p593) after a hike

7 Enjoy a brew in the **Lake Agnes Teahouse** (p604) high above bluer than blue Lake Louise

One Week

Spend the day in **Calgary** exploring the sites from the 1988 Winter Olympics and grab a meal on trendy 17th Ave. The next day, get into dino mode by taking a day trip to Drumheller and visiting the **Royal Tyrrell Museum of Palaeontology**. Back in Calgary, go for a wander through the neighborhoods of Kensington and Inglewood and fight for a table at world-class **Rouge**.

Wake early and head west. Stop first in **Canmore** before continuing into Banff National Park and arriving in **Banff Town**. Hike up Sulphur Mountain, ride back down on the **Banff Gondola** and finish off at the bottom with a soak in **Banff Upper Hot Springs**.

After a stay in Banff, continue north to **Lake Louise**, stopping for the view outside the Chateau. Find time for the short, steep hike to the **Lake Agnes Teahouse**, then continue the drive to the **Columbia Icefield**. Get ready to stop every five minutes to take yet another amazing photograph.

Roll into **Jasper** and splash out on the **Park Place Inn**. After some much-needed sleep, stop off at **Maligne Canyon** on the way to **Maligne Lake**, where a short hike might bag you a bear or a moose. Escape the mountains and head to **Edmonton**. Once there dive into the **Old Strathcona** neighborhood, finishing your Alberta adventure with a plate of smoking hot jambalaya at **Da-De-O**.

The Complete Rockies

Follow the One Week itinerary, but include side trips into **Kananaskis Country**, the **Icefields Parkway** and north to **Grande Cache** to see the start of the mountains. Also tack on some time down south heading to **Waterton Lakes National Park**, experiencing this less-visited mountain paradise.

History

Things may have started off slowly in Alberta, but it's making up for lost time. Human habitation in the province dates back 7500 years – the aboriginal peoples of the Blackfoot, Kainaiwa (Blood), Siksika, Peigan, Atsina (also called Gros Ventre), Cree, Tsuu T'ina (Sarcee) and Assiniboine tribes all settled here in prehistoric times, and their descendants still do. These nomadic peoples roamed the southern plains of the province in relative peace and harmony until the middle of the 17th century, when the first Europeans began to arrive.

With the arrival of the Europeans, Alberta began to change and evolve – the impact of these new arrivals was felt immediately. Trading cheap whiskey for buffalo skins saw the start of the decline of both the buffalo and the traditional ways of the indigenous people. Within a generation, the aboriginal peoples were restricted to reserves and the buffalo all but extinct.

In the 1820s, the Hudson's Bay Company set up shop in the area and European settlers continued to trickle in. By 1870 the North West Mounted Police (NWMP) – the predecessor of the Royal Canadian Mounted Police (RCMP) – had built forts within the province to control the whiskey trade and maintain order. And it was a good thing they did, because 10 years later the railway reached Alberta and the trickle of settlers turned into a gush.

These new residents were mostly farmers, and farming became the basis of the economy for the next century. Vast riches of oil and gas were discovered in the early 20th century, but it took time to develop them. At the conclusion of WWII there were 500 oil wells; by 1960, there were 10,000, by which time the petroleum business was the biggest in town.

From humble pastoral beginnings to one of the strongest economies in the world, Alberta has done alright for itself.

Land & Climate

The prairies to the east give way to the towering Rocky Mountains that form the western edge of Alberta. That mountainous spine forms the iconic scenery for which the province is known. The eastern foothills eventually peter out, melding into the flatland.

Alberta is a sunny sort of place; any time of year you can expect the sun to be out. Winters can be cold, when the temperature can plummet to a bone-chilling -20°C. Climate change has started to influence snowfall, with the cities receiving less and less every year.

Summers tend to be hot and dry, with the warmest months being July and August, where the temperature sits at a comfortable 25°C. The 'June Monsoon' is, as you'd expect from the nickname, often rain-filled, while the cooler temperatures and fall colors of September are spectacular.

Chinook winds often kick up in the winter months. These warm westerly winds blow in from the coast, deposit their moisture on the mountains and give Albertans a reprieve from the winter chill, sometimes increasing temperatures by as much as 20°C in one day!

ℹ Getting There & Around

Alberta is easily accessible by bus, car, train and air. The province shares an international border with Montana, USA (for details about crossing the border, see p881) and provincial borders with the Northwest Territories (NWT), British Columbia (BC) and Saskatchewan.

Air

The two major airports are in Edmonton and Calgary, and there are daily flights to both from major hubs across the world. Carriers serving the province include Air Canada, American Airlines, British Airways, Delta, Horizon Air, KLM, United Airlines and WestJet. For further details, see p000 and p002.

Bus

Greyhound Canada (p884) has bus services to Alberta from neighboring provinces and Greyhound (p881) has services from the USA. Destinations from Edmonton include Winnipeg ($148, 18 hours, three daily), Vancouver ($133, 17 hours, five daily), Prince George ($84, 10 hours, daily), Hay River ($173, 16 hours, six times weekly) and Whitehorse ($191, 29 hours, one daily). From Calgary, destinations include Kamloops ($82, 10 hours, four daily), Regina ($71, 10 hours, two daily), Saskatoon ($87, nine hours, four daily), Vancouver ($90, 15 hours, five daily) and Winnipeg ($152, 20 hours, two daily). Times can vary greatly, based upon connections, and fares can be reduced by booking in advance.

Moose Travel Network (p888) runs a variety of trips in western Canada. Most start and finish in Vancouver, but along the way hit the highlights of the mountain parks and other Alberta must-sees. In winter it operates ski-focused tours that are a great option for carless ski bums. During the summer months trips depart daily and for the winter season a few times per week.

Car

Alberta was designed with the automobile and an unlimited supply of oil in mind. There are high-quality, well-maintained highways and a network of back roads to explore. Towns for the most part will have services, regardless of the population. Be aware that in more remote areas, especially in the north, those services could be a large distance apart. Fill up the gas tank where possible and be prepared.

In winter, driving can be a real challenge; roadways are maintained, but expect them to be snow covered after a snowfall. Drivers here are hardy, so roads rarely close. Use common sense, slow down and check the forecast and road conditions before venturing out.

Train

Despite years of hard labor, countless work-related deaths and its aura as one of the great feats of 19th-century engineering, Alberta's contemporary rail network has been whittled down to just two regular passenger train services. **VIA Rail** (www.via.ca) runs the thrice-weekly *Canadian* from Vancouver to Toronto which passes through Jasper and Edmonton in both directions. Edmonton to Vancouver costs $225 and takes 27 hours; Edmonton to Toronto costs $405 and takes 55 hours. The Toronto-bound train stops in Saskatoon, Winnipeg and Sudbury Junction.

The thrice-weekly *Skeena* travels from Jasper to Prince Rupert, BC ($117, 32 hours).

The legendary Canadian Pacific Railway, the western section of which operates from Calgary to Vancouver via Banff, is primarily a freight line these days. Its only 'passenger service' is on luxury train journeys run by **Royal Canadian Pacific** (www.royalcanadianpacific.com) and **Rocky Mountaineer** (www.rocky mountaineer.com) costing from $2000 for six-day excursions.

ALBERTA GETTING THERE & AROUND

ALBERTA FAST FACTS

» Population: 3,724,832

» Area: 642,317 sq km

» Capital: Edmonton

» Quirky fact: The Albertosaurus was a relative of the T-Rex that was first discovered in the Horseshoe Canyon in 1884

EDMONTON

POP 730,000

First-time visitors to Alberta bracing themselves for another underwhelming central Canadian city are often flummoxed by Edmonton. Despite advance publicity regaling everything from dirty oil sands to North America's largest mall, Alberta's often ignored capital is more refined than many outsiders imagine. Sure, there are the glitzy petroleum-funded towers of downtown, predictable urban sprawl and plenty of SUV-clogged highways to negotiate, but in contrast to its longtime archrival to the south (Calgary), Edmonton has carved a distinctive cultural niche. Count on a large annual calendar of festivals, the redbrick and vaguely bohemian neighborhood of Old Strathcona, some little-heralded Ukrainian heritage, and a huge swath of riverside parkland that cuts through the downtown district like a pair of green lungs.

The North Saskatchewan River divides Edmonton in half. To the north is the downtown area, which is centered on 101st Ave, or Jasper Ave as it is called. To the south is Old Strathcona, once a separate city but now an independently minded neighborhood devoid of high-rises and overflowing with art, culture and style.

Giant-sized West Edmonton Mall is to the west, hidden in suburbia and best experienced in small doses.

History

The Cree and Blackfoot tribes can trace their ancestry to the Edmonton area for 5000 years. It wasn't until the late 18th century that Europeans first arrived in the area. A trade outpost was built by the Hudson's Bay Company in 1795, which was dubbed Fort Edmonton.

Trappers, traders and adventurers frequented the fort, but it wasn't until 1870, when the government purchased Fort Ed and opened up the area for pioneers, that Edmonton saw its first real growth in population. When the railway arrived in Calgary in 1891, growth really started to speed up.

REGIONAL DRIVING DISTANCES

Calgary to Banff: 130km
Banff to Jasper: 290km
Edmonton to Calgary: 300km

Gold was the first big boom for the area – not gold found in Alberta, but gold in the Yukon. Edmonton was the last stop in civilization before dreamers headed north to the Klondike. Some made their fortunes, most did not; some settled in Edmonton and the town began to grow.

In the 1940s, WWII precipitated the construction of the Alaska Hwy and the influx of workers further increased the population. Ukrainians and other Eastern European immigrants came to Edmonton in search of work and enriched the city.

Edmonton is again the hub for those looking to earn their fortune in the north. But it isn't gold or roads this time – it's oil.

⊙ Sights & Activities

Royal Alberta Museum MUSEUM
(Map p553; www.royalalbertamuseum.ca; 12845 102nd Ave; adult/child $10/5; ⊙9am-5pm) Exhibits in Edmonton's leading museum include sections on insects and diamonds, and a lauded display of Alberta's First Nations' culture. The highlight, however, is the 'Wild Alberta' gallery which splits the province into different geographical zones and displays plants and animals from each. The museum – in operation since 1967 – is situated high on a bluff to the west of downtown in a modern granite building that was visited and renamed by Queen Elizabeth II during Alberta's centenary in 2005.

TOP CHOICE **Art Gallery of Alberta** ART GALLERY
(Map p554; www.youraga.ca; 2 Sir Winston Churchill Sq; adult/child $12/8; ⊙11am-7pm Tue-Fri, 10am-5pm Sat & Sun, closed Mon) With the opening of this fantastic new art gallery in January 2010, Edmonton at last gained a modern signature building to emulate any great city and doubled the display space of its less-exalted predecessor, the Edmonton Art Gallery. Looking like a giant glass and metal space helmet, the new futuristic structure in Churchill Sq is an exhibit in its own right that houses over 6000 historical and contemporary works of art, many of which have a strong Canadian bias. Additional plush facilities include a 150-seat theater, shop and restaurant.

FREE **Alberta Government House**
HISTORIC BUILDING
(Map p553; 12845 102nd Ave; tours free; ⊙11am-4:30pm Sun & holidays) When you finish exploring the Royal Alberta Museum head next door (Sundays and holidays only) to Govern-

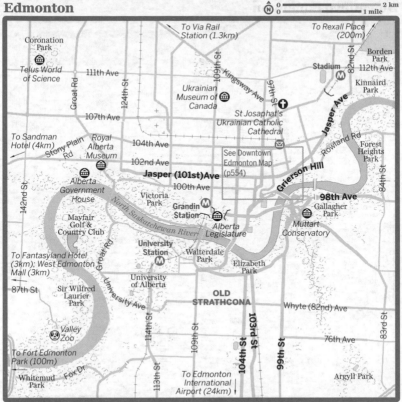

ment House, an opulent mansion and the former residence of the lieutenant governor. Steeped in history and tirelessly preserved, you'd never guess that it's nearing its centennial birthday (in 2013). The artwork alone is worth visiting – the walls are lined with stunning works by Alberta artists.

FREE **Alberta Legislature**   NOTABLE BUILDING
(Map p553; www.assembly.ab.ca; cnr 97th Ave & 107th St; admission free; ⊙8:30am-5pm) Home to politicians, debate and some surprisingly good art is the Alberta Legislature. Where Fort Edmonton once stood, the Leg is a grand old building. With its iconic dome and marble interiors, it has grown to become a local landmark. There are free 45-minute tours (every hour) to take you behind the scenes and the grounds themselves are a splendid place to spend a warm day. To hook up with a tour, head to the interpretive center/gift shop in the pedway at 10820 98th Ave.

Fort Edmonton Park   HISTORIC SITE
(off Map p553; www.fortedmontonpark.ca; cnr Fox & Whitemud Drs; adult/child $13.75/7; ⊙10am-6pm May-Sep; 🚼) Originally built by the Hudson Bay Company in 1795, Fort Edmonton was moved several times before being finally dismantled in 1915. This newer riverside reconstruction began life in the 1960s and captures the fort at its 1846 apex. Onsite are mock-ups of Edmonton's city streets at three points of their historical trajectory: 1885, 1905 and 1920. A vintage steam train and streetcar link all the exhibits, and costumed guides are there to answer questions and add some flavor.

Muttart Conservatory   GARDEN
(Map p553; www.muttartconservatory.ca; 9626 96A St; adult/child $10.50/5.25; ⊙10am-5pm Mon-Fri, 11am-5pm Sat, Sun & holidays) Looking like some sort of pyramid-shaped, glass bomb shelter, the Muttart Conservatory is actually a botanical garden that sits south

ALBERTA EDMONTON

of the river off James MacDonald Bridge. Each of the four pyramids holds a different climate region and corresponding foliage. It's an interesting place to wander about, especially for gardeners, plant fans and those in the mood for something low-key.

Sir Winston Churchill Square LANDMARK (Map p554) The subject of a controversial face-lift designed to tie in with the city's 2005 centennial, this public space is a Europeanlike plaza where people can meet, hang out and relax (outside temperature permitting). The square's former green areas have been replaced with a small amphitheater, a fountain and a cafe. Around the perimeter is a quadrangle of important buildings, including the City Hall, the Provincial Court and the impressive new Art Gallery of Alberta (p552).

Ukrainian Heritage Sites HISTORICAL SITE With a huge Ukrainian population and a long history of immigration, there are a few places

around town to learn about the culture of the old country and its transplantation in Canada. These sites are found north of downtown and can be combined into a single outing:

St Josaphat's Ukrainian Catholic Cathedral (Map p553; www.stjosaphat.ab.ca; 10825 97th St at 108th Ave; admission free; ⏱by appointment)

Ukrainian Canadian Archives & Museum of Alberta (9543 110th Ave; admission by donation; ⏱10am-5pm Tue-Fri, noon-5pm Sat)

Ukrainian Museum of Canada (Map p553; 10611 110th Ave; admission free; ⏱9:30am-4pm Mon-Fri May-Aug)

Alberta Railway Museum MUSEUM (www.railwaymuseum.ab.ca; 24215 34th St; adult/child $5/2; ⏱10am-5pm mid-May–early Sep) This museum, on the northeast edge of the city, has a collection of more than 50 railcars, including steam and diesel locomotives and rolling stock, built and used between 1877 and 1950. It also has a col-

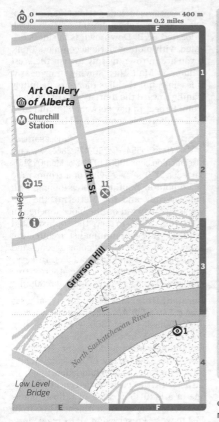

ALBERTA SIGHTS & ACTIVITIES

lection of railway equipment, old train stations, old train stations and related buildings. On weekends, volunteers fire up some of the old engines and you can ride along for $4 (the diesel locomotives run every Sunday in season; the 1913 steam locomotive gets going only on holiday weekends). To get there, drive north on 97th St (Hwy 28) to Hwy 37, turn right and go east for 7km to 34th St, then turn right and go south about 2km.

North Saskatchewan River Valley PARK
Edmonton has more designated urban parkland than any other city in North America, most of it contained within an interconnected riverside green belt that effectively cuts the metropolis in half. The green zone is flecked with lakes, bridges, wild areas, golf courses, ravines and approximately 160km worth of cycling and walking trails. It is easily accessed from downtown.

A fine way to get a glimpse of the downtown core from the river is to take a ride on the **Edmonton Queen** (Map p554; www.edmontonqueen.com; 9734 98th Ave; 1hr cruise from $17.95, dinner cruise $49.95; ☺May-Sep). This modern stern-wheeler will take you for an hour-long cruise up- or downriver, depending on the mood of the captain. There is often onboard live entertainment to keep the mood festive.

West Edmonton Mall SHOPPING MALL
(off Map p553; www.westedmontonmall.com; 170th St; ☺10am-9pm Mon-Fri, to 6pm Sat, noon-6pm Sun; ⊞) A kitsch lover who is tired of Vegas could still have a field day in West Edmonton Mall. Not content to simply be a shopping mall, this urban behemoth has the world's largest waterslides, an equipped indoor wave pool, a full-sized amusement park, a skating rink, two, yes, two minigolf courses, a fake reef with real seals swimming around, a petting zoo, a hotel and 800 stores thrown in as a bonus. Stroll through Chinatown, grab a meal on the delightfully unauthentic Bourbon St, or go for a skate or bungee jump. Then dive into the sea of chain retail shops.

☞ Tours

Several companies offer half-day tours of Edmonton ($40 to $65) or longer tours that explore outlying areas. **Magic Times Tours** (Map p553; ☏780-940-7479; www.magictimes.ca; Suite 309B, 9815 96A St) Does three-hour tours of all the main sights, including the river valley, Alberta Legislature and Old Strathcona.

Edmonton Ghost Tours (www.edmonton ghosttours.com; per person $10; ◷9.30pm Mon-Thu Jul & Aug) Offers spooky walking tours starting from 10322 83rd Ave in Old Strathcona. No booking is required – just turn up 15 minutes early.

🎎 Festivals & Events

Edmonton has many festivals throughout the year. Following are some highlights.

International Street Performers Festival   THEATER

(www.edmontonstreetfest.com; ◷2nd week Jul) Sometimes the best theater is outside – international performers all alfresco.

Edmonton's Capital Ex   FAIR

(www.capitalex.ca; ◷late Jul) For years, Klondike Days was the big summer festival in Edmonton. It has now morphed into the Capital Ex, with less of a focus on gold rush history and a move to contemporary fun. Live music, rides and a nugget's worth of olden days fun are the highlights of this evolving event.

Edmonton Fringe Theatre Festival
THEATER

(www.fringetheatreadventures.ca; ◷mid-Aug) An 11-day program of live alternative theater on three outdoor stages in the parks and on the streets. Many shows are free and no ticket costs more than $10. There's no booking – you choose a theater and stand in line. The festival draws half a million people each year to Old Strathcona.

Canadian Finals Rodeo   RODEO

(www.canadianfinalsrodeo.ca; tickets $16-46; ◷early Nov) The Canadian Finals Rodeo is the biggest indoor pro rodeo in Canada. With good bucking stock and the top cowboys there to test their skills, this is a great event to check out, especially if you missed the Calgary Stampede.

🛏 Sleeping

Edmonton has a better range of independent accommodations than some Canadian cities. Options include a trio of boutique hotels, a couple of cheap hostels and a centrally located B&B. Downtown is business oriented with more generic accommodations. If you are in town mainly to visit the West Edmonton Mall, then staying in or near it is feasible, but the digs there are definitely leaning toward the touristy side of the spectrum. Expect to pay between $90 and $125 for a comfortable room at a midrange place.

TOP CHOICE **Matrix**   BOUTIQUE HOTEL **$$**
(Map p554; ☏780-429-2861; www.matrixedmonton.com; 10001 107th St; r Mon-Fri $135, Sat & Sun $170; ℗@🛜) One of a triumvirate of Edmonton boutique hotels (along with the Varscona and the Metterra), the Matrix is the new kid on the block (opened in 2007) that claims to serve the 'sophisticated traveler,' with cool minimalist architecture punctuated with woody color accents and plenty of handy modern gadgets. In keeping with its boutique image, there's free wine and cheese every evening at 5:30pm.

Fairmont Hotel Macdonald   HOTEL **$$$**
(Map p554; ☏780-424-5181; www.fairmont.com; 10065 100th St; r from $300; ℗@🏊) Stealing the best nook in town (as it always does) Edmonton's historic Fairmont Hotel exhibits the usual array of intricate stucco, Italian marble, ornate chandeliers and lush carpets. In the early 20th century it was one in a luxurious chain of railway hotels that dotted the cross-continental line from east to west. Preserved in all its regal glory, it's still fit for monarchs and for *you* if you can stretch to the $300-plus asking price. The regularly renovated rooms with all the expected amenities are almost worth the premium price.

Varscona   BOUTIQUE HOTEL **$$**
(☏780-434-6111; www.varscona.com; 8208 106th St, cnr Whyte Ave; r from $145; ℗@🛜) Right in the heart of Old Strathcona (Map p554), this charming hotel styles itself as 'casually elegant,' suggesting you can roll up either in a tracksuit or a business suit – or some kind of combination of the two. With the coolest neighborhood in town right on the doorstep, your ability to stick your finger on the collective pulse of Edmonton is made all the easier. Breakfast, parking and evening wine and cheese are thrown in to sweeten the deal.

Metterra   BOUTIQUE HOTEL **$$**
(☏780-465-8150; www.metterra.com; 10454 Whyte Ave; r Mon-Fri $149, Sat & Sun $179; ℗@🛜) If you can wade through the un-

OLD STRATHCONA

A roguish alternative to gigantic West Edmonton Mall and its wannabe satellites, Old Strathcona (Map p553) is what keeps the city interesting, a constantly evolving strip of redbrick 'Victorian' buildings that was saved from the developer's bulldozer in the 1970s and successfully reinvented as an antidote to the big box blandness ubiquitous elsewhere. Centered on 82nd Ave (colloquially known as Whyte Ave), Edmonton's collective pulse palpitates here in bohemian dive bars, cocktail lounges, vegetarian-biased eating joints, fringe theaters, vintage magazine shops and all kinds of other countercultural trends, ideas and fashion statements.

Situated 800m south of the North Saskatchewan River, Old Strathcona began life as a separate settlement in the 1880s with the coming of the Canadian Pacific Railway. Following a series of catastrophic fires in other prairie cities, Strathcona's lawmakers passed a decree in 1902 requiring all future buildings to be made of brick, which means much of the original building stock has survived to the present day intact.

When the Canadian Northern railway reached Edmonton in 1905 much of the town's business moved north and, in 1912, Strathcona residents voted to reluctantly amalgamate with their cocky new sibling. But Strathcona's dwindling importance turned out to be a blessing in disguise. In the 1970s, when Edmonton's downtown was being rebuilt with oil money, Strathcona was mysteriously overlooked. It was an oversight that ultimately saved it. The area enjoyed a cultural renaissance in the late 1980s, and in 2007 its historical value was recognized when it was granted provincial heritage status.

creative hotel brochure blurb ('urban oasis,' 'contemporary decor,' 'traditional hospitality'), you'll find that the Met is actually a decent place to stay and a fitting reflection of the happening entertainment district (Old Strathcona) in which it sits. The modern, luxurious interior is accented with Indonesian artifacts hinting at the owner's secret penchant for all things Eastern.

Union Bank Inn BOUTIQUE HOTEL **$$$**
(Map p554; ☎780-423-3600; www.unionbankinn. com; 10053 Jasper Ave; r from $199; P❄@☎) This posh boutique hotel on Jasper Ave, in a former bank building dating from 1910, is an upmarket masterpiece. With just 34 rooms, the staff will be at your beck and call, and the in-room fireplaces make even Edmonton's frigid winters almost bearable. There's an equally fancy restaurant – Madison's (p559) – on the ground floor.

HI-Edmonton Hostel HOSTEL **$**
(☎780-988-6836, 877-467-8336; www.hihostels. ca; 10647 81st Ave; dm/d $29/65; P@☎) Right in the heart of Old Strathcona, this busy hostel is a safe bet. The rooms are a bit jam-packed with bunks and it feels somewhat like a converted old people's home (which is fitting seeing as it used to be a convent), but the location and price are hard to beat.

Hotel Selkirk HOTEL **$$**
(☎780-496-7227; www.hotelselkirk.com; 1920 St, Fort Edmonton Park; r from $124; P❄☎) If you're into the idea of visiting the past at Fort Edmonton, why not take it to the next level and spend the night? This historic hotel has period decorated rooms from the roaring 20s and staying here gives you free entry into the fort and its surrounds. There's an on-site restaurant and English high tea on offer during the summer.

Alberta Place Suite Hotel HOTEL **$$**
(Map p554; ☎780-423-1565; www.albertaplace. com; 10049 103rd St; studio/ste $112/137; P@☎⛲) What was once an apartment building is now a suite hotel with a range of hotel room–style apartments spanning from studios to family suites. Well located and refreshingly mid-price, all rooms have private kitchen facilities, work desks and well-designed if austere furnishings. On the communal level, there's a pool and fitness center.

Glenora Inn B&B B&B **$$**
(☎780-488-6766; www.glenorabnb.com; 12327 102nd Ave; r without/with bathroom $70/100; P@☎) A B&B of the frilly Victorian variety, Glenora inhabits the burgeoning West End strip of 124th St. The building (of

Edmonton is nothing if not kid friendly and there are plenty of family-oriented things to do. **Telus World of Science** (Map p553; www.edmontonscience.com; 11211 142nd St; adult/child $13.95/11.95; ☉10am-7pm; ⓘ) is a great place to start. With an emphasis on interactive displays, there are a million things to discover, all under one roof. Fight crime with the latest technology, see what living on a spacecraft is all about, go on a dinosaur dig and explore what makes the human body tick. Young and old will have a blast and maybe even learn something at the same time. The center also includes an IMAX theater (extra cost) and an observatory with telescopes (no extra cost).

The **Valley Zoo** (Map p553; www.valleyzoo.ca; 13315 Buena Vista Rd; adult/child $10.50/5.25; ☉9:30am-4pm, to 6pm May-Sep; ⓘ), with more than 100 exotic, endangered and native animals, is another option. Kids will enjoy the petting zoo, camel and pony rides, miniature train, carousel and paddleboats. If you want to brave the zoo in the frigid winter, admission costs are reduced.

Fort Edmonton Park (p553) has a small amusement park for kids, while West Edmonton Mall (p555) could keep even the most hyperactive seven-year-old distracted for weeks.

1912 vintage, meaning it's 'historic' by Edmonton standards, though not technically 'Victorian') also houses a shop and a downstairs bistro where inn dwellers can procure a complimentary breakfast. There's a communal parlor and an outdoor patio for when the weather's less arctic.

Sutton Place Hotel　　　HOTEL **$$**
(Map p554; ☎780-428-7111; www.suttonplace.com; 10235 101st St; s & d from $159; P@☒) Part of a chain – albeit a small one – the upmarket Sutton Place lacks the intimacy of smaller hotels. Aside from classy rooms replete with glitz and glamour there are numerous additional facilities here. The indoor water park is fantastic, and there are restaurants, cocktail lounges and a casino on the grounds. Look out for cheap specials.

Crowne Plaza　　　HOTEL **$$**
(Map p554; ☎780-428-6611; www.chateaulacombe.com; 10111 Bellamy Hill; r from $120; P☀@☒) While aimed at the business crowd, this tidy hotel is a good place to check for some good deals. Make sure you request a room up high with a river view. The rooms are nice with balconies on some, which is great in the summer though pointless come winter.

Fantasyland Hotel　　　HOTEL **$$$**
(off Map p553; ☎780-444-3000, 800-737-3783; www.fantasylandhotel.com; 17700 87th Ave; r $188-288; P☀@☒ⓘ) As if West Ed wasn't surreal enough, this adjoining hotel is

something to behold. There are standard rooms, but the real draw is the themed rooms. With 13 themes to choose from – Africa to igloo, Roman to Polynesian – it's hard to pick just one. Barely staying on the cool side of kitsch, it's a big hit with families. It also has a wide variety of bedding options to suit any imaginable situation. There are bunk beds for kids, sitting beside the Jacuzzi, a round king-sized for mum and dad, and a mirror on the ceiling so everyone can keep an eye on each other – nice.

Go Backpackers　　　HOSTEL **$**
(Map p554; ☎780-423-4146; www.gohostels.ca; 10209 100th Av NW; dm/d $30/88; P@☎) In a new location just south of Jasper Ave, Go has more breathing space than the HI with four- to six-bed dorms, private rooms, a TV room, kitchen and on-site pub.

Sandman Hotel　　　HOTEL **$$**
(off Map p553; ☎780-483-1385; www.sandmanhotels.com; 17635 Stony Plain Rd; r from $119; P@☒) OK, it's a chain, but at least it's a Canadian one. This branch is close to the West Ed Mall and has a swimming pool, restaurant and decent rooms at a good price.

Rainbow Valley Campground & RV Park　　　CAMPGROUND **$**
(☎780-434-5531, 888-434-3991; www.rainbow-valley.com; 13204 45th Ave; tent/RV sites $28/32; ☉mid-Apr–mid-Oct; P) For an inner-city camping spot this one is pretty

good. It's in a good location to get to 'The Mall' and keep some distance from it at the same time.

✗ Eating

Edmonton's food scene reflects its multiculturalism though you're never far from the default dinner, Alberta beef. If you're willing to hunt around, you can get a quality meal at any price, without ever having to succumb to a franchised restaurant. The most varied and economical place to eat is in Old Strathcona on or around its arterial road, Whyte Ave (Map p553). Here, you can traverse the globe gastronomically from Iran to India as well as choose from plenty of good vegetarian options. The best downtown nexus is Jasper Ave, the main road that slices through downtown. The up-and-coming option is the rejuvenated warehouse district centered north of Jasper Ave on 104th St.

Downtown

Taste of Ukraine UKRAINIAN $$
(off Map p554; www.tasteofukraine.com; 12210 Jasper Ave) There's mum in the kitchen, the eldest son behind the bar, the chatty daughter waiting tables, and dad out back updating the books. Taste of Ukraine is a true family affair and a friendly one at that. The real test, of course, is the food but you don't need to be a Tolstoy-reading Cossack to realize that the cabbage rolls, sauerkraut, buckwheat, fresh bread and vodka shots are spot on.

Blue Plate Diner FUSION, VEGETARIAN $$
(Map p554; www.blueplatediner.ca; 10145 104th St; mains $12-18; ✍) In the revitalized 104th St warehouse district, this vegetarian-biased diner serves healthy food in hearty portions. And there's style too. Cool colored lighting and exposed brickwork embellish the atmospheric interior, meaning you can eat your tofu and lentils without feeling as if you've joined a hippy commune. Try the tofu stir-fry or steak sandwich and enjoy larger-than-average plates of crisp, locally grown vegetables.

Madison's Grill FUSION $$$
(Map p554; ☑780-401-2222; www.unionbankinn. com; 10053 Jasper Ave; mains from $26; ◷8am-10pm Mon-Thu, to 11pm Fri & Sat, to 8pm Sun) Located in the Union Bank Inn and continuing the same high standards of service and quality, delicate meats and seafood are prepared here with flair. The dining room

is elegant, the service is top-notch and the wine pairing menu goes for a wallet-stretching $50.

Characters FUSION $$$
(Map p554; ☑780-421-4100; www.characters.ca; 10257 105th St; mains from $27; ◷11:30am-2pm & 5:30-10:30pm Mon-Sat) What you expect is a loud, clamorous family-run restaurant full of old mafiosi hitmen. What you get is an upmarket bistro with a 20-page menu, professional service and dishes such as Chilean sea bass and ahi tuna. Not many characters, but plenty of fancy food.

Hardware Grill STEAKHOUSE $$$
(Map p554; ☑780-423-0969; www.hardwaregrill. com; 9698 Jasper Ave; mains $36-48; ◷5pm-late Mon-Sat) When you really want to impress even yourself, head to this plush oasis high on a bluff above the river in what is traditionally the seedier part of town. The Hardware occupies an old (for Edmonton) redbrick building that has retained its more elegant features and spruced up the rest. Signposts promise an ambitious triumvirate of 'comfort, flavor and panache,' a boast at least partly fulfilled in expertly prepared duck breast, lamb rack and Alberta beef.

Russian Tea Room RUSSIAN $$
(Map p554; www.therussiantearoom.ca; 10312 Jasper Ave; mains $11-18) Bowls of borscht, a vast array of teas and some decent snacks are only half the story here. Darkly lit with an eerie bordello feel, the Russian Tea Room is also the haunt of various psychics who sit at dimly lit tables and tell the fortunes (tarot cards, tea leaves and palm-reading) of superstitious passing punters. It's surprisingly popular.

High Level Diner CANADIAN $
(www.highleveldiner.com; 10912 88th Ave; mains $6-15; ◷8am-10pm Mon-Thu, to 11pm Fri & Sat, 9am-9pm Sun) Want to catch up with some locals over eggs? This friendly, popular eatery right beside the river is a great way to start the day.

Old Strathcona & Around

TOP CHOICE **Da-De-O** CAJUN $$
(www.dadeo.ca; 10548A Whyte Ave; mains $10-16; ◷11:30am-11pm Mon, Tue & Thu-Sat, noon-10pm Sun, closed Wed) A classic diner restaurant serving Cajun food, Da-De-O competes for the prize of Edmonton's most memorable eating joint. With retro jukeboxes, art-deco lighting and some jazz

etchings on the wall, the decor is eye-catching and interesting, while the food – oysters, jambalaya and filling po'boys – is the stuff of Louisiana legend. The perennial highlight is the spice-dusted sweet potato fries. Forget the Big Easy. Save the airfare and eat here.

Café Mosaics   VEGETARIAN $
(10844 Whyte Ave; mains $6-12; ⊙9am-9pm Mon-Sat, 11am-2:30pm Sun; ⏚⏚) A Strathcona institution, this arty, activist-frequented vegetarian-vegan haunt is a meat-free zone that has taken a page out of San Francisco's book: how to make vegetable dishes both interesting and tasty. The results are invariably good. As a litmus test, check the number of carnivores who take a day off meat to come here. Try the tofu curry, cowgirls' breakfast or Moroccan chickpea soup. There's even a special meat-free kids' menu.

Upper Crust Café   CANADIAN $
(www.cafeuppercrust.ca; 10909 86th Ave; mains $8-16; ⊙11am-9pm Mon-Fri, 9am-9pm Sat) What was once just plain old home cooking has now been rebranded as 'comfort food,' ie basic, untechnical flavors and an eating experience that reminds you of your mum, gran – or both. Cottoning on to this nostalgic need, Upper Crust, tucked into the front of a nondescript, shabby-looking apartment building, effortlessly serves up such simple concoctions as chili con carne, pan-fried chicken in mushroom sauce (remember that?) and rainbow trout.

Origin India   INDIAN $$
(www.theoriginindia.com; 10511 Whyte Ave; mains $13-16) Jumping on the burgeoning Indian fusion bandwagon, Origin India embraces a chic modern look while staying true to its origins – *dal makhani,* butter chicken and spicy paneer.

Tokyo Noodle Shop & Sushi Bar   JAPANESE $
(10736 Whyte Ave; mains from $7.25; ⊙11:30am-9:30pm Mon-Thu, to 10:30pm Fri & Sat, noon-9pm Sun) Good sushi and noodles by the gallon. Nothing fancy, but that's the point.

🍷 Drinking

Nightlife is best found either on Whyte Ave (Map p553), with its bohemian feel, or downtown on Jasper Ave, with more inner-city flavored watering holes. The scene is fun and energetic and the locals are keen to integrate.

Three Bananas   CAFE
(Map p554; www.threebananas.ca; Sir Winston Churchill Sq, 9918 102nd Ave) This bookish coffee bar in Churchill Sq with its mosaic walls and Warhol-esque banana prints is a good place to grab a caffeine hit on the way to the new art museum.

Black Dog Freehouse   PUB
(www.blackdog.ca; 10425 Whyte Ave) Insanely popular with all types, the Black Dog is essentially a pub with a couple of hidden extras: a rooftop patio, known as the 'wooftop patio,' with heaters (naturally, this is Alberta), a traditional ground-floor bar (normally packed cheek to jowl on weekday nights), and a basement that features live music and occasional parties. The sum of the three parts has become a rollicking Edmonton institution.

Elephant & Castle   PUB
(www.elephantcastle.com; 10314 Whyte Ave) What passes for damn ordinary in London (where the Elephant & Castle is a rather grotesque shopping center) is strangely exotic in Edmonton. A red phone box, velvety bar stools and the smell of beer emanating from the thick, carpeted floor add British authenticity to this sporty drinking nook where you can watch Man United do battle with Chelsea et al.

Block 1912   CAFE
(10361 Whyte Ave) A regal attempt at a genuine Torinese coffee bar on Whyte Ave, this inviting place allows you to recline on European-style sofas and armchairs and enjoy your coffee with a range of snacks – or even a gelato. There's a small bar open evenings.

Two Rooms Cafe   CAFE
(10324 Whyte Ave) Another laid-back Strathcona joint that could have been transplanted from some libertine European city, Two Rooms has a tiny wood-furnished interior, street-side patio and – most importantly – good coffee.

Devlin's Martini Lounge   BAR
(10507 Whyte Ave) Trendy but with a mixed-age demographic, Delvin's is all black leather couches, fruity cocktails and office escapees on a girls' night out. There's a limited tapas menu and big windows where you can sit and watch the insomniac action on Whyte Ave.

(Continued on page 569)

National Parks

While other countries flaunt medieval castles or ancient Hellenic ruins, Canada has its own 'great wonder': the world's first National Parks Service. Created with the aim of balancing ecological integrity with the right of access and recreation for all, this evolving organization, which numbered six parks at its inception in 1911, has multiplied sevenfold to provide a protective umbrella for 42 natural enclaves with a combined area the size of Italy.

Peyto Lake, Banff National Park, Alberta

Top 5 Parks for History

Long at the forefront of global environmental protection, Canada endowed the world with its third national park – Banff – in 1885 along with numerous other pioneering areas: Yoho, Jasper and Waterton, to name but three. Paradoxically, it is often the country's newer parks that harbor its oldest archeological remains.

Gwaii Haanas

1 Canada's most advanced and best preserved First Nations culture survives on BC's Haida Gwaii (Queen Charlotte Islands; p753). It has protected its heritage in a scattering of abandoned villages, craning totem poles and excavated archeological sites.

Banff

2 Predated only by Yellowstone in the USA and Royal National Parks in Australia, Banff's (p584) history is entwined with the history of the national park movement and the pioneering railways that helped pave its way.

Ukkusiksalik

3 One of Canada's newest parks (p821; inaugurated in 2003) is also one of its most interesting with over 500 archeological sites showcasing the development of Inuit culture from the 11th century to the 1960s.

Jasper

4 Harking back to the early 20th century, Jasper's Yellowhead Museum (p606) exhibits the exploits of European explorers, fur trading posts, and a cross-continental railroad.

Terra Nova

5 Don't expect historical Rome, but Newfoundland's gift to the park system (p475) hides interesting early-20th-century settlement history with remnants of sawmills, shipbuilding and residential quarters evident on a coastal trail contouring Newport Sound.

Right

2. Mt Chephren, Banff National Park, Alberta
3. Sila River, Ukkusiksalik National Park, Nunavut

Top 5 Wilderness Parks

'Space, the final frontier' said Captain Kirk in *Star Trek*. He obviously hadn't been to Northern Canada, where several designated wilderness parks make the South Pole look crowded. You can conquer your agoraphobia and embrace the splendid isolation in any of the following five places:

Quttinirpaaq

1 Frozen onto chilly End, the world's most northerly park (p820) was never going to be busy. Not visited by Europeans until 1875 it is a base for scientific research and a launch pad for North Pole trips.

Auyuittuq

2 A name few Canadians will recognize (or be able to pronounce), Auyiuttuq (p817; the land that never melts) is another leave-your-car-at-home kind of park. Situated on Baffin Island it is ideal for ski touring, climbing or backcountry camping.

Aulavik

3 More people have visited the moon than drop by Aulavik (p808) annually (official annual tourist numbers rarely exceed a hundred). Situated on the Banks Island, this land of foraging musk oxen and 24 hour summer sunlight is the true 'back of beyond'.

Torngat Mountains

4 For residents of Labrador the words 'Torngat' (p500) and 'wilderness' are interchangeable. Charter a plane to drop you in this stark mélange of glaciated mountains and roaming caribou.

Ivvavik

5 No services, no facilities, just miles of untamed tundra. Save some money, hone your backcountry survival skills and live out your expedition fantasies (p786).

Left

1. Hikers, Quttinirpaaq National Park 4. Saglek Fjord, Torngat Mountains National Park, Newfoundland

Top 5 Parks for Wildlife

Non-Canadians, from countries where the original ecosystems have all but disappeared, are often overwhelmed by their first sight of the Serengeti of the north, where giant herds of caribou roam across swathes of chilly tundra and bears are kings of a primeval but ecologically vital food chain.

5

Wapusk

1 Polar bears are Wapusk's (p525) raison d'être (the name means 'white bear' in Cree) and the best place in the world to see these great white beasts in the wild. Book a guided tour and head for Churchill, Manitoba.

Wood Buffalo

2 Aside from being the second largest national park in the world (after Greenland), Wood Buffalo (p801) also protects the planet's last free-roaming herd of wood bison in an area equivalent to the size of Switzerland.

4

Forillon

3 In Gaspé Bay (p298) in Québec province wildlife viewing has entered the realm of the sea with seven different species of whale plying local waters. Whale-watching trips depart during the summer months along a spectacular coastline overlooked by precipitous cliffs.

Yoho

4 Adjacent to Banff and equally spectacular, resplendent Yoho (p737) harbors the sight that every hiker wants to see (as long as it's from a safe distance), the endangered grizzly bear.

Aulavik

5 Few ever see them, but they're still there; remote Aulavik (p808) is home to the world's highest concentration of musk oxen who survive alongside caribou, arctic foxes and arctic hares.

Right
5. Musk ox **4.** Grizzly bear

Top 5 Parks for Hiking

Canada's national parks are visceral places where nature rules and modern mechanical infringements have been kept to a minimum. To successfully see and understand them you're best off dumping your car/motor boat/bush plane and striking out like the erstwhile First Nations and Inuit people – on foot.

Waterton Lakes

1 The Canadian Rockies' forgotten corner is a continuation of the US's Glacier National Park to the south and is notable for its easily accessible high alpine day hikes, many of which start directly from diminutive Waterton townsite (p616).

Riding Mountain

2 A huge array of trails – more than 400km worth – pepper this forested Unesco Biosphere Reserve (p521) that sits like a wooded island amid fertile agricultural land in southern Manitoba. In winter many trails are groomed for cross-country skiing.

Cape Breton Highlands

3 The font of Nova Scotia's once distinct French-Acadian culture, Cape Breton (p365) is best accessed via 25 moderate day ████ ████████████████████████████████ Trail scenic highway.

Jasper

4 The Skyline trail, the Tonquin Valley, the Whistlers and the 'Path of the Glacier'; the names are legendary, the going tough and the scenery intense even by spectacular Rocky Mountain standards (p584).

Pacific Rim

5 This park (p694), bisected by the West Coast Trail, an old coastal path on Vancouver Island that once served as a rescue route for shipwrecked sailors, safeguards one of the finest backcountry hiking experiences on the western littoral.

Left

3. Cape Breton Highlands National Park, Nova Scotia
4. Hiking, Jasper National Park, Alberta

Top 5 Parks for Outdoor Activities

Getting to and around many of Canada's national parks is a taxing enough physical activity. But, if several days of bush-whacking through boreal forest doesn't do it for you, you can try all number of other ambitious activities at your own tempo (and risk).

Kootenay

1 Pioneering European climbers who ran out of Alpine peaks to summit, headed west to Canada's Kootenay range (p732) to a seemingly boundless array of crenulated, technically challenging peaks. Three generations later their great-grandchildren are still at it.

Fundy

2 One of the few parks to juxtapose raw wilderness with slower, more relaxing pursuits, Fundy (p406) mixes rugged backcountry hiking through coastal Acadian forests with tennis, golf and even lawn bowling.

Grasslands

3 A prairie landscape in Saskatchewan close to the US border, Grasslands (p538) is prime horse-riding country. Follow the equestrian legend of Chief Sitting Bull here (where he came post–Battle of Little Bighorn) independently or on an organized trip.

Prince Albert

4 Lake-speckled Prince Albert (p546), also in Saskatchewan, is where the northern boreal forests meet more open continental parkland. It provides an excellent environment to cast a line for trout, pike and walleye.

Glacier

5 For those to whom the words 'ski resort' is anathema, Glacier (p736) provides a rustic antidote with its legendary dumpings of powdery snow ideal for heli-skiing, telemark and backcountry excursions.

Right
4. Anglin Lake, Prince Albert National Park, Saskatchewan
1. Flow Lake, Kootenay National Park, British Columbia

Top 5 Spatially Challenged Parks

In the world's second-biggest country where the largest national park (Wood Buffalo) out-sizes even Switzerland, the notion that 'small is beautiful' might seem a little redundant. But certain parts of Canada's sprawling Park Service have turned their tiny but ecorich landscapes into grand environmental schemes.

Gulf Islands

1 The most southerly dots in the expansive Southern Gulf Islands archipelago between Vancouver Island and BC's Lower Mainland provide much needed 'breathing space' between the two growing metropolises of Vancouver and Victoria (p621).

St Lawrence Islands

2 Canada's smallest national park (p189) measures just 4 sq km and consists of two dozen islands speckled across the St Lawrence River. It plays a key role in highlighting the delicate balance between biodiversity and recreation.

Point Pelee

3 Geographically tiny, but vital to birds (and bird-watchers), Point Pelee (p133) on Canada's most southerly tip, is an important fly-through for over 360 feathered species.

Prince Edward Island

4 PEI (p436) enhances its diminutive stature with dune-backed beaches, narrow wetlands and a gigantic literary legacy enshrined in *Anne of Green Gables*.

Georgian Bay Islands

5 Splayed across Lake Huron in Ontario, these proverbial specks on the map are only accessible by water-based transport, rendering oar-powered excursions to the park's 59 small islands (p146) a physical necessity.

Left

3. Boardwalk, Point Pelee National Park, Ontario
1. Starfish, Gulf Islands National Park, British Columbia

Top 5 Unesco World Heritage Site Parks

Unesco World Heritage sites are synonymous with the pyramids of Giza or Rome's colosseum, but since the inauguration of Nahanni National Park in 1978 the UN body has given *natural* heritage equal billing. Nine Canadian national parks are now Unesco-protected.

Kluane

1 Ranked for its huge glaciers (at least 100 remain unnamed), Kluane (p772) inhabits the icy triangle of land bordering Alaska, BC and the Yukon and provides clues into the process of glacial land moderation.

Nahanni

2 Nahanni (p803) was one of the first *natural* World Heritage sites to be inscribed, in 1978. It is protected for its thunderous rivers, deep canyons, pristine forests and bleak tundra.

Gros Morne

3 A spectacular jumble of fjords, headlands, sheer cliffs, and waterfalls on the Newfoundland coast, Gros Morne (p481) is listed for its importance in understanding the processes of continental drift.

Banff

4 The centerpiece of the communally listed Rocky Mountain Parks, Banff (p584) is the scenic jewel that turned the heads of so many early explorers. It continues to astound with its dagger-shaped mountains, plush railway-era hotel and salubrious hot springs.

Yoho

5 Named for the ancient Cree word for 'shock and 'awe', Yoho (p737) is one of the geological highlights of the Rocky Mountain Parks, with its Burgess Shale fossil deposits exhibiting 120 marine species over a 500-million-year trajectory.

Right
1. Frozen shoreline, Kluane National Park, Yukon Territory **2.** Virginia Falls, Nahanni National Park Reserve, Northwest Territories

MARK NEWMAN

JIM WARK

O'Byrne's PUB

(10616 Whyte Ave) Get lost in the labyrinth of rooms in this popular Irish pub. Lots of varieties on tap and live music keep the place interesting.

Pub 1905 PUB

(Map p554; 10525 Jasper Ave) A popular local watering hole with a happening happy hour and plethora of TVs makes this a choice spot to catch an Oilers game.

☆ Entertainment

See and *Vue* are free local alternative weekly papers with extensive arts and entertainment listings. For daily listings, see the entertainment section of the *Edmonton Journal* newspaper.

For concentrated club-hopping, Whyte Ave and Old Strathcona (Map p553) are the places to head.

Princess Theatre CINEMA

(10337 Whyte Ave; tickets Mon & weekend matinees $5, other times adult/student & child $8/6) The Princess is a grand old theater that defiantly sticks her finger up at the mall-housed multiplexes that are dominant elsewhere. Dating from the pre-talkie days (1915) it screens first-run, art-house and cult classics.

Blues on Whyte LIVE MUSIC

(www.bluesonwhyte.ca; 10329 Whyte Ave) This is the sort of place your mother warned you about: dirty, rough, but still somehow cool. It's a great place to check out some live music; blues and rock are the standards here. The small dance floor is a good place to shake a leg.

Halo Lounge NIGHTCLUB

(Map p554; 10538 Jasper Ave) A small, clamorous basement nightclub with Brit-biased music ranging from mod to alt rock, Halo has a kind of '70s lava lamp feel. The dance floor is compact and rarely empty.

New City Suburbs NIGHTCLUB

(Map p554; www.newcitycompound.com; 10081 Jasper Ave) Taking up residence in an old theater, this nightclub is a great venue for live punk rock, mod sounds, Buzzcocks reunions and straight rock and roll. It has frequent live bands, comedy nights and theme nights that are popular with the college crowd.

Citadel Theatre THEATER

(Map p554; www.citadeltheatre.com; 9828 101A Ave; tickets from $45; ☺Sep-May) Presents contemporary and classic live theater by Edmonton's foremost company.

New Varscona Theatre THEATER

(www.varsconatheatre.com; 10329 83rd Ave; tickets from $14) Hiding in the fringes, the Varscona puts on edgy productions from its Strathcona home base.

Jubilee Auditorium THEATER

(1455 87th Ave) The place to check out the **Edmonton Opera** (☏780-424-4040; www.edmontonopera.com; tickets from $24; ☺Oct-Apr). Otherwise, this is a great venue for live performances of every kind.

Gay & Lesbian Venues

Buddy's Nite Club NIGHTCLUB

(off Map p554; www.buddysedmonton.com; 11725B Jasper Ave) The font of wet T-shirt comps, drag shows and ominous-sounding 'dance your pants off' nights, Buddy's is ever popular with gay men.

Sports

Edmonton Oilers SPORTS

(www.edmontonoilers.com; tickets from $38.50) The Oilers are the local National Hockey League (NHL) team – the season runs from October to April. Games are played at oft-renamed **Rexall Place** (off Map p553; 7424 118th Ave NW), once the stomping ground of 'The Great One,' former ice-hockey pro Wayne Gretzky.

Edmonton Eskimos SPORTS

(www.esks.com; adult/child from $43/21.50) The Eskimos take part in the Canadian Football League (CFL) from July to October at **Commonwealth Stadium** (11000 Stadium Rd).

🛍 Shopping

Old Strathcona (Map p553) is the best area for unique independent stores – vintage magazines, old vinyl, retro furnishings and the like. If you're in search of the opposite – ie big chains selling familiar brands – sift through the 800-plus stores in West Edmonton Mall (p555).

Avenue Guitars MUSIC STORE

(10550 Whyte Ave) You can warm your fingers plucking opening stanzas to 'Stairway to Heaven' in Old Strathcona's premier music store. It sells custom-made and collector's guitars and all the usual suspects.

Old Strathcona Farmers' Market
FOOD & DRINK

(10310 83rd Ave at 103rd St; ☺8am-3pm Sat, noon-5pm Tue Jul & Aug) This not-to-be-missed indoor market offers everything from organic food to arts and crafts, and hosts some 130 vendors. Everyone comes here on Saturday morning – it's quite the scene.

Movie Poster Shop
SOUVENIRS

(8126 Gateway Blvd NW) Essential browsing for anyone who ever fantasized about having a rare black-and-white print of Steve McQueen/Natalie Wood/Mick Jagger on their wall.

Junque Cellar
ACCESSORIES

(10442 Whyte Ave) What is plain old junk to some is retro-cool to others. Sift through the typewriters, lava lamps, old phones, comics, clothes and other flashbacks of erstwhile pop culture.

ℹ Information

Café Dabar (10816 Whyte Ave; internet per hr $5; ☺9am-10pm Mon-Sat, 11am-7pm Sun) Free wi-fi if you buy something.

Custom House Global Foreign Exchange (10104 103rd Ave) Foreign currency exchange.

Edmonton Tourism (9990 Jasper Ave; ☺8am-5pm) Friendly place with tonnes of flyers and brochures.

Main post office (9808 103A Ave)

Police, Ambulance & Fire (☎911)

Police Dispatch Line (☎780-423-4567) For nonemergencies.

Royal Alexandra Hospital (☎780-477-4111; 10240 Kingsway Ave) Has a 24-hour trauma center.

Stanley A Milner Public Library (7 Sir Winston Churchill Sq; ☺9am-9pm Mon-Fri, to 6pm Sat, 1-5pm Sun) Lots of free internet terminals.

ℹ Getting There & Away

Air

Edmonton International Airport (YEG; www.edmontonairports.com) is about 30km south of the city along the Calgary Trail, about a 45-minute drive from downtown.

Bus

The large **bus station** (Map p554; 10324 103rd St) has Greyhound Canada services to numerous destinations, including Jasper ($67, 4½ hours, four daily), Calgary ($51, from 3½ hours, from 10 daily) and Yellowknife (22 hours, one daily). For more information on buses to other provinces in Canada, see p551.

Red Arrow (www.redarrow.ca) buses stop at the Holiday Inn Express hotel (10010 104th St) and serve Calgary ($67, three to 3½ hours, at least four daily), Fort McMurray ($81, five hours, one daily) and Banff ($127, seven hours, two daily). The buses are a step up, with plugs for your laptop, leather seats and more legroom for taller people.

Car

All the major car-rental firms (p886) have offices at the airport and around town. **Driving Force** (www.thedrivingforce.com; 11025 184 St) will rent, lease or sell you a car. Check the website; it often has some good deals.

Train

The small **VIA Rail station** (www.viarail.ca; 12360 121st St) is rather inconveniently situated 5km northwest of the city center near Edmonton City Centre Airport. The *Canadian* travels three times a week east to Saskatoon, Winnipeg and Toronto and west to Jasper, Kamloops and Vancouver. At Jasper, you can connect to Prince George and Prince Rupert. For fares see p551.

ℹ Getting Around

To/From the Airport

City buses unfortunately don't make it all the way to the airport, so your best option is to jump on a **Sky Shuttle Airport Service** (www.edmontonskyshuttle.com; adult/child $18/10). It runs three different routes that service hotels in most areas of town, including downtown and the Strathcona area.

A cab fare from the airport to downtown will cost about $50.

Car & Motorcycle

There is metered parking throughout the city. If you're staying in Old Strathcona, most hotels offer complimentary parking to guests. Visitors can park their car for the day and explore the neighborhood easily on foot. Edmonton also has public parking lots, which cost about $12 per day or $1.50 per half hour; after 6pm you can park for a flat fee of about $2.

Public Transportation

City buses and a 10-stop tram system – the Light Rail Transit (LRT) – cover most of the city. The fare is $2.75 (day passes $8.25). Buses operate at 30-minute intervals between 5:30am and 1:30am. Check out the excellent transit planning resources at www.edmonton.ca. Daytime travel between Churchill and Grandin stations on the LRT is free.

Between mid-May and early October you can cross the High Level Bridge on a streetcar ($4 round-trip, every 30 minutes between 11am and 10pm). The vintage streetcars are a great way to travel to the Old Strathcona Market (103rd St at 94th Ave), where the line stops. Or go from Old Strathcona to the downtown stop, next to the Grandin LRT Station (109th St between 98th and 99th Aves).

Taxi

Two of the many taxi companies are **Yellow Cab** (☎780-462-3456) and **Alberta Co-Op Taxi** (☎780-425-2525). The fare from downtown to the West Edmonton Mall is about $25. Flagfall is $3.60, then it's $0.20 for every 150m.

AROUND EDMONTON

East of Edmonton

When Edmontonians want to get away from it all and retreat back to nature, **Elk Island National Park** (www.pc.gc.ca/eng/pn-np/ab/elkisland/index.aspx; adult/6-16yr/senior $7.80/3.90/6.80; ☉dawn-dusk) is often their first port of call. This 194-sq-km park is home to much native wildlife, such as elk, plains bison and a small herd of the threatened wood bison. At just 45km east of Edmonton on the Yellowhead Hwy (Hwy 16), it's convenient for weekend getaways, meaning the **campgrounds** (tent & RV sites $25.50, campfire permits $8.80) are quite popular. Some of the park's campgrounds close from early October to May.

There is ample opportunity to get some exercise here, too: hiking, canoeing and cycling are popular in the summer, while snowshoeing and cross-country skiing are the things to do after the snow flies. When you arrive plan to hit the visitors center at the entrance to get all the information you might need for enjoying the park.

The **Ukrainian Cultural Heritage Village** (8820 112th St; adult/7-17yr/senior $8/4/7; ☉10am-6pm mid-May–early Sep, 10am-6pm Sat & Sun early Sep–mid-Oct), 50km east of Edmonton on Hwy 16 (3km east of Elk Island National Park), is an exact replica of a turn-of-the-century Ukrainian town, paying homage to the 250,000 Ukrainian immigrants who came to Canada in the late 19th and early 20th centuries. Many settled in central Alberta, where the landscape reminded them of the snowy steppes of home. Among the exhibits are a dozen or so structures, including a restored pioneer home and an impressive Ukrainian Greek Orthodox church. The staff are dressed in period garb and are in character, too, adding a slice of realism and fun to the day.

South of Edmonton

Located halfway between Edmonton and Calgary on Hwy 2 is **Red Deer**. This growing community boasts an agricultural heritage and benefits from its proximity to the two major centers. Beyond being a rest stop and an all-else-fails place to stay during the tourist season, there is very little for the traveler here. Red Deer is about 1½ hours away from either city, and accommodations will not be as tight nor as expensive. For more information, contact the **Red Deer Visitor & Convention Bureau** (www.tourismreddeer.net; 30 Riverview Park), or just drive through the city where you'll have your pick of chain establishments.

West of Edmonton

Heading west from Edmonton toward Jasper, Hwy 16 is a gorgeous drive through rolling wooded hills that are especially beautiful in fall. Accommodations are available along the way. Greyhound buses ply the route.

Hinton is a small, rough-around-the-edges town carved from the bush. The pervasive logging industry keeps the majority of the town's population gainfully employed. There is some good mountain biking to be found here; cruise into the info center for more information on trails. If there is snow on the ground, the **Athabasca Lookout Nordic Centre** offers winter visitors beautiful groomed ski trails up to 25km long. It also has illuminated night skiing on a 1.5km trail, plus a 1km luge run. There's a user fee of $5. For more information, contact the **Hinton Tourist Information Centre** (☎780-865-2777), off Hwy 16.

Just north of Hinton lies the tiny settlement of **Grande Cache**. There is little of interest in this small industry town, only a few overpriced hotels aimed at expense account–wielding natural resources workers. However, the drive along Hwy 40 between Hinton and Grande Cache is spectacular, with rolling forested foothills, lakes and abundant wildlife.

CALGARY

POP 1,065,000

Brash, bold and dripping in oil money, it's easy to pour scorn on flashy Calgary, as some do. A slightly-less-frenetic but colder version of desert Dubai, this nebulous, hard-to-grasp prairie city has grown up so fast that last week (let alone last month) can seem like ancient history.

Livable but sometimes characterless, prosperous but economically precarious, super-modern but not always pretty, 21st-century Calgary isn't a place that any unbiased out-of-towner is likely to fall in love with (although the locals can be fanatically loyal). Most visitors either come here on business and deposit their briefcases in one of a plethora of generic business hotels, or arrive in outdoor garb and use it as a springboard for the more alluring attractions of K-Country and Banff. But itinerants holed up on longer stopovers (unexpected or otherwise) needn't break into a cold sweat. Shoehorned among the Stetsons and SUVs of downtown, there's a decent dining scene, an excellent museum, remnants of the 1988 Winter Olympics and – contrary to popular belief – a good (and expanding) public transportation system.

Cowboys led Calgary's first incarnation in the early 1900s, paving the way for what has become one of the world's biggest rodeos – the Calgary Stampede. The oil barons piled in next, after the first big Alberta oil strike in 1947, and brought with them a boom-bust economic cycle that has been both the city's blessing and curse. These days, the bulk of new arrivals are here to make fast money rather than immerse themselves in Calgary's cultural splendor. If you've arrived looking for the soul of the city it could be a long and fruitless search. If it's youthful nightlife, chic restaurants, clean streets and a well-paid job you're after, you might just get lucky.

History

From humble and relatively recent beginnings, Calgary has been transformed into a cosmopolitan modern city that has hosted an Olympics and continues to wield huge economic clout. Before the growth explosion, the Blackfoot people called the area home for centuries. Eventually they were joined by the Sarcee and Stoney tribes on the banks of the Bow and Elbow Rivers.

By the time the 1870s rolled around, the NWMP built a fort and called it Fort Calgary after Calgary Bay on Scotland's Isle of Mull. The railroad followed a few years later and, buoyed by the promise of free land, settlers started the trek west to make Calgary their home.

Long a center for ranching, the cowboy culture was set to become forever intertwined with the city. For the initial stages of the 20th century, Calgary simmered along, growing slowly. Then in the 1960s everything changed. Overnight, ranching was seen as a thing of the past and oil was the new favorite child. With the 'black gold' seeming to bubble up from the ground nearly everywhere in Alberta, Calgary became the natural choice of place to set up headquarters.

The population exploded and the city began to grow at an alarming rate. As the price of oil continued to skyrocket, it was good times for the people of Cowtown. The '70s boom stopped dead at the '80s bust. Things slowed and the city diversified.

The 21st century began with an even bigger boom. House prices have gone through the roof, there is almost zero unemployment and the economy is growing 40% faster than the rest of Canada. Not bad for a bunch of cowboys.

⊙ Sights

Glenbow Museum MUSEUM
TOP CHOICE (www.glenbow.org; 130 9th Ave SE; adult/student & youth/senior $14/9/10; ⊙9am-5pm Fri-Wed, to 9pm Thu) For a town with such a short history, Calgary does a fine job in telling it at the commendable Glenbow Museum that traces the legacy of Calgary and Alberta both pre- and post-oil. Contemporary art exhibitions and stunning artifacts dating back centuries fill its halls and galleries. With an extensive permanent collection and an ever-changing array of traveling exhibitions, there is always something for the history buff, art lover and pop culture fanatic to ponder. The best museum in the province – hands down.

Fort Calgary Historic Park HISTORIC PARK
(www.fortcalgary.com; 750 9th Ave SE; adult/child/senior $10.50/6.50/9.50; ⊙9am-5pm) In 1875 Calgary was born at Fort Calgary. If only the NWMP who first called Fort Calgary home could see it now. Luckily their efforts have been restored for posterity. There are preserved buildings to walk through,

the chance to dress up like a Mountie and even a jail to get locked up in.

Calgary Zoo
ZOO

(www.calgaryzoo.ab.ca; 1300 Zoo Rd NE; adult/child/senior $18/10/16; ☉9am-6pm) More than 900 animals from around the world, many in enclosures simulating their natural habitats, make this Calgary's most popular attraction. Besides the animals, the zoo has a **Botanical Garden** with changing garden displays, a **tropical rainforest**, a good **butterfly enclosure** and the 6½-hectare **Prehistoric Park**, featuring fossil displays and life-sized dinosaur replicas in natural settings. Picnic areas dot the zoo and a cafe is on-site. During winter, when neither you nor the animals will care to linger outdoors, the admission price is reduced. To get here, take the C-Train east to the Zoo stop.

Heritage Park Historical Village
HISTORIC PARK

(www.heritagepark.ab.ca; 1900 Heritage Dr SW at 14th St SW; adult/child $19/14; ☉9.30am-5pm mid-May–early Sep, 9.30am-5pm Sat & Sun early Sep–mid-Oct) Want to see what Calgary used to look like? Head down to this historical park and step right into the past. With a policy that all buildings within the village are from 1915 or earlier, it really is the opposite of modern Calgary. There are 10 hectares of recreated town to explore, with a fort, grain mill, church, school and lots more. You can ride on the steam train, catch a trolley and even go for a spin on the SS *Moyie*, the resident stern-wheeler, as it churns around the Glenmore Reservoir. Heritage Park has always been a big hit with the kiddies and is a great place to soak up Western culture. To get there, take the C-Train to Heritage station, then bus 20.

FREE Inglewood Bird Sanctuary
NATURE RESERVE

(2425 9th Ave SE; admission free; ☉dawn-dusk) Get the flock over here and look out for some foul play at this nature reserve. With more than 260 bird species calling the sanctuary home, you are assured of meeting some feathered friends. It's a peaceful place with walking paths and benches to observe the residents. There is a small **interpretive center** (admission free, donations appreciated; ☉10am-4pm) to give you some more information about the birds, complete with displays that are popular with the young ones.

FREE Calgary Chinese Cultural Centre
MUSEUM

(197 1st St SW; admission free; ☉9am-9pm) Inside this impressive landmark building, built by skilled Chinese artisans in 1993, you'll find a magnificent 21m-high dome ornately painted with 561 dragons and other imagery. Its design was inspired by Beijing's Temple of Heaven. The 2nd and 3rd floors frequently house changing art and cultural exhibitions. Downstairs, the **museum** (adult/senior & child $2/1; ☉11am-5pm) holds Chinese art and artifacts, including a collection of replica terracotta soldiers.

Prince's Island Park
PARK

For a little slice of Central Park in the heart of Cowtown, take the bridge over to this island, with grassy fields just made for tossing the Frisbee, bike paths and ample space to stretch out. During the summer months, you can catch a Shakespeare production in the park's natural grass amphitheater. Watch yourself around the river: the water is cold and the current is strong and not suitable for swimming. The bridge to the island from downtown is at the north end of 3rd St SW, near the Eau Claire Market shopping area.

Fish Creek Provincial Park
PARK

(admission free; ☉8am-dark) Cradling the southwest edge of Calgary, this huge park is a sanctuary of wilderness hidden within the city limits. Countless trails intertwine to form a labyrinth to the delight of walkers, mountain bikers and the many animals who call the park home. Severe flooding in the park in the mid-2000s washed away many bridges and, in many cases, severely impacted on the landscape. The park is slowly returning to normal with the assistance of the city and Mother Nature. There are numerous access points to the park, which stretches 20km between 37th St in the west and Bow River in the east. From downtown, take bus 3 via Elbow Dr.

Calgary Tower
NOTABLE BUILDING

(101 9th Ave SW; adult/youth $14/10; ☉observation gallery 9am-9pm) This 1968 landmark tower is an iconic feature of the Calgary skyline, though it has now been usurped by six taller buildings. There is little doubt that the aesthetics of this once-proud concrete structure have passed into the realm of kitsch, but, love it or hate it, the slightly

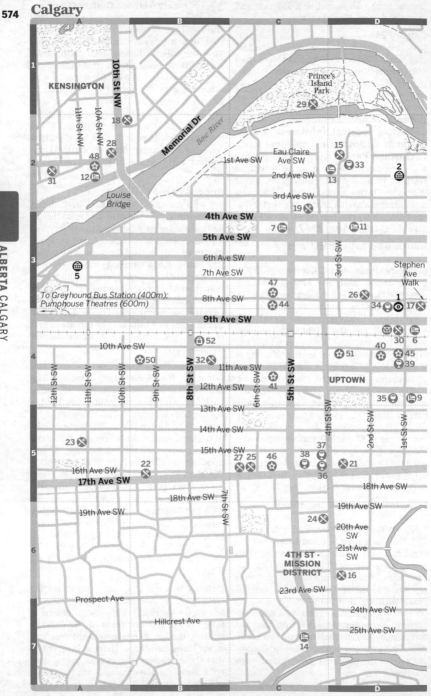

ALBERTA CALGARY

phallic 191m structure is a fixture of the downtown area. The views from the top are fantastic and there is even a revolving restaurant so you won't miss a thing. Back in '88, the Olympic flame burned brightly on top of the tower.

Other Museums
MUSEUMS

For stunning contemporary artwork, stop in at the **Art Gallery of Calgary** (www.art-gallerycalgary.org; 117 8th Ave SW; adult/child $5/2.50; ☺10am-5pm Tue-Sat). What it lacks in floor space, it more than makes up for with the standard of work on display.

To learn the history of Calgary's first inhabitants, the Tsuu T'ina (Sarcee) people, check out the **Tsuu T'ina Culture Museum** (3700 Anderson Rd SW; admission $3; ☺9am-4pm Mon-Fri). Take MacLeod Trail South to Anderson Rd, turn west and follow for 5km to the museum.

Those with an interest in the military will enjoy the **Museum of the Regiments** (4520 Crowchild Trail SW; adult/student $6/3; ☺9:30am-4pm), a very thorough overview of Calgary's military background and its role in Canadian conflicts over the years. Follow Crowchild Trail to Flanders Ave, about 3km south of downtown.

🏃 Activities

Though, ostensibly, it appears to be designed purely for the automobile, Calgary actually has over 400km of trails within its city limits. The best of them parallel the Bow River, meaning you can bisect the city free of road interference. To plan your route, check out the *Calgary Pathway* *(t th htt tt httr) Attt tt tttt) tttttttttt tttt tht* **Calgary Parks & Recreation Department office** (3rd fl, 205 8th Ave SE) and from most bike shops.

For rentals, the **Outdoor Programs Centre** (www.calgaryoutdoorcentre.ca; 2500 University Dr NW) at the University of Calgary, 7km from downtown, has top-quality bikes and just about anything else you might need.

Canada Olympic Park
SPORTS

(www.canadaolympicpark.ca; 88 Canada Olympic Rd SW) In 1988 the Winter Olympics came to Canada for the first time. Calgary played host and many of the events were contested at Canada Olympic Park. Located near the western edge of town along Hwy 1, you won't be able to miss the distinctive 70m and 90m ski jumps crowning the skyline. Check out the **Olympic Hall of Fame** (admission $6; ☺9am-5pm May-Sep, 10am-4pm

ALBERTA ACTIVITIES

Oct-Apr) and learn about some great Canadian athletes and the story of the Calgary games. If you are feeling more daring, you can go for a 60-second **bobsleigh ride** (per ride $135) with a professional driver on a 120kmh Olympic course. It could be the most exhilarating and expensive minute of your life. Alternatively, you can take a trip along a **zip-line** (tickets $55) from the top of the ski jump. In winter you can go for a **ski**, or strap on a **snowboard** and hit the sphincter-tightening super-pipe. Summer is for **mountain biking** (hill ticket/lesson $22), when you can ride the lift-serviced trails till your brakes wear out.

Olympic Oval   ICE SKATING
(www.ucalgary.ca/oval; skating adult/child $6/4) Keeping with the Olympic spirit, head to the University of Calgary and go for a skate on Olympic Oval. Used for the speed skating events at the Olympics, it offers public skating on the long track and has skates available to rent.

☞ Tours

The cheapest way to tour town is to take bus 10 ($2.75) from along 6th Ave. This bus goes on a 2½-hour circular route past old and new areas and the city's highest point, with views to the foothills, the university and some wealthy districts in the northwest.

Hammerhead Tours   CULTURE
(403-590-6930; www.hammerheadtours.com; tours $45-135) Has a variety of tour options to choose from, including city tours and trips to the Columbia Icefield, Drumheller, Banff and more.

✿ Festivals & Events

For a year-round list of the city's events, go to www.tourismcalgary.com/e-cvb/coe/main.cfm. The big festival in Calgary is the annual Calgary Stampede, held every July.

Calgary International Children's Festival   CHILDREN

(www.calgarychildfest.org; Epcor Centre for the Performing Arts, 205 8th Ave SE; admission $9; ⊙late May) Kids have all the fun at this annual event, with music, performers and all sorts of kidding around.

Carifest   CARIBBEAN

(www.carifestcalgary.com; Stephen Ave & Prince's Island Park; ⊙early Jun) The Caribbean comes alive right here in Calgary. Concerts, food stalls, street parties and stuff for the kids.

Calgary Stampede   RODEO

(www.calgarystampede.com; tickets from $24; ⊙2nd week Jul) Billed as the greatest outdoor show on earth and fast approaching its 100th anniversary, Calgary's Stampede is world famous. Events include a daily rodeo with bucking broncos, steer wrestling, barrel racing and, of course, bull riding. At night there's a grandstand show and the ever-popular chuckwagon races. It's a great time to visit Calgary, when civic spirits are on a yearly high with live music, stampede breakfasts and a rowdy party atmosphere permeating the city. Book ahead for accommodations during this event.

Calgary Folk Music Festival   MUSIC

(www.calgaryfolkfest.com; ⊙late Jul) Ray Charles once said that all music is folk music; that statement is celebrated at this annual four-day event featuring great live

music every summer on Prince's Island. Top-quality acts from around the globe make the trek to Cowtown for this groovy event. There's heaps of fun to be had hanging out on the grass listening to the sounds of summer with 12,000 close friends.

🛏 Sleeping

Finding a family-run nonchain hotel in Calgary used to be like finding a water hole in Death Valley, but the opening of a trio of boutique hotels during 2009 and '10 has provided some welcome relief.

Downtown hotels are notoriously expensive, although many run frequent specials. Business-orientated hotels are often cheaper over weekends. Hotels near the western edge of town are concentrated into an area called, appropriately, Motel Village (corner of Crowchild Trail NW and Banff Trail NW). Every chain hotel you can think of has a property here, so if you are looking for a deal, investigate this area.

The prices quoted in this section are normal for summer; during the Stampede, demand causes rates to rise and availability to plummet. If you are heading here during that time be sure to book ahead.

TOP CHOICE ▶ Centro Motel   MOTEL $$

(☎403-288-6658; www.centromotel.com; 4540 16th Ave NW; r from $99; P❋@⊚) A 'boutique motel' sounds like an oxymoron until you descend on the brand-new Centro 7km northwest of Calgary's real 'centro' on the Trans-Canada Hwy (Hwy 1). Taking an old motel building in March 2010 and making it over with modern boutique features, the indie owners have left no detail missing, from light fittings to bathrobes to the

---

CALGARY FOR CHILDREN

Calgary is a very kid-friendly destination, with most attractions having a portion aimed at the younger set. These are some highlights with kids in mind.

You'll wish science class was as fun as the **Telus World of Science** (www.calgaryscience.ca; 701 11th St SW; adult/child/family $15/12/49; ⊙9:30am-5:30pm). Kids get a big bang out of this user-friendly and very interactive science center. There is a giant dome, where light shows depicting the cosmos are projected, and a whole raft of other things to discover. Plans are in the works to move on from the current Bow River location, so it's best to phone ahead.

Children of all ages will enjoy **Calaway Park** (www.calawaypark.com; adult/child/family $27/21/70; ⊙10am-7pm Jul-early Sep, 5-9pm Fri, 10am-7pm Sat & Sun late May-Jul, 11am-6pm Sat & Sun early Sep-early Oct), western Canada's largest outdoor family amusement park. It features 30 rides from wild to mild, live stage entertainment, 22 food vendors, 28 different carnival games, a trout-fishing pond and an interactive maze. To get there, head 10km west of the city on Hwy 1.

flower baskets hanging from the walkways. Additional bonuses include a complimentary breakfast and free phone calls to anywhere in Canada and the US.

Hotel Alma   BOUTIQUE HOTEL $$

(☎403-220-3203; www.hotelalma.ca; 169 University Gate NW; r from $129; ☎) Get ready for something different. Operated and run by the University of Calgary and situated on the campus (7km from downtown), the Alma opened in October 2009 with small Euro-style rooms decked out boutique fashion and located in an old student residence. Guests get access to all on-campus facilities that include everything from a gym to a florist, plus there's free long-distance phone calls (within North America).

Hotel Le Germain   BOUTIQUE HOTEL $$$

(☎403-264-8990; www.germaincalgary.com; 899 Centre St SW; d from $279; P@☎) At last, a posh boutique hotel to counteract the bland assortment of franchise inns that service downtown Calgary. Germain is actually a member of a franchise, albeit a small French-Canadian one, but the style (check out the huge glass wall in reception) is verging on opulent, while the 24-hour gym, in-room massage, complimentary newspapers and funky lounge add luxury touches. Even better, the hotel is efficiently built and has a long list of conservation policies.

Hotel Arts   BOUTIQUE HOTEL $$$

(☎403-266-4611, 800-661-9378; www.hotelarts.ca; 119 12th Ave SW; ste from $250; P✷@☎≋) Setting a new standard in Calgary, this boutique hotel plays hard on the fact that it's not part of an international chain. Aimed at the modern discerning traveler with an aesthetic eye, there are hardwood floors, thread counts Egyptians would be envious of and art on the walls that should be in a gallery.

Fairmont Palliser   HOTEL $$$

(☎403-262-1234, 800-441-1414; www.fairmont.com/palliser; 133 9th Ave SW; r from $200; P@≋) Cut from the same elegant cloth as other Fairmont hotels, the Palliser is easily the most stunning place to bed down in Calgary. With crystal chandeliers, marble columns, wood-inlaid arched ceiling domes and antique furniture, the interior has a deep regal feel to it, unlike anything else within the city limits. Classic, beautiful and worth every penny.

Twin Gables B&B   B&B $$$

(☎403-271-7754; www.twingables.ca; 611 25th Ave SW; s/d $185/225; P@) In a lovely old home, this B&B features hardwood floors, stained-glass windows, Tiffany lamps and antique furnishings. The three rooms are tastefully decorated, and the location across from the Elbow River provides opportunities for serene walks.

International Hotel   HOTEL $$$

(☎403-265-9600; www.internationalhotel.ca; 220 4th Ave SW; ste from $250; P@☎☎) All 35 floors of this property were recently renovated and the results are uplifting. Large living spaces with great city views are standard, while the sweet suites may have the comfiest beds you'll ever pay to sleep on.

Sheraton Suites Calgary Eau Claire
                                HOTEL $$$

(☎403-266-7200, 800-325-3535; www.sheraton.com; 255 Barclay Pde SW; ste from $299; P✷@☎≋) With a great location and overflowing with amenities, this business-oriented hotel should satisfy even the fussiest of travelers. The staff love to go the extra mile in this all-suite hotel. Valet parking, a pool and a beautiful interior top it all off.

HI-Calgary   HOSTEL $

(☎403-269-8239; www.hostellingintl.ca/Alberta; 520 7th Ave SE; dm from $30, r from $75; @☎) For the budget-minded, this pleasant hostel is one of your only options for the price in Calgary. Fairly standard bunk rooms and a few doubles are available. It has a kitchen, laundry, games room and internet facilities; it's a popular crossroads for travelers and a good place to make friends, organize rides and share recommendations. Be careful at night in this area – you are only a couple of blocks from both a homeless shelter and the roughest bar in town.

Carriage House Inn   INN $$

(☎403-253-1101; www.carriagehouse.net; 9030 Macleod Trail S; r from $135; P✷@☎) When you first arrive here, the tired exterior is less than inspiring, but inside things perk up. Recent renovations have done wonders in bringing the Carriage House back up to speed. The rooms are tidy and it's close to lots of eating and shopping options.

Kensington Riverside Inn
                          BOUTIQUE HOTEL $$$

(☎403-228-4442; www.kensingtonriversideinn.com; 1126 Memorial Dr NW; r from $260; P☎) This impressive boutique-style hotel in

Kensington is a delight; a refined attitude permeates the smart-looking, beautifully finished property. The rooms are elegant and sport river views. Highly recommended.

Five
HOTEL $$
(☎403-451-5551; www.5calgary.com; 618 5th Ave SW; r from $89; P@⑦) Five is a middle-of-the-road downtown option with various pros (friendly staff, gym, kitchenettes in rooms) and cons (slightly worn rooms, dodgy 1970s architecture). Weigh them up and make your choice.

Calaway RV Park
CAMPGROUND $
(☎403-240-3822; www.calawaypark.com; Hwy 1; tent & RV sites from $24; P⑦) The youngsters will love camping at the amusement park, not too far from town to drive. During the Stampede it runs a shuttle into town.

Calgary West Campground
CAMPGROUND $
(☎403-288-0411; www.calgarycampground. com; Hwy 1; tent/RV sites $29/42; P@⑦▨) Just west of Calgary, near Canada Olympic Park, this campground is close to the city and has good facilities.

✗ Eating
If Calgary is a 'fast-moving city' then its burgeoning restaurant scene is supersonic. Eating establishments come and go here like thieves in the night making gastronomic Top 10s out-of-date before critics can even tweet them. The overall culinary trend is one of constant improvement in terms of both quality and eclecticism. Where solitary cows once roamed, vegetables and herbs now prosper, meaning that trusty old stalwart, Alberta beef, is no longer the only thing propping up the menu.

You will find good eat streets in the neighborhoods of Kensington, Inglewood, Mission and 17th Ave, and downtown on Stephen St.

Downtown

TOP CHOICE **Catch**
SEAFOOD $$
(☎403-206-0000;www.catchrestaurant. ca; 100 8th Ave SW; mains $17-27) The problem for any saltwater fish restaurant in landlocked Calgary is that, if you're calling it fresh, it can't be local. Overcoming the conundrum, Catch, situated in an old bank building in Stephen St, flies its 'fresh catch' in daily from both coasts (BC and the Maritimes). You can work out the carbon-offsets for your lobster, crab and oysters on one of three different floors: an oyster bar, a dining room or an upstairs atrium.

Rush
FUSION $$$
(☎403-271-7874; www.rushrestaurant.com; 207 9th Av SW; mains from $25) Not to be confused with the so-bad-they're-almost-good Canadian rock band of the same name, Rush the restaurant is a decidedly cooler affair with glass walls, gold millwork and not a long-haired head-banger in sight. Food-wise, this is gastronomy from the top drawer with intelligent wine pairings, and a chef's tasting menu winning almost universal plaudits. Opt for the foie gras or the halibut and enjoy the complimentary canapés and petit fours.

✓ Blink
FUSION $$
(☎403-263-5330; www.blinkcalgary.com; 111 8th Ave SW; mains from $20) Blink multiple times but you still won't miss this trendy city center gastro haven where an acclaimed British chef oversees an ever-evolving menu of fine dishes that yell out that well-practised modern restaurant mantra of 'fresh, seasonal and local.' The decor is all open-plan kitchens and exposed brick, and you can delve even deeper into the culinary process through regular cooking classes (last Sunday of the month; $125).

Peter's Drive-In
BURGERS $
(www.petersdrivein.com; 219 16th Ave NE; mains $2.50-5; ◷9am-midnight) In 1962 Peter's opened its doors and locals have been flocking there ever since to a largely unchanged menu of super-thick shakes, burgers off the grill and fries that make no pretence of being healthy. It's a true drive-in, so either bring the car along or be happy to eat on the lawn out front.

1886 Buffalo Cafe
BREAKFAST $
(187 Barclay Pde SW; ◷6am-3pm Mon-Fri, 7am-3pm Sat & Sun) Calgary needs more places like Buffalo Cafe, a salt-of-the-earth diner in the high-rise dominated city center that the realty lords forgot to knock down. The wooden shack construction dates from the late 19th century and once belonged to the Bow River Lumber Company. These days it's more famous for its huevos rancheros.

Metropolitan Grill
MEDITERRANEAN $$
(☎403-263-5432; www.themetropolitangrill.ca; 317 8th Ave SW; mains from $15; ◷11am-1am) With a prime location on Stephen Ave Walk, the Met Grill is a trendy and tasty place to savor dinner. Specializing in North American dishes with a fancy twist, the patio out front is a perfect location to have some lunch and take in the views of all the beautiful people.

River Café   FUSION $$$

(☑403-261-7670; www.river-cafe.com; Prince's Island Park; mains $24-50; ⊗11am-11pm Mon-Fri, 10am-11pm Sat & Sun) This organic, free-range and undeniably upscale restaurant that has won a litany of culinary awards is situated on the surprisingly leafy confines of Prince's Island in the middle of the Bow River. The menu is eclectic and determined by season and availability of ingredients with everything originating from either Alberta or BC. With 24 hours notice they can prepare you a picnic hamper in the summer months to enjoy in the nearby park.

Caesar's Steak House   STEAKHOUSE $$$

(512 4th Ave SW; steaks from $35; ⊗11am-midnight) Well, why wouldn't you? You're in the heart of beef country, so it's only polite to sink your teeth into some prime Alberta AAA steak.

The King and I   THAI $$

(www.kingandi.ca; 822 11th Ave SW; mains from $12; ⊗11:30am-10:30pm Mon-Thu, to 11:30pm Fri, 4:30-11:30pm Sat, 4:30-9:30pm Sun) Not just a movie with Yul Brynner, but Bangkok-good Thai food, too. This downtown classic with an exotic atmosphere is popular with groups. Try the curries or the pad thai – both are fantastic.

17th Avenue & Mission

Le Chien Chaud   FAST FOOD $

(www.lechienchaud.com; 3-2015 4th St SW; hot dogs $5; ⊗11am-8pm Mon-Sat, noon-6pm Sun) 'Gourmet hot dogs' sounds like a greasy joke, but these ones are rather delicious. With more varieties of tube-steak than anyone previously thought possible, Le Chien Chaud can even cater to vegetarians.

Nellie's Kitchen   BREAKFAST $

(738B 17th Ave SW; mains $6.50-9; ⊗7:30am-3:30pm Mon-Fri, 8am-3:30pm Sat & Sun) Nellie's has long been a favorite place to start the day, catch up with friends and attempt to quell a hangover. Humungous breakfasts, bottomless coffee and funky style are the hallmarks of this 17th Ave stalwart. Nellie's is a growing empire these days, but the original is still the best.

Melrose Café & Bar   CANADIAN $$

(www.melrosecalgary.com; 730 17th Ave SW; mains $9-15; ⊗11am-midnight Mon-Fri, 10am-1am Sat & Sun) Right in the epicenter of Calgary cool on 17th Ave, Melrose has been starting and finishing nights out since it was the in thing to go there and watch

Melrose Place (how times have changed). The gourmet pizzas are good to split over one of the many beers available on tap. The patio is legendary, full of lounging, posing locals.

⦿ Farm   FUSION $$

(www.farm-restaurant.com; 1006 17th Ave SW; shared dish $12-19; ⊗11:30am-10pm Mon-Fri, 10:30am-11pm Sat, 10:30am-10pm Sun) Raising the excitement bar on 17th Ave, Farm is a new 'tasting kitchen' for fine meats, beer, wine and particularly cheese. The menu is about attention to detail, back-to-the-land purity and a genuine love of good food.

Antonio's Garlic Clove   ITALIAN $$

(www.garlicclove.net; 2206 4th St SW; mains from $20; ⊗5pm-late) They take their garlic seriously here – it's in *everything* from the appetizers right through to dessert. Flavorful and obviously aromatic dishes are the hallmark of this authentic Italian eatery. Make sure you try the garlic beer.

Galaxie Diner   BREAKFAST $

(www.galaxiediner.com; 1413 11th St SW; mains $5-9; ⊗7am-3pm Mon-Fri, to 4pm Sat & Sun) Classic no-nonsense '50s-style diner that serves all-day breakfasts. Squeeze into one of the half-dozen tables or grab a pew at the bar.

Cilantro   ITALIAN $$

(www.crmr.com; 17th Ave SW; mains from $16; ⊗11am-10pm Mon-Thu & Sun, to 11pm Fri, 5-11pm Sat) Great Italian food, big wine glasses and nice decor put the finishing touches on a good meal at small and intimate Cilantro.

Kensington

Osteria de Medici   ITALIAN $$$

(☑403-283-5553; www.osteria.ca; 201 10th St NW; mains from $21) Italian restaurants are ubiquitous in North America, but few are as good as their home-country counterparts. Fortunately, the grandiose Medici is one of an authentic minority with uncomplicated renditions of classic Italian dishes such as veal marsala and *linguine alla vongole* (mussels). The secret? The proprietor is from Molise (east of Rome) and half of the clientele are from Hollywood (if you believe the blurb).

Sushi Club   JAPANESE $$

(1240 Kensington Rd NW; mains from $10; ⊗11:30am-2pm & 5-9pm Mon, Wed, Thu & Fri) This could well be the best sushi in town; at the very least it's right up there. It's perhaps a bit on the pricey side, but you get what you pay for. It has a great lunch special, where a massive spread costs under $10.

Broken Plate
MEDITERRANEAN $$
(www.brokenplate.ca; 302 10th St NW; mains from $15) One of three Greek-themed restaurants in the city (all under the same name), this one, in the independently minded neighborhood of Kensington, is the original and best. Excellent pastas, pizzas and traditional Greek fare are enthusiastically consumed in the open, light-filled dining area. And yes, they break plates to dancing waiters Friday and Saturday nights.

Inglewood

Rouge
FUSION $$$
(☎403-531-2767; www.rougecalgary.com; 1240 8th Ave SE; mains $36-80) Calgary cuisine has recently been a tale of two 'R's – Rush (p579) and Rouge, with the latter becoming the city's most celebrated restaurant with its inclusion in the prestigious 2010 S Pellegrino World's Top 100 Restaurants list (rated at No 60 – the highest in Canada). Located in a historic 1891 mansion in Inglewood, it's expensive and hard to get into, but once inside you're on hallowed ground. Enjoy the inspired, creative and sustainable food choices and exceptional fit-for-a-king service.

🍷 Drinking

For bars hit 17th Ave NW, with a slew of martini lounges and crowded pubs, and 4th St SW, with a lively after-work scene. Other notable areas include Kensington Rd NW and Stephen Ave (a six-block downtown stretch of 8th Ave).

Hop In Brew
PUB
(www.hopinbrew.com; 213 12th Ave SW) Imagine if you took an old house, turned it into a dive bar, and then threw a great party every weekend. Tucked down a quiet street just off the main drag, the Hop In Brew has got some style. The converted house has a bar upstairs and down, a pool table up top and winding steps right through the middle. There are good tunes, grungy atmosphere and plenty on tap.

Ming
BAR
(520 17th Ave SW) 'Serving all comrades until 2am' says the sign, hinting that Ming might not be conservative Calgary's most traditional bar. Contrarians, lefties and people with their tongues stuck firmly in their cheeks sit down inside beneath the pop-art image of Chairman Mao and sip on Che Guevara cocktails in what is one of 17th Ave's trendiest watering holes.

Barley Mill
PUB
(www.barleymill.net; 201 Barclay Pde SW) This freestanding structure adjacent to Eau Claire Market is a favorite after-work stop for the downtown working stiffs. There's a big summer patio and the festive atmosphere keeps it popular year-round.

Ship & Anchor
PUB
(534 17th Ave SW) The Ship is an uberclassic Calgary institution, an all-time favorite of uni students, people who think they're hip and indie music fans. With plentiful beers on tap, the shadowy interior is a cozy winter hideaway, while the picnic table-filled patio is Posing Central come summertime.

Flames Central
BAR
(www.flamescentral.com; 219 8th Ave SW) The place to be to catch a hockey game on the big screen. The huge interior of what used to be a cinema has been transformed into the sports bar to end all sports bars. With more TVs than an electronics shop, you'll definitely get a good view of the game, even when they're playing the Oilers. There is an on-site restaurant and it has concerts from time to time.

Rose & Crown
PUB
(www.roseandcrowncalgary.ca; 1503 4th St SW) This British-style pub feels like it could hold most of Britain. Multileveled and popular, it's a good place to meet and greet some new-found friends.

Vicious Circle
BAR
(www.viciouscircle.ca; 1011 1st St SW) Dark and moody, cocktails and martinis, comfy couches and a stylish atmosphere – check it out.

☆ Entertainment

You can see the money walking Calgary's streets after dark: beautiful, well-dressed 20-somethings in stretch limos, noisy stag nights in corporate bars, high-heeled girls in skimpy party dresses defying minus 20°C temperatures. People like to go out here; and they like to dress up, too. Leave your fleece in Vancouver and borrow someone's ironing board.

For complete entertainment guides, pick up a copy of *ffwd*, the city's largest entertainment weekly.

Whiskey
NIGHTCLUB

(www.thewhiskeynightclub.com; 341 10th Ave SW) Here lie all the unbeatable facets of an ubertrendy nightclub: surly bouncers, a big list of entry rules, long freezing cold lines, a chill-out bar, music from the '80s onwards, and plenty of beautiful people showing off on the dance floor.

Broken City
MUSIC VENUE

(www.brokencity.ca; 613 11th Ave SW) If you fancy a bit of rock and roll and are looking for a club with a 4/4 heartbeat, then Broken City is your scene. Indie rock, alt country and punk all do the rounds and get the crowds going. Gigs are usually on Thursday and Friday nights.

HiFi Club
NIGHTCLUB

(www.hificlub.ca; 219 10th Ave SW) The HiFi is a hybrid. Rap, soul, house; electro, funk; the dance floor swells nightly to the sounds of live DJs who specialize in making you sweat. Check out Sunday Skool, the weekly soul and jazz session or Saturday night's showcase for touring bands and DJs.

Kaos
MUSIC VENUE

(718 17th Ave SW) Jazz lovers unite at Kaos for nightly live music. The hip older crowd is a nice relief from the pubescent atmosphere found at some nightspots around town.

Marquee Room
MUSIC VENUE

(www.theuptown.com; 612 8th Ave SW) Upstairs from the Uptown Cinema, this stylish joint is quickly becoming one of Calgary's hot spots. Great for live bands and DJs.

Epcor Centre for the Performing Arts
THEATER

(www.epcorcentre.org; 205 8th Ave SE) This is the hub for live theater in Calgary with four theaters and one of the best concert halls in North America.

Loose Moose Theatre Company
THEATER

(1229 9th Ave SE) Guaranteed to be a fun night out, Loose Moose specializes in improv comedy and audience participation.

Plaza Theatre
CINEMA

(1113 Kensington Rd NW) Right in the heart of Kensington, the Plaza shows art-house flicks and cult classics – it's where you'll end up doing the 'Time Warp' (again!).

Globe Cinema
CINEMA

(617 8th Ave SW) Specializing in foreign films and Canadian cinema, both often hard to find in mainstream movie houses.

Paramount Chinook
CINEMA

(6455 MacLeod Trail SW) Located in Chinook Centre shopping mall, the Paramount has 17 screens, so there must be something on worth seeing. There is an IMAX theater on-site, too.

Pumphouse Theatres
THEATER

(www.pumphousetheatres.ca; 2140 Pumphouse Ave SW) Set in what used to be, you guessed it, the pumphouse, this theater company puts on avant-garde, edgy and entertaining productions.

Jubilee Auditorium
THEATER

(www.jubileeauditorium.com/southern; 1415 14th Ave NW) You can hang with the upper crust at the ballet or rock out to a good concert, all under the one roof.

Gay & Lesbian Venues

Pick up a copy of *Outlooks* (www.outlooks. ca), a gay-oriented monthly newspaper distributed throughout the province. The website offers an extensive gay resource guide to Calgary and beyond.

Twisted Element
NIGHTCLUB

(www.twistedelement.ca; 1006 11th Ave SW) Consistently voted the best gay dance venue by the local community, this club has weekly drag shows, karaoke nights and DJs spinning nightly.

Calgary Eagle
BAR

(www.calgaryeagle.com; 424A 8th Ave SE) Billed as Calgary's leather bar, this place is popular with the fetish-inclined.

Back Lot
BAR

(209 10th Ave SW) This one's for boys mainly. There's a patio and drink specials while you take in the view.

Sports

Calgary Flames
SPORTS

(403-777-0000; tickets from $15) Archrival of the Edmonton Oilers, the Calgary Flames play ice hockey from October to April at the **Saddledome** (Stampede Park). Make sure you wear red to the game and head down to 17th Ave afterwards, or the 'Red Mile' as they call it during playoff time.

Calgary Stampeders
SPORTS

(403-289-0258; tickets from $27; Jul-Sep) The Calgary Stampeders, part of the CFL, play at **McMahon Stadium** (1817 Crowchild Trail NW) in northwest Calgary.

🔒 Shopping

Shopping in Calgary can be a disjointed affair. There are several hot spots, but these districts are reasonably far apart. The Kensington area and 17th Ave SW have a good selection of interesting, fashionable clothing shops and funky trinket outlets. Stephen Ave Walk is another highlight; the pedestrian mall has a good selection of shops, bookstores and atmosphere.

Alberta Boot Co   CLOTHING
(www.albertaboot.com; 50 50th Ave S; boots $235-1700) Visit the factory and store run by the province's only Western boot manufacturer and pick up a pair of your choice made from kangaroo, ostrich, python, rattlesnake, lizard, alligator or boring old cowhide.

Chinook Centre   MALL
(www.chinookcentre.com; 6455 Macleod Trail SW) If you're in need of some retail therapy, Chinook, just south of downtown, is a good place to get your treatment. Chain retail shops, department stores, a movie theater and lots of greasy food are all present and accounted for.

Mountain Equipment Co-Op OUTDOOR GEAR
(MEC; 830 10th Ave SW) MEC is the place to get your outdoor kit sorted before heading into the hills. It has a huge selection of outdoor equipment, travel gear, active clothing and books.

Smithbilt Hats   CLOTHING
(www.smithbilthats.com; 1103 12th St SE) Ever wondered how a cowboy hat is made? Well, here is your chance to find out. Smithbilt has been shaping hats in the traditional way since you parked your horse out front.

ℹ️ Information

Alberta Children's Hospital (☑403-955-7211; 2888 Shaganappi Trail NW) Emergency room open 24 hours.

Calforex (304 8th Ave SW) Currency exchange facilities. Banks seem to live at every corner downtown; look to 17th Ave or Stephen Ave Walk if one isn't within sight. Many branches are open on Saturday and bank machines are open 24/7.

Hard Disk Café (638 11th Ave SW; internet per hr $5; ☉7am-7pm Mon-Thu, to 9pm Fri)

Main post office (207 9th Ave SW)

Police, Ambulance & Fire (☑911)

Police Dispatch Line (☑403-266-1234) For nonemergencies.

Rockyview General Hospital (☑403-943-3000; 7007 14th St SW) Emergency room open 24 hours.

Tourism Calgary (www.tourismcalgary.com; 101 9th Ave SW; ☉8am-5pm) Operates a visitors center in the base of the Calgary Tower. The staff will help you find accommodations. Information booths are also available at both the arrivals and departures levels of the airport.

ℹ️ Getting There & Away

Air

Calgary International Airport (YYC; www.calgaryairport.com) is about 15km northeast of the center off Barlow Trail, a 25-minute drive away. For more information on flights into Calgary, see p551.

Bus

The Greyhound Canada **bus station** (877 Greyhound Way SW) has services to Banff ($29, two hours, six daily) and Edmonton ($51, from 3½ hours, 10 or more daily). It also serves Drumheller and Lethbridge. For information on fares to other parts of Canada, see p570. **Red Arrow** (www.redarrow.pwt.ca; 205 9th Ave SE) runs luxury buses to Edmonton ($60, 3½ hours, seven daily).

Car

All the major car-rental firms are represented at the airport and downtown. For more information on car hire, see p886.

Train

Inexplicably, Calgary welcomes no passenger trains (which bypass the city in favor of Edmonton and Jasper). Instead, you get **Rocky Mountaineer Railtours** (www.rockymountain-███ ████), ████ ██ ███ ██████ █████-████ rail excursions (two-day tours per person from $1400).

ℹ️ Getting Around

To/From the Airport

Sundog Tours (☑403-291-9617; tickets adult/child $15/8) runs every half-hour from around 8:30am to 9:45pm between all the major downtown hotels and the airport.

You can also go between the airport and downtown on public transportation. From the airport, take bus 57 to the Whitehorn stop (northeast of the city center) and transfer to the C-Train; reverse that process coming from downtown. This costs only $2.75, and takes between 45 minutes and an hour.

A taxi to the airport costs about $35 from downtown.

Car & Motorcycle

Parking in downtown Calgary is an absolute nightmare. Luckily, downtown hotels generally have garages, and extortionately high-priced private lots are available for about $20 per day. There is also metered parking at about $1 per 45 minutes (free after 6pm and on Sunday). Thankfully, outside the downtown core, parking is free and easy to find.

Public Transportation

Calgary Transit (www.calgarytransit.com) is efficient and clean. You can choose from the Light Rapid Transit (LRT) rail system, also known as the C-Train, and ordinary buses. One fare entitles you to transfer to other buses or C-Trains. The C-Train is free in the downtown area along 7th Ave, between 10th St SW and 3rd St SE. If you're going further or need a transfer, buy your ticket from a machine on the C-Train platform. Most of the buses run at 15- to 30-minute intervals daily. There is no late-night service. The C-Train and bus fare per single/day is $2.75/8.25. The C-Train is currently adding a new line to access the west of the city, which is due to open in 2012.

Taxi

For a cab, call **Checker Cabs** (☎403-299-9999) or **Yellow Cab** (☎403-974-1111). Fares are $3 for the first 150m, then $0.20 for each additional 150m.

BANFF & JASPER NATIONAL PARKS

While Italy has Venice and Florence, Canada has Banff and Jasper, legendary natural marvels that are as spectacular and vital as anything the ancient Romans ever built. But, don't think these protected areas have no history. Of the thousands of national parks scattered around the world today, Banff, created in 1885, is the third oldest while adjacent Jasper was only 22 years behind. Situated on the eastern side of the Canadian Rockies, the two bordering parks were designated Unesco World Heritage sites in 1984, along with BC's Yoho and Kootenay, for their exceptional natural beauty coupled with their manifestation of important glacial and alluvial geological processes. In contrast to some of North America's wilder parks, they both support small towns that lure between 2 to 5 million visitors each year. Despite all this, the precious balance between humans and nature continues to be delicately maintained – just.

Visiting the Park

Visitors come here for all sorts of reasons: to ski, climb and hike on the mountains, to raft and kayak the rivers, to camp among the trees, or explore on their mountain bikes. But most come simply to look, and to stand in awe of the sheer beauty of this amazing place.

As you pass through this special area, you are under the ever-watchful eye of the animals that call it home. This is the place to see the Canadian Rockies' Big Five: deer, elk, moose, wolf and bear. (But only if you're lucky: they don't pose for everyone's photos.)

The one-day park entry fee (for entry to both parks) is $9.80/4.90 per adult/child; the passes are good until 4pm the following day.

History

Banff National Park, Canada's first park, became the template for conservation. When Jasper joined the park system just over a century ago, this corridor of conservation was complete. Within that protected zone, the small towns of Banff and Jasper have emerged. These two towns, where development is frozen and the idea of ecotourism has been around since the 1880s, have lived in harmony with the surrounding wilderness for decades.

Banff is far from a secret these days – crowds are inevitable and you will have to share those scenic lookouts. But most will agree that's a small price to pay for a part of this country that will remain in your thoughts long after you bid the mountains *au revoir.*

Kananaskis Country

Kananaskis, or K-Country as the locals call it, is a mountainous Shangri-la with all the natural highlights of Banff National Park, but with almost no clamor. Driving the scenic and sparsely trafficked Hwy 40, you are treated to blankets of pine forest interspersed with craggy peaks and the odd moose in the verge. At an impressive 4000 sq km, it's a hefty tract of landscape to try and take in. Luckily, there is a network of hiking trails to get you into the backcountry and away from the roads. Hikers, cross-country skiers, bikers and climbers – mainly in-the-know Albertans – all lust over these hills which are the perfect combination of wild, accessible, unspoiled and inviting.

From the eastern edge of the mountains you can drive the paved Hwy 40 to the ᴋᴀɴᴀɴᴀꜱᴋɪꜱ ʟᴀᴋᴇꜱ, ᴘᴇᴀᴋꜱ ᴛᴜʀɴɪɴɢ, ᴅᴏᴡɴ onto the unsealed Smith-Dorian Rd to complete the drive to Canmore. Or if you can, continue along Hwy 40 all the way to Highwood House – this scenic drive is definitely the road less traveled and well worth exploring; be aware this portion of the road is closed over winter.

🏃 Activities

K-Country is also C-Country. Cowboy-up and go for a ride with **Boundary Ranch** (📞403-591-7171; www.boundaryranch.com; Hwy 40; rides from $40; ⊙mid-May–mid-Oct), which will take you for a trail ride that could last anywhere from an hour to days.

Purpose-built to host the alpine skiing events in the '88 Olympics, **Nakiska** (www.skinakiska.com; Hwy 40), five minutes' drive south of Kananaskis Village, is a racer's

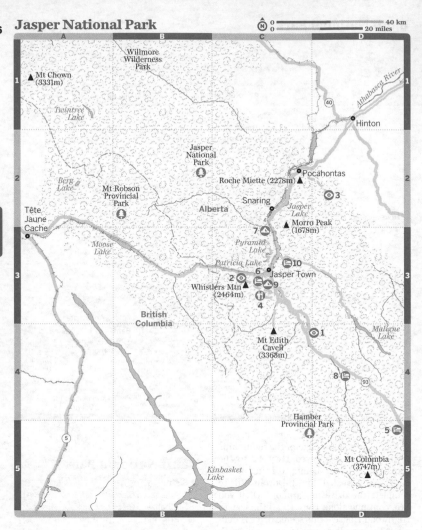

dream and top Canadian skiers still train here. K-Country's other ski resort, Fortress Mountain, has been closed on and off (mainly off) since 2004.

The Kananaskis River has class II and III rapids and is popular with white-water rafting companies operating out of Banff (see p595).

Sleeping & Eating

Proof of Kananaskis' get-away-from-it-all ethos came when it was selected to host the first post-9/11 G8 summit when security was particularly high. The likes of

Tony Blair, Jacques Chirac and Vladimir Putin were bivouacked at the **Delta Lodge at Kananaskis** (403-591-7711; www.delta hotels.com; r from $219). The amazing scenery, tip-top facilities and isolation were a big hit with the world leaders, except Texan George W Bush who, oddly, opted to fly out of cowboy country and return to American soil – every night. Delta's pricey **Fireweed Grill** (Delta Lodge; mains $20-30) does baked river fish and AAA Alberta steak.

If you can't afford G8 prices, get the full Kananaskis experience by sleeping under the stars at the **Boulton Creek Campground** (☑403-591-7226; Kananaskis Lakes Rd; powered/nonpowered sites $20/30; ☉mid-May–Oct).

ⓘ Information

About 8km from Hwy 1 along Hwy 40 is the **Barrier Lake Information Centre** (☑403-673-3985; www.tpr.alberta.ca/parks; Hwy 40; ☉9am-4pm, to 5pm May-Sep), which has loads of info and sells backcountry camping permits.

Canmore

A former mining town, Canmore was once the quiet alternative to the mass tourism of Banff. Then, after one too many 'best kept secret' travel articles, everybody started coming here for a little peace and quiet. Despite the commotion, the soul of the town has remained intact and Canmore, although not national park protected, has been developed sensibly and sustainably – so far. At just 26km from Banff and on the cusp of Kananaskis Country, it's at the crossroads of some of the most magnificent scenery you will ever see. For those seeking a mountain holiday with slightly less glitz, more of a rugged feel and less pretension, Canmore can still cut it.

⊙ Sights & Activities

Canmore excels in two particular mountain activities: cross-country skiing and mountaineering.

Cross-country Skiing
Both winter and summer are prime times at the **Canmore Nordic Centre** (www.canmore nordic.com; 1988 Olympic Way). Used for the cross-country skiing events at the 1988 Olympics, the Nordic Centre is arguably the best facility of its kind in Canada and the training ground for many national champions. It offers ski rentals and lessons for the uninitiated and a network of trails that would keep an Olympian busy for days.

Mountain Biking
Once the snow melts, the Nordic Centre's trails transform into some of the best mountain biking around, with over 80km of off-road to test your skills. Close to here, the Rundle Riverside and Spray River/Goat Creek trails both head north to Banff Town (see p594).

Rock Climbing
Canmore is one of the premier rock-climbing destinations in the Rockies. In the summer, there are numerous climbing crags such as Cougar Creek, Grassi Lakes and Grotto Canyon all within a relatively short distance of each other. For those looking for multipitch rock, the limestone walls of Mt Rundle and Mt Yamnuska are local classics with routes of all grades. In the colder months, Canmore is the place to be for frozen waterfall climbing – learn at the Junkyards, practise on Grotto Falls or take the final exam on The Terminator.

If you are keen to give climbing in any of its forms a try, talk to **Yamnuska Mountain Adventures** (www.yamnuska.com; Suite 200, Summit Centre, 50 Lincoln Park), which will provide expert instruction, qualified guides and all the gear you might need. Yamnuska also offers longer courses for those wanting to gain the skills necessary to spend some serious time in the hills.

🛏 Sleeping

Canmore Clubhouse HOSTEL $
(☑403-678-3200; www.alpineclubofcanada.ca; Indian Flats Rd; dm from $36; ℗) Steeped in climbing history and mountain mystique, the Alpine Club of Canada's beautiful hostel sits on a rise overlooking the valley. You'll find all of the usual hostel amenities here, along with a sauna. The Alpine Club offers classes in mountaineering and maintains several backcountry huts. The Clubhouse is a great place to find climbing partners or just soak up the spirit of adventure. Located 5km south of town, it's an inconvenient 45-minute walk or pleasant five-minute drive away.

Alberta's five national parks are remarkable not just for their environmental steward-ship, but for the pioneering role they have played in the development of Canada's (and the planet's) bid to protect pristine land for future generations. Banff, formed in 1885, was Canada's first and the world's third national park and acted as a meta-phoric litmus test for subsequent ecological management, while Waterton (1895), Jasper (1907), Elk Island (1913) and Wood Buffalo (1922) provided four more testing grounds for Canada's still nascent National Parks Service in the first quarter of the 20th century.

All of Alberta's parks bar Elk Island double up as Unesco World Heritage sites. Yet, despite such impressive billing, Banff, Jasper and Waterton support infrastructures unheard of in many other North American parks, particularly in the US. Common to each are sizeable resort towns, commercial ski areas, thirsty golf courses, popular franchise restaurants and long-running and often feisty debates about how to man-age ecological integrity alongside the right of recreation for all. With the arguments still raging, the fate of Alberta's parks could well be a harbinger for the long-term fu-ture of protected areas worldwide.

Windtower Lodge & Suites   HOTEL **$$**
(☑403-609-6600; www.windtower.ca; 160 Kananaskis Way; d/ste $169/239; ［Ｐ＠❡］) Named for the stunning rock feature only a few kilometers to the east, this modern and well-appointed hotel is a good option. The rooms are a bit small, so spending a bit more on a suite is a good idea. Some rooms have fine views of the Three Sisters and all have access to the hot tub and fit-ness center.

✖ Eating

The Wood   STEAKHOUSE **$$**
(www.thewood.ca; 838 8th St; mains $12-29) Plenty of wood and a big fireplace create a relaxed, sophisticated vibe in this log build-ing in Canmore's town center. If you're hav-ing a day off from AAA Alberta steak (not easy here), plump for the excellent salmon burger with a Dijon tartar relish.

Grizzly Paw   PUB **$$**
(www.thegrizzlypaw.com; 622 Main St; mains $13-20) Yes, it's a microbrewery (offering six year-round beers) and yes, it serves food (including wings, burgers and shep-herd's pie), meaning this funky gastro-pub is a Rocky Mountain rarity.

Quarry   PUB **$$$**
(www.quarrydininglounge.com; 718 Main St; mains $17-32) This posh brasserie with an open kitchen viewable from a wrap-around bar creates European-influenced food with some subtle surprises, includ-ing Moroccan tagine, homemade terrine and spaghetti carbonara.

❶ Information

Canmore Library (950 8th Ave) For free internet and wi-fi; best to book ahead to get a computer.

Canmore Visitor Information Centre (www. discoveralberta.com; 2801 Bow Valley Trail; ⊙8am-8pm) Just off Hwy 1.

❶ Getting There & Away

Canmore is easily accessible from Banff Town and Calgary from Hwy 1. The **Banff Airporter** (www.banffairporter.com) runs up to 10 buses a day to/from Calgary Airport ($52) and Banff ($15). Slightly cheaper is **Greyhound Canada** (www.greyhound.ca) with connections to Down-town Calgary ($25), Banff Town ($12.50) and all stops west as far as Vancouver ($138). The bus stops in 8th St and had no official depot at time of writing. You must buy your tickets online.

Icefields Parkway

Paralleling the Continental Divide for 230km between Lake Louise and Jasper Town, plain old Hwy 93 has been wisely rebranded as the Icefields Parkway (or the slightly more romantic 'Promenade des Glaciers' in French) as a means of somehow preparing people for the majesty of its sur-roundings. And what majesty! The high-light is undoubtedly the humungous Co-lumbia Icefield and its numerous fanning glaciers, and this dynamic lesson in erosive geography is complemented by weeping waterfalls, aquamarine lakes, dramatic mountains and the sudden dart of a bear, an elk, or was it a moose?

Completed in 1940, most people ply the Parkway's asphalt by car, meaning it can get busy in July and August. For a clearer vision consider taking a bus or, even better, tackling it on a bike – the road is wide, never prohibitively steep, and sprinkled with plenty of strategically spaced campgrounds, hostels and hotels.

⊙ Sights

Every bend in the road reveals a view seemingly more stunning than the last. There are lakes and glaciers galore – too many to mention. Here are some favorites.

Peyto Lake   NATURAL SITE

This is the sort of scenery you come to the Canadian Rockies to find. This bluer than blue glacier-fed lake has been photographed more than Brangelina. Don't let the inevitable zoo of people deter you – the view is one of the best anywhere. The lake is best visited in early morning, between the time the sun first illuminates the water and the first tour bus arrives. From the bottom of the lake parking lot, follow a paved trail for 15 minutes up a steady gradual incline to the wooden platform overlooking the lake. From here you can continue up the paved trail, keeping right along the edge of the ridge. At the junction of three trails, follow the middle trail until you reach an unmarked dirt road; if you continue down it for about 2.5km you'll find yourself in a serene rocky bowl with a stream running through the center.

The Weeping Wall   NATURAL SITE

Just before you get to the Big Bend – you'll know it when you get there – you'll come across The Weeping Wall. The towering rock wall sits just above the east side of the highway. In the summer months it is a sea of waterfalls, with tears of liquid pouring from the top creating a veil of moisture. Come winter, it's a whole different story. The water freezes up solid to form an enormous sheet of ice. The vertical football field is a popular playground for ice climbers who travel from around the globe to test their mettle here. Scaling the wall is a feather in the cap for the alpinists lucky enough to clamber to the top. Be sure to observe the ice from the safety of the roadside lookout; falling chunks of ice the size of refrigerators are not uncommon.

Columbia Icefield   MUSEUM

About halfway between Lake Louise Village and Jasper Town you'll encounter the only accessible section of the vast Columbia Icefield, which contains about 30 glaciers and is up to 350m thick. This remnant of the last ice age covers 325 sq km on the plateau between Mt Columbia (3747m) and Mt Athabasca (3491m). It's the largest icefield in the Rockies and feeds the North Saskatchewan, Columbia, Athabasca, Mackenzie and Fraser River systems with its meltwaters.

The mountainous sides of this vast bowl of ice are some of the highest in the Rockies, with nine peaks higher than 3000m.

Be sure to stop here at the **Icefield Centre** (☎780-852-6288; admission free; ☺9am-6pm May–mid-Oct). The downstairs **Glacial Gallery** explains the science of glaciers and provides a comprehensive snapshot of the area's history. On the main level you can have a chat to the rangers from **Parks Canada** (☎780-852-6288), who can advise you on camping options and climbing conditions and answer any questions you might have regarding the park. There's a fairly insipid cafeteria here along with a hotel (see p590).

Athabasca Glacier   NATURAL SITE

The tongue of the Athabasca glacier runs from the Columbia Icefield almost down to the road opposite the Icefield Centre and can be visited on foot or in specially designed buses. The glacier has retreated about 1.6km in the last 150 years. To reach its toe walk or drive 1km to a small parking lot and the start of the 0.6km **Forefield Trail**. While it is permitted to stand on a small roped section of the ice, do not attempt to cross the warning tape. Many do, but the glacier is riddled with crevasses and there are fatalities nearly every year.

The best way to experience the Columbia Icefield is to walk on it. For that you will need the help of **Athabasca Glacier Icewalks** (☎780-852-5595, 800-565-7547; www.icewalks.com; Icefield Centre), which supplies all the gear you'll need and a guide to show you the ropes. It offers a three-hour tour (adult/child $60/30; departing 10:40am daily June to September), and a six-hour option ($70/35) on Sunday and Thursday for those wanting to venture further onto the glacier.

The other far easier (and more popular) way to get on the glacier is via a 'Snocoach' ice tour offered by **Brewster** (✆877-423-7433; www.brewster.ca; adult/child $49/24; ☺tours every 15-30min 9am-5pm May-Oct). For many people this is the defining experience of their Columbia Icefield visit. The large hybrid bus-truck grinds a track onto the ice where it stops to allow you to go for a short walk in a controlled area on the glacier. Dress warmly and wear good shoes. Tickets can be bought at the Icefield Centre or online.

Athabasca Glacier to Jasper Town
SCENIC HIGHWAY

As you snake your way through the mountains on your way to Jasper, there are a few places worth stopping at. **Sunwapta Falls** and **Athabasca Falls**, closer to Jasper, are both worth a stop. The latter is the more voluminous and is at its most ferocious in the summer when it's stoked with glacial meltwater. A less-visited spot is idyllic blue-green **Horseshoe Lake**, revered by ill-advised cliff-divers. Don't be tempted to join them.

At Athabasca Falls, Hwy 93A quietly sneaks off to the left. Take it. Literally the road less traveled, this old route into Jasper offers a blissfully traffic-free experience as it slips serenely through deep, dark woods and past small placid lakes and meadows.

🛏 Sleeping & Eating

The Icefields Parkway is punctuated with a good batch of well-camouflaged hostels and lodges. Most are close to the highway in scenic locations. There are also numerous primitive **campgrounds** (per night $15.70) in the area. Good options are Honeymoon Lake, Joans Creek, Mt Kerkeslin, Waterfowl Lakes and Wilcox Creek Campgrounds.

Mosquito Creek International Hostel
HOSTEL **$**

(✆403-670-7589; www.hihostels.ca; dm member/nonmember $23/27; P) Don't let the name put you off – Mosquito Creek, 26km north of Lake Louise, is a perfect launching pad for backcountry adventures, the sauna is an ideal flop-down-and-do-nothing end to the day and the adjacent river just adds to the atmosphere. The hostel sometimes closes in winter, so call ahead.

Rampart Creek International Hostel
HOSTEL **$**

(✆403-670-7589; www.hihostels.ca; dm member/nonmember $23/27; P) Rampart, 11km north of the Saskatchewan River Crossing, has long been a popular place with climbers, cyclists and other troublemakers. The tiny crag at the back is good fun for a bouldering session, and the 12 bunks and facilities are clean and cozy. Then there's the sauna – more lethargy. Call first in winter in case it's closed.

🛏 Beauty Creek International Hostel
HOSTEL **$**

(Map p586; ✆780-852-3215; www.hihostels.ca; Icefields Parkway; dm member/nonmember $23/27; ☺check-in 5-10pm) Forget the lack of electricity, propane-powered lights, outside loos and well-drawn water, and home in on the all-you-can-eat pancake breakfast and poetry-inspiring scenery.

Sunwapta Falls Resort
HOTEL **$$$**

(Map p586; ✆888-828-5777; www.sunwapta.com; r from $209; P@) A handy Icefields pit stop 53km south of Jasper townsite, Sunwapta offers a comfortable mix of suites and lodge rooms cocooned in pleasant natural surroundings. There's a home-style restaurant and gift shop on-site that are popular with the tour-bus crowd.

Columbia Icefield Chalet
HOTEL **$$$**

(✆877-423-7433; Icefield Centre, Icefields Parkway; r from $260; ☺May-Oct; P) Panoramic views of the glacier are unbelievable at this chalet – if only the windows were a bit bigger. You are in the same complex as the madness of the Icefield Centre, so it can feel like you are staying in a shopping mall at times. But after all the buses go away for the night, you are left in one of the most spectacular places around. A nothing-to-write-home-about cafeteria shares the complex.

Num-Ti-Jah Lodge
INN **$$$**

(✆403-522-2167; www.num-ti-jah.com; d $275; P) Standing like a guardian of Bow Lake, the historic Num-Ti-Jah Lodge is full to the brim with character and backcountry nostalgia. Carved wood interior decor, animal heads and photos from the golden age adorn the walls. The rooms are tidy, if a little small. The lodge restaurant (mains from $14, three-course dinner $45) has an extensive wine list.

Banff Town

Like the province in which it resides, Banff is something of an enigma. A resort town with souvenir shops, nightclubs and fancy restaurants is not something any national park purist would want to claim credit for. But, looks can be misleading. First, Banff is no ordinary town. It developed historically, not as a residential district, but as a service center for the park that surrounds it. Second, the commercialism of Banff Ave is delusory. Wander five minutes in either direction and (though you may not initially realize it) you're in wild country, a primeval food chain of bears, elk, wolves and bighorn sheep. Banff civilized? It's just a rumor.

History

While most mountain towns have their roots in the natural resource industry, Banff was created in the late 1800s with tourism in mind. The railway arrived first, then the Cave and Basin hot springs were discovered and the potential to make some money became evident. First came the hordes of wealthy Victorians, staying at the Banff Springs Hotel and soaking in the soothing waters. Everything changed in 1911 when the road finally reached the town and the doors were flung open to the masses.

Banff continued to grow as more tourists arrived and services aimed at not just the upper class began to take root. Town developers have long been frustrated by the inclusion of the townsite within the national park. This has meant that building restrictions are tight, new development has ceased and the future of building in Banff is both a political and ecological hot potato. Actually living in Banff is a challenge: the federal government owns all the land, only those employed can take up residence and businesses are obligated to provide accommodations for their employees.

Though the infrastructure and size of the town remains fixed, the number of tourists has continued to spiral skywards. For as long as the town has been incorporated, locals have bickered about tourism. While they may pay everyone's wages, the visitors overrun the town and move it away from the quiet mountain town it once was.

◉ Sights

TOP CHOICE **Whyte Museum of the Canadian Rockies** MUSEUM
(www.whyte.org; 111 Bear St; adult/child $8/5; ⊙10am-5pm) The century-old Whyte Museum is more than just a rainy-day option. There is a beautiful gallery displaying some great pieces on an ever-changing basis. The permanent collection tells the story of Banff and the hearty men and women who forged a home among the mountains. Attached to the museum is an archive with thousands of photographs spanning the history of the town and park; these are available for reprint. The museum also gives out leaflets for a self-guided **Banff Culture Walk**.

Banff Gondola LANDMARK
(Mountain Ave; adult/6-15yr $29/14; ⊙8:30am-9pm summer, reduced hours rest of year) In summer or winter you can summit a peak near Banff thanks to the Banff Gondola, whose four-person enclosed cars glide you up to the top of Sulphur Mountain in less than 10 minutes. Named for the thermal springs that emanate from its base, this peak is a perfect viewing point and a tick-box Banff attraction. There are a couple of restaurants on top plus an extended hike on boardwalks to Sanson Peak, an old weather station. Some people hike all the way up on a zigzagging 5.6km trail. You can travel back down on the gondola for half price and recover in the hot springs.

Cave & Basin National Historic Site
HISTORIC SITE
(Cave Ave; adult/child $4/3; ⊙9am-6pm May-Oct, 11am-4pm Mon-Fri 9:30am-5pm Sat & Sun Nov-Apr) Aboriginals have known about this hot spot for 10,000 years. The Cave & Basin is a great place to sniff around and discover how Banff National Park came into being. In 1883, three railway workers found the hot springs and discovered a thermal gold mine. Quickly throwing up a shack to charge bathers for their thermal treatments, the government soon stepped in and decided to declare Banff Canada's first national park in order to preserve the springs. You can't swim here any more, but there's an indoor museum (temporarily closed at the time of research) and an interpretive walk along boardwalks to the springs and cave vent. The 2.5km **Marsh Loop Trail** across the park's only natural river marsh also starts here.

Banff Town

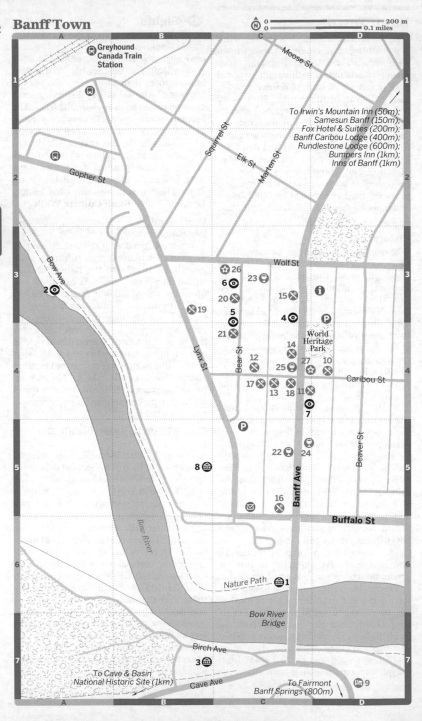

Greyhound Canada Train Station

To Irwin's Mountain Inn (50m);
Samesun Banff (150m);
Fox Hotel & Suites (200m);
Banff Caribou Lodge (400m);
Rundlestone Lodge (600m);
Bumpers Inn (1km);
Inns of Banff (1km)

Moose St

Gopher St

Squirrel St

Elk St

Marten St

Wolf St

Bow Ave

World Heritage Park

Bear St

Lynx St

Caribou St

Beaver St

Banff Ave

Bow River

Buffalo St

Nature Path

Bow River Bridge

Birch Ave

To Cave & Basin National Historic Site (1km)

Cave Ave

To Fairmont Banff Springs (800m)

ALBERTA BANFF TOWN

Banff Upper Hot Springs   SPA
(Mountain Ave; adult/student $7.30/6.30; ⊙9am-11pm May-Sep, 10am-10pm Sun-Thu, 10am-11pm Fri & Sat Oct-Apr) You'll find a soothing (if often crowded) hot pool, steam room, spa and excellent mountain views at these hot springs, near the Banff Gondola, 4km south of town. The water emerges from the spring at 47°C; in winter it has to be cooled to 39°C before entering the pool, but in spring the snowmelt does that job. In addition to the pool, you can indulge in a massage or an aromatherapy wrap. Bathing suits, towels and lockers can be rented.

Lake Minnewanka   NATURAL SITE
Lake Minnewanka, pronounced mini-won-ka, as in Willy Wonka, not mini-wanker, as Australian visitors enjoy saying, sits 13km east of Banff Town, making it a popular escape from downtown. The scenic recreational area features plenty of hiking, swimming, sailing, boating and fishing opportunities. The nonchallenging trail around the lake is a good option for a walk; the path is easy to follow and popular. **Minnewanka Lake Cruises** (www.explorerockies.com/minnewanka; adult/child $44/19; ⊙5-9 departures 10am-6pm mid-May–early Oct) offers a 60-minute interpretive cruise on the lake giving plenty of insight into the region's history and geology. You can also fish here or hike to the Alymer Lookout trail

for spectacular lake and mountain views. A Brewster bus can transport you to the lake for an extra fee. See the Minnewanka Lake Cruises website for details.

Banff Park Museum   MUSEUM
(93 Banff Ave; adult/child $3.95/1.95; ⊙10am-6pm May-Sep, 1-5pm Oct-Apr) Occupying an old wooden Canadian Pacific Railway building dating from 1903, this museum is a national historic site. Its exhibits – a taxidermic collection of animals found in the park, including grizzly and black bear, plus a tree carved with graffiti dating from 1841 – have changed little since the museum opened a century ago.

Buffalo Nations Luxton Museum   MUSEUM
(www.buffalonationsmuseum.ca; 1 Birch Ave; adult/6-12yr/senior & student $8/2.50/6; ⊙11am-6pm) The Luxton Museum tells the story of the first inhabitants of the Banff area with some interesting displays and artifacts. Traditional clothing and historic photographs populate the display cabinets, and there's a life-sized replica of a sun dance ceremony and a few other well-put-together displays.

🏃 Activities
Canoeing & Kayaking
Despite a modern penchant for big cars, canoe travel is still very much a quintessential Canadian method of transportation. The

best options near Banff Town are **Lake Minnewanka** and nearby **Two Jack Lake**, both to the northeast, or – closer to the town itself – the **Vermilion Lakes**. Unless you have your own canoe, you'll need to rent one; try **Blue Canoe** (☎403-760-5007; cnr Wolf St & Bow Ave; rental 1st hr/additional hours $34/20).

Cycling
There are lots of riding options around Banff, both on road and on selected trails. Popular routes around Banff Town include **Sundance** (7.4km round-trip) and **Spray River Loop** (12.5km); either is good for families. **Spray River & Goat Creek** (19km one way) and **Rundle Riverside** (14km one way) are both A to Bs with start/finish points near Canmore. The former is pretty straightforward; the latter is more challenging with ups and downs, and potential for thrills and spills. **Bactrax** (www.snowtips-bactrax.com) can organize a shuttle to the trailheads.

Serious road cyclists should check out Hwy 1A between Banff and Lake Louise; the rolling hills and quiet road here are a roadie's dream. Parks Canada publishes the brochure *Mountain Biking & Cycling Guide – Banff National Park,* which describes trails and regulations.

Snowtips/Bactrax (www.snowtips-bactrax.com; 225 Bear St; rentals per hr/day from $10/35) has a barn full of bikes to rent and will also take you on a tour to one of the plethora of bike trails in the Banff area ($20 per hour).

Hiking
Hiking is Banff's tour de force and the main focus of many travelers' visit to the area. The trails are easy to find, well signposted and maintained enough to be comfortable to walk on, yet rugged enough to still get a wilderness experience.

In general, the closer to Banff Town you are, the more people you can expect to see and the more developed the trail will be. But regardless of where in the park you decide to go walking, you are assured to be rewarded for your efforts.

Before you head out, check at the Banff Information Centre (p599) for trail conditions and possible closures. Keep in mind that trails are often snow-covered much later into the summer season than you might realize, and bear trail closures are a possibility, especially in berry season (June to September).

One of the best hikes from the town center is the **Bow River Falls and the Hoodoos Trail** which starts by the Bow River Bridge and tracks past the falls to the Hoodoos, weird rock spires caused by wind and water erosion. The trail plies its way around the back of Tunnel Mountain through forest and some river meadows and is 10.2km return.

You can track the north shore of Lake Minnewanka for kilometers on a multi-use trail that is sometimes closed due to bear activity. The classic hike is to walk as far as the **Alymer Lookout** just shy of 10km one way. Less taxing is the 5.6km return hike to **Stewart Canyon**, where you can clamber down rocks and boulders to the Cascade River.

Some of the best multiday hikes start at the Sunshine parking lot where skiers grab the gondola in winter. From here you can plan two- to four-day sorties up over Healy Pass and down to **Egypt Lake**, or get a bus up to Sunshine Village where you can cross the border into BC and head out across Sunshine Meadows and **Mount Assiniboine Provincial Park**.

The best backcountry experience is arguably the **Sawback Trail** that travels from Banff up to Lake Louise the back way over 74km, six primitive campsites and three spectacular mountain passes.

Check out Lonely Planet's *Banff, Jasper & Glacier National Parks* guide for more details about more single-day and multiday hikes.

Horseback Riding
Banff's first western explorers – fur traders and railway engineers – penetrated the region primarily on horseback and you can recreate their pioneering spirit on guided rides with **Warner Guiding & Outfitting** (☎403-762-4551; www.horseback.com; 132 Banff Ave; 1hr rides from $40) which will fit you out with a trusty steed and lead you along narrow trails for part of the day. Instruction and guiding are included; a sore backside is more or less mandatory for beginners. Grin and bear it. If you're really into it, opt for the six-day Wildlife Monitoring Adventure Expeditions out to limited-access areas accompanied by a Parks Canada researcher.

Skiing & Snowboarding
Strange though it may seem, there are three ski areas in the national park, two of them in the vicinity of Banff Town. Large, snowy

Sunshine Village is considered world-class. Tiny Norquay, a mere 5km from the center, is your half-day, family-friendly option.

Sunshine Village (www.skibanff.com; day ski passes $75) straddles the Alberta-BC border. Though slightly smaller than Lake Louise in terms of skiable terrain it gets much bigger dumpings of snow, or 'Champagne powder' as Albertans like to call it (up to 9m annually). Aficionados laud Sunshine's advanced runs and lengthy ski season, which lingers until Victoria Day weekend in late May. A high-speed gondola whisks skiers up in 17 minutes to the village which sports Banff's only ski-in hotel, the Sunshine Mountain Lodge.

Ski Banff@Norquay (www.banffnorquay. com; Mt Norquay Rd; lift tickets $46), just 6km north of downtown Banff, has a long history of entertaining Banff visitors. The smallest and least visited of the three local hills, this is a good place to body-swerve the major show-offs and hit the slopes for a succinct half day.

Local buses shuttle riders from Banff hotels to both resorts (and Lake Louise) every half hour during the season.

White-Water Rafting

The best rafting is outside the park (and province) on the Kicking Horse River in Yoho National Park, BC. There are class IV rapids here, meaning big waves, swirling holes and a guaranteed soaking. Lesser rapids are found on the Kananaskis River and the Horseshoe Canyon section of the Bow River. The Bow River around Banff is better suited to mellower float trips.

The following companies all have representation in the park. They offer tours starting at around $79. Factor in $15 more for a Banff pickup.

Canadian Rockies Rafting Company (✆403-763-2007; www.chinookraft.com; 215 Banff Ave)

Hydra River Guides (✆403-762-4554; www. raftbanff.com; 211 Bear St)

Wild Water Adventures (✆403-522-2211; www.wildwater.com) Has a desk at the Chateau Lake Louise, but will pick up from Banff for a fee.

ᗧ Tours

GyPSy Guide   SELF-DRIVE
(✆403-760-8200; www.gpstourscanada.com; Sundance Mall, 215 Banff Ave; per day $40) The future of guided travel is right here in Banff

with GyPSy Guide. The GyPSy is a handheld GPS device that you take in your car and guides you around the area. There is a lively running commentary that broadcasts through your stereo, pointing out highlights as you travel. All you have to do is follow the directions and you get a great self-guided tour of the area – Banff, Lake Louise, Columbia Icefield, Jasper and Calgary are all included on the tour. Best of all, if you get tired of the tour guide you can always turn it off.

Discover Banff Tours   WILDLIFE, SIGHTSEEING
(✆403-760-5007; www.banfftours.com; Sundance Mall, 215 Banff Ave; tours $39-145) Discover Banff has a great selection of tours to choose from: three-hour Banff Town tours, sunrise and evening wildlife tours, Columbia Icefield day trips and even a 10-hour grizzly bear tour, where if you don't see a bear you get your money back.

✹ Festivals & Events

The town's biggest annual event is the dual **Banff Mountain Book Festival** and **Banff Mountain Film Festival** (www.banffcentre. ca/mountainfestival), held consecutively in late October and early November. Attracting the cream of the mountain culture aficionados, this event is a must-do for the armchair adventurer and mountain guru alike.

ᗜ Sleeping

Compared with elsewhere in the province, accommodations in Banff Town are fairly costly and, in summer, often hard to find. The old adage of the early bird catching the worm really holds true here, and booking ahead is strongly recommended.

The Banff/Lake Louise Tourism Bureau tracks vacancies on a daily basis; check the listings at the Banff Information Center. You might also try **Enjoy Banff** (✆1-888-313-6161; www.enjoybanff.com), which books rooms for more than 75 different lodgings.

Camping in Banff National Park is popular and easily accessible. There are 13 campgrounds to choose from, most along the Bow Valley Parkway or near Banff Town.

TOP CHOICE **Fairmont Banff Springs**   HOTEL $$$
(✆403-762-2211; www.fairmont.com/ banffsprings; 405 Spray Ave; r from $337; ᴘ @ 🛜 🌊) Imagine crossing a Scottish castle with a French chateau and then plonking it in the middle of one of the world's most spectacular (and accessible) wilderness

areas. Rising like a Gaelic Balmoral above the trees at the base of Sulphur Mountain and visible from miles away, the Banff Springs is a wonder of early 1920s revivalist architecture and one of Canada's most iconic buildings. Wandering around its museumlike interior, it's easy to forget that it's also a hotel. On a par with its opulent common areas, rooms here are suitably exquisite even if the prices fall into the once-in-a-lifetime 'second-honeymoon' bracket.

Banff Rocky Mountain Resort HOTEL $$
(☑403-762-5531; www.bestofbanff.com; 1029 Banff Ave; r from $119; P🐾🐶≋) Being 4km out of town at the far, far end of Banff Ave is a small price to pay for the preferential prices and excellent all-round facilities here (including a hot tub, pool, tennis courts and cafe-restaurant). Added to this is the greater sense of detachment, quiet tree-filled grounds (it never feels like a 'resort') and generously sized bedrooms with sofas, desks and extra beds. There's a free shuttle into town (hourly) or you can walk or cycle 4km along the Legacy Trail.

Rimrock Resort Hotel HOTEL $$$
(☑403-762-3356; www.rimrockresort.com; 300 Mountain Ave; r queen/king $275/365; P📶🐶≋) Further up the hill but slightly further down the price bracket than the Fairmont is the Rimrock, another plush spectacularly located hotel next door to the hot springs which gets understandably overshadowed by its famous neighbor. Controversially located in a wildlife corridor on the slopes of Sulphur Mountain, the views here are nonetheless inspiring. Mountain decadence coats the chalet-like interior, the restaurant (Eden) is considered fine dining, and the rooms almost match the stunning outdoor vistas. Worth every penny.

Tunnel Mountain Village CAMPGROUND $
(☑877-737-3783; www.pccamping.ca; Tunnel Mountain Rd; tent/RV sites $27.40/38.20; P) It's hard to imagine this campground filling its nearly 1000 sites, but come summer it's bursting at the seams with holidaymakers from around the globe. Located at the top of Tunnel Mountain with sites among the trees, it's not nearly as grim as it sounds. Part of it is open during winter, too, so if you want to sleep under canvas at -20°C, they'll let you do it here.

HI-Banff Alpine Centre HOSTEL $
(☑403-762-4122; www.hihostels.ca; 801 Hidden Ridge Way; dm/d from $40/135; P📶🐶) Banff's best hostel is near the top of Tunnel Mountain and well away from the madness of Banff Ave. Walkers will find the commute a good workout, and their efforts will not go unrewarded. The buildings are finished in classic mountain lodge style but without classic mountain lodge prices. There are clean, comfortable accommodations in bunk rooms and a few doubles; fireplaces in the common areas and good views top it all off. The public bus runs right by the front door, so don't let the location deter you.

Fox Hotel & Suites HOTEL $$$
(☑800-760-8500; www.bestofbanff.com; 461 Banff Ave; d from $220; P@📶🐶≋) Banff's newest hotel opened in 2007 and justifies its four-star billing with an eye for the aesthetic and great attention to detail. Bright, modern rooms have retro-patterned wallpaper and unique interesting wall-prints, while the reception has enough trickling water to invoke flashbacks of Rome. The crème de la crème is the inspired recreation of the Cave & Basin springs in the hot tub area with an open hole in the roof that gives out to the sky. The bar-restaurant is called Chilis and serves, among other things, excellent margaritas. The town is a 10-minute walk away.

Banff Caribou Lodge HOTEL $$
(☑403-762-5887; www.bestofbanff.com; 521 Banff Ave; d/ste $149/229; P@📶🐶≋) One of the posher places in the locally run Banff Lodging Co empire (who don it three-and-a-half stars), the Caribou fits the classic stereotype of a mountain lodge with its log and stone exterior, giant lobby fireplace and general alpine coziness. Aside from 189 comfy rooms, you get free local bus passes here, a heated underground car park, an on-site Keg Steakhouse, and a hard-to-avoid spa with various pools and treatment rooms.

Inns of Banff HOTEL $$
(☑403-762-4581; www.bestofbanff.com; 600 Banff Ave; r from $129; P@📶🐶≋) The last hotel on Banff Ave and slightly out of the hustle and bustle, there are some good deals to be found here. Though the architecture is a little passé, there are loads of facilities including both indoor and outdoor pools, ski and bike rentals, and a Japanese restaurant.

Rundlestone Lodge HOTEL $$$
(☑403-762-2201; www.rundlestone.com; 537 Banff Ave; d/ste from $179/339; P📶≋) This place is filled with pseudo old-English

charm, complete with Masterpiece Theater chairs in the lobby. The standard rooms are fairly, well... standard; but splash out for a family or Honeymoon suite that comes with a kitchen, fireplace and loft. The centrally located indoor pool is a nice feature and the obligatory Banff hotel restaurant – this one's called Toloulous – makes a game attempt at food with a Creole twist.

Samesun Banff
HOSTEL $

(☎403-762-5521; www.banffhostel.com; 449 Banff Ave; dm/d $32/129; P@🖘) One of a quintet of western Canada hostels (the other four are in BC), the Samesun is zanier, edgier and a little cheaper than the other local budget digs. Features include a large central courtyard with barbecue, compact four- or eight-person dorms, an on-site bar, complimentary breakfast plus a selection of hotel-style rooms in an adjacent 'chalet' (they're billed as four-star standard though they're not quite the Fox). The clientele is international, backpacker and young (or young at heart).

Irwin's Mountain Inn
HOTEL $$

(☎403-762-4566; www.irwinsmountaininn.com; 429 Banff Ave; d from $149; P@🖘≋) A marginal drop in price and quality on the upper echelons of Banff Ave lands you in Irwin's where the rooms are verging on motel-like and the decor is more 'plastic' than granite. Not surprisingly, the place is popular with families who take advantage of the hot tub, steam room, fitness center and complimentary continental breakfast.

Banff Y Mountain Lodge
HOSTEL $

(☎403-762-3560; www.ymountainlodge.com; 102 Spray Ave; dm $33, d with shared/private bathroom $88/99; P@🖘) The YWCA is Banff's swankiest hostel option offering dorm rooms along with private family-orientated accommodations down by the river.

Bumpers Inn
MOTEL $$

(☎403-762-3386; www.bumpersinn.com; 603 Banff Ave; r from $125; P🖘) Banff provides a rare no-frills motel in bog standard Bumpers, which offers zero pretension, but plenty of financial savings. The town is a 15-minute walk away.

Two Jack Lakeside
CAMPGROUND $

(Minnewanka Loop Dr; tent sites from $27.40; ☺mid-May–mid-Sep; P) Right on Two Jack Lake and the most scenic of the Banff area campgrounds, Lakeside fills its 74 nonreservable sites quickly.

✗ Eating

Banff dining is more than just hiker food. Sushi and foie gras have long embellished the restaurants of Banff Ave and some of the more elegant places will inspire dirty hikers to return to their hotel rooms and take a shower before pulling up a pew. Aside from the establishments below, many of Banff's hotels have their own excellent on-site restaurants that welcome nonguests. AAA Alberta beef makes an appearance on even the most exotic à la carte.

TOP CHOICE Coyote's Deli & Grill
FUSION $$

(www.coyotesbanff.com; 206 Caribou St; lunch mains $8-14, dinner mains $20; ☺7:30am-10:30pm) Coyote's is best at lunchtime when you can bunk off hiking and choose a treat from the deli and grill menu inflected with a strong southwestern slant. Perch on a stool and listen to the behind-the-bar banter as you order up flatbreads, seafood cakes, quesadillas or some interesting soups (try the sweet potato and corn chowder).

Eddie Burger & Bar
BURGERS $$

(www.theeddieburgerbar.ca; Caribou St; burgers $13) Avoid the stereotypes. The Eddie might appear pretentious (black leather seats and mood lighting), and its name may contain the word 'burger,' but it welcomes all types (including exhausted hikers and kids) and its gourmet meals-in-a-bun are subtler and far less greasy than your standard Albertan patty. Try the Spicy Italian or the Mexican and water it down with a Kokanee beer.

Melissa's Restaurant
STEAKHOUSE $$

(www.melissasrestaurant.com; 218 Lynx St; pizzas/steaks from $18/21; ☺7am-10pm) Melissa's is a casual ketchup-on-the-table type of place in an old heritage building dating from 1928. It's huge in the local community and has an equally huge selection of food and price ranges. Nonetheless, its brunch, dinnertime steaks and deep-dish pizzas are probably its most defining dishes.

Maple Leaf Grille
CANADIAN $$$

(www.banffmapleleaf.com; 137 Banff Ave; mains $20-40) With plenty of local and foreign plaudits, the Maple Leaf eschews all other pretensions in favor of one defining word: 'Canadian.' Hence, the menu is anchored by BC salmon, East Coast cod, Albertan beef and Okanagan Wine Country salad... you get the drift. All very patriotic – and tasty.

Giorgio's Trattoria ITALIAN $$

(www.giorgiosbanff.com; 219 Banff Ave; mains from $16; ◷5-10pm) Slightly fancier than your average salt-of-the-earth trattoria, Giorgio's, nonetheless, serves up authentic Italian classics like osso bucco risotto and a fine pear and gorgonzola pizza mixed with the odd Alberta inflection (Buffalo papardelle!). The interior is elegant and there are prices to go with it (especially the wines).

Bison Mountain Bistro FUSION $$

(www.thebison.ca; 211 Bear St; lunch mains from $11, dinner mains from $18; ◷11am-late Mon-Fri, 10am-late Sat & Sun) The Bison might look like it's full of trendy, well-off Calgarians dressed in expensive hiking gear, but its prices are actually very reasonable (nothing over $20). And rather than saturating the menu with AAA Alberta beef, there are big salads here and weird starch-heavy pizzas with butternut squash and rosemary potato toppings. The modern decor is set off by an outdoor patio and ground-floor boutique deli that serves up gourmet cheese and other such delights.

Le Beaujolais FRENCH $$$

(☏403-762-2712; www.lebeaujolaisbanff.com; Banff Ave at Buffalo St; 3-/6-course meals $68/95; ◷6-10pm) Stick the word 'French' in the marketing lingo and out come the ironed napkins, waiters in ties, snails (billed as 'escargot' because it makes them sound so much more palatable) and elevated prices. Beaujolais might not be everybody's post-hiking cup of tea, but if you just came here to gaze romantically at the mountains, why not do it over wild boar, bison and foie gras.

Evelyn's Coffee Bar CAFE $

(201 Banff Ave; mains $6; ◷6.30am-11pm) Pushing Starbucks onto the periphery, Evelyn's parades four downtown locations all on or within spitting distance of Banff Ave. Dive in to any one of them for wraps, pies and – best of all – its own selection of giant homemade cookies.

Bruno's Cafe & Grill BREAKFAST, BURGERS $

(304 Caribou St; mains from $10; ◷8am-10pm) While other joints stop serving breakfasts at 11am, Bruno's keeps going all day replenishing the appetites of mountain men (and women) as it once replenished its one-time Swiss guide owner, Bruno Engler. A kind of greasy spoon meets pub, the walls are decorated with antique ski gear and the crowd at the next table could well be last night's live band refueling for tonight's gig.

The formidable Mountain Breakfast ($17) is served in a basket and requires a Mt Rundle-sized appetite.

Saltlik STEAKHOUSE $$

(www.saltliksteakhouse.com; 221 Bear St; mains from $18; ◷11am-2am) With rib-eye in citrus rosemary butter and peppercorn NY striploin on the menu, Saltlik is clearly no 'Plain Jane' steakhouse knocking out flavorless T-bones. No, this polished dining room abounds with rustic elegance and a list of steaks the length of many establishments' entire menu. In a town not short on steak-providers, this could be No 1.

Magpie & Stump MEXICAN $$

(203 Caribou St; mains $9-14; ◷noon-2am) Classic musty cantina full of dreadlocked Sol-swigging snowboarders where you feel it's almost your dinnertime duty to demolish an overloaded plate of oven-finished chicken enchiladas with a tangy side relish.

🍴 Wild Flour CAFE $

(www.wildflourbakery.ca; 211 Bear St; mains from $5; ◷7am-7pm; ✍) Banff's antidote to Tim Hortons is heavy on organic, vegan and frankly strange-looking cakes, pastries and cinnamon buns backed up with free-trade, organic coffee. They also bake their own bread.

Cows ICE CREAM $

(www.cows.ca; 134 Banff Ave; ice cream from $3.50; ◷11am-9pm) A Prince Edward Island import, Cow's ice cream is legendary out east but this is one of only two branches in western Canada. Bypass the tacky T-shirts and choose from 32 extra-creamy flavors.

🍷 Drinking & Entertainment

Throw a stone in Banff Ave and you're more likely to hit a gap-year Australian than a local. For drinking and entertainment, follow the Sydney accents to local watering holes or look through the listings in the 'Summit Up' section of the weekly *Banff Crag & Canyon* newspaper.

TOP CHOICE St James's Gate Olde Irish Pub PUB

(www.stjamesgatebanff.com; 205 Wolf St; mains from $10; ◷11am-1am Sun-Thu, to 2am Fri & Sat) As Celts pretty much opened up western Canada and gave their name to the town of Banff, it's hardly surprising to find an Irish pub in the park and rather a good one at that. Aside from stout on tap and a healthy selection of malts, St James's offers classic pub grub such as burgers and stew.

Tommy's Neighbourhood Pub   PUB
(www.tommysneighbourhoodpub.com; 120 Banff Ave) Tommy's pub grub menu stretches to crab cakes and spinach artichoke dip. More importantly for traditionalists there's good draft beer, a darts board, and plenty of opportunity to meet the kind of globe-trotting mavericks who have made Banff their temporary home.

Wild Bill's Legendary Saloon   BAR
(www.wbsaloon.com; 201 Banff Ave) Cowboys – where would Alberta be without them? Check this bar out if you're into line-dancing, calf-roping, karaoke and live music of the twangy Willy Nelson variety. The saloon is named after Wild Bill Peyto, a colorful 'local' character who was actually born and raised in that not-so-famous cowboy county of Kent in England.

Elk & Oarsman   PUB
(www.elkandoarsman.com; 119 Banff Ave) Upstairs with a crow's-nest view of Banff Ave, this is the town's most refined pub. The rooftop patio is prime real estate in the summer and the kitchen will fix you up with some good food if you so desire.

Rose & Crown   PUB
(www.roseandcrown.ca; 202 Banff Ave) Banff's oldest pub (since 1985!) is a fairly standard British-style boozer with pool tables and a rooftop patio. Out of all the town's drinking houses, it is best known for its live music, which raises the rafters seven nights a week everything from Seattle grunge.

Hoodoo Club   NIGHTCLUB
(137 Banff Ave) If you came to Banff to go nightclubbing look no further than this chic joint where you can drink, dance and pose not a mile from where wild animals roam.

Banff Centre   THEATER
(www.banffcentre.ca; 107 Tunnel Mountain Dr) A cultural center in a national park? Banff never ceases to surprise. This is the cultural hub of the Bow Valley – concerts, art exhibitions and the popular Banff Mountain Film Festival are all held here.

Lux Cinema Centre   CINEMA
(229 Bear St) The local movie house screens first-run films.

❶ Information
There are coin-fed internet terminals (per hour $6) in malls and hotels throughout town.

Banff Information Centre (www.parkscanada.gc.ca/banff; 224 Banff Ave; ⊙8am-8pm Jun-Sep, 9am-5pm Oct-May) Offices for Parks Canada.

Banff/Lake Louise Tourism Bureau (www.banfflakelouise.com; ⊙8am-8pm May-Sep, 9am-noon & 1-5pm Oct-Apr) In the same building as the Banff Information Centre; advice on services and activities in and around Banff.

Banff Warden Office Dispatch Line (☎403-762-1470) Open 24 hours for nonemergency backcountry problems.

Custom House Currency Exchange (211 Banff Ave; ⊙9am-10pm) In the Park Ave Mall.

Main Post Office (204 Buffalo St; ⊙8:30am-5:30pm Mon-Fri, 9am-5pm Sat)

Mineral Springs Hospital (☎403-762-2222; 301 Lynx St; ⊙24hr) Emergency medical treatment.

Underground (211 Banff Ave; internet per hr $6) Numerous terminals.

❶ Getting There & Away
The nearest airport is in Calgary.

Greyhound Canada (327 Railway Ave) operates buses to Calgary ($29, two hours, six daily), Vancouver ($130, 14 hours, five daily) and points in between.

Brewster Transportation (www.brewster.ca) will pick you up from your hotel and services Jasper ($66, 4¾ hours, daily) and Lake Louise ($15, one hour, multiple buses daily).

SunDog Tour Co (www.sundogtours.com) also runs transport between Banff and Jasper (around a full day, $60, four hours, daily)

All of the major car-rental companies (see p886) have branches in Banff Town. During summer all the cars might be reserved in advance, so call ahead. If you're flying into Calgary, reserving a car at the airport (where the fleets are huge) may yield a better deal than waiting to pick up a car when you reach Banff Town.

❶ Getting Around
Shuttle buses operate daily year-round between Calgary International Airport and Banff. Buses are less frequent in the spring and fall. Companies include **Brewster Transportation** (www.brewster.ca) and **Banff Airporter** (www.banffairporter.com). The adult fare for both is around $50 one way and $98 round-trip.

Banff Transit (☎403-762-1215) runs four hybrid 'Roam' buses on two main routes. Stops include Tunnel Mountain, the Rimrock Resort Hotel, Banff Upper Hot Springs, Fairmont Banff

LOCAL KNOWLEDGE

ANN MORROW: EXTERNAL RELATIONS OFFICER – BANFF NATIONAL PARK

What challenges does Banff National Park face?

Like every national park, Banff exists to protect the health and sustainability of its natural heritage, while providing opportunities to enjoy the activities and discoveries that are possible in this wild and wonderful place. We have grizzly bears, cougars and wolves in the park, and more than 3 million visitors a year, so one challenge is teaching people how to be 'nature-smart' here in the Rocky Mountains: how to give wild animals the space that they need to survive. To allow wildlife to wander freely through their natural ranges, Parks Canada has also built wildlife overpasses and underpasses all along the Trans-Canada Hwy, which traverses the park.

Does the park actively market for new visitors?

Banff gets a lot of promotion, from national, regional and local tourism organizations to Parks Canada to travel guidebooks. We have something very special here – it's our job to share this treasure with all Canadians, and the world (we're also a Unesco World Heritage site). At the same time we have a legal mandate to protect the ecological health of the park for the future generations. Our park management plan, created in consultation with tourism, environmental, community and aboriginal groups, directs us to meet high standards of resource protection, visitor experience and education in the park.

Is Banff too commercialized?

Some people think so. For others it's the easy accessibility of Banff, and the services the town offers, that make this Canada's favorite (as well as first and most famous) national park. What locals love about Banff is that you can head out and enjoy an awe-inspiring, wilderness experience on any of our 1500km of trails in the park, then return to town for sushi and maybe a ballet.

How do you enjoy Banff?

For me it's about being open to the gifts that nature chooses to give, the magical moments that can happen at any time of year, in any weather or any part of the park. Rocky Mountain nature has its own rules and rhythms that you can only get to know by really paying attention over time, and that's part of the appeal. Even though I've lived here most of my life, every time I get outside I'm inspired in some way.

Springs and all the hotels along Banff Ave. Route maps are printed on all bus stops. Buses start running at 6:30am and finish at 11pm; the fare is $2/1 per adult/child.

Taxis can easily be hailed on the street, especially on Banff Ave. Otherwise call **Banff Taxi** (☑403-762-4444). Taxis are metered.

Lake Louise

Famous for its teahouses, grizzly bears, grand hotel, skiing, Victoria Glacier, hiking and lakes (yes, plural), Lake Louise is what makes Banff National Park the phenomenon it is, an awe-inspiring natural feature that is impossible to describe without resorting to shameless clichés. Yes, there is a placid turquoise-tinted lake

here; yes, the natural world feels (and is) tantalizingly close; and yes, the water is surrounded by an amphitheater of finely chiseled mountains that Michelangelo couldn't have made more aesthetically pleasing. Then there are the much commented-on 'crowds,' plus a strangely congruous (or incongruous – depending on your viewpoint) lump of towering concrete known as Chateau Lake Louise. But, frankly, who cares about the waterside claustrophobia? Lake Louise isn't about dodging other tourists. It's about viewing what should be everyone's god-given right to see.

When you're done with gawping, romancing or pledging undying love to your partner on the shimmering lakeshore, try hiking up into the mountainous amphitheater behind. Lake Louise also has a widely lauded ski resort and some equally enticing cross-country options. Thirteen kilometers to the southeast along a winding seasonal road is another spectacularly located body of water, Moraine Lake that some heretics claim is even more beguiling than its famous sibling.

The village of Lake Louise, just off Hwy 1, is little more than an outdoor shopping mall, a gas station and a handful of hotels. The object of all your yearnings is 5km away by car or an equitable distance on foot along the pleasantly wooded Louise Creek trail, if the bears aren't out on patrol (check at the visitors center).

The **Lake Louise Visitor Centre** (Samson Mall, Lake Louise village; ⊙9am-8pm May-Sep, to 5pm Oct & Apr, to 4pm Nov-Mar) has some good geological displays, a Parks Canada desk and a small film theater.

The Bow Valley Parkway between Banff Town and Lake Louise is a slightly slower but much more scenic drive than Hwy 1.

◉ Sights

Lake Louise   NATURAL SITE
Named for Queen Victoria's otherwise anonymous fourth daughter (who also lent her name to the province), Lake Louise is a place that requires multiple viewings. Aside from the standard picture-postcard shot (blue sky, even bluer lake), try visiting at six in the morning, at dusk in August, in the October rain or after a heavy winter storm.

You can rent an unethically priced canoe from the **Lake Louise Boathouse** (per hr $45; ⊙9am-4pm Jun-Oct) and go for a paddle around the lake. Don't fall overboard – the water is freezing.

Moraine Lake   NATURAL SITE
The scenery will dazzle you long before you reach the spectacular deep-teal colored waters of Moraine Lake. The lake is set in the Valley of the Ten Peaks, and the narrow winding road leading to it offers views of these distant imposing summits. With little hustle or bustle and lots of beauty, many people prefer the more rugged and remote setting of Moraine Lake to Lake Louise. There are some excellent day hikes from the lake, or rent a boat at the **Moraine Lake Boathouse** (per hr $40; ⊙9am-4pm Jun-Oct) and paddle through the glacier-fed waters.

Moraine Lake Rd and its facilities are open from June to early October.

Lake Louise Sightseeing Gondola

LANDMARK
(www.lakelouisegondola.com; 1 Whitehorn Rd; round-trip adult/child $25.95/12.95; ⊙9am-5pm) To the east of Hwy 1, this sightseeing gondola will lever you to the top of Mt Whitehorn, where the views of the lake and Victoria Glacier are phenomenal. At the top, there's a restaurant and a Wildlife Interpretive Centre where you can partake in 45-minute **guided hikes** (per person $5; ⊙11am, 1pm & 3pm).

🏃 Activities

Hiking
In Lake Louise beauty isn't skin-deep. The hikes behind the stunning views are just as impressive. Most of the classic walks start from Lake Louise and Moraine Lake. Some are straightforward, while others will give even the most seasoned alpinist reason to huff and puff.

From Chateau Lake Louise, two popular day walks head out to alpine-style teahouses perched above the lake. The shorter but slightly harder hike is the 3.4km grunt past **Mirror Lake** up to the Lake Agnes Teahouse (see p604) on its eponymous body of water. After tea and scones you can trek 1.6km further and higher to the view-embellished **Big Beehive** lookout and Canada's most unexpectedly sited gazebo. Continue on this path down to the Highline Trail to link up with the **Plain of Six Glaciers**, or approach it independently from Chateau Lake Louise along the lakeshore (5.6km one way). Either way, be sure to get close enough for jaw-dropping views of the Victoria Glacier. There's another teahouse on this route that supplements its brews with thick-cut sandwiches and spirit-lifting mugs of hot chocolate with marshmallows.

From Moraine Lake, the walk to **Sentinel Pass**, via the stunning **Larch Valley**, is best in the fall when the leaves are beginning to turn. A strenuous day walk with outstanding views of Mt Temple and the surrounding peaks, the hike involves a steep scree-covered last push to the pass If you're lucky you might spy some rock climbers scaling The Grand Sentinel – a 200m-tall rock spire nearby.

Shorter and easier, the 6km out-and-back **Consolation Lakes Trail** offers that typical Banff juxtaposition of crowded parking lot disappearing almost instantly into raw, untamed wilderness.

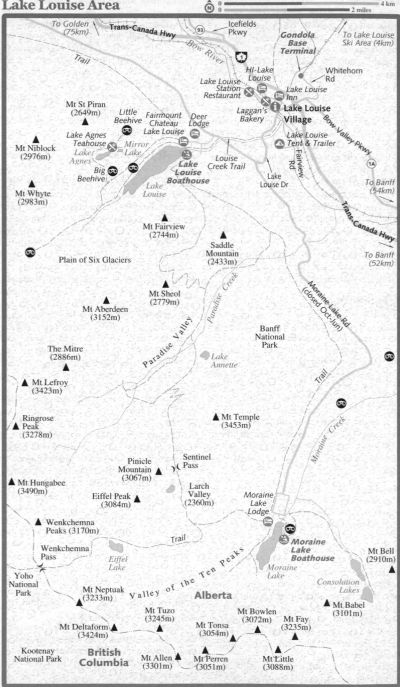

In recent years there has been a lot of bear activity in the Moraine Lake area. Because of this, a minimum group size of four has been imposed by the park on some hikes during berry-gathering season (June to September). If you're arriving solo, check on the noticeboard in the information center in Lake Louise for other hikers looking to make up groups.

Rock Climbing

The **Back of the Lake** is one of the classic crags in the Canadian Rockies. Steep, edgy limestone is the hallmark of this stellar rock-climbing area. The access is a dream: just stroll along the lakeside path until you see a route that tickles your fancy and away you go. There are both traditional climbs and sport routes. For nonclimbers, this is a great area to observe some rock stars at close range and even ask them a few questions. From a climber's perspective, the only downside to this awesome cragging spot are the tourists who insist on watching like you're a zoo animal and the inane questions they ask.

There is a multitude of alpine climbing adventures to be had in the Lake Louise area. Classic snow and ice routes such as Mt Temple and Fairview draw climbers from around the world. Check with Parks Canada for details on conditions and access. For a guided experience, talk to Canmore-based **Yamnuska Mountain Adventures** (☎866-678-4164; www.yamnuska.com). Its staff can meet you in Lake Louise and show you the ropes.

Skiing & Snowboarding

Lake Louise Ski Area (www.skilouise.com; lift tickets from $75), 60km west of Banff Town, is marginally larger than Sunshine Village but gets less natural snow. The ample runs containing plenty of beginner and intermediate terrain are on four separate mountains, so it's closer to a European ski experience than anything else on offer in Canada. The front side is a good place to get your ski legs back with a good selection of simpler stuff and fantastic views. On the backside there are some great challenges to find, from the knee-pulverizing moguls of Paradise Bowl to the high-speed cruising of the Larch area. Make sure you grab a deck burger at the Temple Lodge – it's all part of the whole experience.

🛏 Sleeping

Lake Louise has a campground, a hostel, a couple of mid-priced inns, and a handful of places that fall into the 'special night' category for many travelers.

TOP CHOICE ▷ **Moraine Lake Lodge** HOTEL $$$
(☎800-522-2777; www.morainelake lodge.com; d $345-599; ⊗Jun-Sep; P) Few people would shirk at an opportunity to hang around Moraine Lake for a day or three – and here's your chance. Though nearly as pricey as the Chateau (p603), you'll get a totally different experience here: think small, intimate, personal, private and with famously good service. While billed as rustic (ie no TVs), the rooms and cabins offer mountain-inspired luxury with real fireplaces and balconies overlooking *that* view. There's a fine-dining restaurant on-site which wins equal plaudits.

Fairmont Chateau Lake Louise HOTEL $$$
(☎403-522-3511; www.fairmont.com; Lake Louise Dr; d from $450; P@🛜❄) The opulent twin of Banff Springs enjoys one of the world's most enviable locations on the shores of Lake Louise. Originally built by the Canadian Pacific Railway in the 1890s, the hotel was added to in 1925 and 2004. While opinions differ on its architectural merits, few deny the luxury and romance of its facilities that include a spa, fine dining, a mini-museum, fine views and an unforgettably grandiose decor. Rooms are comfortable, if a little generic.

HI-Lake Louise HOSTEL $
(☎403-522-2200; www.hihostels.ca; Village Rd; dm/d from $34/99; P) This is what a hostel should be – clean, friendly, atmospheric and full of interesting travelers. The building itself is a stunning example of Rockies architecture, with raw timber and stone melding to a rustic aesthetic masterpiece. The dorm rooms are fairly standard, but beware of the private rooms: they are on the small side and a bit overpriced.

Deer Lodge HOTEL $$
(☎403-410-7417; www.crmr.com; 109 Lake Louise Dr; r from $119; P) Tucked demurely behind the Chateau Lake Louise, the Deer Lodge is another historic throwback dating from the 1920s. But, although the rustic exterior and creaky corridors can't have changed much since the days of bobbed hair and F Scott Fitzgerald, the refurbished rooms are another matter, replete with new comfy beds and smart boutique-like furnishings. TV addicts, beware – there aren't any.

Lake Louise Inn
HOTEL $$

(☑403-522-3791; www.lakelouiseinn.com; 210 Village Rd; d from $119; P@🛜🏊) A large, sprawling resort situated close to the village which has its merits, including a pool, restaurant and a tiny historic tearoom. The posher, less motel-like rooms in block five have the best views.

Lake Louise Tent & Trailer
CAMPGROUND $

(☑403-522-3833; off Lake Louise Dr; tent/RV sites $27.40/32.30; ⊘mid-May–Oct; P) This is the closest campground to the village and your best option if you plan to sleep in a million-star hotel. It's a vast place that has great views of Mt Temple. Steer clear of the sites near the railroad tracks as the thundering trains do wonders for keeping you up all night.

✖ Eating

If you can't scrape together the $39 necessary for afternoon tea in the Lakeview Lounge at the Chateau Lake Louise, reconvene to one of the following.

TOP CHOICE Lake Agnes Teahouse
CAFE $

(Lake Agnes Trail; snacks from $3; ⊘Jun-Oct) You thought the view from Lake Louise was good? Wait till you get up to this precariously perched alpine-style teahouse that seems to hang in the clouds beside ethereal Lake Agnes and its adjacent waterfall. The small log cabin runs on gas power and is hike-in only (3.4km uphill from the Chateau). Perhaps it's the thinner air or the seductiveness of the surrounding scenery but the rustic $6 tea and scones here taste just as good as the $39 spread at the Chateau Lake Louise.

Lake Louise Station Restaurant
CANADIAN $$

(mains from $14; ⊘11:30am-9:30pm) Restaurants with a theme have to be handled so carefully – thankfully this railway-inspired eatery, at the end of Sentinel Rd, does it just right. You can either dine in the station among the discarded luggage or in one of the dining cars, which are nothing short of elegant. The food is simple yet effective. A must-stop for trainspotters.

Laggan's Bakery
BAKERY $

(☑403-522-2017; Samson Mall; mains from $5; ⊘6am-8pm) Laggan's (named after Lake Louise's original settlement) is a cafeteria/bakery with limited seating that's famously busy in the summer. The pastries and savories aren't legendary, but they're handy hiking snacks and tend to taste better the hungrier you get. The pizza bagels are worth a special mention.

ℹ Getting There & Around

The bus terminal is basically a marked stop at Samson Mall. The easiest way to get here from Banff is by car or Greyhound bus. See the Banff Town section (p599) for bus service details.

Jasper Town & Around

Take Banff, half the annual visitor count, increase the total land area by 40%, and multiply the number of bears, elk, moose and caribou by the power of three. The result: Jasper, a larger, less-trammeled more wildlife-rich version of the other Rocky Mountains parks whose rugged backcountry wins admiring plaudits for its vertiginous river canyons, adrenaline-charged mountain-bike trails, rampartlike mountain ranges and delicate ecosystems.

Most people enter Jasper Town from the south via the magnificently Gothic Icefields Parkway that meanders up from Lake Louise amid foaming waterfalls and glacier-sculpted mountains, including iconic Mt Edith Cavell, easily visible from the townsite. Another option is to take a legendary VIA train from either Edmonton or BC through foothills imbued with fur-trading and aboriginal history.

Stacked up against Canada's other national parks, Jasper scores highly for its hiking, pioneering history (it's the country's eighth-oldest park), easy-to-view wildlife and hut-to-hut backcountry skiing possibilities. Similarly, bike enthusiasts consistently laud it as having one of the best single-track cycling networks in North America.

◉ Sights

Jasper Tramway
LANDMARK

(Map p586; www.jaspertramway.com; Whistlers Mountain Rd; adult/child $29/15; ⊘Apr-Oct) If the average, boring views from Jasper just aren't blowing your hair back, go for a ride up this sightseeing tramway which is open 9am to 8pm from June to August and closes earlier in the shoulder seasons. The vista is sure to take your breath away, with views, on a clear day, of the Columbia Icefield 75km to the south. From the top of the tram you can take the steep 1.5km hike to the summit of Whistlers Mountain where

Jasper Town

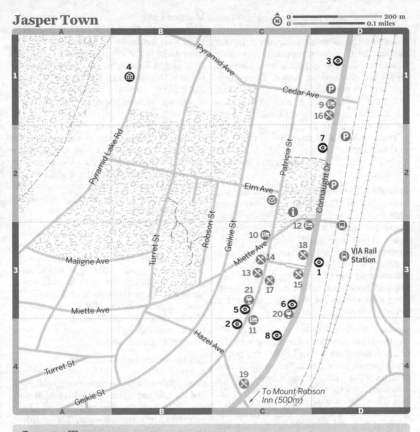

Jasper Town

Sights

1 Brewster Gray Line D3
2 Gravity Gear C4
3 Jasper Adventure Centre D1
   Jasper Walks & Talks .... (see 6)
4 Jasper-Yellowhead Museum &
   Archives B1
5 Maligne Rafting Adventures C3
   Maligne Tours .... (see 6)
6 Rocky Mountain River Guides C3
7 SunDog Tour Company D2
8 Vicious Cycle C4

Sleeping

9 Astoria Hotel D1
10 Athabasca Hotel C3
11 Park Place Inn C4
12 Whistlers Inn C2

Eating

13 Andy's Bistro C3
14 Coco's Café C3
15 Fiddle River Seafood Co C3
16 Jasper Pizza Place D1
17 Something Else C3
18 The Other Paw C3
19 Villa Caruso C4

Drinking

   Atha-B Pub .... (see 10)
20 Jasper Brewing Co C3
21 Pete's On Patricia C3

the outlook is even better. The tramway is about 7km south of Jasper Town along Whistlers Mountain Rd, off the Icefields Parkway.

Miette Hot Springs   SPA
(Map p586; www.parkscanada.gc.ca/hotsprings; Miette Rd; adult/child/family $6.05/5.15/18.45; ☺10:30am-9pm late May-Jun) A good spot for a

soak is the remote Miette Hot Springs, 61km northeast of Jasper off Hwy 16, near the park boundary. The soothing waters are kept at a pleasant 39°C and are especially enjoyable when the fall snow is falling on your head and steam envelops the crowd. There are a couple of hot pools and a cold one, too – just to get the heart going – so it's best to stick a toe in before doing your cannonball. Opening hours are slightly longer in high summer.

You can hike 1km from the parking lot to the **source** of the springs which is overlooked by the original aquacenter built in the 1930s.

Patricia & Pyramid Lakes NATURAL SITE

There's nothing like seeing the mountains reflected in a small deserted alpine lake. These two lakes, a convenient 7km from town, fit that order nicely. Abundant activities are available on the water, with canoes, kayaks and windsurfers available for rent. For those wanting to stay dry, there are hiking and horseback riding trails, too. Keep your eyes peeled for animals – these are prime spotting locations.

Lakes Annette & Edith NATURAL SITE

On the opposite side of the highway to the town, Lakes Annette and Edith are popular for water activities in the summer and skating in the winter. If you're brave and it's very hot, Annette is good for a quick summer dip – just remember the water was in a glacier not too long ago! Edith is more frequented by kayakers and boaters. Both are ringed by cycling/hiking trails and picnic areas. The trail that circumnavigates Lake Annette is wheelchair accessible.

Jasper Town to Maligne Lake SCENIC DRIVE

The inspiring 46km drive between Jasper and Maligne Lake is well worth doing. The road twists and turns and it would seem that at every corner there is an opportunity to see some wildlife. This is one of the best places in Jasper to look for deer, elk, moose and, if you're lucky, bear. The best time to see wildlife is early in the morning.

Maligne Canyon NATURAL SITE

A steep, narrow gorge shaped by a river flowing at its base, this canyon at its narrowest is only a few meters wide and drops a stomach-turning 50m beneath your feet. Crossed by six bridges, various trails lead out from the parking area on Maligne Lake Rd. In the winter, waterfalls freeze solid into sheets of white ice and are popular with ice climbers.

Maligne Lake NATURAL SITE

Almost 50km from Jasper at the end of the road that bears its name, 22km-long Maligne Lake is the recipient of a lot of hype. It is billed as one of the most beautiful lakes within the park and there's no denying its aesthetics: the baby-blue water and a craning circle of rocky, photogenic peaks are feasts for the eyes. Although the north end of the lake is heavy with the summer tour bus brigade, most of the rest of the shoreline is accessible only by foot or boat – hence it's quieter. Numerous campgrounds are available lakeside and are ideal for adventurous kayakers and backcountry hikers. Moose and grizzly bears are also sometimes seen here.

The **Maligne Lake Boathouse** (boat rentals per hr/day $30/90) rents canoes for a paddle around the lake. Not many people paddle all the way to Spirit Island – the lake's most classic view – it would take you all day. If you are really keen to see it, **Maligne Tours** (Map p605; ☎780-852-3370; www.malignelake.com; 627 Patricia St; adult/child $55/27.50; ☺10am-5pm May-Oct) will zip you out there. The company runs a 1½-hour boat tour to the island.

Jasper-Yellowhead Museum & Archives MUSEUM

(Map p605; www.jaspermuseum.org; 400 Pyramid Lake Rd; admission $5; ☺10am-5pm summer, 10am-5pm Thu-Sun rest of year) Poke your head into this museum if it's raining, snowing or too hot. Even if the weather is nice, it does an ample job of telling the Jasper story and the stories of those who arrived here to make it into the town it is today.

🏃 Activities

Cycling

Single-track mountain biking is Jasper's forte and most routes are within striking distance of the townsite. Flatter, on-road options include the long-distance grunt along the Icefields Parkway. The holy grail for experienced off-road bikers is the **Valley of the Five Lakes**, varied and scenic with plenty of places where you can let rip. For more information, get a copy of *Mountain Biking Guide, Jasper National Park* from the Jasper Information Centre.

Vicious Cycle (Map p605; www.viciouscycle-canada.com; 630 Connaught Dr; per day from $24; ☺9am-6pm) can sort out bike rentals and offer additional trail tips.

Hiking

Even when judged against other Canadian national parks, Jasper's trail network is mighty, and with comparatively fewer people than its sister park to the south, you've a better chance of seeing more wildlife and less humans.

Initiate yourself on the interpretative **Discovery Trail**, an 8km easy hike that encircles the townsite highlighting its natural, historical and railway heritage.

Other short, less radical trails include the 3.2km **Mary Schäffer Loop** by Maligne Lake named for one of the earliest European visitors to the area; the **Old Fort Loop** (3.5km) to the site of an old fur-trading post; and the 9km **Mina and Riley Lakes Loop** that leads out directly from the townsite.

Further away and slightly harder is the famous 9.1km **Path of the Glacier Trail** below the impressive face of Mt Edith Cavell that takes you to the foot of the Angel Glacier through the flower-scattered Cavell meadows.

The blue riband multiday hike is the **Skyline Trail**, unusual in that almost all of its 46km are on or above the tree line, affording amazing cross-park views. The hike is usually split over two days, starting at Maligne Lake and emerging near Maligne Canyon on Maligne Lake Rd. You can pitch your tent in a campground or stay in the historic Shovel Pass Lodge.

The leaflet *Day-Hikers' Guide to Jasper National Park* has descriptions of most of the park's easy walks, while the backcountry visitors' guide *Jasper National Park* details longer trails and backcountry campsites and suggests itineraries for hikes of two to 10 days. If you're hiking overnight, you must obtain a backcountry permit (per person per night $10, or buy a season pass for $69) from Parks Canada in the Jasper Information Centre.

Horseback Riding

Incredible fully guided summer pack trips head into the roadless Tonquin Valley where you are bivouacked in the backcountry (but comfortable) Tonquin Amethyst Lake Lodge. The trips are run by **Tonquin Valley Adventures** (www.tonquinadventures.com; 3-/4-/5-day trips $795/1050/1295) and include accommodations, meals and complimentary fishing trips on Amethyst Lake.

Rock Climbing

Despite a preponderance of sedimentary rock, Jasper lures a large number of aspiring rock climbers. If you want a popular crag with an easy approach head out to the **Rock Gardens** located up the trail from 5th Bridge off Maligne Lake Rd. For traditional options, look to **Roche Miette** and **Morro Peak**. The more ambitious opt to summit Mt Edith Cavell. As with most Rockies climbing, a helmet and good route-finding skills are essential.

Those looking to learn the ropes can try **Peter Amann** (☎780-852-3237; www.incentre.net/pamann; 2-day courses $160), something of a Jasper legend who will introduce you to the sport with a two-day beginner course. If you just need equipment, visit **Gravity Gear** (Map p605; www.gravitygearjasper.com; 618 Patricia St).

Skiing & Snowboarding

Jasper National Park's only downhill ski area is **Marmot Basin** (Map p586; www.skimarmot.com; Marmot Basin Rd; full-day pass adult/child $72/58), which lies 19km southwest of town off Hwy 93A. Though not legendary, the presence of 86 runs and the longest high-speed quad chair-lift in the Rockies, mean Marmot is no pushover and its relative isolation compared to the trio of ski areas in Banff means shorter lift lines.

On-site are some cross-country trails and a predictably expensive day lodge, but no overnight accommodations. Seriously cold weather can drift in suddenly off the mountains, so dress with this in mind.

White-Water Rafting

There's nothing like a glacial splashdown to fight the summer heat. The Jasper area has lots of good rafting opportunities, from raging to relaxed on the **Maligne**, **Sunwapta** and **Athabasca Rivers**. The season runs from May to September.

Maligne Rafting Adventures (Map p605; www.raftjasper.com; 616 Patricia St; trips from $59) Everything from float trips to class II and III adventures, plus the option of overnight trips.

Rocky Mountain River Guides (Map p605; www.rmriverguides.com; 626 Connaught Dr; trips from $59) Fun for beginners or experienced river-runners.

☞ Tours

There is a variety of tour companies and booking centers in Jasper. They run a whole

WORTH A TRIP

JASPER IN WINTER

Half of Jasper shuts down in the winter; the other half just adapts and metamorphoses into something just as good (if not better) than its summertime equivalent. Lakes become skating rinks, hiking and biking routes (and some roads) become cross-country skiing trails, waterfalls become ice climbs, and – last but by no means least – prices become far more reasonable.

The best natural outdoor skating rink is on Lac Beauvert in front of the Fairmont Jasper Park Lodge, an area that is floodlit after dark. More skating can be found 6km northeast of the townsite on Pyramid Lake.

The park has an incredible 200km of cross-country skiing trails. Routes less prone to an early snow melt are the **Pyramid Lake Fire Road**, the **Meeting of the Waters** (along a closed section of Hwy 93A), the **Moab Lake Trail** and the **Mt Edith Cavell Road**. Relatively safe, but dramatic backcountry skiing can be found in the Tonquin Valley where you can overnight in a couple of lodges. See www.tonquinvalley.com for more details.

Slightly less athletic is the iconic three-hour **Maligne Canyon Ice-walk** offered by **Jasper Adventure Centre** (Map p605; www.jasperadventurecentre.com; 618 Connaught Dr; adult/child $55/25), a walk through a series of frozen waterfalls viewable from December to April. Extremists tackle these slippery behemoths with rappels and ice axes.

host of tours, including trips to the icefields, train rides, boat rides, wildlife viewing, rafting, horseback riding and more.

Brewster Gray Line   SIGHTSEEING
(Map p605; www.brewster.ca; 607 Connaught Dr)

Jasper Walks & Talks   HIKES
(Map p605; www.walksntalks.com; 626 Connaught Dr)

SunDog Tour Company   SIGHTSEEING
(Map p605; www.sundogtours.com; Connaught Dr)

🛏 Sleeping

Despite its reputation as a quiet antidote to Banff, Jasper's townsite still gets busy in the summer. Book ahead or consider visiting in the less crowded late winter/early spring shoulder season when the deserted mountainscapes (best accessed on cross-country skis) take on a whole new dimension.

Accommodations in Jasper are generally cheaper than Banff, but that's not really saying much. Jasper's 10 park campgrounds are open from mid-May to September/October. One (Wapiti) is partly open year-round. Four of them take reservations. For information, contact **Parks Canada** (☑780-852-6176; 500 Connaught Dr) at the Jasper Information Centre.

Several places outside the town proper offer bungalows (usually wooden cabins)

that are only open in summer. There are considerable winter discounts.

TOP
CHOICE **Park Place Inn**   BOUTIQUE HOTEL **$$$**
(Map p605; ☑780-852-9970; www.parkplaceinn.com; 623 Patricia St; r from $229; @) Giving nothing away behind its rather drab exterior among a parade of downtown shops, the Park Place is a head-turner as soon as you ascend the stairs to its plush open lobby. The 14 self-proclaimed heritage rooms are well deserving of their superior status with marble surfaces, fine local art, claw-foot baths and a general air of refinement and luxury. The service is equally professional.

Fairmont Jasper Park Lodge   HOTEL **$$$**
(☑780-852-3301, 800-441-1414; www.fairmont.com/jasper; 1 Old Lodge Rd; r from $500; P@☏) Sitting on the shore of Lake Beauvert and surrounded by manicured grounds and mountain peaks, this classic old lodge is deservedly popular. With a country-club-meets-1950s-holiday-camp air, the amenity-filled cabins and chalets are a throwback to a more opulent era. The lodge's gem is its main lounge, open to the public, with stupendous lake views. It's filled with log furniture, chandeliers and fireplaces and is the best place in town to write a postcard over a quiet cocktail. There are often off-season discounts.

Tekarra Lodge   HOTEL **$$**
(☑780-852-3058; www.tekarralodge.com; Hwy 93A; d from $169; ⊗May-Oct; P) The most at-

mospheric cabins in the park are set next to the Athabasca River amid tall trees and splendid tranquility. Hardwood floors, wood-paneled walls plus fireplaces and kitchenettes inspire coziness. It's only 1km from the townsite, but has a distinct back-country feel.

Whistlers Inn
HOTEL **$$$**

(Map p605; ☑780-852-9919; www.whistlersinn. com; cnr Connaught Dr & Miette Ave; r $195; @🖜�0️⃣) A central location and above standard rooms give Whistlers an edge over many of its rivals. The rooftop hot tub alone is worth spending the night for – watch the sun dip behind the hills as the recuperative waters soak away the stress of the day. What more could you ask for?

Astoria Hotel
HOTEL **$$$**

(Map p605; ☑780-852-3351; www.astoriahotel. com; 404 Connaught Dr; d from $207; 🖜) With its gabled Bavarian roof the Astoria is one of the town's most distinctive pieces of architecture and one of an original trio of Jasper hotels that has been owned by the same family since the 1920s. Journeyman rooms are functional and comfortable, and are bolstered by the presence of a downstairs bar (De'd Dog) and restaurant (Papa George's).

Athabasca Hotel
HOTEL **$$**

(Map p605; ☑780-852-3386; www.athabascahotel.com; 510 Patricia St; r without/with bathroom $99/175; 🅿@🖜) If you can take the stuffed moose heads, noisy downstairs bar-nightclub and service that is sometimes as fickle as the mountain weather, you'll have no problems at the Athabasca (or Atha-B, as it's known). Centrally located with an attached restaurant and small, but comfortable, rooms (many with shared bathroom) it's been around since 1929 and is probably the best bargain in town.

Coast Pyramid Lake Resort
HOTEL **$$$**

(☑780-852-4900; www.coasthotels.com; Pyramid Lake Rd; d from $249; 🅿) This large property has fantastic views of the lake and great access to it. The design is a bit strange, with a huge swath of concrete driveway bisecting the hotel. The chalet-style buildings fan up the hill, giving most rooms an unencumbered view of the lake. Ample opportunities for lake fun abound, with canoes for rent and a small beach to hang out on. The prices are a bit on the high side and it would do well to improve some of the finishing touches. The resort is closed October to April.

YHA Maligne Canyon
HOSTEL **$**

(Map p586; ☑1-877-852-0781; www.hihostels. ca; Maligne Lake Rd; dm $23; 🅿) Well positioned for winter cross-country skiing and summer sorties along the Skyline Trail, this very basic hostel is poised a little too close to the road to merit a proper 'rustic' tag. Die-hards can get back to nature with six-bed dorms, outhouse toilets and regular visits to the water pump.

Whistlers Campground
CAMPGROUND **$**

(Map p586; Whistlers Rd; tent/RV sites $22/36; 🕗early May–mid-Oct; 🅿) Ever spent the night with 780 other campers? Well, here is your chance. This mini camping city isn't particularly private, but it is the closest option to Jasper Town. Unbelievably, it regularly fills up in the high season. There are interpretive programs, flush toilets and fire pits.

HI-Jasper
HOSTEL **$**

(Map p586; ☑780-852-3215; www.hihostels.ca; Whistlers Mountain Rd; dm/d $26/65; 🅿@🖜) It would be easy not to like this hostel. With dorm rooms that sleep upward of 40 people, giving it that distinctive refugee camp feel, and a location just far enough from town that the walk is a killer, it's already two strikes down. Despite all of this though, it's a great place to stay. The proximity of roommates and relative isolation foster a real community feel, and the nice interior, friendly staff and pristine surroundings make it that much better.

Mount Robson Inn
MOTEL **$$$**

(off Map p605; ☑780-852-3327; www.mount robsoninn.com; 902 Connaught Dr; r from $255; 🅿✱@🖜) A clean, plush place laid out motel-style on the edge of Jasper Town which offers hot tubs, on-site restaurant and a substantial complimentary breakfast.

Snaring River Campground
CAMPGROUND **$**

(Map p586; Hwy 16; tent sites $15; 🕗mid-May–mid-Sep; 🅿) Situated 17km north of Jasper Town, this basic campground – is the park's most primitive and isolated – is the perfect antidote to the busy campgrounds found elsewhere in the park.

✖️ Eating

Jasper's cuisine is mainly hearty post-hiking fare supplemented with a couple of fine-dining spots. Most of the restaurants are located in the town around Connaught Dr and Patricia St. Outlying nexuses such as Maligne Lake and The Whistlers have cafeteria-style restaurants that close in the winter.

TOP CHOICE **The Other Paw**   CAFE, BAKERY **$**
(Map p605; 610 Connaught Dr; mains $2; ☺7am-10pm) An offshoot of The Bear's Paw, a larger cafe around the corner, The Other Paw offers the same insanely addictive mix of breads, pastries, muffins and coffee, but it stays open longer, plus it's right opposite the train station. The aromatic memory of its white chocolate and raspberry scones is enough to jerk your senses into action during the last few kilometers of a lengthy hike/bike/ski.

Fiddle River Seafood Co   SEAFOOD **$$**
(Map p605; 620 Connaught Dr; mains from $18; ☺5-10pm) Being almost 1600km from the sea makes some customers understandably leery, but Jasper's premier seafood joint is no slouch. Pull up a seat near the window and tuck into one of the innovative creations, such as pumpkin seed-crusted trout.

Coco's Café   CAFE **$**
(Map p605; 608 Patricia St; mains from $5; ☺8am-4pm) Coco's versus The Other Paw is a toss-up, though the former might just pip it on the breakfast front. There's not much room inside, but plenty of bodies are content to cram in to plan hikes, trade bear sightings or compare rucksack burns. Ethical eaters are well catered for with tofu scrambles and fair-trade coffee.

Andy's Bistro   FUSION **$$$**
(Map p605; ✆780-852-3323; 622 Patricia St; mains from $22; ☺5-11pm) Following a new trend for fine-dining in outdoor adventure areas (led by Whistler), Andy's is one of two posh Jasper options where you can take off your filthy hiking boots and quaff one of 70 wines. The European-inspired menu (escargot, vol-au-vents, pan-fired veal) has various Indian and Asian inflections.

Something Else   MEDITERRANEAN, STEAKHOUSE **$$**
(Map p605; 621 Patricia St; mains $13-24) Essentially a Greek restaurant, Something Else wears many hats (American, Italian, Cajun) and doesn't always succeed. What it *is* good for is space (even on a Saturday night), decent beer, menu variety, copious kids' options and the good old homemade Greek stuff. Try the lamb or chicken souvlaki.

Jasper Pizza Place   PIZZA **$**
(Map p605; 402 Connaught Dr; mains from $8; ☺11am-11pm) Ask a local (if you can find one) where to grab a cheap meal and, even money, they'll mention this place. There's a method to the queuing madness, if you're prepared to stick around long enough to fight for a table. Not surprisingly, the much-sought-after pizzas are rather good.

View Restaurant   FAST FOOD **$**
(Maligne Lake Lodge; snacks from $4; ☺9am-7pm) On first impressions this aptly named restaurant (behold the view!) at the head of Maligne Lake is just another overpriced cafeteria for tourists. But, beyond the sandwiches, soups and summer jobbers, this place serves up some of the best pastries, muffins and cinnamon buns in the park.

Villa Caruso   STEAKHOUSE **$$**
(Map p605; 640 Connaught Dr; mains from $21; ☺11am-11:30pm) Carnivore, piscatorian and vegetarian needs are all catered for here. Plush wood trimmings and great views are the perfect appetizer for a fine meal out.

Edith Cavell   FUSION **$$$**
(✆780-852-6052; Jasper Park Lodge, 1 Old Lodge Rd; 2-/3-/4-course meals $90/110/130; ☺6-9pm) Fine dining set among the beautiful surroundings of the Jasper Park Lodge with breathtaking views and a menu that is equally awe-inspiring.

Drinking

Pete's on Patricia   NIGHTCLUB
(Map p605; 614 Patricia St) Jasper's most authentic nightclub has some scarily concocted theme nights with a heavy metal vent. DJs spin anything from hip-hop to top 40 – head upstairs after 10pm once it gets going.

Jasper Brewing Co   BREWERY, PUB
(Map p605; www.jasperbrewingco.ca; 624 Connaught Dr) Open since 2005, this brewpub uses glacial water to make its fine ales including the signature Rockhopper IPA or – slightly more adventurous – the Rocket Ridge Raspberry Ale. It's a sit-down affair with TVs and a good food menu.

Atha-B Pub   BAR, NIGHTCLUB
(Map p605; Athabasca Hotel, 510 Patricia St) Nightclubbing in a national park is about as congruous as wildlife-viewing in downtown Toronto. Bear this in mind before you hit the Atha-B, a pub-slash-nightclub off the lobby of the Athabasca Hotel where mullets are still high fashion and the carpet's probably radioactive.

ⓘ Information

Jasper Information Centre (www.parkscan ada.gc.ca/jasper; 500 Connaught Dr; ☺8am-7pm Jun-Sep, 9am-4pm Oct-May) Informative office in historic 'parkitecture' building.

Jasper Municipal Library (500 Robson St; internet per hr $5)

Post office (Map p605; 502 Patricia St, cnr Elm Ave; ⊙9am-5pm Mon-Fri)

Seton General Hospital (Map p605; ☑780-852-3344; 518 Robson St)

❶ Getting There & Around

Bus

The **bus station** (www.greyhound.ca; 607 Connaught Dr) is at the train station. Greyhound buses serve Edmonton ($59, from 4½ hours, four daily), Prince George ($64, five hours, one daily), Kamloops ($70, six hours, two daily) and Vancouver ($115, from 11½ hours, two daily).

Brewster Transportation (www.brewster. ca), departing from the same station, operates express buses to Lake Louise village ($60, 4½ hours, at least one daily) and Banff Town ($70, 5½ hours, at least one daily).

The **Maligne Valley Shuttle** (www.malignelake.com) runs a May to October bus from Jasper Town to Maligne Lake via Maligne Canyon. Fares are one-way/return $20/40.

Car

International car-rental agencies (p886) have offices in Jasper Town.

If you're in need of a taxi, call **Jasper Taxi** (☑780-852-3600), which has metered cabs.

Train

VIA Rail (www.viarail.ca) offers tri-weekly train services west to Vancouver ($168, 20 hours) and east to Toronto ($456, 62 hours). In addition, there is a tri-weekly service to Prince Rupert, BC ($117, 32 hours). Call or check at the **train station** (607 Connaught Dr) for exact schedule and fare details.

SOUTHERN ALBERTA

The national parks of Banff and Jasper and the cities of Calgary and Edmonton grab most of the headlines in Alberta, leaving the expansive south largely forgotten. Here flat farmland is interrupted by deep coulees or canyons that were caused by flooding at the end of the last ice age. Another symbolic feature of the landscape is the towering hoodoos, funky arid sculptures that look like sand-colored Seussian realizations dominating the horizon. History abounds in both the recent Head-Smashed-In Buffalo Jump and the not-so-recent Dinosaur Provincial Park, two areas preserving the past that have attained Unesco World Heritage status.

Natural wonders are plentiful in this sleepy corner of the province. The dusty dry badlands around Drumheller open up into wide open prairies to the east that stretch all the way to the Cyprus Hills of western Saskatchewan. To the west there is Waterton Lakes National Park with some of the most spectacular scenery in the Rockies – yet still under the radar of most visitors.

Drumheller

Founded on coal but now committed to another subterranean resource – dinosaur bones – Drumheller is a small (some would say 'waning') town set amid Alberta's enigmatic badlands that is central axis on the so-called Dinosaur Trail. While paleontology is a serious business here (the nearby Royal Tyrrell Museum is as much research center as tourist site), Drumheller has cashed in on its Jurassic heritage – sometimes shamelessly. Aside from mocked-up stegosauruses on almost every street corner and dino-related prefixes to more than a few business names, there's the large matter of a 26m high fiberglass T-Rex that haunts a large tract of downtown (see p612).

But don't let the paleontological civic pride deter you – once you get beyond the kitsch, the town itself is has a certain je ne sais quoi. The summers are hot and the deep-cut river valley in which Drumheller sits provides a much-needed break to the monotony of the prairies. Hoodoos dominate this badland landscape which has featured in many a movie, Westerns mainly.

The **tourist information center** (00 1st Ave W; ⊙10am-6pm) is close to the aforementioned T-Rex.

⊙ Sights & Activities

Dinosaur Trail, Horseshoe Canyon & Hoodoo Drive   SCENIC DRIVE

Drumheller is on the Dinosaur Trail, a 48km loop that runs northwest from town and includes Hwys 837 and 838; the scenery is quite worth the drive. Badlands and river views await you at every turn. The loop takes you past **Midland Provincial Park** (no camping), where you can take a self-guided hike; across the Red Deer River on the free, cable-operated **Bleriot Ferry**, which has been running since 1913; and to vista points – including the eagle's-eye **Orkney Viewpoint** – overlooking the area's impressive canyons.

Horseshoe Canyon, the most spectacular chasm in the area, is best seen on a short drive west of Drumheller on Hwy 9. A large sign in the parking lot explains the geology of the area, while trails lead down into the canyon for further exploration. There are helicopter rides if you're flush.

The 25km Hoodoo Drive starts about 18km southeast of Drumheller on Hwy 10; the road only goes one way so you must return by the same route. Along this drive you'll find the best examples of **hoodoos**: weird, eroded, mushroomlike columns of sandstone rock. This area was the site of a once-prosperous coal-mining community, and the **Atlas Mine** is now preserved as a provincial historic site. Take the side trip on Hwy 10X (which includes 11 bridges in 6km) from Rosedale to the small community of **Wayne**, population 27 and fast approaching ghost town status.

TOP CHOICE Royal Tyrrell Museum of Palaeontology
MUSEUM

(www.tyrrellmuseum.com; adult/youth $10/6, ⊙9am-9pm mid-May–Sep, 10am-5pm Oct–mid-May) This fantastic museum is one of the preeminent dinosaur museums on the planet. It's not an overstatement to say that no trip to Alberta is complete without a visit to this amazing facility. Children will love the interactive displays and everyone will be in awe of the numerous complete dino-skeletons. There are opportunities to get among the badlands on a guided tour and to discover your own dino treasures either on a guided hike or a dinosaur dig. You'll feel like you've stepped behind the scenes of *Jurassic Park* – and in many ways this is the *real* Jurassic Park.

World's Largest Dinosaur
LANDMARK

(60 1st Ave W; admission $3; ⊙10am-6pm) Warning – cheesy tourist attraction ahead! In a town filled to the brim with dinosaurs, this T-Rex is the king of them all and features in the *Guinness Book of Records*. Standing 26m above a parking lot, it dominates the Drumheller skyline. It's big, not-at-all scary and cost over a million bucks to build, which explains the admission price to go up the 106 steps for the view from its mouth. Kids love it and, truth be told, the view is pretty good. Ironically, the dinosaur isn't even Jurassically accurate; at 46m long, it's about 4.5 times bigger than its extinct counterpart.

🛏 Sleeping

The quality of accommodations is limited in Drumheller, so it's best to book ahead to ensure you're not stuck with something you don't like, or worse, nothing at all.

Heartwood Inn & Spa
INN $$

(☎403-823-6495; www.innsatheartwood.com; 320 N Railway Ave E; d $119-279; @) Standing head and shoulders above most of the accommodations in town, this lovely country inn is awesome. The small rooms are luxurious, comfortable and tastefully done. It has an on-site spa facility that will welcome you like a queen or king. All the rooms have Jacuzzis, and there are romance packages available where the staff decorate your room with candles and rose petals, draw you a bath made for two and let you handle the rest.

River Grove Campground & Cabins
CAMPGROUND $

(☎403-823-6655; www.camprivergrove.com; 25 Poplar St; campsites from $26, cabins from $80, tepees $60; ⊙May-Sep; P☀) Right in town and close to the big dinosaur, this is a pleasant campground with lots of amenities. The tent facilities are alright, with a few shady trees to try and keep you cool in the hot summer sun. You can even rent a tepee for the night, although the Stoney people likely didn't have concrete floors in theirs.

Taste the Past B&B
B&B $$

(☎403-823-5889; 281 2nd St W; s/d $95/115; P) This converted turn-of-the-century house has evolved into a cozy downtown B&B. All rooms have a private bathroom and there is a shared facility downstairs. With only three rooms, this feels more like staying with friends – and by the end of your stay, that's often what it is.

🍴 Eating

TOP CHOICE Last Chance Saloon
BAR $

(Hwy 10X, Wayne; mains from $4.50; ⊙11:30am-midnight) In a land partial to fast-food franchises the words 'there's nowhere else remotely like it' are an underhand compliment. For a taste of something completely different, take the 15-minute drive from Drumheller to the tiny town of Wayne to find this former hell-raising bar-hotel turned Harley Davidson hangout. Last Chance is a classic Western saloon, but without a hint of tourist kitsch. Check out the mining relics, Brownie cameras, old cigarette tins, fully functioning band-box, and the brick that somebody probably tossed through the window circa 1913. The food is almost an afterthought – bog standard burgers with optional beans or fries – but it'll fill you up and give you a little longer to ponder the unique off-beat atmosphere.

Whif's Flapjack House   CANADIAN $
(801 N Dinosaur Trail; mains $6-10; ⊙6am-2pm) The name is the menu: waffles, hamburgers, ice cream, flapjacks and salad. Big portions, a miniature train track suspended from the ceiling, and good value are all found at this local greasy spoon.

Sizzling House   CHINESE, THAI $
(www.sizzlinghouse.com; 160 Centre St; mains from $9; ⊙11am-9pm) The exterior of this unusual Thai and Chinese combo restaurant screams 'run away!' but the redone interior is nice enough and the food surprisingly good. With an exotic mélange of wonton soups, tom yum goong, Manchu beef and Chang Mai vegetables you'll be laughing all the way back to Bangkok – or Beijing.

O'Shea's Eatery & Ale House   PUB $
(www.osheasalehouse.com; 600B, 680 2nd St; mains from $10; ⊙11am-11pm) With everything from Irish-style pub fare to steaks and pasta dishes, everyone will find something to chew on here. Hardwood floors, stained-glass windows and high ceilings give the meal a somewhat unneeded Gothic feel. There is a pub here, too, if you are looking for something more relaxed.

ⓘ Getting There & Away

Greyhound Canada runs buses from the **bus station** (308 Centre St) to Calgary ($38, 1¾ hours, two daily) and Edmonton ($60, 5 hours, two daily).

Hammerhead Tours (p576) runs a full-day tour ($90) from Calgary to the Drumheller badlands and Royal Tyrrell Museum.

Dinosaur Provincial Park

Where *The Lost World* meets *Little House on the Prairie*, **Dinosaur Provincial Park** (www.dinosaurpark.ca; off Hwy 544; admission free; ⊙9am-6pm mid-May–mid-Sep, 10am-5pm mid-Sep–mid-May) isn't just the Grand Canyon in miniature, it's also a Unesco World Heritage site. The final resting place of thousands of dinosaurs, it's a stellar spot to check out some fossils. It's halfway between Calgary and Medicine Hat, and some 48km northeast of Brooks. From Hwy 1, take Secondary Hwy 873 to Hwy 544.

The park comes at you by surprise as the chasm in which it lives opens before your feet from the grassy plain. A dehydrated fantasy landscape, there are hoodoos and colorful rock formations aplenty. Where 75 million years ago dinosaurs cruised around a tropical landscape, it's now a hot and barren place to be. Make sure you dress for the weather with sunscreen and water at the ready.

The 81-sq-km park begs to be explored, with wildflowers, the odd rattler in the rocks and, if you're lucky, maybe even a *T-rex*. This isn't just a tourist attraction, but a hotbed for science; paleontologists have uncovered countless skeletons, which now reside in many of the finest museums around the globe.

There are five short interpretive **hiking trails** to choose from and a **driving loop** runs through part of the park, but to preserve the fossils, access to 70% of the park is restricted. The off-limits areas may be seen only on guided hikes (adult/child $14/8) or bus tours (adult/child $12/8), which operate from late May to October. The hikes and tours are popular, and you should reserve a place by calling ☎403-378-4344.

The park's **visitors center** (☎403-378-4342; adult/child $3/2; ⊙8:30am-5pm mid-May–Sep, 9am-4pm Oct-Apr) has a small yet effective series of dino displays. Some complete skeletons and exhibits on the practicalities of paleontology are worthy of a look.

The park's **campground** (☎403-378-3700; tent/RV sites $23/29, reservations $10; Ⓟ) sits in a hollow by a small creek. The ample tree cover is a welcome reprieve from the volcanic sun. Laundry facilities and hot showers are available, as well as a small shop for last-minute supplies. This is a popular place, especially with the RV set, so best to phone ahead.

Head-Smashed-In Buffalo Jump

The story behind the place with the strangest name of any attraction in Alberta is one of ingenuity and resourcefulness and is key to the First Nations' (and Canada's) cultural heritage. For thousands of years, the Blackfoot people used the cliffs near the town of Fort Macleod to hunt buffalo. **Head-Smashed-In Buffalo Jump** (www.head-smashed-in.com; Spring Point Rd/Secondary Hwy 785; adult/child $9/5; ⊙10am-5pm) was a marvel of simple ingenuity. When the buffalo massed in the open prairie, braves from the tribe would gather and herd them toward the towering cliffs. As the animals got closer, they would be funneled to the edge and made to stampede over it to their doom, thus ensuring the survival of the tribe. For the Blackfoot, the buffalo was sacred; to honor the fallen prey, every part of the animal was used.

The displays at the interpretive centre are fascinating and well presented at this World Heritage Listed site. Despite being slightly out of the way, it's most definitely worth the excursion. The site, about 18km northwest of Fort Macleod and 16km west of Hwy 2, also has a snack bar and a network of walking trails.

Lethbridge

Right in the heart of southern Alberta farming country sits the former coal-mining city of Lethbridge, divided by the distinctive coulees of the Oldman River. Though there isn't a lot to bring you to the city, copious parkland, a couple of good historic sites and an admirable level of civic pride might keep you longer than you first intended. There are ample hiking opportunities in the Oldman River Valley, a 100m-deep coulee bisected by the proverbial Eiffel Tower of steel railway bridges, and the largest of its kind in the world. The downtown area, like many North American downtowns, has made a good stab at preserving its not-so-ancient history. To the east, less-inspiring Mayor McGrath Dr (Hwy 5) is a chain-store-infested drag that could be Anywhere, North America.

⊙ Sights & Activities

Nikka Yuko Japanese Garden   GARDEN
(www.nikkayuko.com; cnr Mayor Mcgrath Dr & 9th Ave S; adult/youth $7/4; ⊙9am-5pm, to 8pm Jul & Aug) The Nikka Yuko Japanese Garden is the perfect antidote if the stresses of the road are starting to show. The immaculate grounds interspersed with ponds, flowing water, bridges, bonsai trees and rock gardens form an oasis of calm amid the bustle of everyday life, and authentic Japanese structures sit among the grassy mounds. Take your time, sit a while and let the Zenlike atmosphere take you on a journey.

Indian Battle Park   PARK
(3rd Ave S) In the coulee between the east and west sides of the city, Indian Battle Park, west of Scenic Dr and named after a

famous 1870 battle between the Blackfoot and the Cree, is no ordinary manicured green space. Instead, this is an expansive, surprisingly wild place astride the Oldman River that is strafed with trails, wildlife and some unsung mining history. Impossible to miss in the middle of it all is 96m-high, 1623m-long **High Level Bridge**, the largest trestle bridge in the world, built in 1909 to carry the railway across the deep coulee to the prairies on the other side.

Almost directly under the bridge, the **Helen Schuler Coulee Centre & Lethbridge Nature Reserve** (admission free; ⊙10am-6pm Jun-Aug, 1-4pm Sep-May) contains a small interpretive center and is the starting point for various nature trails on the reserve's 80 wooded hectares along the river. It runs special nature programs in the summer. At the other end of the car park is the **Coalbanks Interpretive kiosk**, an open-air shelter containing an impressive stash of information on Lethbridge's early mining history. Trails nearby lead to gazebos, picnic areas and viewpoints.

Also within the park is **Fort Whoop-Up** (www.fortwhoopup.com; adult/child $7/3; ⊙10am-5pm Tue-Sat), a replica of Alberta's first and most notorious illegal whiskey trading post. Around 25 of these outposts were set up in the province between 1869 and 1874 to trade whiskey, guns, ammunition and blankets for buffalo hides and furs from the Blackfoot tribes. Their existence led directly to the formation of the NWMP, who arrived in 1874 at Fort Macleod to bring law and order to the Canadian west.

Sir Alexander Galt Museum   MUSEUM
(www.galtmuseum.com; 320 Galt St; adult/child $5/3; ⊙10am-6pm) The story of Lethbridge is continued at the Sir Alexander Galt Museum, encased in an old hospital building (1910) on the bluff high above the river. Interactive kid-oriented displays sit beside a small gallery with contemporary and historical art that will interest the bigger kids. The view from the lobby out onto the coulee is great and free.

⊨ Sleeping

A huge selection of chain hotels from fancy to thrifty can be found on Hwy 5. Take your pick.

Lethbridge Lodge   HOTEL **$$**
(☎403-328-1123; www.lethbridgelodge.com; 320 Scenic Dr S; r from $109; P@☜) Like most Canadian hotels, the rooms here are clean if a little

unmemorable, but the atrium, on the other hand, is something else. All the rooms look down into the fake-foliage-filled interior, complete with winding brick pathways, a kidney-shaped pool and water features. The Cotton Blossom Lounge sits among the jungle and is good fun – the piano player is stranded on a small island – and the pseudo Italian facade of the rooms completes the bizarre picture.

Ramada Hotel & Suites
HOTEL $$
(✆403-380-5050; www.ramadalethbridge. ca; 2375 Hwy 5 S; r from $110; @🐕❄) From a jungle (Lethbridge Hotel) to a 400,000-liter water feature! This slightly-out-of-the-box Ramada has an indoor water park complete with dueling waterslides, wave pool and special kids area. All the standard stuff is here, too, and despite the wacky selling features, the Ramada retains a sense of class. Nonguests can pay to use the water park (adult/child $10/6).

Henderson Lake Campground
CAMPGROUND $
(✆403-328-5452; www.hendersoncampground. com; 3419 Parkside Dr; tent & RV sites from $25; 🅿) It may be in need of a bit of a clean up, but the central location of this campground is hard to beat. Right beside the lake it shares its name with and near to town, you are right among the action. There are tent sites, a shop and a laundry.

✖ Eating

Ric's Grill
STEAKHOUSE $$$
(✆403-317-7427; www.ricsgrill.com; 103 Mayor Mcgrath Dr; mains $19-40) Ever eaten in a water tower – or an ex-water tower to be more precise? Well, here is your chance. Ric's sits 40m high above the prairie in the old Lethbridge water tower (decommissioned in 1999). Turned into a restaurant in 2004, the curved interior affords great views of the city. There is a lounge on one level and a classy dining room upstairs. The steaks are thick and the wine list long; best to reserve a good spot as it's deservedly popular.

Mocha Cabana Café
CAFE $$
(www.mochacabana.ca; 317 4th St; lunch from $12; ⊙7am-9pm, to 11pm Fri & Sat; 🛜) Austere from the outside, the multifunctional Mocha is anything but within. Billing itself as a coffee lounge, wine bar, patio and music venue, it grabs 'best in Lethbridge' prize in each genre. The bright interior has an appealing European ambience and the substantial lunchtime salads are fantastic.

Round Street Café
CAFE $
(427 5th St S; sandwiches $7; ⊙7am-6pm Mon-Sat) A simple but effective indie coffee bar near the Greyhound depot with a fine line in cinnamon buns and thick-cut sandwiches, plus free internet browsing rights.

ℹ Information
Main Post Office (✆403-382-4604; 704 4th Ave S)

Main Tourist Office (www.chinookcountry. com; 2805 Scenic Dr S, at Mayor Mcgrath Dr S; ⊙9am-5pm)

ℹ Getting There & Around
Air
The **Lethbridge airport** (✆403-329-4474; 417 Stubb Ross Rd), a short drive south on Hwy 5, is served by commuter affiliates of Air Canada. Six or seven flights per day go to Calgary.

Bus
Greyhound Canada (✆403-327-1551; 411 5th St S) goes to Calgary ($48, three hours, five daily) and Regina ($103, from 14½ hours, two daily).

For detailed information about local bus services, call the **Lethbridge Transit Infoline** (✆403-320-4978/3885). The downtown bus terminal is on 4th Ave at 6th St. Local bus fares are $2.

Writing-On-Stone Provincial Park

Perhaps the best thing about this **park** (admission free; ⊙tours 9am-6pm mid-May–mid-Sep, 10am-5pm mid-Sep–mid-May) is that it really isn't on the way to *anywhere*. For those willing to get off the main thoroughfare and discover this hidden gem, all efforts will be rewarded. It's named for the extensive carvings and paintings made by the Plains Indians more than 3000 years ago on the sandstone cliffs along the banks of Milk River. There is an excellent self-guided interpretive trail that takes you to some of the more spectacular viewpoints and accessible pictographs.

The best art is found in a restricted area (to protect it from vandalism), which you can only visit on a guided tour with the park ranger. Other activities possible here include canoeing and swimming in the river in summer and cross-country skiing in winter. Park wildlife amounts to more than 160 bird species, 30 kinds of mammals, four kinds of amphibians and three kinds of reptiles, not to mention the fish in the river. Pick up tickets for tours at the park entrance, from the naturalist's office. Tours generally run Saturday and Sunday at 2pm from May to October (adult/child \$12/8).

The park's riverside **campground** (📞403-647-2877; tent/RV sites from \$21/27) has 64 sites, running water, showers and flush toilets and is popular on weekends.

The park is southeast of Lethbridge and close to the US border; the Sweetgrass Hills of northern Montana are visible to the south. To get to the park, take Hwy 501 42km east of Hwy 4 from the town of Milk River.

Waterton Lakes National Park

Who? What? Where? The name **Waterton Lakes National Park** (adult/child & senior per day \$7.80/3.90) is usually prefixed with a vexed question rather than a contented sigh of recognition. While its siblings to the north – Canmore, Banff and Jasper – hemorrhage with tourists and weekend warriors, Waterton is a pocket of tranquility. Sublime. Established in 1895 and now part of a Unesco World Heritage site, Unesco Biosphere Reserve and International Peace Park (with Glacier National Park in the US), 525-sq-km Waterton Lakes lies in Alberta's southwestern corner. Here the prairies meet the mountains and the relief from the flat land is nothing short of uplifting. The park is a sanctuary for numerous iconic animals – grizzlies, elk, deer and cougar – along with 800-odd wildflower species.

The town of **Waterton**, a charming alpine village with a winter population of about 40, provides a marked contrast to larger, tackier Banff and, to a lesser extent, Jasper. There is a lifetime's worth of outdoor adventure to discover here. Highlights include serene Waterton Lake, the regal 1920s-era Prince of Wales Hotel, and the immediacy of the high-alpine hiking terrain; you can be up above the tree line less than one hour from the townsite.

Sitting right on the US border and next to the immense **Glacier National Park**, this is a good spot to forge neighborly relations with the people to the south. You can even flash your passport and do a polycountry backcountry adventure. Together the two parks comprise Waterton-Glacier International Peace Park. Although the name evokes images of binational harmony, in reality each park is operated separately,

and entry to one does not entitle you to entry to the other.

For more information on Glacier National Park, see the excellent US National Park Service website at www.nps.gov/glac.

◉ Sights & Activities

A highlight for many visitors is a boat ride with **Waterton Shoreline Cruises** (www.watertoncruise.com; one way adult/child \$23/12; ⏱May-Oct) across the lake's shimmering waters to the far shore of Goat Haunt, Montana, USA. The 45-minute trip is scenic and there is a lively commentary as you go. Grab your passport before you jump on the often rather full boats, as they dock in the USA for about half an hour.

Those looking to stretch their legs are in luck – Waterton is a hiker's haven. With over 225km of walking tracks, you'll run out of time before you run out of trails. The trails are shared with bikes and horses (where permitted), and once the snow flies, crosscountry skis will get you to the same places. The 17km walk to **Crypt Lake** is a standout – there's a 20m tunnel, a stream that materializes out of the ground and a ladder to negotiate. The only way to get to the trailhead is by boat. Waterton Shoreline Cruises leave the town's marina in the morning and pick up the weary at the Crypt Lake trailhead in the afternoon (adult/child \$18/9).

Another example of Waterton's 'small is beautiful' persona is the 19km **Carthew-Alderson Trail**, often listed as one of the best high alpine day hikes in North America. The Tamarack Shuttle runs every morning in the summer to the trailhead by Cameron Lake (reservations recommended). From here you hike back over the mountains to the townsite.

🛏 Sleeping

The park has three Parks Canada vehicle-accessible campgrounds, none of which takes reservations. Backcountry campsites are limited and should be reserved through the visitors center.

TOP CHOICE **Prince of Wales Hotel**   HOTEL \$\$\$
(📞403-859-2231; www.princeofwaleswaterton.com; Prince of Wales Rd; r from \$234; ⏱mid-May–Sep; 🅿🛜) You can't come to Waterton and not check out this iconic alpine landmark. Situated to take full advantage of the best view in town, this hotel is nothing short of spectacular. When seen from a distance, the serene scene is perhaps the most photogenic in all the Canadian Rockies. Up

close, the old girl is starting to show her age but she's aging like a fine wine. The grand lobby is illuminated with a chandelier worthy of a Scottish castle and the elevator is the oldest working example in North America. The rooms are small but retain the classic feel of this historic hotel. There's antique porcelain in the bathrooms and views that justify the $200-plus asking price.

Bayshore Inn
HOTEL $$$

(☏403-859-2211; www.bayshoreinn.com; 111 Waterton Ave; r $199; ☺Apr–mid-Oct; ℗@⊚) Taking the prize as the biggest hotel in the downtown area, the Bayshore is nothing if not centrally located. With rooms that back right onto the lake and only a couple of steps away from the shops, this is a popular option. The lake views are great, but be sure to book early if you want to see them.

Aspen Village Inn
HOTEL $$

(☏403-859-2255; www.aspenvillageinn.com; 111 Windflower Ave; r from $135; ℗⊚@) Aspen is a more economical, family-friendly version of the Bayshore. Rooms are in two main buildings and several cottage units. Bonuses include a kids' play area, a barbecue and picnic area, and the sight of wild deer grazing the grass outside your room.

Waterton Glacier Suites
HOTEL $$$

(☏403-859-2004; www.watertonsuites.com; 107 Windflower Ave; ste from $225; ℗@⊚≋) With amenities aplenty, these suites have two fireplaces, whirlpool tubs, microwaves and fridges. The rooms are spotless and the rock-and-log exterior looks the part, too. It's open all year round – come winter you'll appreciate those dual fireplaces.

Waterton Townsite Campground
CAMPGROUND $

(☏877-737-3783; Hwy 5; unserviced/full-service $22.50/38.20; ☺mid-May–mid-Oct; ℗) Dominating the southern end of Waterton village, the town campground isn't ideal, but it's a means to an end. Consisting mainly of an enormous gopher hole-infested field aimed at RV campers, it has all the charm of a camping area at a music festival. There are some treed sites near the edges, but by midsummer you'll be lucky to get anything. Book ahead for this one.

HI-Waterton
HOSTEL $

(☏403-859-2151; Cameron Falls Dr at Windflower Ave; dm from $31, r from $93, ☺mid-May–Nov; ℗@≋) If you want a cheap place to stay in the park that isn't under canvas, the hostel

is your sole option. Small dorms that sleep four weary travelers are clean and come with adjoining bathrooms, and there is a small communal kitchen. Check ahead as it's sometimes block-booked.

Bear Mountain Motel
MOTEL $$

(☏403-859-2366; www.bearmountainmotel.com; 208 Mount View Rd; r from $95; ℗) Small, bog-standard motel rooms in a central location. Throw in friendly, knowledgeable owners and you're laughing all the way to the ATM.

Crandell Mountain Campground
CAMPGROUND $

(☏403-859-5133; Red Rock Pkwy; tent & RV sites $22; ☺mid-May–Sep; ℗) For a more rustic alternative to the townsite, head out to this secluded camping spot a few minutes' drive from the park gates.

🍴 Eating

Waterton specializes in unsophisticated but filling cuisine, ideal for topping up your energy both pre- and post-hike. Everything is contained within the townsite.

Zum's Eatery
CANADIAN $$

(116B Waterton Ave; mains from $13) Good home-style cooking of the burger, pizza, and fish and chips variety is brought to you by hard-up students working their summer breaks. The lack of sophisticated flavors is made up for by the character of the decor; several hundred North American license plates embellish almost every centimeter of wall.

Waterton Bagel & Coffee Co
CAFE $

(309 Windflower Ave; bagels from $5; ☺10am–10pm) A godsend if you've just staggered out of the wilderness, this tiny caffeine stop has a handful of window stools, life-saving peanut butter and jam bagels, and refreshing frappuccinos.

Pizza of Waterton
PIZZA $

(103 Fountain Ave; pizzas from $10) Fine pizza 'to go' (the lakeside calls on warm summer evenings), or in the informal interior where you can wash it down with a cold Canadian beer.

🍺 Drinking & Entertainment

Thirsty Bear Saloon
PUB

(www.thirstybearsaloon.com; Main St) Wild nights in the wilderness happen in this large pub/performance space aided by live music, karaoke, good beer and mildly inebriated young ladies in cowboy hats.

ℹ Information

Waterton Visitor Centre (☎403-859-5133; www.parkscanada.gc.ca/waterton; ⊗8am-7pm early May-early Oct) is across the road from the Prince of Wales Hotel. It's the central stop for information.

ℹ Getting There & Around

Waterton lies in Alberta's southwestern corner, 130km from Lethbridge and 156km from Calgary. The one road entrance into the park is in its north-eastern corner along Hwy 5. Most visitors coming from Glacier and the USA reach the junction with Hwy 5 via Hwy 6 (Chief Mountain International Hwy) from the southeast. From Calgary, to the north, Hwy 2 shoots south toward Hwy 5 into the park. From the east, Hwy 5, through Cardston, heads west and then south into the park.

There is no public transportation from Canadian cities outside the park. However, a shuttle service operated by **Glacier Park Inc** (www. glacierparkinc.com) offers daily transport from Prince of Wales Hotel to Glacier Park Lodge in Montana, USA from May to September. Here you can link up with the Amtrak train network.

A hiker's shuttle operates around the park in the summer, linking Cameron Lake with the townsite and the US border at Chief Mountain. It leaves from **Tamarack Outdoor Outfitters** (214 Mount View Rd) in the townsite.

Crowsnest Pass

West of Fort Macleod the Crowsnest Hwy (Hwy 3) heads through the prairies and into the Rocky Mountains to Crowsnest Pass (1396m) and the British Columbian border. The Pass, as it's known, is a string of small communities just to the east of the BC border. Of note is the story of the town of **Frank**. In 1903, Frank was almost completely buried when 30 million cubic meters (some 82 million tonnes worth) of nearby Turtle Mountain collapsed and killed around 70 people. The coal mine dug into the base of the mountain was to blame, some say. But the mining didn't stop; this black gold was the ticket to fortune for the entire region some hundred years ago. Eventually the demand for coal decreased, and after yet more tragedy below the earth, the mines shut down for good.

Frank Slide Interpretive Centre (www. frankslide.com; adult/child $9/5; ⊗10am-5pm), 1.5km off Hwy 3 and 27km east of the BC border, overlooks the Crowsnest Valley. It's an excellent interpretive center that helps put a human face on the tragedy of the Frank landslide, with many interesting displays about mining, the railroad and the early days of this area. There's also a fantastic film dramatizing the tragic events of 1903. Most of the staff can trace their roots to the area and thus the slide.

NORTHERN ALBERTA

Despite the presence of the increasingly infamous oil sands, the top half of Alberta is little visited and even less known. Once you travel north of Edmonton, the population drops off to Siberian levels and the sense of remoteness is almost eerie.

If it's solitude you seek, then this is paradise found. Endless stretches of pine forests seem to go on forever, nighttime brings aurora borealis displays that are better than any chemical hallucinogens, and it is here you can still see herds of buffalo.

This is also where the engine room of the Alberta economy lives. The oil sands near Fort McMurray are one of the largest oil reserves in the world. This helps to import workers from every corner of Canada and export oil earning the province millions of dollars – per hour.

The Cree, Slavey and Dene were the first peoples to inhabit the region, and many of them still depend on fishing, hunting and trapping for survival. The northeast has virtually no roads and is dominated by Wood Buffalo National Park, the Athabasca River and Lake Athabasca. The northwest is more accessible, with a network of highways connecting Alberta with northern BC and the NWT.

Peace River & Around

Alaska here we come! Heading northwest along Hwy 43 leads to the town of Dawson Creek, BC, and mile zero of the Alaska Hwy. Dawson is a whopping 590km from Edmonton, so it's a long way to go to check out this isolated section of northern Alberta. Along the way you'll pass through **Grande Prairie**, the base of operations for the local agricultural industry and home to chuckwagon legend Kelly Sutherland. If you decide to spend the night, most of the accommodations are centered on 100th St and 100th Ave.

Peace River is so named because the warring Cree and Beaver Indians made peace along its banks. The town of **Peace River** sits at the confluence of the Heart, Peace and Smoky Rivers. It has several motels and two campgrounds. Greyhound Canada buses leave daily for the Yukon and NWT. West out of town, Hwy 2 leads to the Mackenzie Hwy.

Mackenzie Highway

The small town of **Grimshaw** is the official starting point of the Mackenzie Hwy (Hwy 35) north to the NWT. There's not much here except for the mile-zero sign and a few shops. The relatively flat and straight road is paved for the most part, though there are stretches of loose gravel or earth where the road is being reconstructed.

The mainly agricultural landscape between Grimshaw and Manning gives way to endless stretches of spruce and pine forest. Come prepared as this is frontier territory and services become fewer (and more expensive) as the road cuts northward through the wilderness. A good basic rule is to fill your tank any time you see a gas station from here north.

High Level, the last settlement of any size before the NWT border, is a center for the timber industry. Workers often stay in the motels in town during the week. The only service station between High Level and Enterprise (in the NWT) is at Indian Cabins.

Lake District

From St Paul, more than 200km northeast of Edmonton, to the NWT border lies Alberta's immense lake district. Fishing is popular (even in winter, when there is ice-fishing) but many of the lakes, especially further north, have no road access and you have to fly in.

St Paul is the place to go if you are looking for little green people. The **flying-saucer landing pad**, which is still awaiting its first customer, is open for business. Residents built the 12m-high circular landing pad in 1967 as part of a centennial project and as a stunt to try to generate tourism (it's billed as the world's largest, and only, UFO landing pad) to the remote region. It worked: UFO enthusiasts have been visiting ever since.

Hwy 63 is the main route into the province's northeastern wilderness interior. The highway, with a few small settlements and campgrounds on the way, leads to **Fort McMurray**, which is 439km northeast of Edmonton. Originally a fur-trading outpost, it is now home to one of the world's largest oilfields. The town is pretty rough and the accommodations are aimed at unhoused oilfield workers, so it's not really a prime holiday spot. The story of how crude oil is extracted from the vast tracts of sand is told at the **Oil Sands Discovery Centre** (515 MacKenzie Blvd; adult/child $6/4; ☺9am-5pm Tue-Sat).

Wood Buffalo National Park

This huge park is best accessed from Fort Smith in the NWT. For more information, see p801.

In Alberta, the only access is via air to Fort Chipewyan. In winter, an ice road leads north to Peace Point (which connects to Fort Smith), and another road links the park to Fort McMurray.

British Columbia

Includes »

Best Places to Eat

- » C Restaurant (p643)
- » Araxi (p666)
- » Bishop's (p646)
- » Red Fish Blue Fish (p678)
- » Tojo's (p646)

Best Places to Stay

- » Wickaninnish Inn (p697)
- » Lake O'Hara Lodge (p738)
- » Free Spirit Spheres (p692)
- » Nita Lake Lodge (p664)
- » Loden Vancouver (p639)

Why Go?

Visitors to British Columbia are never short of superlatives when writing postcards home. It's hard not to be moved by towering mountain ranges, wildlife-packed forests and uncountable kilometers of coastline that slow your heart like a sigh-triggering spa treatment. But Canada's westernmost province is more than a nature-hugging diorama.

Cosmopolitan Vancouver is an animated fusion of cuisines and cultures from Asia and beyond, while vibrant smaller cities like Victoria and Kelowna are increasingly catching up with their own intriguing scenes. And for sheer character, it's hard to beat the province's kaleidoscope of quirky little communities, from rustic northern BC to the laid-back Southern Gulf Islands.

Wherever you head, the great outdoors will always be calling. Don't just point your camera at it. BC is unbeatable for the kind of life-enhancing skiing, kayaking, hiking and biking experiences you'll always remember fondly.

When to Go
Vancouver

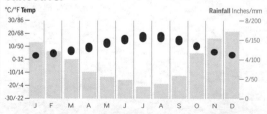

December–March Powder action on the slopes of Whistler and Blackcomb Mountains

July & August Beaches, BBQs and a plethora of outdoor festivals in Vancouver

September & October Great surfing and the start of storm-watching season in Tofino

Getting There & Around

BC's vastness is what strikes most visitors, the majority of whom fly into Vancouver or drive across the US border: it's a scary-sounding 1508km drive from Vancouver to Prince Rupert, for example. But while it's tempting to simply stick around in the big city and avoid the car, you won't really have been to the West Coast unless you head out of town.

Despite the distances, driving remains the most popular method of movement in BC. Plan your routes via the **Drive BC website** (www.drivebc.ca) and check out the 36 services covered by the **BC Ferries** (www.bcferries.com) system.

VIA Rail (www.viarail.com) operates three BC train services. One trundles across the north from the coastline to Jasper. Pick up the second in Jasper for a ride back to Vancouver. The third departs downtown Victoria, weaving up island to Courtenay.

PARKS & WILDLIFE

BC's eight national parks include snow-capped **Glacier** and the Unesco World Heritage sites of **Kootenay** and **Yoho**. The newer **Gulf Islands National Park Reserve** protects a fragile coastal region. Visit the website of **Parks Canada** (www.pc.gc.ca) for information.

The region's 850 provincial parks offer 3000km of hiking trails. Notables include **Strathcona** and remote **Cape Scott**, as well as the Cariboo's canoe-friendly **Bowron Lake** and the Kootenays' Matterhorn-like **Mt Assiniboine**. Check the website of **BC Parks** (www.bcparks.ca) for information.

Expect to spot some amazing wildlife. Ocean visitors should keep an eye out for Pacific gray whales, while land mammals – including elk, moose, wolves, grizzlies and black bear – will have most scrambling for their cameras. And there are around 500 bird varieties, including BC's provincial fowl the Steller's Jay.

Local Culture: Raise a Glass

BC has enjoyed a huge surge in local microbrewed beer, so don't miss out. Steel your taste buds for Surrey's **Central City Brewing** (www.centralcitybrewing.com) and their mildly malty Red Racer ESB. Alternatively, Kelowna's **Tree Brewing** (www.treebeer.com) produces a Hop Head IPA that makes your eyes pop out. To prove that beer doesn't need to pack a punch, **Gulf Islands Brewing** (www.gulfislands brewery.com), based on Salt Spring Island, crafts Heatherdale Ale, an aromatic, heather-infused brew that's subtle, complex and seductive.

Fast Facts

» Population: 4.5 million
» Area: 944,735 sq km
» Capital: Victoria
» Quirky fact: Home of the world's largest hockey stick (Duncan)

It's Official

BC's official flower is the Pacific dogwood. Also officially, its gemstone is jade and its mammal is the Kermode bear.

Resources

» Tourism BC (www.hellobc.com)
» Cycling BC (www.cyclingbc.net)
» British Columbia Beer Guide (www.bcbeer.ca)
» BC Government (www.gov.bc.ca)
» BC Wine Institute (www.winebc.com)
» WaveLength Magazine (www.wavelength magazine.com)
» Van Dop Arts & Cultural Guide (www.art-bc.com)
» Go BC (www.gobc.ca)
» Surfing Vancouver Island (www.surfing vancouverisland.com)

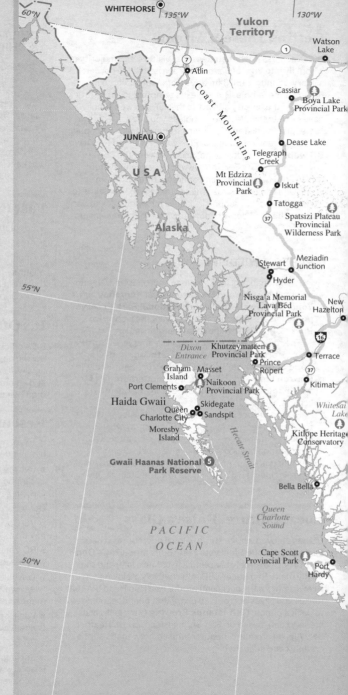

British Columbia Highlights

1 Stretch your legs on a seawall stroll around Vancouver's **Stanley Park** (p627) then enjoy a relaxing sunset at Third Beach

2 Surf up a storm (or just watch a storm) in **Tofino** (p696) on Vancouver Island's wild west coast

3 Slurp some celebrated tipples on an ever-winding **Okanagan Valley** (p716) winery tour

4 Ski the Olympian slopes at **Whistler** (p661) then enjoy a warming après beverage while you rub your aching muscles in the village

5 Explore the ancient and ethereal rainforest of the **Gwaii Haanas National Park Reserve** (p753) and kayak the coastline for a fish-eye view of the region

6 Putter around the lively Saturday Market on **Salt Spring Island** (p708) and scoff more than a few fruit and bakery treats

7 Indulge in some lip-smacking Asian hawker food at the **Summer Night Market** (p657) in Richmond and come away with some spicy takeout

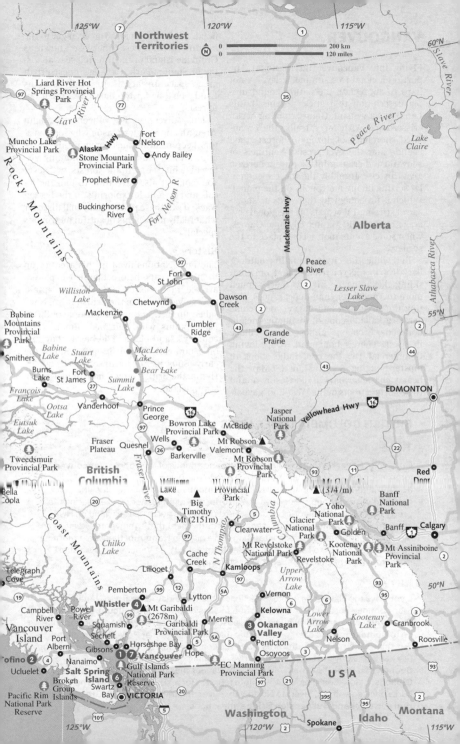

VANCOUVER

Flying into Vancouver International Airport on a cloud-free summer's day, it's not hard to appreciate the nature-bound utopia description that sticks to this 'Lotus Land' like a wetsuit. Gently rippling ocean crisscrossed with ferry trails, the crenulated shorelines of dozens of forest-green islands and the ever-present sentinels of snow-dusted crags glinting on the horizon give this city arguably the most spectacular setting of any metropolis on the planet. Which is probably why there was no shortage of stirring TV visuals for the global coverage of the 2010 Winter Olympic Games, when some events took second place to the scenery.

But while the city's twinkling outdoor backdrop means you're never far from great skiing, kayaking or hiking, there's much more to Vancouver than appearances. Hitting the streets on foot means you'll come across a kaleidoscope of distinctive neighborhoods, each one almost like a village in itself. There's bohemian, coffee-loving Commercial Dr; the cool indie shops of hipster-hugging South Main (SoMa); the hearty character bars of old Gastown; and the colorful streets of the West End 'gayborhood.' And that's before you even get to the bustling artisan nest otherwise known as Granville Island or the forested seawall vistas of Stanley Park, Canada's finest urban green space. In fact, if this really is Lotus Land, you'll be far too busy checking it out to rest.

This diversity is Vancouver's main strength and a major reason why some visitors keep coming back for more. If you're a first timer, soak in the breathtaking vistas and hit the verdant forests whenever you can, but also save time to join the locals and do a little exploring off the beaten track; it's in these places that you'll discover what really makes this beautiful metropolis special.

History

The First Nations lived in this area for up to 16,000 years before Spanish explorers arrived in the late 1500s. When Captain George Vancouver of the British Royal Navy sailed up in 1792, he met a couple of Spanish captains who informed him of their country's land claim. The beach they met on is now called Spanish Banks. But by the early 1800s, as European settlers began arriving, the British crown had an increasing stranglehold.

BRITISH COLUMBIA ITINERARIES

Three Days

Once you've checked out the big-city sights and sounds of metropolis **Vancouver**, jump in the car and drive, via Hwys 99 and 17, to the Tsawwassen ferry terminal for a sigh-triggering boat trip to Swartz Bay on **Vancouver Island**. After docking (not before, please) continue your drive to **Victoria**, overnighting here and exploring the pretty capital and its historic buildings. Next day, drive north up the island on Hwy 1, stopping off at **Chemainus**, a former logging settlement that's reinvented itself as an 'art town.' Continue north for a late lunch and a night in **Nanaimo**, then, next morning, catch the ferry back to the Horseshoe Bay terminal in West Vancouver. It's a short drive from here back to your Vancouver starting point.

One Week

If you have the luxury of a whole week, follow the three-day itinerary to **Nanaimo** then continue north on Hwy 19 to the quaint seaside towns of **Qualicum Beach** and **Parksville**. Walk around, window-shop, absorb the atmosphere, before you continue on to **Comox** and take a ferry back to the mainland, arriving at **Powell River** on the Sunshine Coast. Wind southwards along the coast and forest road, taking a short-hop ferry at Earl's Cove to continue your drive, stopping off at quirky communities like **Sechelt** and **Roberts Creek**. Allow time to wander the charming waterfront village of **Gibsons**, before boarding the 45-minute ferry to Horseshoe Bay. If there's no need to hurry back downtown, divert to North Vancouver and the ever-popular **Grouse Mountain** and **Capilano Suspension Bridge** attractions.

Vancouver

0 —— 4 km
0 —— 2 miles

Bowen Island

To Horseshoe Bay (2km);
Bowen Island (7km);
Whistler (105km)

Lighthouse Park

Burrard Inlet

Sandy West Cove Bay

Upper Levels Fwy

Point Grey

Spanish Banks Beach Park

Jericho Beach

Wreck Beach

Museum of Anthropology

University Of British Columbia

UBC Botanical Garden

Marine Drive Foreshore Park

Musqueam Indian Reserve 2

Iona Island

Sea Island

Strait of Georgia

Coquitlam River

To Buntzen Lake (10km)

Indian Arm Provincial Park

Indian Arm

Mt Seymour Provincial Park

BELCARRA

ANMORE

Belcarra Regional Park

Mossom River

Noons Creek

Barnston Island

PORT COQUITLAM

Mary Hill By-Pass

Douglas Island

To Fort Langley (8km)

Tynehead Regional Park

168th St

176th St

Fraser Hwy

152nd St

SURREY

88th Ave

Green Timbers Urban Forest

King George Hwy

96th Ave

128th St

120th St

72nd Ave

Como Lake Ave

Mundy Park

Austin Ave

COQUITLAM

Burnaby Mountain Conservation Area

BURNABY

Lougheed Hwy

Burnaby Lake Regional Park

Burnaby Village Museum

Deer Lake Park

104th Ave

NEW WESTMINSTER

Canada Way

Kingsway

Annacis Island

Annacis Hwy

Nordel Way

DELTA

Delta Nature Reserve

River Rd

(91)

(99)

Fraser River

North Arm Fraser River

To Tsawwassen (15km); Seattle (USA, 190km)

Richmond Fwy

RICHMOND

Richmond Nature Park

Bridgeport Rd

Mitchell Island

Marine Way

Central Park

Kerr St

Boundary Rd

Rupert St

E Hastings St

Confederation Park

Dollarton Hwy

Mt Seymour Pkwy

Lynn Canyon Park

Capilano Suspension Bridge

To Grouse Mountain (1km)

NORTH VANCOUVER

Marine Dr

Lions Gate Bridge

Stanley Park

First Narrows

Vancouver Harbour

English Bay

See Downtown Vancouver Map (p630)

Granville St

KITSILANO

W Broadway

16th Ave W

W 41st Ave

WEST SIDE

SOUTH MAIN

Queen Elizabeth Park

Cambie St

Oak St

Main St

Knight St

Kingsway

Commercial Dr

Nanaimo St

Lynn Creek

No 1 Rd

Blundell Rd

Westminster Hwy

Steveston Hwy

Kuan Yin Temple

STEVESTON

Gulf of Georgia Cannery

Vancouver International Airport

Fur trading and a feverish gold rush soon redefined the region as a resource-filled Aladdin's cave. By the 1850s, thousands of fortune seekers had arrived, prompting the Brits to officially claim the area as a colony. Local entrepreneur 'Gassy' Jack Deighton seized the initiative in 1867 by opening a bar on the forested shoreline of Burrard Inlet. This triggered a rash of development – nicknamed Gastown – that became the forerunner of modern-day Vancouver.

But not everything went to plan. While Vancouver rapidly reached a population of 1000, its buildings were almost completely destroyed in an 1886 blaze – quickly dubbed the Great Fire, even though it only lasted 20 minutes. A prompt rebuild followed and the new downtown core soon took shape. Buildings from this era still survive, as does Stanley Park. Originally the town's military reserve, it was opened as a public recreation area in 1888.

Relying on its port, the growing city became a hub of industry, importing thousands of immigrant workers to fuel economic development. The Chinatown built at this time is still one of the largest in North America. But WWI and the 1929 Wall St crash brought deep depression and unemployment. The economy recovered during WWII, when shipbuilding and armaments manufacturing added to the traditional economic base of resource exploitation.

Growing steadily throughout the 1950s and 1960s, Vancouver added an NHL (National Hockey League) team and other accoutrements of a midsized North American city. Finally reflecting on its heritage, Gastown – by now a slum – was saved for gentrification in the 1970s, becoming a national historic site in 2010.

In 1986 the city hosted a highly successful Expo world's fair, sparking a wave of new development and adding the first of the mirrored skyscrapers that now define Vancouver's downtown core. A further economic lift was hoped for when the city staged the Olympic and Paralympic Winter Games in 2010. Even bigger than Expo, it was the city's chance to showcase itself to the world.

◉ Sights

Vancouver's most popular attractions are in several easily walkable neighborhoods, especially hot spots like Gastown, Chinatown, Stanley Park and Granville Island. Chichi Yaletown attracts fashionista window shoppers, while the real hipsters and bohemians are more likely to be found cruising SoMa and Commercial Dr. Laidback Kitsilano enjoys great beach access and leads out towards the tree-lined University of British Columbia (UBC) campus, a minitown of its own.

DOWNTOWN

Bordered by water on two sides and with Stanley Park on its tip, downtown Vancouver combines shimmering glass apartment and business towers with the shop-lined attractions of Robson St, the city's central promenade.

VANCOUVER IN...

One Day

Begin with a heaping breakfast at the **Templeton** before heading to the **Vancouver Art Gallery**. Next, take a window-shopping stroll along Robson St, then cut down to the waterfront for some panoramic sea and mountain vistas. Walk west along the **Coal Harbour** seawall and make for the dense trees of **Stanley Park**. Spend the afternoon exploring the beaches, totem poles and **Vancouver Aquarium** here before ambling over to the **West End** for dinner.

Two Days

Follow the one-day itinerary then, the next morning, head to clamorous **Chinatown**. Stop at the towering **Millennium Gate** and duck into the nearby **Dr Sun Yat-Sen Classical Chinese Garden** for a taste of tranquility. Check out the colorful stores (and tempting pork bun snacks) around the neighborhood before strolling south along Main St towards **Science World** for some hands-on fun, then hop on the SkyTrain at the nearby station. Trundle to Waterfront Station and take the scenic SeaBus over to North Vancouver's **Lonsdale Quay public market**. On your way back, drop in at Gastown's **Alibi Room** for a microbrew beer.

Vancouver Art Gallery   ART GALLERY

(Map p630; www.vanartgallery.bc.ca; 750 Hornby St; adult/child $22.50/7.50, by donation 5-9pm Tue; ⊙10am-5pm Wed-Mon, to 9pm Tue) The VAG has dramatically transformed since 2000, becoming a vital part of the city's cultural scene. Contemporary exhibitions – often showcasing Vancouver's renowned photoconceptualists – are now combined with blockbuster international traveling shows. Check out **Fuse** (admission $19.50), a quarterly late-night party where you can hang out with the city's young arties over wine and live music.

Canada Place   NOTABLE BUILDING

(Map p630; www.canadaplace.ca; 999 Canada Place Way) Shaped like a series of sails jutting into the sky over the harbor, this cruise-ship terminal and convention center is also a pier where you can stroll the waterfront for some camera-triggering North Shore mountain views. If you have kids in tow, duck inside for the **Port Authority Interpretation Centre** (www.portvancouver. com; admission free; ⊙8am-5pm Mon-Fri), a hands-on illumination of the city's maritime trade. Check out the grass-roofed expansion next door and the tripod-like **Olympic Cauldron**, a permanent reminder of the 2010 Games.

Bill Reid Gallery of Northwest Coast Art
ART GALLERY

(Map p630; www.billreidgallery.ca; 639 Hornby St; adult/child $10/5; ⊙11am-5pm Wed-Sun) Showcasing carvings, paintings and jewelry from Canada's most revered Haida artist, this is a comprehensive intro to Reid and his fellow First Nations creators. Hit the mezzanine floor and you'll be face-to-face with an 8.5m-long bronze of intertwined magical creatures, complete with impressively long tongues.

BC Place Stadium   NOTABLE BUILDING

(Map p630; www.bcplacestadium.com; 777 Pacific Blvd) Site of 2010's Winter Olympic opening and closing ceremonies, the city's main arena was having a new retractable lid fitted during research for this book. On completion, it will host football's **BC Lions** and soccer's **Vancouver Whitecaps**. The **BC Sports Hall of Fame & Museum** (www. bcsportshalloffame.com) – a kid-friendly celebration of the province's sporting achievements – is also expected to reopen after the refurbishment.

DON'T MISS

GARDENS

» Dr Sun Yat-Sen Classical Chinese Garden (p629)

» VanDusen Botanical Garden (p635)

» Bloedel Floral Conservatory (p635)

» UBC Botanical Garden (p634)

» Nitobe Memorial Garden (p634)

Marine Building   HISTORICAL BUILDING

(Map p630; 335 Burrard St) This elaborate, 22-story art deco gem is a tribute to the city's maritime past. Peruse the exterior of seahorses, lobsters and streamlined ships, then hit the lobby's stained-glass panels, zodiac-inlaid floor and brass-doored elevators. The British Empire's tallest building when completed in 1930, it now houses offices.

Vancouver Lookout   NOTABLE BUILDING

(Map p630; www.vancouverlookout.com; 555 W Hastings St; adult/child $15/7; ⊙8:30am-10:30pm mid-May–Sep, 9am-9pm Oct–mid-May) Atop this 169m-high, needle-like viewing tower – accessed via twin glass elevators – you'll enjoy 360-degree vistas of city, sea and mountains unfurling around you. Tickets are pricey but are valid all day – return for a sunset view to get your money's worth.

STANLEY PARK

This magnificent 404-hectare park combines excellent attractions with a mystical natural aura. Don't miss a stroll or cycle (rentals near the W Georgia St entrance) around the 8.8km seawall: a kind of visual spa treatment fringed by a 150,000-tree temperate rainforest, it'll take you past the park's popular totem poles.

Vancouver Aquarium   AQUARIUM

(www.vanaqua.org; adult/child $27/17, reduced in winter; ⊙9:30am-7pm Jul & Aug, 9:30am-5pm Sep-Jun) Home to 9000 water-loving critters – including wolf eels, beluga whales and mesmerizing jellyfish – there's also a walk-through rainforest of birds, turtles and a statue-still sloth. Check for feeding times and consider an **Animal Encounter trainer tour** (from $24). The newest draw here is the 4D Experience: a 3D movie theater with added wind, mist and aromas.

Miniature Railway `RAILWAY`

(☏604-257-8531; adult/child $6.19/3.10; ⊙10am-6pm Jul-early Sep, reduced off-season) Families looking for a charming alternative to the city's bigger kid-friendly attractions should head to the heart of the park for a 15-minute railway trundle through the trees. This is also one of Vancouver's fave Christmas lures, when the grounds are decorated with Yuletide decorations and dioramas.

Second Beach & Third Beach `BEACH`

Second Beach is an ever-busy, family-friendly area on the park's western side, with a grassy playground, snack bar and a pitch-and-putt golf course. Its main attraction is the seasonal outdoor **swimming pool** on the waterfront. Third Beach is a more laid-back hangout, with plenty of large logs to sit against and catch possibly Vancouver's best sunset.

FREE Lost Lagoon `NATURE RESERVE`

Originally an extension of Coal Harbour, this tranquil, watery oasis is now colonized by indigenous plant and beady-eyed birdlife accessed via a shoreline trail. Drop into the **Nature House** (Map p630; www.stanleyparkecology.ca; admission free; ⊙10am-7pm Tue-Sun May-Sep) for an introduction to the park's ecology and ask about the area **walks** (adult/child $10/5).

WEST END

A dense nest of low-rise older apartment buildings occupying a tangle of well-maintained residential streets, the West End is the city center's lively heart. Dripping with wooden heritage homes and lined on two sides by seawall promenades, it has plenty of dining and shopping options and is also the home of Vancouver's gay community.

Roedde House Museum `MUSEUM`

(Map p630; www.roeddehouse.org; 1415 Barclay St; admission $5; ⊙10am-5pm Tue-Sat, 2-4pm Sun) For a glimpse of pioneer-town Vancouver, drop by this handsome 1893 timber-framed mansion. Packed with antiques, it's a superb re-creation of how well-heeled locals used to live. Sunday entry includes tea and cookies and costs $1 extra. Also check out the surrounding preserved homes in **Barclay Heritage Sq.**

English Bay Beach `BEACH`

(Map p630; cnr Denman & Davie Sts) Whether it's a languid August evening with buskers, sunbathers and volleyballers, or a blustery November day with the dog walkers, this sandy curve is an unmissable highlight. Snap photos of the beach's towering **inukshuk sculpture** or continue along the bustling seawall into neighboring Stanley Park.

YALETOWN

An evocative, brick-lined former warehouse district transformed into swanky bars, restaurants and boutiques in the 1990s, pedestrian-friendly Yaletown is where the city's rich and beautiful come to see and be seen. Roughly bordered by Nelson, Homer, Drake and Pacific Sts, the past is recalled by the old rail tracks still embedded in many of the roads.

Roundhouse Community Arts & Recreation Centre `NOTABLE BUILDING`

(Map p630; www.roundhouse.ca; 181 Roundhouse Mews, cnr Davie St & Pacific Blvd) Yaletown's main cultural and performance space is housed in a refurbished Canadian Pacific Railway repair shed. This train-flavored heritage is recalled in a small on-site **museum** (www.wcra.org/engine374; admission free) housing one of the city's most important artifacts: engine No 374, the locomotive that pulled the first passenger train into Vancouver in 1887.

David Lam Park `PARK`

(Map p630; www.vancouverparks.ca; cnr Drake St & Pacific Blvd) A crooked elbow of landscaped waterfront at the neck of False Creek, this is a popular summertime hangout for Yaletownites. It's also a perfect launch point for a 2km stroll along the north bank of False Creek to Science World. You'll pass public artworks, slick glass towers and visiting birdlife, including blue herons.

FREE Contemporary Art Gallery `ART GALLERY`

(Map p630; www.contemporaryartgallery.ca; 555 Nelson St; ⊙noon-6pm Wed-Sun) Focused on modern art – photography is particularly well represented – this small, purpose-built gallery showcases local and international works.

GASTOWN

Now a national historic site, the cobbled streets of Gastown are where the city began – look out for the jaunty bronze of early resident 'Gassy' Jack Deighton teetering on his whiskey barrel. Many heritage buildings remain, most now housing cool bars, restaurants or trendy shops. The landmark **steam clock** (Map p630) is halfway along Water St. A snapshot favorite, it's actually powered by electricity.

Vancouver Police Museum   MUSEUM
(Map p630; www.vancouverpolicemuseum.ca; 240 E Cordova St; adult/student $7/5; ⊘9am-5pm) Charting the city's murky criminal past – complete with confiscated weapons, counterfeit currencies and a mortuary exhibit lined with wall-mounted tissue samples – this excellent little museum also runs recommended **Sins of the City walking tours** (adult/child $15/12) plus after-hours **Forensics for Adults workshops** ($12).

Science World at TELUS World of Science   MUSEUM
(Map p630; www.scienceworld.ca; 1455 Quebec St; adult/child $21/14.25; ⊘10am-5pm Mon-Fri, 10am-6pm Sat & Sun) The two levels of hands-on science and natural-history exhibits here bring out the kid in everyone. An ideal place to entertain the family, there's also an **Omnimax Theatre** screening large-format documentaries. Explore without the kids at the regular adults-only **After Dark** ($19.75) events. During research, an outdoor science park was also being added to the site.

CHINATOWN
Adjoining Gastown, North America's third-largest Chinatown is a highly wanderable explosion of sight, sound and aromas. Check out the towering **Chinatown Millennium Gate** (cnr W Pender & Taylor Sts), the area's monumental entry point, and don't miss the bustling summer **night market** (Map p630). For more information on the area – including events like the summer festival and the annual New Year parade – visit www.vancouver-chinatown.com.

Dr Sun Yat-Sen Classical Chinese Garden   GARDEN
(Map p630; www.vancouverchinesegarden.com; 578 Carrall St; adult/child $14/10; ⊘9:30am-7pm mid-Jun–Aug, 10am-6pm Sep & May–mid-Jun, 10am-4:30pm Oct-Apr) A tranquil break from clamorous Chinatown, this intimate 'garden of ease' reveals the Taoist symbolism behind the placing of gnarled pine trees and ancient limestone formations. Check out the less elaborate, but free, park next door.

SOUTH MAIN (SOMA) & COMMERCIAL DRIVE
Eschewing the fake tans of Robson St's mainstream shoppers, Vancouver's indie crowd has colonized an area of town that used to be a byword for down-at-heel. Radiating from the intersection of Main St and Broadway, South Main – also known as SoMa – is home

to the city's carefully cultivated young alternative crowd: think skinny jeans and plaid shirts for guys and vintage chic and thick-framed spectacles for girls. Bohemian coffee shops, cool-ass bars, vegetarian eateries and one-of-a-kind boutiques – especially past the 20th Ave intersection – are blooming here.

Urban adventurers should also alight at the Broadway-Commercial SkyTrain station for a stroll north along funky Commercial Dr (www.thedrive.ca), where decades of European immigrants – especially Italians, Greeks and Portuguese – have created a United Nations of restaurants, coffee bars and exotic delis. The best spot in town to watch televised international soccer games among passionate fans, it's also a promenade of espresso-supping patio dwellers on languid afternoons when it's lined with young bohemians and student-types.

Punjabi Market   SHOPPING AREA
Located on Main St, past 48th Ave, and also known as 'Little India,' this enclave of sari stores, bhangra music shops and some of the region's best-value curry buffet restaurants is a good spot for a spicy all-you-can-eat lunch followed by a restorative walkabout.

GRANVILLE ISLAND
Fanning out under the giant iron arches of Granville Bridge, this gentrified former industrial peninsula – it's not actually an island – is one of the best spots to spend a lazy afternoon. Studded with restaurants, bars, theaters and artisan businesses, it's usually crowded on summer weekends, as visitors chill out with the buskers and wrestle the seagulls for their fish and chips. For information and happenings, check www. granvilleisland.com.

Granville Island Public Market   MARKET
(Map p630; Johnston St; ⊘9am-7pm) Granville Island's highlight is the covered Public Market, a multisensory smorgasbord of fish, cheese, fruit and bakery treats. Pick up some fixings for a picnic at nearby Vanier Park or hit the international food court (dine off-peak and you're more likely to snag a table). **Edible BC** (www.edible-british columbia.com; tours $49) offers excellent market tours for the foodie-inclined.

Granville Island Brewing   BREWERY
(Map p630; www.gib.ca; 1441 Cartwright St; tours $9.75; ⊘noon, 2pm & 4pm) A short tour of Canada's oldest microbrewery ends with four sample beers in the Taproom – often

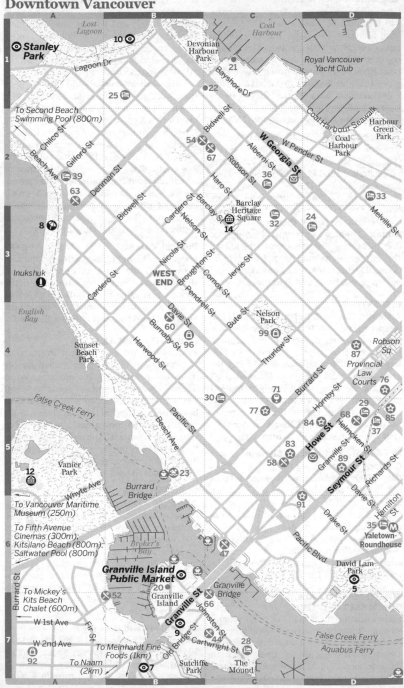

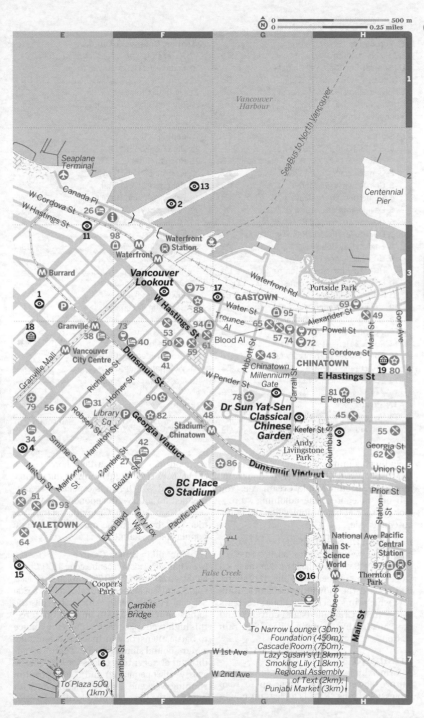

N 0 ____ 500 m
0 ____ 0.25 miles

Vancouver Harbour

SeaBus to North Vancouver

Centennial Pier

Seaplane Terminal

Canada Pl

W Cordova St 26

W Hastings St 11

13

2

Waterfront Station

Waterfront

Burrard

Vancouver Lookout

75 17

88

Waterfront Rd

Portside Park

GASTOWN

Water St 95

69

49

Gore Ave

1

Granville 38

73

40

94

53

50

59

61

Trounce Al

Blood Al

65

57 74

70

72

Alexander St

Powell St

E Cordova St

Main St

18

Vancouver City Centre

43

Abbott St

Chinatown Millennium Gate

CHINATOWN

19 80

Dunsmuir St

Richards St

Homer St

41

W Pender St

Carrall St

E Hastings St

81

E Pender St

45

55

Georgia St

62

79

56

31

Library Sq

90

82

78

48

Dr Sun Yat-Sen Classical Chinese Garden

Keefer St

3

Columbia St

Andy Livingstone Park

34

4

Robson St

Smithe St

Hamilton St

Georgia Viaduct

Stadium-Chinatown

42

27

Beatty St

86

Dunsmuir Viaduct

Union St

Prior St

Cambie St

46

51

93

YALETOWN

64

Expo Blvd

Terry Fox Way

BC Place Stadium

Pacific Blvd

National Ave

Main St-Science World

16

Pacific Central Station

97

Thornton Park

Station St

15

Cooper's Park

Cambie Bridge

False Creek

Quebec St

Main St

6

Cambie St

To Plaza 500 (1km)

W 1st Ave

W 2nd Ave

To Narrow Lounge (30m);
Foundation (450m);
Cascade Room (750m);
Lazy Susan's (1.8km);
Smoking Lily (1.8km);
Regional Assembly
of Text (2km);
Punjabi Market (3km)

BRITISH COLUMBIA VANCOUVER

including summer-favorite Hefeweizen, mildly hopped Brockton IPA or the recommended Kitsilano Maple Cream Ale. You can buy takeout in the adjoining store – look for special-batch tipples like the popular Ginger Ale.

Downtown Historic Railway RAILWAY
(Map p630; www.trams.bc.ca; adult/child $2/1; ⊙noon-6pm Sat, Sun & holidays Jun–mid-Oct) Once you've finished trawling the shops, hop aboard the Downtown Historic Railway, which runs clackety antique streetcars between the Granville Island entrance and the Canada Line Olympic Village SkyTrain station.

KITSILANO
A former hippy haven where the counterculture flower children grew up to reap professional jobs, 'Kits' is a pleasant neighborhood of wooden heritage homes, cozy coffee bars and highly browseable shops. Store-lined W 4th Ave is especially recommended for a lazy afternoon stroll. A short seawall amble from Granville Island, Vanier Park houses three museums and is a popular picnic haunt.

HR MacMillan Space Centre MUSEUM
(www.hrmacmillanspacecentre.com; 1100 Chestnut St; adult/child $15/10.75; ⊙10am-5pm Jul & Aug, 10am-3pm Mon-Fri & 10am-5pm Sat & Sun Sep-Jun) Popular with kids, who hit the hands-on exhibits with maximum force, this high-tech space center offers the chance to battle aliens, design spacecraft and take a Mars-bound simulator ride. There's an additional **observatory** (admission free; ⊙weekends, weather permitting) and a **planetarium** running weekend laser shows ($10.75) with music by the likes of Pink Floyd.

Museum of Vancouver MUSEUM
(MOV; www.museumofvancouver.ca; 1100 Chestnut St; adult/child $12/8; 10am-5pm Tue-Sun, to 8pm Thu) The recently rebranded MOV has upped its game with cool temporary exhibitions and late-opening parties aimed at an adult crowd. There are still colorful displays on local 1950s pop culture and 1960s hippie counterculture, plus plenty of hands-on kids stuff, including weekend scavenger hunts.

Vancouver Maritime Museum MUSEUM
(www.vancouvermaritimemuseum.com; 1905 Ogden Ave; adult/child $11/8.50; 10am-5pm May-Aug, 10am-5pm Tue-Sat & noon-5pm Sun Sep-Apr) Combining dozens of intricate model ships with detailed re-created boat sections and a few historic vessels, the highlight here is the *St Roch*, an arctic patrol vessel that was the first to navigate the Northwest Passage in both directions.

Kitsilano Beach BEACH
(cnr Cornwall Ave & Arbutus St) Attracting a young crowd of buff Frisbee tossers and giggling volleyball players, the water here is fine for a dip but there's also a giant outdoor heated saltwater pool if you prefer.

UNIVERSITY OF BRITISH COLUMBIA
West from Kits on a 400-hectare forested peninsula, UBC (www.ubc.ca) is the province's largest university. Its concrete campus is surrounded by the University Endowment Lands, complete with accessible beach and forest areas and a smattering of visitor attractions.

TOP CHOICE **Museum of Anthropology** MUSEUM
(Map p625; www.moa.ubc.ca; 6393 NW Marine Dr; adult/child $14/12; 10am-5pm Wed-Mon & 10am-9pm Tue, closed Mon mid-Oct–mid-Jan) Recently renovated and expanded,

GREEN YOUR VANCOUVER VISIT

Apart from walking, using transit and picking up a **Green Zebra Guide** (www.green zebraguide.ca), a coupon book that gives you deals at local sustainable businesses, there are a couple of additional ways to add a shiny eco sheen to your Vancouver trip. Spearheaded by the Vancouver Aquarium and a growing menu of city restaurants, **Ocean Wise** (www.oceanwise.ca) encourages sustainable fish and shellfish supplies that minimize environmental impact. Visit its website for an ever-growing list of participating local restaurants and check menus for symbols indicating Ocean Wise dishes. A similar, smaller movement called the **Green Table Network** (www.greentable.net) can help you identify area restaurants that try to source all their supplies – not just seafood – from sustainable, mostly local sources.

Sustainability also has a chatty social side with **Green Drinks** (www.greendrinks. org), a monthly drop-in gathering for anyone interested in environmental issues. The meetings take place at Steamworks Brewing Company (p648) and usually attract more than 100 regulars for beer-fueled discussions on alternative energy, global warming and the sky-high price of tickets to Al Gore events.

For more tips on how to green your trip, check in with the online **Granville Magazine** (www.granvilleonline.ca), which is brimming with eco ideas. And if you need some extra inspiration, check out these cool, locally written books: *100-Mile Diet: A Year of Local Eating* by Alisa Smith and JB Mackinnon (2007), *Greater Vancouver Green Guide* by the UBC Design Centre for Sustainability (2009) and *The Greenpeace to Amchitka* by Robert Hunter (2004), which is a first-hand account of the inaugural protest voyage from Vancouver that kick-started the world's biggest green movement.

Vancouver's best museum houses northwest coast aboriginal artifacts, including Haida houses and totem poles, plus non–First Nations exhibits like European ceramics and Cantonese opera costumes. The free guided tours are highly recommended, as is the excellent artsy gift shop. Give yourself a couple of hours at this museum.

UBC Botanical Garden   GARDEN
(Map p625; www.ubcbotanicalgarden.org; 6804 SW Marine Dr; adult/child $8/4; ⏲9am-4:30pm Mon-Fri, 9:30am-4:30pm Sat & Sun, reduced off-season) A giant collection of rhododendrons, a fascinating apothecary plot and a winter green space of off-season bloomers are highlights of this 28-hectare complex of themed gardens. The additional **Greenheart Canopy Walkway** (www.greenheartcanopywalkway. com; adult/child $20/6; ⏲9am-5pm) lifts visitors 17m above the forest floor on a 308m guided eco tour. Combined entry with Nitobe Memorial Garden is adult/child $12/6.

Nitobe Memorial Garden   GARDEN
(www.nitobe.org; 1895 Lower Mall; adult/child $8/4; ⏲10am-4pm, reduced off-season) Designed by a top Japanese landscape architect, this lovely green space is a perfect example of the Asian nation's symbolic horticultural art form. Aside from some traffic noise and summer bus tours, it's a

tranquil retreat, ideal for quiet meditation. Combined entry with the botanical garden is adult/child $12/6.

Pacific Spirit Regional Park   PARK
(Map p625; cnr Blanca & W 16th Aves) A stunning 763-hectare green space stretching from Burrard Inlet to the North Arm of the Fraser River, this is an idyllic spot to hug some trees and explore the 54km of walking, jogging and cycling trails. Visit the Park Centre on W 16th Ave for maps and further info.

WEST SIDE

A large, catch-all area covering City Hall and the heritage homes of Fairview, plus the strollable stores and restaurants of South Granville and beyond, there are several good reasons to visit this part of the city. And with the opening of the Canada Line SkyTrain link in 2009, it's much easier to reach and explore from downtown.

Queen Elizabeth Park   PARK
(www.vancouverparks.ca) With sports fields, manicured lawns and formal gardens, this 52-hectare spot is a local favorite. Check out the synchronized fountains at the park's summit, where you'll also find a hulking Henry Moore bronze called *Knife Edge – Two Piece*. If you want to be taken out to the

ball game, the recently restored **Nat Bailey Stadium** is a popular summer-afternoon haven for baseball fans.

Bloedel Floral Conservatory   GARDEN
(www.vancouverparks.ca; adult/child $4.76/2.43; ☺9am-8pm Mon-Fri, 10am-9pm Sat & Sun May-Aug, 10am-5pm daily Sep-Apr) Cresting the hill in Queen Elizabeth Park, this domed conservatory has three climate-controlled zones housing 400 plant species, dozens of koi carp and many free-flying tropical birds, including parrots and macaws. At time of writing, the conservatory was under threat of closure so check before heading over.

VanDusen Botanical Garden   GARDEN
(www.vandusengarden.org; 5251 Oak St; adult/child $9.75/5.25; ☺10am-4pm Nov-Feb, 10am-5pm Mar & Oct, 10am-6pm Apr, 10am-8pm May, 10am-9pm Jun-Aug, 10am-7pm Sep) Four blocks west of Queen Elizabeth Park, this garden offers a highly ornamental confection of sculptures, Canadian heritage flowers, rare plants from around the world and a popular hedge maze. The garden is one of Vancouver's top Christmas destinations, complete with thousands of twinkling fairy lights.

 Activities

With a reputation for outdoorsy locals who like nothing better than an early morning 20km jog and a lip-smacking rice-cake breakfast, Vancouver is all about being active. Popular pastimes include running, biking and kayaking, while you're also just a short hop from some serious winter-sport action in North Vancouver and West Vancouver.

Hiking & Running

For arm-swinging strolls or heart-pounding runs, the 8.8km Stanley Park seawall is mostly flat – apart from a couple of uphills where you could hang onto a passing

bike. UBC's Pacific Spirit Regional Park (p634) is also a popular running spot, with tree-lined trails marked throughout the area. If you really want a workout, try North Vancouver's **Grouse Grind**, a steep, sweat-triggering slog up the side of Grouse Mountain that's been nicknamed 'Mother Nature's Stairmaster.' You can reward yourself at the top with free-access to the resort's facilities – although you'll have to pay $10 to get down on the Skyride gondola.

Cycling

Joggers share the busy Stanley Park seawall with cyclists (and in-line skaters), necessitating a one-way traffic system to prevent bloody pileups. The sea-to-sky vistas are breathtaking, but the exposed route can be hit with crashing waves and icy winds in winter. Since slow moving, camera-wielding tourists crowd the route in summer, it's best to come early in the morning or late in the afternoon.

BRITISH COLUMBIA ACTIVITIES

COAL HARBOUR SEAWALL STROLL

An idyllic waterfront weave starting at **Canada Place** and ending at **Stanley Park** (it's about 2km), this is a perfect, sigh-triggering amble for a sunny afternoon. You'll pass the new convention centre expansion, a gaggle of bobbling floatplanes and the grassy nook of **Harbour Green Park**, where you can catch a breathtaking mountain-framed vista that will have you pulling out your camera and setting it to 'panoramic' mode. Continue past the handsome *Light Shed* artwork – a replica of one of the many marine shacks that once lined this area – then look out for the cozy houseboats bobbling in the marina near the Westin Bayshore, the hotel where Howard Hughes holed up for three months in 1972. You'll soon be on the doorstep of Stanley Park, where you can extend your walk for 8.8km around the shoreline perimeter or retire for dinner to the restaurants crowding nearby Denman St.

VANCOUVER FOR CHILDREN

Family-friendly Vancouver is stuffed with things to do with vacationing kids. Pick up a copy of the free *Kids' Guide Vancouver* flyer from racks around town and visit www.kidsvancouver.com for tips, resources and family-focused events. Car-hire companies rent car seats – legally required for young children here – for a few dollars per day, but you'll need to reserve in advance. If you're traveling around the city without a car, make sure you hop on the SkyTrain or SeaBus transit services or the miniferry to Granville Island; kids love 'em, especially the new SkyTrain cars, where they can sit up front and pretend they're driving. Children under five travel free on all transit. Childcare equipment – strollers, booster seats, cribs, baby monitors, toys etc – can be rented from the friendly folk at **Wee Travel** (☎604-222-4722; www.weetravel.ca). Your hotel can usually recommend a licensed and bonded babysitting service.

Stanley Park (p627) can keep most families occupied for a full day. If it's hot, make sure you hit the water park at Lumberman's Arch or try the swimming pool at Second Beach; also consider the **miniature railway** (p628). The park is a great place to bring a picnic, and its beaches – especially Third Beach – are highly kid-friendly. Save time for the **Vancouver Aquarium** (p627) and, if your kids have been good, consider a behind-the-scenes trainer tour.

The city's other educational family-friendly attractions include **Science World** (p629) and the **HR MacMillan Space Centre** (p632). If it's raining, you can also duck inside Canada Place for the hands-on **Port Authority Interpretation Centre** (p627).

If you time your visit right, the city has an array of family-friendly festivals, including the **Pacific National Exhibition** (p637), the **Vancouver International Children's Festival** (p637) and the fireworks fiesta known as the **Celebration of Light** (p637).

After circling the park to English Bay, energetic cyclists can continue along the north side of False Creek towards Science World, where the route heads up the south side of False Creek towards Granville Island, Vanier Park, Kitsilano Beach and, finally, UBC. This extended route, including Stanley Park, is around 25km. If you still have some energy, UBC's Pacific Spirit Regional Park (p634) has great forested bike trails, some of them with challenging uphills.

There's a plethora of bike and blade rental stores near Stanley Park's W Georgia St entrance, especially around the intersection with Denman St. One of these, **Spokes Bicycle Rentals** (Map p630; www.vancouverbikerental.com; 1798 W Georgia St), offers a handy free route map. Also pick up the *Greater Vancouver Cycling Map* ($3.95) from local convenience stores. It highlights designated routes around the region and includes resources for visiting bikers.

Kayaking & Windsurfing

It's hard to beat the joy of an early evening paddle around the coastline here, with the sun sliding languidly down the mirrored glass towers that forest the city like modern-day totem poles. With its calm waters, Vancouver is a popular spot for both veteran and novice kayakers.

Headquartered on Granville Island, the friendly folk at **Ecomarine Ocean Kayak Centre** (Map p630; www.ecomarine.com; 1668 Duranleau St; rentals 2hr/day $36/69; ⊙9am-6pm Sun-Thu & 9am-9pm Fri & Sat Jun-Aug, 10am-6pm daily Sep-May) offer equipment rentals and guided tours. Its **Jericho Beach branch** (Jericho Sailing Centre, 1300 Discovery St; ⊙9am-dusk daily May-Aug, 9am-dusk Sat & Sun Sep) organizes events and seminars where you can rub shoulders with local paddle nuts.

For those who want to be at one with the sea breeze, **Windsure Adventure Watersports** (www.windsure.com; Jericho Sailing Centre, 1300 Discovery St; surfboard/skimboard rentals per hr $18.58/4.64; ⊙9am-8pm Apr-Sep) specializes in kiteboarding, windsurfing and skimboarding and offers lessons and equipment rentals from its Jericho Beach base.

Swimming

Vancouver's best **beaches** – English Bay, Kitsilano Beach, Jericho Beach and Stanley Park's Second Beach and Third Beach – bristle with ocean swimmers in summer. For the nakedly inclined, UBC's Wreck Beach is the city's naturist haven.

Popular with families, there's an excellent – though often crowded – outdoor **swimming pool** near Second Beach in Stanley Park. Alternatively, Kitsilano Beach has a large heated outdoor **saltwater pool** (2305 Cornwall Ave; adult/child $5.10/2.52; ☺7am-8:45pm mid-May–mid-Sep). If it's raining, you'll likely prefer the indoor **Vancouver Aquatic Centre** (Map p630; 1050 Beach Ave; adult/child $5.10/2.52; ☺6:30am-9:30pm Mon-Fri, 8am-9pm Sat & Sun), which also has a sauna, whirlpool and diving tank.

☞ Tours

Architectural Institute of BC WALK
(☎604-683-8588 ext 333; www.aibc.ca; tours $5; ☺1pm Tue-Sat Jul & Aug) Two-hour guided walks around the buildings of historic neighborhoods. Six tours available.

Vancouver Urban Adventures BIKE
(☎604-451-1600, 877-451-1777; www.vancouverurbanadventures.com; tours from $25) Alongside its extensive walking-tour program, it offers a five-hour guided bike ride ($75) around the city.

Accent Cruises BOAT
(Map p630; ☎604-688-6625; www.accentcruises.ca; 1698 Duranleau St; dinner cruise $60; ☺May–mid-Oct) Popular sunset boat cruises with salmon buffet option. Departs from Granville Island.

Vancouver Trolley Company BUS
(☎604-801-5515, 888-451-5581; www.vancouvertrolley.com; adult/child $38/20) Red replica trolley buses offering hop-on-hop-off transportation around popular city stops.

Vancouver Tour Guys WALK
(☎604-690-5909; www.tourguys.ca) The scheduled walking tours of three area neighborhoods are free but gratuities (in the $5 to $10 range) are highly encouraged. Check the website for the ever-changing itinerary.

Harbour Cruises BOAT
(Map p630; ☎604-688-7246, 800-663-1500; www.boatcruises.com; north end of Denman St; adult/child $30/10; ☺May-Oct) View the city, and some unexpected wildlife, from the water on a 75-minute harbor boat tour. Dinner cruises also available.

Big Bus BUS
(☎604-299-0700, 877-299-0701; www.bigbus.ca; adult/child $38/20) Hop-on-hop-off tourist bus covering 23 attractions. Two-day option also available.

★ Festivals & Events

Dine Out Vancouver FOOD
(www.tourismvancouver.com) Two weeks of three-course tasting menus ($18, $28 or $38) at area restaurants. Mid-January.

Chinese New Year COMMUNITY
(www.vancouver-chinatown.com) Festive kaleidoscope of dancing, parades and great food held in January or February.

Winterruption ARTS
(www.winterruption.com) Granville Island brushes off the winter blues with a music and performance festival around mid-February.

Vancouver Playhouse International Wine Festival WINE
(www.playhousewinefest.com) The city's oldest and best annual wine celebration takes place in late March.

Vancouver Craft Beer Week BEER
(www.vancouvercraftbeerweek.com) The first week of May sees a boozy roster of tastings, pairing dinners and tipple-fueled shenanigans.

Vancouver International Children's Festival CHILDREN'S
(www.childrensfestival.ca) Storytelling, performance and activities in the tents at Vanier Park in mid-May.

Bard on the Beach ARTS
(www.bardonthebeach.org) A season (June to September) of four Shakespeare-related plays in Vanier Park tents.

Vancouver International Jazz Festival MUSIC
(www.coastaljazz.ca) City-wide cornucopia of superstar shows and free outdoor events from mid-June.

Car Free Vancouver Day COMMUNITY
(www.carfreevancouver.org) Neighborhoods across the city turn over their main streets around mid-June for food, music and market stalls.

Dragon Boat Festival BOAT
(www.dragonboatbc.ca) In the third week of June, a two-day splashathon of boat-racing fun.

Vancouver Folk Music Festival MUSIC
(www.thefestival.bc.ca) Folk and world music shows at Jericho Beach in mid-July.

Celebration of Light FIREWORKS
(www.celebration-of-light.com) Free international fireworks extravaganza in English Bay from late July.

Walking Tour
Stanley Park

❯ Overlooking the glassy waters of ❶ **Coal Harbour**, follow the curving seawall path into the park, looking out for cyclists and in-line skaters who haven't yet grasped the route's dual-lane system. Keeping your gaze on the water, and looking for beady-eyed blue herons along the way, you'll soon reach the ❷ **Stanley Park Information Centre**, where you can pick up a map (and maybe an ice cream) for the rest of your trek. Pull out your camera for some photos of the nearby brightly painted ❸ **totem poles**, then turn around and shoot the downtown towers and maybe a floatplane or two skittering into the harbor. Continue on towards the ❹ **Nine O'clock Gun**, which still booms across the city every night, then wind northwards to ❺ **Brockton Point** with its little white-and-red lighthouse. This is where Arnold Schwarzenegger handed the torch to Sebastian Coe just before the Winter Olympics in 2010. The adjoining downhill stretch will bring you to the oft-photographed ❻ **Girl in a Wetsuit**

sculpture and then the looming under-carriage of the towering ❼ **Lions Gate Bridge**. You'll get a blast of sea breeze as you round ❽ **Prospect Point** as well as some spectacular sea-to-sky vistas; pause here to reflect on the 2006 storm that up-rooted many of the old trees in this area. Take out your camera again for some shots of ❾ **Siwash Rock**, a slender offshore outcrop that's part of First Nations legend. If your legs are feeling wobbly, it might be time for a break soon – a good opportunity to dig into that picnic you brought along (what do you mean you forgot?). Back on your feet, push on to ❿ **Third Beach**, where you can relax on a log and let the panoramic sea views roll over you. Pick up the pace after this break, strolling past the ⓫ **swimming pool at Second Beach** and hitting the home stretch to ⓬ **English Bay**, where ice-cream shops and restorative restaurants abound.

Pride Week COMMUNITY
(www.vancouverpride.ca) From late July, parties, concerts and fashion shows culminate in a giant pride parade.

MusicFest Vancouver MUSIC
(www.musicfestvancouver.com) Showcase of choral, opera, classical, jazz and world music performances in mid-August.

Pacific National Exhibition COMMUNITY
(www.pne.bc.ca) Family-friendly shows, music concerts and a fairground from mid-August.

Vancouver International Fringe Festival ARTS
(www.vancouverfringe.com) Wild and wacky theatricals at mainstream and unconventional Granville Island venues in mid-September.

Vancouver International Film Festival ARTS
(www.viff.org) Popular two-week showcase (from late September) of Canadian and international movies.

Vancouver International Writers & Readers Festival ARTS
(www.writersfest.bc.ca) Local and international scribblers populate literary seminars, galas and public forums from mid-October.

Eastside Culture Crawl ARTS
(www.eastsideculturecrawl.com) East Vancouver artists open their studios for three days of wandering visitors in late November.

Santa Claus Parade COMMUNITY
(www.rogerssantaclausparade.com) Christmas procession in mid-November, complete with the great man himself.

🛏 Sleeping

With around 25,000 metro Vancouver hotel, hostel and B&B rooms available, the region has plenty of options to suit all tastes and budgets. While rates peak in the summer months, there are some great deals available in fall and early spring, when the weather is often amenable and the tourist crowds reduced. The **Tourism Vancouver** (www.tourismvancouver.com) website lists options and packages while the province's **Hello BC** (www.hellobc.com) service provides further information and bookings. Be aware that hotels often charge $10 to $20 for overnight parking.

DOWNTOWN

Loden Vancouver BOUTIQUE HOTEL $$$
(Map p630; 📞604-669-5060, 877-225-6336; www.theloden.com; 1177 Melville St; r from $249; ✳🔊) The definition of class, the stylish Loden is the real designer deal. Its 70 rooms combine a knowing contemporary élan with luxe accoutrements like marble-lined bathrooms and those oh-so-civilized heated floors. The attentive service is top-notch, while the glam Voya is one of the city's best hotel bars. Hit the town in style in the hotel's complimentary London taxicab.

Fairmont Pacific Rim HOTEL $$$
(Map p630; 📞604-695-5300, 888-264-6877; www.fairmont.com/pacificrim; 1038 Canada Pl; r from $350; ✳🔊🏊) This chic 400-room property opened just in time for the Olympics. Check out the wraparound text-art installation on the exterior, then nip inside to the elegant white lobby. Many rooms have city views, while the ones with waterfront vistas will blow you away as you sit in your jetted tub. High-tech flourishes include iPod docks and Nespresso machines.

Victorian Hotel HOTEL $$
(Map p630; 📞604-681-6369, 877-681-6369; www.victorianhotel.ca; 514 Homer St; r with private bathroom from $149, with shared bathroom from $129) Housed in a pair of renovated older properties, the high-ceilinged rooms at this Euro-style pension combine glossy hardwood floors, a sprinkling of antiques, an occasional bay window and plenty of heritage charm. Most are en suite, with TVs and summer fans provided, but the best rooms are in the newer extension, complete with marble-floored bathrooms.

Urban Hideaway Guesthouse GUESTHOUSE $$
(Map p630; 📞604-694-0600; www.urban-hideaway.com; 581 Richards St; d/tw/loft $109/129/149; @) This supremely cozy home-away-from-home is a good-value, word-of-mouth favorite. Tuck yourself into one of the seven comfy rooms (the loft is our favorite) or spend your time in the lounge areas downstairs. Breakfast fixings (eggs, bacon et al) are provided: you cook it yourself in the well-equipped kitchen. Bathrooms are mostly shared, although the loft is en suite.

St Regis Hotel BOUTIQUE HOTEL $$$
(Map p630; 📞604-681-1135, 800-770-7929; www.stregishotel.com; 602 Dunsmuir St; r from $220; ✳@🔊) The rooms at this art-lined

boutique sleepover in the heart of downtown exhibit a loungey élan, with leather-look wallpaper, earth-tone bedspreads, flat-screen TVs and multimedia hubs. Check out the furniture, too: it's mostly reclaimed and refinished from the old Hotel Georgia. Rates include breakfast, a business center with free-use computers and access to the nearby gym.

Samesun Backpackers Lodge HOSTEL $
(Map p630; ☎604-682-8226, 877-972-6378; www.samesun.com; 1018 Granville St; dm/r $29.50/71; @❞) Expect a party atmosphere at this lively hostel in the heart of the Granville nightclub area – there's also a hopping on-site bar if you don't quite make it out the door. The dorms, complete with funky paint jobs, are comfortably small and there's a large kitchen plus a strong lineup of social events. Free continental breakfast.

Moda Hotel BOUTIQUE HOTEL $$
(Map p630; ☎604-683-4251, 877-683-5522; www.modahotel.ca; 900 Seymour St; d from $159; ❞) The old Dufferin Hotel has been reinvented as this white-fronted, designer-flecked boutique property one block from the Granville St party area. The new rooms have loungey flourishes like mod furnishings and bold paintwork, and the bathrooms have been given a swanky makeover.

HI Vancouver Central HOSTEL $
(Map p630; ☎604-685-5335, 888-203-8333; www.hihostels.ca/vancouver; 1025 Granville St; dm/r $33.50/83; ✽@❞) Opposite the Samesun, this labyrinthine former hotel has a calmer ambience, small dorms with sinks and many private rooms – some with en suites. Continental breakfast included.

L'Hermitage Hotel BOUTIQUE HOTEL $$$
(Map p630; ☎778-327-4100, 888-855-1050; www.lhermitagevancouver.com; 788 Richards St; r from $190; ✽) Another new boutique sleepover, the look is typically designer here but there are also some handy suites with full kitchens.

WEST END

TOP CHOICE **Sylvia Hotel** HOTEL $$
(Map p630; ☎604-681-9321; www.sylviahotel.com; 1154 Gilford St; s/d/ste from $110/165/195) Generations of guests keep coming back to this ivy-covered gem for a dollop of old-world charm followed by a side order of first-name service. The lobby decor resembles a Bavarian pension – stained-glass windows and dark-wood paneling – and there's a wide array of comfortable room configurations to suit every need. The best are the 12 apartment suites, which include full kitchens and English Bay panoramas. If you don't have a room with a view, decamp to the main floor lounge to nurse a beer and watch the sunset.

Listel Vancouver BOUTIQUE HOTEL $$
(Map p630; ☎604-684-8461, 800-663-5491; www.thelistelhotel.com; 1300 Robson St; d from $169; ✽) Vancouver's self-described 'art hotel' is a graceful cut above the other properties at this end of Robson St. Attracting a grown-up gaggle of sophisticates with its gallery-style art installations (check the little hidden art space just off the lobby), the mood-lit rooms are suffused with a relaxing west-coast ambience. Adding to the artsy appeal, the on-site O'Doul's resto-bar hosts nightly live jazz.

Buchan Hotel HOTEL $$
(Map p630; ☎604-685-5354, 800-668-6654; www.buchanhotel.com; 1906 Haro St; r from $86) This cheery, tidy and good-value heritage sleepover near Stanley Park combines cheaper rooms – many with shared bathrooms, elderly furnishings and older blankets – with higher-quality and pricier en suites. The smiley front-desk staff is excellent and there are storage facilities for bikes and skis.

Riviera Hotel HOTEL $$
(Map p630; ☎604-685-1301, 888-699-5222; www.rivieraonrobson.com; 1431 Robson St; r from $119; ❞) Best of the slightly dinged but well-located apartment-style hotels crowding the Robson and Broughton intersection, the finest deals at this midsized concrete tower are the spacious one-bedroom suites. Complete with full kitchens and slightly scuffed furnishings, they easily fit small families. Free parking.

HI Vancouver Downtown HOSTEL $
(Map p630; ☎604-684-4565, 888-203-4302; www.hihostels.ca/vancouver; 1114 Burnaby St; dm/r $33.50/83.25) This quiet, purpose-built hostel has a more institutional feel than its Granville St brother (p640). Dorms are all small and rates include continental breakfast.

Blue Horizon Hotel HOTEL $$
(Map p630; ☎604-688-1411, 800-663-1333; www.bluehorizonhotel.com; 1225 Robson St; d from $159; ✽@✈) Sleek and comfortable, this slender tower-block property has

Vancouver's gay and lesbian scene is part of the city's culture rather than a subsection of it. The legalization of same-sex marriages in BC has resulted in a huge number of couples using Vancouver as a kind of gay Vegas for their destination nuptials. For more information on tying the knot, visit www.vs.gov.bc.ca/marriage/howto.html.

Vancouver's West End district – complete with its pink-painted bus shelters, fluttering rainbow flags and hand-holding locals – houses western Canada's largest 'gayborhood,' while the city's lesbian contingent is centered more on Commercial Dr.

Pick up a free copy of *Xtra!* for a crash course on the local scene, and check www.gayvancouver.net, www.gayvan.com, and www.superdyke.com for pertinent listings and resources. In the evening, start your night off at the **Fountainhead Pub** (www.thefountainheadpub.com; 1025 Davie St), the West End's loudest and proudest gay bar, with its sometimes-raucous patio. Later, move on to the scenes biggest club: **Celebrities** (Map p630; www.celebritiesnightclub.com; 1022 Davie St). For an even bigger party, don't miss the giant annual **Pride Week** (p637) in late July, which includes Vancouver's biggest street parade.

Check the online directory of the **Gay & Lesbian Business Association of BC** (www.glba.org) or pick up its glossy free brochure for listings on all manner of local businesses, from dentists to spas and hotels. You can also drop in and tap the local community at the popular **Little Sister's Book & Art Emporium** (Map p630; www.littlesisters.ca; 1238 Davie St).

business hotel–like rooms. All are corner suites with balconies.

YALETOWN
Opus Hotel Vancouver   BOUTIQUE HOTEL **$$$**
(Map p630; ☎604-642-6787, 866-642-6787; www.opushotel.com; 322 Davie St; d/ste from $210/400; ❄☎) Celebs looking for a place to be seen should look no further. The city's original designer boutique sleepover has been welcoming the likes of Justin Timberlake and that bald bloke from REM for years. The paparazzi magnets come for the chic suites, including feng-shui bed placements and luxe bathrooms with clear windows overlooking the streets (visiting exhibitionists take note). There's a stylish on-site resto-bar plus a small gym.

YWCA Hotel   HOTEL **$$**
(Map p630; ☎604-895-5830, 800-663-1424; www.ywcahotel.com; 733 Beatty St; s/d/tr $69/86/111; ❄☎⛹) One of Canada's best Ys, this popular tower near Yaletown is a useful option for those on a budget. Accommodating men, women, couples and families, it's a bustling place with a communal kitchen on every other floor and rooms ranging from compact singles to group-friendly larger quarters. All are a little institutionalized – think student study bedroom – but each has a sink and refrigerator.

Georgian Court Hotel   HOTEL **$$**
(Map p630; ☎604-682-5555, 800-663-1155; www.georgiancourt.com; 773 Beatty St; r from $160; ❄☎) A recent makeover for this discreet, European-style property hasn't changed its classic approach to high service levels and solid, dependable amenities. The spruced-up standard rooms have new carpets and curtains but the apartment-style corner suites, with their quiet, recessed bedrooms, are recommended. There's a small on-site fitness room and the Swiss-flavored William Tell Restaurant draws plenty of outside diners.

GRANVILLE ISLAND & KITSILANO
Granville Island Hotel   BOUTIQUE HOTEL **$$**
(Map p630; ☎604-683-7373, 800-663-1840; www.granvilleislandhotel.com; 1253 Johnston St; d from $159; ❄@☎) Hugging the quiet eastern tip of Granville Island, you'll be a five-minute walk from the public market here, with plenty of additional dining, shopping and theater options right on your doorstep. Characterized by contemporary west-coast decor, the rooms feature exposed wood and soothing earth tones. There's also a cool rooftop Jacuzzi, while the on-site brewpub makes its own distinctive beer (Jamaican Lager recommended).

Kitsilano Suites   APARTMENT **$$**
(☎778-833-0334; www.kitsilanosuites.com; 2465 W 6th Ave; ste $149-229; ☎) Pretend you're a

Kits local at this shingle-sided arts-and-crafts house divided into three smashing self-catering suites. Although a century old, each is lined with modern appliances without spoiling their heritage feel: think hardwood floors, claw-foot bathtubs and stained-glass windows. Each has a full kitchen (a welcome pack is included so you can chef-up your first breakfast); there are shops and restaurants nearby on W 4th Ave.

HI Vancouver Jericho Beach HOSTEL $
(☑604-224-3208, 888-203-4303; www.hihostels. ca/vancouver; 1515 Discovery St; dm/r $20/76.25; ☺May-early Oct; @☎) Resembling a Victorian hospital from the outside, this large hostel has a great outdoorsy location – especially if you're here for the sun-kissed Kitsilano vibe and the activities at nearby Jericho Beach (downtown is a 20-minute bus ride away). Rooms are basic, but extras include a large kitchen, licensed Jerry's Cove Café and bike rentals. Plan ahead and book one of the nine sought-after private rooms.

Mickey's Kits Beach Chalet B&B $$
(☑604-739-3342, 888-739-3342; www.mickeys bandb.com; 2142 W 1st Ave; d $135-175; ☎⛱) Eschewing the heritage-home approach of most Kitsilano B&Bs, this modern, Whistler-style chalet has three rooms and a tranquil, hedged-in garden terrace. Rooms – including the gabled, top-floor York Room – are decorated in a comfortable contemporary style, but only the York has an en suite bathroom. It's a family-friendly place: the hosts can supply toys, cribs and help arrange babysitters. Includes continental breakfast.

UBC & WEST SIDE
Shaughnessy Village HOTEL $$
(☑604-736-5511; www.shaughnessyvillage.com; 1125 W 12th Ave; s/d $79/101; ☒) This entertainingly kitsch sleepover – pink carpets, flowery sofas and nautical memorabilia – describes itself as a tower-block 'B&B resort.' Despite the old-school approach, it's perfectly shipshape, right down to its well-maintained rooms, which, like boat cabins, are lined with wooden cupboards and include microwaves, refrigerators and tiny en suites. Extras include cooked breakfasts, an outdoor pool and a large laundry room.

University of British Columbia Housing
HOSTEL, HOTEL $
(☑604-822-1000, 888-822-1030; www.ubccon ferences.com; hostel r from $35, apt from $49, ste from $179; ☎) You can pretend you're still a student by staying on campus at UBC. The wide variety of room types includes good-value one- or two-bed spots at the Pacific Spirit Hostel, private rooms in shared four-to six-bed apartments at Gage Towers (most with great views), and the impressive, hotel-style West Coast Suites with flat-screen TVs and slick wood-and-stone interiors. Most rooms available May to August only.

Plaza 500 HOTEL $$
(☑604-873-1811, 800-473-1811; www.plaza500. com; 500 W 12th Ave; r from $159; ❋☎) With some great views overlooking the downtown towers and the looming North Shore mountains, rooms at the Plaza 500 have a contemporary business-hotel feel. It's a mod look that's taken to the max in Fig-Mint, the property's Euro-chic resto-bar. Rates include passes to a local gym, while the nearby Canada Line SkyTrain station can have you downtown in minutes.

✗ Eating
Celebrated for an international diversity that even rival foodie cities like Toronto and Montréal can't match, Vancouver visitors can fill up on great ethnic dishes before they even start on the region's flourishing west-coast cuisine. To sample the best, just combine both approaches: try some of North America's finest sushi for lunch, then sample Fraser Valley duck or Vancouver Island lamb for a sophisticated dinner. Whatever you choose, don't miss the seafood – it's BC's greatest culinary asset.

With the city in the midst of a restaurant renaissance – barely a week goes by without a new eatery launching itself on the scene – you can tap into the latest vibe with the online reviews at www.urbandiner.ca or pick up a free copy of either *Eat Magazine* or *City Food*.

DOWNTOWN
Chambar EUROPEAN $$
(Map p630; ☑604-879-7119; www.chambar.com; 562 Beatty St; mains $14-29) This romantic, brick-lined cave – atmospherically lit by candles at night – is a great place for a lively chat among Vancouver's urban professionals. The sophisticated Euro menu includes perfectly prepared highlights like pan-seared scallops and velvet-soft lamb shank but delectable *moules et frites* are the way to go. An impressive wine and cocktail list (try a Blue Fig Martini) is coupled with a great Belgian beer menu. For more casual

fare, check out Medina Café, Chambar's daytime-only sister next door.

Templeton
BREAKFAST, BURGERS **$**

(Map p630; www.thetempleton.blogspot.com; 1087 Granville St; mains $8-12) A funky chrome-and-vinyl '50s diner with a twist, Templeton chefs up plus-sized organic burgers, addictive fries, vegetarian quesadillas and perhaps the best hangover cure in town – the 'Big Ass Breakfast.' Sadly, the mini-jukeboxes on the tables don't work, but you can console yourself with a waistline-busting chocolate-ice-cream float. Beer here is of the local microbrew variety. Avoid busy weekend peak times or you'll be queuing for ages.

C Restaurant
SEAFOOD **$$$**

(Map p630; ☎604-681-1164; www.crestaurant.com; 1600 Howe St; mains $28-40) This pioneering west-coast seafood restaurant overlooking False Creek isn't cheap (lunch is cheaper, though) but its revelatory approach to fish and shellfish makes it possibly the city's best seafood dine-out. You'll be hard-pressed to find smoked salmon with cucumber jelly served anywhere else, but there's also a reverence for simple preparation that reveals the delicate flavors in dishes such as local side-stripe prawns and northern BC scallops.

Finch's
CAFE **$**

(Map p630; www.finchteahouse.com; 353 W Pender St; mains $3-8) Arrive off-peak and you might find a seat at one of the dinged old dining tables studding this buzzing corner cafe that has a 'granny-chic' look of creaky wooden floors and junk-shop bric-a-brac. You'll be joining in the know hipsters and creative types who've been calling this their local for years. They come for good-value breakfasts (egg and soldiers from $2.50) and a range of fresh-prepared baguette sandwiches and house-made soups.

La Bodega
MEDITERRANEAN **$$**

(Map p630; www.labodegavancouver.com; 1277 Howe St; small plates $8-12) It's all about the tasting plates at this country-style tapas bar, one of the most authentic Spanish restaurants in Vancouver. Pull up a chair, order a jug of sangria and decide on a few shareable treats from the extensive menu – if you're feeling spicy, the chorizo sausage hits the spot and the Spanish meatballs are justifiably popular. There's a great atmosphere, so don't be surprised if you find yourself staying for more than a few hours.

Japadog
ASIAN FUSION **$**

(Map p630; www.japadog.com; 520 Robson St; hotdogs $8-12) You'll have spotted the patient lineups at Vancouver's three Japadog fusion hotdog stands, but these celebrated, ever-*genki* Japanese expats have now opened a small storefront with a handful of tables. The short menu is almost the same – think turkey smokies with miso-mayo sauce and bratwursts with onion, daiko and soy – but there's also a naughty choc-banana dessert dog. Cash only.

Gallery Café
CAFE **$**

(Map p630; www.thegallerycafe.ca; 750 Hornby St; mains $5-10) The mezzanine level of the Vancouver Art Gallery is home to a chatty indoor dining area complemented by one of downtown's best and biggest outdoor patios. The food is generally of the salad and sandwiches variety, but it's well worth stopping in for a drink, especially if you take your coffee (or bottled beer) out to the parasol-forested outdoor area to top up your tan.

Gorilla Food
VEGETARIAN **$**

(Map p630; www.gorillafood.com; 436 Richards St; mains $4-7.50; ☑) This smashing little subterranean eatery is lined with woodsy flourishes and the kind of fresh-faced, healthy-living vegans who will make you want to adopt a new lifestyle. Organic raw food is the approach, which means treats such as seaweed wraps and pizza made from a dehydrated seed crust topped with tomato sauce, tenderized zucchini and mashed avocado.

WEST END

Raincity Grill
WEST COAST **$$$**

(Map p630; ☎604-685-7337; www.raincitygrill.com; 1193 Denman St; mains $17-30) This excellent English Bay restaurant was sourcing and serving unique BC ingredients long before the fashion for Fanny Bay oysters and Salt Spring Island lamb took hold. It's a great showcase for fine west-coast cuisine: the $30 three-course tasting menu (served between 5pm and 6pm) is a bargain and the weekend brunch is a local legend. If you're on the move, drop by the takeout window and pick up gourmet fish and chips for $10, then head to English Bay Beach for a picnic. Excellent wine list.

Guu With Garlic
JAPANESE **$$**

(Map p630; www.guu-izakaya.com; 1689 Robson St; mains $8-14) One of the many authentic Asian bistros, sushi spots and noodle joints at Robson St's West End tip, you'll be chilling with the ESL students at this cool-ass and ultra-welcoming *izakaya* (Japanese-style pub). Heaping hot pots and steaming noodle bowls are on offer but it's best to experiment with a few Japanese bar tapas plates like black cod with miso mayo, deep-fried egg pumpkin balls or a finger-lickin' basket of *tori-karaage* chicken that will make you turn your back on KFC forever.

Lolita's
MEXICAN $$
(Map p630; www.lolitasrestaurant.com; 1326 Davie St; mains $18-25) This lively cantina is ever-popular with in-the-know West Enders for good reason: a great place to find yourself late at night, its warm and mellow party vibe makes you feel like you're hanging out with friends in a bar at the beach. Turn your taste buds on with a few rounds of gold tequila or a fruity cocktail or three, but make sure you take a booze respite with some spicy, fusionesque fare, including the wonderful halibut tacos.

Sushi Mart
JAPANESE $
(Map p630; www.sushimart.com; 1686 Robson St; mains $6-10) You'll be rubbing shoulders with chatty young Asians at the large communal dining table here, one of the best spots in town for a sushi feast in a casual setting. Check the fresh-sheet blackboard showing what's available and then tuck into expertly prepared and well-priced shareable platters of all your fave *nigiri*, *maki* and sashimi treats.

YALETOWN

Blue Water Café
SEAFOOD $$$
(Map p630; ☎604-688-8078; www.bluewatercafe.net; 1095 Hamilton St; mains $22-44) Under chef Frank Pabst's expert eye, this high-concept seafood restaurant has become Vancouver's best posh oyster bar and the pinnacle of Yaletown fine dining. House music gently percolates through the brick-lined, cobalt-blue interior, while seafood towers, arctic char and BC sablefish grace the tables inside and on the patio outside. If you feel like an adventure, head for the semicircular raw bar and watch the whirling blades prepare delectable sushi and sashimi, served with the restaurant's signature soy-seaweed dipping sauce.

Glowbal Grill Steaks & Satay
FUSION $$
(Map p630; www.glowbalgrill.com; 1079 Mainland St; mains $17-40) Casting a wide net that catches the power-lunch, after-work

and late-night fashionista crowds, this hip but unpretentious joint has a comfortable, lounge-like feel. Its menu of classy dishes fuses west-coast ingredients with Asian and Mediterranean flourishes – the prawn linguine is ace and the finger-licking satay sticks are a recommended starter. Check the glass-walled meat cellar on the counter and choose your desired steak cut.

Regional Tasting Lounge
FUSION $$
(Map p630; www.r.tl; 1130 Mainland St) An intimate, mood-lit dining room with an innovative menu approach: every three months it adds a new regional focus, which brings taste-bud-hugging treats from different parts of the world. Foodie focuses have included Italy, Spain, Greece and New Orleans, but there's always a selection of Pacific Northwest classics if you want to taste-trip BC, too. There's a three-course $29 tasting menu available daily.

GASTOWN

TOP CHOICE Judas Goat
FUSION $$
(Map p630; www.judasgoat.ca; 27 Blood Alley; small plates $6-10) This smashing 28-seat, mosaic-and-marble nook became a local foodie favorite soon after its 2010 opening. Named after the goats used to lead sheep off slaughterhouse trucks, it's nailed the art of small, simply prepared but invitingly gourmet tapas treats like beef brisket meatballs, lamb cheek wrapped in savoy cabbage and scallop tartare with pork rinds. Like its Salt Tasting Room brother next door, you'll find a good (although much shorter) wine and Spanish sherry drinks list. Arrive off-peak to avoid lineups: there's a 90-minute time limit for diners.

Acme Café
CAFE $
(Map p630; www.acmecafe.ca; 51 W Hastings St; mains $8-10) The black-and-white deco-style interior here is enough to warm up anyone on a rainy day – or maybe it's the retro-cool U-shaped counter. But it's not just about looks at this new neighborhood fixture. The hipsters flock here for good-value hearty breakfasts and heaping comfort-food lunches flavored with a gourmet flourish: meatloaf, chicken club and shrimp guacamole sandwiches are grand but why not drop by for an afternoon coffee and some house-baked fruit pie?

La Taqueria
MEXICAN $
(Map p630; www.lataqueria.ca; 322 W Hastings St; taco platters $7.50-9.50;✈) Arrive off-peak

to avoid the crush at this delightful hole-in-the-wall and you'll be able to grab a perch at the turquoise-colored counter. Listening to the grassroots Mexican soundtrack is the perfect accompaniment to a few superbly prepared soft tacos: go for the four-part combo (around $10) and choose from fillings like grilled fish, pork cheeks and house-marinated beef. Vegetarians have some tasty choices (the veggie combo is cheaper). Save room for a glass of cinnamony *horchata*.

Salt Tasting Room　　　CHEESE & CHARCUTERIE **$$**
(Map p630; www.salttastingroom.com; Blood Alley; small plates $8-15) Tucked along a cobbled back alley reputedly named after the area's former butcher trade, this atmospheric brick-lined wine bar offers around 100 interesting tipples, most of which are unusually offered by the glass. Beer fans will also find a small menu of treats, including the excellent Anchor Liberty Ale. From your communal table perch, peruse the giant blackboard of house-cured meats and regional cheeses, then go for a $15 tasting plate of three, served with piquant condiments – sharp, Brit-style piccalilli is best.

Nuba　　　MIDDLE EASTERN **$$**
(Map p630; www.nuba.ca; 207 W Hastings St; mains $8-19; 🗋) This hopping subterranean Lebanese restaurant attracts budget noshers and cool hipsters in equal measure. Try the good-value falafel plate ($9), heaped with hummus, tabbouleh, salad, pita and brown rice. It'll make you realize what wholesome, made-from-scratch food is supposed to taste like. More substantial fare – grilled lamb, Cornish hen etc – has also been added since the eatery moved from its hole-in-the-wall site across the street. Excellent service.

Deacon's Corner　　　CAFE **$**
(Map p630; www.deaconscorner.ca; 101 Main St; mains $6-13) The perfect Gastown combination of new gentrification and old-school good value, this lively neighborhood diner has been luring Vancouverites to a grubby part of town since opening day. They come for the large, hangover-busting breakfasts (biscuits with sausage, gravy and eggs is recommended if you want your weekly calorie intake in a single meal), while lunch options include good-value grilled sandwiches (go for the pulled pork) plus heaping fish and chips.

CHINATOWN

Bao Bei　　　ASIAN FUSION **$$**
(Map p630; www.bao-bei.ca; 163 Keefer St; mains $10-18) This chic-but-welcoming Chinese brasserie quickly hooked the hipsters when it opened in 2010. From its prawn and chive dumplings to its addictive short-rib-filled buns, it's brought a unique contemporary flair to eating out in the area, combined with an innovative approach to ingredients: top-of-the-range organic meat and sustainable seafood is used throughout. It's easy to find yourself seduced by the relaxed, candlelit ambience, especially if you hit the excellent cocktail menu.

Phnom Penh　　　VIETNAMESE **$$**
(Map p630; 244 E Georgia St; mains $8-18) Arrive early or late to avoid the queues at this locals' favorite eatery. The dishes here are split between Cambodian and Vietnamese soul food classics, such as crispy frog legs, spicy garlic crab and prawn- and sprout-filled pancakes. Don't leave without sampling a steamed rice cake, stuffed with pork, shrimp, coconut and scallions, and washed down with an ice-cold bottle of Tsingtao.

Hon's Wun-Tun House　　　CHINESE **$$**
(Map p630; www.hons.ca; 268 E Keefer St; mains $6-18) Part of the city's favorite Chinese restaurant minichain, Hon's flagship Chinatown branch is suffused with inviting cooking smells and clamorously noisy diners. The giant, 300-plus items menu ranges from satisfying dim sum brunches to steaming wonton soups bobbing with juicy dumplings. For something different, try the congee rice porridge, a fancy rice, soul-food dish in seafood, chicken and beef varieties.

SOUTH MAIN (SOMA) & COMMERCIAL DRIVE

Chutney Villa　　　INDIAN **$$**
(www.chutneyvilla.com; 147 E Broadway; mains $8-18) Don't be surprised to get a hug from the owner when entering this warmly enveloping South Indian restaurant that lures savvy SoMa-ites with its lusciously spiced curries (lamb *poriyal* is a favorite), best served with fluffy dosas to mop them up. There's an outstanding Sunday-brunch combo of veggie curries and piping-hot Indian coffee, plus a drinks list of bottled Indian beers, on-tap BC brews and fresh lime cordial. Come hungry and expect to share and stay long.

Foundation
VEGETARIAN **$$**

(2301 Main St; mains $6-14; 🖉) This lively vegetarian (mostly vegan) noshery is where artsy students and chin-stroking young intellectuals like to hang. Despite the clientele, it's not at all pretentious (apart from the philosophical quotes on the walls) and its mismatched Formica tables are often topped with dishes like heaping Utopian Nachos, spicy black bean burgers or hearty house-made curries – called Revolutionary Rations on the menu. Vancouver's Storm Brewing beers are also served.

Havana
LATIN, FUSION **$$**

(www.havanarestaurant.ca; 1212 Commercial Dr; mains $10-20) The granddaddy of Drive dining has still got it, hence its buzzing patio on most summer nights. Combining a rustic Latin American ambience – peruse the graffiti signatures scratched into the walls – with a roster of satisfying Afro-Cuban-southern soul-food dishes, highlights range from yam fries to slow-roasted lamb curry and perfect platters of clams, mussels and oysters.

Reef
CARIBBEAN **$$**

(www.thereefrestaurant.com; 1018 Commercial Dr; mains $11-17) With its funkily bright interior, this is a perfect rainy-night haunt. The Caribbean soul-food menu includes heaping dishes like Bajan fried chicken and eye-poppingly spicy Jamaican curries, but don't ignore the cornmeal johnny cakes that usually arrive free at the table: you'll be planning your next visit as soon as you've finished them.

GRANVILLE ISLAND

Go Fish
SEAFOOD **$$**

(Map p630; 1505 W 1st Ave; mains $8-13) A two-minute walk west along the seawall from the Granville Island entrance, this wildly popular seafood shack is one of the city's best fish-and-chip joints, offering a choice of halibut, salmon or cod encased in crispy golden batter. The smashing (and lighter) fish tacos are highly recommended, while the ever-changing daily specials – brought in by the nearby fishing boats – often include praiseworthy scallop burgers or ahi tuna sandwiches. There's not much of a seating area, so pack your grub and continue along the seawall to Vanier Park for a picnic with the ever-watchful seagulls.

Agro Café
CAFE **$**

(Map p630; www.agrocafe.org; 1363 Railspur Alley; mains $6-10) Seemingly known only to locals and Emily Carr Uni students, this slightly hidden cafe is a smashing coffee stop with a Fair Trade commitment. But there's much more on offer here: tuck into a BC-brewed Back Hand of God Stout or a bulging ciabatta sandwich. And if you're hungry for a good start to the day, the heaping brekkies are a great fill-up (and a genuine good deal). In summer, sip your Americano outside and watch the Granville Island world go by.

Sandbar
SEAFOOD **$$$**

(Map p630; ☎604-669-9030; www.vancouverdine.com; 1535 Johnston St; mains $18-35) West-coast seafood dominates at this adult-oriented, high-ceilinged restaurant under the Granville St Bridge. The oysters, best enjoyed on the rooftop deck, are recommended and the 1800-strong wine list is something to write home about. Live music is served up Thursday to Saturday when the urban professionals drop by to loosen their ties.

KITSILANO & WEST SIDE

Maenam
THAI **$$**

(www.maenam.ca; 1938 W 4th Ave; mains $15-18) A swish, contemporary reinvention of the Thai restaurant model, this is probably unlike any Thai eatery you've been to. Sophisticated, subtle and complex traditional and international influences flavor the menu in a room with a laid-back modern lounge feel. Inviting exploration, try the *geng panaeng neua* beef curry, a sweet, salty and nutty treat suffused with aromatic basil. The mains are great value, but why not share a few smaller plates (around the $8 to $10 range) instead?

Bishop's
WEST COAST **$$$**

(☎604-738-2025; www.bishopsonline.com; 2183 W 4th Ave; mains $28-38) A pioneer of superb west-coast cuisine long before the 'locavore' fashion took hold, modest but legendary chef-owner John Bishop – he'll almost certainly drop by your table to say hi – is still at the top of his game in this charming, art-lined little restaurant. Served in an elegant, white-tablecloth room, the weekly changing menu can include stuffed rabbit loin, steamed smoked sablefish and the kind of crisp, seasonal veggies that taste like they've just been plucked from the ground.

Tojo's
JAPANESE **$$$**

(☎604-872-8050; www.tojos.com; 1133 W Broadway; mains $19-26) Hidekazu Tojo's legendary skill with the sushi knife has created one of North America's most revered sushi restaurants. Among his exquisite dishes are favorites like lightly steamed monkfish, sautéed halibut cheeks and fried red tuna wrapped with seaweed and served with plum sauce. The maplewood sushi bar seats are more sought after than a couple of front-row Stanley Cup tickets, so reserve as early as possible and make sure you sample a selection or two from the sake menu.

Vij's
INDIAN $$

(www.vijs.ca; 1480 W 11th Ave; mains $18-26) Just off S Granville St, Vij's is the high-water mark of contemporary East Indian cuisine, fusing regional ingredients, subtle global flourishes and classic ethnic dishes to produce an array of innovative flavors. The unique results range from signature wine-marinated 'lamb popsicles' to savor-worthy dishes like halibut, mussels and crab in a tomato-ginger curry. Reservations not accepted.

Naam
VEGETARIAN $$

(www.thenaam.com; 2724 W 4th Ave; mains $8-14;) Luring city vegetarians for 30 years, this casual 24-hour eatery still has the ambience of a cozy hippy hangout. But the menu and weekend brunch queues show that these guys mean business, encouraging legions of repeat diners who keep coming back for stuffed quesadillas, hearty farmers breakfasts and sesame-fried potatoes with miso gravy. Live music is a nightly fixture and there's a convivial covered patio.

Bistrot Bistro
FRENCH $$

(www.bistrotbistro.com; 1961 W 4th Ave; mains $14-19) A charming, snob-free neighborhood bistro with a casual contemporary feel, the menu here combines traditional French recipes with seasonal local ingredients and simple, flavor-revealing preparations. Ex-pect hearty nosh like apple-sweetened pork tenderloin still simmering in its skillet and the kind of robust *boeuf bourguignon* that makes lesser chefs weep.

Drinking

Distinctive new lounges and pubs are springing up in Vancouver like persistent drunks at an open bar. Wherever you end up imbibing, check out some of the region's excellent craft brews, including tasty tipples from Driftwood Brewing, Howe Sound Brewing and Central City Brewing. Granville St, from Robson to Davie Sts, is a party district of mainstream haunts, but Gastown is your best bet for brick-lined character bars.

Alibi Room
PUB

(Map p630; www.alibi.ca; 157 Alexander St) Vancouver's favorite craft-brew bar, this hopping brick-walled contemporary tavern stocks a changing roster of about 25 mostly BC beers from celebrated breweries like Phillips, Driftwood, Old Yale, Crannog, Central City and beyond. Adventurous taste-trippers, Main St hipsters and old-lag Camra (Campaign for Real Ale) drinkers alike, enjoy the $9 'frat bat' of four sample tipples: choose your own or ask to be surprised. Food-wise, go for skinny fries with chili garlic vinegar or a bulging, Pemberton-sourced burger.

Six Acres
BAR

(Map p630; www.sixacres.ca; 203 Carrall St) Perfect for a shared plate of finger food, it's just as easy to cover all the necessary food groups with the extensive beer selection here. There's a small, animated patio out front but inside is great for hiding in a candlelit corner and working your way through some exotic bottled brews, often including London Porter and the rather marvelous Draft Dodger from Phillips Brewing. Vancouver's coziest tavern, you can pull a board game from the shelf for an extended stay.

Railway Club
PUB

(Map p630; www.therailwayclub.com; 579 Dunsmuir St) Accessed via an unobtrusive wooden door next to a 7-11, this is one of the city's friendliest drinkeries and you'll fit right in as soon as you roll up to the bar – unusually for Vancouver, you have to order at the counter. Expect regional microbrews from the likes of Tree Brewing and Central City (go for its ESB) and hit the hole-in-the-wall kitchen for late-night nosh, including burgers and quesadillas. There's an eclectic roster of live music every night

Three Lions Café
PUB

(www.threelionscafe.ca; 1 E Broadway) This small, Brit-owned gastropub has a dedicated local following. Pulling both Tetley and London Pride on tap, as well as a good array of bottled ciders, the service is excellent and the food (including great pies, Indian-style curries and a truly smashing lamb burger) is made to order from locally sourced ingredients. Drop by for its excellent weekend breakfast or try the ever-popular quiz night held every second Tuesday. Good spot to watch TV soccer games.

Cascade Room
BAR

(www.thecascade.ca; 2616 Main St) A warm and chat-noisy spot that's the perfect contemporary reinvention of a trad neighborhood bar. Choice bottled beers feature but the excellent 50-strong cocktail list is best:

try a Cascade Room Cocktail of bourbon, pressed apple, lime juice, vanilla bean, bitters and egg white. Food is of fine gastropub quality, with the wine-braised beef and bubble and squeak recommended. Drop by on Mondays for quiz night.

Irish Heather   PUB
(Map p630; www.irishheather.com; 210 Carrall St) One of Vancouver's best gastropubs, pull up a chair on the bar side – the floor is reclaimed Guinness barrels – and dip into a great list of Irish drafts and international bottled brews. Or head to the narrow room next door where the regular Long Table Series – beer and dinner for under $15 – has become a runaway success. A great spot for charcuterie plates or hearty, homemade fare like bangers and mash or steak and Guinness pie.

Narrow Lounge   BAR
(www.narrowlounge.com; 1893 Main St) Enter just around the corner on 3rd Ave – the red light above the door tells you if it's open – then descend into Vancouver's coolest small bar. Little bigger than a train carriage and lined with stuffed animal heads and junk-shop pictures, it's an atmospheric nook where the absence of windows means it always feels like midnight. Ask the friendly bar staff for recommendations – cocktails like the Bramble or beers such as Blue Buck Ale are popular.

UVA   BAR
(Map p630; www.uvawinebar.ca; 900 Seymour St) Possibly the city's best wine bar, this little nook combines a heritage mosaic floor and swanky white vinyl chairs that add a dash of mod class. Despite the cool look, there's a snob-free approach that will have you happily taste-tripping through a boutique drinks list carefully selected from old- and new-world delights. Combine with tasting plates from charcuterie to tangy cheese.

Steamworks Brewing Company   BREWERY
(Map p630; www.steamworks.com; 375 Water St) A giant Gastown microbrewery in a cavernous converted brick warehouse. The signature beer here is Lions Gate Lager, a good summer tipple. A favorite place for the city's after-work crowd, the pub downstairs can get noisy while the upstairs is all about serene views across to the North Shore. The menu is packed with pub classics, but the pizzas are a stand-out.

St. Augustine's   PUB
(www.staugustinesvancouver.com; 2630 Commercial Dr) Looking like a regular neighbor-

hood sports bar from the outside, step inside for Vancouver's largest array of on-tap microbrews. Most are from BC but there's usually an intriguing selection or three from south of the border. Drop by for Monday evening's cask night and you'll find an extra special tipple on offer. Food is of the standard pub-grub variety.

Diamond   BAR
(Map p630; www.di6mond.com; 6 Powell St) Look for the unassuming entrance and head upstairs and you'll suddenly find yourself in one of Vancouver's best cocktail bars. This high-ceilinged heritage room is popular with local hipsters but it's never pretentious. Try the list of perfectly nailed cocktails plus some intriguing, Asian-focused tapas plates.

☆ Entertainment

Pick up the free *Georgia Straight* – or check www.straight.com – to tap local happenings. Event tickets are available from **Ticketmaster** (www.ticketmaster.ca) but **Tickets Tonight** (www.ticketstonight.ca) also sells half-price day-of-entry tickets. Clubbers should peruse the listings at www.clubvibes.com and www.clubzone.com. Live music shows are listed in the *Straight* and at www.livevan.com. For cinema listings, visit www.cinemaclock.com.

Nightclubs

Fortune Sound Club   NIGHTCLUB
(Map p630; www.fortunesoundclub.com; 147 E Pender St) The city's best club has transformed a grungy old Eastside location – formerly the legendary Ming's Chinese Restaurant – into a slick space with the kind of genuine staff and younger, hipster-cool crowd rarely seen in Vancouver nightspots. Slide inside and you'll find a giant dance floor bristling with party-loving locals out to have a great time. Expect a long wait to get in on weekends: it's worth it, though, for Happy Ending Fridays when you'll possibly dance your ass off.

Caprice   NIGHTCLUB
(Map p630; www.capricenightclub.com; 967 Granville St) Originally a movie theater – hence the giant screen evoking its Tinseltown past – upscale Caprice is one of the Granville strip's best mainstream haunts. The cavernous two-level venue is a thumping magnet for all the local preppies and their miniskirted girlfriends, while the adjoining resto-lounge is great if you need to rest your eardrums and grab a restorative cocktail and bite to eat. Expect to line up here on weekends

when the under-25s visiting from the suburbs dominate.

Republic NIGHTCLUB
(Map p630; www.donnellynightclubs.ca; 958 Granville St) If you make it this far up Granville, you're in for a loungey change of pace from the noisy clubs at the Robson St end: Republic attracts those sophisticated over-25s who have strayed all the way from Yaletown. Start your visit with a cocktail on the 2nd-floor patio while you look over the human wreckage of staggering late-night drunks. Then hit the dance floor, open nightly. Sunday is reggae and ska classics, while Saturday offers pulsing dance shenanigans.

Shine NIGHTCLUB
(Map p630; www.shinenightclub.com; 364 Water St) With music from electro to funky house and hip-hop, Gastown's sexy subterranean Shine attracts a younger crowd and is divided into a noisy main blue room and an intimate cozy-cave red room with a 40ft chill-out sofa. The club's Bonafide Saturday indie disco and electro rave night is justifiably popular, while Wednesday's reggae, glitch and dubstep is slightly more chill.

Live Music

Biltmore Cabaret LIVE MUSIC
(www.biltmorecabaret.com; 395 Kingsway) One of Vancouver's best alternative venues has only been open in its present incarnation for a few years but it's already a firm favorite. The SoMa crowd comes for the nightly changing smorgasbord of Vancouver and visiting indie bands that run range from the Wintermitts to Tribal Soiree and Attack in Black (what do you mean you've never heard of them?). When there are no bands, DJ, poetry and film nights keep things lively, as well as Sunday's highly popular Kitty Nights burlesque show.

Commodore LIVE MUSIC
(Map p630; www.livenation.com; 868 Granville St) Up-and-coming local bands know they've finally made it when they play the city's best midsized music venue, a lovingly restored art deco ballroom that still has the bounciest dance floor in town – courtesy of stacks of tires placed under its floorboards. If you need a break from your moshing shenanigans, collapse at one of the tables lining the perimeter, catch your breath with a bottled Stella from the back bar then plunge back in.

Media Club LIVE MUSIC
(Map p630; www.themediaclub.ca; 695 Cambie St) This intimate, low-ceilinged indie space tucked underneath the back of the Queen Elizabeth Theatre books inventive local acts that mix and match the genres, so you may have the chance to see electro-symphonic or acoustic metal groups alongside power pop, hip-hop and country bands – although probably not on the same night. A great place for a loud night out (earplugs not supplied), this rivals the Railway Club and the Rickshaw for catching up-and-coming Vancouver acts.

Yale LIVE MUSIC
(Map p630; www.theyale.ca; 1300 Granville St) Blues fans should head along Granville to the Yale, a blowsy, unpretentious joint with a large stage, devoted clientele and beer-sticky dance floor. Many shows are free – check the website for details.

Cellar Restaurant & Jazz Club LIVE MUSIC
(www.cellarjazz.com; 3611 W Broadway) Chin-stroking jazz nuts might find themselves drawn to the subterranean Cellar Restaurant & Jazz Club, where serious tunes are reverentially performed. Tuesday entry is free and there are good beer specials.

Cinemas

Scotiabank Theatre CINEMA
(Map p630; www.cineplex.com; 900 Burrard St) Modern, nine-screen multiplex.

Cinemark Tinseltown CINEMA
(Map p630; www.cinemark.com; 88 W Pender St) Popular multiplex combining blockbusters and art-house films.

Pacific Cinémathéque CINEMA
(Map p630; www.cinematheque.bc.ca; 1131 Howe St) Art-house cinema screening foreign and underground movies.

Vancity Theatre CINEMA
(Map p630; www.viff.org; 1181 Seymour St) State-of-the-art facility screening festival and art-house fare.

Fifth Avenue Cinemas CINEMA
(www.festivalcinemas.ca; 2110 Burrard St) Popular venue screening indie, foreign flicks and blockbuster movies.

Theater & Classical Music

Vancouver Playhouse THEATER
(Map p630; www.vancouverplayhouse.com; cnr Hamilton & Dunsmuir Sts) Presenting a six-play season at its large civic venue.

Arts Club Theatre Company THEATER
(www.artsclub.com) Popular classics and works by contemporary Canadian playwrights are at three venues around town.

Firehall Arts Centre THEATER
(Map p630; www.firehallartscentre.ca; 280 E Cordova St) An intimate studio venue presenting 'difficult' works to an artsy crowd.

Vancouver Symphony Orchestra LIVE MUSIC
(www.vancouversymphony.ca) Fusing complex and stirring recitals with crossover shows of movie music, opera and even Shakespearean sonnets. At venues around the city.

Sports

Vancouver Canucks SPORTS
(www.canucks.com) The city's NHL team is Vancouver's leading sports franchise. Book ahead for games at downtown's Rogers Arena, also known as GM Place (Map p630).

Vancouver Whitecaps SPORTS
(www.whitecapsfc.com) Playing at the temporary Empire Field stadium until BC Place is renovated, the city's professional soccer team hits the MLS big league in 2011.

BC Lions SPORTS
(www.bclions.com) Also playing at Empire Field until BC Place is ready, Vancouver's Canadian Football League (CFL) side is ever-hungry for Grey Cup triumph.

Vancouver Canadians SPORTS
(www.canadiansbaseball.com) Watching this fun baseball team play at Nat Bailey Stadium is all about hanging out in the sun with beer and a hotdog.

🔒 Shopping

Robson St is ideal for wanton chain-store browsing, but if you're aiming your credit cards at independent retailers in Vancouver, you'll have to dig a little deeper. If you prefer an edgier look, it's hard to beat the quirky SoMa boutiques between 19th and 23rd Aves. For window shopping, Granville Island, South Granville (especially from Broadway onwards) and Kitsilano's W 4th Ave usually hit the spot. But it's Gastown that's the up-and-comer: check out the streets radiating from Maple Tree Sq for some cool hipster shopping.

Regional Assembly of Text ACCESSORIES
(www.assemblyoftext.com; 3934 Main St) The epitome of South Main eccentricity, this ironic antidote to the digital age was founded by pen-and-paper-loving art-school grads. Ink-stained fans flock here to stock up on Little Otsu journals, handmade pencil boxes and American Apparel T-shirts printed with typewriter motifs. Check out the tiny under-the-stairs reading room showcasing cool underground art, and don't miss the monthly letter-writing club (7pm, first Thursday of every month), where you can sip tea, scoff cookies and hammer away on those vintage typewriters.

John Fluevog Shoes CLOTHING
(Map p630; www.fluevog.com; 65 Water St) The cavernous Gastown flagship of Vancouver's fave shoe designer (the smaller original store still operates on Granville), Fluevog's funky shoes, sandals and thigh-hugging boots have been a fashion legend since 1970. It's tempting to try something on – some of the footwear looks like Doc Martens on acid, while others could poke your eye out from 20 paces – but beware: falling in love can happen in an instant.

Mountain Equipment Co-op OUTDOOR GEAR
(www.mec.ca; 130 W Broadway) The cavernous granddaddy of Vancouver outdoor stores, with an amazing selection of mostly own-brand clothing, kayaks, sleeping bags and clever camping gadgets: MEC has been turning campers into fully fledged outdoor enthusiasts for years. You'll have to be a member to buy, but that's easy to arrange and only costs $5. Equipment – canoes, kayaks, camping gear etc – can also be rented here.

Smoking Lily CLOTHING
(www.smokinglily.com; 3634 Main St) Quirky art-school cool is the approach at this SoMa store, where skirts, belts and halter tops are whimsically accented with prints of ants, skulls or the periodic table. Men's clothing is slowly creeping into the mix, with some fish, skull and tractor T-shirts and ties. A fun spot to browse (the staff are friendly and chatty), it's hard to imagine a better souvenir than the silk tea cozy printed with a Pierre Trudeau likeness.

Deluxe Junk CLOTHING
(Map p630; www.deluxejunk.com; 310 Cordova St) A treasure trove of antique glories, from flapper dresses to sparkly evening shoes and even the occasional old-school wedding outfit, this one of the city's best vintage-clothing stores. Mostly serving discerning females, there are also essential outfits for passing blokes, including cummerbunds and Hawaiian shirts (not usually worn to-

A tasty cornucopia of BC farm produce hits the stalls around Vancouver from June to October. Seasonal highlights include crunchy apples, lush peaches and juicy blueberries, while home-baked cakes and treats are frequent accompaniments. Don't be surprised to see zesty local cheese and a few arts and crafts added to the mix. To check out what's on offer, visit www.eatlocal.org.

» **East Vancouver Farmers Market** (Trout Lake Park north parking lot; ⊘9am-2pm Sat mid-May–mid-Oct)

» **Kitsilano Farmers Market** (Kitsilano Community Centre, 2690 Larch St; ⊘10am-2pm Sun mid-May–mid-Oct)

» **Main Street Station Farmers Market** (Map p630; Thornton Park, 1100 Station St; ⊘3-7pm Wed early Jun-Sep)

» **UBC Farm Market** (UBC; ⊘9am-1pm Sat mid-Jun–Sep)

» **West End Farmers Market** (Map p630; Nelson Park, btwn Bute & Thurlow Sts; ⊘9am-1pm Sat mid-Jun–mid-Oct)

» **Winter Farmers Market** (Wise Hall, 1882 Adanac St; ⊘10am-2pm 2nd & 4th Sat of month Nov-Apr)

gether). Check out the vintage cigarette holders – perfect for that 1940s dinner party you're time traveling back to.

Mink Chocolates   FOOD & DRINK
(Map p630; www.minkchocolates.com; 863 W Hastings St) Avoid the usual Canuck souvenirs of maple-syrup cookies and vacuum-packed salmon at this decadent designer chocolate shop in the downtown core. Trouble is, once you've selected a handful of choccy bonbons – little edible artworks embossed with prints of trees and coffee cups – you'll be lured to the drinks bar for a velvety hot chocolate. Next stop; years of addiction therapy.

Gravity Pope   CLOTHING
(www.gravitypope.com; 2205 W 4th Ave) One of a clutch of cool clothing stores strung along Kitsilano's highly browseable W 4th Ave, this unisex shop includes ultracool footwear on one side and and designer clothing for the pale and interesting set (think ironic tweed ties and printed halter tops) on the other. Don't spend all your dosh here, though: check out nearby **Vivid** and **Urban Rack**, too.

Rubber Rainbow Condom Company
                                     ACCESSORIES
(3851 Main St) Doing brisk business in its South Main location, this fun, funky condom and lube store serves all manner of experiment-inviting accessories, including studded, vibrating and 'full-fitting strawberry flavored' varieties. Ask for a selection pack if you're going to be in town for a while – you never know how lucky you might get.

Coastal Peoples Fine Arts Gallery
                                      SOUVENIRS
(Map p630; www.coastalpeoples.com; 1024 Mainland St) This sumptuous Yaletown gallery showcases a fine selection of Inuit and northwest coast aboriginal jewelry, carvings and prints. Focusing on the high-art side of aboriginal crafts, you'll find some exquisite items here that will likely have your credit card sweating within minutes.

Meinhardt Fine Foods   FOOD & DRINK
(www.meinhardt.com; 3002 Granville St) There's a great deli and a handy next-door takeout service at this South Granville cuisine-lover's paradise – the culinary equivalent of a sex shop for fine-food fans. Check out the narrow aisles of international condiments, then start building your ideal picnic from the impressive bread, cheese and cold-cuts selection.

Red Cat Records   MUSIC STORE
(www.redcat.ca; 4332 Main St) *High Fidelity*-style record store that's a 101 intro to Vancouver's underground music scene.

Wanderlust   BOOKSTORE
(www.wanderlustore.com; 1924 W 4th Ave) Extensive travel guides, maps and accessories.

Lazy Susan's   ACCESSORIES
(www.lazysusansonline.com; 3467 Main St) A fabulous display of must-have kitsch from 1950s greetings cards to sushi-shaped building blocks and Scrabble-tile rings and cufflinks.

Barbara-Jo's Books to Cooks BOOKSTORE
(Map p630; www.bookstocooks.com; 1740 W
2nd Ave) Foodie bookstore with a menu
of cooking classes.

Information
Internet Access
Internet Coffee (104 Davie St; per hr $3.25;
⊘9am-1:30am) Twenty terminals plus fax, CD-
burning and printing services.

Vancouver Public Library (www.vpl.vancouver.
bc.ca; 350 W Georgia St; free; ⊘10am-9pm
Mon-Thu, 10am-6pm Fri & Sat, noon-5pm Sun;
@⊚) Free internet access on library computers
plus free wi-fi access with a guest card from the
information desk.

Media & Internet Resources
CBC Radio One 88.1 FM (www.cbc.ca/bc)
Canadian Broadcasting Corporation's commer-
cial-free news, talk and music station.

City of Vancouver (www.vancouver.ca)
Resource-packed official city site with downloadable maps.

CKNW 980AM (www.cknw.com) News, traffic
and talk radio station.

Georgia Straight (www.straight.com) Free
listings newspaper.

Inside Vancouver (www.insidevancouver.ca)
Stories on what to do in and around the city.

Miss 604 (www.miss604.com) Vancouver's
favorite blogger.

Tyee (www.thetyee.ca) Local online news
source.

Vancouver is Awesome (www.vancouveri
sawesome.com) Vibrant, arts-focused online
magazine.

Vancouver Magazine (www.vanmag.com)
Glossy local trend mag.

Vancouver Sun (www.vancouversun.com)
City's main daily newspaper.

Medical Services
St Paul's Hospital (1081 Burrard St; ⊘24hr)
Downtown accident and emergency.
Shoppers Drug Mart (www.shoppersdrugmart.
ca; 1125 Davie St; ⊘24hr) Pharmacy chain.

Ultima Medicentre (www.ultimamedicentre.
ca; Bentall Centre, Plaza Level, 1055 Dunsmuir
St; ⊘8am-5pm Mon-Fri) Walk-in clinic, appoint-
ments unnecessary.

Money
RBC Royal Bank (www.rbc.com; 1025 W Georgia St; ⊘9am-5pm Mon-Fri) Main bank branch
with money-exchange services.

Vancouver Bullion & Currency Exchange
(www.vbce.ca; 800 W Pender St; ⊘9am-5pm
Mon-Fri) Often the best exchange rates in town.

Post
Canada Post main outlet (349 W Georgia St;
⊘8:30am-5:30pm Mon-Fri)

Georgia Post Plus (1358 W Georgia St;
⊘9:30am-6pm Mon-Fri, 10am-4pm Sat)

Howe Street postal outlet (732 Davie St;
⊘9am-7pm Mon-Fri, 10am-5pm Sat)

Tourist Information
Tourism Vancouver visitor centre (www.tour
ismvancouver.com; 200 Burrard St; ⊘8:30am-
6pm daily Jun-Aug, 8:30am-5pm Mon-Sat
Sep-May) Free maps, city and wider BC visitor
guides and a half-price theater ticket booth.

Getting There & Away
Air
Vancouver International Airport (www.yvr.ca) is
the main west-coast hub for airlines from Canada,
the US and international locales. It's in Richmond,
a 13km (30-minute) drive from downtown.

Domestic flights arriving here include regular
Westjet (www.westjet.com) and **Air Canada**
(www.aircanada.com) services. Linked to the
main airport by free shuttle bus, the South
Terminal receives BC-only flights from smaller
airlines and floatplane operators.

Several handy floatplane services can also
deliver you directly to the Vancouver waterfront's
Seaplane Terminal. These include frequent **Harbour Air Seaplanes** (www.harbour-air.com) and
West Coast Air (www.westcoastair.com) services
from Victoria's centrally located Inner Harbour.

Boat
BC Ferries (www.bcferries.com) services arrive at Tsawwassen – an hour's drive south of
downtown – from Vancouver Island's Swartz
Bay (passenger/vehicle $14/46.75, 1½ hours)
and Nanaimo's Duke Point (passenger/vehicle
$14/46.75, two hours). Services also arrive here
from the Southern Gulf Islands (p706).

Ferries also arrive at West Vancouver's Horseshoe Bay – 30 minutes from downtown – from
Nanaimo's Departure Bay (passenger/vehicle
$14/46.75, 1½ hours), Bowen Island (passenger/
vehicle $9.75/27.90, 20 minutes) and Langdale
(passenger/vehicle $12.85/43.20, 40 minutes)
on the Sunshine Coast.

Bus
Most out-of-town buses grind to a halt at Vancouver's **Pacific Central Station** (1150 Station
St). **Greyhound Canada** (www.greyhound.ca)
services arrive from Whistler (from $25, 2¾
hours), Kelowna (from $48, six hours) and Cal-
gary (from $79, 14 to 17 hours), among others.
Traveling via the BC Ferries Swartz Bay–Tsawwassen route, frequent **Pacific Coach Lines**
(www.pacificcoach.com) services trundle in
here from downtown Victoria (from $28.75, 3½

hours). PCL also operates services between Whistler, Vancouver and Vancouver International Airport (from $35, from 3½ hours). **Snowbus** (www.snowbus.com) also offers a winter-only ski bus service to and from Whistler ($30.95, three hours).

Quick Coach Lines (www.quickcoach.com) runs an express shuttle between Seattle and Vancouver, departing from downtown Seattle (US$40.85, four hours) and the city's Sea-Tac International Airport (US$54.15, 3½ hours).

Car & Motorcycle

If you're coming from Washington State in the US, you'll be on the I-5 until you hit the border town of Blaine, then on Hwy 99 in Canada. It's about an hour's drive from here to downtown Vancouver. Hwy 99 continues through downtown, across the Lions Gate Bridge to Horseshoe Bay, Squamish and Whistler.

If you're coming from the east, you'll probably be on the Trans-Canada Hwy (Hwy 1), which snakes through the city's eastern end, eventually meeting with Hastings St. If you want to go downtown, turn left onto Hastings and follow it into the city center, or continue on along the North Shore toward Whistler.

If you're coming from Horseshoe Bay, Hwy 1 heads through West Vancouver and North Vancouver before going over the Second Narrows Bridge into Burnaby. If you're heading downtown, leave the highway at the Taylor Way exit in West Vancouver and follow it over the Lions Gate Bridge toward the city center.

All the recognized car rental chains have Vancouver branches. Avis, Budget, Hertz and Thrifty also have airport branches.

Train

Trains trundle in from across Canada and the US at **Pacific Central Station** (1150 Station St). The Main Street-Science World SkyTrain station is just across the street for connections to downtown and the suburbs.

VIA Rail (www.viarail.com) services arrive from Kamloops North ($86, 10 hours), Jasper ($179, 20 hours) and Edmonton ($241, 27 hours), among others.

Amtrak (www.amtrak.com) US services arrive from Eugene (from US$67, 13½ hours), Portland (from US$50, eight hours) and Seattle (from US$35, 3½ hours).

ℹ Getting Around
To/From the Airport
SkyTrain's 16-station Canada Line (adult one-way fare to downtown $7.50 to $8.75) operates a rapid-transit train service from the airport to downtown. Trains run every eight to 20 minutes and take around 25 minutes to reach downtown's Waterfront Station.

If you prefer to cab it, budget $30 to $40 for the 30-minute taxi ride from the airport to your downtown hotel. For $10 to $20 more, consider arriving in style in a limo from **Aerocar Service** (www.aerocar.ca).

Bicycle
With routes running across town, Vancouver is a relatively good cycling city. Pick up a *Greater Vancouver Cycling Map* ($3.95) at convenience stores. Cyclists can take their bikes for free on SkyTrains, SeaBuses and rack-fitted transit buses. Additional maps and resources are available at the **City of Vancouver** (www.vancouver.ca/cycling) website.

Boat
Running mini vessels (some big enough to carry bikes) between the foot of Hornby St and Granville Island, **Aquabus Ferries** (www.theaquabus.com) services spots along False Creek as far as Science World. Its cutthroat rival is **False Creek Ferries** (www.granvilleislandferries.bc.ca), which operates a similar Granville Island service from the Aquatic Centre, plus additional ports of call around False Creek.

Car & Motorcycle
The rush-hour vehicle lineup to cross the Lions Gate Bridge to the North Shore frequently snakes far up W Georgia St. Try the alternative Second Narrows Bridge. Other peak-time hot spots to avoid are the George Massey Tunnel and Hwy 1 to Surrey.

Parking is at a premium downtown: there are few free spots available on residential side streets and traffic wardens are predictably predatory. Some streets have metered parking, but pay-parking lots (from $4 per hour) are a better proposition – arrive before 9am at some for early-bird discounts. Underground parking at either Pacific Centre shopping mall or the Central Library will have you in the heart of the city.

Public Transportation
The website for **TransLink** (www.translink.bc.ca) bus, SkyTrain and SeaBus services has a useful trip-planning tool, or you can buy the handy *Getting Around* route map ($1.95) from convenience stores.

A ticket bought on any of the three services is valid for 1½ hours of travel on the entire network, depending on the zone you intend to travel in. The three zones become progressively more expensive the further you journey. One-zone tickets are adult/child $2.50/1.75, two-zone tickets $3.75/2.50 and three-zone tickets $5/3.50. An all-day, all-zone pass costs $9/7. If you're traveling after 6:30pm or on weekends or holidays, all trips are classed as one-zone fares and cost $2.50/1.75. Children under five travel free on all transit services.

Bus

The bus network is extensive in central areas and many vehicles have bike racks. All are wheelchair accessible. Exact change is required since all buses use fare machines and change is not given.

99B-Line express buses operate between the Commercial-Broadway SkyTrain station and UBC. These buses have their own limited arrival and departure points and do not use the regular bus stops.

There is also a handy night-bus system that runs every 30 minutes between 1:30am and 4am across the Lower Mainland. The last bus leaves downtown Vancouver at 3:10am. Look for the night-bus signs at designated stops.

SeaBus

The aquatic shuttle SeaBus operates every 15 to 30 minutes throughout the day, taking 12 minutes to cross the Burrard Inlet between Waterfront Station and Lonsdale Quay. At Lonsdale there's a bus terminal servicing routes throughout North Vancouver and West Vancouver. Services depart from Waterfront Station between 6:16am and 1:22am Monday to Saturday (8:16am to 11:16pm Sunday). Vessels are wheelchair accessible and bike-friendly.

SkyTrain

The SkyTrain rapid-transit network consists of three routes and is a great way to move around the region: consider taking a spin on it, even if you don't have anywhere to go.

The original 35-minute Expo Line goes to and from downtown Vancouver and Surrey, via stops throughout Burnaby and New Westminster. The Millennium Line alights near shopping malls and suburban residential districts in Coquitlam and Burnaby. Opened in late 2009, the new Canada Line links the city to the airport and Richmond.

Expo Line trains run every two to eight minutes, with services departing Waterfront Station between 5:35am and 1:15am Monday to Friday (6:50am to 1:15am Saturday; 7:15am to 12:15am Sunday). Millennium Line trains run every five to eight minutes, with services departing Waterfront Station between 5:54am and 12:31am Monday to Friday (6:54am to 12:31am Saturday; 7:54am to 11:31pm Sunday). Canada Line trains run every eight to 20 minutes throughout the day. Services run from the airport to downtown between 5:10am and 12:57am and from Waterfront Station to the airport between 4:50am and 1:05am. If you're heading for the airport from the city, make sure you board a YVR-bound train – some are heading to Richmond, not the airport.

While SkyTrain ticket prices mirror the zones used across the TransLink network, there is one notable exception. Passengers departing on Canada Line trains from the airport are charged an extra $5 AddFare when purchasing their ticket from station vending machines. You do not have to pay this extra charge when traveling to the airport from downtown.

Taxi

Flagging a downtown cab shouldn't take long, but it's easier to get your hotel to call you one. Operators include **Vancouver Taxi** (☑604-871-1111), **Black Top & Checker Cabs** (☑604-731-1111) and **Yellow Cab** (☑604-681-1111). Taxi meters start at $3.05 and add $1.73 per kilometer.

LOWER MAINLAND

Metro Vancouver – often referred to as Greater Vancouver or the Lower Mainland – is chock-full of looming mountains, crenulated coastal parks, wildlife sanctuaries, historic attractions and characterful communities, mostly within a 45-minute drive of downtown Vancouver. North Vancouver and West Vancouver together make up the North Shore, located across Burrard Inlet from Vancouver proper. For more information on the North Shore, visit www.van couversnorthshore.com.

In contrast, Richmond (and its charming Steveston enclave) lies directly south of Vancouver via Hwy 99. It's now easily accessible from the city via the Canada Line SkyTrain route .

North Vancouver

POP 45,000

A commuter 'burb for downtown professionals, the city of 'North Van' rises from the waterfront from the SeaBus stop at Lonsdale Quay, where you'll find a popular public market. It also houses a couple of the region's top visitor attractions. For information on what to do here, visit the municipal website (www.cnv.org) or pick up the free *North Shore News* paper.

◉ Sights & Activities

Capilano Suspension Bridge   PARK
(Map p625; www.capbridge.com; 3735 Capilano Rd; adult/child $29.95/10; ☺8:30am-8pm Jun-Aug, 9am-7pm May & Sep, reduced off-season) Walking gingerly across the world's longest (140m) and highest (70m) suspension bridge, swaying gently over the roiling waters of Capilano Canyon, remember that the steel cables you are gripping are embedded in huge concrete blocks on either side. That should steady your feet – unless the teenagers are stamp-

ing their way across. The region's most popular attraction – hence the summertime crowds – the grounds here include rainforest walks, totem poles and some smaller bridges strung between the trees.

Grouse Mountain
PARK
(www.grousemountain.com; 6400 Nancy Greene Way; adult/child $39/13.95; ⊙9am-10pm) This mountaintop perch is one of the region's most popular outdoor hangouts. In summer, Skyride gondola tickets to the top include access to lumberjack shows, alpine hiking trails and a grizzly-bear refuge. Pay extra for the zipline course ($105) or the new Eye of the Wind tour ($25), which takes you to the top of a 20-story wind turbine tower for spectacular views. In winter, Grouse is also a magnet for skiers and snowboarders.

FREE Lynn Canyon Park
PARK
(Map p625; Park Rd; ⊙7am-9pm May-Aug, 7am-7pm Sep-Apr) This free alternative to Capilano is a verdant North Van spot with its own slightly smaller suspension bridge. There are also plenty of excellent hiking trails and some great tree-hugging picnic spots. Check out the park's **Ecology Centre** (www.dnv.org/ecology; 3663 Park Rd; admission by donation; ⊙10am-5pm Jun-Sep, 10am-5pm Mon-Fri, noon-4pm Sat & Sun Oct-May) for displays on the area's rich biodiversity.

Mt Seymour Provincial Park
PARK
(Map p625; www.bcparks.ca; 1700 Mt Seymour Rd) A popular nature escape from the city, this ruggedly lovely, tree-lined park is suffused with summertime hiking trails that suit walkers of all abilities. Like Grouse, the area transforms in winter, when **Mt Seymour Resorts** (www.mountseymour.com) runs three lifts to take you skiing or snowboarding on its 21 runs. There's also a toboggan area and snow-tubing course.

Vancouver Eco Tours
BUS TOUR
(☑604-290-0145; www.vancouverecotours.com; adult/child $65/55) Trundle around North Shore sights – Deep Cove, Grouse Mountain etc – in green biofuel vans. See the website for free tour options.

🛏 Sleeping & Eating

Pinnacle Hotel at the Pier
HOTEL $$
(☑604-986-7437; www.pinnaclehotelatthepier.com; 138 Victory Ship Way; r from $169; ❋ 🖥 🐕) North Van's swanky new Pinnacle is an excellent option if you want to stay on this side of the water and hop over to the city center on the SeaBus, just a few minutes' walk

away. Rooms are furnished with understated elegance – the hotel balances itself nicely between business and leisure travelers – with calming pastel hues favored over bold colors. Fitness buffs will enjoy the property's large gym and pool. Harbor-view rooms are recommended but they cost a little extra.

Grouse Inn
MOTEL $$
(☑604-988-1701, 800-779-7888; www.grouseinn.com; 1633 Capilano Rd; s/d/ste from $79/99/129; ❋ 🖥) While it looks like a small shopping mall from the outside, this family-friendly motel is favored by winter skiers and summer wilderness explorers and is stuffed with amenities. It has a playground, outdoor pool and free continental breakfast. Rooms have bright and breezy interiors – especially if you like busy, 1980s-style bedspreads – and come in a wide array of configurations, including Jacuzzi suites and larger rooms for groups.

Burgoo Bistro
FUSION $$
(www.burgoo.ca; 3 Lonsdale Ave; mains $8-16) With the feel of a cozy, rustic cabin, Burgoo's menu of comfort foods with a twist aims to warm up those North Van winter nights: the Guinness-infused Irish stew, spicy apricot lamb tagine or smile-triggering butter chicken with brown basmati rice would thaw a glacier from 50 paces. If all you fancy is a few beers, dip into the dark and hoppy Burgoo Brew or the blackcurranty Middle Mountain Black Mead. Live jazz on Sunday nights.

Observatory
WEST COAST $$$
(☑604-998-4403; www.grousemountain.com; Grouse Mountain; mains $35-40) Clinging gamely to the top of Grouse Mountain, this fine dining spot serves up dishes of seared scallops and beef tenderloin along with the region's best views of nighttime Vancouver, twinkling in the valley far below.

Altitudes Bistro
BURGERS, CANADIAN $$
(www.grousemountain.com; Grouse Mountain; mains $8-17) Adjoining the Observatory, the views here are almost as good and the atmosphere is decidedly more laid-back. Quality pub food in a ski-lodge setting.

ℹ Getting There & Around
SeaBus vessels arrive at Lonsdale Quay from Vancouver's Waterfront Station ($3.50, 12 minutes) every 15 to 30 minutes throughout the day. From the bus terminal at the quay, bus 236 runs to Capilano Suspension Bridge then on to the base of Grouse Mountain.

Rocky Mountaineer Vacations runs its popular **Whistler Sea to Sky Climb** (www.rockymountaineer.com) train into North Vancouver from Whistler (from $129, three hours, once daily May to mid-October).

West Vancouver

POP 42,000

Adjoining North Vancouver, the considerably more wealthy 'West Van' is studded with multilevel mansions that cling to the cliff tops and look down – in more ways than one – across the region. It's a stop-off point on the drive from downtown to the Horseshoe Bay ferry terminal and points north to Whistler. You can check out all the parochial intrigue at the city council website (www.westvancouver.ca).

⊙ Sights & Activities

Cypress Provincial Park   PARK
(www.bcparks.ca; Cypress Bowl Rd) Around 8km north of West Van along Hwy 99, Cypress Provincial Park offers great summertime hiking trails, including the fairly challenging Black Mountain Loop. In winter, the park's **Cypress Mountain** (www.cypressmountain.com) attracts well-insulated sporty types with its 38 ski runs and popular snowshoe trails. Site of the snowboard and freestyle skiing events at the 2010 Winter Olympic and Paralympic Games, it's one of the city's favorite snowbound playgrounds.

Lighthouse Park   PARK
(Map p625; cnr Beacon Lane & Marine Dr) Some of the region's oldest and most spectacular trees live within the 75-hectare Lighthouse Park, including a rare stand of original coastal forest and plenty of copper-trunked arbutus trees. About 13km of hiking trails crisscross the area, including a recommended trek that leads to Point Atkinson Lighthouse and some shimmering views across lovely Burrard Inlet. If you're driving from downtown, turn left on Marine Dr after crossing the Lions Gate Bridge.

Sewell's Sea Safari   TOUR
(604-921-3474; www.sewellsmarina.com; 6409 Bay St; adult/child $79/69; ◇Apr-Oct) Head to the marina near Horseshoe Bay to get a seat on a rigid-hulled inflatable for a two-hour high-speed ride out to sea. With the spray in your face and the wind rattling your sunglasses, keep your eyes open for possible whale-pod sightings – barking seals and soaring eagles are almost guaranteed.

🛏 Sleeping & Eating

Lighthouse Park B&B   B&B $$
(604-926-5959, 800-926-0262; www.lighthousepark.com; 4875 Water Lane; ste from $175) This elegant two-suite sleepover, complete with private entrances and a flower-decked courtyard, will have you feeling like a West Van aristo in no time. Each suite has a fridge and DVD player, as well as a decanter of sherry for that essential alfresco evening tipple. You can sober up with a stroll to nearby Point Atkinson Lighthouse.

Fraiche   WEST COAST $$$
(www.fraicherestaurant.ca; 2240 Chippendale Rd; mains $28-40) You'll fall in love with the panoramic shoreline views over the city even before you start eating at this swanky locals' favorite. Perfect Pacific Northwest is the approach here, with typical highlights on the seasonal menu including roasted Steelhead or Qualicum Bay scallops served with lobster ravioli. If you fancy a taste of the high life without the price, drop in for lunch when many dishes are under $20, or try the weekend brunch (Dungeness crab cakes recommended).

Salmon House on the Hill   SEAFOOD $$$
(www.salmonhouse.com; 2229 Folkestone Way; mains $22-30) The buttery-soft salmon dishes are always excellent, but there's also an ever-changing array of seasonal BC seafood, including delectable Fanny Bay oysters and Hecate Strait halibut.

DON'T MISS

WATERFRONT WALK FEST

Take bus 250 from downtown Vancouver and hop off along West Van's Marine Dr at the intersection with 24th St. Peruse the charming clutch of stores and coffee shops in Dundarave Village, then stroll downhill to the waterfront. Drink in the panoramic coastline views from Dundarave Pier, then weave eastwards along the shore-hugging Centennial Seawalk. On West Van's favorite promenade, you'll pass joggers, blue herons and public artworks before the 2km paved walkway comes to a stop. From here, head back up to the Marine Dr shops or weave over to Ambleside Park where you'll find a dramatic First Nations welcome figure facing the water.

Thai Pudpong THAI $
(www.thaipudpong.com; 1474 Marine Dr; mains
$8-14) Locals' fave with sweet-and-sour
classics like stir-fried squid and the excellent red curry beef.

Burnaby

POP 203,000

East of Vancouver, no-nonsense Burnaby is
a residential suburb with a strip-mall feel.
In addition, a handful of attractions aim to
keep you away from the shops.

Offering a peaceful environment, mi-
nus the hectic energy of downtown, the
pathways of **Deer Lake Park** (Map p625)
crisscross the meadows and woodlands,
circling the lake where fowl and other
wildlife hang out. The adjoining **Burnaby
Village Museum** (Map p625; www.burnaby
villagemuseum.ca; 6501 Deer Lake Ave; adult/
child/youth $10/5/7.50; ⊙11am-4:30pm May-
Aug) colorfully recreates a BC pioneer town,
complete with replica homes, businesses
and a handsome 1912 carousel. To get directly there, take the Sperling Ave exit off
Hwy 1 and follow the museum signs.

An ever-expanding homage to materi-
alism, **Metropolis at Metrotown** (www.
metropolisatmetrotown.com; ⊙10am-9pm
Mon-Fri, 9:30am-9pm Sat, 11am-6pm Sun) is
BC's biggest mall, with 470 wallet-luring
stores. Savvy shoppers arrive early in the
morning to beat the crowds then rest
their weary credit cards at the sprawling
food court ¬ Indian, Japanese and Chinese cuisines are recommended. The mall
is a 20-minute SkyTrain ride from downtown Vancouver; the mall is big enough to
warrant its own eponymous station.

For information on the area, contact
Tourism Burnaby (☑604-419-0377; www.
tourismburnaby.com).

Richmond & Steveston

POP 174,000

The new Canada Line SkyTrain link has
made the region's modern-day Chinatown
much easier to reach from downtown
Vancouver. Hop aboard and head down the
line for a half-day of Asian shopping malls –
centered on the Golden Village area –
followed by a taste-trip through Chinese,
Japanese and Vietnamese restaurants.

And don't miss the city's charming historic waterfront Steveston village, a popu-

lar destination for sunset-viewing locals
with a penchant for great fish and chips.
For information on both areas, log on to
www.tour ismrichond.com.

◉ Sights & Activities

TOP **Gulf of Georgia Cannery** MUSEUM
CHOICE (Map p625; www.gulfofgeorgiacannery.com;
12138 4th Ave; adult/child $7.80/3.90; ⊙10am-5pm
Feb-Oct) Illuminating the sights and sounds
(and smells) of the region's bygone era of
labor-intensive fish processing, this is an excellent museum in a former working cannery.
Most of the machinery remains and there's
an evocative focus on the people who used to
work here. You'll hear recorded testimonies
from old 'slimers' percolating through the
air like ghosts and see large black-and-white
blow-ups of the real staff who spent their days
immersed in entrails. Take one of the free
hourly tours, often run by former employees.

Summer Night Market MARKET
(www.summernightmarket.com; 12631 Vulcan
Way; ⊙7pm-1am Fri & Sat, 7pm-midnight Sun
mid-May–early Oct) Much larger than downtown's Chinatown version, thousands of
hungry locals are lured here every weekend
to check out the tacky vendor stands and –
more importantly – the dozens of hawker
food stalls. Don't eat before arriving and
you can taste-trip through steaming Malaysian, Korean, Japanese and Chinese treats.

Britannia Shipyard MUSEUM
(www.britannia-hss.ca; 5180 Westwater Dr;
⊙10am-6pm Tue-Sun May-Sep, 10am-4pm
Sat & Sun Oct-Apr) This fascinating
museum site of creaky old sheds housing
dusty tools, boats and reminders of the
region's gritty maritime past.

Kuan Yin Temple NOTABLE BUILDING
(Map p625; www.buddhisttemple.ca; 9160 Steveston Hwy; admission free; ⊙9:30am-5:30pm)
Modeled on Beijing's Forbidden City, this
temple's highlight is its sumptuous Gracious Hall, complete with deep-red and
gold exterior walls and a gently flaring
orange porcelain roof.

🛏 Sleeping & Eating

Fairmont Vancouver Airport HOTEL $$
(☑604-207-5200, 866-540-1414; www.fairmont.
com/vancouverairport; Vancouver International
Airport; r from $169; ❈ ☞ ☒) You can't stay
any closer to the airport than this luxury,
amenity-laden hotel, reached via a walk-
way from the US departure hall. A great

IDYLLIC ISLAND JAUNT

Just because you've found yourself running out of road in shoreline West Vancouver, it doesn't mean you have to end your adventures. You can hit the Horseshoe Bay ferry terminal – with or without your car – for a quick hop over to **Bowen Island**. Once a favored summertime retreat for colonials looking for a seaside escape from the hard work of building the province, it's now populated by a friendly clutch of writers and artists.

Once you're there – the breathtaking crossing over the glassy, tree-lined water takes around 20 minutes – you'll find yourself in a rustically charming little community that suddenly feels a million miles from big city life. Drop into the **visitor centre** (www.bowenchamber.com; 432 Cardena Rd; ⊙10am-5pm Thu-Sun mid-May–early Sep, reduced off-season) for a crash course in what to do...then set about doing it.

Scenic kayaking tours are offered by **Bowen Island Sea Kayaking** (☑604-947-9266, 800-605-2925; www.bowenislandkayaking.com; rentals 3hr/day $45/70, tours from $65). But just strolling the many relatively easy forest trails – and stopping for a picnic overlooking the waterfront – is always a good idea.

You'll likely spend a lot of time clattering along the boardwalk area near the ferry dock. This is where you'll find **Doc Morgan's Restaurant & Pub** (mains $8-22), where the chatty patios overlook the park and the harbor. Pub grub is the main focus here and the fish and chips are recommended. If you enjoy yourself so much that you decide to stay, you're only a short stroll from the **Lodge at the Old Dorm** (☑604-947-0947; www.lodgeattheolddorm.com; 460 Melmore Rd; r $95-150), a character-filled B&B dripping with art deco and arts-and-crafts accents. The six rooms are bright and comfortable – the Lady Alexandra room with its own private garden is our favorite – and the continental buffet breakfast, served on a central counter in the kitchen, is full of yummy home-baked treats. In fact, you'll probably already be considering moving here permanently.

option for boarding your long-haul flight in a trance-like state of calm. The rooms are elegantly furnished with high-end flourishes, including remote-controlled drapes and marble-lined bathrooms.

Stone Hedge B&B　　　　B&B $$
(☑604-274-1070; www.thestonehedge.com; 5511 Cathay Rd; s/d from $125/140; ▩) This surprisingly peaceful B&B is named after the large stone wall and formidable cedar hedge surrounding the property. Rooms are tastefully lined with reproduction antiques and landscape paintings. The best feature is the chintzy guest lounge, which opens directly onto a large, secluded swimming pool.

Pajo's　　　　SEAFOOD $
(www.pajos.com; the Wharf, Steveston; mains $6-9) It's hard to think of a better spot to enjoy fish and chips than Steveston's boat-bobbling wharf. Luckily, this floating, family-run local legend fully delivers. Peruse the fresh catches on the backs of the nearby fishing boats, then follow your nose down the ramp to Pajo's little ordering hatch. You'll be greeted by a friendly face and a menu more extensive than your average chippy. Go the traditional fresh-fried cod,

salmon or halibut route (with secret-recipe tartar sauce) or mix things up with a yellowfin tuna burger and zucchini sticks.

Shanghai River Restaurant　　CHINESE $$
(7381 Westminster Hwy; mains $6-18) Grab a seat overlooking the kitchen window at this cavernous contemporary northern Chinese eatery and you'll be mesmerized by the work that goes into folding what are among the best Vancouver-area dim-sum dumplings. Order shareable plates – one dish per person is best – and be careful not to squirt everyone with the delicate but ultrajuicy pork or shrimp dumplings. The braised duck and ham soup is a great winter warmer.

SEA TO SKY HIGHWAY

Otherwise known as Hwy 99, this picturesque cliffside roadway links the communities between West Vancouver and Lillooet and is the main route to Whistler from Vancouver and the Lower Mainland. Recently upgraded for the Olympics, the winding route has several worthwhile stops – especially if you're an outdoor-activity fan, history buff or lover of BC's variegated mountain landscape. 'The Mountain' radio station (107.1FM in Squamish, 102.1FM in Whistler) provides handy traffic and road-condition updates en route.

Squamish & Around

POP 15,000

Situated midway between Vancouver and Whistler, Squamish sits at the meeting point of ocean, river and alpine forest. Originally just a grungy logging town, it's now a popular base for outdoor activities, especially in summer. Head to the slick visitor center, named the **Squamish Adventure Centre** (☑604-815-4994, 866-333-2010; www.tourismsquamish.com; 38551 Loggers Lane; ☑8am-8pm Jun-Sep, 9am-6pm Oct-May), to see what's on offer. It has lots of good info and maps on area hiking and biking trails.

◉ Sights & Activities

Just before town, on Hwy 99, the **Britannia Mine Museum** (www.britanniaminemuseum. ca; adult/child $19.75/12.75; ☑9am-4:30pm) is a popular stop. Once the British Empire's largest copper mine, it's been preserved with an impressive recent restoration. The underground train tour into the pitch-black mine tunnels is a highlight and there are plenty of additional kid-friendly exhibits – including gold panning – as well as a large artsy gift shop. Plans are afoot for enhanced attractions and facilities in the next few years, so check ahead to see what's new.

About 4km before you reach Squamish, you'll hear the rushing waters of **Shannon Falls Provincial Park** (www.bcparks.ca). Pull into the parking lot and stroll the short trail to BC's third-highest waterfall, where water cascades down a 335m drop. A few picnic tables make this a good stopping point for an alfresco lunch.

Continuing your drive, you'll soon see a sheer, 652m-high granite rock face looming ahead. Attracting hardy climbers, it's called 'The Chief' and it's the highlight of **Stawamus Chief Provincial Park** (www.bcparks. ca). You don't have to be geared up to experience the summit's breathtaking vistas: there are hiking routes up the back for anyone who wants to have a go. Consider **Squamish Rock Guides** (www.squamishrockguides.com; guided climbs half-/full day from $75/115) for climbing assistance or lessons.

The 100 or so trails around Squamish draw plenty of mountain-bike enthusiasts. The **Cheekeye Fan trail** near Brackendale has some easy forested rides, while downhill thrill seekers will prefer the **Diamond**

WORTH A TRIP

WHERE BC BEGAN

Little Fort Langley's tree-lined streets and 19th-century storefronts make it one of the Lower Mainland's most picturesque historic villages, ideal for an afternoon away from Vancouver. Its main historic highlight is the colorful **Fort Langley National Historic Site** (www.pc.gc.ca/fortlangley; 23433 Mavis Ave; adult/child $7.80/3.90; ☑9am-8pm Jul & Aug, 10am-5pm Sep-Jun), perhaps the region's most important old-school landmark.

A fortified trading post since 1827, this is where James Douglas announced the creation of BC in 1858, giving the site a legitimate claim to being the province's birthplace. With costumed reenactors, re-created artisan workshops and a gold-panning area that's very popular with kids (they also enjoy charging around the wooden battlements) this is an ideal place for families who want to add a little education to their trips.

If you need an introduction before you start wading into the buildings, there's a surprisingly entertaining time-travel-themed movie presentation on offer. And make sure you check the website before you arrive: there's a wide array of events that bring the past evocatively back to life, including a summertime evening campfire program that will take you right back to the pioneer days of the 1800s.

If you're driving from Vancouver, take Hwy 1 east for 40km, then take the 232nd St exit north. Follow the signs along 232nd St until you reach the stop sign at Glover Rd. Turn right here, and continue into the village. Turn right again on Mavis Ave, just before the railway tracks. The fort's parking lot is at the end of the street.

If traveling by transit, take the SkyTrain from downtown to Surrey Central Station, then transfer to bus 501, 502 or 320 to Langley. Transfer in Langley to the C62 and alight at the intersection of 96 Ave and Glover Rd. The fort is a signposted 400m walk from here.

Head/Power Smart area, where the routes have inviting names like **Dope Slope** and **Icy Hole of Death**. Drop in on **Corsa Cycles** (www.corsacycles.com; 830-1200 Hunter Pl; bike rental per day $45; ⊙9:30am-5:30pm) for rentals and trail advice. Also check the website of the **Squamish Off Road Cycling Association** (www.sorca.ca).

Historic-train nuts should continue just past town to the smashing **West Coast Railway Heritage Park** (www.wcra.org; 39645 Government Rd; adult/child $15/10; ⊙10am-5pm). This large, mostly alfresco museum is the final resting place of BC's legendary *Royal Hudson* steam engine and has around 90 other historic railcars, including 10 working engines and the original prototype SkyTrain car. Check out the handsome new Roundhouse building, housing the park's most precious trains and artifacts.

If you prefer to travel under your own steam, **Squamish Spit** is a kiteboarding (and windsurfing) hot spot; the season runs from May to October. The website of the **Squamish Windsports Society** (www.squamishwindsports.com) is your first point of contact for weather and water conditions and information on access to the spit.

🍴 Sleeping & Eating

Howe Sound Inn & Brewing Company

INN $$

(☑604-892-2603; www.howesound.com; 37801 Cleveland Ave; r $119; 🐾) Quality rustic is the approach at this comfortable sleepover: rooms are warm and inviting with plenty of woodsy touches. There's an outdoor climbing wall where you can train for your attempt on the nearby Stawamus Chief and a sauna where you can recover afterwards. The downstairs brewpub is worth a visit even if you're not staying – yam fries and Oatmeal Stout are recommended.

Alice Lake Provincial Park   CAMPGROUND $

(☑800-689-9025; www.discovercamping.ca; campsites from $24) A large, family-friendly campground, 13km north of Squamish, with more than 100 sites. There are two shower buildings with flush toilets, and campers often indulge in activities like swimming, hiking and biking (rentals available). Consider an interpretive ranger tour through the woods (July and August only). Reserve ahead – this is one of BC's most popular campsites.

Squamish Inn on the Water   HOTEL $$

(☑604-892-9240, 800-449-8614; www.innonthewater.com; 38222 Hwy 99; d/r/ste from $28.50/79/139; 🐾) This attractive, lodge-style hotel, complete with hardwood floors and a sun-bathed riverfront patio, is just a short walk (via tunnel) to the downtown core. The lodge suites and rooms are contemporary and comfortable and there are also a few small, good-value dorm rooms with large bathrooms – you'll have to ask about these (and book ahead) since the hotel doesn't advertise them.

Grilled Fromage   SANDWICH SHOP $

(www.grilledfromage.com; 38134 Cleveland Ave; mains $4-9) If you thought a grilled cheese sandwich was just that, step inside this funkily painted spot and peruse the menu of more than 50 varieties. The Napoleon (Camembert and bacon on sourdough) is popular but go for the decadent High Roller (lobster and smoked Gruyère).

Sunflower Bakery Cafe   CAFE $

(www.sunflowerbakerycafe.com; 38086 Cleveland Ave; mains $4-9) This bright and breezy spot serves fresh wraps and bagel sandwiches plus an array of chunky cakes and bulging fruit pies that will have you committing to some heavy exercise. Good coffee pit stop.

ℹ Getting There & Away

Greyhound Canada (www.greyhound.ca) buses arrive in Squamish from Vancouver ($17, 1½ hours, seven daily) and Whistler ($14, one hour, eight daily). Slightly more salubrious **Pacific Coach Lines** (www.pacificcoach.com) buses also arrive here from downtown Vancouver ($39.20, 1½ hours, up to eight daily).

Garibaldi Provincial Park

Visiting outdoor types often make a beeline for the 1950-sq-km **Garibaldi Provincial Park** (www.bcparks.ca), justly renowned for hiking trails colored by diverse flora, abundant wildlife and panoramic wilderness vistas. Summer hikers seem magnetically drawn here but the trails also double as cross-country ski routes in winter. There are five main trail areas – directions to each are marked by the blue-and-white signs you'll see off Hwy 99.

Among the park's most popular trails, the **Cheakamus Lake hike** (3km) is relatively easy with minimal elevation. Also in this area, and just outside the provincial park, the BC Forest Service's 30-sq-km **Whistler Interpretive Forest** offers a lot of summer activities, including kayaking, fishing and mountain biking. The trailhead is 8.5km from Hwy 99, opposite Function Junction at the south end of Whistler.

The **Elfin Lakes trail** (11km) is a lovely, relatively easy day hike. For overnighters, the trail continues on to the extinct volcano of Opal Cone. There's a first-come, first-served overnight shelter once you reach Elfin, and backcountry camping ($5) is available at Red Heather, 5km from the parking lot. The trailhead parking lot is 16km east of Hwy 99.

The **Garibaldi Lake hike** (9km) is an outstanding introduction to 'Beautiful BC' wilderness, fusing scenic alpine meadows and breathtaking mountain vistas. The bright aqua hue of the undisturbed lake contrasts with the dark, jagged peak of Black Tusk rising behind it. Backcountry campsites ($5) are further up the trail at Taylor Meadows, on the lake's western shoreline.

Brandywine Falls Provincial Park

A few kilometers north of Squamish and adjacent to Hwy 99, this tree-lined 143-hectare **park** (www.bcparks.ca) is centered on a spectacular 70m waterfall. A short stroll through the forest leads to a leg-jellying platform overlooking the top of the falls, where water drops suddenly out of the trees like a giant faucet. There are also great vistas over Daisy Lake and the mountains of Garibaldi Provincial Park. A 7km looped trail leads further through the dense forest and ancient lava beds to Cal-Cheak Suspension Bridge.

WHISTLER

POP 9200

Named for the furry marmots that populate the area and whistle like deflating balloons, this gabled alpine village is one of the world's most popular ski resorts. It was home to many of the outdoor events at the 2010 Winter Olympic and Paralympic Games, so feel free to slip on your skis and aim (if only in your imagination) for a gold medal of your own.

Nestled in the shade of the formidable Whistler and Blackcomb Mountains, the wintertime village has a frosted, Christmas card look. But summer is also a popular time, with Vancouverites and international travelers lured to the lakes and crags by a wide array of activities, from mountain biking to scream-triggering zipline runs.

Centered on four main neighborhoods – approaching via Hwy 99 from the south, you'll hit Creekside first – Whistler Village is the key hub for hotels, restaurants and shops. You'll find humbler B&B-type accommodations in the quieter Village North, while the Upper Village is home to some swanky hotels, clustered around the base of Blackcomb. Don't be surprised if you get lost when you're wandering around on foot, though there are plenty of street signs and lots of people around to help with directions.

⊙ Sights

The dramatic wood-beamed **Squamish Lil'wat Cultural Centre** (www.slcc.ca; 4854 Blackcomb Way; adult/child/youth $18/8/11; ☉9:30am-5pm) showcases two quite different First Nations groups – one coastal and one interior based – with museum exhibits and artisan presentations. Entry starts with a 15-minute movie and includes a self-guided tour illuminating the heritage and modern-day indigenous communities of the region. There's a wealth of art and crafts on display (check out the amazing two-headed sea serpent carving near the entrance) and the energetic young staff encourage plenty of questions about their twin cultures.

Perched just above the village on Blackcomb, **Whistler Sliding Centre** (www.whistler slidingcentre.com; 4910 Glacier Lane; adult/child $7/free; ☉10am-5pm) hosted Olympic bobsled, luge and skeleton events and is now open to the public. You can wander exhibits and check out video footage from the track or take a general tour (adult/child $15/free) or behind-the-scenes tour (adult/child $69/59).

The recently revamped **Whistler Museum** (www.whistlermuseum.org; 4333 Main St; adult/child $7/4; ☉11am-5pm) traces the area's dramatic development, with some colorful exhibits plus evocative photos of old skiing gear and the region's pre-resort days. There's also plenty of information on the 2010 Olympics if you missed it (as well as recollections of the previous Games bid).

If you're here in summer, head to the Upper Village and the plaza in front of the Fairmont Chateau Whistler for the lively **Whistler Farmers Market** (www.whistler farmersmarket.org; ☉11am-4pm Sun, mid-Jun–mid-Oct), where you can peruse the arts and crafts and stuff your face with seasonal fruits and bakery treats.

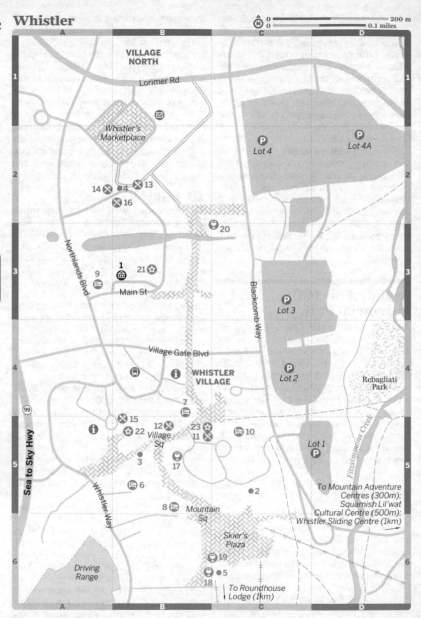

BRITISH COLUMBIA WHISTLER

☆ Activities
Skiing & Snowboarding

Comprising 38 lifts and almost 34 sq km of skiable terrain, criss-crossed with over 200 runs (more than half aimed at intermediate-level skiers), the **Whistler-Blackcomb** (www.whistlerblackcomb.com; 1-day lift ticket adult/child/youth $93/46/78) sister mountains were physically linked for the first time in 2009. The resort's mammoth 4.4km **Peak 2 Peak Gondola** includes the world's longest unsupported span and takes 11 minutes to shuttle wide-eyed powder hogs between the two high alpine areas, so you can hit the slopes on both mountains on the same day.

The winter season kicks off here in late November and runs to April on Whistler and June on Blackcomb – December to February is the peak. If you want to emulate your fave Olympic ski heroes, Whistler Creekside was the setting for all the 2010 downhill skiing events.

You can beat the crowds with an early-morning **Fresh Tracks ticket** (adult/child $17.25/12.60), which must be bought in advance at Whistler Village Gondola Guest Relations. The price includes a buffet breakfast at the Roundhouse Lodge up top. Night owls might prefer the evening **Night Moves** (adult/child $18/12) program operated via Blackcomb's Magic Chair lift after 5pm.

Snowboard fans should also check out the freestyle terrain parks, mostly located on Blackcomb, including the Snow Cross and the Big Easy Terrain Garden. There's also the popular Habitat Terrain Park on Whistler.

If you didn't bring you own gear, **Mountain Adventure Centres** (www.whistlerblackcomb.com/rentals; 1-day ski or snowboard rental adult/child from $46/32) has several equipment rental outlets around town. It offers online reservations – choose your favorite gear before you arrive – as well as lessons for ski and snowboard first timers.

Cross-country Skiing & Snowshoeing

A pleasant stroll or free shuttle bus away from the village, **Lost Lake** (www.crosscount

ryconnection.bc.ca; day pass adult/child/youth $17/8.50/10; ◔8am-9pm) is the hub for 22km of wooded cross-country ski trails, suitable for novices and experts alike. Around 4km of the trail is lit for nighttime skiing until 10pm and there's a handy 'warming hut' providing lessons and equipment rentals. Snowshoers are also well served in this area: you can stomp off on your own on 10km of trails or rent equipment and guides.

The **Whistler Olympic Park** (www.whistlerolympicpark.com; 5 Callaghan Valley Rd, Callaghan Valley) is 16km southwest of the village via Hwy 99. It hosted the 2010 Olympic biathlon, Nordic combined, cross-country skiing and ski jumping events. While the site was still being prepared on our visit after the Games, it's expected to become a prime area for public cross-country skiing and snowshoeing. Check the venue's website for the latest information.

For snowshoeing tours – including a three-hour fondue excursion – check in with **Outdoor Adventures Whistler** (www.adventureswhistler.com; 4205 Village Sq; adult/child from $69/39). Prices include equipment rentals and the company also offers a wide array of other tours and activities.

Mountain Biking

Taking over the melted ski slopes in summer and accessed via the lift at the village's south end, **Whistler Mountain Bike Park** (www.whistlerbike.com; 1-day pass adult/child/youth $53/29/47; ◔10am-8pm mid-Jun–Aug, 10am-5pm May–mid-Jun & Sep–mid-Oct) offers barreling downhill runs and an orgy of jumps, beams and bridges twisting through 200km of well-maintained forested trails. You don't have to be a bike courier to stand the knee-buckling pace: easier routes are marked in green, while blue intermediate trails and black-diamond advanced paths are offered if you want to **Crank It Up** – the name of one of the park's most popular routes. The park stages well-attended **women's nights** on Mondays and Wednesdays.

Outside the park area, winding trails around the region include **Comfortably Numb** (a tough 26km with steep climbs and bridges), **A River Runs Through It** (suitable for all skill levels, it has teeter-totters and log obstacles), and the gentle **Valley Trail**, an easy 14km loop that encircles the village and its lake, meadow and mountain-chateau surroundings – this is recommended for first timers.

Hiking

With more than 40km of flower-and-forest alpine trails, most accessed via the Whistler Village Gondola, the region is ideal for those who like nature of the strollable variety. Favorite routes include the **High Note Trail** (8km), which traverses pristine meadows and has stunning views of the blue-green waters of Cheakamus Lake. Route maps are available at the visitor centre. Guided hikes are also offered by the friendly folk at **Whistler Alpine Guides Bureau** (www.whistlerguides.com; 19-4314 Main St; guided hikes adult/child from $79/59), who can also help with rock-climbing and rap-jumping excursions.

Rafting

Tumbling waterfalls, dense forest and a menagerie of wildlife are some of what you might see as you lurch along the Elaho or Squamish Rivers on an adrenalin-charged half- or full-day rafting trip. **Whistler River Adventures** (www.whistlerriver.com; Whistler Village Gondola; adult/child/youth from $95/59/75) offers five paddle-like-crazy-or-you'll-never-make-it excursions, including the popular Green River trip, a white-water roller-coaster that'll have you whimpering and getting your pants wet just like a baby.

⭐ Festivals & Events

WinterPRIDE   COMMUNITY
(www.gaywhistler.com) A week of gay-friendly snow action and late-night partying in early February.

TELUS World Ski & Snowboard Festival   SKIING
(www.wssf.com) In mid-April, a nine-day showcase of pro ski and snowboard competitions.

Kokanee Crankworx   BIKING
(www.crankworx.com) An adrenalin-filled celebration of bike stunts, speed and shenanigans in mid-July.

Cornucopia   FOOD, WINE
(www.whistlercornucopia.com) Bacchanalian mid-November food and wine fest.

Whistler Film Festival   ARTS
(www.whistlerfilmfestival.com) Four days of Canadian and independent movie screenings, plus industry schmoozing, in late November.

🛏 Sleeping

Winter is the peak for prices here, but last-minute deals can still be had if you're planning an impromptu overnight from Vancouver – check the website of **Tourism Whistler** (www.whistler.com) for room sales and packages. Most hotels extort parking fees (up to $20 daily) and some also slap on resort fees (up to $25 daily) – confirm these before you book.

TOP CHOICE **Nita Lake Lodge**   HOTEL $$$
(☉604-966-5700, 888-755-6482; www.nitalakelodge.com; 2135 Lake Placid Rd; r from $250; ☎) Adjoining Creekside train station – handy if you're coming up on the Rocky Mountaineer Sea to Sky Climb – this swanky timber-framed lodge is perfect for a pampering retreat. Hugging the lakeside, the chic but cozy rooms feature individual patios, rock fireplaces and bathrooms with heated floors and large tubs – they also have little kitchenettes with microwaves and fridges. There's a good on-site restaurant but a free shuttle can whisk you to the village if you want to dine further afield. Creekside lifts are a walkable few minutes away.

Adara Hotel   HOTEL $$
(☏604-905-4665, 866-502-3272; www.adarahotel.com; 4122 Village Green; r from $160; ❄☎) Unlike all those smaller lodges now claiming to be boutique hotels, the sophisticated and centrally located Adara was built from scratch as the real deal. Lined with sparse but knowing designer details – including fake antler horns in the lobby – the accommodations have spa-like bathrooms, flat-screen TVs and iPod docking stations (the

DON'T MISS

WIRED FOR FUN

Stepping out into thin air 70m above the forest floor might seem like a normal activity for a cartoon character but ziplining turns out to be one of the best ways to encounter the Whistler wilderness. Attached via a body harness to the cable you're about to slide down, you soon overcome your fear of flying solo. By the end of your time in the trees, you'll be turning midair summersaults and whooping like a banshee. The two cool courses operated by **Ziptrek Ecotours** (www.ziptrek.com; adult/child from $99/79) are strung between Whistler and Blackcomb mountains and operate in both winter and summer seasons. Its newer **TreeTrek guided canopy walk** (adult/child $39/29) is a gentle web of walkways and suspension bridges for those who prefer to keep their feet on something a little more solid than air. It's ideal for families.

front desk will loan you an iPod if you've left yours at home). Despite the ultracool aesthetics, service is warm and relaxed.

HI Whistler Hostel HOSTEL $
(☑604-962-0025; www.hihostels.ca; 1035 Legacy Way; dm/r $39/153; ⊛@) Replacing Whistler's former too-small HI, this smashing new hostel repurposes part of the 2010 Olympic athletes village near Function Junction – it's 7km south of town with transit bus access. The large, lodge-like building with its IKEA-esque furnishings includes 188 beds in four-bed dorms as well as 14 sought-after en suite private rooms. There's a well-equipped kitchen plus a BBQ deck and cafe.

Riverside RV Resort & Campground
CAMPGROUND $
(☑604-905-5533; www.whistlercamping.com; 8018 Mons Rd; tent sites/cabins/yurts $35/159/99; ⊛) This warm and friendly RV property, a few minutes' drive past Whistler on Hwy 99, recently restored its tent camping spots and has also added some cool new yurts to its cozy cabins. The yurts have basic furnishings and electricity (bring your own sleeping bag) and they also have a dedicated service block with hot showers. The resort's on-site Junction Café serves great breakfasts (have the salmon eggs Benedict).

Crystal Lodge HOTEL $$
(☑604-932-2221, 800-667-3363; www.crystal-lodge.com; 4154 Village Stroll; d/ste from $130/175; ⊛⊛⊛) Not all rooms are created equal at the Crystal, a central sleepover forged from the fusion of two quite different hotel towers. Cheaper rooms in the South Tower are standard motel-style – baths and fridges are the highlight – but those in the Lodge Wing match the splendid rock-and-beam lobby, complete with small balconies. Both share excellent proximity to village restaurants and are less than 100m from the main ski lift.

Chalet Luise B&B $$
(☑604-932-4187, 800-665-1998; www.chaletluise.com; 7461 Ambassador Cres; r from $125; ⊛) A five-minute trail walk from the village, this recently renovated, Bavarian-look pension has eight bright and sunny rooms – think pine furnishings and crisp white duvets – and a flower garden that's ideal for a spot of evening wine quaffing. Or you can just hop in the hot tub and dream about the large buffet breakfast coming your way in the morning. Free parking.

Edgewater Lodge HOTEL $$
(☑604-932-0688, 888-870-9065; www.edgewater-lodge.com; 8020 Alpine Way; r from $150; ⊛) A few minutes' drive past Whistler on Hwy 99, this 12-room lakeside lodge is a nature lover's idyll and has a celebrated on-site restaurant. Each room overlooks the glassy water through a large picture window – sit in your padded window alcove and watch the ospreys or hit the surface with a kayak rental.

Blackcomb Lodge HOTEL $$
(☑604-935-1177, 888-621-1117; www.whistlerpremier.com; 4220 Gateway Dr; r/ste from $109/139; ⊛@⊛) With an excellent Village Sq location, the top rooms here have deep leather sofas, dark-wood furnishings and full kitchens, while the standard rooms without kitchens are almost as comfortable. Very close to grocery and liquor stores.

UBC Whistler Lodge HOSTEL $
(☑604-822-5851; www.ubcwhistlerlodge.com; 2124 Nordic Dr; dm summer/winter $30/40) Up a steep hill in the Nordic residential neighborhood, facilities are basic and quirky (bunks are built into the walls; rooms are separated by curtains) but the rates are a bargain.

Fairmont Chateau Whistler   HOTEL **$$$**
(☑604-938-8000, 800-606-8244; www.fairmont.
com/whistler; 4599 Chateau Blvd; r from $350)
Dramatic baronial lodge lobbies and comfortably palatial rooms, many with mountain views. Close enough to enjoy ski-in, ski-out privileges on Blackcomb.

Whistler Village Inn & Suites   HOTEL **$$**
(☑604-932-4004, 800-663-6418; www.whistler
villageinnandsuites.com; 4429 Sundial Pl; d/ste
$119/139; ☒☷) Recently renovated twin-lodge sleepover with rustic chic rooms and a free breakfast buffet. Good central location.

Pinnacle International Hotel   HOTEL **$$**
(☑604-938-3218, 888-999-8986; www.whistler
pinnacle.com; 4319 Main St; d from $139; ☏☒☷)
Friendly, well-established, adult-oriented lodge with Jacuzzi tubs in most rooms.

✖ Eating

RimRock Café   WEST COAST **$$**
(☑604-932-5565; www.rimrockwhistler.com; 2117
Whistler Rd; mains $16-22) On the edge of Creekside and accessible just off Hwy 99, the menu at this locals' favorite includes highlights like seared scallops, venison tenderloin and a recommended Seafood Trio of grilled prawns, ahi tuna and nut-crusted sablefish. All are served in an intimate room with two fireplaces and a large, flower-lined patio where you can laugh at the harried highway drivers zipping past.

Araxi Restaurant & Lounge
                  WEST COAST **$$$**
(☑604-932-4540; www.toptable.ca; 4222 Village
Sq; mains $30-45) Whistler's best splurge restaurant, Araxi chefs up an inventive and exquisite Pacific Northwest menu plus charming and courteous service. Try the BC halibut and drain the 15,000-bottle wine selection but save room for a dessert: a regional cheese plate or the amazing Okanagan apple cheesecake...or both.

Christine's Mountain Top Dining
                  CANADIAN **$$**
(☑604-938-7437; Rendezvous Lodge, Blackcomb
Mountain; mains $12-22) The best of the handful of places to eat while you're enjoying a summertime summit stroll or winter ski day on the slopes at Blackcomb Mountain. Socked into the Rendezvous Lodge, try for a view-tastic patio table and tuck into a seasonal seafood grill or a lovely applewood smoked cheddar grilled cheese sandwich. Reservations recommended.

Crepe Montagne   FRENCH **$$**
(www.crepemontagne.com; 4368 Main St; mains
$8-14) This small, authentic creperie – hence the French accents percolating among the staff – offers a bewildering array of sweet and savory buckwheat crepes with fillings including ham, brie, asparagus, banana, strawberries and more. Good breakfast spot: go the waffle route and you'll be perfectly set up for a day on the slopes.

Beet Root Café   CAFE **$**
(29-4340 Lorimer Rd; light mains $6-11) The best home-style hangout in town, pull up a cushion by the window, make yourself at home and tuck into fresh-made soup, bulging sandwiches or the excellent breakfast burritos. Stick around until you smell the cookies emerging from the oven, then scoff yourself into a happy stupor.

Gone Village Eatery   CANADIAN **$**
(www.gonevillageeatery.com; 4205 Village Sq; mains
$6-12; ☏) Hidden behind Armchair Books, this chatty, wood-floored haunt serves hearty breakfast grub (have the omelet burrito), lunch specials (sandwiches, falafel or the $10 burger-and-beer deal do the trick) and any-time-of-day baked treats (snag a chewy toffee cookie). Also a good spot to fire up your laptop and update your travel blog.

Roundhouse Lodge   FAST FOOD **$**
(Whistler Mountain; mains from $6) Handily located at the junction of several ski lifts, most powder hogs hit the Roundhouse at least once during their day atop Whistler Mountain. The giant, food-court-style approach delivers plenty of choice, so you shouldn't have any trouble stuffing your face with burgers, pizza and fish and chips. Alternatively, kick it up a notch with **Steeps Grill**, a full-service Roundhouse joint with great views and lip-smacking seafood chowder.

Sachi Sushi   JAPANESE **$$**
(106-4359 Main St; mains $8-22) Whistler's best sushi spot doesn't stop at California rolls. Serving everything from crispy popcorn shrimp to seafood salads and stomach-warming udon noodles (the tempura noodle bowl is best), this bright and breezy eatery is a relaxing après hangout. Consider a glass of hot sake on a cold winter day.

21 Steps Kitchen & Bar   CANADIAN **$$**
(www.21steps.ca; St Andrews House; mains
$14-22) With small plates for nibblers, the main dishes at this cozy upstairs spot have

a high-end comfort-food approach. Not a great place for vegetarians – unless you like stuffed Portobello mushroom – with steak, chops and seafood featuring heavily. Check out the great attic bar, a Whistlerite favorite.

Drinking & Entertainment

Garibaldi Lift Company
PUB

(Whistler Village Gondola) The closest bar to the slopes – watch the powder geeks or bike nuts on Whistler Mountain skid to a halt from the patio – the GLC is a rock-lined cave of a place. It's the ideal spot to absorb a Kootenay Mountain Ale and a bulging GLC burger while you rub your muscles and exchange exaggerated stories about your epic battles with the mountain.

Whistler Brewhouse
BREWERY

(www.markjamesgroup.com; 4355 Blackcomb Way) This lodge-like drinkery crafts its own beer on the premises and, like any artwork, the natural surroundings inspire the masterpieces, with names like Lifty Lager and Twin Peaks Pale Ale. It's an ideal pub if you want to hear yourself think, or if you just want to watch the game on one of the TVs. The food, including pasta, pizza and fish and chips, is superior to standard pub grub.

Amsterdam Café Pub
PUB

(www.amsterdampub.com; Village Sq) A brick-lined party joint with a neighborhood-pub vibe, this bar is in the heart of the village action and offers lots of drinks specials – the Alexander Keith's Pale Ale is recommended. You can treat your hangover to a late-night feast the next day or coming in for a good-value fry-up.

Longhorn Saloon & Grill
PUB

(www.longhornsaloon.ca; 4290 Mountain Sq) Fanning out near the base of Whistler Mountain with a patio that threatens to take over the town, this local legend feels like it's been here since the first skier turned up. The pub food is nothing special but it's hard to beat the atmosphere on a hopping winter evening.

Garfinkels
NIGHTCLUB

(www.garfswhistler.com; 1-4308 Main St) Mixing mainstream dance grooves with a few live bands, Whistler's biggest club is ever-popular. Arrive early on weekends when it's especially packed.

Moe Joe's
NIGHTCLUB

(www.moejoes.com; 4155 Golfer's Approach) More intimate than Garfinkels, this is the best place in town if you like dancing

yourself into a drooling heap. It's always crowded on Friday nights.

Village 8 Cinema
CINEMA

(www.village8.ca; Village Stroll) Shows first-run flicks in the heart of the village.

Information

Pick up the *Pique* or *Whistler Question* newspapers for further local insights.

Armchair Books (www.whistlerbooks.com; 4205 Village Sq; ☺9am-9pm) Central bookstore with strong travel section.

Custom House Currency Exchange (4227 Village Stroll; ☺9am-5pm May-Sep, 9am-6pm Oct-Apr) Handy central exchange.

Northlands Medical Clinic (www.northlands clinic.com; 4359 Main St; ☺9am-5:30pm) Walk-in medical center.

Post office (106-4360 Lorimer Rd; ☺8am-5pm Mon-Fri, 8am-noon Sat)

Public Library (www.whistlerlibrary.ca; 4329 Main St; ☺11am-7pm Mon-Sat, 11am-4pm Sun; ⓦ) Internet access per 10 minutes $2.50; register at front desk.

Whistler Activity Centre (4010 Whistler Way; ☺10am-6pm) Recommendations and bookings for local activities.

Whistler visitor center (www.whistler.com; 4230 Gateway Dr; ☺8am-8pm) Flyer-lined visitor center with friendly staff.

Getting There & Around

While most visitors arrive by road from Vancouver via Hwy 99, you can also fly in on a **Whistler Air** (www.whistlerair.ca) floatplane to Green Lake (round-trip $149; 51 minutes; two daily May to September).

Greyhound Canada (www.greyhound.ca) buses arrive at Creekside and Whistler Village from Vancouver (from $25, 2¾ hours, seven daily) and Squamish ($14, one hour, eight daily).

SkyLynx motor coach services from **Pacific Coach Lines** (www.pacificcoach.com) also arrive from Vancouver (from $35, 3½ hours, six daily) and Vancouver International Airport and drop off at Whistler hotels. **Snowbus** (www.snowbus.com) operates a winter-only service from Vancouver ($21, three hours, two daily).

Train spotters can trundle into town on Rocky Mountaineer Vacations' **Whistler Sea to Sky Climb** (www.rockmountaineer.com), which winds along a picturesque coastal route from North Vancouver (from $129, three hours, one daily May to mid-October).

Whistler's **WAVE** (www.busonline.ca) public buses (adult/child/one-day pass $2/1.50/5) are equipped with ski and bike racks. In summer, there's a free service from the village to Lost Lake.

SUNSHINE COAST

Stretching 139km along the water from Langdale to Lund, the Sunshine Coast – separated from the Lower Mainland by the Coast Mountains and the Strait of Georgia – has an independent, island-like mentality that belies the fact that it's only a 40-minute ferry ride from Horseshoe Bay. With Hwy 101 linking key communities like Gibsons, Sechelt and Powell River, it's an easy and convivial region to explore and there are plenty of available activities to keep things lively: think kayaking and scuba diving with a side order of artists' studios for good measure. Check the website of **Sunshine Coast Tourism** (www.sunshinecoast canada.com) for information and pick up a copy of the *Recreation Map & Attractions Guides* ($3) for activities around the region.

❶ Getting There & Around

BC Ferries (www.bcferries.com) services arrive at Langdale, 6km northeast of Gibsons, from West Vancouver's Horseshoe Bay (passenger/vehicle $12.85/43.20, 40 minutes, eight daily). Reservations recommended in summer. **Sunshine Coast Transit System** (www.busonline.ca; adult/child $2.25/1.75) runs bus services from the terminal into Gibsons, Roberts Creek and Sechelt.

Malaspina Coach Lines (www.malaspinacoach. com) buses arrive twice daily (once a day off-season) from Vancouver, via the ferry, in Gibsons ($30, two hours), Roberts Creek ($32, 2½ hours), Sechelt ($40, three hours) and Powell River ($58, five to six hours). Rates include the ferry fare.

Gibsons

POP 4100

Your first port of call after docking in Langdale and driving on to town, Gibsons' pretty waterfront strip is named Gibsons Landing and it's a rainbow of painted wooden buildings perched over the marina. Famous across Canada as the setting for *The Beachcombers,* a TV show filmed here in the 1970s that fictionalized a town full of eccentrics, the place hasn't changed much since. Head up the incline from the water and you'll hit the shops on the main drag of Upper Gibsons and Hwy 101.

Once you've finished wandering the town, kayak rentals and tours are available from the friendly folk at **Sunshine Kayaking** (www.sunshinekayaking.com; Molly's Lane; rentals 4hr/24hr $40/75; ☉9am-6pm Mon-Fri, 8am-6pm Sat & Sun). Its guided sunset ($65) and full-moon ($65) tours are especially recommended.

Your best bet for a bed in the area is **Soames Point B&B** (☑604-886-8599, 877-604-2672; www.soamespointbb.com; 1000B Marine Dr; d from $159), an immaculate and tranquil sleepover with breathtaking waterfront views. The large suite has a private entrance, vaulted ceilings and its own deck, a great spot for breakfast. At the end of the day, you can head down to the water where another deck, complete with seats and a BBQ, is ideal for a glass of wine.

While the best spot in town for a hearty breakfast and comfort food of the fish-

---

WORTH A TRIP

DETOUR TO COWBOY COUNTRY

The next town after Whistler on Hwy 99, friendly **Pemberton** (www.pemberton.ca) has a welcoming vibe and a distinctive provenance as a farming and cowboy region – which explains why the town's kitsch-cool mascot is a potato in a neckerchief called Potato Jack. Mosey on in and you'll find the area's valley location creates a milder climate than Whistler in winter – it's often much warmer in summer, too. Visitors, generally outdoorsy types, spend their time horse riding, with operators including **Pemberton Stables** (www.pembertonstables.ca; tours $45-120) and **Adventures on Horseback** (www.adventuresonhorseback.ca; 2hr tours from $75). But consider a little flying she-nanigans instead: **Pemberton Soaring Centre** (www.pembertonsoaring.com) offers 15-minute taster trips in two-person gliders (the pilot does all the work) for $94, while a spectacular 50-minute glide over the glaciers and snowcapped peaks costs $237. Sliding silently over the toy-town meadows and checking out the imposing mountains close up will likely be one of the highlights of your BC visit. Visit the town's website for a few more activity ideas. Better still, just drop into the ever-animated **Pony Espresso** (www.ponyespresso.ca; 1392 Portage Rd; mains $8-14), where the locals will be hanging out and chatting over fresh-made pasta and sandwich dishes. Time your visit for Thursday evening's beer and pizza night and you'll likely meet every Pembertonian in town.

and-chips variety is **Molly's Reach** (www. mollysreach.ca; 647 School Rd; mains $7-12), where you should certainly aim for a window seat, gourmet seafood fans shouldn't miss **Smitty's Oyster House** (www.smittys oysterhouse.com; 643 School Rd; mains $12-26), tucked just underneath. Regionally sourced and perfectly prepared treats here include Fanny Bay oysters and golden halibut fritters.

Drop by the **visitor centre** (604-886-2374, 866-222-3806; www.gibsonschamber.com; 417 Marine Dr; 9am-5pm Jul & Aug, reduced off-season) for information and resources.

Roberts Creek

POP 3100

Roberts Creek Rd, off Hwy 101, leads to the center of this former hippy enclave that retains a distinctly laid-back vibe. Follow the road through the village and amble out onto **Roberts Creek Pier**, overlooking the Strait of Georgia. Backed by a large waterfront park (there's a beach here at low tide), it's an idyllic spot to watch the natural world float by. West of town, **Roberts Creek Provincial Park** (www.bcparks.ca) is another beachfront picnic spot.

Exactly what a great hostel should be, the laid-back **Up the Creek Backpackers** (604-885-0384, 877-885-8100; www.up thecreek.ca; 1261 Roberts Creek Rd; dm/r $26/75; @) has small dorms, one private room and a predilection for recycling. The local bus stops just around the corner so you're encouraged to arrive here by transit – loaner bikes are offered to get you around once you've unpacked.

For something a little more upmarket, the **Artist & the Quiltmaker B&B** (604-741-0702, 866-570-0702; www.theartistandthequilt maker.com; 3173 Mossy Rock Rd; d from $125) is a three-room, Victorian-style property that's well worth a stop. Its large upstairs suite, complete with kitchenette, is popular with families but the lovely Renaissance Room is perfect for romantic canoodling.

For sustenance, the ever-popular **Gumboot Restaurant** (1041 Roberts Creek Rd; mains $7-14) is ideal for rubbing shoulders with the locals and scoffing a hearty dinner – check out those organic buffalo burgers and bulging, veggie-friendly Gumboot Garden sandwiches.

For more information on the area, visit www.robertscreek.com.

Sechelt

POP 8500

A useful base for active travelers, with plenty of hiking, biking, kayaking and diving opportunities, Sechelt is the second-largest town on the Sunshine Coast. It also has plenty of pit-stop amenities if you're just passing through.

With a good kayak launch site and a sandy, stroll-worthy beach, fir- and-cedar-forested **Porpoise Bay Provincial Park** (www.bcparks.ca) is 4km north of Sechelt along East Porpoise Bay Rd. There are trails throughout the park and an 84-site **camp ground** (www.discovercamping.ca; campsite $24) with handy hot showers.

For visiting paddlers (and pedalers), **Pedals & Paddles** (www.pedalspaddles.com; Tillicum Bay Marina; rentals 4hr/24hr $40/75) organizes kayak rentals or takes you on one of the tours of the inlet's wonderfully tranquil waters.

Alternatively, chat with local artists and growers at the summertime **Sechelt Farmers & Artisans Market** (www.secheltmarket. com; 8:30am-1:30pm Sat Apr-Sep), in the parking lot of the Raven's Cry Theatre, or stick around for the mid-August **Sunshine Coast Festival of the Written Arts** (www. writersfestival.ca).

If you feel like splurging on a sleepover, it's worth continuing your drive along Hwy 101 past Sechelt to **Rockwater Secret Cove Resort** (604-885-7038, 877-296-4593; www.rockwatersecretcoveresort.com; 5356 Ole's Cove Rd; r/cabin/ste/tent $209/209/249/419;) where the highlight accommodations are luxury tent suites perched like nests on a steep cliff. About as far from camping as you can get, each canvas-walled cabin has a heated rock floor, Jacuzzi tub and a private deck overlooking the bay. The resort has a good west-coast restaurant (mains $16 to $28), but if you want to hang out with the locals, head to the **Lighthouse Pub** (5764 Wharf Rd; mains $8-16), a lively neighborhood haunt where you can eavesdrop on debates about whether Gibsons is better than Powell River, while feasting on hearty pub grub and boat-bobbling waterfront vistas.

For information, drop by the **visitor centre** (604-885-1036, 877-885-1036; www. secheltvisitorcentre.com; 5790 Teredo St; 9am-5pm daily Jul & Aug, 9am-5pm Mon-Sat Jun & Sep, 10am-4pm Mon-Sat Oct-May).

ℹ SUNSHINE COAST GALLERY CRAWL

While you're pootling along Hwy 101, keep your eyes peeled for a jaunty purple flag or two fluttering in the breeze. The flags indicate that an artist is at work on the adjoining property. Pick up the *Sunshine Coast Purple Banner* flyer from area visitor centers and galleries and it will tell you where the artists are located – just in case you miss the flags – and if they're available for a drop-in visit – some prefer that you call ahead. The region is studded with art and crafts creators, working with wood, glass, clay, jewelry and just about everything else. For further information, check www.suncoastarts.com.

Powell River

POP 13,000

A short ferry hop along Hwy 101 brings you to this vibrant former resource town, which has a strong claim to being the heart and soul of the Sunshine Coast. Funkier than Sechelt and busier than Gibsons, Powell River is well worth a sleepover and is a hot spot for outdoor activities – drop by the **visitor centre** (☑604-485-4701, 877-817-8669; www.discoverpowellriver.com; 111-4871 Joyce Ave; ☺9am-9pm Mon-Fri, 10am-6pm Sat & Sun May-Sep, 9am-5pm Mon-Fri Oct-Apr) for tips and information.

West of downtown, **Willingdon Beach City Park** is ideal for a waterfront picnic. The fascinating **Powell River Museum** (www.powellrivermuseum.ca; 4798 Marine Ave; adult/child $2/1; ☺9am-4:30pm Jun-Aug, 9am-4:30pm Mon-Fri Sep-May) nearby houses a shack once occupied by Billy Goat Smith, a hermit who lived here (with his goats) in the early 1900s. Alternatively, hit the water with a kayak from **Powell River Sea Kayak** (www.bcseakayak.com; 3hr/12hr rental $35/44).

For a quirky, creaky-floored sleepover, the character-packed **Old Courthouse Inn** (☑604-483-4000, 877-483-4777; www.oldcourt houseinn.ca; 6243 Walnut St; s/d $94/109) occupies the town's former court chambers and police station. In keeping with the historic theme, its rooms are handsomely decorated with antique furnishings.

At the end of a long day of exploring, it's hard to beat a brew and a hearty meal at the **Shinglemill Pub & Bistro** (www.shin glemill.net; 6233 Powell Pl; mains $8-16). But if you're looking for something a little bit fancier, try the **Alchemist Restaurant** (www.alchemistrestaurant.com; 4680 Marine Ave; mains $19-33), where local seasonal ingredients are fused with French Mediterranean approaches to produce mouthwatering mains such as pan-seared scallops and rack of lamb served with goat-cheese ravioli. Save some room and time to sit back with the artisan cheese plate.

VANCOUVER ISLAND

The largest populated landmass off the North American coast – it's around 500km long and 100km wide – Vancouver Island is laced with colorful, often quirky communities, many founded on logging or fishing and featuring the word 'Port' in their name.

Despite the general distaste among residents for the 'too busy' mainland – a distaste that often comes from people who've never actually left the island – the locals are usually a friendly and welcoming bunch, proud of their region and its distinct differences. If you want to make a good impression, don't refer to the place as 'Victoria Island,' a frequent mistake that usually provokes involuntary eye rolls and an almost imperceptible downgrading of your welcome.

While Victoria itself – the history-wrapped BC capital that's stuffed with attractions – is the first port of call for many, it should not be the only place you visit here. Food and wine fans will enjoy weaving through the verdant Cowichan Valley farm region; those craving a laid-back, family-friendly enclave should hit the twin seaside towns of Parksville and Qualicum; outdoor-activity enthusiasts shouldn't miss the surf-loving west-coast area; and those who fancy remote backcountry far from the madding crowds should make for the north island region, an undiscovered gem that's among BC's most rewarding wilderness areas.

For an introduction to the island, contact **Tourism Vancouver Island** (☑250-754-3500; www.vancouverisland.travel) for listings and resources.

Victoria

POP 78,000

With a population approaching 350,000 when you add in the suburbs, this picture-postcard provincial capital was long touted as North America's most English city. This was a surprise to anyone who actually came from Britain, since Victoria promulgated a dreamy version of England that never really was: every garden (complete with the occasional palm tree) was immaculate; every flagpole was adorned with a Union Jack; and every afternoon was spent quaffing tea from bone-china cups.

Thankfully this tired theme-park version of Ye Olde England has gradually faded in recent years. Fuelled by an increasingly younger demographic, a quiet revolution has seen lame tourist pubs, eateries and stores transformed into the kind of bright-painted bohemian shops, wood-floored coffee bars and surprisingly innovative restaurants that would make any city proud. It's worth seeking out these enclaves on foot but activity fans should also hop on their bikes: Victoria has more cycle routes than any other Canadian city. Once you've finished exploring, there's also BC's best museum, a park that's licked with a windswept seafront and outdoor activities that include whale-watching and kayak adventures.

Sights

TOP CHOICE **Royal BC Museum** MUSEUM
(Map p676; www.royalbcmuseum.bc.ca; 675 Belleville St; adult/child $14.29/9.06; ◎10am-5pm) At the province's best museum, start at the 2nd-floor natural-history showcase fronted by a beady-eyed woolly mammoth and lined with realistic dioramas – the forest of elk and grizzlies peeking from behind trees is highly evocative. Then peruse the First Peoples exhibit and its deep exploration of indigenous culture, including a fascinating mask gallery (look for the ferret-faced white man). The best area, though, is the walk-through recreated street that re-animates the early colonial city, complete with a chatty Chinatown, highly detailed stores and a little movie house showing Charlie Chaplin films. The museum also has an **IMAX theatre**.

FREE **Parliament Buildings** HISTORICAL BUILDING
(Map p676; www.leg.bc.ca; 501 Belleville St; ◎8:30am-5pm daily May-Sep, 8:30am-5pm Mon-Fri Oct-Apr) Across from the museum, this surprisingly handsome (despite its glorious confection of turrets, domes and stained glass) building is the province's working legislature but it's also open to history-loving visitors. Peek behind the facade on a colorful 30-minute **tour** led by costumed Victorians, then stop for lunch at the 'secret' politicians' restaurant (see p679). Come back in the evening when the building's handsome exterior is lit up like a Christmas tree.

Art Gallery of Greater Victoria ART GALLERY
(Map p674; www.aggv.bc.ca; 1040 Moss St; adult/child $13/2.50; ◎10am-5pm Mon-Wed, Fri & Sat, 10am-9pm Thu, noon-5pm Sun) Head east of downtown on Fort St and follow the gallery signs to find one of Canada's best Emily Carr collections. Aside from Carr's swirling nature canvases, you'll find an ever-changing array of temporary exhibitions. Check online for events, including lectures, presentations and even singles' nights for lonely arts fans.

Craigdarroch Castle MUSEUM
(Map p674; www.thecastle.ca; 1050 Joan Cres; adult/child $13.75/5; ◎9am-7pm mid-Jun–Aug, 10am-4:30pm Sep–mid-Jun) If you're in this part of town checking out the gallery, don't miss this elegant turreted mansion a few minutes' walk away. A handsome, 39-room landmark built by a 19th-century coal baron with money to burn, it's dripping with period architecture and antique-packed rooms. Climb the tower's 87 steps (check out the stained-glass windows en route) for views of the snowcapped Olympic Mountains.

Victoria Bug Zoo ZOO
(Map p676; www.bugzoo.com; 631 Courtney St; adult/child/youth $9/6/8; ◎10am-5pm Mon-Sat, 11am-5pm Sun, reduced off-season) The most fun your wide-eyed kids will have in Victoria without even realizing it's educational, step inside the bright-painted main room for a cornucopia of show-and-tell insect encounters. The excellent guides handle and talk about critters like frog beetles, dragon-headed crickets and the disturbingly large three-horned scarab beetles, before releasing their audience (not the insects) into the gift shop.

Beacon Hill Park PARK
(Map p676) Fringed by the crashing ocean, this dramatic green space is a great spot to weather a wild storm – check out the windswept trees along the cliff top. You'll also find one of the world's tallest totem poles, a Victorian cricket pitch and a marker for

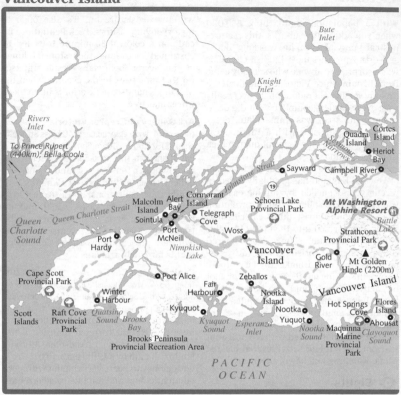

Mile 0 of Hwy 1, alongside a statue of Terry Fox, the one-legged runner whose attempted cross-Canada trek gripped the nation in 1981. If you're here with kids, check out the **children's farm** with its baby goats and wandering peacocks.

Emily Carr House   MUSEUM
(Map p674; www.emilycarr.com; 207 Government St; admission by donation; ⏱11am-4pm Tue-Sat May-Sep) The birthplace of BC's best-known painter, this bright-yellow, gingerbread-style house has plenty of period rooms and displays on the artist's life and work. There's an ever-changing array of local contemporary works on display but head to the **Art Gallery of Greater Victoria** (p671) if you want to see more of Carr's paintings.

🏃 Activities
Whale-watching
Raincoat-clad tourists head out by the boatload from Victoria throughout the May-to-October viewing season. The whales don't always show, so most excursions also visit the local haunts of elephant seal and sea lions.

Operators include the following:

Prince of Whales
(Map p676; ☎250-383-4884, 888-383-4884; www.princeofwhales.com; 812 Wharf St; adult/child $100/80) Long-established local operator.

Springtide Charters
(Map p676; ☎250-384-4444, 800-470-3474; www.springtidecharters.com; 1111 Wharf St; adult/child $99/69) Popular local operator.

Kayaking
Ambling around the coast of Vancouver Island by kayak is the perfect way to see the region, especially if you come across a few soaring eagles, lolling seals and an occasional starfish-studded beach. You can rent equipment for your own trek or join a tour of the area's watery highlights.

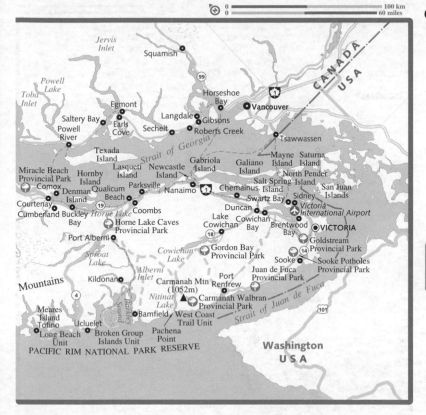

Some operators:

Ocean River Sports
(Map p676; ☎250-381-4233; www.oceanriver. com; 1824 Store St; rental 2 hr/24hr $30/48; ⏱9:30am-6pm Mon-Wed & Sat, 9:30am-8pm Thu & Fri, 10am-5pm Sun) Popular 2½-hour harbor tours ($65).

Sports Rent
(Map p676; ☎250-385-7368; www.portsrentbc. com; 1950 Government St; canoe rental 5hr/24hr $39/49; ⏱9am-5:30pm Mon-Thu, 9am-6pm Fri, 9am-5pm Sat, 10am-5pm Sun) Rents equipment like canoes as well as bikes, tents, wetsuits etc.

Scuba Diving
The region's dive-friendly underwater eco-system includes many popular spots such as Ogden Point Breakwater and 10 Mile Point.

Some established equipment rental and guide operators:

Frank Whites Dive Store
(Map p676; ☎250-385-4713; 1620 Blanshard St; www.frankwhites.com; ⏱9am-5:30pm) Scuba equipment rentals and courses.

Ogden Point Dive Centre
(☎250-380-9119, 888-701-1177; www.divevictoria. com; 199 Dallas Rd; ⏱9am-6pm) Courses, rentals etc a few minutes from the Inner Harbour.

☞ Tours

Architectural Institute of BC   WALK
(Map p676; ☎604-683-8588 ext 333, 800-667-0753; www.aibc.ca; 1001 Douglas St; tours $5; ⏱1pm Tue-Sat Jul & Aug) Five great-value, building-themed walking tours covering angles from art deco to ecclesiastical.

Harbour Air Seaplanes   PLANE
(Map p676; ☎800-665-0212, 604-274-1277; www.harbour-air.com; tours from $99) For a bird's-eye Victoria view, the 30-minute

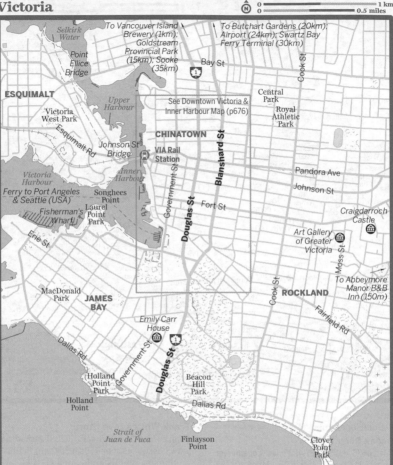

N 0 ———————— 1 km
0 ———————— 0.5 miles

floatplane tour from the Inner Harbour is fab – especially when it dive-bombs the water on landing.

Cycle Treks BIKE
(Map p676; ☎250-386-2277, 877-733-6722; www.cycletreks.com; 1000 Wharf St; tours from $99; ⊙9:30am-6pm Mon-Sat) Leads six-hour seafront-themed cycling tours.

Vancouver Island Brewery BREWERY
(Map p674; ☎250-361-0005; www.vanisland-brewery.com; 2330 Government St; tour $6; ⊙3pm Fri & Sat) Offers 30-minute tours of the plant followed by four-sample tasting.

Big Bus Victoria BUS
(Map p676; ☎250-389-2229, 888-434-2229; www.bigbusvictoria.ca; 811 Government St; adult/child $35/17) Offers 90-minute hop-on, hop-off tours around 22 local points of interest.

🎆 Festivals & Events

Dine Around Stay in Town FOOD
(www.tourismvictoria.com/dinearound) Three weeks of bargain *prix fixe* meals at many restaurants around the city; mid-February.

DON'T MISS

STROLLABLE 'HOODS

Sometimes you just need to abandon the guidebook and go for a wander. Luckily, compact and highly walkable downtown Victoria is ideal for that. Start your amble in **Chinatown**, at the handsome gate near the corner of Government and Fisgard Sts. One of Canada's oldest Asian neighborhoods, this tiny strip of businesses is studded with neon signs and traditional grocery stores, while **Fan Tan Alley** – a narrow passageway between Fisgard St and Pandora Ave – is a miniwarren of traditional and trendy stores hawking cheap and cheerful trinkets, cool used records and funky artworks. Consider a guided amble with **Hidden Dragon Tours** (www.oldchinatown. com; adult/child $29/14.50). Its three-hour evening lantern tour will tell you all about the area's historic opium dens and the hardships of 19th-century immigration.

Next up, head over to **Bastion Sq**, located between Government and Wharf Sts. Occupying the site of the old Fort Victoria, this pedestrianized plaza of scrubbed colonial strongholds is also home to the **Maritime Museum of British Columbia** (Map p676; www.mmbc.bc.ca; 28 Bastion Sq; adult/child/youth $12/6/7; ☺9:30am-5pm mid-Jun–mid-Sep, 9:30am-4:30pm mid-Sep–mid-Jun), where 400 model ships illuminate the region's rich and salty nautical heritage.

Victoria Day Parade FIESTA
Mid-May street fiesta shenanigans with dancers and marching bands.

Victoria SkaFest MUSIC
(www.victoriaskafest.ca) Canada's largest ska music event, held in mid-July.

Victoria International Jazzfest JAZZ
(www.jazzvictoria.ca) Nine days of jazz performance in late June.

Moss Street Paint-In ART
(www.aggv.bc.ca) In mid-July 100 artists demonstrate their skills at this popular one-day community event.

Victoria Fringe Theater Festival THEATER
(www.victoriafringe.com) Two weeks of quirky short plays staged throughout the city in late August.

🛏 Sleeping

From heritage B&Bs to midrange motels and swanky high-end sleepovers, Victoria is stuffed with accommodations options for all budgets. Off-season sees some great deals and Tourism Victoria's **room reservation service** (✆250-953-2033, 800-663-3883; www.tourismvictoria.com) can let you know what's available.

Swans Suite Hotel HOTEL $$$
(Map p676; ✆250-361-3310, 800-668-7926; www.swanshotel.com; 506 Pandora Ave; d/ste $199/289; 🛜) Across the street from the tiny railway station – you'll hear the train toot into town twice a day – this former old brick warehouse has been transformed into an art-lined boutique sleepover. Most rooms are spacious loft suites where you climb upstairs to bed in a gabled nook, and each is decorated with a comfy combination of wood beams, rustic chic furniture and deep leather sofas. The full kitchens are handy but continental breakfast is included.

Fairmont Empress Hotel HOTEL $$$
(Map p676; ✆250-384-8111, 866-540-4429; www.fairmont.com/empress; 721 Government St; r from $189; ❅@🛜) Rooms at this ivy-covered, century-old Inner Harbour landmark are elegant but conservative and some are quite small, but the overall effect is grand and glossy – from the Raj-style curry restaurant to the high tea sipped while overlooking the waterfront. Even if you don't stay, make sure you stroll through and soak up the ambience.

Parkside Victoria Resort & Spa HOTEL $$$
(Map p676; ✆250-716-2651, 866-941-4175; www.parksidevictoria.com; 810 Humboldt St; ste from $269; 🛜🐾) A slick new apartment-style hotel a couple of blocks from the Inner Harbour, with the comfortable, well-equipped rooms ideal if you want a home-style base steps from the city center. Full kitchens, balconies and a gym might make you want to move in permanently. There's also an on-site mini-cinema screening nightly free flicks.

Hotel Rialto HOTEL $$
(Map p676; ✆250-382-4157, 800-332-9981; www.hotelrialto.ca; 653 Pandora Ave; r $139-249; 🛜) Completely refurbished from the faded former budget hotel it used to be, the new

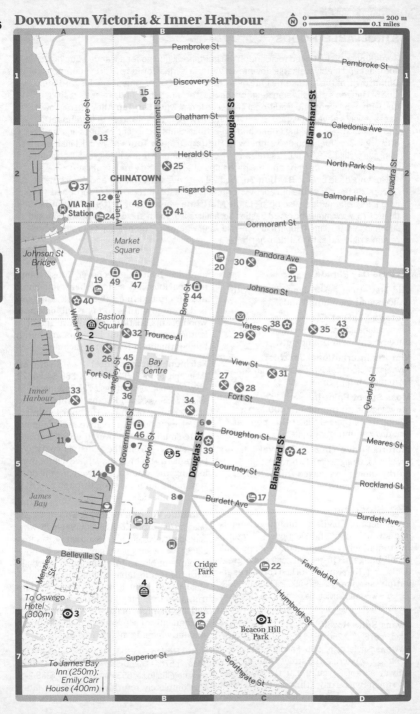

N
0 — 200 m
0 — 0.1 miles

Pembroke St
Pembroke St
Discovery St
Store St
Government St
Douglas St
Blanshard St
Quadra St
15
Chatham St
Caledonia Ave
13
10
Herald St
North Park St
25
CHINATOWN
Balmoral Rd
Fisgard St
37
12
48
41
Fan Tan Al
VIA Rail
Station
24
Cormorant St
Johnson St
Bridge
Market
Square
Pandora Ave
20
30
21
19
49
47
Johnson St
40
Broad St
44
Wharf St
Bastion
Square
2
32 Trounce Al
Yates St 38 35 43
29
16
26 45
Langley St
Bay
Centre
View St
31
Fort St
36
27
28
Inner
Harbour
33
Fort St
9
34
6
11
46
Broughton St
7
39
42
14
5
Courtney St
James
Bay
8
Burdett Ave
18
17

Belleville St
Cridge
Park
22
Fairfield Rd
Menzies St
To Oswego
Hotel
(300m)
4
3
Humboldt St
23
1
Beacon Hill
Park
Superior St
Southgate St
To James Bay
Inn (250m);
Emily Carr
House (400m)

BRITISH COLUMBIA VICTORIA

Rialto is a well-located downtown option in an attractive century-old heritage building. Each of the 38 mod-decorated rooms has a fridge, microwave and flat-screen TV and some have tubs as well as showers. The lobby's tapas lounge is justifiably popular, whether or not you're staying here.

Oswego Hotel HOTEL $$
(☏250-294-7500, 877-767-9346; www.oswegov ictoria.com; 500 Oswego St; d/ste from $159/229) Victoria's swankiest newer hotel is a designer lounge sleepover in a quiet residential location. Rooms come with granite floors, cedar beams and (in most units) small balconies. All have kitchens (think stainless steel) and deep baths, making them more like apartments than hotel suites. Cleverly, the smaller studio rooms have space-saving high-end Murphy beds.

Spinnakers Guesthouses B&B $$
(☏250-384-2739; www.spinnakers.com; 308 Catherine St; r/ste from $159/259; ☏) A short stumble from its own celebrated brewpub (p680), this clutch of adult-oriented guesthouses combines luxury details with pampering home comforts. The Heritage House is a restored 1884 family home with antiques, fireplaces and private patios. The larger Garden Suites have a contemporary feel and a smattering of Asian design flourishes. Gourmet continental breakfast is included.

James Bay Inn INN $$
(☏250-384-7151, 800-836-2649; www.jamesbay inn.com; 270 Government St; r from $129) A few minutes' walk from the Emily Carr House, this quirky charmer has a well-maintained, retro feel. The charm might wear off when

you realize there's no elevator but once you lug your bags up the stairs, you'll find a vast array of room types: most have busy-patterned carpets and furniture that's old but not quite antique. There are some kitchenettes but the downstairs neighborhood bar also serves decent pub grub.

Ocean Island Inn HOSTEL $
(Map p676; ☎250-385-1788, 888-888-4180; www.oceanisland.com; 791 Pandora Ave; dm/s/d from $27.50/30/55; @🛜) This funky, multicolored sleepover is a labyrinth of dorms and private rooms – ask for one with a window. There's a large communal kitchen on the ground floor and a licensed lounge for quiz nights and open mikes. It also offers private, self-catering suites across town in a James Bay character house (from $128) – see www.oisuites.com for information.

HI Victoria Hostel HOSTEL $
(Map p676; ☎250-385-4511, 888-883-0099; www.hihostels.ca; 516 Yates St; dm/d $31.50/78; @🛜) A well-located, quiet hostel with two large single-sex dorms, three small co-eds and a couple of private rooms. While an extensive reno was being planned at the time of our visit, it's currently a little institutionalized with basic dorms, a large games room and a book-lined reading area. Free weekly city tours are offered.

Abbeymoore Manor B&B $$
(☎250-370-1470, 888-801-1811; www.abbey moore.com; 1470 Rockland Ave; r from $165; 🛜) A romantic 1912 arts-and-crafts mansion, Abbeymoore's handsome colonial exterior hides seven antique-lined rooms furnished with Victorian knickknacks. Some rooms have kitchens and jetted tubs.

Queen Victoria HOTEL $$
(Map p676; ☎250-386-1312, 800-663-7007; www.qvhotel.com; 655 Douglas St; d/ste from $133/152; ❄🏊) A well-maintained tower-block property near the Inner Harbour with rooms that have a business-hotel feel. All have balconies and handy fridges; some also have kitchenettes.

Chateau Victoria Hotel & Suites
HOTEL $$
(Map p676 ☎250-382-4221, 800-663-5891; www.chateauvictoria.com; 740 Burdett Ave; d/ste/penthouse from $152/202/400; ❄@🏊) There's a well-maintained '80s feel at this perfectly located tower-block hotel but the rooms are clean and many have handy kitchens. The hotel's top-floor restaurant has breathtaking views.

✖ Eating

Formerly dominated by tourist traps serving nothing but poor-quality fish and chips, Victoria's dining scene has radically transformed in recent years. Pick up *Eat Magazine* (free) to see what's on the menu and keep in mind that hours are often extended ad hoc in summer.

TOP CHOICE Fort Café CANADIAN $
(Map p676; 742 Fort St; mains $6-10; 🛜) This warm and inviting subterranean hipster haunt offers the perfect combination of great comfort food and cool digs. Among the heaping fresh-made nosh, the turkey avocado wraps and hot pepper beef sandwiches are stand-outs, while there's also a rare offering of all the Salt Spring Brewing beers on draft. Check out the Atari game system around the corner at the back, or drop in for Friday's massively popular quiz night (doors open 7:30pm). If you miss it, there's a shelf of board games to keep you busy. Also check out its cool-ass coffee-shop satellite called **Picnic** (506 Fort St).

Hernandéz MEXICAN $
(Map p676; www.hernandezcocina.com; just off 750 Yates St; mains $5-8) Inauspiciously hidden in a covered passageway between Yates and View Sts, Victoria's best Mexican hole-in-the-wall has a queue of slavering locals as soon as it opens. Vegetarian options abound but the *huarache de pollo* – thick tortilla with chicken – is legendary and goes perfectly with a local Phillips Brewing beer. There are never enough available tables, so consider packing your butcher-paper parcel and heading to Beacon Hill Park for a picnic. Cash only.

Red Fish Blue Fish SEAFOOD $
(Map p676; www.redfish-bluefish.com; 1006 Wharf St; mains $6-10) On the waterfront boardwalk at the foot of Broughton St, this freight-container takeout shack serves a loyal clientele who just can't get enough of its fresh-made sustainable seafood. Highlights like scallop tacones, wild salmon sandwiches, tempura battered fish and chips and the signature chunky Pacific Rim chowder all hit the spot: find a waterfront perch to enjoy your nosh but watch for hovering seagull mobsters.

Camille's WEST COAST $$
(Map p676; ☎250-381-3433; www.camilles restaurant.com; 45 Bastion Sq; mains $18-26) A charming subterranean dining room with a lively, ever-changing menu reflecting what-

ever the chef can source locally and seasonally, perhaps ranging from pan-seared BC duck and sweet spot prawns to breathtaking desserts packed with local fruits and berries. With a great wine menu, this spot invites adventurous foodies to linger. Recommended for a romantic night out.

John's Place BREAKFAST, CANADIAN $$
(Map p676; www.johnsplace.ca; 723 Pandora Ave; mains $7-17) Victoria's best weekend brunch spot, this wood-floored, high-ceilinged heritage room is lined with funky memorabilia and the menu is a cut above standard diner fare. It'll start you off with a basket of addictive house-made bread, but save room for heaping pasta dishes or a Belgian waffle breakfast. And don't leave without trying a thick slab of pie from the case at the front.

Brasserie L'Ecole FRENCH $$
(Map p676; ✆250-475-6260; www.lecole.ca; 1715 Government St; mains $20-24) This country-style French bistro has a warm, casual atmosphere and a delectable menu. Locally sourced produce is de rigueur, so the dishes constantly change to reflect seasonal highlights like figs, salmonberries and heirloom tomatoes. We recommend the lamb shank, served with mustard-creamed root vegetables and braised chard. Beer fans will also love the bottled French, Belgian and Quebec brews.

Dutch Bakery BAKERY $
(Map p676; www.thedutchbakery.com; 718 Fort St; mains $4-7) A charming downtown institution that's been packing them in for decades with its Formica counter tops, old lady ambience and simple light meals and cream-packed cakes. Chat up the regulars and they'll recommend a beef pie with potato salad followed by a fruit-pie chaser. Peruse the handmade candies near the entrance and pick up some marzipan teeth or sprinkle-topped chocolate coins for the road.

Pig BBQ Joint SANDWICH SHOP $
(Map p676; www.pigbbqjoint.com; 749 View St; sandwiches $5-6) This vegetarian-free hole-in-the-wall is all about the meat, specifically bulging, Texas-style pulled-pork sandwiches (beef brisket and smoked-chicken variations are also offered). Expect lunchtime queues (better to arrive early or late) and consider perking up your order with a side of succulent cornbread or pail of house-made ice tea. Plans were afoot to open a second larger venue around the corner at the time of our visit – stay tuned.

Tibetan Kitchen ASIAN FUSION $
(Map p676; www.tibetankitchen.ca; 680 Broughton St; mains $7-15) Lunch specials are an excellent deal (check the board outside) at this cozy, wood-lined South Asian eatery. Start with some shareable openers like veggie pakoras and paneer poppers, then move on to fresh-made noodle and curry mains; there are plenty of vegetarian options but the slow-cooked, ginger-infused Shepta Beef is highly recommended. Whatever you end up trying, wash it down with a lip-smacking lychee lassi.

Legislative Dining Room CANADIAN $$
(Map p676; room 606 Parliament Buildings; mains $6-16) One of Victoria's best-kept dining secrets, the Parliament Buildings has its own subsidized restaurant where MLAs (and the public) can drop by for a silver-service menu of regional dishes, ranging from smoked tofu salads to velvety steaks and shrimp quesadillas. It's cash only and entry is via the security desk just inside the building's main entrance.

Zambri's ITALIAN $$
(Map p676; www.zambris.ca; 820 Yates St; mains $20-25) Run by a second-generation Italian chef, the menu here is far from traditional trattoria fare. Unassuming from the outside, the ever-changing dishes might range from a hearty squash soup with butter-fried sage to a mouth-melting sablefish, served with rapini and poached eggs. Consider the nightly three-course tasting menu or, for the budget minded, drop by for lunch instead.

ReBar VEGETARIAN, FUSION $$
(Map p676; www.rebarmodernfood.com; 50 Bastion Sq; mains $9-16; ✍) A laid-back local legend, ReBar mixes colorful interiors with a natty, mostly vegetarian menu. Carnivores will be just as happy to eat here, though, with hearty savory dishes such as shitake-tofu pot stickers, Thai green curry and heaping brunches – the salmon-topped bagel melt is great. There's also a wholesome specialty juice selection (try the orange, pear and cranberry).

 Drinking
One of BC's best beer towns, Victoria offers local craft brews and a frothy array of great watering holes. Look out for tipples by local lads Phillips Brewing and Driftwood Brewery. Repeated first-hand research was undertaken for these reviews.

Spinnakers Gastro Brewpub PUB

(www.spinnakers.com; 308 Catherine St) A pioneering craft brewer, this wood-floored smasher is a short hop from the Inner Harbour but it's worth it for tongue ticklers like copper-colored Nut Brown Ale and hoppy Blue Bridge Double IPA – named after the sky-blue span that delivers most quaffers to the door. Save room to eat: the seasonal dishes – many designed for beer pairing – often include sharable platters piled high with everything from wild salmon to Cortez Island clams.

Big Bad John's PUB

(Map p676; www.strathconahotel.com; 919 Douglas St) Easily missed from the outside because of the regulars piling into the much larger but fairly generic Sticky Wicket pub adjoining it, this evocative little hillbilly theme bar feels like you've stepped into the backwoods. But rather than some dodgy banjo players with mismatched ears, you'll find good-time locals enjoying the cave-like ambience of peanut-shell-covered floors and a ceiling dotted with grubby bras. Likely the most fun you'll have in any Victoria bar.

Canoe Brewpub PUB

(Map p676; www.canoebrewpub.com; 450 Swift St) The cavernous brick-lined interior here is popular on rainy days but the patio is the best in the city with its (usually) sunny views across to the Johnson St Bridge. Indulge in on-site-brewed treats like the hoppy Red Canoe Lager and the summer-friendly Siren's Song Pale Ale. Grub is also high on the menu here with stomach-stuffing lamb potpie and wild salmon tacos recommended.

Bard & Banker PUB

(Map p676; www.bardandbanker.com; 1022 Government St) This cavernous Victorian repro pub is handsomely lined with cut-glass lamps, open fireplaces and a long granite bar topped with 30 brass beer taps. Pull up a stool and taste-test Phillips Blue Buck, Nova Scotia's Alexander Keith's and the house-brand Robert Service Ale. There's nightly live music plus a nosh menu ranging from elevated pub standards to crisp-fried squid and an artisan cheese board.

Swans Brewpub PUB

(Map p676; www.swanshotel.com; 506 Pandora Ave) This chatty, wood-beamed brewpub was formerly a grain warehouse where freight trains rolled right into the building. Great tipples include the malty Appleton Brown Ale, a distinctive brew that'll make you permanently turn your back on Budweiser. Make room for a naughty beer pairing of Riley Scotch Ale and dark chocolate truffles.

☆ Entertainment

Check the freebie *Monday Magazine* weekly for listings or head online to www.livevictoria.com.

Live Music & Nightclubs

Lucky Bar NIGHTCLUB

(Map p676; www.luckybar.ca; 517 Yates St) A Victoria institution, downtown's eclectic Lucky Bar offers live music from ska and indie to electroclash. There are bands here at least twice a week, while the remaining evenings are occupied by dance-floor club nights, including Wednesday's mod fest and Saturday's mix night.

Logan's Pub LIVE MUSIC

(www.loganspub.com; 1821 Cook St) A 10-minute walk from downtown, in Cook St Village, this sports pub looks like nothing special from the outside, but its roster of shows is a fixture of the local indie scene. Fridays and Saturdays are your best bet for performances but other nights are frequently also booked – check the online calendar to see what's coming up.

Sugar LIVE MUSIC

(Map p676; www.sugarnightclub.ca; 858 Yates St) A popular, long-standing club that's been hosting a wide array of local and visiting bands for years – expect everything from Bob Marley tribute acts to a thundering visit from the Dayglo Abortions. Usually only open Thursday to Saturday, the two-floored joint hosts DJ club nights when there's no live act on board.

Element NIGHTCLUB

(Map p676; www.elementnightclub.ca; 919 Douglas St) Conveniently located under the Sticky Wicket and Big Bad John's, Element is a mainstream club hangout known for its Saturday top 40, hip-hop and R&B night. Friday is also popular and there are additional fairly regular live acts.

Theater & Cinemas

Victoria's main stages, **McPherson Playhouse** (Map p676; www.rmts.bc.ca; 3 Centennial Sq) and the rococo-interiored **Royal Theatre** (Map p676; www.rmts.bc.ca; 805 Broughton St), each offer mainstream visiting shows and performances. The latter is also home of the **Victoria Symphony** (www.victoriasymphony.bc.ca) and **Pacific Opera Victoria** (www.pov.bc.ca). A 20-minute stroll from downtown, the celebrated **Belfry Theatre** (www.belfry.bc.ca; 1291 Gladstone Ave) showcases contemporary plays in its lovely former-church-building venue.

The city's main first-run cinema is **Cineplex Odeon** (Map p676; www.cineplex.com; 780 Yates St). Art-house flicks hit the screen at UVic's **Cinecenta** (www.cinecenta.com; University of Victoria), while the Royal BC Museum's **IMAX Theatre** (Map p676; www.imaxvictoria.com) shows larger-than-life documentaries and Hollywood blockbusters.

 Shopping

While Government St is a magnet for souvenir shoppers, those looking for more original purchases should head to the Johnson St stretch between Store and Government. Now designated as 'LoJo' (Lower Johnson), this old-town area is a hotbed of independent stores.

Smoking Lilly   CLOTHING
(Map p676; www.smokinglily.com; 569 Johnson St) LoJo's signature shop is an almost-too-tiny boutique stuffed with eclectic garments and accessories that define art-school chic. Tops and skirts with insect prints are hot items, but there are also lots of cute handbags, socks and brooches to tempt your credit card.

Ditch Records   MUSIC
(Map p676; www.ditchrecords.com; 635 Johnson St) This narrow, *High Fidelity*-style shop is lined with tempting vinyl and furtive musos perusing the homemade racks of releases by bands like the Meatmen and Nightmares on Wax. With its threadbare carpet and cave-like feel, it's an ideal wet Monday afternoon hangout. And if it suddenly feels like time to socialize, you can book gig tickets here, too.

Munro's Books   BOOKSTORE
(Map p676; www.munrobooks.com; 1108 Government St) Like a cathedral to reading, this high-ceilinged local legend lures browsers who just like to hang out among the shelves. There's a good array of local-interest tomes as well as a fairly extensive travel section at the back on the left. Check out the racks of bargain books, too – they're not all copies of *How to Eat String* from 1972.

Rogers' Chocolates   FOOD & DRINK
(Map p676; www.rogerschocolates.com; 913 Government St) This charming, museum-like confectioner has the best ice-cream bars in town but repeat offenders usually spend their time hitting the menu of rich Victoria Creams, one of which is usually enough to substitute for lunch. Flavors range from peppermint to chocolate nut and they're good souvenirs, so long as you don't scoff them all before you get home.

Silk Road   FOOD & DRINK
(Map p676; www.silkroadtea.com; 1624 Government St) A pilgrimage spot for regular and exotic tea fans, you can pick up all manner of leafy paraphernalia here. Alternatively, sidle up to the tasting bar to quaff some adventurous brews. There's also a small on-site spa where you can indulge in oil treatments and aromatherapy.

Salt Spring Soapworks   ACCESSORIES
(Map p676; www.saltspringsoapworks.com; 575 Johnson St) Like a candy shop for soap fans, this kaleidoscopically colored nook is stuffed with pampering bath bombs, body butters and soaps, all made just across the water on Salt Spring. If you're looking for an unexpected souvenir for that bloke in your life, the tangy wild rhubarb soap is the top seller for men.

 Information

Downtown Medical Centre (622 Courtney St; ⊘8:30am-5pm) Handy walk-in clinic.

Main post office (Map p676; 706 Yates St; ⊘ ... between ... near the corner of Yates and Douglas Sts.

Stain Internet Café (609 Yates St; per hr $3.50; ⊘10am-2am) Central and late-opening internet spot.

Visitor centre (Map p676; www.tourismvictoria.com; 812 Wharf St; ⊘8:30am-8:30pm Jun-Aug, 9am-5pm Sep-May) Busy, flyer-lined visitor center overlooking the Inner Harbour.

 Getting There & Away

Air

Victoria International Airport (www.victoriaairport.com) is 26km north of the city via Hwy 17. **Air Canada** (www.aircanada.com) services arrive here from Vancouver (from $73, 25 minutes, up to 21 daily) while **Westjet** (www.westjet.com) flights arrive from Calgary (from $129, 1½ hours, six daily). Both airlines offer competing connections across Canada.

Harbour Air Seaplanes (www.harbour-air.com) arrive in the Inner Harbour from downtown

Vancouver ($145, 35 minutes) throughout the day. Similar **Helijet** (www.helijet.com) helicopters arrive from Vancouver (from $149, 35 minutes).

Boat

BC Ferries (www.bcferries.com) arrive from mainland Tsawwassen (adult/child/vehicle $14/7/46.75, 1½ hours) at Swartz Bay, 27km north of Victoria via Hwy 17. Services arrive hourly throughout the day in summer but are reduced off-season.

Victoria Clipper (www.clippervacations.com) services arrive in the Inner Harbour from Seattle (adult/child US$93/46, three hours, up to three a day). **Black Ball Transport** (www.ferrytovictoria.com) boats also arrive from Port Angeles (adult/child/vehicle US$15.50/7.75/$55, 1½ hours, up to four daily) as do passenger-only **Victoria Express** (www.victoriaexpress.com) services (US$10, one hour, up to three daily).

Bus

Services terminating at the city's main **bus station** (Map p676; 700 Douglas St) include **Greyhound Canada** (www.greyhound.ca) routes from Nanaimo ($23.30, 2½ hours, four daily) and Port Alberni ($40.30, four to five hours, two daily), along with frequent **Pacific Coach Lines** (www.pacificcoach.com) services from Vancouver (from $28.75, 3½ hours) and Vancouver International Airport ($40.25, four hours).

Car & Motorcycle

Budget (www.budgetvictoria.com; 757 Douglas St)

Hertz (www.hertz.ca; 2253 Douglas St)

Train

The charming **VIA Rail** (www.viarail.com) *Malahat* train arrives in the city on the Johnson St Bridge from Courtenay ($53, five hours, once a day), with additional island stops in Nanaimo, Parksville and Chemainus, among others.

ⓘ Getting Around

To/From the Airport

AKAL Airporter (www.victoriaairporter.com) minibuses run between the airport and area hotels ($19, 30 minutes). The service meets all incoming and outgoing flights. In contrast, a taxi to downtown costs around $50, while transit bus 70 takes around 35 minutes, runs throughout the day and costs $2.50.

Bicycle

Victoria is a great cycling capital with plenty of routes criss-crossing the city and beyond. Check the website of the **Greater Victoria Cycling Coalition** (www.gvcc.bc.ca) for local resources. Bike rentals are offered by **Cycle BC Rentals** (Map p676; www.cyclebc.ca; 685 Humboldt St; per hr/day $7/24; ⊙9am-6pm).

Boat

Victoria Harbour Ferry (Map p676; www.victoriaharbourferry.com; tickets from $5) covers the Inner Harbour, Songhees Park (for Spinnakers Brewpub), Reeson's Landing (for the LoJo shopping area) and other stops along the Gorge Waterway with its colorful armada of bath-sized little boats.

Public Transportation & Taxi

Victoria Regional Transit (www.busonline.ca) buses (tickets adult/child $2.50/1.65) cover a wide area from Sidney to Sooke, with some routes served by modern-day double deckers. Day passes (adult/child $7.75/5.50) are also available from convenience and grocery stores. Under-fives travel free.

Established taxi providers:

BlueBird Cabs (☑250-382-2222, 800-665-7055; www.taxicab.com)

Yellow Cab (☑250-381-2222, 800-808-6881; www.yellowcabofvictoria.ca)

Southern Vancouver Island

Not far from Victoria's madding crowds, southern Vancouver Island is a laid-back region of quirky little towns that are never far from tree-lined cycle routes, waterfront hiking trails and rocky outcrops bristling with gnarly Garry oaks. The wildlife here is abundant and impressive and you'll likely spot bald eagles swooping overhead, sea otters cavorting on the beaches and perhaps the occasional orca sliding silently by just off the coast.

SAANICH PENINSULA & AROUND

Home of Vancouver Island's main regional airport and its much busier ferry terminal, this peninsula north of Victoria has more to offer than just a way to get from here to there. A languid day trip from Victoria, waterfront Sidney offers bookstore browsing, while further afield you'll find BC's most popular garden attraction.

SIDNEY

At the northern end of Saanich Peninsula, seafront Sidney is studded with around a dozen used bookstores, enabling it to call itself the region's only 'Booktown.'

If the book angle floats your boat, you can spend a leisurely afternoon ducking into the likes of **Tanner's** (2436 Beacon Ave), with its massive magazine and large travel-book sections; and **Beacon Books** (2372 Beacon Ave), with its huge array of used tomes, all guarded by Rosabelle, the portly store cat.

ON YER BIKE

Bring your bike across on the ferry from the mainland and when you arrive in Swartz Bay you can hop on to the easily accessible and well-marked **Lochside Regional Trail** to downtown Victoria. The 29km mostly flat route is not at all challenging – there are only a couple of overpasses – and it's an idyllic, predominantly paved ride through small urban areas, waterfront stretches, rolling farmland and forested countryside. There are several spots to pick up lunch en route and, if you adopt a leisurely pace, you'll be in town within four hours or so. If you've been bitten by the biking bug, consider extending your trek past Victoria on the 55km **Galloping Goose Regional Trail**. Colonizing a former 1920s railway line, it's one of the island's most popular bike routes and it will take you all the way to rustic, waterfront Sooke. While longer than its sibling, it's similarly flat most of the way, which makes it popular with the not-quite-so-hardcore biking fraternity. You can access the trail by crossing over the Johnson St Bridge from downtown Victoria; the trailhead is on your right.

The cracking **Shaw Ocean Discovery Centre** (www.oceandiscovery.ca; 9811 Seaport Pl; adult/child $12/6; ⊙noon-5pm) is the town's kid-luring highlight. Enter through a dramatic Disney-style entrance – it makes you think you're descending below the waves – then step into a gallery of aquatic exhibits, including mesmerizing iridescent jellyfish, spiky sea cucumbers and a large touch tank brimming with purple starfish and gelatinous anemones. Continue your marine education aboard a whale-watching boat trek with Sidney's **Sea Quest Adventures** (www.seaquestadventures.com; 2537 Beacon Ave; adult/child $95/79), located a few steps away.

If the sight of fish just makes you hungry, head to the end of the town's short pier and tuck into some halibut and chips at **Pier Bistro** (2950 Beacon Ave; mains $10-18), which serves lovely waterfront views along with its nosh. Avoid deep-fried seafood altogether with an authentic Mexican alternative – the $9.95 three-part taco plate is best – at the cheery **Carlos Express** (2527 Beacon Ave; mains $8-10) nearby. It runs a larger sit-down eatery a couple of blocks away if you're ready for dinner. You can also join the gossiping locals at the art-lined **Red Brick Café** (2423 Beacon Ave; mains 4-8), where coffee and a large ginger snap makes for an ideal pit stop: the house-made soups, chili and pizzas are deservedly popular – check the specials board before you order.

If you decide to stick around, the new **Sidney Pier Hotel and Spa** (☑250-655-9445, 866-659-9445; www.sidneypier.com; 9805 Seaport Pl; d/ste $159/299; @) on the waterfront fuses west-coast lounge cool with beach pastel colors. Many rooms have shoreline views – some side-on – and each has local artworks lining the walls. Also check out the lobby's unmissable artifact: a large chunk of the *Sea Shepherd* Greenpeace vessel.

On your way into 'book town', drop by the **visitor centre** (☑250-656-7102; www.sidney.ca; 2295 Ocean Ave; ⊙10am-4pm) for tips on bookish and non-bookish pursuits.

Victoria Regional Transit (www.busonline. ca) bus 70 trundles into Sidney from Victoria ($2.50, one hour) throughout the day.

BRENTWOOD BAY

A 30-minute drive from Victoria via West Saanich Rd, the rolling farmlands of waterfront Brentwood Bay are chiefly known for **Butchart Gardens** (www.butchartgardens.com; 800 Benvenuto Ave; adult/child/youth $28.10/2.86/14.05; ⊙9am-10pm mid-Jun–Aug, reduced off-season), Vancouver Island's top visitor attraction. The immaculate grounds are divided into separate gardens where there's always something in bloom. Summer is crowded, with tour buses rolling in relentlessly, but evening music performances and Saturday night fireworks (July and August) make it all worthwhile. Tea fans take note: the **Dining Room Restaurant** serves a smashing afternoon tea, complete with roast-vegetable quiches and Grand Marnier truffles...leave your diet at the door.

If you have time, also consider nearby **Victoria Butterfly Gardens** (www.butterflygardens.com; 1461 Benvenuto Ave; adult/child/youth $12.50/6.50/11.50; ⊙9am-5.30pm May-Aug, reduced off-season), which offers a kaleidoscope of thousands of fluttering critters (from around 75 species) in a free-flying environment. As well as watching them flit about and land on your head, you can learn about ecosystem life cycles, as well as eye-balling exotic fish, plants and birds. Look out for Spike, the red-crowned puna ibis bird that likes strutting around the trails as if he owns the place.

SOOKE & AROUND

Rounding Vancouver Island's rustic southern tip towards Sooke (a 45-minute drive from Victoria), Hwy 14 is lined with twisted Garry oaks and unkempt hedgerows, while the houses – many of them artisan workshops or homely B&Bs – seem spookily hidden in the forest shadows.

Sharing the same building (and hours) as the visitor center, the fascinating **Sooke Region Museum** illuminates the area's rugged pioneer days. Check out Moss Cottage in the museum grounds: built in 1869, it's the oldest residence west of Victoria.

If you're also craving a few thrills, find your inner screamer on the eight-run forested zipline course (plus two suspension bridges) operated by **Adrena LINE** (www.adrenalinezip.com; 5128 Sooke Rd; adult/child $95/85). Its monthly full-moon zips are the most fun and if you don't have your own transport, it'll pick you up from Victoria.

A more relaxed way to encounter the natural world is the **Sooke Potholes Provincial Park** (www.bcparks.ca), a 5km drive from Hwy 14 (the turnoff is east of Sooke). With rock pools and potholes carved into the river base during the last ice age, it's a popular spot for swimming and tube floating and is ideal for a summer picnic. Camp-

ing is available through the website of the **Land Conservancy** (www.conservancy.bc.ca; tent site $21; ⊙May-Sep).

You'll find B&Bs dotted along the route here but, for one of the province's most delightful and splurge-worthy sleepovers, head to Whiffen Spit and **Sooke Harbour House** (☎250-642-3421, 800-889-9688; www.sookeharbourhouse.com; 1528 Whiffen Spit Rd; ste from $399). Paintings, sculptures and carved wood line its interiors. Some of the 28 rooms have fireplaces and steam showers and all have views across the wildlife-strewn waterfront – look for gamboling sea otters and swooping cranes.

You won't be disappointed with the hotel's celebrated restaurant but also consider checking the town's **Edge Restaurant** (6686 Sooke Rd; mains $9-19), an inauspicious-looking eatery that turns out to be a gourmet revelation. Seasonal regional ingredients are the approach and everything is made from scratch. The menu is ever-changing – spend some time perusing the chalkboard – but it often includes delectables like crispy tuna or braised beef short rib. The desserts (think apple spring rolls with whipped cream cheese) are dangerously good.

For local info, chat up the friendly folk at the **Sooke visitor centre** (☎250-642-6351, 866-888-4748; www.sooke-portrenfrew.com; 2070 Philips Rd; ⊙9am-5pm, closed Mon in winter).

JUAN DE FUCA PROVINCIAL PARK

The 47km **Juan de Fuca Marine Trail** (www.juandefucamarinetrail.com) in **Juan de Fuca Provincial Park** (www.bcparks.ca) rivals the West Coast Trail (p695) as a must-do trek for outdoorsy island visitors. From east to

---

WORTH A TRIP

TIME FOR A HIKE?

About 16km from Victoria, on the Island Hwy, abundantly scenic **Goldstream Provincial Park** (www.bcparks.ca), at the base of Malahat Mountain, makes for a restorative nature-themed day trip from the city. Dripping with ancient, moss-covered cedar trees and a moist carpet of plant life, it's known for its chum salmon spawning season (late October to December). Hungry bald eagles are attracted to the fish and birdwatchers come ready with their cameras. Head to the park's **Freeman King visitor centre** (☎250-478-9414; ⊙9am-4:30pm) for area info and natural history exhibits.

Aside from nature watching, you'll also find great hiking here: marked trails range from tough to easy and some are wheelchair accessible. Recommended treks include the hike to 47.5m-high Niagara Falls (not *that* one) and the steep, strenuous route to the top of Mt Finlayson, one of the region's highest promontories. The visitor center can advise on trails and will also tell you how to find the park's forested **campground** (☎604-689-9025, 800-689-9025; www.discovercamping.ca; campsites $24) if you feel like staying over.

west, its trailhead access points are China Beach, Sombrio Beach, Parkinson Creek and Botanical Beach.

It takes around four days to complete the route – the most difficult stretch is between Bear Beach and China Beach – but you don't have to go the whole hog if you want to take things easier. Be aware that some sections are often muddy and difficult to hike, while bear sightings and swift weather changes are not uncommon.

The route has several basic backcountry campsites and you can pay your camping fee ($5 per person) at any of the trailheads. The most popular spot to pitch your tent is the slightly more salubrious, family-friendly **China Beach Campground** (☑604-689-9025, 800-689-9025; www.discovercamping.ca; tent sites $24), which has pit toilets and cold-water taps but no showers. There's a waterfall at the western end of the beach and booking ahead in summer is essential.

Booking ahead is also required on the **West Coast Trail Express** (☑250-477-8700, 888-999-2288; www.trailbus.com) minibus that runs between Victoria, the trailheads and Port Renfrew (from $55, daily from May to September in each direction).

Conveniently nestled between the Juan de Fuca and West Coast Trails, Port Renfrew is a great access point for either route. Quiet and often stormy during the off-season, it's usually dripping with preparing or recuperating hikers in summer.

If you've had enough of your sleeping bag, try **Port Renfrew Resorts** (☑250-04/-5541; www.portrenfrewresorts.com; 17310 Parkinson Rd; d from $159), a recently refurbished waterfront miniresort with motel-style rooms and some luxurious, wood-lined cabins. Wherever you lay your head, save time for dinner and a few brews on its pub-style restaurant patio.

For a respite from campground mystery-meat pasta, the nearby **Coastal Kitchen Café** (17245 Parkinson Rd; mains $8-14) serves fresh salads and sandwiches, plus burgers and pizzas. The seafood is the star attraction, especially the Dungeness crab and chips. Hikers are often found lolling around outside on the picnic tables here.

Port renfrew has several spots to stock up on supplies or just fraternize with other trekkers and it's worth dropping by the **visitor centre** (www.portrenfrew.com; ⊙10am-6pm May-Sep) on your left as you enter town.

Cowichan Valley

A swift Hwy 1 drive northwest of Victoria, the verdant Cowichan Valley region is ripe for discovery, especially if you're a traveling foodie or you're craving some outdoor activities. Contact **Tourism Cowichan** (☑250-746-1099, 888-303-3337; www.tourismcowichan.com) for maps and information.

DUNCAN
POP 5000

Originally an isolated logging-industry railroad stop – the gabled station now houses a little museum – Duncan is the Cowichan Valley's main town (officially, it's a city). A useful base for exploring the region, it's known for its dozens of totem poles, which dot the downtown core like sentinels. Sports fans should also check out the community center, which is fronted by a latter-day totem: the recently refurbished World's Largest Hockey Stick (plus puck).

If your First Nations curiosity is piqued, head to the **Quw'utsun' Cultural & Conference Centre** (www.quwutsun.ca; 200 Cowichan Way; adult/child $13/6; ⊙10am-4pm Mon-Sat Jun-Sep) to learn about carving, beading and traditional salmon runs. Its **Riverwalk Café** serves authentic First Nations cuisine.

Alternatively, drive 3km north of town to the **BC Forest Discovery Centre** (www.discoveryforest.com; 2892 Drinkwater Rd; adult/child $15/10; ⊙10am-4:30pm Jun-early Sep, reduced off-season), complete with its pioneer-era buildings, logging machinery and a working steam train.

If you're hungry, time your visit well and sample some of the region's abundant produce (and baked treats) at downtown's giant **Duncan Farmers Market** (www.marketinthesquare.net; cnr Ingram St & Market Sq; ⊙9am-2pm Sat May-Nov).

The area's chatty hub, **Duncan Garage** (3330 Duncan St; mains $4-9) is a refurbished heritage building housing a bookshop, an organic grocery store and a lively cafe where brunches, baked treats and light lunches draw locals. For more substantial fare, **Craig Street Brew Pub** (www.craigstreet.ca; 25 Craig St; mains $11-15) is a wood-floored resto-bar serving quality comfort food like jambalaya pizza and excellent own-brewed beer – try the Shawnigan Irish Ale.

LAKE COWICHAN & AROUND

West of Duncan on Hwy 18, the waterfront town of Lake Cowichan is an ideal destination for outdoorsy types. Hugging the eastern end of the lake and the adjoining Cowichan River, the town marks the end of the **Trans-Canada Trail**, a mammoth hiking and biking route that runs across the country from Newfoundland. While you probably won't be taking on the whole thing, you can take a photo at the grand wooden marker and tell everyone back home that you did.

It's worth taking a few deep breaths at the ultraclear, tree-fringed lakefront – look out for elk and perhaps the occasional black bear – and you should also consider a swim or area hike here. Alternatively, check in for a kayak excursion with the friendly folks at **Warm Rapids Inn & Kayak Centre** (250-709-5543; www.warmrapidsinn.com). A great spot to learn kayaking, they'll take you out for a full-day, fully equipped course ($150) on the nearby river, tailored to your skill level. They also offer good-value homestyle **B&B accommodation** (r $65-110), plus a cool self-contained yurt in the woods ($150).

COWICHAN BAY

'Cow Bay' to the locals, the region's most attractive pit stop is a colorful string of wooden buildings perched on stilts over a mountain-shadowed ocean inlet. It's well worth an afternoon of your time, although it might take that long to find parking on a busy summer day. Arrive hungry and drop into **Hilary's Artisan Cheese** (www.hilaryscheese.com; 1737 Cowichan Bay Rd) and **True Grain Bread** (www.truegrain.ca; 1725 Cowichan Bay Rd) for the makings of a great picnic.

Alternatively, let someone else do all the work with some hearty fish and chips from **Rock Cod Café** (www.rockcodcafe.com; 1759 Cowichan Bay Rd; mains $8-16), or push out the boat – not literally – with a multicourse regional tasting feast on the patio deck of the lovely **Masthead Restaurant** (www.themastheadrestaurant.com; 1705 Cowichan Bay Rd; mains $22-29), where seafood treats like prosciutto-wrapped snapper combine with sterling views and a great Cowichan Valley wine list.

After you're fully fueled, duck into the **Maritime Centre** (www.classicboats.org; 1761 Cowichan Bay Rd; admission by donation; 9am-dusk) to peruse some salty boat-building exhibits and intricate models. And if you

really can't tear yourself away, stay for the night overlooking the water at the ever-friendly **Cowichan Oceanview B&B** (250-746-5669; www.cowichanoceanviewbb.com; 1778 Fenwick Rd; d $85-130;), where your smashing host Lorraine chefs up a great breakfast: if you're lucky it will include a blackberry smoothie of locally picked fruit. There are two rooms available, but the Lighthouse Room is recommended for its panoramic bay vista and giant bathroom.

CARMANAH WALBRAN PROVINCIAL PARK

Home to some of BC's most elderly residents, the old-growth spruce and cedar trees in this magnificent but remote **park** (www.bcparks.ca) frequently exceed 1000 years. With an ancient and mythical ambience, it's a half-hour walk down the valley to commune with the tallest trees. However, the trails are primitive and are not intended for the unprepared.

COWICHAN WINE (& CIDER) COUNTRY

Eyebrows were raised when the Cowichan Valley region began proclaiming itself as Vancouver Island's version of Provence a few years back, but the wine snobs have been choking on their words ever since.

Favorite stops include **Cherry Point Vineyards** (www.cherrypointvineyards.com; 840 Cherry Point Rd, Cobble Hill; 10am-5pm), with its lip-smacking blackberry port; **Averill Creek** (www.averillcreek.ca; 6552 North Rd, Duncan; 11am-5pm May-Oct), with its viewtastic patio and lovely pinot noirs; and the ever-popular **Merridale Estate Cidery** (www.merridalecider.com; 1230 Merridale Rd, Cobble Hill; 10:30am-4:30pm), an inviting apple-cider producer offering six varieties as well as a new brandy-distilling operation.

If you can, time your visit for the three-day **Cowichan Wine & Culinary Festival** (www.wines.cowichan.net) in September, when regional producers showcase their wares in a series of tasty events.

For more information on the wineries of this area and throughout Vancouver Island, check www.wineislands.ca.

For those without a map looking for the main Carmanah Valley trailhead, follow South Shore Rd from Lake Cowichan to Nitinat Main Rd and bear left. Then follow Nitinat Main to Nitinat Junction and turn left onto South Main. Continue to the Caycus River Bridge and, just south of the bridge, turn right and follow Rosander Main (blue-and-white BC Parks signs reassuringly point the way) for 29km to the trailhead. Be aware that these are active logging roads, which means bumpy, often narrow tracks and the promise of a rumbling approach from a scary log truck – they have the right of way, so don't give them a hard time.

CHEMAINUS
POP 4500

After the last sawmill shut down in 1983, tiny Chemainus became the model for BC communities dealing with declining resource jobs. Instead of submitting to a slow death, town officials commissioned a giant wall mural depicting local history. More than three dozen additional artworks were later added and a new tourism industry was born. A popular day trip by train from Victoria, the town introduced its own currency in 2010 – pick up your Chemainus Dollars at local banks and you can use them around the area.

Stroll the Chemainus streets on a mural hunt and you'll pass artsy boutiques and tempting ice-cream shops. In the evening, the surprisingly large **Chemainus Theatre** (www.chemainustheatrefestival.ca; 9737 Chemainus Rd) stages professional productions – mostly popular plays and musicals to keep you occupied.

Developed in partnership with the theater – ask about show packages – the town's **Chemainus Festival Inn** (250-246-4181, 877-246-4181; www.festivalinn.ca; 9573 Chemainus Rd; r $139-249; ✲) is like a midrange business hotel from a much larger town. Rooms are slick and comfortable and many include kitchens.

You can chat with the locals over coffee at the **Dancing Bean Cafe** (www.dancingbean.ca; 9885 Maple St; mains $6-9.50), an animated hangout with light meals (chicken sandwich recommended), live music most Saturdays and a good-value $2.22 breakfast special.

Check in at the **visitor centre** (250-246-3944; www.chemainus.bc.ca; 9796 Willow St; 9am-5pm May-Oct, reduced off-season) for mural maps and further information.

Nanaimo
POP 79,000

Maligned for years as Vancouver Island's grubby second city, Nanaimo will never have the allure of tourist-magnet Victoria. But the 'Harbour City' has undergone its own quiet renaissance since the 1990s, with the downtown emergence of some good shops and eateries and a slick new museum. With its own ferry service from the mainland, the city is also a handy hub for exploring up-island.

◉ Sights & Activities

Nanaimo Museum   MUSEUM
(www.nanaimomuseum.ca; 100 Museum Way; adult/child/youth $2/0.75/1.75; ☺10am-5pm mid-May–Aug, 10am-5pm Tue-Sat Sep–mid-May) Just off the Commercial St main drag, this shiny new museum showcases the region's heritage, from First Nations to colonial, maritime, sporting and beyond. Highlights include a strong Coast Salish focus and a walk-through evocation of a coal mine that's popular with kids. Ask at the front desk about summertime pub and cemetery tours.

Newcastle Island Marine Provincial Park   PARK
(www.newcastleisland.ca) Nanaimo's rustic outdoor gem offers tranquil hiking and cycling, as well as beaches and wildlife-spotting opportunities. Settled by the Coast Salish – and still part of their traditional territory – it was the site of shipyards and coal mines before becoming a popular short-hop summer excursion in the 1930s, when a teahouse was added. Accessed by a 10-minute ferry from the harbor (adult/child $4/3), there's a seasonal eatery and regular First Nations dancing displays.

Bastion   HISTORICAL BUILDING
(www.nanaimomuseum.ca; cnr Front & Bastion Sts; adult/child $1/free; ☺10am-3pm Jun-Aug, reduced hrs May & Sep) Undergoing a renovation at the time of our visit, this waterfront wooden tower was built as a fortification by the Hudson's Bay Company in 1853 and moved to this spot in 1974. A brief but charming ceremony sees one of its cannons fired for tourists at noon – the polystyrene 'cannonball' can still shake a few ribs. Nearby is the site of the weekly **Nanaimo Downtown Farmers Market** (www.nanaimofarmersmarket.com; ☺10am-2pm Fri May-Oct).

Nanaimo

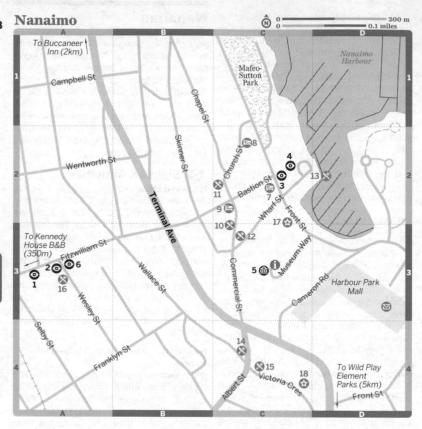

Old City Quarter
NEIGHBORHOOD

(www.oldcityquarter.com; cnr Fitzwilliam & Wesley Sts) Amble uphill from the waterfront and within minutes you'll arrive at a few blocks of strollable heritage buildings colonized by independent stores, galleries and eateries. Highlights include **Artzi Stuff** (309B Wesley St), with its local jewelry and own-made silk scarves, and **A Wee Cupcakery** (www.aweecupcakery.com; 407 Fitzwilliam St), with its irresistible array of all-butter cakes, including a naughty Nanaimo Bar variety.

Just Dive In Adventures
TOUR

(☑250-754-2241; www.justdiveinadventures.com; dive excursions/boat tours $95/79) Possibly the most fun you'll have in the water, snorkeling with seals is this operator's most popular excursion. You'll likely spot dozens of the playful critters and – possibly – a killer whale or two. Scuba diving is also offered: the regional waters are among the best in Canada for diving and wolf eels and Pacific octopus sightings are common. If you prefer to watch without doing any work, try a marine safari boat tour instead.

Wild Play Element Parks
AMUSEMENT PARK

(www.wildplay.com; 35 Nanaimo River Rd; adult/child from $40/20; ⊘10am-6pm mid-Jun–Aug, reduced off-season) This former bungee-jumping site has reinvented itself with five obstacle courses strung between the trees. Once you're harnessed, you can hit zip lines, rope bridges, tunnels and Tarzan swings, each aimed at different ability levels.

🛏 Sleeping

Painted Turtle Guesthouse
HOSTEL $

(☑250-753-4432, 866-309-4432; www.paintedturtle.ca; 121 Bastion St; dm $26.12, r $45-98; @🤶) This exemplary budget property in the heart of downtown combines four-bed dorms with family and private rooms. Hardwood floors and IKEA-esque furnishings abound, while facilities range from a large and welcoming kitchen to a laundry room and en suite showers. You can book local activities through the front desk but you might spend most of your time hanging around the fireplace in the lounge playing table football instead.

Kennedy House B&B   B&B **$$**
(☑250-754-3389, 877-750-3389; www.kenne dyhouse.ca; 305 Kennedy St; r $85-125) Uphill from the waterfront, this is one of the few Nanaimo B&Bs nearish to the city center – in fact, it's close to the VIA Rail stop and the Old City Quarter. A restored and outwardly imposing 1913 heritage mansion, it has two lovely rooms, combining antique knickknacks and contemporary flourishes. Elegant, quiet and adult-oriented, there's a smashing cooked breakfast to rouse you from your morning slumber.

Buccaneer Inn   MOTEL **$$**
(☑250-753-1246, 877-282-6337; www.buccaneer inn.com; 1577 Stewart Ave; s/ste from $79/149; ☏) Handy for the Departure Bay ferry terminal, this family-run motel has an immaculate white paint job. The neat and tidy approach is carried over into the maritime-themed rooms, many of which have kitchenettes. Splurge on a spacious suite and you'll have a fireplace, full kitchen and flat-screen TV.

Coast Bastion Inn   HOTEL **$$**
(☑250-753-6601, 800-663-1144; www.coastho tels.com; 11 Bastion St; r from $139; ☏) Downtown's leading hotel has an unbeatable location overlooking the harbor, with most rooms having good views. Rooms have been refurbished with a lounge-modern élan in recent years, adding flat-screen

TVs and (in most rooms) small fridges. The lobby resto-bar is a popular hangout but there's also an on-site spa if you want to chillax.

Dorchester Hotel   HOTEL **$$**
(☑250-754-6835, 800-661-2449; www.dorches ternanaimo.com; 70 Church St; r/ste from $119/129; ☏) Waterfront tower hotel with business-hotel-style rooms and an exceedingly slow elevator.

Grand Hotel Nanaimo   HOTEL **$$**
(☑250-758-3000, 877-414-7263; www.the grandhotelnanaimo.ca; 4898 Rutherford Rd; r from $149; @☒) Edge-of-town business-style accommodation with some superior suites.

✕ Eating

TOP
CHOICE **Gabriel's Café**   FUSION **$**
(183 Commercial St; mains $4-8; ☑) This well-located hole-in-the-wall is a revelation. Chat with the man himself behind the counter, then tuck into made-from-scratch treats like pulled-pork sandwiches with apple-cider BBQ sauce or the popular Thai green chili coconut curry, inspired by the owner's global travels. Vegetarians are well looked after – try the black-bean burger – while off-menu vegan dishes can be made on request. There's not much room to sit so consider a takeout: pick up a smoked salmon and cream-cheese breakfast bun and scoff it on the nearby waterfront. Don't miss the homemade green mint raspberry iced tea.

Penny's Palapa   MEXICAN **$$**
(10 Wharf St H Dock; mains $8-12; ☉Apr-Oct) This tiny, flower-and-flag-decked floating hut and patio in the harbor is a lovely spot

First run in 1967 to mark the city's centennial, and now overseen by the Loyal Nanaimo Bathtub Society, the **World Championship Bathtub Race** (www.bathtubbing.com) is the region's biggest summer draw. In late July, the four days of marine-themed shenanigans include a street fair, a parade and a giant fireworks extravaganza, but the main event remains the big race where hundreds of salty sea dogs jump into customized bath-sized crafts – some adapted for upwards of $3000 – and embark on a grueling 58km course. Whizzing around Entrance and Winchelsea Islands, they finish – if they make it – at Departure Bay. Speedboat engines are standard for the 90-minute sprint, with thousands of spectators lining the bay for the spectacular finish. A dip in the tub will never seem the same again.

for an alfresco meal among the jostling boats. An inventive, well-priced menu of Mexican delights includes seasonal seafood specials – the signature halibut tacos are recommended – plus some good vegetarian options. Arrive early: the dining area fills rapidly on balmy summer evenings. Drinks-wise: it's all about the margaritas.

Wesley Street Restaurant   WEST COAST **$$**
(www.wesleycafe.com; 321 Wesley St; mains $15-29; ⊙lunch & dinner Tue-Sat) Like a transplant from Victoria, Nanaimo's best splurge-worthy dine-out showcases BC-sourced ingredients prepared with contemporary flair. The oft-changing menu is seasonal, but look out for Haida Gwaii salmon, Qualicum Bay scallops and Cowichan Valley duck. Take your time and savor. And if you're looking for a dinner deal, there's a three-course $30 special from Tuesday to Thursday.

Pirate Chips   FAST FOOD **$**
(1 Commercial St; mains $4-10) Locals originally came here for the best fries in town – the curry topping is recommended – but they keep coming back for the funky ambience and quirky pirate-themed decor. It's an excellent late-night hangout: you can even indulge in poutine and deep-fried chocolate bars – although preferably not together: see p691 for the hospital location if you do.

Thirsty Camel Café   MIDDLE EASTERN **$$**
(www.thirstycamelcafe.ca; 14 Victoria Cres; mains $8-14) Partake of a lip-smacking Middle Eastern feast at this sunny little family-owned joint, tucked into an elbow of Victoria Cres. Everything's house-prepared from scratch, which makes for hearty falafel pitas, addictive hummus and some spicy winter soups. The shareable platters (especially the spice-encrusted Persian chicken) are recommended and there are several excellent vegetarian options that even meat eaters will love.

Mon Petit Choux Café & Bakery   BAKERY **$**
(120 Commercial St; mains $7-9) A chatty neighborhood hangout that has a surprisingly gourmet approach to its light meals. French-flecked favorites include roast chicken and cranberry compote sandwiches and an amazing Alsace pizza of smoked bacon and caramelized onions. Drop in for afternoon coffee and a dangerous roster of delectable bakery treats like cherry chocolate strudel and *pan au chocolat*.

Modern Café'   CANADIAN **$$**
(221 Commercial St; mains $9-19; ⊙9am-11pm) This reinvented old coffee shop has cool loungey interiors combining exposed brick and comfy booths or, if it's sunny, a sun-warmed outdoor patio. The menu has wraps, burgers and sandwiches that are a cut above standard diner fare and there are some small-plate options for those who just want to snack. It also recently opened a nightclub upstairs.

🍷 Drinking & Entertainment

Longwood Brewpub   BREWERY
(www.longwoodbrewpub.com; 5775 Turner Rd) Incongruously located in a new strip mall development, this handsome stone and gabled resto-pub combines a surprisingly good food menu with some lip-smacking own-brewed beers. Try for a deck table and decide between recommended mains like Cajun chicken quesadilla or halibut and prawn wraps – vegetarians should hit the roasted vegetable lasagna. Beer-wise, you can't go wrong with the four 6oz taster glasses for $6.63 – make sure one of them is Russian Imperial Stout.

Dinghy Dock Pub   PUB
(www.dinghydockpub.com; 8 Pirates Lane) Accessed via a mini-ferry hop, this lively pub and restaurant combo floating offshore

from Protection Island is an ideal place to rub shoulders with salty locals and knock back a few malty brews on the deck. The menu doesn't stretch far beyond classic pub fare but there's live music on weekends to keep your toes tapping. To get to the pub, take the 10-minute ferry (return $9) from the harbor.

Queen's Hotel LIVE MUSIC
(www.thequeens.ca; 34 Victoria Cres) The city's best live music and dance spot, hosting an eclectic roster of performances and club nights, ranging from indie to jazz and country.

Port Theatre THEATER
(www.porttheatre.com; 125 Front St) Presenting local and touring live-theater shows.

Avalon Cinema Centre CINEMA
(Woodgrove Centre, 6631 N Island Hwy) Nanaimo's favorite blockbuster movie house is this 10-screen multiplex.

ℹ Information

Nanaimo Maps & Charts (☎250-754-2513; 8 Church St; ⊙9am-5:30pm Mon-Sat, 10am-4pm Sat) Excellent bookstore with good array of maps and travel guides.

Nanaimo Regional General Hospital (☎250-754-2121; 1200 Dufferin Cres)

Post office (☎250-267-1177; Harbour Park Mall; ⊙8:30am-5pm Mon-Fri)

Tourism Nanaimo (☎250-754-8141; www.tourismnanaimo.com; 2290 Bowen Rd; ⊙9am-6pm May-Aug, reduced off-season) Edge-of-town site, with downtown satellite operation in the visitor information office.

ℹ Getting There & Away
Air

Nanaimo Airport (www.nanaimoairport.com) is 18km south of town via Hwy 1. **Air Canada** (www.aircanada.com) flights arrive here from Vancouver (from $98, 25 minutes) throughout the day.

Frequent **Harbour Air Seaplanes** (www.harbour-air.com) services arrive in the inner harbor from downtown Vancouver ($79, 25 minutes) and Vancouver International Airport ($67, 20 minutes).

Boat

BC Ferries (www.bcferries.com) from Tsawwassen (passenger/vehicle $14/46.75, two hours) arrive at Duke Point, 14km south of Nanaimo. Services from West Vancouver's Horseshoe Bay (passenger/vehicle $14/46.75, one hour 35 minutes) arrive at Departure Bay, 3km north of the city center via Hwy 1.

Bus

Greyhound Canada (www.greyhound.ca) buses arrive from Victoria ($23.30, 2½ hours, four daily), Campbell River ($30.80, three hours, two daily), Port Alberni ($25.80, 1½ hours, two daily) and Tofino ($46.30, four hours, two daily).

Train

The daily **VIA Rail** (www.viarail.com) *Malahat* train trundles in from Victoria ($27, 2½ hours), Parksville ($20, 35 minutes) and Courtenay ($27, two hours), among other places.

ℹ Getting Around

Downtown Nanaimo, around the harbor, is highly walkable, but after that the city spreads out and a car or strong bike legs are required. Be aware that taxis are expensive here.

Nanaimo Regional Transit (www.busonline.ca) buses (single trip/day pass $2.25/5.75) stop along Gordon St, west of Harbour Park Mall. Bus 2 goes to the Departure Bay ferry terminal. No city buses run to Duke Point.

Nanaimo Airporter (www.nanaimoairporter.com) provides door-to-door service ($26) to downtown from both ferry terminals.

Parksville & Qualicum

Previously called Oceanside, this mid-island region has reverted to using its twin main towns as its moniker, mainly because no one could tell where Oceanside was just by hearing its name.

◉ Sights & Activities

Coombs Old Country Market MARKET
(www.oldcountrymarket.com; 2326 Alberni Hwy, Coombs; ⊙9am-7pm Jul & Aug, reduced off-season) The mother of all pit stops, this ever-expanding menagerie of food and crafts is centered on a large store stuffed with bakery and produce delectables. It attracts huge numbers of visitors on balmy summer days, when cameras are pointed at the grassy roof where a herd of goats spends the season. Nip inside for giant ice-cream cones, heaping pizzas and the deli makings of a great picnic, then spend an hour wandering the attendant stores clustered around the site.

Milner Gardens & Woodland GARDEN
(www.milnergardens.org; adult/child/youth $10/free/6; 2179 W Island Hwy, Qualicum Beach; ⊙10am-5pm daily May-Aug, 10am-5pm Thu-Sun Apr & Sep) An idyllic summertime attraction combining rambling forest trails shaded by centuries-old trees and flower-packed gardens planted with magnificent

rhododendrons. Meander down to the 1930s **tearoom** on a stunning bluff overlooking the water. Tuck into afternoon tea ($8.75, 1pm to 4pm) on the porch and drink in views of the bird-lined shore and snow-capped peaks shimmering on the horizon.

World Parrot Refuge NATURE RESERVE
(www.worldparrotrefuge.org; 2116 Alberni Hwy, Coombs; adult/child $12/8; ☉10am-4pm) Rescuing exotic birds from captivity and nursing them back to health, this excellent educational facility preaches the mantra that parrots are not pets. Pick up your earplugs at reception and stroll among the enclosures, each alive with recovering (and very noisy) birds. Don't be surprised when some screech a chirpy 'hello' as you stroll by.

Horne Lake Caves Provincial Park PARK
(www.hornelake.com; tours adult/child from $20/17; ☉10am-5pm Jul & Aug, reduced off-season) Horne Lake Caves Provincial Park is a 45-minute drive from Parksville (take Hwy 19 towards Courtenay, then exit 75 and proceed for 12km on the gravel road) but it's worth it for BC's best spelunking. Two caves are open to the public for self-exploring, or you can take a guided tour of the spectacular Riverbend Cave – look out for the 'howling wolf' and 'smiling Buddha' formations.

🍴 Sleeping & Eating

TOP CHOICE Free Spirit Spheres CABINS **$$**
(☎250-757-9445; www.freespiritspheres.com; 420 Horne Lake Rd, Qualicum Bay; cabins from $125) Suspended by cables in the trees, this clutch of three spherical treehouses enables guests to cocoon themselves in the forest canopy. Compact inside, Eve is smaller and basic, while Eryn and Melody are lined like little boats with built-in cabins, nooks and mp3 speakers. Sleeping here is all about communing with nature (TVs are replaced with books), but that doesn't mean you have to give up creature comforts: guests receive a basket of baked goodies on arrival and there's a ground-level facilities block with sauna, BBQ and hotel-like showers. Book early for summer.

Inn the Estuary B&B **$$**
(☎250-468-9983; www.inntheestuary.com; 2991 Northwest Bay Rd, Nanoose Bay; ste $175; 🛜) Hidden off the road, this lovely, retreat-style B&B is as close to waterfront nature as you can get: its two self-contained suites have huge picture windows overlooking the bay's wildlife sanctuary wetlands and all you'll be able to hear are chirping birds and the rustle of occasional deer in the woods. The contemporary chic rooms have fireplaces, kitchens and jetted outdoor tubs, while free loaner bikes and kayaks are also available.

Crown Mansion BOUTIQUE HOTEL **$$**
(☎250-752-5776; www.crownmansion.com; 292 E Crescent Rd, Qualicum Beach; r from $145; 🛜) A sumptuous family home built in 1912, this handsome white-painted mansion was restored to its former glory and opened as a unique hotel in 2009. Recall past guests Bing Crosby and John Wayne as you check out the family crest in the library fireplace, then retire to your elegant room with its heated bathroom floor and giant bed. Rates include continental breakfast – arrive early and snag the window table.

Blue Willow Guest House B&B **$$**
(☎250-752-9052; www.bluewillowguesthouse.com; 524 Quatna Rd, Qualicum Beach; s/d/ste

---

WORTH A TRIP

SAY CHEESE...AND THEN MOO

Nibble on the region's 'locavore' credentials at **Morningstar Farm** (www.morningstarfarm.ca; 403 Lowry's Rd, Parksville; admission free; ☉9am-5pm Mon-Sat), a small working farmstead that's also a family-friendly visitor attraction. Let your kids run wild checking out the cowsheds and cheese makers – most will quickly fall in love with the roaming pigs, goats and chickens so you can expect some unusual Christmas pressie requests when you get back home. But it's not just for youngsters here: head to the **Little Qualicum Cheeseworks** shop, where samples of the farm's curdy treats (as well as its own-cured bacon) are provided – this is a great place to pick up picnic supplies. The creamy, slightly mushroomy brie is a bestseller but the Qualicum Spice is recommended: it's flavored with onion, garlic and sweet red pepper. Better still, the farm recently opened **Mooberry Winery**, where you can pair your cheese with blueberry, cranberry or gooseberry fruit wines.

$120/130/140) A surprisingly spacious Victorian-style cottage, this lovely B&B has a book-lined lounge, exposed beams and a fragrant country garden. The two rooms and one self-contained suite are lined with antiques and each is extremely homely. The attention to detail carries over to the gourmet breakfast: served in the conservatory, it's accompanied by finger-licking home-baked treats.

Fish Tales Café SEAFOOD **$$**
(www.fishtalescafe.com; 336 W Island Hwy, Qualicum Beach; mains $8-21) This Qualicum fixture has the look of an old-school English teashop but it's been reeling in visitors with its perfect fish and chips for years. It's worth exploring the non-deep-fried dishes – the two-person platter of scallops, shrimp, smoked salmon and mussels is recommended – and, if you arrive early enough, you can grab a table in the garden.

Shady Rest CANADIAN **$$**
(3109 W Island Hwy, Qualicum Beach; mains $10-19) A laid-back neighborhood bar perched over the shell-strewn beach on Qualicum's main drag, this casual hangout is popular with locals and visitors. Drop by for some perfectly prepared pub grub – try the excellent halibut burger – and a couple of restorative beers (Sea Dog Amber Ale is recommended). Hearty weekend brunches are also available.

ⓘ Information

Find out more about the region – which also includes rustic Bowen – by checking with the local **tourism board** (☑250-248-6300, 888-799-3222; www.visitparksvillequalicumbeach.com) or visiting the friendly folks at **Qualicum Beach visitor centre** (☑250-752-95326; www.qualicum.bc.ca; 2711 W Island Hwy; ☉8:30am-6:30pm mid-May–mid-Sep, 9am-4pm Mon-Sat mid-Sep–mid-May).

ⓘ Getting There & Away

Greyhound Canada (www.greyhound.ca) services arrive in Parksville from Victoria ($35.80, three to four hours, five daily), Nanaimo ($14.90, 40 minutes, four daily) and Campbell River ($27.30, two hours, two daily), among other towns. The same buses, with similar times and rates, serve Qualicum Beach.

The daily **VIA Rail** (www.viarail.com) *Malahat* train arrives in Parksville from Victoria ($34, 3½ hours), Nanaimo ($20, 40 minutes) and Courtenay ($20, one hour 20 minutes), among others. The same train, with similar times and rates, serves Qualicum Beach.

Port Alberni

POP 17,500

Although its key fishing and forestry sectors have been declining for decades, Alberni – handily located on Hwy 4 between the island's east and west coasts – is a good location for outdoor exploration. Additionally, there are some intriguing historic attractions and an unexpected winery.

ⓞ Sights & Activities

Cathedral Grove PARK
(www.bcparks.ca) Between Parksville and Port Alberni, the spiritual home of tree huggers is a mystical highlight of MacMillan Provincial Park. Often overrun with summer visitors – try not to knock them down as they scamper across the highway in front of you – its accessible forest trails wind through a dense canopy of vegetation, offering glimpses of some of BC's oldest trees, including centuries-old Douglas firs more than 3m in diameter. Try hugging that.

Alberni Valley Museum MUSEUM
(www.alberniheritage.com; 4255 Wallace St; admission by donation; ☉10am-5pm Tue-Sat, to 8pm Thu) Lined with eclectic aboriginal and pioneer-era exhibits, this is a fascinating local attraction. The section on the West Coast Trail shows how the route was once a life-saving trail for shipwreck victims. History fans should also hop aboard the town's **Alberni Pacific Railway** (adult/child/youth $30/15/22.50) to **McLean Mill**. A national historic site, it's Canada's only working steam-powered sawmill.

Emerald Coast Vineyards Wine Shop WINERY
(www.emeraldcoastvineyards.ca; 2787 Alberni Hwy; ☉noon-5pm Tue-Sun May-Sep, noon-4pm Thu-Sat Oct-Apr) This handsome wood-gabled, family-run winery building looks like it should be somewhere else but it's an indication that Alberni is moving on from its gritty past. Step inside for free tastings made from locally grown grapes: the dessert-like blueberry port is well worth a sip or three.

Wild West Watersports WATERSPORTS
(www.wildwestwatersports.com; 4255 Wallace St) Colonizing a grubby former corner of the old waterfront mill site, this local operator is taking full advantage of the area's predilection for exposed wind currents with kiteboarding and windsurfing rentals and lessons. Kayak rentals are also available.

BRITISH COLUMBIA PORT ALBERNI

MV Francis Barkley TOUR
(www.ladyrosemarine.com; 5425 Argyle St; return trip $50-74) With the sale of the venerable *Lady Rose*, it's left to the *MV Francis Barkley* to take passengers on idyllic day cruises up Barkley Sound.

Batstar Adventure Tours TOUR
(www.batstar.com; 4785 Beaver Creek Rd) From guided bike trips into the wilderness to multiday kayak odysseys around the Broken Group Islands, these guys can get you outdoors...and then some.

Sleeping & Eating

Hummingbird Guesthouse B&B $$
(☎250-720-2111, 888-720-2114; www.hummingbirdguesthouse.com; 5769 River Rd; ste $125-160; 🕸) With four large suites and a giant deck (complete with hot tub), this modern B&B has a home-away-from-home feel – just ask Jasper the languid house cat. There's a shared kitchen on each of the two floors but the substantial cooked breakfast should keep you full for hours. Each suite has satellite TV, one has its own sauna and there's a teen-friendly games room out back.

Fat Salmon Backpackers HOSTEL $
(☎250-723-6924; www.fatsalmonbackpackers.com; 3250 Third Ave; dm $21-25; @🕸) Driven by energetic, highly welcoming owners, this funky, eclectic backpacker joint offers four- to eight-bed dorms with names like 'Knickerbocker' and 'Mullet Room.' There are lots of books, free tea and coffee and a kitchen bristling with utensils. Make sure you say hi to Lily, the world-famous house dog.

Arrowvale Riverside Campground & Cottages CAMPGROUND $
(☎250-723-7948; www.arrowvale.ca; 5955 Hector Rd; campsite/cottage $25/149) About 6km west of Alberni, along the Somass River, the Arrowvale offers showers, a playground and heaping fruit pies in its on-site cafe. For those who've had enough of camping, there are two comparatively luxe river-view cottages with fireplaces and Jacuzzi tubs. Kids will enjoy the farm animals (check their bags for smuggled baby goats when you leave).

All Mex'd Up MEXICAN $
(5440 Argyle St; mains $3-9; ☉May-Sep) A funky and highly colorful little Mexican shack near the waterfront – it's decorated with chili-shaped fairy lights – with everything made from scratch. Pull up a stool and tuck into a classic array of made-with-love tacos, quesadillas and big-ass burritos.

❶ Information
For tips, visit the **Alberni Valley visitor centre** (☉250-724-6535; www.albernivalleytourism.com; 2533 Port Alberni Hwy; ☉8am-6pm mid-May–Aug, reduced off-season) on your way into town.

❶ Getting There & Away
Greyhound Canada (www.greyhound.ca) buses arrive here from Victoria ($46.30, four to five hours, three daily), Nanaimo ($25.80, 1½ hours, two daily) and Tofino ($29.40, two hours, two daily), among others.

Pacific Rim National Park Reserve
A wave-crashing waterfront and brooding, mist-covered trees ensure that the **Pacific Rim National Park Reserve** (www.pc.gc.ca/pacificrim; park pass adult/child $7.80/3.90) is among BC's most popular outdoor attractions. The 500-sq-km park comprises the northern Long Beach Unit, between Tofino and Ucluelet; the Broken Group Islands in Barkley Sound; and, to the south, the ever-popular West Coast Trail.

LONG BEACH UNIT
Attracting the lion's share of visitors, Long Beach Unit is easily accessible by car along the Pacific Rim Hwy. Wide sandy beaches, untamed surf, lots of beachcombing nooks and a living museum of old-growth rainforest are the main reasons for the summer tourist clamor.

The **Wickaninnish Interpretive Centre** (Wick Rd; admission included with park pass fee) was being redesigned during our visit to the region: check ahead and consider a visit if it's open, since it's a great introduction to the park.

If you're inspired to take a stroll, try one of the following trails, keeping your eyes peeled for swooping bald eagles and shockingly large banana slugs. Safety precautions apply on all trails in the region: tread carefully over slippery surfaces and never turn your back on the mischievous surf.

Long Beach Great scenery along the sandy shore (1.2km; easy).

Rainforest Trail Two interpretive loops through old-growth forest (1km; moderate).

Schooner Trail Through old- and second-growth forests with beach access (1km; moderate).

Shorepine Bog Loops around a moss-layered bog (800m; easy and wheelchair-accessible).

South Beach Through forest to a pebble beach (800m; easy to moderate).

Spruce Fringe Trail Loop trail featuring hardy Sitka spruce (1.5km; moderate).

Wickaninnish Trail Shoreline and forest trail (2.5km; easy to moderate).

🛏 Sleeping & Eating

Green Point Campground CAMPGROUND **$** (☑250-689-9025, 877-737-3783; www.pccamping.ca; campsites $34.40; ⊘mid-Mar–mid-Oct) Between Ucluelet and Tofino, on the Pacific Rim Hwy, Green Point Campground encourages lots of novice campers to try their first night under the stars. Extremely popular in the summer peak (book ahead), its 105 tent sites are located on a forested terrace, with trail access to the beach. Expect fairly basic facilities: the faucets are cold but the toilets are flush.

Wickaninnish Restaurant WEST COAST **$$** (www.wickaninnish.ca; mains $16-28) You can make up for roughing it with a rewarding meal in the interpretive centre at the Wickaninnish Restaurant, where the crashing surf views are served with fresh-catch local seafood. If you're just passing through, drop by the complex's **Beachfront Café** (snacks $3-5; ⊘9am-6pm Mar-Sep) for a snack or an ice-cold Wickaccino.

ℹ Information

First-timers should drop by the **Pacific Rim visitor centre** (☑250-726-4600; www.pacificrimvisitor.ca; 2791 Pacific Rim Hwy; ⊘10am-4pm, reduced off-season) for maps and advice on exploring this spectacular region. If you're stopping in the park, you'll need to pay and display a pass, available here or from the yellow dispensers dotted along the highway.

ℹ Getting There & Around

Tofino Bus (www.tofinobus.com; one way/return/day pass $10/15/21) runs a 'Beach Bus' service linking points throughout the area.

BROKEN GROUP ISLANDS UNIT

Comprising some 300 islands and rocks scattered across 80 sq km around the entrance to Barkley Sound, the Broken Group is a serene natural wilderness beloved of visiting kayakers – especially those who enjoy close-up views of gray whales, harbor porpoises and multitudinous birdlife. Com-

passes are required for navigating here, unless you fancy paddling to Hawaii.

If you're up for a trek, **Lady Rose Marine Services** (www.ladyrosemarine.com) will ship you and your kayak from Port Alberni to its Sechart Whaling Station Lodge (three hours away) in Barkley Sound on the *MV Francis Barkley*. The lodge rents kayaks (per day $40 to $60) if you'd rather travel light and it offers accommodation (single/double $150/235, including all meals).

From there, popular paddle destinations include Gibraltar Island, one hour away, with its sheltered campground and explorable beaches and tidal pools. Willis Island (1½ hours from Sechart) is also popular. It has a campground and, at low tide, you can walk to the surrounding islands. Remote Benson Island (four hours from Sechart) has a campground, grazing deer and a blowhole.

Camping fees are $9.80 per night, payable at Sechart or to the boat-based staff who patrol the region – they can collect additional fees from you if you decide to stay longer. The campgrounds are predictably basic and have solar composting toilets, but you must carry out all your garbage. Bring your own drinking water since island creeks are often dry in summer.

WEST COAST TRAIL UNIT

Restored after a major 2006 storm, the 75km West Coast Trail is BC's best-known hiking route. It's also one of the toughest. Not for the uninitiated, there are two things you'll need to know before tackling it: it will hurt and you'll want to do it again next year.

Winding along the wave-licked rainforest shoreline between trailhead information centers at Pachena Bay, 5km south of Bamfield on the north end, and Gordon River, 5km north of Port Renfrew on the southern tip, the entire stretch takes between six and seven days to complete. Open May to September, access to the route is limited to up to 60 overnight backpackers each day. All overnighters must pay a trail-user fee ($127.50) plus $30 to cover the two short ferry crossings on the route. **Reservations** (☑250-387-1642, 800-435-5466; www.parkscanada.gc.ca/pacificrim; nonrefundable reservation fee $24.50) are required for the mid-June to mid-September peak season but not for the off-peak periods. All overnighters must attend a 1½-hour orientation session before departing.

If you don't have a reservation, some permits are kept back for a daily wait-list system: six of each day's 26 available spaces are set aside at 1pm to be used on a first-come, first-served basis at each trailhead. If you win this lottery you can begin hiking that day, but keep in mind that you might wait a day or two to get a permit this way in the peak season.

If you don't want to go the whole hog (you wimp), you can do a day hike or even hike half the trail from Pachena Bay, considered the easier end of the route. Overnight hikers who only hike this end of the trail can leave from Nitinat Lake. Day hikers are exempt from the large trail-user fee but they need to get a free day-use permit at one of the trailheads.

West Coast Trailers are a hardy bunch and must be able to manage rough, slippery terrain, stream crossings and adverse, suddenly changing weather. There are also more than 100 little (and some not-so-little) bridges and 70 ladders. Be prepared to treat or boil all water and cook on a lightweight camping stove (you'll be bringing in all your own food). Hikers can rest their weary muscles at any of the basic campsites along the route, most of which have solar-composting outhouses. It's recommended that you set out from a trailhead at least five hours before sundown to ensure you reach a campsite before nightfall – stumbling around in the dark is the prime cause of accidents on this route.

West Coast Trail Express (www.trailbus. com) runs a daily shuttle (May to September) to Panchena Bay from Victoria ($85, six hours) and Nanaimo ($95, four hours). It also runs a service to Gordon River from Victoria ($60, 2½ hours) and Bamfield ($75, 3½ hours). Check the website for additional stops and reserve ahead in summer.

Tofino

POP 1650

Transforming rapidly in recent years from a sleepy hippy hangout into a soft-eco resort town (it's like the Whistler of Vancouver Island), Tofino is the region's most popular outdoor hangout. It's not surprising that surf fans and other visitors keep coming: packed with activities and blessed with stunning beaches, Tofino sits on Clayoquot (clay-kwot) Sound, where forested mounds rise from roiling waves

that batter the coastline in a dramatic, ongoing spectacle. A short drive south of town, the **visitor centre** (☑250-725-3414; www.tourismtofino.com; 1426 Pacific Rim Hwy; ☺10am-6pm May-Sep, reduced off-season) has detailed information on area accommodations, hiking trails and hot surf spots. There's also a satellite branch in town at 455 Campbell St.

◉ Sights

Tofino Botanical Gardens   GARDEN
(www.tbgf.org; 1084 Pacific Rim Hwy; 3-day admission adult/child/youth $10/free/6; ☺9am-dusk) Check out what coastal temperate rainforests are all about by exploring the flora and fauna at the Tofino Botanical Gardens, complete with a frog pond, forest boardwalk, native plants and an ongoing program of workshops and field trips. There's a $1 discount for car-free arrivals. This is also the new home of the **Raincoast Interpretive Centre** (www.raincoast education.org).

Maquinna Marine Provincial Park   PARK
(www.bcparks.ca) One of the most popular day trips from Tofino, the highlight here is **Hot Spring Cove**. Tranquility-minded trekkers travel to the park by Zodiac boat or seaplane, watching for whales and other sea critters en route. From the boat landing, 2km of boardwalks lead to the natural hot pools.

Meares Island   PARK
Visible through the mist and accessible via kayak or tour boat from the Tofino waterfront, Meares Island is home to the Big Tree Trail, a 400m boardwalk through old-growth forest that includes a stunning 1500-year-old red cedar. The island was the site of the key 1984 Clayoquot Sound antilogging protest that kicked off the region's latter-day environmental movement.

Ahousat   PARK
Situated on remote Flores Island and accessed by tour boat or kayak, Ahousat is the mystical location of the spectacular Wild Side Heritage Trail, a moderately difficult path that traverses 10km of forests, beaches and headlands between Ahousat and Cow Bay. There's a natural warm spring on the island and it's also home to a First Nations band. A popular destination for kayakers, camping of the no-facilities variety is allowed here.

✖ Activities

Surfing

Live to Surf
(www.livetosurf.com; 1180 Pacific Rim Hwy; board rental 6hr $25) Tofino's original surf shop also supplies skates and skimboards.

Pacific Surf School
(www.pacificsurfschool.com; 430 Campbell St; board rental 6hr/24hr $15/20) Offering rentals, camps and lessons for beginners.

Surf Sister
(www.surfsister.com; 625 Campbell St) Introductory lessons for boys and girls plus women-only multiday courses.

Kayaking

Rainforest Kayak Adventures
(www.rainforestkayak.com; 316 Main St; multiday courses & tours from $685) Specializes in four-to-six-day guided tours and courses.

Remote Passages
(www.remotepassages.com; Wharf St; tours from $64) Gives short guided kayaking tours around Clayoquot Sound and the islands.

Tofino Sea Kayaking Co
(www.tofino-kayaking.com; 320 Main St; tours from $60) Offers short guided paddles, including a popular four-hour Meares Island trip, plus rentals (from $40).

Boat tours

Jamie's Whaling Station
(www.jamies.com; 606 Campbell St; adult/child $99/65) Whale, bear and sea-lion spotting tours.

Ocean Outfitters
(www.oceanoutfitters.bc.ca; 421 Main St; adult/child $79/59) Popular whale-watching tours, with bear and hot-springs treks also offered.

Tla-ook Cultural Adventures
(www.tlaook.com; tours from $44) Learn about aboriginal culture by paddling an authentic dugout canoe.

🛏 Sleeping

Wickaninnish Inn   HOTEL $$$
(☎250-725-3100, 800-333-4604; www.wickinn. com; Chesterman Beach; r from $399) Cornering the market in luxury winter storm-watching packages, 'the Wick' is worth a stay any time of year. Embodying nature with its recycled wood furnishings, natural stone tiles and the ambience of a place grown rather than constructed, the sump-

tuous guest rooms have push-button gas fireplaces, two-person hot tubs and floor-to-ceiling windows. The region's most romantic sleepover, it's high-end but never pretentious and has a truly awesome waterfront restaurant.

Pacific Sands Beach Resort   HOTEL $$$
(☎250-725-3322, 800-565-23224; www.pacif icsands.com; 1421 Pacific Rim Hwy; r/villa from $220/450) The chic but nevertheless laid-back Pacific Sands has great lodge rooms but its stunning waterfront villas are even better. Great for groups, these huge timber-framed houses open directly onto the beach and include kitchens, stone fireplaces, slate and wood floors and ocean-view bedrooms with private decks. Built on pillars to preserve rainforest root systems, it also has energy-efficient heating systems. It'll drop you off and pick you up in town with its courtesy cars.

Chesterman Beach B&B   B&B $$$
(☎250-725-3726; www.chestermanbeach.net; 1345 Chesterman Beach Rd; ste from $185; 🛜) Located among a string of B&Bs, this classy, adult-oriented spot leads the way. The two main rooms have their own private entrances and amazing access to the beach just a few steps away (you'll be lulled to sleep by the waves at night). The smaller Lookout suite is our favorite, with its cozy, wood-lined ambience and mesmerizing beach vistas. There's also a separate cottage at the back of the property that's good for small groups.

Inn at Tough City   HOTEL $$
(☎250-725-2021; www.toughcity.com; 350 Main St; d $169-229; 🛜) Near the heart of the action and monikered after the town's old nickname, this quirky brick-built waterfront inn offers eight wood-floored en suite rooms, most with balconies and some with those all-important Jacuzzi tubs. Room five has the best views – look out for the bright-red First Nations longhouse across the water. Built from recycled wood, bricks and stained-glass windows from as far away as Scotland (ask co-owner Crazy Ron about the project), there's also an excellent on-site sushi bar.

Sauna House B&B   B&B $$
(☎250-725-2113; www.saunahouse.net; 1286 Lynn Rd; r/cabin $115/135) On a tree-lined street of secluded B&Bs just across from Chesterman Beach, this rustic nook includes a gabled loft above the main property and a small,

self-contained cabin out back. The tranquil, wood-lined cabin is recommended: it has a small kitchenette, a sunny deck that's great for breakfast (included in rates and usually featuring home-baked muffins) and its own compact sauna – the perfect place to end a strenuous day of hiking.

Whalers on the Point Guesthouse
HOSTEL $

(☎250-725-3443; www.tofinohostel.com; 81 West St; dm $32, r $85-135; @🗢) This excellent HI hostel is the Cadillac of backpacker joints. Close to the center of town, but with a secluded waterfront location, it's a comfy wood-lined place with a lounge overlooking the shoreline that is an idyllic spot to watch the natural world drift by. The dorms are mercifully small and some double-bed private rooms are also available. Facilities include a granite-countered kitchen, BBQ patio, games room and a wet sauna. Reservations essential in summer.

Clayoquot Field Station
HOSTEL $$

(☎250-725-1220; www.tbgf.org; 1084 Pacific Rim Hwy; dm/r $32/85; @🗢) In the grounds of the botanical gardens, this immaculate and quiet wood-built education center has a selection of four-bed dorm rooms, a large kitchen and an on-site laundry. There are also two private suites (the larger one has a kitchen and is ideal for families). A great sleepover for nature lovers, with rates including entry to the gardens.

✗ Eating

TOP CHOICE TacoFino
MEXICAN $

(www.tacofino.com; 1180 Pacific Rim Hwy; mains $4-10) Arrive off-peak at this massively popular, orange-painted taco truck or you'll be waiting a while for your made-from-scratch nosh. It's worth it, though: these guys have nailed the art of great Mexican comfort food. Pull up an overturned yellow bucket – that's the seating – and tuck into sustainable fish tacos or bulging burritos stuffed with chicken. Even better are the tasty pulled-pork *gringas* and the ever-popular taco soup. Whatever you have, wash it down with a zinging lime-mint freshie: it's so sharply minty, your eyes will pop out.

Sobo
SEAFOOD $$

(www.sobo.ca; 311 Neill St; mains $6-14) Before TacoFino ruled the vending-cart world, Sobo – it means 'sophisticated bohemian' – was the king with its legendary purple truck. It was so successful it's now upgrad-

ed to its own wildly popular bistro-style restaurant. Fish tacos and crispy shrimp cakes remain, but new treats at the table include Vancouver Island seafood stew and roasted duck confit pizza.

Shelter
WEST COAST $$$

(www.shelterrestaurant.com; 601 Campbell St; mains $25-39) An exquisite west-coast eatery with international accents. Our menu favorite here is the shrimp and crab dumplings. There's a strong commitment to local, sustainable ingredients – the salmon is wild and the sablefish is trap-caught – and there are plenty of nonfishy options for traveling carnivores, including a delectable char-grilled pork chop dish.

Schooner on Second
SEAFOOD $$

(www.schoonerrestaurant.ca; 331 Campbell St; mains $12-28) Family-owned for 50 years, this local legend has uncovered many new ways to prepare the region's seafood: halibut stuffed with shrimp, brie and pine nuts is recommended (as are the giant breakfasts). Or try the giant Captain's Plate blowout of salmon, scallops et al.

ⓘ Getting There & Around

Orca Airways (www.flyorcaair.com) flights arrive at Tofino Airport from Vancouver International Airport's South Terminal ($206, 55 minutes, one to four daily).

Greyhound Canada (www.greyhound.ca) buses arrive from Port Alberni ($29.40, two hours, two daily), Nanaimo ($46.30, four hours, two daily) and Victoria ($70.70, six to seven hours, three daily), among other towns.

Tofino Bus (www.tofinobus.com) 'Beach Bus' services roll in along Hwy 4 from Ucluelet ($15, 40 minutes, up to three daily).

Ucluelet
POP 1500

Driving on Hwy 4's winding mountain stretch to the west coast, you'll suddenly arrive at a junction sign proclaiming that Tofino is 33km to your right, while just 8km to your left is Ucluelet (yew-klew-let). Sadly, most still take the right-hand turn. Which is a shame, since sleepier 'Ukee' – often regarded as the ugly sister of the two – has more than a few charms of its own and is a good reminder of what Tofino used to be like before tourism took over. For information, head to the **visitor centre** (☎250-726-2485; www.ucluelet.travel; 200 Main St; ◷9:30am-4:30pm), hidden up the ramp at the back of the building.

⊙ Sights & Activities

Tucked in a little waterfront cabin, **Ucluelet Aquarium** (www.uclueletaquarium.org; Main St Waterfront Promenade; adult/child $5/2; ☺10am-6pm Mar-Oct) is an excellent small attraction, often crammed with wide-eyed kids. The emphasis is on biodiversity education, using pinkie-finger touch tanks teeming with colorful local marine life, including purple starfish and alien-like anemones – the octopus is the star attraction, though. All the critters are here temporarily on a catch-and-release program. Bold plans are afoot for a much bigger facility – watch this space.

Starting at the intersection of Peninsula and Coast Guard Rds, then winding around the wave-slapped cliffs past the lighthouse (get your camera out here) and along the craggy shoreline fringing the town, the 8.5km **Wild Pacific Trail** (www.wildpacific trail.com) offers smashing views for hikers of Barkley Sound and the Broken Group Islands. Seabirds are abundant and it's a good storm-watching spot – stick to the trail or the crashing waves might pluck you from the cliffs.

If you're not too tired, **Majestic Ocean Kayaking** (www.oceankayaking.com; 1167 Helen Rd; tours from $67) can lead you around the harbor or Barkley Sound on a bobbling kayak trek. And if you want to practice the ways of surfing, check in with **Relic Surf Shop** (www.relicsurfshop.com; 1998 Peninsula Rd; 3hr lesson/rentals per day from $74/40); it offers lessons and rentals. Alternatively, rent some wheels from the friendly team at **Ukee Bikes** (www.ukeebikes.com; 1559 Imperial Lane; per hr/24hr $5/25) and cycle over to Tofino to see what all the fuss is about.

🛏 Sleeping & Eating

Surfs Inn Guesthouse   HOSTEL $
(☎250-726-4426; www.surfsinn.ca; 1874 Peninsula Rd; dm/ste/cottage $28/159/259; 🕾) While this blue-painted clapboard house on a small hill contains three homey little dorm rooms, a well-equipped kitchen and is high on friendliness, it's the two refurbished cabins out the back that attract many: one is larger, self-contained and great for groups of up to six; while the other is divided into two suites with kitchenettes. Each cottage has a BBQ and surf packages are available if you want to hit the waves.

Black Rock Oceanfront Resort   HOTEL $$$
(☎250-726-4800, 877-762-5011; www.blackrock resort.com; 596 Marine Dr; r from $179) Just to prove that Tofino doesn't have all the swanky resorts, this slick new sleepover combines lodge, cottage and beach-house accommodation, all wrapped in a contemporary wood and stone west-coast look. Many rooms have great views of the often dramatically stormy surf and there's also a vista-hugging restaurant specializing in regional nosh.

C&N Backpackers   HOSTEL $
(☎250-726-7416, 888-434-6060; www.cnnback packers.com; 2081 Peninsula Rd; dm/r $25/65; 🕾) They're very protective of their hardwood floors here, so take off your shoes at the door of this calm and well-maintained hostel. The dorms are mostly small and predictably basic, but private rooms are also available and there's a spacious downstairs kitchen. The highlight is the landscaped, lounge-worthy garden overlooking the inlet, complete with hammocks and a rope swing.

Ukee Dogs   CANADIAN $
(1576 Imperial Lane; mains $4-7) Focused on home-baked treats and comfort foods, this bright and breezy, good-value eatery offers hotdogs of the gourmet variety (go for the Canuck dog) and great pies from steak and curry to salmon wellington. Drop by in the afternoon for coffee and sprinkle-topped cakes and come back in the morning for the best breakfast in town: the sausage scram-ble! Yum.

ℹ Getting There & Around

Greyhound Canada (www.greyhound.ca) buses arrive from Port Alberni ($27.30, 1½ hours, two daily), Nanaimo ($46.30, three to four hours, two daily) and Victoria ($64.70, five to seven hours, three daily), among others.

Tofino Bus (www.tofinobus.com) 'Beach Bus' services roll in along Hwy 4 from Tofino ($15, 40 minutes, up to three daily).

Denman & Hornby Islands

Regarded as the main Northern Gulf Islands, **Denman** (www.denmanisland.com) and **Hornby** (www.hornbyisland.net) share laid-back attitudes, artistic flair and some tranquil outdoor activities. You'll arrive by ferry at Denman first from Buckley Bay on Vancouver Island, then you hop from Denman across to Hornby. Stop at **Denman Village**, near the first ferry dock, and pick up a free map for both islands

Denman has three provincial parks: **Fillongley**, with easy hiking and beachcombing; **Boyle Point**, with a beautiful walk to the lighthouse; and **Sandy Island**, only accessible by water from north Denman. Consider timing your visit for a free Saturday tour of **Denman Island Chocolate Factory** (www.denmanislandchocolate.com), which must be reserved in advance. Note, though: there are no samples on offer.

Among Hornby's provincial parks, **Tribune Bay** features a long sandy beach with safe swimming, while **Helliwell** offers notable hiking. **Ford's Cove**, on Hornby's south coast, offers the chance for divers to swim with six-gill sharks. The island's large **Mt Geoffrey Regional Park** is criss-crossed with hiking and mountain-biking trails.

For kayaking rentals contact **Denman Hornby Canoes & Kayaks** (www.denman paddling.ca; 4005 East Rd, Denman Island; 3/6hr $35/50), or **Hornby Island Outdoor Sports** (www.hornbyoutdoors.com; 5875 Central Rd, Hornby Island) for kayak (per three hours $42) and bike rentals (per hour/day $15/45).

Sleeping & Eating

Sea Breeze Lodge
HOTEL **$$**
(☏250-335-2321, 888-516-2321; www.seabreeze lodge.com; 5205 Fowler Rd, Hornby Island; adult/child/youth $165/75/115; 🐾) This 12-acre retreat, with 16 cottages overlooking the ocean, has the feel of a Spanish villa with a Pacific Rim twist. Rooms are comfortable rather than palatial and some have fireplaces and full kitchens. You can swim, kayak and fish or just flop lazily around in the cliff-side hot tub. Rates – reduced for those under 17 – are per person and include three daily meals.

Hawthorn House B&B
B&B **$$**
(☏250-335-0905; 3375 Kirk Rd, Denman Island; r $95-110) Handily located near the ferry dock and a short walk from the main Denman Village shops and services, this rustic garden property has three cozy rooms that can each be adapted for small groups. The best is the cottage room, located in a separate cabin and with a little kitchenette and an ocean-view porch. Cooked breakfast included.

Cardboard House
BAKERY **$**
(2205 Central Rd, Hornby Island; mains $4-8) It's easy to lose track of time at this old shingle-sided farmhouse that combines a hearty bakery, pizza shop and cozy cafe. It's impossible not to stock up on a bag full of oven-fresh muffins, cookies and croissants for the road, but stick around for an alfresco lunch in the adjoining orchard, which also stages live music Wednesday and Sunday evenings in summer.

Island Time Café
CAFE **$**
(3464 Denman Rd, Denman Island; mains $7-9) This village hangout specializes in fresh-from-the-oven bakery treats like muffins and scones (plus organic coffee), as well as bulging breakfast wraps and hearty house-made soups. The pizza is particularly recommended, and all is served with a side order of gossip from the chatty locals. If the sun is cooperating, sit outside and catch some rays.

ℹ️ Getting There & Away

BC Ferries (www.bcferries.com) services arrive throughout the day at Denman from Buckley Bay (passenger/vehicle $8.35/19.55, 10 minutes). Hornby Island is accessed by ferry from Denman (passenger/vehicle $8.35/19.55, 10 minutes).

Comox Valley

Comprising the towns of Comox, Courtenay and Cumberland, this is a temperate region of rolling mountains, alpine meadows and colorful communities. A good base for outdoor adventures, its activity-triggering highlight is Mt Washington. Drop by the area **visitor centre** (☏250-334-3234, 888-357-4471; www.discovercomoxvalley.com; 2040 Cliffe Ave, Comox; ⊙9am-5pm mid-May–Aug, 9am-5pm Mon-Sat Sep–mid-May) for tips.

◎ Sights & Activities

The main reason for winter visits, **Mt Washington Alpine Resort** (www.mount washington.ca; lift ticket adult/child winter $59/31, summer $37.50/25) is the island's skiing mecca, with its 60 runs, snowshoeing park and 55km of cross-country ski trails. But there are also some great summer activities here, including horseback riding, fly-fishing and some of the region's best biking and alpine hiking trails. Visit www.discovermountwashington.com for more activity suggestions.

Known for its life-sized replica of an elasmosaur – a prehistoric marine reptile first discovered in the area – the excellent **Courtenay & District Museum & Palaeontology Centre** (www.courtenaymuseum.ca; 207 Fourth St; admission by donation; ⊙10am-

5pm Mon-Sat, noon-4pm Sun mid-May–mid-Sep, 10am-5pm Tue-Sat mid-Sep–mid May) also houses First Nations exhibits and provides a colorful introduction to the region's pioneering past. You can hunt for your own fossils along the banks of the Puntledge River on a guided summertime **fossil tour** (adult/child $25/15).

Outdoor types should also make for **Miracle Beach Provincial Park** (www.bcparks.ca), home to some excellent hiking trails and tranquil beaches. Alternatively, Courtenay's **Pacific Pro Dive & Surf** (www.scubashark.com; 2270 Cliffe Ave; scuba package rental per day $75) can help with scuba lessons and equipment rentals, while Comox's **Simon's Cycles** (www.simoncycle.com; 1841 Comox Ave; rental $30) offers bike rentals.

🛏 Sleeping & Eating

Riding Fool Hostel　　　　　HOSTEL $
(☎250-336-8250, 888-313-3665; www.ridingfool.com; 2705 Dunsmuir Ave, Cumberland; dm/r $23/55; @🛜) One of Vancouver Island's best backpacker joints, Riding Fool is a restored heritage building with immaculate wooden interiors, a large kitchen and lounge area and the kind of neat and tidy private rooms often found in hotels. Bicycle rentals are available at the downstairs shop: this is a great hostel in which to hang out with the mountain-bike crowd.

Shantz Haus Hostel　　　　　HOSTEL $
(☎250-703-2060, 866-603-2060; www.shantzhostel.com; 530 Fifth St, Courtenay; dm/r $25/58; @🛜🐾) This peaceful little hostel feels like staying in a favorite aunt's house. Luckily, she's quite a cool aunt: her two dorms are small and cozy, while her two private rooms are ideal for families. The bathrooms are the antithesis of institutionalized hostels and there's a full kitchen, fireplace common room and sunny deck with BBQ. Give Jake the house cat a little attention.

Mad Chef Café　　CANADIAN, FUSION $$
(www.madchefcafe.net; 492 Fitzgerald Ave, Courtenay; mains $8-20) Bright and colorful neighborhood eatery serving a great selection of made-from-scratch meals: this is a good place for a salad, since they're heaping and crispy-fresh. Sharers should go for the Mediterranean plate, piled high with olives, hummus, pitta and lovely own-made bruschetta. Gourmet duck or salmon burgers are also popular.

Atlas Café　　　　　　　FUSION $$
(www.atlascafe.ca; 250 Sixth St, Courtenay; mains $12-18) Courtenay's favorite dine-out has a pleasing modern bistro feel with a taste-tripping global menu fusing Asian, Mexican and Mediterranean flourishes. Check out the gourmet fish tacos plus ever-changing seasonal treats. Good vegetarian options, too.

Kingfisher Oceanside Resort　　HOTEL $$
(☎250-338-1323, 800-663-7929; www.kingfisherspa.com; 4330 Island Hwy, Courtenay; r/ste $145/220; @🛜) Comfortable waterfront lodge with spa. Many rooms have full kitchens and shoreline balconies.

Cona Hostel　　　　　　　HOSTEL $
(☎250-331-0991, 877-490-2662; www.theconahostel.com; 440 Anderton Ave, Courtenay; d/r $25/58; @🛜) Cozy, orange-painted riverfront hostel with large kitchen and BBQ patio. Runs a Mt Washington shuttle in winter.

Waverley Hotel Pub　　　　BURGERS $$
(www.waverleyhotel.ca; 2692 Dunsmuir Ave, Cumberland; mains $8-14) Come for hearty pub grub and stick around for live bands on the kick-ass little stage.

Campbell River

POP 29,500

Southerners will tell you this marks the end of civilization on Vancouver Island, but Campbell River is a handy drop-off point for wilderness tourism in Strathcona Provincial Park and is large enough to have plenty of attractions and services of its own. The **visitor center** (☎1-250-683-0115, 877-286-5705; www.campbellriver.travel; 1235 Shoppers Row; ⊙9am-6pm Mon-Sat, 10am-4pm Sun) can fill you in.

◉ Sights & Activities

The recommended **Museum at Campbell River** (www.crmuseum.ca; 470 Island Hwy; adult/child $6/4; ⊙10am-5pm daily May-Sep, noon-5pm Tue-Sun Oct-Apr) showcases aboriginal masks, an 1890s pioneer cabin and video footage of the world's largest artificial, non-nuclear blast: an underwater mountain in Seymour Narrows that caused dozens of shipwrecks before it was blown apart in a controlled explosion 1958.

Since locals claim the town as the 'Salmon Capital of the World' you should wet your line off the downtown **Discovery Pier** (rod rentals $6 per day) or just stroll along with the crowds and see what everyone else has caught. Much easier than catching your own lunch, you can also buy fish and chips here.

🛏 Sleeping & Eating

Heron's Landing
HOTEL $$

(☎250-923-2848, 888-923-2849; www.herons landinghotel.com; 492 S Island Hwy; r from $145; @🛜) Superior motel-style accommodation with renovated rooms, including large loft suites ideal for families.

Heritage River Inn
MOTEL $$

(☎250-286-6295, 800-567-2007; www.heritage riverinn.com; 2140 N Island Hwy; r from $80; ❄) Quiet motel north of downtown with sauna, Jacuzzi and gazebo-covered BBQs. Rates include continental breakfast.

Royal Coachman Inn
BURGERS $$

(84 Dogwood St; mains $8-18) Brit-style pub serving BC and cross-Canada brews and a large array of grub from burgers to Thai ginger salad.

ℹ Getting There & Around

Campbell River Airport (www.crairport.ca) gets **Pacific Coastal Airlines** (www.pacific-coastal. com) flights from Vancouver International Airport ($208, 45 minutes, up to seven daily).

Greyhound Canada (www.greyhound.ca) services arrive from Port Hardy, ($48.30, 3½ hours, daily), Nanaimo ($35.80, three hours, two daily), Victoria ($57.60, six to 10 hours, three daily) and beyond.

Campbell River Transit (www.buslonline.ca; adult/child $1.75/1.50) operates local buses throughout the area.

Strathcona Provincial Park

Driving inland from Campbell River on Hwy 28, you'll soon come to BC's oldest protected area and also Vancouver Island's largest **park** (www.bcparks.ca). Centered on Mt Golden Hinde, the island's highest point (2200m), Strathcona is a magnificent pristine wilderness criss-crossed with trail systems that deliver you to waterfalls, alpine meadows, glacial lakes and looming mountain crags.

On arrival at the main entrance, get your bearings at **Strathcona Park Lodge & Outdoor Education Centre** (www.strathcona.bc.ca). A one-stop shop for park activities, including kayaking, guided treks, yoga camps, ziplining and rock climbing (all-in adventure packages are available, some aimed specifically at families), this is a great place to rub shoulders with other outdoorsy types – head to the **Whale Dining Room** or **Canoe Club Café** eateries for a fuel up.

The lodge also offers good **accommodation** (r/cabin from $136/175), which, in keeping with its low-impact approach to nature and commitment to eco-education, is sans telephones and TVs. Rooms range from basic college-style bedrooms to secluded timber-framed cottages. If you are a true back-to-nature fan, there are also several campsites available in the park. Alternatively, consider pitching your tent at **Buttle Lake Campground** (☎604-689-9025, 800-689-9025; www.

WORTH A TRIP

QUADRA ISLAND HOP

A short skip across the water with **BC Ferries** (www.bcferries.com; passenger/vehicle $8.35/19.55), rustic Quadra is a popular jaunt from Campbell River. Drop into the **visitor information booth** (www.quadraisland.ca; ⊗9am-4pm Jun-Sep) in the parking lot of the Quadra Credit Union near the ferry dock for some tips on your visit.

The island's fascinating **Nuyumbalees Cultural Centre** (www.nuyumbalees.com; 34 Weway Rd; adult/child $10/5; ⊗10am-5pm May-Sep) illuminates the heritage and traditions of the local Kwakwaka'wakw First Nations people, showcasing carvings and artifacts and staging traditional dance performances. Alternatively, the sandy beaches and clear waters of **Rebecca Spit Provincial Park** (www.bcparks.ca) offer idyllic swimming. For paddle nuts, **Quadra Island Kayaks** (www.quadraislandkayaks. com; tours from $59, rentals per day $40) can get you out on the glassy waters around the coastline; it provides rentals as well as lessons and guided tours (sunset paddle recommended). If you just want to hang out with the locals, head to **Spirit Sqare** where, in summer, performers entertain alfresco.

If you've fallen in love and want to stay, the handsome **Heriot Bay Inn & Marina** (☎250-285-3322, 888-605-4545; www.heriotbayinn.com; Heriot Bay; r/tent site from $99/24) has motel-style rooms, rustic cabins and tent spots, while the lovely, wood-lined **Quadra Island Boutique Hostel** (☎250-285-3198; www.quadraislandhostel. com; 653 Green Rd; dm/r $28/60) has small rooms, friendly hosts, a hot tub and a tree-fringed BBQ deck. What are you waiting for?

discovercamping.ca; tent site $24). The swimming area and playground here make this a good choice for families.

Notable park hiking trails include **Paradise Meadows Loop** (2.2km), an easy amble in a delicate wildflower and evergreen ecosystem; and **Mt Becher** (5km), with its great views over the Comox Valley and mountain-lined Strait of Georgia. The 9km **Comox Glacier Trail** is quite an adventure but is only recommended for advanced hikers. Around Buttle Lake, easier walks include **Lady Falls** (900m) and the trail along **Karst Creek** (2km), which winds past sinkholes, percolating streams and tumbling waterfalls.

North Vancouver Island

Down-islanders (which means anyone below Campbell River) will tell you, 'There's nothing up there worth seeing,' while locals here will respond, 'They would say that, wouldn't they?' Parochial rivalries aside, what this giant region, covering nearly half the island, lacks in towns, infrastructure and population, it more than makes up for in rugged natural beauty. Despite the remoteness, some areas are remarkably accessible to hardy hikers, especially along the North Coast Trail.

Spotting black bears feasting on roadside berries soon becomes commonplace up here, but you'll also appreciate many of the quirky locals who color the region: northerners have a hardy, independent streak that marks them out from the south-island softies. For further information on the region, check in with **Vancouver Island North** (www.vancouverislandnorth.ca).

TELEGRAPH COVE

Originally just a one-shack telegraph station, charming Telegraph Cove has successfully reinvented itself in recent decades as a visitor magnet. Its pioneer-outpost feel is enhanced by the dozens of wooden buildings standing around the marina on stilts, but the place can get ultracrowded in summer. The road into the area was paved a few years back, encouraging a new hotel and housing development.

Head first along the boardwalk to the smashing **Whale Interpretive Centre** (www.killerwhalecentre.org; suggested donation $2; ☺May-Sep), bristling with hands-on artifacts and artfully displayed skeletons of cougars, sea otters and a giant fin whale.

You can also see whales of the live variety just offshore: this is one of the island's top marine-life viewing regions and **Stubbs Island Whale Watching** (www.stubbs-island.com; adult/child $94/84; ☺May-Sep) will get you up close with the orcas on a boat trek – you might also see humpbacks, dolphins and sea lions. Its sunset cruise is a highlight. For a bear alternative, **Tide Rip Grizzly Tours** (www.tiderip.com; $288; ☺mid-May–Sep)

AND FINALLY...THE NORTH COAST TRAIL

If your response to the famed West Coast Trail (p695) is 'been there, done that,' it's time to strap on your hiking boots for the north-island equivalent, a 43km route that opened to itchy hikers in 2008. You can start on the western end at Nissen Bight, but you'll have to hike in 15km on the established (and relatively easy) Cape Scott Trail to get there. From Nissen Bight, the trail winds eastwards to Shushartie Bay. You'll be passing sandy coves, deserted beaches and dense, wind-whipped rainforest woodland, as well as a couple of river crossings on little cable cars. The trail is muddy and swampy in places so there are boardwalks to make things easier. The area is home to elk, deer, cougars, wolves and black bears (make sure you know how to handle an encounter before you set off), while offshore you're likely to spot seals, sea lions, sea otters and grey whales. Like its west-coast sibling, the North Coast Trail is for experienced and well-equipped hikers only. There are backcountry campsites at Nissen Bight, Laura Creek and Shuttleworth Bight and the route should take five to eight days.

The Holberg Cape Scott trailhead is 63km from Port Hardy and is accessible on well-used logging roads. You can drive there yourself or take the dedicated **North Coast Trail Shuttle** (www.northcoasttrailsshuttle.com; $70). Once you're done at the Shushartie Bay end, you can pick up a **Cape Scott Water Taxi** (www.capescottwatertaxi.ca; $80) back to Port Hardy. You must book both the shuttle and the boat ahead of time – the shuttle company can also help you book the water taxi.

Reservations are not required for the North Coast Trail.

BEST LITTLE COOKHOUSE IN THE NORTH

The winding, tree-lined Hwy 19 stretch between mid-island Campbell River and north-island Port Hardy is studded with little communities (as well as a few black bears feasting on roadside berries). If it's mealtime when you arrive around tiny Sayward, drop into the legendary **Cable Cookhouse** (1741 Sayward Rd; mains $8-20). This seemingly age-old cafe is uniquely cocooned in 2.7km of steel logging cables, a reminder of the area's hardy resource-industry past. Inside, cool 1950s frescoes of logging-camp scenes adorn the back walls. But you haven't just come here to look, so make sure you unnotch your belt and hit the menu. An ideal spot to kick-start your day, tuck into the heaping Loggers Breakfast of eggs, bacon et al. Better still, drop by for lunch: the salmon melt sandwich and oyster burger are excellent. And if you can resist the thick slabs of own-made fruit pie on the counter, you're doing better than most. In fact, the Cable Cookhouse is where many diets come to die.

leads full-day trips to local beaches and inlets in search of the area's furry residents.

The established **Telegraph Cove Resorts** (☑250-928-3131, 800-200-4665; www.telegraphcoveresort.com; campsite/cabin from $27/115) provides accommodations in forested tent spaces and a string of rustic cabins on stilts overlooking the marina. The nearby and much newer **Dockside 29** (☑250-928-3163, 877-835-2683; www.telegraph cove.ca; r $140-175) is a good, motel-style alternative. Its rooms have kitchenettes with hardwood floors and waterfront views.

The **Killer Whale Café** (mains $14-18; ☺May-Sep) is the cove's best eatery – the salmon, mussel and prawn linguini is recommended. The adjoining **Old Saltery Pub** is an atmospheric, wood-lined nook with a cozy central fireplace and tasty Killer Whale Pale Ale. It's a good spot to sit in a corner and pretend you're an old sea salt – eye patch and wooden leg optional.

PORT MCNEILL
POP 2600

Barreling down the hill almost into Broughton Straight, Port McNeill is the north island's second-largest community, making it a useful supply stop for travelers.

More a superior motel than a resort, the hilltop **Black Bear Resort** (☑250-956-4900, 866-956-4900; www.port-mcneill -accommodation.com; 1812 Campbell Way; d/tw/ste $135/155/235; @🛜🛋) overlooks the town and is conveniently located across from shops and restaurants. The standard rooms are small but clean and include microwaves and fridges; full-kitchen units are also available and there's a new on-site spa. Rates include a large continental-breakfast buffet.

If you're still hungry, the nearby **Bo-Banees** (1705 Campbell Way; mains $7-15) restaurant serves burritos, burgers and Lucky Lager – the logger's favorite beer. The chicken quesadilla is a winner here.

Drop by the gabled **visitor center** (☑250-956-3131; www.portmcneill.net; 1594 Beach Dr; ☺9am-5pm Mon-Fri, 10am-3pm Sat, reduced off-season) for regional info, then stop in at the **museum** (351 Shelley Cres; ☺10am-5pm Jul-Sep, 1-3pm Sat & Sun Oct-Jun) to learn about the area's logging-industry heritage.

Greyhound Canada (www.greyhound. ca) buses arrive in Port McNeill from Port Hardy ($14.90, 30 minutes, daily), Campbell River ($42, 2½ hours, daily) and Nanaimo ($70.70, six hours, daily).

Regular **BC Ferries** (www.bcferries.com) services also arrive from Alert Bay and Sointula (passenger/vehicle $9.75/22.75) but times and schedules vary – see the website for details.

ALERT BAY
POP 550

Located on Cormorant Island, this visitor-friendly village has an ancient and mythical appeal. Its First Nations community and traditions are still prevalent, but its blend with an old pioneer fishing settlement makes it an even more fascinating day trip from Port McNeill. Drop by the **visitor center** (☑250-974-5024; www.alertbay. ca; 116 Fir St; ☺9am-4:30pm Mon-Fri, reduced off-season) for an introduction.

The highly recommended **U'mista Cultural Centre** (☑250-974-5403; www. umista.ca; 1 Front St; adult/child $8/1; ☺9am-5pm daily May-Aug, 9am-5pm Tue-Sat Sep-Apr) showcases an impressive collection of Kwakwaka'wakw masks and other potlatch items originally confiscated by Canada's federal government. Singing, dancing and BBQs are often held here, while modern-day totem-pole carvers usually work their magic out front. One of the world's tallest totem poles was carved on site in the 1960s and is appropriately placed on the front lawn of the **Big House**, which hosts traditional dances in July and August. Also drop into **Culture Shock Interactive Gallery** (www.cultureshockgallery.ca; 10A Front St) for some exquisite artwork souvenirs.

If the ocean is calling you, **Seasmoke Whale Watching** (www.seaorca.com; adult/child $95/85) offers a five-hour whale-watching trek on its yacht, including afternoon tea.

PORT HARDY
POP 3800

Settled by Europeans in the early 1800s, this small north-island settlement is best known as the arrival/departure point for BC Ferries Inside Passage trips. It's also a handy gear-up spot for the North Coast Trail.

☉ Sights & Activities

Before you leave town on a long hike, check into the new **Quatse Salmon Stewardship Centre** (www.thesalmoncentre.org; 8400 Byng Rd; adult/child $5/2; ☉10am-5pm Wed-Sun mid-May–Sep) to learn all about the life cycle of local salmon. The kid-friendly facility has lots of critters in tanks and was also working on a new theater room at the time of our visit. The friendly staff will answer all your salmon-related questions.

Port Hardy is a great access point for exploring the north-island wilderness and hikers can book a customized guided tour with the friendly folk at **North Island Daytrippers** (www.islanddaytrippers.com). For those who prefer to paddle, **Odyssey Kayaking** (www.odysseykayaking.com; rentals/tours from $40/99) can take you on guided tours around Malei Island, Bear Cove and Alder Bay or leave you to your own devices with a full-day rental. For dive fans, **Catala Charters** (www.catalacharters.net; dive trips from $150) options include trips to Browning Passage. Dripping with octopus, wolf eels and corals, it's one of BC's top cold-water dive sites.

🛏 Sleeping & Eating

Ecoscape Cabins   CABIN $$
(☎250-949-8524; www.ecoscapecabins.com; 6305 Jensen Cove Rd; cabins $125-175; ☎) A clutch of immaculate cedar-wood cabins, divided between three compact units –

with flat-screens, microwaves and sunny porches (ideal for couples) – and three roomier hilltop units with swankier furnishings, BBQs and expansive views. There's a tranquil retreat feel to staying here and you should expect to see eagles swooping around the nearby trees. Deer are not uncommon, too.

North Coast Trail Backpackers Hostel   HOSTEL $
(☎250-949-9441, 866-448-6303; www.porthardyhostel.webs.com; 8635 Granville St; dm/r from $24/58) Colonizing a former downtown storefront, this labyrinthine hostel is a warren of small and larger dorms, overseen by a friendly couple with plenty of tips about how to encounter the region – they'll even pick you up from the ferry if you call ahead. The hostel's hub (a hangout for house dog Luke) is a large rec room and, while the kitchen is small, a coffee shop was being added at the time of our visit.

Bear Cove Cottages   CABIN $$
(☎250-949-7939, 877-949-7339; www.bearcovecottages.ca; 6715 Bear Cove Hwy; d $149; ☎) A string of eight comfy cabins, all with kitchenettes and views across the water (and the road) from your deck . There's a well-maintained motel feel but the rooms have handy extras like small Jacuzzi tubs and corner fireplaces – you can also borrow a BBQ to make full use of your patio.

Escape Bistro & Gallery   CANADIAN $$
(8405 Byng Rd; mains $16-22) Just across from the Salmon Stewardship Centre, this excellent reinvention of a once-tired resto-bar is a revelation. The old-school dining room (try for a booth) has been enlivened with local artworks and there's live Friday and Saturday guitar music to keep things animated. The menu combines simple home-cooked dishes with lip-smacking European fare like Hungarian goulash and Vienna schnitzel – go for Friday's pork-roast special. Excellent service.

Café Guido   CAFE $
(7135 Market St; mains $5-7; ☎) A friendly locals' hangout where you'll easily end up sticking around for an hour or two, especially if you hit the loungey sofas with a tome purchased from the bookstore downstairs. Grilled paninis are the way to go for lunch (try the Nero) but there's always a good soup special. Then nip upstairs to the surprisingly large and diverse craft shop.

ℹ️ Information

Head to the **visitor center** (☎250-949-7622; www.porthardy.travel; 7250 Market St; h9am-5pm Jun-Aug, 9am-5pm Mon-Fri Sep-May) for local info, including comprehensive North Coast Trail maps ($9.95). Say hi to the stuffed otter while you're checking your email at the terminal (per half-hour $2.50).

ℹ️ Getting There & Around

Pacific Coastal Airlines (www.pacific-coastal.com) services arrive from Vancouver ($235, 1¼ hours, up to three daily).

Greyhound Canada (www.greyhound.ca) buses roll in from Port McNeill ($14.90, 45 minutes, daily), Campbell River ($48.30, 3½ hours, daily) and Nanaimo ($73, seven hours, daily).

BC Ferries (www.bcferries.com) arrive from Prince Rupert (passenger/vehicle $170/390, 15 hours, schedules vary) through the spectacular Inside Passage.

North Island Transportation (nit@island.net) operates a handy shuttle ($8) to/from the ferry terminal via area hotels.

CAPE SCOTT PROVINCIAL PARK

It's more than 550km from the comparatively metropolis-like streets of down-island Victoria to the nature-hugging trailhead of this remote **park** (www.bcparks.ca) on Vancouver Island's crenulated northern tip. But if you really want to experience the raw, ravishing beauty of BC – especially its unkempt shorelines, breeze-licked rainforests and stunning sandy bays animated with tumbling waves and beady-eyed seabirds – this should be your number-one destination.

Hike the well-maintained, relatively easy 2.5km San Josef Bay Trail and you'll stroll from the shady confines of the trees right onto one of the best beaches in BC; a breathtaking, windswept expanse of roiling water, forested crags and the kind of age-old caves that could easily harbor lost smugglers. You can camp right here on the beach or just admire the passing ospreys before plunging back into the trees.

With several wooded trails to tempt you – most are aimed at well-prepared hikers with plenty of gumption – the forest offers moss-covered yew trees, centuries-old cedars and a soft carpet of sun-dappled ferns covering every square centimeter.

Between the giant slugs that seem to own the place, you'll also spot historic plaques showing that this unlikely area was once settled by Scandinavian pioneers who arrived here from Europe on a promise from the government of a main road link from down-island. Now mostly reclaimed by the forest, the evocative, crumbling shacks of these settlers, most of whom eventually left when the promised road failed to materialize, can still be seen almost hidden in the dense undergrowth.

One of the area's shortest trails (2km), in adjoining **Raft Cove Provincial Park** (www.bcparks.ca), brings you to the wide, crescent beach and beautiful lagoons of Raft Cove. You're likely to have the entire 1.3km expanse to yourself, although the locals also like to surf here (it's their secret, so don't tell anyone).

Hiking much further in the region is not for the uninitiated or unprepared. But if you really want to go for it, consider hitting the relatively new **North Coast Trail** (p703).

SOUTHERN GULF ISLANDS

Stressed-out Vancouverites tired of languishing on their favorite Stanley Park beach or trying to find the city's best sushi restaurants often seek solace in the restorative arms of the rustic Southern Gulf Islands, conveniently strung like a necklace of enticing pearls between the mainland and Vancouver Island. Once colonized by hippy-dippy Canadian dropouts and fugitive US draft dodgers, Salt Spring, Galiano, Mayne, Saturna and North and South Pender Islands are the natural retreat of choice for many in the region.

Not all the islands are created equal, of course. Salt Spring is recommended if you want a sojourn where you don't have to sacrifice on great restaurants; Galiano is popular if you fancy a wood cabin, scenic nooks and outdoor activities; and remote Saturna is ideal if you really need to escape from the tourist hordes dogging your every step. Wherever you decide to head, the soothing relaxation begins once you step on the ferry to get here: time suddenly slows, your heart rate drops to hibernation level and the scenery of forested isles and glassy water slides by like a slow-motion nature documentary.

During your ferry trip, pick up a free copy of the *Gulf Islands Driftwood* (www.gulfislandsdriftwood.com) newspaper for local info, listings and happenings.

Southern Gulf Islands

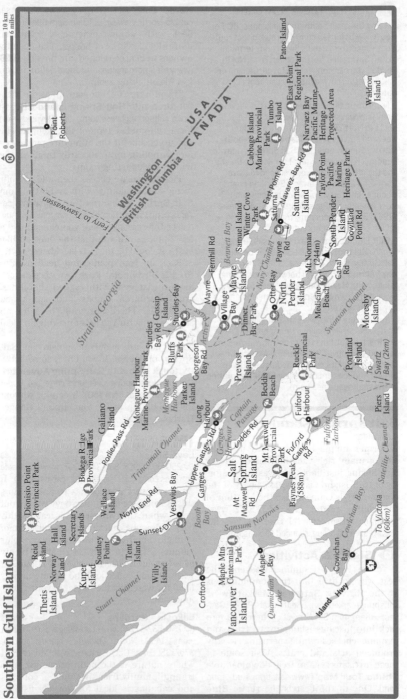

BRITISH COLUMBIA

10 km
6 miles

Point Roberts

Patos Island

Waldron Island

East Point Regional Park

Cabbage Island Marine Provincial Park

Tumbo Island

Narvaez Bay Pacific Marine Heritage Protected Area

Samuel Island

Winter Cove Park

East Point Rd

Saturna

Navarez Bay Rd

Saturna Island

Taylor Point Pacific Marine Heritage Park

Washington
British Columbia

U S A
C A N A D A

Ferry to Tsawwassen

Bennett Bay

Fernhill Rd

Mayne

Mayne Island

Otter Bay

Payne Rd

Mt Norman (244m)

South Pender Island

Gowlland Point Rd

Canal Rd

Village

Dinner Bay Park

North Pender Island

Medicine Beach

Strait of Georgia

Gossip Island

Sturdies Bay

Sturdies Bay Rd

Bluffs Park

Parker Island

Georgeson Bay Rd

Prevost Island

Swanson Channel

Moresby Island

Montague Harbour

Montague Harbour Marine Provincial Park

Galiano Island

Potlie Pass Rd

Bodega Ridge Provincial Park

Dionisio Point Provincial Park

Long Harbour

Montague Harbour

Georges

Beddis Beach

Captain Passage

Trincomali Channel

Ruckle Provincial Park

Portland Island

To Swartz Bay (2km)

Piers Island

Upper Ganges Rd

Ganges

Leddis Rd

Salt Spring Island

Mt Maxwell Provincial Park

Fulford Ganges Rd

Fulford Harbour

Fulford Harbour

Satellite Channel

Wallace Island

Secretary Islands

North End Rd

Vesuvius Bay

Booth Bay

Mt Maxwell Rd

Baynes Peak (588m)

Reid Island

Hall Island

Sunset Dr

Southey Point

Tent Island

Kuper Island

Norway Island

Thetis Island

Willy Island

Crofton

Maple Mtn Centennial Park

Maple Bay

Sansum Narrows

Sansum Narrows

Quamichan Lake

Cowichan Bay

Cowichan Bay

To Victoria (60km)

Island Hwy

Vancouver Island

Stuart Channel

ℹ Getting There & Around

Serving the main Southern Gulf Islands, **BC Ferries** (www.bcferries.com) operates direct routes from Vancouver Island's Swartz Bay terminal to Salt Spring and North Pender. From North Pender, you can connect to Mayne, Galiano or Salt Spring. From Mayne, you can connect to Saturna.

From the mainland, there is a direct service from Tsawwassen to Galiano, which then connects to North Pender. There are also direct weekend services from Tsawwassen to both Mayne (Sunday only) and Salt Spring (Friday to Sunday). For more frequent services to these and the other islands, you will need to travel from Tsawwassen to Swartz Bay, then board a connecting ferry. For island hopping, consider a handy SailPass (four-/seven-day pass $199/239). It covers ferry travel around the region on 20 different routes.

Gulf Islands Water Taxi (www.saltspring.com/watertaxi) runs walk-on ferries between Salt Spring, North Pender and Saturna (one way/return $15/25) and between Salt Spring, Galiano and Mayne (one way/return $15/25), twice daily from September to June and once a day in July and August.

Salt Spring Air (www.saltspringair.com) floatplane services arrive throughout the Southern Gulf Islands from downtown Vancouver and Vancouver International Airport. Check the website for its many schedules and fares. Similar services are offered by **Seair Seaplanes** (www.seairseaplanes.com).

Salt Spring Island

POP 10,500

A former hippie enclave that's now the site of many rich vacation homes, pretty Salt Spring justifiably receives the majority of Gulf Island visitors. The heart of the community is Ganges, also the location of the **visitor center** (☎250-537-5252; www.saltspringtourism.com; 121 Lower Ganges Rd; ⊗9am-5pm Jul & Aug, reduced off-season).

◉ Sights & Activities

If you arrive on a summer weekend, the best way to dive into the community is at the thriving **Saturday Market** (www.saltspringmarket.com; Centennial Park, Ganges; ⊗8am-4pm Sat Apr-Oct), where you can tuck into luscious island-grown fruit and piquant cheeses while perusing locally produced arts and crafts. Visit some of these artisans via a free downloadable **Studio Tour Map** (www.saltspringstudiotour.com). One of the best is the rustic **Blue**

Horse Folk Art Gallery (www.bluehorse.ca; 175 North View Dr; ⊗10am-5pm Sun-Fri Mar-Dec), with, among other cool creations, its funky carvings of horses. The friendly owners recently opened an on-site **B&B** (www.bloomorganicbandb.com; d $150) if you feel like sticking around.

If you haven't eaten your fill at the market, drop into **Salt Spring Island Cheese** (www.saltspringcheese.com; 285 Reynolds Rd) for a self-guided tour of the facilities. Be sure to check out the miniature ponies before sampling up to 10 curdy treats in the winery-style tasting room.

Pick a favorite cheese then add to your picnic-in-the-making with a bottle from **Salt Spring Vineyards** (www.saltspringvineyards.com; 151 Lee Rd; ⊗11am-5pm mid-Jun–Aug, reduced off-season), where you can sample a few tipples until you find the one you like best – it could be the rich blackberry port.

Pack up your picnic and head over to **Ruckle Provincial Park** (www.bcparks.ca), a southeast gem with ragged shorelines, gnarly arbutus forests and sun-kissed farmlands. There are trails here for all skill levels, with Yeo Point making an ideal pit stop.

It's not all about hedonism on Salt Spring, of course. If you crave some activity, touch base with **Salt Spring Adventure Co** (www.saltspringadventures.com; 124 Upper Ganges Rd; tours from $50). It can kit you out for a bobbling kayak tour around Ganges Harbour.

🛏 Sleeping

Love Shack　　　　　　　　CABIN **$$**
(☎250-653-0007, 866-341-0007; www.oceansidecottages.com; 521 Isabella Rd; cabins $135) If Austin Powers ever comes to Salt Spring, this is where he'll stay. A groovy waterfront nook, where the hardest part is leaving, this cozy cottage has a lava lamp, a collection of vintage cameras and a record player plus albums (Abba to Stan Getz). With plenty of artsy flourishes, the kitchen is stocked with organic coffee and the private deck is ideal for watching the sunset in your velour jumpsuit.

Lakeside Gardens　　　　　CABIN **$$**
(☎250-537-5773; www.lakesidegardens resort .com; 1450 North End Rd; cabana/cottage $75/135; ⊗Apr-Oct) A rustic wooded retreat where nature is the main attraction, this tranquil, family-friendly clutch of cottages and cabanas is ideal for low-key fishing,

swimming and boating. The cabanas are basic – think camping in a cabin – with fridges, outdoor BBQs and solar-heated outdoor showers, while the larger cottages have TVs, en suites and full kitchens.

Wisteria Guest House
B&B $$

($250-537-5899, 888-537-5899; www.wisteria guesthouse.com; 268 Park Dr; r/cottage $129/159) A home-style B&B with welcoming cats and dogs, there are six guest rooms here (some with shared bathrooms) and a pair of private-entrance studios, plus a small cottage space that has its own compact kitchen facilities. The property is surrounded by a rambling, flower-strewn garden that lends an air of tranquility. An excellent cooked breakfast is served in the large communal lounge.

Harbour House Hotel
HOTEL $$

($250-537-5571, 888-799-5571; www.salt springharbourhouse.com; 121 Upper Ganges Rd; s & d from $129; @) Great Ganges location and a combination of motel-style and superior rooms with Jacuzzis.

Seabreeze Inne
MOTEL $$

($250-537-4145, 800-434-4112; www.sea breezeinne.com; 101 Bittancourt Rd; s & d from $119; @) Immaculate motel up the hill from Ganges; rates include continental breakfast and outdoor hot tub.

✖ Eating & Drinking

Tree House Café
CAFE $$

(www.treehousecafe.ca; 106 Purvis Lane; mains $11-18) A magical outdoor cafe in the heart of Ganges; you'll be sitting in the shade of a large plum tree as you choose from a menu of comfort pastas, Mexican specialties and gourmet burgers – the Teriyaki salmon burger is recommended, washed down with a hoppy bottle of Salt Spring Pale Ale. Live music every night in summer.

Barb's Buns
CAFE $

(121 McPhillips Ave; mains $6-9) Good wholesome treats are the menu mainstays here, with heaping pizza slices, hearty soups and bulging sandwiches drawing the lunch crowd, many of them grateful vegetarians. Others repeatedly fail to resist the mid-afternoon lure of organic coffee, cookies, cakes and, of course, Barb's lovely buns.

Raven Street Market Café
CANADIAN $$

(www.ravenstreet.ca; 321 Fernwood Rd; mains $8.50-18) A favorite haunt of north-island locals, this neighborhood eatery has a comfort-food

menu with a gourmet twist. Adventurous pizzas include herbed lamb and artichoke, while the awesome seafood-and-sausage gumbo combines mussels, tiger prawns and chorizo sausage with a secret Creole recipe. There's a little shop here, too, so you can pick up some local wine for breakfast.

Restaurant House Piccolo
WEST COAST $$$

(www.housepiccolo.com; 108 Hereford Ave; mains $20-28) White tablecloth dining – duck is recommended – along with Salt Spring's best wine list.

Oystercatcher Seafood Bar & Grill
SEAFOOD $$

(100 Manson Rd; mains $8-16) Delectable local seafood, especially the oysters and salmon.

ℹ Getting There & Around

BC Ferries, Gulf Island Water Taxis and Salt Spring Air operate services to Salt Spring (see p708). The island's three ferry docks are at Long Harbour, Fulford Harbour and Vesuvius Bay. Water taxis and floatplanes arrive in Ganges Harbour.

If you don't have your own car, **Salt Spring Island Transit** (www.busonline.ca; adult/under-5 $2/free) runs a five-route mini-shuttle service around the island, connecting to all three ferry docks. Bus 4 runs from Long Harbour to Ganges. Alternatively, **Amber Taxi Co** ($250-537-3277) provides a local cab service.

North & South Pender Islands
POP 2200

Once joined by a sandy isthmus, the North and South Penders are far quieter than Salt Spring and attract those looking for a quiet, retreat approach to their vacation. With pioneer farms, old-time orchards and almost 40 coves and beaches, the Penders – now linked by a single-lane bridge – are a good spot for bikers and hikers. For visitor information check www.penderislandchamber.com.

◉ Sights & Activities

Enjoy the sand at **Medicine Beach** and **Clam Bay** on North Pender as well as **Gowlland Point** on the east coast of South Pender. Just over the bridge to South Pender is **Mt Norman Regional Park**, complete with a couple of hikes that promise grand views of the surrounding islands. There's a regular Saturday **farmers market** (⊙Apr-Nov) in the community hall and a smaller one at the Driftwood Centre, the region's not-very-big commercial hub.

Dozens of artists call Pender home and you can chat with them in their galleries and studios by downloading a pair of free maps from **Pender Creatives** (www.pender creatives.com) that reveal exactly where they're all at. Not surprisingly, most are on North Pender.

You can hit the water with a paddle (and hopefully a boat) with the friendly team at **Pender Island Kayak Adventures** (www. kayakpenderisland.com; Otter Bay Marina; tours adult/child from $45/30). If you prefer recreation of the bottled variety, consider a tasting at **Morning Bay Vineyard** (www. morningbay.ca; 6621 Harbour Hill; ⏰10am-5pm Wed-Sun, reduced off-season), a handsome post-and-beam-built winery where the grapes are grown on a steep 20-step terrace. Its recommended Gewurztraminer-Riesling blend is light and crisp.

🛏 Sleeping

Poet's Cove Resort & Spa   HOTEL $$$
(☎250-629-2100, 888-512-7638; www.poetscove. com; 9801 Spalding Rd, Bedwell Harbour, South Pender; r from $250; ▓) A luxurious harborfront lodge with arts-and-crafts-accented rooms, most with great views across the glassy water. Some of Chichi extras include a full-service spa and an activity center that books ecotours and fishing excursions around the area. There's also an elegant west coast restaurant (Aurora), where you can dine in style. As well as this, the resort offers kayak treks plus a full-treatment spa, complete with that all-important steam cave.

Inn on Pender Island   HOTEL $$
(☎250-629-3353; 800-550-0172; www.innon pender.com; 4709 Canal Rd; r/cabins $99/149) A rustic lodge with motel-style rooms and a couple of cozy, wood-lined cabins, you're surrounded here by verdant woodland, which explains the frequent appearance of wandering deer. The lodge rooms are neat and clean and share an outdoor hot tub, but the waterfront cabins have barrel-vaulted ceilings, full kitchens and little porches out front. There's also an on-site restaurant.

Shangri-La Oceanfront B&B   B&B $$$
(☎250-629-3808, 877-629-2800; www.pend-erislandshangrila.com; 5909 Pirate's Rd; d from $185) It's all about escaping and relaxing at this three-unit waterfront property where each room has its own outdoor hot tub for drinking in the sunset through the trees. You'll have your own private entrance plus pampering extras like thick robes, large individual decks and a sumptuous breakfast. Our fave room is the Lost in Space suite, where the walls are painted with a glowing galaxy theme.

Arcadia by the Sea   CABIN $$
(☎250-629-3221, 877-470-8439; www.arca diabythesea.com; 1329 MacKinnon Rd; d $125-225; ⏰May-Sep; ▓) Tranquil, adults-only sleepover with three homely cottages (each with kitchen and deck). Free ferry pickup.

Pior Centennial Park   CAMPGROUND $
(☎604-689-9025, 800-689-9025; www.discov ercamping.ca; campsite from $15; ⏰mid-May–mid-Oct) Nestled among trees, this fairly basic campground has a cold-water pump, pit toilets and picnic tables.

🍴 Eating

Pender Island Bakery Café   BAKERY $
(Driftwood Centre, 1105 Stanley Point Dr; mains $6-16) The locals' fave coffeehouse, there's much more to this chatty nook than regular joe. For a start, the java is organic, as are many of the bakery treats, including some giant cinnamon buns that will have you wrestling an islander for the last one. Gourmet pizzas are a highlight – the Gulf Islander (smoked oysters, anchovies, spinach and three cheeses) is best – while heartier fare includes spinach and pine nut pie and a bulging seafood lasagna.

Hope Bay Café   SEAFOOD $$
(4301 Bedwell Harbour Rd; mains $16-24) Seafood rules (closely followed by the sterling views across Plumper Sound) at this laidback, bistro-like spot a few minutes from the Otter Bay ferry dock. The fish and chips are predictably good but dig deeper into the menu for less-expected treats like stuffed pork shoulder, herb-crusted wild BC salmon and the excellent bouillabaisse that's brimming with mussels, scallops, salmon and cod.

Aurora   WEST COAST $$$
(☎250-629-2115; www.poetscove.com; Poet's Cove Resort & Spa; mains $18-34) Seasonal and regional are the operative words at this fine-dining eatery. Allow yourself to be tempted by a Salt Spring goat-cheese tart starter but save room for main dishes like the local seafood medley of crab, scallops and mussels. Dinner reservations are recommended, but if you can't get in here, head to the resort's Syrens lounge bar.

ℹ Getting There & Around

BC Ferries, Gulf Island Water Taxis and Salt Spring Air operate services to Pender (see p708). Ferries stop at North Pender's Otter Bay, where most of the islands' population resides. If you don't have a car, and your accommodations can't pick you up, catch a **Pender Island Taxi** (☎250-629-3555).

Saturna Island

POP 325

Small and suffused with tranquility, Saturna is a lovely nature retreat that's remote enough to deter casual visitors. Almost half the island, laced with curving bays, stunning rock bluffs and towering arbutus trees, is part of the Gulf Islands National Park Reserve and the only crowds you're likely to come across are the feral goats that have called this their munchable home for decades. If you've had enough of civilization, this is the place to be. The **Saturna Island Tourism Association** (www.saturna tourism.com) website has a downloadable map. Bring cash with you – there are no ATMs (and only two shops) here.

On the north side of the island, **Winter Cove Park** has a white-sand beach that's popular for swimming, boating and fishing. If you're here for Canada Day (July 1), you should also partake of the island's main annual event in the adjoining Hunter Field. This communal **Lamb Barbeque** (www.saturnalambbarbeque.com; adult/child $20/10) complete with live music, sack races, beer garden and a smashing meat-lovers feast, is centered on a pagan fire pit surrounded by dozens of staked-out, slow-roasting sheep.

Walk off your meat belly the next day with a hike up **Mt Warburton Pike** (497m), where you'll spot wild goats, soaring eagles and restorative panoramic views of the surrounding islands: focus your binoculars and you might spy a whale or two sailing quietly along the coast.

Wine fans can also partake of tastings and tours at **Saturna Island Winery** (www.saturnavineyards.com; 8 Quarry Rd; ◷11:30am-4:30pm), which also has an on-site **bistro** that's only open for lunch.

If you're been inspired by the gentler pace of life to stick around, **Breezy Bay B&B** (☎250-539-5957; www.saturnacan.net/breezy; 131 Payne Rd; d $95) is a century-old still-working farmhouse property with its own private beach. The main house has wooden floors, stone fireplaces and even an old library, while your room – with shared bathroom – will be fairly basic but clean and comfortable. Breakfast is in a window-lined room overlooking a garden. Alternatively, **Saturna Lodge** (◷250-539-2254, 866-539-2254; www.saturna.ca; 130 Payne Rd; d $119-149; ☏) is an elegant, six-room country inn, combining landscaped gardens with close proximity to the waterfront. Rates include breakfast.

ℹ Getting There & Around

BC Ferries, Gulf Island Water Taxis and Salt Spring Air operate services to Saturna (see p708). The ferry docks at Lyall Harbour on the west of the island. A car is not essential here since some lodgings are near the ferry terminal, but there are no taxis or shuttle services to get you around. Only bring your bike if you like a challenge: Saturna is a little too hilly for casual pedalers.

Mayne Island

POP 900

Once a stopover for gold rush miners (who nicknamed it 'Little Hell') on their way to the mainland, Mayne is the region's most historic island. Long past its importance as a commercial hub, it now houses a colorful clutch of resident artists. For further information, visit www.mayneislandchamber.ca.

The heritage **Agricultural Hall** in Miners Bay hosts the lively farmers market (◷10am-1pm Sat Jul-Sep) of local crafts and produce, while the nearby **Plumper Pass Lock-up** (◷11am-3pm Fri-Mon late Jun-early Sep) is a tiny museum that originally served as a jailhouse.

Among the most visit-worthy galleries and artisan studios on the island is **Mayne Island Glass Foundry** (www.mayne islandglass.com; ◷10am-5pm Jun-Sep, reduced off-season), where recycled glass is used to fashion new jewelry and ornaments – pick up a cool green-glass slug for the road.

The south shore's **Dinner Bay Park** has a lovely sandy beach, as well as a **Japanese Garden**. Built by locals to commemorate early-20th-century Japanese residents, it's immaculately landscaped and is lit up with fairy lights at Christmas.

For paddlers and pedalers, **Mayne Island Kayaking** (www.kayakmayneisland.com; 563

Arbutus Dr; rentals 2hr/8hr from $40/60, tours from $50) offers rentals and tours.

If it's time to eat, head to **Wild Fennel Restaurant** (574 Fernhill Rd; mains $16-20), which specializes in seasonal fresh ingredients. The menu changes constantly, but hope for the Crab Three Ways – crab served in salad, bisque and lollipop form.

If you're just too lazy to head back to the mainland, **Mayne Island Resort** (☑866-539-5399; www.mayneislandresort.com; 494 Arbutus Dr; r/cottage from $99/225; 🛏🐾) combines ocean-view rooms in a century-old inn with swanky new luxe beach cottages. There's also a large resto-bar and a new spa.

❶ Getting There & Around

BC Ferries, Gulf Island Water Taxis and Salt Spring Air operate services to Mayne (see p708). For transportation around the island, call **MIDAS Taxi** (☑250-539-3132).

Galiano Island

POP 1100

Named after a Spanish explorer who visited in the 1790s, the bustling ferry end of Galiano is markedly different to the rest of the island, which becomes ever more forested and tranquil as you continue your drive from the dock. Supporting the widest ecological diversity of the Southern Gulf Islands – and regarded by some as the most beautiful – this skinny landmass offers a bounty of activities for visiting marine enthusiasts and landlubbers alike.

Once you've got your bearings – ie driven off the ferry – head for **Montague Harbour Marine Provincial Park** for trails to beaches, meadows and a cliff carved by glaciers. In contrast, **Bodega Ridge Provincial Park** is renowned for its eagle, loon and cormorant bird life and has some spectacular drop-off viewpoints.

The protected waters of **Trincomali Channel** and the more chaotic waters of **Active Pass** satisfy paddlers of all skill levels. **Gulf Island Kayaking** (www.seakayak.ca; 3hr/day rental from $38/75, tours from $55) can help with rentals and guided tours.

If you're without a car, or you just want to stretch your legs, you can explore the island with a bike from **Galiano Bicycle** (www.galianoisland.com/galianobicycle; 4hr/day $25/30).

Fuel up on food and local gossip at **Daystar Market Café** (96 Georgeson Bay Rd; mains $4-10), a funky hangout that serves hearty salads, thick sandwiches and fruit smoothies. Alternatively, down a pint or three at the venerable **Hummingbird Pub** (www.hummingbirdpub.com; 47 Sturdies Bay Rd; mains $8-12), where pub grub on the patio is always a good idea.

Among the places to sleep on the island, sophisticates will enjoy **Galiano Inn** (☑250-539-3388, 877-530-3939; www.galianoinn.com; 134 Madrona Dr; r $249-299; 📶), a Tuscan-style villa with 10 elegant rooms, each with a fireplace and romantic oceanfront terrace. Adult, sophisticated and soothing, it's close to the Sturdies Bay ferry dock. Those craving a nature-hugging retreat will likely enjoy **Bodega Ridge** (☑250-539-2677, 877-604-2677; www.bodegaridge.com; 120 Manastee Rd; d $200; 📶), a tranquil woodland clutch of seven cabins at the other end of the island. Each has three bedrooms and is furnished in rustic country fashion.

The main clutch of businesses and services is around the ferry dock at Sturdies Bay and includes a garage, post office, bookstore and **visitor info booth** (www.galianoisland.com; 2590 Sturdies Bay Rd; ⊙Jul & Aug).

❶ Getting There & Around

BC Ferries, Gulf Island Water Taxis and Salt Spring Air operate services to Galiano (see p708). Ferries arrives at the Sturdies Bay dock.

FRASER & THOMPSON VALLEYS

Vancouverites looking for an inland escape shoot east on Hwy 1 through the fertile plains of places like Abbotsford. Most just whiz past this farmland and you should too – unless you have a hankering to see a turnip in the rough.

About 150km east of Vancouver, Hope has a good **visitor center** (☑604-869-2021; www.hope.ca; 919 Water Ave; ⊙9am-5pm) with plenty of information about the local provincial parks and the region. This is also where the road does a three-way split. Hwy 1 continues spectacularly north, literally through the vertical walls of the beautiful Fraser Canyon. From Lytton, it follows the Thompson River and the terrain slowly smoothes out and becomes drier, foreshadowing the ranchlands of the Cariboo region to the north beyond Cache Creek. Hwy 5 shoots its multilane expanse 200km northeast to the commercial center of Kamloops. The Crowsnest Hwy (Hwy 3) takes a circuitous and pretty course east through rugged EC Manning Provincial Park and on to Osoyoos and the southern Okanagan Valley.

Note that on weekends and other busy times, Hwy 1 west of Hope can get traffic-clogged.

EC Manning Provincial Park

After the farmlands of the Lower Mainland, this 708-sq-km **provincial park** (☎604-795-6169; www.bcparks.ca), 30km southeast of Hope, is a hint of bigger – much bigger – things to come in the east (think Rocky Mountains). It packs in a lot: dry valleys; dark, mountainous forests; roiling rivers; and alpine meadows. It makes a good pause along Hwy 3 but don't expect solitude as there are scores of folk from the burgs west seeking the same.

The following hiking choices are easily reached from Hwy 3:

Dry Ridge Trail Crosses from dry interior to alpine climate; excellent views and wildflowers (3km round trip, one hour).

Canyon Nature Trail Nice loop trail with a river crossing on a bridge (2km, 45 minutes).

Lightning Lake Loop The perfect intro: a level loop around this central lake. Look for critters in the evening (9km, two hours).

Manning is a four-seasons playground. **Manning Park Resort** (☎250-840-8822, 800-330-3321; www.manningpark.com) offers downhill skiing and snowboarding (adult/child day pass $45/30) and 100km of groomed trails for cross-country skiing and snowshoeing. It also has the only indoor accommodations throughout the park. The 73 somewhat-pricey units (from $150) are a mix of rooms in the lodge and cabins. All provide the use of the requisite hot tub.

You can pitch your tent at **Coldspring**, **Hampton** or **Mule campgrounds** (campsites $21) or the more popular **Lightning Lake campground** (☎reservations 800-689-9025; www.discovercamping.ca; campsites $28), which takes reservations. There are 10 **backcountry campgrounds** (campsites per person $5) for overnight hikers that are normally not accessible before late June.

The park's **visitor center** (⊙8:30am-4:30pm Jun-Sep, 8:30am-4pm Mon-Fri Oct-May) is 30km inside the western boundary and has detailed hiking descriptions and a relief model of the park and nearby beaver ponds.

Greyhound Canada (☎800-661-8747; www.greyhound.ca) has buses from Vancouver ($46, three to four hours, two daily).

Fraser River Canyon

The name alone makes Spuzzum a fun stop along Hwy 1 on its way to Cache Creek, 85km west of Kamloops. The road shadows the swiftly flowing Fraser River and, as you'd expect, white-water rafting is huge here. The grand scenery and several good provincial parks make this a winning trip.

Just north of Spuzzum, **Alexandra Bridge Provincial Park** (☎604-795-6169; www.bcparks.ca) makes a scenic stop; you can picnic while gazing at the historic 1926 span. Further north, the ecologically diverse **Stein Valley Nlaka'pamux Heritage Park** (www.bcparks.ca) is managed with the Lytton First Nation. It offers some excellent long-distance hiking through dry valleys and snow-clad peaks amid one of the best-preserved watersheds in lower BC.

Fraser & Thompson Valleys

White-water rafting down the Fraser and its tributaries' fast-flowing rapids is popular and a number of companies near Lytton lead trips. One-day trips cost from $120 per adult.

Kumsheen Rafting Resort (☎800-663-6667; www.kumsheen.com) offers a variety of trips and funky accommodations in tent-cabins ($100). **Hyak River Rafting** (☎800-663-7238; www.hyak.com) covers all the main waterways.

Kamloops

POP 83,200

If you've opted to follow Hwy 1 to the east to the Rockies and Banff, Kamloops makes a useful break in the journey. Motels abound and there's a walkable historic center. Historically, the Shuswap First Nation found the many rivers and lakes useful for transportation and salmon fishing. Traders set up camp for fur hunting in 1811.

Hwy 1 cuts eastwest through town, linking Vancouver with the Rockies, while Yellowhead Hwy (Hwy 5) heads northeast to Jasper and southwest to Vancouver via Merritt (this stretch is called the Coquihalla Hwy). The focus of the downtown area is tree-lined Victoria St, which is a lively place on sunny days; very busy train tracks separate the wide Thompson River from the downtown area. Franchises and malls line the highlands along Hwy 1.

◉ Sights & Activities

Using Victoria St as your anchor, stroll downtown, stopping at the art gallery and museum.

Kamloops Museum MUSEUM
(☎250-828-3576; www.kamloops.ca/museum; cnr Seymour St & 2nd Ave; adult/child $3/1; ◷9:30am-4:30pm Tue-Sat, until 7:30pm Thu) Kamloops Museum is in a vintage building and has a suitably vintage collection of historic photographs. Come here for the scoop on river-namesake David Thompson and a new floor dedicated to kids.

Kamloops Heritage Railway HISTORIC TRAIN
(☎250-374-2141; www.kamrail.com; 510 Lorne St; adult/child from $17/10) Across the train tracks from downtown, the Kamloops Heritage Railway runs 70-minute train rides powered by steam engine.

Kamloops Art Gallery ART GALLERY
(☎250-377-2400; www.kag.bc.ca; 465 Victoria St; adult/child $5/3; ◷10am-5pm Mon-Wed, Fri & Sat, 10am-9pm Thu) Suitably loft-like in feel, the Kamloops Art Gallery has an emphasis on contemporary Western and aboriginal works by regional artists.

British Columbia Wildlife Park ZOO
(☎250-573-3242; www.bczoo.org; adult/child $13/10; ◷9:30am-4:30pm) Parents may look longingly at the cages used to corral unruly critters at the British Columbia Wildlife Park, 17km east of Kamloops on Hwy 1. Captives include bears and cougars.

Paul Lake Provincial Park PARK
(☎250-819-7376; www.bcparks.ca) On the often-hot summer days, the beach at Paul Lake Provincial Park beckons and you may spot falcons and coyotes. There is a 20km mountain-biking loop. It's 24km north of Kamloops via Hwy 5.

⏢ Sleeping

Older and cheaper motels can be found along a stretch of Hwy 1 east of downtown. Columbia St, from the center up to Hwy 1 above town, has another gaggle of chain and indie motels. The nearby parks have good camping.

TOP CHOICE **Plaza Heritage Hotel** HOTEL $$
(☎250-377-8075, 877-977-5292; www.plazaheritagehotel.com; 405 Victoria St; r $110-250; ☞☀☎) You'll think you've fallen into a Laura Ashley seconds bin at this 66-room six-story classic that's little changed since its opening in 1928. In a town of bland modernity in the lodging department, the Plaza reeks character. Excellent free breakfasts.

South Thompson Inn INN $$
(☎250-573-3777, 800-797-7713; www.stigr.com; 3438 Shuswap Rd; r $140-300; ☀☎☒) Some 20km west of town (via Hwy 1), this ranch-like waterfront sleepover is perched on the banks of the South Thompson and set amid rolling grasslands. Its 57 rooms are spread between the wood-framed main building, a small manor house and some converted stables.

Scott's Inn MOTEL $$
(☎250-372-8221; www.scottsinn.kamloops.com; cnr 11th Ave & Columbia St; r from $90; ☀@☎☒) Unlike many budget competitors, Scott's is close to the center. The 51 rooms are motel-standard but extras include an indoor pool, hot tub, cafe and rooftop sun deck.

DESTINATION	FARE	DURATION	FREQUENCY (PER DAY)
Vancouver	$64	5hr	7
Calgary	$90	10hr	4
Jasper	$61	6hr	2
Prince George	$77	7hr	4
Kelowna	$34	2½-4hr	3

✗ Eating & Drinking

Look for the free booklet *Farm Fresh*, which details the many local producers you can visit. Local farmers markets are held in the morning on Wednesday (corner of 5th Ave and Victoria St) and Saturday (corner of 2nd Ave and St Paul St). Victoria St is the place for nightlife.

Hello Toast   CAFE $
(☎250-372-9322; 428 Victoria St; mains $5-9; ☺8am-5pm Mon-Sat; ✍) As opposed to Good Morning Croissant, this veggie-friendly, organic cafe offers whole grains for some, and fried combos of bacon and eggs or burgers for others. Nice open front and sidewalk tables.

Chapter's Viewpoint Restaurant   FUSION $$
(☎250-374-3224; 610 Columbia St; mains $14-24; ☺11:30am-10pm Mon-Fri, 5-10pm Sat & Sun) The patio overlooking Kamloops is the best place to be on a balmy summer evening. The menu features sirloin steak and poached salmon but the New Mexican route is recommended.

Commodore   PUB $$
(☎250-851-3100; 369 Victoria St; ☺5pm-late Mon-Wed & Sat, from 11am Thu-Fri) Old-feeling pub with a long menu that highlights fondue, the Com is the place on Friday nights for live jazz and funk. Other nights, DJs spin pretty much anything.

Kelly O'Bryan's   PUB $
(☎250-828-1559; 244 Victoria St; meals $8-10; ☺noon-late) A classic fake-Irish bar (yes, that's a real category these days), this one has solid bar chow, good pints and a laughable number of employees wearing kilts (Scottish? Irish? Whatever!).

❶ Information

The **visitor center** (☎250-374-3377, 800-662-1994; www.tourismkamloops.com; 1290 W Hwy 1, exit 368; ☺8am-6pm daily summer, 9am-6pm Mon-Fri rest of year; 🛜) is just off Hwy 1, overlooking town. There's internet access here ($1 per 10 minutes, free wi-fi).

❶ Getting There & Around

Seven kilometers northwest of town, **Kamloops Airport** (YKA; ☎250-376-3613; www.kamloops airport.com) has daily service to/from Vancouver and Calgary.

Greyhound Canada (☎800-661-8747; www.greyhound.ca) is about 1km southwest of the center off Columbia St W.

VIA Rail (☎888-842-7245; www.viarail.ca) serves Kamloops North Station – 11km from town – with the tri-weekly *Canadian* on its run from Vancouver (9½ hours) to Jasper (9½ hours) and beyond. Fares vary greatly by season and class of service.

Kamloops Transit System (☎250-376-1216; www.transitbc.com/regions/kam; adult/child $2/1.50) runs local buses.

For a taxi, call **Yellow Cabs** (☎250-374-3333).

Around Kamloops

The hills looming northeast of Kamloops are home to **Sun Peaks Resort** (☎800-807-3257; www.sunpeaksresort.com; lift ticket adult/child $73/36). This ever-growing resort boasts 122 ski runs (including some 8km-long powder trails), 11 lifts and a pleasant base-area village. In summer, lifts (adult/child $39/23) provide access to more than two dozen mountain-bike trails.

Those saving their cash for the slopes and/or trails choose the **Sun Peaks Hostel** (☎250-578-0057; www.sunpeakshostel. com; 1140 Sun Peaks Rd; dm/d from $30/70; 🛜) over the various lodges, B&Bs and luxury condos.

Past the resort road, Hwy 5 continues north toward the Alberta border and Jasper National Park (440km from Kamloops). Along the way (125km from Kamloops) it passes near Wells Gray Provincial Park (p748), one of BC's finest and a haven for those who really want to get away from civilization.

OKANAGAN VALLEY

It is hard to know which harvest is growing faster in this fertile and beautiful valley: tourists or fruit. Certainly, bounty abounds in this ever-more-popular lovely swath midway between Vancouver and Alberta. The moniker 'Canada's Napa Valley' is oft repeated and somewhat apt. The 180km-long Okanagan Valley is home to dozens of excellent wineries, whose vines spread across the terraced hills, soaking up some of Canada's sunniest weather.

This recent emphasis on highbrow refreshments contrasts with the valley's traditional role as a summertime escape for generations of Canadians, who frolic in the string of lakes linking the Okanagan's towns. And while retirees mature slowly in the sun, so do orchards of peaches, apricots and other fruits that may not have the cachet of grapes but which give the air a perfumery redolence at the peak of summer.

Near the US border, Osoyoos is almost arid but things soon become greener heading north. Near the center, Kelowna is one of the fastest growing cities in Canada. It's a heady mix of culture, lakeside beauty and fun. In July and August, however, the entire valley can seem as overburdened as a grapevine right before the harvest. For many, the best time to visit is late spring and early fall, when the crowds are manageable.

Summer days are usually dry and hot, with the nights pleasantly cool. Winters are snowy but dry, making nearby Big White an attraction for skiers and snowboarders.

Osoyoos

POP 5100

Once-modest Osoyoos is on the brink of change, as it embraces an upscale and developed future as part of the new Okanagan Valley. The town takes its name from the First Nations word 'soyoos,' which means 'sand bar across,' and if the translation is a bit rough, the definition is not: much of the town is indeed on a narrow spit of land that divides Osoyoos Lake. It is ringed with beaches and the waters irrigate the lush farms, orchards and vineyards that line Hwy 97 going north out of town.

Nature's bounty aside, this is the arid end of the valley and locals like to say that the town marks the northern end of Mexico's Sonoran Desert; much of the town is done up in a manner that loses something across two borders. From the cactus-speckled sands to the town's cheesy faux tile-and-stucco architecture, it's a big change from the BC image of pine trees and mountains found in both directions on Hwy 3.

⊙ Sights & Activities

Osoyoos Lake is one of the warmest in the country. That, together with the sandy beaches, means great swimming. Many lakeside motels and campgrounds hire out kayaks, canoes and small boats. For sweeping valley views go just 3km east of town up Hwy 3. About 8km west of town on Hwy 3, look for **Spotted Lake**, a weird natural phenomenon that once would have made a kitschy roadside attraction. In the hot summer sun, the lake's water begins to evaporate, causing its high mineral content to crystallize and leave white-rimmed circles of green on the water.

TOP CHOICE **Osoyoos Desert Centre** NATURE PARK (☏250-495-2470; www.desert.org; off Hwy 97; adult/child $7/5; ☉9:30am-4:30pm mid-May–mid-Sep, call other times) Hear the rattle of a snake and the songs of birds at the Osoyoos Desert Centre, 3km north of town, which has interpretive kiosks along raised boardwalks that meander through the dry land. The nonprofit center offers 90-minute guided tours throughout the day. Special gardens focus on delights like delicate wildflowers. Note that, even here, condo development encroaches like sand dunes.

Nk'Mip Desert & Heritage Centre MUSEUM (☏250-495-7901; www.nkmipdesert.com; 1000 Rancher Creek Rd; adult/child $12/8; ☉9:30am-8pm Jul & Aug, to 4pm Jun & Sep, call other times) Part of a First Nations empire, the Nk'Mip Desert & Heritage Centre, off 45th St north of Hwy 3, features cultural demonstrations and guided tours of the sandy highlights. It also has a desert golf course, a noted winery, a resort and more.

🛏 Sleeping

The eastern edge of the lake is lined with campgrounds. More than a dozen modest motels line the narrow strip of land that splits Osoyoos Lake (beware of shabby older properties). Many cluster around Hwy 3 and there's another clump on the southwest shore near the border. Chains can be found at the junction. Rates plummet in winter.

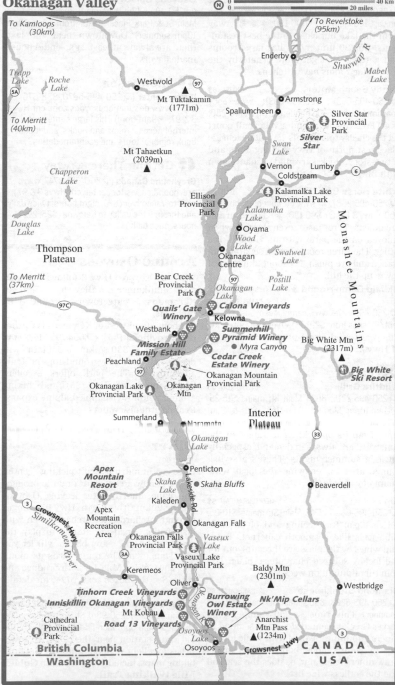

Avalon Inn MOTEL $$
(☎250-495-6334, 800-264-5999; www.avalon inn.ca; 9106 Main St; r $100-180; ✳@🛜) Away from the lake but close to the best restaurants, this 20-unit motel has large rooms and gardens that get more ornate by the year. Some rooms have kitchens.

Sandy Beach Motel MOTEL $$
(☎250-495-6931, 866-495-6931; www.sandy beachmotel.com; 6706 Ponderosa Dr; r $140-280; ✳@) Free rowboats and a volleyball court set the cheery tone at this 25-unit beachside place just north of Hwy 3. Bungalows and a two-story block surround a shady lawn with BBQs.

White Horse B&B B&B $$
(☎250-495-2887; www.thewhitehorsebb.com; 8000 Hwy 3 East; r $90-130; ✳) The gourmet breakfasts here taste even better when enjoyed on the patio with its views of the valley. The three rooms have a separate entrance and are plush. It's about 2km east of town, up the hill.

Nk'Mip Campground & RV Resort
CAMPGROUND $
(☎250-495-7279; www.campingosoyoos.com; tent/RV sites from $29/38) Over 300 sites at this year-round resort off 45th St north of Hwy 3.

✗ Eating

Wildfire Grill FUSION $$
(☎250-495-2215; 8526 Main St; mains $15-25; ⊙11am-10pm Mon-Fri, 9am-11pm Sat & Sun) Wildfire serves up a range of global cuisines from its open kitchen. Tables in the courtyard are always in demand, especially on long summer nights. There's a stylish lounge area for enjoying the local wine bounty by the glass.

Bibo MEDITERRANEAN $$
(☎250-495-6686; 8316 Main St; mains $10-25; ⊙11am-10pm) Rich-feeling and oh-so-dark, Bibo feels like a smooth cabernet. Tapas and wines by the glass are the stars; opt for the locally sourced charcuterie plate. DJs spin till midnight on weekends.

Diamond Steakhouse STEAKHOUSE $$
(☎250-495-6223; 8903 Main St; mains $15-25; ⊙dinner) This timeless '60s supper club serves Greek-accented steak and seafood to diners humming Dean Martin while lounging in commodious booths. The steaks draw diners from afar, as does the seafood and the endless wine list.

Osoyoos Gelato GELATO $
(☎250-495-5425; Watermark Beach Resort, cnr Main St & Park Place; treats from $2; ⊙10am-10pm summer) Downtown near the lake, there are always at least 24 splendid housemade flavors.

❶ Information

Visitor center (☎250-495-5070, 888-676-9667; www.destinationosoyoos.com; cnr Hwys 3 & 97; ⊙9am-5pm) This large center has internet access, maps and books, and it can book regional tours and accommodation.

❶ Getting There & Away

Greyhound Canada (☎800-661-8747; www. greyhound.ca; visitor center, cnr Hwys 3 & 97) runs to Vancouver ($70, eight hours, twice daily) and through the valley to Kelowna ($25, 2½ hours, once daily).

Around Osoyoos

West of Osoyoos, Hwy 3 follows the rugged Similkameen Valley for 47km to **Keremeos**, a cute town surrounded by orchards.

About 30km west of Keremeos is **Cathedral Provincial Park** (☎604-795-6169; www. bcparks.ca), a 330-sq-km mountain wilderness that's a playground for the truly adventurous. The park offers excellent backcountry camping ($5) and hiking around wildflower-dappled alpine expanses and turquoise waters.

Oliver

POP 4500

Once a humdrum fruit-picking center, Oliver is now a center for organic produce and wine. Shortly after leaving Osoyoos for the 20km drive north, Hwy 97 plunges through orchard after orchard laden with lush fruits. Roadside stands display the ripe bounty and many places will let you pick your own. The route earns its moniker 'The Golden Mile' for both produce and wine. See the boxed text, p724, for details on the latter.

The **visitor center** (☎250-498-6321; www. sochamber.ca; 36250 93rd St; ⊙9am-5pm daily May-Sep, 9am-5pm Mon-Fri Oct-Apr) is in the old train station near the center of town. It has excellent regional info and walking/ biking maps, including of the 10km **Golden Mile Walking Trail**.

The small roads through the vineyards around Oliver are made for exploring on a bike. **Double O Bikes** (☑250-498-8348; www. doublebikes.com; 35653 Main St; per day from $15; ⊘9:30am-5pm Tue-Sat) has tons of advice.

🛏 Sleeping & Eating

Oliver's vibrant **farmers market** (Lion's Park; ⊘8:30am-12:30pm Sat Jul-Sep) showcases local foodstuffs and is just off Hwy 97.

Burrowing Owl Guest House
BOUTIQUE HOTEL **$$$**
(☑250-498-0620, 877-498-0620; www.bovwine. ca; Road 22; r $180-350; 🅿@🛜🏊) One of the Okanagan's best wineries has 10 rooms with patios facing southwest over the vineyards. There's a big pool, hot tub, king-size beds and corporate mission-style decor. The **Sonora Room** (mains $12-25) is noted for its fusion cuisine. It's 13km south of Oliver, off Hwy 97.

Mount View Motel
MOTEL **$**
(☑250-498-3446; www.mountviewmotel.net; 34426 97th St; r $70-120; 🅿🛜) Close to the center of town, seven units sunbathe around a flower-bedecked motor court. All have kitchens – and corkscrews.

Cantaloupe Annie's
CAFE **$**
(☑250-498-2955; 34845 97th St; meals from $6; ⊘9:30am-5:30pm Mon-Sat, 11am-3pm Sun summer; 🛜) For a splendid picnic, peruse the deli cases at this cafe famous for its local specials, smoked meats and fruit-based desserts.

Medici's Gelateria
GELATO **$**
(☑250-498-2228; 9932 350th Ave; treats from $2; ⊘8am-6pm) Frozen delights so good, you'll want to worship – and you can easily, given this is an old church. Good coffee plus soups, paninis and more made with local produce.

Oliver to Penticton

About 10km north of Oliver on Hwy 97, nature reasserts itself. **Vaseux Wildlife Centre** (☑250-494-6500; ⊘dawn-dusk) has a 300m boardwalk for viewing oodles of birds (it's not just humans migrating here), bighorn sheep, mountain goats or some of the 14 species of bat. You can also hike to the **Bighorn National Wildlife Area** and the **Vaseux Lake National Migratory Bird Sanctuary**, with more than 160 bird species. The lake itself is an azure gem, well framed by sheer granite cliffs.

If you're not in a hurry, small roads on the east side of Skaha Lake between Okanagan Falls and Penticton are much more interesting (wineries and views) than Hwy 97.

Penticton
POP 32,900

Not as frenetic as Kelowna, Penticton combines the idle pleasures of a beach resort with its own edgy vibe. Long a final stop in life for Canadian retirees (which added a certain spin to its Salish-derived name Pen-Tak-Tin, meaning 'place to stay forever'), the town today is growing fast, along with the rest of the valley.

Penticton makes a good base for your valley pleasures. There are plenty of activities and diversions to fill your days even when you don't travel further afield. Ditch Hwy 97, which runs west of the center, for Main St and the attractively walkable downtown area, which extends about 10 blocks southward from the picture-perfect lakefront; avert your eyes from the long stretch of strip malls and high-rise condos further south.

👁 Sights

Okanagan Beach boasts about 1300m of sand, with average summer water temperatures of about 22°C. If things are jammed, there's often quieter shores at 1.5km-long **Skaha Beach**, south of the center.

IT'S TIME FOR FRUIT

Roadside stands and farms where you can pick your own fruit line Hwy 97 between Osoyoos and Penticton. Major Okanagan Valley crops and their harvest times:

Strawberries Mid-June to early July

Raspberries Early to mid-July

Cherries Mid-June to mid-August

Apricots Mid-July to mid-August

Peaches Mid-July to mid-September

Pears Mid-August to late September

Apples Early September to late October

Table Grapes Early September to late October

SS Sicamous
HISTORICAL SITE

(☎250-492-0405; 1099 Lakeshore Dr W; adult/child $5/1; ☉9am-9pm May-Oct, 10am-4pm Mon-Fri Nov-Apr) Right on the sand, the SS *Sicamous* hauled passengers and freight on Okanagan Lake from 1914 to 1936. Now restored and beached, it has been joined by the equally old tugboat, *SS Naramata*.

Casabella Princess
BOAT TOUR

(☎250-492-4090; www.casabellaprincess.com; adult/child $20/10; ☉varies, May-Sep) If the *Sicamous* stimulates your inner seaman, enjoy a one-hour, open-air lake tour on a faux stern-wheeler. There are multiple daily sailings at summer's peak.

Penticton Museum
MUSEUM

(☎250-490-2451; 785 Main St; admission by donation; ☉10am-5pm Tue-Sat) Inside the library, the Penticton Museum has delightfully eclectic displays, including the de rigueur natural-history exhibit with stuffed animals and birds plus everything you'd want to know about the Peach Festival.

Art Gallery of Southern Okanagan
ART GALLERY

(☎250-493-2928; 199 Marina Way; admission $2; ☉10am-5pm Tue-Sat) The beachfront Art Gallery of Southern Okanagan displays a diverse collection of regional, provincial and national artists.

🏃 Activities

The paved **Okanagan River Channel Biking & Jogging Path** follows the rather arid channel that links Okanagan Lake to Skaha Lake. But why pound the pavement when you can float? Classic cheesy resort diversions like minigolf await at the west end of Okanagan Beach.

Watersports

Coyote Cruises (☎250-492-2115; 215 Riverside Dr; rental & shuttle $11; ☉10am-4:30pm Jun-Aug) rents out inner tubes that you can float to a midway point on the channel. Coyote Cruises buses you back to the start near Okanagan Lake (if you have your own floatable, it's $5 for the bus ride).

There are several watersports rental places on Okanagan Lake. If it floats you can rent it, including kayaks for $20 an hour and ski boats for $280 for four hours.

Castaways (☎250-490-2033; Penticton Lakeside Resort, 21 Lakeshore Dr)

Pier Water Sports (☎250-493-8864; Rotary Park, Lakeshore Dr W)

Mountain Biking & Cycling

Long dry days and rolling hills add up to perfect conditions for mountain biking. Get to popular rides by heading east out of town, toward Naramata (p722). Follow signs to the city dump and Campbell's Mountain, where you'll find a single-track and dual-slalom course, both of which aren't too technical. Once you get there, the riding is mostly on the right-hand side, but once you pass the cattle guard, it opens up and you can ride anywhere.

For cycling, try the route through Naramata and onto the Kettle Valley Rail Trail (p722); other good options are the small, winery-lined roads south of town and east of Skaha Lake.

Rent bikes and pick up a wealth of information at **Freedom – The Bike Shop** (☎250-493-0686; www.freedombikeshop.com; 533 Main St; bikes per day $40). **Fun City** (☎250-462-1151; 1070 Lakeshore Dr; bikes per day $40) lives up the promise of its name with maps of self-guiding tours.

Rock Climbing

Propelled by the dry weather and compact gneiss rock, climbers from all over the world come to the **Skaha Bluffs** to enjoy a seven-month climbing season on more than 400 bolted routes. The local climbing group, **Skaha.org** (www.skaha.org), has comprehensive info on the bluffs, which are on Smythe Dr off Lakeside Rd on the east side of Skaha Lake. In 2010, **BC Parks** (www.bcparks.ca) assumed control of the site; learn more of future plans online.

Skaha Rock Adventures (☎250-493-1765; www.skaharockclimbing.com; 1-day intros from $120) offers advanced, technical instruction and introductory courses for anyone venturing into a harness for the first time.

Skiing & Snowboarding

Apex Mountain Resort (☎877-777-2739, conditions 250-487-4848; www.apexresort.com; lift tickets adult/child $60/37), 37km west of Penticton off Green Mountain Rd, is one of Canada's best small ski resorts. It has more than 68 downhill runs for all ability levels, but the mountain is known for its plethora of double-black-diamond and technical runs (the drop is over 600m). It is usually quieter than nearby Big White Mountain.

✨ Festivals & Events

It seems like Penticton has nothing but crowd-drawing festivals all summer long.

Elvis Festival CULTURAL
(www.pentictonelvisfestival.com) Dozens of Elvis impersonators could be your idea of heaven or hound-dog hell, especially the afternoon of open-mike sing-alongs. Held in late June.

Peach Festival FRUIT
(✆800-663-5052; www.peachfest.com) The city's premier event is basically a week-long party in early August that has taken place since 1948, loosely centered on crowning a Peach Queen.

Pentastic Jazz Festival MUSIC
(✆250-770-3494; www.pentasticjazz.com) More than a dozen bands perform at five venues over three days in early September.

🛏 Sleeping

Lakeshore Dr West and South Main St/Skaha Lake Rd are home to most of the local motels. The Okanagan Beach strip is the most popular area. The visitor center has a long list of B&Bs. Expect off-season discounts.

Spiller Estate B&B B&B $$
(✆250-490-4162, 800-610-3794; www.holman langwineries.com; 475 Upper Bench Rd; r $140; ☺May-Oct; ❀) Just 2km east of the centre, on the road to Naramata, this four-room half-timbered 1930s lodge is on the grounds of its namesake winery. You can smell the peaches ripening from the shady grounds, which are a short hike from Munson Mountain.

Rochester Resort MOTEL $$
(✆250-493-1128, 800-567-4904; www.pentic ton.com/rochester-resort; 970 Lakeshore Dr W; r $140-300; ❀❀❀) The unassuming 1970s design extends to the modest beige and avocado decor. But you'll have little time to linger indoors, what with all the fun nearby. All 36 units have kitchens. Some have two bedrooms, others have lake views from their balconies.

Tiki Shores Beach Resort MOTEL $$
(✆250-492-8769, 866-492-8769; www.tikishores .com; 914 Lakeshore Dr W; condos $140-300; ❀❀❀) This lively resort has 40 condo-style units with separate bedrooms and kitchens. Throw your own toga party in one of the 'Roman theme units,' and throw your soiled post-bacchanalia ware into the handy guest laundry.

Park Royal RV Resort CAMPGROUND $
(✆250-492-7051; www.parkroyal.ipenticton.com; 240 Riverside Dr; RV sites from $45) Right near the busy end of Okanagan Beach, the 40 sites here are set among shady lawns.

HI Penticton Hostel HOSTEL $
(✆250-492-3992; www.hihostels.ca; 464 Ellis St; dm/r from $24/60; ❀@❀) This 47-bed hostel is near the center in a heavily used old house; it arranges all sorts of activities, including wine tours.

🍴 Eating

Penticton definitely has its share of good eats. Stroll around Main and Front Sts in the center and you will find numerous choices. The **farmers market** (✆250-583-9933; Main St; ☺8am-noon Sat May-Oct) hosts large numbers of local organic producers and runs a few blocks south of the lake.

[TOP CHOICE] Amante Bistro FUSION $$
(✆250-493-1961; www.amantebistro.com; 483 Main St; mains $10-30; ☺11am-2pm & 5-10pm Mon-Sat) There's intimate dining for those who want to enjoy a changing seasonal menu of carefully prepared dishes like small pizzas with Poplar Grove blue cheese or a slow-roasted pork belly with scallops; local produce stars. Excellent Okanagan wine list.

Salty's Beachouse SEAFOOD $$
(✆250-493-5001; 1000 Lakeshore Dr W; mains $12-25; ☺5-10pm Apr-Oct) You expect deep-fried but what you get is a nuanced menu of seafood with global accents. Typical is Cayman Island chowder, which is rich and multifaceted. Dine under the stars on the patio or enjoy the lake views from the upper level.

Il Vecchio Deli DELI $
(✆250-492-7610; 317 Robinson St; sandwiches $5; ☺10am-4pm Mon-Sat) The smell that greets you as you enter confirms your choice. The best lunch sandwiches in town can be consumed at a couple of tables in this atmospheric deli but will taste better on a picnic. Choices are amazing; we like the garlic salami with marinated eggplant sandwich.

Fibonacci CAFE $
(✆250-770-1913; 219 Main St; meals from $7; ☺8am-10pm Mon-Sat; ❀) You see the large brass coffee roaster right when you enter this downtown cafe that serves up lots of healthy Mediterranean fare. Thin-crust pizzas are made with local produce. At night there's a rotating line-up of art-house films, comedy acoustic and open mike.

Dream Cafe FUSION $$
(☎250-490-9012; 67 Front St; mains $8-26; ⊙8am-late Tue-Sun) The heady aroma of spices envelopes your, well, head as you enter this pillow-bedecked, upscale-yet-funky bistro. Asian and Indian flavors mix on the menu, which has many veggie options. On many nights there's live acoustic guitar by touring pros; tables outside hum all summer long.

Theo's GREEK $$
(☎250-492-4019; www.eatsquid.com; 687 Main St; mains $10-25; ⊙11am-10pm) The place for locals on match.com second dates, serving up authentic Greek island cuisine in the atmospheric dark and fire-lit interior or out on the patio. The Garithes Uvetsi is a symphony of starters that will please two.

🍷 Drinking & Entertainment
Look for local Cannery Brewing beers around town; the seasonal Blackberry Porter is fresh and smooth. Many dinner places also feature live entertainment some nights and most have good lounges.

The **Hooded Merganser** (☎250-493-8221; Penticton Lakeside Resort, 21 Lakeshore Dr) is a stylish over-the-water pub with walls of glass overlooking docks and the lake. It's popular through the year. Just ashore, the **Barking Parrot** (☎250-493-8221; Penticton Lakeside Resort, 21 Lakeshore Dr) has a vast patio with heaters that extend the season almost to winter. Cover bands rock the weekends.

🛍 Shopping
Purchase the best local artistic efforts at the **Lloyd Gallery** (☎250-492-4484; 18 Front St; ⊙9:30am-5:30pm Mon-Sat), which bursts with the colors of the valley and is one of several on the block. Stock up on reading material amid the stacks of used titles at the appropriately named **Book Shop** (☎250-492-6661; 242 Main St).

ℹ Information
The **visitor center** (☎250-493-4055, 800-663-5052; www.tourismpenticton.com; 553 Railway St, cnr Hwy 97 & Eckhardt Ave W;⊙8am-8pm May-Sep, 10am-6pm Oct-Apr) is one of BC's best. There's free internet and a whole room devoted to the BC Wine Information Centre with regional wine information, tasting and sales.

ℹ Getting There & Around
Penticton Regional Airport (YYF; ☎250-492-6042; www.cyyf.org) Daily flights by Air Canada Jazz to Vancouver (one hour).

Greyhound Canada (☎800-661-8747; www.greyhound.ca; 307 Ellis St) Services within the Okanagan Valley as well as routes to Vancouver ($76, seven hours, two daily) and Kamloops ($50, four hours, one daily).

Penticton Transit (☎250-492-5602; www.bctransit.com; single trip/day pass $2/4) Runs between both waterfronts.

Penticton to Kelowna
A lakeside resort town 18km north of Penticton on Hwy 97, **Summerland** features some fine 19th-century heritage buildings on the hillside above the ever-widening and busy highway. The **Kettle Valley Steam Railway** (☎877-494-8424; www.kettlevalleyrail.org; 18404 Bathville Rd; adult/child $21/13; ⊙mid-May–mid-Oct) is an operating 16km remnant of the famous railway (p722). Ride behind old steam locomotives in open-air cars and enjoy orchard views.

Hugging the lake below Hwy 97, some 25km south of Kelowna, the little town of **Peachland** is good for a quick, breezy stroll. Smart stoppers will pause longer at the **Blind Angler Grill** (☎250-767-9264; 5899A Beach Ave; mains $8-25; ⊙9am-9pm), a shack-like place overlooking a small marina. What's lost in structural integrity is more than made up for in food quality: breakfasts shine, burgers are superb and night-time ribs and halibut are sublime.

Between Peachland and Kelowna, urban sprawl becomes unavoidable, especially through the billboard-lined nightmare of **Westbank**.

WORTH A TRIP

SCENIC DRIVE TO NARAMATA

On all but the busiest summer weekends, you can escape many of Penticton's mobs by taking the road less traveled, 18km north from town along the east shore of Okanagan Lake. The route is lined with more than 20 wineries as well as farms producing organic lavender and the like. There's lots of places to hike, picnic, bird-watch or do whatever else occurs to you in beautiful and often secluded surroundings. **Naramata** is a cute little village. This is a good route for cycling and at several points you can access the **Kettle Valley Rail Trail** (p722).

Kelowna

POP 120,300

A kayaker paddles past scores of new tract houses on a hillside: it's an iconic image for fast-growing Kelowna, the unofficial 'capital' of the Okanagan and the sprawling centre of all that's good and not-so-good with the region.

Entering from the north, the ever-lengthening urban sprawl of tree-lined Hwy 97/ Harvey Ave seems to go on forever. Once past the ceaseless waves of chains and strip malls, the downtown is a welcome reward. Museums, culture, nightlife and the park-lined lakefront feature. About 2km south of the center, along Pandosy Ave, is Pandosy Village, a charming and upscale lakeside enclave.

Kelowna, an Interior Salish word meaning 'grizzly bear,' owes its settlement to a number of missionaries who arrived in 1858, hoping to 'convert the Natives.' Settlers followed and in 1892 the town was established. Industrial fruit production was the norm until the wine industry took off 20 years ago.

⊙ Sights

CITY PARK & PROMENADE

The focal point of the city's shoreline, this immaculate downtown park is home to manicured gardens, water features and **Hot Sands Beach**, where the water is a respite from the summer air. Among the many statues (the visitor center has a good guide) look for the one of the **Ogopogo**, the lake's mythical and hokey - monster. Restaurants and pubs take advantage of the uninterrupted views of the lake and forested shore opposite. North of the marina, **Waterfront Park** has a variegated shoreline and a popular open-air stage.

CULTURAL DISTRICT

Be sure to pick up the Cultural District walking-tour and public-art brochures at the visitor center and visit www.kelowna museums.ca.

Located in the old Laurel Packing House, the **BC Orchard Industry Museum** (☑250-763-0433; 1304 Ellis St; admission by donation; ◷10am-5pm Mon-Sat) recounts the Okanagan Valley from its ranchland past, grazed by cows, to its present, grazed by tourists. The old fruit packing-crate labels are works of art. It was due to reopen in 2011 after a major restoration.

In the same building, the knowledgeable staff at the **Wine Museum** (☑250-868-0441; admission free; ◷10am-6pm Mon-Sat, 11am-5pm Sun) can recommend tours, steer you to the best wineries for tastings and help you fill your trunk with the many local wines on sale.

The airy **Kelowna Art Gallery** (☑250-979-0888; www.kelownaartgallery.com; 1315 Water St; admission $3; ◷10am-5pm Tue, Wed, Fri & Sat, 10am-9pm Thu, 1-4pm Sun) features local works. Nearby, **Turtle Island Gallery** (☑250-717-8235; 115-1295 Cannery Lane) sells and displays works by Aboriginal artists.

The **Okanagan Heritage Museum** (☑250-763-2417; 470 Queensway Ave; admission by donation; ◷10am-5pm Mon-Sat) looks at centuries of local culture in an engaging manner that includes a First Nations pit house, a Chinese grocery and a Pandosy-era trading post.

Behind the museum, the exquisite grounds of **Kasugai Gardens** (admission free; ◷9am-6pm) are good for a peaceful stroll.

🏃 Activities

The balmy weather makes Kelowna ideal for fresh-air fun, whether on the lake or in the surrounding hills.

You can rent speedboats (starting at $60 per hour), arrange fishing trips and cruises or rent windsurfing gear at **Kelowna Marina** (☑250-861-8001; www.kelownamarina.ca), at the lake end of Queensway Ave. Windsurfers take to the water from the old seaplane terminal, near the corner of Water St and Cawston Ave.

You'll find great hiking and mountain-bike riding all around town. The 17km **Mission Creek Greenway** is a meandering, wooded path following the creek along the south edge of town. The western half is a wide and easy expanse, but to the east the route becomes sinuous as it climbs into the hills.

Knox Mountain, which sits at the northern end of the city, is another good place to hike or ride. Along with bobcats and snakes, the 235-hectare park has well-maintained trails and rewards visitors with excellent views from the top.

👉 Tours

TOP CHOICE **Monashee Adventure Tours** (☑250-762-9253; www.monasheeadventure tours.com) Offers scores of biking and hiking tours of the valley, parks, Kettle Valley Rail Trail (from $80) and wineries. Many tours are accompanied by entertaining lo-

OKANAGAN VALLEY WINERIES

The abundance of sunshine, fertile soil and cool winters have allowed the local wine industry to thrive. Kelowna and the region north are known for whites like pinot grigio. South, near Penticton and Oliver, reds are the stars, especially the ever-popular merlots.

A majority of the over 100 wineries are close to Hwy 97, which makes tasting a breeze. Most offer tours and all will gladly sell you a bottle or 20 (in fact many of the best wines are only sold at the wineries). A growing number feature excellent cafes and bistros that offer fine views and complex regional fare to complement what's in the glass.

Festivals

Okanagan seasonal **wine festivals** (www.thewinefestivals.com) are major events, especially the one in fall. For more on the winter festival and ice wine, see p854.

The usual dates are fall (early October), winter (mid-January), spring (early M) and summer (early August).

Information

Two good sources of information on Okanagan Valley wines are the **BC Wine Information Centre** (p722) in Penticton's visitor center and the **Wine Museum** (p723) in Kelowna. *John Schreiner's Okanagan Wine Tour Guide* is an authoritative guidebook.

Tours

There are numerous companies that let you do the sipping while they do the driving.

Club Wine Tours (☎250-762-9951, 866-386-9463; www.clubwinetours.com; 3-7hr tours $65-125) The signature tour includes four wineries and lunch in a vineyard.

Distinctly Kelowna Tours (☎250-979-1211, 866-979-1211; www.wildflowersandwine.com; 3-7hr tours $80-140) Offers winery tours by valley region, plus hikes through the scenic hills followed by a winery lunch and agricultural tours.

Visiting the Wineries

At wineries open for visitors, you can expect to taste wine, but the experience varies greatly. Some places have just a couple of wines on offer, others offer dozens of vintages. Some tasting rooms are just glorified sales areas, others have magnificent views of the vineyards, valley and lakes. Some charge, others are free.

Among the dozens of options, the following (listed north to south) are recommended. Summerhill Pyramid and Cedar Creek Estate are south of Kelowna along the lake's east shore. The rest of the wineries can be reached via Hwy 97.

cal guides. Prices include a bike, lunch and shuttle to the route. The same shuttle can also be used by independent riders looking for one-way transport. In winter, snowshoe tours are offered.

🛏 Sleeping

As in the rest of the Okanagan Valley, accommodations here can be difficult to find in summer if you haven't booked. At other times, look for bargains. The visitor center lists dozens of area B&Bs. Chain motels dominate Harvey Ave/Hwy 97 going east. Rates fall as you head along the strip but you pay the price by being in less-than-salubrious surroundings.

Hotel Eldorado HOTEL **$$$**
(☎250-763-7500, 866-608-7500; www.hotelel doradokelowna.com; 500 Cook Rd; r $180-400; ❄@🔊🏊) This historic lakeshore retreat, south of Pandosy Village, has 19 heritage rooms where you can bask in antique-filled luxury. A modern low-key wing has 30 more rooms and six opulent waterfront suites. It's classy, artful and funky all at once. Definitely the choice spot for a luxurious getaway.

Royal Anne Hotel HOTEL **$$**
(☎250-763-2277, 888-811-3400; www.royalan nehotel.com; 348 Bernard Ave; r $100-200; ❄@🔊) Location, location, location are the three amenities that count at this otherwise unexciting, older five-story motel in the heart of

Calona Vineyards (☎250-762-3332; www.calonavineyards.ca; 1125 Richter St, Kelowna; ☺9am-6pm summer, 10am-5pm winter) Near Kelowna's Cultural District, and one of BC's largest producers, Calona was the first in the Okanagan Valley (it started in 1932).

Summerhill Pyramid Winery (☎250-764-8000; www.summerhill.bc.ca; 4870 Chute Lake Rd, Kelowna) On Kelowna's eastern shore, wines are aged in a huge pyramid.

Cedar Creek Estate Winery (☎250-764-8866; www.cedarcreek.bc.ca; 5445 Lakeshore Rd, Kelowna; ☺10am-6pm Apr-Oct, 11am-5pm Nov-Mar) Known for excellent tours as well as Ehrenfelser, a refreshing fruity white wine. The **Vineyard Terrace** (mains $10-15; ☺11:30am-3pm Jun–mid-Sep) is good for lunch.

Quails' Gate Winery (☎250-769-4451; www.quailsgate.com; 3303 Boucherie Rd, Kelowna; ☺10am-5pm) A small winery with a huge reputation; known for its pinot noir and sauvignon blanc. The **Old Vines Restaurant** (mains $10-20; ☺11am-9pm) is among the best.

Mission Hill Family Estate (☎250-768-7611; www.missionhillwinery.com; 1730 Mission Hill Rd, Westbank; ☺10am-5pm) Go for a taste of one of the blended reds (try the Bordeaux) or the thirst-quenching pinot gris. Luncheons at the **Terrace** (mains $24-27; ☺11am-3pm mid-May–mid-Sep) are a seasonal treat.

Tinhorn Creek Vineyards (☎250-498-3743; www.tinhorn.com; 32830 Tinhorn Creek Rd, Oliver; ☺9am-5pm) Near the junction of Hwy 97 and Road 7 on the Golden Mile. Notable reds and whites include the top-tier Oldfield series, namesake of owner Sandra Oldfield.

Inniskillin Okanagan Vineyards (☎250-498-6663; www.inniskillin.com; Road 11 W, Oliver; ☺10am-6pm May-Oct, 10am-5pm Mon-Fri Nov-Apr) BC's first producer of Zinfandel is also home to the elixirs known as ice wines.

Road 13 Vineyards (☎250-498-8330; www.road13vineyards.com; 13140 316A Ave, Road 13, Oliver; ☺10am-5:30pm Apr-Oct) Its very drinkable reds and whites win plaudits. The no-frills vibe extends to the picnic tables with gorgeous views and the motto: 'It's all about dirt.'

Burrowing Owl Estate Winery (☎250-498-0620; www.bovwine.ca; 100 Burrowing Owl Pl, Oliver; ☺10am-5pm Apr-Oct) Wine with an eco-accent that includes organic grapes. This Golden Mile landmark includes a hotel and the Sonora Room restaurant (p719).

Nk'Mip Cellars (☎250-495-2985; www.nkmipcellars.com; 1400 Rancher Creek Rd, Osoyoos; ☺) Excellent winery owned by an entrepreneurial First Nations band. Simple meals with aboriginal touches this continental are served at the **Patio** (mains $16-18; ☺11:30am-8pm May-Sep).

town. Rooms have standard modern decor, fridges and huge, openable windows.

Travelodge Kelowna MOTEL $$
(☎250-763-7771, 800-578-7878; www.travelodge.com; 1627 Abbott St; r $90-180; ❄@☎☲) Perfectly located downtown and across from City Park, this 52-room motel is as unadorned as a grapevine in winter. There is a decent outdoor pool and a hot tub.

Prestige Hotel MOTEL $$
(☎250-860-7900, 877-737-8443; www.prestigeinn.com; 1675 Abbott St; r $120-250; ❄@☎☲) This 66-room place has a great location across from City Park and once you're inside, you can't see the rather hideous exterior. The rooms are just fine, in an upscale-motel sort

of way (nice soap, LCD TVs, piles of decorative pillows etc).

Willow Creek Family Campground CAMPGROUND $
(☎250-762-6302; www.willowcreekcampground.ca; 3316 Lakeshore Rd; tent/RV site $30/45; ☎) Close to Pandosy Village and a beach, this 87-site facility has a laundry; tent sites are on a grassy verge.

Kelowna SameSun International Hostel HOSTEL $
(☎250-763-9814, 877-562-2783; www.samesun.com; 245 Harvey Ave; dm/r from $28/80; ❄@☎) Near the center and the lake, this purpose-built hostel has 88 dorm beds plus private rooms. Activities include BBQs year-round.

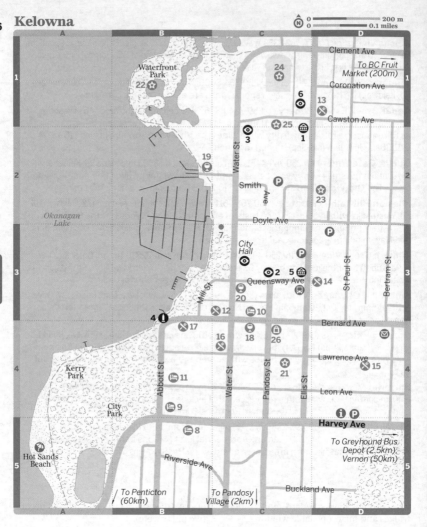

Eating

Many of Kelowna's restaurants take full advantage of the local bounty of foodstuffs. But don't let the feel of Vancouver East cause you to go all continental in your dining time: 8pm is late. The local microbrewer, **Tree Brewing**, has an excellent range of beers that are widely sold around

Food Purveyors

The **farmers market** (☎250-878-5029; cnr Springfield Rd & Dilworth Dr; ⊙8am-1pm Wed & Sat Apr-Oct) has over 150 vendors, including many with prepared foods. Local artisans also display their wares. It's off Hwy 97. Another **market** (⊙4-8pm Thu) is held at the Dolphins statue parking lot.

TOP CHOICE **BC Fruit Market** (☎250-763-8872; 816 Clement Ave; ⊙9am-5pm Mon-Sat) is like a county fair. Right inside the local fruit-packing cooperative, with dozens upon dozens of the Okanagan's best fruits on display and available for tasting; prices are half that in supermarkets.

At first glance, **Guisachan Village** (2355 Gordon Dr) may look like a humdrum strip mall but closer inspection reveals that it is a culinary mecca of fine-food purveyors, including the following:

Codfathers Seafood Market   SEAFOOD $
(☎250-763-3474; ⊙9am-7pm) There's fresh fish of course but picnickers love the array of smoked salmon and other smoked goods. A small cafe serves chowders, fish and chips etc.

L&D Meats & Deli   DELI $
(☎250-717-1007; ⊙9:30am-6pm Mon-Sat) Arrays of smoked meats and other deli items; good choice of deliciously good sandwiches.

Okanagan Grocery   BAKERY $
(☎250-862-2811; ⊙9:30am-5:30pm Tue-Sat) Artisan and organic bakery with breads from baguettes to croissants.

Restaurants & Cafes

TOP CHOICE RauDZ   FUSION $$
(☎250-868-8805; www.raudz.com; 1560 Water St; mains $12-25; ⊙5-10pm) Noted chef Rod Butters returns with this casual bistro that is a temple to Okanagan produce and wine. The dining room is as airy and open as the kitchen and the seasonal menu takes global inspiration for Med-infused dishes good for sharing, as well as steaks and seafood. Suppliers include locally renowned Carmelis goat cheese.

Rotten Grape   TAPAS $$
(☎250-717-8466; 231 Bernard Ave; mains $8-15; ⊙5pm-midnight Wed-Sun) Enjoy flights of local wines without the fru-fru in the heart of town. If you utter 'tannin, the hobgoblin of pinot' at any point, be quiet and eat some of the tasty tapas (from $10).

Mamma Rosa   ITALIAN $$
(☎250-763-4114; 561 Lawrence Ave; mains $12-25; ⊙5-10pm Tue-Sun) Okay, the red and white checked tablecloths are plastic, but that just makes wiping up your slobber that much easier. And slobber you will over big bowls of excellent homemade pasta (about 100 varieties it seems) and more. Customize by adding meatballs, broccoli, anchovies etc.

Bean Scene   CAFE $
(☎250-763-1814; 274 Bernard Ave; coffee $2; ⊙6:30am-10pm; 🛜) Has a great bulletin board to check up on local happenings while you munch on a muffin. A quieter location, **Bean Scene North** (☎250-763-4022; 1289 Ellis St; ⊙6am-6pm; 🛜), offers caffeinated respite in the Cultural District.

La Bussola   ITALIAN $$
(☎250-763-3110; 1451 Ellis St; mains $15-30; ⊙5-10pm Mon-Sat) The Cultural District location is fitting. Since 1974 Franco and Lauretta Coccaro have worked to perfect their Italian supper house. The menu

DON'T MISS

KETTLE VALLEY RAIL TRAIL

The famous **Kettle Valley Rail Trail** vies with wine drinking and peach picking as the attraction of choice for visitors (smart ones do all three).

Once stretching 525km in curving, meandering length, the railway was built so that silver ore could be transported from the southern Kootenays to Vancouver. Finished in 1916, it remains one of the most expensive railways ever built on a per-kilometer basis. It was entirely shut by 1989 but it wasn't long before its easy grades (never over 2.2%) and dozens of bridges were incorporated into the Trans Canada Trail.

Of the entire KVR Trail, the most spectacular stretch is close to Kelowna. The 24km section through the **Myra Canyon** has fantastic views of the sinuous canyon from **18 trestles** that span the gorge for the cliff-hugging path. That you can enjoy the route at all is something of a miracle as 12 of the wooden trestles were destroyed by fire in 2003. But all are rebuilt; much credit goes to the **Myra Canyon Trestle Restoration Society** (www.myratrestles.com). The broad views take in Kelowna and the lake. Although much fire damage remains, you can see alpine meadows reclaiming the landscape.

To reach the area closest to the most spectacular trestles, follow Harvey Ave (Hwy 97) east to Gordon Dr. Turn south and then go east 2.6km on KLO Rd and then join McCulloch Rd for 7.4km after the junction. Look for the Myra Forest Service Rd, turn south and make a winding 8.7km climb on a car-friendly gravel road to the parking lot.

Myra Canyon is just part of an overall 174km network of trails in the Okanagan that follow the old railway through tunnels, past Naramata and as far south as Penticton and beyond. You can easily access the trail at many points or book hiking and cycling tours (p723). **Myra Canyon Bike Rentals** (☎250-878-8763; www.myracanyonrental. com; half-day from $40; ☺May–mid-Sep) has bike rentals; confirm by calling in advance.

spans the boot, from pesto to red sauce, veal to seafood. Dine on the flower-bedecked sidewalk tables or in the stylish dining room.

🍷 Drinking

Sturgeon Hall PUB
(☎250-860-3055; 1481 Water St; ☺11am-midnight Mon-Sat) Fanatical fans of hockey's Kelowna Rockets feast on excellent burgers and thin-crust pizza while quaffing brews at the bar or outside at sidewalk tables. In season, every TV shows hockey.

Doc Willoughby's PUB
(☎250-868-8288; 353 Bernard Ave; ☺11:30am-2am) Right downtown, this pub boasts a vaulted interior lined with wood and tables on the street; perfect for a drink or a meal. The beer selection is excellent, including brews from Tree Brewing and Penticton's Cannery Brewing.

Rose's Waterfront Pub PUB
(☎250-860-1141; Delta Grand Okanagan Hotel, 1352 Water St) Part of the upscale end of the waterfront, the vast lakeside terrace is the place for sunset drinks and snacks – from several hours before to several hours after.

☆ Entertainment

Downtown Kelowna boasts several ever-changing clubs, mostly at the west end of Leon and Lawrence Aves. Free summer nighttime concerts take place in **Kerry Park** on Friday and Saturday and on Waterfront Park's **Island Stage** on Wednesday.

Blue Gator LIVE MUSIC
(☎250-860-1529; www.bluegator.net; 441 Lawrence Ave; ☺Tue-Sun) Blues, rock, acoustic jam and more at the valley's sweaty temple of live music and cold beer.

Kelowna Rockets SPORTS
(☎250-860-7825; www.kelownarockets.com; tickets from $20) Kelowna Rockets is the much-beloved local WHL hockey team, playing in the flashy 6000-seat **Prospera Place Arena** (☎250-979-0888; cnr Water St & Cawston Ave).

Kelowna Actors Studio THEATER
(☎250-862-2867; www.kelownaactorsstudio. com; 1379 Ellis St; tickets from $45) Enjoy works as diverse as *The Producers* and *Same Time Next Year* at this dinner theater with serious ambitions.

Rotary Centre for the Performing Arts VENUE

(☎250-717-5304, tickets 250-763-1849; 421 Cawston Ave) There's galleries, a theatre, cafe, craft workshops and live classical music.

🔒 Shopping

The many food purveyors offer locally produced items that make excellent gifts. **Mosaic Books** (☎250-763-4418; 411 Bernard Ave) is an excellent independent bookstore, selling maps (including topographic ones) and travel guides, plus books on aboriginal history and culture.

ℹ Information

Many downtown cafes have wi-fi access.

Kelowna General Hospital (☎250-862-4000; 2268 Pandosy St, cnr Royal Ave; ☺24hr)

Kelowna Library (☎250-762-2800; 1380 Ellis St; ☺10am-5:30pm Mon, Fri & Sat, 10am-9pm Tue-Thu, noon-4pm Sun Oct-Mar) Visitors enjoy one hour of free online access.

Postal outlet (☎250-868-8480; 571 Bernard Ave; ☺9am-5pm Mon-Sat)

Visitor center (☎250-861-1515, 800-663-4345; www.tourismkelowna.com; 544 Harvey Ave; ☺8am-7pm daily summer, 8am-5pm Mon-Fri & 10am-3pm Sat & Sun winter) Near the corner of Ellis St; excellent touring maps.

ℹ Getting There & Away

From **Kelowna airport** (YLW; ☎250-765-5125; www.kelownaairport.com), **Westjet** (www.westjet.com) serves Vancouver, Victoria, Edmonton, Calgary and Toronto. **Air Canada Jazz** (www.aircanada.com) serves Vancouver and Calgary. **Horizon Air** (www.alaskaair.com) serves Seattle. The airport is a long 20km north of the center on Hwy 97.

Greyhound Canada (☎800-661-8747; www.greyhound.ca; 2366 Leckie Rd) is inconveniently east of the downtown area, off Hwy 97. City buses 9 and 10 make the run from Queensway station in the downtown (every 30 minutes between 6:30am and 9:45pm).

ℹ Getting Around

To/From the Airport

Kelowna Airport Shuttle (☎250-888-434-8687; www.kelownashuttle.com) costs $12 to $15 per person. Cabs cost about $30.

Bus

Kelowna Regional Transit System (☎250-860-8121; www.busonline.ca) runs local bus services. The one-way fare in the central zone is $2. A day pass for all three zones costs $5.50. All the downtown buses pass through **Queensway station** (Queensway Ave, btwn Pandosy & Ellis Sts). Service is not especially convenient.

Car & Taxi

All major car-rental companies are at Kelowna airport. Taxi companies include **Kelowna Cabs** (☎250-762-4444/2222).

Big White Ski Resort

Perfect powder is the big deal at **Big White Ski Resort** (☎250-765-8888, 800-663-2772, snow report 250-765-7669; www.bigwhite.com; 1-day lift pass adult/child $71/35), located 55km east of Kelowna off Hwy 33. With a vertical drop of 777m, it features 16 lifts and 118 runs that offer excellent downhill and backcountry skiing, while deep gullies make for killer snowboarding. Because of Big White's isolation, most people stay up here. The resort includes numerous restaurants, bars, hotels, condos, rental homes and a hostel. The resort has lodging info and details of the ski-season Kelowna shuttle.

Vernon

POP 59,200

The Okanagan glitz starts to fade before you reach Vernon. Maybe it's the weather. Winters have more of the traditional inland BC bite and wineries are few. But that doesn't mean the area is without its charms. The orchard-scented valley is surrounded by three lakes – Kalamalka,

REGIONAL BUS DISTANCES FROM KELOWNA

DESTINATION	FARE	DURATION	FREQUENCY (PER DAY)
Penticton	$22	1¼hr	4
Kamloops	$39	3hr	3
Vancouver	$78	6hr	6
Calgary	$110	10hr	1

Okanagan and Swan – that attract fun seekers all summer long. Downtown Vernon has some good eateries and is enlivened by over 30 wall murals ranging from schmaltzy to artistic. Most of the shops are found along 30th Ave (known as Main St). Confusingly, 30th Ave is intersected by 30th St in the middle of downtown, so mind your streets and avenues.

⊙ Sights & Activities

The beautiful 9-sq-km **Kalamalka Lake Provincial Park** (☎250-545-1560; www.bcparks.ca) south of town lies on the eastern side of this warm, shallow lake. The park offers great swimming at Jade and Kalamalka Beaches, good fishing and a network of mountain-biking and hiking trails. There's also excellent rock climbing at cougar-free Cougar Canyon.

Ellison Provincial Park, 16km southwest of Vernon on Okanagan Lake, is western Canada's only freshwater marine park; scuba diving is popular here and gear (scuba, snorkeling and kayaks) can be rented from **Innerspace Watersports** (☎250-549-2040; www.innerspacewatersports.com; 3103 32nd St). Ellison is also known for its world-class rock climbing. To get to Ellison from downtown, go west on 25th Ave, which soon becomes Okanagan Landing Rd. Follow that and look for signs to the park.

Two fun attractions make hay from local agriculture. **Davison Orchards** (☎250-549-3266; www.davisonorchards.ca; 3111 Davison Rd; ⊙daylight hrs May-Oct) has tractor rides, homemade ice cream, fresh apple juice, winsome barnyard animals and more.

Next door, **Planet Bee** (☎250-542-8088; www.planetbee.com; 5011 Bella Vista Rd; admission free; ⊙daylight hrs May-Oct) is a working honey farm where you can learn all the sweet secrets of the nectar and see a working hive up close. Follow 25th Ave west, turn north briefly on 41st St, then go west on Bella Vista Rd and watch for signs.

🛏 Sleeping

Accommodations are available in all price ranges. The visitor center has information on local B&Bs.

Beaver Lake Mountain Resort
CAMPGROUND, INN $
(☎250-762-2225; www.beaverlakeresort.com; 6350 Beaver Lake Rd; campsites from $27, cabins $55-170; 🐾) Set high in the hills east of

Hwy 97, about midway between Vernon and Kelowna, this postcard-perfect lakeside resort has a range of rustic log and more luxurious cabins that sleep up to six people.

Tiki Village Motel
MOTEL $$
(☎250-503-5566, 800-661-8454; www.tikivillagevernon.com; 2408 34th St; r $80-150; ❄🐾🏊) Hide your brother's Game Boy in the pool wall and he'll never find it again. Another ode to the glory days of concrete blocks, the Tiki has suitably expansive plantings and 30 rooms with an unintended *Mad Men* vibe.

Schell Motel
MOTEL $
(☎250-545-1351, 888-772-4355; www.schellmotel.ca; 2810 35th St; r $70-140; ❄🐾🏊) Another vision in artful concrete blocks, this immaculate indie motel has a welcoming pool, BBQ, a sauna, fridges and some kitchens. The 32 rooms are ideally central but out of range of the 32nd St roar.

Ellison Provincial Park
CAMPGROUND $
(☎800-689-9025, information only 250-494-6500; www.discovercamping.ca; campsites $30; ⊙Apr-Oct) Some 16km southwest of Vernon on Okanagan Landing Rd, this is a great place. The 71 campsites fill up early, so be serve.

✗ Eating

The evening **farmers market** (☎250-546-6267; cnr 48th Ave & 27th St; ⊙4-8pm Fri) adds class to the Village Green Mall parking lot at the north end of town. There are also morning **markets** (3445 43rd Ave; ⊙8am-noon Mon & Thu), just west of Hwy 97.

Talkin Donkey
CAFE $
(☎250-545-2286; 3923 32nd St; meals $7; ⊙7am-9pm, until 11pm Fri; 🐾) When they talk about 'drinking responsibly' at this local institution, they mean ensuring that your coffee is fair trade. A good chunk of the proceeds at this funky coffeehouse with a spiritual edge goes to charity. Tap your Birkenstock-clad toes to Friday-night folk music.

Blue Heron Waterfront Pub
CAFE $$
(☎250-542-5550; 7673 Okanagan Landing Rd; mains $8-25; ⊙11am-late Apr-Oct) Southwest of town, sweeping views of Okanagan Lake from the big patio keep things hopping all summer long. The meaty fare of excellent steaks and burgers is leavened by cheesy fare such as nachos.

DESTINATION	FARE	DURATION	FREQUENCY (PER DAY)
Kelowna	$19	1hr	6
Kamloops	$30	2hr	3
Vancouver	$75	7½hr	3
Calgary	$85	9hr	1

Eclectic Med   MEDITERRANEAN $$
(☑250-558-4646; 2915 30th Ave; mains $12-25; ⊙noon-9pm) The name sums up the menu, which brings a Mediterranean accent to local standards like Alberta steaks, lake fish and lots of valley veggies. Plates are artfully presented.

🔒 Shopping

Bookland   BOOKSTORE
(☑250-545-1885; 3400 30th Ave) Topo maps, travel guides and books on activities in the Okanagan Valley and BC. Excellent selection of local works, magazines and newspapers.

ℹ Information

Visitor center (☑250-545-3016, 800-665-0795; www.tourismvernon.com; 701 Hwy 97 S; ⊙8:30am-6pm May-Oct, 10am-4pm Nov-Apr) The office is 2km south of the town centre.

ℹ Getting There & Around

Greyhound Canada (☑800-661-8747; www.greyhound.ca; 3102 30th St, cnr 31st Ave) runs services listed in box.

Vernon Regional Transit System (☑250-545-7221; fares $2) buses leave downtown from the bus stop at the corner of 31st St and 30th Ave. For Kalamalka Lake, catch bus 1 or 6; for Okanagan Lake, bus 7.

North of Vernon

Attractions are few in this area, which is more notable for its major highway connections. Just north of Vernon, beautiful Hwy 97 heads northwest to Kamloops via tree-clad valleys punctuated by lakes, while equally lovely Hwy 97A continues northeast to Sicamous and Hwy 1. **Armstrong**, 23km north of Vernon, is a cute little village.

SILVER STAR

Classic inland BC dry powder makes **Silver Star** (☑250-542-0224, 800-663-4431; snow report 250-542-1745; www.skisilverstar.com; 1-day lift ticket adult/child $71/35) a very popular ski resort. The 115 runs have a vertical drop of 760m; snowboarders enjoy a half-pipe and a terrain park. In June the lifts haul mountain bikers and hikers up to the lofty green vistas.

All manner of accommodations can be reserved through the resort. **Samesun Lodge** (☑250-545-8933, 877-562-2783; www.samesun.com; 9898 Pinnacles Rd; dm/r from $30/80; @🛜) runs a very popular and almost posh backpacker hotel.

To reach Silver Star, take 48th Ave off Hwy 97. The resort is 20km northeast of Vernon.

SHUSWAP REGION

Rorschach-test-like **Shuswap Lake** anchors a somewhat bland but pleasing region of green, wooded hills, farms and two small towns, Sicamous and Salmon Arm. The latter has the area's main **visitor center** (☑250-832-2230, 877-725-6667; www.shuswap.bc.ca; 200 Hwy 1; ⊙8am-8pm daily May-Aug, 10am-5pm Mon-Fri Sep-Apr).

The area is home to several lake-based provincial parks and is a popular destination for families looking for outdoor fun. The main attraction, though, is the annual spawning of sockeye salmon at **Roderick Haig-Brown Provincial Park** (☑250-851-3000; www.bcparks.ca), just off the highway via Squilax. This 10.59-sq-km park protects both sides of the Adams River between Shuswap Lake and Adams Lake, a natural bottleneck for the bright-red sockeye when they run upriver every October. The fish population peaks every four years, when as many as four million salmon crowd the Adams' shallow riverbed – the next big spawn is due in 2014.

Puttering about the lake on a **houseboat** is a convivial way to explore the Shuswap, especially during the height of summer, when the lake fills with people hoping to wash away their urban cares. Most rent by the week (from $2000) and can sleep upward of 10 people. Contact the visitor center for listings of houseboat operators.

THE KOOTENAYS & THE ROCKIES

Ahhhh. You just can't help saying it as you ponder the plethora of snow-covered peaks in the Kootenay Region of BC. Deep river valleys cleaved by white-water rivers, impossibly sheer rock faces, alpine meadows and a sawtooth of white-dappled mountains stretching across the horizon inspire awe, action or mere contemplation.

Coming from the west, the mountain majesty builds as if choreographed from above. The roughly parallel ranges of the Monashees and the Selkirks striate the West Kootenays with the Arrow Lakes adding texture. Appealing towns like Revelstoke and Nelson nestle against the mountains and are centers of year-round outdoor fun. The East Kootenays cover the Purcell Mountains region below Golden, taking in Radium Hot Springs and delightful Fernie. The Rockies climb high in the sky to the border with Alberta.

BC's Rocky Mountains parks (Mt Revelstoke, Glacier, Yoho and Kootenay) don't have the – no pun intended – high profile of Banff and Jasper National Parks over the border, but for many that's an advantage. Each has its own spectacular qualities, often relatively unexploited by the Banff-bound hordes.

Across this richly textured region, look for grizzly and black bear, elk, moose, deer, beaver, mountain goats and much more. Pause to make your own discoveries.

Revelstoke

POP 8000

Gateway to serious mountains, Revelstoke doesn't need to toot its own horn – the ceaseless procession of trains through the center does all the tooting anyone needs. Built as an important point on the Canadian Pacific transcontinental railroad that first linked eastern and western Canada, Revelstoke echoes not just with whistles but with history. The compact center is lined with heritage buildings yet it's not a museum piece; there's a vibrant local arts community and most locals take full advantage of the boundless opportunities for hiking, kayaking and, most of all, skiing. It's more than worth a long pause as you pass on Hwy 1, which bypasses the town

centre to the northeast. The main streets include 1st St and Mackenzie Ave.

⊙ Sights

Grizzly Plaza, between Mackenzie and Orton Aves, is a pedestrian precinct and the heart of downtown, where free live-music performances take place in the evenings throughout July and August. While outdoor activities are Revelstoke's real draw card, a stroll of the center and a pause at the museums is a must.

TOP CHOICE Revelstoke Railway Museum

MUSEUM

(☑250-837-6060; www.railwaymuseum.com; adult/child $10/2; ⊙9am-8pm summer, 11am-4pm Fri-Tue winter) Revelstoke Railway Museum, in an attractive building across the tracks from the town center, contains restored steam locomotives, including one of the largest steam engines ever used on Canadian Pacific Railway (CPR) lines. Photographs and artifacts document the construction of the CPR, which was instrumental – actually essential – in linking eastern and western Canada.

Revelstoke Museum

MUSEUM

(☑250-837-3067; 315 1st St W; adult/child $4/2; ⊙9am-5pm Mon-Sat, 1-4pm Sun May-Sep, 1-4pm Mon-Fri Oct-Apr) Revelstoke Museum holds a permanent collection of furniture and historical odds and ends, including mining, logging and railway artifacts that date back to the town's establishment in the 1880s. Also keep a look out for the many historical plaques mounted on buildings around town.

🏃 Activities

Winter

Sandwiched between the vast but relatively unknown Selkirk and Monashee mountain ranges, Revelstoke draws serious snow buffs looking for vast landscapes of crowd-free powder. It's where North America's first ski jump was built (1915).

Just 6km southeast of town, the **Revelstoke Mountain Resort** (☑888-837-2188; www.revelstokemountainresort.com; 1-day lift ticket adult/child $75/26) has ambitions to become the biggest ski resort this side of the Alps. But given its seemingly endless virgin slopes only opened in 2008, it has a ways to go. In the meantime you can, in one run (out of 52), ski both 700m of bowl and 700m of trees. The vertical drop is 1713m, greater than Whistler's.

Although the resort is making bowls accessible that were once helicopter or cat only, there are myriad more that are still remote. **Mica Heliskiing** (✆877-837-6191; www.micaheli.com; 207 Mackenzie Ave) is one of several companies offering trips; costs begin at $1200 per day.

For **cross-country skiing** (www.revelstokenordic.org), head to the Mt MacPherson Ski Area, 7km south of town on Hwy 23. You'll pay a mere $6 to use the 22km of groomed trails.

Free Spirit Sports (✆250-837-9453; 203 1st St W) rents a wide variety of winter gear, including essential avalanche equipment.

Summer

All that white snow turns into white water come spring and rafting is big. **Apex Rafting Co** (✆250-837-6376, 888-232-6666; www.apexrafting.com; 112 1st St E; adult/child $85/69) runs kid-friendly two-hour guided trips on the Illecillewaet River in spring and summer. **Natural Escapes Kayaking** (✆250-837-7883; www.naturalescapes.ca) leads tours, offers lessons and rent kayaks ($35 for two hours).

Mountain biking is huge here, as it is across the region. Pick up a copy of the *Biking Trail Map* from the visitor center or **Skookum Cycle & Ski** (✆250-814-0090; www.skookumcycle.com; 118 Mackenzie Ave), where you can rent bikes.

🛏 Sleeping

Revelstoke has a good selection of places to stay. Only truck spotters will gravitate to those out on Hwy 1. Several motels and cute B&Bs (the visitor center has lists) are right in the center.

Swiss Chalet Motel MOTEL $$
(✆250-837-4650, 888-272-4538; www.swisschaletmotel.com; 1101 Victoria Rd; r $80-160; ❄@🐾🤶) It's a short walk to the center from this cheery family-run motel, which includes an especially generous continental breakfast (one of the muffins here would make a dozen at many chains). The 22 rooms have fridges.

Regent Inn HOTEL $$
(✆250-837-2107, 888-245-5523; www.regentinn.com; 112 1st St E; r $120-200; ❄🤶🐾) The poshest place in town is not lavish but is comfy. The 50 modern rooms bear no traces of the hotel's 1914 roots (and exterior). The restaurant and lounge are both good and popular. Many bob the night away in the outdoor hot tub.

Revelstoke Lodge MOTEL $$
(✆250-837-2181; 888-559-1979; www.revelstokelodge.com; 601 1st St W; r $70-150; ❄@🐾🤶) This 42-room, pink-hued motel overcomes its inherent flaws, such as an all-encompassing parking area and stark cinder-block construction, thanks to its location. Check out a room or two to find one with recent paint and watch out for dark ones.

Blanket Creek Provincial Park
CAMPGROUND $
(✆800-689-9025; www.discovercamping.ca; campsites $21) This park, 25km south of Revelstoke along Hwy 23, includes over 60 campsites with flush toilets and running water. There's a playground and a waterfall is nearby.

SameSun Budget Lodge HOSTEL $
(✆250-837-4050, 877-562-2783; www.samesun.ca; 400 2nd St W; dm/r from $25/60; @🤶) Ramble though the numerous rooms in this perennial backpacker favorite. The 80 beds are often full, so book ahead. Expanded patios fill with a jovial international crowd.

🍴 Eating & Drinking

The **farmers market** (⊙8am-1pm Sat) sprawls across Grizzly Plaza. Mt Begbie Brewing makes good local microbrews that are available around town.

TOP CHOICE **Woolsey Creek** FUSION $$
(✆250-837-5500; 604 2nd St W; mains $10-20; ⊙5-10pm) The food at this lively and fun place is the artistic result of two women, Sylvie and Sophie, and their passion for inventive fare. There are global influences across the menu (you won't go wrong with the prosciutto-stuffed chicken) and a fine wine list. Excellent starters encourage sharing and lingering on the large patio.

La Baguette BAKERY $
(✆250-814-7088; Garden St; snacks from $3; ⊙7am-7pm Thu-Tue) Delicious new bakery near Victoria Rd has luscious, French-style goods plus paninis and coffees.

Modern Bakeshop & Café CAFE $
(✆250-837-6886; 212 Mackenzie Ave; mains from $5; ⊙7am-5pm Mon-Sat; 🤶) Try a *croque-monsieur* (grilled ham-and-cheese sandwich) or an elaborate pastry for a taste of Europe at this cute art moderne cafe. Many items are made with organic ingredients.

The Cabin BAR $
(✆250-837-2144; 200 E 1st St; ⊙5pm-midnight) Bowling alley, bar, outdoor gear store and

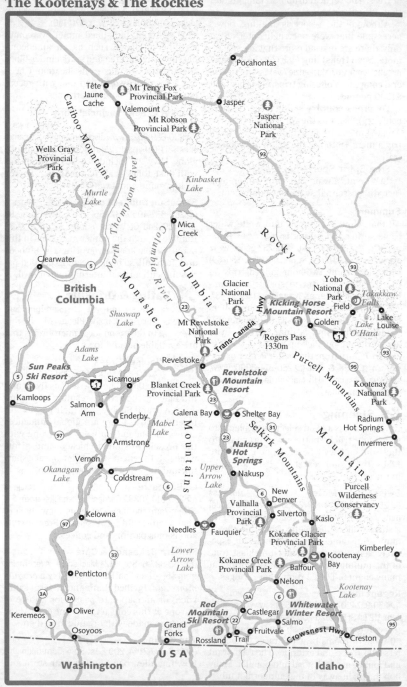

art gallery. A groovy chill spot with a few snacks to go with the beers.

ℹ Information

The main **visitor center** (☏250-837-5345, 800-487-1493; www.seerevelstoke.com; 206 Campbell Ave; ⊙9am-4pm Mon-Fri) is open year-round. But during summer, go to the larger seasonal **visitor center** (110 Mackenzie Ave; ⊙9am-9pm Jun-Aug, 10am-6pm May & Sep). It has parking and internet access ($1 per 10 minutes).

A **Parks Canada regional office** (☏250-837-7500; revglacier.reception@pc.gc.ca; 301 3rd St; ⊙8am-4:30pm Mon-Fri) has in-depth info about nearby Mt Revelstoke and Glacier National Parks.

ℹ Getting There & Away

Greyhound Canada (☏800-661-8747; www.greyhound.ca; 1899 Fraser Dr) is west of town, just off Hwy 1. It has storage lockers. Buses go east to Calgary ($62, six hours, three daily) via Banff, and west to Vancouver ($95, 10 hours, three daily) via Kamloops or Kelowna.

Revelstoke Shuttle (☏888-569-1969; www.revelstokeconnection.com) has daily shuttles to/from Kelowna ($84, 2½ hours).

Mt Revelstoke National Park

Grand in beauty if not in size (only 260 sq km), this **national park** (www.pc.gc.ca/revelstoke), just northeast of its namesake town, is a vision of peaks and valleys – many all but untrod.

From the 2223m summit of Mt Revelstoke, the views of the mountains and the Columbia River valley are excellent. To ascend here, take the 26km **Meadows in the Sky Parkway**, 1.5km east of Revelstoke off the Trans-Canada Hwy (Hwy 1). Open after the thaw (usually June to September), this paved road winds through lush cedar forests and alpine meadows and ends at

BRITISH COLUMBIA MT REVELSTOKE NATIONAL PARK

> **DON'T MISS**
>
> ## TWO PERFECT WALKS
>
> Easily accessible, **Skunk Cabbage Trail**, 28km east of Revelstoke on Hwy 1, is a 1.2km boardwalk along the Illecillewaet River. It is lined with its huge namesakes. Another 4km east, the **Giant Cedars Boardwalk** winds a 500m course up and down and all around a grove of huge old-growth cedars.

ⓘ AVALANCHE WARNING

The Kootenays are the heart of avalanche country, which kill more people in BC each year than any other natural phenomenon. The toll is high every year; a 2010 disaster at an extreme snow-mobiling meet near Revelstoke claimed three lives and injured at least 30.

Avalanches can occur at any time and even on terrain that seems relatively flat. Roughly half the people caught in them don't survive. It's vital that people venturing out onto the snow make inquiries about conditions first; if an area is closed don't go there. Whether you're backcountry ski touring or simply hiking in the alpine region, you'll want to rent a homing beacon; most outdoor shops can supply one.

In Revelstoke, the Canadian Avalanche Centre is operated by the **Canadian Avalanche Association** (CAA; ☎250-837-2435, 24hr info 800-667-1105; www.avalanche.ca). It analyzes avalanche trends, weather patterns and issues forecasts for the Kootenays and beyond.

BRITISH COLUMBIA THE KOOTENAYS & THE ROCKIES

Balsam Lake, within 2km of the peak. From here, walk to the top or take the free shuttle, which runs from 10am to 4pm daily.

There are several good hiking trails from the summit. You can camp only in designated backcountry campsites, and you must have a $10 Wilderness Pass camping permit (in addition to your park pass), which, along with lots of useful information, is available from **Parks Canada in Revelstoke** (p735) or from the **Rogers Pass Centre** (p736) inside Glacier National Park. Admission to both Mt Revelstoke and Glacier National Parks (the two are administered jointly) is adult/child $8/4 per day.

Glacier National Park

To be really accurate, this 1350-sq-km **park** (www.pc.gc.ca/glacier) should be called 430 Glaciers National Park; the annual snowfall here can be as much as 23m. Because of the sheer mountain slopes, this is one of the world's most active avalanche areas. For this reason, skiing, caving and mountaineering are regulated; you must register

with park wardens before venturing into the backcountry. Call for a daily **avalanche report** (☎250-837-6867) in season. Admission to this and Mt Revelstoke National Park (the two are administered jointly) is adult/child $8/4 per day.

Whether you travel by car, bus, trail or bicycle (more power to you), Rogers Pass will likely rank as one of the most beautiful mountain passes you'll ever traverse. Be sure to pause at the **Hemlock Grove Trail**, 54km west of Revelstoke, where a 400m boardwalk winds through an ancient hemlock rainforest.

Spend some time with the CPR dioramas at the informative **Rogers Pass Centre** (☎250-814-5233; ⏱8am-8pm mid-June–Aug, 7am-5pm other times), 72km east of Revelstoke. The center shows films about the park and organizes guided walks in summer. As a bonus, there's an excellent bookstore run by the **Friends of Mt Revelstoke & Glacier National Parks** (www.friendsrevglacier.com).

Across from the center, the 50-room **Glacier Park Lodge** (☎250-837-2126, 888-567-4477; www.glacierparklodge.ca; r $100-140; ❄☎☀) has a cafe, gas station and coin laundry.

Not far from here are the park's two campgrounds: **Illecillewaet** and **Loop Brook** (per campsite $22; ⏱Jul-Sep). Both have running water and flush toilets.

Golden

POP 3900

Golden is well situated for the national parks – there are six nearby – and for more immediate pleasures, like white-water rafting – the Kicking Horse River converges with the Columbia here. Don't just breeze past the strip of franchised yuck on Hwy 1 or you'll miss the tidy little town center down by the tumbling river.

Expect delays for years to come on Hwy 1 east of Golden as the road is reconstructed from scratch (see www.kickinghorse canyon.ca).

🏃 Activities

Golden is the center for **white-water rafting** trips on the turbulent and chilly Kicking Horse River. Powerful grade III and IV rapids, and breathtaking scenery along the sheer walls of the Kicking Horse Valley, make this rafting experience one of

North America's best. Full-day trips on the river average about $105; half-day trips are about $65. Local operators include **Alpine Rafting** (☎250-344-6778, 888-599-5299; www.alpinerafting.com).

Over 60% of the 106 ski runs at **Kicking Horse Mountain Resort** (☎250-439-5400, 866-754-5425; www.kickinghorseresort.com; 1-day lift pass adult/child from $74/35) are rated advanced or expert. With 1260 vertical meters and a snowy position between the Rockies and the Purcells, the resort's popularity grows each year. It's 14km from Golden on Kicking Horse Trail.

🛏 Sleeping & Eating
There are scores of chain motels along Hwy 1; check with the chamber of commerce for B&Bs. In the walkable center, 9th Ave N is good for cafes, bakeries and shops. The **farmers market** (⊙2-7pm Wed Jul & Aug) is next to the chamber of commerce.

Chancellor Peak Chalets INN $$$
(☎800-644-8888, 250-344-7038; www.chancellorpeakchalets.com; 2924 Kicking Horse Rd; cabins $195-265) 'What a find!' is a common response among guests to this riverside retreat. The 18 log chalets have two levels and sleep up to six. There are soaker tubs, full kitchens and all the nature you can breathe in. The chalets are 25km east of Golden, off Hwy 1.

Mary's Motel MOTEL $$
(☎250-344-7111, 866-234-6279; www.marysmotel.com; 603 8th Ave N; r $80-140; ☀🐾🖥) In town, right on the roaring river, Mary's has 81 rooms spread across several buildings; get one with a patio. There are more choices nearby.

Sander Lake Campground CAMPGROUND $
(☎250-344-6517; www.rockies.net/~bsander; campsites $15-18) This campground, located 12km southwest of Golden off Hwy 95, has a bucolic location amid trees and hills. There are 27 sites and three log cabins ($80).

Kicking Horse Grill CANADIAN $$
(☎250-344-2330; www.thekickinghorsegrill.ca; 1105 9th St S; mains $20-30; ⊙5-9pm) Dishes at this creative log cabin change depending on the season, although excellent steaks and trout are always on the menu. See if you can try for a table outside under the huge tree.

ⓘ WINTER ROAD CONDITIONS

For up-to-date road conditions on the Trans-Canada Hwy (Hwy 1) and across the province, consult **DriveBC** (☎800-550-4997; www.drivebc.ca). This is essential in winter when storms can close roads for extended periods.

ⓘ Information
Unfortunately, the shiny **visitor center** (☎250-344-7711; ⊙9am-6pm), 1km east on Hwy 1 from the Hwy 95 turnoff into Golden, mostly ignores the immediate region. For local info, visit the **Golden Chamber of Commerce** (☎250-344-7125, 800-622-4653; www.goldenchamber.bc.ca; 500 10th Ave N; ⊙10am-6pm Mon-Sat Jun-Aug, 10am-4pm Mon-Fri Sep-May).

ⓘ Getting There & Away
Greyhound Canada (☎800-661-8747; www.greyhound.ca; Husky Travel Centre, 1050 Trans-Canada Hwy) serves Vancouver ($124, 11 to 13 hours, three daily) and Calgary ($48, four hours, three daily) via Banff.

Yoho National Park
Fed by glaciers, the ice-blue Kicking Horse River plows through the valley of the same name. The surging waters are an apt image for this dramatic **national park** (☎250-343-6783; www.pc.gc.ca/yoho; adult/child $10/5), home to looming peaks, pounding waterfalls, glacial lakes and patches of pretty meadows.

Although the smallest (1310 sq km) of the four national parks in the Rockies, Yoho is a diamond in the (very) rough. This wilderness is the real deal; it's some of the continent's least tarnished.

East of Field on Hwy 1 is the **Takakkaw Falls road** (⊙late Jun-early Oct). At 254m, Takakkaw is one of the highest waterfalls in Canada. From here **Iceline**, a 20km hiking loop, passes many glaciers and spectacular scenery.

This World Heritage site protects the amazing Cambrian-age **fossil beds** on Mt Stephen and Mt Field. These 515-million-year-old fossils preserve the remains of marine creatures that were some of the earliest forms of life on earth. You can only get to the fossil beds by guided hikes, which

NORTHERN LIGHTS WOLF CENTRE

The **Northern Lights Wolf Centre** (☎250-344-6798; www.northernlight-swildlife.com; adult/child $10/6; ◷10am-6pm) is a refuge in the wild for wolves born into captivity. Visitors can expect to meet a resident wolf or two and learn about their complex and human-like family structure. The goal of the centre is to educate people about wolves, which are still being hunted to extinction to protect both cattle and even other endangered species. The centre is just west of Golden, 5km off the Trans-Canada. Look for signs or call.

are led by naturalists from the **Yoho Shale Geoscience Foundation** (☎800-343-3006; www.burgess-shale.bc.ca; tours from $75). Reservations are essential.

Near the south gate of the park, you can reach pretty **Wapta Falls** along a 2.4km trail. The easy walk takes about 45 minutes each way.

The three campgrounds within Yoho all close from October to April. Only the **Kicking Horse Campground** (campsites $28) has showers, making its 88 sites the most popular. Nearby, right at the turnoff to Yoho Valley Rd, the quieter **Monarch Campground** (campsites $18) offers 44 basic sites. Appealing **Takakkaw Falls Campground** (campsites $18), 13km along the gravel Yoho Valley Rd, has 35 walk-in (200m) campsites for tents only.

The isolated **HI-Yoho National Park** (Whiskey Jack Hostel; ☎403-670-7580, 866-762-4122; www.hihostels.ca; dm $26-28; ◷Jul-Sep) offers 27 dorm-style beds. It's 13km off Hwy 1 on Yoho Valley Rd, just before the Takakkaw Falls Campground and close to the falls itself.

LAKE O'HARA

Perched high in the mountains east of Field, **Lake O'Hara** is worth the significant hassle involved in reaching the place, which is an encapsulation of the whole Rockies. Compact wooded hillsides, alpine meadows, snow-covered passes, mountain vistas and glaciers are all wrapped around the stunning lake. A basic day trip is worthwhile, but stay overnight in the backcountry and you'll be able to access many more trails, some quite difficult, all quite spectacular. The **Alpine Circuit** (12km) has a bit of everything.

To reach the lake, you can take the **shuttle bus** (adult/child $15/7.50; ◷mid-Jun–early Oct) from the Lake O'Hara parking lot, 15km east of Field on Hwy 1. A quota system governs bus access to the lake and limits permits for the 30 backcountry campsites. You can freely walk the 11km from the parking area, but no bikes are allowed. The area around Lake O'Hara usually remains snow-covered or very muddy until mid-July.

Make reservations for the **bus trip** (☎250-343-6433) or for **camping** (backcountry permit adult $10) up to three months in advance. Given the popularity of Lake O'Hara, reservations are basically mandatory (unless you want to walk). However, if you don't have advance reservations, six day-use seats on the bus and three to five campsites are set aside for 'standby' users. To try to snare these, call ☎250-343-6433 at 8am the day before.

Lake O'Hara Lodge (☎250-343-6418; www.lakeohara.com; r per person per night from $280, 2-night minimum) has been leaving guests slack jawed for over 80 years. The only place to stay at the lake tent-free, the lodge is luxurious in a rustic way. Its environmental practices are lauded.

FIELD

Don't go past Field without stopping. Right off Hwy 1, this historic railroad town has a dramatic overlook of the river and is a quaint yet unfussy place. Many of its buildings date from the early days of the railways, when it was the Canadian Pacific Railway's headquarters for exploration and, later, for strategic planning when engineers were trying to solve the problem of moving trains over Kicking Horse Pass (see the results from a Hwy 1 lookout 8km east of Field).

Field has more than 20 B&Bs. **Fireweed Hostel** (☎250-343-6999, 877-343-6999; www.fireweedhostel.com; 313 Stephen Ave; dm $30-40, r $80-160; @⊛) has four spotless rooms.

TOP CHOICE **Truffle Pigs Bistro and Kicking Horse Lodge** (☎250-343-6303; www.trufflepigs.com; 100 Centre St; r $100-200, mains $8-25; ⊛) is a legendary cafe serving inventive, high-concept bistro fare that's locally sourced and usually organic. The inn across the street has 14 rooms with the same cheeky style as the bistro.

Greyhound Canada buses stop at the park info center on Hwy 1 on their trips west to Golden ($20, 1½ hours, three daily) and beyond and east to Banff ($25, 1½ hours, three daily).

ℹ Information

At **Yoho National Park Information Centre** (📞250-343-6783; off Hwy 1, Field; ⊘9am-4pm Sep-Apr, 9am-5pm May & Jun, 9am-7pm Jul & Aug), pick up the free *Backcountry Guide*; its map and trail descriptions give an excellent overview. Rangers can advise on itineraries and conditions. Alberta Tourism staffs a desk here in summer.

Mt Assiniboine Provincial Park

Between Kootenay and Banff National Parks lies this lesser-known and smaller (39-sq-km) **provincial park** (www.bcparks.ca), part of the Rockies' Unesco World Heritage site. The pointed peak of Mt Assiniboine (3618m) – often referred to as Canada's Matterhorn – and its near neighbors have become a magnet for experienced rock climbers and mountaineers. Backcountry hikers revel in its meadows and glaciers.

The park's main focus is crystal-clear **Lake Magog**, which is reachable on a 27km trek from Banff National Park. At the lake there's the commercially operated **Mt Assiniboine Lodge** (📞403-678-2883; www.canadianrockies.net/assiniboine; r per person from $260), a **campground** (campsites $10) and some **huts** (per person $20), which may be reserved through the lodge. Helicopter transport is $130 to $160 each way.

Kootenay National Park

Shaped like a lightning bolt, **Kootenay National Park** (📞250-347-9505; www.pc.gc.ca/kootenay; adult/child $10/5) is centered on a long, wide, tree-covered valley shadowed by cold, gray peaks. Encompassing 1406 sq km, Kootenay has a more moderate climate than the other Rocky Mountains parks and, in the southern regions especially, summers can be hot and dry (which is a factor in the frequent fires). It's the only national park in Canada to contain both

glaciers and cacti. From BC you can create a fine driving loop via Kootenay and Yoho National Parks. See p739 for details on the main park visitor center.

The short interpretive **Fireweed Trail** loops through the surrounding forest at the north end of Hwy 93. Panels explain how nature here is recovering from a 1968 fire. Some 7km further on, **Marble Canyon** has a pounding creek flowing through a nascent forest. Another 3km south on the main road is the short, easy trail through forest to ochre pools known as the **Paint Pots**. Panels describe both the mining history of this rusty earth and its past importance to Aboriginal people.

Learn how the park's appearance has changed over time at the **Kootenay Valley Viewpoint**, where informative panels vie with the view. Just 3km south, **Olive Lake** makes a perfect picnic or rest stop. A lakeside interpretive trail describes some of the visitors who've come before you.

Radium Hot Springs

Lying just outside the southwest corner of Kootenay National Park, Radium Hot Springs is a major gateway to the whole Rocky Mountains national park area. The **Kootenay National Park & Radium Hot Springs Visitor Center** (📞250-347-9331, 800-347-9704; www.radiumhotsprings.com; 7556 Main St E/Hwy 93/95; ⊘9am-7pm May-Sep, 9am-5pm Oct-Apr) has internet access, an excellent display on the parks and is staffed with Parks Canada rangers.

Radium boasts a large resident population of **bighorn sheep**, which often wander through town, but the big attraction is the **hot springs** (📞250-347-9485; adult/child $7/6; ⊘9am-11pm mid-May–early Oct, noon-9pm rest of yr), 3km north of town. The hot springs' pools are quite modern and can get very busy in summer. The water comes from the ground at 44°C, enters the first pool at 39°C and hits the final one at 29°C.

Radium glows with lodging – some 30 motels at last count. Highly recommended is **Misty River Lodge B&B** (📞250-347-9912; www.mistyriverlodge.bc.ca; 5036 Hwy 93; r $60-100). Directly outside the park gate, this five-room B&B has owners who are enthusiastic about the parks and ready to share their knowledge with guests; bicyclists are welcomed.

Radium Hot Springs to Fernie

South from Radium Hot Springs, Hwy 93/95 follows the wide Columbia River valley between the Purcell and Rocky Mountains. It's not especially interesting, unless you're into the area's industry (building ski resorts), agriculture (golf courses) or wild game (condo buyers).

At Skookumchuk, 90km south of Radium Hot Springs, a gravel road heads eastwards to **Top of the World Provincial Park** (📞250-422-4200; www.bcparks.ca), which has hiking trails and backcountry camping ($5) and cabins ($15 to $30). The highlight is a 6km hike or bike ride from the end of the road to the simply named **Fish Lake**, which is filled with just that.

South of Skookumchuk, the road forks. Go left and after 31km you'll reach Hwy 3 for Fernie. Go left on Hwy 95A and you'll come to **Fort Steele Heritage Town** (📞250-426-7342; www.fortsteele.ca; adult/child summer $15/5, less other times; ⊙9:30am-6:30pm Jul & Aug, 9:30am-5pm Apr-Jun, Sep & Oct, 10am-4pm Nov-Mar), a re-created 1880s town that's an order of magnitude less irritating than many of similar ilk.

From here it's 95km to Fernie along Hwys 93 and 3.

Fernie

POP 4700

Surrounded by mountains on four sides – that's the sheer Lizard Range you see looking west – Fernie defines cool. Once devoted solely to lumber and coal, the town has used its sensational setting to branch out. Skiers love the more-than-8m of dry powder that annually hits the runs easily seen from town. In summer this same dramatic setting lures scores of hikers and mountain bikers.

Despite the town's discovery by pleasure seekers, it still retains a down-to-earth vibe, best felt in the cafes, bars, shops and galleries along Victoria/2nd Ave in the historic center, three blocks south of Hwy 3/7th Ave. Fernie was the location of *Hot Tub Time Machine*, a farcical 2010 film that starred John Cusack and Chevy Chase.

◉ Sights

Fernie experienced a devastating fire in 1908 (one of many disasters), which resulted in a brick-and-stone building code.

Thus today you'll see numerous fine **early-20th-century buildings**, many of which were built out of local yellow brick, giving the town an appearance unique in the East Kootenays. Get a copy of *Heritage Walking Tour* ($5), a superb booklet produced by the **Fernie Museum** (📞250-423-7016; 491 2nd Ave; admission by donation; ⊙10am-5:30pm).

Located in the old CPR train station, the **Arts Station** (📞250-423-4842; 601 1st Ave; ⊙vary) has a small stage, galleries and studios for some of the many local artists.

🏃 Activities

In fall, eyes turn to the mountains for more than their beauty: they're looking for snow. A five-minute drive from downtown Fernie, fast-growing **Fernie Alpine Resort** (📞250-423-4655, 877-333-2339, snow conditions 250-423-3555; www.skifernie.com; 1-day pass adult/child $75/25) boasts 114 runs, five bowls and almost endless dumps of powder. Most hotels run shuttles here daily.

Mountain biking is almost as big as skiing. From easy jaunts in **Mt Fernie Provincial Park** (www.bcparks.ca), which is a mere 3km from town, to legendary rides up and down the hills in and around the ski resort (which runs lifts in summer), Fernie has lots for riders. Many come just to tackle the legendary **Al Matador**, which drops over 900m before finishing in the terrific Three Kings trail. Get a copy of the widely available *Fernie Mountain Bike Map* and check out the **Crank Fernie** (www.crankfernie.com) website. **Ski & Bike Base** (📞250-423-6464; www.skibase.com; 432 2nd Ave) is but one of many excellent gear-rental and supply places along 2nd Ave. Mountain bikes start at $30 per day.

The Elk River is a classic white-water river, with three grade IV rapids and 11 more grade IIIs. It passes through beautiful country and you can often see large wildlife. Several outfits, such as **Mountain High River Adventures** (📞250-423-5008, 877-423-4555; www.raftfernie.com), offer day trips for about $120 or half-day floats for $60.

Great hiking trails radiate in all directions from Fernie. The excellent and challenging **Three Sisters hike** (20km) winds through forests and wildflower-covered meadows, along limestone cliffs and scree slopes. Get directions at the visitor center.

🛏 Sleeping

Being a big ski town, Fernie's high season is winter. You'll have most fun staying in the center, otherwise **Fernie Central Reservations** (⌨800-622-5007; www.ferniecentralreservations.com) can book you a room at the ski resort.

HI Raging Elk Hostel HOSTEL $
(⌨250-423-6811; www.ragingelk.com; 892 6th Ave; dm/r from $26/60; ⊚) Wide decks allow plenty of inspirational mountain gazing at this well-run central hostel that has good advice for those hoping to mix time on the slopes and/or trails with seasonal work. The pub is a hoot.

Mt Fernie Provincial Park CAMPGROUND $
(⌨800-689-9025; www.discovercamping.ca; campsites $21) Only 3km from town, it has 40 sites, flush toilets, waterfalls and access to mountain-bike trails.

Park Place Lodge HOTEL $$
(⌨250-423-6871, 888-381-7275; www.parkplacelodge.com; 742 Hwy 3; r $90-200; ❄⊚⊛) The nicest lodging close to the center, its 64 comfortable rooms have high-speed internet, fridges, microwaves and access to an indoor pool. Some have balconies and views.

Red Tree Lodge MOTEL $$
(⌨250-423-4622, 800-977-2977; www.redtreelodge.com; 1101 7th Ave; r $80-150; ❄⊚⊛) Unprepossessing but ideally located, this two-story motel has refurbished rooms, with a touch of style. There's a hot tub, a full shared kitchen, some balconies and lots of mountain views.

🍴 Eating & Drinking

Cincott Farms Organic Market (⌨250-423-5564; 851 7th Ave; ⊙8am-8pm) is like a daily farmers market. Look for the good ales of Fernie Brewing Co at most local pubs. The Arts Station sometimes has live music by local bands.

Blue Toque Diner CAFE $
(⌨250-423-4637; 500 Hwy 3; mains $8; ⊙8:30am-3:30pm) Part of the Arts Station; the menu features lots of seasonal and organic vegetarian specials. This is the place for breakfast.

Rip 'n' Richards Eatery PIZZA $$
(⌨250-423-3002; 301 Hwy 3; mains $10-15; ⊙11am-11pm) Enjoy the views of the Elk River and surrounding peaks from the deck. But save some attention for the long menu of good burgers, salads and pizza.

Mug Shots Bistro BAKERY $
(⌨250-423-8018; 591 3rd Ave; mains $5; ⊙8am-5pm; @⊚) Always buzzing, it offers coffee, baked goods, sandwiches and internet access.

🛍 Shopping

Polar Peek Books BOOKSTORE
(⌨250-423-3736; 592 2nd Ave) An eclectic mix of books, with a good section of local interest. Great recommendations.

ℹ Information

The **visitor center** (⌨250-423-6868; www.ferniechamber.com; 102 Commerce Rd; ⊙9am-6pm summer, 9am-5pm Mon-Fri winter) is east of town off Hwy 3, just past the Elk River crossing. Good displays about the area; the Fernie Museum is also a good info source.

ℹ Getting There & Around

Shuttles operate between town and the ski resort.

Airport Shuttle Express (www.airportshuttleexpress.com) To/from Calgary airport (adult/child $114/94, four hours) in ski season.

Greyhound Canada (⌨250-423-6811; HI Raging Elk Hostel, 892 6th Ave) Buses west to Kelowna ($115, 11½ hours, two daily) via Cranbrook and Nelson ($68, six hours, two daily) and east to Calgary ($70, 5½ to seven hours, two daily).

The Shuttle (⌨250-423-4023; theshuttle-fernie@hotmail.com) To/from Calgary airport (adult/child $120/90, 4½ hours) in winter.

Kimberley

POP 5900

When big-time mining left Kimberley in 1973, a plan was hatched to turn the little mountain village (altitude 1113m) into a tourist destination with a Bavarian theme. The center was turned into a pedestrian zone named the **Platzl**, locals were encouraged to prance about in lederhosen and dirndls and sausage was added to many a menu. Now, over three decades later, the shtick is fading like memories of the war. There's still a bit of fake half-timbering about, you can get a schnitzel and there is summertime dancing aimed at the tour-bus crowds, but mostly it's a diverse place that makes a worthwhile detour off Hwy 95 between Cranbrook and Radium Hot Springs.

The **visitor center** (☎250-427-3666; www.kimberleychamber.com; 270 Kimberley Ave; ☺10am-6pm daily Jun-Aug, 10am-6pm Mon-Sat Sep-May) sits in the large parking area behind the Platzl.

Take a 15km ride on **Kimberley's Underground Mining Railway** (☎250-427-7365; www.kimberleysundergroundmining railway.ca; Gerry Sorensen Way; adult/child $18/7; ☺11am-3:30pm mid-May–mid-Sep) as the tiny train putters through the steep-walled Mark Creek Valley toward some sweeping mountain vistas. At the end of the line, you can take a chairlift up to the **Kimberley Alpine Resort** (☎250-427-4881, 877-754-5462; www.skikimberley.com; 1-day lift pass adult/child $65/18). In winter, the resort has over 700 hectares of skiable terrain, mild weather and 80 runs.

Cranbrook

POP 19,800

The area's main center, 31km southeast of Kimberley, **Cranbrook** is a dusty crossroads. However, it has one great reason for stopping: the **Canadian Museum of Rail Travel** (☎250-489-3918; www.trains deluxe.com; adult/child $16/8; ☺10am-6pm summer, 10am-5pm Tue-Sat winter), which has some fine examples of classic Canadian trains, including the luxurious 1929 edition of the *Trans-Canada Limited,* a legendary train that ran from Montréal to Vancouver.

Hwy 3/95 bisects the town and is a grim, treeless strip of motels. But just south, **Elizabeth Lake Lodge** (☎250-426-6114; www.elizabethlakelodge.com; 590 Van Horn St S/Hwy3/95; campsites/r from $24/90; ❋@☎) stars with its lakeside location, stylish

CHECK YOUR WATCH

It is a constant source of confusion that the East Kootenays lie in the Mountain Time Zone along with Alberta – unlike the rest of BC, which falls within the Pacific Time Zone. West on Hwy 1 from Golden, the time changes at the east gate of Glacier National Park. Going west on Hwy 3, the time changes between Cranbrook and Creston. Mountain Time is one hour ahead of Pacific Time.

rooms and fun-filled mini-golf course based on BC history.

Cranbrook to Rossland

Hwy 3 twists and turns its way 300km from Cranbrook to Osoyoos at the south end of the Okanagan Valley. Along the way it hugs the hills close to the US border and passes eight border crossings. As such, it's a road of great usefulness, even if the sights never quite live up to the promise.

Creston, 123km west of Cranbrook, is known for its many orchards and as the home of Columbia Brewing Co's Kokanee True Ale. But both of these products are mostly shipped out, so you should do the same. Hwy 3A heads north from here for a scenic 80km to the Kootenay Lake Ferry (see the boxed text, p745), which connects to Nelson. This is a fun journey.

The **Creston Valley Wildlife Management Area** (☎250-402-6900; www.creston wildlife.ca; admission free; ☺dawn-dusk), 11km west of Creston, is a good place to spot oodles of birds, including blue herons, from the 1km boardwalk.

Some 85km west of Creston, **Salmo** is notable mostly as the junction with Hwy 6, which runs north for a bland 40km to Nelson. The Crowsnest Hwy splits 10km west. Hwy 3 bumps north through **Castlegar**, which is notable for having the closest large airport to Nelson and a very large pulp mill. Hwy 3B dips down through the cute little cafe-filled town of **Fruitvale** and industrial **Trail**.

Rossland

POP 3500

About 10km west of Trail, Rossland is a world apart. High in the Southern Monashee Mountains (1023m), this old mining village is one of Canada's best places for mountain biking. A long history of mining has left the hills crisscrossed with old trails and abandoned rail lines – all of which are prefect for riding.

The **visitor center** (☎250-362-7722, 888-448-7444; www.rossland.com; ☺9am-5pm mid-May–mid-Sep) is located in the **Rossland Museum** building, at the junction of Hwy 22 (from the US border) and Hwy 3B.

Mountain biking is the reason many come to Rossland. Free-riding is all the rage as the ridgelines are easily accessed and there are lots of rocky paths for plunging downhill. The **Seven Summits Trail** is a 30.4km single track along the crest of the Rossland Range. The **Kootenay Columbia Trails Society** (www.kcts.ca) has tons of info, including downloadable maps.

Good in summer for riding, **Red Mountain Ski Resort** (250-362-7384, 800-663-0105, snow report 250-362-5500; www.redresort.com; 1-day lift pass adult/child $64/32) draws plenty of ski bums in winter. Red, as it's called, includes the 1590m-high Red Mountain and 2040m-high Granite Mountain, for a total of 485 hectares of challenging, powdery terrain.

Hwy 3B curves through awesome alpine scenery before rejoining Hwy 3 28km northwest of Rossland. The road then wends its way 170km west to Osoyoos through increasingly arid terrain.

Nelson

POP 9300

Nelson is reason enough to visit the Kootenays and should be on any itinerary in the region. Tidy brick buildings climb the side of a hill overlooking the west arm of deep-blue Kootenay Lake, and the waterfront is lined with parks and beaches. The thriving cafe, art and nightlife culture is simply a bonus. However, what really propels Nelson over the top is its personality: a funky mix of hippies, characters, creative types and rugged individualists. You can find all these along Baker St, the pedestrian-friendly main drag where wafts of patchouli mingle with hints of fresh-roasted coffee.

Born as a mining town in the late 1800s, in 1977 a decades-long heritage-preservation project began. Today there are more than 350 carefully preserved and restored period buildings. Nelson is an excellent base for hiking, skiing and kayaking the nearby lakes and hills.

◉ Sights

Almost a third of Nelson's **historic buildings** have been restored to their high- and late-Victorian architectural splendor. Pick up the superb *Heritage Walking Tour* booklet from the visitor center. It gives details of over two dozen buildings in the center and offers a good lesson in Victorian architecture. The *Artwalk* brochure lists the many public-art displays.

Touchstones Nelson (250-352-9813; 502 Vernon St; adult/child $10/4; ⊙10am-5pm Mon-Wed, Fri & Sat, to 8pm Thu, noon-4pm Sun Jun-Aug, closed Mon Sep-May) combines engaging historical displays with art in Nelson's grand old city hall (1902).

By the iconic Nelson Bridge, **Lakeside Park** is both a flower-filled, shady park and a beach. From the center, follow the **Waterfront Pathway**, which runs all along the shore (its western extremity past the airport has a remote river vantage). You can walk one way to the park and ride **Streetcar 23** (adult/child $3/2; ⊙11am-5pm daily Jun–mid-Sep, Sat & Sun May & mid-Sep–mid-Oct) the other way. It follows a 2km track from Lakeside Park to the wharf at Hall St.

🏃 Activities

Kayaking

The natural (meaning undammed) waters of Kootenay Lake are a major habitat for kayaks. **ROAM** (250-354-2056; www.roamshop.com; 639 Baker St) sells gear, offers advice and works with the noted **Kootenay Kayak Company** (250-505-4549; www.kootenaykayak.com; rentals per day from $40, tours from $80). Kayaks can be picked up at ROAM or Lakeside Park.

Hiking

The two-hour climb to **Pulpit Rock**, practically in town, affords fine views of Nelson and Kootenay Lake, and excellent hikes abound in two parks in the Selkirk Mountains. Nearby north of town, **Kokanee Creek Provincial Park** (250-825-4212; www.bcparks.ca), 20km northeast off Hwy 3A, has several trails heading away from the visitor center. **Kokanee Glacier Provincial Park** (trail conditions 250-825-3500; www.bcparks.ca) boasts 85km of some of the area's most superb hiking trails. The fantastic 4km (two-hour) hike to Kokanee Lake on a well-marked trail can be continued to the treeless, boulder-strewn expanse around the glacier.

Mountain Biking

Mountain-bike trails wind up from Kootenay Lake along steep and challenging hills, followed by vertigo-inducing downhills. Pick up *Roots Rocks Rhythm* ($15), which details 70 trails, from **Sacred Ride** (250-362-5688; www.sacredride.ca; 213B Baker St; rentals per day $45-55).

Skiing & Snowboarding

Known for its heavy powdery snowfall, **Whitewater Winter Resort** (☎250-354-4944, 800-666-9420, snow report 250-352-7669; www.skiwhitewater.com; 1-day lift ticket adult/child $57/35), 12km south of Nelson off Hwy 6, has the same small-town charm as Nelson. Lifts are few but so are the crowds, who enjoy a drop of 396m on 46 runs.

🛏 Sleeping

By all means stay in the heart of Nelson so you can fully enjoy the city's beat. The visitor center has lists of B&Bs in heritage homes near the center.

TOP CHOICE Hume Hotel   HOTEL $$
(☎250-352-5331, 877-568-0888; www.humehotel.com; 422 Vernon St; r $80-150; @🛜) This 1898 classic hotel is reclaiming its former grandeur. The 43 rooms (beware of airless ones overlooking the kitchen on sultry nights) vary in quality; ask for the huge corner rooms with views of the hills and lake. Rates include a delicious breakfast, and it has several appealing nightlife venues (see p745).

HI Dancing Bear Inn   HOSTEL $
(☎250-352-7573, 877-352-7573; www.dancingbearinn.com; 171 Baker St; dm $22-26, r $50-60; ☺@🛜) The brilliant management here offers advice and smoothes the stay of guests in the 14 shared and private rooms (all share bathrooms). Gourmet kitchen and a library.

Cloudside Inn   INN $$
(☎250-352-3226, 800-596-2337; www.cloudside.ca; 408 Victoria St; r $100-160; ❄@🛜) Live like a silver baron at this vintage mansion where the six rooms are named after trees. Luxuries abound, and a fine patio looks over the terraced gardens.

Victoria Falls Guest House   INN $$
(☎250-352-2297; www.victoriafallsguesthouse.com; cnr Victoria & Falls Sts; r $110-130; 🛜) The wide porch wraps right around this festive yellow renovated Victorian. The four rooms have sitting areas and cooking facilities. Decor ranges from cozy antique to family-friendly bunk beds.

Mountain Hound Inn   GUESTHOUSE $$
(☎250-352-6490, 866-452-6490; www.mountainhound.com; 621 Baker St; r $80-110; ❄@) The 19 rooms are small but have an industrial edge – to go with the cement-block walls. It also offers in-room high-speed internet.

WhiteHouse Backpacker Lodge   HOSTEL $
(☎250-352-0505; www.white-house.ca; 816 Vernon St; dm $25, r from $50-60; @🛜) Relax on the broad porch overlooking the lake at this comfy heritage house. You'll get all the pancakes you can cook yourself for breakfast.

City Tourist Park   CAMPGROUND $
(☎250-352-7618; campnels@telus.net; 90 High St; campsites from $20; ☺May-Oct) Just a five-minute walk from Baker St, this small campground has 40 shady sites.

🍴 Eating

Stroll the Baker St environs and you'll find a vibrant mix of eateries.

Nelson has two **farmers markets**: one is in the **centre** (cnr Josephine & Baker Sts; ☺9:30am-3pm Wed Jul-Sep); the other in **Cottonwood Falls Park** (☺8am-2pm Sat May-Oct) is both the largest in the region and next to a waterfall.

TOP CHOICE All Seasons Cafe   FUSION $$
(☎250-352-0101; www.allseasonscafe.com; 620 Herridge Lane; mains $15-30; ☺5-10pm Mon-Sat) Sitting on the patio under the little lights twinkling in the huge maple above is a Nelson highlight (in winter, candles provide the same romantic flair). The eclectic menu changes with the seasons. The wine list is iconic.

Bibo   FUSION $$
(☎250-352-2744; 518 Hall St; mains $10-25; ☺noon-11pm) Bibo is all exposed brick inside, while outside, a hillside terrace looks down to the lake. Small plates celebrate local produce: go nuts and design your own cheese and charcuterie plate. The short list of mains includes steaks and seafood.

Dominion Cafe   BAKERY $
(☎250-352-1904; 334 Baker St; mains $5) A little gem of a bakery-cafe, the chairs are as rickety as the ancient decor; the metaphors continue as the dining area is as small as the menu. But items like the organic, vegan bumbleberry square are sublime.

Oso Negro   CAFE $
(☎250-532-7761; 604 Ward St; coffee from $2; ☺7am-5pm; @) This local favorite corner cafe roasts its own coffee. Outside there are tables in a garden that burbles with water features amid statues.

Busaba Thai Cafe   THAI $$
(☎250-352-2185; 524 Victoria St; mains $10-20; ☺11am-10pm) The iced Thai coffee here can turn around a hot day. The rich details of the interior have the lush elegance of a

Bangkok gift shop where you'd actually buy something. The food is authentic and best enjoyed on the patio under the stars.

 Drinking

Look for the organic ales of the Nelson Brewing Co.

Library Lounge   BAR
(☏250-352-5331; Hume Hotel, 422 Vernon St; ⏰11am-late) This refined space in the classic hotel (p744) has some good sidewalk tables where you can ponder the passing parade. There's live jazz most nights. Downstairs, the Spiritbar nightclub aspires to something more metropolitan.

The Royal   PUB
(☏250-352-1269; 330 Baker St; ⏰11am-2am) A popular bar right on Baker St. Listen to bands under the high ceilings inside or kick back on the deck.

 Shopping

Otter Books   BOOKSTORE
(☏250-352-7525; 398 Baker St) New books and maps.

Isis Exotica   ACCESSORIES
(☏250-352-0666; 582 Ward St) The place to feel the local vibe: sex toys and oils in a feminist setting.

 Information

The **visitor center** (☏250-352-3433, 877-663-5706; www.discovernelson.com; 225 Hall St; ⏰8:30am-6pm daily May-Oct, 8:30am-5pm Mon-Fri Nov-Apr) contains good information about the region.

Many cafes have internet access. **Nelson Library** (☏250-352-6333; 602 Stanley St; ⏰11am-8pm Mon & Wed, 11am-6pm Tue & Thu-Sat) has free access.

Listen to the Nelson beat on **Kootenay Co-op Radio** (FM93.5).

 Getting There & Around

Castlegar Airport (YCG; www.castlegar.ca/airport.php) Closest airport to Nelson.

Greyhound Canada (☏250-352-3939; Chahko-Mika Mall, 1128 Lakeside Dr) Buses to Calgary ($120, 11 to 13 hours, two daily) via various south Kootenays cities, and Vancouver ($130, 12 to 13 hours, two daily) via Kelowna ($65, 5½ hours).

Nelson Transit System Buses (☏250-352-8201; www.bctransit.ca; fare $1.75) Main stop: the corner of Ward and Baker Sts. Buses 2 and 10 serve Chahko-Mika Mall and Lakeside Park.

Queen City Shuttle (☏250-352-9829; www.kootenayshuttle.com; one way adult/child $24/12) Links with Castlegar Airport (one hour).

Nelson to Revelstoke

Heading north from Nelson, there are two options – both scenic – for reaching Revelstoke. Hwy 6 heads west for 16km before turning north at South Slocan. The road eventually runs alongside pretty Slocan Lake for about 30km before reaching New Denver. You'll see mining drama all the way.

KOOTENAY FERRIES

The long Kootenay and Upper and Lower Arrow Lakes necessitate some scenic ferry travel. All **ferries** (www.th.gov.bc.ca/marine/ferry_schedules.htm) are free. On busy summer weekends you may have to wait in a long line for a sailing or two before you get passage.

Kootenay Lake Ferry (☏250-229-4215) sails between Balfour on the west arm of Kootenay Lake (34km northeast of Nelson) and Kootenay Bay, where you can follow Hwy 3A for the pretty 80km ride south to Creston. It is a 35-minute crossing. In summer the ferry leaves Balfour every 50 minutes between 6:30am and 9:40pm, and Kootenay Lake from 7:10am to 10:20pm.

Needles Ferry (☏250-837-8418) crosses Lower Arrow Lake between Fauquier (57km south of Nakusp) and Needles (135km east of Vernon) on Hwy 6; the trip takes five minutes and runs every 30 minutes in each direction. This is a good link between the Okanagan Valley and the Kootenays.

Upper Arrow Lake Ferry (☏250-837-8418) runs year-round between Galena Bay (49km south of Revelstoke) and Shelter Bay (49km north of Nakusp) on Hwy 23. The trip takes 20 minutes and runs from 6am to 11pm every hour on the hour from Shelter Bay and every hour on the half-hour between 6:30am and 11:30pm from Galena Bay.

cool vistas of snow-clad peaks rising from the lake and little else with this option, which is 97km in total between Nelson and New Denver.

Heading north and east from Nelson on Hwy 3A is probably the most interesting route. After 34km there is the dock for the **Kootenay Lake Ferry** (p745) at Balfour. This ride is worth it even if you're not going anywhere, because of the long lake vistas of blue mountains rising sharply from the water.

At Balfour the road becomes Hwy 31 and follows the lake 34km north to Kaslo, passing cute little towns along the way.

KASLO

A cute little lake town that's a good stop, Kaslo is a low-key gem. The **visitor center** (☑250-353-2525; www.klhs.bc.ca; 324 Front St; ☺9am-5pm mid-May–mid-Oct) can help with info on the myriad ways to kayak and canoe the sparkling blue waters right outside. Next door, the 1898 **SS Moyie** (adult/child $8/4; ☺9am-5pm mid-May–mid-Oct) has been restored. There's a range of accommodations in and around town, plus some good ice-cream stands.

NEW DENVER

Wild mountain streams are just some of the natural highlights on Hwy 31A, which goes up and over some rugged hills. At the end of this twisting 47km road, you reach New Denver, which seems about five years away from ghost-town status. But that's not bad as this historic little gem slumbers away peacefully right on the clear waters of Slocan Lake. The **Silvery Slocan Museum** (☑250-358-2201; www.newdenver.ca; 202 6th Ave; ☺9am-5pm mid-Jun–Sep) is also home to the very helpful visitor center. Housed in the 1897 Bank of Montreal building, it features well-done displays from the booming mining days, a tiny vault and an untouched tin ceiling.

Both New Denver and the equally sleepy old mining town of **Silverton**, just south, have excellent cafes. They are also good for arranging access to **Valhalla Provincial Park** (www.bcparks.ca), a 496-sq-km area that's one of BC's most attractive and under-appreciated parks. Like the famous photo of Diana sitting alone in front of the Taj Mahal, the park sits in grand isolation on the west side of Slocan Lake: you'll need a boat to access the many trails and remote campsites.

Making the loop from Nelson via Hwys 6 and 31 through New Denver is an excel-lent day trip. Otherwise, if you're headed to Revelstoke, continue north 47km on Hwy 6 from New Denver to Nakusp through somewhat bland rolling countryside.

NAKUSP

Right on Upper Arrow Lake, both Nakusp and the chain of lakes were forever changed by BC's orgy of dam building in the 1950s and 1960s. The water level here was raised and the town had to be moved, which is why it now has a sort of 1960s-era look. It does have some attractive cafes and a tiny museum.

Nakusp Hot Springs (☑250-265-4528; www.nakusphotsprings.com; adult/child $9/free; ☺9:30am-9:30pm), 12km northeast of Nakusp off Hwy 23, feel a bit artificial after a revamp. However, you'll forget this as you soak away your cares amid an amphitheater of trees. Ditch the car and walk here on the beautiful 8km **Kuskanax Interpretive Trail** from Nakusp.

From Nakusp you could head west on Hwy 6 to Vernon (p729) in the Okanagan Valley – a 245km drive that includes the Needles Ferry. Or head north 55km on Hwy 23 to the Upper Arrow Lake Ferry (p745) and the final 48km to Revelstoke.

CARIBOO, CHILCOTIN & COAST

This vast and beautiful region covers a huge swath of BC north of the Whistler tourist hordes. It comprises three very distinct areas. The **Cariboo** region includes numerous ranches and terrain that's little changed from the 1850s when the 'Gold Rush Trail' passed through from Lillooet to Barkerville. There are two noteworthy provincial parks here: untamed Wells Gray and canoe-happy Bowron Lake.

Populated with more moose than people, the **Chilcotin** lies to the west of Hwy 97, the region's north–south spine. Its mostly wild, rolling landscape has a few ranches and some aboriginal villages. Hwy 20 travels west from Williams Lake to the spectacular Bella Coola Valley – a bear-and-wildlife-filled inlet along the coast.

Much of the region can be reached via Hwy 97 and you can build a circle itinerary to other parts of BC via Prince George in the north. The Bella Coola Valley is served by ferry from Port Hardy on Vancouver Island (p705), which makes for cool circle-route itineraries.

There is a daily **Greyhound Canada** (☎800-661-8747; www.greyhound.ca) service along Hwy 97 to/from Prince George.

Williams Lake to Prince George

Cattle and lumber have shaped **Williams Lake**, the hub for the region. Some 206km north of the junction of Hwys 1 and 97, this small town has a pair of small museums and numerous motels. The best reason to stop is the superb **Discovery Centre** (☎250-392-5025; www.williamslakechamber.com; 1660 Broadway S, off Hwy 97; ⊙9am-5pm summer, 9am-4pm rest of year), a visitor center in a huge log building. It has full regional info and the lowdown for trips west to the coast on Hwy 20.

Quesnel, 124km north of Williams Lake on Hwy 97, is all about logging. There are some good motels and cafes in the tidy, flower-lined center. From Quesnel, Hwy 26

leads east to the area's main attractions, Barkerville Historic Park (p747) and Bowron Lake Provincial Park (p747).

North of Quesnel it's 116km on Hwy 97 to Prince George (p757).

Barkerville & Around

In 1862 Billy Barker, previously of Cornwall, struck gold deep in the Cariboo. Soon Barkerville sprung up, populated by the usual fly-by-night crowds of whores, dupes, tricksters and just plain prospectors. Today you can visit more than 125 restored heritage buildings in **Barkerville Historic Town** (☎888-994-3332; www.barkerville.ca; adult/child $14/4.25; ⊙8am-8pm mid-May–Sep). In summer, people dressed in period garb roam through town, and if you can tune out the crowds it feels more authentic than forced. It has cafes and a couple of B&Bs. At other times of year you can visit the town for free but don't expect to find much open – possibly a plus.

BOWRON LAKE PROVINCIAL PARK

The place heaven-bound canoeists go when they die, **Bowron Lake Provincial Park** (www.bcparks.ca) is a fantasyland of 10 lakes surrounded by snowcapped peaks. Forming a natural circle with sections of the Isaac, Cariboo and Bowron Rivers, its 116km canoe circuit is one of the world's finest. There are eight portages, with the longest (2km) over well-defined trails.

The whole circuit takes between six and 10 days, and you'll need to be completely self-sufficient. It's generally open mid-May to October. September is an excellent choice, both for the bold colors of changing leaves and lack of summertime crowds.

The BC Parks website has a downloadable document with everything you'll need to know for planning your trip, including mandatory reservations (which book up months in advance).

If you'd rather leave the details to others, **Whitegold Adventures** (☎250-994-2345, 866-994-2345; www.whitegold.ca; Hwy 26, Wells) offers four- to eight-day guided paddles of Bowron Lake. A full circuit costs $1800 per person.

To get to the park by car, turn off Hwy 26 just before Barkerville and follow the 28km gravel Bowron Lake Rd.

Sleeping

All the following are near the start of the circuit. The lodges rent gear, kayaks and canoes.

» **Bowron Lake Provincial Park Campground** (campsites $16) Has 25 simple sites.

» **Bowron Lake Lodge** (☎250-992-2733, 800-519-3399; www.bowronlakelodge.com; campsites $28, r $40-80; ⊙May-Sep) Picture-perfect and right on the lake, there are cabins and motel rooms.

» **Becker's Lodge** (☎250-992-8864, 800-808-4761; www.beckerslodge.ca; r 2 nights $80-220) Log chalets are inviting inside and out.

Near Barkerville, quirky **Wells** has accommodations, restaurants and a general store. The **visitor center** (☎250-994-2323, 877-451-9355; www.wellsbc.com; 4120 Pooley St; ⊗9am-6pm May-Sep), in an old storefront, has details.

Barkerville is 82km east of Quesnel, at the end of Hwy 26.

Wells Gray Provincial Park

Plunging 141m onto rocks below, **Helmcken Falls** – Canada's fourth-highest – is but one of the undiscovered facets of **Wells Gray Provincial Park** (www.bcparks.ca), itself an undiscovered gem.

BC's fourth-largest park is bounded by the Clearwater River and its tributaries, which define the park's boundaries. Highlights for visitors include five major lakes, two large river systems, scores of waterfalls and most every kind of BC land-based wildlife.

Most people enter the park via the town of **Clearwater** on Hwy 5, 123km north of Kamloops. From here a 36km paved road runs to the park's south entrance. Part-gravel, Wells Gray Rd then runs 29km into the heart of the park. Many hiking trails and sights such as Helmcken Falls are accessible off this road, which ends at Clearwater Lake.

You'll find opportunities for **hiking**, **cross-country skiing** or **horseback riding** along more than 20 trails of varying lengths. Rustic backcountry campgrounds dot the area around four of the lakes. To rent canoes, contact **Clearwater Lake Tours** (☎250-674-2121; www.clearwaterlaketours.com; canoes per day from $50), which also leads treks.

There are three vehicle-accessible **campgrounds** (☎250-674-2194; campsites $14) in the park, all with pit toilets but no showers. One of the woodsiest, the 50-site **Pyramid Campground** (⊗May-Oct) is just 5km north of the park's south entrance and close to Helmcken Falls. There's plenty of **backcountry camping** (per person $5).

Clearwater has stores, restaurants and a slew of motels, including **Dutch Lake Resort** (☎250-674-3351, 888-884-4424; www.dutchlake.com; 361 Ridge Dr, Clearwater; campsites from $25, r $100-220), which has cabins, motel units and 65 campsites. Rent a canoe and practice for greater fun in the park.

Wells Gray Guest Ranch (☎250-674-2792, 866-467-4346; www.wellsgrayranch.com; campsites $15, r $75-130) has 12 cozy rooms in cabins and the main lodge building. It's 27km north of Clearwater.

The **Clearwater visitor center** (☎250-674-2646; www.wellsgray.ca; 425 E Yellowhead Hwy, cnr Clearwater Valley Rd; ⊗9am-7pm daily Jul & Aug, 9am-7pm Mon-Fri Apr-Jun & Sep-Dec; ☏) is a vital info stop for the park; it books rooms.

Chilcotin: Highway 20

Meandering over the lonely hills west of the Chilcotin, Hwy 20 runs 450km from Williams Lake to the Bella Coola Valley. Long spoken about by drivers in the sort of hushed tones doctors use when describing a worrisome stool specimen, the road has been steadily improved and today is more than 90% paved. However, the section that's not is a doozy. Known as the **Hill**, this perilous 30km stretch of gravel is 386km west of Williams Lake. It descends 1524m from Heckman's Pass to the valley (nearly sea level) through a series of tortuous switchbacks and 10% to 18% grades. However, by taking your time and using low gear you'll actually enjoy the stunning views (just make certain that's not as you plunge over the side). And it's safe for all vehicles – tourists engorged with testosterone from their SUVs (sport-utility vehicles) are humbled when a local in a Chevy beater zips past.

Driving the road in one go will take about six hours. You'll come across a few aboriginal villages as well as gravel roads that lead off to the odd provincial park and deserted lake. Check with the visitor center at Williams Lake (p747) for details of these and available services.

Bella Coola Valley

Leaving the dry expanses of the Chilcotin, you're in for a surprise when you reach the bottom of the hill. The Bella Coola Valley is at the heart of Great Bear Rainforest (p749), a lush land of huge stands of trees, surging white water and lots of bears. It almost feels like Shangri-La – without the monks. But it is a spiritual place: Nuxalk First Nations artists are active here, and for many creative types from elsewhere this is literally the end of the road.

The valley stretches 53km to the shores of the North Bentinck Arm, a deep, glacier-fed fjord that runs 40km inland from the Pacific Ocean. The two main towns, **Bella Coola** on the water and **Hagensborg** 15km

THE GREAT BEAR RAINFOREST

It's the last major tract of coastal temperate rainforest left on the planet. The Great Bear Rainforest is a wild region of islands, fjords and towering peaks. Covering 64,000 sq km (or 7% of BC), it stretches south from Alaska along the BC coast and Haida Gwaii to roughly Campbell River on Vancouver Island (which isn't part of the forest). The forests and waters are remarkably rich in life: whales, salmon, eagles, elk, otter and more thrive here. Remote river valleys are lined with forests of old Sitka spruce, Pacific silver fir and various cedars that are often 100m tall and 1500 years old.

As vast as it is, however, the Great Bear is under great threat. Less than 40% is protected and the BC government keeps missing deadlines for protection plans. Meanwhile mineral and logging companies are eyeing the forest, while others want to build a huge pipeline. Among the many groups fighting to save this irreplaceable habitat is the **Raincoast Conservation Foundation** (www.raincoast.org). The website www.savethegreatbear.org is a good source of info.

From Bella Coola, you can arrange boat trips and treks to magical places in the Great Bear, including hidden rivers where you might see a rare Kermode bear, a white-furred offshoot of the black bear known in tribal legend as the 'spirit bear' and the namesake of the rainforest.

east, almost seem as one, with most places of interest in or between the two. Most places aimed at visitors are open May to September; check for dates beyond that. Both the visitor center and your accommodations can point you to guides and gear for skiing, mountain biking, fishing, rafting and much more. Services like car repair, ATMs, laundry and groceries are available.

◉ Sights & Activities

Spanning the Chilcotin and the east end of the valley, the southern portion of **Tweedsmuir Provincial Park** (☑250-398-4414; www bcparks.ca) is the second-largest provincial park in BC. It's a seemingly barely charted place perfect for challenging backcountry adventures. Many hikes and canoe circuits can only be reached by floatplane. Get details at the Williams Lake (p747) or Bella Coola Valley (p750) visitor centers. **Day hikes** off Hwy 20 in the valley follow trails into lush and untouched coastal rainforest.

A good, short hike just west of Hagensborg can be found at **Walker Island Park** on the edge of the wide and rocky Bella Coola River floodplain. Leaving the parking area you are immediately in the middle of a grove of cedars that are 500 years old. But there's really no limit to your activities here. You can hike into the hills and valleys starting from roads or at points only reachable by boat along the craggy coast.

The valley is renowned for bears. **Kynoch West Coast Adventures** (☑250-982-2298; www.coastmountainlodge.com) specializes in critter-spotting float trips down local rivers (from $80) and wilderness hikes.

🛏 Sleeping & Eating

There are dozens of B&Bs and small lodges along Hwy 20. Many offer evening meals; otherwise there are a couple of cafes and motels in Bella Coola.

Coast Mountain Lodge   INN $$
(☑250-982-2298; www.coastmountainlodge. com; 1900 Hwy 20, Hagensborg; r $95-150; @�) The 14 rooms are huge, and many have a location convenient. There is also a little coffee bar with an internet terminal. The owners also run Kynoch West Coast Adventures, and guests can rent minivans (per day $55).

Bella Coola's Eagle Lodge   GUESTHOUSE $$
(☑250-799-5587, 866-799-5587; www.eaglelodgebc.com; 1103 Hwy 20, Bella Coola; campsites $10-18, r $80-190; @�) Experts in the local area own this three-room lodge. It overlooks a verdant expanse; there are 10 campsites.

Bailey Bridge Campsite & Cabins   CAMPGROUND $
(☑250-982-2342; www.baileybridge.ca; Salloompt River Rd; campsites $18-25, cabins from $70) Near the namesake bridge, 27 nicely shaded campsites and six cabins dot the riverbank. A small store will sell gear and supplies.

ℹ Information

Bella Coola Valley Visitor Information (☏250-799-5202, 866-799-5202; www.bellacoola.ca; 628 Cliff St, Bella Coola; ⊘8am-4:30pm mid-Jun–mid-Sep Sun-Fri) can help you sort out the many joys of the valley.

ℹ Getting There & Away

BC Ferries (☏888-223-3779; www.bcferries. com; adult/child $170/8, car from $340) runs the Discovery Coast route, which links Bella Coola and Port Hardy on Vancouver Island several times a week in summer. The journey takes from 13 to 34 hours, depending on stops. Best are the direct 13-hour trips as the usual boat, the aging *Queen of Chilliwack*, does not have cabins. Unfortunately, BC Ferries seems to be doing its best to ignore this route (except for raising fares substantially).

There are no buses along Hwy 20 to Williams Lake, although you can go by charter plane. **Pacific Coastal Airlines** (☏800-663-2872; www.pacificcoastal.com) has daily flights to/from Vancouver (one way from $234, one hour).

NORTHERN BC

Northern BC is where you will truly feel that you've crossed that ethereal border to some place different. Nowhere else are the rich cultures of Canada's Aboriginal people so keenly felt, from the Haida on Haida Gwaii to the Tsimshians on the mainland. Nowhere else does land so exude mystery, whether it's the storm-shrouded coast and islands or the silent majesty of glaciers carving passages through entire mountain ranges.

And nowhere else has this kind of promise. Highways like the fabled Alaska or the awe-inspiring Stewart-Cassiar inspire adventure, discovery or even a new life. Here, your place next to nature will never be in doubt; you'll revel in your own insignificance.

Prince Rupert

POP 14,700

People are always 'discovering Prince Rupert.' And what a find it is. This fascinating city with a gorgeous harbor is not just a transportation hub (ferries go south to Vancouver Island, west to Haida Gwaii and north to Alaska) but a destination in its own right. It has two excellent museums,

fine restaurants and a culture that draws much from its aboriginal heritage.

It may rain 220 days a year but that doesn't stop the drip-dry locals enjoying activities in the misty mountains and waterways. Originally the dream of Charles Hays (who built the railroad here before going to a watery grave on the *Titanic*), Rupert (as it's called) always seems one step behind a bright future. But finally its ship may have come in – literally. A new container port speeds cheap tat from China to bargain-desperate Americans and each year huge cruise ships on the Inside Passage circuit drop off their hordes to 'discover' Rupert's authentic appeal.

◉ Sights

A short walk from the center, **Cow Bay** is a delightful place for a stroll. The eponymous spotted decor is everywhere but somehow avoids seeming clichéd. There are shops, cafes and a good view of the waterfront, especially from the cruise ship docks at the Atlin Terminal.

⌐TOP⌐ **Museum of Northern BC**   MUSEUM
⌐CHOICE⌐ (☏250-624-3207; www.museumof northernbc.com; 100 1st Ave W; adult/child $6/2; ⊘9am-5pm mid-May–Aug, 9am-5pm Tue-Sat Sep–mid-May) Don't miss the Museum of Northern BC, which resides in a building styled after an aboriginal longhouse. The museum shows how local civilizations enjoyed sustainable cultures that lasted for thousands of years – you might say they were ahead of their time. The displays include a wealth of excellent Haida, Gitksan and Tsimshian art and plenty of info on totem poles. Special tours of the museum and the bookshop are excellent.

Totem Poles   MONUMENT
You'll see totems all around town: two flank the statue of Charlie Hays beside City Hall on 3rd Ave. To witness totembuilding in action, stop by the **Carving Shed**, next door to the courthouse. For more, see p754.

🏃 Activities

Skeena Kayaking (☏250-624-5246; www. skeenakayaking.ca; rentals per 24hr $90) offers both rentals and custom tours of the area, which has a seemingly infinite variety of places to put in the water.

Beginning at a parking lot on the Yellowhead Hwy, 3km south of town, a flat

4km loop trail to **Butze Rapids** has interpretive signs. Other walks here are more demanding.

Pike Island (Laxspa'aws) is a small island past Digby Island, outside of the harbor. Thriving villages were based there as long as 2000 years ago, and remnants and evidence can be seen today. Further afield, **Khutzeymateen Grizzly Bear Sanctuary** is home to more than 50 of the giants. Both can only be reached with tours.

☞ Tours

Prince Rupert Adventure Tours

BOAT, WILDLIFE

(☎250-627-9166; www.adventuretours.net; Atlin Terminal; adult/child from $55/50) Offers boat tours that circle Kaien Island (May to October) plus whale tours. Its Khutzeymateen trips are amazing.

Seashore Charters

BOAT, WILDLIFE

(☎250-624-5645, 800-667-4393; www.seashorecharters.com; Atlin Terminal; adult/child from $60/44) Half-day trips to Laxspa'aws that include a 40-minute boat ride each way; also offers Khutzeymateen, harbor, whale and wildlife tours.

🛏 Sleeping

Rupert has a range of accommodations, including more than a dozen B&Bs, but when all three ferries have pulled in, competition gets fierce: book ahead.

Crest Hotel

HOTEL $$

(☎250-624-6771, 800-663-8150; www.cresthotel.bc.ca; 222 1st Ave W; r $100-300; ❄@🕸) Prince Rupert's premier hotel has harborview rooms that are worth every penny, right down to the built-in bay-window seats. Avoid the smallish rooms overlooking the parking lot. Suites are downright opulent.

Eagle Bluff B&B

B&B $$

(☎250-627-4955; www.eaglebluff.ca; 201 Cow Bay Rd; r $50-120; @) Ideally located on Cow Bay, this B&B on a pier is in a heritage building that has a striking red and white paint job. Inside, however, the seven rooms have decor best described as home-style; some share bathrooms.

Inn on the Harbour

MOTEL $$

(☎250-624-9107, 800-663-8155; www.innontheharbour.com; 720 1st Ave W; r $85-160; 🕸) Sunsets may dazzle you to the point that you

NORTH PACIFIC HISTORIC FISHING MUSEUM

About 20km south of Prince Rupert, the **North Pacific Historic Fishing Museum** (☎250-628-3538; www.cannery.ca; 1889 Skeena Dr; adult/child $12/6; ⊙noon-4:30pm Tue-Sun May, Jun & Sep, 11am-5pm Jul & Aug), near the town of Port Edward, explores the history of fishing and canning along the Skeena River. The fascinating all-wood complex was used from 1889 to 1968; exhibits document the miserable conditions of the workers. Hours are not always reliable so confirm before your visit. Prince Rupert Transit has bus service to the site.

don't notice the humdrum exterior at this modern, harbor-view motel. The 49 rooms have been revamped.

Pioneer Hostel

HOSTEL $

(☎250-624-2334, 888-794-9998; www.pioneerhostel.com; 167 3rd Ave E; dm $25-30, r $50-60; ⊜🕸) Spotless compact rooms, accented with vibrant colors. Small kitchen and BBQ facilities out back; provides free bikes and ferry/train pickups.

Black Rooster Roadhouse

HOSTEL $

(☎250-627-5337; www.blackrooster.ca; 501 6th Ave W; dm $25, r $25-85; @🕸) Renovated house just up the hill from the center, with a patio and a bright common room. Call for shuttle pickup.

Prince Rupert RV Campground

CAMPGROUND $

(☎250-624-5861; www.princerupertrv.com; 1750 Park Ave; tent/RV sites from $27/35; @) Located near the ferry terminal, it has 88 sites, hot showers, laundry and flush toilets.

🍴 Eating & Drinking

Halibut and salmon fresh from the fishing fleet appear on menus all over town.

Charley's Lounge

PUB $$

(☎250-624-6771; Crest Hotel, 222 1st Ave W; mains $8-20; ⊙noon-late) Locals flock to trade gossip while gazing out over the harbor from the heated patio. The pub menu features some of Rupert's best seafood.

Cow Bay Café FUSION $$

(☑250-627-1212; 205 Cow Bay Rd; mains $10-20; ☺11:30am-9pm) The inventive menu at this well-known bistro changes twice daily; there are always a half-dozen mains and desserts to tempt. Dine outside on the harbor.

Smiles Seafood SEAFOOD $

(☑250-624-3072; 113 Cow Bay Rd; mains $6-20; ☺11am-9pm) Since 1934 Smiles has served classic, casual seafood meals. Slide into a vinyl booth or sit out on the deck.

Cowpuccino's CAFE $

(☑250-627-1395; 25 Cow Bay Rd; coffee $2; ☺7am-8pm) A funky local cafe where the coffee will make you forget the rain.

Breakers Pub PUB $

(☑250-624-5990; 117 George Hills Way; meals $8; ☺11am-late; 🛜) Right on the water at Cow Bay, take in the big views of the fishing boats while the skippers grouse at the bar. The food is fine (good fish sandwiches) and you can play darts or shoot pool.

 Shopping

See the bounty of Rupert's vibrant creative community at the artist-run **Ice House Gallery** (☑250-624-4546; Atlin Terminal; ☺noon-5pm Tue-Sun). **Rainforest Books** (☑250-624-4195; 251 3rd Ave W) has a good selection of new and used.

❶ **Information**

Java Dot Cup (☑250-622-2822; 516 3rd Ave W; per hr $3; ☺7:30am-9pm; 🛜) Internet access plus a decent cafe.

Visitor center (☑250-624-5637, 800-667-1994; www.tourismprincerupert.com; Museum of Northern BC, 100 1st Ave W; ☺9am-5pm daily mid-May–Aug, 9am-5pm Tue-Sat Sep–mid-May) Visitor services are limited to a rack of brochures and the front desk at the museum.

❶ **Getting There & Away**

The ferry and train terminals are 3km southwest of the center.

Air

Prince Rupert Airport (YPR; ☑250-622-2222; www.ypr.ca) is on Digby Island, across the harbor from town. The trip involves a bus and ferry; pickup is at the Highliner Hotel (815 1st Ave) two hours before flight time. Confirm all the details with your airline or the airport.

Air Canada Jazz (☑888-247-2262; www.aircanada.com) and **Hawkair** (☑800-487-1216; www.hawkair.ca). Check-in for the former is at the airport; for the latter, at Highliner Hotel.

Bus

Greyhound Canada (☑800-661-8747; www.greyhound.ca; 112 6th St) buses depart for Prince George ($120, 10 hours) once a day.

Ferry

Alaska Marine Highway System (☑250-627-1744, 800-642-0066; www.ferryalaska.com) has one or two ferries each week to the Yukon gateways of Haines (passenger/car $160/374, cabins from $120) and Skagway, Alaska: a spectacular albeit infrequent service (see the boxed text, p759).

BC Ferries (☑250-386-3431; www.bcferries.com) Inside Passage run to Port Hardy (adult $100-170, child fare 50%, car $220-390, cabin from $85, 15 to 25 hours) is hailed for its amazing scenery. There are three services per week in summer, one per week in winter on the new *Northern Expedition*. The Haida Gwaii service goes to Skidegate Landing (adult $33-39, child fare 50%, car $115-140, seven hours) six times per week in summer and three times a week in winter on the *Northern Adventure*.

Train

VIA Rail (www.viarail.ca; BC Ferries Terminal) operates tri-weekly to/from Prince George (12½ hours) and, after an overnight stop, Jasper in the Rockies.

❶ **Getting Around**

Prince Rupert Transit (☑250-624-3343; www.bctransit.com; adult/child $1.25/1) Infrequent service to the ferry port and North Pacific Historic Fishing Village ($2.50). The main bus stop is at the ratty Rupert Square Mall on 2nd Ave.

Skeena Taxi (☑250-624-5318) To/from the ferries is about $12.

Haida Gwaii

Haida Gwaii, which means 'Islands of the People,' offers a magical trip for those who make the effort. Attention has long focused on their many unique species of flora and fauna to the extent that 'Canada's Galapagos' is a popular moniker. But each year it becomes more apparent that the real soul of the islands is the Haida culture itself. Long one of the most advanced and powerful First Nations, the Haida suffered terribly after Westerners arrived.

Now, however, their culture is resurgent and can be found across the islands in myriad ways beyond their iconic totem poles. Haida reverence for the environment is protecting the last stands of superb old-growth rainforests, where the spruce and cedars are some of the world's largest. Amidst this sparsely populated, wild and rainy place are bald eagles, bears and much more wildlife. Offshore, sea lions, whales and orcas abound.

In 2010 two events further confirmed the islands' resurgence. The name used by Europeans since their arrival in the 18th century, Queen Charlotte Islands, was officially ditched; and the federal government moved forward with its plans to make the waters off Haida Gwaii a marine preserve.

A visit to the islands rewards those who invest time to get caught up in their allure, their culture and their people – plan on a long stay. The number-one attraction here is remote **Gwaii Haanas National Park Reserve**, which makes up the bottom third of the archipelago. Named the top park in North America by *National Geographic Traveler* for being 'beautiful and intact,' it is a lost world of Haida culture and superb natural beauty.

Haida Gwaii forms a dagger-shaped archipelago of some 450 islands lying 80km west of the BC coast, and about 50km from the southern tip of Alaska. Mainland ferries dock at Skidegate Landing on Graham Island, the main island for 80% of the 5000 residents and commerce. The principal town is Queen Charlotte City (QCC), 7km west of Skidegate. The main road on Graham Island is Hwy 16, which is fully paved. It links Skidegate with Masset, 101km north, passing the small towns of Tlell and Port Clements.

Graham Island is linked to Moresby Island to the south by a ferry from Skidegate Landing. The airport is in Sandspit on Moresby Island, 12km east of the ferry landing at Aliford Bay. The only way to get to Gwaii Haanas National Park Reserve, which covers the south part of Moresby Island, is by boat or floatplane.

⊙ Sights & Activities

The Haida Gwaii portion of the **Yellowhead Hwy** (Hwy 16) heads 110km north from QCC past Skidegate, Tlell and Port Clements. The latter was where the famous golden spruce tree on the banks of the Yakoun River was cut down by a demented forester in 1997. The incident is detailed in the best-selling *The Golden Spruce* by John Vaillant, one of the best books on the islands and the Haida culture in print.

All along the road to **Masset**, look for little seaside pullouts, oddball boutiques and funky cafes that are typical of the islands' character.

TOP CHOICE **Gwaii Haanas National Park Reserve & Haida Heritage Site**

PARK

This huge Unesco World Heritage site encompasses Moresby and 137 smaller islands at the southern end of the islands. It combines a time-capsule look at abandoned Haida villages, hot springs, amazing natural beauty and some of the continent's best kayaking.

Archaeological finds have documented more than 500 ancient Haida sites, including villages and burial caves throughout the islands. The most famous village is **SGaang Gwaii (Ninstints)** on Anthony Island, where rows of weathered **totem poles** stare eerily out to sea. Other major sights include the ancient village of **Skedans**, on Louise Island, and **Hotspring Island**, where you can soak away the bone-chilling cold in natural springs. The sites are protected by Haida Gwaii watchmen, who live on the islands in summer.

Access to the park is by boat or plane only. A visit demands a decent amount of advance planning and usually requires several days. From May to September, you must obtain a reservation, unless you're with a tour operator.

Contact **Parks Canada** (✆250-559-8818; www.pc.gc.ca/gwaiihaanas; Haida Heritage Centre at Qay'llnagaay, Skidegate; ⏰8:30am-noon & 1-4:30pm Mon-Fri) with questions. The

DON'T MISS

HAIDA HERITAGE CENTRE AT QAY'LLNAGAAY

One of the top attractions in the north is this marvelous **cultural centre** (✆250-559-7885; www.haidaheritage centre.com; Skidegate; adult/child $15/5; ⏰9am-6pm Jun-Aug, 11am-5pm Tue-Sat Sep-May). With exhibits on history, wildlife and culture, just by itself it would be enough reason to visit the islands. The rich traditions of the Haida are fully explored in galleries, programs and work areas where contemporary artists create new works such as the totem poles lining the shore.

website has links to the **essential annual trip planner**. Anyone who has not visited the park during the previous three years must attend a free orientation at the park office (all visitors also must register).

The number of daily **reservations** (☎877-559-8818) is limited: plan well in advance. There are user fees (adult/child $20/10 per night). Nightly fees are waived if you have a Parks Canada Season Excursion Pass. A few much-coveted standby spaces are made available daily: call Parks Canada.

The easiest way to get into the park is with a tour company. Parks Canada can provide you with lists of operators; tours last from one day to two weeks. Many can also set you up with **rental kayaks** (average per day/week $60/300) and gear for independent travel.

Moresby Explorers (☎250-637-2215, 800-806-7633; www.moresbyexplorers.com; Sandspit) has one-day tours from $205 as well as much longer ones. It rents kayaks and gear.

Queen Charlotte Adventures (☎250-559-8990, 800-668-4288; www.queencharlotte adventures.com) offers lots of one- to 10-day trips using boats and kayaks. It has a six-day kayak trip to the remote south for $1620. It rents kayaks and gear.

Yakoun Lake   NATURAL ATTRACTION
Hike about 20 minutes through ancient stands of spruce and cedar to pristine **Yakoun Lake**, a large wilderness lake towards the west side of Graham Island. A small beach near the trail is shaded by gnarly Sitka alders. Dare to take a dip in the bracing waters or just enjoy the sweeping views.

The trailhead to the lake is at the end of a rough track that is off a branch from the main dirt and gravel logging road between QCC and Port Clements. It runs for 70km, watch for signs for the lake; on weekdays check in by phone (☎250-557-6810) for logging trucks.

Naikoon Provincial Park   PARK
(☎250-626-5115; www.bcparks.ca) Much of the island's northeastern side is devoted to the beautiful 726-sq-km Naikoon Provincial Park, which combines sand dunes and low sphagnum bogs, surrounded by stunted

---

ONE TALL TALE

Though most Aboriginal groups on the northwest coast lack formal written history as we know it, centuries of traditions manage to live on through artistic creations such as totem poles.

Carved from a single cedar trunk, totems identify a household's lineage in the same way a family crest might identify a group or clan in Britain, although the totem pole is more of a historical pictograph depicting the entire ancestry.

Unless you're an expert, it's not easy to decipher a totem. But you can start by looking for the creatures that are key to the narrative. Try to pick out the following.

Beaver Symbolizes industriousness, wisdom and determined independence.

Black bear Serves as a protector, guardian and spiritual link between humans and animals.

Eagle Signifies intelligence and power.

Frog Represents adaptability, the ability to live in both natural and supernatural worlds.

Hummingbird Embodies love, beauty and unity with nature.

Killer whale Symbolizes dignity and strength (often depicted as a reincarnated spirit of a great chief).

Raven Signifies mischievousness and cunning.

Salmon Typifies dependable sustenance, longevity and perseverance.

Shark Exemplifies an ominous and fierce solitude.

Thunderbird Represents the wisdom of proud ancestors.

Two excellent places both to see totem poles and learn more are the Haida Heritage Centre at Qay'llnagaay (p753) at Skidegate and the Museum of Northern BC (see p750) in Prince Rupert.

and gnarled lodgepole pine, and red and yellow cedar. The **beaches** on the north coast feature strong winds, pounding surf and flotsam from across the Pacific. They can be reached via the stunning 26km-long Tow Hill Rd, east of Masset. A 21km loop **trail** traverses a good bit of the park to/from Fife Beach at the end of the road.

🛏 Sleeping

Small inns and B&Bs are mostly found on Graham Island. There are numerous choices in QCC and Masset, with many in between and along the spectacular north coast. Naikoon Provincial Park has two **campgrounds** (campsites $16), including a dramatic windswept one on deserted Agate Beach, 23km east of Masset.

Premier Creek Lodging INN $
(☑250-559-8415, 888-322-3388; www.qcislands.net/premier; 3101 3rd Ave, QCC; dm $25, r $35-100; @) Dating from 1910, this friendly lodge has eight beds in a hostel building out back and 12 rooms in the main building, ranging from tiny but great-value singles to spacious rooms with views and porches. There's high-speed internet.

All The Beach You Can Eat CABINS $$
(☑604-313-6192; www.allthebeachyoucaneat.com; 15km marker Tow Hill Rd; cabins $85-120) On beautiful North Beach, two cabins are perched in the dunes, back from the wide swath of sand that runs for miles east and west. One, the sweet little Sweety Pie, has views that seem to reach to Japan. Like two other properties with rental cabins out here, there is no electricity; you cook and see with propane. It's off the grid and out of this world.

Copper Beech House B&B $$
(☑250-626-5441; www.copperbeechhouse.com; 1590 Delkatla Rd, Masset; r from $100) David Phillips has created a legendary B&B in a rambling old house on Masset Harbor. It has three unique rooms and there's always something amazing cooking in the kitchen.

🍴 Eating & Drinking

The best selection of restaurants is in QCC, although there are also a few in Skidegate, Tlell and Masset. Ask at the visitor center about local Haida feasts, where you'll enjoy the best salmon, blueberries and more you've ever had. Good supermarkets are found in Skidegate and Masset.

Queen B's CAFE $
(☑250-559-4463; 3201 Wharf St, QCC; mains $3-10; ⊙9am-5pm) This funky place excels at baked goods, which emerge from the oven all day long. There are tables with water views outside and lots of local art inside.

Ocean View Restaurant SEAFOOD $$
(☑250-559-8503; Sea Raven Motel, 3301 3rd Ave, QCC; mains $10-25; ⊙11am-9pm) Good fresh seafood (try the halibut) is the specialty at this casual dining room, where some tables look out to the harbor.

Rising Tide Bakery BAKERY, CAFE $
(☑250-557-4677; ⊙8am-5pm Wed-Sun Jun-Aug; 🛜) Loved by locals and visitors alike for its cliché-defying cinnamon rolls made with flour ground on site. Also delicious soups and sandwiches.

Moon Over Naikoon BAKERY $
(☑250-626-5064; 17km marker Tow Hill Rd; ⊙8am-5pm Jun-Aug) Embodying the spirit of this road to the end of everything, this tiny community center–cum–bakery has a kaleidoscopic collection of artworks and stuff found on the beach.

ℹ Information

Either download or pick up a free copy of the encyclopedic annual *Guide to the Haida Gwaii* (www.queencharlotteislandsguide.com). A good website for information is www.haidagwaiitourism.ca. **Parks Canada** (www.pc.gc.ca/gwaiihaanas) also has much information online.

QCC visitor center (☑250-559-8316; www.qcinfo.ca; 3220 Wharf St, QCC; ⊙8:30am-9pm daily Jul & Aug, 9am-5pm Tue Sat Oct Apr, 9am-5pm May, Jun & Sep) is handy, although there's been a recent encroachment of gift items. Get a free copy of *Art Route*, a guide to more than 40 studios and galleries. A desk at Sandspit Airport opens for incoming flights.

ℹ Getting There & Away

The BC Ferries service from Prince Rupert is the most popular way to reach the islands.

Air

The main airport for Haida Gwaii is at **Sandspit** (YZP; ☑250-559-0052) on Moresby Island. Note that reaching the airport from Graham Island is time-consuming: if your flight is at 3:30pm, you need to line up at the car ferry at Skidegate Landing at 12:30pm (earlier in summer). There's also a small airport at **Masset** (YMT; ☑250-626-3995).

Air Canada Jazz (☑888-247-2262; www.aircanada.com) Daily between Sandspit and Vancouver.

Hawkair (📞800-487-1216; www.hawkair.ca) Daily service from Sandspit to Vancouver.

North Pacific Seaplanes (📞800-689-4234; www.northpacificseaplanes.com) Links Prince Rupert with Masset (from $260) and anyplace else a floatplane can land.

Pacific Coastal Airlines (📞800-663-2872; www.pacific-coastal.com) Masset to Vancouver several times per week.

Ferry
BC Ferries (📞250-386-3431; www.bcferries. com) Prince Rupert to/from Skidegate Landing (adult $33-39, child fare 50%, car $115-140, seven hours) runs six times a week in summer, three per week in winter on the *Northern Adventure*. Cabins are useful for overnight schedules (from $85).

ℹ Getting Around

Off Hwy 16, most roads are gravel or worse.

BC Ferries (adult/child $9/4.50, cars from $20, 20 minutes, almost hourly 7am to 10pm) operates a small car ferry linking the two main islands at Skidegate Landing and Alliford Bay. Schedules seem designed to inconvenience air passengers.

Eagle Transit (📞877-747-4461; www.haidag waii.net/eagle) meets flights and ferries. The fare from the airport to QCC is $27.

Renting a car can be as expensive ($60 to $100 per day) as bringing one over on the ferry. **Budget** (📞250-637-5688; www.budget.com) has locations at the airport and QCC. **Rustic Car Rentals** (📞250-559-4641, 877-559-4641; citires@qcislands.net; 605 Hwy 33, QCC) is also in Masset.

Prince Rupert to Prince George

You can cover the 725km on Hwy 16 between BC's Princes in a day or a week. There's nothing that's an absolute must-see, but there's much to divert and cause you to pause if so inclined. Scenery along much of the road (with a notable exception) won't fill your memory card but it is a pleasing mix of mountains and rivers.

PRINCE RUPERT TO SMITHERS

For the first 150km, Hwy 16 hugs the wide and wild **Skeena River**. This is four-star scenic driving and you'll see glaciers and jagged peaks across the waters. However, tatty **Terrace** is nobody's idea of a reward at the end of the stretch.

From Terrace, Hwy 16 continues 93km east to Kitwanga, where the **Stewart-Cas-**siar Hwy (Hwy 37) strikes north towards the Yukon and Alaska.

Just east of Kitwanga you reach the **Hazelton** area (comprising New Hazelton, Hazelton and South Hazelton), the center of some interesting aboriginal sites, including **'Ksan Historical Village & Museum** (📞250-842-5544; www.ksan.org; admission $2; ☉9:30am-4:30pm Mon-Fri Oct-May, 9am-5pm Apr-Sep). This re-created village of the Gitksan people features longhouses, a museum, various outbuildings and totem poles.

SMITHERS

Smithers, a largish town with a cute old downtown, is roughly halfway between the Princes. The **visitor center** (📞250-847-5072, 800-542-6673; www.tourismsmith ers.com; 1411 Court St; ☉9am-6pm May-Sep, 9am-5pm Mon-Fri Oct-Apr) can steer you to excellent mountain biking, white-water rafting and climbing. Great hiking is found at nearby **Babine Mountains Provincial Park** (📞250-847-7329; www.bcparks.ca; backcountry campsites per person $5), a 324-sq-km park with trails to glacier-fed lakes and subalpine meadows.

The **Smithers Guesthouse** (📞250-847-4862; www.smithersguesthouse.com; 1766 Main St; dm from $24, r $60-82; @🖥🛜) is close to the center. Rooms are basic, but the welcome is warm. Main St has several good cafes. **Mountain Eagle Books & Bistro** (📞250-847-5245; 3775 3rd St; ☉9am-6pm Mon-Sat; 🛜) has books and info on the area's thriving folk-music scene. The tiny cafe has veggie soup and lunches.

SMITHERS TO PRINCE GEORGE

South and west of Smithers, after 146km you pass through **Burns Lake**, the center of a popular fishing district. After another 128km, at **Vanderhoof**, Hwy 27 heads 66km north to **Fort St James National Historic Site** (📞250-996-7191; www.pc.gc.ca; adult/child $8/4; ☉9am-5pm May-Sep), a former Hudson's Bay Company trading post that's on the tranquil southeastern shore of Stuart Lake and has been restored to its 1896 glory. From Vanderhoof, the 100km to Prince George passes through a region filled with the dead trees seen across the north. These bright-red specimens are victims of mountain pine beetles, whose explosive population growth is linked to comparatively milder winters due to climate change.

Prince George

POP 84,300

In First Nations times, before outsiders arrived, Prince George was called Lheidli T'Enneh, which means 'people of the confluence,' an appropriate name given that the Nechako and Fraser Rivers converged here. Today the name would be just as fitting, although it's the confluence of highways that matters most. A lumber town since 1807, it is a vital BC crossroads and you're unlikely to visit the north without passing through at least once.

Hwy 97 from the south cuts through the center of town on its way north to Dawson Creek (360km) and the Alaska Hwy. Hwy 16 becomes Victoria St as it runs through town westward to Prince Rupert (724km), and east to Jasper (380km) and Edmonton. The downtown, no beauty-contest winner, is compact and has some good restaurants. Still, you'll do well to nab your 40 winks, enjoy some chow and hit the road.

⊙ Sights

Exploration Place (✆250-562-1612; www. theexplorationplace.com; Fort George Park; adult/child $9/6; ⊙9am-6pm), southeast of downtown (follow 20th Ave east of Gorse St), has various kid-friendly galleries devoted to science plus natural and cultural history.

Cottonwood Island Nature Park has walks alongside the river and is home to the small **Prince George Railway & Forestry Museum** (✆250-563-7351; www.pgrfm.bc.ca; 850 River Rd; adult/child $6/3; ⊙10am-5pm mid-May–mid-Oct), which honors choo-choos, the beaver and local lore.

⊨ Sleeping

Hwy 97/Central St makes an arc around the center, where you'll find legions of motels and big-box stores. The **Bed & Breakfast Hotline** (✆250-562-2222, 877-562-2626; www. princegeorgebnb.com) arranges bookings in your price range (from $50 to $100). Most provide transportation from the train or bus station.

Economy Inn   MOTEL $
(✆250-563-7106, 888-566-6333; www.economy inn.ca; 1915 3rd Ave; r $60-95; ✳🐾) Close to the center, this simple blue-and-white motel has 30 clean rooms and a whirlpool. Celebrate your savings with a scrumptious Dairy Queen Peanut Buster Parfait across the street.

Esther's Inn   MOTEL $$
(✆250-562-4131, 800-663-6844; www.esthers inn.com; 1151 Commercial Cres; r $80-120; ✳@🐾) Do you seek a tiki? The faux Polynesian theme extends through the 118 rooms. Have hot times in the three Jacuzzis. It's out on the Hwy 97 bypass.

Travelodge Goldcap   MOTEL $$
(✆250-563-0666, 800-663-8239; www.travel odgeprincegeorge.com; 1458 7th Ave; r $75-130; ✳@🐾) A real barker in the beauty department, the Travelodge is nicer on the inside (isn't everything?). The 77 rooms are motel-standard but huge. Better yet, it's steps from good restaurants and bars.

Bee Lazee Campground   CAMPGROUND $
(✆250-963-7263, 866-679-6699; www. beelazee.ca; 15910 Hwy 97S; campsites $20-27; ⊙May-Sep; 🐾🐾) About 10km south of town, this RV-centric place features full facilities, including free hot showers, a pool and laundry.

✗ Eating & Drinking

The **farmers market** (cnr George St & 3rd Ave; ⊙8:30am-2pm Sat May-Sep) is a good place to sample some of the array of local foods and produce.

Cimo   MEDITERRANEAN $$
(✆250-564-7975; 601 Victoria St; mains $10-25; ⊙noon-2pm Mon-Fri, 5-10pm Mon-Thu, until 11pm Fri & Sat) The fresh and often excellent Mediterranean dishes here never disappoint. Dine (or enjoy just a glass of BC wine) in the stylish interior or out on the patio. There's live jazz heard here many nights.

Thanh Vu   ASIAN $
(✆250-564-2255; 1778 Hwy 97 S; mains $8-15; ⊙11am-9pm) This local favorite is situated out on the Hwy 97 strip. The Vietnamese food is tasty and fresh – it's better than most Asian food you'll find north of greater Vancouver.

White Goose Bistro   FUSION $$
(✆250-561-1002; 1205 3rd Ave; mains $8-25; ⊙11:30am-10pm) A touch of class downtown, chef Ryan Cyre cooks up surprising treats like lobster nachos in addition to more classic bistro fare at this white-tablecloth restaurant. Lunch sees salads, sandwiches and pastas.

REGIONAL BUS DISTANCES FROM PRINCE GEORGE

DESTINATION	FARE	DURATION	FREQUENCY (PER DAY)
Dawson Creek	$72	5-6½hr	2
Jasper	$65	5hr	1
Prince Rupert	$120	10hr	1
Vancouver	$96	12hr	2

🛍 Shopping

Books & Company BOOKSTORE
(☑250-563-6637; 1685 3rd Ave; ⊙8am-6pm
Mon, Wed & Sat, 8am-9pm Thu, 8am-10pm Fri,
10am-5pm Sun; ☎) The best bookstore in
northern BC; it has a convivial cafe.

ℹ Information

Visitor center (www.tourismpg.com) Station
(☑250-562-3700, 800-668-7646; VIA Rail
Station, 1300 1st Ave; ⊙8am-8pm May-Sep,
8:30am-5pm Oct-Apr); branch (☑250-563-
5493; cnr Hwy 97 & Hwy 16; ⊙8am-8pm May-
Aug) The excellent train station visitor center
can make bookings like ferry tickets. Internet
access per 30 minutes is $3.50.

ℹ Getting There & Away

Prince George Airport (YXS; ☑250-963-2400;
www.pgairport.ca) is on Airport Rd, off Hwy
97. **Air Canada Jazz** (www.aircanada.com) and
Westjet (www.westjet.com) serve Vancouver.

Greyhound Canada (☑800-661-8747; www.
greyhound.ca; 1566 12th Ave)

VIA Rail (www.viarail.ca; 1300 1st Ave) heads
west three times a week to Prince Rupert (12½
hours) and east three times a week to Jasper
(7½ hours) and further east; through passengers must overnight in Prince George.

ℹ Getting Around

Major car rental agencies have offices at the
airport.
Prince George Transit (☑250-563-0011; www.
busonline.ca; fare $2) Operates local buses.
Prince George Taxi (☑250-564-4444)

Prince George to Alberta

Look for lots of wildlife along the 380km
stretch of Hwy 16 that links Prince George
with Jasper, just over the Alberta border.
The major attraction along the route actually abuts Jasper National Park, but on
the BC side of the border. **Mt Robson Provincial Park** (☑250-964-2243; www.bcparks.

ca) has steep glaciers, prolific wildlife and
backcountry hiking that is unfortunately
overshadowed by its famous neighbor. **Mc-
Bride** is good for a pause.

Stewart-Cassiar Highway

Like the promises of a politician, the
Stewart-Cassiar Hwy (Hwy 37) just gets
better each year. But unlike those promises, it's not full of holes. Much improved,
this 700km road is a viable and ever-more-
popular route between BC and the Yukon
and Alaska (see the boxed text, p759). But
it's more than just a means to get from Hwy
16 (Meziadin Junction) in BC to the Alaska
Hwy in the Yukon (7km west of Watson
Lake), it's a window onto one of the largest remaining wild and wooly parts of the
province. And it's the road to Stewart, the
very worthwhile detour to glaciers, and
more (see boxed text, p760).

Less than 2% of the road is unsealed
gravel and it's suitable for all vehicles. At
any point you should not be surprised to
see bears, moose and other large mammals.

There's never a distance greater than
150km between gas stations and you'll find
the occasional lodge and campground. But
note that many places keep erratic hours
and are only open in summer. The **Stewart-
Cassiar Tourism Council** (www.stewart
cassiar.com) is a good source of info. BC
provides **road condition reports** (☑800-
550-4997; www.drivebc.ca). When it's dry in
summer, people drive from Stewart or even
Smithers to Watson Lake in a single day,
taking advantage of the long hours of daylight. But this a real haul, so prepare.

Dease Lake, 488km north of Meziadin
Junction, is the largest town and has year-
round motels, stores and services.

Among the many natural wonders, **Spat-
sizi Plateau Provincial Wilderness Park**
(☑250-771-4591; www.bcparks.ca) is accessed
by a rough, 28km gravel road from Tatogga,

about 150km north of Meziadin Junction. The park is undeveloped and isolated. The trails are often little more than vague notions across the untouched landscape. You'll need to be both highly experienced and self-sufficient to tackle this one.

Boya Lake Provincial Park (📞250-771-4591; www.bcparks.ca; campsites $16) is less than 90km from the provincial border. This serene little park surrounds Boya Lake, which seems to glow turquoise. You can camp on the shore.

Alaska Highway

As you travel north from Prince George along Hwy 97, the mountains and forests give way to gentle rolling hills and farmland. Nearing Dawson Creek (360km) the landscape resembles the prairies of Alberta. There's no need to dawdle.

From **Chetwynd** you can take Hwy 29 along the wide vistas of the Peace River valley north via Hudson's Hope to join the Alaska Hwy north of Fort St John.

Dawson Creek is notable as the starting point (Mile 0) for the Alaska Hwy and it capitalizes on this at the **Alaska Highway House** (📞250-782-4714; 10201 10th St; admission by donation; ⏰9am-5pm daily May-Sep, 9am-5pm Mon-Fri Oct-Apr), an engaging little museum in a vintage building overlooking the milepost. (For more on the Alaska Hwy, see p770.) The nearby downtown blocks make a good stroll and there is a walking tour of the old buildings. The **visitor center** (📞250-782-9595, 866-645-3022; www.tourismdawsoncreek.com; 900 Alaska Ave; ⏰8am-5:30pm May-Aug, 10am-5pm Tue-Sat Sep-Apr; 📶) has the usual listings of accommodations. Note that this corner of BC stays on Mountain Standard Time year-round, so in winter the time is the same as Alberta, one hour later than BC. In summer the time is the same as Vancouver.

Now begins the big drive (see the boxed text, p759). Heading northwest from Dawson Creek, Fort St John is a stop best not started; in fact the entire 430km to **Fort Nelson** gives little hint of the wonders to come.

NORTH TO THE YUKON

From BC there are three main ways to go north (or south!) by vehicle. All are potentially good choices, so you have several ways of creating a circle itinerary to the Yukon and possibly Alaska.

Alaska Highway

Fabled and historic, the Alaska Hwy (p759), from its start point in Dawson City (via Hwy 97 north of Prince George) through northeast BC to Watson Lake (944km), is being somewhat eclipsed by the Stewart-Cassiar Hwy. Still, it's an epic drive, even if the sections to Fort Nelson are bland. It's most convenient for those coming from Edmonton and the east.

Stewart-Cassiar Highway

The Stewart-Cassiar (Hwy 37; see p758) runs 700km through wild scenery from the junction with Hwy 16, 240km east of Prince Rupert and 468km west of Prince George. A side trip to the incomparable glaciers around Stewart is easy. This route is convenient for people from most of BC, Alberta and the western US. It ends at the Alaska Hwy, near Watson Lake in the Yukon.

Alaska Marine Highway System

We love the car ferries run by the state of Alaska along the **Inside Passage** (www.ferryalaska.com). Free of frills, they let you simply relax and view one of the world's great shows of marine life while enjoying the same scenery cruise-ship passengers spend thousands more to see. You can take a three-day ride on boats from Bellingham, Washington (north of Seattle) to Haines (p774) and Skagway (p775) in southeast Alaska, on the Yukon border. Or catch the ferries in Prince Rupert (see p752) for service to the same two towns (you could link this to the BC Ferries route from Port Hardy). The ferries – especially cabins – fill up fast in summer, so reserve.

WORTH THE TRIP: STEWART & HYDER

Awesome. Yes it's almost an automatic cliché, but when you gaze upon the **Salmon Glacier**, you'll understand why it was coined in the first place. This horizon-spanning expanse of ice is more than enough reason to make the 67km detour off Hwy 37 (the turnoff is 158km north of Meziadin Junction). In fact, your first confirmation comes when you encounter the iridescent blue expanse of the **Bear Glacier** looming over Hwy 37A.

The sibling border towns of **Stewart, BC** and **Hyder, Alaska** sit on the coast at the head of the Portland Canal. Stewart, the more business-like of the pair, has the **visitor center** (☎250-636-9224, 888-366-5999; www.stewart-hyder.com; 222 5th Ave; ☺9am-6pm Jun-Sep, limited hr winter) and excellent places to stay and eat.

Among several campgrounds and motels, the real star is **Ripley Creek Inn** (☎250-636-2344; www.ripleycreekinn.com; 306 5th Ave; r $55-125; @🖨). The 39 rooms are stylishly decorated with new and old items and there's a huge collection of vintage toasters (!) and the excellent **Bitter Creek Cafe**.

Hyder ekes out an existence as a 'ghost town.' Some 40,000 tourists come through every summer, avoiding any border hassle from US customs officers because there aren't any (although going back to Stewart you'll pass through beady-eyed Canadian customs). It has muddy streets and two businesses of note: the **Glacier Inn**, a bar you'll enjoy if you ignore the touristy 'get Hyderized' shot-swilling shtick and **Seafood Express** (☎250-636-9011), which has the tastiest seafood ever cooked in a school bus (*this* is Hyder).

The Salmon Glacier is 33km beyond Hyder, up a winding dirt road that's okay for cars when it's dry. Some 3km into the drive, you'll pass the **Fish Creek viewpoint**, an area alive with bear and doomed salmon in late summer.

Fort Nelson's **visitor center** (☎250-774-2541; www.northernrockies.ca; 5500 50th Ave N; ☺8am-8pm daily May-Sep, 8:30am-4:30pm Mon-Fri Oct-Apr) has good regional information for the drive ahead. The town itself is in the midst of a boom brought on by the exploitation of the region's vast oil-filled lands. This is the last place of any size on the Alaska Hwy until Whitehorse – most 'towns' along the route are little more than a gas station and motel or two.

Around 140km west of Fort Nelson, **Stone Mountain Provincial Park** (☎250-427-5452; www.bcparks.ca; campsites $14) has hiking trails with backcountry camping and a campground. The stretches of road here often have dense concentrations of wildlife: moose, bears, bison, wolves, elk and much more. The Alaska Hwy now rewards whatever effort it took getting this far.

A further 75km brings you to **Muncho Lake Provincial Park** (www.bcparks.ca; camp sites $16), centered on the emerald-green lake of the same name and boasting spruce forests, vast rolling mountains and some truly breathtaking scenery. There are two campgrounds by the lake, plus a few lodges scattered along the highway through the park, including **Northern Rockies Lodge** (☎250-776-3481, 800-663-5269; www.northern-rockies-lodge.com; campsites from $35, r $80-200).

Finally, **Liard River Hot Springs Provincial Park** (☎250-427-5452; www.bcparks.ca) has a steamy ecosystem that allows a whopping 250 species of plants to thrive (and, after a long day in the car, you will too, in the soothing waters). The park's **campground** (☎800-689-9025; www.discovercamping.ca; campsites $17) has 52 campsites. From here it's 220km to Watson Lake (p771) and the Yukon.

Yukon Territory

Best Places to Eat

» Drunken Goat Taverna (p782)

» Klondike Kate's (p783)

» Klondike Rib & Salmon Bake (p768)

» Giorgio's Cucina (p768)

Best Places to Stay

» High Country Inn (p768)

» Edgewater Hotel (p768)

» Bombay Peggy's (p782)

» Klondike Kate's (p782)

Why Go?

The name Yukon is evocative as well as descriptive: adventure, the far north, wilderness, moose. How can you even hear 'Yukon' and not feel a stirring within? This vast and thinly populated wilderness – most four-legged species far outnumber humans – has a grandeur and beauty only appreciated by experience.

Few places in the world today have been so unchanged over the course of time. Aboriginal people, having eked out survival for thousands of years, hunt and trap as they always have. The Klondike Gold Rush of 1898 was the Yukon's high point of population, yet even its heritage is ephemeral, easily erased by time.

Any visit will mean much time outdoors. Canada's five tallest mountains and the world's largest ice fields below the Arctic are all within Kluane National Park. Canoe expeditions down the Yukon River are epic. You'll appreciate the people; join the offbeat vibe of Dawson City and the bustle of Whitehorse.

When to Go
Dawson City

Winter Days of snowy solitude from November to April end when the river ice breaks up.

Summer Summers, spanning June to August, are short but warm, even hot.

September You can feel the north winds coming. Trees erupt in color, crowds thin, things close.

Beaufort Sea

Arctic National Wildlife Refuge

Herschel Island (Qiqiktaruk) Territorial Park

Ivvavik National Park

Vuntut National Park

Eskimo Lakes

Old Crow

Inuvik

135°W   130°W   125°W

0 ——— 200 km
0 ——— 120 miles

N

Richardson

Ogilvie Mountains

Porcupine River

Eagle Plains ⑤

Arctic Circle

Great Bear Lake

Peel River

Mountains

Bonnet Plume River

Mackenzie River

65°N

Dempster Hwy

65°N

Top of the World Hwy

⑨

① **Dawson City**

⑤ **Tombstone Territorial Park**

Elsa ●● Keno

Mayo Lake

⑪ Mayo

Northwest Territories

Selwyn Mountains

Stewart River

Stewart Crossing

Silver Trail

White River

④ **Yukon River**

②

Pelly Crossing

Minto ●

Yukon Territory

Beaver Creek

Nisling River

①

Carmacks ●

Robert Campbell Hwy

Faro

④ Ross River

Canol Rd ⑥

Tungsten

Nahanni National Park

Burwash Landing ●● Destruction Bay

Kluane Lake

Aishihik Lake

③ **Klondike Highway**

Teslin R

Nahanni Range Rd

Mt Logan (5959m) ▲ ⑥

Kluane National Park

Alaska Hwy

Haines Junction ●

Lake Laberge

⑥

Logan Mtns

60°N

Wrangell-St Elias National Park

Haines Hwy

Kusawa Lake

② **WHITEHORSE**

① Johnson's Crossing

④ Upper Liard

Watson Lake

Tatshenshini-Alsek Provincial Park

Carcross ●

①

Teslin ●

①

⑨⑦

Alaska Hwy

White Pass & Yukon Route

⑦

Skagway ●

Teslin Lake

③⑦

140°W   135°W   130°W   125°W

Alaska (USA) / CANADA

Highlights

① Get caught up in the modern vibe of **Dawson City** (p778), Canada's funkiest historic town

② Spend an extra day in surprising **Whitehorse** (p764), where culture abounds

③ Count moose on the **Klondike Highway** (p775) – they may outnumber cars

④ Live the dream of kayakers and canoeists by paddling the legendary **Yukon River** (p766)

⑤ Lose yourself – not literally! – in **Tombstone Territorial Park** (p785), where the grandeur of the north envelops you

⑥ Find one of the 100 unnamed glaciers in **Kluane**

National Park (p772) and give it a name

⑦ Sit back and enjoy the ride on the fabled **White Pass & Yukon Route** (p776)

YUKON TERRITORY FAST FACTS

» Population: 32,000

» Area: 483,450 sq km

» Capital: Whitehorse

» Quirky fact: Home to Robert Service, the poet who immortalized the Yukon through works like *The Shooting of Dan McGrew* and *The Cremation of Sam McGee*

History

There's evidence that humans were eating animals in the Yukon some 15,000 to 30,000 years ago, depending on your carbon-dating method of choice. However, it's widely agreed that these people were descended from those who crossed over today's Siberia while the land bridge was in place. There's little recorded history otherwise, although it's known that a volcanic eruption in AD 800 covered much of the southern Yukon in ash. Similarities to the Athapaskan people of the southwest US have suggested that these groups may have left the Yukon after the volcano ruined hunting and fishing.

In the 1840s Robert Campbell, a Hudson's Bay Company explorer, was the first European to travel the district. Fur traders, prospectors, whalers and missionaries all followed. In 1870 the region became part of the Northwest Territories (NWT). But it was in 1896 when the Yukon literally hit the map, after gold was found in a tributary of the Klondike River, near what was to become Dawson City. The ensuing gold rush attracted upwards of 40,000 hopefuls from around the world. Towns sprouted overnight to support the numerous wealth-seekers, who were quite unprepared for the ensuing depravities (see the boxed text, p777).

In 1898 the Yukon became a separate territory, with Dawson City as its capital. Building the Alaska Hwy (Hwy 1) in 1942 opened up the territory to development. In 1953 Whitehorse became the capital, because it had the railway and the highway. Mining continues to be the main industry, followed by tourism.

Local Culture

The 30,000-plus hardy souls who live in the Yukon Territory take the phrase 'rugged individualist' to heart. It's hard to stereotype but safe to say that the average Yukoner enjoys the outdoors (in all weather conditions!), relishes eating meats seldom found on menus to the south and has a crack in their truck's windshield (caused by one of the many dodgy roads).

Of course the independence of Yukoners comes at a price to the rest of Canada. More than 70% of the territory's annual revenue each year comes from the federal government and it has been used to fund all manner of services at relatively comfortable levels. Whitehorse, for instance, has a range of cultural and recreational facilities that are the envy of southern Canadian communities many times its size. More than 5000 people have government jobs.

Thanks to the Yukon's long isolation before WWII, the 14 First Nations groups have maintained their relationship to the land and their traditional culture, compared to groups forced to assimilate in other parts of Canada. They can be found across the territory and in isolated places like Old Crow, living lives not fundamentally changed in centuries. It's not uncommon to hear various aboriginal dialects spoken by elders.

Light – or the lack thereof – does play an important role in local life. Many people adjust to the radical variations in daylight

EXTREME YUKON

Tough conditions spawn tough contests.

» **Yukon Quest** (www.yukonquest. com) This legendary 1600km dog-sled race goes from Whitehorse to Fairbanks, Alaska, through February darkness and -50°C temperatures. Record time: 10 days, 2 hours, 37 minutes.

» **Yukon River Quest** (www.yukon riverquest.com) The world's premier canoe and kayak race, which covers the classic 742km run of the Yukon River from Whitehorse to Dawson City in June. Record times include team canoe (39 hours, 32 minutes) and solo kayak (44 hours, 14 minutes).

» **Klondike Trail of '98 Road Relay** (www.klondikeroadrelay.com) Some 100 running teams of 10 each complete the overnight course from Skagway to Whitehorse in September.

KILL YOUR DINNER...

Worried that the increasing sophistication of Whitehorse was causing Yukoners to become too citified (read: Southern or south of the Yukon border), *Up Here,* the award-winning magazine of Canada's North, offered the following suggestions to avoid going soft.

Be Northern. Build a house out of town. Wear moosehide and sealskin. Park your car in your yard. Pee by the highway. Take your dog to work. Smoke 'em if you've got 'em. Say 'the Yukon' (What gutless bureaucrat dropped the 'the'?). Jaywalk. Commute on your quad. Look people in the eye. Don't shave – and ladies, that goes for you. Curse. Spit. Enter without knocking. Eat bannock, dry-meat and tea. Build campfires in your yard. Shop at the dump. Call the rest of the world 'Outside.' Kill your cellphone. Kill your dinner. And stop acting like a goddamn Southerner.

Up Here (www.uphere.ca)

through the year just fine but others do not. Every year you hear of long-time residents and newcomers alike who one day (often in February) announced enough was enough and moved south for good.

Parks

The Yukon has a major Unesco World Heritage site. Raw and forbidding, Kluane National Park sits solidly within the Yukon abutting Tatshenshini-Alsek Provincial Park in British Columbia (BC), while Glacier Bay and Wrangell-St Elias National Parks are found in adjoining Alaska.

The Yukon has four territorial parks (www.yukonparks.ca), but much of the territory itself is park-like and government campgrounds can be found throughout. Tombstone Territorial Park is both remote yet accessible via the Dempster Hwy, so that you can absorb the horizon-sweeping beauty of the tundra and majesty of vast mountain ranges.

ℹ Information

There are excellent visitor information centers (VICs) covering every entry point in the Yukon: Beaver Creek, Carcross, Dawson City, Haines Junction, Watson Lake and Whitehorse.

Thanks to its generous support by the Canadian taxpayer, the Yukon government produces enough literature and information to supply a holiday's worth of reading. Among the highlights are *Camping on Yukon Time, Art Adventures on Yukon Time* and lavish walking guides to pretty much every town with a population greater than 50. Start your collection at the various visitor centers online (www.travelyukon. com). Another good internet resource is www. yukoninfo.com.

A great way to get a feel for the Yukon and its larger-than-life stories is to read some of

the vast body of Yukon novels. Start with Jack London, *Call of the Wild* is free online at www. online-literature.com.

ℹ Getting There & Around

Whitehorse is linked by **air** to Vancouver, Calgary, Edmonton and Alaska. There are even flights direct to Germany during summer. Dawson City has flights to Inuvik in the NWT and to Alaska.

There are three major ways to reach the Yukon by road: first by **ferry** to the entry points of Skagway and Haines, Alaska, by the Alaska Hwy from Dawson Creek, BC, and by the Stewart-Cassiar Hwy from northwest BC that joins the Alaska Hwy near Watson Lake.

You can reach Whitehorse from BC by bus. From there a patchwork of companies provides links to Skagway and Alaska (but nothing to Dawson!). Rental cars (and RVs) are expensive and only available in Whitehorse. The Alaska Hwy and Klondike Hwy are paved and have services every 100km to 200km.

Check road conditions in the Yukon (☎511; www.511yukon.ca).

WHITEHORSE

POP 23,800

The leading city and capital of the Yukon, Whitehorse will likely have a prominent role in your journey. The territory's two great highways, the Alaska and the Klondike, cross here; it's a hub for transport. You'll find all manner of outfitters and services for explorations across the territory. Most of its residents have government-related jobs, but they flee for the outdoors no matter what the season.

Utility aside, Whitehorse can delight. It has a well-funded arts community, good restaurants and a range of motels. Exploring the sights within earshot of the rushing Yukon River can easily take a day or more. Look past bland commercial buildings and you'll see a fair number of heritage ones awaiting your discovery.

Whitehorse has always been a transportation hub, first as a terminus for the White Pass & Yukon Route railway from Skagway in the early 1900s. During WWII it was a major center for work on the Alaska Hwy. In 1953, Whitehorse was made the capital of the territory, to the continuing regret of much smaller and isolated Dawson City.

◉ Sights

Museums

SS Klondike   HISTORICAL SITE
(☑867-667-4511; South Access Rd & 2nd Ave; adult/child $6/2; ☺9am-5pm mid-May–mid-Sep) Carefully restored, this was one of the largest sternwheelers used on the Yukon River. Built in 1937, it made its final run upriver to Dawson in 1955 and is now a national historic site. Try not to wish it was making the run now.

MacBride Museum   MUSEUM
(☑867-667-2709; www.mcbridemuseum.com; cnr 1st Ave & Wood St; adult/child $8/4.50; ☺9am-6pm mid-May–Sep, noon-4pm Tue-Sat Oct–mid-May) The Yukon's attic covers the gold rush, First Nations, intrepid Mounties and more. Old photos vie with old stuffed critters, all under a sod roof.

Old Log Church   HISTORICAL BUILDING
(☑867-668-2555; www.oldlogchurchmuseum.ca; 303 Elliott St; adult/child $6/5; ☺10am-6pm mid-May–Aug) The only log-cabin-style cathedral in the world is a 1900 downtown gem. Displays include the compelling story of Rev Isaac Stringer, who boiled and ate his boots while lost in the wilderness for 51 days. Fittingly, all that's left is his sole.

Yukon Beringia Interpretive Centre
                    MUSEUM
(☑867-667-8855; www.beringia.com; Km1473 Alaska Hwy; adult/child $6/4; ☺9am-6pm) This place focuses on Beringia, a mostly ice-free area that encompassed the Yukon, Alaska and eastern Siberia during the last ice age. Engaging exhibits re-create the time, right down to the giant beaver by the door. It's just south of the airport.

Yukon Transportation Museum   MUSEUM
(☑867-668-4792; www.goytm.ca; 30 Electra Circle; adult/child $6/3; ☺10am-6pm mid-May–Aug)

Find out what the Alaska Hwy was really like back in the day and let's just say mud was a dirty word. Exhibits cover planes, trains and dog-sleds. The museum adjoins the Beringia Centre.

Waterfront

One look at the majestic Yukon River and you'll understand why the waterfront is being reborn. The beautiful **White Pass & Yukon Route Station** (Front St) has been restored and anchors the area.

At the north end of the waterfront, **Shipyards Park** has a growing collection of historic structures gathered territory-wide and a skateboard track and toboggan hill. Linking it all is a cute little **waterfront trolley** (adult/child $2/free; ☺9am-9pm Jun-Aug).

Whitehorse Fishway

Stare down a salmon at the **Whitehorse Fishway** (☑867-633-5965; admission by donation; ☺9am-9pm Jun-Aug), a 366m wooden fish ladder (the world's longest) past the hydroelectric plant south of town. Large viewing windows let you see chinook salmon swim past starting in late July (before that it's grayling). Outside, amidst the thunderous roar of the river's spillway, there's usually a tent where you can learn about the ingenious aboriginal fishing methods. Note that salmon counts and average sizes are decreasing, a feared result of climate change.

The fishway is easily reached on foot from town; see p767.

Art Galleries

Whitehorse is at the center of the Yukon's robust arts community.

Arts Underground   GALLERY
(☑867-667-4080; Hougen Centre lower level, 305 Main St; ☺9am-5:30pm Mon-Sat) Operated by the Yukon Arts Society. There are carefully selected and well-mounted rotating exhibits.

Yukon Artists@Work   GALLERY
(☑867-393-4848; 120 Industrial Rd; ☺noon-5pm daily Jun-Aug, Fri-Sun Sep-May) Operated by 35 local artists, some of whom may be busyily creating when you visit. It's just situated north of the big box shopping area.

Midnight Sun Gallery & Gifts
                    GALLERY, SHOP
(☑867-668-4350; 205C Main St; ☺9am-8pm) Has good selections of Yukon arts, crafts and products.

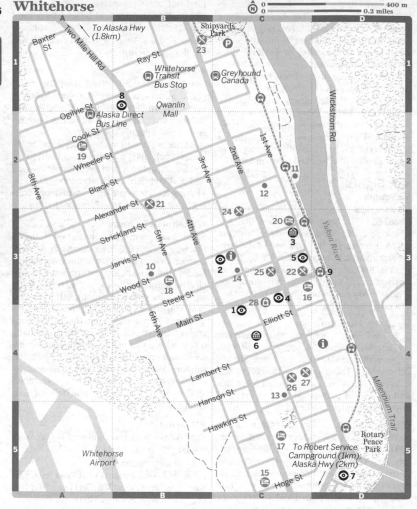

North End Gallery GALLERY
(☎867-393-3590; 1116 1st Ave; ◷10am-6pm Mon-Sat) High-end Canadian art.

Sundog Carving Studio & Gallery GALLERY
(☎867-633-4186; 4194 4th Ave; ◷9am-4:30pm Mon-Fri) First Nations artists sell their own works at this cooperative store.

🕴 Activities

The VIC can guide you to numerous local hikes and activities year-round. Otherwise, Whitehorse is a major outfitting center for adventures on Yukon waterways.

Canoeing & Kayaking

Whitehorse is the starting place for popular canoeing and kayaking trips to Carmacks or on to Dawson City. It's an average of eight days to the former and 16 days to the latter. Outfitters offer rentals that include transport back to Whitehorse. Canoe/kayak to Carmacks is about $210/300, to Whitehorse $350/500. Most paddlers use the map *The Yukon River: Marsh Lake to Dawson City* available at www.yukonbooks.com.

Kanoe People   ADVENTURE TOURS
(☎867-668-4899; www.kanoepeople.com; cnr
1st Ave & Strickland St) At the river's edge.
Can arrange any type of trip including
paddles down Teslin and Big Salmon
Rivers. Gear, maps and guides for sale,
bikes for rent.

Up North Adventures   ADVENTURE TOURS
(☎867-667-7035; www.upnorthadventures.com;
103 Strickland St) Offers rentals and transport on the major rivers. Also paddling
lessons, guided mountain-bike trips and
winter sports.

Cycling

Whitehorse has scores of **bike trails** along
the Yukon River and into the surrounding
hills. The VIC has maps. For bike rentals,
try **Cadence Cycle** (☎867-633-5600; 508
Wood St) which has good used mountain
bikes from $20 per day. It also does repairs.

Walking & Hiking

You can walk a scenic 5km loop around
Whitehorse's waters that includes a stop at
the fishway. From the SS *Klondike* go south
on the **Millennium Trail** until you reach the
Robert Service Campground and the Rotary
Centennial Footbridge over the river. The
fishway is just south. Head north along the
water and cross the Robert Campbell Bridge
and you are back in the town center.

Tours

**Yukon Historical & Museums
Association**   WALKING TOURS
(☎867-667-4704; 3126 3rd Ave; admission $4;
⏲9am-3pm Mon-Sat Jun-Aug) Offers quirky
and interesting downtown walking tours
four times daily. Meet at its office in the
1904 Donneworth House. Ask your guide
to show you the WWII-era American
latrines that's still not winning any hearts
and minds.

 Yukon Conservation Society HIKING
TOURS
(☎867-668-5678; www.yukonconservation.org;
302 Hawkins St; ⏲Jul & Aug) Discover the
natural beauty all around Whitehorse
with a free Yukon Conservation Society
nature hike. There are 10 itineraries ranging from easy to hard.

Festivals & Events

See p763 for some legendary Yukon events
that include Whitehorse.

Sleeping

Whitehorse can get almost full during the
peak of summer, so book ahead. The VIC
has lists of B&Bs. Whitehorse has a lot of
midrange motels that earn the sobriquet
'veteran.' Check a room first before you
commit.

High Country Inn
HOTEL $$

(☎867-667-4471, 800-554-4471; www.highcoun tryinn.ca; 4051 4th Ave; r $90-220; ❀@☎) Towering over Whitehorse (four stories!), the High Country is popular with business travelers and high-end groups. The 84 rooms are large – some have huge whirlpools right in the room. A deranged-looking 40ft Mountie stands guard in the parking lot.

Edgewater Hotel
HOTEL $$

(☎867-667-2572, 877-484-3334; www.edgewater hotelwhitehorse.com; 101 Main St; r $90-190; ❀@☎) Much updated, the Edgewater has a dash of style. The 30 rooms are smallish (some lack air-con) but have flat-screen TVs. Better rooms have river views, some have kitchens.

Robert Service Campground
CAMPGROUND $

(☎867-668-3721; www.robertservicecampground. com; Robert Service Way; sites $18; ☀mid-May-Sep; @☎) It's a pretty 15-minute walk from town on the Millennium Trail to the 70 sites at this tents-only campground on the river 1km south of town. Excellent coffee, baked goods and ice cream in the cafe.

Historical House B&B
B&B $$

(☎867-668-2526; www.yukongold.com; cnr 5th Ave & Wood St; r $85-110; ❀@) A classic wooden home from 1907, there are three rooms here. Top-floor ones have individual bathrooms down the hall and angled ceilings. A larger unit has a huge kitchen. The common area has a wood stove. There's high-speed internet and a nice garden.

Midnight Sun Inn
B&B $$

(☎867-667-2255, 800-284-4448; www.midnight sunbb.com; 6188 6th Ave; r $100-135; ❀@) A modern B&B in a sort of overgrown suburban-style house with four themed rooms. The Sun is downtown, has high-speed internet and serves big breakfasts.

Beez Kneez Bakpakers
HOSTEL $

(☎867-456-2333; www.bzkneez.com; 408 Hoge St; dm/r $30/65; @☎) Like the home you've left behind, this cheery hostel has a garden, deck, grill and free bikes. Two cabins ($65) are much in demand.

River View Hotel
MOTEL $$

(Canada's Best Value Inn; ☎867-667-7801, 888-315-2378; www.riverviewhotel.ca; 102 Wood St; r $90-150; @☎) The floors sound hollow here but many of the 53 rooms have the views implied by the name and all are very large. It's close to everything, yet on a quiet street.

Hi Country RV Park
CAMPGROUND $

(☎867-667-7445; www.hicountryrvyukon.com; 91374 Alaska Hwy; tent/RV $18/36; @☎) At the top of Robert Service Way, this woodsy campground offers hookups, showers, laundry and a playground.

✖ Eating

Ignore the influx of chains and enjoy one of Whitehorse's excellent downtown restaurants. There's a great range; look for fresh Yukon salmon in season. The **Fireweed Community Market** (Shipyards Park; ☀3-8pm Thu mid-May–mid-Sep) draws vendors from the region; the berries are fabulous.

TOP CHOICE Klondike Rib & Salmon Bake
CANADIAN $$

(☎867-667-7554; 2116 2nd Ave; mains $12-25; ☀4-9pm) It looks touristy and it seems touristy and it *is* touristy, but the food is excellent at this sprawling casual place with two decks. Besides the namesakes, fresh halibut also wins raves.

Giorgio's Cucina
ITALIAN $$

(☎867-668-4050; 206 Jarvis St; mains $12-30; ☀11:30am-2pm & 5-10pm) The best place in town for Italian has creative specials. The semi-open kitchen flames things up and the steaks are prime. Portions are mother lode size – make certain your room has a fridge.

Yukon Meat & Sausage
DELI $

(☎867-667-6077; 203 Hanson St; sandwiches $6; ☀9am-5:30pm Mon-Sat) The smell of smoked meat wafts out to the street and you walk right in; there's a huge selection of prepared items and custom-made sandwiches. Great for picnics, or eat in.

Sanchez Cantina
MEXICAN $$

(☎867-668-5858; 211 Hanson St; mains $10-20; ☀11:30am-3pm & 5-9:30pm) You have to head south across two borders to find Mexican this authentic. Burritos are the thing – get them with the spicy mix of red and green sauces. Settle in for what may be a wait on the broad patio.

Baked Café
CAFE $

(☎867-633-6291; 100 Main St; snacks $4; ☀7am-7pm; ☎) In summer, the outdoor tables at this stylish cafe attract swells in shades who you'd think would be reading *Daily Variety*. Smoothies, soups, daily lunch specials, baked goods and more.

Alpine Bakery
BAKERY $

(☎867-668-6871; 411 Alexander St; snacks from $6; ☀8am-6pm Mon-Sat) Everything is organic at this serious bakery where there are daily whole-grain and lunch specials. Fresh juices are the thing to cool down on that one hot summer day.

Drinking

Whitehorse has a fair number of grotty old boozers. But you can find enjoyable and atmospheric bars in the Edgewater Hotel and High Country Inn . Look for the tasty brews of the local Yukon Brewing Co.

All summer, there are free lunchtime concerts by Yukon musicians and artists at **LePage Park** (cnr Wood St & 3rd Ave; ⊙noon, Mon-Fri May-Sep).

Coasters (☑867-633-2788; 206 Jarvis St; ⊙3pm-late) has deejays and bands playing rockabilly, hip-hop or something trendy from Vancouver. Sunday is open mike.

🔒 Shopping

Many of the galleries listed in Sights are excellent sources of local items.

TOP CHOICE **Mac's Fireweed Books** BOOKSTORE (☑867-668-2434; www.yukonbooks.com; 203 Main St; ⊙8am-midnight May-Sep, to 9pm Oct-Apr) Mac's has an unrivaled selection of Yukon titles. It also stocks topographical maps, road maps, magazines and newspapers.

ℹ️ Information

Among local newspapers, the *Yukon News* is feisty, while *What's Up Yukon* (www. whatsupyukon.com) is the source for entertainment listings.

Tourism Whitehorse (☑867-668-8629; www.visitwhitehorse.com; 3128 3rd Ave; ⊙9am-4:30pm Mon-Fri) Located next to the Yukon Historical & Museums Association in a 1905 house. Strictly for the city; good website.

VIC (☑867-667-3084; 100 Hanson St; ⊙8am-8pm May–mid-Sep, 9am-4:30pm Mon-Fri mid-Sep–May) Essential; has territory-wide information.

Whitehorse General Hospital (☑867-393-8700; 5 Hospital Rd; ⊙24hr)

ℹ️ Getting There & Away

Whitehorse is the transportation hub of the Yukon.

Air

Whitehorse airport (YXY; ☑867-667-8440; www.gov.yk.ca/yxy/) Five minutes west of downtown off the Alaska Hwy.

Air Canada (☑888-247-2262; www.aircanada.com) Serves Vancouver.

Air North (☑800-661-0407; www.flyairnorth.com) Locally owned, serves Dawson City, Old Crow, Inuvik in the NWT, Fairbanks in Alaska, and Vancouver, Edmonton and Calgary.

Condor (☑800-364-1667, in Germany 01805 707 202; www.condor.com) Has twice-weekly flights to/from Frankfurt in summer.

Bus

Bus services, er, come and go; check the latest with the VIC.

Alaska Direct Bus Line (☑867-668-4833; www.alaskadirectbusline.com; 501 Ogilvie St) Service (two/three times weekly winter/summer) to Fairbanks and Anchorage, Alaska via the Alaska Hwy including Haines Junction (US$75, two hours) and Tok, Alaska (US$135, 9½ hours).

Greyhound Canada (☑867-667-2223, 800-661-8747; www.greyhound.ca; 2191 2nd Ave) Service south along the Alaska Hwy to Dawson Creek ($240, 20 hours, three times per week); connects with buses for the rest of BC and Canada.

White Pass & Yukon Route (☑867-633-5710; www.wpyr.com; Whitehorse ticket office, 1109 Front St; ⊙9am-5pm Mon-Sat mid-May–mid-Sep) Offers an enjoyable and scenic rail and bus connection to/from Skagway (adult/child from US$116/58, 4½ hours) via Fraser, BC. There is an option for a longer train ride with the bus transfer at Carcross.

ℹ️ Getting Around

To/From the Airport

Yellow Cab (☑867-668-4811) About $18 from the center for the 10-minute ride.

Bus

Whitehorse Transit System (☑867-668-7433; ⊙Mon-Sat) Main transfer point at the Qwanlin Mall. Route 2 (ticket $2.50, every 30 to 70 minutes) serves the airport, the center and the Robert Service Campground.

Car & RV

Check your rate very carefully as it's common for a mileage charge to be added after the first 100km, which will not get you far in the Yukon. Also understand your insurance coverage and whether damage from Yukon's rugged roads is covered. There's a reason you see all those ads for windshield replacement.

Budget (☑867-667-6200; www.budget.com), **Hertz** (☑867-668-4224; www.hertz.com) and **National/NorCan** (☑867-456-2277; www.national.com) are at the airport.

Whitehorse Subaru (☑867-393-6550; www.whitehorsesubaru.com; 17 Chilkoot Way) Can usually beat the biggies on price.

Fraserway RV Rentals (☑867-668-3438; www.fraserwayrvrentals.com; 9039 Quartz Rd) Rents all shapes and sizes of RV from $80 to $300 per day depending on size (it matters) and season. Mileage extra.

ALASKA HIGHWAY

It may be called the Alaska Hwy but given that its longest stretch is in the Yukon (958km) perhaps another name is in order...

Roughly 2450km in length from Dawson Creek, BC, to Delta Junction, far inside Alaska, the Alaska Hwy has a meaning well beyond just a road. Sure it's a way to get from point A to point B, but it's also a badge, an honor, an accomplishment. Even though today it's a modern road, the very name still evokes images of big adventure and getting away from it all.

As you drive the Alaska Hwy in the Yukon, know that you're on the most scenic and varied part of the road. From little villages to the city of Whitehorse, from meandering rivers to the upthrust drama of the St Elias Mountains, the scenery will overwhelm you.

BC to Whitehorse

You'll never be far from an excuse to stop on this stretch of the Alcan. Towns, small parks and various roadside attractions appear at regular intervals. None are massively compelling but overall it's a pleasant drive. See p770 for details of the Alaska Hwy in BC.

WORTH A TRIP

LET THERE BE HIGHWAY

Nowadays the aura of the Alaska Hwy is psychological rather than physical. In every way it's a modern two-lane road, with smooth curves, broad sight lines and paving from one end to another, but that has not always been the case. A famous 1943 photo shows a jeep seemingly being sucked down to China through a morass of mud while soldiers look on helplessly.

With the outbreak of WWII, Canada and the US decided that years of debate should end and that a proper road was needed to link Alaska and the Yukon to the rest of Canada and the US.

That a road – any road – could be carved out of the raw tundra and wilderness of the north in a little over a year was a miracle, although unlimited money and manpower (US soldiers and Canadian civilians, including Aboriginal people) helped. The 2450km gravel highway ran between Dawson Creek in BC and Fairbanks in Alaska. The route chosen for the highway followed a series of existing airfields – Fort St John, Fort Nelson, Watson Lake and Whitehorse – known as the Northwest Staging Route.

In April 1946 the Canadian section of the road (1965km) was officially handed over to Canada. In the meantime, private contractors were busy widening, graveling and straightening the highway, leveling its steep grades and replacing temporary bridges with permanent steel ones – a process that has continued since, creating the modern road you drive today.

Known variously as the Alaskan International Hwy, the Alaska Military Hwy and the Alcan (short for Alaska-Canada) Hwy, it's now called the Alaska Hwy. It has transformed both the Yukon and Alaska, opening up the north to year-round travel and forever changing the way of life of the First Nations along the route.

The Alaska Hwy begins at 'Mile 0' in Dawson Creek in northeastern BC and goes to Fairbanks, Alaska, although the official end is at Delta Junction, about 155km southeast of Fairbanks.

Mileposts long served as reference points, but improvements shortening the road and Canada's adoption of the metric system have made mileage references archaic. Historic numbers persist in the names of some businesses and attractions.

For more on the Alaska Hwy and its harrowing past, check out the **Watson Lake VIC** (p784), the **Yukon Transportation Museum** (p765) in Whitehorse and the **Alaska Highway House** in Dawson Creek, BC (p760). For a minutely detailed guide to every feature, including seemingly every pothole and moose turd, look for the *Milepost*, a legendary annual publication.

WATSON LAKE

Originally named after Frank Watson, a British trapper, Watson Lake is the first town in the Yukon on the Alaska Hwy and is just over the border from BC. It's mostly a good rest stop except for the superb **VIC** (☎867-536-7469; www.watsonlake.ca; ☺8am-8pm summer), which has a good museum about the highway and a passel of territory-wide info. The town offers campgrounds, motels, full services and a Greyhound Canada stop.

The town is famous for its **Sign Post Forest** just outside the VIC. The first sign-post, 'Danville, Illinois,' was nailed up in 1942. Others were added and now there are 68,000 signs, many purloined late at night from municipalities worldwide.

Twenty-six kilometers west of Watson Lake is the junction with the Stewart-Cassiar Hwy (Hwy 37), which heads south into BC (p760). For a discussion of the various routes into the Yukon, see p759.

Just west of the junction, family-run **Nugget City** (☎867-536-2307, 888-536-2307; www.nuggetcity.com; campsites from $20, cabins from $80; ☎) has accommodations and food that's three cuts above the Alaska Hwy norm. Stop just for the baked goods, especially the berry pie.

Another 110km west, past the 1112km marker, look for the **Rancheria Falls Recreation Site**. A boardwalk leads to powerful twin waterfalls. It's an excellent stop.

TESLIN

Teslin, on the long, narrow lake of the same name, is a settlement of distinction. Long a home to the Tlingits (lin-*kits*), the Alaska Hwy brought both prosperity and rapid change to this aboriginal population. The engrossing **George Johnston Museum** (☎867-390-2550; www.gjmuseum.yk.net; Km 1294 Alaska Hwy; adult/child $6/3; ☺9am-5pm mid-May–early Sep) details the life and culture of a 20th-century Tlingits leader through photographs, displays and artifacts.

JOHNSON'S CROSSING

Some 53km north of Teslin is Johnson's Crossing, at the junction of the Alaska Hwy and Canol Rd (Hwy 6). During WWII the US army built the Canol pipeline at tremendous human and financial expense to pump oil from Norman Wells in the NWT to Whitehorse. Like any good military boondoggle, it was abandoned after countless hundreds of millions of dollars (in 1943 money, no less) were spent.

WORTH A TRIP

ROBERT CAMPBELL HWY

To get right off the beaten path, consider this lonely gravel road (Hwy 4) which runs 588km from Watson Lake north and west to Carmacks (p778), where you can join the Klondike Hwy for Dawson City. Along its length, the highway parallels various rivers and lakes. Wilderness campers will be thrilled.

Ross River, 373km from Watson Lake at the junction with the Canol Rd (Hwy 6), is home to the Kaska First Nation and a supply center for the local mining industry. There are campgrounds and motels in town.

Whitehorse to Alaska

For long segments west of Whitehorse, the Alaska Hwy has been modernized to the point of blandness. Fortunately, this ends abruptly in Haines Junction. From here the road parallels legendary Kluane National Forest and the St Elias Mountains. The 300km to Beaver Creek is the most scenic part of the entire highway.

HAINES JUNCTION

It's goodbye flatlands when you reach Haines Junction and see the sweep of imposing peaks looming over town. You've reached the stunning Kluane National Park and this is the gateway. The town makes an excellent base for exploring the park or staging a serious four-star mountaineering, backcountry or river adventure. German travelers will hear their language spoken all over town.

The magnificent Haines Hwy heads south from here to Alaska (p774).

Yukon Tourism (☎867-634-2345; www.hainesjunctionyukon.com; ☺10am-6pm May & Sep, 8am-8pm Jun-Aug) and **Parks Canada** (☎867-634-7250; www.parkscanada.gc.ca/kluane; ☺10am-6pm mid-May–Aug, to 4pm Sep–mid-May) share the **VIC** (Logan St) in the Kluane National Park headquarters building. There's lots of info from the two agencies and a good model of the local terrain. In summer, rangers give regular nature talks.

All shops, lodging and services are clustered around the Alaska and Haines Hwys junction. And that thing that looks like an acid-trip cupcake? It's a **sculpture** meant to be a winsome tableau of local characters and critters.

🏃 Activities

Even the spectacular ridges surrounding Haines Junction don't begin to hint at the beauty of Kluane National Park. Although the park should be your focus, there are some good activities locally.

For a hike after hours of driving, there's a pretty 5.5km **nature walk** along Dezadeash River where Hwy 3 crosses it at the south end of town.

Paddlewheel Adventures (🖉867-634-2683; www.paddlewheeladventures.com; 116 Kathleen St), opposite the VIC, arranges Tatshenshini rafting trips ($125 per person, includes lunch), scenic white-water trips and guided interpretive hikes ($55 to $125). It rents mountain bikes or canoes ($30 per day) and provides local transportation.

Owned by a longtime park warden and guide, **Kruda Ché Boat Tours** (🖉867-634-2378; www.krudache.com) will arrange any number of custom tours by boat and on foot within Kluane National Park. Wildlife, history and aboriginal culture are among the themes.

🛏 Sleeping & Eating

There's a cluster of motels and RV parks in Haines Junction. There's a beach and shade at **Pine Lake**, a territorial campground 6km east of town on the Alaska Hwy. Cerulean waters highlight **Kathleen Lake** (sites $15), a Parks Canada campground 24km south of Haines Junction off the Haines Hwy.

Raven Motel   INN $$
(🖉867-634-2500; www.ravenhotelyukon.com; 181 Alaska Hwy; r $130-160; ❋🛜) There are 12 comfortable motel-style rooms here and guests can partake of a vast German-style break buffet. But the real star is the restaurant, which has the best food between Whitehorse and Alaska. Menus are complex and continental (meals $35 to $50).

Alcan Motor Inn   MOTEL $$
(🖉867-634-2371, 888-265-1018; www.alcanmotorinn.com; s & d $90-150; ❋🛜) The modern two-story Alcan has 23 large rooms with great views of the jagged Auriol Range. Some have full kitchens and there's a cafe.

Village Bakery & Deli   BAKERY/CAFE $
(🖉867-634-2867; Logan St; mains $6-10; ⊘7am-9pm May-Aug; 🛜) Across from the VIC, the bakery here turns out excellent goods all day, while the deli counter has tasty sandwiches you can enjoy on the huge deck. On Friday night there's a popular barbecue with live folk music.

Frosty Freeze   BURGERS $
(🖉867-634-7070; Alaska Hwy; mains $6; ⊘11am-10pm May-Sep) What looks like a humdrum fast-food joint is several orders of magnitude better. The shakes are made with real ice cream, the sundaes feature fresh berries and the burgers (try the mushroom-Swiss number) are huge and juicy.

ℹ Information

Parks Canada has two information centers. One is in Haines Junction and the other at **Tachal Dhal** (Sheep Mountain; Alaska Hwy; ⊘9am-3:30pm late May-early Sep), 130km west of Haines Junction. Get a copy of the *Recreation Guide,* which shows the scope of the park (and how little is actually easily accessible). The map shows hikes ranging from 10 minutes to 10 days.

ℹ Getting There & Away

Alaska Direct Bus Line (🖉867-668-4833; www.alaskadirectbusline.com; 501 Ogilvie St) Service (two/three times weekly winter/summer) to Fairbanks and Anchorage in Alaska via the Alaska Hwy through Tok (US$125, 7½ hours); east to Whitehorse (US$75, two hours).

KLUANE NATIONAL PARK & RESERVE

Unesco-recognized as an 'empire of mountains and ice,' Kluane National Park & Reserve looms south of the Alaska Hwy much of the way to the Alaska border. This rugged and magnificent wilderness covers 22,015 sq km of the southwest corner of the territory. Kluane (kloo-wah-neee) gets its far-too-modest name from the Southern Tutchone word for 'lake with many fish.'

With British Columbia's Tatshenshini-Alsek Provincial Park to the south and Alaska's Wrangell-St Elias National Park to the west, this is one of the largest protected wilderness areas in the world. Deep beyond the mountains you see from the Alaska Hwy are over 100 named glaciers and as many unnamed ones.

Winters are long and harsh. Summers are short, making mid-June to early September the best time to visit. Note that winter conditions can occur at any time, especially in the backcountry. See Haines Junction for the park's campground.

⊙ Sights

The park consists primarily of the **St Elias Mountains** and the world's largest nonpolar **ice fields**. Two-thirds of the park is glacier interspersed with valleys, glacial lakes, alpine forest, meadows and tundra. The **Kluane Ranges** (averaging a height of 2500m) are seen along the western edge of the Alaska Hwy. A greenbelt wraps around the base where most of the animals and vegetation live. Turquoise **Kluane Lake** is the Yukon's largest. Hidden are the immense ice fields and towering peaks, including **Mt Logan** (5959m), Canada's highest mountain, and **Mt St Elias** (5488m), the second highest. Partial glimpses of the interior peaks can be found at the Km 1622 **viewpoint** on the Alaska Hwy and also around the Donjek River Bridge, but the best views are from the air. You can arrange charters of planes or helicopters in Haines Junction.

🏃 Activities

There's excellent **hiking** in the forested lands at the base of the mountains, along either marked trails or less-defined routes. There are about a dozen in each category, some following old mining roads, others traditional aboriginal paths. Detailed trail guides and topographical maps are available at the information centers. Talk to the rangers before setting out. They will help select a hike and can provide updates on areas that may be closed due to bear activity. Overnight hikes require backcountry permits ($10 per person per night).

The Tachal Dhal information center is the starting point for **Slims West**, a popular 60km round-trip trek to **Kaskawulsh** Nlou ler - one of the 8 wildland can be reached on foot. This is a difficult route that takes from three to five days to complete and includes sweeping views from Observation Mountain (2114m). An easy overnight trip is the 15km **Auriol** loop, which goes from spruce forest to subalpine barrens and includes a wilderness campground. It's 7km south of Haines Junction.

Fishing is good and **wildlife-watching** plentiful. Most noteworthy are the thousands of Dall sheep that can be seen on Sheep Mountain in April, May and September. There's a large and diverse population of grizzly bear, as well as black bear, moose, caribou, goats and 150 varieties of birds, among them eagles and the rare peregrine falcon.

Many enjoy **skiing** or **snowshoeing**, beginning in February.

DESTRUCTION BAY

This small village on the shore of huge Kluane Lake is 107km north of Haines Junction. It was given its evocative name after a storm tore through the area during construction of the highway. Most of the residents are First Nations, who live off the land through the year. **Congdon Creek** is 17km east of town on the Alaska Hwy and has an 81-site territorial campground and a fine lakeside setting.

BURWASH LANDING

Commune with an enormous, albeit stuffed, moose at the excellent **Kluane Museum** (📞867-841-5561; adult/child $4/2; ⊗9am-8pm mid-May–early Sep). Enjoy intriguing wildlife exhibits and displays on natural and aboriginal history. There's **boating** on Kluane Lake, including a good 10km paddle to the wildlife-filled mouth of the Kluane River.

BEAVER CREEK

Wide-spot-in-the-road Beaver Creek is a beacon for sleepy travelers or those who want to get gas – certainly its lackluster

BEETLES RIP?

Even as beetles wreak havoc on forests across BC and the Rockies, the forests of the Yukon may be recovering. Certainly you can't miss the vast swaths of brown as you drive the Alaska Hwy past Kluane National Park: millions upon millions of dead trees killed by the spruce beetle, starting in 1994.

Many reasons for this disaster center on climate change, including warmer winters allowing far more beetles than usual to survive from one year to the next.

In recent years, however, several factors are now working against the beetles: dead trees mean less food, a very cold winter killed many beetles and there is now a population explosion of beetle-eaters. New attacks on trees have plummeted toward historic levels. Meanwhile, nature has opened the door to other trees; birch and alder, which grow fast and are favored by a burgeoning population of moose and other critters.

To get a sense of the devastation caused by beetles in the last decade stop at the short **Spruce Beetle Loop**, 17km northwest of Haines Junction, just off the highway.

eateries will ensure the latter. The Canadian border checkpoint is just north of town; the US border checkpoint is 27km further west. Both are open 24 hours.

The **VIC** (☑867-862-7321; Km 1202 Alaska Hwy; ◉8am-8pm May-Sep) has information on all of the Yukon. A strange **sculpture garden** just north tempts the silly (or intoxicated) into unnatural acts.

Of the four motels in town, the **1202 Motor Inn** (☑867-862-7600, 800-661-0540; 1202 Alaska Hwy; r from $60) is the least offensive. The 30 rooms are basic and functional. Get one away from the idling trucks.

ALASKA

Note that the incredible scenery of the Alaska Hwy dims a bit once you cross into its namesake state. The Alaska Hwy department leaves the road much more despoiled than the pristine conditions in the Yukon.

From the US border, it's 63km (39 miles) to **Tetlin National Wildlife Refuge** (tetlin. fws.gov) on the Alaska Hwy. About 117km past Tetlin, you'll reach the junction with the Taylor Hwy (Hwy 5) which connects north with the Top of the World Hwy (p784) to Dawson City.

HAINES HIGHWAY

If you're doing only a short loop between Haines and Skagway via Whitehorse, this 259km road might be the highlight of your trip. In fact, no matter what length your Yukon adventure, the Haines Hwy (Hwy 3) might be the high point. In a relatively short distance you see glaciers, looming snow-clad peaks, lush and wild river valleys, windswept Alpine meadows and a bald-eagle-laced river delta.

Heading south of Haines Junction, look west for a close-up of the St Elias Mountains, those glaciers glimpsed at the top stretch all the way to the Pacific Ocean. About 80km south, look for the **Tatshenshini River viewpoint**. This white-water river flows through protected bear country and a valley that seems timeless.

About 10km further, look for **Million Dollar Falls**. For once the sight lives up to the billing, as water thunders through a narrow chasm. Let the roar lull you to sleep at the nearby territorial **campground**.

The highway crosses into BC for a mere 70km but you'll hope for more as you traverse high and barren alpine wilderness, where sudden snow squalls happen year-round. At the 1070m Chilkat Pass, an ancient aboriginal route into the Yukon, the road suddenly plunges down for a steep descent into Alaska. The US border is 72km north of Haines, along the wide **Chilkat River Delta**.

Home to scores of **bald eagles** year-round, the handsome birds flock like pigeons each fall when they mass in the trees overlooking the rivers drawn by the comparatively mild weather and steady supply of fish.

Pullouts line the Haines Hwy (Hwy 7 in Alaska), especially between mileposts 19 and 26. Take your time driving and find a place to park. Just a few feet from the road it's quiet, and when you see a small tree covered with 20 pensive – and sizable – bald eagles, you can enjoy your own raptor version of *The Birds*.

Haines (Alaska)

Unlike Skagway just across the Lynn Canal, Haines has escaped the cruise-ship mobs and it's all the better for it. It's a real community with a real downtown close to the working waterfront. There are good shops, a couple of small museums and a historic fort. You can easily walk around much of the town in a few scenic hours. As you gaze out over the beautiful mountain-backed waters – possibly with a relaxing beverage in hand – you're unlikely to be jealous of those aboard the conga line of cruise ships puffing (and we mean puffing, the pollution is deplorable) their way to the next port.

Coming from the south on the Alaska Marine Highway ferries, Haines is definitely the port of choice for accessing the Yukon. For more coverage of Haines and southeast Alaska, see Lonely Planet's *Alaska*.

◉ Sights & Activities

Walk the center and waterfront and then amble over to **Fort Seward**, an old army post dating back 100 years. Now a national historic site, the many mannered buildings have been given a range of new uses, from art galleries to funky stores to B&Bs.

Haines makes the most of its feathered residents and has an **eagle festival** (http://baldeaglefest.org) in their honor every November. Numerous local guides will take you to see the birds in ways you can't do from the side of the Haines Hwy.

📥 Sleeping & Eating

The Haines CVB has oodles of choices at all price ranges.

Captain's Choice Motel MOTEL $$
(📞907-766-3111, 800-478-2345; www.capchoice.com; 108 2nd Ave N; r US$100-180; ❀🐾) An admiral might even choose this place, as many of the 37 rooms have sweeping water views and all are large. It's right in the center.

Portage Cove State Recreation Site
CAMPGROUND $
(Beach Rd; tent sites US$5; ⊙15 May-Aug) It's worth losing your car so you can stay at this cyclist- and backpacker-friendly campground on the water 1.6km south of town. Light a campfire and let the mist roll in.

Fireweed FUSION $$
(📞907-766-3838; Bldg 37 Blacksmith Rd; mains US$10-20; ⊙11am-10pm; 🐾) In Fort Seward, Fireweed is an oasis of organic and creative cuisine. Enjoy the excellent pizzas, salads, chowders and seafood out on the deck overlooking the Lynn Canal. We swoon over the Haines Brewing Spruce Tip Ale.

Mountain Market & Spirits MARKET $
(📞907-766-3340; 151 3rd Ave; meals US$4-10; ⊙7am-7pm; 🐾) Get your Haines Hwy or Alaska ferry picnic here. Treats include excellent coffee, baked goods, big sandwiches and lots of organic prepared foods.

ℹ️ Information

Prices for Haines are in US$. Haines is on Alaska time, one hour earlier than Yukon time.

Haines Convention & Visitors Bureau (📞007 766-2234, 800-458-3579; www.haines.ak.us; 122 2nd Ave; ⊙9am-5pm May-Sep) Publishes a hugely useful vacation planner and has trail maps plus Yukon info.

ℹ️ Getting There & Away

There's no public transportation from Haines into the Yukon.

Alaska Maritime Highway System (📞800-642-0066; www.ferryalaska.com) Superb service links Haines and the Yukon to BC and the US. Car ferries serve Skagway, the Inside Passage and importantly, Prince Rupert in BC (p753); also Bellingham, Washington in the US. For more information, see p759. The ferry terminal is situated 6.5km south of town.

Haines-Skagway Fast Ferry (📞907-766-2100, 888-766-2103; www.hainesskagwayfastferry.com) Carries passengers only (adult/child US$35/18, 45 minutes, three or more per day, June to September) and docks near the center.

KLONDIKE HIGHWAY

Beginning seaside in Skagway, Alaska, the 716km Klondike Hwy climbs high to the forbidding Chilkoot Pass before crossing into stunning alpine scenery on the way to Carcross. For much of its length, the road generally follows the **Gold Rush Trail**, the route of the Klondike prospectors. You'll have a much easier time of it than they did (p777).

North of Whitehorse, the road passes through often-gentle terrain that has been scorched by wildfires through the years. Signs showing the dates let you chart nature's recovery.

Skagway (Alaska)

Skagway has been both delighting and horrifying travelers for over 100 years. In 1898 rogues of all kinds preyed upon arriving miners bound for Dawson. Today it's T-shirt vendors preying on tourists. When several huge cruise ships show up at once, the streets swarm with day-trippers.

However, behind the tat there's a real town that has many preserved attractions. At night, after the cruise ships have sailed, Skagway has its own quiet charm. Still, there's no need to linger, as the Yukon beckons. Although it's in the US, it can only be reached by car on the Klondike Hwy from the Yukon (with a short stretch in BC). It's the starting point for the famed Chilkoot Trail and the White Pass & Yukon Route.

Skagway is the last stop on the Alaska Marine Highway System's inland passage service from the south and as such is an important entry point for the Yukon. Lonely Planet's *Alaska* has extensive coverage of Skagway and the rest of Southeast Alaska.

Prices below are in US$. Skagway is on Alaska time, one hour earlier than the Yukon. Most places close outside of summer.

👁 Sights

A seven-block corridor along Broadway, part of the **Klondike Gold Rush National Historic Park**, is home to restored buildings, false fronts and wooden sidewalks from Skagway's gold rush era. The Park Service has tours, a museum and info.

The **White Pass & Yukon Route** (WP&YR; 📞907-983-2217, 800-343-7373; www.wpyr.com; cnr 2nd Ave & Spring St; adult/child US$110/55; ⊙early May-late Sep) is the stunning reason most people visit Skagway (other than T-shirts). The line twists up the tortuous route to the namesake White Pass, tracing the notorious White Pass trail used during the Klondike Gold Rush.

Sleeping

Reservations are strongly recommended during July and August. The CVB has comprehensive accommodations lists.

Sergeant Preston's Lodge MOTEL $$ (☎907-983-2521; www.sgtprestonslodge.com; 370 6th Ave; r US$80-120; ☞) The 40 bright and clean rooms are right in the historic center. Call for ferry pick-up.

Pullen Creek RV Park CAMPGROUND $ (☎907-983-2768, 800-936-3731; www.pullen creekrv.com; 501 Congress St; tent/RV US$22/36) This park is right next to the ferry terminal.

North Eden CAFE $ (☎907-983-2784; 21st Ave at State St; meals $4-8; ☉7am-2pm) Located inside the You Say Tomato Natural Foods store, stop here for a hearty coffee before you head up the Klondike Hwy or lay in some healthy eats before the ferry south.

ℹ Information

Chilkoot Trail Centre (cnr Broadway & 2nd Ave; ☉8am-5pm Jun-Aug) Run by Parks Canada (☎800-661-0486; www.pc.gc.ca/chilkoot) and the US National Park Service (☎907-983-3655; www.nps.gov/klgo), this place provides advice, permits, maps and a list of transportation options to/from the Chilkoot Trail.

Skagway Convention & Visitors Bureau (☎907-983-2854, 888-762-1898; www.skag way.com; 245 Broadway; ☉8am-6pm) Complete area details inside a landmark building.

US National Park Service (☎907-983-2921; cnr Broadway & 2nd Ave; ☉8am-6pm) Pick up the *Skagway Trail Map* for area hikes; has full details on the Klondike Gold Rush National Historic Park.

ℹ Getting There & Away

From Skagway to Whitehorse on the Klondike Hwy (Hwy 2) is 177km. Customs at the border usually moves fairly quickly.

Boat

Alaska Maritime Highway System (☎800-642-0066; www.ferryalaska.com) Superb service links Haines and the Yukon to BC and the US. Car ferries serve Haines, the Inside Passage and importantly, Prince Rupert in BC

(p753); also Bellingham, Washington in the US. For more information, see p759. The ferry terminal is right in the center.

Haines-Skagway Fast Ferry (☎907-766-2100, 888-766-2103; www.hainesskagwayfastferry. com) Carries passengers only (adult/child US$35/18, 45 minutes, three or more per day, June to September) and docks near the center.

Bus & Train

White Pass & Yukon Route (☎907-983-2217, 800-343-7373; www.wpyr.com; cnr 2nd Ave & Spring St; adult/child from US$116/58, 4½ hours; ☉Mon-Sat mid-May–mid-Sep) Offers an enjoyable and scenic rail and bus connection to/from Whitehorse via Fraser, BC. There is an option for a longer train ride with the bus transfer at Carcross.

Chilkoot Trail

Arduous at best and deadly at worst in 1898, the Chilkoot Trail was the route most prospectors took to get over the 1110m Chilkoot Pass from Skagway and into the Yukon. Today, hikers reserve spots months in advance to travel the same route.

The well-marked 53km trail begins near **Dyea**, 14km northwest of Skagway, and heads northeast over the pass. It then follows the Taiya River to Lake Bennett in BC, and takes three to five days to hike. It's a hard route in good weather and often treacherous in bad. You must be in good physical condition and come fully equipped. Layers of warm clothes and rain gear are essential.

Hardware, tools and supplies dumped by the prospectors still litter the trail. At several places there are wooden shacks where you can put up for the night, but these are usually full, so a tent and sleeping bag are required. There are 10 designated campgrounds along the route, each with bear caches.

At the Canadian end you can either take the White Pass & Yukon Route train from Bennett back to Skagway or further up the line to Fraser in BC, where you can connect with a bus for Whitehorse.

The Chilkoot Trail is a primary feature of the **Klondike Gold Rush International Historic Park**, a series of sites managed by both Parks Canada and the US National Park Service that stretches from Seattle, Washington, to Dawson City. Each Chilkoot hiker must obtain one of the 50 permits available for each day in summer; reserve well in advance. Parks Canada/US National Park Service charge $53 for a permit plus $12 for a reservation. Each day eight permits are issued on a first-come, first-served basis. For information, contact the **Chilkoot Trail Centre** in Skagway (p776) or go online. Necessary pre-planning includes determining which campsites you'll use each night.

Carcross

Long a forgotten gold-rush town, cute little Carcross, 74km southeast of Whitehorse, is on a roll. There are daily trains in summer from Skagway on the **White Pass & Yukon Route** (p776; one-way adult/child $170/85). Some old buildings are being restored and the site on Lake Bennett is superb. (Although Klondike prospectors who had to build boats here to cross the lake didn't think so.)

The **VIC** (☎867-821-4431; ⊙8am-8pm May-Sep) is in the old train station and has an excellent walking tour booklet of the town. The station also has good displays on local history and directly behind is a hall where local artists show their wares.

Carcross Desert, the world's smallest, is the exposed sandy bed of a glacial lake. It's 2km north of town.

Whitehorse to Carmacks

Leaving Whitehorse by the Klondike Hwy is none too exciting. There's land with low trees and a few cattle ranches. After about 40km, however, look for serene **Lake Laberge**, which has a beach, followed by **Fox Lake**, 24km further north, and **Twin Lakes**, 23km south of Carmacks. Each has a government campground with shelters and pump water.

FOOLHARDY & FUTILE

The Klondike Gold Rush continues to be the defining moment for the Yukon. Certainly it was the population high point. Some 40,000 gold seekers washed ashore (some literally) in Skagway, hoping to strike it rich in the gold fields of Dawson City, some 700km north.

To say that most were ill-prepared for the adventure is an understatement. Although some were veterans of other gold rushes, a high percentage were American men looking for adventure. Clerks, lawyers and waiters were just some of those who thought they'd just pop up North and get rich. The reality was different. Landing in Skagway, they were set upon by all manner of flimflam artists, most working for the incorrigible Soapy Smith. Next came dozens of trips hefting their 1000lb of required supplies over the frozen Chilkoot Pass. Then they had to build boats from scratch and make their way across lakes and the Yukon River to Dawson. Scores died trying.

Besides more scamsters, there was another harsh reality awaiting in Dawson: by the summer of 1897 when the first ships reached the west coast of the US with news of the discoveries on Dawson's Bonanza Creek, the best sites had all been claimed. The Klondike Gold Rush mobs were mostly too late to the action by at least a year. Sick and broke, the survivors glumly made their way back to the US. Few found any gold and most sold their gear for pennies to merchants who in turn resold it to incoming gold seekers for top dollar. Several family fortunes in the Yukon today can be traced to this trade.

Today, even the hardiest folk seem like couch potatoes when compared to these harrowing stories. The depravation, disease and heartbreak of these 'dudes' of the day make for fascinating reading. Among the many books about the Klondike Gold Rush, the following are recommended (and easily found in the Yukon):

» *The Klondike Fever* by Pierre Berton is the classic on the gold rush.

» *Sailor on Snowshoes* by Dick North traces Jack London's time in the Yukon and the hunt for his cabin. London's stories of the gold rush made his name as a writer.

» *Soapy Smith* by Stan Sauerwein is a delightful tale about the Skagway scalawag for whom the word incorrigible was invented.

The **Klondike Hwy** from Skagway via Whitehorse and as far as Minto follows what Parks Canada calls the Gold Rush Trail. To stay on the course of the gold seekers from there you'll need to paddle the Yukon River.

Carmacks

This village of 400 sits right on the Yukon River and is named for one of the discoverers of gold in 1896, George Washington Carmacks. A rogue seaman wandering the Yukon, it was almost by luck that Carmacks (with Robert Henderson, Tagish Charlie and Keish – aka Skookum Jim Mason) made their claim on Bonanza Creek. Soon he was living the high life and it wasn't long before he abandoned his First Nations family and headed south to the US.

Given his record as a husband and father, it's fitting that Carmacks be honored by this uninspired collection of gas stations and places to stay. The main reason to stop is the excellent **Tage Cho Hudan Interpretive Centre** (☏867-863-5830; admission by donation; ☺9am-4pm May-Sep). Volunteers explain aboriginal life past and present. Like elsewhere in the territory, residents here are keenly attuned to the land, which supplies them with game and fish throughout the year. A pretty 15-minute interpretive walk by the river provides a glimmer of insight into this life.

This is also the junction with the Robert Campbell Hwy (p771).

About 25km north of Carmacks, the **Five Finger Recreation Site** has excellent views of the treacherous stretch of the rapids that tested the wits of riverboat captains traveling between Whitehorse and Dawson. There's a steep 1.5km walk down to the rapids.

Minto

Easily missed – unless you're toting a canoe or kayak – Minto is where the Klondike Hwy leaves the route of the Gold Rush Trail. This is a popular place to put in for the four- to five-day trip down the Yukon River to Dawson City. It's about 72km north of Carmacks.

Stewart Crossing

Another popular place to get your canoe wet, Stewart Crossing is on the Stewart River, which affords a narrow and somewhat more rugged experience before it joins the Yukon to the west for the trip to Dawson.

Otherwise unexceptional, the village is the junction of the Klondike Hwy (Hwy 2) and the Silver Trail (Hwy 11).

North of Stewart Crossing the Klondike Hwy continues for 139 bland kilometers to the junction with the Dempster Hwy. From here it's only 40km to Dawson City.

DAWSON CITY

If you didn't know its history, Dawson would be a delightful place to pause for a while, plunging into its quirky culture and falling for its seductive, funky vibe. That it's one of the most historic and beautiful towns in Canada is like gold dust on a cake: unnecessary but damn nice.

Set on a narrow shelf at the confluence of the Yukon and Klondike Rivers, a mere 240km south of the Arctic Circle, Dawson City was the center of the Klondike Gold Rush.

Today, you can wander the dirt streets of Dawson, passing old buildings with dubious permafrost foundations leaning on each other for support (that's in comparison to the real drunks you'll see leaning on each other for support outside the local saloons). There's a rich cultural life, with many people finding Dawson the perfect place for free expression (that person doing a shot on the next bar stool may be a dancer, filmmaker, painter or a miner).

Dawson can be busy in the summer, especially during its festivals. But by September the days are getting short, the seasonal workers have fled south and the 2000 year-round residents (professionals, miners, First Nations, dreamers, artists and those who aren't sure where they fit) are settling in for another long and quiet winter.

History

In 1898 more than 30,000 prospectors milled the streets of Dawson – a few newly rich, but most without prospects and at odds with themselves and the world. Shops, bars and prostitutes relieved these hordes of what money they had, but Dawson's fortunes were tied to the gold miners and, as the boom ended, the town began a decades-long slow fade.

The territorial capital was moved to Whitehorse in 1952 and the town lingered on, surviving on the low-key but ongoing gold-mining industry. By 1970 the population was under 900. But then a funny thing happened on the way to Dawson's demise: it was rediscovered. Improvements to the Klondike Hwy and links to Alaska allowed the first major influx of summertime tourists, who found a charmingly moldering time capsule from the gold rush. Parks Canada designated much of the town as historic and began restorations.

◉ Sights

Dawson is small enough to walk around in a few hours, but you can easily fill three or more days with the many local things to see and do. If the summertime hordes get you down, head uphill for a few blocks where you'll find timeless old houses and streets.

Like a gold nugget on a tapped-out creek, street numbers are a rarity in Dawson. Unless noted otherwise, opening hours and times given here cover the period from mid-May to early September. For the rest of the year, most sights, attractions and many businesses are closed.

In a real boon to families, almost all attractions are free for kids 12 and under.

Klondike National Historic Sites
HISTORIC PARK
It's easy to relive the gold rush at myriad preserved and restored places. **Parks Canada** (www.pc.gc.ca/dawson) does an excellent job of providing information and tours. In addition to the individual sight and tour fees listed here, there are various good-value Parks Canada **passes** (adult $14-32); buy tickets and passes at the beautiful **Palace Grand Theatre** (King St; ◷9:30am-5:30pm), between 2nd and 3rd Aves.

For information, go to the Parks Canada desk in the VIC. See p780 for details on Dredge No 4.

Robert Service Cabin
(cnr 8th Ave & Hanson St; admission free; ◷2:30-4:30pm) Called the 'Bard of the Yukon,' poet and writer Robert W Service lived in this typical gold-rush cabin from 1909 to 1912. Don't miss the **dramatic readings** (adult $7; ◷1:30pm & 7pm).

Commissioner's Residence
(Font St; adult $7; ◷10am-5pm, tour times vary) Built in 1901 to house the territorial commissioner, this proud building was designed to give potential civic investors confidence in the city. The building was the longtime home of Martha Black, who came to the Yukon in 1898, owned a lumberyard and was elected to the Canadian Parliament at age 70. (*Martha Black* by Flo Whyard is a great book about this amazing woman.)

SS KenoYukon
(adult $7; ◷10am-6pm) The SS *Keno* was one of a fleet of paddle wheelers that worked the Yukon's rivers for more than half a century. Grounded along the waterfront, the boat re-creates a time before any highways.

Harrington's Store
(cnr 3rd Ave & Princess St; admission free; ◷9am-4:30pm) This old shop has historic photos from Dawson's heyday.

TOP CHOICE Jack London Interpretive Centre
MUSEUM
(Firth St; admission $5; ◷11am-6pm) In 1898 Jack London lived in the Yukon, the setting for his most popular stories, including *Call of the Wild* and *White Fang*. At the writer's cabin there are daily interpretive talks. A labor of love by historian Dick North, Dawne Mitchell and others, this place is a treasure trove of stories – including the search for the original cabin.

Dänojà Zho Cultural Centre CULTURAL CENTER
(☎867-993-6768; www.trondek.com; Front St; adult $5; ◷10am-6pm Mon-Sat) Inside this beautiful riverfront wood building there are displays and interpretative talks on the *Hän Hwëch'in* (River People) First Nations. The collection includes traditional artifacts and a re-creation of a 19th-century fishing camp. Check on the schedule for cultural tours and performances of authentic dances.

Dawson City Museum
MUSEUM
(☎867-993-5291; 5th Ave; adult $9; ◷10am-6pm) Make your own discoveries among the 25,000 gold rush artifacts at this museum. Engaging exhibits walk you through the grim lives of the miners. The museum is housed in the landmark 1901 Old Territorial Administration building.

Midnight Dome
PARK
The slide-scarred face of this hill overlooks the town to the north, but to reach the top you must travel south of town about 1km, turn left off the Klondike Hwy onto New Dome Rd, and continue for about 7km. The Midnight Dome, at 880m above sea level, offers great views of the Klondike Valley, Yukon River and Dawson City. There's also a steep **trail** that takes 90 minutes from Judge St in town; maps are available at the VIC.

Crocus Bluff & Cemeteries
MONUMENTS
A 15-minute walk up King St and Mary McCloud Rd near town leads to 10 **cemeteries**

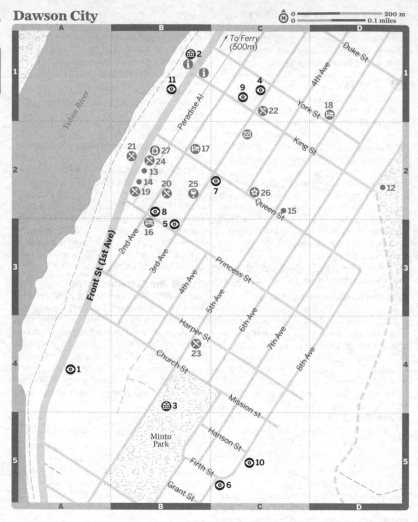

that are literally filled with characters. Among them: Joe Vogler, who fought to have Alaska secede from the US. He was buried here in 1993, having vowed not to be buried in an Alaska that wasn't free. Todd Palin (husband of Sarah) is among his acolytes.

Near the cemeteries, a short path out to pretty **Crocus Bluff** has excellent views of Dawson and the Klondike and Yukon Rivers. It is a short walk up King St from town. If driving, take New Dome Rd and turn at Mary McLeod Rd (ignoring the 'No Exit' signs).

Mines

The deeply scarred valleys around Dawson speak of the vast amounts of toil that went into the gold hunt. **Dredge No 4** (Bonanza Creek Rd; adult $7; ⊙10am-4pm, tour times vary), 13km off the Klondike Hwy, is a massive dredging machine that tore up the Klondike Valley and left the tailings, which remain as a vast, rippled blight on the landscape. The Parks Canada tours are absorbing.

Just 1.5km further up the valley, the Bonanza Creek **Discovery Site** is roughly where gold was first found in 1897. It's a quiet site today with a little water burbling through the rubble.

Galleries

Dawson has a thriving arts community. The **Klondike Institute for Art & Culture** (KIAC; ☑867-993-5005; cnr 3rd Ave & Queen St) has an impressive studio building, galleries and educational programs.

KIAC's exhibition space, the **ODD Gallery** (☑867-993-5005; cnr 2nd Ave & Princess St; ⊙hrs vary), shows local works.

Fortymile Gold Workshop/Studio (☑867-993-5690; 3rd Ave btwn York & King Sts) has gold creations from 30 local artists. Watch as jewelry is made from local refined gold, which is silky and has a rich yellow color, as opposed to the bling you see peddled on late-night TV.

🏃 Activities

Besides arriving by **canoe** or **kayak**, many people also exit Dawson via the Yukon River. A popular trip good for novices goes from Dawson for three days and 168km downstream to Eagle City, Alaska.

Dawson Trading Post (☑867-993-5316; Front St; canoe per day $30) rents out canoes and arranges longer trips. Dawson City River Hostel (p782), across the river, is the local agent for **Eagle Canoe Rentals** (www.eaglecanoerentals.com), with canoe rental for the three- to four-day trip to Eagle, plus return transport from US$125.

Besides the walks above town listed under Sights, a three-hour **hike to Moosehead**, an old First Nations village, is popular. The trail follows hillsides above the river north of town. Be sure to get a map at the VIC.

You can explore much of the Dawson area by bike, including the **Ridge Road Heritage Trail**, which winds through the gold fields south of town. Rent bikes at **Circle Cycle** (☑867-993-6270; cnr King St & 7th Ave; bikes per day $30) or the Dawson City River Hostel.

👉 Tours

Parks Canada docents, often in period garb, lead excellent **walking tours** (adult $7; ⊙daily) of Dawson. Learn about individual buildings and the many characters that walked the streets (many of whom could be called 'street-walkers'). You can also take a self-guided **audio tour** (adult $7; ◷9:30am-4:30pm).

TOP CHOICE Goldbottom Tours (☑867-993-5750; www.goldbottom.com; ticket office Front St; ◷daily) is run by the legendary Millar mining family. Tour their mine 15km up Hunker Creek Rd, which meets Hwy 2 just north of the airport. The 3½-hour tours cost $30 (children free) or you can include transport to/from Dawson for $40. You get to keep what you find. They also provide a shuttle to sites outside Dawson (Midnight Dome, Dredge No 4 etc) for $40.

Sail the Yukon on the **Klondike Spirit** (☑867-993-5323; www.klondikespirit.com; tickets Triple J Hotel, cnr 5th Ave & Queen St; tours from $50), a modern re-created paddle wheeler that offers day and dinner cruises.

✹ Festivals & Events

See p763 for Yukon events that include Dawson.

Dawson City Music Festival (☑867-993-5384; www.dcmf.com) Popular – tickets sell out two months in advance and the city fills up; reservations are essential (late July).

Discovery Days Celebrates the you-know-what of 1896. On the third Monday in August there are parades and picnics. Events begin days before, including an excellent art show.

🛏 Sleeping

Reservations are a good idea in July and August, although the VIC can help. Many places will pick you up at the airport; ask in advance. Unless otherwise stated, the following are open all year.

TOP CHOICE Bombay Peggy's INN **$$** (☑867-993-6969; www.bombaypeggys.com; cnr 2nd Ave & Princess St; r $90-200; ◷Mar-Dec; ❋◉) A renovated brothel, Peggy's allure is its period furnishings and spunky attitude. Budget 'snug' rooms share bathrooms. Rooms are plush in a way that will make you want to wear a garter. The bar is a classy oasis.

⊘ Klondike Kate's INN **$$** (☑867-993-6527; www.klondikekates.ca; cnr King St & 3rd Ave; cabins $120-140; ◷Apr-Sep; ◉) The 15 cabins behind the excellent restaurant of the same name are rustic without the rusticisms. High-speed internet, microwaves and fridges ensure comfort.

The porches are perfect for decompressing. Green practices are many.

Dawson City River Hostel HOTEL **$** (summer ☑867-993-6823; www.yukonhostels.com; dm $18-22, r from $46; ◷mid-May–Sep) This delightfully eccentric hostel is across the river from town and five minutes up the hill from the ferry landing. It has good views, cabins, platforms for tents and a communal bathhouse. Tent sites are $14. Owner Dieter Reinmuth is a noted Yukon author.

Aurora Inn INN **$** (☑867-993-6860; www.aurorainn.ca; 5th Ave; r $120-170; ◉) All 20 rooms in this European-style inn are large and comfortable. And if there's such a thing as Old World cleanliness, it's here: the admonishments to remove your (invariably) muddy shoes start at the entrance.

Downtown Hotel HOTEL **$$** (☑867-993-5346, 800-661-0514; www.downtownhotel.ca; cnr Queen St & 2nd Ave; r $95-150; ❋◉❈) A landmark hotel on a prominent corner, the fittingly named Downtown has 34 rooms in the main heritage building and 25 more in a modern annex. Not all have air-con; ask to see a couple as some are small and/or frumpy.

Yukon River Campground CAMPGROUND **$** (sites $12) On the western side of the river about 250m up the road to the right after you get off the ferry, this territorial campground has 98 shady sites.

Gold Rush Campground RV Park CAMPGROUND **$** (☑867-993-5247; 866-330-5006; www.goldrushcampground.com; cnr 5th Ave & York St; sites $20-40; ◷mid-May–mid-Sep; ❈) Convenience trumps atmosphere at this 83-site gravel parking lot for RVs.

✕ Eating

Picnickers, hikers and backcountry campers will find two good grocery stores in town. A **farmers market** (◷11am-5pm Sat mid-May–mid-Sep) thrives by the iconic waterfront gazebo. The sweet-as-candy carrots are the product of very cold nights. Try some birch syrup.

With exceptions noted below, most places close outside of summer.

TOP CHOICE Drunken Goat Taverna GREEK **$$** (☑867-993-5800; 2nd Ave; mains $12-25; ◷noon-9pm) Follow your eyes to the flowers, your ears to the Aegean music and your nose to the excellent Greek food, run 12-months-a-year by Tony Dovas. Out back there's a simple take-out with beer-absorbing pizzas in the evening ($10).

Klondike Kate's   FUSION $$
(☑867-993-6527; cnr King St & 3rd Ave; mains $8-25; ⊙8am-9pm Apr-Sep) Two ways to know spring has arrived: the river cracks up and Kate's reopens. Locals in the know prefer the latter. The long and inventive menu has fine sandwiches, pastas and fresh Yukon fish. Look for great specials. This is *the* place for breakfast.

La Table on 5th   FUSION $$
(☑867-993-6860; Aurora Inn, 5th Ave; mains $15-35; ⊙5-9pm) Ponder a passel of schnitzels or a bevy of steaks at this slightly formal continental restaurant. Make arrangements in advance and a local storyteller will join you at your table.

Cheechako's Bake Shop   BAKERY $
(☑867-993-6590; cnr Front & Princess Sts; meals $4-8; ⊙7am-7pm) A real bakery and a good one, on the main strip. Muffins, cookies and treats vie with sandwiches made on homemade bread for your attention.

River West   CAFE $
(☑867-993-6339; near cnr Front & Queen Sts; meals $4-7; ⊙7am-7pm Mar-Oct) Busy throughout the day, this excellent coffeehouse, bakery and cafe looks out on the Front St action. Grab an outside table.

🍺 Drinking

The spirit of the prospectors lives on in several saloons in Dawson City. On summer nights the action goes on until dawn, which would mean something if it weren't light all night.

TOP CHOICE **Bombay Peggy's**   PUB
(☑867-993-6969; cnr 2nd Ave & Princess St; ⊙11am-11pm) There's always a hint of pleasures to come swirling around the tables of Dawson's most inviting bar. Enjoy good beers, wines and mixed drinks inside or out.

Bars at Westminster Hotel   BARS
(3rd Ave; ⊙noon-late) These two bars carry the mostly affectionate monikers 'Snakepit,' 'Armpit' or simply 'Pit.' The places for serious drinkers, with live music many nights.

Billy Goat   PUB
(☑867-993-5800; 2nd Ave; ⊙5pm-1am) Not a branch of the famed Chicago original

but a nice, mannered lounge from Tony of Drunken Goat fame.

Downtown Hotel   PUB
(☑867-993-5346; cnr Queen St & 2nd Ave; ⊙11am-late) This unremarkable bar comes to life at 9pm in summer for what can best be called the 'Sourtoe Schtick.' Tourists line up to drink a shot of booze ($10) that has a pickled human toe floating in it. It's a long-running gag that's delightfully chronicled in Dieter Reinmuth's *The Saga of the Sourtoe*. (That the toe – it *is* real – looks much like a bit of beef jerky should give pause to anyone used to late-night Slim Jim jonesing...)

☆ Entertainment

TOP CHOICE **Diamond Tooth Gertie's Gambling Hall**   CASINO
(☑867-993-5575; cnr Queen St & 4th Ave; $6; ⊙7pm-2am mid-May–mid-Sep) This popular re-creation of an 1898 saloon is complete with small-time gambling, a honky-tonk piano and dancing girls. The casino helps promote the town and fund culture. Each night there are three floor shows heavy on corn and kicking legs.

🛍 Shopping

Maximilian's   BOOKSTORE
(☑867-993-6537; Front St; ⊙8am-8pm) Has an excellent selection of regional books, magazines, out-of-town newspapers and topographical and river maps.

Dawson Trading Post   CURIOS/OUTDOOR GEAR
(☑867-993-5316; Front St; ⊙9am-7pm) Sells interesting old mining gadgets, bear traps ($500) and old mammoth tusks so you can take up carving. It has a good bulletin board.

ℹ Information

Much of Dawson is closed October to May. The biweekly, volunteer-run *Klondike Sun* covers special events and activities.

CIBC ATM (2nd Ave) Near Queen St.

Dawson City Community Library (☑867-993-5571; cnr 5th Ave & Queen St; ⊙11am-8pm Tue-Sat but can vary) Has internet access.

Dawson Medical Clinic (☑867-993-5744; Church St; ⊙9am-noon & 1-5pm Mon-Fri) A private clinic near 6th Ave; nurses are always on call at the adjoining government clinic (☑867-993-4444).

Post office (☑867-993-5342; 3rd Ave; ⊙8:30am-5:30pm Mon-Fri, 11:30am-2:30pm Sat) Between King and Queen Sts.

TastyByte Internet Cafe (☑867-993-6105; Front St; per hr $12; ☺8am-4pm) Good coffee and wi-fi access.

VIC (☑867-993-5566; cnr Front & King Sts; ☺8am-8pm May-Sep) Parks Canada information is split between here and the Palace Grand Theatre on King St between 2nd and 3rd Aves.

Western Arctic Information Centre (☑867-993-6167; Front St; ☺8am-8pm mid-May–mid-Sep) Maps and information on the NWT and the Dempster Hwy.

ℹ Getting There & Away

Dawson City is 527km from Whitehorse. Public transport to/from Whitehorse is an ongoing problem – there usually is none as you can see by the pleas for rides on the bulletin board by River West. Should you fly in, note there are no rental cars either.

Dawson City airport (YDA)About 19km east of town off the Klondike Hwy.

Air North (☑800-661-0407; www.flyairnorth. com) Serves Whitehorse, Old Crow, Inuvik in the NWT and Fairbanks in Alaska.

Alaska/Yukon Trails (☑800-770-7275; www. alaskashuttle.com) Runs shuttles between Dawson and Tok, Alaska via the Top of the World Hwy and Chicken, Alaska, but confirm all details in advance.

Dawson City to Alaska

From Dawson City, the free ferry crosses the Yukon River to the scenic **Top of the World Hwy** (Hwy 9). Only open in summer, the mostly paved 106km-long ridge-top road to the US border has superb vistas across the region.

You'll continue to feel on top of the world as you cross the border. The land is barren alpine meadows with jutting rocks and often grazing caribou. The **border crossing** (☺9am-9pm Yukon time/8am-8pm Alaska time 15 May–15 Sep) has strict hours – if you're late you'll have to wait until the next day.

On the US side, Alaska shows its xenophobic side, as the 19km connection to the Taylor Hwy (Hwy 5) is mostly dirt and often impassable after storms (expect to get dirt in parts of your vehicle and person you didn't think possible). The old gold-mining town of **Eagle** on the Yukon River is 105km north. Some 47km south over somewhat better roads, you encounter **Chicken**, a delightful place of free-thinkers happy to sell you a stupid T-shirt at one of the gas station-cafes or offer their views regarding government bureaucrats. Another 124km

south and you reach the Alaska Hwy, where a turn east takes you to the Yukon. Just a tick west, **Tok** has services and motels. Alaska time is one hour earlier than the Yukon.

DEMPSTER HIGHWAY

Rather than name this road for an obscure Mountie (William Dempster), this road should be named the Firestone Hwy or the Goodyear Hwy, for the number of tires it's sent to an explosive demise. This 736km thrill ride is one of North America's great adventure roads, winding through stark mountains and emerald valleys, across huge tracts of tundra and passing Tombstone Territorial Park.

The Dempster (Hwy 5 in the Yukon, Hwy 8 in the NWT) starts 40km southeast of Dawson City off the Klondike Hwy and heads north over the Ogilvie and Richardson mountains beyond the Arctic Circle and on to Inuvik in the NWT, near the shores of the Beaufort Sea.

Road Conditions

Built on a thick base of gravel to insulate the permafrost underneath (which would otherwise melt, causing the road to sink without a trace), the Dempster is open most of the year, but the best time to travel is between June and early September, when the ferries over the Peel and Mackenzie Rivers operate. In winter, ice forms a natural bridge over the rivers, which become ice roads. The Dempster is closed during the spring thaw and the winter freeze-up; the timing of these vary by the year and can occur from mid-April to June and mid-October to December, respectively.

Graveled almost its entire length, the highway has a well-deserved reputation for being rough on vehicles. Travel with extra gas and tires and expect to use them. Check road conditions in the Yukon (☑511; www.511yukon.ca) and the NWT (☑800-661-0750; www.dot.gov.nt.ca); the Western Arctic Information Centre (p784) in Dawson City is a good resource. It takes 10 to 12 hours to drive to Inuvik without stopping for a break. (Given that William Dempster regularly made 700km dog-sled journeys in sub-zero weather, this rugged and challenging road is properly named after all.)

TOMBSTONE TERRITORIAL PARK

Shades of green and charcoal color the wide valleys here and steep ridges are dotted with small glaciers and alpine lakes. Summer feels tentative but makes its statement with a burst of purple wildflowers in July. Clouds sweep across the tundra, bringing squalls punctuated by brilliant sun. Stand amid this and you'll know the meaning of the sound of silence.

Tombstone Territorial Park (www.yukonparks.ca) lies along Dempster Hwy for about 50km. The park's only formal **campground** (sites $12) has a new and excellent **Interpretive Centre** (◷9am–5pm late May–mid-Sep), which offers walks and talks. It's 71km from the start of the highway and is set in along the headwaters of the Yukon River just before **Tombstone Mountain**, the point where the trees run out and the truly wild northern scenery begins.

There are good **day hikes** near the campground, as well as longer, more rigorous **treks** for experienced wilderness hikers. Permits are required for backcountry camping, especially at several lakes popular in summer. (The park's backcountry camping guide shows refreshing honesty in its answer to this frequently asked question: 'Will you come looking for me if I don't return?' 'No.')

Tombstone is an easy day trip from Dawson City (112km each way). With preparations, however, a multiday park adventure could be the highlight of your trip. The 2011 movie *The Big Year* with Steve Martin, Owen Wilson and Jack Black was partly shot in the park.

Sleeping & Eating

Accommodations and vehicle services along the route are few. The **Klondike River Lodge** (☑867-993-6892) at the south junction rents jerry cans for gas that you can take north and return on the way back.

The next available services are 369km north in Eagle Plains. The **Eagle Plains Hotel** (☑867-993-2453; eagleplains@northwestel. net; r $100-130) is open year-round and offers 32 rooms. The next service station is 180km further at **Fort McPherson** in the NWT. From there it's 216km to Inuvik.

The Yukon government has three campgrounds – at **Tombstone Mountain** (72km from the start of the highway), **Engineer Creek** (194km) and **Rock River** (447km). There's also a NWT government campground at **Nitainlaii Territorial Park**, 9km south of Fort McPherson. Sites at these campgrounds are $12.

ARCTIC PARKS

North of the Arctic Circle, the Yukon's population numbers a few hundred. It's a lonely land with little evidence of humans and only the hardiest venture here during the short summers.

The 280-person village of **Old Crow** (www. oldcrow.ca) is home to the Vuntut Gwitch'in First Nations and is unreachable by vehicle. Residents subsist on caribou from the legendary 130,000-strong Porcupine · herd, which migrates each year between the Arctic National Wildlife Refuge (ANWR) in Alaska and the Yukon. Not surprisingly, the locals are against the perennial threat of oil drilling on the US side of the border in the ANWR.

On the Yukon side of this vast flat arctic tundra, a large swath of land is now protected in two adjoining national parks, Vuntut and Ivvavik. Information on both can be obtained from the Parks Canada office in Inuvik, NWT (p807), where you can get information on the very limited options for organizing visits to the parks (think chartered planes, long treks over land and water, and total self-sufficiency). There are no facilities of any kind in the parks.

Vuntut National Park

Vuntut, a Gwitch'in word meaning 'among the lakes,' is about 100km north of Old Crow, where there is a one-person **park office** (☑867-667-3910; www.pc.gc.ca/vuntut). The 4345-sq-km park was declared a national park in 1993. It lives up to its name with scores of lakes and ponds and is home to 500,000 waterbirds in late summer.

THE YUKON IS MELTING, MELTING...

The Yukon could serve as exhibit one in the case for climate change. Every corner of the territory is experiencing rapid changes in the environment because it's getting warmer a lot quicker than anybody ever imagined. In the far north, Herschel Island (p786) is literally dissolving as the permafrost thaws. One gruesome sign: long-buried coffins floating to the surface of the melting earth. Unesco has listed it as one of the world's most threatened historic sites.

In Dawson City locals have for decades bet on the day each spring when the Yukon River suddenly breaks up and begins flowing. Detailed records show that the mean date for this has moved one week earlier in the last century to May 5, with the pace accelerating.

Perhaps the most easily seen is the beetle devastation in Kluane National Park (p773). Preparing the Yukon for a radically different and warmer future is now a major political topic, even if nobody has the answers.

Archaeological sites contain fossils of ancient animals such as mammoths, plus evidence of early humans.

Ivvavik National Park

Ivvavik, meaning 'a place for giving birth to and raising the young,' is situated along the Beaufort Sea adjoining Alaska and covers 10,170 sq km. The park (www.pc.gc.ca/ivvavik) is one of the calving grounds for the Porcupine caribou herd; thousands are born over a three-week period beginning in late May.

The park holds one of the world's great white-water rivers, the **Firth River**, which can be navigated for 130km from Margaret Lake near the Alaskan border north to the Beaufort Sea. When the river meets Joe Creek, the valley narrows to a canyon and there are numerous areas of white water rated Class II and III+.

Herschel Island (Qiqiktaruk) Territorial Park

Its aboriginal name means 'it is island' and indeed it is. Barely rising above the waters of Mackenzie Bay on the Beaufort Sea, **Herschel Island** (☑867-667-5648; www.yukonparks.ca) has a long tradition of human habitation. The Inuvialuit lived here for thousands of years, making the most of the prime position on the seal-rich waters. In the late 1800s American whalers set up shop at **Pauline Cove**, a natural port deep enough for ocean vessels and protected from northerly winds and drifting pack ice.

Abandoned in 1907, the whalers left behind several wooden buildings which survive today, often appearing ghost-like out of the gloom. Evidence can also be found of missionaries, whose position as redeemers of souls was never embraced locally. Today Inuvialuit families use the island for traditional hunting.

There are no permanent residents, although in summer a growing number of scientists set up shop, monitoring the island's steady disintegration as it melts away (p786).

Summer visits to the island are possible via daytime tours from Inuvik. The flight across the Mackenzie Delta to reach the island is spectacular and park rangers often give tours. Backcountry camping during the short summer season (from late June to August) is possible. There are fire rings, wind shelters, pit toilets and limited water. Others visit the island at the end of a kayak trip in Ivvavik National Park.

Northwest Territories

Includes »

Why Go?

On a planet containing seven billion people, it's difficult to imagine that there are still places as empty as the Northwest Territories (NWT), a vast swathe of boreal forest and arctic tundra five times the size of the United Kingdom but with a population of a small provincial town. Nineteenth-century gold prospectors passed it over as too remote, modern Canadians (if they head north at all) prefer to romanticize about the iconic Nunavut or the grandiose Yukon; while more people orbit the earth each year than visit lonely Aulavik, one of the territory's four national parks.

What they're missing is esoteric and unique, a potent combo of epic, accessible terrain and singular aboriginal culture that contains one of the world's greatest waterfalls, North America's deepest lake and enough brutal wilderness to keep a modern-day David Livingstone happy for a couple of lifetimes.

Best Places to Eat

» Bullocks (p795)
» Fuego International Restaurant (p795)
» Wildcat Café (p795)
» Tonimoes (p808)

Best Places to Stay

» Arctic Chalet (p807)
» Fort of the Forks (p803)
» Embleton House B&B (p794)
» Heritage Hotel (p806)

When to Go

Yellowknife

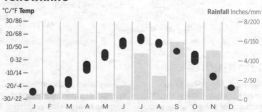

June See the midnight sun at the Summer Solstice Festival in Yellowknife

July–August Hyperactive summer season; good for fishing and canoeing in lakes and rivers

December–March Best time for aurora borealis viewing with long nights and dark skies

Highlights

① Pack two spare tires and more film than you can fathom for the gobsmacking drive from Inuvik along the **Dempster Highway** (p807)

② Rent a kayak and go for a float on the **Great Slave Lake** (p793) amid technicolor houseboats and barnstorming floatplanes

③ J-stroke past gorgeous hot springs, haunted gorges and gorging bears in the paddlers' paradise of **Nahanni National Park Reserve** (p804)

④ Be buffaloed by mating snakes, vanishing rivers and the eponymous ungulates of **Wood Buffalo National Park** (p802)

⑤ Go to the dogs during a husky-team ride near **Yellowknife** (p794) beneath the aurora borealis or the midnight sun

⑥ Hit road and water on a summer excursion along the **Ingraham Trail** (p797)

⑦ Go where few have gone before and hike part or all of the **Canol Heritage Trail** (p806)

NORTHWEST TERRITORIES FAST FACTS

» Population: 43,529

» Area: 1,346,106 km sq

» Capital: Yellowknife

» Quirky fact: The world's first grolar bear (grizzly/polar bear hybrid) was discovered in the wild in the NWT in 2006.

History

Archaeologists say the first NWT residents, ancestors of today's Dene, tramped here from Asia about 14,000 years ago. The Inuvialuit, who migrated from Alaska, showed up more recently.

With the prospect of wealth from the fur trade, Europeans penetrated northern Canada in the 18th and 19th centuries, and on their heels came missionaries. Even well into the 1900s the region was largely the fiefdom of competing churches and the Hudson's Bay Company.

After oil turned up near Tulita in the 1920s, a territorial government was formed. In the '30s, gold near Yellowknife and radium near Great Bear Lake brought an influx of non-Aboriginals. Federal health, welfare and education programs began in earnest in the 1950s and '60s. In the 1970s the Dene and Inuvialuit emerged as a political force, demanding a say in – and benefits from – resource extraction on their land.

In 1999 the territory was cut in half, with the eastern and central Arctic becoming Nunavut. The remaining population is evenly divided between Aboriginals and non-Aboriginals. The latter group, and to a smaller extent the former, have benefited from the recent oil, gas and diamond development, which have thrown the territorial economy into hyperdrive.

Land & Climate

The NWT is a supersized wilderness reaching poleward from the 60th parallel. The south is evergreen flatlands, the east is the boulderscape of the Canadian Shield, and toothy mountains rear up from the west. Canada's jumbo river, the Mackenzie, bisects the territory, draining two gargantuan lakes, Great Slave and Great Bear. In the North the territory hurdles the treeline and gathers in a few bleak High Arctic islands.

Weatherwise, summers range from miserable to stupendous. In Yellowknife and Inuvik, highs average 20°C, but on any given day you could find yourself sweltering or shivering. One sure thing is daylight: from May through July there's no end of it. June's the driest summer month, but lake ice can linger until the month's end. Most visitors come in July and August.

Winters are long, dark and punishing. In January, lows in Yellowknife collapse to -40°C and daylight is feeble. If you're keen on visiting in the snowy season, try March or April, when the sun climbs and the mercury follows suit.

❶ Getting There & Away

AIR

For air travelers, Edmonton is the main gateway to the NWT. **First Air** (www.firstair.ca), **Canadian North** (www.canadiannorth.com) and **Air Canada** (www.aircanada.com) fly daily from there to Yellowknife, starting at around $600 return. Canadian North also flies from Edmonton to Hay River (about $670 return). **Northwestern Air Lease** (www.nwal.ca) serves Fort Smith direct from Edmonton (around $1010 return).

From Whitehorse, Yukon, First Air flies to Yellowknife (about $1100 return, via Fort Simpson), while **Air North** (www.flyairnorth.com) goes to Inuvik ($570 return).

From Iqaluit, Nunavut, both First Air and Canadian North depart for Yellowknife (about $1800 return).

BUS

The sole bus link to the southern NWT is provided by Greyhound Canada (p884), which runs year-round from Edmonton to Hay River for $173 one way. From there, a regional carrier connects to other communities (see p796).

❶ NWT INFORMATION PORTAL

Northwest Territories Tourism (www.explorenwt.com) is the portal for official visitor info. It's got a dashing and detailed website, can field off-the-wall inquiries, and will distribute all manner of tourism literature, including the annual *NWT Explorers' Guide*. If you plan to drive extensively in the NWT, grab a copy of the staggeringly comprehensive *Milepost Guide*, the bible of Northern motoring, available at most bookstores.

CAR & MOTORCYCLE

There are two overland routes to the southern NWT. From Edmonton, a long (and, frankly, monotonous) day's drive up Hwy 35 brings you to the NWT border, 84km shy of Enterprise. Alternatively, from Fort Nelson, British Columbia (on the Alaska Hwy), the Liard Trail runs 137 potholed (but paved) kilometers to the border. Fort Liard is another 38km north.

If you're heading up to the Mackenzie Delta, you can set out from Dawson City, Yukon, on the shockingly scenic Dempster Hwy, which reaches the NWT boundary after 465km.

❶ Getting Around

AIR

Half of the NWT's 32 communities are fly-in only, accessed from hub airports in Yellowknife, Norman Wells and Inuvik. Service in the North Slave region is provided by **Air Tindi** (www.airtindi.com), in the Mackenzie Valley by **North-Wright Air** (www.north-wrightairways.com), and in the Mackenzie Delta by **Aklak Air** (www.aklakair.ca).

BUS

Frontier Coachlines (frontiercoach@nt.sympatico.ca) meets Greyhound Canada in Hay River, and offers connecting buses to Yellowknife (five times a week), Fort Smith (three times a week) and Fort Simpson (twice a week).

CAR & MOTORCYCLE

To best appreciate the NWT, you need wheels. Automobiles can be rented in major communities. For Yellowknife car-rental agencies, see p797; for other towns, contact the local tourism office for information.

The territory has two highway networks: a southern system, linking most communities in the North Slave, South Slave and Deh Cho regions; and the Dempster Hwy, which winds through the Mackenzie Delta. Getting to the Delta from southern NWT requires a two-day detour through BC and the Yukon.

In summer, free ferries cross several rivers; in winter, vehicles drive across on 4ft-thick ice. Travel is interrupted for several weeks during 'break-up' (April and May) and, often, 'freeze-up' (December or January). For ferry information, call ☎800-661-0750. The major crossing, at the Mackenzie River on Hwy 3, may soon be obviated by construction of a $150 million bridge.

Before traveling, call ☎800-661-0750 for highway reports. See also p886 for general information about driving safely in Canada.

Yellowknife

Adrift amid the droning bush planes and paint-peeled houseboats of Yellowknife's Old Town, it's still possible to detect a palpable frontier spirit. It's as if you're standing on the edge of a large, undiscovered and barely comprehensible wilderness – and realistically (you can scratch that simile), you *are*. Draw a line north from Yellowknife to the Arctic Ocean and you won't cross a single road.

Subarctic Yellowknife supports 50% of the population of the NWT (20,000), a spicy if sometimes discordant stew of Dene and Métis from across the territory; Inuit and Inuvialuit from further north; grizzled

---

NORTHWEST TERRITORIES ITINERARIES

One Week

After flying to **Yellowknife**, spend the morning getting the scoop on the NWT at the **Prince of Wales Northern Heritage Centre**. Then amble down to **Old Town**, grab lunch at the famous **Wildcat Café** and summit **Bush Pilot's Monument**. The lake looks inviting, eh? Rent a canoe and leisurely circumnavigate Latham Island, gawking at the shacks, mansions, floatplanes, and houseboats. Righteously fatigued, repair to **Bullock's Bistro** to sip beer, sup on whitefish and watch the sun not set.

Next morning, rent a car, pack hiking boots and a fishing rod, and explore lake-lined **Ingraham Trail**. Break out the picnic basket at Cameron Falls.

Now motor west toward the **Mackenzie Bison Sanctuary** and get close-up snapshots of these woolly behemoths. Car-camp your way along the **Waterfalls Route**, then backtrack to **Fort Simpson**. Join a flightseeing tour into **Nahanni National Park Reserve** and lunch at the legendary Virginia Falls.

Two Weeks

Skip the road trip. Fly from Yellowknife to Fort Simpson, meet your outfitter and spend 10 days paddling the paradisiacal **South Nahanni River**.

non-Aboriginal pioneers; get-rich-quick newcomers from southern Canada; plus Armenians, Somalis and other more recent immigrants.

Named Somba K'e (Place of Money) in the local Tlicho language, the city has served as territorial capital since 1967 and a mining hub for a good three decades longer. Diamonds have now replaced gold as the main regional pocket-liner, but the settlement is happy to be stuck in its own frigid time-warp and remains more geographically isolated than its initial demeanor suggests.

The black, cryogenic winters can break your spirit, but in the hyperactive summers Yellowknife is doable in shorts and a large dousing of insect repellent. Not surprisingly, the territory's greatest diversity of shops and restaurants are here.

History

When the first Europeans reached Great Slave Lake in 1771, the north shore was home to the Tetsot'ine who were dubbed the Yellowknives due to their penchant for copper blades. Wars and foreign diseases eradicated them, but on the map the moniker remained.

More than a century later, Klondike-bound prospectors on Yellowknife Bay unearthed a different yellow metal: hard-rock gold. By the mid-1930s, bush planes had made the area accessible to commercial mining. Yellowknife became a boomtown.

In 1967, when Ottawa decided to devolve management of the NWT, Yellowknife, as the most populous town was picked as capital. The community began to shift from hardscrabble outpost to buttoned-down bureaucratic hub. That shift accelerated horrifically in 1992 when a bitter labor dispute at Giant Mine led to the underground-bombing death of nine strikebreakers. Roger Warren, an unemployed miner, went to jail for life.

Since then, gold mining has ceased in Yellowknife. Four fly-in kimberlite mines north of town are now fueling a new boom, making diamonds the city's best friend.

◉ Sights

DOWNTOWN

Uphill from the Old Town, Yellowknife's downtown was built – quite literally – on gold in the 1940s and '50s. Things really took off post 1967 when the city became the NWT's territorial capital.

FREE **Prince of Wales Northern Heritage Centre** MUSEUM
(www.pwnhc.ca; ◷10:30am-5pm Mon-Fri, noon-5pm Sat & Sun Sep-May) Acting as a historical and cultural archive for the whole NWT, the well laid-out and exhaustive Northern Heritage Centre, opened by the Prince of Wales in 1979, is pleasantly situated overlooking Frame Lake. Here, expertly assembled displays address natural history, European exploration, Northern aviation and, especially, Dene and Inuit ways. And, unusually for super-expensive Yellowknife, it's free.

FREE **Legislative Assembly**
NOTABLE BUILDING
(www.assembly.gov.nt.ca; ◷9am-6pm Mon-Fri, tours given at 10:30am) In 1993 the NWT government coughed up $25 million to build the impressive, igloo-shaped Legislative Assembly, which is also off 48th St and near Frame Lake. You can learn about the territory's aboriginal-style government by joining a free hour-long tour. There's also excellent Northern art throughout.

OLD TOWN

There are plenty of living people older than the city of Yellowknife but, although haphazard 'Old Town' only dates from the mid 1930s, its ramshackle streets wedged between Back and Yellowknife Bays have a tangible gold-rush-era atmosphere. Here funky cabins and eye-catching subarctic-style mansions share views with B&Bs, floating homes and a couple of legendary fish shacks, namely the Wild Cat and Bullocks. At the tip of Old Town, N'Dilo (dee-lo, meaning 'end of the road') is Yellowknife's aboriginal village.

You can procure a leaflet outlining an Old Town heritage walking tour from the Northern Frontier Visitor Centre.

Bush Pilot's Monument MONUMENT
Perched atop 'The Rock,' a large outcrop right before the bridge to Latham Island, this simple needle pays homage to the gutsy bush pilots who opened up the NWT. Climb the stairs to the viewpoint where you can watch modern floatplane traffic and envy the people on polychromatic houseboats in the bay. Summer sunsets – if you can stay up that late – are stunning.

The Wild Cat Café HISTORICAL BUILDING
An original town structure dating from 1937, this tiny log cabin has been preserved

NORTHWEST TERRITORIES

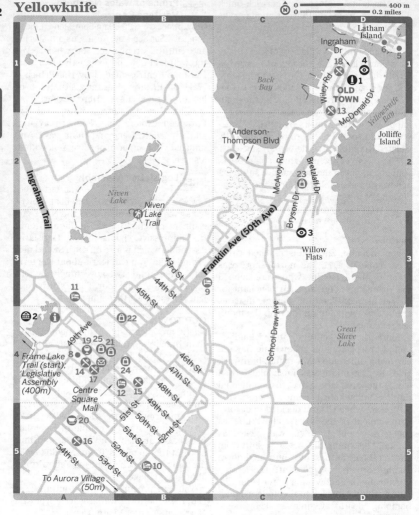

and turned into one of the city's most well-known restaurants, the Wild Cat. Debate raged recently when the new French-Canadian vendor tried to change its name to Le Wild Cat. The moral: don't mess with tradition.

Ragged Ass Rd   LANDMARK
Named by gold-rush-era prospectors who had gone stony broke (ragged ass), this road was immortalized in a song and album by Canadian rock musician Tom Cochrane (himself the son of a bush pilot) in 1995. The street sign subsequently went missing so many times that the city authorities start-

ing selling copies as souvenirs. Mansions now outnumber the sagging gold-rush-era cabins on the street.

🏃 Activities
Cross-country Skiing
The nexus for ski activities is **Yellowknife Ski Club** (www.skiyellowknife.com), whose operations are based on Hwy 3 2km north of the Explorer Hotel on the north side of town. There are 14km of groomed and lit trails here. Alternatively you can don skis and sally forth across the frozen Yellowknife Bay.

Yellowknife

Hiking

There are various hikes in and around town. The longest and best is the 9km **Frame Lake Trail**, around the eponymous lake. Starting downtown in Capital Area Park proceed clockwise past the Northern Heritage Centre and Legislative Assembly. On the northern side of the lake the trail goes off-piste over rocky outcrops and boreal forest typical of the Canadian Shield. By branching off near the hospital on the lake's western side you can join the 1.2km **Range Lake Trail**. Additional spurs connect to the precipitous **Jackfish Lake Trail** and the groomed **Niven Lake Trail**, which is more of a suburban stroll.

In popular **Fred Henne Territorial Park** (☉mid-May–mid-Sep), opposite the airport off Hwy 3, there's chilly swimming at **Long Lake Beach** and hiking on the 4km **Prospector's Trail**. Get the map from the park office, as the trail's not always clear.

Knackered backpackers can shower at **Ruth Inch Memorial Pool** (6001 Franklin Ave; ☉6am-11pm Mon-Thu, 6am-10:30pm Fri, noon-9:30pm Sat, noon-11pm Sun), which has a whirlpool and steam room.

Kayaking

On hot, bug-infested days, the water is the best place to be. **Narwal Adventure Training & Tours** (www.narwal.ca; 4702 Anderson-Thompson Blvd), run out of a B&B on Back Bay (part of the Great Slave Lake), rents canoes, kayaks ($45 per day) and bikes (per

hour/day $5/20), and also offers tours and lessons. Call ahead.

Overlander Sports (www.overlandersports.com; 4909 50th St; ☉9:30am-6pm Mon-Sat), Yellowknife's main outfitter store, rents canoes and kayaks (per day/week $45/200) in summer and cross-country skis ($25 per day) in winter.

☞ Tours

Dog-sledding, an invitation to a Dene fish barbecue, overnighting in a trapper's tent, sightseeing from a bush plane; Yellowknife offers plenty of 'only-in-the-NWT' experiences. Check out the *Explorers' Guide*, available from the Northern Frontier Visitors Centre for more options.

Air Tindi   SIGHTSEEING
(☎867-669-8200; www.airtindi.com; 35 Mitchell Rd) Offers excellent 30-minute tours over the city, the Ingraham Trail and Yellowknife Bay ($225 for up to three people, $495 for four to nine people). There's also a dramatic four-hour tour to Great Slave Lake's cliff-flanked East Arm, with an hour-long stop for hiking ($1565 for up to three people, $3015 for four to eight people).

Arctic Escapes   SIGHTSEEING
(☎867-445-2829; www.aetravel.ca) Conducts a leisurely 1½-hour walking tour of historic Old Town for $29 per person, or 30-minute bush plane ride for $85 per person.

North Star Adventures ADVENTURE
(☎867-446-2900; www.northstaradventures.ca)
This aboriginal-owned and -operated company offers excellent cultural trips, including a fish camp package ($199 per person), an overnight Trapper's Tent package ($249 per person), three-hour aurora-viewing boat trips ($150 per person), and snowmobile trips on Great Slave Lake ($50 per hour).

Beck's Kennels DOG-SLEDDING
(☎867-873-5603; www.beckskennels.com; 124 Curry Dr) The Becks are the NWT's mushing royalty. In winter, go for an 8km guided dog-sled tour ($60) or learn to drive your own team ($85). In summer the dogs pull wheeled sleds.

Bluefish Services FISHING
(☎867-873-4818; www.bluefishservices.ca) Bluefish takes fisherfolk out on Great Slave Lake to battle grayling, pike and lake trout. Prices range from $125 for 4½ hours up to $275 for 10 hours. It also offers simple one-hour boat tours ($39), and 2½-hour bird-watching excursions ($110).

Aurora Village AURORA-VIEWING
(☎867-669-0006; www.auroravillage.com; 5203 54th St) These guys are specialists in aurora-viewing trips on special heated seats ($120 including transport, drinks and snacks). They also offer dog-sledding ($90), snowmobiling ($95), and snowshoeing ($95).

✵ Festivals & Events

For a capital city, Yellowknife has few quality festivals. The stellar exception is **Folk on the Rocks** (www.folkontherocks.com; day/weekend pass $45/65; ⊙3 days mid-Jul), a groovefest on Long Lake featuring everything from hip-hop to Dene drumming. It draws musicians from northern and southern Canada.

The **Summer Solstice Festival** (www.solsticefestival.ca; ⊙late Jun) is actually a series of unrelated events, including cultural performances on National Aboriginal Day (June 21), and, most years, Raven Mad Daze, a downtown street fair.

The city's official winter bash, **Caribou Carnival** (www.cariboucarnival.com; ⊙Mar), feels a bit like tired self-parody. Held on frozen Frame Lake, it involves cabin-feverish locals competing in contests such as moose calling. Far more vibrant is the **Snowking Winter Festival** (www.snowking.ca; ⊙Mar), run by a grizzled houseboater who hosts concerts, theatrical performances and hockey games at a giant ice-palace he builds on Yellowknife Bay.

Also in March is the **Diavik 150**, the NWT's top sled-dog race, which takes place over three days on Great Slave Lake.

🛏 Sleeping

When it comes to accommodations, Yellowknife is functional at best. It has few raveworthy lodgings of any kind and no hostels, making camping the only budget option. In general, B&Bs are the best deals and Old Town has quite a few. Enquire at the visitors centre.

TOP CHOICE **Embleton House B&B** B&B $$
(☎867-873-2892; 5203 52nd St; s/d with shared bathroom $85/125, with private bathroom $148/170; @🛜) Convenient to downtown, this well-kitted-out B&B offers two options: three rooms with a shared bathroom and kitchen, or four decorative themed suites with private whirlpool baths, complimentary computers and kitchenettes (with breakfast ingredients included). The owners are extremely congenial and both the price and facilities outweigh any downtown hotel.

Arnica Inn MOTEL $$
(☎867-873-8511; www.arnicainn.com; 4115 Franklin Ave; r $149; ✳🛜) The former Red Coach Inn is looking a little plusher these days after some recent upgrading but is still locally run. Rooms are clean, large and motel-style and service is laid-back but friendly. Location-wise it's handily placed halfway between downtown and Old Town.

Explorer Hotel HOTEL $$$
(☎867-873-3531; www.explorerhotel.ca; 4825 49th Ave; r $198-210; 🛜) Looming over downtown, this generic high-rise has comfortable modern rooms, great views, a restaurant and a lounge. A shuttle is available from the airport.

Yellowknife Inn HOTEL $$
(☎867-873-2601; www.yellowknifeinn.com; 5010 49th St; r from $150; 🛜) Trying hard to nab the billing as Yellowknife's fanciest hotel, this recently revamped inn still falls a few yards wide of boutique status. Attached to the Centre Square Mall it also runs the adjacent Latitudes Restaurant and MacKenzie Lounge.

Fred Henne Territorial Park CAMPGROUND $
(☎867-920-2472; www.campingnwt.ca; off Hwy 3; walk-in/nonpowered/powered sites $15/22/28; ⊙mid-May–mid-Sep) This is the closest campground to town. Opposite the airport, it has full facilities, including showers and toilets. You can walk to downtown in under 40

minutes using the Jackfish and Frame Lake trails. Those with their own transport can also camp along the Ingraham Trail

✕ Eating

First the bad news: almost half the restaurant franchises in Yellowknife are run by the same chef. Now the good news: he's Québecois, the next best thing to French. While the food quality here is good for a town of approximately 20,000, beware of inflated prices. Basic sandwiches or salads start at $12 a pop.

Bar a couple of quirky gems in the Old Town, most restaurants are on or just off Franklin Ave.

TOP CHOICE Bullock's Bistro   SEAFOOD $$

(cnr Ingraham Dr & Wiley Rd; mains $17-28; ⊙noon-9pm Mon-Sat, 2-9pm Sun, often closed Oct) Take away Bullocks and you take away half of Yellowknife's personality – this scruffy old fish shack is insanely popular despite abrupt (verging on rude) service, lack of printed menus, a help-yourself drinks fridge and ridiculously expensive prices. The secret: fantastically fresh fish, whale-sized portions, loads of character and the exciting notion that you never know what's going to happen next. The decor is backwoods cabin meets *Hell's Kitchen* and the clientele is bush pilots mingled with thick-skinned locals. Arrive early and prepare to be yelled at.

Fuego International Restaurant

MEDITERRANEAN $$$

(4915 50th St; mains from $25) This new-ish very un-Yellowknife restaurant stands in marked ▓▓▓▓▓▓▓▓ ▓▓ ▓▓▓ ▓▓▓ ▓▓▓▓▓ ▓▓ ▓▓▓ ▓▓▓▓▓ ▓▓▓ cy Fuego wouldn't look out of place in Toronto, with its plush furnishings and mood lighting. The food is modern fusion with Spanish inflections and there's live music most nights to fill the gaps between courses. Upstairs is the more casual Twist Lounge.

Wildcat Café   CANADIAN $$

(cnr Wiley Rd & Doornbos Ln; ⊙Jun-Sep) A bit of history that's worth a visit in its own right, the Wildcat has been churning food out of this modest Old Town log cabin since 1937. Saved from demolition in 1976, it currently operates under a different vendor each summer, meaning the menu, prices and opening hours vary. There's a pleasant summer deck and a popular ice-cream window.

Nico's Café   CAFE $

(480 Range Lake Rd; ⊙7am-6pm Mon-Fri, 9am-6pm Sat) This new cafe in the equally new Centre Ice Plaza is part of Nico's Market. A vital cog

in Chef Pierre's burgeoning culinary empire, it serves tasty European-style snacks and cappuccino in real porcelain cups.

Surly Bob's   CANADIAN $$

(4910 Franklin Ave; mains from $12) Yes the proprietor's named Bob and yes, he's sometimes surly; but you don't come to this subterranean sports bar for pleases and thank-yous. You come instead for legendary chicken wings, a varied menu and some infamous Yellowknife backwards-coming-forwards bonhomie.

Le Frolic Bistro Bar   FRENCH $$

(5019 49th St; mains $12-35; ⊙11am-11pm Mon-Sat) Toujours Français. This Euro-style bistro feels more like a traditional pub until the food arrives: escargots, creative salads, a memorable artichoke dip and excellent (expensive) desserts.

Le Stock Pot   SANDWICH SHOP $

(5012 53rd St; sandwiches $7-10, ⊙8am-6pm Mon-Wed, 8am-8pm Thu & Fri, 10am-6pm Sat) Yellowknife's delectable deli offers fresh sandwiches, wraps, salads, baked goods and – wait for it – croque-monsieur. All this plus a sunny patio equals the best lunch spot in town.

Sushi North   JAPANESE $$

(4910 Franklin Ave; mains $8-14; ⊙11am-7pm Mon-Sat) Hopping during the lunch hour, this excellent place does sushi with a polar spin: the raw fish is Arctic char.

Drinking

Maybe it's the cold, the wintertime dark or the fact that nearby villages and mines restrict liquor. Whatever the reason, thirsty Yellowknifers have long found solace in the town's bars. Not surprisingly, there are plenty of them, from swanky to foul. Follow the warm smell of beer.

Sam's Monkey Tree Pub   PUB

(483 Range Lake Rd) Adrift from the downtown strip, the Monkey is a little less rough around the edges than other Yellowknife bars, offering pub grub with a good selection of beers. The large interior is furnished with appropriately large TV screens, all the better for watching big sports games.

Black Knight Pub   PUB

(4910 49th St; ⊙11am-2am) Among the more straight-laced drinkeries, the local favorite is the Black Knight, which has an English-Irish-Scottish theme to its brews and decor. The Top Knight dance club is upstairs.

Javaroma   CAFE
(5201 Franklin Ave; ⊘7am-10pm Mon-Fri, 9am-
10pm Sat, 10am-10pm Sun; @🛜) The only coffee bar you'd want to linger in has good joe,
comfy couches, wi-fi, a TV, sandwiches and
large iced cinnamon buns. Get out of the
cold and hunker down.

🛍 Shopping

Surprise! Yellowknife contains numerous
shops and galleries and is the best place
in Canada to buy Northern art, crafts and
clothing. If you can't find what you want
(say, a size XL moose-hide vest), request
contact information for artisans, who often
work on commission.

Northern Images   ACCESSORIES
(www.northernim ages.ca; 4801 Franklin Ave;
⊘10am-6pm Mon-Sat) Jointly owned by
Northern aboriginal art-and-crafts cooper-
atives, this excellent place carries the famed
Inuit print collections from Cape Dorset,
Pangnirtung and Ulukhaktok, along with
Dene specialties such as birchbark baskets.

Gallery of the Midnight Sun   SOUVENIRS
(www.gallerymidnightsun.com; 5005 Bryson Dr,
⊘10am-6pm Mon-Sat, noon-5pm Sun) This gallery has an ample supply of aboriginal art,
including ornately decorated Dene moccasins and jackets. It also stocks souvenirs
made in southern Canada.

Dawn Oman Art Studio   SOUVENIRS
(www.dawnoman.com; 4911 47th St; ⊘noon-6pm)
Dawn Oman, a nationally lauded Métis
painter, renders Northern themes in vivid
primary colors. Her work appears on canvas,
silk, mouse pads etc in her at-home gallery.

Birchwood Gallery   SOUVENIRS
(www.birchwoodgallery.com; 4810 Franklin Ave;
⊘10am-6pm Mon-Sat) In the YK Centre Mall,
this high-end spot focuses on large-scale local paintings and often features guest artists working in the gallery.

Yellowknife Book Cellar   BOOKSTORE
(4923 49th St; ⊘9:30am-6pm Mon-Wed & Sat,
9:30am-8pm Thu & Fri, noon-5pm Sun) Contains
the best selection of Northern and aboriginal titles.

ℹ Information

Emergency
Note that ☎911 is not the emergency number
in the NWT.
Ambulance & Fire (☎867-873-2222) For
emergencies.

Police (☎emergencies 867-669-1111, nonemergencies 867-669-5100; 5010 49th Ave)

Library
Yellowknife Public Library (2nd fl, Centre
Square Mall; ⊘10am-9pm Mon-Thu, to 6pm Fri,
to 5pm Sat) An ample Northern book collection, free internet, rowdy youths.

Medical
Stanton Territorial Hospital (☎867-669-4111;
off Old Airport Rd; ⊘24hr) Just off the Frame
Lake Trail.

Money
You'll find all the big banks (Scotia Bank, TD
Bank and CIBC) downtown on Franklin Ave.

Post
Main post office (4902 Franklin Ave)

Tourist Information
Northern Frontier Visitors Centre (www.
northernfrontier.com; 4807 49th St; internet
access per 15min $1; ⊘8:30am-6pm May-Sep)
The visitors center has reams of maps and brochures, plus the indispensable *Explorers' Guide*,
published annually by NWT Arctic Tourism.
Inside are exhibits on the NWT environment,
but the most powerful display is the parking lot
itself, deformed by melting permafrost.

ℹ Getting There & Away

Air
Yellowknife is the NWT's air hub. Most flights
from outside the territory land here, and most
headed to smaller NWT communities depart
from here. Brace yourself for high prices. **First
Air** (www.firstair.ca) serves Hay River ($283 one
way, 45 minutes, Sunday to Friday), Fort Simpson
($453 one way, one hour, Sunday to Friday) and
Inuvik ($593 one way, 1¾ hours, Sunday, Monday,
Wednesday and Friday), while **Canadian North**
(www.canadiannorth.com) flies to Inuvik ($593
one way, 2½ hours, daily) and Norman Wells
($506 one way, one hour, daily). Smaller airlines
sometimes offer good special fares. **Northwestern Air Lease** (www.nwal.ca) goes to Fort Smith
($350 one way, one hour, Sunday to Friday),
Buffalo Airways (www.buffaloairways.com) flies
to Hay River ($200 one way, 45 minutes, Sunday
to Friday). **Air Tindi** (www.airtindi.com) lands in
Fort Simpson ($385 one way from Monday to Fri-
day but just $180 one way Saturday and Sunday,
80 minutes) and the small Tlicho and Chipewyan
communities around Great Slave Lake.

Bus
Inconveniently, Frontier Coachlines is at 113
Kam Lake Rd, in Yellowknife's industrial boon-
docks. Buses depart Monday through Friday,
stopping in Rae ($30, 80 minutes), Fort Provi-
dence ($74, four hours) and Enterprise ($90,

seven hours) en route to Hay River ($98, eight hours). From there, connections can be made to Edmonton, Fort Smith or Fort Simpson.

Car

Renting a car in Yellowknife isn't cheap. A small car typically costs about $75/450 per day/week, *plus* 30 cents per kilometer, with 250 free kilometers thrown in with weekly rentals only.

Rent-a-Relic ([☎]867-873-3400; 356 Old Airport Rd; [⊙]variable, call ahead) is dirt cheap, but you pretty much need a car just to get there. Downtown, try **Yellowknife Motors** ([☎]867-766-5000; cnr 49th Ave & 48th St). Big-name agencies (see p886) are at the airport.

① Getting Around

Much of Yellowknife is easily walkable (or bike-able in the summer). From downtown to Old Town is about 2km, or a 20-minute walk. Bikes can be rented from Narwal Adventure Training & Tours from June to August.

To/From the Airport

Yellowknife's airport is opposite Long Lake, a couple of kilometers west of downtown. Taxis operate around the clock, charging about $15 for a ride downtown. A regular free shuttle bus deposits guests at the Explorer Hotel, Yellowstone Inn and Arnica Inn.

Car

With its prominent landmarks, Yellowknife is easy to navigate. Parking around Franklin Ave is metered; free spots are a few blocks away on side streets. Ask at the visitors center about the three-day parking pass for tourists.

Bus

Yellowknife City Transit ([☎]867-873-4693; adult/child $2/1.50) runs three routes. Route 1 serves Old Airport Rd and downtown. Route 2 connects downtown and Old Town. The summer-only Rte 3 melds the above two routes together. Most buses run every half-hour, roughly 6:30am to 7:30pm Monday to Friday and for just a few hours on Saturday.

Taxi

Cabs are plentiful. Fares are $3 plus $1.60 per kilometer. The biggest company is **City Cab** ([☎]867-873-4444).

AROUND YELLOWKNIFE

Ingraham Trail

The Ingraham Trail (Hwy 4), winding 69km northeast of Yellowknife, is where locals go to play. The route reveals sce-

nic, lake-dotted, jack-pine-lined Canadian Shield topography, and offers good fishing, hiking, camping, paddling, picnicking and, in winter, skiing and snowmobiling.

The trail begins inauspiciously, weaving past the rotting infrastructure of **Giant Mine**. A few kilometers later is the 11km access road to **Dettah**, a tiny, quiet Dene settlement.

Prelude Lake, 28km from Yellowknife, is a busy, family-oriented weekend spot. It has a vast **campground** (walk-in/powered $15/28; [⊙]mid-May–Sep 15), a boat launch and nature trails.

At **Hidden Lake Territorial Park**, 46km from Yellowknife, a 1.2km trail leads to popular **Cameron Falls**. You can cross the upstream footbridge and crawl to the brink of this marvelous cascade. Another 9km down the Ingraham Trail, just before the highway bridge, a 400m trail goes to Cameron River Ramparts, a small but pretty cousin of Cameron Falls.

At **Reid Lake**, 61km from Yellowknife, you can swim, canoe or fish for pike, whitefish and trout. The **campground** (walk-in/powered $15/28; [⊙]mid-May–Sep 15) is busy on weekends; otherwise it's quiet. It has a good beach and walking trail, plus campsites on the ridge with views of Pickerel Lake.

In summer, the trail ends at **Tibbitt Lake** where, fittingly, there's a stop sign. The lake has good fishing and is the start of some fine canoe routes – ask for details at the Northern Frontier Visitors Centre. In winter, this is the beginning of the 570km ice road to the diamond mines. There are no services on the ice road and non-industrial traffic is highly discouraged.

NORTH SLAVE

This region, between Great Slave and Great Bear Lakes, is rocky, lake-strewn and rich in minerals. Save for the people in Yellowknife, most people here are Tlicho, living traditional (and nontourist-oriented) lives.

Highway 3

From Yellowknife, paved Hwy 3 runs 98km northwest to Behchokó (formerly Rae-Edzo), rounds the North Arm of Great Slave Lake, and dives 214km to Fort Providence.

The Yellowknife–Behchokó stretch winds through the bogs, taiga and pinkish

WHERE THE GOLD WAS PAVED WITH STREETS

Amid the featureless topography of the Great Slave Lake region, the disused Giant gold mine stands out as a stark reminder of a short-lived and often tempestuous era. Passed over by Klondike-bound prospectors in the 1890s as being too inaccessible, the NWT's first significant gold strike was made in 1935 by two opportunistic canoeists, Johnny Baker and Herb Baker. But it wasn't until after WWII that the fever went viral with a massive staking boom based on seams that ran beneath the town itself, a discovery that inspired the wry comment that Yellowknife was a city 'where the gold was paved with streets'.

Yellowknife's (literal) golden years had two distinct peaks split by a protracted downturn in the 1970s, when the worldwide price of gold fell low. As prices became more volatile in the early 1990s the industry was blighted by Canada's worst-ever industrial dispute between the mine's then-owners, Royal Oak, and the Smelter and Allied Workers Union, which culminated in the 1992 bombing of a mine shaft, an outrage that killed nine flown-in strikebreakers. A former mine worker and union member was ultimately convicted of planting the bomb; he had apparently acted alone.

Controversy continued in the late '90s as productivity dropped and, in 1999, Giant went into receivership. It was bought out by Miramar, owners of the nearby Con mine. Con closed in 2003 and Giant ceased production a year later when extracting further gold became unprofitable but, miraculously, Yellowknife's economy was saved by the discovery of another precious commodity: diamonds.

Despite ongoing controversy surrounding environmentally unfriendly tailing ponds and contamination from arsenic trioxide, gold's legacy has been carefully preserved by the NWT Mining Heritage Society. Formed in 2000, the group is preparing to open a NWT Mining and Geological Museum on Hwy 3 on the former Giant mine premises.

outcrops of the Canadian Shield. There's little to see in **Behchokó** (population 1834), 10km north of Hwy 3 on an access road. Though it's among the NWT's largest communities – and by far the biggest aboriginal settlement – it's very insular and tourists may feel out of place. It has a basic service station, a cafe and a convenience store.

Across the Hwy 3 bridge, the outcrops vanish and the land becomes flat boreal forest, which is ubiquitous in the southern NWT. The road also changes, becoming wide, straight and smooth. If you're tempted to gun it, beware: the **Mackenzie Bison Sanctuary**, with the world's largest herd of free-ranging, pure wood bison, is just east of here. The animals that graze along the road outweigh your car and have tempers, so be observant. There are no trails or visitor facilities in the sanctuary.

On the south side of the sanctuary, a 5km access road leads to Fort Providence. Bypassing that, you'll come to a service station, a sometimes-open visitor information booth and, a few kilometers beyond, the free car-ferry **MV Merv Hardie** (☑800-661-0750; ⊗6am-midnight). In winter there's an ice bridge. Work on the controversially expensive Deh Cho Bridge, designed to enable year-round crossing of the Mackenzie River, started in 2008. It is due to open to traffic in late 2011.

Fort Providence

This low-key Slavey community (population 750), near the head of the Mackenzie River, was settled in 1861 with the establishment of a Roman Catholic mission. Halfway along the access road to the community is the pretty (and often quite crowded) **Fort Providence Territorial Park** (powered sites $28; ⊗mid-May–Sep 15). It has pit toilets and riverfront sites.

Fort Providence is a bucolic place – just ask the buffalo grazing in the grassy lots. There are good picnic benches atop the 10m-high riverbanks and past the beautiful wooden church is a boat launch. The fishing's good, and pike, walleye and sometimes grayling can be caught from shore. If nothing is biting, outfitters can take you on the water.

At the entrance to town, the **Snowshoe Inn** (☑867-699-3511; www.ssimicro.com/snowshoe; s/d $140/170; ☎) has decent, modern, waterfront rooms. Across the road, the short-order **Snowshoe Inn Restaurant** (dishes $6-18; ⊗7am-8pm Mon-Sat, 10am-8pm Sun; ☎) whips up sandwiches and smooth milkshakes. Photos on the wall depict local history. Close by, a fine craft shop features the area's specialty: moose-hair tufting.

SOUTH SLAVE

The South Slave Region, encompassing the area south of Great Slave Lake, is mostly flat forestland, cut through by big rivers and numerous spectacular waterfalls. The communities here feel more 'southern' – and aboriginal culture is less evident – than elsewhere in the territory.

Mackenzie Highway

From the Hwy 3 junction, 23km south of the Mackenzie River, the Mackenzie Hwy (Hwy 1) branches west into the Deh Cho region and southeast into the South Slave. This latter branch is well traveled and well paved. It runs 186km to the Alberta border (and thence to Edmonton) and is dubbed the **Waterfalls Route**, due to some stunning roadside cascades.

First up on this route is **Lady Evelyn Falls Territorial Park** (nonpowered/powered sites $22.50/28; ⊙mid-May–Sep 15), 7km off Mackenzie Hwy on the Kakisa access road. There's a short path to the 17m falls, which pour over an ancient, crescent-shaped coral reef. Another trail leads to the Kakisa River beneath the falls, which is a good fishing spot. The campground has showers, towering pines and, on weekends, lots of anglers. Another 8km down the access road is the tiny settlement of **Kakisa** (population 52).

From the Kakisa access road it's 83km to the service-station hodgepodge of **Enterprise** (population 97-ish). **Twin Falls Inn** (☏867-984-3711; s/d $94/99), at the junction of Hwys 1 and 2, offers gas, snacks and utilitarian rooms. Around the bend is **Winnie's** (☏867-984-3211; meals $5-10; ⊙7am-5pm Mon-Sat, 8am-5pm Sun), where greasy breakfasts lubricate the local gossip.

South on the Mackenzie Hwy the road parallels impressive **Twin Falls Gorge Territorial Park** (⊙mid-May–Sep 15). The eponymous pair of falls are linked by a 2km forested trail, which makes for a lovely hike or cycling route. At the north end of the trail is the tiered, 15m **Louise Falls** on the Hay River. There are numerous **campsites** (walk-in/nonpowered/powered sites $15/22.50/28) nestled in a boreal glade,

plus toilets and showers. At the trail's south end, impressive **Alexandra Falls** (33m) involves a lot of liquid losing a lot of height; it has a lookout and a picnic shelter.

At the Alberta border, 72km south, is the **60th Parallel Territorial Park**. At the **Visitors Centre** (⊙8:30am-8:30pm mid-May–Sep 15), staff dispense pamphlets, coffee and hit-or-miss advice. There are also displays of aboriginal crafts such as beaded moccasins, and a **campground** (nonpowered sites $22.50) with toilets and showers.

Hay River

POP 3648

A hard-working, hard-bitten town, Hay River has little to offer visitors superficially, though there's good fishing, boating, dogsledding and even an 18-hole golf course located here. This is the NWT's second-largest community and the North's freight distribution center; it's the terminus of Canada's northernmost railroad, the depot for Arctic-bound barges and the port of the Great Slave commercial fishery.

⊙ Sights & Activities

If it's a hot and sunny day, head to the Vale Island **beach**, which fronts oceanic Great Slave Lake. The interpretive **Kiwanis Nature Trail** starts in Riverview Drive and runs along the banks of the Hay River and the West Channel of Great Slave Lake. The visitor center can provide additional information on hiking, flightseeing, fishing, golf and canoe rentals. For an indoor diversion, you might want to check out the **Hay River Heritage Centre** (☏867-874-3872; cnr Mackenzie Dr & 102nd Ave; ⊙call ahead) in the town's old Hudson's Bay Company trading post.

🛏 Sleeping

Ptarmigan Inn   HOTEL $$
(☏867-874-6781; www.ptarmiganinn.com; 10J Gagnier St; r $139; ✻🛜) In the heart of downtown, Hay River's only true hotel has clean, well-appointed rooms, a pub, dining room (called 'Keys') and fitness center.

Hay River Territorial Park Campground
CAMPGROUND $
(☏867-874-3772; nonpowered/powered sites $22.50/28; ⊙mid-May–mid-Sep) A Frisbee's throw from the beach, this densely wooded campground has hot showers, a barbecue area and a children's playground. It's off 104th St on Vale Island.

Paradise Gardens & Campground

CAMPGROUND $

(☑867-875-4430; 82 Paradise Rd; walk-in/non-powered/powered $15/22.50/28) A half-hour south of town on one of the NWT's few farms, this place has 15 campsites and offers harvest-it-yourself berry picking.

Harbour House B&B

B&B $$

(☑867-874-2233; 2 Lakeshore Dr; s/d $80/90) On flood-cheating pilings above a beach-front lot, this sunny, eight-room B&B has a curious nautical/polar/religious vibe. There's a good continental breakfast.

✖ Eating

Back Eddy Cocktail Lounge & Restaurant

SEAFOOD $$

(☑867-874-6680; 6 Courtoreille St; mains $15-20; ☺11am-2:30pm & 5pm-late Mon-Sat) This low-lit dining room is probably the best in town. Featured is fresh-caught Great Slave Lake fish, including pan-fried whitefish topped with scallops and shrimp ($18).

Fisherman's Wharf

MARKET $

(cnr 101st St & 100th Ave; ☺10am-2pm Sat mid-Jun–mid-Sep) A weekly outdoor market with fresh fish and Northern-grown produce.

Sub on the Hub

FAST FOOD $

(☑867-874-6898; 73 Woodland Dr; fast food $5-8; ☺9am-9pm Mon-Fri, 10am-9pm Sat, noon-9pm Sun) Dispensing pizza and burgers from a take-out window in the recreation complex downtown, this place doesn't so much cook as heat things up.

ℹ Information

The **Visitor Information Centre** (cnr Macken-zie Hwy & McBryan Dr; ☺9am-9pm Sat-Wed May-Sep) has brochures and runs walking tours along local nature trails in the summer. In the off-season, stop by the town hall, a block north on Commercial Dr. The **library** (☺10am-5pm & 7-9pm Mon-Thu, 1-5pm Fri-Sun) next door has free internet access.

ℹ Getting There & Away

Air

Flying to Yellowknife nearly daily (about $200 one way, 45 minutes) are locally based Buffalo Airways along with First Air. Northwestern Air Lease flies to Edmonton from $350.

Bus

Greyhound Canada has nearly daily service to Edmonton ($165 one way, 16 hours). Frontier Coachlines goes to Yellowknife ($98, eight hours), Fort Smith ($71, three hours) and Fort Simpson ($91, six hours). The depot is just north of the Vale Island Bridge.

Car & Motorcycle

By road, it's a paved 38km to Enterprise. Along the way is the Paradise Garden farming settle-ment and the turn-off to Hwy 5, leading 267 partially paved kilometers to Fort Smith.

ℹ Getting Around

Once Hwy 2 enters town it's called the Mackenzie Hwy and becomes the main drag. On Vale Island it changes names again, to 100th Ave. Both Vale Island and downtown are walkable, but they're a couple of kilometers apart, making wheels desir-able. You can pick up a street map at the visitors center at the entrance to town. **Reliable Cabs** (☑867-974-4444) provides a taxi service.

Fort Smith

POP 2360

On a high bluff above the Slave River, Fort Smith is absurdly friendly, idyllic – and somewhat un-Northern. Maybe it's the brick homes, ball fields and water tower, or the fact that the town abuts Alberta. For years this was the gateway to the North, sit-uated at the end of a portage route around the Slave River rapids. The Hudson's Bay Company set up shop here in 1874, and until Yellowknife became the territorial capital in 1967, this was the administrative center for most of Canada's northern territories. Today the town remains a peaceful, appeal-ing government hub and headquarters of Wood Buffalo National Park. Two-thirds of the residents are Cree, Chipewyan or Métis.

⊙ Sights

FREE Northern Life Museum

MUSEUM

(☑867-872-2859; cnr King St & McDougal Rd; ☺1-5pm) The Northern Life Museum is the North's best small-town museum, with intriguing displays on local history and cul-ture, plus the corpse of Canus, a whooping crane sire whose sexual efforts helped save his species from extinction.

Fort Smith Mission Historic Park

HISTORIC PARK

(cnr Breynat St & Mercredi Ave; admission free; ☺May-Sep) Weedy Fort Smith Mission His-toric Park commemorates the days when this was Roman Catholicism's beachhead into the North. Self-guided tour maps are available from the visitors center; at the museum, you can arrange for a guided tour.

Activities

In addition to Wood Buffalo National Park, there are several worthwhile activities near town. The **rapids** in the area are famous for two things: the northernmost nesting colony of white pelicans, which can be seen fishing from midriver islands, and world-class **paddling**.

The Rapids of the Drowned, in front of the town, are accessible from a stairway off Wolf Ave. Upriver, the Mountain, Pelican and Cassette rapids can be viewed by **hiking** Fort Smith's 30km stretch of the Trans Canada Trail (TCT), or by shorter **walks** beginning along the 24km road to Fort Fitzgerald. A trail guide can be acquired at the visitors center.

Sleeping & Eating

Thebacha B&B   B&B $$
(☎867-872-2060; www.taigatour.com/bandb.htm; 53 Portage Ave; s/d $80/100; @) One of three local B&Bs, Thebacha offers clean, wood-paneled rooms in a pine-tree-shaded home near the heart of town. The proprietors also run Taiga Tour Company (p802) and rent outdoor gear. Bike use is complimentary.

Pelican Rapids Inn   HOTEL $$
(☎867-872-2789; 152 McDougal Rd; r $125-155) Across from the park visitors center, the town's only hotel has 31 standard rooms, cheery help and a restaurant (mains $7 to $20) with tolerable repasts, ranging from steak to Chinese.

Queen Elizabeth Territorial Park
                                       CAMPGROUND $
(☎867-872-2607; powered sites $28; ☉mid-May–Sep 15) At the end of Tipi Trail, 4km west of the town center, this idyllic and usually empty campground lies near the river bluff. Showers and firewood are available.

Ed's Express   FAST FOOD $
(195 McDougal Rd; mains $5-9; ☉11am-11pm Mon-Sat) Blessedly, this spartan fast-food eatery does better with its burgers, pizza and donairs than with its decor.

Information

The **Visitor Information Centre** (www.fortsmith.ca; 108 King St; ☉8:30am-6pm) is in the recreation complex. It has lots of tourist literature, free internet terminals and a manager who'll talk your ear off. McDougal Rd and Portage Ave have most of the eateries, hotels and shops, including **North of 60 Books** (66 Portage Ave; ☉1-5:30pm Tue-Sat). While you're in town,

you may also want to visit the Visitors Reception Centre for Wood Buffalo National Park.

Getting There & Around

Northwestern Air Lease offers flights to Yellowknife ($350 one way, one hour, Sunday to Friday) and Edmonton ($497 one way, two hours, five weekly). Frontier Coachlines runs buses to Hay River ($71, three hours, three weekly). In the winter months, an ice road runs to Fort McMurray, Alberta.

From Hay River, partially paved Hwy 5 cuts through the top of Wood Buffalo National Park. Fort Smith proper is walkable and McDougal Rd is the main drag. For a taxi service, try **Portage Cabs** (☎867-872-3333).

Wood Buffalo National Park

Straddling the Alberta–NWT border, Canada's biggest national park isn't spectacular, but it *is* weird. In this Switzerland-sized boreal flatland are salt-springs that encrust the landscape, rivers that disappear underground and balls of mating snakes.

The park was established in 1922 to protect wood buffalo – a large, dark, distinctly Northern subspecies of bison. About 5500 of them now inhabit the region and you'll likely see them grazing along roadsides or wallowing in the dust.

Also protected here are whooping cranes – the last wild migratory flock on Earth. These giant birds nearly disappeared, but are rebounding thanks to international safeguards. They, along with millions of ducks and geese, avail themselves of park wetlands, including the enormous Peace-Athabasca Delta. Moose, caribou, bears, lynx and wolves are also residents, along with countless mosquitoes and horseflies. Come prepared for battle.

Sights & Activities

Along Hwy 5, roadside points of interest include the karst topography at **Angus Sinkhole**, the disappearing **Nyarling River** and, just outside the park boundary, sudsy **Little Buffalo River Falls**. Further on, there's a 13km dirt side road to the **Salt Plains Lookout**, where a half-kilometer walk leads to a vast white field formed by saltwater burbling from an ancient seabed.

Along the Peace Point road is the **Salt River Day-Use Area**, home to the continent's northernmost snake hibernaculum (alas, they only have group sex in late April), and the trailhead for excellent **day hikes** to salt flats and sinkholes. Down the road 36km, at popular **Pine Lake Campground** (tent sites $15.70; ⊘late May–mid-Sep), you can swim and bask on white-sand beaches. This is the only roadside campground in the park.

For the adventurous, there are a half-dozen **backcountry hiking** trails, plus **paddling** on the historical fur-trade routes along the Athabasca, Peace and Slave Rivers. Contact the park for details, permits and info on guided walks and outdoor programs.

☞ Tours

Taiga Tour Company (☎867-872-2060; www.taigatour.com; 53 Portage Ave) is the park's only licensed outfitter, offering wildlife-watching, dog-sledding and fishing.

Reliance Airways (☎867-872-4004; www.relianceairways.ca) does flightseeing over the park, including half-hour fly-bys of the salt plains and sinkholes and two-hour over-flights of the Peace River Delta to see wood bison and whooping cranes.

ⓘ Information

Park entry is free. The park headquarters are in Fort Smith, where there's an excellent **Visitors Reception Centre** (☎867-872-7960; www.pc.gc.ca/buffalo; 149 McDougal Rd; ⊘9am–noon & 1-5pm Mon-Fri, 1-5pm Sat & Sun). It offers a slide show, hiking maps and displays on the park's quirky features.

DEH CHO

Deh cho means 'big river' in the local Slavey tongue, and this region in the southwestern NWT is awash in waterways – most notably the Mackenzie, Liard and Nahanni. The area is also blessed with mountains, comparatively warm temperatures and rich aboriginal culture.

Mackenzie Highway

From the Hwy 3 junction, 30km south of Fort Providence, the gravel Mackenzie Hwy (Hwy 1) cuts west through 288km of flat boreal forest to Fort Simpson. This is a lobotomizingly dull drive, with few views or points of interest.

The blessed exception is **Sambaa Deh Falls Territorial Park** (nonpowered sites $22.50; ⊘mid-May–Sep 15), which is halfway to Fort Simpson. It features a marvelous roadside waterfall, a fishing spot 10 minutes' walk downstream through multihued muskeg (look out for the hidden waterfall) and the smaller Coral Falls. The pleasant, clean campground also has showers.

Another 90km further on, at the junction of the Mackenzie Hwy and Hwy 7, is the **Checkpoint**, a service station, restaurant and motel complex that may or may not be in business by the time you visit.

Here, the Mackenzie Hwy becomes paved. A free car-ferry, the **MV Lafferty** (☎800-661-0750; ⊘8am-11:45pm mid-May–late Oct), crosses the Liard River just south of Fort Simpson. In winter there's an ice bridge. Traffic halts during freeze-up and thaw.

From Fort Simpson, the Mackenzie Hwy continues a rugged 222km north into rolling mountains, reaching the Dene settlement of **Wrigley** (population 122). Hunting, fishing and trapping remain the basis of this mainly log-cabin village. A winter ice road continues to Tulita.

Fort Simpson

In Slavey, Fort Simpson (population 1216) is *Liidlii Kue* – 'where two rivers meet'. The voluminous Liard and Mackenzie converge here, and for thousands of years so have the people of the southwestern NWT. Permanent settlement began with a fur-trading post in 1803, and Fort Simpson was soon the Hudson's Bay Company's district headquarters. Today, with an easygoing blend of Slavey, Métis and European cultures, it's the administrative and transport hub of the region and the gateway to nearby Nahanni National Park Reserve.

The **Visitor Information Centre** (☎867-695-3182; ⊘9am-8pm Mon-Fri, noon-8pm Sat & Sun May-Sep), at the entrance to town, has helpful staff and brochures. Also in town are a grocery store, a gas station, a craft shop, ATMs, a library with free internet and a bank.

◉ Sights & Activities

There's a **walk** along the Mackenzie riverfront with views of the driftwood-laden water and of Papal Flats, where thousands gathered to welcome the Pope in 1987. Historic **McPherson House** and the **cabin** of eccentric trapper Albert Faille are also nearby. They can be viewed only from the outside unless you join a **historical tour**

(⊙1pm daily summer); ask at the visitor center for details.

Around Canada Day is the **Open Sky Festival** (www.openskyfestival.ca), a three-day music-and-arts festival that attracts a variety of performers and craftspeople from across the NWT.

🛏 Sleeping & Eating

Fort of the Forks HOTEL $$
(☎867-695-2700; www.fortoftheforks.com; Mackenzie Hwy 1; r $175; 🛜) It's not often the NWT gets a new hotel, so be sure to make the most of this unique 'truck stop' where executive rooms are provided in modern trailers – of all places. There's also an on-site store, gas station and the Dehcho Grill restaurant.

Bannockland Inn B&B $$
(☎867-695-3337; www.bbcanada.com/1831. html; s/d $155/165; ❄🛜) This posh B&B, located 4.6km east of town off the Mackenzie Hwy, overlooks the sweeping intersection of the rivers. It's a prime choice if you have a car or another way into town.

Fort Simpson Territorial Campground CAMPGROUND $
(nonpowered/powered sites $22.50/28; ⊙mid-May–Sep 15) In the woods between the visitors center and Papal Flats, the campground has showers, pit toilets and 32 pleasant campsites.

Dehcho Grill CANADIAN $$$
(www.fortoftheforks.com; MacKenzie Hwy 1; meals $20-40) Food in the Fort of the Forks mixes international standards (NY Steak and Chicken Parmigiano) with local sensations (Arctic char and salmon). If you're not up for the full spread, try the egg-biased breakfasts or the burgers (famous, apparently).

ℹ Getting There & Around

Operating from Yellowknife are Air Tindi ($325 one way from Monday to Friday, $180 one way Saturday and Sunday, 80 minutes) and First Air ($333 one way, one hour, Sunday to Friday). The latter also flies from Whitehorse ($687 one way, two hours, three a week). Frontier Coachlines goes from Hay River ($91 one way, six hours, twice a week). Fort Simpson town is easily walkable.

Nahanni National Park Reserve

To many, Nahanni *means* wilderness. Situated in the southwestern NWT near the Yukon border, this 4766-sq-km park embraces its namesake, the epic South Nahanni River. This untamed river tumbles more than 500km through the jagged Mackenzie Mountains.

Dene stories of giants in the area go back thousands of years. Since the early 1900s outsiders have added their own tales about wild tribes, lost gold and mysterious deaths, including the legendary decapitation of two treasure-seeking brothers. Place names such as the Headless Range and Deadmen Valley underscore this mythology.

Appropriately, the Nahanni is a Canadian Heritage river, and the park is a Unesco World Heritage site – the first place given that designation in Canada. In 2007 Canada's federal government announced plans to protect more of the Nahanni watershed by doubling the park's size. The eventual settlement of the region's aboriginal land claim could result in an even bigger park expansion.

◉ Sights & Activities

Near its midpoint, the Nahanni River drops 30 stories over Canada's premier cascade, **Virginia Falls**; elsewhere it's framed by canyons, flanked by caves and warmed by **Rabbitkettle Hot Springs**. Moose, wolves, grizzly bears, Dall sheep and mountain goats patrol the landscape.

Paddling is what Nahanni is all about. If you plan to do this independently, you should be a capable whitewater paddler (in Class IV rapids). This is no pleasure float; people have died here. Consult with the park office for advice, warnings and recommendations on good maps and books. Contact the tour companies for assistance or renting canoes or rafts.

🧭 Tours
Flightseeing
The easiest way to see the park is to join a flightseeing tour. A typical six-hour excursion departs Fort Simpson aboard a floatplane, follows the Nahanni upriver through steep-walled canyons and then lands just above Virginia Falls. Two hours of hiking and picnicking ensue. On these tours, you pay for the plane: about $1900 for a four-passenger craft, and $2800 for six. To find fellow travelers to split the cost, phone the air companies in advance, or ask around town. Flightseeing companies based in Fort Simpson are all located on Antoine Drive near the in-town airstrip.

Simpson Air FLIGHTSEEING
(☑867-695-2505; www.simpson-air.ca)

Wolverine Air FLIGHTSEEING
(☑867-695-2263; www.wolverineair.com)

Paddling

Raft or canoe trips can be arranged with a licensed outfitter. Prices range from $3600 to $5700, depending on distance. Trips should be prebooked, preferably months in advance. Canoes are best for people with basic experience; rafts, which are helmed by a guide, are more relaxing and suitable for all skill levels.

Nahanni Wilderness Adventures

WILDERNESS TRIP
(☑403-678-3374; www.nahanniwild.com) Most trips begin at Moose Ponds, Rabbitkettle Lake or Virginia Falls, because those are where floatplanes can land. From the Moose Ponds to Rabbitkettle is about 160km, much of it Class III whitewater. For the 118km from Rabbitkettle to the falls, the river meanders placidly through broad valleys. Once the falls are portaged, it's another 252km to Blackstone Territorial Park, first through steep-sided, turbulent canyons, and then along the broad Liard River. The lower-river trip requires seven to 10 days. From Rabbitkettle it's around 14 days, while from the Moose Ponds it's 21.

Black Feather WILDERNESS TRIP
(☑705-746-1372; www.blackfeather.com) Includes special family and women-only trips.

Nahanni River Adventures WILDERNESS TRIP
(☑867-668-3180; www.nahanni.com)

🛏 Sleeping

Camping is allowed along the riverbanks. There are only four designated campgrounds; the one at Virginia Falls is staffed and has a dock for canoes and floatplanes, as well as composting toilets exposed to the grandeur of nature. The campground at Rabbitkettle Lake is also staffed.

ℹ Information

You can't get here by road, yet about 1000 people visit yearly. Half are paddlers on epic white-water expeditions; the others are mostly with fly-in day tours to the falls and hot springs. Admission quotas are strict: 12 guided and 12 unguided visitors per night at the Virginia Falls campground, with a maximum two-night stay. For unguided visitors (particularly big groups), it's wise to reserve months in advance.

You can obtain park information and permits in Fort Simpson at **Parks Canada** (☑867-695-3151; www.parkscanada.gc.ca/nahanni; cnr 100 St & 100 Ave; ☺8:30am-noon & 1-5pm Jun 15–Sep 15, 8:30am-noon & 1-5pm Mon-Fri Sep 16–Jun 14). The day-use fee is $24.50; longer-term visitors pay a flat fee of $147.20.

Getting There & Away

If you are traveling independently, you'll need to charter an airplane into the park by contacting a flightseeing company.

Liard Trail

At the Checkpoint, 63km south of Fort Simpson, the dirt Liard Trail (Hwy 7) branches off the Mackenzie Hwy (Hwy 1) and heads south through the Liard Valley, with the Mackenzie Mountains appearing to the west. Black bear and bison abound. The only gas station is at Fort Liard. South of there, at the British Columbia border, pavement starts. The trail links with the Alaska Hwy near Fort Nelson, making a loop through British Columbia, the NWT and Alberta possible. From Fort Simpson to Fort Nelson is 487km. Beware: in wet weather, this road turns to goo.

Halfway between the Checkpoint and Fort Liard is **Blackstone Territorial Park** (nonpowered sites $22.50; ☺mid-May–Sep 15) with information, a campground, short hiking trails and terrific views of the mountains and the confluence of the Liard and Nahanni. Most trips down the South Nahanni end here.

Across the Liard from Blackstone is **Nahanni Butte** (population 115), a Slavey village accessible only by air charter or boat, or by ice road in winter. It has a general store, a motel, river-taxi services – and more mosquitoes than anywhere else on Earth.

FORT LIARD

Fort Liard has lush forests, prim log homes and the balmiest weather in the NWT. This Dene village still values its traditions, such as weaving birch-bark baskets, which are ornately decorated with porcupine quills. These can be bought at one of the NWT's finest craft shops, **Acho Dene Native Crafts** (www.adnc.ca; cnr Main St & Poplar Rd; ☺9am-7pm Mon-Sat, to 5pm Sun), in the middle of town. It doubles as the visitors center.

Before you reach the village of nearly 600 souls, the free, rudimentary **Hay Lake Community Campground** has drinking water and an outhouse. The **Liard Valley General Store & Motel** (📞867-770-4441; cnr Main St & Black Water Rd; s/d $125/150; ❄), on the far side of town, has 12 rooms. It's often full, so make reservations.

A cafe and a service station are across the road from Acho Dene Native Crafts. The British Columbia border is 38km south.

SAHTU

Lamentably, or perhaps blessedly, mountain-studded Sahtu is the only region of the NWT inaccessible by road. The Mackenzie, swollen by water draining from one-fifth of Canada, cuts its way through here; in places it's more than 3km wide. On either side of it, baldheaded peaks arise, guarding some of the wildest country – and best hiking and paddling – left in the world.

Norman Wells

For the NWT, this historic oil town is a rare bird – a non-aboriginal settlement springing from the boreal frontier, halfway between Fort Simpson and Inuvik. The community itself is mainly of interest to hikers keen on the Canol Heritage Trail. Other than by the trail, the town is only reachable by plane or boat.

Clearly a labor of love, the **Norman Wells Historical Centre** (www.normanwellsmuseum.com; Mackenzie Dr; admission free; ⏰10am-5:30pm Mon-Fri, to 4pm Sat) is a mini-museum showcasing regional history, geology, arts and crafts, and information on the rivers and the Canol Heritage Trail. There's a pretty cool giftshop too.

◉ Sights & Activities

Hikers can explore fossil-laden areas such as **Fossil Canyon**; picnicking and canoeing are possible at **Jackfish Lake**. If that doesn't keep you busy, you can make a trip to the town dump at dusk to look for black bears.

The town is used as a jumping-off point for several canoeable rivers, including the Mountain, Keele and Natla. **Canoe North Adventures** (www.canoenorthadventures.com), run by two Ontarians but based out of Norman Wells from June to September, has nearly two decades of experience in organizing rugged canoeing trips. It has recently also added some hikes to their itinerary, including exploratory forays along the Canol Heritage Trail (see p805).

🛏 Sleeping & Eating

Annoyingly, the **campground** (sites free) is exiled a few kilometers upriver from town. Campers often just pitch their tents on the riverbanks in front of the town proper.

Heritage Hotel   HOTEL $$$
(📞867-587-5000; www.heritagehotelnwt.com; Mackenzie Dr; r $245; 🛜) This clean, minimalist, rather posh hotel seems out of place in the working-class Wells. Many of the 32 sparkling rooms have river views plus there's a spa, an adjacent 4-hole golf course, and the Ventures dining room, which, with mains like Thai-marinated steak ($22), is the best eatery in town – no contest.

Mackenzie Valley Hotel   HOTEL $$$
(📞867-587-3035; www.mackenzievalleyhotel.com; Mackenzie Dr; r from $180) has a shabby older section and a more expensive, immaculate new wing that overlooks the river. The restaurant does decent caribou burgers, pizza and some OK wines.

ℹ Getting There & Around

Canadian North (www.canadiannorth.com) stops on daily flights between Yellowknife and Inuvik. **North-Wright Airways** (www.north-wrightairways.com) serves Yellowknife and Inuvik (indirectly), as well as the more isolated communities along the river.

WESTERN ARCTIC

Comprising the Mackenzie Delta, the Richardson Mountains and several High Arctic islands, this is the NWT's most diverse region. Several national parks are here, plus a scattering of aboriginal hamlets and the prefabricated polis of Inuvik, which can be driven to via the heart-wrenchingly beautiful Dempster Hwy.

Inuvik

POP 3484

Inuvik, a few dozen kilometers from the mouth of the Mackenzie River, is the NWT's third-largest town and the Paris (ahem!) of the Western Arctic. The town was artificially

WORTH A TRIP

CANOL HERITAGE TRAIL

Norman Wells' main attraction is the **Canol Heritage Trail**, a national historic site that leads 372km southwest to the Yukon border. From there, a road goes to Ross River and the Yukon highway system. The trail was built at enormous monetary and human cost during WWII to transport oil to Whitehorse; Canol is shorthand for 'Canadian Oil.' However, the huge project was abandoned in 1945 because the war was almost over and there were cheaper sources of oil.

The route traverses peaks, canyons and barrens. Wildlife is abundant and there are numerous deep river crossings along the trail. There are no facilities, although you can get a little shelter in some of the old Quonset huts. Hiking the whole length takes three to four weeks and most people need to arrange food drops. The beginning of the trail is flat and swampy, so day hikes from Norman Wells are not recommended. Some visitors use helicopters, available from Norman Wells, to reach the most interesting parts of the trail; ask at the **Village Office** (☑867-587-3700; www.normanwells.com), which has a list of local outfitters offering this type of service. A couple of dozen stout souls hike the entire trail each year.

erected in 1955 to serve as a government administrative post and with its rainbow-colored rows of houses and warren of above-ground heated pipes, it still feels like a work in progress. From late May through late July, Inuvik has ceaseless daylight. During that time, lots of visitors arrive via the rugged, awesome 747km Dempster Hwy from the Yukon. When winter sets in, ice-roads open up, including a virtual superhighway north to Tuktoyaktuk.

◉ Sights & Activities

Our Lady of Victory Church   LANDMARK
(Mackenzie Rd) The town landmark is Our Lady of Victory Church, also called the Igloo Church, with a resplendent white dome and a lovely interior (though the place is often locked).

Jàk Park   PARK
Jàk Park, 6km south of town, has a good lookout tower for viewing the subarctic terrain.

Northern Images   ART GALLERY
(☑867-777-2786; 115 Mackenzie Rd; ◷9am-5:30pm Mon-Fri, 10am-5:30pm Sat) Northern Images, in an octagonal log-cabin, is *the* gallery in town. There are scads of Northern art and crafts here, including $170 beaver-skin caps and $3600 Inuit carvings.

Dempster Highway   SCENIC HIGHWAY
After checking out the above sights, the best thing you can do in Inuvik is get out of town. The easiest way is to drive the Dempster Hwy, a ribbon of gravel that

reaches westward into some of the most stunning alpine scenery available. You can rent a 4X4 Jeep Cherokee Dempster-ready pickup from **Arctic Chalet** (www.arctic chalet.com; 25 Carn St) for $95 per day plus 100 free kilometers. It also rents kayaks and canoes for $100 and $200 per week respectively.

⛵ Tours

Most tours involve flights over the braided Mackenzie Delta and the weather-beaten Arctic coast, where trees peter out and the landscape becomes riddled with pingos: ice-cored hills that erupt from the tundra. Photographers should try for a seat at the rear of the plane.

Arctic Chalet   ADVENTURE
(☑867-777-3535; www.arcticchalet.com; 25 Carn St) Provides year-round adventure services in addition to its comfy cabins. In winter, dog-sled tours are run daily ($125). Participants are given the opportunity to command the teams of snow-white huskies over the trails.

Up North Tours   SIGHTSEEING
(☑867-777-2204; www.upnorthtours.ca; 69 MacKenzie Rd) Up North offers numerous tours, the most popular being a flight to Tuktoyaktuk on the Arctic coast ($385 per person) to view pingos and ice-houses. It also has boating in the Mackenzie Delta ($165 per person) in the summer and snowmobile tours in the winter.

✤ Festivals & Events

Sunrise Festival　　　　　　FIREWORKS
(📞867-777-2607; ⊘early Jan) Brings the locals together for fireworks on the ice to greet the first sunrise after 30 days of darkness.

Great Northern Arts Festival　　ARTS
(www.gnaf.org; ⊘late Jul) The North's top art festival, drawing scores of carvers, painters and other creators from across the circumpolar world. This is an ideal place to buy Arctic art, watch it being made, or participate in workshops and cultural presentations.

🛏 Sleeping

Arctic Chalet　　　　　　HOTEL $$

TOP CHOICE (📞867-777-3535; www.arcticchalet.com; 25 Carn St; r shared/private bathroom $110/130 📶) The Arctic Chalet, with its sunny cabins in a boreal glade, is the best place to stay in Inuvik. Each building has simple kitchen facilities. The energetic owners rent canoes, kayaks and cars, run dog-sledding tours and are objective sources of local info. The Chalet is about 3km from town. There's a rustic cabin sans facilities ($50) for travelers who want a true pioneering experience.

Mackenzie Hotel　　　　　　HOTEL $$$
(📞867-777-2861; www.mackenziehotel.com; 185 Mackenzie Rd; s/d $189/204; @) Recently overhauled, this is the town's high-end hotel, with chandeliers in the lobby and nice art in the spanking-new rooms. The place is also home to Tonimoes restaurant and Shivers lounge. The hotel also operates the cheaper **Eskimo Inn** (s/d $119/129) down the road.

Jàk Park Campground　　CAMPGROUND $
(📞867-777-3613; nonpowered/powered sites $22.50/28; ⊘Jun-Aug) This pretty government-operated campground, about 6km south of town on the Dempster Hwy, provides hot showers and firewood. There's a good view of the delta and the breeze keeps the mosquitoes at bay a bit.

Polar B&B　　　　　　　　B&B $$
(📞867-777-2554; www.inuvik.net/polar; 75 Mackenzie Rd; r from $95) Upstairs from the bookstore, this B&B has four large rooms with shared bathroom, common area and kitchen. It's very centrally located – perhaps a little too much so.

Happy Valley Campground　CAMPGROUND $
(📞867-777-3652; Franklin Road; nonpowered/powered sites $22.50/28; ⊘Jun-Aug) Practically downtown, this campground offers the same services as Jàk Park. Stay here if you're without a car and on a budget; otherwise, choose Jàk.

🍴 Eating & Drinking

In recent years, Inuvik's culinary situation has become dire. You'd be wise to self-cater. Occupying a full block of downtown, Northmart is the town's big grocery.

Tonimoes　　　　　　　CANADIAN $$
TOP CHOICE (185 Mackenzie Rd; lunch mains $10-13, dinner mains $12-36; ⊘7am-2pm & 5-9pm) With standard breakfasts, burger-y lunches and a surf-and-turf dinner menu, this low-lit dining room is the town's sole respectable eatery.

Shivers　　　　　　　　　　PUB $$
(185 Mackenzie Rd; ⊘11am-12:30am Mon-Sat) Despite the inane name, this spacious, low-key pub, located opposite Tonimoes in the Mackenzie Hotel, is a fine place to tipple.

Café Gallery　　　　　　　CAFE $
(90 Mackenzie Rd; meals $5-12; ⊘9am-5pm Mon-Fri, noon-5pm Sat) Belying its name, this is a charmless joint where locals join for joe. There are also espressos, muffins, soups and sandwiches.

ℹ Information

CIBC Bank (134 Mackenzie Rd) Has an ATM

Inuvik Centennial Library (100 Mackenzie Rd; ⊘10am-6pm & 7-9pm Mon-Thu, 10am-6pm Fri, 1-5pm Sat & Sun) Free internet access, a used-book exchange and an excellent selection of Northern books.

Inuvik Regional Hospital (📞867-777-8000; 285 Mackenzie Rd; ⊘24hr) That blue, red and yellow Lego structure opposite the visitors center.

Parks Canada (📞867-777-8800; 187 Mackenzie Rd; ⊘8:30am-5pm Jun-Aug, call ahead at other times) This office has info on Tuktut Nogait, Ivvavik and Aulavik National Parks, as well as the Pingo Canadian Landmark. Park visitors must register and deregister here.

Post office (187 Mackenzie Rd)

Western Arctic Visitors Centre (www.inuvik. ca; 284 Mackenzie Rd; ⊘9am-7pm Jun–mid-Sep) Has tourism literature, eager staff, plus a stuffed caribou and other displays. Parks Canada holds summer interpretive programs here; enquire for the schedule.

ℹ Getting There & Away

Air

Mike Zubko Airport is 14km south of town. **Town Cab** (☑867-777-4777) charges $25 between there and downtown.

Air North operates flights to Dawson City, Old Crow and Whitehorse. **Aklak Air** (www.aklakair. ca) has scheduled services to Tuktoyaktuk, Paulatuk and Sachs Harbour and provides charters to the national parks. Canadian North services Norman Wells (daily) and Yellowknife (daily), where you can make connecting flights to Calgary and Edmonton. First Air operates flights to Yellowknife, where there are connections throughout the North.

Car

Arctic Chalet Car Rental (www.arcticchalet. com; 25 Carn St) rents a range of vehicles and has a counter at the airport. **NorCan** (☑867-777-2346) also has an airport counter. If you are driving, it's vital that you check Dempster Hwy road and ferry conditions (☑800-661-0750).

Tuktoyaktuk

POP 870

About 140km northeast of Inuvik on the storm-battered coast is Tuktoyaktuk, perhaps the most-visited community in the Canadian Arctic. Commonly known as Tuk (hence the 'Tuk U' T-shirts you'll be likely to see across the territory), this has long been the home of the whale-hunting Inuit and is now also a land base for Beaufort Sea oil and gas explorations.

Pods of beluga whales can sometimes be seen in July and early August. Visible year-round are pingos, of which the Tuk Peninsula has the world's highest concentration. Some 1400 of these huge mounds of earth and ice dot the land and have been designated the **Pingo Canadian Landmark**. The **hamlet office** (☑867-977-2286) can provide more information on the area and services.

There is an old **military base** here, dating from the cold war, as well as old **whaling buildings**, and two charming little **churches** dating from the time when the Catholic and Anglican churches battled to proselytize the Aboriginal people. Land access is limited to a winter ice road, and most tourists arrive by air in the summer as part of half-day tours from Inuvik (p806).

Paulatuk

This small Inuvialuit community of 300 residents is on the Arctic coast near the mouth of the Hornaday River, about 400km east of Inuvik. The town's name means 'soot of coal'; one of the main attractions is the **Smoking Hills**, which contain smoldering sulfide-rich slate. For more information, contact the **hamlet office** (☑867-580-3531).

TUKTUT NOGAIT NATIONAL PARK

Paulatuk is the closest settlement to this park, a wild place about 45km east that's a major calving ground for Bluenose caribou. There are no services or facilities here; however a small visitors center for the park is open for inspection in town during the summer. For information, contact **Parks Canada** (☑867-777-8800; 187 Mackenzie Rd; ☺8:30am-5pm Jun-Aug, call ahead at other times) in Inuvik.

Banks Island

Lying in the Arctic Ocean to the north of Paulatuk, Banks Island may have been first inhabited 3500 years ago. By polar standards wildlife is abundant and this is one of the best places on Earth to see musk ox. The island also has two bird sanctuaries with flocks of snow geese and seabirds in the summer. **Sachs Harbour**, an Inuvialuit community of about 120, is the only settlement. Contact the **hamlet office** (☑867-690-4351) for information. There is a scheduled air service to Sachs Harbour from Inuvik.

AULAVIK NATIONAL PARK

On the north end of Banks Island, this seldom-visited park (annual visits usually number less than a dozen) covers 12,275 sq km. It has the world's largest concentration of musk ox as well as badlands, tundra and archaeological sites. The name means 'place where people travel' and that's what you'll have to do to get there. Contact **Parks Canada** (☑867-777-8800; www.pc.gc.ca; 187 Mackenzie Rd; ☺8:30am-5pm Jun-Aug, call ahead at other times) in Inuvik for details about visiting.

Nunavut

Includes »

Best Places to Eat

» Granite Room (p814)

» Water's Edge Restaurant (p814)

» Gallery (p814)

» Sugar Rush Café (p821)

Best Places to Stay

» Frobisher Inn (p813)

» Nova Inn (p813)

» Cape Dorset Suites (p818)

» Nanuq Lodge (p821)

Why Go?

Picture a treeless, ice-encrusted wilderness lashed by unrelenting inclement weather with a population density that makes Greenland seem claustrophobic. Now add polar bears, beluga whales and a scattering of hard-core Aboriginals who have successfully mastered a landscape so harsh that foreigners dared not colonize it.

Nunavut (created out of the Northwest Territories in 1999) is Canada's newest, largest and most lightly populated geographical subdivision, a mythical assortment of uninhabited islands and frigid ocean that exists on the planet's climatic and geographic extremes. Visitors here face multiple obstacles, not least perennial blizzards, a nonexistent road network, and a travel budget that would stretch the wallet of a Toronto-based property tycoon. But those that do get through have the privilege of joining a small band of intrepid trail blazers, only in the know halcyon days the year, setting foot where few people have ever trodden before.

When to Go

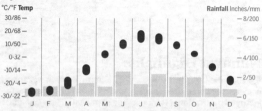

July & August Prime visiting time is during the short hyperactive summer season

April & May The ideal time for dog-sledding and other snow sports

June The midnight sun coincides with Iqaluit's Alianait Arts Festival

Nunavut Highlights

1 Feel small beside the planet's most precipitous cliffs in **Auyuittuq National Park** (p817)

2 Encounter soapstone polar bears – but watch out for real ones – in the Inuit art mecca of **Cape Dorset** (p817)

3 Chomp char, chew caribou and munch musk ox at one of the many eateries in Canada's most curious capital, **Iqaluit** (p812)

4 Moonwalk across awesomely lunar **Resolute** (p819), where nothing grows despite four months of midnight sun

5 Splash amid the cascades, caribou and canoe-friendly currents of the Edenic **Soper River** (p815)

6 Home in on Pond Inlet to organize logistics for sorties to the bird sanctuaries of **Sirmilik National Park** (p819)

History

Nunavut has been populated for about 4000 years, though the Inuit arrived just a millennium ago, migrating from Alaska. For countless generations they lived here nomadically, pursuing game as the season dictated and devising an ingenious material culture to cope with the conditions.

Though Vikings may have visited Baffin Island (Helluland in the sagas), the first definitive European arrival was in 1576, when Martin Frobisher came seeking the Northwest Passage. For the next 375 years the Arctic saw more explorers (including Sir John Franklin, who disappeared here in 1845), whalers, traders and missionaries. In a vast land, these visits had comparatively little impact on the Inuit people.

Then, after WWII, Nunavut's history went supersonic. Canada finally took interest in the Arctic, recognizing its strategic importance. In the 1950s and '60s Inuit were settled into villages and, in some cases, relocated to the High Arctic to bolster national sovereignty.

In the 1960s and '70s rising political awareness among the Inuit inspired dreams of self-government. After years of negotiations, Canada's map was redrawn in 1999. Nunavut split from the Northwest Territories and became a separate territory. Many of the Inuit who now govern here were born in igloos and raised nomadically.

Language

Inuktitut, English versus Inuktitut Inuktitut is king. It's the primary tongue of 70% of Nunavummiut, and the only language for many elders and children. It's not easy to grasp, being guttural as well as polysynthetic (meaning words morph together to form paragraph-sized monsters), and it's also hard to read, because it's mostly written in syllabics (an inscrutable orthographic system based on syllables instead of letters).

You'll get by fine if you combine English, hand gestures and a sense of humor. Still, a few local words will help bridge the cultural divide:

How are you?	Qanuippit?	ka-*nwee*-peet?
I am fine	Qanuingi	ka-*nweeng*-ee
Thank you	Qujannamiik	coy-*ahn*-nah-meek
You're welcome	Ilaali	ee-*lah*-lee
Yes	Ii	ee
No	Aakka	*ah*-kah
Good morning	Ullaakkut	ood-*lahk*-kut
Good afternoon	Unnusakkut	oo-noo-*sahk*-koot

Land & Climate

Gargantuan Nunavut sprawls over North America's northeastern flank. About half – the part on Canada's mainland – is the 'Barrenlands,' an expanse of undulating rock and tundra cut through by legendary rivers like the Thelon and the Kazan. Even more barren is the rest of the territory – mostly the Arctic archipelago, which scatters north to Ellesmere Island, just shy of the Pole, and east to Baffin, home to sky-scraping mountains and half of Nunavut's population.

Unsurprisingly, the territory is chilly. Snow holds sway from September to early June; relentless winds create hard-to-fathom chill factors, such as the -92°C once recorded at Kugaaruk. July to mid-August is summer, when the seas thaw beneath perpetual sun. During this time highs average 12°C in Iqaluit and 7°C further north in Resolute. Much warmer temps – even above 30°C – occur, but so too do mid-July blizzards.

ℹ Getting There & Around

Ditch the car. Nunavut is basically roadless, so the only way to get here is via (impoverishingly pricey) flights. Iqaluit has nearly daily arrivals from Montréal and Ottawa aboard **First Air** (www.firstair.ca) and **Canadian North** (www. canadiannorth.com) starting at $1900 return. Both airlines serve Iqaluit from Yellowknife for about $2500 return.

Rankin Inlet is linked to Winnipeg by **Calm Air** (www.calmair.com), **Kivalliq Air** (www.kival liqair.com) and First Air starting at $1300 return. Cambridge Bay is accessible from Yellowknife on First Air and Canadian North for about $1400 return.

Smaller communities are reached by air from three hubs. From Iqaluit, First Air and **Kenn Borek Air** (www.borekair.com) serve the High Arctic and Baffin Island. From Rankin Inlet, Calm Air and Kivalliq Air cover the Kivalliq region. From Cambridge Bay, First Air and Canadian North cover the Kitikmeot region.

NUNAVUT FAST FACTS

» Population: 32,900

» Area: 2,093,190 km sq

» Capital: Iqaluit

» Quirky fact: Hans Island, a 1.3 sq km nodule of land wedged between Ellesmere Island (Nunavut) and Greenland, is the subject of a long-running border dispute between Canada and Denmark

One Week

After arriving in **Iqaluit**, revel in contemporary Inuit art at the **Nunatta Sunakkutaan-git Museum**, the **Legislative Assembly** and **galleries**. By now parched and famished, join half of Iqaluit for beer and a burger at the **Storehouse Bar & Grill**.

On the second day, get out of town – first, aboard a boat tour to **Qaummaarviit Historic Park** and then by stalking fox and snowy owls in **Sylvia Grinnell Territorial Park**.

On the third day, make a splash in **Katannilik Territorial Park**: rent a canoe from an Iqaluit outfitter and fly to the **Soper River**. For the next five days, float through a polar paradise, bathing under waterfalls and slipping silently past caribou on the riverbank.

Two Weeks

After exercising your arms on the Soper, it's time to work those legs. Fly to **Pangnirtung**, check out the **Uqqurmiut Centre for Arts & Crafts** then catch a boat ride to **Auyuittuq National Park**. Hike pristine, surreal **Akshayuk Pass** beneath icy spires and the tallest cliffs you'll ever see.

IQALUIT

Nunavut's seat of government, Iqaluit (ee-*kal*-oo-eet) is Canada's culture-clash capital, at once futuristic and primeval, worldly and Third Worldly, utterly bizarre and tediously banal. Unlike the territory's parochial villages, this is a boomtown of Johnny-come-latelies: Ottawa paper-pushers and grunts from Newfoundland, plus Inuit professionals and politicians from around the Arctic. Many of these Inuit walk in two worlds (as the cliché goes), wearing sealskin vests over tailored suits and yammering into cellphones about whale-hunting.

The dusty, debris-strewn townscape of Iqaluit, with its moon-base buildings and tangle of above-ground pipes, is perversely fascinating for a while, and there are some sights, restaurants and shops worth a stop. However, real life here takes place on the land, and most visitors head out of town,

hiking along the Sylvia Grinnell River or taking a boat tour to Qaummaarviit Historic Park.

History

Each summer for centuries, nomadic Inuit trekked to the Sylvia Grinnell River to spear char in the roiling waters. They called the area Iqaluit: place of fish.

In 1576 Martin Frobisher showed up. The English naval captain, on a quest for the fabled Northwest Passage, had made a wrong turn into what's now Frobisher Bay. There he unearthed glittering yellow ore, mined it, and sailed home with a million-plus pounds of worthless fool's gold.

For another 350 years local Inuit kept fishing, interrupted occasionally by whalers, explorers and missionaries. Then, during WWII, American servicemen established an airbase here. After the war, Canadian forces stayed on, and the outpost, named Frobisher Bay, became the administrative center of the eastern Arctic.

In 1987 the community officially changed its name to Iqaluit, and in 1995 voters picked it (over Rankin Inlet) to be Nunavut's capital. In the past decade the population has doubled (to more than 6000).

⊙ Sights

FREE **Legislative Assembly** NOTABLE BUILDING
(Federal Rd; ⊙9am-5pm Mon-Fri, tours 1:30pm Mon-Fri Jun-Aug or by appointment) Nunavut's prefab Legislative Assembly is no marble-columned parliament, but has

WEBSITES

Iqaluit-based **Nunavut Tourism** (☎866-686-2828; www.nunavuttourism.com) is the territory's official oracle of visitor info. It's got a splashy and comprehensive website, and can answer queries, and mail you the swell *Nunavut Travel Planner*. Another good website is **Explore Nunavut** (www.explorenunavut.com).

touches such as sealskin benches and a narwhal-tusk ceremonial mace. Local art is displayed in the foyer.

FREE Nunatta Sunakkutaangit Museum
MUSEUM

(Sinaa St; ☺1-5pm) Nunatta Sunakkutaangit Museum, though itty-bitty, is worth a look. It has a permanent gallery of Inuit artifacts, a fine little gift shop and, best of all, temporary exhibits such as Pangnirtung's famed annual print collection.

Waterfront
LANDMARK
The waterfront, between the breakwater and Coast Guard Station, is the locus of traditional Inuit activity. Amid the old snowmobiles and fuel cans, hunters butcher seals and build boats and sleds. Ask before taking photos.

Apex Beach
NOTABLE BUILDING
(Bill Mackenzie Rd) Apex Beach is the site of the photogenic red-and-white **Hudson Bay Trading Post** complex, though the only structure you can enter is the refurbished Gallery By the Red Boat (p815).

🏃 Activities

Despite the spongy, ankle-bending terrain, Iqaluit's wide-open landscapes make **hiking** a delight. Trails are few, but the absence of trees means it's difficult to get lost. There are sometimes caribou and fox at **Sylvia Grinnell Territorial Park** (Iqaluit Rd; admission free), where paths lead to a waterfall, rapids and escarpments. The park is 2km out of town: head towards the airport, then follow the signs. Other excellent hikes include tracing the waterfront from downtown to Apex or, at low tide, exploring Tarr Inlet beyond Apex.

Not keen on perambulating? All-terrain vehicles and, in winter, snowmobiles are available for rent from **Qairrulik Outfitting** (☎867-979-6280; www.qairrulikoutfitting.com; snowmobiles/ATVs per day from $220/275). Alas, no one currently rents kayaks, but this may change. It's worth asking around because Koojesse and Tarr inlets offer great paddling.

Blueberry picking is a tasty way to get familiar with the exquisite, delicate tundra. Berries flourish near the river and above Apex. Take a container or gobble as you go.

☞ Tours

Though outfitters vary from year to year, there are usually a handful of tours available, from helicopter flights to dog-sled journeys. Consult the *Nunavut Travel Planner* or the staff at the visitors center for specifics. Most tours require minimum numbers, so bring friends or reserve early so other visitors can be rounded up.

Polynya Adventure
OUTDOOR ACTIVITIES
(☎867-979-6260; www.polynya.ca) Polynya Adventure designs a variety of offerings, including city historical tours, summer boat excursions in Frobisher Bay and dog-sledding in winter. It, or other outfitters, can take you to the recommended Qaummaarviit Historic Park, 12km from town. The park preserves a 750-year-old Inuit winter camp. Sod houses – and human bones – are still there.

Northwinds Arctic Adventures
OUTDOOR ACTIVITIES
(☎867-979-0551; www.northwinds-arctic.com) These seasoned pros lead arctic expeditions and dog-sledding programs and have worked with everyone from BBC's *Top Gear* to *Canadian Geographic*.

🎪 Festivals

Alianait Arts Festival
ARTS, CULTURE
(www.alianait.ca; ☺late June) A midsummer celebration of Inuit culture encompassing art, music, film, story-telling, food and a circus. People travel from across Canada for this week-and-a-half extravaganza in late June.

🛏 Sleeping

Camping is the only cheap option. For everything else, book ahead and prepare to hemorrhage cash.

TOP CHOICE Frobisher Inn
HOTEL $$$
(☎867-979-2222; www.frobisherinn.com; Astro Hill Terrace; r $260; ☎) Up on the hill, the 'Frobe' has modern, bayside rooms with marvelous views. There's a good restaurant, and the Astro Hill complex has a coffeeshop, pool, bar and cinema.

Nova Inn
HOTEL $$$
(☎867-979-6684; www.novainniqaluit.com; 923 Federal Rd; d/ste $195/250; P @) What would be a bog-standard lower-bracket business hotel in the south becomes bloody luxury up here, even if the prices are closer to a five-star Fairmont. Get ready to acquaint yourself with the 'downtown' Nova Inn which comes with complimentary newspapers, an Inuit craft shop and even a gym to save you suffering those frostbite-inducing morning jogs.

Discovery Lodge Hotel
HOTEL $$$
(☎867-979-4433; www.discoverylodge.com; 1056 Mivvik St; s/d $230/245; @) The town's premier hotel is comfortable but no-frills, highlighting the usual Nunavut conundrum of motel-standard rooms at Paris Ritz prices. It is most notable for its restaurant (see p814). There's also a handy airport shuttle.

Rannva's Bed & Breakfast
B&B $$
(☎867-979-3183; Bldg 3102, Helen Maksagak Dr; r per person incl breakfast $125; 🖎) In the bright 'old nursing station' in atmospheric but out-of-the-way Apex, Faroese seamstress Rannva Simonsen crafts snazzy sealskin garments and lodges guests.

Sylvia Grinnell Territorial Park
CAMPGROUND $
(Iqaluit Rd; tent sites free) There are no facilities here except pit toilets.

✖ Eating

Iqaluit has Nunavut's broadest range of culinary options, including several places that serve 'country food.' Most of the best places are in the posher hotels. You can expect big portions but at hugely inflated prices (most stuff is flown in). Shame on any Arctic tourist who fails to gorge on caribou!

TOP CHOICE Granite Room
FUSION $$$
(☎867-979-4433; www.discoverylodge.com; Mivvik St; mains $30-47) Nunavut's top restaurant in the Discovery Lodge Hotel has an extensive wine list and luscious local cuisine, like poached Arctic char ($44) and caribou steak in peppercorn sauce ($45). The homemade ice cream gets raves.

Water's Edge Restaurant
STEAKHOUSE $$$
(www.novainniqaluit.com; 923 Federal Rd; mains from $22) Being in the running for the 'best restaurant in Nunavut' probably isn't going to prompt any *Food Network* producers to fly north, but this steakhouse in the Nova Inn does a good job in replicating the comfort food that is par for the course down south. And such huge portions!

Gallery
CANADIAN $$$
(☎867-979-2222; The Astro Hill Terrace; mains $25-42; ⊗7am-2pm & 5-8:30pm Mon-Fri, 8am-2pm & 5-8:30pm Sat & Sun) A popular, palatable dining room at the Frobisher Inn offering pasta, steak and Northern cuisine, including caribou stew ($27) and grilled Davis Strait char ($34). In the evening, artists hawk their wares in the dining room.

Snack
FAST FOOD $$
(Nipisa St; ⊗6am-8pm) Unashamedly greasy, Snack has burnt down twice in recent years, most recently in June 2007, but it has arisen from the ashes. Back in business, this Francophone-run diner serves up 1950s kitsch and cheap, mainstream meals (including poutine) on paper plates.

Café Northern Lights
CAFE $
(cnr Queen Elizabeth Way & Niaqunngusiaq Rd; lunch $6-12; ⊗8am-5pm Mon-Fri) In the Royal Bank building, this fast, cheap, popular lunch spot does soup-and-sandwich specials ($9) and stir-fries ($12).

Caribrew Café
CAFE $
(www.frobisherinn.com; The Astro Hill Terrace; snacks from $5; ⊗7am-5pm Mon-Fri, 9am-4pm Sat & Sun) This warm, inviting cafe in the Frobisher Inn is the closest Nunavut gets to Starbucks (with lunch options) which will be either a shock or a relief, depending on your allegiance.

🍷 Drinking

In Iqaluit, almost all crimes, as well as the astronomical suicide rate, are linked to drinking. To combat this, the town clamps down on alcohol. Beer and wine can be had with a meal at several restaurants, but there's no liquor store and only one public bar (though the latter may soon change).

Grind & Brew
CAFE
(Sinaa St; ⊗7am-5:30pm or 6pm) Cappuccinos be damned: Iqaluit's blue-collar, beachfront coffeeshop, just down the road from the museum, offers basic joe, a few pastries, and picnic tables from which to watch doings on the waterfront.

Fantasy Palace
CAFE
(Bldg 1085E, Mivvik St; ⊗7am-5pm Mon-Fri, 10am-5pm Sat, 11am-5pm Sun) A short stroll from the airport, this is a decent place to get a wrap, some java or, on those hot Arctic days, an ice cream cone ($2.25).

Storehouse Bar & Grill
BAR
(The Astro Hill Terrace; ⊗5pm-1am) As befits the only drinkery in town, this big, new, well-appointed watering hole in the Frobisher Inn is a little bit of everything: pub, pool hall, sports bar and disco. The food (pizza and burgers) is also good.

Shopping

Inuit prints, carvings and tapestries are world renowned and are widely available in Iqaluit. For deals on less-refined pieces, dine at the Frobisher Inn, where artists circulate through the dining room offering their works for sale.

Iqaluit Fine Arts Studio
SOUVENIRS

(☑867-979-5578; www.iqaluitfinearts.com; Bldg 1127 Mivvik St; ☺11am-5pm Mon-Sat) Right across from the airport terminal, this gallery has carvings of everything from $12 inukshuks (tacky) to $7000 shamans in soapstone (transcendent).

Malikkaat
ACCESSORIES

(☑867-979-6426; 1083, Mivvik St; ☺10am-6pm Mon-Fri, 10am-4pm Sat) Tiny yet diverse, this giftshop sells traditional sealskin mitts and knit caps along with some unorthodox carvings.

Rannva Design
CLOTHING, ACCESSORIES

(☑867-979-3183; www.rannva.com; Bldg 3102 Helen Maksagak Dr; ☺by appointment Mon-Fri, 2-5pm Sat & Sun) In her Apex studio, Rannva Simonsen sews together the ancient and the chic, generating hip fur garments.

Gallery By the Red Boat
SOUVENIRS

(☑867-979-2055; www.bytheredboat.ca; Bill Mackenzie Rd; ☺vary or by appointment) In an old Hudson's Bay building on Apex Beach, this spartan gallery showcases Saila Kipanek's masterful, costly carvings.

ⓘ Information

Ambulance & Fire (☑867-979-4422) For emergencies. Note that 911 is not the emergency number in Nunavut.

Arctic Ventures (Queen Elizabeth Way; ☺10am-10pm Mon-Sat, 1-10pm Sun) Tucked away upstairs is a spectacular selection of Arctic books and CDs.

Baffin Regional Hospital (☑867-979-7300; Niaqunngusiaq Rd; ☺24hr)

Iqaluit Centennial Library (Sinaa St; ☺1-6pm Mon & Wed, 3-8pm Tue & Thu, 3-6pm Fri, 1-4pm Sat & Sun) In the visitors center building, with free internet.

Police (☑emergencies 867-979-1111, nonemergencies 867-975-0123) Note that 911 is not the emergency number in Nunavut.

Royal Bank of Canada (cnr Queen Elizabeth Way & Niaqunngusiaq Rd) This bank is at the Four Corners intersection. Nearby is the CIBC bank.

Unikkaarvik Regional Visitors Centre (☑867-979-4636; Sinaa St; ☺9am-6pm Mon-Fri, 1-4pm Sat & Sun) Might not have the most knowledgeable staff, but offers ample pamphlets, an informative minimuseum and a reference collection of Nunavut books and videos.

ⓘ Getting There & Around

Most flights from outside the territory land here (p811) and flights to the smaller Baffin communities depart from here. First Air serves all communities on the island, plus Resolute and Rankin Inlet. Kenn Borek Air operates services to fewer destinations but is often cheaper. Canadian North goes to Rankin.

Iqaluit is compact and thoroughly walkable. Even the airport is an easy stroll from downtown, about half a kilometer along Mivvik St. The city is also awash with cabs that charge $6 to anywhere. Expect to share: drivers often load to capacity before making drop-offs. Try **Pai-Pa Taxi** (☑867-979-5222).

BAFFIN REGION

The Baffin region comprises Nunavut's constellation of eastern and High Arctic

---

EXTREME FACTS

» At 2,093,190 sq km, Nunavut is significantly larger than many of the world's most populous nations including Mexico and Indonesia. If it were an independent country, it would be the world's 15th largest.

» Supporting an estimated 30,000 people, its total population is the same as the British Overseas Territory of Gibraltar (6.8 sq km).

» Nunavut has the highest birth rate of any Canadian province or territory.

» The territory has only 21km of roads and an equal paucity of trees.

» It is home to nearly half of the world's polar bear population.

» Alert on Ellesmere Island is the northernmost permanently inhabited settlement on the planet with a registered population of just five people.

» The total number of annual visitors for Nunavut's four expansive national parks is approximately 800. Many of these come by boat and don't disembark.

islands. It reaches from the swampy, forested isles of James Bay to the jagged peaks of Ellesmere Island, 3000km north. Half of Nunavut's population lives in this region, and visitors will find the best scenery, outdoor opportunities and tourism infrastructure here.

Katannilik Territorial Park

One of the finest parks in Nunavut is just a few dozen kilometers - by foot, flight or snowmobile - from Iqaluit. *Katannilik* means 'place of waterfalls,' and comprises two main features: the Soper River and the Itijjagiaq Trail.

A Canadian Heritage waterway, the aquamarine **Soper River** splashes 50 navigable kilometers through a deep, fertile valley, past cascades, caribou, gemstone deposits and dwarf-willow forest to the community of Kimmirut (population 411). Paddlers usually spend three days to a week floating and exploring.

Hikers and skiers can opt for the **Itijjagiaq Trail**, a traditional 120km route over the tablelands of the Meta Incognita Peninsula and through the Soper valley. The hike usually takes 10 or 12 days. The trailhead is on Frobisher Bay, about 10km west of Iqaluit. For more details, contact **Parks Nunavut** (☑867-975-7700; www.nunavutparks.com).

Most paddlers charter a plane from Iqaluit to the riverside airstrip at Mt Joy, float from the put-in to Kimmirut, and then fly back to Iqaluit. Kenn Borek Air charges about $1300 from Iqaluit to Mt Joy and can carry approximately 1100kg of people and gear. For hikers, you can hire an Iqaluit outfitter to take you to the trailhead by boat; ask for names at the **Unikkaarvik Regional Visitors Centre** (☑867-979-4636; Sinaa St; ☉9am-6pm Mon-Fri, 1-4pm Sat & Sun) in Iqaluit.

First Air flies from Kimmirut to Iqaluit four times weekly ($178 one way).

Pangnirtung

Among Nunavut's outlying communities, Pangnirtung, or 'Pang' (population 1325), is the best destination, with art and outdoor opportunities galore. Located 40km south of the Arctic Circle, Pang hugs a stunning fjord and is the gateway to Auyuittuq National Park.

Sights

Uqqurmiut Centre for Arts & Crafts   ART GALLERY

(☑867-473-8870; www.uqqurmiut.com; ☉9am-noon & 1-5pm Mon-Fri) The town is famous for tapestries, prints and woven hats, all available at the Uqqurmiut Centre for Arts & Crafts, opposite the interpretive center. Artists in the printshop and weaving studio often show off their techniques and wares; ask first before snapping photos.

Kekerten Historic Park   HISTORIC PARK

About 50km south of town is Kekerten Historic Park, an old whaling station on an island. A trail leads past the remains of 19th-century houses, tools and graves. A boat tour here (around $180 per person for a minimum of four people) is a full-day trip. Outfitters can also take you wildlife-watching or fishing. For any of these, Joavee of **Alivaktuk Outfitting Services** (☑867-473-8721; jalivaktuk@nv.sympatico.ca) is highly recommended.

⚡ Activities

Pang supposedly has two **hiking paths**, detailed on a map available at the interpretive center. One ill-defined trail follows the Duval River's north side and another departs from the campground on the river's south side, hugs the bank until reaching a waterfall and then wanders off overland.

🛏 Sleeping & Eating

Of all the small towns in Nunavut, you'd think Pangnirtung would have decent lodging, but alas, options are actually rather limited.

Auyuittuq Lodge (☑867-473-8955; www.pangnirtunghotel.com; r per person $225), Pang's only hotel, is just down the street from the interpretive center, and has rudimentary rooms, shared bathrooms, neglectful service and noxious food.

Other lodging options include a campground above town beside the river (watch out for theft and for howling windstorms, which turn tents to ribbons) and **homestays** (per person $80, incl meals $120), which let you bunk with a local Inuit family; contact the interpretive center for details.

Wise souls self-cater from **Northern Store** (☑867-473-8935; ☉10am-6pm Mon-Sat, noon-5pm Sun), just down the road from the hotel.

ⓘ Information

Angmarlik Interpretive Centre (☑867-473-8737; oarnaqaq1@gov.nu.ca; ☉8:30am-8pm

Mon-Fri, 10:30am-8pm Sat, 11:30am-8pm Sun)
Has displays on Inuit and whaling history, a
massive whale skull and information on local
guides and outfitters.

Parks Canada (✆867-473-2500; www.park
scanada.gc.ca; ⏱8:30am-noon & 1-5pm Jul &
Aug, 8:30am-noon & 1-5pm Mon-Fri Sep-Jun)
Next door to the interpretive center.

Qimiruvik Library (✆867-473-8678; ⏱4-8pm
Mon-Fri; ☷) In the Angmarlik Centre, has free
internet.

ⓘ Getting There & Away

From Iqaluit, there are daily flights to Pang run
by Kenn Borek Air and First Air (from $438
return).

Auyuittuq National Park

Among the globe's most flabbergasting
places, Auyuittuq (ah-you-*ee*-tuk) means
'the land that never melts.' Appropriately, there are plenty of glaciers in this
19,500-sq-km park, plus jagged peaks, vertiginous cliffs and deep valleys. Hikers trek
along the 97km **Akshayuk Pass** (crossing
the Arctic Circle) between late June and
early September, when it's snow-free. Nearby, climbers scale **Mt Thor** (1500m), the
earth's highest sheer cliff. Camp wherever
you can find a safe, wind-proof, ecologically
appropriate spot. Nine emergency shelters
dot the pass.

Parks Canada (✆867-473-2500; www.
parkscanada.gc.ca; ⏱8:30am-noon & 1-5pm Jul
& Aug, 8:30am-noon & 1-5pm Mon-Fri Sep-Jun)
Is in Pangnirtung, next to the Angmarlik
Interpretive Centre. You must register here
and pay the park entry fee (bizarrely set at
$24.76 per night, up to $148).

The south end of the pass is 30km from
Pangnirtung. In summer you can hike
there in two days, or, more commonly, have
an outfitter take you by boat (about $110,
two-person minimum). For about $175 per
person, through-hikers can arrange to be
picked up at the other end by an outfitter
from Qikiqtarjuaq, which is served by First
Air and Kenn Borek Air.

While wondrous, Auyuittuq is also brutal, isolated and sometimes polar bear-
ridden. Only wilderness veterans should
conduct self-guided treks here; other people
can sign on with the park's only licensed
tour company, **Black Feather** (www.black-
feather.com), which offers 10-, 14- and 16-day
hikes, ranging from $3100 to $3800.

Cape Dorset

Cape Dorset (population 1236), on the
rocky shore of Baffin Island's Foxe Peninsula, is the epicenter of Inuit art. A half-
century ago the residents here pioneered
modern Arctic carving and printmaking,
marketing it to the world with remarkable
success.

The **Mallikjuaq Park Visitor Centre**
(✆867-897-8996) has artifacts portraying
the history of Cape Dorset and the Mallikjuaq Islands, and can help arrange a visit
to the park.

◎ Sights & Activities

West Baffin Eskimo Cooperative
ART GALLERY
(✆867-897-8944; ⏱9am-5pm Mon-Fri) Though
many Inuit communities now generate
world-class artworks, Cape Dorset's remain
the most revered. Just around the corner
from the hotel, the West Baffin Eskimo
Cooperative has a fine gallery plus an intriguing studio where you can watch artists work. (In summer, though, the place is
pretty empty and sometimes closed, so call
ahead.) The Kingnait Inn also sells sculptures, and you can often find artists carving
outside their homes.

Mallikjuaq Historic Park   HISTORIC PARK
You can hike to Mallikjuaq Historic Park
in about 45 minutes, but only at low tide.
Otherwise, hire an outfitter to take you
there by boat. The park features ruins of
thousand-year-old pre-Inuit stone houses,
hiking trails, wildlife and tundra flowers.
Ask at the visitor center or the Kingnait Inn
about other hiking routes near town.

⎔ Tours

Huit Huit Tours   OUTDOOR ACTIVITIES
(✆867-897-8806;   www.capedorsettours.com)
Huit Huit Tours offers multiday dog-sled

ⓘ POLAR BEARS

Polar bears aren't just on Nunavut's
license plates. *Nanuq* (the Inuit name)
is an inveterate wanderer and can turn
up just about anywhere, any time of
year. Worse, unlike grizzlies and black
bears, they actively prey on people.
Inquire about bear sightings before
trudging out of town, or go with a
shotgun-toting guide.

NICE PACKAGES

Independent travel offers the intrepid the chance for trailblazing, saving cash and seeing the real guts of a place. Except, perhaps, in Nunavut. Here more than anywhere else in Canada you should consider a package tour: only big groups can achieve the economies of scale that make the Arctic affordable. Sure, a $4000 cruise is spendy, but on a per-day basis, it's little costlier – and a lot more fun – than hunkering down in a High Arctic hotel. Nunavut package tours are numerous, ranging from guided hiking in Auyuittuq National Park to taking a nuclear-powered icebreaker to the Pole. For a rundown of tour operators and outfitters, see the annual travel planner from **Nunavut Tourism** (867-979-6551, 866-686-2888; www.nunavuttourism.com).

adventures in winter and summertime excursions focusing on wildlife and Inuit culture.

🛏 Sleeping & Eating

Kingnait Inn　　　　　　　　HOTEL $$$
(867-897-8863; s/d $200/325, incl meals $260/385) Just around the bend from the Eskimo Cooperative is Cape Dorset's local hotel, which offers meals and spartan rooms. You may have to share a room if the place fills up.

Cape Dorset Suites　　　　HOTEL $$$
(867-897-8806; www.dorsetsuites.com; r per person $200; 🖥) Recent upgrades at Cape Dorset have added one-bedroom suites and conference facilities at a new location. Still surprising guests with warm wood furnishings and ample space are the three-bedroom Guest House, and aptly named two-bedroom White House and the slightly more surreally named Beach House. All suites have kitchens, laundry and cable TV.

ℹ Getting There & Away

Each weekday, First Air flies here from Iqaluit ($610 return); six days per week Kenn Borek makes the same trip.

Pond Inlet

POP 1315

On Baffin Island's north coast, Pond Inlet is in Tununiq, 'the place facing away from the sun'. Perhaps for that reason, locals seem more insular and unfriendly than in other Nunavut towns. Non-Inuit originally arrived here for whaling and trading opportunities; now they come to kayak, hunt and gaze slack-jawed at the mountainscape. Make arrangements with outfitters before arriving; this is not a place to wing it.

🏃 Activities

Hiking

For a short hike, head a few kilometers out of town to Salmon Creek and the remains of an old Inuit village. The more ambitious trek is to **Mt Herodier** (765m), 15km east of town. Along the coast, there's fishing for Arctic char in July and August.

Boat & Kayak Trips

Polar Sea Adventures (867-899-8870; www.polarseaadventures.com) conducts paddling expeditions and can rent kayaks and paddling gear. It and other outfitters guide whale-watching expeditions and late-spring wildlife-viewing adventures to the floe edge, the biologically rich area where the sea ice meets the open water. Durations and costs vary; expect to pay up to $4000 for a week at the floe edge.

🛏 Sleeping & Eating

Tamaarvik Park　　　　CAMPGROUND $
(tent sites free) Camping is available here, located 4km south of town via the Water Lake Rd.

Sauniq Inn　　　　　　　　HOTEL $$$
(867-899-6500; www.pondinlethotel.com; r from $225; 🖥) Another Inns North Hotel operated by Arctic Cooperatives Ltd (ACL), an aboriginal organization, the Sauniq offers the usual cozy, if a little austere, facilities at typically weighty Nunavut rates. It can organize an airport shuttle, car rental and put you in touch with all the local outfitters and tour agents. There's an onsite restaurant, laundry and meeting room.

ℹ Information

Nattinnak Centre (867-899-8225; 🕙10am-noon & 1-5pm Tue Thu & Fri, 1-5pm & 7-9pm Wed, 2-4pm Sun) has information on area activities and outfitters, plus a tiny giftshop and a fine little minimuseum with info, maps and displays on wildlife and local culture. Check out the life-size dioramas and the very cool fish-skin baskets. If you are really lucky you might catch some throat-singing or drum dancing.

❶ Getting There & Away
First Air flies to/from Iqaluit almost daily ($1400 return), and twice per week Kenn Borek Air serves Resolute ($792 return).

Sirmilik National Park
Near Pond Inlet is the Sirmilik National Park, inaugurated in 1999, and strewn with spires, glaciers and hoodoos (weird eroded red sandstone towers). The terrain provides a breeding ground for countless seabirds including the planet's largest flock of snow geese. The park is made up of three main areas: Bylot Island, a bird sanctuary and one of world's largest uninhabited islands; Oliver Sound, a fiord with exciting canoeing opportunities; and the Borden Peninsula with its striking hoodoos.

Experiencing Sirmilik on your own is a challenge, so most people choose to go on some kind of package tour. **Parks Canada** (✆867-899-8092; www.parkscanada.gc.ca; ◷8.30am-noon & 1-5pm Mon-Fri) maintains an office in Pond Inlet with a list of outfitters and is where you must register and pay the entrance fee ($24.50 per night, up to $147.20).

Resolute
POP 229

The upside of living in Resolute, on Cornwallis Island, is you don't have to mow your lawn. The downside is everything else. A clutch of minuscule homes in a wind-lashed gravel desert, Canada's worst-climate community was founded when the feds lured the Inuit here to shore up national sovereignty. Most visitors are just passing through to get to Quttinirpaaq National Park, the North Pole, or the only more-northerly community in Canada, scenic Grise Fiord.

If you have time, try local hiking or fly to the national historic site, **Beechey Island**, about 80km east; charter flights for around 10 people cost at least $2100. This desolate place was where the ill-fated Franklin expedition wintered in 1845–46 before vanishing forever. Traces of the 128 men and their unsuccessful rescuers remain. Ask at Resolute's hotels for information on tours and outfitters.

Given the likelihood of being 'weathered in' at Resolute for days, it's fortuitous there are two great hotels. **Qausuittuq Inns North** (✆867-252-3900; www.resolutebay.com; r $225, incl meals $430; @) is a lodge with almost embarrassingly doting service, plus good home cooking. **South Camp Inn** (✆867-252-3737; www.southcampinn.com; r $245; @☎), Resolute's nerve centre, is labyrinthine, well appointed and run by Aziz Kheraj, a Tanzanian who, improbably,

---

WORTH A TRIP

THELON RIVER

Among the big Barrenland rivers in Nunavut's Kivalliq region, the most notable – and floatable – is the legendary Thelon. A Canadian Heritage river, the waterway wends some 1000km through utterly wild country, starting in the Northwest Territories just east of Great Slave Lake and emptying into saltwater near the Nunavut community of Baker Lake. Much of its length is protected by the Thelon Wildlife Sanctuary, and there's talk of guarding its headwaters with a national park. Caribou, grizzly, wolf, musk ox and gyrfalcon abound here, as do – weirdly – spruce trees, springing up far north of the normal treeline. Though Inuit seldom travel these waters today, their ancient campsites flank the riverbanks.

In any given summer – we're talking mid-July to mid-August – a hundred or so people paddle the Thelon. If you're keen to be among them, you'll need to plan carefully. Canoeing the river doesn't require remarkable paddling skills, but it *does* demand wilderness savvy. Floating the entirety would take many weeks; most people opt to paddle just a portion and charter a plane to drop them off and pick them up. A simpler option is to sign on with an outfitter, such as **Canoe Arctic** (✆867-872-2308; www.canoearctic.com) or others listed in the annual travel planner from **Nunavut Tourism** (✆867-979-6551, 866-686-2888; www.nunavuttourism.com).

INUIT CULTURE

In Canada's cultural stew, Nunavut is the most exotic ingredient. Most residents are Inuit – the legendary 'Eskimos' (the term is considered embarrassingly archaic) who are only a generation removed from *Nanook of the North*.

Nowadays, superficially at least, modernity has engulfed them. Tourists seeking childlike, nose-rubbing indigenes will be out of luck. Town life has trumped nomadism; plywood homes have obviated igloos; snowmobiles outnumber dog-teams a hundred-fold. Everyone watches the same stupid TV shows we all do.

And yet the place is wild. Inuit remain at heart hunter-gatherers. Though the tools of their trade have changed, nature and its rhythms still hold sway. Harvesting animals remains a holy sacrament. Discussions with locals here invariably revolve around wildlife and weather and it's clear there are mixed feelings about no longer being 'on the land.'

In addition to being Inuit-dominated, Nunavut culture is profoundly rural. Except in Iqaluit, there are zero urban refinements. Communities are ramshackle, roads are mud-rutted, yards are festooned with junk. Dysfunction is everywhere, from graffiti to suicide. People can seem sullen or aloof, though seldom hostile. The best advice for enjoying the place is to slow down, chill out and check your southern standards at the door.

is the High Arctic's kingpin. Surprisingly good meals are included in the room price.

First Air flies to/from Iqaluit four times weekly ($2800 return), while Kenn Borek Air serves small High Arctic towns and does charters.

Quttinirpaaq National Park

If you have a fortune to squander, a fun way would be to visit Canada's second-biggest park, way up on northern Ellesmere Island. A chartered plane from Resolute costs $23,500 (one way) for about six people. If you'd like a pick-up, you can double that price.

Highlights include **Cape Columbia**, the continent's northernmost point, **Mt Barbeau**, which at 2616m is the highest peak in eastern North America, and **Lake Hazen Basin**, a thermal oasis where animals, due to their unfamiliarity with humans, appear strangely tame. For park information, contact **Parks Canada** (☎867-975-4673; nunavut. info@pc.gc.ca).

KIVALLIQ REGION

The Kivalliq region takes in the Hudson Bay coast and the Barrenlands to the west. This is a flat, windswept area, thick with caribou and waterfowl, and cut through by wild rivers such as the Back, Kazan and Thelon. Nunavut's newest national park, Ukkusiksalik, is here with bears, whales and, thus far, almost zero infrastructure or visitorship.

Rankin Inlet

POP 2358

Muddy, dusty, littered and busy, Rankin was founded in 1955 as a mining center and is now the Kivalliq's largest community and the regional government and transport center. From here you can go fishing in the bay or in the many rivers and lakes.

⊙ Sights & Activities

Inukshuk & Waterfront　　　　MONUMENT
Rankin's famed Inukshuk (stone cairn of human form) is probably the most-photographed in Nunavut. It lords over the community like a giant turned to stone. That and the sometimes-bustling waterfront are what pass for in-town sights in Rankin Inlet.

**Iqalugaarjuup Nunanga
Territorial Park**　　　　NATURE RESERVE
Formerly known as plain old Ijiraliq Territorial Park, this tongue-twister of a park (the name means: 'the land around the river of little fish') is located 10km from town and is popular for hiking and berry picking. Near the Meliadine River's mouth are archeological sites where the Dorset people, who preceded the Inuit, used to live.

Marble Island
HISTORICAL SITE

In Hudson Bay, 50km east of Rankin, is uninhabited Marble Island, a graveyard for James Knight and his crew, who sought the Northwest Passage in the 18th century. Some wrecks of 19th-century whaling ships are there too. Ask at the visitor center or hotel to learn if anyone's offering tours there.

🛏 Sleeping & Eating

Nanuq Lodge
B&B $$$

(📞867-645-2650; www.nanuqlodge.com; s/d $150/200; @) This big, friendly, sunny B&B is the best place to stay in the region. It rents kayaks, loans bicycles and happily arranges tours, including dog-sled rides. Enjoy the comfortable rooms adorned with Inuit art and equipped with TVs, or trade polar-bear stories in the communal sitting room. Breakfast includes fresh baked bread.

Siniktarvik Hotel
HOTEL $$$

(📞867-645-2807; www.siniktarvik.ca; s/d $205/250; 📶) A rambling, aluminium-clad hotel on Rankin's main street, it's the nexus of much of the town's activity and is passable by polar standards. Meals are $60-plus per day.

Sugar Rush Café
CAFE $

(📞867-645-3373; sandwiches $7-10) This may be Earth's only diner with both rock 'n' roll kitsch and caribou jerky strips ($2.50).

🔒 Shopping

The shopping's decent: **Matchbox Gallery** (📞867-645-2674; www.matchboxgallery.com; ⊘vary) is a small space famed for having pioneered Inuit ceramic art (on sale for serious bucks), while **Ivalu** (📞867-645-3400; ⊘10am-5pm Mon-Fri) is more of a gift shop, with everything from frozen musk ox sirloin tips to $300 sealskin mitts.

ℹ Information

The **Rankin Inlet Visitors Centre** (📞867-645-3838; ⊘8:30am-7pm Mon-Fri), located at the airport, has perfunctory information and historical displays and even-more-perfunctory help.

ℹ Getting There & Away

Canadian North and First Air operate services to/from Yellowknife ($1600 return) and Iqaluit ($1600 return), and First Air, Calm Air and Kivalliq Air run flights to Winnipeg (from $1300 return). Calm Air and Kivalliq Air provide services to the region's smaller communities.

KITIKMEOT REGION

The Kitikmeot is Nunavut's least-populated and probably least-visited region, occupying the mainland's arctic coast and the islands north of there. Between them runs the fabled – and usually frozen – Northwest Passage.

WORTH A TRIP

THE BACK OF BEYOND

Surrounding Wager Bay, a large inlet off Hudson Bay, **Ukkusiksalik National Park** (www.pc.gc.ca) is the newest of Nunavut's Parks Canada quartet, inaugurated in 2003. Comprising 20,500 sq km of bleak uninhabited tundra, the park is notoriously difficult to visit, though expensive, weather-dependent trips sometimes occur in July and August, flying in through Winnipeg, Rankin Inlet and Baker Lake. The park's only accommodation is the lonely **Sila Lodge**, a warm but basic abode built by three Inuit friends in 1987 and taken over by the park in 2003. It consists of a main building and five individual cabins each equipped with three bedrooms and a sitting area. In the surrounding wilderness – a vast tundra punctuated by a few dwarf birch 'trees' – lives a surprising array of wildlife, including caribou, arctic hare, peregrine falcon and, most notably, polar bear. Indeed, outside Churchill, Manitoba, the park is one of the best places in the world to view these predatory creatures in their wild state. Another curiosity is the isolated former Hudson's Bay Company supply post at nearby **Ford Lake** abandoned in the 1940s. Ukkusiksalik was closed for the 2010 season but was scheduled to reopen in summer 2011. Phone 📞867-462-4500 to check current status.

Cambridge Bay

POP 1477

Say 'Cambridge Bay' and even Nunavut residents shiver. This wind-wracked settlement on southeast Victoria Island is the regional administrative and transport center.

Explorers seeking the Northwest Passage often took shelter here; you can see what remains of Roald Amundsen's schooner *Maud* in the harbor. **Ovayok Territorial Park** (formerly Mt Pelly Territorial Park), accessible over a rough road or via a half-day hike (15km), is a prime place to see musk ox and offers good views from **Mt Pelly** (200m). It has interpretive signage, walking trails and camping spots. South across the passage is **Queen Maud Bird Sanctuary**, the world's largest migratory bird refuge.

Arctic Coast Visitors Centre (☑867-983-22224; 1 Omingmak St; ⊙9am-5pm Mon-Fri) organizes tours, has displays about exploration, rents bicycles and offers showers. **Arctic Island Lodge** (☑867-983-2345; www.cambridgebayhotel.com; s/d $225/325) is swanky by Nunavut standards. Meals cost an extra $35 and up per day.

Canadian North and First Air fly to/from Yellowknife for about $1400 return. First Air flies from Cambridge Bay to the Kitikmeot's other communities.

Understand
Canada

population per sq km

CANADA   USA   FRANCE

♦ ≈ 4 people

Canada Today

Loonie Boons

The Canadian economy kicked butt from 1993 to 2007. That's the year the Loonie reached parity with the greenback for the first time in three decades. Oil and natural gas were the reasons. But like many countries, the GFC brought things to a halt. The economy fell into recession, and Ottawa posted its first fiscal deficit in 2009 after 12 years of surplus.

And then: Canadian banks bounced back, thanks to their tradition of conservative lending. Even with a pesky deficit, Canada is doing a-OK compared to its global brethren. The International Monetary Fund predicts it'll be the only one of the seven major industrialized democracies to return to surplus by 2015.

The High Price of Oil

Voltaire may have written off Canada as 'a few acres of snow' back in the mid-18th century, but those 'few acres' have yielded vast amounts of oil, timber and other natural resources, that in turn have propelled Canada to a very enviable standard of living.

The only issue: extracting and developing the resources comes with an ecological price, and Canadians debate what to do about it. Oil is a conundrum. Northern Alberta's Athabasca Tar Sands are the world's second-biggest oil reserves, and they've done a big job boosting the economy. They also produce 5% of Canada's greenhouse gas emissions, according to Environment Canada. Environmentalists say the sands are massive polluters. The pro-industry camp says improvements are being made and, when compared to other oil producers such as Saudi

Top Culture Resources

» **Canadian Broadcasting Corporation** (CBC; www. cbc.ca) The country's main purveyor of news and cultural programming via TV and radio.

» **Polaris Music Prize** (www.polarismusicprize.ca) Fetes the best Canadian music-maker (based on merit); the website provides links to uber-cool album downloads.

» **Juno Awards** (www. junoawards.ca) Honors the best Canadian music-makers (based on sales); a good indicator of who's currently popular.

belief systems
(% of population)

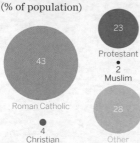

43 — Roman Catholic

4 — Christian

23 — Protestant

2 — Muslim

28 — Other

if Canada were 100 people

28 would be of British Isles origin
23 would be of French origin
15 would be of European origin
34 would be of Other origin

Arabia and Venezuela, the oil sands measure up, especially when human rights issues and decreased transportation distances are factored in (most of Canada's oil goes to the USA).

Table Talk

The nation's much-cherished, but ailing, universal health care system sparks serious table talk. Although no one will admit it, a two-tiered system is in place, and those with deep pockets can access additional, often quicker care in private facilities. People like Newfoundland premier and millionaire Danny Williams, for instance. He went to Florida in 2010 for heart surgery that was available in Canada, which sent newspaper headlines screaming.

Still, a free, portable health care system that's available to everyone is quite a feat. To many citizens, it's at the very root of what makes Canada great. So are progressive views on same-sex marriage, immigration and marijuana use.

Politics

In 2006, the Conservative Party took over from the Liberals for the first time in 12 years. Stephen Harper became the new prime minister, but he led Canada's smallest minority government since Confederation. In 2008 he called an early election, hoping to boost the Conservatives' grip. It did, but only 22% of Canadians voted, the lowest in history.

Amid controversy, Harper suspended parliament twice in 2009. The first time to avoid a no-confidence vote by opposition parties, which

» Population: 33.5 million

» Unemployment rate: 8.3%

» Median family income: $63,900

» Hours TV watched per week: 21.4

» Life expectancy: women 83.9 years, men 78.7 years

Top Films

» **National Film Board of Canada** (www.nfb.ca) Produces quality documentaries and animation; watch them online or on your iPhone.

» **Bon Cop, Bad Cop** (2006, dir Eric Canuel) An Anglophone and Francophone join forces; top grossing Canadian movie ever.

» **The Sweet Hereafter** (1997, dir Atom Egoyan) A small BC town copes with a deadly bus crash.

» **Away from Her** (2006, dir Sarah Polley) Alzheimer's breaks apart a rural Ontario couple.

worked. The second time to deal with the economy, he said. Opponents say he did it to muzzle allegations of Afghan detainee torture. (Reports had surfaced that the Canadian government and troops knew about torture going on at the hand of Afghan troops, but didn't do anything about it.) That the government shutdown occurred before the Olympics started in Vancouver added fuel to the fire.

Top Books

» **Beautiful Losers** (Leonard Cohen) Experimental oddity involving love, sex and Aboriginals.

» **The Apprenticeship of Duddy Kravitz** (Mordechai Richler) A Montréal Jew quests to make money.

History

The Aboriginals, French, British and Americans are the main characters in Canadian history. The tale begins some 15,000 years ago, when Aboriginal societies took shape and spread throughout the land. Europeans entered the picture next, arriving in the late 15th century, for the most part. By the mid-1700s, the country was plowing full-steam ahead toward development.

You'll hear some familiar themes throughout the ages: conflicts between Aboriginals and European settlers, colonial fights over the land and its resources, governing a large, multicultural group in a way that keeps everyone happy. These issues have shaped Canadian history from the get-go, and they're still in play today.

The government has designated 956 national historic sites across the country, from forts to battlefields to famous homes. Parks Canada runs about one-fifth of them, which often have costumed interpreters and are pretty darn cool.

The First Inhabitants

Canada's first inhabitants were most likely hunter-nomads who, in hungry pursuit of caribou, elk and bison, crossed over from Asia on the land bridge that once linked Siberia and Alaska. As the earth warmed and the glaciers retreated, these immigrants began to trickle all across the Americas.

About 4500 years ago, a second major wave of migration from Siberia brought the ancestors of the Inuit to Canada. The new arrivals took one look at the North, sized it up as a tasty icebox filled with fish-and-seal dinners, and decided to hang around. These early Inuit were members of the Dorset Culture, named after Cape Dorset on Baffin Island, where its remains were first unearthed. Around AD 1000 a separate Inuit culture, the whale-hunting Thule of northern Alaska, began making its way east through the Canadian Arctic. As these people spread, they

---

Top Historic Sites

» L'Anse aux Meadows, Newfoundland

» Louisbourg, Nova Scotia

» Batouche, Saskatchewan

» Province House, PEI

» Québec City, Québec

» Klondike sites, Yukon

» Head-Smashed-In Buffalo Jump, Alberta

» Alexander Graham Bell site, Nova Scotia

TIMELINE	**Circa 70 million BC**	**Circa 25,000 BC**	**1000 BC**
	Dinosaurs enjoy the warm, coastal climate that exists in southern Alberta at this time (the hefty creatures think of it like today's Victoria).	Hot on the hoofs of juicy caribou and bison, the first humans arrive in Canada by crossing over the land bridge that once connected Siberia to North America.	After hanging around for a few thousand years, the Maritime Archaic Indians, known for their ceremonial burials at sites like Port aux Choix, inexplicably disappear.

overtook the Dorset Culture. The Thule are the direct ancestors of the modern Inuit.

By the late 15th century, when the first Europeans arrived, Aboriginal peoples had spread beyond the Arctic into four other major locations across Canada: the Pacific, the Plains, the southern Ontario/St Lawrence River area and the Northeast woodlands. For more on their history, see the Aboriginal Cultures chapter (p845).

Age of Discovery

Viking celebrity Leif Eriksson was the first European to reach Canada's shores. In fact, he and his tribe of Scandinavian seafarers were the first Europeans in all of North America. Around AD 1000 they poked around the eastern shores of Canada, establishing winter settlements and way stations for repairing ships and restocking supplies, such as at L'Anse Aux Meadows (p485) in Newfoundland. The local tribes didn't exactly roll out the welcome mat for these intruders, who eventually tired of the hostilities and went home. There would be no more visits from the outside for another 300 to 400 years.

The action heated up again in the late 15th century. In 1492, backed by the Spanish crown, Christopher Columbus went searching for a western sea route to Asia and instead stumbled upon some small islands in the Bahamas. Other European monarchs, excited by his 'discovery,' quickly sponsored expeditions of their own. In 1497, Giovanni Caboto, better known as John Cabot, sailed under a British flag as far west as Newfoundland and Cape Breton.

Cabot didn't find a passage to China, but he did find cod, a much-coveted commodity in Europe at the time. In short order, hundreds of boats were shuttling between Europe and the fertile new fishing grounds. Basques whalers from northern Spain soon followed. Several were based at Red Bay (p499) in Labrador, which became the biggest whaling port in the world during the 16th century.

King François I of France looked over the fence at his neighbors, stroked his beard, then snapped his fingers and ordered Jacques Cartier to appear before him. By this time, the hunt was on not only for the Northwest Passage but also for gold, given the findings by Spanish conquistadors among the Aztec and Inca civilizations. François hoped for similar riches in the frosty North.

Upon arrival in Labrador, Cartier found only 'stones and horrible rugged rocks,' as he wrote in his journal in 1534. He dutifully kept exploring and soon went ashore on Québec's Gaspé Peninsula to claim the land for France. The local Iroquois thought he was a good neighbor at first, until he kidnapped two of the chief's sons and took them back to Europe. To his credit, Cartier returned them a year later when

---

For the whole enchilada, watch *Canada: A People's History* (2000–01), a 17-episode CBC TV series. Don't have an extra 32 hours in your schedule? Trawl the website (www.cbc.ca/history) for bite-sized historical summaries.

In *Canadian History for Dummies*, best-selling author Will Ferguson uses his irreverent, opinionated and energetic style to take you on an entertaining cruise through his country's wild and wacky past.

1000	1497	1528	1534
Viking Leif Eriksson and crew wash up at L'Anse aux Meadows, where they build sod houses. They're the first Europeans in North America, beating Columbus by 500 years.	John Cabot sails over from Britain and finds Newfoundland instead of China. It's not a bad trade-off because the waters are filled with fat, delicious codfish.	St John's, Newfoundland, bobs up as North America's first town. It belongs to no nation; rather it serves fishing fleets from all over Europe.	Jacques Cartier sails into what is now Québec. He searches for gold and precious metals, but gets only chilled rocks. He claims the land for France anyway.

sailing up the St Lawrence River to Stadacona (present-day Québec City) and Hochelaga (today's Montréal). Here he got wind of a land called Saguenay that was full of gold and silver. The rumor prompted Cartier's third voyage, in 1541, but alas, the mythical riches remained elusive.

Fur Trade Ignites

King François I got bored with his distant colony, since it wasn't producing the bling. But his interest perked back up a few decades later when felt hats became all the rage. Everyone who was anyone was wearing a furry hat and, as the fashion mavens knew, there was no finer chapeau than one made from beaver pelts. With beavers pretty much extinct in the Old World, the demand for a fresh supply was strong.

In 1588, the French crown granted the first trading monopoly in Canada, only to have other merchants promptly challenge the claim. And so the race for control of the fur trade was officially on. The economic value of this enterprise and, by extension, its role in shaping Canadian history, cannot be underestimated. It was the main reason behind the country's European settlement, at the root of the struggle for dominance between the French and the British, and the source of strife and division between Aboriginal groups. All because of a silly hat!

In order to gain control of the distant lands, the first order of business was to put European bodies on the ground. In the summer of 1604, a group of French pioneers established a tentative foothold on Île Ste-Croix (a tiny islet in the river on the present US border with Maine). They moved to Port Royal (today's Annapolis Royal) in Nova Scotia the following spring. Exposed and difficult to defend, neither site made a good base for controlling the inland fur trade. As the would-be colonists moved up the St Lawrence River, they finally came upon a spot their leader, Samuel de Champlain, considered prime real estate – where today's Québec City stands. It was 1608 and 'New France' had become a reality.

French vs English

The French enjoyed their plush fur monopoly for several decades, but in 1670 the British mounted a formidable challenge. They caught a lucky break when a pair of disillusioned French explorers, Radisson and Des Groseilliers, confided that the best fur country actually lay to the north and west of Lake Superior, which was easily accessible via Hudson Bay. King Charles II quickly formed the Hudson's Bay Company and granted it a trade monopoly over all the lands whose rivers and streams

Canadian Inventions

» Foghorn (1854)
» Basketball (1892)
» Insulin (1922)
» Easy-Off Oven Cleaner (1932)
» Plastic garbage bag (circa 1950)
» Blackberry smartphone (1999)

Explorer Jacques Cartier bestowed Canada with its name. Scholars say it comes from *kanata*, a Huron-Iroquois word for 'village' or 'settlement,' which was written in Cartier's journal and later transformed by mapmakers to 'Canada.'

1603	1608	1610	1670
After King James strands British naval officer Peter Easton in Newfoundland without pay, Easton becomes Canada's first pirate. Soon he commands 40 ships and 5000 men.	After four years of moving around, Samuel de Champlain finds his dream-home site, putting down stakes at Québec City and giving New France its first permanent settlement.	The British take their turn: merchant John Guy builds a plantation at Cupids, Newfoundland. It's England's first colony in Canada (and second in the New World after Jamestown).	King Charles II creates the Hudson's Bay Company to shore up the local fur trade for the Brits. Years later, the company morphs into The Bay department store chain.

drained into the bay. This vast territory, called Rupert's Land, encompassed about 40% of present-day Canada, including Labrador, western Québec, northwestern Ontario, Manitoba, most of Saskatchewan and Alberta, and part of the Northwest Territories.

The English infuriated the French with such moves, and so the French kept right on galling the English by settling further inland. Both countries had claims to the land, but each wanted regional dominance. They skirmished back and forth in hostilities that mirrored those in Europe, where wars raged throughout the first half of the 18th century.

Things came to a head with the Treaty of Utrecht, which ended Queen Anne's War (1701–13) overseas. Under its provisions, the French had to officially recognize British claims to Hudson Bay and Newfoundland, and give up all of Nova Scotia (then called Acadia) except for Cape Breton Island.

The conflict simmered for a few decades, then ramped up to a new level in 1754 when the two countries battled each other in the French and Indian Wars (also known as the Seven Years' War). The tide soon turned in the Brit's favor with the capture of the Louisbourg fortress (p374), giving them control of a strategically important entrance to the St Lawrence River.

In 1759 they besieged Québec, scaling the cliffs in a surprise attack and quickly defeating the stunned French; it was one of Canada's bloodiest and most famous battles, and left both commanding generals dead. At the Treaty of Paris (1763), France handed Canada over to Britain.

Growing Pains

Managing the newly acquired territory presented quite a challenge for the British. First, they had to quell uprisings by the Aboriginal tribes, such as the attack on Detroit by Ottawa Chief Pontiac. So the British government issued the Royal Proclamation of 1763, which prevented colonists from settling west of the Appalachian Mountains and regulated purchases of aboriginal land. Though well-intentioned, the proclamation was largely ignored.

The French Canadians caused the next headache. Tensions rose when the new rulers imposed British law that heavily restricted the rights of Roman Catholics (the religion of the French), including the rights to vote and hold office. The British hoped their discriminatory policy would launch a mass exodus and make it easier to anglicize the remaining settlers. The plan didn't work – the French just crossed their arms and dug in their heels further.

As if the tribes and French weren't problems enough, the American colonies started making revolutionary rumbles to the south. The Brit-

Unofficial Canadian National Anthems

» 'The Hockey Song' (Stompin' Tom Connors)

» 'Lovers in a Dangerous Time' (performed by writer Bruce Cockburn or the Barenaked Ladies, take your pick)

» 'Mon Pays' (Gilles Vignault)

1755	1759	1763	1775
The English deport some 14,000 French Acadians from the Bay of Fundy region. They're forced onto ships during the Great Expulsion; many head to Louisiana in the USA.	Canada's most famous battle, a beauty between the French and English, happens on the Plains of Abraham at Québec City. It lasts less than an hour. France loses.	The Treaty of Paris boots France out of Canada after France loses the Seven Years' War. Thus, Canada ceases to ping-pong between power-mongering France and Britain.	At the start of the American Revolution, American rebels invade Canada and try to entice Québec to join the revolt against the British, but the locals refuse.

ish governor, Guy Carleton, wisely reasoned that winning the French settlers' political allegiance was more valuable than turning them into tea drinkers. This led to the passage of the Québec Act of 1774. The Act confirmed French Canadians' right to their religion, allowed them to assume political office and restored the use of French civil law. Indeed, during the American Revolution (1775–83) most French Canadians refused to take up arms for the American cause, although not many willingly defended the British either.

After the Revolution, the English-speaking population exploded when some 50,000 settlers from the newly independent America migrated northward. Called United Empire Loyalists due to their presumed allegiance to Britain, many settlers were motivated more by cheap land than by actual love of king and crown. The majority ended up in Nova Scotia and New Brunswick, while a smaller group settled along the northern shore of Lake Ontario and in the Ottawa River Valley (forming the nucleus of what became Ontario). About 8000 people moved to Québec, creating the first sizeable anglophone community in the French-speaking bastion.

Empire of the Bay: The Company of Adventurers That Seized a Continent (2000), by Peter C Newman, relays the blustering Hudson's Bay Company story, from its fur-trading origins to today's The Bay department stores.

Splitsville: Upper & Lower Canada

Partly in order to accommodate the interests of Loyalist settlers, the British government passed the Constitutional Act of 1791, which divided the colony into Upper Canada (today's southern Ontario) and Lower Canada (now southern Québec). Lower Canada retained French civil laws, but both provinces were governed by the British criminal code.

The British crown installed a governor to direct each colony. The governor in turn appointed the members of his 'cabinet,' then called the Executive Council. The legislative branch consisted of an appointed Legislative Council and an elected Assembly, which ostensibly represented the interests of the colonists. In reality, though,

THE MAPLE LEAF SYMBOL

It's on the penny, on Air Canada planes, on Toronto hockey team jerseys – you can't escape the maple leaf. It has been considered a national symbol for almost two centuries. In 1836, *Le Canadien*, a newspaper published in Lower Canada, wrote about it as a suitable emblem for the nation. Ontario and Québec both were using it on their coat of arms by 1868. The Canadian Armed Forces used it during the World Wars. Finally, after much wrangling over the design (one leaf? three leaves? 13 points on it?), the current 11-point leaf was granted national symbol status and went on the flag in 1965.

1793	1818	1858	1864
Explorer Alexander Mackenzie makes the first transcontinental journey across the land. He scrawls 'from Canada by land' on a rock near Bella Coola, BC.	The USA and Britain hash out the Treaty of 1818. The upshot: Canada's border is defined as the 49th Parallel from Lake of the Woods to the Rocky Mountains.	Yee-haw! Prospectors discover gold along the Fraser River in BC, spurring thousands of get-rich-quick dreamers to move north and start panning. Most remain poor.	The Fathers of the Confederation meet in Charlottetown, PEI, and mould a new country called Canada from the group of loosely knit colonies that now comprise the land.

the Assembly held very little power, since the governor could veto its decisions. Not surprisingly, this was a recipe for friction and resentment. This was especially the case in Lower Canada, where an English governor and an English-dominated Council held sway over a French-dominated Assembly.

Rampant cronyism made matters even worse. Members of the conservative British merchant elite dominated the Executive and Legislative Councils and showed little interest in French-Canadian matters. Called the Family Compact in Upper Canada and the Château Clique in Lower Canada, their ranks included brewer John Molson and university founder James McGill. The groups' influence grew especially strong after the War of 1812, an ultimately futile attempt by the USA to take over its northern neighbor.

In 1837, frustration over these entrenched elites reached boiling point. Parti Canadien leader Louis-Joseph Papineau and his Upper Canadian counterpart, Reform Party leader William Lyon Mackenzie, launched open rebellions against the government. Although both uprisings were quickly crushed, the incident signaled to the British that the status quo wasn't going to cut it any longer.

Cautious Reunion

The British dispatched John Lambton, the Earl of Durham, to investigate the rebellions' causes. He correctly identified ethnic tensions as the root of the problem, calling the French and British 'two nations warring in the bosom of a single state.' He then earned the nickname 'Radical Jack' by asserting that French culture and society were inferior and obstacles to expansion and greatness – only assimilation of British laws, language and institutions would quash French nationalism and bring long-lasting peace to the colonies. These ideas were adopted into the Union Act of 1840.

Upper and Lower Canada soon merged into the Province of Canada and became governed by a single legislature, the new Parliament of Canada. Each ex-colony had the same number of representatives, which wasn't exactly fair to Lower Canada (ie Québec), where the population was much larger. On the plus side, the new system brought responsible government that restricted the governor's powers and eliminated nepotism.

While most British Canadians welcomed the new system, the French were less than thrilled. If anything, the union's underlying objective of destroying French culture, language and identity made Francophones cling together even more tenaciously. The provisions of the Act left deep wounds that still haven't fully healed (see the boxed text, p837).

France retains a token of its early exploits in Canada: St-Pierre and Miquelon, two small islands off Newfoundland's coast, remain staunchly French to this day.

1867	1873	1885	1893
It's official: the British North America Act unites the colonies under the Dominion of Canada, a card-carrying member of the British Empire. Queen Victoria celebrates with Canadian bacon for breakfast.	The Mounties are formed, showing the world that crime-fighting can happen politely (as Dudley Do-Right attests).	Canada's first national park opens in Banff, Alberta; meanwhile, in Craigellachie, BC, workers drive in the spike that completes the Canadian Pacific Railway.	The Montréal AAA hockey team accepts the first Stanley Cup (donated by one Lord Stanley of Preston). It's now the oldest trophy North American pro sports teams compete for.

Thus the united province was built on slippery ground. The decade or so following unification was marked by political instability as one government replaced another in fairly rapid succession. Meanwhile, the USA had grown into a self-confident economic powerhouse, while British North America was still a loose patchwork of independent colonies. The American Civil War (1861–65) and the USA's purchase of Alaska from Russia in 1867 raised fears of annexation. It became clear that only a less volatile political system would stave off these challenges, and the movement toward federal union gained momentum.

Canada Confederates

In 1864, Charlottetown, Prince Edward Island (PEI), served as the birthing room for modern Canada. At the town's Province House (p424), the 'Fathers of Confederation' – a group of representatives from Nova Scotia, New Brunswick, PEI, Ontario and Québec – got together and hammered out the framework for a new nation. It took two more meetings before Parliament passed the British North America Act in 1867. And so began the modern, self-governing state of Canada, originally known as the Dominion of Canada. The day the act became official, July 1, is celebrated as Canada's national holiday; it was called Dominion Day until it was renamed Canada Day in 1982.

How the West was Won

Task one on the infant dominion's to-do list was to bring the remaining land and colonies into the confederation. Under its first prime minister, John A Macdonald, the government acquired vast Rupert's Land in 1869 for the paltry sum of £300,000 (about $11.5 million in today's money) from the Hudson's Bay Company. Now called the Northwest Territories (NWT), the land was only sparsely populated, mostly by Plains First Nations and several thousand Métis (may-*tee*), a racial blend of Cree, Ojibwe or Saulteaux and French-Canadian or Scottish fur traders, who spoke French as their main language. Their biggest settlement was the Red River Colony around Fort Garry (today's Winnipeg).

The Canadian government immediately clashed with the Métis people over land and rights, causing the latter to form a provisional government led by the charismatic Louis Riel. He sent the Ottawa-appointed governor packing and, in November 1869, seized control of Upper Fort Garry, thereby forcing Ottawa to the negotiating table. However, with his delegation already en route, Riel impulsively and for no good reason executed a Canadian prisoner he was holding at the fort. Although the murder caused widespread uproar in Canada, the government was so

Searching for your Cajun roots? The Acadian Genealogy Homepage (www.acadian.org) has compiled census reports harking back to 1671, plus maps and histories of local Acadian communities.

1896	1913	1917	1922
Prospectors find more of the shiny stuff, this time in the Yukon. The Klondike Gold Rush is on, with 40,000 hopefuls bringing their picks and pans to Dawson City.	Immigration to Canada crests, with more than 400,000 people embracing the maple leaf. Most are Americans and Eastern Europeans, who can't resist the call of the nation's fertile prairies.	Canada introduces the draft to replenish forces fighting for England in WWI. French Canadians, in particular, oppose the call-up, foreshadowing tensions to come.	Joseph-Armand Bombardier invents a snowmobile prototype in his workshop in Valcourt, Québec. The first model has a propeller. His company eventually goes on to design aircraft.

The USA has invaded Canada twice – in 1775 and 1812 – both times to no avail.

keen to bring the west into the fold it agreed to most of Riel's demands, including special language and religious protections for the Métis. As a result, the then-pint-sized province of Manitoba was carved out of the NWT and entered the dominion in July 1870. Macdonald sent troops after Riel but he narrowly managed to escape to the USA. He was formally exiled for five years in 1875.

British Columbia (BC), created in 1866 by merging the colonies of New Caledonia and Vancouver Island, was the next frontier. The discovery of gold along the Fraser River in 1858 and in the Cariboo region in 1862 had brought an enormous influx of settlers to such goldmine boomtowns as Williams Lake and Barkerville (p748). Once the gold mines petered out, though, BC was plunged into poverty. In 1871 it joined the dominion in exchange for the Canadian government assuming all its debt and promising to link it with the east within 10 years via a transcontinental railroad.

The construction of the Canadian Pacific Railway is one of the most impressive chapters in Canadian history. Macdonald rightly regarded the railroad as crucial in unifying the country, spurring immigration and stimulating business and manufacturing. It was a costly proposition, made even more challenging by the rough and rugged terrain the tracks had to traverse. To entice investors, the government offered major benefits, including vast land grants in western Canada. Workers drove the final spike into the track at Craigellachie, BC, on November 7, 1885.

To bring law and order to the 'wild west,' the government created the North-West Mounted Police (NWMP) in 1873, which later became the Royal Canadian Mounted Police (RCMP). Nicknamed 'Mounties,' they still serve as Canada's national police force today. Although they were effective, the NWMP couldn't prevent trouble from brewing on the prairies, where the Plains First Nations had been forced to sign various treaties relegating them to reserves. It wasn't long before these groups began to challenge their status.

The Canadian Military History Gateway (www. cmhg.gc.ca) provides access to digitized resources on Canada's military history, including audio links to old CBC war broadcasts.

Meanwhile, many Métis had moved to Saskatchewan and settled around Batoche (p546). As in Manitoba, they quickly clashed with government surveyors over land issues. In 1884, after their repeated appeals to Ottawa had been ignored, they coaxed Louis Riel out of exile to represent their cause. Rebuffed, Riel responded the only way he knew: by forming a provisional government and leading the Métis in revolt. Riel had the backing of the Cree, but times had changed: with the railroad nearly complete, government troops arrived within days. Riel surrendered in May and was hanged for treason later that year.

1931	1933	1942	early 1960s
The residential school system peaks. Aboriginal, Inuit and Métis children are removed from their communities and forced to attend schools (most operated by churches) far from home to 'assimilate.'	Three out of 10 people are out of work, as Canada feels the effects of the Great Depression. The Prairies are especially hard hit by the drought-induced Dust Bowl.	Newfoundland becomes the only North American site directly attacked by German forces during WWII, when a U-boat launches a torpedo that strikes inland at Bell Island.	It's a time of change: the 'Quiet Revolution' modernizes, secularizes and liberalizes Québec, while Aboriginal peoples are finally granted citizenship nationwide.

Cutting Ties to England

Canada rang in the 20th century on a high note. Industrialization was in full swing, prospectors had discovered gold in the Yukon, and Canadian resources – from wheat to lumber – were increasingly in demand. In addition, the new railroad opened the floodgates to immigration.

Between 1885 and 1914 about 4.5 million people arrived in Canada. This included large groups of Americans and Eastern Europeans, especially Ukrainians, who went to work cultivating the prairies. Optimism reigned: a buoyant Prime Minister Wilfrid Laurier said 'The 19th century was the century of the United States. I think we can claim that it is Canada that shall fill the 20th century.' It was only natural that this new-found self-confidence would put the country on track to autonomy from Britain. The issue took on even greater urgency when WWI broke out in 1914.

Canada – as a member of the British Empire – found itself automatically drawn into the conflict. In the war's first years, more than 300,000 volunteers went off to European battlefields. As the war dragged on and thousands of soldiers returned in coffins, recruitment ground to a halt. The government, intent on replenishing its depleted forces, introduced the draft in 1917. It proved to be a very unpopular move, to say the least, especially among French Canadians. Animosity toward Ottawa was already at an all-time high since the government had recently abolished bilingual schools in Manitoba and restricted the use of French in Ontario's schools. The conscription issue fanned the flames of nationalism even more. Thousands of Québecois took to the streets in protest, and the issue left Canada divided and Canadians distrustful of their government.

By the time the guns of WWI fell silent in 1918, most Canadians were fed up with sending their sons and husbands to fight in distant wars for

> Delegates to the Charlottetown Conference in 1864 had to sleep on their steamships because the circus was in town and all of the inns were fully booked.

EXTREME MAKEOVER: THE IMAGE OF LOUIS RIEL

Rebel, murderer, traitor – Métis leader Louis Riel was called many things, and not many of them were compliments, in 1885, when he was hanged for treason. But today, a growing number of Canadians see him as a hero who defended the rights of the oppressed against an unjust government. Statues of Riel now stand on Parliament Hill in Ottawa and outside the Manitoba Legislature in Winnipeg, where his boyhood home and grave have become places of pilgrimage. The government's 1998 Statement of Reconciliation to Canada's Aboriginal peoples even included an apology for Riel's execution. For more on his life and related historical sites, see p510.

1961	1962	1963	1964
The kind and neighborly folks of Saskatchewan introduce the first universal healthcare plan, an idea that soon spreads to the rest of Canada.	Canada becomes the third nation in space, after the Soviet Union and the USA, when it launches the Alouette satellite into the stratosphere.	After smoothing a whole lot of concrete, workers lay the final touches on the Trans-Canada Hwy, spanning 7821km from Saint John's, Newfoundland, to Victoria, BC.	Tim Horton's, started by the eponymous ice hockey defenceman, serves its first donut and cup of coffee in Hamilton, Ontario. Timmy's is now Canada's largest restaurant chain.

Britain. Under the government of William Lyon Mackenzie King, an eccentric fellow who communicated with spirits and worshipped his dead mother, Canada began asserting its independence. Mackenzie King made it clear that Britain could no longer automatically draw upon the Canadian military, started signing treaties without British approval, and sent a Canadian ambassador to Washington. This forcefulness led to the Statute of Westminster, passed by the British Parliament in 1931. The statute formalized the independence of Canada and other Commonwealth nations, although Britain retained the right to pass amendments to those countries' constitutions.

Oddly, that right remained on the books for another half century. It was removed only with the 1982 Canada Act, which Queen Elizabeth II signed into law on Parliament Hill in Ottawa on April 17. Today, Canada is a constitutional monarchy with a parliament consisting of an appointed upper house, or Senate, and an elected lower house, the House of Commons. The British monarch remains Canada's head of state, although this is predominantly a ceremonial role and does not diminish the country's sovereignty. Within Canada, the appointed governor general is the monarch's representative.

Lil' Canada All Grown Up

The period after WWII brought another wave of economic expansion and immigration, especially from Europe.

Newfoundland finally joined Canada in 1949. Joey Smallwood, the politician who persuaded the island to sign up, claimed it would bring economic prosperity. Once he became Newfoundland's premier, he helped this prosperity along by forcing a resettlement program upon citizens. People living in small, isolated fishing communities (aka outports) were strongly 'encouraged' to pack up and move inland where the government could deliver schools, health care and other services more economically. One method for 'encouraging' villagers was to cut ferry services to their communities, thus making them inaccessible since there were no roads.

The only province truly left behind during the 1950s boom years was Québec. For a quarter century, it remained in the grip of ultraconservative Maurice Duplessis and his Union Nationale party, with support from the Catholic Church and various business interests. Only after Duplessis' death did the province finally start getting up to speed during the 'Quiet Revolution' of the 1960s. Advances included expanding the public sector, investing in public education and nationalizing the provincial hydroelectric companies. Still, progress wasn't swift enough for radical nationalists who claimed independence was

More than one million Canadians served in the armed forces during WWII from a population of approximately 11.5 million; 42,000 died.

Manual laborers from China built much of the railroad's western stretch. They earned $0.75 to $1.25 per day, not including expenses, and often were given the most dangerous, explosive-laden jobs.

1967	1982	1990	1992
The Great Canadian Oil Sands plant opens at Fort McMurray, Alberta, and starts pumping out black gold. It's reputed to hold more oil than all of Saudi Arabia.	Queen Elizabeth II signs the Canada Act, giving Canada complete sovereignty. However, she retains the right to keep her mug on the money and appoint a governor general.	The Oka Crisis occurs, a violent standoff between the government and a band of Mohawk activists near Montréal, sparked by a land claim over a golf course. One person dies.	The government imposes the Atlantic cod moratorium, and thousands of fisherfolk lose their livelihoods. The ban was supposed to be lifted within a few years, but depleted stocks never rebounded.

VIVE LE QUÉBEC LIBRE

Québec's separatism movement began in earnest in the 1968, when René Lévesque founded the sovereignist Parti Québecois (PQ).

The issue intensified quickly. In October 1970, the most radical wing of the movement, the Front de Libération du Québec (FLQ; Québec Liberation Front), kidnapped Québec's labor minister Pierre Laporte and a British trade official in an attempt to force the independence issue. Prime Minister Pierre Trudeau declared a state of emergency and called in the army to protect government officials. Two weeks later, Laporte's body was found in the trunk of a car. The murder discredited the FLQ in the eyes of many erstwhile supporters and the movement quickly faded away.

Lévesque's PQ won the 1976 Québec provincial election and quickly pushed through a bill that made French the province's sole official language. His 1980 referendum on secession, however, was resoundingly defeated, with almost 60% voting *non*. The issue was put on the back burner for much of the 1980s.

Lévesque's successor, Robert Bourassa, agreed to a constitution-led solution – but only if Québec was recognized as a 'distinct society' with special rights. In 1987 Prime Minister Brian Mulroney unveiled an accord that met most of Québec's demands. To take effect, the so-called Meech Lake Accord needed to be ratified by all 10 provinces and both houses of parliament by 1990. Dissenting premiers in three provinces eventually pledged their support but, incredibly, the accord collapsed when a single member of Manitoba's legislature refused to sign. Mulroney and Bourassa drafted a new, expanded accord, but the separatists picked it apart and it too was trounced.

Relations between Anglos and Francophones hit new lows, and support for independence was rekindled. Only one year after returning to power in 1994, the PQ, under Premier Lucien Bouchard, launched a second referendum. This was a cliff-hanger: Québecois decided by 52,000 votes – a majority of less than 1% – to remain within Canada.

The issue has continued to wax and wane in recent years.

the only way to ensure Francophone rights. Québec has spent the ensuing years flirting with separatism (see the boxed text, p837).

In 1960, Canada's Aboriginal peoples were finally granted Canadian citizenship. In 1985, Canada became the first country in the world to pass a national multicultural act and establish a federal department of multiculturalism. Today 40% of Canadians claim their origins are in places other than Britain or France.

1998	1999	2003	2005
The Canadian government apologizes to Aboriginal peoples, saying 'attitudes of racial and cultural superiority led to a suppression of Aboriginal culture and values.' It vows not to repeat past mistakes.	Nunavut, Canada's newest province, is chiseled from the icy eastern Arctic, giving about one-fifth of Canadian soil to the 28,000 Inuit who live there.	Canada becomes the world's third-largest diamond producer (after Botswana and Russia), thanks to riches discovered in the NWT. The baubles spark a modern-day boom similar to gold rush times.	Canada legalizes gay marriage throughout the country. Most provinces and territories permitted it anyway, but now hold-outs Alberta, PEI, Nunavut and the NWT have to join the ranks.

Outdoor Activities

No matter what your ability, no matter what your taste, Canada has action for you. And you don't always have to drive for days to find it (unless you're looking for seaside surf in Saskatchewan!).

Sweetest Slopes

» Whistler-Blackcomb, Whistler, BC

» Le Massif, Baie-Saint-Paul, Québec

» Sunshine Village, Banff, Alberta

» Big White, Kelowna, BC

» Fernie Resort, Fernie, BC

Skiing & Snowboarding

These adrenaline boosters are top draws in Canada, and the big hills are found in two main regions: the west (the Canadian Rockies, Columbia Mountains and Coast Mountains) and Québec's eastern mountains.

Québec boasts big slopes – Le Massif, near Québec City, has a vertical drop of 770m (2526ft) – that are close to cities. Most of these nonalpine hills, like Mont-Tremblant, are a day's drive from Toronto and less than an hour from Québec City and Montréal. Ski areas in Québec's Eastern Townships, such as Sutton and Owl's Head, offer renowned gladed runs – runs that weave through a thinned forest.

Out west, it's all about big mountains and a lot of alpine terrain. You'll slip down gargantuan slopes at Whistler-Blackcomb, which has the highest vertical drop (and cost), *and* the most impressive terrain variation in North America. You'll also ride into stunning postcard landscapes in the Canadian Rockies (eg Sunshine, Lake Louise, Marmot). Between the 2500m peaks of Whistler and the Rockies, you'll find an abundance of lift-serviced ski/snowboard areas.

In BC's Okanagan Valley resorts like Big White and Apex boast good snow year after year (no droughts here). Snowpack ranges from 2m to 6m-plus, depending on how close the resort is to the Pacific Ocean.

Travelers in search of the deepest, driest snow in the world should check out areas in BC's Kootenay Region, such as Nelson's Whitewater, Rossland's Red Mountain or Fernie's Alpine Resort. As an alternative, powder-seekers can pay a little extra for guaranteed and untouched deeps with BC's world-renowned helicopter and cat-ski operators (pioneered by www.canadianmountainholidays.com), which offer a range of experiences for intermediate and expert riders.

For cross-country skiing, Canmore, Alberta (www.canmorenordic.com), is a-swish with popular trails that were the site of 1988 Olympics. Urban areas that get lots of winter snow – like Montréal, Winnipeg, Edmonton and Ottawa – convert their park's walking trails into ski routes, and many bike shops convert their stock into Nordic skis and rent equipment.

The Canadian Ski Council (www.skicanada.org) can offer more information.

The world's longest ice-skating rink is the 7km portion of the Rideau Canal that glides through Ottawa. Winnipeg, Manitoba, notorious for chilly winters, clears 3km of ice on the Assiniboine and Red rivers for its outdoor rink.

Hiking

Trails that range from gentle jaunts around an interpretive path to breath-sapping slogs up a mountain crisscross Canada's national and provincial parks. Even the most confirmed couch-dweller will be able to find somewhere suitable to trek.

Canada's hiking hot spot is Lake Louise in Alberta's Banff National Park. From here you can march through dense spruce and pine forests that burst into a stunning bright-yellow canopy in the fall. Then ascend into alpine meadows that are carpeted with wildflowers and surrounded by crumbling glaciers and azure lakes. Also in the region: Wilcox Ridge and Parker Ridge, near Jasper, which offer unbelievable glacier views.

In BC's Yoho National Park you'll find the extension of this hiking wonderland at Lake O'Hara (accessible by bus reservation). The trail network weaves together pristine lakes with some of the largest peaks in the Rockies. And BC's provincial parks system (www.bcparks.ca) contains over 100 parks. Winners include Garibaldi Park's landscape of ancient volcanoes (not far from Whistler) and Mt Robson Park's popular Berg Lake alpine trail (in BC but near Alberta's Jasper).

Out east awe-inspiring trails crosshatch the landscape, too. Cape Breton Highlands National Park offers exquisite hiking over stark, dramatic coastline. Newfoundland's trails make for fantastic hiking since most clutch the shoreline and often provide whale views. The East Coast Trail (www.eastcoasttrail.com) on the Avalon Peninsula is renowned for its vistas.

In southern Ontario, the Bruce Trail (www.brucetrail.org) tracks from Niagara Falls to Tobermory. It's the oldest and longest continuous footpath in Canada and spans more than 850km. Though portions are near cities like Hamilton and Toronto, it's surprisingly serene.

In fact, while many wild places and parks exist across Canada, you needn't go far from its urban centers for a walk in the woods. There are many good trails within Montréal's Parc du Mont-Royal or in the 361 sq km of wooded hills in Gatineau Park, just outside Ottawa. Edmonton is known as the greenest city in Canada and is bisected by the North Saskatchewan River's steep-sided river bank, a perfect place for escaping the city under a comforting canopy of trees. Most famous of all is Vancouver's Stanley Park. Right next to corporate towers, an idyllic peninsula of gigantic trees surrounded on three sides by the lapping ocean.

Paddlesports

Paddling Canada (www.paddlingcanada.com) has general information on kayaking and canoeing, with links to courses and events.

Kayaking & Rafting

The Canadian Arctic, kayaking's motherland, still remains one of its special places: cruise the polar fjords of Ellesmere Island and watch narwhals and walruses during the fuse-short summer. Further south, slide silently past ancient forests and totem poles in BC's Gwaii Haanas National Park Reserve, or in the province's Johnstone Strait and watch orcas breaching. The east coast has sea kayaking galore. Trips in Witless Bay or Gros Morne, Newfoundland, often glide alongside whales.

Unlike sea kayaks, white-water kayaks have changed dramatically. Playboats – tiny plastic kayaks with flat hulls like surfboards – are designed to surf on a river's stationary and recirculating waves. The world's playboating mecca, serving up some of the biggest waves and hundreds of beginner-friendly, warm-water bumps, is just upstream of the nation's capital, near Beachburg on the Ottawa River.

Top Day Hikes

» Lake Louise, Banff, Alberta

» Skyline Trail, Cape Breton Highlands, Nova Scotia

» Parker Ridge, Jasper, Alberta

» Stanley Park, Vancouver, BC

» Bruce Trail, Ontario

OUTDOOR ACTIVITIES HIKING

Playboating's gnarly brother, creekboating, uses rounder boats with more flotation to help paddlers career down steep, narrow, waterfall-riddled rivers. Make sure you have a solid Eskimo Roll for righting yourself when you flip. Go with a team of safety-conscious boaters as you try BC creeks like Callaghan Creek (near Whistler), Kuskanax Creek (in Nakusp, near Revelstoke) and the Kicking Horse River (in Golden). Or take a shot at the Taureau, near Québec City on the Jacques-Cartier River, dubbed the 'toughest run in the east.'

For a similar thrill without the years of practice, take a trip on one of Canada's rivers in a guided raft. You can test the Ottawa's big rapids, rage down Golden BC's Kicking Horse or spend a week on the Yukon's glacial Tatshenshini River (near Whitehorse).

Canoeing

As old as kayaking, and equally Canadian, is the canoe. Because of the country's water-soaked landscape, it's possible to paddle from one side to the other with only two major portages: Methye and Grand Portage.

Start by canoeing in flatwater in Ontario's Algonquin or Quetico Provincial Parks (www.ontarioparks.com), or under the mountains on BC's Bowron Lakes chain (www.bowronlakes.com).

Once you've gathered moving-water skills, paddle one of 33 Canadian Heritage Rivers (www.chrs.ca). Some of the best include the Northwest Territories' South Nahanni River (near Fort Simpson) and Ontario's French River (near Sudbury).

Mountain Biking & Cycling

Cold winters and long distances have shaped cycling in Canada: it's less lifestyle-oriented (like riding to work) and more for recreation. That said, Canada has revolutionized mountain biking and provides an expansive landscape for two-wheeled exploration.

To start gently, BC's Kettle Valley Rail Trail (KVR; www.kettle valleyrailway.ca), near Kelowna, has no more than a 2% grade. This dramatic segment of a 600km converted railbed barrels across wooden trestle bridges and through canyon tunnels. It's one piece of a grow

Top Places to Paddle

» South Nahanni River, Northwest Territories

» Kicking Horse River, Golden, BC

» Beachburg, Ottawa River, Ontario

» Johnstone Strait, BC

» Gwaii Haanas National Park, BC

BACKCOUNTRY BENDERS

Canada has more sublime, multiday treks than you can shake a (hiking) stick at. Here are some of our favorites:

» **Skyline Trail** (Jasper National Park, Alberta) Four days above the tree line on this intermediate crest trail is one of Canada's classic mountain treks.

» **Long Range Traverse** (Gros Morne National Park, Newfoundland) Start this challenging four-day walk from the edge of a magical, fjord-like lake. Take a compass and GPS; the alpine plateau is crisscrossed by a web of caribou trails.

» **Donjek Route** (Kluane National Park, Yukon) Take this super-challenging week-long 100km vision quest into the wildest alpine and glacier landscape in Canada.

» **Crypt Lake Trail** (Waterton National Park, Alberta) Climb through a tunnel and up to an eerie crystal lake. This challenging 18km route is actually a long day-hike; it's only accessible by ferryboat.

» **West Coast Trail** (Pacific Rim National Park Reserve, BC) It's a rugged, salty, six- to eight-day trek on Vancouver Island's wild side, where a raging ocean meets a Paul Bunyan wilderness.

» **Trans Canada Trail** (www.tctrail.ca) One of the most ambitious paths ever conceived, the 18,078km ribbon runs from Cape Spear in Newfoundland all the way to Victoria, British Columbia. It's still a work in progress, but provincial trails sometimes coincide with it.

ing rail-to-trail system that offers cyclists the perfect chance to explore quiet areas without the worry of traffic – or steep hills.

The KVR is just a tiny section of something much, much bigger: the Trans Canada Trail (www.tctrail.ca). *The* trail – one of the most ambitious trail projects ever undertaken – is not complete, but many thousands of kilometers of this future record-breaking trail, like the KVR, have been incorporated into it. The entire 18,078km trail (some of it river routes) will link 600 communities from coast to coast to coast and provide for multi-use access to cyclists, snowmobilers, horseback riders and hikers.

Prefer the verticals? On Vancouver's North Shore (www.nsmba.ca), you'll be riding on much narrower and steeper 'trestles.' Birthplace of 'freeride' mountain biking (which combines downhill and dirt jumping), this area offers some of the most unique innovations: elevated bridges, log rides and skinny planks that loft over the wet undergrowth. Since the explosive rise in popularity of this kind of riding, BC ski areas have taken on mountain biking and now offer lift-serviced, North Shore–inspired trails. Most popular ski areas like Panorama (www.panorama resort.com), Apex (www.apexresort.com) and Sun Peaks (www.sunpeaks resort.com) offer well-built trails for a reasonable fee.

If you like mixing ups with your downs, try Ontario's Hardwood Hills (www.hardwoodhills.ca), located an hour north of Toronto. Or slam over one of the International Mountain Biking Association's 'Epic' rides (www.imba.com/epics), such as Rossland, BC's 30km Seven Summits ridge-top trail (www.kcts.ca).

For road touring, Canada's east coast, with more small towns and less emptiness, is a fantastic place to pedal, either as a single-day road ride or a multi-day trip. Circle Québec's Lac St Jean, or try any part of the 4000km Route Verte (www.routeverte.com), the longest network of bicycle paths in the Americas. Or follow PEI's bucolic red roads and its Confederation Trail (www.tourismpei.com/pei-cycling).

Best Biking
» Heritage roads & Confederation Trail, PEI
» Kettle Valley Rail Trail, Kelowna, BC
» North Shore, Vancouver, BC
» Seven Summits, Rossland, BC
» Route Verte, Québec

Climbing

Lots of mountains equal lots of great places to climb, especially in the Rockies. PeakFinder (www.peakfinder.com) categorizes 1500 of the western beauties.

Rock Climbing

Canmore, just outside Banff, is the ideal place for beginners and beyond. Climbing shops, a climbing school (www.yamnuska.com) and thousands of limestone sport climbs within a 30-minute radius of town make this a one-stop vacation that's sure to rock.

The Skaha Bluffs (www.skaha.org) in BC's semi-arid Okanagan Valley draw all levels of climbers for the 700-plus gneiss (and nice, too!) sport climbs.

Slicing northwest from Canada's other wine region in Niagara, Ontario is a limestone escarpment that's littered with sport climbs. Go up Rattlesnake Point, Kelso Park, or above the azure waters overhanging Georgian Bay in Lion's Head on the Bruce Peninsula (www.thebruce peninsula/lionshead).

Once you're ready – really ready – to expose yourself, try climbing the granite monolith deemed 'the Chief.' It pops out of the Pacific Ocean like a gladiator's furious fist in Squamish, BC, Canada's climbing capital. If you can manage the Chief's Apron, you'll reach the Grand Wall of this 'Yosemite North.' But don't fret if the Chief has you quaking – there are plenty of surrounding cliffs with a variety of opportunities. Squamish Rock Guides (www.squamishrockguides.com) has details.

For similar big walls in the alpine style, brave the granite Bugaboo Spires in the Purcell range, near Golden, BC.

Ice Climbing

When the summer rock-climbing season ends, Canadians don't stop climbing. They just don a pair of warm mitts, a down jacket, crampons and an ice axe, and are ready to take on the most abundant and consistent ice climbing in the world.

Northern Ontario's Orient Bay (near Thunder Bay) is a spectacular ice-laced escarpment with more than 100 single-pitch climbs for all levels. Québec's Pont-Rouge, northwest of Québec City, produces some of the best ice climbers in the world. Rouge's annual Festiglace (www.festiglace.com) highlights this region's delights.

But the world's ice palace is the Canadian Rockies. Banff, Kootenay, Yoho and Jasper national parks remain frozen for six months a year, and by early November notorious routes like Polar Circus and Curtain Call are in full form. If those are a little out of your league, step into Louise Falls (Lake Louise) or Professor Falls (Banff). As in summer, Canmore is the place to get started and take a lesson.

Mountain Climbing

Top Climbs

» The Chief,
Squamish, BC

» Mt Logan,
Yukon

» Canmore,
Alberta

» Pont-Rouge,
Québec

» Skaha Bluffs,
Okanagan Valley,
BC

» Bugaboo Spire,
near Golden, BC

Mountaineering in Canada began in the late 1800s when CP Rail, which owned a couple of swanky hotels in Banff National Park, hired Swiss mountain guides to make sure adventure-seeking guests would return to pay their bar tabs. Mountains such as Lake Louise's Mt Victoria remain prized peaks in one of the world's most impressive climbing regions.

If you prefer the European approach, climb the Matterhorn of Canada, BC's Mt Assiniboine – from a full-service lodge and an alpine hut. Other western classics include Alberta's Mt Edith Cavell, in Jasper; BC's Mt Robson and Sir Donald in the Rockies; and Garibaldi Peak, in Garibaldi Provincial Park, near Whistler.

The most legendary climb is also the highest: the Yukon's Mt Logan. Give yourself a couple of weeks to work your way up this 5959m, ice-riddled Kluane National Park massif.

While there aren't as many Swiss guides left, you'll still find Canadian guides (www.alpineclubofcanada.ca) to be the best in the business as they follow in the footsteps of their forebears.

HOCKEY: THE NATIONAL PASTIME

Canadians aren't fooling around when it comes to hockey. They play a lot, and they play well – as their 2010 team gold medal proves.

Grassroots hockey, aka pond hockey, takes place in communities across the country every night on a frozen surface. All you need is a puck, a hockey stick and a few friends to live the dream. Plaster Rock, New Brunswick hosts the annual World Pond Hockey Tournament (www.worldpondhockey.com), where if you register early enough, you and your mates can face off with the Boston Danglers, Skateful Dead, Boiled Owls and other amateur teams on an iced-up lake.

If you'd rather watch than play, Vancouver, Edmonton, Calgary, Toronto, Ottawa and Montréal all have NHL (www.nhl.com) teams who skate hard and lose the odd tooth. Minor pro teams and junior hockey clubs fill many more arenas with rabid fans; check the Canadian Hockey League (www.chl.ca) and American Hockey League (www.theahl.com) for local stick wielders.

Fishing

Canada is swimming with an abundance of walleye, pike, rainbow and lake trout, and muskie. Northern Saskatchewan contains some of the most productive lakes, and many are serviced by fishing lodges. North of 60 degrees latitude – the Canadian North – is also a pretty sure bet to catching your supper, albeit a little pricier to access. But you'd be surprised how lucky you can get by just fishing in the lake at the side of the road.

Check local, provincial and federal fishing regulations wherever you are; most hardware or fishing shops can tell you everything there is to know.

Canada also has the longest coastline in the world and over 52,000 islands, so it's no wonder that saltwater fishing is also top-shelf. West-coast salmon are the usual draw on the Pacific, while it's not uncommon to catch a dozen mackerel or flounder in the Atlantic's many bays and inlets in places like Lunenburg, Nova Scotia. It's always a good idea to hire a guide; weather and seas can change dramatically over a short period of time, and local experts can help you find what you came looking for: a big fight.

Surfing, Windsurfing & Kiteboarding

Wind and wave sports in Canada have one thing in common – chilly water. But with the abundance of high-quality gear, you won't notice temperatures while you're ripping up world-class wind and waves on unpopulated beaches and lakes.

Surfing

In Pacific Rim National Park Reserve, on Vancouver Island's 'Wild Side' (the west coast), you don't have to deal with any line-up fisticuffs. Locals here are pretty laissez-faire, because when the fog rises there's an endless sand beach, and behind the last footprints the landscape becomes enveloped by a gigantic, dark cedar jungle. June and September are best for mere mortals, but if you want to test some of the fiercest storms the Pacific can dish out, try surfing in winter. Tofino, outside the park, has a superb choice of surf schools. Surfing Vancouver Island (www.surfingvancouverisland.com) has the latest news.

Eight thousand kilometers east, Nova Scotia can also dish out some serious surf. The US south coast's hurricane season (August to November) brings Canadians steep fast breaks, snappy right and left point breaks, and offshore reef and shoal breaks in areas like Lawrencetown, just outside Halifax, as well as the entire south shore region. There are a

Good Fishin' Holes

» Miramichi River, New Brunswick

» La Ronge & Far North, Saskatchewan

» Lunenburg, Nova Scotia

» Great Slave Lake, Northwest Territories

SNOWY ADVENTURES

It's a long season, so to make sure you don't get bored with plain ol' skiing, snowboarding and ice skating, here are some beyond-the-norm cold-weather activities:

» **Dog-sledding** Guided trips will let you mush your own team for a day or on overnight trips. Yellowknife in the Northwest Territories has the huskies, as does Temagami in northern Ontario.

» **Snow-kiting** It's a sort of windsurfing-meets-snowboarding endeavor. Outfitters at Marble Mountain, on Newfoundland's west coast, can harness you to the wind-propelled contraption.

» **Snow touring** For the hut-to-hut ski pilgrimage dubbed 'The Canadian Haute Route,' Banff and Yoho National Parks have four Alpine Club huts (www.alpineclubofcanada.ca) on the breathtaking Wapta ice cap. Québec's Parc de la Gaspésie has a system of 14 ski-in huts in the Chic Choc Mountains.

couple of surf schools here. Scotia Surfer has the lowdown (www.scotia surfer.com).

Windsurfing & Kiteboarding

Top Places to Surf & Windsurf

» Tofino, Vancouver Island, BC

» Lawrencetown, Nova Scotia

» Nitinat Lake, Vancouver Island, BC

» Howe Sound, Squamish, BC

» Magdalen Islands, Québec

Vancouver Island's freshwater Nitinat Lake offers one of the most consistent wind locations on the planet, with daily thermal flows coming in off the ocean. Squamish, BC, benefits greatly from a wind-funneling venturi effect, which gets wild in Howe Sound.

No trees hold back the wind at Alberta's Oldman River Reservoir, and only power-generating wind farms compete for a chunk of the gust. In the center of Canada, surfers have four Great Lakes and the gigantic Georgian Bay (try access through Midland, Ontario) to choose from.

It would seem that Québec's Magdalen Islands – a small chain in the Gulf of St Lawrence, accessible by ferry from Québec or Prince Edward Island – were made for wind sports. It's the kind of place so blessed that if the wind is blowing the wrong way, you can drive a few minutes down to another beach where it's just perfect. Sheltered lagoons offer safe learning locations for testing kiteboards or seeking shelter during heavy days.

Horseback Riding

Alberta is the premier place to get in the saddle. In Banff and Jasper national parks, outfitters can set you up for a weeklong pack trip where you'll sleep in canvas, stove-warmed tents; cross swift creeks; tie the diamond hitch; hear old-time music; and eat some of the best home-cooked meals outside Mom's house. Or kick up dust on the Cowboy Trail (www.thecowboytrail.com) in the sacred Porcupine Hills, south of Calgary, for a genuine ranch experience of cattle drives and roundups.

SUMMER BLASTS

» **Tidal bore rafting** The explosive force of the famous Fundy tides makes this activity one-of-a-kind in Maitland, Nova Scotia. Depending on the moon's phase, your whitewater trip (www.tidalborerafting.com) can be wild or mild. Either way, you'll get very, very wet.

» **Ziplining** Strap in to a body harness and glide through the trees, high above the ground (whooping like a banshee is optional). Several provinces have zipline outfitters, including BC's Ziptrek Ecotours (www.ziptrek.com) in Whistler, and Newfoundland's Marble Zip Tours (www.marbleziptours.com) near Corner Brook.

» **Scuba diving** In BC's 'Emerald Sea' divers can plunge into world-class sites like Race Rocks (www.racerocks.com) in Victoria or Porteau Cove Provincial Park (www.bcparks.ca) near Vancouver. You'll see whales, wolf eel, sea lions, octopus, harbor seals, dolphins and much more in an aquarium of life. Or try freshwater diving at Ontario's Fathom Five National Marine Park (www.pc.gc.ca/fathomfive). It's off the Bruce Peninsula and boasts crystal-clear water, underwater cliffs and caves, and more than 20 wrecks.

Aboriginal Cultures

Canada's original inhabitants began living on the land more than 15,000 years ago. The term 'Aboriginal' refers to the descendants of these earliest residents, which now comprise three groups: First Nations (those of North American Indian descent), Métis (those with 'mixed blood' ancestry) and Inuit (those in the Arctic). Together they make up almost 4% of Canada's total population.

The People

First Nations

This broad term applies to all Aboriginal groups *except* the Métis and Inuit (see the separate headings for each of those groups on p847). Almost 700,000 First Nations people live in Canada (about 2% of the total population), comprising more than 600 communities (sometimes called bands). About 40% of First Nations people live on reserves.

British Columbia is home to the most First Nations (198 groups), while Ontario is second (126 groups). The remaining communities are spread mostly in Saskatchewan, Manitoba, Alberta, Québec and the Northwest Territories.

The groups vary widely by region.

Pacific

Historically, the people along the Pacific coast built cedar-plank houses and carved elaborate totem poles and canoes. The potlatch, a ritual feast where the host gives away lavish gifts and possessions, is a renowned facet of many local cultures. The Canadian government banned the practice from 1885 to 1951 for being 'uncivilized.'

The Haida of Haida Gwaii, a group of islands off BC's northern shore, are perhaps the region's best-known First Nations group. They're extraordinary artists, famed for their wood carvings, totem poles and stylized prints of animals.

The Tsimshians on the mainland and matrilineal Tlingit, who spread into Alaska, have similar art forms.

Plains

The Plains First Nations, which traditionally included the Sioux, Cree and Blackfoot, occupied the prairies from Lake Winnipeg to the Rocky Mountain foothills. Primarily buffalo hunters, they cunningly killed their prey by driving them over cliffs, such as at Head-Smashed-In Buffalo Jump in southern Alberta. The buffalo provided sustenance, and the hides were used for tipis and clothes.

The Plains today still have a strong First Nations (and Métis) pres-

---

Aboriginal Peoples

» Pacific – Haida, Tsimshians, Tlingit

» Plains – Sioux, Cree, Blackfoot

» Great Lakes/ St Lawrence – Ojibwe, Huron

» Maritimes – Mi'kmaq, Maliseet

» N Québec & Labrador – Innu

» Northern ON, MB & SK – Cree

» Yukon & NWT Dene, Gwich'in

» Arctic – Inuit

The Long Exile (2007), by Melanie McGrath, follows three Inuit families who were forced to relocate to staggeringly bleak Ellesmere Island in the high Arctic, as Canada tried to stake its claim during the Cold War.

ence. Winnipeg has the largest number of First Nations people in Canada, with Edmonton not far behind. In Regina, First Nations University of Canada (www.firstnationsuniversity.ca) is the only First Nations–run institution of higher learning in the country.

Great Lakes & St Lawrence River area

Present-day southern Ontario and the area along the St Lawrence River are the time-honored home of the Iroquoian-speaking peoples, who were once divided into the Five Nations (including the Mohawk, Oneida and Seneca), the Huron, the Erie and the Neutral confederacies. Although often at war with each other, they were a sophisticated lot who lived in large farming communities, built sturdy longhouses and traded with other tribes.

Today Manitoulin Island, floating in Lake Huron, preserves Ojibwe culture through its several reserves, where visitors can attend powwows and follow the Great Spirit Circle Trail (www.circletrail.com). Wendake, outside Québec City, is an active Huron reserve. It was the first reserve to have its own bank (in 1960); today, it provides employment for other tribes.

Maritime Provinces

The Mi'kmaqs and Maliseets are the main First Nations in the Maritimes, accounting for just over 1% of the total population there. Traditionally they fished the shores in summer, and moved inland to hunt moose and caribou in winter.

In New Brunswick, the Maliseets (renowned basket makers) live in the upper Saint John River valley in the west, while the Mi'kmaqs live to the east. In Nova Scotia, the Mi'kmaqs live in 14 communities, mostly around Bras d'Or Lake on Cape Breton and near Truro. A small group also lives on Prince Edward Island.

During the past two decades a revitalization movement has emerged, encouraging a revival of traditional song and dance, language programs, and healing and ritual ceremonies. Public powwows often take place, especially around Truro.

Northeastern Québec & Labrador

The Innu are the long-time inhabitants of the cold boreal forest stretching across the north of Québec and Labrador. The Innu often are confused with the Inuit, but they are not related. Rather, two First Nations – the Naskapi and the Montagnais – make up the Innu. In the past, they were fairly nomadic, and survived by hunting caribou and moose for food and skins. A popular traditional craft is the Innu tea doll, a toy made of caribou hide that served the dual purpose of being a plaything but also a method of transporting tea leaves during long journeys.

About 80% of Innu live in Québec, with 20% in Labrador.

Northern Ontario, Manitoba & Saskatchewan

The Cree dominate this chilly landscape. As one of Canada's largest First Nations, they also extend west into the Plains and east into Québec. There's a well-known reserve in Ontario at Moose Factory (a former Hudson Bay fur trading post), which built the hemisphere's first Aboriginal eco-lodge. Many Cree also live in polar bear epicenter Churchill, Manitoba, where they make up about one-third of the local population; it's not uncommon to hear people speaking Cree in Churchill.

Historically, the Cree have a reputation for being gifted healers.

Yukon & Northwest Territories

The Dene were the first people to settle in what is now the Northwest Territories. Today many live in Yellowknife, as well as villages through-

Cities with Most Aboriginals

» Winnipeg 68,380
» Edmonton 52,100
» Vancouver 40,310
» Calgary 26,575
» Toronto 26,575
» Saskatoon 21,535
» Ottawa 20,590
» Montréal 17,865
» Regina 17,105
» Prince Albert 13,565

Percentage of Population that's Aboriginal

» Nunavut 85%
» Northwest Territories 50%
» Yukon Territory 25%
» Manitoba 15%
» Saskatchewan 15%
» Alberta 6%
» BC 5%
» Ontario 2%

out the Mackenzie Delta, west into the Yukon and Alaska, east toward Nunavut and south into the prairies. Traditionally they're hunters, fishers and trappers and known for their birch-bark basket weaving.

The Gwich'in First Nations people live farther north and rely on caribou for a major part of their diet and lifestyle. They've actively protested drilling in the Arctic National Wildlife Refuge, saying it will deplete the caribou herd there that they depend on for food. The economy of their communities is based mostly on hunting and fishing.

Métis

Métis is the French word for 'mixed blood.' Historically, the term was applied to the children of French fur traders and Cree women in the prairies, and English and Scottish traders and Dene women in the north. Today the term is used broadly to describe people with mixed First Nations and European ancestry.

Métis account for about one-third of the overall Aboriginal population. They are largely based in western Canada. Winnipeg and Edmonton are the cities with the highest number of Métis.

Louis Riel is the culture's most famous individual. He battled for the rights of Métis, who were often trampled during Canada's westward expansion. Riel led two resistance movements against the government, the last at Batoche, Saskatchewan, in 1885. He was caught and convicted of treason, though today he's considered a hero to most Canadians.

Unlike First Nations, Métis have never lived on reserves.

Inuit

The Inuit are Arctic Canada's natives. Today they number 56,000 (4% of the overall Aboriginal population) and are spread throughout four Arctic regions: Nunavut, the Inuvialuit area in the Northwest Territories, Nunavik (northern Québec) and Nunatsiavut (Labrador). All in all, they cover one-third of Canada.

Inuit have never lived on reserves, preferring small communities instead: 38% of their villages have a population of less than 500 people. About 29% have between 500 and 999 people, while 33% have 1000 or more residents.

Traditionally Inuit hunted whales and big game, traveled by kayak and dog sled, and spent winters in igloos. Snowmobiles and houses have replaced the sleds and igloos these days, but subsistence hunting is still a big part of the economy, as is traditional soapstone carving and printmaking.

The Inuit language is Inuktitut, a system of syllabics versus letters.

Recent History

Toward Reconciliation

Canada never experienced the all-out massacres that marred the European/Native American clashes in the USA. Nevertheless, Canada's Aboriginal population still suffered discrimination, loss of territory and civil rights violations throughout the country's history.

In 1990, Aboriginal frustration over these issues reached a boiling point with the Oka Crisis, a violent standoff between the government and a band of Mohawk activists near Montréal. The conflict was sparked by a land claim: the town of Oka was planning to expand a golf course onto land that the Mohawk considered sacred. A 78-day clash ensued, and one policeman died of gunshot wounds. The event shook Canada, and focused national attention on Aboriginal human rights violations and outstanding land claims.

In the aftermath of Oka, a Royal Commission on Aboriginal Peoples issued a report recommending a complete overhaul of relations between the government and indigenous peoples. Slow to respond at

Top First Nations Cultural Centers

» Haida Heritage Centre (www. haidaheritagecentre.com), BC

» Dänojà Zho Centre (www. trondek.com), YK

» Museum of Northern BC (www.museumofnorthernbc. com), BC

» Wanuskewin Heritage Park (www. wanuskewin. com), SK

Louis Riel: A Comic Strip Biography (2003) by Chester Brown, an unusual graphic novel and powerful landmark work, tells the fascinating story of Manitoba's charismatic 19th-century Métis leader.

first, in 1998 the Ministry of Indian and Northern Affairs issued an official Statement of Reconciliation that accepted responsibility for past injustices toward Aboriginal peoples. It specifically apologized for the policy of removing children from their families and educating them in underfunded government schools in the name of assimilation. Most importantly, though, it pledged to give indigenous peoples greater control over their land, resources, government and economy.

Land Claim Issues

Most Aboriginals didn't see land as an owned commodity when they signed treaties with early Europeans – they felt the land and its resources would be shared. But the colonists saw treaties as a trade of land for compensation.

More than 50 treaties were signed, first with the British and then the Canadian governments. Not all First Nations, Inuit or Métis signed treaties. Among those who did, many did not receive the land, money, food, medicine or housing they were promised. Since the 1970s Aboriginal people have made land claims against the federal and provincial governments, an issue that gained urgency as plans were made to develop northern resources. Where no treaties were signed, land claims now involve roughly half the total area of Canada. Treaties are important because they acknowledge that native people have certain rights as the nation's original occupants, as recognized in the Constitution Act of 1982.

Resolution of land claims is complicated, as two levels of government are involved with all the ensuing debates surrounding land ownership and how treaties should be interpreted. Some cases remain unresolved after half a century and frustration has mounted. In the 1980s and '90s the fight to settle land claims became increasingly vocal and sometimes violent. A 1985 blockade by the Haida of British Columbia against logging an old-growth forest finally resolved a 13-year land claims battle. There have been armed standoffs between Aboriginals and police like that at an Ontario reserve called Camp Ipperwash in 1995, where police shot and killed Chippewa protestor Anthony Dudley George.

In November 1975, after conflict with the Cree and Inuit of northern Québec over plans to construct a series of hydroelectric dams, the governments of Canada and Québec signed the James Bay and Northern Québec Agreement, granting exclusive hunting and fishing rights to about 170,000 sq km of territory. It was the first modern-day land-claim settlement. But in 1988 Hydro-Québec signed a $17-billion contract with the New York Power Authority to export electricity from a second phase of dams called the Great Whale Project, which would flood Cree and Inuit treaty land. Grand Chief Matthew Coon Come launched a high-profile media battle in 1990 that included the support of Robert Kennedy Jr; Cree and Inuit paddled a traditional canoe from Hudson's Bay to Manhattan. New York State cancelled the deal, and Québec cancelled the project.

In 1993 Canada's biggest land claim was settled when Prime Minister Brian Mulroney signed into existence the new territory of Nunavut, which took effect in 1999, giving the Inuit self-government after more than 20 years of negotiations. The 28,000 people of the far north now had control over about one-fifth of Canadian soil.

Since the creation of Nunavut there has been widespread mineral exploration that gives the territory the potential for much-needed revenue. Likewise, in 2002 most of the land claims had been settled with the Dene, Inuit and Métis of the Northwest Territories' Mackenzie Valley, where there are plans for an oil and gas pipeline.

Aboriginal land claims continue to capture the front page of Canadian newspapers. To draw attention to their battles and to the poor condition of reserves, in 2007 First Nations blocked the main highway between Toronto and Montréal on Canada Day weekend. But there is

'Eskimo' was the term given to Inuit by European explorers and is now rarely used in Canada. It is derived from an Algonquian term meaning 'raw meat eaters,' and many find it offensive.

It was Newfoundland's Beothuk Aboriginals and their ceremonially ochre-coated faces who were dubbed 'red men' by arriving Europeans, a name soon applied to all of North America's indigenous groups. The Beothuk died out by 1829.

also hope; later that month, the Québec government signed an agreement with their northern Cree that would grant them the right to run their own justice and community affairs.

Arctic Apology

Another notable apology came in 2010, when the government said it was sorry for the relocation of Inuit families to the high Arctic during the 1950s. At the time, the government promised the families a better life by moving to the region, but it didn't follow through in providing them with necessary supports like adequate shelter and supplies. As a result, the families struggled greatly to survive. Many have argued the government moved the families not to help them, as stated, but to establish Canada's Arctic sovereignty during the Cold War. The apology was a follow up to a 1996 settlement, in which the government agreed to pay $10 million into a trust fund to compensate the families.

Aboriginal Arts

The shared history of Aboriginal and non-Aboriginal cultures in Canada is most immediately perceived through the visual arts. In the mid-19th century, Paul Kane and Cornelius Krieghoff both painted Aboriginal subjects; works by them can be seen at Toronto's Royal Ontario Museum (www.rom.on.ca) and Ottawa's National Gallery (www.gallery.ca). Emily Carr visited First Nations villages in northern BC and her vivid paintings of totem poles, architecture and nature, some of which are displayed at the Vancouver Art Gallery (www.vanartgallery.bc.ca), are inspired by Aboriginal art and spirituality – 'Indian art broadened my seeing,' she wrote in her posthumously published 1946 autobiography.

Since the mid-20th century there has been strong appreciation of and a market for Aboriginal art, in particular Inuit sculpture. The small, wintry town of Cape Dorset on Nunavut's Baffin Island is the epicenter, and you can see soapstone carvers in action at local studios and co-ops. Much of the Inuit art for sale around the country comes from Cape Dorset.

While some Aboriginal artists work in a collective environment, others pursue a more individualistic path. Influential Haida artist Bill Reid's awe-inspiring sculptures are on display at the University of British Columbia's Museum of Anthropology in Vancouver, as well as at the city's Bill Reid Gallery of Northwest Coast Art (www.billreidgallery.ca). Also look out for colorful paintings of Ojibwa legends by Norval Morriseau; mixed-media works by Saskatchewan-born Edward Poitras; and younger artists such as Marianne Nicholson and Brian Jungen.

Aboriginal Tourism

From learning to paddle a traditional canoe in Tofino, BC, to sampling bannock bread in a Mi'kmaq cafe on Prince Edward Island's Lennox Island, to trying your hand at driving a dog team in Nunavut, the growing popularity of Aboriginal tourism is an indicator of native people's determination to retain or regain their traditional cultural roots. In 2001, businesses owned or operated by Canada's First Nations, Métis and Inuit employed more than 10,000 people and generated $862 million – an important source of income, especially in remote regions where 'town jobs' are rare.

The further north in Canada you head, the more your travel dollars benefit Aboriginals. First Air (www.firstair.ca) and Air Creebec (www.aircreebec.ca) are Aboriginal-owned, as are Inns North hotels (www.innsnorth.com), located in 19 communities throughout Nunavut and the Northwest Territories. Cruise North (www.cruisenorthexpeditions.com) is an Inuit-owned leisure cruise operation that offers wildlife safaris deep into Labrador's Torngat Mountains National Park and other icy journeys.

Increasingly, Aboriginals are opening their lives to visitors. Dine on maktaaq, smoked whitefish and caribou stew in the Tuktoyaktuk home

Top Museums for Aboriginal Arts

» Art Gallery of Ontario (www.ago.net), Toronto

» Museum of Civilization (www.civilization.ca), Gatineau

» National Gallery (www.gallery.ca), Ottawa

» UBC Museum of Anthropology (www.moa.ubc.ca), Vancouver

Several scientists recently traveled by dogsled around Baffin and Ellesmere islands in Canada's far north to interview Inuit families and document personal accounts of climate change. Their website (www.globalwarming101.com) has photos and podcasts.

The Golden Spruce (2005), John Vaillant's nonfiction book about an ancient tree that's cut down, provides an excellent look at the Haida culture and Haida Gwaii.

of a traditional hunter, or try a homestay with an Iqaluit family. The experience can be as varied as a walk in Sylvia Grinnell Territorial Park (www.nunavutparks.com) in Iqaluit, perusing the Great Northern Arts Festival (www.gnaf.org) in Inuvik in the Northwest Territories, taking a moccasin-making workshop at Head-Smashed-In Buffalo Jump (www.head-smashed-in.com) in Alberta, or wine tasting and even a round of golf at Nk'Mip (www.nkmip.com) in Osoyoos, BC.

Several places encourage a longer immersion in local cultures. Gwaii Haanas National Park Reserve & Haida Heritage Site (www.pc.gc.ca/gwaiihaanas) consists of ancient Haida villages, burial caves and eerie totem poles spread over more than 100 islands. Many visitors stay for several days to kayak among them. Moose Factory, in northern Ontario, is a spirited Cree reservation that offers tours and the northern hemisphere's first Aboriginal-owned eco-lodge (www.creevillage.com). The design reflects traditional Cree values and uses organic wool and cotton in its furnishings, among other earth-friendly features.

A good website with links to Aboriginal tourism opportunities nationwide is http://canada.travelall.com/promos/Aboriginal.htm. BC has its own Aboriginal Tourism Association (www.aboriginalbc.com), with the lowdown on 60 Aboriginal-owned businesses in the province.

ABORIGINAL MEDIA

News
» **First Nations Drum** (www.firstnationsdrum.com) National newspaper.
» **First Perspective** (www.firstperspective.ca) Online news source.
» **CBC Aboriginal** (www.cbc.ca/Aboriginal) The broadcaster's online site devoted to Aboriginal news and culture, with links to regional programming in native languages.

TV
» **Aboriginal Peoples Television Network** (APTN; www.aptn.ca) National cable/satellite network that produces and airs Aboriginal programming.
» **Cooking with the Wolfman** (www.cookingwiththewolfman.com) Chef David Wolfman hosts this show on APTN in which he prepares traditional foods with a modern twist, say elk medallions with scallops or moose moussaka; the website has recipes.

Films
» **Octobre** (1994) Drama by provocative Québecois filmmaker Pierre Falardeau that looks at the terrorist abduction and murder of Pierre Laporte during the 1970 October Crisis from the kidnappers' viewpoint.
» **Rocks at Whiskey Trench** (2000) Documentary by Alanis Obomsawin observing the events surrounding the 1990 Oka Crisis and its effects on the Mohawk community.

Music
» **CBC Radio 3** (www.radio3.cbc.ca) Look for the weekly podcast 'Ab-Originals' (tagline: a musical podlatch) on this indie music station, accessible online or via satellite radio.
» **Canadian Aboriginal Music Awards** (www.canab.com) See who won for best rock, blues and hip-hop albums, but also for best traditional flute, powwow and hand drum music; there are links to the artists and their tunes.

Books
» **Theytus Books** (www.theytus.com) BC-based company publishing across genres: fiction, children's books, memoirs and journals of poetry and short stories, among others.

General
» **Aboriginal Canada Portal** (www.aboriginalcanada.gc.ca) The federal government's site, with the mother lode of resources and links.

Wine Regions

While many international visitors – especially those who think Canadians live under a permanent blanket of snow – are surprised to learn that wine is produced here, their suspicion is always tempered after a drink or two. Canada's wines have gained ever-greater kudos in recent years and while smaller-scale production and the industry dominance of other wine regions means they'll never be a global market leader, there are some truly lip-smacking surprises waiting for thirsty grape lovers.

And since the best way to sample any wine is to head straight to the source – where you can taste the region in the glass – consider doing a little homework and locating the nearest vineyards on your Canada visit. You won't want to miss the multitude of top table wineries in Ontario's Niagara region or British Columbia's Okanagan Valley – the country's leading producers – but a visit to the smaller, often rustic wineries of Québec and the charming boutique operations of Nova Scotia and Vancouver Island's Cowichan Valley can be just as rewarding.

Wherever your tipple-craving crawl takes you (with a designated driver of course), drink widely and deeply and prepare to be surprised. And make sure you have plenty of room in your suitcase – packing materials are always available, but you'll probably drink everything before you make it to the airport anyway.

> Hundreds of Canadian wineries are sampled at the Wines of Canada website (www.winesofcanada.com), which also explores tipple history and regional varietals.

ONLY HERE FOR THE BEER?

Before you start thinking that Canadians only drink wine, it's worth noting that beer is at least as important a national beverage here. And while you'll soon come across the innocuous, mass-produced fizz made by brewing behemoths Labatt and Molson, a little digging uncovers a thriving regional and local microbrewing scene that's dripping with fantastic ales, bitters and lagers.

Midsized breweries like Moosehead in New Brunswick, Alexander Keith's in Nova Scotia, Sleemans in Ontario, Big Rock in Alberta and Okanagan Springs in BC produce some easy-to-find, highly quaffable tipples. It's worth noting that several of these have been taken over by the two big boys in recent years, although they haven't been stupid enough to change much about these successful operations.

It's at the local level where you'll find the real treats. Canada is suffused with a foamy head of excellent small-batch brewers and visiting beer geeks should make a point of searching these out by asking for the local beer wherever they find themselves drinking. Some highlights to look out for include Québec's Boréale, Alberta's Wild Rose Brewery and Nova Scotia's Propeller Brewing. In Ontario, keep your tongue alert for beers from Wellington Brewery, Kawartha Lake Brewing Company and Steam Whistler Brewing. And in BC, it's all about Phillips Brewing, Tree Brewing and Central City Brewing, among many others. Cheers!

Regional Wine List

Depending on how thirsty you are, you're rarely too far from a wine region in Canada. Which means that most visitors can easily add a mini taste-tripping tour to their visit if they'd like to meet a few producers and sample some intriguing local flavors. Here's a rundown of the best areas, including the magnum-sized larger regions and the thimble-sized smaller locales – why not stay all summer and visit them all?

Find out more about Nova Scotia's wine region, including information on courses and festivals, at www.winesofnovascotia.ca.

Okanagan Valley

The rolling hills of this lakeside BC region are well worth the five-hour drive from Vancouver. Studded among the vine-striped slopes are more than 100 wineries enjoying a diverse climate that fosters both crisp whites and bold reds. With varietals including pinot noir, pinot gris, pinot blanc, merlot and chardonnay, there's a wine here to suit almost every palate. Most visitors base themselves in Kelowna, the Okanagan's wine capital, before fanning out to well-known blockbuster wineries like Mission Hill, Quail's Gate, Cedar Creek and Summerhill Pyramid Winery (yes, it has a pyramid). Many of them also have excellent vista-hugging restaurants. For more, see p724.

Find out more about BC's wine regions and annual festivals – and download free touring maps – at www.winebc.com.

Golden Mile

Some of BC's best Okanagan wineries are centered south of the valley around the historic town of Oliver, where the Golden Mile's hot climate fosters a long, warm growing season. Combined with gravel, clay and sandy soils, this area is ideally suited to varietals like merlot, chardonnay, gewürztraminer and cabernet sauvignon. While the 20 or so wineries here are not actually crammed into one mile – it's more like 20km – the proximity of celebrated producers like Burrowing Owl, Tinhorn Creek and Road 13 Vineyards makes this an ideal touring area. And if you're still thirsty, continue south to Osoyoos and check out Nk'Mip Cellars, a First Nations winery on the edge of a dessert.

Niagara Peninsula

This picture-perfect Ontario region of country inns and charming old towns offers more than 60 wineries and grows more than three-quarters of Canada's grapes. Neatly divided between the low-lying Niagara-on-the-Lake area and the higher Niagara Escarpment, its complex mix of soils and climates – often likened to the Loire Valley – is ideal for chardonnay, riesling, pinot noir and cabernet-franc varietals. This is also the production center for Canadian icewine, that potently sweet dessert drink made from grapes frozen on the vine. Home to some of Canada's biggest and best wineries, including Inniskillin, Jackson-Triggs and Peller Estates, don't miss smaller pit-stops like Magnotta and Cave Spring Cellars in the Escarpment area.

BC'S ISLAND APERITIF

Long-established as a farming area, Vancouver Island's verdant Cowichan Valley is also home to some great little wineries. A short drive from Victoria, you'll find Averill Creek, Blue Grouse, Cherry Point Vineyards and Venturie-Schulze. Also consider Merridale Estate Cidery, which produces six celebrated ciders on its gently-sloped orchard grounds. For information on the wineries here, visit www.wineislands.ca.

Prince Edward County

Proving that not all Ontario's wineries are clustered in Niagara, this comparatively new grape-growing region – located in the province's southeastern corner and almost three hours drive from Toronto – is a charming alternative if you want to avoid the tour buses winding through the main wine area. A long-established fruit-growing district with generally lower temperatures than Niagara, cooler-climate wines are favored here – including chardonnay and pinot noir. The most intriguing wineries include Closson Chase, Black Prince Winery and Grange of Prince Edward. If your tastebuds are piqued, consider checking out other Ontario wine regions like Pelee Island and Lake Erie North Shore.

Eastern Townships

Starting around 80km southeast of Montréal, this idyllic patchwork farmland region in Québec is studded with quiet villages, leafy woodlands, crystal clear lakes and winding countryside roads. A rising tide of wineries has joined the traditional farm operations here in recent years, with rieslings and chardonnays particularly suited to the area's cool climate and soil conditions. But it's the local icewines, dessert wines and fruit wines that are the area's main specialties, so make sure you come with a sweet tooth. Wineries to perk up your taste-buds here include Domaine Félibre, Vignoble de L'Orpailleur and Vignoble le Cep d'Argent.

Montérégie

The dominant player in Québec's wider Eastern Townships, this bumpy and bucolic area is packed with vineyards and orchards (not to mention a surfeit of maple groves). A major fruit farming region – this is an ideal spot to try ciders and flavor-packed fruit wines – growers here are happy to try just about any red or white varietal, but it's their rosés that are particularly memorable. Recommended wineries include Domaine St-Jacques, Les Petits Cailloux and Vignoble des Pins; and keep in mind that Québec restaurants often encourage diners to bring their own bottles, so fill your car as you explore the region.

Nova Scotia

Divided into six boutique wine-producing regions – from the warm shoreline of Northumberland Strait to the verdant Annapolis Valley – Nova Scotia's two-dozen wineries are mostly just a couple of hours drive from big city Halifax. One of the world's coldest grape-growing areas, cool-climate whites are a staple here, including a unique varietal known as l'Acadie Blanc. Innovative sparkling wines are a Nova Scotia specialty and they tend to dominate the drops that are on offer at the popular stops such as the excellent Benjamin Bridge Vineyards. Other highly recommended destinations to fill up your glass include Gaspereau Vineyards, Jost Vineyards and Domaine De Grand Pre.

Festivals

Canada is dripping with palate-pleasing wine events, which makes it especially important to check the dates of your trip: raising a few glasses with celebratory locals is one of the best ways to encounter the country. If you're in BC, it's hard to miss one of the Okanagan's four main festivals – one for each season. They include the 10-day, 165-event **Fall Wine Festival** staged in October and the highly

Books

» *John Schreiner's Okanagan Wine Tour Guide*, by John Schreiner (2010)

» *Crush on Niagara: The Definitive Wine Tour Guide for Niagara, Lake Erie North Shore, Pelee Island and Prince Edward County*, by Andrew Brooks (2010)

» *Wine Atlas of Canada*, by Tony Aspler (2006)

» *Wineries and Wine Country of Nova Scotia*, by Sean Wood (2006)

» *British Columbia Wine Country*, by John Schreiner and Kevin Miller (2007)

Tasty wine blogs

» On the Road with the Grape Guy (www. ontheroad withgrapeguy. blogspot.com)

» Basic Juice (www.basicjuice. blogs.com)

» Canadian Wine Guy (www. canadianwineguy. com)

» John Schreiner on Wine (www. johnschreiner. blogspot.com)

» Dr Vino (www. drvino.com)

» Grape Guy (www.ontheroad withgrapeguy. blogspot.com)

» Basic Juice (www.basicjuice. blogs.com)

» Canadian Wine Guy (www. canadianwine guy.com)

» John Schreiner on Wine (www. johnschreiner. blogspot.com)

» Dr Vino (www. drvino.com)

enjoyable **Winter Festival of Wine**, held every January at Sun Peaks ski resort. For more information on these events, visit www. thewinefestivals.com. If you prefer not to leave the big city, check out March's **Vancouver Playhouse International Wine Festival** (www. playhousewinefest.com) or July's Taste: **Victoria's Festival of Food and Wine** (www.victoriataste.com).

Across the country in Ontario, Niagara also stages more than one annual event to celebrate its winey wealth, including January's **Icewine festival**, June's **New Vintage Festival** and September's giant, nine-day **Niagara Wine Festival**. For information on these events, visit www. niagarawinefestival.com.

Alternatively, Québec-bound grape nuts should drop into the annual **Montréal Passion Vin** (www.montrealpassionvin.ca), a swish two-day charity fundraiser focused on unique and rare vintages. Focused instead on regional food as well as wine, the Eastern Townships' Magog-Orford area hosts the multiday **Fête des Vendanges** (www.fetedes vendanges.com) in September.

Visitors to the east coast are not left out of the fun. Nova Scotia hosts a **Winter Icewine Festival** (www.nsicewinefestival.ca) in February, as well as larger, 50-event **Fall Wine Festival** (www.nsfallwinefestival.ca) in mid-September.

Lip-smacking Tours

If weaving around on your own searching for great places to drink seems a little random, there are some handy operators here who can guide you in your quest for a quality vino. In Nova Scotia, the friendly folks at **Go North Tours** (www.gonorthtours.com) offers five regional tipple treks, driving its small groups around wineries across the province. In Ontario, consider a wine tour with a difference: by bike. **Niagara Wine Tours International** (www.niagara worldwinetours.com) operates several guided cycling trips that are tailored to all fitness levels. And if you're on the road in British Columbia, **Top Cat Tours** (www.topcattours.com) presents a tempting menu of full-day options if you want to explore the Okanagan. These include a Great Estates tour that drives you to the region's biggest wineries as well as a South Okanagan Tour that includes the Golden Mile.

DOWNING ICEWINE IN THE SNOW

There are many good reasons to visit the Okanagan's **Winter Festival of Wine** – accessible educational seminars, lip-smacking dinner events, cozy alpine lodge ambience and some of BC's best outdoor winter activities – but the evening Progressive Tasting is the best. Twenty wineries set up their stalls and offer more than 100 wines at locations throughout the Christmas card village, while increasingly tipsy visitors slip, slide and tumble their way between them in an attempt to keep their glasses as full as possible.

Staged in the third week of January, the annual festival is particularly renowned for celebrating a distinctive tipple that's become a signature of Canadian wineries. Made from grapes frozen on the vine below -8°C – there are plenty of fakes on the market that don't meet this simple criterion – Canadian icewine is a premium, ubersweet dessert drink sold in distinctive slender bottles at upwards of $50 a pop. While Austria, Germany and other countries produce their own icewines, it's a product that reflects Canada's enduring international image as a snowy, winter wonderland.

Tasty Classes

If you're a little jealous of those people who confidently swirl their glasses before airily proclaiming their wine is oaky with a hint of Old Spice and pine nuts, consider getting your own back by learning some wine snob tricks of your own. If you have the time and money, you could consider a full-on sommelier course. But if you're looking for something a little less grueling (and expensive), check out some of the fun and affordable short courses staged at wine stores across the country.

Vancouver's Firefly Fine Wines & Ales (www.fireflyfinewinesandales. com) offers regular evening events where you'll learn about and taste a few wines based around a theme – often a country like Spain or Chile – in a convivial setting with a dozen or so others.

In Toronto, where the vast majority of liquor stores are run by the Liquor Control Board of Ontario (www.lcbo.com), shops across the region run an active and ever-changing roster of wine appreciation classes. Mostly aimed at non-experts who'd like to learn something new about what they're drinking, they cover themes like An Introduction to Wine Appreciation or Wines of the Old World. The courses are good value and must be booked in advance. They also run tutored tastings and cooking classes.

Explore Ontario further by downloading a free map and wine country visitor guide from www. winesofontario. org.

Cuisines of Canada

When the *Globe and Mail* newspaper recently asked salivating Canadians to nominate the country's national dish, its website comments form heated up faster than a frying egg on a mid-summer Toronto sidewalk. Poutine – golden fries drowned in gravy and cheese curds – dominated the exercise, while Montréal-style bagels, salmon jerky, pierogies, donairs, California rolls and even ketchup-flavored potato chips jostled for taste-bud attention. Aside from showing that Canadians love their comfort food, the unscientific poll indicated that the national menu is as diverse as the locals, reflecting a casserole of food cultures whisked together from centuries of immigration.

But before you start thinking that Canadians only eat to lag themselves for the winter or that a sophisticated dinner event is a night-out at a Tim Hortons donut outlet (go for the Maple Cream), there's much more to scoffing here than your appetite might imagine. Big cities like Montréal, Toronto and Vancouver have developed internationally renowned fine-dining scenes rivaling any major metropolis. At the same time, regions across the country have rediscovered the unique ingredients grown, foraged and produced on their doorsteps – bringing distinctive seafood, piquant cheeses and lip-smacking fruits and veggies to the mouths of curious locavores...which explains why any Canadian area with a population of more than two seems to have its own farmers market.

But don't just take our word for it. Wherever you aim for on your travels here, sink your teeth into the wide array of available homegrown flavors and make dining like a Canadian a key focus of your trip. Now, un-notch that belt and get scoffing.

Local Flavors

From east coast lobster to prairie pierogies and west coast spot prawns, some distinctive dishes and ingredients will always define Canada's regions. These provincial soul foods directly reflect local ingredients and the diverse influences of their cooks. And for hungry visitors in search of sustenance, it's often these foods that are the true tastes of the nation.

If you're starting from the east, the main dish of the Maritime provinces is lobster – boiled in the pot and served with a little butter – and the best place to get stuck into it is a community hall 'kitchen party' on Prince Edward Island. Dip into some chunky potato salad and hearty seafood chowder while waiting for your kill to arrive, but don't eat too much; you'll need room for the mountainous fruit pie coming your way afterwards.

Next door, Nova Scotia visitors should save their appetites for butter-soft Digby scallops and rustic Lunenberg sausage, while the favored food of nearby Newfoundland and Labrador often combines rib-sticking dishes of cod cheeks and sweet snow crab. If you're feeling really ravenous, gnaw on a slice of seal flipper pie – a dish you're unlikely to forget in a hurry.

Along with broiled Atlantic salmon (if you want to start a fight on either coastline, take a stance on west versus east coast salmon), the French-influenced region of New Brunswick serves-up *poutine râpée,* potatoes stuffed with pork and boiled for a few hours. It's been filling the bellies of locals here for decades and is highly recommended if you haven't eaten for a week or two.

'if you want to start a fight on either coastline, take a stance on west versus east coast salmon'

Québec is the world's largest maple syrup producer, processing around 6.5 million gallons of the sweet pancake accompaniment every year.

In the French-influenced province of Québec, fine food seems to be a lifeblood for the locals, who will happily sit down for four-hour *joie de vivre* dinners where accompanying wine and conversation flow in equal measures.

The province's cosmopolitan Montréal has long claimed to be the nation's fine-dining capital, but there's an appreciation of food here at all levels that also includes hearty pea soups, exquisite cheeses and tasty pâtés sold at bustling markets. In addition, there's also that national dish poutine waiting to clog your arteries plus smoked meat deli sandwiches so large you'll have to dislocate your jaw to fit them in your mouth.

Ontario – especially Toronto – is a microcosm of Canada's melting pot of cuisines. Like Québec, maple syrup is a super-sweet flavoring of choice here, and it's found in decadent desserts such as beavertails (fried, sugared dough) and on breakfast pancakes that are the size of Frisbees. Head south to the Niagara Peninsula wine region and you'll also discover restaurants fusing contemporary approaches and traditional local ingredients, such as fish from the Great Lakes.

Far north from here, Nunavut in the Arctic Circle is Canada's newest territory but it has a long history of Inuit food, offering a real culinary adventure for extreme cuisine travelers. Served in some restaurants (but more often in family homes – make friends with locals and they may invite you in for a feast), regional specialties include boiled seal, raw frozen char and maktaaq – whale skin cut into small pieces and swallowed whole.

In fact, Canada's Aboriginal people have many fascinating and accessible culinary traditions. Reliant on meat and seafood – try a juicy

ON THE ROAD IN BC'S FARM REGION

Ask Vancouverites where the food on their tables comes from and most will point vacantly at a nearby supermarket, while others will confidently tell you about the Fraser Valley. This lush interior region starts about 50km from the city and has been studded with busy farms for decades. In recent years, farmers and the people they feed have started to get to know one another on a series of six Circle Farm Tours. These self-guided driving tours take you around the communities of Langley, Abbotsford, Chilliwack, Mission, Agassiz & Harrison Mills and Maple Ridge & Pitt Meadows, pointing out recommended pit-stops – farms, markets, wineries and dining suggestions – along the way. Adding a cool foodie adventure to your BC trip, the tour maps can be downloaded free at www.circlefarmtour.ca.

halibut stew on BC's Haida Gwaii – there's also a First Nations tradition of bannock bread, imported by the Scots and appropriated by Canada's original locals. And if you think you're an expert on desserts, try some 'Indian ice-cream.' Made from whipped soapberries, it's sweetened with sugar to assuage its bitter edge.

In contrast, the central provinces of Manitoba, Saskatchewan and Alberta have their own deep-seated culinary ways. The latter, Canada's cowboy country, is the nation's beef capital – you'll find top-notch Alberta steak on menus at leading restaurants across the country. If you're offered 'prairie oysters' here, though, you might want to know (or maybe you'd prefer not to) that they're bull's testicles prepared in a variety of ways designed to take your mind of their origin.

> *'Lobster, an Eastern Canada specialty, contains less cholesterol and saturated fat than beef or pork'*

There's an old Eastern European influence over the border in Manitoba, where immigrant Ukrainians have made comfort food staples of pierogies and thick, spicy sausages. Head next door to prairie-land Saskatchewan for dessert, though. The province's heaping fruit pies are its most striking culinary contribution, especially when prepared with tart Saskatoon berries. These berries are often so abundant, you'll find them sneaked into sweet and savory dishes – and maybe also your shoes – when you dine out here.

In the far west, British Columbians have traditionally fed themselves from the sea and the fertile farmlands of the interior. Indeed, lobster, an Eastern Canada specialty, contains less cholesterol and saturated fat than beef or pork...until you dip it in butter, of course.

The Okanagan Valley's peaches, cherries and blueberries – best purchased from seasonal roadside stands throughout the region – are the staple of many summer diets. In fact, you might find the occasional

---

TASTE-TRIPPING COOKING COURSES

Culinary tourism has spread like an overturned bowl of blueberries here in recent years. If you're hungry for a side dish of foodie education on your trip, check out the following courses or contact your destination's tourism organization to see what's on offer.

Amateurs and pros alike will find a course to suit their level at Vancouver's popular **Dirty Apron Cooking School** (www.dirtyapron.com). An ever-changing smorgasbord of regional cuisines is the approach and the classes – mostly taught by French-influenced chef David Robertson – aim to make students feel comfortable about mastering the required skills for a wide array of ingredient-based cooking.

One of Toronto's best options, the two-hour hands-on courses offered by **Great Cooks** (www.greatcooks.ca) feature loquacious visiting chefs and gregarious foodies talking you through sauce-making, French-Canadian bistro skills or Japanese sushi rolling, among many others.

You can learn all about the heights of Canadian culinary expertise on an immersive weekend residential course at Nova Scotia's celebrated **Trout Point Cooking and Wine School** (www.troutpoint.com). The programs – including Nova Scotia seafood cooking and cheese and cheesemaking masterclasses – are held at a sumptuous wilderness resort and are among Canada's most popular cooking vacations.

If you're more attracted to Vancouver Island's produce cornucopia, consider an educational tour of the verdant Cowichan Valley farm region, offered by **Travel With Taste** (www.travelwithtaste.com). You'll meet and sample with artisan cheese makers and boutique vintners before tucking into a gourmet lunch of wild BC salmon. The company also offers lip-smacking guided tours around Victoria and Salt Spring Island.

giddy local slumped against a tree with fruit-stained lips and a big smile. But it's the seafood that attracts the lion's share of culinary fans. Tuck into succulent wild salmon, juicy Fanny Bay oysters and velvet-soft scallops and you may decide you've stumbled on foodie nirvana.

Geoduck (pronounced 'gooey duck') is BC's most unusual aquatic dish. A giant saltwater clam, it's a delicacy in Chinese restaurants and is shipped to chefs around the world.

Showcasing Canada's burgeoning **100 Mile Diet** (www.100milediet. org) movement, this website tells you all you need to know about the value of eating local.

Canadian bacon is a North America–wide name for back bacon. The term is much more commonly used in the US than in Canada, though.

Top Dining Neighborhoods

Ask anyone in Toronto, Montréal or Vancouver to name Canada's leading foodie city and they'll likely inform you that you've just found it. But while each of the big three claims to be at the top table when it comes to dining, their strengths are so diverse they're more accurately defined as complimentary courses in one great meal – in fact, if you jog between them, you might work off a little of that belt-challenging excess.

'If Montréal serves as an ideal starter, that makes Toronto the main course'

First dish on the table is Montréal, which was Canada's sole dine-out capital long before the upstarts threw off their donut-based shackles. Renowned for bringing North America's finest French-influenced cuisine to local palates, it hasn't given up its crown lightly. Chefs here are often treated like rock stars as they challenge old world conventions with daring, even artistic approaches – expect clever, fusionesque gastronomy. You should also expect a great restaurant experience: Montréalers have a bacchanalian love for eating out, with lively rooms ranging from cozy old town heritage restaurants to the animated patios of Rue St Arthur and the sophisticated, often funky eateries of the Plateau.

If Montréal serves as an ideal starter, that makes Toronto the main course – although that's a reflection of its recent elevation rather than its prominence. Fusion is also the default approach in Canada's largest city, although it's been taken even further here with a wave of contemporary immigration adding modern influences from Asia to a foundation of British, Greek and Italian cuisines. With a bewildering 7000 restaurants to choose from, though, it can be a tough choice figuring out where to unleash your top-end dining budget. The best approach is to hit the neighborhoods: both the Financial District and Old York areas are studded with classy, high-end joints where swank is a typical side-dish.

And while that appears to make Vancouver the dessert, it could easily be argued that this glass-towered west coast metropolis is the best of the bunch. In recent years, some of the country's most innovative chefs have set up shop here, inspired by the twin influences of an abundant local larder of unique flavors and the most cosmopolitan – especially Asian – population in Canada. Fusion is the starting point here in fine-dining districts like Yaletown and Kistilano. But there's also a high-level of authenticity in top-notch ethnic dining: the best sushi bars and Japanese izakayas outside Tokyo jostle for attention with superb Vietnamese and Korean eateries that feel like they've been transported from halfway around the world.

Food-lovers books

» *An Edible Journey: Exploring the Islands' Fine Food, Farms & Vineyards,* by Elizabeth Levinson (2009)

» *Flavours of Canada,* by Anita Stewart (2006)

» *Ocean Wise Cookbook,* by Jane Mundy (2010)

» *The Boreal Gourmet: Adventures in Northern Cooking,* by Michele Genest (2010)

» *Flavours of Prince Edward Island: A Culinary Journey,* by Jeff McCourt, Alan Williams and Austin Clement (2010)

Festivals & Events

Food is often the foundation for good times in Canada and many regions celebrate their cuisines with festivals. If you're lucky enough to stumble on one or two during your visit, don't miss out: they're among the best ways to hang out and get to know the locals.

Recommended events – large and small – include **Prince Edward Island's International Shellfish Festival** (www.peishellfish.com); **New Brunswick's Shediac Lobster Festival** (www.shediaclobsterfestival.ca); **Québec's Fête du Chocolat de Bromont** (www.feteduchocolat.ca); **Toronto's Salut Wine & Food Festival** (www.salutwinefestival.com); and Vancouver Island's **Cowichan Wine & Culinary Festival** (www.wines.cowichan.net).

Alongside these great events, Canadians rarely need an excuse to celebrate with food at home. Languid summer barbecues, fall's feast-like Thanksgiving and Christmas time's family get-togethers traditionally center on tables groaning with heaping salad bowls, aromatic meat dishes and diet-denying fruit desserts. If you're lucky enough to be invited over, ask what you can bring along to contribute to the revelries.

Wildlife

Whether you've come to glimpse polar bear, grizzly bear, whale or moose, Canada delivers. With 35% of its landscape covered by boreal forest, and 202,000km of coastline (the world's longest), the country has heaps of habitat for wildlife spotting.

On Land

Moose

Moose nibble shrubs throughout Canada. They're part of the deer family, but far more humungous, with skinny, ballerina-like legs that support a hulking body. Males weigh up to 534kg, all put on by a vegetarian diet of twigs and leaves. Despite their odd shape, moose can move it: they run up to 56km per hour, and in water, they can swim as fast as two men paddling a canoe.

Males grow a spectacular rack of antlers every summer, only to discard it in November. You'll spot moose foraging near lakes, muskegs and streams, as well as in the forests of the western mountain ranges in the Rockies and the Yukon. Newfoundland is perhaps the moosiest place of all. In 1904, the province imported and released four beasts into the wild. They enjoyed the good life of shrub-eating and hot sex, ultimately spawning the 120,000 Bullwinkles that now roam the woods.

Moose generally are not aggressive, and they often will pose for photographs. They can be unpredictable, though, so don't startle them. During mating season (September), the males can become belligerent, so keep your distance.

Black & Grizzly Bear

If you're lucky enough to spot a bear in the wild, it will most likely be a black bear. About half a million of these furry critters patrol the forests and bushland just about everywhere except Prince Edward Island, southern Alberta and southern Saskatchewan.

Ursus arctos horribilis, better known as the grizzly bear, makes its home on the higher slopes of the Rocky and Selkirk Mountains of British Columbia, Alberta and the Yukon. The endangered creature stands up to a fearsome 3m tall and has a distinctive hump between its shoulders. Grizzlies are solitary animals with no natural enemies except humans. Although they enjoy an occasional snack of elk, moose or caribou, they usually fill their bellies with berries and other vegetation.

Just to confuse you, black bear are sometimes brown and some grizzlies are almost black. The way to tell them apart is to look for certain distinguishing characteristics: the grizzly has a dish-shaped face, small and rounded ears and that aforementioned shoulder hump.

In 1994, coastal BC's Khutzeymateen Grizzly Bear Sanctuary (near Prince Rupert, BC) was protected. Over 50 grizzlies live on this 45,000-hectare refuge. A few eco-tour operators have permits for

Best Moose-Viewing

» Northern Peninsula, Newfoundland

» Cape Breton Highlands National Park, Nova Scotia

» Algonquin Provincial Park, Ontario

» Maligne Lake, Jasper National Park, Alberta

Serious birders can put their efforts to good use by logging their counts and helping science at www.ebird.org.

viewing the animals. The mountain national parks (Banff, Jasper, Kootenay, Yoho) also offer a chance to see these rare omnivores as you drive or hike in the region.

Polar Bear

The fiercest member of the bear family, polar bears weigh less than 1kg at birth but grow to be as heavy as 600kg or more. The premier place to observe them is Churchill, Manitoba, on the shores of Hudson Bay, from late September to early November. About 900 of the world's roughly 20,000 white-furred beasts prowl the tundra here – it's one of their major maternity denning grounds.

Operators will tour you around the polar bear capital of the world in elevated tundra buggies. Just don't step out – these carnivorous predators look at you as if you're a walking filet mignon. Unlike grizzly and black bear, polar bear actively prey on people.

Nunavut is home to nearly half of the world's polar bear population, though bear-rich spots such as Ukkusiksalik National Park are notoriously difficult to visit.

Polar bear occasionally show up on Newfoundland's Northern Peninsula and Labrador's coastal towns, coming to shore from the drifting pack ice.

Caribou, Elk & Deer

The white-tailed deer can be found anywhere from Nova Scotia's Cape Breton to the Northwest Territories' Great Slave Lake. Its bigger relative, the caribou, is unusual in that both males and females sport enormous antlers. Barren-ground caribou feed on lichen and spend most of the year on the tundra from Baffin Island to Alaska. Woodland caribou roam farther south, with some of the mightiest herds trekking across northern Québec and Labrador. The beasts also show up in BC's and Newfoundland's mountainous parks, which is where many visitors catch their glimpse.

Elk *(wapiti),* another of the deer species, is a formidable creature whose 'bugling' roars can scare the bejeezus out of you. Their relatively small herds roam around western Canada, especially the Kootenays and Vancouver Island in BC, although quite a few also hang out in the national parks of Banff and Jasper (Alberta), as well as Waterton Lakes (Alberta), Riding Mountain (Manitoba) and Prince Albert (Saskatchewan). Like moose, elk generally are not aggressive, except during mating season in September/October.

Bison

The huge, heavy-shouldered, shaggy bison (buffalo) that once roamed the prairies in vast herds now exists only in parks. It is said that there were once as many as 60 million bison in North America. Their herds would often take days to pass by a single point. Their 19th-century slaughter – often by chartered trainloads of 'sportsmen' who left the carcasses to rot – is one of the great tragedies of the North American west, affecting the very survival of Aboriginal peoples. To check out the largest herd of bison, take a trip to Wood Buffalo National Park, close to the Alberta–Northwest Territories border. Smaller herds roam the national parks of Waterton Lakes and Elk Island in Alberta, Prince Albert in Saskatchewan and Riding Mountain in Manitoba.

Wolf

The wolf can be every bit as fierce and cunning as is portrayed in fairy tales, although it rarely attack humans. Wolf hunt in packs and aren't afraid to take on animals much larger than themselves, includ-

---

Best Bear-Spotting

» Churchill, MB – polar bears

» Prince Rupert, BC – Khutzeymateen Grizzly Bear Sanctuary

» Rocky Mountain National Parks (Banff/Jasper, AB; Kootenay/Yoho, BC) – grizzly, black bears

---

The white hairs on a polar bear are hollow and trap sunlight to help keep the animal warm in frigid temperatures.

ing moose and bison. They're still fairly common in sparsely populated areas between Labrador and the Yukon. If you're out in the bush, you may hear them howling at the moon. At Ontario's Algonquin Provincial Park (www.algonquinpark.on.ca) you can actually take part in a public 'howl.' Wolves will readily respond to human imitations of their calls, so the park's staff conducts communal sessions on various summer evenings to give visitors a 'wail' of an experience.

In the Water

East Coast

More than 22 species of whale and porpoise lurk offshore throughout Atlantic Canada, drawn to the rich fishy feeding waters like Homer Simpson to donuts. Among the standouts: the humpback whale, which averages 15m and 36 tons – serious heft to be launching up and out of the water for their playful breaching; the North Atlantic right whale, the world's most endangered leviathan, with an estimated population of just 350; and the mighty blue whale, the largest animal on earth at 25m and a good 100 tons. Finback aren't much smaller. You can spot them by their jaw's asymmetrical coloring (white or yellowish on the right side and black on the left side). Then there's the little guy, the minke, which grows to 10m and often approaches boats, delighting passengers with acrobatics as it, too, breaches and shows off.

Whale watch boat operators are ubiquitous and will bring you close to the creatures. Popular tour areas include Cape Breton's Cabot Trail coastline, with over 20 operators in the region, especially around Pleasant Bay; the most common sightings are humpback, minke and pilot whale. In the Bay of Fundy excellent whale watching concentrates around Nova Scotia's Digby Neck and New Brunswick's Fundy Isles; this is where you'll have the best shot at seeing rare right whale as well as blue whale. Newfoundland pretty much has whales swimming all around its shores, with humpback and minke commonly seen; tour operators cluster near Witless Bay Ecological Reserve and Twillingate.

Tadoussac, Québec, on the St Lawrence River, is another outstanding area for viewing. Not only do finback, blue, humpback and minke patrol the water, but also beluga whale. The white cuties here are the only population outside of the Arctic.

Those friggin' black flies aren't just bothering you with their itchy, painful bites – they're all over moose, caribou and other animals, too, from April to July (a bit later in colder climates).

WILDLIFE IN THE WATER

TRYING TO HANG ON

There are 602 endangered species in Canada, according to the Committee on the Status of Endangered Wildlife. Hunting, pollution and destruction of habitat are the main factors behind their disappearance. Some of the most fragile creatures include:

» **Vancouver Island marmot** This squirrel family member is found only on – that's right – Vancouver Island, BC. In the mid-1980s, the population was 300 animals; by 2001, it had declined to less than 75, of which only 25 marmots remained in the wild. Through a captive breeding program and other recovery efforts, the wild population is now back to around 220. Strathcona Provincial Park is one of the release sites.

» **Whooping crane** A group of 220 whoopers nests in Wood Buffalo National Park, on the Alberta–Northwest Territories border, and migrates south each year to the Texas Gulf Coast. Thanks to conservation efforts the flock has increased by 35% in the last 10 years.

» **Eastern cougar** It once crept through forests in Ontario, Québec, New Brunswick and Nova Scotia – and may still, though scientists can't be sure. Recent (but unverified) sightings in New Brunswick keep hope alive that the big cat has not disappeared forever. Cougars still survive in western Canada.

And while whale watch tours are great, never underestimate what you can see from shore, especially from places like Cape Breton's Cabot Trail, Newfoundland's Avalon Peninsula and Tadoussac.

West Coast

Orca, gray whale and humpback whale are the west's claim to fame.

Orca are the only creature in the water that fears no enemy other than humans, and their diet includes seal, beluga and other whales (hence the 'killer whale' nickname). Their aerodynamic bodies, signature black-and-white coloration and incredible speed (up to 40km/h) make them the Ferraris of the aquatic world. The waters around Vancouver Island, particularly in the Johnstone Strait, teem with orcas in summer. Much of the waterway has been preserved as the Robson Bight Ecological Preserve. It's Canada's only killer whale sanctuary, and it's the best place in the world for viewing them. Access is via Telegraph Cove. Resident orcas also swim near Victoria, from which several tours depart.

A major gray whale migration occurs off Vancouver Island's west coast near Tofino each winter. Approximately 20,000 behemoths leave the Baja Peninsula to journey north to Alaska, cruising right past Vancouver Island en route. The journey peaks in late March, which is when the Pacific Rim Whale Festival (www.pacificrimwhalefestival.com) takes place. You can see the whales from shore, as they swim in very close. Several pods spend the summer months in Clayoquot Sound, along with humpbacks. Seals and sea lions hang around, too.

North Coast

Beluga glide in Arctic waters. The white whales are one of the smallest members of the whale family, typically measuring no more than 4m and weighing about one ton. They are chatty fellows who squeak, groan and peep while traveling in closely knit family pods. In Churchill, Manitoba, you can see them by boat or kayak tour, or don a wetsuit and go snorkeling with them.

Early explorers called narwhals 'unicorns of the sea' for the large tusk growing off their forehead (it's actually a tooth). They swim in the far north and are rare to see.

In the Air

Canadian skies are home to 462 bird species, with BC and Ontario boasting the greatest diversity. The most famous feathered resident is the common loon, Canada's national bird. It's a waterbird whose

---

Whale Hot Spots

» Witless Bay, Newfoundland

» Grand Manan Island, New Brunswick

» Digby Neck, Nova Scotia

» Cabot Trail, Nova Scotia

» Victoria, BC

» Tofino, BC

» Tadoussac, Québec

To hear west coast orcas doing their heavy-breathing thing, go to www. orcasound.net. To hear east coast whales singing songs, go to http://new -brunswick.net/ new-brunswick/ whales/avi.html.

SALMON RUNS

British Columbia has the best seats for viewing the bizarre, annual spectacle.

» Every fall between October and December, you'll see chum salmon fight the current for egg laying – and their inevitable death – in Vancouver Island's Goldstream Provincial Park (www.goldstreampark.com). Afterward, eagles flock to feast on the carcasses, filling their plates until February.

» Every four years, some of the 15 million sockeye salmon reach the Adams River near Chase, BC. You'll see red if you're around in the fall of 2014, 2018, 2022...

» Each August Chinook salmon – the largest Pacific species, at 5ft long – swim 1200 grueling kilometers upstream in the Fraser River, only to be met by Rearguard Falls. Watching them battle to leap over the waterway is a sight to behold. Rearguard Falls Provincial Park, near Valemount, BC, has a ringside viewing platform.

mournful yet beautiful call often rings out across quiet backcountry lakes early or late in the day.

What's all the flap about? Well, if you're a Canada goose, it can be up to 1000km a day. Flying in their distinctive V formation, some of these geese have made the trip from northern Québec to the USA in a single day!

Seabirds flock to Atlantic Canada to breed. You'll be able to feast your eyes upon razorbill, kittiwake, arctic tern, common murre and yes, puffin. Everyone loves these cute little guys, a sort of waddling penguin-meets-parrot, with black-and-white feathers and an orange beak. They nest around Newfoundland, in particular.

The seabird colonies can be up to one million strong, their shrieks deafening and their smell, well, not so fresh. Still, it's an amazing sight to behold. The preeminent places to get feathered are New Brunswick's Grand Manan Island and Newfoundland's Witless Bay and Cape St Mary's (both on the Avalon Peninsula near St John's). The best time is May through August, before the birds fly away for the winter.

Bald eagle swoop throughout Canada and remain the true rulers of the sky. Their wingspan can reach more than 2m. Good viewings sites include Brackendale, near Squamish, BC, where up to 4000 eagles nest in winter; around Bras d'Or Lake in Cape Breton, Nova Scotia; and on Vancouver Island's southern and western shores in BC.

Ontario's Point Pelee National Park is a birders' bonanza in spring and fall, when migratory songbirds flit by; more than 370 kinds have been spotted.

Best Bird-Watching

» Cape St Mary's, Newfoundland

» Witless Bay, Newfoundland

» Point Pelee National Park, Ontario

» Grand Manan Island, New Brunswick

» Brackendale, BC

WILDLIFE IN THE AIR

Survival Guide

Directory A-Z

Accommodations

In Canada, you'll be choosing from a wide range of B&Bs, chain motels, hotels and hostels. Provincial tourist offices publish comprehensive directories of accommodations, and some take bookings online.

Seasons

» Peak season is summer, from late May to early September, when prices are highest.

» It's best to book ahead during summer, as well as during ski season at winter resorts, and during holidays and major events, as rooms can be scarce.

Prices

» Prices listed in this book are for peak-season travel and, unless stated otherwise, do not include taxes (which can be up to 17%). If breakfast is included and/or a bathroom is shared, that information is included in our listing.

» The budget category comprises campgrounds, hostels and simple hotels and B&Bs where you'll likely share

a bathroom. Rates rarely exceed $80 for a double.

» Midrange accommodations, such as most B&Bs, inns (auberges in French), motels and some hotels, generally offer the best value for money. Expect to pay between $80 and $180 for a comfortable, decent-sized double with a private bathroom and TV.

» Top-end accommodations (more than $180 per double) offer an international standard of amenities, including fitness and business centers and other upmarket facilities.

Amenities

» Most properties offer in-room wi-fi. It's typically free in budget and midrange lodgings, while top-end hotels often charge a fee.

» Many smaller properties, especially B&Bs, ban smoking. Marriott and Westin brand hotels are 100% smoke free. All other properties have rooms set aside for nonsmokers. In this book, we have used the nonsmoking icon (☻) to mean that all rooms within a property are nonsmoking.

» Air-conditioning is not a standard amenity at most

budget and midrange places. If you want it, be sure to ask about it when you book.

Discounts

» In winter, prices can plummet by as much as 50%.

» Membership in the American Automobile Association (AAA) or an associated automobile association, American Association of Retired Persons (AARP) or other organizations also yields modest savings (usually 10%).

» Check the hotel websites listed throughout this book for special online rates. The usual suspects also offer discounted room prices throughout Canada:

Priceline (www.priceline.com)
Hotwire (www.hotwire.com)
Expedia (www.expedia.com)
Travelocity (www.travelocity.com)
Tripadvisor (www.tripadvisor.com)

B&Bs

» **Bed & Breakfast Online** (www.bbcanada.com) is the main booking agency for properties nationwide.

» In Canada, B&Bs (gîtes in French) are essentially converted private homes whose owners live on site. People who value privacy may find B&Bs too intimate, as walls are rarely soundproof and it's usual to mingle with your hosts and other guests.

» Standards vary widely, sometimes even within a single B&B. The cheapest rooms tend to be small with few amenities and a shared bathroom. Nicer ones have added features such as a balcony, a fireplace and an en suite bathroom. Breakfast is always included in the rates (though it might be continental instead of a full cooked affair).

» Not all B&Bs accept children.

» Minimum stays (usually two nights) are common, and many B&Bs are only open seasonally.

PRACTICALITIES

» The most widely available newspaper is the Toronto-based *Globe and Mail*. Other principal dailies are the *Montréal Gazette*, *Ottawa Citizen*, *Toronto Star* and *Vancouver Sun*.

» *Maclean's* (www.macleans.ca) is Canada's weekly news magazine.

» The Canadian Broadcasting Corporation (CBC) is the dominant nationwide network for both radio and TV. The Canadian Television Network (CTN) is the major competition.

» Canada officially uses the metric system, but imperial measurements are used for many day-to-day purposes. To convert between the two systems, see the chart on the inside front cover.

» Smoking is banned in all restaurants, bars and other public venues nationwide.

Camping

» Canada is filled with campgrounds – some federal or provincial, others privately owned.

» The official season runs from May to September, but exact dates vary by location.

» Facilities vary widely. Backcountry sites offer little more than pit toilets and fire rings, and have no potable water. Unserviced (tent) campgrounds come with access to drinking water and a washroom with toilets and sometimes showers. The best-equipped sites feature flush toilets and hot showers, and water, electrical and sewer hookups for recreational vehicles (RVs).

» Private campgrounds sometimes cater only to trailers (caravans) and RVs, and may feature convenience stores, playgrounds and swimming pools. It is a good idea to phone ahead to make sure the size of sites and the services provided at a particular campground are suitable for your vehicle.

» Most government-run sites are available on a first-come first-served basis and fill up quickly, especially in July and August. Several national parks participate in Parks Canada's **camping**

reservation program (☑877-737-3783; www.pc camping.ca; reservation fees $10.80), which is a convenient way to make sure you get a spot. Provincial park reservation information is provided in destination chapters throughout this book.

» Nightly camping fees in national and provincial parks range from about $20 to $30 for tents up to $39 for full hookup sites; fire permits often cost a few dollars extra. Backcountry camping costs about $14 per night. Private campgrounds tend to be a bit pricier. BC's parks, in particular, have seen a hefty rate increase in recent years.

» Some campgrounds remain open for maintenance year-round and may let you camp at a reduced rate in the off-season. This can be great in late autumn or early spring when there's hardly a soul about. Winter camping, though, is only for the hardy.

Homestays

How do you feel about staying on the couch of a perfect stranger? If it's not a problem, consider joining an organization that arranges homestays. The groups following charge no fees to become a member, and the stay itself is also free.

Couch Surfing (www.couchsurfing.com)

Hospitality Club (www.hospitalityclub.org)

Hostels

Canada has independent hostels as well as those affiliated with Hostelling International (HI). All have dorms ($25 to $35 per person on average), which can sleep from two to 10 people, and many have private rooms (from $60) for couples and families. Rooms in HI hostels are gender segregated and alcohol and smoking are prohibited; non-members pay a surcharge of about $4 per night.

Bathrooms are usually shared, and facilities include a kitchen, lockers, internet access, laundry room and a shared TV room. Most hostels, especially those in the big cities, are open 24 hours a day. If they are not, ask if you can make special arrangements if you are arriving late.

For additional information and online reservations:

Backpackers Hostels Canada (www.backpackers. ca) Independent hostels.

Hostelling International Canada (www.hihostels.ca)

Hostels.com (www.hostels. com) Includes independent and HI hostels.

BOOK YOUR STAY ONLINE

For more accommodation reviews by Lonely Planet authors, check out hotels.lonelyplanet.com/Canada. You'll find independent reviews, as well as recommendations on the best places to stay. Best of all, you can book online.

Most hotels are part of international chains, and the newer ones are designed for either the luxury market or businesspeople. Rooms have cable TV and wi-fi; many also have swimming pools and fitness and business centers. Rooms with two double or queen-sized beds sleep up to four people, although there is usually a small surcharge for the third and fourth person. Many places advertise that 'kids stay free' but sometimes you have to pay extra for a crib or a rollaway (portable bed).

In Canada, like the USA (both lands of the automobile), motels are ubiquitous. They dot the highways and cluster in groups on the outskirts of towns and cities. Although most motel rooms won't win any style awards, they're usually clean and comfortable and offer good value for travelers. Many regional motels remain your typical 'mom and pop' operations, but plenty of North American chains have also opened up around the region.

University Accommodations

In the lecture-free summer months, some universities and colleges rent beds in their student dormitories to travelers of all ages. Most rooms are quite basic, but with rates ranging from $25 to $40 per night, and often including breakfast, you know you're not getting the Ritz. Students can usually qualify for small discounts.

Activities

Snowboarding, sea kayaking, mountain biking – there's so much to do we've devoted a whole chapter to Canada's Outdoor Activities (see p838).

THE CHAIN GANG

Budget
Days Inn (☎800-329-7466; www.daysinn.com)
Econo Lodge (☎877-424-6423; www.econolodge.com)
Super 8 (☎800-800-8000; www.super8.com)

Midrange
Best Western (☎800-780-7234; www.bestwestern.com)
Clarion Hotel (☎877-424-6423; www.clarionhotel.com)
Comfort Inn (☎877-424-6423; www.comfortinn.com)
Fairfield Inn (☎800-228-2800; www.fairfieldinn.com)
Hampton Inn (☎800-426-7866; www.hamptoninn.com)
Holiday Inn (☎888-465-4329; www.holidayinn.com)
Howard Johnson (☎800-446-4656; www.hojo.com)
Quality Inn & Suites (☎877-424-6423; www.qualityinn.com)
Travelodge/Thriftlodge (☎800-578-7878; www.travelodge.com)

Top End
Delta (☎877-814-7706; www.deltahotels.com)
Fairmont (☎800-257-7544; www.fairmont.com)
Hilton (☎800-445-8667; www.hilton.com)
Hyatt (☎888-591-1234; www.hyatt.com)
Marriott (☎888-236-2427; www.marriott.com)
Radisson (☎888-201-1718; www.radisson.com)
Ramada (☎800-272-6232; www.ramada.com)
Sheraton (☎800-325-3535; www.sheraton.com)
Westin (☎800-937-8461; www.westin.com)

Other resources:
Parks Canada (www.pc.gc.ca) National park action.
Canada Trails (www.canadatrails.ca) Hiking, biking and cross-country skiing.
Canadian Ski Council (www.skicanada.org) Skiing and snowboarding.
Paddling Canada (www.paddlingcanada.com) Kayaking and canoeing.
Alpine Club of Canada (www.alpineclubofcanada.ca) Climbing and mountaineering.

Business Hours

The list below provides 'normal' opening hours for businesses. Reviews throughout this book show specific hours only if they vary from these standards. Note, too, that hours can vary by season. Our listings depict peak season operating times.

Banks 10am-5pm Mon-Fri; some open 9am-noon Sat
General office hours 9am-5pm Mon-Fri
Museums 10am-5pm daily, sometimes closed on Mon
Restaurants breakfast 8am-11am, lunch 11:30am-2:30pm Mon-Fri, dinner 5-9:30pm daily; some open for brunch 8am-1pm Sat & Sun
Bars 5pm-2am daily
Clubs 9pm-2am Wed-Sat
Shops 10am-6pm Mon-Sat, noon-5pm Sun, some open to 8 or 9pm Thu and/or Fri
Supermarkets 9am-8pm, some open 24hr

Customs Regulations

The **Canada Border Services Agency** (CBSA; www.cbsa.gc.ca) has the customs lowdown. A few regulations to note:

Alcohol You can bring in 1.5L of wine, 1.14L of liquor or 24 355mL beers duty free.

Gifts You can bring in gifts totaling up to $60.

Money You can bring in/take out up to $10,000; larger amounts must be reported to customs.

Personal effects Camping gear, sports equipment, cameras and laptop computers can be brought in without much trouble. Declaring these to customs as you cross the border might save you some hassle when you leave, especially if you'll be crossing the US–Canadian border multiple times.

Pets You must carry a signed and dated certificate from a veterinarian to prove your dog or cat has had a rabies shot in the past 36 months.

Prescription drugs You can bring in/take out a 90-day supply for personal use (though if you're bringing it to the USA, know it's technically illegal but overlooked for individuals).

Tobacco You can bring in 200 cigarettes, 50 cigars, 200g of tobacco and 200 tobacco sticks duty free.

Discount Cards

Discounts are commonly offered for seniors, children, families and people with disabilities, though no special cards are issued (you get the savings on site when you pay). AAA and other automobile association members can also receive various travel-related discounts.

International Student Identity Card (ISIC; www.isiccard.com) Provides students with discounts on travel insurance and admission to museums and other sights. There are also cards for those who are under 26 but not students, and for full-time teachers.

Parks Canada Discovery Pass (www.pc.gc.ca/voyage-travel/carte-pass/index_e.asp; adult/child 6-16yr/family $68/33/136) Provides access to 27 national parks and 77 historic sites for a year. Can pay for itself in as few as seven visits over daily entry fees; also provides quicker entry into sites. Many cities have discount cards for local attractions; see destinations for details.

» Montréal Museum Pass
» Ottawa Culture Passport
» UBC Attractions Passport (Vancouver)
» Winnipass (Winnipeg)

Embassies & Consulates

All countries have their embassies in Ottawa and maintain consulates in such cities as Montréal, Vancouver, Calgary and Toronto. Contact the relevant embassy to find out which consulate is closest to you.

Australia (☑613-236-0841; www.ahc-ottawa.org; Suite 710, 50 O'Connor St, Ottawa, ON K1P 6L2)

France (☑613 780 1708; www.ambafrance-ca.org; 42 Sussex Dr, Ottawa, ON K1M 2C9)

Germany (☑613-232-1101; www.ottawa.diplo.de; 1 Waverley St, Ottawa, ON K2P 0T8)

Ireland (☑613-233-6281; www.embassyofireland.ca; 130 Albert St, Ottawa, ON K1P 5G4)

Italy (☑613-232-2401; www.ambottawa.esteri.it; 21st fl, 275 Slater St, Ottawa, ON K1P 5H9)

Japan (☑613-241-8541; www.ca.emb-japan.go.jp; 255 Sussex Dr, Ottawa, ON K1N 9E6)

Mexico (☑613-233-8988; www.embamexican.com; Suite 1500, 45 O'Connor St, Ottawa, ON K1P 1A4)

Netherlands (☑613-237-5030; www.netherlands embassy.ca; Suite 2020, 350 Albert St, Ottawa, ON K1R 1A4)

New Zealand (☑613-238-5991; www.nzembassy.com; Suite 727, 99 Bank St, Ottawa, ON K1P 6G3)

UK (☑613-237-2008; www.ukincanada.fco.gov.uk; 80 Elgin St, Ottawa, ON K1P 5K7)

USA (☑613-238-5335; http://ottawa.usembassy.gov; 490 Sussex Dr, Ottawa, ON K1N 1G8)

Electricity

120v/60hz

120v/60hz

Gay & Lesbian Travelers

Canada is tolerant when it comes to gays and lesbians, though this outlook is more common in the big cities than in rural areas. Same-sex marriage is legal throughout the country (Canada is one of only 10 nations worldwide that permits this).

Montréal, Toronto and Vancouver are by far Canada's gayest cities, each with a humming nightlife scene, publications and lots of associations and support groups. All have sizeable Pride celebrations, too, which attract big crowds. For more details, see the boxed texts on p239, p69 and p641.

Attitudes remain more conservative in the northern regions. Throughout Nunavut, and to a lesser extent in the aboriginal communities of the Northwest Territories, there are some retrogressive attitudes toward homosexuality. The Yukon, in contrast, is more like British Columbia, with a live-and-let-live west coast attitude.

The following are good resources for gay travel; they include Canadian information, though not all are exclusive to the region:

Damron (www.damron.com) Publishes several travel guides, including *Men's Travel Guide, Women's Traveller* and *Damron Accommodations*; gay-friendly tour operators are listed on the website, too.

Gay Canada (www.gaycanada.com) Search by province or city for queer-friendly businesses and resources.

Gay Travel News (www.gaytravelnews.com) Website listing gay-friendly destinations and hotels.

Out Traveler (www.outtraveler.com) Gay travel magazine.

Purple Roofs (www.purpleroofs.com) Website listing queer accommodations, travel agencies and tours worldwide.

Queer Canada (www.queercanada.ca) A general resource.

Xtra (www.xtra.ca) Source for gay and lesbian news nationwide.

Health

BEFORE YOU GO
INSURANCE

Canada offers some of the finest health care in the world. The problem is that, unless you are a Canadian citizen, it can be prohibitively expensive. It's essential to purchase travel health insurance if your regular policy doesn't cover you when you're abroad. Check www.lonelyplanet.com/travel_services for supplemental insurance information.

Bring medications you may need clearly labeled in their original containers. A signed, dated letter from your physician that describes your medical conditions and medications, including generic names, is also a good idea.

RECOMMENDED VACCINATIONS

No special vaccines are required or recommended for travel to Canada. All travelers should be up to date on routine immunizations.

MEDICAL CHECKLIST

» acetaminophen (eg Tylenol) or aspirin
» anti-inflammatory drugs (eg ibuprofen)
» antihistamines (for hay fever and allergic reactions)
» antibacterial ointment (eg Neosporin) for cuts and abrasions
» steroid cream or cortisone (for poison ivy and other allergic rashes)
» bandages, gauze, gauze rolls
» adhesive or paper tape
» safety pins, tweezers
» thermometer

MEDICAL CHECKLIST

VACCINE	RECOMMENDED FOR	DOSAGE	SIDE EFFECTS
tetanus-diphtheria	all travelers who haven't had booster within 10 years	one dose lasts 10 years	soreness at injection site
measles	travelers born after 1956 who've had only one measles vaccination	one dose	fever, rash, joint pains, allergic reactions
chickenpox	travelers who've never had chickenpox	two doses one month apart	fever, mild case of chickenpox soreness at the
influenza	all travelers during flu season (November through March)	one dose	soreness at the injection site, fever

» DEET-containing insect repellent for the skin

» permethrin-containing insect spray for clothing, tents and bed nets

» sunblock

» motion-sickness medication

WEBSITES

Canadian resources:
Public Health Agency of Canada
(www.publichealth.gc.ca)
General resources:
MD Travel Health
(www.mdtravelhealth.com)
World Health Organization (www.who.int)
Government travel health websites:
Australia
(www.smarttraveller.gov.au)
United Kingdom
(www.nhs.gov/healthcare abroad)
United States
(www.cdc.gov/travel/)

IN CANADA

AVAILABILITY & COST OF HEALTH CARE

Medical services are widely available. For emergencies, the best bet is to find the nearest hospital and go to its emergency room. If the problem isn't urgent, call a nearby hospital and ask for a referral to a local physician, which is usually cheaper than a trip to the emergency room (where costs can be $500 or so before any treatment).

Pharmacies are abundant, but prescriptions can be expensive without insurance. However, Americans may find Canadian prescription drugs to be cheaper than drugs at home. You're allowed to take out a 90-day supply for personal use (though know it's technically illegal to bring them into the USA, but overlooked for individuals).

INFECTIOUS DISEASES

Most are acquired by mosquito or tick bites, or environmental exposure. The

Public Health Agency of Canada (www.publichealth.gc.ca) has details on all listed below.

Giardiasis Intestinal infection. Avoid drinking directly from lakes, ponds, streams and rivers.

Lyme Disease Occurs mostly in southern Canada. Transmitted by deer ticks in late spring and summer. Perform a tick check after you've been outdoors.

Severe Acute Respiratory Syndrome (SARS) At the time of writing, SARS has been brought under control in Canada.

West Nile Virus Mosquito-transmitted in late summer and early fall. Prevent by keeping covered (wear long sleeves, long pants, hats, and shoes rather than sandals) and apply a good insect repellent, preferably one containing DEET, to exposed skin and clothing.

ENVIRONMENTAL HAZARDS

Cold exposure This can be a significant problem, especially in the northern regions. Keep all body surfaces covered, including the head and neck. Watch out for the 'Umbles' – stumbles, mumbles, fumbles and grumbles – which are signs of impending hypothermia.

Heat exhaustion Dehydration is the main contributor. Symptoms include feeling weak, headache, nausea and sweaty skin. Lay the victim flat with their legs raised, apply cool, wet cloths to the skin, and rehydrate.

Insurance

See p872 for health insurance and p885 for car insurance.

Travel Insurance

Make sure you have adequate travel insurance, whatever the length of your trip. At a minimum, you need coverage for medical emergencies and treatment, including hospital stays and an emergency flight home. Medical treatment for non-Canadians is very expensive.

Also consider insurance for luggage theft or loss. If you already have a homeowners or renters policy, check what it will cover and only get supplemental insurance to protect against the rest. If you have prepaid a large portion of your vacation, trip cancellation insurance is worthwhile.

Worldwide travel insurance is available at www.lonelyplanet.com/travel_services. You can buy, extend and claim online at anytime – even if you're already on the road. Also check the following providers:

Insure.com (www.insure.com)
Travel Guard (www.travelguard.com)
Travelex (www.travelex.com)

Internet Access

» It's easy to find internet access. Libraries, schools and community agencies in practically every town provide free high-speed internet terminals for public use, travellers included. The only downsides are that usage time is limited (usually 30 minutes), facilities have erratic hours and you may not be able to upload photos (it depends on the facility). The government's **Community Access Program** (C@P) provides the services.

» Internet cafes are limited to the main tourist areas, and access generally costs $3 to $4 per hour.

» Wi-fi is widely available. Most lodgings have it (in-room, with good speed), as do many urban coffee shops and bars. We've identified sleeping, eating and drinking listings that have wi-fi with a 🛜. We've denoted lodgings that offer internet terminals for guest use with a @.

» Check the regional Information sections throughout the book for suggested facilities where you can go online.

Legal Matters
Police
» If you're arrested or charged with an offense, you have the right to keep your mouth shut and to hire any lawyer you wish (contact your embassy for a referral, if necessary). If you cannot afford one, ask to be represented by public counsel. There is a presumption of innocence.

Drugs & Alcohol
» The blood-alcohol limit is 0.08% and driving cars, motorcycles, boats and snowmobiles while drunk is a criminal offense. If you are caught, you may face stiff fines, license suspension and other nasty consequences.
» Consuming alcohol anywhere other than at a residence or licensed premises is also a no-no, which puts parks, beaches and the rest of the great outdoors off limits, at least officially.
» Avoid illegal drugs, as penalties may entail heavy fines, possible jail time and a criminal record. The only exception is the use of marijuana for medical purposes, which became legal in 2001. Meanwhile, the decriminalization of pot possession for personal use remains a subject of ongoing debate

among the general public and in parliament.

Other
» Abortion is legal.
» Travelers should note that they can be prosecuted under the law of their home country regarding age of consent, even when abroad.

Maps
» Most tourist offices distribute free provincial road maps.
» For extended hikes or multiday backcountry treks, it's a good idea to carry a topographic map. The best are the series of 1:50,000 scale maps published by the government's **Centre for Topographic Information** (http://maps.nrcan.gc.ca). These are sold by around 900 map dealers around the country; check the website for vendors.
» You can also download and print maps from **GeoBase** (www.geobase.ca).

Money
» All prices quoted in this book are in Canadian dollars ($), unless stated otherwise.
» Canadian coins come in 1¢ (penny), 5¢ (nickel), 10¢ (dime), 25¢ (quarter), $1 (loonie) and $2 (toonie or twoonie) denominations. The gold-colored loonie features the loon, a common Canadian water bird, while

the two-toned toonie is decorated with a polar bear.
» Paper currency comes in $5 (blue), $10 (purple), $20 (green) and $50 (red) denominations. The $100 (brown) and larger bills are less common, and are tough to change.
» The Canadian dollar has seen fluctuations over the last decade, though since 2007 it has tracked quite closely to the US dollar.
» For changing money in the larger cities, currency exchange offices may offer better conditions than banks.
» See p19 for exchange rates and costs.

ATMs
Many grocery and convenience stores, airports, and bus, train and ferry stations have ATMs. Most are linked to international networks, the most common being Cirrus, Plus, Star and Maestro.

Most ATMs also spit out cash if you use a major credit card. This method tends to be more expensive because, in addition to a service fee, you'll be charged interest immediately (in other words, there's no interest-free period as with purchases). For exact fees, check with your own bank or credit card company.

Visitors heading to Canada's more remote regions (such as in Newfoundland) won't find an abundance of ATMs, so it is wise to cash up beforehand.

Scotiabank, common throughout Canada, is part of the Global ATM Alliance. If your home bank is a member, fees may be less if you withdraw from Scotiabank ATMs.

Cash
Most Canadians don't carry large amounts of cash for everyday use, relying instead on credit and debit cards. Still, carrying some cash, say $100 or less, comes in handy when making small purchases. In some cases,

---

LEGAL AGE
» Driving a car: 16
» Smoking tobacco: 18 (19 in British Columbia, Ontario and the Atlantic provinces)
» Homosexual consent (for males): 18
» Consent for other sexual activity: 16
» Voting in an election: 18
» Drinking alcoholic beverages: 19 (18 in Alberta, Manitoba and Québec)

cash is necessary to pay for rural B&Bs and shuttle vans; inquire in advance to avoid surprises. Shops and businesses rarely accept personal checks.

Credit Cards

Major credit cards such as MasterCard, Visa and American Express are widely accepted in Canada, except in remote, rural communities where cash is king. You'll find it difficult or impossible to rent a car, book a room or order tickets over the phone without having a piece of plastic. Note that some credit card companies charge a 'transaction fee' (around 3% of whatever you purchased); check with your provider to avoid surprises.

For lost or stolen cards, these numbers operate 24 hours:

American Express (☑866-296-5198; www.american express.com)

MasterCard (☑800-307-7309; www.mastercard.com)

Visa (☑800-847-2911; www.visa.com)

TAXES & REFUNDS

TAX RATES (GST + PST)	RECOMMENDED FOR
Alberta	5%
British Columbia*	12%
Manitoba	12%
New Brunswick*	13%
Newfoundland*	13%
Nova Scotia*	15%
Ontario*	13%
PEI	15%
Québec	13.5%
Saskatchewan	10%

*has a combined HST

Taxes & Refunds

Canada's federal goods and services tax (GST), variously known as the 'gouge and screw' or 'grab and steal' tax, adds 5% to just about every transaction. Most provinces also charge a provincial sales tax (PST) on top of it. Several provinces have combined the GST and PST into a harmonized sales tax (HST). Whatever the methodology, expect to pay 10% to 15% in all. Unless otherwise stated, taxes are not included in prices given. You might be eligible for a rebate on some of the taxes. If you've booked your accommodations in conjunction with a rental car, plane ticket or other service (ie if it all appears on the same bill from a 'tour operator'), you should be eligible to get 50% of the tax refunded from your accommodations. Fill out the GST/HST Refund Application for Tour Packages form available from the **Canada Revenue Agency** (☑902-432-5608, 800-668-4748; www.cra-arc.gc.ca/E/pbg/gf/gst115).

Tipping

Tipping is a standard practice.

Traveler's Checks

Traveler's checks are becoming more and more obsolete in the age of ATMs. Traveler's checks issued in Canadian dollars are generally treated like cash by businesses. Traveler's checks in most other currencies must be exchanged for Canadian dollars at a bank or foreign currency office. The most common issuers:

American Express (www.americanexpress.com)

MasterCard (www.mastercard.com)

Visa (www.visa.com)

Post

Canada's national postal service, **Canada Post/Postes Canada** (www.canadapost.ca),

TIPPING RATES

TIPPING RATES	RECOMMENDED FOR
Restaurant waitstaff	15% to 20%
Bar staff	$1 per drink
Hotel bellhop	$1 to $2 per bag
Hotel room cleaners $2 per day	13%
Taxis	10% to 15%

is neither quick nor cheap, but it is reliable. Stamps are available at post offices, drugstores, convenience stores and hotels.

Postcards or standard letters cost 57¢ within Canada, $1 to the USA and $1.70 to all other countries. Travelers often find they have to pay high duties on items sent to them while in Canada, so beware.

Public Holidays

Canada observes 10 national public holidays and more at the provincial level. Banks, schools and government offices close on these days.

National Holidays

New Year's Day January 1

Good Friday March or April

Easter Monday March or April

Victoria Day Monday before May 25

Canada Day July 1; called Memorial Day in Newfoundland

Labour Day First Monday of September

Thanksgiving Second Monday of October

Remembrance Day November 11

Christmas Day December 25

Boxing Day December 26

Provincial Holidays

Some provinces also observe local holidays, with Newfoundland leading the pack.

Family Day Third Monday of February in Alberta, Ontario, Saskatchewan and Manitoba; known as Louis Riel Day in Manitoba

St Patrick's Day Monday nearest March 17

St George's Day Monday nearest April 23

National Day Monday nearest June 24 in Newfoundland; June 24 in Québec (aka St-Jean-Baptiste Day)

Orangemen's Day Monday nearest July 12 in Newfoundland

Civic Holiday First Monday of August everywhere *except* Newfoundland, PEI, Québec and Yukon Territory

Discovery Day Third Monday of August in Yukon Territory

School Holidays

Kids break for summer holidays in late June and don't return to school until early September. University students get even more time off, usually from May to early or mid-September. Most people take their big annual vacation during these months.

Telephone

Canada's phone system is almost identical to the USA's system.

Domestic & International Dialing

Canadian phone numbers consist of a three-digit area code followed by a seven-digit local number. In many parts of Canada, you must dial all 10 digits preceded by ☑1, even if you're calling across the street. In other parts of the country, when you're calling within the same area code, you can dial the seven-digit number only, but this is slowly changing. The pay phone or phone book where you are should make it clear which system is used.

For direct international calls, dial ☑011 + country code + area code + local phone number. The country code for Canada is ☑1 (the same as for the USA, although international rates still apply for all calls made between the two countries).

Toll-free numbers begin with ☑800, ☑877 or ☑866 and must be preceded by 1. Some of these numbers are good throughout Canada and the USA, others only work within Canada, and some work in just one province.

Emergency Numbers

Dial ☑911. This is *not* the emergency number in the Yukon, Northwest Territories or Nunavut (see those chapters for emergency numbers).

Cell Phones

Local SIM cards can be used in European and Australian phones. Other phones must be set to roaming.

If you have a European, Australian or other type of unlocked GSM phone, buy a SIM card from local providers such as **Telus** (www.telus.com), **Rogers** (www.rogers.com) or **Bell** (www.bell.ca).

US residents can often upgrade their domestic cell phone plan to extend to Canada. **Verizon** (www.verizonwireless.com) provides good results.

Reception is poor in rural areas no matter who your service provider is.

Public Phones

Coin-operated public pay phones are fairly plentiful. Local calls cost 25¢ (sometimes 35¢); many phones also accept prepaid phonecards and credit cards. Dialing the operator (☑0) or directory assistance (☑411 for local calls, 1 + area code + 555-1212 for long-distance calls) is free of charge from public phones; it may incur a charge from private phones.

Phonecards

Prepaid phonecards usually offer the best per-minute rates for long-distance and international calling. They come in denominations of $5, $10 or $20 and are widely sold in drugstores, supermarkets and convenience stores. Beware of cards with hidden charges such as 'activation fees' or a per-call connection fee. A surcharge ranging from 30¢ to 85¢ for calls made from public pay phones is common.

POSTAL ABBREVIATIONS

PROVINCES & TERRITORIES	ABBREVIATIONS
Alberta	AB
British Columbia	BC
Manitoba	MB
New Brunswick	NB
Newfoundland & Labrador	NL
Northwest Territories	NT
Nova Scotia	NS
Nunavut	NU
Ontario	ON
Prince Edward Island	PE
Québec	QC
Saskatchewan	SK
Yukon Territory	YT

UNIQUELY CANADIAN CELEBRATIONS

» **National Flag Day** (February 15) Commemorates the first time the maple-leaf flag was raised above Parliament Hill in Ottawa, at the stroke of noon on February 15, 1965.

» **Victoria Day** (late May) This day was established in 1845 to observe the birthday of Queen Victoria and now celebrates the birthday of the British sovereign who's still Canada's titular head of state. Victoria Day marks the official beginning of the summer season (which ends with Labour Day on the first Monday of September). Some communities hold fireworks.

» **National Aboriginal Day** (June 31) Created in 1996, it celebrates the contributions of Aboriginal peoples to Canada. Coinciding with the summer solstice, festivities are organized locally and may include traditional dancing, singing and drumming; storytelling; arts and crafts shows; canoe races; and lots more.

» **Canada Day** (July 1) Known as Dominion Day until 1982, Canada Day was created in 1869 to commemorate the creation of Canada two years earlier. All over the country, people celebrate with barbecues, parades, concerts and fireworks.

» **Thanksgiving Day** (mid-October) First celebrated in 1578 in what is now Newfoundland by explorer Martin Frobisher to give thanks for surviving his Atlantic crossing, Thanksgiving became an official Canadian holiday in 1872 to celebrate the recovery of the Prince of Wales from a long illness. These days, it's essentially a harvest festival involving a special family dinner of roast turkey and pumpkin, very much as it is practiced in the US.

Time

Canada spans six of the world's 24 time zones. The Eastern zone in Newfoundland is unusual in that it's only 30 minutes different from the adjacent zone. The time difference from coast to coast is 4½ hours.

Canada observes daylight saving time, which comes into effect on the second Sunday in March, when clocks are put forward one hour, and ends on the first Sunday in November. Saskatchewan and small pockets of Québec, Ontario and BC are the only areas that do not switch to daylight saving time.

In Québec especially, times for shop hours, train schedules, film screenings etc are usually indicated by the 24-hour clock.

Tourist Information

» The **Canadian Tourism Commission** (www.canada.travel) is loaded with general information, packages and links.

» All provincial tourist offices maintain comprehensive websites packed with information helpful in planning your trip.
Staff also field telephone inquiries and, on request, will mail out free maps and directories about accommodations, attractions and events. Some offices can also help with making hotel, tour or other reservations.

» For detailed information about a specific area, contact the local tourist office, aka visitors center. Just about every city and town has at least a seasonal branch with helpful staff, racks of free pamphlets and books and maps for sale. Visitor center addresses are listed in the Information sections for individual destinations throughout this book.

Provincial tourist offices:
Newfoundland & Labrador Tourism (☑800-563-6353; www.newfoundlandlabrador.com)

Northwest Territories (NWT) Tourism (☑800-661-0788; www.spectacularnwt.com)

Nunavut Tourism (☑866-686-2888; www.nunavuttourism.com)

Ontario Tourism (☑800-668-2746; www.ontariotravel.net)

Prince Edward Island Tourism (☑800-463-4734; www.peiplay.com)

Tourism British Columbia (☑800-435-5622; www.hellobc.com)

Tourism New Brunswick (☑800-561-0123; www.tourismnewbrunswick.ca)

TIME

TIME DIFFERENCE BETWEEN CITIES

Vancouver	3pm
New York City	6pm
Montréal	6pm
Newfoundland	7:30pm
London	11pm

Tourism Nova Scotia (☎800-565-0000; www.novascotia.com)

Tourism Saskatchewan (☎877-237-2273; www.sasktourism.com)

Tourisme Québec (☎877-266-5687; www.bonjourquebec.com)

Travel Alberta (☎800-252-3782; www.travelalberta.com)

Travel Manitoba (☎800-665-0040; www.travelmanitoba.com)

Yukon Department of Tourism (☎800-661-0494; www.travelyukon.com)

Travelers with Disabilities

Canada is making progress when it comes to easing the everyday challenges facing people with disabilities, especially the mobility impaired.

» Many public buildings, including museums, tourist offices, train stations, shopping malls and cinemas, have access ramps and/or lifts. Most public restrooms feature extra-wide stalls equipped with hand rails. Many pedestrian crossings have sloping curbs.

» Newer and recently remodeled hotels, especially chain hotels, have rooms with extra-wide doors and spacious bathrooms.

» Interpretive centers at national and provincial parks are usually accessible, and many parks have trails that can be navigated in wheelchairs.

» Car rental agencies offer hand-controlled vehicles and vans with wheelchair lifts at no additional charge, but you must reserve them well in advance. See p886 for a list of rental agencies.

» For accessible air, bus, rail and ferry transportation check **Access to Travel** (www.accesstotravel.gc.ca), the federal government's website. In general, most transportation agencies can accommodate people with disabilities if you make your needs known when booking.

Other organizations specializing in the needs of travelers with disabilities:

Access-Able Travel Source (www.access-able.com) Lists accessible lodging, transport, attractions and equipment rental by province.

Canadian National Institute for the Blind (www.cnib.ca)

Canadian Paraplegic Association (www.canparaplegic.org) Information about facilities for mobility-impaired travelers in Canada.

Mobility International (www.miusa.org) Advises travelers with disabilities on mobility issues and runs an educational exchange program.

Society for Accessible Travel & Hospitality (www.sath.org) Travelers with disabilities share tips and blogs.

Visas

For information about passport requirements, see p880.

Citizens of dozens of countries – including the USA, most Western European nations, Australia, New Zealand, Japan and South Korea – do not need visas to enter Canada for stays of up to 180 days. US permanent residents are also exempt. **Citizenship & Immigration Canada** (CIC; www.cic.gc.ca) has the details.

Nationals of other countries – including China, India and South Africa – must apply to the Canadian visa office in their home country for a temporary resident visa (TRV). A separate visa is required if you plan to study or work in Canada.

Single-entry TRVs ($75) are usually valid for a maximum stay of six months from the date of your arrival in Canada. Multiple-entry TRVs ($150) allow you to enter Canada from all other countries multiple times while the visa is valid (usually two or three years), provided no single stay exceeds six months.

Visa extensions ($75) need to be filed with the **CIC Visitor Case Processing Centre** (☎888-242-2100; ⊙8am-4pm Mon-Fri) in Alberta at least one month before your current visa expires.

Visiting the USA

Admission requirements are subject to rapid change. The **US State Department** (www.travel.state.gov) has the latest information, or check with a US consulate in your home country.

Under the US visa-waiver program, visas are not required for citizens of 36 countries – including most EU members, Australia and New Zealand – for visits of up to 90 days (no extensions allowed), as long as you can present a machine-readable passport and are approved under the **Electronic System for Travel Authorization** (ESTA; www.cbp.gov/esta). Note you must register at least 72 hours before arrival, and there's a $14 fee for processing and authorization.

Canadians do not need visas, though they do need a passport or document approved by the **Western Hemisphere Travel Initiative** (www.getyouhome.gov). Citizens of all other countries need to apply for a US visa in their home country before arriving in Canada.

All foreign visitors (except Canadians) must pay a US$6 'processing fee' when entering at land borders. Note that you don't need a Canadian multiple-entry TRV for repeated entries into Canada from the USA, unless you have visited a third country.

Volunteering

Volunteering provides the opportunity to interact with local folks and the land in ways you never would just passing through. Many organizations charge a fee, which varies depending on the program's length and the type of food and lodging it provides. The fees usually do not cover travel to Canada. Groups that use volunteers:

Churchill Northern Studies Centre (www.churchill science.ca) Volunteer for six hours per day (anything from stringing wires to cleaning) and get free room and board at this center for polar bear and other wildlife research.

Earthwatch (www.earth watch.org) Help scientists track whales off the coast of British Columbia, track moose and deer in Nova Scotia, and monitor climate change in Churchill, Manitoba or the Mackenzie Mountains of the Northwest Territories. Trips last from seven to 14 days and cost from $2250 to $5050.

Volunteers for Peace (www.vfp.org) Offers tutoring stints in Aboriginal communities the Yukon's far north, as well as projects in Québec.

World-Wide Opportunities on Organic Farms (www.wwoof.ca; application fee $45) Work on an organic farm, usually in exchange for free room and board; check the website for locations throughout Canada.

Women Travelers

Canada is generally a safe place for women to travel, even alone and even in the cities. Simply use the same common sense as you would at home.

In bars and nightclubs, solo women are likely to attract a lot of attention, but if you don't want company, most men will respect a firm 'no thank you.' If you feel threatened, protesting loudly will often make the offender slink away – or will at least spur other people to come to your defense. Note that carrying mace or pepper spray is illegal in Canada.

Physical attack is unlikely, but if you are assaulted, call the police immediately (☎911 except in the Yukon, Northwest Territories and Nunavut; see individual chapters for their emergency numbers) or contact a rape crisis center. A complete list is available from the **Canadian Association of Sexual Assault Centres** (☎604-876-2622; www.casac. ca). Hotlines in some of the major cities:

Calgary (☎403-237-5888)
Halifax (☎902-425-0122)
Montréal (☎514-934-4504)
Toronto (☎416-597-8808)
Vancouver (☎604-255-6344)

Resources for women travelers include:

Journeywoman (www.journeywoman.com)

Her Own Way (www.voyage. gc.ca/publications/woman -guide_voyager-feminin-eng. asp) Published by the Canadian government for Canadian travelers, but it contains a great deal of general advice.

Work

Permits

In almost all cases, you need a valid work permit to work in Canada. Obtaining one may be difficult, as employment opportunities go to Canadians first. Before you can even apply, you need a specific job offer from an employer who in turn must have been granted permission from the government to give the position to a foreign national. Applications must be filed at a visa office of a Canadian embassy or consulate in your home country. Some jobs are exempt from the permit requirement. For full details, check with **Citizenship & Immigration Canada** (www.cic.gc.ca/ english/work/index.asp).

Employers hiring temporary service workers (hotel, bar, restaurant, resort) and construction, farm or forestry workers sometimes don't ask for a permit. If you get caught, however, you can kiss Canada goodbye.

Finding Work

Students aged 18 to 30 from more than a dozen countries, including the USA, UK, Australia, New Zealand, Ireland and South Africa, are eligible to apply for a spot in the **Student Work Abroad Program** (SWAP; www.swap.ca). If successful, you get a six-month to one-year, nonextendable visa that allows you to work anywhere in Canada in any job you can get. Most 'SWAPpers' find work in the service industry as wait staff or bartenders.

Even if you're not a student, you may be able to spend up to a year in Canada on a 'working holiday program' with **International Experience Canada** (www. international.gc.ca/iyp-pij/ intro_incoming-intro_entrant. aspx). The Canadian government has an arrangement with several countries for people aged 18 to 35 to come over and get a job; check the website for participants. The Canadian embassy in each country runs the program, but basically there are quotas and spaces are filled on a first-come first-served basis.

Transportation

GETTING THERE & AWAY

Flights, tours and rail tickets can be booked online at www.lonelyplanet.com/travel_services.

Entering the Country

Entering Canada is pretty straightforward. First, you will show your passport (and your visa if you need one; see p878). The border officer will ask you a few questions about the purpose and length of your visit. After that, you'll go through customs. See Going to Canada (www.goingtocanada.gc.ca) for details.

US citizens at land and sea borders have other options besides using a passport, such as an enhanced driver's license or passport card. See the Western Hemisphere Travel Initiative (www.getyouhome.gov) for approved identification documents.

Note that questioning may be more intense at land border crossings and your car may be searched.

For updates (particularly regarding land-border crossing rules), check the websites for the US State Department (www.travel.state.gov) and Citizenship & Immigration Canada (www.cic.gc.ca).

Air

Airports

Toronto is far and away the busiest airport, followed by Vancouver. The international gateways you're most likely to arrive at include:

Calgary (YYC; www.calgaryairport.com)

Edmonton (YEG; www.flyeia.com)

Halifax (YHZ; www.hiaa.ca)

Montréal (Trudeau; YUL; www.admtl.com)

Ottawa (YOW; www.ottawa-airport.ca)

St John's (YYT; www.stjohnsairport.com)

Toronto (Pearson; YYZ; www.gtaa.ca)

Vancouver (YVR; www.yvr.ca)

Winnipeg (YWG; www.waa.ca)

Airlines

Air Canada, the national flagship carrier, is considered one of the world's safest airlines. Other companies based in Canada and serving international destinations are the discount airline WestJet, the short-haul carrier Porter, and the charter airlines Air Transat and Sunwing.

Air Canada (www.aircanada.com)

Air France (www.airfrance.com/ca)

Air New Zealand (www.airnewzealand.ca)

Air Transat (www.airtransat.com) Charter airline from major Canadian cities to holiday destinations (ie southern USA and Caribbean in winter, Europe in summer).

Alaska Air & Horizon Air (www.alaskaair.com)

Alitalia (www.alitalia.com/ca_en)

American Airlines (www.aa.com)

ANA (www.anaskyweb.com)

British Airways (www.ba.com)

Cathay Pacific (www.cathaypacific.com)

China Airlines (www.china-airlines.com)

Continental Airlines (www.continental.com)

Condor (www.condor.com) German charter airline that flies to Vancouver and Whitehorse.

Delta Airlines (www.delta.com)

Eva Air (www.evaair.com)

KLM (www.klm.com)

Japan Airlines (www.ar.jal.com)

Lufthansa (www.lufthansa.com)

Philippine Airlines (www.philippineairlines.com)

Porter Airlines (www.flyporter.com) Flies in eastern Canada and internationally to Boston, Chicago and New York.

Qantas (www.qantas.com.au)

Singapore Airlines (www.singaporeair.com)

Sunwing Airlines (www.flysunwing.com) Charter

airline from major Canadian cities to holiday destinations in the USA, Mexico and Caribbean.

Swiss Air (www.swiss.com)

United Airlines (www.united.ca)

US Airways (www.usairways.com)

WestJet (www.westjet.com)

Land

Border Crossings

There are 22 official border crossings along the US–Canadian border, from New Brunswick to British Columbia.

The website of the **Canadian Border Services Agency** (www.cbsa-asfc.gc.ca/general/times/menu-e.html) shows current wait times at each. You can also access it via the government's wireless portal (www.wap.gc.ca) or on Twitter (@CBSA_BWT).

In general, waits rarely exceed 30 minutes, except during the peak summer season, and on Friday and Sunday afternoons, especially on holiday weekends, when you might get stuck at the border for several hours. Some entry points are especially busy:

» Windsor, Ontario, to Detroit, Michigan

» Fort Erie, Ontario, to Buffalo, New York State

» Niagara Falls, Ontario, to Niagara Falls, New York State

» Québec to Rouse's Point/Champlain, New York State

» Surrey, British Columbia, to Blaine, Washington State

Other border points tend to be quieter, sometimes so quiet that the officers have nothing to do except tear apart your luggage. When approaching the border, turn off any music, take off your sunglasses and be exceptionally polite. Most officers do not welcome casual conversation, jokes or clever remarks.

When returning to the USA, check the website for the US Department for Homeland Security (http://apps.cbp.gov/bwt/) for border wait times.

All foreign visitors (except Canadians) must pay a $6 'processing fee' when entering the USA by land; credit cards are not accepted.

For information on documents needed to enter Canada, see p880.

Bus

Greyhound (www.greyhound.com) and its Canadian equivalent, **Greyhound Canada** (www.greyhound.ca), operate the largest bus network in North America. There are direct connections between main cities in the USA and Canada, but you usually have to transfer to a different bus at the border (where it takes a good hour for all passengers to clear customs/immigration). Most international buses have free wi-fi on board. See the table (p882) for sample fares and durations.

Other notable international bus companies (with free wi-fi) include:

Megabus (www.megabus.com) Runs between Toronto and New York City, and Toronto and Philadelphia; usually cheaper than Greyhound. Tickets can only be purchased online.

Quick Coach (www.quickcoach.com) Runs between Seattle and Vancouver; typically a bit quicker than Greyhound.

Car & Motorcycle

The highway system of the continental USA connects directly with the Canadian highway system at numerous points along the border. These Canadian highways then meet up with the east–west Trans-Canada Hwy further north. Between the Yukon Territory and Alaska, the main routes are the Alaska, Klondike and Haines Hwys.

If you're driving into Canada, you'll need the vehicle's registration papers, proof of liability insurance and your home driver's license. Cars rented in the USA can usually be driven into Canada and back, but make sure your rental agreement says so in case you are questioned by border officials. If you're driving a car registered in someone else's name, bring a letter from the owner authorizing use of the vehicle in Canada. For details about driving within Canada, see p885.

CLIMATE CHANGE & TRAVEL

Every form of transport that relies on carbon-based fuel generates CO_2, the main cause of human-induced climate change. Modern travel is dependent on aeroplanes, which might use less fuel per kilometer per person than most cars but travel much greater distances. The altitude at which aircraft emit gases (including CO_2) and particles also contributes to their climate change impact. Many websites offer 'carbon calculators' that allow people to estimate the carbon emissions generated by their journey and, for those who wish to do so, to offset the impact of the greenhouse gases emitted with contributions to portfolios of climate-friendly initiatives throughout the world. Lonely Planet offsets the carbon footprint of all staff and author travel.

GREYHOUND BUS ROUTES & FARES

ROUTE	DURATION	FREQUENCY	FARE (US$)
Boston–Montréal	from 7hr	up to 8 daily	105
Detroit–Toronto	from 5½hr	up to 5 daily	73
New York–Montréal	10hr	up to 2 daily	84
Seattle–Vancouver	4hr	up to 5 daily	38

Train

Amtrak (www.amtrak.com) and VIA Rail Canada (www.viarail.ca) run three routes between the USA and Canada. Customs inspections happen at the border, not upon boarding.

Sea

Ferry

Various ferry services on the coasts connect the US and Canada.

Bar Harbor, Maine–Yarmouth, NS Service halted in 2010 but due to start again in 2011; check Bay Ferries (www.nfl-bay.com).

Eastport, Maine–Deer Island, NB East Coast Ferries (www.eastcoastferries.nb.ca); see p397.

Seattle–Victoria, BC Victoria Clipper (www.clippervacations.com); see p682.

Alaska–Port Hardy, BC Alaska Marine Highway System (www.ferryalaska.com); see p706.

Alaska–Prince Rupert, BC BC Ferries (www.bcferries.com); see p753.

Freighters

An adventurous, though not necessarily inexpensive, way to travel to or from Canada is aboard a cargo ship. Freighters carry between three and 12 passengers and, though considerably less luxurious than cruise ships, they give a salty taste of life at sea.

For more information on the ever-changing routes:

Cruise & Freighter Travel Association (www.travltips.com)

Freighter World Cruises (www.freighterworld.com)

GETTING AROUND

Air

Airlines in Canada

Air Canada operates the largest domestic-flight network serving some 150 destinations together with its regional subsidiary, Air Canada Jazz.

Low-cost, low-frills carriers are chasing Air Canada's wings. The biggest is Calgary-based WestJet. In response, Air Canada entered the discount game by introducing inexpensive 'Tango' fares, which sometimes undercut even the discount carriers, on its regular flights.

The Canadian aviation arena also includes many independent regional and local airlines, which tend to focus on small, often-remote regions, mostly in the North. Depending on the destination, fares in such noncompetitive markets can be high.

Air Canada (☑888-247-2262; www.aircanada.com) Nationwide flights.

Air Canada Jazz (☑888-247-2262; www.aircanada.com) Regional flights throughout western and eastern Canada.

Air Creebec (☑800-567-6567; www.aircreebec.ca) Serves northern Québec and Ontario, including Chisasibi and Chibougamau from Montréal and other cities.

Air Inuit (☑888-247-2262; www.airinuit.com) Flies from Montréal to all 14 Inuit communities in Nunavik (northern Québec), including Kuujjuaq and Puvirnituq.

Air Labrador (☑800-563-3042; www.airlabrador.com) Flies mostly within Labrador.

Air North (☑in Canada 867-668-2228, in USA 800-661-0407; www.flyairnorth.com)

TRAIN ROUTES & FARES

ROUTE	DURATION	FREQUENCY	FARE (US$)
New York–Toronto (*Maple Leaf*)	14hr	1 daily	125
New York–Montréal (*Adirondack*)	11hr	1 daily	62
Seattle–Vancouver (*Cascades*)	4hr	2 daily	44

com) Flies from the Yukon to British Columbia, Alberta, Northwest Territories and Alaska.

Air St-Pierre (☎902-873-3566, 877-277-7765; www. airsaintpierre.com) Flies from eastern Canada to the French territories off Newfoundland's coast.

Air Tindi (☎867-669-8260; www.airtindi.com) Serves the Northwest Territories' North Slave region.

Aklak Air (☎866-707-4977; www.aklakair.ca) Serves the Northwest Territories' Mackenzie Delta.

Bearskin Airlines (☎800-465-2327; www. bearskinairlines.com) Serves destinations throughout Ontario and eastern Manitoba.

Calm Air (☎204-778-6471, 800-839-2256; www.calmair. com) Flights throughout Manitoba and Nunavut.

Canadian North (☎800-661-1505; www.canadiannorth. com) Flights to, from and within the Northwest Territories and Nunavut.

Central Mountain Air (☎888-865-8585; www.flycma. com) Destinations throughout British Columbia and Alberta.

First Air (☎800-267-1247; www.firstair.ca) Flies from Ottawa, Montréal, Winnipeg and Edmonton to 24 Arctic destinations, including Iqaluit.

Harbour Air (☎800-665-0212; www.harbour-air.com) Seaplane service from the city of Vancouver to Vancouver Island, Gulf Islands and the Sunshine Coast.

Hawkair (☎866-429-5247; www.hawkair.ca) Serves northern British Columbia from Vancouver and Victoria.

Kenn Borek Air (☎867-252-3845; www.borekair. com) Serves Iqaluit and other communities around Nunavut.

Kivalliq Air (☎204-888-5619, 877-855-1500; www. kivalliqair.com) Flies from Winnipeg to Churchill and Nunavut.

Northwestern Air Lease (☎877-872-2216; www.nwal. ca) Flies in Alberta and Northwest Territories.

North-Wright Air (☎867-587-2333; www.north -wrightairways.com) Serves the Northwest Territories' Mackenzie Valley.

Pacific Coastal Airlines (☎800-663-2872; www.pacific -coastal.com) Vancouver-based airline with service to many British Columbia locales.

Porter Airlines (☎888-619-8622; www.flyporter.com) Flies turboprop planes from Montréal, Halifax and Ottawa to Toronto's quicker, more convenient City Centre Airport downtown.

Provincial Airlines (☎800-563-2800; www.provincialair lines.com) St John's-based airline with service throughout Newfoundland and to Labrador.

Seair Seaplanes (☎604-273-3900, 800-447-3247; www.seairseaplanes.com) Flies from Vancouver to Nanaimo and the Southern Gulf Islands in British Columbia.

Transwest Air (☎800-667-9356; www.transwestair.com) Service within Saskatchewan.

West Coast Air (☎800-347-2222; www.westcoastair. com) Seaplane service from Vancouver city to Vancouver Island and the Sunshine Coast.

WestJet (☎800-538-5696, 888-937-8538; www.westjet. com) Calgary-based low-cost carrier serving destinations throughout Canada.

Air Passes

Star Alliance (www.star alliance.com) members Air Canada, Continental Airlines, United Airlines and US Airways have teamed up to offer the North American Airpass, which is available to anyone not residing in the USA, Canada, Mexico, Bermuda or the Caribbean. It's sold only in conjunction with an international flight operated by any Star Alliance-member airline. You can buy as few as three coupons (US$399) or as many as 10 (US$1099).

Air North has an **Arctic Circle Air Pass** (www.flyair north.com/DealsAndNews/Arctic CircleAirPass.aspx) for those traveling around the Yukon and Northwest Territories.

Bicycle

Much of Canada is great for cycling. Long-distance trips can be done entirely on quiet back roads, and many cities (including Edmonton, Montréal, Ottawa, Toronto and Vancouver) have designated bike routes.

» Cyclists must follow the same rules of the road as vehicles, but don't expect drivers to always respect your right of way.

» Helmets are mandatory for all cyclists in British Columbia, New Brunswick, Prince Edward Island and Nova Scotia, as well as for anyone under 18 in Alberta and Ontario.

» The **Better World Club** (☎866-238-1137; www.better worldclub.com) provides emergency roadside assistance. Membership costs $40 per year, plus a $12 enrollment fee, and entitles you to two free pick-ups, and transport to the nearest repair shop, or home, within a 50km radius of where you're picked up.

» For information on Canada's sweetest mountain biking and cycling trails, see p840.

Transportation

» By air: most airlines will carry bikes as checked luggage without charge on international flights, as long as they're in a box. On domestic flights they usually charge between $30 and

$65. Always check details before you buy the ticket.

» By bus: you must ship your bike as freight on Greyhound Canada. In addition to a bike box ($10), you'll be charged according to the weight of the bike, plus an oversize charge ($30) and GST. Bikes only travel on the same bus as the passenger if there's enough space. To ensure that yours arrives at the same time as (or before) you do, ship it a day early.

» By train: VIA Rail will transport your bicycle for $20, but only on trains offering checked-baggage service (which includes all long-distance and many regional trains).

Rental

Outfitters renting bicycles exist in most tourist towns; many are listed throughout this book.

» Rentals cost around $15 per day for touring bikes and $25 per day for mountain bikes. The price usually includes a helmet and lock.

» Most companies require a security deposit of $20 to $200.

Purchase

Buying a bike is easy, as is reselling it before you leave. Specialist bike shops have the best selection and advice, but general sporting-goods stores may have lower prices. Some bicycle stores and rental outfitters also sell used bicycles. To sniff out the best bargains, scour flea markets, garage sales and thrift shops, or check the notice boards in hostels and universities. These are also the best places to sell your bike.

Boat

Ferry services are extensive, especially throughout the Atlantic provinces and in British Columbia. For schedule information, see the Getting There & Away and Getting Around sections of the destination chapters.

Walk-ons and cyclists should be able to get aboard at any time, but call ahead for vehicle reservations or if you require a cabin berth. This is especially important during summer peak season and holidays. Main operators include:

Bay Ferries (☎888-249-7245; www.bayferries.com) Year-round service between Saint John, New Brunswick, and Digby, Nova Scotia.

BC Ferries (☎250-386-3431, 888-223-3779; www.bcferries.com) Huge passenger-ferry systems with 25 routes and 46 ports of call, including Vancouver Island, the Gulf Islands, the Sechelt Peninsula along the Sunshine Coast and the Queen Charlotte Islands, all in British Columbia.

Coastal Transport (☎506-662-3724; www.coastaltransport.ca) Ferry from Blacks Harbour to Grand Manan in the Fundy Isles, New Brunswick.

CTMA Ferries (☎418-986-3278, 888-986-3278; www.ctma.ca) Daily ferries to Québec's Îles de la Madeleine from Souris, Prince Edward Island.

East Coast Ferries (☎506-747-2159, 877-747-2159; www.eastcoastferries.nb.ca) Connects Deer Island to Campobello Island, both in the Fundy Isles, New Brunswick.

Labrador Marine (☎709-535-0810, 866-535-2567; www.labradormarine.com) Connects Newfoundland to Labrador.

Marine Atlantic (☎800-341-7981; www.marine-atlantic.ca) Connects Port aux Basques and Argentia in Newfoundland with North Sydney, Nova Scotia.

Northumberland Ferries (☎902-566-3838, 888-249-7245; www.peiferry.com) Connects Wood Islands, Prince Edward Island and Caribou, Nova Scotia.

Provincial Ferry Services (www.gov.nl.ca/ferryservices) Operates coastal ferries throughout Newfoundland.

Bus

Greyhound Canada (☎800-661-8747; www.greyhound.ca) is the king, plowing along an extensive network in central and western Canada, as well as to/from the USA. In eastern Canada, it is part of an alliance of regional carriers, including Orléans Express in Québec and Acadian Lines in the Maritime provinces. You can usually transfer from one carrier to another on a single ticket.

Buses are generally clean, comfortable and reliable. Amenities may include onboard toilets, air-conditioning (bring a sweater), reclining seats and onboard movies. Smoking is not permitted. On long journeys, buses make meal stops every few hours, usually at highway service stations.

Acadian Lines (☎800-567-5151; www.acadianbus.com) Service throughout New Brunswick, Nova Scotia and Prince Edward Island.

Autobus Maheux (☎888-797-0011; www.autobusmaheux.qc.ca) Service from Montréal to Québec's northwest regions.

Coach Canada (☎800-461-7661; www.coachcanada.com) Scheduled service within Ontario and from Toronto to Montréal.

DRL Coachlines (☎709-263-2171; www.drl-lr.com) Service throughout Newfoundland.

Intercar (☎888-861-4592; www.intercar.qc.ca) Connects Québec City, Montréal and Tadoussac, among other towns in Québec.

Limocar (☎866-700-8899; www.limocar.com) Regional service in Québec.

Malaspina Coach Lines (☎604-886-7742, 877-227-8287; www.malaspinacoach.com) Service between Vancouver and the Sunshine Coast in British Columbia.

Megabus (www.megabus.com) Service between Toronto and Montréal via Kingston; tickets can only be purchased online.

Ontario Northland (☎800-461-8558; www.ontarionorthland.ca) Operates bus and train routes that service northern Ontario from Toronto.

Orléans Express (☎888-999-3977; www.orleansexpress.com) Service to eastern Québec.

Pacific Coach Lines (☎250-385-4411, 800-661-1725; www.pacificcoach.com) Service between Vancouver Island and mainland British Columbia.

Saskatchewan Transportation Company (STC; ☎800-663-7181; www.stcbus.com) Service within Saskatchewan.

Voyageur (☎800-661-8747; www.greyhound.ca) Operates within Ontario and Québec.

For information about traveling on buses that are operated by tour companies, see p887.

Bus Passes

Greyhound's **Discovery Pass** (www.discoverypass.com) is valid for travel in both the USA and Canada. Note that for short-haul trips, the pass is not necessarily more economical than buying individual tickets. However, it can be worthwhile for onward, long-haul travel.

The pass allows unlimited travel from coast to coast, within periods ranging from seven to 60 days.

You must purchase the pass 14 to 21 days before departure, so it can be mailed to you (although if your trav-

els are beginning in the USA, you can buy it onsite at the terminal two hours before departure).

Costs

Bus travel is cheaper than other means of transport. Advance purchases (four, seven or 14 days) save quite a bit, too. For specific route and fare information, see the Getting There & Away sections in the regional chapters.

Reservations

Greyhound and most other bus lines don't take reservations, and even buying tickets in advance does not guarantee you a seat on any particular bus. Show up at least 45 minutes to one hour prior to the scheduled departure time, and chances are pretty good you'll get on. Allow more time on Friday and Sunday afternoons and around holidays.

Car & Motorcycle

Automobile Associations

Auto-club membership is a handy thing to have in Canada. The **Canadian Automobile Association** (CAA; ☎800-268-3750; www.caa.ca) offers services, including 24-hour emergency roadside assistance, to members of international affiliates such as AAA in the USA, AA in the UK and ADAC in Germany. The club also offers trip-planning advice, free maps, travel-agency services and a range of discounts on hotels, car rentals etc.

The **Better World Club** (☎866-238-1137; www.betterworldclub.com), which donates 1% of its annual revenue to environmental cleanup efforts, has emerged as an alternative. It offers service throughout the USA and Canada, and has a roadside-assistance program for bicycles (see p883).

Bring Your Own Vehicle

There's minimal hassle driving into Canada from the USA as long as you have your vehicle's registration papers, proof of liability insurance and your home driver's license.

Driver's License

In most provinces visitors can legally drive for up to three months with their home driver's license. In some, such as British Columbia, this is extended to six months.

If you're spending considerable time in Canada, think about getting an International Driving Permit (IDP), which is valid for one year. Your automobile association at home can issue one for a small fee. Always carry your home license together with the IDP.

Fuel

Gas is sold in liters. At the time of writing, the average for midgrade fuel was $1.08 per liter (about C$4.10 per US gallon). Prices are higher in remote areas, with Yellowknife usually setting the national record; drivers in Calgary typically pay the least for gas.

Fuel prices in Canada are usually higher than in the USA, so fill up south of the border.

Insurance

Canadian law requires liability insurance for all vehicles, to cover you for damage caused to property and people.

» The minimum requirement is $200,000 in all provinces except Québec, where it is $50,000.

» Americans traveling to Canada in their own car should ask their insurance company for a Nonresident Interprovince Motor Vehicle Liability Insurance Card (commonly known as a 'yellow card'), which is accepted

LONG-DISTANCE BUS FARES

ROUTE	STANDARD FARE	7-DAY FARE	DURATION
Vancouver–Calgary	$137	$86	14-17hr
Montréal–Toronto	$63	$29	8-10hr
Toronto–Vancouver	$243	$199	65-70hr

as evidence of financial responsibility anywhere in Canada. Although not mandatory, it may come in handy in an accident.

» Car-rental agencies offer liability insurance. Collision Damage Waivers (CDW) reduce or eliminate the amount you'll have to reimburse the rental company if there's damage to the car itself. Some credit cards cover CDW for a certain rental period, if you use the card to pay for the rental, and decline the policy offered by the rental company. Always check with your card issuer to see what coverage it offers in Canada.

» Personal accident insurance (PAI) covers you and any passengers for medical costs incurred as a result of an accident. If your travel insurance or your health-insurance policy at home does this as well (and most do, but check), then this is one expense you can do without.

Rental

CAR

To rent a car in Canada you generally need to:

» be at least 25 years old
» hold a valid driver's license (an international one may be required if you're not from an English- or French-speaking country
» have a major credit card

Some companies will rent to drivers between the ages of 21 and 24 for an additional charge.

You should be able to get an economy-sized vehicle for about $35 to $65 per day.

Child safety seats are compulsory (reserve them when you book) and cost about $8 per day.

Major international car-rental companies usually have branches at airports, train stations and in city centers.

Avis (☑800-437-0358; www. avis.com)

Budget (☑800-268-8900; www.budget.com)

Dollar (☑800-800-4000; www.dollar.com)

Enterprise (☑800-736-8222; www.enterprise.com)

Hertz (☑800-263-0600; www.hertz.com)

National (☑800-227-7368; www.nationalcar.com)

Thrifty (☑800-847-4389; www.thrifty.com)

Practicar (☑800-327-0116; www.practicar.ca) Formerly known as Rent a Wreck, often has lower rates. It's also affiliated with Backpackers Hotels Canada and Hostelling International.

In Canada, on-the-spot rentals often are more expensive than pre-booked packages (ie cars booked with a flight).

MOTORCYCLE

Several companies offer motorcycle rentals and tours. A Harley Heritage Softail Classic costs about $210 per day, including liability insurance and 200km mileage. Some companies have minimum rental periods, which can be as much as seven days. Riding a hog is especially popular in British Columbia.

Coastline Motorcycle Tours & Rentals (☑250-335-1837, 866-338-0344; www.coastlinemc.com) Out of

Victoria and Vancouver in British Columbia.

McScoots Motorcycle & Scooter Rentals (☑250-763-4668; www.mcscoots.com) Big selection of Harleys, also operates motorcycle tours, based in Kelowna, British Columbia.

Open Road Adventure (☑250-494-5409; www. canadamotorcyclerentals.com) Rentals and tours out of Summerland, near Kelowna, British Columbia.

RECREATIONAL VEHICLES

The RV market is biggest in the west, with specialized agencies in Calgary, Edmonton, Whitehorse and Vancouver. For summer travel, book as early as possible. The base cost is roughly $160 to $265 per day in high season for midsized vehicles, although insurance, fees and taxes add a hefty chunk. Diesel-fueled RVs have considerably lower running costs.

Some recommended companies:

Canadream Campers (☑403-291-1000, 800-461-7368; www.canadream.com) Based in Calgary with rentals (including one-ways) in eight cities, including Vancouver, Whitehorse, Toronto and Halifax.

Go West Campers (☑800-661-8813; www.go-west.com) Rents out of Calgary and Coquitlam, British Columbia (near Vancouver).

Road Conditions & Hazards

Road conditions are generally good, but keep in mind:

» Fierce winters can leave potholes the size of landmine craters. Be prepared to swerve. Winter travel in general can be hazardous due to heavy snow and ice, which may cause roads and bridges to close periodically. **Transport Canada** (☎800-387-4999; www.tc.gc.ca/road) provides links to road conditions and construction zones for each province.

» If you're driving in winter or in remote areas, make sure your vehicle is equipped with four-seasonal radial or snow tires, and emergency supplies in case you're stranded.

» Distances between services can be long in sparsely populated areas such as the Yukon, Newfoundland or northern Québec, so keep your gas topped up whenever possible.

» Moose, deer and elk are common on rural roadways, especially at night. There's no contest between a 534kg bull moose and a Subaru, so keep your eyes peeled.

Road Rules

» Canadians drive on the right-hand side of the road.

» Seat belt use is compulsory. Children under 18kg must be strapped in child booster seats, except infants, who must be in a rear-facing safety seat.

» Motorcyclists must wear helmets and drive with their headlights on.

» Distances and speed limits are posted in kilometers. The speed limit is generally:

• 40km/h to 50km/h in cities
• 90km/h to 110km/h outside town

» Slow down to 60km/h when passing emergency vehicles (such as police cars and ambulances) stopped on the roadside with their lights flashing.

» Turning right at red lights after coming to a full stop is permitted in all provinces (except where road signs prohibit it, and on the island of Montréal, where it's always a no-no). There's a national propensity for running red lights, however, so don't take your 'right of way' at intersections for granted.

» Driving while using a hand-held cell phone is illegal in British Columbia, Newfoundland, Nova Scotia, Ontario, PEI, Québec and Saskatchewan.

» Radar detectors are not allowed in most of Canada (Alberta, British Columbia and Saskatchewan are the exceptions). If you're caught driving with a radar detector, even one that isn't being operated, you could receive a fine of $1000 and your device may be confiscated.

» The blood-alcohol limit for drivers is 0.08%. Driving while drunk is a criminal offense.

Hitchhiking & Ride-Sharing

Hitching is never entirely safe in any country and we don't recommend it. That said, in remote and rural areas in Canada it is not uncommon to see people thumbing for a ride.

» If you do decide to hitch, understand that you are taking a small but potentially serious risk. Remember that it's safer to travel in pairs and let someone know where you are planning to go.

» Hitchhiking is illegal on some highways (ie the 400 series roads in Ontario), as well as in the provinces of Nova Scotia and New Brunswick.

» **Digihitch** (www.canada.digihitch.com) is a decent, if dated, resource.

» Ride-share services offer an alternative to hitching. **Autotaxi** (www.autotaxi.com) lists rides within Canada and to the USA. You can advertise a ride yourself or make arrangements with drivers going to your destinations.

In Québec, **Allô Stop** (www.allostop.com) does much the same.

Local Transportation

For fares and other details, see Getting Around under city and town listings throughout this book.

Bicycle

Cycling is a popular means of getting around during the warmer months, and many cities have hundreds of kilometers of dedicated bike paths. Bicycles typically can be taken on public transportation (although some cities have restrictions during peak travel times). All the major cities rent bikes.

Bus

Buses are the most ubiquitous form of public transportation, and practically all towns have their own systems. Most are commuter oriented, and offer only limited or no services in the evenings and on weekends.

Train

Toronto and Montréal are the two Canadian cities with subway systems. Vancouver's version is mostly an above-ground monorail. Calgary, Edmonton and Ottawa have efficient light rail systems. Route maps are posted in all stations.

Taxi

Most of the main cities have taxis. They are usually metered, with a flag-fall fee of roughly $2.70 and a per-kilometer charge around $1.75. Drivers expect a tip of between 10% and 15%. Taxis can be flagged down or ordered by phone.

Tours

Tour companies are another way to get around this great big country. We've listed several in the Tours sections for destinations throughout this book. Reliable companies operating in multiple provinces across Canada include:

Arctic Odysseys (☑20 6-325-1977, 800-574-3021; www.arcticodysseys.com) Experience Arctic Canada close up on tours chasing the northern lights in the Northwest Territories, heli-skiing on Baffin Island or polar-bear spotting on Hudson Bay.

Backroads (☑510-527-1555, 800-462-2848; www.back roads.com) Guided cycling, walking and/or paddling tours in the Rockies, Nova Scotia and Québec.

Moose Travel Network (☑in eastern Canada 416-504-7514, 888-816-6673, in western Canada 604-777-9905, 888-244-6673; www.moosenetwork. com) Operates backpacker-type tours in small buses throughout British Columbia, Alberta, Québec, Ontario, Nova Scotia and PEI. The two- to 19-day trips hit Whistler, Banff, Jasper, Calgary, Toronto, Montréal and Halifax, among others, and you can jump on or off anywhere along the route. In winter, various skiing and snowboarding packages are available.

Nahanni River Adventures (☑867-668-3180, 800-297-6927; www.nahanni.com) Operates rafting and kayaking expeditions in the Yukon, British Columbia and Alaska, including trips on the Firth, Alsek and Babine Rivers, as well as down the Tatshenshini-Alsek watershed.

Road Scholar (☑800-454-5768; www.roadscholar. org) This is the new name for the programs run by Elderhostel. The nonprofit organization offers study tours in nearly all provinces for active people over 55, including train trips, cruises, and bus and walking tours.

Routes to Learning (☑613-530-2222, 866-745-1690; www. routestolearning.ca) From bird-watching in the Rockies to trekking around Québec City to walking in the footsteps of Vikings on Newfoundland, this nonprofit group has dozens of educational tours throughout Canada.

Salty Bear Adventure Tours (☑902-202-3636, 888-425-2327; www.saltybear. ca) Backpacker-oriented van tours through the Maritimes with jump-on/jump-off flexibility. There's a three-day circuit around Cape Breton, Nova Scotia, and a five-day route that goes into PEI.

Trek America (☑in USA 800-221-0596, ☑in UK 0870-444-8735; www.trekamerica. com) Active camping, hiking and canoeing tours in small groups, geared primarily for people between 18 and 38, although some are open to all ages.

Train

VIA Rail (☑888-842-7245; www.viarail.ca) operates most of Canada's intercity and transcontinental passenger trains, chugging over 14,000km of track. In some remote parts of the country, such as Churchill, Manitoba, trains provide the only overland access.

» Rail service is most efficient in the corridor between Québec City and Windsor, Ontario – particularly between Montréal and Toronto, the two major hubs.

» The rail network does not extend to Newfoundland, Prince Edward Island or the Northern Territories.

» Free wi-fi is available on trains in the corridor. Via Rail was set to expand the service to additional trains in fall 2010.

» Smoking is prohibited on all trains.

Classes

There are four main classes:
» Economy class buys you a fairly basic, if indeed quite comfortable, reclining seat with a headrest. Blankets and pillows are provided for overnight travel.

» Business class operates in the southern Ontario/ Québec corridor. Seats are more spacious and have outlets for plugging in laptops. You also get a meal and priority boarding.

» Sleeper class is available on shorter overnight routes. You can choose from compartments with upper or lower pullout berths, and private single, double or triple roomettes, all with a bathroom.

» Touring class is available on long-distance routes and includes sleeper class accommodations plus meals, access to the sightseeing car and sometimes a tour guide.

Costs

Taking the train is more expensive than the bus, but most people find it a more comfortable way to travel. June to mid-October is peak season, when prices are about 40% higher. Buying tickets in advance (even just five days before) can yield significant savings.

Long-Distance Routes

VIA Rail has several classic trains:

Canadian A 1950s stainless-steel beauty between Toronto and Vancouver, zipping through the northern Ontario lake country, the western plains via Winnipeg and Saskatoon, and Jasper in the Rockies over three days.

Hudson Bay From the prairie (slowly) to the subarctic: Winnipeg to polar-bear hangout Churchill.

Malahat Carves through Vancouver Island's magnificent countryside; get off and back on as many times as you'd like.

Ocean Chugs from Montréal along the St Lawrence River through New Brunswick and Nova Scotia.

LONG-DISTANCE TRAIN ROUTES

ROUTE	DURATION	FREQUENCY	FARE (US$)
Toronto–Vancouver (Canadian)	87hr	3 weekly	890
Winnipeg–Churchill (Hudson Bay)	43hr	2 weekly	309
Victoria–Courtenay (Malahat)	4½hr	1 daily	59
Halifax–Montréal (Ocean)	22hr	1 daily (except none Tue)	258
Prince Rupert–Jasper (Skeena)	33hr	3 weekly	206

Skeena An all-daylight route from Jasper, Alberta, to coastal Prince Rupert, British Columbia; there's an overnight stop in Prince George (you make your own hotel reservations).

Privately run regional train companies offer additional rail-touring opportunities:

Algoma Central Railway (www.algomacentralrailway. com) Access to northern Ontario wilderness areas; see p169.

Ontario Northland (www. ontarionorthland.ca) Operates the *Northlander* from Toronto to Cochrane in northern Ontario and the seasonal *Polar Bear Ex-*
ᴵᴵᴵᴾᴺˢˢ ᴵᴵᴵᴵᴵᴵᴵᴵᴵ,ᴵᴵᴵ ᴵᴵᴵ ᴬᴵᴵᴾ ᴵᴵᴵ
Moosonee on Hudson Bay; see p98.

Royal Canadian Pacific (www.royalcanadianpacific. com) Another cruise-ship-like luxury line between and around the Rockies via Calgary p551.

Rocky Mountaineer Railtours (www.rockymountain eer.com) Gape at Canadian Rockies scenery on swanky trains between Vancouver, Kamloops and Calgary; see p583.

White Pass & Yukon Route (www.wpyr.com) Gorgeous route paralleling the original White Pass trail from Whitehorse, Yukon, to Fraser, British Columbia; see p775.

Reservations

Seat reservations are highly recommended, especially in summer, on weekends and around holidays. During peak sᴇᴀsᴏᴵᴵ ᴵᴵᴵᴵᴾ ᴵᴵ ᴵᴵᴵᴵᴵᴵᵉ October), some of the most popular sleeping arrangements are sold out months in advance, especially on long-distance trains such as the *Canadian*. The *Hudson Bay* often books solid during polar-bear season (around late September to early November).

Train Passes

VIA Rail offers a couple of passes that provide good savings:

» The Canrailpass-System is good for seven trips on any train during a 21-day period. All seats are in economy class; upgrades are not permitted. You must book each leg at least three days in advance (you can do this online). It costs $941/588 in high/low season.

» The Canrailpass-Corridor is good for seven trips ᴵᴵᴵᴵᴵᴵᴵᴵ ᴰ ᴵᴵᴵ-ᴵᴵᴬᴵᴵ ᴵᴵᴾᴵᴵᴵᴵᴵᴵᴵᴵ trains in the Québec City–Windsor corridor (which includes Montréal, Toronto and Niagara). It costs $337 year-round.

Language

WANT MORE?

For in-depth language information and handy phrases, check out Lonely Planet's *French Phrasebook*. You'll find it at **shop.lonelyplanet.com**, or you can buy Lonely Planet's iPhone phrasebooks at the Apple App Store.

English and French are the two official languages of Canada. You'll see both on highway signs, maps, tourist brochures, packaging etc. In Québec the preservation of French is a primary concern and fuels the separatist movement. Here, English can be hard to find, and road signs and visitor information will often be in French only. Outside Montréal and Québec City, French will be necessary at least some of the time.

New Brunswick is the only officially bilingual province. French is widely spoken, particularly in the north and east. It is somewhat different from the French of Québec. Nova Scotia and Manitoba also have significant French-speaking populations, and there are pockets in most other provinces. In the west of Canada, French isn't as prevalent

The French spoken in Canada is essentially the same as what you'd hear in France. Although many English-speaking (and most French-speaking) students in Québec are still taught the French of France, the local tongue is known as 'Québecois' or *joual*. Announcers and broadcasters on Québec TV and radio tend to speak a more refined, European style of French, as does the upper class. Québecois people will have no problem understanding more formal French.

The sounds used in spoken French can almost all be found in English. There are a few exceptions: nasal vowels (represented in our pronunciation guides by o or u followed by an almost inaudible nasal consonant sound m, n or ng), the 'funny' *u* (ew in our guides) and the deep-in-the-throat r. Bearing these few points in mind and reading the pronunciation guides in this chapter as if they were English, you'll be understood just fine.

BASICS

French has two words for 'you' – use the polite form *vous* unless you're talking to close friends or children, in which case you'd use the informal *tu*. You can also use *tu* when a person invites you to use *tu*.

All nouns in French are either masculine or feminine, and so are the articles *le/la* (the) and *un/une* (a) and adjectives that go with the nouns. We've included masculine and femine forms where necessary, marked with 'm/f'.

Hello.	Bonjour.	bon·zhoor
Goodbye.	Au revoir.	o·rer·vwa
Excuse me.	Excusez-moi.	ek·skew·zay·mwa
Sorry.	Pardon.	par·don
Yes./No.	Oui./Non.	wee/non
Please.	S'il vous plaît.	seel voo play
Thank you.	Merci.	mair·see
You're welcome.	De rien.	der ree·en

How are you?
Comment allez-vous? — ko·mon ta·lay·voo

Fine, and you?
Bien, merci. Et vous? — byun mair·see ay voo

My name is ...
Je m'appelle ... — zher ma·pel ...

What's your name?
Comment vous appelez-vous? — ko·mon voo·za·play voo

Do you speak English?
Parlez-vous anglais? — par·lay·voo ong·glay

I don't understand.
Je ne comprends pas. — zher ner kom·pron pa

ACCOMMODATIONS

Do you have any rooms available?
Est-ce que vous avez   es·ker voo za·vay
des chambres libres?   day shom·brer lee·brer

How much is it per night/person?
Quel est le prix   kel ay ler pree
par nuit/personne?   par nwee/per·son

Is breakfast included?
Est-ce que le petit   es·ker ler per·tee
déjeuner est inclus?   day·zher·nay ayt en·klew

campsite	*camping*	kom·peeng
dorm	*dortoir*	dor·twar
guesthouse	*pension*	pon·syon
hotel	*hôtel*	o·tel
youth hostel	*auberge de jeunesse*	o·berzh der zher·nes
a ... room	*une chambre ...*	ewn shom·brer ...
single	*à un lit*	a un lee
double	*avec un grand lit*	a·vek un gron lee
air-con	*climatiseur*	klee·ma·tee·zer
bathroom	*salle de bains*	sal der bun
window	*fenêtre*	fer·nay·trer

DIRECTIONS

Where's ...?
Où est ...?   oo ay ...

What's the address?
Quelle est l'adresse?   kel ay la·dres

Could you write the address, please?
Est-ce que vous pourriez   es·ker voo poo·ryay
écrire l'adresse,   ay·kreer la·dres
s'il vous plaît?   seel voo play

Can you show me (on the map)?
Pouvez-vous m'indiquer   poo·vay·voo mun·dee·kay
(sur la carte)?   (sewr la kart)

at the corner	*au coin*	o kwun
at the traffic lights	*aux feux*	o fer
behind	*derrière*	dair·ryair
in front of	*devant*	der·von
far (from ...)	*loin (de ...)*	lwun (der ...)
left	*gauche*	gosh
near (to ...)	*près (de ...)*	pray (der ...)
next to ...	*à côté de ...*	a ko·tay der...
opposite ...	*en face de ...*	on fas der ...
right	*droite*	drwat
straight ahead	*tout droit*	too drwa

KEY PATTERNS

To get by in French, mix and match these simple patterns with words of your choice:

Where's (the entry)?
Où est (l'entrée)?   oo ay (lon·tray)

Where can I (buy a ticket)?
Où est-ce que je   oo es·ker zher
peux (acheter   per (ash·tay
un billet)?   un bee·yay)

When's (the next train)?
Quand est   kon ay
(le prochain train)?   (ler pro·shun trun)

How much is (a room)?
C'est combien pour   say kom·buyn poor
(une chambre)?   (ewn shom·brer)

Do you have (a map)?
Avez-vous (une carte)?   a·vay voo (ewn kart)

Is there (a toilet)?
Y a-t-il (des toilettes)?   ee a teel (day twa·let)

I'd like (to book a room).
Je voudrais   zher voo·dray
(réserver   (ray·ser·vay
(une chambre).   ewn shom·brer)

Can I (enter)?
Puis-je (entrer)?   pweezh (on·tray)

Could you please (help)?
Pouvez-vous   poo·vay voo
(m'aider),   (may·day)
s'il vous plaît?   seel voo play

Do I have to (book a seat)?
Faut-il (réserver   fo·teel (ray·ser·vay
une place)?   ewn plas)

EATING & DRINKING

A table for (two), please.
Une table pour (deux),   ewn ta·bler poor (der)
s'il vous plaît.   seel voo play

What would you recommend?
Qu'est-ce que vous   kes·ker voo
conseillez?   kon·say·yay

What's in that dish?
Quels sont les   kel son lay
ingrédients?   zun·gray·dyon

I'm a vegetarian.
Je suis végétarien/   zher swee vay·zhay·ta·ryun/
végétarienne.   vay·zhay·ta·ryen (m/f)

I don't eat ...
Je ne mange pas ...   zher ner monzh pa ...

Cheers!
Santé!   son·tay

That was delicious.
C'était délicieux!   say·tay day·lee·syer

Please bring the bill.
Apportez-moi   a·por·tay·mwa
l'addition,   la·dee·syon
s'il vous plaît.   seel voo play

Signs

Entrée	Entrance
Femmes	Women
Fermé	Closed
Hommes	Men
Interdit	Prohibited
Ouvert	Open
Renseignements	Information
Sortie	Exit
Toilettes/WC	Toilets

Key Words

appetiser	entrée	on·tray
bottle	bouteille	boo·tay
breakfast	déjeuner	day·zher·nay
children's menu	menu pour enfants	mer·new poor on·fon
cold	froid	frwa
delicatessen	traiteur	tray·ter
dinner	souper	soo·pay
dish	plat	pla
food	nourriture	noo·ree·tewr
fork	fourchette	foor·shet
glass	verre	vair
grocery store	épicerie	ay·pees·ree
highchair	chaise haute	shay zot
hot	chaud	sho
knife	couteau	koo·to
local speciality	spécialité locale	spay·sya·lee·tay lo·kal
lunch	dîner	dee·nay
main course	plat principal	pla prun·see·pal
market	marché	mar·shay
menu (in English)	carte (en anglais)	kart (on ong·glay)
plate	assiette	a·syet
spoon	cuillère	kwee·yair
wine list	carte des vins	kart day vun
with/without	avec/sans	a·vek/son

Meat & Fish

beef	bœuf	berf
chicken	poulet	poo·lay
fish	poisson	pwa·son
lamb	agneau	a·nyo
pork	porc	por
turkey	dinde	dund
veal	veau	vo

Fruit & Vegetables

apple	pomme	pom
apricot	abricot	ab·ree·ko
asparagus	asperge	a·spairzh
beans	haricots	a·ree·ko
beetroot	betterave	be·trav
cabbage	chou	shoo
celery	céleri	sel·ree
cherry	cerise	ser·reez
corn	maïs	ma·ees
cucumber	concombre	kong·kom·brer
gherkin (pickle)	cornichon	kor·nee·shon
grape	raisin	ray·zun
leek	poireau	pwa·ro
lemon	citron	see·tron
lettuce	laitue	lay·tew
mushroom	champignon	shom·pee·nyon
peach	pêche	pesh
peas	petit pois	per·tee pwa
(red/green) pepper	poivron (rouge/vert)	pwa·vron (roozh/vair)
pineapple	ananas	a·na·nas
plum	prune	prewn
potato	pomme de terre	pom der tair
prune	pruneau	prew·no
pumpkin	citrouille	see·troo·yer
shallot	échalote	eh·sha·lot
spinach	épinards	eh·pee·nar
strawberry	fraise	frez
tomato	tomate	to·mat
turnip	navet	na·vay
vegetable	légume	lay·gewm

Other

bread	pain	pun
butter	beurre	ber
cheese	fromage	fro·mazh
egg	œuf	erf
honey	miel	myel
jam	confiture	kon·fee·tewr
lentils	lentilles	lon·tee·yer
oil	huile	weel
pasta/noodles	pâtes	pat
pepper	poivre	pwa·vrer
rice	riz	ree
salt	sel	sel
sugar	sucre	sew·krer
vinegar	vinaigre	vee·nay·grer

Drinks

beer	*bière*	bee·yair
coffee	*café*	ka·fay
(orange) juice	*jus (d'orange)*	zhew (do·ronzh)
milk	*lait*	lay
tea	*thé*	tay
(mineral) water	*eau (minérale)*	o (mee·nay·ral)
(red) wine	*vin (rouge)*	vun (roozh)
(white) wine	*vin (blanc)*	vun (blong)

EMERGENCIES

Help!
Au secours! — o skoor

I'm lost.
Je suis perdu/perdue. — zhe swee pair·dew (m/f)

Leave me alone!
Fichez-moi la paix! — fee·shay·mwa la pay

There's been an accident.
Il y a eu un accident. — eel ya ew un ak·see·don

Call a doctor.
Appelez un médecin. — a·play un mayd·sun

Call the police.
Appelez la police. — a·play la po·lees

I'm ill.
Je suis malade. — zher swee ma·lad

It hurts here.
J'ai une douleur ici. — zhay ewn doo·ler ee·see

I'm allergic to ...
Je suis allergique ... — zher swee za·lair·zheek ...

SHOPPING & SERVICES

I'd like to buy ...
Je voudrais acheter ... — zher voo·dray ash·tay ...

May I look at it?
Est-ce que je peux le voir? — es·ker zher per ler vwar

I'm just looking.
Je regarde. — zher rer·gard

I don't like it.
Cela ne me plaît pas. — ser·la ner mer play pa

How much is it?
C'est combien? — say kom·byun

It's too expensive.
C'est trop cher. — say tro shair

Question Words

How?	*Comment?*	ko·mon
What?	*Quoi?*	kwa
When?	*Quand?*	kon
Where?	*Où?*	oo
Who?	*Qui?*	kee
Why?	*Pourquoi?*	poor·kwa

Can you lower the price?
Vous pouvez baisser le prix? — voo poo·vay bay·say ler pree

There's a mistake in the bill.
Il y a une erreur dans la note. — eel ya ewn ay·rer don la not

ATM	*guichet automatique de banque*	gee·shay o·to·ma·teek der bonk
credit card	*carte de crédit*	kart der kray·dee
internet cafe	*cybercafé*	see·bair·ka·fay
post office	*bureau de poste*	bew·ro der post
tourist office	*office de tourisme*	o·fees der too·rees·mer

TIME & DATES

What time is it?
Quelle heure est-il? — kel er ay til

It's (eight) o'clock.
Il est (huit) heures. — il ay (weet) er

It's half past (10).
Il est (dix) heures et demie. — il ay (deez) er ay day·mee

morning	*matin*	ma·tun
afternoon	*après-midi*	a·pray·mee·dee
evening	*soir*	swar
yesterday	*hier*	yair
today	*aujourd'hui*	o·zhoor·dwee
tomorrow	*demain*	der·mun

Monday	*lundi*	lun·dee
Tuesday	*mardi*	mar·dee
Wednesday	*mercredi*	mair·krer·dee
Thursday	*jeudi*	zher·dee
Friday	*vendredi*	von·drer·dee
Saturday	*samedi*	sam·dee
Sunday	*dimanche*	dee·monsh

January	*janvier*	zhon·vyay
February	*février*	fayv·ryay
March	*mars*	mars
April	*avril*	a·vreel
May	*mai*	may
June	*juin*	zhwun
July	*juillet*	zhwee·yay
August	*août*	oot
September	*septembre*	sep·tom·brer
October	*octobre*	ok·to·brer
November	*novembre*	no·vom·brer
December	*décembre*	day·som·brer

Numbers

1	*un*	un
2	*deux*	der
3	*trois*	trwa
4	*quatre*	ka·trer
5	*cinq*	sungk
6	*six*	sees
7	*sept*	set
8	*huit*	weet
9	*neuf*	nerf
10	*dix*	dees
20	*vingt*	vung
30	*trente*	tront
40	*quarante*	ka·ront
50	*cinquante*	sung·kont
60	*soixante*	swa·sont
70	*soixante-dix*	swa·son·dees
80	*quatre-vingts*	ka·trer·vung
90	*quatre-vingt-dix*	ka·trer·vung·dees
100	*cent*	son
1000	*mille*	meel

TRANSPORTATION

Public Transportation

boat	*bateau*	ba·to
bus	*bus*	bews
plane	*avion*	a·vyon
train	*train*	trun

I want to go to ...
Je voudrais aller à ...   zher voo·dray a·lay a ...

Does it stop at (Amboise)?
Est-ce qu'il s'arrête à   es·kil sa·ret a
(Amboise)?   (om·bwaz)

At what time does it leave/arrive?
À quelle heure est-ce   a kel er es
qu'il part/arrive?   kil par/a·reev

Can you tell me when we get to ...?
Pouvez-vous me   poo·vay·voo mer
dire quand   deer kon
nous arrivons à ...?   noo za·ree·von a ...

I want to get off here.
Je veux descendre   zher ver day·son·drer
ici.   ee·see

first	*premier*	prer·myay
last	*dernier*	dair·nyay
next	*prochain*	pro·shun

a ... ticket	*un billet ...*	un bee·yay ...
1st-class	*de première classe*	der prem·yair klas
2nd-class	*de deuxième classe*	der der·zyem las
one-way	*simple*	sum·pler
return	*aller et retour*	a·lay ay rer·toor

aisle seat	*côté couloir*	ko·tay kool·war
delayed	*en retard*	on rer·tar
cancelled	*annulé*	a·new·lay
platform	*quai*	kay
ticket office	*guichet*	gee·shay
timetable	*horaire*	o·rair
train station	*gare*	gar
window seat	*côté fenêtre*	ko·tay fe·ne·trer

Driving & Cycling

I'd like to hire a ...   *Je voudrais louer ...*   zher voo·dray loo·way ...

4WD	*un quatre-quatre*	un kat·kat
car	*une voiture*	ewn vwa·tewr
bicycle	*un vélo*	un vay·lo
motorcycle	*une moto*	ewn mo·to

child seat	*siège-enfant*	syezh·on·fon
diesel	*diesel*	dyay·zel
helmet	*casque*	kask
mechanic	*mécanicien*	may·ka·nee·syun
petrol/gas	*essence*	ay·sons
service station	*station-service*	sta·syon·ser·vees

Is this the road to ...?
C'est la route pour ...?   say la root poor ...

(How long) Can I park here?
(Combien de temps)   (kom·byun der tom)
Est-ce que je peux   es·ker zher per
stationner ici?   sta·syo·nay ee·see

The car/motorbike has broken down (at ...).
La voiture/moto est   la vwa·tewr/mo·to ay
tombée en panne (à ...).   tom·bay on pan (a ...)

I have a flat tyre.
Mon pneu est à plat.   mom pner ay ta pla

I've run out of petrol.
Je suis en panne   zher swee zon pan
d'essence.   day·sons

I've lost my car keys.
J'ai perdu les clés de   zhay per·dew lay klay der
ma voiture.   ma vwa·tewr

behind the scenes

SEND US YOUR FEEDBACK

We love to hear from travelers – your comments keep us on our toes and help make our books better. Our well-traveled team reads every word on what you loved or loathed about this book. Although we cannot reply individually to postal submissions, we always guarantee that your feedback goes straight to the appropriate authors, in time for the next edition. Each person who sends us information is thanked in the next edition – and the most useful submissions are rewarded with a free book.

Visit **lonelyplanet.com/contact** to submit your updates and suggestions or to ask for help. Our award-winning website also features inspirational travel stories, news and discussions.

Note: We may edit, reproduce and incorporate your comments in Lonely Planet products such as guidebooks, websites and digital products, so let us know if you don't want your comments reproduced or your name acknowledged. For a copy of our privacy policy visit lonelyplanet.com/privacy.

OUR READERS

Many thanks to the travelers who used the last edition and wrote to us with helpful hints, useful advice and interesting anecdotes:

Poul Aasø, Ewa Affinito, Carole Bennett, Kate Berry, Marieke Bouwman, Christina, Steven Coole, Tony Copp, Jacques Coté, Olivia Cozens, Sangini Crane, Sarah De Clermont, Chris Drysdale, Christopher Dunlap, Gerardo Durand-chastel, Frank Eisenhuth, Christina Engels, James Falk, Christian Felsch, Lauren Finger, Rosalind Foley, Joanna Fowler, Andrea Gaebel, Matt Hawker, Gary Hellen, Daniel Herbert, Gwen Holt, Marjorey Hope, John Hopkinson, Eric Houston, Jo Hughes, Ineke Imbo, Lea Kitler, John Kriz, Kathleen Lizotte, Edgar Locke, Amanda Mallon, Marianna Martin, Trevor Mazzucchelli, Ann Mccarry, Ursa Mekis, Morena Menegatti, John Mirehouse, Gabor Mlinko, Basil Moser, Dorothy Mul, Colleen Mulhall, Maria, Richard Newton, Gary Nielsen, Marco Pagura, Jordan Payne, Aina Ranke, Nicholas Read, Raphael Richards, Claire Ridgwell, Duurt Rijkels, Amelie Robitaille, Lynne Romano, Anita Schneider, Leanna Sharp, Kris Sloane, Gord Smoker, Ivan Stephen, Robert Strauch, Kate Sullivan, Helen Sutton, Frank & Tamara Van Egmond, Natasha Verkerk, Riaz Virani, Helen Waters, Dominique P Weber, Robert White, Jeannine Winkel, Beat Zenklusen

AUTHOR THANKS

Karla Zimmerman

Thanks to St John's gurus Bryan Curtis and Sarah Mathieson; Harvey in Bonavista; Gillian Marx and Laura Walbourne at Newfoundland Tourism; and the countless locals who stopped to tell me their tales. Thanks to rightnbook babe Liza Worth for worhun ing the wheel once again. Über gratitude to fellow scribes Catherine, Celeste, John, Emily, Brandon, Sarah, Brendan and RVB for kick-ass work. Mega-gratefulness to Jennye, Bruce and the editorial crew. Thanks most to Eric Markowitz, the world's best partner-for-life.

Catherine Bodry

I'd like to thank Jennye Garibaldi for taking a chance, and Karla Zimmerman for being on top of my random questions. I heart Canadians, but a few in particular made my trip fabulous: Gord Johns and Kim, random strangers on the street, now good friends; LinLyn Liu for great recs; Norman Hardie for time and a floor; and Lana Mau, my new bestie and research companion. As always, thanks to Lael and my family and friends back home, without whose support I could never make a go of this.

Celeste Brash

Thanks to tourism's best: Emily Kimber at Destination Halifax and Pamela Beck with PEI Tourism. Special thanks to crazy hitchhikers Caitlin and Courtney, the folks of Digby Backpackers

BEHIND THE SCENES

and Kiwi Kaboodle, John Tattrie, Darcy in Cape d'Or, Doug in Guysburough, Cailin O'Neill in Halifax, John Bil in PEI, the Tysons in Parsborro and Sandra in Creignish. I wish I could work with Karla Zimmerman and Jennye Garibaldi on every book. Meanwhile husband Josh moved our life to the US in the whirlwind and my dad Trace picked up many trailing details.

John Lee
Enormous thanks to all those locals and ever-friendly Visitor Centre staff who took the time to stop, chat and help at various points around the province, especially those on Vancouver Island. Thanks also to my nephew Christopher for joining me on that leg of the trip and making it a lot of fun. Finally, thanks to my Dad for coming out from the UK to test-drive the book: he gets the first copy.

Emily Matchar
Big thanks to Jennye Garibaldi and Karla Zimmerman, who made this thing happen, and to the rest of the Lonely Planet team in California and Oz. Thanks to all the New Brunswickers who pointed me towards the best hikes, hidden beaches, pubs and poutine râpée. Thanks to Jamin Asay, the best travel (and life) companion anyone could ask for. And thanks to my grandmother, Evelyn Matchar, who passed away during the writing of this book, for imparting her sense of wonder and her deep-seated appreciation for the unconventional.

Brandon Presser
My research trips back home to Canada would not be possible without the love and support of my family – big hugs to Jack & Sheila, Chas & Brenda, Mo & Wendy, Cindy & Joey, and Steve & Linda. Special thank yous to Rob Gregorini, Lloyd Jones and travel pal Dan B. Thanks also to Kattrin Sieber, Jantine Van Kregten, and Caroline & Dave. In Lonely Planet-land, props to my Ontario co-captain Catherine, CA mamma Karla, and savvy editrix Jennye G.

Sarah Richards
Thank you to my husband, Benjamin, and son, Noah, for their undying support and patience. I'm grateful to all the friendly Quebecers I met along my travels, especially Greg at Maison Historique James Thompson, Sylvie at ALT Québec and Marie-Line at the Manoir Richelieu, for all of their excellent advice and warm hospitality. Thanks to Lonely Planet for sending me to Québec and supporting my *pain au chocolat* habit.

Brendan Sainsbury
Thanks to all the untold bus drivers, tourist info volunteers, restaurateurs, dinosaur experts and innocent bystanders who helped me during research, particularly to Jennye Garibaldi for offering me the gig in the first place and Karla Zimmerman for being a supportive coordinating author. Special thanks to Ann Morrow in Banff for granting me a spontaneous interview and opening my eyes to the beauty of the park. Thanks also to my wife Liz and Kieran for their company on the road.

Ryan Ver Berkmoes
The number of folks to thank outnumber Kermode bears but here's a few: Jim 'kootchie-kootchie' Kemshead never fails to deliver both beer and drama. In BC, Prince Rupert's Bruce Wishart is good for both info and drinks of all kinds. Karla Zimmerman was simply ace. It's always good to share a title page with John Lee and folks at Lonely Planet like Jennye, Alison and Bruce are pure delight. Of course, Erin put the Sweety in the pie.

ACKNOWLEDGMENTS

Cover photograph: Polar bears, Churchill, Manitoba, T. Davis/W. Bilenduke/Getty.

Many of the images in this guide are available for licensing from Lonely Planet Images: www.lonelyplanetimages.com.

THIS BOOK
For this 11th edition of *Canada*, Karla Zimmerman once again coordinated an outstanding author team (see Our Writers, p910). This guidebook was commissioned in Lonely Planet's Oakland office and produced by the following:

Commissioning Editor Jennye Garibaldi

Coordinating Editor Justin Flynn

Coordinating Cartographer Corey Hutchison

Coordinating Layout Designer Adrian Blackburn

Managing Editors Sasha Baskett, Bruce Evans

Managing Cartographers David Connolly, Alison Lyall

Managing Layout Designer Indra Kilfoyle

Assisting Editors Janet Austin, Andrew Bain, Kate Daly, Andrea Dobbin, Carly Hall, Anne Mulvaney, Sally O'Brien, Gabbi Stefanos, Elizabeth Swan

Assisting Cartographers Ildiko Bogdanovits, Andrew Smith

Assisting Layout Designers Paul Iacono, Jessica Rose, Jacqui Saunders, Kerrianne Southway

Cover Research Naomi Parker

Internal Image Research Sabrina Dalbesio

Thanks to Joanne, Emily Wolman, Heather Dickson, Lisa Knights, Jocelyn Harewood, Anna Metcalfe, Averil Robertson, Laura Stansfeld, Branislava Vladisavljevic, Annelies Mertens, Jeanette Wall, Mark Adams, Stefanie Di Trocchio, Janine Eberle, Brigitte Ellemor, Joshua Geoghegan, Mark Germanchis, Michelle Glynn, Liz Heynes, Lauren Hunt, Laura Jane, David Kemp, Nic Lehman, John Mazzocchi, Wayne Murphy, Piers Pickard, Lachlan Ross, Michael Ruff, Julie Sheridan, John Taufa, Sam Trafford, Juan Winata, Emily K Wolman, Celia Wood, Nick Wood

index

Map Pages **p000**
Photo Pages **p000**

Map Pages **p000**
Photo Pages **p000**

how to use this book

These symbols will help you find the listings you want:

- 👁 Sights
- 🏃 Activities
- 🎓 Courses
- 👉 Tours
- 🎊 Festivals & Events
- 🛏 Sleeping
- 🍴 Eating
- 🍷 Drinking
- ⭐ Entertainment
- 🛍 Shopping
- ℹ Information/Transport

Look out for these icons:

- **TOP CHOICE** Our author's recommendation
- **FREE** No payment required
- 🍃 A green or sustainable option

Our authors have nominated these places as demonstrating a strong commitment to sustainability – for example by supporting local communities and producers, operating in an environmentally friendly way, or supporting conservation projects.

These symbols give you the vital information for each listing:

- 📞 Telephone Numbers
- 🕐 Opening Hours
- 🅿 Parking
- 🚭 Nonsmoking
- ❄ Air-Conditioning
- @ Internet Access
- 📶 Wi-Fi Access
- 🏊 Swimming Pool
- 🥗 Vegetarian Selection
- 📖 English-Language Menu
- 👪 Family-Friendly
- 🐾 Pet-Friendly
- 🚌 Bus
- ⛴ Ferry
- Ⓜ Metro
- Ⓢ Subway
- ⊖ London Tube
- 🚊 Tram
- 🚆 Train

Reviews are organised by author preference.

Map Legend

Sights
- Beach
- Buddhist
- Castle
- Christian
- Hindu
- Islamic
- Jewish
- Monument
- Museum/Gallery
- Ruin
- Winery/Vineyard
- Zoo
- Other Sight

Activities, Courses & Tours
- Diving/Snorkelling
- Canoeing/Kayaking
- Skiing
- Surfing
- Swimming/Pool
- Walking
- Windsurfing
- Other Activity/Course/Tour

Sleeping
- Sleeping
- Camping

Eating
- Eating

Drinking
- Drinking
- Cafe

Entertainment
- Entertainment

Shopping
- Shopping

Information
- Post Office
- Tourist Information

Transport
- Airport
- Border Crossing
- Bus
- Cable Car/Funicular
- Cycling
- Ferry
- Metro
- Monorail
- Parking
- S-Bahn
- Taxi
- Train/Railway
- Tram
- Tube Station
- U-Bahn
- Other Transport

Routes
- Tollway
- Freeway
- Primary
- Secondary
- Tertiary
- Lane
- Unsealed Road
- Plaza/Mall
- Steps
- Tunnel
- Pedestrian Overpass
- Walking Tour
- Walking Tour Detour
- Path

Boundaries
- International
- State/Province
- Disputed
- Regional/Suburb
- Marine Park
- Cliff
- Wall

Population
- Capital (National)
- Capital (State/Province)
- City/Large Town
- Town/Village

Geographic
- Hut/Shelter
- Lighthouse
- Lookout
- Mountain/Volcano
- Oasis
- Park
- Pass
- Picnic Area
- Waterfall

Hydrography
- River/Creek
- Intermittent River
- Swamp/Mangrove
- Reef
- Canal
- Water
- Dry/Salt/Intermittent Lake
- Glacier

Areas
- Beach/Desert
- Cemetery (Christian)
- Cemetery (Other)
- Park/Forest
- Sportsground
- Sight (Building)
- Top Sight (Building)

John Lee

British Columbia, Cuisines of Canada, Wine Regions **Originally from St Albans in the UK, John** moved to Canada's West Coast to study at the University of Victoria in the 1990s, moving to Vancouver and launching a full-time independent travel-writing career in 1999. Since then, he's been covering the region (and beyond) for major newspapers and magazines around the world. Becoming a Lonely Planet author in 2005, he has contributed to 18 titles, including writing the most recent editions of the *Vancouver City Guide* and penning a daily blog for the LP website from the 2010 Olympic Winter Games. To read his latest stories and see what he's up to next, visit www.johnleewriter.com.

Emily Matchar

New Brunswick **Though American by birth, Emily has** long suffered acute Canada-envy (and not just for the healthcare, either!). She's had some of her best adventures in the True North, from paddling with seals off the coast of British Columbia to eating poutine at 3am in Montréal to hanging out with canoe-makers in rural New Brunswick. These days, she makes her home quite a bit further south, in Chapel Hill, North Carolina, where she writes for a variety of magazines, newspapers and websites. She's contributed to half a dozen Lonely Planet guides, including *USA*, *Mexico* and *Trips: The Carolinas, Georgia and the South*.

Brandon Presser

Ontario **For this, his second time** coauthoring the *Canada* guide, Brandon had the distinct honor of tracing his father's old trucking route through the moose-clad recesses of northern Ontario. Brandon is himself no stranger to the area – he was born in Ottawa and spent much of his childhood in the region. After living in Paris, Tokyo and Boston, Brandon strapped on a backpack and joined the glamorous ranks of eternal nomadism. As a fulltime freelance travel writer he's contributed to over 20 Lonely Planet titles from *Iceland* to *Thailand* and many '-lands' in between.

Sarah Richards

Québec **Loyal to the mountains** and forests of her native BC, Sarah vowed never to love another Canadian province. But when she started her undergraduate degree at McGill University, a torrid love affair with the enticing vibe of Québec threatened to break her ties with home forever. After graduation, she roamed Asia and Europe for six years, before finding her way back into the arms of Montréal. She blames the soft scents of freshly baked croissants in the wind and the sinful delights of the city's vibrant nightlife for her betrayal.

Brendan Sainsbury

Alberta, Northwest Territories, Nunavut, National Parks **An expat Brit from** Hampshire, England, Brendan is a former fitness instructor, volunteer teacher, wannabe musician and travel guide who now writes about travel full-time. In 2003 he met a Canadian girl from Saskatoon while in Spain. After romancing in Cuba and getting married in Mexico, they now live (with their son, Kieran) in White Rock, BC. Brendan is a long-time lover of Alberta's national parks and is the coauthor of Lonely Planet's current *Banff, Jasper & Glacier National Parks* guide.

Ryan Ver Berkmoes

British Columbia, Manitoba, Saskatchewan, Yukon Territory **Ryan's** been bouncing around BC and the Yukon for more than two decades. This time he added Manitoba and Saskatchewan. But what he really added was more critter-spotting than he'd ever imagined possible. But it's fitting given Ryan's background with moose. At his first newspaper job he was tasked with placing random moose jokes in the classifieds to pique reader interest (eg What's a moose's favorite philosopher? Cam-moose). For better jokes than that, surf over to ryanverberkmoes.com.

OUR STORY

A beat-up old car, a few dollars in the pocket and a sense of adventure. In 1972 that's all Tony and Maureen Wheeler needed for the trip of a lifetime – across Europe and Asia overland to Australia. It took several months, and at the end – broke but inspired – they sat at their kitchen table writing and stapling together their first travel guide, *Across Asia on the Cheap*. Within a week they'd sold 1500 copies. Lonely Planet was born.

Today, Lonely Planet has offices in Melbourne, London and Oakland, with more than 600 staff and writers. We share Tony's belief that 'a great guidebook should do three things: inform, educate and amuse'.

OUR WRITERS

Karla Zimmerman

Coordinating Author, Newfoundland & Labrador During her years covering Canada coast to coast for Lonely Planet, Karla has become an honorary Newfoundlander (with a rum-soaked certificate to prove it), an honorary Vancouverite (with a sushi addiction to prove it), and some would say an honorary Canadian (with a Tim Horton's fixation to prove it). On her most recent trip to The Rock, she heard a quote that pretty much sums it up: 'Moose? They're like boats — they're *every*where.' When she's not north of the border, Karla lives in Chicago, where the donuts are good but not Canadian good. She writes travel features for newspapers, books, magazines and websites.

Catherine Bodry

Ontario Catherine grew up just below the Canadian border, in Washington State, and has made countless trips to visit her northern neighbors. During her youth she camped on Vancouver Island, and when she got a little older she snuck across the border for the coveted 19-year-old drinking age. Since then, she's driven the Alaska Highway five times, explored the western coast by ferry, and filled her belly repeatedly across Ontario's farmland. Writing for Lonely Planet feeds (and often fuels) her wanderlust: you'll find her in Lonely Planet's *Alaska*, *Pacific Northwest Trips* and *Thailand*. Check out www.catherinebodry.com for more of her work.

Celeste Brash

Nova Scotia, Prince Edward Island, Travel with Children 'This is where people from Tahiti go on vacation?' – this question is often asked of Celeste during her voyages through the Maritimes. Lighthouses and lupine are a far cry from palm trees and hibiscus of her island home of 15 years, but Celeste became certain long ago that Atlantic lobster is the best food on Earth, fell in love with the crisp air and is an unabashed Anne fan. After this trip she moved from the tropics to a similar latitude in Oregon to start more temperate adventures involving salmon and blackberries.

OVER PAGE | MORE WRITERS

Published by Lonely Planet Publications Pty Ltd
ABN 36 005 607 983
11th edition – March 2011
ISBN 978 1 7417 9234 8
© Lonely Planet 2011   Photographs © as indicated 2011
10 9 8 7 6 5 4 3 2 1
Printed in Singapore

Although the authors and Lonely Planet have taken all reasonable care in preparing this book, we make no warranty about the accuracy or completeness of its content and, to the maximum extent permitted, disclaim all liability arising from its use.